45°E

60°E

Black Sea

Caspian Sea

Aral Sea

Aras River

Amu Darya (Oxus River)

Toros Dağları

Kuhha-ye Zāgros

Reshteh-ye Alborz

Hindu Kush

Cyprus

Tigris River

Mesopotamia

Dasht-e Kavor (Salt Desert)

Euphrates River

Jordan River

Syrian Desert

Iranian Plateau

Dead Sea

Dasht-e Lut (Sand Desert)

Sinai

Nafud

Persian Gulf

Najd

Gulf of Oman

al-Hijaz

Red Sea

Arabian Peninsula

Nubian Desert

al-Rub al-Khali

Atbara River

Arabian Sea

Blue Nile River

Nile River

Gulf of Aden

Socotra

Nile River

INDIAN OCEAN

N

For Reference

Not to be taken from this room

0   200   400 mi.

0   200   400 km

ENCYCLOPEDIA OF THE
MODERN
MIDDLE EAST &
NORTH AFRICA
SECOND EDITION

ENCYCLOPEDIA OF THE
MODERN
MIDDLE EAST &
NORTH AFRICA
SECOND EDITION

VOLUME 2

Dabbagh — Kuwait University

Philip Mattar

EDITOR IN CHIEF

MACMILLAN REFERENCE USA

An imprint of Thomson Gale, a part of The Thomson Corporation

Detroit • New York • San Francisco • San Diego • New Haven, Conn. • Waterville, Maine • London • Munich

The Encyclopedia of the Modern Middle East and North Africa, 2nd Edition

Philip Mattar

For permission to use material from this product, submit your request via Web at http://www.gale-edit.com/permissions, or you may download our Permissions Request form and sumbit your request by fax or mail to:

Thomson Gale
27500 Drake Rd.
Farmington Hills, MI 48331-3535
Permissions Hotline:
248-699-8006 or 800-877-4253, ext. 8006
Fax: 248-699-8074 or 800-762-4058

Cover photographs reproduced by permission of Corbis, and AP/Wide World Photos.

Since this page cannot legibly accommodate all copyright notices, the acknowledgements constitute an extension of the copyright notice.

While every effort has been made to ensure the reliability of the information presented in this publication, Thomson Gale does not guarantee the accuracy of the data contained herein. Thomson Gale accepts no payment for listing; and inclusion in the publication of any organization, agency, institution, publication, service, or individual does not imply endorsement of the editors or publisher. Errors brought to the attention of the publisher and verified to the satisfaction of the publisher will be corrected in future editions.

LIBRARY OF CONGRESS CATALOGING-IN-PUBLICATION DATA

Encyclopedia of the modern Middle East and North Africa / edited by Philip Mattar.— 2nd ed.
p. cm.
Includes bibliographical references and index.
ISBN 0-02-865769-1 (set : alk. paper) — ISBN 0-02-865770-5 (v. 1 : alk. paper) — ISBN 0-02-865771-3 (v. 2 : alk. paper) — ISBN 0-02-865772-1 (v. 3 : alk. paper) — ISBN 0-02-865773-X (v. 4 : alk. paper)
1. Middle East—Encyclopedias. 2. Africa, North—Encyclopedias. I. Mattar, Philip, 1944-

DS43.E53 2004
956'.003—dc22   2004005650

This title is also avalable as an e-book.
ISBN 0-02-865987-2 (set)
Contact your Gale sales representative for ordering information.

Printed in the United States of America
10 9 8 7 6 5 4 3

DABBAGH, MARZIEH
[c. 1942–]

Islamist activist in Iran.

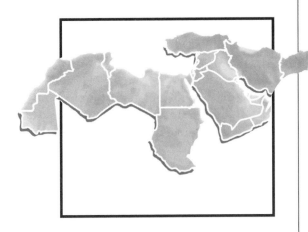

D

Marzieh Dabbagh was born in Hamadan, Iran, in the early 1940s. She was married at the age of thirteen, gave birth to eight children, and moved to Tehran. There she joined the circle of Ayatollah Saidi, a protégé of Ayatollah Ruhollah Khomeini, and became a dedicated Islamist. In 1972, she was arrested by the SAVAK and severely tortured. After a second arrest, when her health began to fail, she was released. Dabbagh left Iran for Europe. In England and France, she participated in hunger strikes on behalf of Iranian prisoners. In Saudi Arabia, she distributed Khomeini's clandestine fliers among Muslim pilgrims to Mecca. In Syria, she helped set up a military camp where anti-Shah combatants were trained. With the help of the dissident Shiʿite cleric Imam Musa Sadr, an Iranian who was mobilizing the Shiʿa of Lebanon, Dabbagh trained a new generation of young Iranian combatants in paramilitary tactics. She was a confidant and bodyguard of Khomeini in Paris in 1978. After the Iranian Revolution, she participated in the Iran–Iraq War (1980–1988) and served as a military commander. She joined the Pasdaran paramilitary group and took an active role in destroying all rival organizations, from the Kurdish Komeleh and Democrat parties to the secret cells of the Fedaʾiyan and Mojahedin organizations. In the late 1980s, she went to Moscow as part of a delegation to negotiate with Mikhail Gorbachev. In the 1980s and 1990s, she headed the Islamist Women's Society. She served four terms in the Iranian parliament (the First, the Second, and the Fifth Majles) until 2000, when she was not elected to the more reformist Sixth Majles.

See also IRANIAN REVOLUTION (1979); IRAN–IRAQ WAR (1980–1988); KHOMEINI, RUHOLLAH.

Bibliography

Afary, Janet, "Portraits of Two Islamist Women: Escape from Freedom or from Tradition?" *Critique* 19 (Fall 2001): 47–77.

JANET AFARY

DABBAS, CHARLES
[1885–1935]

President of Lebanon.

Charles Dabbas (also Debbas), born to a Greek Orthodox family, earned a law degree. His close association with French interests in the Middle East led France to select him to be the first "elected" president of Lebanon before independence. He assumed the presidency in 1926, during the French mandate. The selection of a Greek Orthodox as president was intended to appease the Muslims, who were displeased with the idea of Lebanon's separation from Syria.

Dabbas's judicial and administrative background and his French wife made him extremely acceptable to the French mandate authorities. His rule was facilitated by his strong alliance with the Sunni Muslim speaker of the Senate, Shaykh Muhammad al-Jisr. Dabbas worked to extend the authority of the government to areas outside of Beirut. He made trips to the Shuf and to the south, and he criticized the low standard of state services—or their absence in some cases. Ultimately disillusioned, he resigned in 1933 and moved to Paris, where he died two years later.

See also SHUF; SUNNI ISLAM.

AS'AD ABUKHALIL

DADDAH, MOKHTAR OULD
[1924–2003]

First president of Mauritania, 1960–1978.

Mokhtar Ould Daddah was born 25 December 1924 in Boutilimit in the Trarza district, southwestern Mauritania, 60 miles southeast of Nouakchott. A member of a prestigious Marabout tribe, he became Mauritania's first university graduate, earning a law degree in Paris. During the late 1950s he assumed a leadership role in organizing Mauritania's independence. In 1961 Daddah officially became head of state as well as head of government under a newly established presidential regime. Central to his efforts at nation building was the idea of a unique desert civilization, encompassing Spanish Sahara (now Western Sahara), southern Morocco, and Mauritania, to the banks of the Senegal River.

In the mid-1970s Daddah drew Mauritania closer to both France and Morocco, against the background of the Western Sahara conflict. In 1976 Mauritania and Morocco agreed on the partition of Western Sahara following its evacuation by Spain. But the ensuing war there with Algerian-backed Polisario forces placed inordinate stress on Mauritania, and Daddah lost the support of key sectors of the society. He was overthrown by a military committee in a bloodless coup on 10 July 1978 and placed under arrest.

In 1980 Daddah was allowed to leave, going briefly to Tunisia and then to Nice, France, where he kept a low profile for many years. As Mauritanian political life slowly opened up during the mid-1990s, Daddah began to speak out against the regime. His brother Ahmed headed the leading opposition group. Daddah returned to Mauritania on 17 July 2001.

See also MAURITANIA; WESTERN SAHARA.

Bibliography

Hodges, Tony. *Western Sahara: Roots of a Desert War.* Westport, CT: Lawrence Hill, 1983.

BRUCE MADDY-WEITZMAN

DAFTARI, AHMAD MATIN
[1896–1971]

Iranian politician.

The son-in-law of Mohammad Mossadegh and father of the cleric Hedayatollah Matin Daftari (a leading member of Mojahedin-e Khalq, the Baghdad-based opposition group), Ahmad Matin Daftari was born to an Iranian vizierial family. In 1929, he was sent to Europe by the Iranian government to study law. He was Reza Shah Pahlavi's minister of justice in 1936 and prime minister in 1939. Throughout his political career, Daftari also taught at Tehran University, as a member of the faculty of law, and wrote several books on the subject of law. His participation in politics was stalled in 1962 because of his opposition to the price hikes imposed by Mohammad Reza Shah Pahlavi's government and the political activism of his two sons, who opposed the shah's regime. Daftari died in Tehran.

See also MOJAHEDIN-E KHALQ; MOSSADEGH, MOHAMMAD; PAHLAVI, MOHAMMAD REZA; PAHLAVI, REZA.

NEGUIN YAVARI

DAĞLARCA, FAZIL HÜSNÜ

[1914–]

Prolific Turkish poet.

The son and grandson of army officers, Fazil Hüsnü Dağlarca was educated at the Küleli Military Lycée in Istanbul. He won his first poetry prize at age thirteen. From 1933 his poems appeared in leading journals and newspapers, and his first collection was published the day of his graduation from Mekteb-i Harbiye (the war academy) in Ankara (1935). He continued publishing during fifteen years as an army officer and seven as a Ministry of Labor inspector. In 1959 he became a bookstore owner and publisher in Istanbul and edited a monthly literary journal between 1960 and 1964. His shop was a gathering place for leading literary figures until he closed it to devote himself fully to literature (1970). He has won numerous Turkish and foreign awards. In 1967 a five-man jury of Turkish writers named him Turkey's leading poet, and he received the International Poetry Forum's Turkish Award in 1968.

In general, critics connect him to no literary school (Turkish or foreign), noting his highly developed individuality and originality, even in the formative years. Some liken his method to that of free association. His profound influence led to a new Turkish surrealism. He has written in diverse forms, from epic to quatrain, and his verses range from lyric and inspirational to satire and social criticism.

Among the themes in the poetry that built his reputation are the individual's relationship to God, the cosmos, nature, and fellow human beings; the beginnings of the Ottoman Empire; Turkish heroism at the Turkish Straits and in the war of independence; and praise of Mustafa Kemal Atatürk. In the 1950s, Dağlarca turned to social and political criticism, protesting the plight of the Turkish villager over the centuries and denouncing the West for colonialism and exploitation, taking up, for example, events in Algeria, the atom bomb, and in *Vietnam Savaşimiz* (Our Vietnam war, 1966), expressing the strong anti-American feelings of the day.

Some have taken him to task for sacrificing his art to politics, arguing that his social and political poetry lacks the significance of his earlier work. In all, Dağlarca has published some fifty books, including a number for children.

See also ATATÜRK, MUSTAFA KEMAL; LITERATURE: TURKISH.

Bibliography

Dağlarca, Fazil Hüsnü. *Selected Poems,* translated by Talât Sait Halman. Pittsburgh, PA: University of Pittsburgh Press, 1969.

Menemencioğlu, Nermin, ed. (in collaboration with Fahir İz). *The Penguin Book of Turkish Verse.* Harmondsworth, U.K., and New York: Penguin, 1978.

KATHLEEN R. F. BURRILL

DAHLAN, MUHAMMAD

[1961–]

Palestinian activist and security official in the Palestinian Authority.

Born in Khan Yunis refugee camp in Gaza, Muhammad Dahlan later headed Shabiba, the youth movement of al-Fatah, in the West Bank during the 1980s. He was imprisoned by Israel on numerous occasions between 1981 and 1986, was active in the first Intifada, and was eventually deported in 1988. In exile in Tunis, Dahlan helped the Palestine Liberation Organization (PLO) coordinate the Intifada.

Upon the establishment of the Palestinian Authority (PA) in 1994, Dahlan returned from exile and headed the Gaza branch of the Preventative Security Forces. A frequent participant in Israeli-Palestinian negotiations during the 1990s, he became one of the most powerful figures in the PA. With the breakdown of the peace process, he ran into political difficulties. His crackdown on groups such as HAMAS that were opposed to the peace process, and his good working relationship with Israel and the United States, angered some Palestinians. His call for PA political reform angered Arafat. Dahlan resigned in June 2002 but was appointed minister of state for security affairs in the spring of 2003 by PA prime minister Mahmud Abbas. During the power struggle between Abbas and Arafat in the summer of 2003, Dahlan found himself pitted against Jibril Rajub, former West Bank head of the Preventative Security Forces, whom Arafat had appointed his national security adviser.

See also ABBAS, MAHMUD; FATAH, AL-; IN-
TIFADA (1987–1991); PALESTINE LIBERATION
ORGANIZATION (PLO); PALESTINIAN AU-
THORITY; RAJUB, JIBRIL; WEST BANK.

MICHAEL R. FISCHBACH

DAMANHUR

City of the Nile delta.

Damanhur is the capital of Buhayra (Beheira) governorate; it is southeast of Alexandria, Egypt. Its
original name was Timinhur (city of Horus), and it
was called Hermopolis Parva in Byzantine times. It
has been the seat of a Coptic bishop since the fourth
century C.E. It became a commercial center during
the early spread of Islam and was made the residence
of a senior Mamluk officer because it commanded
the entire Nile delta region and was a major stage
on the post road from Alexandria on the Mediterranean Sea to Cairo on the Nile River. In April
1799, its inhabitants destroyed a company of
Napoléon's troops.

Now a major station on the railroad and the
center of a network of secondary rail routes within
the delta, it is an important market center for cotton and rice. Its population was estimated at about
222,000 in 1992.

See also BUHAYRA; COPTS; MAMLUKS.

Bibliography

Atiya, Aziz S., ed. *The Coptic Encyclopedia.* New York:
Macmillan, 1991.

ARTHUR GOLDSCHMIDT

DAMASCUS

Syria's capital and largest city.

Damascus is situated on the edge of an ancient oasis, al-Ghuta, where the Barada River runs along
the eastern base of the Anti-Lebanon mountains.
The city is mentioned by name as early as the fifteenth century B.C.E., when it was captured by the
Egyptian pharaoh Thutmoses III. It was subsequently occupied by the Israelites, Assyrians, Babylonians, Greeks, and Nabataeans before being
conquered by Rome, whose governors constructed

the network of streets, plazas, walls, and gates that
continues to define the contours of the Old City.
When the Byzantines took charge of Damascus
around 395 C.E., they consecrated the massive temple to Jupiter in the center of the city as the Church
of Saint John the Baptist. The largely Monophysite
population remained hostile to the Melkite rulers
of Byzantium and welcomed the Sassanid army that
occupied the city in 612.

Byzantine forces retook Damascus around 627,
but after a brief siege the city opened its gates to the
Arab Muslims led by Khalid ibn al-Walid in September 635. Byzantium's counterattack was crushed
on the banks of the Yarmuk River the following
summer, and in December 636 an Arab/Muslim
army commanded by Abu Ubayda ibn al-Jarra
marched into the city once again. Upon the death
of the governor Yazid ibn Abi Sufyan three years
later, Yazid's brother Mu'awiya assumed command
of the Arab Muslim forces based in Damascus.
Mu'awiya succeeded Ali as caliph, or leader, of the
Muslims after a series of confrontations in 658–661
and designated the city as the capital of the new
Umayyad dynasty.

During the Umayyad era from 661 to 750,
Damascus constituted the center of a political and
economic domain stretching from Spain in the west
to Khorasan in the east. The third Umayyad ruler,
al-Walid, transformed the comparatively modest
mosque that had been built on the grounds of the
Church of Saint John into a much grander structure, known as the Umayyad Mosque. This building and other monuments constructed by the
Umayyads were ransacked when an Abbasid army occupied the city in the spring of 750. Damascus fell
into relative obscurity after the Abbasid dynasty
transferred the Muslim capital to Iraq; its inhabitants repeatedly rose in revolt, but Abbasid forces
crushed each of these insurrections. The powerful
governor of Egypt, Ahmad ibn Tulun, incorporated
Damascus into his domain in 878, as did a powerful Turkic confederation, the Ikhshidids, sixty years
later.

By the late tenth century, Damascus stood at the
intersection of conflicts involving the Fatimid rulers
of Egypt, the Hamdanids of Aleppo, the Byzantines
to the west, various Turkoman tribes from the
north, and the collapsing Abbasid Empire in the

east. Continual raids and occupations severely disrupted the city's trade and destroyed whole commercial and residential districts. A series of Seljuk governors struggled to gain control of the city during the last quarter of the eleventh century, but it was only when the military commander (*atabeg*) Zahir al-Din Tughtaqin seized power in 1104 that a modicum of order returned. Tughtaqin's successors, the Burids, oversaw a marked recovery of the Damascene economy and the establishment of several new suburbs, although the dynasty faced a combination of internal challenges from the Batiniyya and external threats from the Crusaders and the Zangids of Aleppo until the last Burid ruler was supplanted by Nur al-Din Mahmud in 1154.

Nur al-Din reestablished Damascus as the capital of Syria. New fortifications were constructed; religious schools and foundations proliferated. The city fell into the hands of Nur al-Din's former lieutenant, Salah al-Din ibn al-Ayyubi, in 1176 and remained an important Ayyubid center for the next half century. During these decades, European merchants turned the silk brocade, copper wares, and leather goods manufactured in the city into lucrative items of international commerce. Profits generated by the burgeoning trade with Europe enabled the court to patronize large numbers of prominent scholars and artisans. This illustrious era ended only when the Mongols overran the city in the spring of 1260. In the wake of the Mongol defeat at Ayn Jalut, Damascus became subordinated to the Mamluk rulers of Egypt, for whom it served first as a forward base of operations against Mongol incursions and later as a provincial capital.

Damascus put up little resistance to the Ottomans, who occupied the city in September 1516. When Sultan Selim I died five years later, however, the long-standing governor Janbirdi al-Ghazali declared the city independent. Janissaries quickly suppressed the revolt, pillaging and burning whole neighborhoods. Thereafter, Damascus lost much of its political and economic importance and became the seat of one of three Ottoman governorates (*vilayets*) in Syria. The city's fortunes rose whenever local families captured the office of governor, most notably during the period of al-Azm rule in the early eighteenth century, but fell when such families relinquished power to outsiders. Throughout the Ottoman era, Damascus served as a key way sta-

Umayyed Mosque, originally a pagan temple, then a church, now a mosque representing the fourth holiest Islamic site, overlooks nearby structures in Damascus, the capital of Syria. © CHARLES & JOSETTE LENARS/CORBIS. REPRODUCED BY PERMISSION.

tion along the pilgrimage route between Anatolia and Mecca. The governor of the city assumed the office of commander of the pilgrimage (*amir al-hajj*) for the arduous trip south across the Syrian desert, a position from which both his administration and his fellow Damascenes derived considerable revenue. The link to the Hijaz was reinforced with the opening of a railway line between Damascus and Medina in 1908.

By the first years of the twentieth century, Damascus had become a major center of agitation against the Ottoman regime. The reformist governor Midhat Paşa not only tolerated the growth of Arab nationalist sentiment, but also inaugurated improvements in the city's roads and commercial districts that strengthened the local bourgeoisie. The liberal atmosphere encouraged Damascenes to demonstrate in support of the 1908 revolution in Istanbul, but the outbreak of World War I brought a reassertion of Ottoman authority. The wartime governor Cemal Paşa cracked down on Arab nationalists, most famously by hanging twenty-one prominent leaders in the main squares of Damascus and Beirut on 6 May 1916. The Ottoman troops did not withdraw from Damascus until the end of September 1918, and on 1 October Arab forces led by Amir Faisal I ibn Hussein of the Hijaz marched into the city alongside British imperial units.

Faisal immediately set up a military government in Damascus then supervised the formation of a general Syrian congress, which on 7 March 1920 declared Syria a sovereign state with Faisal as king. When the establishment of the new civilian administration went unacknowledged by the European powers meeting in San Remo the following month, and France was given charge of the country's affairs by way of a mandate from the League of Nations to prepare the country for eventual independence, Damascus exploded in rioting; the general congress declared a state of emergency and ordered the formation of a militia to assist in restoring order. Despite the efforts of the Syrian authorities, popular unrest persisted, prompting the French army to occupy the city at the end of July 1920 and exile King Faisal. Strikes and demonstrations continued throughout the mandate period; the rebel Druze leader Sultan al-Atrash managed to gain a foothold in the southern suburbs during the revolt of 1925. French commanders responded by bombarding Damascus twice, in October 1925 and April 1926. Nineteen years later, on the eve of France's final evacuation and Syria's independence, the city was bombarded yet again.

With a population (2002) of 1,368,300, contemporary Damascus is not only the largest city and capital of the Syrian Arab Republic but also a major industrial and commercial center. Damascus University, founded in 1923, remains the country's most prestigious institution of higher education, and al-Asad Library houses Syria's largest collection of printed materials. An annual international trade fair, initiated in 1954, promotes a wide range of Syrian-made goods, while encouraging the city's influential business community to establish closer connections with the outside world.

See also ATRASH, SULTAN PASHA AL-; CEMAL PAŞA; DAMASCUS UNIVERSITY; FAISAL I IBN HUSSEIN; JANISSARIES; MAMLUKS; MIDHAT PAŞA; UMAYYAD MOSQUE.

Bibliography

Hinnebusch, Raymond A., Jr. *A Political Organization in Syria: A Case of Mobilization Politics.* Pittsburgh, PA: University of Pittsburgh Press, 1975.

Hopwood, Derek. *Syria 1945–1986: Politics and Society.* Boston: Unwin Hyman, 1988.

Keenan, Brigit, and Bedon, Tim (photographer). *Damascus: Hidden Treasures of the Old City.* New York: Thames and Hudson, 2000.

Khoury, Philip S. *Syria and the French Mandate: The Politics of Arab Nationalism.* Princeton, NJ: Princeton University Press, 1987.

Khoury, Philip S. *Urban Notables and Arab Nationalism: The Politics of Damascus, 1860–1920.* Cambridge, MA: Cambridge University Press, 1983.

FRED H. LAWSON

DAMASCUS AFFAIR (1840)

Blood libel accusation leveled by Christians at the Jews of Damascus.

On 5 February 1840 a Capuchin friar named Thomas disappeared from Damascus with his Muslim servant, Ibrahim. Their whereabouts were never discovered. The friar was under the jurisdiction of the recently appointed French consul, Count Ratti-Menton, who supported the accusation of local Christians that the Jews were responsible for the alleged murders in order to obtain blood to make their matzot for Passover. Several prominent Jews of Damascus were thereupon rounded up and subjected to torture; several died, one converted to Islam, and a confession of guilt was extracted.

In March, the Jews of Istanbul, alarmed at the libel of Damascus and a simultaneous libel in Rhodes, alerted western Jewish leaders to the events. An international campaign to rescue the Jews of Damascus and to pressure the Egyptian governor of Damascus, Sharif Pasha, was organized in England. The defense efforts were spearheaded by Moses Montefiore of England and Albert Crémieux of France. Press coverage and parliamentary condemnations of injustices in the East heightened public interest in the Jewish plight in general and Ottoman judicial malpractice in particular. Interventions by Queen Victoria, Lord Henry Palmerston, U.S. Secretary of State John Forsyth, and Klemens von Metternich of Austria to obtain a release of the victims were of no avail.

In the summer of 1840, Montefiore and Crémieux set off for Egypt and Syria to win the freedom of the Jews of Damascus. The fate of the delegation was monitored by the European press as the Damascus affair became a cause célèbre. Newly emancipated European Jewry was haunted by the specter of a return to medieval anti-Jewish prejudice. British parliamentary liberals were also concerned about the continued use of torture and the need for Ottoman judicial reform. Great Britain, additionally, expressed an interest in protecting the Jews of the East as a counterbalance to French and Russian protection of Roman Catholics and Orthodox Christians in the Muslim world. In August, Montefiore and Crémieux won the release of the tortured Jews of Damascus, but Muhammad Ali refused to exonerate them. Montefiore then proceeded to Istanbul to obtain the sultan's condemnation of the libel and future protection for Ottoman Jewry. The Ferman of Abdülmecit I of 6 November 1840 denounced the blood libel and stressed "that the charges made against them and their religion are nothing but pure calumny." The sultan further specified that Jews were to be specifically included in the reforms embodied in the Hatt-i Serif of Gülhane and that "the Jewish nation shall possess the same advantages and enjoy the same privileges as are granted to the numerous other nations who submit to our authority. The Jewish nation shall be protected and defended."

Despite Montefiore's success and the imperial rescript, blood libels recurred throughout the Middle East. Libels in Damascus (nine occurred there between 1840 and 1900), Aleppo, Beirut, Chios, Safad, the Dardanelles, Gallipoli, Cairo, Alexandria, Dayr al-Qamar, Hamadan in Iran, Salonika, Smyrna, and elsewhere were instigated by Armenians and Greeks as well as Muslims. The havoc wrought by these repeated accusations was partially responsible for the decline and emigration of Ottoman Jewry beginning in the late nineteenth century. The vulnerability of Ottoman Jewry led as well to the formation of the Alliance Israélite Universelle in 1860.

See also ALLIANCE ISRAÉLITE UNIVERSELLE (AIU); FERMAN.

Bibliography

Dundes, Alan, ed. *The Blood Libel Legend: A Casebook in Anti-Semitic Folklore.* Madison: University of Wisconsin Press, 1991.

Gerber, Jane S. "The Damascus Blood Libel: Jewish Perceptions and Responses." *Proceedings of the Eighth World Congress of Jewish Studies.* Jerusalem: Institute of Contemporary Jewry, 1983.

Parfitt, Tudor. "The Year of the Pride of Israel: Montefiore and the Blood Libel of 1840." In *The Century of Moses Montefiore,* edited by Sonia Lipman and V. D. Lipman. Oxford and New York: Oxford University Press, 1985.

JANE GERBER
UPDATED BY MICHAEL R. FISCHBACH

DAMASCUS UNIVERSITY

Oldest of the present four universities in Syria.

Damascus University is one of four universities currently operating in Syria; the other three are the University of Aleppo, the University of Tishrin (at Latakia), and the University of the Ba'th (at Homs). The earliest institutions of higher learning in Ottoman Syria were the Institute of Medicine (Ma'had al-Tibb) established in Damascus in 1903 and the School of Law (Madrasa al-Huquq) established in Beirut in 1913. After the end of Ottoman rule in Syria in 1918 and the establishment of the Arab government of King Faisal in Damascus (1918–1920), the Institute of Medicine and the School of Law, which had experienced difficulties and closures during World War I, were newly opened in Damascus in 1919. The Institute of Medicine was then renamed the Arab Institute of Medicine (al-Ma'had al-Tibbi al-Arabi) and was headed by Dr. Rida Sa'id, who became president of the newly established Syrian University from 1923 to 1936.

On 15 June 1923, the head of the Union of Syrian States, created by the mandatory authorities of France, issued a decree establishing the Syrian University (al-Jami'a al-Suriyya) which was to include medicine and law in addition to the Arab Scientific Academy (al-Majma al-Ilmi al-Arabi), and the Arab Directorate of Antiquities (Dar al-Athar al-Arabiyya). On 15 March 1926, the academy and the Directorate of Antiquities were removed from the Syrian University. A School of Higher Literary Studies (Madrasat al-Durus al-Adabiyya al-Ulya) was established in 1928 and attached to the university. The school taught Arabic language and literature and Arabic philosophy and sociology over a period of three years. In 1929, it was renamed the School of Higher Letters (Madrasat al-Adab al-Ulya); between 1935 and 1956, it was closed.

The number of students in medicine and law rose from 180 (1919–1920) to 1,094 (1944–1945). Women first enrolled in medicine and law from

1922 to 1923. Their numbers in 1945 were 72 in medicine and 12 in law.

After Syria became independent in 1945, faculties of sciences and arts and a Higher Institute for Teachers were established the following year in the Syrian University. A Faculty of Engineering was opened in Aleppo the same year as part of the Syrian University. This faculty later became the nucleus of the University of Aleppo, established in 1958. In 1954, a Faculty of Islamic Law (*shariʿa*) was established in the Syrian University. In 1956, the Institute of Commerce was established and attached to the Faculty of Law, becoming the Faculty of Commerce (1959–1960).

On 19 October 1958, during the union between Syria and Egypt, a new law was issued regulating the affairs of the universities. The Syrian University changed its name to Damascus University. Two new faculties for engineering and dentistry were added to it from 1959 to 1960.

Under the Baʿth party, which has been ruling Syria since 1963, and especially after the Correctionist Movement of President Hafiz al-Asad in 1970, university education expanded tremendously and the number of both students and faculty increased. The University of Tishrin was established in 1971 and the University of the Baʿth in 1979. In 2002 Damascus University included fourteen faculties plus the Institute for Administrative Development, as well as several teaching hospitals, a nursing school, and language centers. The university offers M.A. and Ph.D. programs in various disciplines. Enrollment for the 1998–1999 academic year was more than 23,000.

See also ALEPPO; ASAD, HAFIZ AL-; BAʿTH, AL-; FAISAL I IBN HUSSEIN; HOMS; LATAKIA.

ABDUL-KARIM RAFEQ

DAMMAM, AL-

Saudi Arabian port on the Persian Gulf.

Al-Damman is a city on Saudi Arabia's gulf coast and capital of the Eastern Province since 1952. Transformed by the discovery of oil at nearby Dhahran, al-Dammam boasts a major port (built in 1950) and the terminus of the Riyadh railroad. An Anglo-Saudi conference in al-Dammam in 1952 failed to produce agreement on Saudi-Qatar and Saudi-Abu Dhabi frontiers. Al-Dammam's population has surged as a result of the steady economic growth in the Eastern Province, although no reliable figures are available. The city, in combination with the Saudi Arabian American Oil Company (ARAMCO) headquarters at Dhahran and the residential town of al-Khubar, lies at the center of a commercial, industrial, and petroleum hub. King Faisal University is located in al-Dammam. The nearby King Fahd Causeway provides the only land link with Bahrain, and the King Fahd Airport, the newest of the kingdom's three international airports, was opened in 1999, replacing an older facility at Dhahran.

Bibliography

Nawwab, Ismail I., et al., eds. *Saudi Aranco and Its World: Arabia and the Middle East.* Dhahran: Saudi Aramco, 1995.

J. E. PETERSON

DANCE

A social activity that takes on a multitude of forms within sacred and everyday contexts in Middle Eastern societies.

The Middle East abounds in forms of dance and stylized movement ranging from those associated with ritualized religious ceremonies, such as the Semaʾa of the mystical Sufi Whirling Dervishes, to more spontaneous dancing, such as belly dancing, that occurs in informal everyday contexts. One of the earliest documents of Middle Eastern expressive arts is the multivolume tome written by Abu Faraj al-Isfahan in the tenth century, *Kitab al-Aghrani* (The book of songs), which indicates that the realm of the arts has always been highly cosmopolitan. Various courts had ethnically and religiously diverse dance troupes that regularly accompanied musicians. Their participation was considered a necessary element in creating *tarab*—the joy that is felt by performers and audience members during musical events.

Far from being merely a pastime, dance in the Middle East carries heavy symbolic meaning. Although some Middle Eastern communities adhere closely to interpretations of religious texts that warn against the carnal aspects of music and dance, other communities cannot conceive of celebrating life's important moments without music and its by-product, dance. In the Middle East, one's ability to dance can signify a number of things. In some countries such as Morocco, for example, a woman's dance style is read as a text from which spectators make assumptions about her personality: If she shows little interest in dancing at a wedding, others may conclude that she is not sincere in her happiness for the union of the couple, or that she is not fun-loving. Small flourishes taken from international pop stars and included in one's own locally based repertoire speak volumes about taste and the cultural influences absorbed through media. And although male dancers in the Middle East have been able to reach a sort of professional (*maʿalim*) status, the same has not always been true for women. Sources such as Isfahan's indicate that women have been performers as long as there has been music and dance, but female performers have often been stigmatized. Although displaying a talent for dance among family and friends is desirable and in some cases required, dancing as a profession is often discouraged, and paid performers are not always accorded high social status.

Most mainstream communities in the Middle East attach a great deal of importance to dance as a necessary component to any significant celebration. Although traditions vary from region to region, dance may be present at engagement ceremonies, weddings, births and naming ceremonies, seasonal harvests, holidays (both national and religious), festivals, and circumcisions, not to mention the day-to-day visits among close friends and family that are common among women. Some religious scholars very deliberately delineate the boundaries between sacred and profane contexts, but patterned bodily movement may occur as well during Sufi *dhikr* ceremonies, visits to saints' shrines, and local religious ceremonies that may blend Islamic and pre-Islamic syncretic elements. In many instances there is an overlap between Christian, Jewish, and Muslim celebratory practices, as these communities have lived side by side for many centuries and have imparted their individual artistic expression to other faith groups. The Fez Festival of World Sacred Music is a case in point. Created after the first Gulf War

A crowd gathers to dance the *freylekhs*, a traditional Jewish dance of celebration. © HULTON-DEUTSCH COLLECTION/CORBIS. REPRODUCED BY PERMISSION.

(1991), the festival featured music and arts from around the world in order to underscore the common features of shared traditions. Such world music festivals are sites of great innovation and provide impetus for the cultural preservation and reinvention of traditions.

Among the better-known forms of dance in the Middle East are the hora, the debka, and Israeli dance, which blend the cultural traditions of the various ethnic groups living in Israel. These dance traditions are done in groups and reinforce familial and community bonds rather than showcase an individual dancer's skill. The debka (also, dabka), is performed on joyous occasions in Greater Syria. Dancers (traditionally, young men) join hands in an open circle and move slowly in step to drumbeats. The steps become faster at specific intervals, with intermittent bounces. The dancers are usually accompanied by a single dancer waving a cloth or a stick. A modified version may be performed by a new husband and wife at their wedding celebration. Similar styles of dance occur in Turkey as well. The debka is originally an Arab dance, but Israelis have created many versions of it that are performed at Israeli national festivals.

Exotic belly dancers provide nighttime entertainment in an Istanbul hotel. © DAVID LEES/CORBIS. REPRODUCED BY PERMISSION.

Emigrants from the Middle East take their dance traditions with them, and many Middle Eastern dance groups exist outside the region. The origins of the Hora can be traced back to the Balkans, but it was brought to Palestine after World War I by Baruch Agadati, an actor of Romanian origin. Many Israeli composers have written music using the rhythm of the Hora. Because the Balkans were once Ottoman territories, similar forms of dance exist in many regions of Turkey. In Turkey, high-school students practice various folk-dance forms and perform in traditional costumes on a Youth Day, which was created by Mustafa Kemal Atatürk in the early days of the Turkish Republic. Turkey's preservation of pre-Ottoman Turkish culture spawned a national interest in folkloric dance genres that still thrives today. Jews moving to Palestine during the twentieth century brought with them a variety of folk dances of national and local origin, including the dances of Yemenite Jews and Hasidim, and the hora, which became Israel's national dance. Dancing, with a strong folk emphasis, is a popular recreation on kibbutzim in Israel.

Raqs Sharqi, or belly dancing, was made famous in the Middle East and beyond primarily through Egyptian television. There are many variations of belly dancing throughout the Middle East, but all share an emphasis on rythmically moving the stomach, pelvis, and hips. The range of movement depends on the individual dancer's ability, and can be done casually among friends or in entertainment settings with elaborate costumes and acrobatic flourishes.

See also MUSIC.

Bibliography

Kapchan, Deborah. *Gender on the Market: Moroccan Women and the Revoicing of Tradition.* Philadelphia: University of Pennsylvania Press, 1996.

Lynch, David. "Staging the Sacred in Morocco: The Fes Festival of World Sacred Music." Master's thesis, University of Texas at Austin, 2000.

Racy, Ali Jihad. *Music in the Genius of Arab Civilization,* 2d edition. Cambridge, MA: MIT Press, 1983.

Stokes, Martin. *The Arabesk Debate: Music and Musicians in Modern Turkey.* Oxford, U.K.: Clarendon Press, 1992.

Sugarman, Jane C. *Engendering Song: Singing and Subjectivity at Prespa Albanian Weddings.* Chicago: University of Chicago Press, 1997.

Van Nieuwkerk, Karin. *A Trade Like Any Other: Female Singers and Dancers in Egypt.* Austin: University of Texas Press, 1995.

MARIA F. CURTIS

DANESHVAR, SIMIN
[1921–]

Prominent Iranian fiction writer.

Simin Daneshvar was born in Shiraz. In the late 1930s she moved to Tehran to study at the then new Tehran University, from which she received a Ph.D. in Persian literature in 1949. Her collection of short stories, *Atash-e Khamush* (Quenched fire; 1948), was the first such publication by a woman in Iran. In 1950, she married Jalal Al-e Ahmad (1923–1969). She spent two academic years (1952–1954) as a Fulbright scholar at Stanford University in the United States. Upon returning to Iran, she was hired as a lecturer by the Archaeology Department of Tehran University and taught there for twenty-five years. However, she never received tenure because the government considered both her and her husband too critical of conditions under the rule of Mohammad Reza Shah Pahlavi.

Daneshvar's most famous work is *Savushun* (Mourners of Siyavosh), which was published in 1969, the first novel by an Iranian woman; it subsequently was translated into English. Throughout the 1970s, 1980s, and 1990s, she continued to write short stories and novels. In addition, her Persian translations of major American and European novelists have contributed to the corpus of works available in Persian literature.

See also AL-E AHMAD, JALAL; PAHLAVI, MOHAMMAD REZA.

Bibliography

Daneshvar, Simin. *Daneshvar's Playhouse: A Collection of Stories*, translated by Maryam Mafi. Washington, DC: Mage, 1989.

Daneshvar, Simin. *Savushun: A Novel about Modern Iran*, translated by M. R. Ghanoonparvar. Washington, DC: Mage, 1990.

MICHAEL C. HILLMAN
UPDATED BY ERIC HOOGLUND

DAR AL-DAʿWA WA AL-IRSHAD

Shaykh Rashid Rida opened this Institute of Propaganda and Guidance in Cairo, Egypt, in 1912 as a reformist Islamic school.

As a youth in Tripoli (now in Lebanon), Rashid Rida had seen American missionaries use a bookshop to proselytize, and his master, Muhammad Abduh, had commented similarly on a Capuchin monastery-school in Sicily. Egypt's higher state schools ignored Islam, and Abduh was unable to reform the mosque-university of al-Azhar. When he died in 1905, Abduh was trying to found his own reformist Islamic school.

Rida's efforts to found such a school in Constantinople (now Istanbul) in 1909 fell through. The Cairo Dar al-Daʿwa offered free room, board, and tuition to Muslims aged twenty to twenty-five, with preference to students from distant lands. Three years of study were to qualify one as a guide (*murshid*) fit to preach and teach among Muslims; six years were to qualify one as a missionary (*daʿi*) to non-Muslims. Although World War I closed the school, its example was presumably not lost on Rida's later admirers among the Muslim Brotherhood.

See also ABDUH, MUHAMMAD; RIDA, RASHID.

Bibliography

Adams, Charles C. *Islam and Modernism in Egypt: A Study of the Modern Reform Movement Inaugurated by Muhammad ʿAbduh.* New York: Russell and Russell, 1968. Reprint of 1933 edition.

DONALD MALCOLM REID

DAR AL-FONUN

One of the first secular institutions of higher education, established on the European model, in Iran.

The Dar al-Fonun (Abode of Arts) was founded in 1851 in Tehran, Iran, by Mirza Taqi Khan Amir Kabir, one of the chief reform-minded ministers of the long-ruling Qajar dynasty king Naser al-Din Shah.

As elsewhere in the Middle East, the establishment of the school was stimulated by the desire to import European science and technology, especially military technology, and to train army officers and civil servants. Dar al-Fonun's teachers were usually Europeans. Its first cadre included seven Austrians who were hired to give military training in the cavalry, infantry, and artillery divisions, and courses in engineering, medicine, pharmaceuticals, agriculture, and mineralogy, as well as foreign languages. The first efforts at translation of Western books into Persian as well as the publication of the first Persian textbooks is also associated with the Dar al-Fonun. The students of the Dar al-Fonun were usually sons of the aristocracy, some of whom, upon graduation, were sent to Europe to pursue further education, and who came to assume important positions later in their careers.

See also AMIR KABIR, MIRZA TAQI KHAN; NASER AL-DIN SHAH.

Bibliography

Keddie, Nikki R. *Roots of Revolution: An Interpretive History of Modern Iran.* New Haven, CT: Yale University Press, 1981.

PARVANEH POURSHARIATI

DAR AL-ISLAM

An abode, country, territory, or land where Islamic sovereignty prevails.

In Dar al-Islam, the citizenry abide by the ordinances, rules, edicts, and assembly of Islam. The Muslim state guarantees the safety of life, property, and religious status (only if the religion is not idolatrous) of minorities (*ahl al-dhimma*) provided they have submitted to Muslim control.

Dar al-Harb (the abode of war) provides the contrast to Dar al-Islam. *Shariʿa* (Islamic) law divides the world into these two abodes. Dar al-Harb denotes territory that is not governed by the assembly of Islam, and is directly contiguous to the abode of Islam. Warfare (jihad) can be invoked in order to convert the abode of war into the abode of Islam, or to rescue the bordering abode. Theoretically, an abode of war can extend ad infinitum. Muslim states, in order to avoid conditions requiring constant jihad, yield to the decision of legal experts (*ulama*), who, based on certain criteria, accept or reject the notion that an area has converted from, or needs to be reconfigured into, Dar al-Islam. These are as follows: (1) the edicts of unbelievers have gained ascendancy; (2) unprotected Muslims and peoples of the book must be rescued; (3) territorial proximity to unbelievers has become repugnant.

Of the above conditions, the first is probably the most important since even if a single edict of Islam is observed, a territory cannot be deemed Dar al-Harb. Further, jihad can be invoked for the sole purpose of turning Dar al-Harb into Dar al-Islam—in other words, to allow for the prevalence of Islamic edicts and the protection of Muslims.

CYRUS MOSHAVER

DAR AL-KUTUB AL-MISRIYYA

The Egyptian national library.

The Dar al-Kutub al-Misriyya library was founded in 1870 in Cairo as the Khedivial Library by Ali Mubarak, Khedive Ismaʿil's minister of education. German orientalists directed the library until World War I, when Egyptians took over. In 1904, along with the Museum of Arab Art, "the Dar" was installed in a neo-Islamic-style building. The Dar was

moved again in the 1970s to new quarters on the Nile in Bulaq. President Husni Mubarak's wife Suzanne made a personal commitment to expanding literacy and reading, promoting the opening of numerous additional libraries throughout the country.

Bibliography

Crabbs, Jack A., Jr. *The Writing of History in Nineteenth-Century Egypt: A Study in National Transformation.* Cairo: American University in Cairo Press, 1984.

DONALD MALCOLM REID

DAR AL-MOʿALLAMIN

Teacher-training school in Afghanistan.

The first Dar al-Moʿallamin (House of teachers) teacher-training school was established in Kabul in 1914 by Amir Habibollah (1901–1909), who sought to bring the secular European pedagogy and curriculum to Afghanistan. Initially, students received three years of instruction after having had six years of primary-school education, but the system was changed during the reign of King Amanollah (1919–1929) so that students enter the Dar al-Moʿallamin after nine years of primary school.

Dar al-Moʿallamins were established in other major provincial centers of Afghanistan and by 1970 there were fourteen institutions teaching more than 5,000 students annually. Because most of the Dar al-Moʿallamins were boarding schools, they have played an important part in educating rural youth sent to provincial centers to be educated. They have also served a political function in Afghanistan because public-school teachers form an important segment of the Afghan intelligentsia and have been an influential political force. Dar al-Moʿallamin students participated in the student demonstrations during the late 1970s. As a result, the Dar al-Moʿallamins were closed for some time. During the chaos of the fighting of 1980s and the Taliban rule of the 1990s the students and the teachers of the Dar al-Moʿallamins fled or were unable to teach, and the Dar al-Moʿallamins ceased to function, as did all of Afghanistan's educational system. Although teacher training is again a high priority for the Afghan government, the old Dar al-Moʿallamin system has been largely abandoned and teacher training has been taken over by the University of Kabul School of Education.

Bibliography

Adamec, Ludwig W. *Historical Dictionary of Afghanistan*, 2d edition. Lanham, MD: Scarecrow Press, 1997.

GRANT FARR

DAR AL-ULUM

Teacher-training school in Egypt.

Khedive Isma'il Pasha and Minister of Education Ali Mubarak opened Dar al-Ulum in 1871 to train teachers of Arabic for Egypt's new state schools. Its mixed curriculum included both the religious subjects of Islam taught at al-Azhar and "modern" subjects such as history, geography, and mathematics. A college of Cairo University since 1946, Dar al-Ulum in 2003 had 108 faculty and nearly 9,000 students.

See also AZHAR, AL-; CAIRO UNIVERSITY.

Bibliography

Aroian, Lois A. *The Nationalization of Arabic and Islamic Education in Egypt: Dar al-Ulum and al-Azhar.* New York: American University in Cairo, 1983.

DONALD MALCOLM REID

D'ARCY CONCESSION (1901)

Oil concession granted by the Iran to British national D'Arcy in 1901.

William Knox D'Arcy (1849–1917) was a successful British entrepreneur who in 1901 obtained from the government of Iran a sixty-year concession to search for and produce petroleum in an area of central and southern Iran covering 480,000 square miles. In return, the Iranian government received 20,000 British pounds in cash, paid-up shares of an equal value, and a promise of 16 percent of the annual net profits. In 1905, after failing to find oil and having spent most of his capital, D'Arcy assigned his concession rights to Burma Oil, in return for 170,000 barrels of petroleum. Oil was discovered in commercial quantity at Masjed-e Soleyman in 1908, and Burma was reincorporated the following year as the Anglo-Persian Oil Company (APOC, later, the Anglo-Iranian Oil Company, then British Petroleum). In 1914, the British navy decided to convert its ships from the use of coal to oil as fuel, and in tandem the British government became a majority shareholder in APOC. The concession subsequently proved highly profitable for Great Britain. Up to Iran's nationalization of the concession in 1951, APOC paid nearly $600 million in profits and $700 million in corporate taxes to the British government; the Iranian government received a total of $310 million in royalties.

See also PETROLEUM, OIL, AND NATURAL GAS; PETROLEUM RESERVES AND PRODUCTION.

Bibliography

Ferrier, Ronald W. *The History of the British Petroleum Company*, Vol. 1: *The Developing Years, 1901–1932.* New York; Cambridge, U.K.: Cambridge University Press, 1982.

DANIEL E. SPECTOR
UPDATED BY ERIC HOOGLUND

DARDANELLES, TREATY OF THE (1809)

Officially known as "The Treaty of Peace, Commerce, and Secret Alliance: Great Britain and the Ottoman Empire, 5 January 1809," with ratifications exchanged in Istanbul on 27 July 1809.

The Treaty of the Dardanelles grew out of the international rivalries surrounding the Napoleonic wars. The one constant rivalry during this period was that between Great Britain and France. The other European powers sided with one or the other as their military fortunes ebbed and flowed. Until 1805, Russia and France were allies. After Russia joined the Third Coalition against Napoléon, France endeavored to involve the Ottoman Empire in a war with Russia as a distraction. This war began in 1806 and lasted until 1812. Now allied with Russia, Britain sent a naval expedition against Istanbul in 1807; although Britain was able to force its way through the Dardanelles, the Ottomans pushed them back with a loss of two ships. Britain also occupied Alexandria but was forced to withdraw. Except for Britain, France was able to defeat the Third Coalition powers, and in 1807 Russia once more allied with France while continuing its war against the Ottomans. This set the stage for a change in British relations with the Ottomans, now fighting an ally of their perpetual enemy, France.

Sir Robert Adair led the British negotiations with the Sublime Porte that led to the 1809 treaty. The treaty contained eleven articles to which were appended four "separate and secret articles" and one "additional and secret article." The basic articles addressed the recent war between the two powers. They provided for an end to hostilities between Great Britain and the Ottomans with the exchange of prisoners; restoration of any Ottoman fortresses in British possession; mutual restoration of the property of British and Ottoman citizens seized by either side during the war; continuation of the 1675 Treaty of Capitulations; mutual good treatment of the merchants of both countries; an Ottoman tariff set at 3 percent; customary honors to the ambassadors of each nation on the same basis as all other ambassadors; appointment of consuls to facilitate trade; British agreement not to appoint Ottoman subjects as consuls nor to grant patents of protection to Ottoman subjects; and recognition of Ottoman authority to prohibit ships of war passing through the straits in time of peace. This latter was of special significance as it marked Britain as the first European power to recognize this Ottoman prerogative. General recognition of this did not, however, occur until 1841.

The "separate and secret articles" dealt primarily with France and Russia. Britain pledged to support the Ottomans should France declare war on them, including sending a fleet to the Mediterranean for that purpose. Britain also agreed to provide military supplies if France threatened the Ottomans short of declaring war. Regarding Russia, Britain offered to help secure a peace with Russia should this be possible before the Ottomans were able to end their war. This part of the treaty also included a provision for adjudication of the claims of both parties surrounding the British invasion and retreat from Alexandria.

The "additional and secret article" promised 300,000 pounds sterling to the Ottomans as a confirmation of friendship. Although Britain ratified this article, it was not to be presented for exchange unless France began a war with the Ottomans, which never took place.

In addition to ending the war between Britain and the Ottomans, recognizing the right of the Ottomans to close the straits, creating an alliance against France, and reconfirming the capitulations, the treaty is of particular interest because of its language. Normally, treaties are drawn in the language of the parties negotiating them. Because the Ottomans had a limited knowledge of English, however, they insisted that the treaty be drawn in Turkish and French, with which they were much more comfortable. This was a matter of some discussion in the foreign office, but the Ottoman position prevailed.

See also BONAPARTE, NAPOLÉON; SUBLIME PORTE.

Bibliography

Adair, Robert. *The Negotiations for the Peace of the Dardanelles, in 1808–9: With Dispatches and Official Documents.* 2 vols. London: Longman, Brown, Green, and Longmans, 1845.

Hurewitz, J. C., ed. *Diplomacy in the Near and Middle East: A Documentary Record, 1535–1914.* New York: Octagon Books, 1972.

DANIEL E. SPECTOR

DARÜLFÜNÜN

The Darülfünün (Imperial Ottoman University) was the first institution of higher learning in the Middle East modeled along Western lines.

As a prominent symbol of the Tanzimat reforms, the Darülfünün the was the frequent victim of the Ottoman Empire's domestic politics in early years and suffered repeated closures. Its creation was first proposed in 1846 by Mustafa Reşid Paşa, but the school did not actually open until 1870, and then only for one year. On the impetus of the minister of education, Ahmet Cevdet Paşa, it was open again between 1874 and 1881. Then it remained closed until opening permanently in the fall of 1900, largely because of the efforts of a leading Ottoman politician, Mehmet Küçük Sait Paşa. Its curriculum included law, mathematics, chemistry, biology, philosophy, and the humanities, as well as courses on the Qur'an, the *hadith* (traditions of Muhammad), and other aspects of Islam. In 1933, the Darülfünün was renamed Istanbul University, and it remains one of the preeminent universities in the Middle East.

See also CEVDET, AHMET; ISTANBUL UNIVERSITY; MUSTAFA REŞID; TANZIMAT.

Bibliography

Lewis, Bernard. *The Emergence of Modern Turkey*, 3d edition. New York: Oxford University Press, 2002.

Shaw, Stanford, and Shaw, Ezel Kural. *History of the Ottoman Empire and Modern Turkey.* 2 vols. Cambridge, U.K., and New York: Cambridge University Press, 1976–1977.

ZACHARY KARABELL

DARWAZA, MUHAMMAD IZZAT

[1889–1975]

Palestinian politician and historian.

Muhammad Izzat Darwaza, born in Nablus, was an Ottoman bureaucrat in Palestine and Lebanon. He was a major figure in several Arab nationalist organizations, including al-Fatat, during the waning years of the Ottoman Empire, and helped organize the first Arab Congress (Paris, 1913). A pan-Arab nationalist who believed in the unity of Greater Syria after the Ottoman defeat and the establishment of the British and French mandates, Darwaza was also concerned with resisting Zionism.

During the British Mandate in Palestine, Darwaza became a leading figure in the Istiqlal (Independence) Party, a pan-Arab nationalist party reestablished in Palestine in 1932. When the Palestine Arab Revolt that began in 1936 flared up in 1937, Darwaza coordinated guerrilla activities from Damascus for the Arab Higher Committee.

He was a member of the reconstituted Arab Higher Committee for one year in 1947, then retired from active politics to write on Arab, Islamic, and Palestinian history.

See also ARAB HIGHER COMMITTEE (PALESTINE); FATAT, AL-; ISTIQLAL PARTY: PALESTINE; PALESTINE ARAB REVOLT (1936–1939).

Bibliography

Khalidi, Rashid. *Palestinian Identity: The Construction of Modern National Consciousness.* New York: Columbia University Press, 1997.

Khalidi, Rashid, ed. *The Origins of Arab Nationalism.* New York: Columbia University Press, 1991.

Kimmerling, Baruch, and Migdal, Joel. *The Palestinian People: A History.* Cambridge, MA: Harvard University Press, 2003.

Porath, Yehoshua. *The Emergence of the Palestinian-Arab National Movement, 1918–1929.* London: Cass, 1974.

MICHAEL R. FISCHBACH

DARWISH, ISHAQ

[1896–1974]

Palestinian politician.

The nephew of Jerusalem mufti Amin al-Husayni, Muhammad Ishaq Darwish was born in Jerusalem. He went to Beirut for his higher education, and was a soldier in the Ottoman army during World War I. Darwish's long career in politics began after the war, when he joined the Arab Club and supported pan-Arabism and the regime of King Faisal I in Damascus, Syria. With Faisal's fall, however, Darwish turned toward Palestine-centered nationalism and in the early 1920s became the first secretary of the Palestine-wide Muslim–Christian Association, headquartered in Jerusalem. He joined the Palestine Arab party after it was founded in 1923, and was one of the founders of the Istiqlal Party in 1932. Through most of these years, Darwish was an aide to his uncle, the mufti. In 1947, he was elected to the Fourth Arab Higher Committee, which that year staged a protest strike and boycotted UNSCOP, the UN committee researching plans for the partition for Palestine. Darwish lived with his uncle in Lebanon and London, England, briefly in the 1960s and returned to Jerusalem before his death.

See also FAISAL I IBN HUSSEIN; HUSAYNI FAMILY, AL-; HUSAYNI, MUHAMMAD AMIN AL-; ISTIQLAL PARTY: PALESTINE; PAN-ARABISM.

Bibliography

Muslih, Muhammad Y. *The Origins of Palestinian Nationalism.* New York: Columbia University Press, 1988.

Porath, Yehoshua. *The Emergence of the Palestinian-Arab National Movement, 1918–1929.* London: Frank Cass, 1974.

ELIZABETH THOMPSON

DARWISH, MAHMUD

[1942–]

Palestinian poet.

Mahmud Darwish, recognized since the mid-1960s as the leading national poet of the Palestinian people, was born to a peasant family in al-Birwa, east of

Mahmud Darwish, one of the most acclaimed poets of the Arab world, wrote of the lives of his fellow Palestinians under Israeli rule. In the 1960s, as Darwish's popularity began to spread, the Israeli military placed him under house arrest on several occasions. © ROBERT H. TAYLOR, UNIVERSITY OF OKLAHOMA. REPRODUCED BY PERMISSION.

Acre. The village was destroyed by Israeli troops in 1948, causing Darwish's family to flee to Lebanon, the first of the poet's many displacements. Darwish returned to his homeland two years later, under the care of an uncle, but it was too late to be included in the census of Palestinians who had stayed through the war.

Darwish became a refugee, a "present-absent alien," and the peculiar status of Palestinians under Israeli dominion became the subject of many of his early poems, including "Identity Card," perhaps his most famous. Darwish began to recite his poetry at festivals and rallies, exciting the interest of the Israeli military. Between 1961 and 1969, Darwish was imprisoned several times, but he continued to write, publishing his first collection of poems, *Leaves of Olive,* in 1964. He also published articles for *al-Ittihad* and

al-Jadid, periodicals of the Arab faction of the Israeli Communist Party (RAKAH).

In 1967 four of Darwish's poems were published in Yusuf al-Khal's prestigious literary magazine, *al-Sh'ir,* marking the first time many critics in the Arab world had read poetry written by Palestinians living under Israeli rule. This new genre of writing—which borrowed its strident, self-affirmative tone from Palestinian poets such as Ibrahim Tuqan and Abd al-Rahim Mahmud—was dubbed "resistance poetry," and Darwish became its best-known practitioner. By the end of the decade, translations of his poetry were reaching international audiences, and in 1969 the Afro-Asian Writer's Union awarded him its Lotus Prize.

After a year in Moscow, where he studied political economy, Darwish moved to Cairo and wrote for *al-Ahram.* Two years later, in 1973, Darwish settled in Beirut and became editor of *Shu'un Filistiniyya,* a journal of the Palestine Research Center. In 1981 he founded the internationalist literary journal *al-Karmil,* which he continues to edit. After Israel's siege of Beirut in 1982, Darwish was evacuated with the Palestinian forces. From a new exile, in Paris, he wrote weekly columns for *al-Yawm al-Sabi* as well as several new volumes of poems. In 1986 he published his prose memoir of the days of siege in *al-Karmil,* and the text was later published as a book, *Memory for Forgetfulness.* Darwish's memoir is a modernist blend of diary, literary criticism, political commentary, and visionary narrative; it is one of the most singular and ambitious works of modern Arabic prose.

Darwish joined the Palestine Liberation Organization (PLO) in 1973 and became a member of its executive committee in 1987. In 1993, after the government of Israel and the PLO signed the Declaration of Principles, Darwish resigned from his position and distanced himself from the newly created Palestinian Authority. In 1996 he moved to Ramallah.

Darwish's early poetry is characterized by its uncompromising postures, political directness, and, at times, a sloganlike simplicity. His later work shows much greater range. In poems like "Intensive Care Unit," a personal intimacy balances the heroism; and Darwish has become more adept in his handling of history and myth, especially in the poems of *Mural*

(2000), his twentieth volume. Throughout his oeuvre, the trope of writing has a privileged place in Darwish's thinking about the existential situation of the Palestinian people. Writing is at once an insufficient weapon in the battle for national self-determination, as well as a necessary tool for recording the history of that battle; it is a concrete mark, and an erasable trace. As Darwish promises in "We Date Our Days with the Butterflies": "We will write our names to reveal their roots east of our bodies. / We will write what the bird writes in the open spaces, and forget the signatures of our feet."

Bibliography

Boullata, Issa J., trans. and ed. *Modern Arab Poets, 1950–1975.* Washington, DC: Three Continents Press; London: Heinemann, 1976.

Darwish, Mahmud. *The Adam of Two Edens: Selected Poems,* edited by Munir Akash and Daniel Moore. Syracuse, NY: Syracuse University Press, 2000.

Darwish, Mahmud. *Memory for Forgetfulness: August, Beirut, 1982,* translated by Ibrahim Muhawi. Berkeley: University of California Press, 1995.

Darwish, Mahmud. *Unfortunately, It Was Paradise: Selected Poems,* edited and translated by Munir Akash and Carolyn Forché. Berkeley: University of California Press, 2003.

Jayyusi, Salma Khadra, ed. *Anthology of Modern Palestinian Literature.* New York: Columbia Univeristy Press, 1992.

Udhari, Abdullah al-, trans. *Victims of a Map: Mahmud Darwish, Samih al-Qasim, Adonis.* London: Al Saqi Books, 1984.

KAMAL BOULLATTA
UPDATED BY ROBYN CRESWELL

DARWISH, SAYYID

[1892–1923]

Egyptian composer and singer.

During his short life, Sayyid Darwish composed thirty musical plays and dozens of other songs, including light strophic tunes, virtuosic love songs, and religious songs. His work drew upon the language, songs, and images of working-class Egypt. He took Arabic song in a new direction by laying the foundation for Egyptian populist musical expression that endured throughout the twentieth century and has been heard echoing in the compositions of

Zakariyya Ahmad and Sayyid Makkawi. As a consequence, he remains a dominating figure in Egyptian cultural life.

He was born in Alexandria and around 1917 moved to Cairo, where he composed for the theatrical troupes of George Abyad, Ali al-Kassar, Munira al-Mahdiyya, the Ukkasha Brothers, and Najib al-Rihani, often in collaboration with his friend, the poet Badi Khayri. Together they helped develop a colloquial comic theater based on indigenous language, music, and characters. Sayyid Darwish infused his compositions with the anti-imperialist political sentiments of his day and with pride in an Egyptian heritage. He and his music expressed sentiments widely shared by the Egyptian people at the time of the Revolution of 1919, and they remain identified with attitudes of popular resistance to the present day.

Among Sayyid Darwish's best-known works are "al-Ashara al-Tayyiba," a play mocking Turkish governance written by Muhammad Taymur, and songs such as "Zuruni Kull Sana Marra" (Visit me once every year). His "Biladi, Biladi" (My country), with a text derived from a speech by nationalist leader Mustafa Kamil and an arrangement by lyricist Yunis al-Qadi, was adopted as the Egyptian national anthem in 1977.

See also KAMIL, MUSTAFA.

VIRGINIA DANIELSON

DASHNAK PARTY

Translated as the Armenian Revolutionary Federation (ARF), the Dashnak Party sought to improve the lives of Armenians in the Ottoman Empire, eventually embracing Armenian nationalism.

The Dashnak Party was founded in 1890 by Armenians in Tbilisi, Georgia, then part of the Russian empire. The initial focus of its attention was western Armenia or so-called Turkish Armenia, the sector of historic Armenia in the Ottoman Empire. In the early twentieth century, it also began to organize seriously in eastern Armenia in the Russian empire, as well as in Armenian communities across Russia, Turkey, and Iran. Between 1918 and 1920, during the period of the independent Republic of Armenia, its activities were centered in the new country. After Sovietization, the ARF moved abroad, first fleeing to Iran and eventually settling in Beirut, Lebanon, from where it guided Armenian political life in the Middle East until the Lebanese civil war began in 1975.

The ARF was organized to gather and coordinate the efforts of numerous small groups of Armenians in the Caucasus region involved in revolutionary activity. Bringing together a literate elite, local activists, and peasant guerrillas into a single party was probably its principal ideological achievement. With its leadership schooled in the Russian educational system and its revolutionary, nationalist, populist, and socialist ideas, the ARF articulated the goals of these numerous strands of Armenian society into coherent collective national objectives.

Relieving the plight of the Armenians in the Ottoman provinces as its primary objective, the ARF concentrated on organizing, educating, and arming the population in the countryside to resist the arbitrary rule of Ottoman administrators. Eventually it resolved to assassinate Sultan Abdülhamit II, who was held responsible for a series of brutal massacres in the 1890s. The overthrow of the sultan by the Young Turks and the restoration of the Ottoman constitution in 1908 seemed to affirm that the struggle against the sultan's regime, despite the increased brutalization of the Armenian population by the army, police, and the Hamidiye corps, had been worth the price. The 1909 massacres of Armenians in Adana province soon reversed expectations and revived tensions.

Reluctant to divide its energy and its attention, initially the ARF had chosen to sidestep the problem of autocracy in the Russian Empire. Events leading up to the 1905 revolution, however, precipitated the decision to oppose the tsar also as a despotic ruler devising and implementing policies oppressive to the Armenians. Crossing that threshold proved decisive because the consequences of World War I compelled the ARF to reconsider its objectives. With the decimation of the Armenian population in the Ottoman Empire, the ARF goal of seeing a national home secured in the Armenian-inhabited eastern provinces of the Ottoman Empire was voided. The breakup of the tsarist empire in 1918 instead provided an opportunity to develop the former Russian province of Yerevan, which was de-

clared an independent republic, into the nucleus of an Armenian state. ARF members virtually ran the entire government of the Armenian republic. This close association had its drawbacks for the Armenian state in that Western powers were unsympathetic to a government run by a party whose platform advocated socialism. Conversely, its nationalist program made it a foe of Bolshevism and hence subjected it to the enmity of the Soviet regime. Banished from Soviet Armenia in 1920, the ARF assumed the mantle of a nationalist government-in-exile. When it reorganized in the diaspora, the ARF completely lost its Russian-Armenian character as it found a new basis for its existence among the exile communities in the Middle East, mostly composed of the survivors of the former Armenian population of the Ottoman state.

Part of the success of the ARF is explained by the fact that from 1890 to 1920 it attracted a sizable contingent of the Armenian intellectual elite. Whether as party members, advocates, or supporters, they created a huge body of nationalist literature. The practice was started by its founders, Kristapor Mikayelian (1859–1905); Stepan Zorian (1867–1919), known as Rostom; and Simon Zavarian (1866–1913). The party organ, *Droshak* (Banner), was the leading journal of Armenian political thought. During the independent republic, many distinguished figures from Russian-Armenian society became associated with the ARF. Avetis Aharonian, famed as a writer, became president and traveled to Paris to negotiate with the Allies. Alexander Khatisian, one-time mayor of Tbilisi, became prime minister. Others who rose to prominence during this period, such as Simon Vratsian, Nigol Aghbalian, and Levon Shant, remained central figures in the Armenian diaspora and its endeavors to educate a new generation of Armenians in exile. The ARF also attracted numerous guerrilla leaders and frontline revolutionaries into its ranks. Papken Siuni led the capture of the Ottoman Bank in 1896 in Constantinople. Men like Andranik, Aram Manoogian, and Drastamard Kanayan, called Dro, led organized armed defense of Armenian communities and of the Armenian republic. In diaspora, the ARF has been less successful in finding the kind of charismatic leadership that once distinguished it as the leading Armenian political organization. From this standpoint, the evocation of past leadership has become an important feature sustaining the organization in diaspora communities.

From an organizational standpoint, the ARF bridged two major gulfs in late nineteenth- and early twentieth-century Armenian society: It created an alliance between Turkish Armenians and Russian Armenians, who had become divided by a boundary, and between the rural population and the urban population, who inhabited completely separate spaces as the Armenian bourgeoisie lived outside the Armenian heartland. To maintain a network that spanned so widely both socially and geographically, the ARF developed a highly decentralized organization that empowered regional bureaus with the privilege of devising policy.

Throughout its existence, the ARF has relied on direct financial support from Armenian society. With a large following and popular base, the organization has maintained a substantial infrastructure. Despite the destruction of innumerable Armenian communities, the ARF continuously maintained its operations and reorganized its network as Armenians migrated across the Middle East. Though based in urban Armenian communities and deriving support from the lower and middle classes, the ARF program addressed principally the condition of the Armenians in the Turkish provinces and of the agrarian population in general. Beyond equal treatment before the law and structural reform in the Ottoman government, the ARF placed great emphasis on improving the lot of Armenian farmers. An economic program therefore always formed a vital part of its doctrine. With many socialists among its ranks, the party as a whole was still slow to adopt socialism as the party platform despite its ideological currency in Russia. Ideas of the kind seemed remote from Armenian reality in the distant provinces of the Ottoman and Russian Empires. Consequently, despite its urban base, the ARF did not agitate as strongly among industrial workers, who tended to be drawn to social democratic groups, but rather concentrated on the program of national liberation.

Because Armenians constituted a subject minority unequipped to resolve its own problems, in the judgment of the ARF Armenian emancipation depended on the attention of the European powers. Their sympathetic influence was required to compel the reluctant Ottomans to introduce reforms. This policy remained controversial throughout the period as outside powers involved themselves with the Armenian question on their own timetable of interests and as the Ottoman government in its state of weakness looked upon the strategy with enormous suspicion. The persecution of Armenians in the Ottoman Empire during World War I, resulting in the Armenian Genocide, finally aligned the Western powers on the side of the Armenian republic. The Western failure to extend sufficient assistance to make a difference in preserving Armenian statehood, however, raised the question of whether the ARF had not misplaced its trust.

The ARF regards itself as a vanguard organization. In its early decades, its membership consisted of professional revolutionaries who published its papers, organized its cells, manufactured weapons, led guerrilla operations, and briefly ran a government. Its constituency has not been restricted to any class because it derived its strength from its popular nationalist program. The ARF constituency remains the larger segment of the Armenian diaspora though it no longer draws the same level of critical support from the professional class as it once did.

With its main political mission defused by 1920, the ARF devoted considerable attention to resurrecting Armenian communal life among the exile communities. The emergence of a new independent Republic of Armenia has posed special challenges to the organization, which for long sustained itself with the myth of national leadership. The rise in the 1980s of a major nationalist movement in Armenia independent of the ARF left the party somewhat stranded. These problems combined with earlier difficulties when its principal base was destroyed by the civil war in Lebanon. The largest and most dynamic diaspora community in the Middle East had provided the ARF a secure home in the post–World War II decades. Even so, with the independence of Armenia in 1991 and the conflict over Nagorno Karabagh, the ARF redirected its attention toward supporting domestic change in Armenia and enlisting international support for the Armenian struggle for sovereignty and self-government.

See also ARMENIAN GENOCIDE; ARMENIAN REVOLUTIONARY MOVEMENT; HUNCHAK PARTY; OTTOMAN EMPIRE: OVERVIEW.

Bibliography

Adalian, Rouben P. *Historical Dictionary of Armenia.* Lanham, MD: Scarecrow Press, 2002.

Atamian, Sarkis. *The Armenian Community: The Historical Development of a Social and Ideological Conflict.* New York: Philosophical Library, 1955.

Hovannisian, Richard G. *The Republic of Armenia,* 4 vols. Berkeley: University of California Press, 1971–1996.

ROUBEN P. ADALIAN

DASHTI, ALI
[1896–1981]

An Iranian writer, member of parliament, and ambassador.

Born near Bushehr and trained in Muslim religious studies at Karbala, Iraq, Ali Dashti became a journalist upon his return to Iran in 1918. He established the paper *Shafaq-e Sorkh* (Red twilight) in 1922, and for several years the paper supported the policies of Reza Shah Pahlavi. After Dashti became disillusioned with and his paper critical of the shah in the late 1920s, he was taken to prison on several occasions. His first book, a collection of articles titled *Prison Days,* described his incarcerations. From 1928 to 1978 he spent many terms in the parliament, first as an elected deputy and from the mid-1950s as a senator appointed by the shah. During the 1940s, he was the leader of the Justice Party, a political group that opposed the Tudeh Party and supported a constitutional monarchy. In 1948, the shah named him Iranian ambassador to Egypt and Lebanon. In the 1950s, Dashti published several novels treating the plight of upper-class Iranian women. His book on Hāfez's poetry, the first of a series of important impressionistic critiques of major classical poets of Persian literature, appeared in 1957. *In Search of Omar Khayyam* (1971) typifies his literary, critical, and scholarly work. Dashti's Pahlavi-era political career led to his harassment and incarceration after the Iranian Revolution (1979). *Twenty-Three Years: A Study of the Prophetic Career of Mohammad,* published posthumously in 1985, illustrates his secular concerns about Islam in the modern world.

See also IRANIAN REVOLUTION (1979); LITERATURE: PERSIAN; PAHLAVI, REZA; TUDEH PARTY.

Bibliography

Knorzer, J. E., ed. *Ali Dashti's Prison Days: Life under Reza Shah.* Costa Mesa, CA: Mazda, 1994.

MICHAEL C. HILLMANN
UPDATED BY ERIC HOOGLUND

DATES

Throughout history, the date palm has satisfied the needs—from food to fuel to construction materials—of those who live in desert and tropical regions. Now, the importance of its cultivation is waning.

Since the dawn of recorded history, the date palm has been associated with the Middle East. It has featured prominently in the rituals of the religions of antiquity, Judaism, Christianity, and Islam. Perfectly suited to the climate of the region, the date palm can endure desert heat, withstand long periods of flooding, and tolerate high levels of salinity. In general, a plentiful supply of water together with prolonged periods of high temperatures are ideal for the growth of the tree and for the ripening of its fruit. An average tree will produce approximately fifty pounds of fruit each year. The date palm has been for the settled Arabs what the camel has been for the nomads, providing a commercial crop to exchange for imported necessities, material for construction, bedding, and an important source of fuel. Beneath its shade they can grow other fruit trees, vines, and aromatic plants, and beneath these cultivate vegetables, melons, and fodder crops. For many it provides a staple food, rich in calories and with appreciable amounts of vitamins. The fruit can be easily packed and transported, while the seeds are ground up and used as camel food.

Date-palm cultivation is labor intensive. Trees may be grown from seed but are usually grown from shoots, suckers, or buds. Soil preparation for date-palm cultivation involves a multistage process, and an elaborate system of irrigation requiring regular maintenance is essential. Because half of all trees grown from seeds are male and unproductive, sophisticated means of growing plants, relying most especially on artificial pollination, have been practiced from ancient times. Each tree requires special care and pruning for optimum yields. Harvesting of dates usually occurs in September and October but may begin as early as mid-August and continue until December, depending on the variety. In Iraq, the unique art of date cultivation has, since antiquity, been acknowledged legally by awarding to tenant cultivators hereditary property rights to the tree independent of the rights attached to the land on which it is grown. Contractual arrangements between cultivators and landowners vary according to differences in the inputs of skill and capital. Tenure practices and juristic ramifications associated with date cultivation are therefore complex.

Dates are most prolific in Iraq where there are 627 varieties. The groves along the Shatt al-Arab make up the largest single area of date cultivation, at one time covering over 100 square miles (260 sq km). Their harvest season long determined trade patterns in the Persian (Arabian) Gulf and much of the Indian Ocean. Until World War II, Iraq provided some 80 percent of the world's date crop, and dates constituted its largest export earnings. With the growth of the oil industry, the importance of dates in Iraq and elsewhere in the Middle East has declined. Greater oil earnings have reduced dependence on date palms for necessities, the attraction of other more remunerative and less arduous employments has depleted the pool of skilled cultivators, while the pollution associated with oil and modernization generally has had a detrimental effect on date palms.

See also SHATT AL-ARAB.

Bibliography

Dowson, V. H. W. "The Date and the Arab." *Journal of the Royal Central Asian Society* 36 (1949): 34–41.

Lennie, A. B. "Agriculture in Mesopotamia in Ancient and Modern Times." *Scottish Geographical Magazine* 52 (1936): 33–46.

ALBERTINE JWAIDEH

DAUD, MUHAMMAD
[1909–1978]

President of Afghanistan, 1973–1978.

Muhammad Daud, who earned the nickname of Sardar-i Diwana (the crazy prince) because of his hot temper and ruthlessness, was born in Kabul. His father, Sardar (Prince) Mohammad Aziz Khan, was a half brother of King Mohammad Nadir Barakzai (1929–1933), the founder of the Musahiban ruling dynasty of the Mohammadzai clan, of the Barakzai

family of the Pashtuns (or Pakhtun) who dominated national politics in Afghanistan since the early 1800s. Daud attended Habibia and Amania schools in Kabul before continuing his education in France from 1921 to 1930. He returned to Kabul and after a one-year course at the Infantry Officers School, was appointed a major general and commanding officer of the armed forces in Mashriqi province, eastern Afghanistan (1932–1935). In 1933, Daud's uncle, King Nadir Shah, and his father, the Afghan envoy in Berlin, were assassinated separately as a result of political and family feuds. Nadir Shah's son, Mohammad Zahir, assumed the Afghan throne, and in 1934 Daud married the sister of Zahir Shah. Between 1935 and 1953, Daud rose from governor and general commanding officer in the western provinces to minister of defense and interior.

Daud was prime minister from 1953 to 1963. An ardent secular nationalist, Daud made strong military and economic progress his top priority. Initially denied assistance by the United States and the West, he turned to the Soviets. With their help he created a mechanized military force and adopted an *etatist* (state socialist) economic policy that concentrated on transportation and communication infrastructures and the expansion of education. Exploiting Pushtun nationalism, Daud pursued an aggressive territorial claim (for Pushtunistan) against Pakistan, which resulted in greater trade and with economic and military dependence on the Soviet Union. An alleged rift within the royal household over this issue culminated in Daud's resignation as prime minister in March 1963. He spent the next decade in retirement, unhappy with the constitutional developments in 1964 that curtailed participation of royal family members in government and political processes. Assisted by a group of junior military officers active in the pro-Soviet Parcham (Banner) Communist party, Daud returned to power on 17 July 1973 and proclaimed himself president of the Republic of Afghanistan, thus ending the monarchy.

Shortly thereafter, Daud consolidated power by relying on his old networks and persecuting his perceived enemies, among whom were members of the Islamist political movements. Toward the end of his rule, he appeared to distance himself from his old ally, the Soviet Union, in favor of closer ties with Iran and the Gulf States, while striving to improve relations with Pakistan. In spite of these attempts, his presidency proved to be a period of confusion, contradictions, and indecision. In the end, Daud met his death at the hands of pro-Soviet Afghan communists, whom he had protected and nurtured during the previous decades.

In retrospect, some remember him as a patriot who single-handedly sought, but failed, to bring about progress and economic development in Afghanistan. Although intelligent, he was also a stubborn dictator and was ill informed about Soviet thinking and long-term goals in the region. Thus, he allowed himself to be used as a conduit for communism and Soviet influence, which led to ongoing strife.

See also BARAKZAI DYNASTY; NADIR BARAKZAI, MOHAMMAD; PARCHAM; ZAHIR SHAH.

Bibliography

Arnold, Anthony. *Afghanistan: The Soviet Invasion in Perspective*, revised edition. Stanford, CA: Hoover Institution Press, 1985.

Dupree, Louis. *Afghanistan.* Oxford and New York: Oxford University Press, 1997.

M. NAZIF SHAHRANI

DA'UD PASHA

[1812–1872]

Ottoman official in Lebanon.

Da'ud Pasha was born in Constantinople (now Istanbul; some sources say in 1816 and others say in 1818) to an Armenian Catholic family. He received his education at a French school and then attended a French college in Vienna, where he earned a law degree. He then entered the foreign service, and his first post was in Berlin. He wrote a book on Western jurisprudence and was known as a doctor of law. Da'ud Pasha also served as consul general in Vienna and later was director of publications and then director of post and telegraphic services in Constantinople. His French education brought him close to French circles in Constantinople. He was the first *mutasarrif* in Lebanon after the 1861 *mutasarrifiyya* order was designed for Lebanon by the Great Powers and the Ottoman Empire.

Before he began his mission in Lebanon, Da'ud Pasha was promoted to the rank of minister, thus becoming the highest-ranking Christian working for the Ottoman government. He improved tax collection in Lebanon and established public schools. He also founded a school for the Druze, in an attempt to appease that community after the end of the Druze–Maronite armed conflict. His mission was abruptly ended in 1868 after he became embroiled in the politics of Lebanon and tried to expand the area of "Lebanon." He then held various administrative positions in Constantinople. He died in Switzerland.

AS'AD ABUKHALIL

DAVAR

See NEWSPAPERS AND PRINT MEDIA: ISRAEL

DA'WA AL-ISLAMIYYA, AL-

Iraqi Shi'ite political party, whose name means Call to Islam.

Al-Da'wa al-Islamiyya was formed by Shi'ite clerical figures in the 1960s to combat secularist tendencies among the Iraqi elites. It operated underground, since religious expression was suppressed by the secular socialist Ba'th Party, which came to power in 1968, attempted to control the national religious life and internal structure of the Shi'ite clergy. Members of the clergy, including Ayatullah Muhammad Baqir al-Sadr and Ayatullah Muhsin Hakim, backed or helped in the creation of the party, which organized antigovernment demonstrations on behalf of the deprived Shi'ite population of southern Iraq in the early 1970s. With the Shi'ite clergy in power in Iran after the revolution of 1979, the party became more politically active and received funding and backing from Iran. This led to heavy persecution and mass imprisonment and executions by Saddam Hussein's government. In turn, the Da'wa Party launched attempts to assassinate government officials. In 1985, various Shi'ite parties, including the Da'wa Party, formed in Tehran the Supreme Assembly for the Islamic Revolution in Iraq. But the Da'wa Party was weakened by the counter-efforts of the Iraqi government to court the Shi'ite masses with economic and religious concessions, and by the Iraqi Shi'a's lack of identification with their Iranian coreligionists.

After the 1991 Gulf War, the Daʿwa Party led a rebellion against the government of Saddam Hussein, but it was ruthlessly crushed. Party members established a London branch, which joined the coalition of Iraqi opposition groups aligning themselves with the United States. After the U.S. invasion of Iraq in 2003, the Daʿwa Party was revived within Iraq, but political differences seem to have surfaced between the London branch and the Iraqi branch regarding the U.S. occupation of Iraq. The party cooperated with the U.S. forces and its leader, Abd al-Zahra Uthman Muhammad (editor of several newspapers and magazines), joined the Iraqi Governing Council appointed in July 2003 by Paul Bremer, the official leader of the U.S. civil administration of Iraq.

Although the party is supported by Ayatullah Kazim al-Haʾiri, many within it look to the guidance of other ayatollahs as well, including the powerful Grand Ayatollah Ali al-Sistani. Despite their differences, the various branches seem to be united in their desire to swiftly end the U.S. occupation, and in creating an Islamic state in Iraq, though not necessarily along the Iranian lines of clergy domination.

See also Baʿth, al-; Hussein, Saddam; Shiʿism; War in Iraq (2003).

Bibliography

Batatu, Hanna. "Shiʿism Organization in Iraq: Al-Daʿwah al Islamiyya and al Mujahidin." In *Shiʿism and Social Protest,* edited by Juan Cole and Nikki Keddie. New Haven, CT: Yale University Press, 1986.

Wiley, Joyce N. *The Islamic Movement of Iraqi Shiʿas.* Boulder, CO: Lynne Rienner, 1992.

Maysam J. al-Faruqi

DAWASIR TRIBE

See Tribes and Tribalism: Dawasir Tribe

DAYAN, MOSHE

[1915–1981]

Israeli military leader and politician.

Moshe Dayan was born at Kibbutz Degania in the Jordan valley. His family left in 1920 to join the founders of Nahalal, the first *moshav* (cooperative settlement) in the Jezreel valley, where Dayan was educated at an agricultural school. During the Arab revolt, Dayan served in a Jewish patrol unit (*notrim*) of Britain's mandatory police in Palestine under the command of Captain Orde Wingate. As a member of Haganah—the defense force of the Jewish national institutions in Palestine—and a student of its officers' school, he was arrested in 1940 by the British. Released after fifteen months in jail, Dayan commanded an advance unit of the Haganah that was sent by the Allies into Syria, then controlled by Vichy France. It was here that he lost an eye in battle, and the black patch that he subsequently wore became his trademark. The injury put a temporary halt to Dayan's military career. In 1946, he received his first political assignment, representing the MAPAI (Labor) at the World Zionist Congress in Basel.

At the beginning of the Arab–Israel War of 1948, Dayan served as an officer for Arab affairs at Haganah headquarters. In May he was given his first combat position—organizing the defense of the kibbutzim on the Kinneret (Sea of Galilee) front. He next led a mobile commando regiment that captured the city of Lydda. In July 1948, Dayan was named commander of Jerusalem. In this position, he negotiated a cease-fire in the Jerusalem area and an armistice with Jordan. He and Reuven Shiloah drew up a draft of principles for a territorial agreement with King Abdullah of Jordan; it was not negotiated, however, because the king refused to be the only Arab ruler to sign a peace treaty with Israel.

Between 1949 and 1953, Dayan held several senior positions in Israel's army. Appointed chief of staff in December 1953, he reshaped Israel's army as a fighting force. The greatest achievement of the army under Dayan's direct command was the Sinai campaign of 1956, in which it took over the entire Sinai peninsula in a week. Dayan objected to Prime Minister David Ben-Gurion's decision to withdraw Israel's forces from all positions in Sinai in response to U.S. pressure and Soviet threats, and in return for Western guarantees of free passage in the Strait of Tiran and the placement of UN observers in Sharm al-Shaykh and Gaza. Dayan resigned from the army in January 1958. Following two years of study at the Hebrew University of Jerusalem, he was elected a MAPAI member of the Knesset and named minister of agriculture in Ben-Gurion's government

Moshe Dayan (1915–1981) had a distinctive military career, culminating in his election as chief of staff of the armed forces. In 1958, Dayan left the military to take up a career in politics. He played a role in negotiating the landmark Israeli-Egyptian peace treaty of 1979. © DAVID RUBINGER/CORBIS. REPRODUCED BY PERMISSION.

(1959). With Shimon Peres, Dayan became prominent in MAPAI's young leadership club, which aspired to democratize the party and take over its leadership. Although Ben-Gurion had encouraged their entry into politics and the government, his veteran associates, including Levi Eshkol and Golda Meir, felt threatened by the younger group and were alienated by its criticism of the party. Eshkol succeeded Ben-Gurion as prime minister in June 1963. In November 1964, Dayan resigned from the Eshkol government to protest what he described as the prime minister's lack of confidence in him.

Prior to the 1965 elections, Dayan joined Ben-Gurion's Rafi Party. His greatest political hour came in the Arab–Israel War of 1967. Criticism of Eshkol's hesitancy to react forcefully to Egypt's blocking the Strait of Tiran to Israel's shipping and its rapid military buildup in Sinai created pressure for Dayan's appointment as defense minister and the formation of a national unity government. Dayan led the army as a civilian. He was reluctant to occupy the Golan Heights but succumbed to pressure from the government. He also did not want Israel's forces to reach the Suez Canal but did not prevent it. After the war, Dayan was put in charge of the territories occupied by Israel—the Golan Heights, the West Bank, and the Gaza Strip. He promulgated the economic integration of the territories, Israeli settlement there, and the maintenance of open bridges over the Jordan River.

The 1967 war and its aftermath made Dayan a leading, though controversial, national political contender. In 1968, Rafi joined MAPAI to form the Labor Party. Dayan supported the merger but kept alive his option to run as an independent until the Arab–Israel War of 1973, which severely undermined his public support. The coordinated attack by Egypt and Syria, which caught Israel unprepared, shattered Dayan's leadership credibility and produced demands for his and Prime Minister Meir's resignations. The Labor party managed to win the next election (31 December 1973), though with decreased representation. Although a state commission of inquiry (the Agranat commission) found no personal negligence in the conduct of the war, criticism did not wane. A large segment of the public was not prepared to put all the blame for the army's lack of preparedness on military officers. Israel's advantageous military position at the end of the war, and the beginning of diplomatic negotiations, did not put an end to criticism.

Prime Minister Meir resigned on 18 January 1974, and Dayan refused to serve in the Labor government headed by Yitzhak Rabin. In the 1977 elections, Dayan ran on the Labor party's Knesset list; he had first negotiated with the Likud and had contemplated an independent run. Following Likud's electoral victory, its leader, Menachem Begin, invited Dayan to serve as foreign minister in his government. In this position, Dayan launched the secret talks with Egypt that eventually led to President Anwar al-Sadat's visit to Jerusalem, and he is largely credited with playing a major role in the

Camp David Accords between Israel and Egypt (1978), and the subsequent peace treaty with Egypt (1979). Nevertheless, he resigned from the Begin government on 23 October 1979, criticizing its handling of the talks with Egypt on the implementation of the Camp David autonomy plan for the Palestinians in the occupied territories. He believed that Israel should have negotiated more vigorously, unencumbered by internal political restraints. Subsequently, Dayan advocated unilateral implementation of the autonomy plan. Under this banner he ran as an independent in the 1981 elections, but his list (Telem) received meager support. He died soon afterward. An accomplished amateur archaeologist, Dayan also was a prolific writer.

See also ARAB–ISRAEL WAR (1948); ARAB–ISRAEL WAR (1967); ARAB–ISRAEL WAR (1973); BEN-GURION, DAVID; CAMP DAVID ACCORDS (1978); ISRAEL: POLITICAL PARTIES IN; MEIR, GOLDA; PERES, SHIMON.

Bibliography

Dayan, Moshe. *Breakthrough: A Personal Account of the Egypt–Israel Peace Negotiations*. New York: Knopf, 1981.

Dayan, Moshe. *Diary of the Sinai Campaign*. New York: Harper and Row, 1966.

Dayan, Moshe. *Living with the Bible*. New York: Morrow, 1978.

Dayan, Moshe. *Story of My Life*. New York: Morrow, 1976.

Slater, Robert. *Warrior Statesman: The Life of Moshe Dayan*. New York: St. Martin's, 1991.

Teveth, Shabtai. *Moshe Dayan: The Soldier, the Man, the Legend*, translated by Leah and David Zinder. Boston: Houghton Mifflin, 1973.

NATHAN YANAI

DAYAN, YAEL

[1939–]

Israeli writer and civil rights activist.

Yael (also Ya'el) Dayan was born in Afula to Moshe Dayan, who later became chief of staff of the Israel Defense Force (IDF) and defense and foreign minister, and Rahel (also Rachel) Dayan, a well-known social activist specializing in immigrant absorption. Yael studied international relations at the Hebrew University and biology at the Open University. She

served as an officer in the IDF Spokesman Unit and covered the June War of 1967 in that capacity. There she met her husband, General Dov Sion (1924–2003). In the 1980s, already a well-established author and commentator on public issues, she entered politics and was elected to the Knesset in 1992 as a Labor Party member. Her three terms in the Knesset were marked by intensive and outspoken attempts to promote the rights of minority groups, chief among them Israeli Arabs, gays, and lesbians. She was also active in Arab-Israeli peace causes and was involved in various efforts to intensify rapprochement between the two peoples after the signing of the September 1993 Oslo Accord. In the 2003 elections she was not included on the Labor party list and joined the Meretz Party list of candidates but was not reelected.

A prolific writer, she has written several novels and memoirs, some of which have been translated into English, including *New Face in the Mirror*, 1959, *Death Has Two Sons*, 1967, *Dust*, 1963, and *Envy the Frightened*, 1960 (fiction); and *A Soldier's Diary: Sinai 1967*, 1968, *Three Weeks in October*, 1979, and *My Father, His Daughter*, 1983 (nonfiction), as well as many articles and film scripts dealing with women's issues, peace, and social criticism.

See also DAYAN, MOSHE; GENDER: GENDER AND LAW; GENDER: GENDER AND POLITICS; ISRAEL: OVERVIEW; ISRAEL: POLITICAL PARTIES IN; OSLO ACCORD (1993).

MERON MEDZINI

DAYR AL-ZAWR PROVINCE

Province in eastern Syria on the Euphrates River named after its major town, Dayr al-Zawr.

The name Dayr al-Zawr means literally the convent of the grove where clusters of tamarisks grow alongside the river. Apparently, a convent was originally established there. The town of Dayr al-Zawr is located on the right bank of the Euphrates River 640 feet (195 m) above sea level. The river is crossed by a suspension bridge 1,476 feet (450 m) long, completed in 1931.

The province of Dayr al-Zawr (or al-Furat), according to official data, in 1982 included 29 villages and 261 farms spreading over 3 *qadas* (subprovinces) currently referred to as *mintaqas*: Dayr al-Zawr, Abu Kamal, and al-Mayadin. They are divided into 14 *nahiyas* (smaller administrative units).

The total population of the province in 2002 was 1,311,700, and of the town of Dayr al-Zawr, 216,200.

ABDUL-KARIM RAFEQ

DAYR YASIN

Palestinian village.

Dayr Yasin (Deir Yasin), 3 miles (5 km) on the outskirts of Jerusalem, was attacked by Jewish paramilitary units during the civil war between Palestinians and Jews in the period between announcement of the United Nations partition plan in November 1947 and proclamation of the state of Israel in May 1948. Although only one of a number of incidents in which Jewish forces attacked Palestinian civilians, the Dayr Yasin massacre became the most notorious and the longest remembered because of the unusually large number of deaths, Palestinian loss of the village, and the extent to which the reports of the massive loss of lives that circulated through the Palestinian community exacerbated fears that led to mass flight of Palestinians.

The attack on Dayr Yasin occurred on 9 April 1948, and was initiated by the Irgun Zvaʾi Leʾumi, or Etzel (National Military Organization), and Lohamei Herut Yisrael, or Lehi (Fighters for the Freedom of Israel), which was also known as the Stern Gang. Etzel, which was headed by Menachem Begin (who would later become Israel's prime minister), was a dissident faction of the Haganah, the quasi-official defense organization of the Palestinian Jewish community, or Yishuv. Although Dayr Yasin's residents had not been involved in any significant incident against the Yishuv, and had signed a nonaggression pact with the Haganah, the leaders of Etzel and Lehi justified their surprise attack by charging that the village had been a base for Palestinian guerrillas, an accusation that was not substantiated by the Haganah. During the attack about 105 men, women, and children were murdered, although a figure of 250 is often cited; many bodies were mutilated and thrown into a well. There was some armed resistance to the attack.

The leaders of the Yishuv, including David Ben-Gurion (who would later become Israel's first prime minister), strenuously denounced the attack and disclaimed any responsibility for it. However, there is credible evidence that the Haganah had been informed of the impending attack in advance and that a Haganah unit had provided covering fire for Etzel and Lehi. During the incident, residents of Dayr Yasin who were not slain were driven from the village, and most of it was destroyed. Later, the remains of the village were taken over and occupied by the Haganah.

Dayr Yasin symbolized the extent to which the struggle between Palestinian and Jewish communities in Palestine was becoming an all-out civil war with civilian casualties. It thus contributed to the panic that led to the collapse and mass flight of the Palestinian community.

See also BEGIN, MENACHEM; HAGANAH; IRGUN ZVAʾI LEʾUMI (IZL); LOHAMEI HERUT YISRAEL.

Bibliography

Begin, Menachem. *The Revolt: Story of the Irgun.* New York: Henry Schuman, 1951.

Khalidi, Walid. *From Haven to Conquest: Readings in Zionism and the Palestine Problem until 1948.* Beirut: Institute for Palestine Studies, 1971.

McGowan, Daniel, and Ellis, Marc H., eds. *Remembering Deir Yassin: The Future of Israel and Palestine.* Brooklyn, NY: Olive Branch Press, 1998.

Rogan, Eugene L., and Shlaim, Avi, eds. *The War for Palestine: Rewriting the History of 1948.* Cambridge, U.K.: Cambridge University Press, 2001.

DON PERETZ

DEAD SEA

Salt-water lake situated between Jordan, the West Bank, and Israel.

The Dead Sea (Arabic, Bahr al-Lut; ancient Greco-Romano, Lacus Asphaltites), the lowest surface point on the planet (the actual lowest point is under the ocean), is situated in the 350-mile-long (560 km) Jordan–Dead Sea rift valley, bordered by the Hashimite Kingdom of Jordan to its east, the

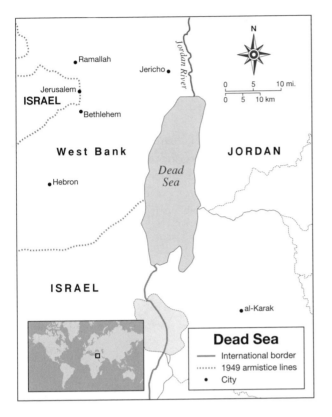

MAP BY XNR PRODUCTIONS, INC. THE GALE GROUP.

State of Israel to its southwest, and the West Bank to its northwest. The surface of the Dead Sea is 1,302 feet (397 m) below Mediterranean sea level, with an area of about 395 square miles (1,020 sq km). It is 51 miles (82 km) long.

This inland lake is the world's saltiest; its water contains about 25 percent solid concentrates, as compared to ocean concentrates of some 4 to 6 percent. The lake has no outlet and is fed from the north by waters of the Jordan River and *wadis* (streams that are usually dry but fill during the rainy season). In its middle, it is divided by the Lisan (tongue), which stretches across some 75 percent of the lake's width from Jordan toward Israel. Economically, the Dead Sea is important to the bordering regions, since each uses it for tourism—many visitors seek its purported medicinal properties and spas exist to allow such visits, especially in Israel. The land near its shores is also cultivated, with sweet irrigation water brought to those fields. From the Dead Sea's brine, both Jordan and Israel extract potash, an important component of agricultural fertilizer.

Bibliography

Davila, James R., ed. *The Dead Sea Scrolls as Background to Post-biblical Judaism and Early Christianity: Papers from an International Conference at St. Andrews in 2001.* Boston, MA: Brill, 2003.

Hodge, Stephen. *The Dead Sea Scrolls Rediscovered: An Updated Look at One of Archaeology's Greatest Mysteries.* Berkeley, CA: Seastone, 2003.

Let the Dead Sea Live; Concept Document: Moving towards a Dead Sea Basin Biosphere Reserve and World Heritage Listings. Prepared by Friends of the Earth Middle East Consultant Team: Mike Turner, Gaith Fariz, Husan Abu Faris FoEME Team: Sefan Hoermann, Gidon Bromberg, 1 November 1999.

Magness, Jodi. *The Archaeology of Qumran and the Dead Sea Scrolls.* Grand Rapids, MI: Eerdmans 2003.

PETER GUBSER

DEAD SEA SCROLLS

Ancient religious documents.

The Dead Sea Scrolls are ancient manuscripts found at Khirbat Qumran, in caves in the Judean desert near the Dead Sea, 7.5 miles (12 km) from Jericho. The scrolls were uncovered in 1947. Archaeologists later discovered a cemetery of over one thousand graves, a central building, and central caves containing fragments of old documents. The area was apparently destroyed by an earthquake in 31 B.C.E. and then rebuilt. The authors of the scrolls lived there until 68 C.E. The contents of the scrolls and other evidence show that the authors belonged to a Jewish sect. The scrolls or fragments include two complete copies of Isaiah and fragments of nearly every other book of the Bible. Their discovery advanced the study of the Hebrew Bible, since the earliest versions before the scrolls were discovered dated to the Middle Ages. Fragments of the Apocrypha and the Pseudepigrapha and other unknown books were also found, including the Book of Tobit, the Hebrew version of Jubilees, and the Aramaic version of the Book of Enoch. The scrolls include sectarian books as well, including a commentary on Habakkuk, parts of a commentary on Micah and Nahum, and others. These commentaries explain the prophetic writings in relation to the history of the sect. Other scrolls deal with the sect's organization and theological doctrines. They also contain fragments of the Zadokite documents that were found in Cairo. The Temple scroll minutely details the Temple. The sect responsible for the scrolls was assumed to have been the Essenes, but recent scholarship has placed this thesis in doubt. They beheld the power of good ruling in a world in opposition to the power of evil, and they saw themselves as the chosen "sons of light."

Their apocalyptic circles, among whom Enoch was composed, probably influenced the beginnings of Christianity, especially those close to Paul and John the Evangelist.

Some of the scrolls came into the possession of Hebrew University through E. L. Sukenik, who was responsible for the first publication of selections. Others went to the United States where they were published by Burrows, Brownlee and were subsequently purchased for the government of Israel through the agency of Sukenik's son, Yigael Yadin. They are housed in the Shrine of the Book in the Israel Museum. The publication of the many fragments was entrusted to a group of scholars whose slow progress generated international controversy. In 1991, the system was overhauled to ensure speedy publication. The Huntington Library in San Marino, California, in the interim, published photographs of the collection and made them available without restrictions.

See also YADIN, YIGAEL.

Bibliography

Charlesworth, James, ed. *The Dead Sea Scrolls: Hebrew, Aramaic, and Greek Texts with English Translations: Pseudepigraphic and Non-Masoretic Psalms and Prayers (Dead Sea Scrolls, No. 4, Part A).* Louisville, KY: Westminster/John Knox Press, 1998.

Davies, Philip R. *The Complete World of the Dead Sea Scrolls.* New York: Thames and Hudson, 2002.

Garcia, Florentíno Martínez, and Tigchelaar, Eibert, eds. *The Dead Sea Scrolls Study Edition.* Grand Rapids, MI: Eerdmans, 2000.

Reed, Stephen A. *The Dead Sea Scrolls Catalogue: Documents, Photographs and Museum Inventory Numbers.* Atlanta, GA: Scholars, 1994.

MIA BLOOM

DEBKA

See DANCE

DE BUNSEN, MAURICE
[1852–1932]

British diplomat.

Maurice De Bunsen entered the diplomatic service in 1877 and helped settle the dispute between France and Spain over Morocco in 1911 and 1912. In 1915, Prime Minister H. H. Asquith appointed him head of a committee to determine British wartime policy toward the Ottoman Empire in Asia. The resulting report of the De Bunsen committee established the foundation for British policy in the Middle East.

Bibliography

Hurewitz, J. C., trans. and ed. *The Middle East and North Africa in World Politics,* 2d edition. New Haven, CT: Yale University Press, 1975.

ZACHARY KARABELL

DECENTRALIZATION PARTY

Political party of the Ottoman Empire from 1912 to 1916.

The Ottoman Administrative Decentralization Party was founded in Egypt in December 1912 by Muslim and non-Muslim Syrian émigré intellectuals. Party leaders included Rafiq al-Azm (president), Iskandar Ammun (vice-president), Rashid Rida, and Muhibb al-Din al-Khatib. The party espoused a program of decentralization for the multiethnic and multireligious empire. But it formed branches only in Arab areas and lacked official status. Along with the empirewide Ottoman Liberty and Entente Party, it sought wider powers for provincial councils in education, financial affairs, religious foundations, and public works. It advocated local military service and two official languages in each region, Turkish and the local language. The party maintained close links with the reform societies that emerged in Arab cities in 1912 and 1913. Despite dissension in its ranks after the Arab Congress (June 1913), the party survived until World War I as the coordinator of Arab autonomist movements. The dominant Committee for Union and Progress implied that party members advocated separatism and pro-Western treason. Cemal Paşa sentenced prominent members to death in 1915 and 1916.

See also CEMAL PAŞA; COMMITTEE FOR UNION AND PROGRESS; RIDA, RASHID.

Bibliography

Duri, A. A. *The Historical Formation of the Arab Nation: A Study in Identity and Consciousness,* translated by Lawrence I. Conrad. London and New York: Croom Helm, 1987.

HASAN KAYALI

DECLARATION OF LA CELLE ST. CLOUD

Agreement by France to allow Morocco independence.

In August 1953, France deposed the Moroccan sultan, Sidi Muhammad bin Yusuf. Until then, the Moroccan opposition had been divided, but the exile of the monarch united the country. A wave of strikes, violence, and disturbances swept the country, accompanied by demands for the sultan's return and the immediate independence of Morocco. The French government of Prime Minister Pierre Mendès-France finally recognized that Morocco would not be pacified, except at a cost far greater than the French were willing to pay. In October 1955, the exiled sultan went to France, and the Declaration of La Celle St. Cloud was issued by the French foreign minister, Antoine Pinay, on November 6. Under its terms, France agreed to grant Morocco independence in accord with the principle of Franco–Moroccan interdependence. This concept raised some concern in Morocco about the sincerity of the French, but in March 1956, the promise enshrined in the declaration became fact, with the former sultan becoming King Muhammad V, ruler of the new state.

See also MUHAMMAD V.

Bibliography

Mansfield, Peter. *The Arabs,* 3d edition. New York: Penguin, 1985.

ZACHARY KARABELL

DEDE ZEKAI

[1825–1899]

Ottoman Turkish composer.

Dede Zekai, also known as Hoca Zekai Dede Efendi and Mehmet Zekai Dede, was born in the Eyub dis-

trict of Istanbul. His father was a teacher and imam of the local mosque. As a child, he was schooled in singing, calligraphy, and memorization of the Qur'an; his music teachers included Hammamzade Ismail Dede and Dellalzade İsmail. At the age of thirteen, he went to Egypt where he was a court musician in Cairo. He acquired the title "dede" after studying Sufism, and the title "hoca" for teaching music at the Darüşşafaka. Among his students were Subhi Ezgi, Rauf Yekta Bey, and Ahmet Rasim. Over 260 of his compositions survive today. Half of these are religious compositions; the other half were composed in the *beste, ağir semai, yürük semai,* and *şarki* genres. Fifty-five of his pieces are melodies, and 182 of his compositions were published in a four-volume collection.

See also AHMET RASIM; DELLALZADE İSMAIL.

DAVID WALDNER

DEEDES, WYNDHAM

[1883–1956]

British colonial official in the Middle East.

After serving in World War I, the British Brigadier General Sir Wyndham Henry Deedes was posted to Istanbul as a military attaché and to Cairo, then a British protectorate, as public security director. From 1920 to 1922 he served as chief secretary to British High Commissioner Sir Herbert Samuel in Palestine, then under British mandate. Although known for his pro-Zionist sympathies, Deedes played a role in promoting the Supreme Muslim Council as an Arab counterweight to the Jewish Agency.

See also JEWISH AGENCY FOR PALESTINE; SAMUEL, HERBERT LOUIS; SUPREME MUSLIM COUNCIL.

Bibliography

Ingrams, Doreen. *Palestine Papers 1917–1922: Seeds of Conflict.* London: J. Murray, 1972.

Porath, Yehoshua. *The Emergence of the Palestinian-Arab National Movement, 1918–1929.* London: Cass, 1974.

Wasserstein, Bernard. *The British in Palestine: The Mandatory Government and Arab–Jewish Conflict, 1917–1929.* Oxford, U.K., and Cambridge, MA: B. Blackwell, 1991.

ELIZABETH THOMPSON

DE GAULLE, CHARLES
[1890–1970]

President of France, 1958 to 1969; instrumental in ending French colonialism in the Middle East and North Africa.

Charles de Gaulle, one of republican France's great statesmen, earned his place in French history by the spirited exercise of leadership in the face of national adversity—first when he placed himself at the head of the Free French movement in 1940 to meet the challenges of the German occupation in World War II, and again when he took the lead in reshaping French political institutions in 1958 to meet the challenges of the Algerian war of independence, European integration, and the cold war. Faced, in both periods, with the contradiction of ensuring France's well-being in Europe and sustaining a precarious hold on remnants of the French Empire, de Gaulle did not deviate from his primary objective for long. The relative ease, therefore, with which he could divest France of claims to empire helped pave the way for full independence in the Middle Eastern mandates of Lebanon and Syria by 1945 and for the decolonization of Algeria by 1962.

De Gaulle established this priority early in his military career when he reluctantly deferred his passionate interest in French defense strategies to complete a tour of duty in the Middle East from 1929 to 1931. While there, he hinted at the charismatic didacticism that was to become the hallmark of his speeches. This was when, overriding the contradictions that separated colonial administrators from the political aspirations of their subjects, he urged Lebanon's youth to build a progressive state with the help of France. Returning to the Middle East during World War II, after its liberation in 1941 by British and Free French forces, General de Gaulle was incensed when he saw how Britain, with tacit American backing, was exploiting French weaknesses to support the Lebanese and Syrian nationalist movements. Ultimately, however, he refrained from exerting what would have been a corrosive resistance to Allied demands for France's retreat from empire in the area.

When de Gaulle returned to power in 1958, he had to deal with the French army's repression of Algeria's nationalist struggle against a colonial social order. This morally and materially debilitating war also affected France's relations with neighboring Arab states as well as with the United States, Britain, and the international community. De Gaulle initially mapped out a progressive future for what was to be a felicitously integrated Franco–Algerian society. He concentrated, however, on turning the sometimes dangerously rebellious military around to building France up as a nuclear power independent of its erstwhile allies and able to lead with Germany in the development of the European community. With these priorities uppermost in his mind, de Gaulle agreed in 1962 to the nationalist demand for a fully independent Algeria, and France subsequently closed this chapter in the history of empire with the absorption of a massive flight of colonists from across the Mediterranean.

In the aftermath of the Algerian peace, de Gaulle favored a resolution with the Arab world to complement French links with Israel. In the last years before he resigned his presidency in 1969, he assumed France's heightened stature would justify the role of arbiter in the Arab–Israel conflict, but he failed to make allowances for the complexity of the problem and the greater involvement of the superpowers.

Bibliography

De Gaulle, Charles. *Memoirs of Hope: Renewal and Endeavor*, translated by Terence Kilmartin. New York: Simon and Schuster, 1971.

Lacouture, Jean. *Charles De Gaulle*. Vol. 1: *The Rebel, 1890–1944*, translated by Patrick O'Brian. Vol. 2: *The Ruler, 1945–1970*, translated by Alan Sheridan. New York: Norton, 1990–1992.

JOHN P. SPAGNOLO

DE HAAN, YA'AKOV YISRAEL
[1881–1924]

Dutch-born poet and journalist who was assassinated because of his anti-Zionist activities.

Ya'akov Yisrael de Haan was assassinated on 30 June 1924 near the Sha'are Tzedek Hospital in Jerusalem by two members of the Haganah. He joined the Mizrahi Zionist movement early in his career, but after moving to Palestine he eschewed Zionism, joined the Agudat Israel, and became the spokesman for the Ashkenazi Council. He wrote increasingly anti-Zionist articles and sent pro-Arab reports to the League of Nations and the British mandatory authorities. These activities made de Haan an enemy of the Yishuv leadership and led to his assassination.

See also AGUDAT ISRAEL; ASHKENAZIM; YISHUV; ZIONISM.

BRYAN DAVES

DEHKHODA, ALI AKBAR
[1880–1956]

A leading reformist voice during Iran's Constitutional Revolution, 1905–1911; lexicographer.

Ali Akbar Dehkhoda's journalistic and satirical prose—for example, in *Charand Parand* (Balderdash) and in *engagé* (politically concerned) verse (collected in his Divan)—influenced later writers of Persian literature.

During the Pahlavi era (1925–1941), like some other literary intellectuals, Dehkhoda left politics to work on academic projects. In the early 1940s, he returned as an administrator to his old secondary school, which had become the Faculty of Law at Tehran University. With the approval and support of Iran's parliament, in 1945 he began work on his Persian encyclopedic dictionary called *Loghat'nameh* (Book of words). Some twenty thousand pages later and years after his death, the work reached completion in 1980.

See also LITERATURE: PERSIAN.

Bibliography

Losensky, P. "Inshallah Gurbah Ast: God Willing, It's a Cat." *Iranian Studies* 19 (1986).

MICHAEL C. HILLMANN

DELLALZADE İSMAIL
[1797–1869]

Ottoman Turkish singer and composer.

Dellalzade İsmail, the son of a palace official, was born in the Fath district of Istanbul. Upon finishing primary school, his musical talents were noticed, and he became a student of the great Dede Zekai Efendi. At the age of nineteen, he joined the palace orchestra as a singer; later, he became the companion and chief prayer caller of Sultan Mahmud II. In 1846, Sultan Abdülmecit appointed him singing instructor in the newly established Academy of Music. Dellalzade is considered one of the musical geniuses of a period in which the flowering of Turkish classical music was met by the increasing popularity of Western music. He composed more than seventy pieces, including solemn folk tunes (*semai*) and ballads (*şarki*). Among his most well-known compositions are *Yegah Ağir Semai, Suznak Beste,* and *Şehnaz Şarki.*

See also ABDÜLMECIT I; DEDE ZEKAI; MAHMUD II.

DAVID WALDNER

DELOUVRIER, PAUL
[1914–1995]

Delegate general of the French government in Algeria in the 1950s technocrat.

Born in Remiremont, Vosges, in France, Paul Delouvrier was a financial specialist, a member of the French Underground in World War II, and an associate of Jean Monnet, who pioneered European economic integration. While serving in the European Coal and Steel Union, President Charles de Gaulle appointed Delouvrier delegate general to Algeria, a difficult position because of the ongoing Algerian War of Independence and France's complex internal politics. Delouvrier's chief task—where he had considerable success—was to supervise social and economic projects of the Constantine Plan (outlined by de Gaulle in in a speech in October 1958), which aimed to accelerate Algeria's development. Nevertheless, Delouvrier's authority disintegrated during this fitful period of decolonization, and he resigned in 1960. After his return to France, de Gaulle tapped him in 1961 as delegate general to rejuvenate Paris and its environs—a responsibility covering three departments. This was one of the great urban projects in modern French history. Delouvrier succeeded in creating satellite cities and in linking suburban rail systems with Paris's métro. He was prefect of the Paris region from 1966 to 1969. He headed France's electricity board from 1969 to 1979 and promoted its nuclearization. He served on the Conseil Economique et Social until he retired in 1984.

Bibliography

Horne, Alistair. *A Savage War of Peace: Algeria, 1954–1962*, 2d edition. New York: Viking, 1987.

Saxon, Wolfgang. "Paul Delouvrier, French Official in Paris and Algiers, Dies at 80." *New York Times*. 18 January 1995.

PHILLIP C. NAYLOR

DELTA

Often called Lower Egypt, the land between the mouths of the Nile.

The delta is a triangular area (shaped like the Greek letter Δ) that has been built up by the silt carried within the waters of the Nile River. When the Nile approaches the Mediterranean, much of the solid wastes and organic matter picked up during its long trip to the sea is screened out at the marshy estuaries and left behind to build more delta land. Although in ancient Egypt the Nile delta had seven mouths, today it has two—the Damietta on the east and Rosetta on the west—and many small channels. The broad coastal rim of the delta measures about 150 miles (240 km) from Alexandria in the west to Port Sa'id in the east. It is about 100 miles (160 km) from the Mediterranean coast south to Cairo, Egypt's capital.

The delta landscape is flat and mostly fertile, but the area nearest the coast is marshy, dominated by brackish inlets and lagoons. Since the construction of the Delta Barrages in the early nineteenth century, most of the farmland has been converted from basin to perennial irrigation, which supports two or three crops per year instead of one. Almost half the inhabitants are small landowners, sharecroppers, or peasants working for wages who live in villages surrounded by the lands they till. The others live in towns or cities. Fruits, vegetables, and cotton are the important delta crops. Delta Egyptians have generally had more contact with the outside world than have Upper Egyptians and are therefore more Westernized.

Bibliography

Metz, Helen Chapin, ed. *Egypt: A Country Study*, 5th edition. Washington, DC: U.S. Government Printing Office, 1991.

ARTHUR GOLDSCHMIDT

DELTA BARRAGES

A special type of dam on the Nile.

Delta Barrages are designed to regulate the upstream level but not the flow of water in the two distributary branches of the Nile, so that when the river is low, water can still flow into irrigation canals.

Construction of the original Rosetta and Damietta Barrages, 70 miles north of Cairo, Egypt, proposed by Linant de Bellefonds Pasha, a Belgian engineer in the employ of Muhammad Ali Pasha, viceroy of Egypt, was started in 1833 and completed in 1843. This ultimately permitted conversion of over 754,000 acres of the Nile delta from basin irrigation to perennial irrigation, lengthening the growing season and dramatically increasing agricultural output. Muhammad Ali originally proposed using stones from the nearby Giza pyramids as building material for the barrages, but was dissuaded by Linant, who argued that it would be too costly. Poorly constructed, the barrages were rebuilt during the British occupation. Additional barrages were subsequently constructed at Idfina (1915) and Zifta (1943) in the delta. Three major barrages were later built on the main Nile between Cairo and Aswan.

Bibliography

Hurst, Harold E. *The Nile: A General Account of the River and the Utilization of Its Waters.* London: Constable, 1952.

Nyrop, Richard F., ed. *Egypt: A Country Study,* 4th edition. Washington, DC: U.S. Government Printing Office, 1983.

Waterbury, John. *Egypt: Burdens of the Past, Options for the Future.* Bloomington: Indiana University Press, 1978.

DAVID WALDNER
UPDATED BY GREGORY B. BAECHER

DE MENASCE FAMILY

Sephardic family who arrived in Egypt during the eighteenth century, via Palestine and Morocco.

The leading member of the family in the nineteenth century was Jacob De Menasce (1807–1887), who began his career in Cairo as a money changer (*sarraf*) and banker and gradually emerged as the private banker of the Khedive Isma'il. He was one of the earliest entrepreneurs in Egypt to recognize the opportunities offered by European trade and, with

Jacob Cattaoui, opened the banking and trading establishment of J. L. Menasce et Fils with branches in England, France, and Turkey. In 1872 and 1873, De Menasce was granted Austro-Hungarian protection and subsequently was given the title of baron by the Austro-Hungarian Empire, along with Hungarian citizenship. In 1871, he moved to Alexandria, the new and permanent seat of the family. His son, Béhor Levi, continued in the family's financial enterprises, but his grandson, Baron Jacques Béhor De Menasce (1850–1916), deserted the banking profession in favor of the cotton and sugar businesses. In 1890, Jacques served as the president of Alexandria's Jewish community and remained in that capacity for about twenty-five years. His younger brother Félix Béhor (1865–1943) became concerned with Zionism and was a personal friend of Dr. Chaim Weizmann, then president of the World Zionist Organization. In September 1921, Félix represented the Egyptian Zionist organization in Carlsbad at the twelfth World Zionist Congress; in later years he served as Alexandria's Jewish community president. The De Menasce family was not merely wealthy. It was European-educated and Western-oriented and led the Alexandria community from the early 1870s into the 1930s.

See also WEIZMANN, CHAIM; WORLD ZIONIST ORGANIZATION (WZO).

Bibliography

Krämer, Gudrun. *The Jews in Modern Egypt: 1914–1952.* Seattle: University of Washington Press, 1989.

Landau, Jacob M. *Jews in Nineteenth-Century Egypt.* New York: New York University Press, 1969.

Mizrahi, Maurice. "The Role of Jews in Economic Development." In *The Jews of Egypt: A Mediterranean Society in Modern Times,* edited by Shimon Shamir. Boulder, CO: Westview, 1987.

MICHAEL M. LASKIER

DEMETRIUS II

[?–1870]

111th Coptic patriarch of Egypt, 1862–1870.

Because Khedive Sa'id Pasha had likely ordered the murder of Demetrius II's predecessor, Cyril IV (for his pursuit of closer associations with foreign churches without the viceroy's approval), Demetrius

adopted a modest domestic agenda. His sometimes obsequious loyalty to the khedive guaranteed that his tenure was trouble-free but undistinguished. He continued Cyril's support of education for the clergy but had little of his interest in church reform, which was eagerly sought by the progressive laity, specifically in matters of finance and land management. As a result, the Coptic populace's long-held mistrust of the conservative clergy, having been suspended during Cyril's enlightened tenure, was renewed in intensity and has flared intermittently to the present. After Demetrius's death, the patriarchate went empty for almost five years.

See also COPTS; CYRIL IV.

Bibliography

Atiya, Aziz S. *A History of Eastern Christianity,* revised edition. Millwood, NY: Kraus Reprint, 1980.

DONALD SPANEL

DEMIREL, SÜLEYMAN

[1924–]

The Republic of Turkey's ninth president.

Born in Islamköy, Isparta, Süleyman Demirel graduated from the Department of Civil Engineering of Istanbul Technical University in 1949, after which he was employed at the Istanbul Administration of Electricity. In 1954, he went to the United States as an Eisenhower Fellow to conduct research on dam construction, irrigation, and electrification. Upon his return, he was appointed general director of the State Irrigation Administration, where he supervised the construction a series of dams. From 1962 through 1964, he taught hydro-engineering at Middle East Technical University.

Demirel joined the Justice Party (JP) in 1962 and was elected chairperson upon the sudden death of its founder in 1964. In the general elections of October 1965, the JP won 248 seats in the National Assembly and Demirel became Turkey's twenty-ninth prime minister. In the next general elections, in October 1969, the JP gained 46.53 percent of the vote and 256 seats, retaining its predominant position in the parliament. Nevertheless, Demirel's new cabinet failed to resolve the problems posed by the radical student movements, and he was forced by the military to resign in March 1971.

Turkish president Süleyman Demirel votes in the 1999 local and general elections. Two nationalist parties received the most votes, guaranteeing a continuance of a three-party government, but afterwards there were many reports of irregularities and abuses in the election process. © AFP/CORBIS. REPRODUCED BY PERMISSION.

In 1974, Demirel formed the first National Front government with several rightist parties. In 1977, hyperinflation and escalating civil strife resulted in an early general election. Having won 213 parliamentary seats, the Republican People's Party formed a minority government under the leadership of Bülent Ecevit. When Ecevit's cabinet resigned after ten months, Demirel once again became prime minister of a coalition government with the National Salvation Party and the National Action Party. The new cabinet remained in power for only six months and resigned after failing to obtain a vote of confidence in December 1978. Two years later, Demirel formed his third National Front government with the National Salvation Party and the National Action Party. However, growing domestic violence, ethnic clashes, economic bottlenecks, and the parliament's inability to elect a president paved the way for another military intervention on 12 September 1980. Demirel was taken for his

"personal safety" to Hamzaköy and was deprived of his political rights for the following ten years.

In the early 1980s, Demirel was placed under house arrest by the ruling military junta and sent to Zincirbozan for four months. During the 1986 general elections he supported the True Path Party (DYP) and after his political ban was lifted in 1987 he became its chairperson. In the elections of 1991, the DYP won a parliamentary plurality (178 out of 450 seats) and Demirel formed Turkey's first rightist/leftist coalition government with the Social Democratic Populist Party. Upon the sudden death of President Turgut Ozal on 17 April 1993, Demirel was elected ninth president of the Republic and resigned from his post in the DYP.

Demirel served the full seven-year presidential term. He believed that the head of state should foster effective coordination among the public institutions, including the military, state organizations, the government, and the parliament, and therefore achieve "the smooth functioning of the state" with minimum interference on his/her part. Demirel never hesitated to use his presidential powers toward this objective. For instance, on the occasion of his meeting with the members of the opposition within the DYP, he asserted that he was trying to establish the stability of the political system. The stability of political parties, including the DYP, would, for him, contribute to the stability of the system as a whole.

Demirel left the office on 16 May 2000, when the National Assembly rejected a constitutional amendment that would have allowed him to serve a second term. He later joined the international Mitchell Committee on the Middle Eastern peace process and did not return to active involvement in Turkish politics.

See also ECEVIT, BÜLENT; JUSTICE PARTY; MIDDLE EAST TECHNICAL UNIVERSITY; SOCIAL DEMOCRATIC POPULIST PARTY; TRUE PATH PARTY.

Bibliography

Arat, Yeşim. "Demirel: National Will and Beyond." In *Political Leaders and Democracy in Turkey,* edited by Metin Heper and Sabri Sayari. Lanham, MD: Lexington Books, 2002.

Heper, Metin, and Menderes, Çinar. "Parliamentary Government with a Strong President: The Post-1989 Turkish Experience." *Political Science Quarterly* III, no. 3 (1996): 483–503.

Lombardi, Ben. "Turkey: Return of the Reluctant Generals?" *Political Science Quarterly* 112, no. 2 (1997): 191–215.

Sherwood, W.B. "The Rise of the Justice Party in Turkey." *World Politics* 20, no. 1 (1977): 54–65.

NERMIN ABADAN-UNAT
UPDATED BY BURÇAK KESKIN-KOZAT

DEMOCRATIC ORGANIZATION OF AFGHAN WOMEN (1965)

A Marxist-oriented political group active between 1965 and 1992.

The Democratic Organization of Afghan Women (DOAW) was founded in 1965 as a component of the People's Democratic Party of Afghanistan (PDPA) by Anahita Ratebzad, who served as its first president. After the PDPA seized power in the military coup of April 1978, DOAW became an important organization in the Democratic Republic of Afghanistan (DRA). Ratebzad announced that the DOAW's primary objective was to fight against feudalism and Western imperialism in defense of the objectives of the "Saur (April 1978) Revolution." In 1979 President Taraki (1978–1979) changed the name of the organization to the Khalq (People's) Organization of Afghan Women (KOAW). In 1980 the organization retook its original name and started a monthly journal, *Zanan-i-Afghanistan* (Women of Afghanistan), to publicize its objectives. It also expanded its activities in the provinces and launched a literacy campaign to make education available to women of all ages and to inform them of the objectives of the Saur Revolution. In 1981 the DOAW claimed nineteen district and seven municipal committees and 209 primary organizations whose main function was to attract women to the organization in support of revolution. When Najibullah came to power in 1986 he eliminated all Marxist rhetoric in an effort to lessen growing opposition to the PDPA regime. In line with this policy, the organization's name was changed from *Sazman-i-Democratic-i-Zanan-i-Afghanistan* (Democratic Organization of Afghan Women) to *Shura-i-Sarasari-Zanan-i-Afghanistan* (All Afghanistan Women's Council), and Ratebzad was replaced by Firuza Wardak as president of the organization.

See also AFGHANISTAN: OVERVIEW; AFGHANISTAN: SOVIET INTERVENTION IN; ARAB SOCIALISM; GENDER: GENDER AND THE LAW.

Bibliography

Moghadam, Valentine M. *Modernizing Women: Gender and Social Change in the Middle East.* Boulder, CO: Lynne Rienner Publishers, 1993.

SENZIL NAWID

DEMOCRATIC PARTY OF AZERBAIJAN

Political party that supported autonomy for Iranian Azerbaijan.

The Democratic Party of Azerbaijan (DPA) was created in September 1945 in Tabriz (Iranian Azerbaijan) under the leadership of Ja'far Pishevari. He and other DPA leaders were Azerbaijani Turks of middle-class or landowning origin. Earlier, many had been involved in communist movements (Gilan or Khiyabani revolts, 1920); some had lived or been educated in Soviet Azerbaijan or Moscow. DPA, however, was an independent organization established to secure autonomy for Azerbaijan within Iran. The local branch of the communist Tudeh Party dissolved itself and joined DPA.

Reacting against the brutal policies of economic neglect and Persianization by Reza Shah Pahlavi's dynasty, a DPA-led All Peoples Grand National Assembly (in Tabriz, November 1945, just after World War II) declared rights to national self-determination within sovereign Iran, to retain a just share of their tax revenues, and to use Azerbaijani Turkish (called Türki) as the official language of an autonomous province of Azerbaijan. Elections in December produced an all-DPA *majles* (parliament); Pishevari formed a government that enfranchised women, began land reform, and established Azerbaijani Turkish as the official language.

The autonomy movement had the support of the occupying Soviet troops, which prevented the forces of Mohammad Reza Shah Pahlavi from entering the province to suppress it. Western observers interpreted the DPA, therefore, as a Soviet puppet. In June 1946, after Soviet forces were withdrawn, Tabriz and Iran signed an agreement that fulfilled most DPA demands. In December 1946, however, Iranian forces entered Azerbaijan and suppressed the DPA government and autonomy movement, so the June agreement was abrogated. Pishevari fled to Baku and died there the following year after mysterious complications from an automobile accident.

See also AZERBAIJAN; PAHLAVI, MOHAMMAD REZA; PAHLAVI, REZA; TUDEH PARTY; TURKISH LANGUAGE.

Bibliography

Abrahamian, Ervand. *Iran between Two Revolutions.* Princeton, NJ: Princeton University Press, 1982.

Emami-Yeganeh, Jody. "Iran vs. Azerbaijan (1945–46): Divorce, Separation or Reconciliation?" In *Central Asian Survey.* Oxford: Oxford Microform Publications, 1984.

Fatemi, Faramarz S. *The USSR in Iran: The Background History of Russian and Anglo–American Conflict in Iran, Its Effects on Iranian Nationalism and the Fall of the Shah.* South Brunswick, NJ: A.S. Barnes, 1980.

Swietochowski, Tadeusz. *Russia and Azerbaijan: A Borderland in Transition.* New York: Columbia University Press, 1995.

AUDREY L. ALTSTADT

DEMOCRATIC PARTY OF KURDISTAN (IRAN; KDP)

Political party that organized 1945–1946 revolt to form an autonomous republic for Kurds in Iran.

The Democratic Party of Kurdistan, Iran (KDP), was formed in 1945 by Kurdish nationalists in Mahabad, a predominently Kurdish town in West Azerbaijan province, a region that came under Soviet military occupation following the joint Anglo-Soviet invasion of Iran in 1941. While declaring its desire to remain within Iran, the party demanded the use of the Kurdish language in state schools and government offices in Kurdish areas; the retention of tax revenues for the benefit of the region; and the establishment of provincial assemblies as upheld by the constitution. The party claimed for Kurds a "distinct national identity" based on language, history, and culture. Finding the government unresponsive to its demands, the party, with the help of local tribes, launched a revolt and declared the formation of the independent Republic of Kurdistan in December 1945. The Soviet army did not oppose

the move, nor a similar effort by Azerbaijan Turks in the provincial capital at Tabriz. In fact, Soviet occupation forces prevented the central government in Tehran from suppressing the revolts during the first half of 1946. Nevertheless, under the central government's Royal Army attack, the Mahabad government fell in December 1946.

During the revolutionary upheavals of 1979 Kurdish intellectuals from the Kurdish Democratic Party formed councils (*shuras*) that held local power in conjunction with the leading cleric in Mahabad, Shaykh Ezz al-Din Hosseini, and his followers. They also boycotted the referendum on the country's new constitution. The party and its activities have been suppressed since 1980. On 13 July 1989 Abdul Rahman Ghassemlou, secretary-general of KDP, and two other high-ranking party members were assassinated in Vienna, Austria. Ghassemlou's successor, Sadegh Sharafkandi, met with a similar fate on 17 September 1992 in Berlin.

See also AZERBAIJAN CRISIS; KURDS.

Bibliography

Eagleton, William. *The Kurdish Republic of 1946.* New York; London, U.K.: 1963.

Entessar, Nader. *Kurdish Ethnonationalism.* Boulder, CO: Lynne Rienner, 1992.

PARVANEH POURSHARIATI

DEMOCRATIC PARTY OF KURDISTAN (IRAQ)

Political party advocating the autonomy of the Iraqi Kurds.

The Kurdistan Democratic Party (KDP) was founded on 16 August 1946 at the suggestion of Mullah Mustafa Barzani, who was then in the Kurdish republic of Mahabad. Its creation sanctioned the split of the national movement of the Kurds into different, sometimes opposing, Iranian and Iraqi organizations.

In the absence of Barzani, who went into exile in the Soviet Union, KDP became a progressive party, led by Kurdish intellectuals quite close to the Iraqi Communist Party. After he returned in 1958, the party was shaken by a severe crisis, opposing Barzani's acceptance to the political bureau, along with Ibrahim Ahmad and his son-in-law Jalal Talabani. KDP never fully recovered from these events of 1964 and became a mere instrument of Barzani.

After the collapse of the Kurdish movement in 1975 and discredited by Barzani's decision to stop the resistance, KDP lost the monopoly it had enjoyed for thirty years. Today, the KDP led by Mas'ud al-Barzani must share leadership of the movement in Iraq with its rival, Talabani's Patriotic Union of Kurdistan, and several smaller organizations.

See also BARZANI FAMILY; KURDS; PATRIOTIC UNION OF KURDISTAN (PUK); TALABANI, JALAL.

CHRIS KUTSCHERA

DEMOCRATIC WOMEN'S ASSOCIATION (TUNISIA)

Tunisian organization promoting women's rights.

Formally created in 1989, the Association Tunisienne des Femmes Démocrates (ATFD) is an autonomous activist women's organization dedicated to the elimination of all forms of discrimination against women, the transformation of patriarchal attitudes, the defense of women's acquired rights, and the participation of women in all aspects of political and civil rights. Based in Tunis, the ATFD is comprised of approximately 200 volunteer members, the majority of whom are educated and professional women in their thirties and forties. Like those involved in the broader human rights movement, both the organization and individual activists continue to face significant opposition to their activities.

On International Women's Day 1993, the ATFD opened the first domestic violence center in Tunisia, staffing both a listening center and a hotline. To provide women with a safe environment to discuss their situations, the ATFD center is dedicated to validation, confidentiality, resource referral, and empowerment. The ATFD also works with other Tunisian and international organizations, both governmental and nongovernmental, to increase awareness of domestic violence and provide services to a larger sector of the population. Finally, the ATFD works on improving the legal status of women and sponsoring educational campaigns dedicated to women's rights in Tunisia.

See also GENDER: GENDER AND THE LAW; HUMAN RIGHTS.

ANGEL M. FOSTER

DEMOCRAT PARTY

Turkish political party.

Four members of the Republican People's Party (RPP)—Celal Bayar, Adnan Menderes, Mehmet Fuat Köprülü, and Refik Koraltan—founded the Democrat Party (DP; Demokrat Parti) on 7 January 1946. The immediate impetus for the establishment of the party was to oppose an RPP-sponsored land reform bill. More generally, the DP founders criticized the government for being authoritarian and arbitrary, and for its extensive control of the economy. The DP campaigned on a platform of economic, political, and cultural liberalism.

The DP participated in the elections of 1946, which were held before the party had a chance to build a national organization or make known its candidates. The party gained only 64 out of 465 seats. Over the next four years, party leaders built a strong organization and attracted the support of many groups that had become alienated from the RPP over the previous decade and a half. In the 1950 elections, the DP received 53.3 percent of the popular vote and 86.2 percent of the seats in the Grand National Assembly. On 29 May 1950 the DP formed its first government as the new assembly elected Bayar as president, Menderes prime minister, and Köprülü foreign minister. In the 1954 elections, the DP increased its share of the vote to 56.6 percent, capturing 408 out of 503 assembly seats. In the 1957 general elections, held in the context of growing economic crisis, the DP still managed to garner 325 seats.

Despite encouraging the private sector, DP policies maintained wide latitude for state control over the economy, particularly through investments in the state manufacturing sector. Between 1950 and 1953, inflows of foreign aid and high prices for agricultural goods induced the DP government to encourage agricultural production and exports. A diverse array of policies increased peasant incomes, helping to cement DP popularity in the countryside. After 1953, a combination of declining world prices and a growing shortage of foreign exchange led the DP to implement trade policies that encouraged import-substituting industrialization. Despite growing investment and manufacturing output, large government deficits and the lack of coherent policy led to severe economic problems, and by 1958, the government was forced to impose austerity measures.

The DP pursued a staunchly pro-West foreign policy, joining the North Atlantic Treaty Organization in February 1952 and, on several occasions, siding with the West, even at the expense of creating tensions with its neighbors. Turkey's support for the Baghdad Pact, for example, prompted the Egyptian government to label Turkey a Western surrogate in the region.

As economic conditions deteriorated, the DP became increasingly authoritarian. A series of antidemocratic laws, designed to cripple the RPP while muzzling dissent in the press and in universities, alienated the liberal intelligentsia and the liberal wing within the party. In early 1960, to stifle growing opposition, the government passed some unconstitutional measures. When these measures only catalyzed further opposition, the government declared martial law. At this point, the DP paid the price for never having established harmonious relations with the military: The combination of economic crisis and increasing authoritarianism triggered a military coup that deposed the DP government on 27 May 1960. The leading members of the DP were subsequently placed on trial for treason. On 15 September 1961, fifteen of them were sentenced to death. Twelve of these sentences were commuted, but Menderes and two of his top ministers were executed.

See also BAGHDAD PACT (1955); BAYAR, CELAL; KOPRÜLÜ, MEHMET FUAT; MENDERES, ADNAN; NORTH ATLANTIC TREATY ORGANIZATION (NATO); REPUBLICAN PEOPLE'S PARTY (RPP); TURKISH GRAND NATIONAL ASSEMBLY.

Bibliography

Ahmad, Feroz. The Making of Modern Turkey. London and New York: Routledge, 1993.

Ahmad, Feroz. The Turkish Experiment in Democracy, 1950–1975. London: C. Hurst for the Royal Institute of National Affairs, 1977.

Saribay, Ali Yasar. "The Democratic Party." In Political Parties and Democracy in Turkey, edited by Metin Heper and Jacob M. Landau. London and New York: I.B. Tauris, 1991.

DAVID WALDNER

DENKTASH, RAUF
[1924–]

Turkish Cypriot statesman.

Rauf Denktash (also Denktaş) was born in Paphos, Cyprus, in 1924. His father was a judge. After graduating from the English school in Nicosia, he worked briefly as a columnist for Halkin Sesi (The people's voice), a Turkish Cypriot newspaper founded in 1940 by Dr. Fazil Küçük, the veteran leader of the Turkish Cypriot community. In 1944, Denktash went to study law in England, and in 1947, he was called to the bar.

Upon his return to Cyprus, which was then a British crown colony, Denktash became a barrister, serving from 1949 to 1957 as junior crown counsel, crown counsel, and acting solicitor general. During this time, he also embarked on a political career. He became Küçük's chief aide and served his community as a member of the Consultative Assembly (1948–1960) and as a member of the assembly's Turkish Affairs Committee. He was also elected president of the Federation of Turkish Cypriot Associations, a voluntary organization for the purpose of coordinating the social and economic life of the Turkish Cypriots and organizing their resistance to Greek Cypriot agitation for enosis (union of Cyprus with Greece).

In 1954, the efforts of the Greek Cypriot leaders, Archbishop Makarios III and Georgios Grivas, to achieve enosis and hellenize Cyprus culminated in a full-fledged guerrilla war against the British colonial administration and all those who opposed the Greek Cypriot aims. Denktash helped organize the Turkish resistance movement (TMT) to protect his community.

Küçük and Denktash represented the Turkish Cypriot community at the London Conference of 1959, which resulted in an agreement to establish an independent partnership state in Cyprus. Shortly thereafter, Denktash represented his community on the Constitutional Committee, which drafted a constitution for the new state, and at the Athens Conference, which specified how the Treaty of Alliance and the Treaty of Guarantee (which were to provide security for the new state) were to be implemented. Denktash, therefore, was one of the chief architects of the bicommunal Republic of Cyprus, which came into being in 1960. That year, Denktash was elected president of the Turkish Cypriot Communal Chamber.

In December 1963, Küçük (who had been elected vice president of Cyprus) and Denktash both opposed the proposal by Archbishop Makarios (who had been elected president of Cyprus) to amend the Constitution of 1960 on the grounds that the projected changes would pave the way for enosis. As a consequence, all Turkish Cypriot officials and parliamentary deputies were dismissed, attacks were carried out against Turkish Cypriot enclaves, and the Turkish Cypriots were forced to evacuate 103 villages.

Early in 1964, Denktash flew to New York to present his community's case before the United Nations (UN) Security Council, but he was not allowed to return to Cyprus and remained in what he termed "de facto banishment" for several years. In October 1967, when he returned to Cyprus secretly, he was arrested but then freed as a result of international pressure. After his release, he resumed his position as president of the Turkish Cypriot Communal Chamber (April 1968). Since the Turkish Cypriot community was no longer being represented in the national government, the Communal Chamber had become the backbone of what was gradually becoming an autonomous Turkish Cypriot administration.

Denktash was one of the founders of the provisional Turkish Federated State of Cyprus, which was established in northern Cyprus in February 1975, following the overthrow of the Makarios regime by the Greek junta and the military intervention of Turkey, which the overthrow precipitated (July–August 1974). In June 1976, Denktash was elected as the federated state's first president. In June 1981, he was reelected.

Denktash was also one of the founders of the secessionist Turkish Republic of Northern Cyprus, which was established in November 1983, following

the collapse of negotiations with the head of the Greek Cypriot government, Spyros Kyprianou. In June 1985, Denktash was elected as the republic's first president; he was reelected to that position in June 1990.

Denktash has been a strong advocate of a federal solution to the Cyprus problem, championing the establishment of a bizonal, bicommunal partnership state on the island. He has also been one of the chief promoters of the UN-sponsored intercommunal talks, which have taken place at various intervals since 1975.

Denktash is the author of numerous articles and several books. His best-known work is *The Cyprus Triangle* (London, 1982).

See also GRIVAS, GEORGIOS THEODOROS.

Bibliography

Oberling, Pierre. *The Cyprus Tragedy.* Nicosia, Cyprus: K. Rustem, 1989.

Oberling, Pierre. *Negotiating for Survival.* Princeton, NJ: Aldington, 1991.

Oberling, Pierre. *The Road to Bellapais: The Turkish Cypriot Exodus to Northern Cyprus.* Boulder, CO: Social Science Monographs, distributed by Columbia University Press, New York, 1982.

PIERRE OBERLING

DENTZ, HENRI-FERNAND
[1881–1945]

Vichy French high commissioner and commander in Syria and Lebanon.

Appointed an officer in 1927, Dentz climbed the upper echelons of the French Army in the 1930s, and was appointed high commissioner and commander-in-chief in the Levant in December 1940 by the Vichy government. In May 1941 the premier of Vichy France, Philippe Pétain, ordered Dentz to arm the Iraqi leader Rashid Ali al-Kaylani and to support the Luftwaffe; latest research suggests that Dentz refused the latter order because he was concerned about keeping his troops loyal. On 8 June 1941 the British and the Free French—provoked by Pétain's decision—invaded. Dentz counterattacked, but surrendered to the British in July after receiving guarantees that soldiers would be repatriated to France rather than compelled to join Charles de Gaulle. Condemned to death in 1945, he died in prison the same year.

See also DE GAULLE, CHARLES; KAYLANI, RASHID ALI AL-; WORLD WAR II.

Bibliography

Thomas, Martin. *The French Empire at War, 1940–45.* Manchester: Manchester University Press, 1998.

GEORGE R. WILKES

DERAKHSHANDEH, PURAN
[1949–]

Iranian film director.

Puran Derakhshandeh is credited as being the first woman prior to the Iranian Revolution (1979) to direct a feature-length film. Her most daring film, *Love Across Frontiers* (2000), about an American woman married to an Iranian man, was the first post-revolution film to show a woman without Islamic veiling as well as physical contact between a man and a woman (in this case, a hug)—both of which are forbidden by the codes of morality enforced in Iranian filmmaking after the revolution. Derakhshandeh began her career in television and has continued to make socially aware, women-centered films since the 1980s.

See also BANI-ETEMAD, RAKSAN; MILANI, TAHMINEH.

ROXANNE VARZI

DERB

See GLOSSARY

DERGAH

See NEWSPAPERS AND PRINT MEDIA: TURKEY

DESALINIZATION

A solution to hydrate the arid Middle East.

Desalinization, also referred to as desalination, is the removal of salts and dissolved solids from brackish water or seawater. In the past three decades, due to increasing water demand and increasing resource scarcity, desalinization has become a critical, relatively drought-proof, resource of potable, irrigation, and industrial water in arid regions of the globe. In the Arab countries, which have 5 percent of the world population but only 0.9 percent of the water resources, water shortages are a constant challenge, and desalinization is playing an increasing role. Once so prohibitively expensive and technologically troublesome as to be totally impractical, it is now often the solution of choice in conditions of unreliable water resources. Capital investments and costs of production are going down as innovations improve the technologies involved.

The desalinization plant at Jubail, Saudi Arabia, was the largest such facility in the world when it was photographed for the first time by foreign news media, in 1991. One of several plants along the Persian (Arabian) Gulf, between Kuwait and Qatar, it was then capable of processing 230 million imperial gallons of seawater into drinking water per day. © BETTMANN/CORBIS. REPRODUCED BY PERMISSION.

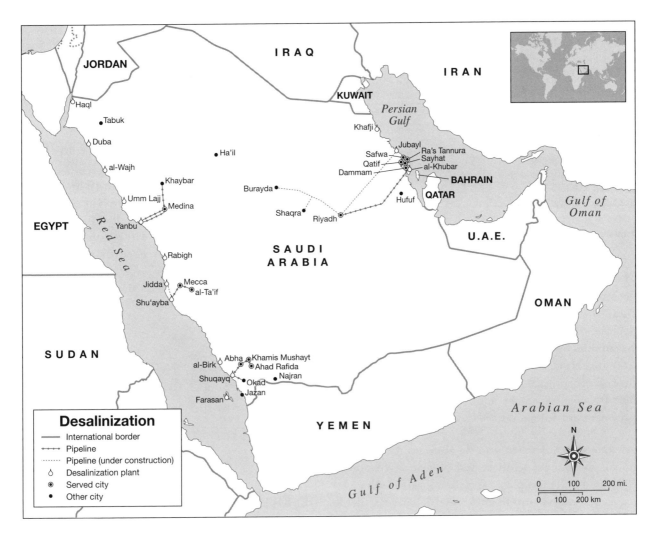

MAP BY XNR PRODUCTIONS, INC. THE GALE GROUP.

Of the more than 12,500 desalinization plants in operation or in construction worldwide, 60 percent are located in the Middle East and North Africa (MENA). The Shuʿayba Plant Phase II in Jeddah, Saudi Arabia, for a time the world's largest plant, supplies the daily water needs of 1.5 million people. Saudi Arabia, whose desalinization output exceeded one billion cubic meters in 2002 to provide 70 percent of its water needs, is the largest desalinated water producer in the world, contributing to 30 percent of global output. Desalinized seawater currently constitutes Saudi Arabia's main source for potable water. This water is transported in a network of 1,550-mile pipelines, 21 pumping stations, 131 depots, and 10 stations for mixing the desalinated water with underground water. Around 1972, the MENA region "ran out of water" as the con-

sumption surpassed the rate of resource renewal. Since then, MENA has relied heavily on desalinization, and is poised to remain for the foreseeable future the largest desalinization market in the world.

Desalinization systems can be membrane-based, such as Reverse Osmosis (RO) and Electro-Dialysis Reversal (EDR), or thermal, such as multi-stage flash (MSF) and multiple-effect distillation (MED). Boiling, leading to desalinization through evaporation, a process of thermal distillation, was known and practiced from ancient times. However, now most desalinization plants use membrane-based reverse osmosis, a process that allows the separation of 99 percent of dissolved salts and impurities from water, by means of pressure exerted on a semipermeable membrane. Between 15 and 50 percent

Bahrain's installed desalination capacity (July 2000)

Facility	Date of commissioning	Capacity (MGD)	Technology
Sitra power and water plant (I, II, III)	1974, 1984, 1985	27.5	MSF
Ras Abu Jarjur RO plant	1984	12.5	RO
Addur RO plant	1992	3	RO
Hidd power and water plant	2000	30	MSF
Total installed capacity	—	73	—

SOURCE: *Ministry of Electricity and Water, Bahrain.*

TABLE BY GGS INFORMATION SERVICES, THE GALE GROUP.

of seawater intake into a plant is purified; the rest becomes brine, or high-salt water, in need of dilution, then dumping. Environmental regulations dealing with the impact of desalinization on the environment vary from country to country. In addition to brine, other effluents include discharged process chemicals used for defouling, and toxic metals, as well as small amounts of solid waste (spent pretreatment filters, filtered solid particles, etc.).

Energy requirements for desalinization are high, mostly to power machinery and to heat feed-water. RO and distillation plants are often located with energy generation plants to improve efficiency. In such cases, additional environmental impacts have to be taken into account on a case-by-case basis. Fortunately, many of the water-starved countries such as Saudi Arabia, Kuwait, the United Arab Emirates, and Libya are major oil and gas producers and have significant reserves. They have invested heavily in desalinization from early on. The first plant in Saudi Arabia was inaugurated in 1954. The Saline Water Corporation in Saudi Arabia is the largest investor in, and operator of, desalinization plants in the world.

Cost reduction is the single most important factor necessary to increase the implementation of desalination. Capital investment unit costs range from $1,000 to $2,000 per cubic meter of capacity, and can be amortized over 20 to 30 years. Unit production costs per cubic meter range from $0.50 for large plants to over $1.50 for small plants, or about one-half the cost of desalinated water in the recent past. It is not economical to operate a plant part time. Economies of scale play an important role in invest-

ment decision-making but are more easily achieved in distillation than in RO process. The Middle East Desalination Research Center (MEDRC), established in 1996 in Muscat, Oman, has been conducting basic and applied research to reduce the cost of water desalinization.

Bahrain, Jordan, and Kuwait were the only water-scarce countries in the region in 1950s. In 2003, twelve countries have water scarcity, and by 2023, six more countries will suffer the same vulnerability, including Israel and Palestine. If the participants in the Palestine–Israel conflict do not exploit water as a unilateral security issue and insist upon retaining control over water resources in the Occupied Territories, the desalinization option may contribute to a solution.

Bibliography

Rogers, Peter, and Lydon, Peter. *Water in the Arab World: Perspectives and Prognoses.* Cambridge, MA: Harvard University Press, 1994.

JOHN F. KOLARS
UPDATED BY KARIM HAMDY

DESERT MOBILE FORCE

See ARAB LEGION

DESERTS

Predominant landscape of the Middle East and North Africa.

Stretching from the Atlantic coast in the west to Pakistan in the east, a band of arid land (15° and 30° north latitude) dominates this region. The North African expanse is generally known as the Sahara, although subdivisions within it have individual names indicating the nature of the surface. The terms *erg* (as in the Great Eastern Erg of Algeria) and *serir* (as the Serir of Kalanshu in Libya) indicate a region of sand dunes. Where the surface is rocky underfoot the terms used are *reg* or *hamada* (for example, the Hamada of Dra south of the Anti-Atlas mountains). Individual areas may also be given the name desert, the Western Desert and the Eastern Desert in Egypt, although they are smaller parts of the whole. On the peninsula of the same name, the Arabian Desert is an extension of the Sahara and is divided into the Rub al-Khali (Empty Quarter, a region of vast sand dunes) and the Nafud and Najd. To the north is the Syrian Desert, and to the east the two deserts of the Iranian plateau are known as the Dasht-e Kavir and the Dasht-e Lut.

The term *desert* is one in common usage and therefore difficult to define. Most experts prefer to speak of "drylands" or "arid lands" and to define such places through various measures of the availability of water for plant growth (implying that not all deserts are hot.) A common definition of desert, however, is those regions of Earth's surface having fewer than 10 inches (250 mm) of precipitation annually and extreme high temperatures. This classical approach relates such measures to areas with types of vegetation adapted to hot, arid conditions. In areas with much sunshine and small amounts of precipitation and/or natural moisture from the soil, only plants called *xerophytes* survive—those adapted to such conditions. In certain hyperarid locations, precipitation may be even less and no vegetation of any kind is found.

Desert rainfall is not only sparse but is also extremely variable in time and space as well as in quantity. Such variance means that human occupancy of the desert must depend for survival on reliable springs and rivers for irrigation rather than on precipitation. Traditional pastoral nomadism, located on the desert margins, was adapted to this environment by moving its productive units (i.e., herds and flocks) to where grass and water seasonally occurred. But even nomads ventured into the true desert only for travel as transporters and raiders. The few permanent inhabitants of the deserts were those oasis dwellers dependent upon perennial springs for intensive agriculture and the growing of date palms.

Desert soils are usually of poor quality except for those in the valleys of rivers where alluvial deposits have accumulated. True desert soils—called *aridisols*—have low biomass, very sparse or no organic acids and gases, few or no bacteria, and are essentially mineral in character. Any rain or sheet flooding and runoff that percolate beneath the surface rapidly evaporate. As a result, soluble salts are precipitated and redeposited, forming a crusty layer on the surface or just beneath it. Repeated leaching and

Women in veils approach the town of Shibam, filled with skyscrapers and known as the "Manhattan of the Desert." Shibam is located in the desert Valley of Hadhramout, and is one of the most fertile areas of Yemen. © WOLFGANG KAEHLER/CORBIS. REPRODUCED BY PERMISSION.

deposition can result in concentrations of sodium chloride (NaCl), white alkali (salt), or similar deposits of sodium carbonate (Na_2CO_3), black alkali, which poison the soil and make agriculture impossible. Under desert conditions agriculture is extremely difficult, and even the use of irrigation water can cause salinity, through evaporation and the precipitation of the dissolved salts it may carry, which leads to the abandonment of such farmland.

The natural xerophytic vegetation found in deserts has adapted to conditions of high temperatures and scant and irregular amounts of precipitation. Xerophytes often occur as drought-resisting plants with heavy cuticles, which reduce transpiration, or with stomata, which can be closed for the same purpose. Other xerophytes reduce water use by shedding their leaves and remaining leafless during the dry season. Among these plants are the euphorbia and the cacti, the latter originally found only in the Western Hemisphere.

Phreatphytes constitute another class of desert vegetation, which includes palms. These plants have developed long taproots, which reach the water table, allowing them to survive the driest of surface conditions. Other plants evade drought by flowering and seeding only during brief rainy periods.

During the intervening months and years of drought, the seeds remain dormant.

Desert vegetation under such conditions is sparse, and soil-forming conditions (including the creation of humus) are poor. Rainstorms can be intense, although of short duration, and often soil particles are carried away from desert surfaces by sheet flooding. The result of these conditions is erosion—which results in hills lacking deep layers of soil. Their profiles are characteristically steep sided with thick strata forming cliff faces rising vertically from the surrounding plains. Flat-topped mesas and steep buttes dominate the landscape, while valleys are flat bottomed with vertical side slopes. Wind erosion and deposition are also significant factors in desert landscape formation. Crescent-shaped barchan dunes are found where sands are insufficient to completely mantle the underlying surface. Copious sands form "seas," with longitudinal sief dunes and star-shaped rhourd dunes. Such seas, however, are the exceptions and rocky desert surfaces are common.

In desert areas, underground supplies of water assume great importance. Porous and permeable strata deep beneath the surface sometimes contain large quantities of water. Such aquifers may have impervious layers (aquicludes) above and below them that confine the water and keep it from escaping except in limited amounts at oases. Other aquifers occur in unconsolidated alluvial materials in river valleys (Arabic, *wadis*). This water is recharged from river seepage and/or rainfall. In the Middle East, most of the major aquifers are nonrenewable and contain fossil water, which once used—extracted or mined—will not be replaced. Desert countries, such as Libya and Saudi Arabia, with few or no surface streams have in the last two decades turned to the exploitation of such aquifers as part of their economic development plans. An ambitious agricultural program in Saudi Arabia has used tube wells and central pivot irrigation to produce bumper wheat crops in an otherwise hostile desert environment. Libya is engaged in constructing a "Great Manmade River"—actually a gigantic system of pumps and pipelines—with which to bring water from aquifers beneath the central Sahara to coastal locations, for municipal and agricultural use. In both these cases and others, the critical element is the quantity of water available and whether it will last long enough to justify such expensive projects. Many experts counsel caution in undertaking such attempts to remake, or "green," the desert.

See also CLIMATE; DESALINIZATION; EASTERN DESERT; GEOGRAPHY; NAFUD DESERT; SYRIAN DESERT; WATER.

Bibliography

Beaumont, Peter. *Environmental Management and Development in Drylands.* London and New York: Routledge, 1989.

Goudie, Andrew, and Wilkinson, John. *The Warm Desert Environment.* Cambridge, U.K., and New York: Cambridge University Press, 1977.

Whitehead, Emily E.; Hutchinson, Charles F.; Timmerman, Barbara N.; et al., eds. *Arid Lands: Today and Tomorrow: Proceedings of an International Research and Development Conference.* Boulder, CO: Westview Press, 1988.

JOHN F. KOLARS

DESERT SHIELD

See GULF WAR (1991)

DESERT STORM

See GULF WAR (1991)

DEVRIM, IZZET MELIH
[1887–1966]

Turkish novelist.

Born in Jerusalem, the son of an Ottoman administrator, Izzet Melih Devrim was graduated from the prestigious Galatasaray School in Istanbul and worked at various commercial jobs. His first literary effort was a volume of prose poetry, titled *Çocuklara Mahsus Gazete* (The children's newspaper), published in 1898, but he did not receive public recognition until 1905 when he was the runner-up in a competition sponsored by a French literary journal. Many of his subsequent works were published in French, and in 1938, he was awarded a doctorate from the Faculty of Letters in Paris. Among Devrim's principal works are *Leyla* (1912), *Sermed* (1918), and *Hüzün ve Tebessüm* (Sadness and a smile, 1922).

See also GALATASARAY LYCÉE.

DAVID WALDNER

DEY

See GLOSSARY

DHAHRAN

Town that is the center of Saudi Arabian oil production.

Dhahran (al-Zahran) is a town of the Eastern Province of Saudi Arabia of perhaps 100,000, not far from al-Dammam and the gulf coast. There was no settlement at Dhahran before Saudi Arabia's first oil strike was made there in 1935. Since then, Dhahran has grown to incorporate the headquarters of the Saudi Arabian American Oil Company (Saudi ARAMCO) and hosts the King Fahd University of Petroleum and Minerals. From 1946 to 1962, the United States operated an air force base at Dhahran that subsequently became a major base for the Royal Saudi Air Force. An international airport at Dhahran was closed after completion of a new airport at al-Dammam.

Bibliography

Nawwab, Ismail I., et al., eds. *Saudi Aramco and Its World: Arabia and the Middle East.* Dhahran: Saudi Aramco, 1995.

J. E. PETERSON

DHIMMA

The legal status of monotheistic non-Muslims and Zoroastrians under Islamic rule which they, collectively or individually, expressly accept.

Dhimma is based on verse 9:29 of the Qur'an and finds precedent in the conquest of Mecca. Caliph Umar's pact with non-Muslims, granting them life and property protection, constitutes the detailed provisions of the institution. Under this status, minorities enjoyed exemption from military service, freedom of religion, freedom to practice their religious duties, and the right to renovate, although not to erect, houses of worship.

In return, a poll tax (*jizya*) was levied; in addition, *dhimmis* were prohibited from criticizing the Qur'an, expressing disrespect to the Prophet or to Islam, conducting missionary activity, or having sexual relations with or marrying Muslim women.

They were not allowed to make their crosses, wine, and pork conspicuous, or to conduct their funerals in public. Riding horses was prohibited, as was erecting houses taller than those of the Muslims. *Dhimmis* were required to wear clothes that made them recognizable and were barred from holding certain public positions.

Modernity has posed for Muslims problems of equality, freedom of religion, and human rights, which seem to originate in an ever-increasing contact with the West, free communication, and multiculturalism. Historically speaking, *dhimma* was conceived during the Islamic conquest but diminished when foreign powers gained the upper hand, especially during the reign of the later Ottoman period and the rise of nationalism. Since the late second half of the twentieth century, the "clash of civilizations," and the increase of Muslims in foreign countries, it has become a symbol for the relationship between Islam and the rest of the world.

The institution of the *dhimma* remains controversial, and there is an extensive debate over whether to abolish it altogether, amend it, or maintain it. The more traditional thinkers reject any thought of changing the institution. Their views range from denying the principle of equality to religions other than Islam, through blocking certain positions of influence in the state to non-Muslims, to reiterating their rights and Islam's traditional liberal attitude according to the *sunna*, especially by comparison to European historical record. Some even go as far as to offer "Islamic citizenship" to non-Muslims. Others claim that the distinction between Muslim and non-Muslim is one of political administration, not of human rights, according *dhimma* to all religionists. The debate over *dhimma* includes political issues: Some of the minorities are accused of having abused it internally, and the West has been accused of having created and exacerbated the entire problem of "minorities."

Bibliography

Ameer, Ali. "Islamism versus the Secularist Weltanschauung." *Journal of Muslim Minority Affairs* Abingdon 21 (2001): 171–174.

Doi, Abd al-Rahman I. *Non-Muslims under Shariah (Islamic Law).* Brentwood, MD: International Graphics, 1979.

Kotb, Sayed. *Social Justice in Islam,* translated by John B. Hardie. New York: Octagon, 1970.

Maududi, Abul A'la. *Rights of Non-Muslims in Islamic State.* Lahore: Islamic Publications, 1961.

Mayer, E. *Islam and Human Rights: Tradition and Politics.* Boulder, CO: Westview Press, 1999.

Na'im, Abdulahi Ahmed, an-. "Religious Freedom in Egypt: Under the Shadow of the Islamic *Dhimma* System." In *Religious Liberty and Human Rights in Nations and in Religions,* edited by Leonard Swidler. Philadelphia: Ecumenical Press, Temple University, 1986.

Nielsen, H. S. "Contemporary Discussions on Religious Minorities in Islam." *Brigham Young University Law Review,* no. 2 (2002): 353–369.

Noor, Farish A. "Toward an Islamic Reformation: Civil Liberties, Human Rights and International Law." *Journal of Muslim Minority Affairs* 20 (2000): 376–379.

Rahmat Allah, Malihah. *The Treatment of the Dhimmis in Ummayyad and Abbassid Periods.* Baghdad: Baghdad University, 1963.

Sanasarian, Elizabeth. *Religious Minorities in Iran.* Cambridge and New York: Cambridge University Press, 2000.

Tabamdeh, Sultanhussein. *A Muslim Commentary on the Universal Declaration of Human Rights,* translated by F. J. Goulding. Guildford: F. J. Goulding, 1970.

Tibi, B. "Religious Minorities under Islamic Law and the Limits of Cultural Relativism." *Human Rights Quarterly* 9, no. 1 (1987): 1–18.

Tritton, Arthur S. *The Caliphs and Their non-Muslim Subjects: A Critical Study of the Covenant of Umar.* London: Frank Cass, 1970.

ILIA ALON

DHOW

A term, probably of Swahili origin, referring to several types of sailing vessels (many now outfitted with motors) common to the Gulf Arab states.

Arabs refer to dhows by names specific to each type, determined principally by size and hull design. Four kinds of dhows account for most of these vessels. The *sambuk* (or *sambook*), perhaps the most widely represented, is a graceful craft with a tapered bow and a high, squared stern; it was often used for pearling, and today is used for fishing and commerce. A larger vessel, the *boom,* is still common in the Gulf. It ranges from 50 to 120 feet (15–35 m) in length, 15 to 30 (5–9 m) feet in width, and up to 400 tons (363 metric tons) displacement. Like early Arab ships it is double-ended (pointed at both ends) with a straight stem post. It is important in Gulf commerce. Now rare is another large ship, the *baggala,* formerly an important deep-sea vessel. Sometimes over 300 tons (272 metric tons) and with a crew of 150, it was built with a high, squared poop, reflecting the influence of sixteenth- and seventeenth-century Portuguese vessels. Like the *sambuk* and *baggala,* it has two masts. The *jalboot,* a single-masted vessel and much smaller (20–50 tons [18–45 metric tons]), formerly was widely used on the pearling banks of the Gulf. Its name and its features, notably an upright bow stem and transom stern, indicate its probable derivation from the British jolly boat. Other smaller craft, all single masted, occasionally found in Gulf or adjacent waters include the *bedan, shuʿi,* and *zarook.*

Dhows were well adapted to Gulf waters because of their shallow draft and maneuverability. Their lateen sails, long stems, and sharp bows equipped them well for running before the monsoon winds of the Indian Ocean, toward India in summer and toward Africa in winter. Wood for planking and masts was imported from the Malabar Coast of India or from East Africa. Traditionally no nails were used; cord made from coconut husks was used to lash together the planks of the decks and gunwales. By the eighth century Arab fleets of such ships were part of a commercial maritime network not matched or superseded until the European circumnavigation of the globe. In the latter part of the eighteenth century, the Qawasim Emirate of the lower Gulf created a maritime empire that displaced earlier Omani dominance. Their power rested on the large fleets of dhows and the skill and ferocity of their crews. The attacks of these "pirates" on Anglo–Indian shipping brought Britain's naval intervention in the early nineteenth century and the eventual establishment of a trucial system under Britain's oversight. Until the 1930s hundreds of dhows made up the fleets that sailed over the pearling banks from June to September. Today a considerable number of commercial cargoes are carried in motorized dhows between Dubai, especially as a transshipment point, and Iran. Some dhows are used for recreational purposes. Traditionally the Gulf's most important manufacturing industry was the construction and outfitting of dhows. In the early twentieth century there were some 2,000 dhows in Bahrain alone, and 130 were built there yearly. Small numbers continue to be built in Bahrain and elsewhere in the Gulf, still with the planks of the hull formed into a shell and the ribs then fitted to them.

Bibliography

Kay, Shirley. *Bahrain: Island Heritage.* Dubai, United Arab Emirates: Motivate, 1989.

Vine, Peter. *Pearls in Arabian Waters: The Heritage of Bahrain.* London: Immel, 1986.

MALCOLM C. PECK

DHUFAR

Southern geographic region and governate of Oman.

Dhufar comprises about one-third of the total area of Oman and is environmentally and ethnically distinct from the rest of the sultanate. Its mountainous interior receives monsoon winds, resulting in a wet, temperate climate suited to cattle grazing. Dhufar also produces frankincense and possesses several oil fields. Many of the 125,600 (1993 census) residents speak ancient South Arabian dialects that predate, but are similar to, Arabic.

After a period of nominal control beginning in the 1820s, the Al Bu Sa'id dynasty of Oman began to assert more permanent authority over Dhufar in the 1890s. The province remained administratively distinct, even having its own coinage. An uprising erupted in the late 1960s due to Dhufari dissatisfaction with Al Bu Sa'id rule. The more enlightened reign of Sultan Qabus ibn Sa'id after 1970 removed much of that dissatisfaction, and by 1976 the separatists were defeated. The province, along with Muscat and Masandam, remains under a governor who reports directly to the sultan, but it has been integrated more fully into Oman through economic and social development. Salala serves as a secondary capital and Raysut is now the second largest port in Oman.

See also DHUFAR REBELLION.

Bibliography

Allen, Calvin H., Jr., and Rigsbee, W. Lynn. *Oman under Qaboos: From Coup to Constitution, 1970–1996.* Portland, OR; London: Frank Cass, 2000.

Anthony, John Duke. *Historical and Cultural Dictionary of the Sultanate of Oman and the Emirates of Eastern Arabia.* Metuchen, NJ: Scarecrow Press, 1976.

MALCOLM C. PECK
UPDATED BY CALVIN H. ALLEN, JR.

DHUFAR REBELLION

Armed insurrection against the ruler of Oman in the southern province of Dhufar (1965–1975).

In 1965, the Dhufar Liberation Front (DFL) initiated an uprising against the rule of Sultan Sa'id bin Taymur Al Bu Sa'id of Oman, whose neglect of social and economic development in the Dhufar region was especially pronounced. At first the uprising was primarily a tribal separatist movement, organized by the DFL in a part of Oman never meaningfully integrated with the rest of the sultanate, and it received encouragement from Egypt and Saudi Arabia.

The course of the rebellion changed dramatically in 1968 after a Marxist state had emerged in neighboring and newly independent South Yemen (People's Democratic Republic of Yemen; PDRY). The uprising then had a secure PDRY base and a steady flow of money and weapons from the Soviet Union, China, and other Communist states that also offered training to the rebels. The movement's goals were reflected in its new name, Popular Front for the Liberation of the Occupied Arabian Gulf (PFLOAG). By the end of 1969, PFLOAG controlled all of Dhufar except for a coastal enclave around the capital, Salala. When another rebel movement, the National Democratic Front for the Liberation of Oman and the Arab Gulf (ND-FLOAG), emerged in northern Oman in 1970, disaffected Omanis, including the sultan's exiled uncle, conspired with military advisers from Britain and with Qabus ibn Sa'id Al Bu Sa'id, the sultan's son, to depose Sa'id. Qabus, who came to power in July 1970, made defeating the Dhufar rebellion his first priority.

Support from Britain, especially in the form of seconded and contract military officers, was crucial, and Iran's supplies of material and manpower were important in countering a determined insurgency in mountainous terrain where, for half the year, monsoon weather severely reduced visibility. Also significant were Jordan's loan of military officers and large financial infusions from the United Arab Emirates, Kuwait, and Saudi Arabia, all of which feared the radical leftist threat.

In 1971 PFLOAG and NDFLOAG merged, becoming the Popular Front for the Liberation of Oman and the Arab Gulf. The insurgency, however, succumbed over the next four years to Qabus's combined military, political, and economic initiatives, including, importantly, amnesty for rebels who laid down their arms. The success of the government's counteroffensive was reflected in the rebel movement's assumption of the more modest title Popular Front for the Liberation of Oman (PFLO) in 1974. By the end of the following year, only isolated pockets of resistance remained in the rugged interior, and the rebellion essentially ended.

See also AL BU SAʿID, QABUS IBN SAʿID; DHUFAR; IBADIYYA; NATIONAL DEMOCRATIC FRONT FOR THE LIBERATION OF OMAN AND THE ARAB GULF; PEOPLE'S DEMOCRATIC REPUBLIC OF YEMEN; POPULAR FRONT FOR THE LIBERATION OF THE OCCUPIED ARABIAN GULF.

Bibliography

Allen, Calvin H., Jr. *Oman: The Modernization of the Sultanate.* London: Croom Helm; Boulder, CO: Westview Press, 1987.

Halliday, Fred. *Arabia without Sultans.* Baltimore; Harmondsworth, U.K: Penguin, 1974.

MALCOLM C. PECK
UPDATED BY ERIC HOOGLUND

DIASPORA

The dispersal of ethnonational groups.

The term *diaspora* is derived from the Greek verb *speiro* (to sow) and the Greek preposition *dia* (over). All diasporas have in common significant characteristics: They result from both voluntary and imposed migration; their members wish to and are able to maintain their ethnonational identity, which is the basis for continued solidarity; core members establish in their host countries intricate organizations that are intended to protect the rights of their members and to encourage participation in the cultural, political, social, and economic spheres; and members maintain continuous contacts with their homelands and other dispersed segments of the same nation.

Ethnonational diasporism is a widespread perennial phenomenon not confined to the Jews, although in many contexts the term is presumed to refer specifically to the Jewish diaspora. Some ethnonational diasporas are dwindling or disappearing, but other historical, modern, and incipient diasporas are multiplying and flourishing all over the world, including in the Middle East.

Middle Easterners of various ethnic backgrounds permanently reside in foreign host countries within or outside the region; simultaneuosly, Middle Eastern states host diasporas. The larger diaspora communities in the Middle East include Palestinians, Egyptians, Yemenis, and guest workers from elsewhere (Chinese, Pakistanis, Koreans, Vietnamese, and Filipinos) who reside in the Gulf states and in Saudi Arabia; Armenians, Druze, and guest workers from Romania, Turkey, the former Soviet Union, Thailand, the Philippines, and African countries residing in Israel; Palestinians, Druze, and Armenians in Lebanon; Palestinians, Druze, and Armenians in Syria; and Sudanese, Palestinians, and a small number of Greeks in Egypt. Some of these diapsoras, such as the Armenians, come from established states, while others, such as the Kurds, Druze, Gypsies, and the Palestinians, are stateless.

Age, dispersal in and outside the region, group size, status, organization, and connection (or lack thereof) to their homelands influence each of these diasporas' positions in and strategies toward host countries an d homelands. Because of globalization and growth in worldwide migration, their economic and political roles have become increasingly significant.

Bibliography

Ma'oz, Moshe, and Sheffer, Gabriel, eds. *Middle Eastern Minorities and Diasporas.* Brighton, U.K.: Sussex Academic Press, 2002.

GABRIEL SHEFFER

DIBA, FARAH
[1938–]

Queen of Iran, 1959–1979.

Farah Diba, born on 14 October 1938, was the only daughter of Sohrab Diba from Azerbaijan and his wife, Farideh Ghotbi, from Gilan on the Caspian coast. Diba's mother supervised her schooling at Tehran's Jeanne d'Arc and Razi schools, and then at the Ecole d'Architecture in Paris, where she was studying when she met Shah Mohammad Reza Pahlavi. Diba became his third wife on 20 December 1959, after he had divorced successively queens Fawzia and Soraya, neither of whom had borne him an heir. As queen, Diba had four children: Cyrus Reza in 1960, Yamina Farahnaz in 1963, Alireza in 1966, and Leila in 1970. Crowned *shahbanou* in 1967, she and the shah hosted a celebration of 2,500 years of monarchy at Persepolis in 1971. Although the event showcased Iran's history to world leaders, detractors criticized its excesses, given the country's underdevelopment. Queen Farah supported her husband's modernization of Iran, championing the arts, education, and women's issues. The revolution of 1978 to 1979 sent her and the shah into exile; he died in Cairo in 1980. Diba since has lived in the United States and France. Although she rarely seeks the spotlight, she remains a patron of the arts and an advocate for children in Iran and around the world.

See also IRANIAN REVOLUTION (1979); PAHLAVI, MOHAMMAD REZA.

Bibliography

Pahlavi, Farah. *An Enduring Love, My Life with the Shah: A Memoir*. New York: Miramax, 2004.

Shawcross, William. *The Shah's Last Ride: The Fate of an Ally*. New York: Simon and Schuster, 1988.

HALEH VAZIRI

DIB, MOHAMMED
[1920–2003]

Algerian novelist and poet.

Mohammed Dib was born into a middle-class family in Tlemcen. He was educated there and in Oujda. Before devoting his time to a literary career, Dib was a teacher and journalist. He was forced to leave Algeria in 1959 and subsequently settled in France. Dib's works chronicle Algeria's decolonization and postcolonial periods. A theme in his writings is the search for authentic self or identity. Dib's body of work illustrates the common pursuit of human dignity.

Dib earned his literary reputation as a result of a remarkable series of novels: *La grande maison* (1952; The great house); *L'incendie* (1954; The fire); *Le métier à tisser* (1957; The weaving loom); *Un été Africain* (1959; An African summer); *Qui se souvient de la mer* (1962; Who remembers the sea), *Cours sur la rive sauvage* (1964; Run on the wild shore); *La danse du roi* (1968; The dance of the king); *Dieu en Barbarie* (1970; God in Barbary); *Le maître de chasse* (1973; The master of hunting); *Habel* (1979; Habel); *Les terrasses d'Orsol* (1985; The terraces of Orsol); *Le sommeil d'Eve* (1989; The sleep of Eve); *Neiges de marbre* (1990; Snows of marble); *Le désert sans détour* (1992; The straightaway desert); *L'infante maure* (1994; The Moorish infanta); *L'arbre à dires* (1989; The tree with statements); *Si diable veut* (1998; IF the devil wants); *Comme un bruit d'abeilles* (2001; Like a sound of bees); *L.A. Trip* (2003), and *Simorgh* (2003; Simorch). Dib also crafted short stories, including the collections *Au café* (1955; At the cafe); *Le talisman* (1966; The talisman); and *La nuit sauvage* (1995; The savage night).

Dib primarily perceived himself as a poet. His poetry collections include *L'ombre gardienne* (1961; The shade guardian); *Formulaires* (1970; Forms); *Omneros* (1975; Omneros); *Feu beau feu* (1979; Fire, beautiful fire); *O vive* (1987; Oh, live); *L'enfant-jazz* (1998; The jazz child, which received the Prix Mallarmé); and *Coeur insulaire: Poèmes* (2000; Insular heart). He also wrote several children's books. Dib is distinguished as a leading member of the Generation of 1954, which also included Kateb Yacine, Mouloud Mammeri, Malek Haddad, and Mouloud Feraoun.

See also LITERATURE: ARABIC, NORTH AFRICAN.

Bibliography

Naylor, Phillip C. *Historical Dictionary of Algeria*, 3d edition. Lanham, MD: Scarecrow Press, 2005.

PHILLIP C. NAYLOR

DIDOUCHE, MOURAD
[1922–1955]

A historic chief of the Algerian revolution.

Mourad Didouche was born into a relatively prosperous family in Algiers. He was a member of Messali Hadj's Parti du Peuple Algérien (PPA; Algerian People's Party) and Mouvement pour le Triomphe des Libertés Démocratiques (MTLD; Movement for the Triumph of Democratic Liberties). He became a leader in the north Constantine region of the Organisation Spéciale (OS; Special Organization). After the OS's suppression, he fled Algeria and collaborated with Mohamed Boudiaf in Paris. He was a prominent member of the Committee of 22 and the Comité Révolutionnaire d'Unité et d'Action (CRUA; Revolutionary Committee for Unity and Action), earning his inclusion among the nine historic chiefs (chefs historiques) of the Algerian revolution. Didouche also edited the Front de Libération Nationale's (FLN; National Liberation Front) Proclamation of I November 1954, inaugurating the war of liberation. He died in combat. After the war, the Algerian government renamed rue Michelet in downtown Algiers as Didouche Mourad.

See also BOUDIAF, MOHAMED; COMITÉ RÉVO-LUTIONNAIRE D'UNITÉ ET D'ACTION (CRUA); FRONT DE LIBÉRATION NATIONALE (FLN); HADJ, MESSALI AL-; MOUVEMENT POUR LE TRIOMPHE DES LIBERTÉS DÉMOCRATIQUES; PARTI DU PEUPLE ALGÉRIEN (PPA).

PHILLIP C. NAYLOR

DILMUN

Prehistoric society of about 2000 B.C.E. that existed in the Persian/Arabian Gulf region, especially on the island of Bahrain.

The search for Dilmun was undertaken by Dr. Geoffrey Bibby and his 1953 Danish archaeological expedition to Bahrain. His excavation of 100,000 burial mounds yielded dates and documents about Dilmun as a rich seafaring civilization. It extended from Kuwait in the north to Oman at the south end of the Persian/Arabian Gulf. Bahrain is believed to have been the center of that civilization.

Bibliography

Bibby, Geoffrey. *Looking for Dilmun.* London: Collins; New York: Knopf, 1970.

EMILE A. NAKHLEH

DIMONA

Israeli frontier city.

Located 22 miles southeast of Beersheba and about 7 miles east of Yeruham, in Israel's southern re-gion, the city is named after the biblical Dimona, a Judean city in the Negev. Initially a residential area serving the Dead Sea Industries workforce in Sodom and the operators of the potash works at Oron, Dimona was originally settled by thirty-six Moroccan immigrant families, joined later by additional newcomers. During the period between 1978 and 1988 it registered a negative immigration balance. Subsequently, however, additional immigrants were brought in (in 1991 Dimona absorbed 1,500 families from Russia and Ethiopia).

Dimona is also home to the Hebrew Israelites, a group of some 2,000 African Americans who initially settled in Dimona in 1969 and who consider their immigration to Israel the final destination of their journey home. Their leader, Ben Ami Ben Israel Carter, supervises the group's communal life. Because, in their view, religions constitute a rift among people, the Hebrew Israelites do not consider themselves disciples of any religion.

Dimona is neither particularly large nor strategically located. Its population in 2002 was 33,700. It is, however, immensely important to Israel because it is home to scientists stationed at the nearby nuclear reactor. The Dimona reactor was built with the aid of the French; during the mid-1960s, it became a source of concern to both the Arabs and the United States, who feared that the reactor would be used to produce nuclear-weapons-grade plutonium. The Israelis gave assurances that the Dimona reactor was for peaceful use, but suspicions remained. In 1980 the International Atomic Energy Agency confirmed that the Dimona reactor was capable of producing weapons-grade ore. Though it has never been publicly acknowledged, it is likely that the Israelis have used the Dimona reactor to help develop nuclear weapons.

In September 1986 Mordechai Vanunu, a former technician at the Dimona nuclear reactor, disclosed to the world that Israel had secretly produced 100 to 200 nuclear warheads. Before the publication of this information in the *New York Times,* Vanunu was kidnapped by the Israeli secret service. At a trial held in camera in Israel he was convicted of treason and espionage and was sentenced to eighteen years in prison; the first eleven and a half years were spent in solitary confinement. His petition for an early release was denied.

Bibliography

Cohen, Avner. *Israel and the Bomb.* New York: Columbia University Press, 1998.

ZACHARY KARABELL
UPDATED BY YEHUDA GRADUS

DINAR

See GLOSSARY

DINKA

A people of Sudan.

The Dinka are a Nilotic people in the Republic of Sudan. Numbering over two million, they are the most numerous ethnic group, inhabiting about a tenth of its 1 million square miles (2.6 million sq km). The land of the Dinka is rich savanna broken by the Nile River, its tributaries, and the Sudd, the great swamps of the Nile that flood the grasslands during the rainy season (May to October) and fall during the dry season (November to April). The Dinka are separated by these rivers and swamps into some twenty-five independent groups. In the past they were governed by lineages rather than any single authority.

Their physical characteristics, ethnic pride, and striking cultural uniformity bind the Dinka together as one people, despite their widespread geographical dispersion. They call themselves not Dinka but Monyjang, which means "the man," or "the husband of men." They are convinced of their superiority to all others, whom they call "foreigners" (*juur*; singular, *jur*).

The Dinka are devoted to their cattle, which provide them with many of their worldly and spiritual needs, from dairy products (supplemented by fish and grain) to protection against illness or death. Cattle are the social cement for "bride wealth" (for marriage) and "blood wealth" (to resolve disputes). The Dinka are a proud people who, despite the ravages of civil war in Sudan, will nevertheless continue to survive.

See also NILE RIVER; SUDD.

ROBERT O. COLLINS

DINSHAWAY INCIDENT (1906)

British atrocity committed in June 1906 against Egyptian peasants accused of assaulting British officers.

Some British officers were hunting pigeons near Dinshaway village in Minufiyya province. One officer died, most probably of sunstroke, but the villagers were accused of assaulting him. As the news spread, the British assumed that a national insurrection might occur, so they called for exemplary punishment of the villagers. The accused assailants were arrested and hastily tried by a special tribunal; some were sentenced to death, some to public flogging or imprisonment.

Their sentences led to widespread protests in Europe and in Egypt. The summary public execution of the convicted peasants caused the rise of Egypt's National Party and the retirement of Britain's consul general, Lord Cromer (born Evelyn Baring). For Egyptians, it remains a black mark against Britain's rule.

See also BARING, EVELYN; NATIONAL PARTY (EGYPT).

Bibliography

Blunt, Wilfrid Scawen. *Atrocities of Justice under British Rule in Egypt.* London: Unwin, 1907.

Marlowe, John. *Cromer in Egypt.* London: Elek; and New York: Praeger, 1970.

Sayyid-Marsot, Afaf Lutfi. *Egypt and Cromer: A Study in Anglo–Egyptian Relations.* London: Murray; New York: Praeger, 1968.

ARTHUR GOLDSCHMIDT

DIRHAM

See GLOSSARY

DISEASES

Major diseases in the Middle East since 1800.

Endemic and epidemic diseases spread in the modern Middle East and North Africa in the wake of expanding European political and economic power. Political and medical responses to diseases changed over time according to the interests of the imperial and local powers and influenced the allocation of resources to research and policies governing medical intervention. Plague, syphilis, malaria, schistosomiasis, and cholera led to the establishment of new forms of government control and modern medical and public health infrastructures.

Plague epidemics decimated the Middle East and North Africa from the sixth through the nineteenth centuries. In Egypt, famine usually followed plague outbreaks because without intense maintenance normally undertaken by the fellahin (peasantry), the irrigation canals became overgrown with reeds and silted up. Plague and famine were largely responsible for a population decline from perhaps 8 million in 1347 at the onset of plague to 3 million in 1805 when Muhammad Ali became viceroy. Bedouin, however, were able to outrun the disease by fleeing into the desert and their numbers remained constant at about several hundred thousand. Outbreaks continued to decimate urban and rural populations in the Middle East until the nineteenth century when Ottoman and Egyptian authorities took steps to introduce quarantines and other public health controls. In then underpopulated Egypt, when Muhammad Ali, the Ottoman viceroy, learned in 1812 that plague had broken out in Istanbul, he promptly imposed strict quarantine on Ottoman ships. The plague did not arrive. When plague again broke out in the eastern Mediterranean Muhammad Ali established a quarantine station at the port city of Damietta. The time the travelers evaded the quarantine and plague broke out in other port cities. Muhammad Ali imposed a cordon sanitaire around Alexandria and ordered his police and troops to imprison plague victims and burn their possessions. Battling widespread resistance, the authorities rounded up poor families and imprisoned them in quarantine stations on the edge of town, shot heads of households who refused to report sick members, and isolated the wealthy in their homes. Families went to great lengths to bury their dead in secret to evade the draconian measures and plague soon spread up the Nile. About a seventh of the Egyptian population and many European residents of Egypt perished. In a secondary outbreak in 1841 Muhammad Ali stiffened the quarantines and soldiers had orders to shoot to kill villagers who attempted to evade them. Fallahin were rounded up, men and women separated and forced to bathe under the supervision of male and female medical personnel, and given clean clothing. Egypt was plague free for three generations.

Between 1894 and 1898 Drs. Shibasaburo Kitasato, Alexander Yersin, and Paul Lewis Simond discovered the plague bacillus and the role of the rat flea in transmitting the disease. Quarantines, rat control, and antibiotics now control plague in most regions of the Middle East and North Africa, but it remains a threat in remote regions of Algeria, Egypt, Iran, Iraq, Libya, Morocco, Tunisia, and Turkey.

Muhammad Ali was equally concerned with syphilis, which also afflicted his troops and impaired the efficacy of his army. Muhammad Ali recruited Antoine-Barthelme Clot (Bey) to organize a Western-style teaching hospital, which opened in 1827. In an attempt to control the disease, he had Clot Bey organize a school to train women medical practitioners (hakimat). The hakimat vaccinated people against smallpox, reported on and treated the prostitute population for syphilis, registered midwives, and performed postmortem exams.

The British occupied Egypt in 1882 and proceeded to further develop Egyptian agriculture. British engineers completed a dam at Aswan in 1902 and in subsequent years raised it and built and expanded a series of barrages to better control the Nile river flow. The Nile Delta was converted from basin to perennial irrigation enabling fellahin to produce three crops a year but at the same time allowing schistosomiasis (bilharzia), hookworm, and other waterborne diseases to spread to formerly uninfected areas.

In 1913 a Rockefeller Foundation survey of Egypt found that about 60 percent of the population was infected with hookworm, bilharzia, non-falciparum malaria, and other parasitic diseases. World War I and the Great Depression exacerbated the disease load in Egypt and many suffered from typhus, typhoid fever, and plague. In 1936 the now independent Egyptian authorities upgraded the Department of Public Health to the Ministry of Health but funding remained limited. In 1940 a leading medical researcher estimated that 75 percent of the Egyptian people had bilharzia, 50 percent ancylostomiasis, 50 percent other parasitic diseases, 90 percent trachoma, 25 percent malaria, 7 percent pellagra, and nearly all had severe childhood diseases. Life expectancy was thirty-one years for men and thirty-six years for women.

In 1942 a severe malaria epidemic broke out in Egypt. Malaria, caused by the *Plasmodium falciparum* parasite, is transmitted to human beings by the anopheles mosquito. The mosquitoes can breed in standing water in irrigation channels, rainfall pools, streams, marshes, and oases, and malaria has been reported in all regions of the Middle East and North Africa, including oases in the Arabian Peninsula and the Sahara. In 1942 nationalist Egyptians insisted that British military aircraft had imported malaria from Sudan, where malaria was endemic. Others connected the disease with the expansion of irrigation. Subsequent research suggested that the mosquito vector might have traveled downriver by boat. Because hundreds of thousands of British troops were in Egypt the British asked the Rockefeller Foundation to launch a malaria control project. Working closely with the Egyptian Ministry of Health the foundation eradicated the disease.

In 1950 and 1951 malaria appeared in Jidda and Mecca, with the increased pilgrim traffic apparently facilitating the spread of the anopheles mosquito. The World Health Organization, the Rockefeller Foundation, and other assistance programs in coordination with national ministries of health, utilized DDT and other pesticides to eradicate the disease almost completely. In recent years, however, newly resistant strains of malaria have reappeared in the Arabian Peninsula, Egypt, Lebanon, Libya, Morocco, and southern Sudan, where it is the leading killer.

Schistosomiasis is endemic in the Nile Valley of Egypt and Sudan and in irrigated regions of Iraq. Schistosomes (blood flukes or parasitic worms) grow in freshwater snails which, when adult, leave the snail and survive in the water for forty-eight hours. The schistosomes may enter the skin of persons wading, washing, or swimming in contaminated water or through the lining of the mouth or intestinal tract of persons who drink contaminated water. The schistosomes grow inside the blood vessels of the body and produces eggs. The eggs travel to the bladder or intestine and are excreted. The infected person must urinate into water infected with freshwater snails for the lifecycle of the schistosomes to be continued. The body's reaction to the parasite's eggs

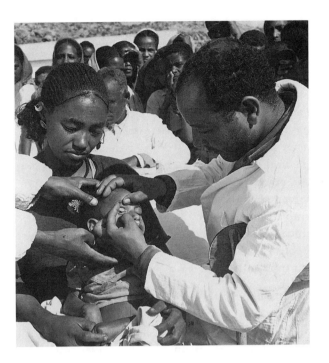

A doctor examines an Ethiopian boy for symptoms of trachoma, a highly contagious eye infection. Outbreaks of malaria are common in North Africa, and the region's medical personnel are also inundated with cases of AIDS, tuberculosis, and various parasitic diseases such as the fly-borne kala azar. © BETTMANN/CORBIS. REPRODUCED BY PERMISSION.

may cause rash, fever, cough, muscle aches, or general debilitation and can damage the liver, intestines, lungs, and bladder. The opening of the Aswan High Dam in 1970 increased land under irrigation by more than 30 percent but also spread schistosomiasis into new regions. A study done in al-Ayaysha, a village on open water in the Nile Delta, found that children swimming in the Nile acquired the disease through repeated contact with contaminated water. They were treated with chemotherapy (Praziquantel), educated about the disease, taught appropriate sanitation procedures, and retested annually. Reinfection rates dropped markedly, but similar intervention throughout the infected region is prohibitively expensive.

Six pandemics of cholera spread between 1817 and 1923 with increased trade, travel, and troop movements from south Asia where the disease is endemic. Cholera is transmitted by contaminated water or food and causes massive diarrhea, dehydration, anuria, acidosis and shock. The fact that the disease was new led Muslim physicians to consult European medical sources. Ottoman physicians began translating medical works from European languages in the early nineteenth century. In 1819 the Ottoman physician Sanizade Atallah studied medicine in the Muslim medical school and then in Padua. He wrote a medical book based on a Viennese source and added sections from other European works. In 1831 Mustafa Behcet, head of the medical college in Istanbul, published a treatise on cholera based on an Austrian source, which Ottoman authorities distributed free throughout the empire. Ottoman authorities established a quarantine service in about 1832 and had religious leaders publish treatises showing that quarantines were not contrary to Islamic law.

In the early nineteenth century European physicians were no better at treating cholera and other diseases than were traditionally trained Muslim physicians. Westernizing Muslim rulers had deducted from the demonstrably superior European weaponry and other scientific and technological advances that European medicine ought to be superior as well. In addition, European physicians were useful for political purposes and by the mid-nineteenth century had largely displaced their Muslim counterparts.

Cholera again spread in 1883, 1896, and 1902. In each of the epidemics, pilgrims returning from Mecca apparently carried the disease with them. In 1883 while working in Cairo, Robert Koch discovered the causative agent, *vibrio cholerae*. Following the cholera epidemics and outbreaks of plague from 1898 to 1905 the British authorities upgraded the al-Tawr quarantine station, which the Egyptian government had established in 1855 and used for the first time in 1862. The discovery of the cholera vibrio and the means of transmission led to improved public health and quarantine procedures in Mecca and throughout the region, which nearly ended the pandemics. The last major epidemic occurred in Egypt in 1947. The outbreak occurred near a British base where troops returning from India were quartered and Egyptians accused the British of having introduced the disease, creating a major and unresolved political controversy. Cholera is treated effectively with oral rehydration solutions to replace lost fluid and rarely is seen in epidemic form. In recent years the al-Tawr cholera vibrio has appeared in sporadic outbreaks.

Tuberculosis was widespread throughout the region but since the 1950s WHO and UNICEF helped ministries of health to vaccinate their populations and the rate of infection dropped significantly. The Egyptian Organization for Human Rights (EOHR) and the Human Rights Center for the Assistance of Prisoners (HRCAP) recently has reported that severe overcrowding, poor ventilation and sanitation, and inadequate nutrition in Egyptian prisons has led to the rapid spread of tuberculosis and other diseases among the prison population.

Eye diseases leading to impaired vision and blindness are common throughout the Middle East and North Africa. Trachoma, the most serious of them, is caused by the bacterium Chlamydia trachomatis. The Chlamydia bacterium infects the conjunctiva and inflammation may result in scarring and even blindness. The disease is spread through secretions from the infected eye spread directly or through common use of towels or bed clothing. Trachoma is prevalent in hot, dry climates with poor sanitary conditions and water shortages. The disease can be treated with tetracycline, but surgery is often necessary to repair damage to the eye. Improved public health and personal hygiene has reduced the incidence of trachoma, but it remains a threat in many parts of the Middle East and North Africa.

Pellagra, caused by inadequate niacin in the diet, is often seen in impoverished regions where corn is a staple and intake of varied plant and animal foods limited. Pellagra causes a distinctive reddish rash and lesions on the neck and is easily prevented by dietary supplements or vitamins. Other debilitating conditions resulting from nutritional deficiencies, such as anemia, are widespread and result directly from poverty.

Hepatitis A, a viral infection of the liver transmitted by the fecal oral route, is endemic throughout the region but can be avoided by consuming only well-cooked food and potable water. Hepatitis B, a viral infection of the liver, is transmitted primarily through behaviors that result in the exchange of blood or body fluids containing blood. Vaccinations are available for Hepatitis A and B. Hepatitis C, also a viral infection of the liver, is endemic in many regions. Recent research suggests that efforts to prevent schistosomiasis may have contributed to its

Blind children in Iraq. The major cause of blindness in developing countries is xerophthalmia, a disease associated with a lack of vitamin A in the diet. If untreated, xerophthalmia leads to keratomalacia, a deterioration and ulceration of the cornea. © J.B. RUSSELL/CORBIS SYGMA. REPRODUCED BY PERMISSION.

spread. Improperly sterilized needles often were used to administer medications for schistosomiasis and apparently transmitted Hepatitis C, which is now a major health problem.

Changes in lifestyle resulting in part from urbanization, increased smoking, a high-fat diet, lack of exercise, and increased obesity have resulted in exceptionally high rates of diabetes. Diabetes is a major public health challenge in Egypt and much of the Eastern Mediterranean region.

AIDS/HIV infection rates in the Middle East and North Africa are relatively low compared with Asia, Europe, and sub-Saharan Africa, but the incidence is rising rapidly and deaths from AIDS have increased since the early 1990s. The disease is most often spread through heterosexual intercourse and to a lesser extent through the transfer of blood and other bodily fluids from an infected person to an uninfected person. Early intervention is crucial be-cause the disease spreads widely once a threshold is reached. Safe sex education, public information programs, greater use of condoms, convenient voluntary testing services, and treatment of sexually transmitted diseases can avert much suffering and crippling medical expenses. Yet the vast majority of infected persons live in the developing world where poverty, malnutrition, and limited education complicate preventive efforts. In addition, some Muslim authorities believe that safe sex education encourages or implies promiscuity and view the disease as a punishment for immoral behavior. In an effort to encourage preventive action, the World Bank, WHO/EMRO and UNAIDS, recently prepared a report titled "Overview of the HIV/AIDS Situation in the Middle East and North Africa and Eastern Mediterranean Region." The report encourages governments to establish national plans for prevention and management of the disease. The government of Morocco is one of the first to prepare a National AIDS action plan and has received funds from the Global Fund to Fight AIDS, TB and Malaria to launch its program. Islamic reformers are advancing the concept of *darar* (the sin of harming others) to argue that men and women are each other's protectors and that spouses are obliged to protect their partners and in turn are entitled to self-protection from exposure to the disease. Recognizing the limits of law enforcement programs, Indonesia and Iran have introduced needle exchange programs to curtail transmission of HIV and hepatitis. Lebanese and other women in the region have argued that women's status must be raised through education, training, and economic independence to enable women to avoid contracting and transmitting the disease by gaining control over their sex lives.

In recent years, the most serious recurrence of disease was in Iraq where the eight-year war with Iran, the 1991 Gulf War, the twelve years of sanctions, and the 2003 U.S. and British occupation resulted in deteriorating conditions, especially for children and the elderly. During the 1990s about 5,000 children died every month from acute diarrheal diseases caused by bacteria, viruses, helminths, or protozoa. In most regions of the world, oral rehydration solution, a mixture of water, glucose, sodium, potassium, and electrolytes, greatly reduced infant mortality rates. The solution, distributed throughout the region by ministries of health, the World Health Organization, the United Nations Children's Fund (UNICEF), and nongovernmental organizations, helps children retain vital fluids and nutrients leading to full recovery. In Iraq, however, potable water and oral rehydration therapy were unobtainable and one in eight children died before his or her fifth birthday. Cholera, easily treated with oral rehydration, also appeared in parts of Iraq and chronic diseases went untreated. The percentage of underweight children increased by over 400 percent, and one in four children under age five was chronically malnourished. After the war UNICEF shipped thousands of tons of emergency medical and water supplies for the prevention and cure of waterborne diseases and high-protein food to fight malnutrition, but unstable conditions greatly impeded distribution.

In the Occupied Territories of Palestine nearly 10 percent of Palestinian children suffer from acute and 13 percent from chronic malnutrition. Malnutrition impairs physical and mental development and when combined with the trauma that Palestinian children have suffered from being exposed to gunfire, tank and helicopter attacks, tear gas, and house demolitions, will have serious long-term consequences. The Israeli reoccupation of Palestinian territories undermined the Palestinian health system and economy; severe overcrowding, poor sanitary conditions, shortage of health facilities, and political unrest have resulted in a massive public health crisis.

Despite setbacks, most regions of the Middle East and North Africa have in recent years experienced substantially decreased infant mortality and increased life expectancy. The current life expectancy now exceeds 65 years of age and is increasing. Noncommunicable diseases are more prevalent than communicable diseases and public health policy makers must adapt their priorities and strategies to the new disease patterns.

See also MEDICINE AND PUBLIC HEALTH.

Bibliography

Barlow, Robin, and Brown, Joseph W., eds. *Reproductive Health and Infectious Disease in the Middle East.* Brookfield, VT: Ashgate Publishing, 1998.

Fahmy, Khaled. "Women, Medicine, and Power in Nineteenth-Century Egypt." In *Remaking Women: Feminism and Modernity in the Middle East,* edited by Lila Abu-Lughod. Princeton, NJ: Princeton University Press, 1998.

Gallagher, Nancy. *Egypt's Other Wars: Epidemics and the Politics of Public Health.* Syracuse, NY: Syracuse University Press, 1990.

Gallagher, Nancy. *Medicine and Power in Tunisia.* New York: Cambridge University Press, 2002.

El Katsha, Samiha, and Watts, Susan. *Gender, Behavior, and Health: Schistosomiasis Transmission and Control in Rural Egypt.* New York and Cairo: American University in Cairo Press, 2002.

Kuhnke, Laverne. *Lives at Risk: Public Health in Nineteenth-Century Egypt.* Berkeley and Los Angeles: University of California Press, 1990.

Rahman, Fazlur. *Health and Medicine in the Islamic Tradition: Change and Identity.* Chicago and Lahore: Kazi Publications, 1998.

NANCY GALLAGHER

DISENGAGEMENT AGREEMENTS

See ARAB–ISRAEL WAR (1973)

DISHDASHA

See CLOTHING

DIWAN

Pronounced "divan" in Persian and Turkish; a term that has been used in a variety of senses.

The term *diwan* has been used to mean all of the following:

- A collection of poetry or prose written by one author.

- A register of census, from the Arabic *awwana,* to collect. The first diwan was the *diwan al-jund,* the register that covered the people of Medina, Medina's military forces, émigrés and their families during the time of Muhammad.

- Ministries from the Umayyad period onward in the Arab world and in India and Iran. Three basic *diwans* corresponded to the three essential needs of the state: chancellery and state secretariat (*diwan al-rasaʾil*), finance (*diwan al-amal),* and the army (*diwan al-jaysh).*

- The imperial privy council of the Ottoman Empire.

- Place of meeting, understood as a separate apartment or sitting room.

- A council chamber or a smoking room.

- A large couch or sofa without a back or arms, often used as a bed.

MIA BLOOM

DIYARBAKIR

City and province in southeastern Turkey.

Diyarbakir province is bounded on the north by the Bitlis Mountains and on the west by the Euphrates River. The province comprises thirteen districts with a total area of 15,355 square kilometers. Its total population is 1,282,628 (2000 census).

The city of Diyarbakir, known in former times as Amida and Kara-Amid, is the principal urban center and capital of the province, which is populated mostly by Kurds. Located on the Tigris River, the city is renowned for its distinctive black basalt fortification walls that date from the fourth century C.E. The walls, with a circumference of 5.5 kilometers, are 12 meters high and 3.5 meters thick.

Diyarbakir has grown rapidly since 1950, when its population was 45,495. After 1984 the city's population multiplied as a result of the army's forcible relocation of Kurdish villagers in an effort to suppress an armed insurrection by the Kurdistan Workers Party. According to the 2000 census, the population had reached 818,396.

During the nineteenth century, Diyarbakir had strong economic links with cities that now are in Iraq and Iran, but these were severed after 1918. Contemporary Diyarbakir is an agricultural market center known also for its cotton textiles, leather products, and trade in grain, mohair, and wool. It has long been known for its goldsmith and silversmith work. The city is linked to western Turkey by railroad and is also the site of an air base.

See also KURDISTAN WORKERS PARTY (PKK); KURDS.

ELIZABETH THOMPSON
UPDATED BY ERIC HOOGLUND

DIYOJEN

See NEWSPAPERS AND PRINT MEDIA: TURKEY

DJAOUT, TAHER
[1954–1993]

Algerian poet, novelist, and journalist.

Taher Djaout was born on 11 January 1954 in Azzefoun, Great Kabylia. After he studied political science and journalism, he worked at the weekly *Algérie-actualité* until his assassination in 1993.

Djaout, who wrote in French, was deeply anchored in his country's history. Algeria is always in the background of his writings, whether they evoke the growing pains of a poor boy during the colonial period in *Les rets de l'oiseleur* (1983; The hunter's net), or tackle the more complex situations of the post-independence years. Many of these themes are central to his first novel, *L'exproprié* (1981; The expropriated).

Djaout began his literary activity as a poet. His collection of poems, *Solstice barbelé* (1975; Thorny solstice), revealed a solid poet who believed in creative freedom. He achieved fame, however, through his fiction, particularly *Les chercheurs d'os* (1984; The bones seekers), which won the Duca Foundation Prize. Like other Algerian writers, in this work Djaout deplores the abuse of the martyrs' memory in postindependence Algeria. His next novel, *L'invention du désert* (1987; Inventing the desert), contracts history with present-day ordinary activities, particularly the problems of a journalist like himself. The novel raises questions dealing with the search for identity and the ordeal of exile.

It is in his last novel, *Les vigiles* (1991; The vigils), that Djaout steps into present-day Algeria, revealing the early signs of religious fervor as an escape and a solution to insurmountable daily problems on the administrative, political, and economic levels. There are also memories of the Algerian war of independence, which continue to haunt Algerian writers.

See also LITERATURE: ARABIC, NORTH AFRICAN.

AIDA A. BAMIA

DJEBAR, ASSIA

[1936–]

Algerian francophone novelist and filmmaker.

Assia Djebar (Fatima Zohra Imaleyene) received her earliest education in Blida and Algiers and went on to study at the L'École Normale Supérieure de Sèvres, the first Algerian woman to be admitted there. She participated in the Algerian War of Independence by interviewing Algerian refugees in neighboring countries for the National Liberation Front newspaper *al-Moudjahid*, work that structures her most famous novel, *L'amour, la fantasie* (1985; published in English as *Fantasia: An Algerian Cavalcade*, 1993). Her first novel, *La soif* (1957), was written during the 1956 student uprising; it was followed by *Les impatients* (1958), *L'enfants du nouveau monde* (1962), *Les alouettes naïves* (1968), and a trilogy composed of *Fantasia, Ombre sultane* (1987; published in English as *A Sister to*

Scheherazade, 1988), and *Femmes d'Alger dans leur appartement* (1980; published in English as *Women of Algiers in Their Apartment*, 1992). Her novel *Loin de Medine* (1991; published in English as *Far from Medina*, 1994) imaginatively renders the earliest Muslim society, putting its women at the center and lyrically evoking pre-Muslim Arab heroines. Most of the other novels focus on the experience of the civil war, offering a view of women's participation that counters the portrayal given by Franz Fanon and others. A novel, *So Vast Is the Prisona* (*Vaste est la prison: Roman*, 1995), appeared in English in 1999. The memoiristic *Algerian White* (*Le blanc de l'Algérie: récit*) appeared in English in 2002.

Djebar has worked extensively in cinema; her best-known film was her first, *La nouba des femmes du Mont Chenoua*, winner of the 1979 Venice Bienniale Critics' Prize. Another is *La Zerda et les chants de l'oubli* (1982). She uses Algerian dialect in these films, making a nationalist as well as feminist statement in her focus on women's conditions and agency. She has taught at the University of Rabat, the University of Algiers, Louisiana State University, and New York University, having chosen self-exile since the outbreak of civil war in Algeria. She has won several literary prizes, including the Neustadt International Prize for Literature (1996) and the Fonlon-Nichols Prize of the African Literary Association (1997).

See also ALGERIAN WAR OF INDEPENDENCE; FILM; FRONT DE LIBÉRATION NATIONALE.

Bibliography

Elia, Nada. "The Fourth Language: Subaltern Expression in Djebar's *Fantasia*." In *Intersections: Gender, Nation, and Community in Arab Women's Novels*, edited by Lisa Suhair Majaj, Paula W. Sunderland, and Therese Saliba. Syracuse, NY: Syracuse University Press, 2002.

World Literature Today: Special Issue on Assia Djebar 70, no. 4 (Autumn 1996).

MARILYN BOOTH

DJEMAʿA

Constituent assembly, usually regulating the village or clan but occasionally tribe or confederation; also the place where its members gather, usually daily.

The traditional form of governance in rural communities in North Africa, the djemaʿa (jamaʿa) consists of the heads of landholding families or lineages. Its head (*amghar* in most Berber-speaking areas) is chosen, usually annually, on a rotating basis by the members. Decisions are made by consensus, typically after considerable consultation. Its responsibilities include maintaining roads and paths, water and irrigation systems, and the local mosque and its school; hiring the school's teacher; ensuring hospitality for visitors; organizing community support for families needing manpower (especially in plowing and harvesting); organizing community festivities; assigning communal land to families for cereal production; and setting times and rules for wood collection, grazing, and beginning the harvest. In the past, the djemaʿa had greater judicial functions: In accordance with the local *qanun*—essentially a list of fines and punishments for a wide variety of misdeeds—it regulated community life and ensured equal justice, responsibility, and benefit.

See also QANUN.

THOMAS G. PENCHOEN

DJERBA

An island off the southeast coast of Tunisia, near the Libyan border.

The island of Djerba (Jarba) is 198 square miles (514 sq km), shaped like a molar tooth, and connected to the mainland of Tunisia on the southeast by a ferry at Adjim and on the southwest by a bridge that dates from the Roman Empire. Between Djerba and the mainland is the shallow inland sea of Bou Grara. The island's elevation is low—barely 188 feet (54 m) above sea level at its highest point—and is surrounded by shallow beaches of fine sand and palm trees, especially in the northeast. The principal population center is Houmt-Souk, a market and fishing port on the north coast. Since Tunisian independence in 1956, dozens of tourist hotels and an airport have been built on Djerba.

Djerba is reputed to be the island of the lotus eaters in Homer's *Odyssey*. Djerba's early history is one of contact with many peoples—Berbers, Carthaginians, Greeks, Romans, Vandals, Byzantines, and others. Companions of the prophet Muhammad brought the Arabic language and religion of Islam to Djerba in 665 C.E. Berber Kharijites, considered heretics by many orthodox Muslims, took refuge in southern Djerba after the Almohads expelled them from western Algeria. Since then the southern part of the island has tended to be Berber and Kharijite, the northeast Arab and Malekite, and the center mixed in population.

During the Middle Ages, Djerba was the scene of continuous persecutions, conquests, revolts, reconquests, civil wars, and plagues. Spaniards, Sicilians, Hafsids, Corsairs, and Ottoman Turks controlled the island at various times. In the eighteenth century, Tunis eventually won the contest with Tripoli for jurisdiction under the Ottoman Empire over Djerba. During the French protectorate, Djerba was under military administration from 1881 to 1890, then French civil administration until independence in 1956. The island is today part of the Tunisian Governorship of Medenine, and its population is a mix of Arab and Berber, plus elements of black African, Turkish, and Maltese origin.

The center and southeast of Djerba and portions of the nearby mainland are among the rare areas of Tunisia where a Berber language is spoken, although it is highly mixed with Arabic vocabulary.

An inside view of the *Griba* (wonderful) synagogue, located on the Isle of Djerba off the coast of southern Tunisia. Built in the time of Ezra (fifth century B.C.E.), it is believed that Ezra visited the island and that relics from the Temple of Jerusalem are within the synagogue's walls. Pilgrimages are still made in honor of Rabbi Simeon bar Yohai, the Talmudic sage attributed with writing the Zohar, a mystical book. The synagogue was the target of a terrorist attack on 11 April 2002 that took the lives of several German tourists. © FULVIO ROITER/CORBIS. REPRODUCED BY PERMISSION.

Midoun Jerba (or Djerba) passersby fill this Tunisian street on a sunny day. Djerba is an island in the central Mediterranean Sea, off the southeast coast of Tunisia. The island contains the remains of an ancient Roman civilization and is a popular tourist destination. © NIK WHEELER/CORBIS. REPRODUCED BY PERMISSION.

According to Arab historian Ibn Khaldun (1332–1406) "Djerba" originally referred to a branch of the Lemata Berbers.

Djerba is home to one of the few remaining Jewish communities in North Africa, the towns of Hara Sghira and Hara Kebira. According to local tradition, the Jewish community of Djerba dates from after the Babylonian captivity in 586 B.C.E.; others claim that Judeo-Berbers migrated to the island in the late eighth century C.E., following the Arab conquest of North Africa. The town of Hara Sghira is the site of the Ghriba—a Jewish synagogue, shrine, and site of a popular annual pilgrimage.

Djerba has low and irregular rainfall—averaging 8 inches (21 cm) per year—and high humidity. The only freshwater sources on the island are a few wells in the northeast and rainwater captured by cisterns. This limits local agriculture to date palms of mediocre quality, olive trees, fruit trees, and some grains and legumes.

In the twentieth and twenty-first centuries, the pressures of increasing population on this ecologically marginal island have gradually forced people out of the traditional occupations of agriculture, fishing, weaving, and pottery-marking. As the island's population increased from 31,800 in 1906 to 62,445 in 1956 to more than 82,000 in 1991, Djerbians began to rotate between the island and the mainland as shopkeepers. In reaction to anti-commercial policies of the Ben Salah government of the 1960s, Djerbians increasingly turned to international migration, and many of them have become successful shopkeepers and businessmen in the Paris area. The 2002 population of Djerba was estimated to have decreased to 60,300.

See also ARABIC; BEN SALAH, AHMED; BERBER; ISLAM; OTTOMAN EMPIRE; TUNISIA.

LAURENCE MICHALAK

DLIMI, AHMED

[1931–1983]

Moroccan military officer.

Ahmed Dlimi achieved dubious prominence during the Ben Barka affair of 1965 and 1966, when he was acquitted in a Paris trial. By the mid-1970s, he was King Hassan II's closest military adviser; as a colonel, he was given command of the military seizure of the contested former Spanish colony of Western Sahara in 1974 and 1975. Promoted to general and given full control over theater operations, from 1979 to 1980 Dlimi oversaw the building of the "wall" in Western Sahara—a fortified sand barrier stretching across nearly 25 percent of the northern border. In early 1983, with relations souring between the military and the throne, Dlimi died in a mysterious auto accident.

See also BEN BARKA, MEHDI; HASSAN II.

Bibliography

Hodges, Tony. *Western Sahara: The Roots of a Desert War.* Westport, CT: L. Hill, 1983.

MATTHEW S. GORDON

DO'AR HA-YOM

See NEWSPAPERS AND PRINT MEDIA: ISRAEL

DOHA

Capital and largest city of Qatar.

Situated almost midway down the east coast of the Qatari peninsula, Doha is the country's center of administration, finance, culture, transportation, and social services. The modern city grew from the fishing and pearling port of al-Bida, which at the end of the nineteenth century had around 12,000 inhabitants. The town's economy depended to a large extent on pearling, and the busy port had some 300 pearling ships in 1939, just before the industry collapsed. After oil revenues began enriching the emirate in the 1960s, the city grew rapidly. Its simple one- and two-story stone, mud, coral block, and timber dwellings were replaced by high-rise apartments and offices, palatial villas, and tree-lined subdivisions supported by modern infrastructure. The city's waterfront is lined by a gracefully curving roadway and landscaped walkway, or corniche. Although the oil and gas industry dominate the local economy, fishing and trade also bring activity to the port town. According to the 1997 census the city had 264,009 inhabitants. Because most of the city's residents are non-Qataris, the character of the city resembles others in the Persian Gulf such as Abu Dhabi, Dubai, and Dhahran, where there are large numbers of Iranians, Indians, Pakistanis, Filipinos, and Bangladeshis who influence the types of restaurants and the items sold in the markets.

Bibliography

Crystal, Jill. *Oil and Politics in the Gulf: Rulers and Merchants in Kuwait and Qatar.* New York; Cambridge, U.K.: Cambridge University Press, 1995.

Zahlan, Rosemarie Said. *The Creation of Qatar.* New York: Barnes and Noble; London: Croom Helm, 1979.

MALCOM C. PECK
UPDATED BY ANTHONY B. TOTH

DOLMA

See FOOD

DOLMABAHÇE PALACE

Ottoman sultan's palace.

Built in 1853 by Sultan Abdülmecit I, Dolmabahçe is located on the banks of the Bosporus in Beşiktaş, north of the centuries-old sultanic residence Topkapi. The new palace, built in a mixture of European styles, replaced an older one on the site, where Sultan Mahmud II had moved in 1815. While it was used for official functions through most of the nineteenth century, Dolmabahçe was the sultan's official residence for only a few years, as Abdülmecit soon moved to Çağiran Palace and Abdülaziz moved to a newer palace on the hill above it at Yildiz. Mustafa Kemal Atatürk died at Dolmabahçe on 8 November 1938.

See also ABDÜLAZIZ; ABDÜLMECIT I; ATATÜRK, MUSTAFA KEMAL; MAHMUD II; TOPKAPI PALACE.

Bibliography

Shaw, Stanford, and Shaw, Ezel Kural. *History of the Ottoman Empire and Modern Turkey,* Vol. 2: *Reform, Revolution, and Republic: The Rise of Modern Turkey, 1808–1975.* Cambridge, U.K., and New York: Cambridge University Press, 1977.

ELIZABETH THOMPSON

DONANMA

See NEWSPAPERS AND PRINT MEDIA: TURKEY

DÖNME

A group in Turkey descended from followers of the mystical messiah Shabbetai Tzevi (1626–1676) who converted from Judaism to Islam.

By the mid-seventeenth century the apocalyptic events of the early modern era (expulsions, persecutions, the rise and fall of empires) inspired many to expect the messiah soon. Shabbetai Tzevi, a descendant of Iberian (Sephardic) exiles, was steeped in Kabbalistic beliefs that sought to hasten messianic redemption. In 1665 his followers proclaimed him the messiah. He eventually acquired a following greater than any other Jewish messianic movement since Christianity. In 1666 Shabbetai Tzevi tried to overthrow the sultan. Thwarted, to avoid execution, he converted. At this point most abandoned him, but a minority did not. His loyalists remained, at least outwardly, Jews, but a few converted. Those who converted still maintained contact with a larger support system of secret allies within the Jewish community. They also were close to an important Sufi order, the Bektashis, who promoted doctrines, notably *taqiya* (religious dissimulation), that provided an Islamic rationale for contradictory beliefs.

After Shabbetai's death, his followers flocked to the major Jewish center in the Ottoman Empire, Salonika. Outwardly good Muslims, with great secrecy they conducted Sabbatean prayers, initially in Hebrew and later in Ladino (Judeo-Spanish), until late the nineteenth century, when they adopted Turkish. The Dönme became a significant element in Salonika. They may have accounted for as much as half of its Muslim population.

During the twilight of the Ottoman Empire, Salonika was the birthplace of the Committee for Union and Progress (CUP) and of Mustafa Kemal (Atatürk). Cavit Bey, a direct descendant of an early disciple and a leader in his own right, was an important minister in the CUP government. Atatürk had studied in a progressive school founded by a Dönme educator. Although the claim that Atatürk was a Dönme is untrue, their complex and sophisticated values shaped the environment of his youth.

In 1924, following the Treaty of Lausanne, the entire Muslim population of Salonika—including the Dönme—was deported to Turkey. In 1925 all Sufi orders were abolished. Shorn of the Dönme support system, intermarriage and assimilation eroded the community. In 1924 Ahmed Emin Yalman, a prominent journalist, had publicly renounced all ties to the sect and called for its complete integration into Turkish national life. Although some are still identified as Salonikli (often a code for Dönme), there is no evidence that their distinctive beliefs and practices survive today.

See also BEKTASHIS; SUFISM AND THE SUFI ORDERS.

Bibliography

Scholem, Gershom. *The Messianic Idea in Judaism and Other Essays on Jewish Spirituality.* New York: Schocken Books, 1995.

BENJAMIN BRAUDE

DOR DE'A

Jewish educational reform movement.

The Dor De'a (Hebrew; Generation of Knowledge) was a Jewish enlightenment movement founded by Hayyim Habshush (?–1899) and Rabbi Yihye ben Solomon Qafih (1850–1932) in San'a, Yemen, in the late nineteenth century. The two men were inspired in part by their personal contacts with the European Jewish scholars, Joseph Halévy and later Edouard Glaser, who explored Yemen.

Dor De'a aimed at reforming Jewish education by purging it of Cabalistic elements (a mystical interpretation of Scriptures) and by introducing a small amount of modern secular subjects and vocational training. From 1910 to 1915, Rabbi Qafih operated a modern school that included the Turkish language as well as Hebrew and Arabic. He was encouraged by the Alliance Israélite Universelle, whose support he had sought. The movement faced strong opposition from conservative elements led by Rabbi Isaac Yiyha (?–1932), supported by the imam of Yemen. The community remained split into opposing factions, which called each other derisively the Darade'a (a mocking Arabic plural derived from Dor De'a) and the Iggeshim (the crooked ones) until their mass emigration to Israel.

See also ALLIANCE ISRAÉLITE UNIVERSELLE (AIU); QAFIH, YIHYE BEN SOLOMON.

Bibliography

Ahroni, Reuben. *Yemenite Jewry: Origins, Culture, and Literature.* Bloomington: Indiana University Press, 1968.

NORMAN STILLMAN

DORNER, DALIA

[1934–]

Israeli jurist, member of Israel's Supreme Court.

Born in Turkey, Dalia Dorner came to Israel in 1944 and studied in a Youth Immigration institution. In 1951, she graduated from the exclusive Reali High School in Haifa. As a teenager, she was active in a leftwing youth movement and fought for egalitarian causes. She enrolled in the Faculty of Law of the Hebrew University of Jerusalem and was awarded an M.J. degree in 1956. Between 1960 and

1973, she served in the Judge Advocate General Corps of the Israel Defense Force (IDF), specializing in defending soldiers. She also served as command defense attorney, deputy judge advocate general, and chief defense attorney of the IDF. Between 1973 and 1979, she was president of the Central Command District Military Court and was later appointed judge in the Military Appeals Court.

Discharged with the rank of colonel, she served for five years as a judge on the Beersheba District Court (1979–1984) and for ten years on the Jerusalem District Court (1984–1994). Appointed to the Supreme Court in 1994, she earned a reputation for being on the liberal wing of the court. She wrote a pioneering decision recognizing the rights of a same sex-mate and she opposed discrimination based on sex. She based her ruling in part on the basic law: human freedom and dignity. She was in the minority in a case dealing with the continued detention of Hizbullah leaders such as Shaykh Abd al-Karim Ubayd seized by Israel as hostages for the return of Israeli prisoners and those missing in action. She argued that this act contradicted the laws of war in the framework of international law and that no one should lose his or her freedom except as punishment or to prevent clear and evident danger. But she supported moderate use of force by the General Security Services to extract confessions. She retired from the court in 2004.

See also GENDER: GENDER AND LAW; GENDER: GENDER AND POLITICS.

MERON MEDZINI

DOST MOHAMMAD BARAKZAI
[1792–1863]

Amir of Afghanistan, 1826–1838, 1842–1863.

Dost Mohammad Barazkai, also called the Great Amir (Amir Kabir), was born in Kandahar in the Mohammadzai branch of the Durrani Pushtun subtribe. Considered the founder of the Mohammadzai dynasty that ruled Afghanistan until 1973, Dost Mohammad first became ruler of Afghanistan in 1826 after a period of civil war. After battling even his own brothers for control, he gradually united the country. He also attempted to regain Afghan territory lost to the Sikhs, who ruled Peshawar at that time. Having defeated the Sikhs at the Battle of Jumrud (1837), he assumed the title Amir al-Mu'minin (Commander of the Faithful).

In the 1830s, Dost Mohammad began to turn away from the British and to make overtures to Persia and Russia. As a result the British invaded Afghanistan (1839) in the first Anglo–Afghan war. Once they had defeated Dost Mohammad and taken him as a hostage to India (1840), the British placed Dost Mohammad's rival Shah Shuja on the throne. The occupation of Afghanistan soon turned into a disaster for the British, however, and they were forced to retreat from Kabul in the winter of 1842, losing almost all of their troops in the process. In 1842, Dost Mohammad returned to the throne and ruled for another twenty years. Three of his twenty-seven sons became rulers of Afghanistan, although only Sher Ali ruled for a prolonged period.

See also ANGLO–AFGHAN WARS.

Bibliography

Adamec, Ludwig. *Historical Dictionary of Afghanistan,* 2d edition. Lanham, MD: Scarecrow Press, 1997.

GRANT FARR

DOU'AJI, ALI AL-
[1909–1949]

Tunisian short story writer, dramatist, and painter.

Ali al-Dou'aji, born in Tunis, worked for literary journals, contributing articles mainly to *al-Alam al-Adabi.* He joined the group of bohemian writers known as Jama'at Taht al-Sur (Group under the wall), which was active between the two world wars. Many of them indulged in drinking and drugs to escape the harsh realities of their lives.

Al-Dou'aji's short stories and essays deal with the problems of the poor and struggling classes. The pessimism of the subjects is tempered by the subtle humor of the writer. He often used dialect in the dialogue of his short stories for a more truthful portrayal of life. His collection of short stories *Sahirtu minhu al-Layali* (1969; Sleepless nights) concerns Tunisia's society and its social ills. His sketches *Jawlatun bayna Hanat al-Bahr al-Abyad al-Mutawassit* (1973; A Tour around the bars of the Mediterranean) reveal his humor, his powers of observation, and his capacity to portray human ridicule.

See also LITERATURE: ARABIC, NORTH AFRICAN.

AIDA A. BAMIA

DOUGHTY, CHARLES
[1843–1926]

English author and traveler in Arabia.

Born in Suffolk to an Anglican cleric, Charles Montagu Doughty studied geology at Cambridge University. Motivated by a desire to examine ancient inscriptions and to explore the origins of humanity in what he considered its primitive setting, from 1876 to 1878 he traveled among the bedouin, whom he considered the original people. Though dressed and living as a simple wanderer in central and western Arabia, he never disguised himself as a native. He was the first literary traveler openly to proclaim his Englishness and never to deny his Christianity, to the point of imagining himself a Christlike figure.

In undertaking his voyage, Doughty benefited from Europe's economic and political penetration of the Middle East. But as he approached what he believed was the beginning of time, that very world of wealth, industry, and capital was interfering with his quest. Remote Anaizah in Central Arabia was by now the home to merchants who discussed Otto von Bismarck and Czar Alexander and life under English rule in Bombay. Hundreds of Najdis had gone down to Egypt "to dig for wages in the work of the Suez Canal," which Doughty called "this moral quagmire."

The result of his labor, *Travels in Arabia Deserta,* published in 1888, did not gain popular success until after World War I. T. E. Lawrence, whose *Seven Pillars of Wisdom* had made him an international literary star, rescued Doughty's book from neglect by arranging for a handsome second edition, which he endorsed with a ten-page introduction. Doughty also wrote patriotic poetry but, unlike his champion, he played little role in public affairs.

See also LAWRENCE, T. E.

Bibliography

Doughty, Charles M. *Travels in Arabia Deserta,* 2 vols. Cambridge, U.K.: Cambridge University Press, 1888.

Hogarth, D. G. *The Life of Charles M. Doughty.* Garden City, NY: Doubleday, Doran, 1929.

BENJAMIN BRAUDE

DOWLATABADI, MAHMOUD
[1940–]

An Iranian writer and actor.

Mahmoud Dowlatabadi was born in Dowlatabad, a village in northwestern Khorasan province. His parents were peasants, and as a child Dowlatabadi learned the various tasks associated with farming and tending livestock. There was no secondary school in his village and after finishing primary school Dowlatabadi went to Sabzevar to continue his education. By the time he was in his late teens, he had to work full-time and thus could not finish high school. He held various jobs in Sabzevar before moving to Mashhad for work, and eventually to Tehran. While in Sabzevar, he developed a great love for reading, especially American and European fiction that had been translated into Persian. By the mid-1960s, he had begun to write short stories. Rural Khorasan—and the social problems intertwined with its relative poverty—is the background for his fiction. By the early 1970s, he was acquiring a reputation as a serious writer who used social realism. He was arrested in 1974, apparently because the SAVAK believed his fiction represented implicit criticism of Mohammad Reza Shah Pahlavi's government. He began writing his epic 3,000-page novel, *Klidar,* in 1978 and did not complete the fifth and final volume until 1983.

Klidar established Dowlatabadi as one of Iran's most significant literary figures in the second half of the twentieth century. Yet his background set him apart from the country's other famous writers, the majority of whom came from middle- or upper-class urban families, had attended college—often outside Iran—and had began their careers by translating foreign works into Persian. Dowlatabadi's contributions to Persian literature since the completion of *Klidar* include essays, novels, short stories, and screenplays. In 1994, he was one of the 133 writers who signed a declaration calling for freedom of expression in Iran. In 2000, he was among twenty-nine intellectuals arrested and charged with anti-state activities for participating in a conference in

Berlin on the reform movement in Iran; he was acquitted in January 2001.

See also PAHLAVI, MOHAMMAD REZA.

Bibliography

Emami, Karim, and Yavari, Houra. "On *Klidar*: A Symposium," in *Iranian Studies*, 22, no. 4 (1989): 82–97.

ERIC HOOGLUND

DRAGOMANS

Translators of Turkish, Persian, and Arabic into European languages.

When the Ottoman Empire began commercial dealings with the Europeans, translators were employed by European agents and diplomats in the capital, Istanbul. As no business could be conducted without these translators, they fulfilled a vital intermediary role in European–Ottoman relations, both political and commercial. Known as dragomans, these translators were usually Christians and often Greeks from the Phanar district of Istanbul. By the nineteenth century, they occupied a position of power and influence in Istanbul.

The Ottoman ministry for foreign affairs employed an official dragoman, and many European diplomats dealt with him or his deputies rather than directly with Ottoman administrators. Ottoman embassies in Europe also employed dragomans. After the Greek revolt in 1821, part of the Greek War of Independence, Muslims and Turks began to act as dragomans, and some became important figures during the Tanzimat reform period of the mid-1800s. One of the many Tanzimat reforms was the creation of a bureau of translation in the Ottoman Ministry of Foreign Affairs, which centralized and incorporated the dragomans.

See also GREEK WAR OF INDEPENDENCE; TANZIMAT.

Bibliography

Lewis, Bernard. *The Emergence of Modern Turkey*, 3d edition. New York: Oxford University Press, 2002.

Shaw, Stanford, and Shaw, Ezel Kural. *History of the Ottoman Empire and Modern Turkey*. 2 vols. Cambridge, U.K., and New York: Cambridge University Press, 1976–1977.

ZACHARY KARABELL

DREYFUS AFFAIR

Famous turn-of-the-century case of French antisemitism.

In 1894 Alfred Dreyfus, a Jewish captain in the French army, was convicted in a secret military court-martial of espionage on behalf of Germany and was sentenced to life imprisonment on Devil's Island in French Guyana, off the coast of South America. His alleged espionage prompted virulent antisemitism and was cited by some French editorialists as but one manifestation of widespread Jewish perfidy. Two years later, an army intelligence investigator concluded that Dreyfus was innocent and the guilty party was Major Walsin Esterhazy. The army at first resisted reopening the case; when it did, it acquitted Esterhazy despite the blatant evidence against him. Later that year the new head of army intelligence confessed he had forged documents implicating Dreyfus and subsequently committed suicide in his jail cell.

A number of prominent liberals and leaders on the Left united in support of Dreyfus, whose conviction they viewed as an unholy antisemitic alliance of France's political Right and the church leadership. The novelist Emile Zola published his famous letter, "J'accuse," in which he vociferously denounced both the military and civil authorities, forcing the investigation into Dreyfus's conviction. A second court martial reiterated Dreyfus's guilt, but shortly thereafter he was pardoned. A number of years later he was declared innocent and returned to his former military rank.

The brazen corruption and antisemitism led to the end of the rightist government in France and, later, the firm separation of church and state there. The antisemitism that manifested itself in many liberal as well as rightist quarters deepened the ties of some Jewish intellectuals to the nascent Zionist Organization. The Viennese journalist Theodor Herzl, who had previously taken some interest in the organization, reported on the trial and, along with his colleague Max Nordau, became totally committed to Zionism.

See also HERZL, THEODOR; NORDAU, MAX.

Bibiography

Bredin, Jean-Denis. *The Affair: The Case of Alfred Dreyfus*, translated by Jeffrey Mehlman. New York: Braziller, 1986.

Burns, Michael. *Dreyfus: A Family Affair, 1789–1945.* New York: HarperCollins, 1991.

Derfler, Leslie. *The Dreyfus Affair.* Westport, CT: Greenwood, 2002.

Stanislawski, Michael. *Zionism and the Fin-de-Siècle: Cosmopolitanism and Nationalism from Nordau to Jabotinsky.* Berkeley: University of California Press, 2001.

CHAIM I. WAXMAN

DROBLES PLAN

See ISRAELI SETTLEMENTS

DRUGS AND NARCOTICS

Drugs have long played a prominent role in the affairs of the Middle East.

The Middle East is ideally suited to profit from all phases of the drug trade. Climate, geography, and, more recently, politics have combined to make the

Two dealers of opium, an illegal drug produced from the poppy flower, openly weigh the drug in the marketplace.
© BETTMANN/CORBIS. REPRODUCED BY PERMISSION.

region an important source and transit point of drugs destined for Europe, the United States, and many of the countries of the Middle East itself. Traditionally, the most important drugs in the Middle East have been opium and marijuana, which provide the raw material for the heroin and hashish that form the staple of the illicit drug trade in the region. Both the opium poppy *(Papaver somniferum)* and marijuana *(Cannabis sativa)* grow easily in many parts of the Middle East and North Africa, and the centuries-old trade routes that crisscross the region give illicit drug producers ready access to the major international drug markets. Although the drug trade is driven largely by the profits inherent in any lucrative criminal activity, in the Middle East it has taken on an important political dimension as rival groups have used enormous drug revenues to pay for the arms necessary to pursue their political ambitions. With a metric ton of heroin worth between $100 million and $600 million, retail, on the streets of the United States, drug sales are an appealing source of immediate, vast revenues for clandestine or criminal activities.

The importance of the Middle East in the international drug trade has varied according to the demand for certain illicit drugs. The taste for drugs is cyclical, alternating between periods of demand for stimulants such as cocaine and amphetamines, and times when the drug-abusing public seeks depressants such as opiates (e.g., morphine, heroin, and other opium derivatives) and hashish. Because the Middle East primarily produces depressants, its importance as a drug source increases when opiates are in demand, as in the 1930s, 1970s, and 1990s.

Opiates

Because *Papaver somniferum* grows best at higher altitudes, Turkey, Afghanistan, Iran, and more recently Lebanon, have at different times been major sources of heroin and other opiates. In the late 1960s and early 1970s, Turkey gained international notoriety as the principal source of the heroin that fed an epidemic of drug abuse in the United States and Europe. In 1973, as part of an agreement with the United States, Turkey first banned, then allowed only very restricted cultivation of opium poppies for medicinal purposes. This is still the only successful drug-crop-control program of its kind, with virtually no leakage into illicit channels.

With Turkey effectively eliminated as a source in the mid-1970s, the center of illicit opiate production shifted eastward to Afghanistan, Lebanon, and, to a lesser extent, Iran. In both Afghanistan and Lebanon, the chaos created by civil war, coupled with the absence of a strong central government and rival combatants' desire for a source of revenue for arms purchases, led to an explosion of opium cultivation. By 1992, Afghanistan had become second only to Myanmar (Burma) in the production of illicit opium. The U.S. government estimated that at the end of 1992, Afghanistan had over 48,000 acres (nearly 19,500 ha) of opium poppy under cultivation, capable of producing 705 tons (640 metric tons) of opium or 70 tons (64 metric tons) of heroin. This would be enough to satisfy estimated heroin needs in the United States six times over and to pump between $6.4 billion and $38.4 billion into the underworld economy. While a large percentage of these opiates is probably consumed by addicts in Afghanistan, Iran, and Pakistan, the remainder flows into the international drug trade through Iran for transshipment to heroin refineries in Turkey and Lebanon. There is also evidence that Afghan opium is flowing northward into new routes opened in central Asia following the collapse of the Soviet Union in 1991.

Although not an opium producer on the scale of Afghanistan, Lebanon is an important country in the international heroin trade. Following Syria's occupation of the Biqa valley in 1976, eastern Lebanon became a center of opium cultivation and heroin refining. The Lebanese government has blamed the Syrian military for the Biqa valley drug trade, which in 1991 had the capacity to produce an estimated 37 tons (34 metric tons) of opium (or 3.7 tons [3.4 metric tons] of heroin) from an estimated nearly 8,400 acres (3,400 ha). Subsequently, a combination of harsh weather and joint Syrian–Lebanese eradication efforts have reduced cultivation to an estimated nearly 1,100 acres (440 ha) in late 1993, though clandestine laboratories may be refining more than 5.5 tons (5 metric tons) a year of heroin from Afghan opium.

Despite Iranian government efforts to ban the opium poppy in 1980, Iran in 1992 was still an important potential source of opium. The U.S. government estimated that nearly 8,650 acres (3,500 ha) of *Papaver somniferum* were under cultivation at the

An Afghan poppy farmer carries an assault rifle while combing through his crop. Poppy growers have been encouraged to cultivate wheat instead of the illicit poppies, the flower used for making opium and heroin. Some farmers are angry because the profit margin for wheat is considerably lower than that for the opium poppy crop. © REZA/WEBISTAN/CORBIS. REPRODUCED BY PERMISSION.

end of the year. There are indications, however, that Iran's addicts consume most domestic opium production. Iran continues to be a conduit for Afghan and Pakistani opiates moving to Turkey and onward along the Balkan route into Europe.

Hashish

Although there is cannabis cultivation in nearly every country of the Middle East, only Morocco and Lebanon are significant hashish producers and exporters. Hashish is simple to manufacture, requiring little of the intensive labor and none of the chemicals needed to refine opiates. And while it does not generate profits on the same scale as opiates, hashish production is a multimillion-dollar criminal enterprise. In 1992, Morocco's nearly 74,000 acres (30,000 ha) of cannabis potentially yielded nearly 9,918 tons (9,000 metric tons) of hashish, most of which was destined for Europe. Lebanon, with an estimated nearly 38,800 acres (15,700 ha) of cannabis under cultivation in 1993, potentially had 623 tons (565 metric tons) of hashish available for export. Cannabis may be sold and used legally in many countries so most governments accord cannabis control a relatively low priority. The hashish trade is likely to remain steady therefore, even as the governments of the Middle East intensify efforts to suppress illicit opiates and stimulants.

See also BIQA VALLEY; CLIMATE; GEOGRAPHY.

Bibliography

Ehrenfeld, Rachel. *Narco-Terrorism.* New York: Basic Books, 1990.

U.S. Congress. Senate. Committee on the Judiciary. *Poppy Politics. Hearings before the Subcommittee to Investigate Juvenile Delinquency.* Washington, DC: U.S. Government Printing Office, 1975.

U.S. Department of Justice. Drug Enforcement Administration. *Illegal Drug Price/Purity Report: January 1989–December 1992.* Washington, DC: U.S. Government Printing Office, 1993.

U.S. Department of Justice. Drug Enforcement Administration. *Illicit Drug Trafficking and Use in the United States.* Washington, DC: U.S. Government Printing Office, 1993.

U.S. Department of Justice. Drug Enforcement Administration. *The NNICC Report 1992: The Supply of Illicit Drugs to the United States.* Washington, DC: U.S. Government Printing Office, 1993.

U.S. Department of State. *International Narcotics Control Strategy Report, April 1993.* Washington, DC: U.S. Government Printing Office, 1993.

W. KENNETH THOMPSON

DRUMMOND–WOLFF CONVENTION

Abortive pact (1885) between Britain and the Ottoman Empire.

Sir Henry Drummond-Wolff negotiated an agreement with Sultan Abdülhamit II at the behest of British Foreign Secretary Lord Robert Salisbury; the pact was to terminate Britain's occupation of Egypt after a three-year period. Because the agreement would have empowered Britain to reenter Egypt under certain conditions, the French and Russian ambassadors in Istanbul persuaded the sultan to withdraw his approval. Consequently, the British occupation of Egypt was greatly prolonged.

See also ABDÜLHAMIT II.

Bibliography

Hornik, F. P. "Mission of Sir Henry Drummond-Wolff to Constantinople 1885–1887." *English Historical Review* 55 (1940): 598–623.

ARTHUR GOLDSCHMIDT

DRUZE

A small religious community that emerged in eleventh-century Cairo and spread to what is today Lebanon, Syria, and Israel.

The name *Druze* (in Arabic *Duruz*, meaning Druzes) was given to the community by outsiders based on the name of al-Darazi, an early convert who came to Cairo in the year 1015, joined the missionary ranks, and was eventually killed or executed in 1019. The Druze manuscripts consider him an apostate and refer to members of the community as Unitarians (*Muwwahhidun*) or People of Unitarianism (*Ahl al-Tawhid*). The Druzes are also known as Sons of Mercy or Sons of Beneficence (*Banu Ma'ruf*). In addition, the word *Ma'ruf* is derived from the Arabic words *arafa* (to know); thus, Druzes are often mentioned in their manuscripts as *A'raf* (those who possess knowledge).

Druze Communities

There are approximately one million Druzes in the world today with 85 to 90 percent of them living in the Middle East. Smaller communities can be found in Australia, Canada, Europe, the Philippines, South America, West Africa, and the United States. Within Druze villages and small towns in the Middle East, the predominant occupation has always been farming, and two classes of landowners and peasants have dominated the Druze economic landscape for centuries. Although most Druzes remain predominantly rural, rapid urbanization and modernization have not only transformed Druze village economics but also facilitated increases in educational levels and professional training.

Despite these recent transformations, social and religious authority among the Druzes remains persistent and comes from a religious elite that has an extraordinary influence on Druze communities. Thus, it may be said that Druzism both unites Druzes into socially cohesive communities and divides them into two main classes: the initiated or wise (uqqal) and the uninitiated or, literally, "ignorant" (juhhal). Only those believers who demonstrate piety and devotion and who have withstood the lengthy process of candidacy are initiated into the esoteric teachings and oral traditions of the faith. Women initiates undergo a less rigorous training because the Druze doctrine considers women to be more spiritually prepared and therefore not in need of the arduous initiation process that men are required to undertake.

The initiated persons are further subdivided based on their spiritual level of advancement. Only a small group of the most devout of the initiated members are called ajawid, meaning the selected, or, literally, "the good." In the eyes of the rest of the community, the ajawid serve as models for righteous behavior, truthfulness, and wisdom; they reinforce the cultural attributes of the entire community. Uninitiated persons comprise the majority of Druze society. They may seek initiation at any age, but their acceptance is based on their character, which is assessed by the initiated ones. Although the uninitiated are indeed "ignorant" of the Druze doctrine, their behavior is expected to conform to certain prescriptions both spiritual (e.g., fealty to God, His prophets, and His luminaries) and moral (e.g., respect for elders, honor for women, and care for children).

Emergence of Druzism (996–1043)

Druzism is traced to Fatimid-Isma'ili-Shi'ite Egypt, and more specifically to the sixth Fatimid caliph al-Hakim bi-Amr Allah (r. 996–1021). Druze history may be divided into three main phases: the emergence of Druzism (996–1043), the era of emirates (1040s–1840s), and recent times (since the 1840s). Although almost all sources date the beginning of Druzism to 1017, the year 996 was not only the beginning of al-Hakim's rule but also, and more importantly, there is evidence of covert preparatory activity between 996 and 1017. The nearly fifty-year period of the emergence of Druzism revolves around

During the Lebanese Civil War, Walid Jumblatt took over leadership of the Druze after the assassination of his father, Kamal, in 1977. Walid's forces fared well during the confrontation, which lasted fifteen years and resulted in an estimated 140,000 deaths. © AP/WIDE WORLD PHOTOS. REPRODUCED BY PERMISSION.

three main leaders, al-Hakim bi-Amr Allah, Hamza ibn Ali al-Zawzani, and Baha al-Din al-Samuqi. In the eyes of many historians, al-Hakim was the most controversial among Fatimi caliphs due to a claim for divinity, which apparently he never made but others attributed to him, and because of his early rigid or unacceptable resolutions against the social and religious practices of Sunnis, Christians, and Jews. Although al-Hakim's attitude toward the Druze faith is not fully discernible from the available sources, it can be concluded that al-Hakim did not prevent Druze missionaries from propagating their doctrine; on the contrary, he appears to have allowed their proselytizing activities, approved their writings, and protected their followers.

Hamza ibn Ali is the central authority behind Druze teachings and as such is considered by some writers to be the actual founder of Druzism. He came to Cairo in December 1016, met the Druze missionaries in the Ridan Mosque, and then proclaimed the new movement in 1017. Four years later, in 1021, al-Hakim left on one of his routine

Druze rebels in Lebanon during the 1958 revolts when the Progressive Socialist Party, led by Kamal Jumblatt, demanded social and political reforms for all sects in Lebanon. Today, the Druze are one of seventeen recognized sects in the country, which requires all citizens to carry a government-issued identification card encoded with his or her religion. © HULTON-DEUTSCH COLLECTION/CORBIS. REPRODUCED BY PERMISSION.

trips to the hills of al-Muqattam east of Cairo but never returned. In the same year, Hamza and his close associates went into retreat, announcing that a period of persecution by al-Hakim's successor, the seventh Fatimid caliph al-Zahir, had begun, and that the affairs of the community were delegated to Baha al-Din. After the hardship years of 1021 to 1026, Baha al-Din resumed missionary activity and wrote epistles until the closing of Druzism in 1043, when he departed to an undisclosed location. Since then, no one has been permitted to join the Druze movement.

Era of Emirates (1040s–1840s)

The second phase of Druze history is represented in three emirates—the Buhturis, Ma'nis, and Shihabis—that played important roles in providing leadership to the Druze masses. The Buhturis (1040s–1507) are a branch of the Tanukhis, who had origins in Arabia but migrated to northern Syria and then settled in Mount Lebanon beginning in the middle of the eighth century. In the first half of the eleventh century some of the Tanukhi princes joined the Druze faith. The relationship of the Buhturi amirs with the Islamic central governments was at times affected by the Islamic power struggles. For example, the Mamluks and Ayyubids fought not only each other, but also the Mongols. Nevertheless, the Buhturis remained in power until the takeover of the Arab lands in 1516 by the Ottoman Sultan Selim I (r. 1512–1520), who is said to have been encouraged by the Druze Ma'ni Prince Fakhr al-Din I.

With the help of the Buhturis, the forefather of the Ma'nis, Prince Ma'n, moved with his supporters to the Shuf in 1120. This Ma'ni clan remained relatively insignificant until the emergence of their prince Fakhr al-Din I (r. 1507–1544). Although he was asked to support the Mamluks, Fakhr al-Din instead joined the Ottoman forces of Sultan Selim, whose army defeated the Mamluks in 1516 in the decisive battle of Marj Dabiq. Subsequently, the Ottomans allowed the Ma'nis to have independent political control within the region, as long as taxes reached Istanbul promptly. With the continued support of the Ottomans, another Druze prince, Fakhr al-Din II (r. 1585/1590–1635), extended the Ma'ni principality north to the Syrian city of Palmyra and south to the Sinai Peninsula. Although he initially re-established good relations with the Ottoman Empire, he also signed treaties with the Grand Duke of Tuscany (1606–1608). As a result, the Ottomans became gradually suspicious of Fakhr al-Din II's overt ambition; they mobilized against him and defeated his army at Hasbayya in 1635. He was then executed with his two sons in Istanbul, but the Ma'ni amirs were allowed to rule until 1697, when the emirate was transferred to the Shihabi house.

With the transfer of power from the Ma'nis to the Shihabis, the Druzes as a whole continued to enjoy a relatively high degree of autonomy. But within a decade, Druzes became divided and eventually turned against each other. At the battle of Ain Dara in 1711 two Druze factions fought—the Qaysis of northern Arabian origin and the Yamanis of southern origin. The decisive victory of the Qaysis caused many of the Yamanis to flee to the Hawran region, reducing Druze influence in Mount Lebanon. The Shihabi principality slowly fell under the political and military control of external rulers. Sectarianism began to take root and religious consciousness was on the rise. Moreover, in the late eighteenth century the Shihabis converted to Christianity, which further reduced the Druze influence in Mount Lebanon.

Modern History (1840s to the Present)

The reign of the last of the Shihabi amirs, Bashir II (1788–1840), reinforced a strong central authority exercised over Mount Lebanon and the areas adjacent to it. However, Bashir II was constrained by the Egyptian rulers and a decade of Egyptian occupation; this led to his fall and, subsequently, to the end of the Shihabi emirate and the beginning of internal civil strife in the early 1840s. In 1843 European foreign powers convinced the Ottoman sultan to pacify the area, and to relinquish affairs in the north to the French-supported Maronites and in the south to the British-backed Druzes. The uneasiness in Mount Lebanon grew and finally exploded into open confrontation, beginning with the Maronite peasants rising against their Maronite landlords in 1858 and then against their Druze landlords in 1860. The bloody events of that year ended in the special autonomous administration of Mount Lebanon within the Ottoman Empire. This arrangement quickly failed and was replaced by a political regime known as *Mutasarrifiyya*, headed by a *mutasarrif* (governor) that imposed a ruler from outside Lebanon who was a subject of the Ottoman sultan. The French mandate replaced the *Mutasarrifiyya* in 1918, and the Druzes in Syria and Lebanon came under the French rule; the Druzes in Palestine and Jordan came under the British mandate. The 1920s and 1930s marked a period of revolts and unrest in the entire region, leading to the independence of Lebanon (1943), Syria (1944), and Israel (1948), and the separation of Druze communities by new national boundaries.

The Syrian Druzes have participated in politics largely through the Atrash family and its recent prominent figure Sultan Pasha al-Atrash. An Arab nationalist symbol of the 1925 to 1927 Jabal Druze revolt against the French forces, Sultan al-Atrash continued to influence local and national politics amongst Druzes until his death in 1982. In the 1967 war between Israel and the Arab states, Israel conquered vast lands, including the Syrian Golan Heights, where four Druze villages have resisted Israeli attempts for annexation; they continue to reassert their Syrian identity, and wish to reunite one day with their relatives in Syria.

The Druzes in Palestine in the 1930s and 1940s were a part of the Arab Legion forces despite their feuds with the surrounding Muslim populations. But in 1947 to 1948 a split took place in the Druze community, and some Druzes voluntarily enlisted in the Israeli army, while others resisted any form of cooperation with the Israeli forces. Subsequently, the first faction prevailed, and in 1956 Israel passed a law requiring three years of military service for all Druze males. Since the 1970s the social and political standings of Druzes in Israel have been gradually improving.

The Druzes in Lebanon have participated in the politics of the country through the two major factions of Jumblattis and Arslanis. In 1958 Kamal Jumblatt and his Progressive Socialist Party, which he founded in 1949, demanded political and social reforms for all Lebanese sects. This crisis led to the deployment of U.S. Marines in Lebanon for seven months to help the national government to restore the peace. Two decades later, however, Lebanon faced a military confrontation that erupted into a full-scale civil war in the spring of 1975. At the beginning of the war the Druzes were a part of a loose coalition of Sunnis, Shiʿa, and Greek Orthodox that fought the Maronite Christian militias, but while the war was still raging, Kamal Jumblatt was assassinated in 1977 and his son Walid took his place. Walid Jumblatt's forces regained previously lost towns, established control over the Shuf Mountain, and emerged victorious in the eyes of the community. In the war many Christians were displaced and it was only in the 1990s that arrangements were made for their return.

Finally, the Lebanese civil war of 1975 to 1990 forced Druzes in Lebanon and elsewhere to put aside their factional politics and to focus on their community's welfare. Furthermore, the civil war also promoted interactions between the Lebanese, Syrian, Israeli, and Jordanian Druze communities. Druzes are likely to continue being loyal to the countries in which they live while doing what is necessary to protect their local and regional communities.

See also ATRASH, SULTAN PASHA AL-; GOLAN HEIGHTS; ISRAEL: OVERVIEW; JABAL DRUZE;

Jordan; Jumblatt Family; Jumblatt, Kamal; Jumblatt, Walid; Lebanese Civil War (1975–1990); Lebanon; Lebanon, Mount; Maronites; Progressive Socialist Party; Shuf; Syria.

Bibliography

Abu Izzeddin, Nejla M. *The Druzes.* Leiden, Neth.: Brill, 1984; 1993.

Ben-Dor, Gabriel. *The Druzes in Israel: A Political Study.* Jerusalem: Magnes, 1981.

Betts, Robert Benton. *The Druze.* New Haven, CT: Yale University Press, 1988.

Firro, Kais. *The Druzes in the Jewish State.* Leiden, Neth.: Brill, 2001.

Firro, Kais. *A History of the Druzes.* Leiden, Neth.: Brill, 1992.

Hitti, Philip K. *The Origins of the Druze People and Religion.* New York: AMS Press, 1928.

Makarem, Sami Nasib. *The Druze Faith.* New York: Delmar, 1974.

Swayd, Samy. *The Druzes: An Annotated Bibliography.* Kirkland, WA, and Los Angeles, CA: ISES Publications, 1998.

Swayd, Samy. *A Historical Dictionary of the Druzes.* Lanham, MD, and London: Scarecrow Press, 2004.

ROBERT BETTS
UPDATED BY SAMY S. SWAYD

DRUZE REVOLTS

Druze uprisings in Syria and Lebanon in the 1830s.

These large-scale revolts erupted among the Druze (particularly in Hawran) beginning in 1837, when Ibrahim Pasha ibn Muhammad Ali sought to force conscription in the region to support his adventures and those of his father. The Egyptian force sent from Damascus to suppress the rebels was defeated. The Druze of Hawran were soon aided by those from Shuf and Wadi al-Taym, and by Muslims from Mount Nablus in Palestine, who also were subject to conscription. During the revolt, a Druze warrior named Shibli al-Aryan became a national hero. Ibrahim Pasha's frustration in dealing with Druze rebels led him to request Bashir II to send Christian fighters to quell the rebellion. The Christian soldiers were under the command of Bashir's son

Khalil, which reinforced Druze suspicions about Bashir's sectarian biases. The revolt failed, but it resulted in intensified sectarian animosities in the mountain regions for years to come.

See also DRUZE; IBRAHIM IBN MUHAMMAD ALI.

AS'AD ABUKHALIL

DUAL CONTAINMENT

U.S. policy toward Iran and Iraq from 1993 to 1997.

In May 1993, the U.S. administration of President William Clinton announced a new policy to contain two countries—Iran and Iraq—that it claimed were threats to U.S. interests in the Middle East. Since Iraq effectively was contained by United Nations sanctions and daily aerial patrols of two no-fly zones in the north and south of the country, the real focus of dual containment was Iran. The stated objective was to apply sufficient international diplomatic and economic pressure on Iran to induce its government to modify its behavior in five areas alleged by the United States: its acquisition of weapons of mass destruction; its repression of domestic political dissent; its support for international terrorism; its efforts to destabilize governments in the Middle East; and its opposition to the Middle East peace process. Although key U.S. allies supported efforts to contain Iraq, they criticized the confrontational approach toward Iran and generally declined to cooperate with the U.S. efforts to isolate it. After 1997, U.S. officials stopped using the term *dual containment,* and the de facto policy became one of finding ways to engage in dialogue with Iran to discuss U.S. concerns. In 2001, the new administration of George W. Bush reverted to viewing Iran as a threat to U.S. interests, although it did not revive the term *dual containment.*

Bibliography

Hooglund, Eric. "Mythology versus Reality: Iranian Political Economy and the Clinton Administration." *Critique,* no. 11 (Fall 1997): 37–51.

F. GREGORY GAUSE III
UPDATED BY ERIC HOOGLUND

DUAL CONTROL

Joint British–French supervision of Egyptian government revenues and disbursements from 1878 to 1882, supplementing the supervision provided by the Caisse de la Dette Publique set up in 1876.

The first controllers were members of the so-called European cabinet, in which a British subject was finance minister and a Frenchman held the portfolio for public works. This cabinet, appointed by Egypt's Khedive Isma'il in August 1878, under pressure from his European creditors, lasted only six months because of its fiscal stringencies, which included placing many Egyptian army officers on half pay. Four months later Khedive Isma'il was deposed in favor of his son, Tawfiq.

The British and French governments appointed their controllers: Sir Evelyn Baring (later Lord Cromer), who had served on the Caisse, and de Blignières, the former Egyptian works minister. They drew up what would become the 1880 liquidation law, which reduced Egyptian government indebtedness by strictly limiting government expenditure. This caused either antiforeign sentiment or feelings of nationalism among Egyptian officers and officials, leading to the 1881 and 1882 Urabi revolution.

Once the cabinet headed by Mahmud Sami al-Barudi took control in February 1882, the controllers could no longer direct the budget. Dual Control was formally terminated when the British occupied Egypt in September 1882. Without access to military force, which Britain and France refused to apply until the Urabi revolution, Dual Control could not impose its program on Egypt's economy and body politic.

See also BARING, EVELYN; ISMA'IL IBN IBRAHIM; URABI, AHMAD.

Bibliography

Marlowe, John. *Cromer in Egypt.* London: Elek; New York: Praeger, 1970.

Schölch, Alexander. *Egypt for the Egyptians! The Socio-Political Crisis in Egypt, 1878–1882.* London: Ithaca Press, 1981.

ARTHUR GOLDSCHMIDT

DUBAI

The second largest and second wealthiest of the seven emirates in the United Arab Emirates; also, the city of the same name.

The story of the emirate of Dubai revolves around that of Dubai City. The emirate was established by the Al Maktum ruling family around 1833 when the family's clan, the Al Bu Falasa, broke away from the Bani Yas tribal confederation that dominated the region of Abu Dhabi. In its early years Dubai was a small fishing village on the best natural harbor (called Dubai Creek) in the region. Under the Al Maktum rulers it became an important pearling port, and by the early years of the twentieth century it was second only to Kuwait among the commercial ports on the Arab side of the Persian Gulf.

Dubai's rulers historically have encouraged commercial development, attracting merchants from around the region to the city. Consequently, large and visible expatriate communities from Iran, South Asia, and around the world give the city a vibrant, colorful, and cosmopolitan character. The largest city in the United Arab Emirates and its commercial capital, Dubai had an estimated population in 2000 of 886,000. In addition to its port and massive dry dock facilities, the city has one of the region's busiest airports. In 1999 the city boasted the world's tallest hotel, the Burj al-Arab, or Tower of the Arabs.

See also ABU DHABI.

Bibliography

Noor, Ali Rashid. *Dubai: Life and Times.* London: Motivate Publishing, 1997.

Peck, Malcolm C. *Historical Dictionary of the Gulf Arab States.* London: Scarecrow Press, 1977.

MALCOLM C. PECK
UPDATED BY ANTHONY B. TOTH

DUBS, ADOLPH
[1920–1979]

U.S. ambassador to Afghanistan, 1977–1979; assassinated in Kabul.

Ambassador Adolph ("Spike") Dubs was the American ambassador to Afghanistan at the time of the Saur Revolution in April 1978. On 14 February 1979, Dubs was kidnapped in Kabul and held hostage by unidentified people claiming to be opponents of the Afghan Marxist government. He was shot to death after a few hours by police allegedly trying to free him. His death had a deleterious effect on relations between Afghanistan and the United States.

Bibliography

Arnold, Anthony. *Afghanistan's Two-Party Communism: Parcham and Khalq.* Stanford, CA: Hoover Institution Press, 1983.

GRANT FARR

DUFFERIN REPORT (1883)

Report commending reorganization of Egyptian government under British occupation.

Lord Dufferin, the British ambassador to the Ottoman Empire in Constantinople (now Istanbul), was sent to Egypt following the defeat of the Urabi revolt to recommend policies for the administration of Britain's occupation. His report on the reorganization of the Egyptian government was issued on 6 February 1883. Recognizing the importance of the rising tide of Egyptian nationalism, Lord Dufferin sought middle ground between the restoration of Egyptian sovereignty and full annexation by England. British officials were to take advisory positions in key offices within the Egyptian administration, including the ministries of finance, interior, public works and irrigation, justice, police, and the army. Other specific measures and reforms discussed in the report were the establishment of an elected government under the khedive (ruler of Egypt, viceroy of the sultan of the Ottoman Empire), the promulgation of civil and criminal codes for the Native Tribunals, the abolishment of forced labor, and putting an end to the use of whippings to collect taxes and obtain evidence of crimes. As a result of Dufferin's report, a Legislative Council and a General Assembly were established, changing the contours of Egyptian politics. Contrary to Dufferin's intention of minimizing British control over the Egyptian government, the reforms discussed in his report increased British presence in Egypt and enhanced Egyptian opposition to the occupation.

See also URABI, AHMAD.

Bibliography

Goldschmidt, Arthur, Jr. *Modern Egypt: The Formation of a Nation-State.* Boulder, CO: Westview Press, 1988.

Vatikiotis, P. J. *The History of Modern Egypt: From Muhammad Ali to Mubarak,* 4th edition. Baltimore, MD: Johns Hopkins University Press, 1991.

DAVID WALDNER

DUKAN DAM

The dam was built on Iraq's Little Zab River to control flooding and to provide irrigation and hydroelectric power.

Severe, recurrent flooding of the Little Zab River to northeastern Iraq was formerly commonplace. The rate of flow in this river as it passes through the Dukan gorge is about 34 cubic yards (26 cu m) per minute during the dry season, rising to more than 4,000 cubic yards (3,000 cu m) per minutes at flood time. Iraq's Development Board was already considering major flood control, drainage, and irrigation schemes throughout the country when the Little Zab gave rise to a series of major floods in 1941, 1946, 1949, 1953, and 1954. The highest flood levels were recorded in this latest year when the river's rate of flow reached 4,800 cubic yards (3,660 cu m) per minute despite a normal average daily rainfall.

In 1954, to control further flooding of the Little Zab and to provide water for irrigation in northeastern Iraq, the Development Board awarded a contract to a French consortium for the construction of an arch dam at Dukan gorge on the Little Zab, some 37 miles (60 km) northwest of Sulaymaniya and 60 miles (100 km) northeast of Kirkuk. Between 1,000 and 1,200 families, representing the population of some fifty villages in the adjacent region, were moved and settled to the northwest at Sanga Sir. The Dukan dam and reservoir were completed in 1959 although structural problems necessitated ongoing repairs and further expense. As part of the Dukan project, a series of regulators and dams were built on the Little Zab and adjacent Udayn River, while a spillway conveying water from the Little Zab to the Udayn provided irrigation to the Ghurfa lands and the lands on the right bank of the Udayn River.

The project was tested almost immediately when the Little Zab flooded in 1959, depositing over 2.6

billion cubic yards (2 billion cu m) of water into the reservoir. This allowed a constant runoff for irrigation during the dry season from August to November. Over 20 billion cubic yards (15 billion cu m) of water were processed through the reservoir during the first six years of its operation.

The dam itself is an enormous structure, 382 feet (116.5 m) high and 1,180 feet (360 m) long. It is 20 feet (6.2 m) wide at the top and 107 feet (32.5 m) wide at its base. The reservoir behind it, covering an area of some 104 square miles (270 sq km) or more, has an estimated usual capacity of 8.9 billion cubic yards (6.8 billion cu m), but a maximum capacity of 10.9 billion cubic yards (8.3 billion cu m). The complex serves multiple purposes including flood control, the provision of hydroelectric power (originally rated at 200,000 kilowatts), and the storage of water for lean periods when the Tigris is low. Indeed, the water contained in the reservoir is intended chiefly for the Kirkuk irrigation project whereby over 890,000 acres (360,000 ha) of land around Irbil, Kirkuk, and Diyala districts are to be brought under cultivation, almost 494,000 acres (200,000 ha) around Kirkuk alone.

See also IRAQ; KIRKUK; SULAYMANIYA; ZAB RIVERS.

Bibliography

Ali, Hassan Mohammad. *Land Reclamation and Settlement in Iraq.* Baghdad: Baghdad Printing Press, 1955.

Salter, Arthur. *The Development of Iraq: A Plan of Action.* London, 1955.

ALBERTINE JWAIDEH

DULLES, JOHN FOSTER
[1888–1959]

U.S. secretary of state, 1953–1959.

John Foster Dulles came to public service after a long and successful legal career that afforded him valuable experience in international affairs. He was a senior adviser to the U.S. delegation to the 1945 founding conference of the United Nations Organization in San Francisco, and a member of the U.S. delegation to the first UN General Assembly in 1948. In 1950 and 1951 he earned the praises of

U.S. secretary of state Dean Acheson for negotiating a "peace of reconciliation" with Japan.

As President Dwight D. Eisenhower's secretary of state from 1953 to 1959, Dulles directed U.S. foreign policy in tandem with the president. The USSR was their focus because communism was considered an immoral and dangerous system. Concerned with the strategic northern tier of Middle Eastern countries bordering on the USSR, Dulles supported conservative pro-American rulers such as Reza Shah Pahlavi in Iran, the Hashimites and Nuri al-Saʿid in Iraq, and Adnan Menderes in Turkey. Although he supported the British-sponsored Baghdad Pact of 1955, Dulles held back from fully committing the United States to membership in the alliance. When Iran's Prime Minister Mohammad Mossadegh threatened to supplant the shah in 1953, Dulles advocated the removal of the prime minister. Together with his brother, CIA director Allen W. Dulles, he organized Operation AJAX, which contributed significantly to Mossadegh's fall in August 1953. In August 1955, in accordance with a secret Anglo-American plot to encourage Israeli-Egyptian talks (Operation ALPHA), Dulles proposed a solution to the Arab–Israel conflict based on resettlement of the Palestinian refugees, treaties to establish permanent frontiers, and guarantees of security for both sides.

Dulles distrusted the attempts of various Middle Eastern states, particularly Egypt, to remain neutral in the Cold War between the superpowers. In 1955 he responded favorably to Egypt's request for funding of the Aswan High Dam, but was disconcerted when Egypt's president Gamal Abdel Nasser made an arms deal with the USSR, via its client Czechoslovakia, in September 1955. Nasser's aspirations to lead the bloc of nonaligned nations, his failure to respond positively to Operation ALPHA, and his recognition of Communist China in May 1956 further alienated Dulles's sympathies.

In July 1956 Dulles decided, with Eisenhower's approval, to revoke the funding offer for the dam project. The withdrawal of funds led to Nasser's nationalization of the Suez Canal, which in turn precipitated an international crisis that culminated in the Arab–Israel War of October 1956. Dulles refused to support the actions of Israel, France, and

Great Britain in their joint attack on Egypt aimed at seizing the canal and toppling Nasser. In early 1957 Dulles participated in the formulation of the Eisenhower Doctrine, which offered U.S. military aid to any Middle East state threatened by the USSR. Invoking the doctrine, Dulles and Eisenhower sent U.S. troops into Lebanon in July 1958 in the wake of the revolution in Iraq.

Struggling against the onset of cancer, Dulles resigned his government position in April 1959 and died in May.

See also ALPHA, OPERATION; BAGHDAD PACT (1955); MENDERES, ADNAN; MOSSADEGH, MOHAMMAD; PAHLAVI, REZA; SUEZ CRISIS.

Bibliography

Finer, Herman. *Dulles over Suez: The Theory and Practice of his Diplomacy.* Chicago: Quadrangle Books, 1964.

Hoopes, Townshend. *The Devil and John Foster Dulles.* Boston: Little, Brown, 1973.

Immerman, Richard H., ed. *John Foster Dulles and the Diplomacy of the Cold War.* Princeton, NJ: Princeton University Press, 1990.

Immerman, Richard H., ed. *John Foster Dulles: Piety, Pragmatism, and Power in U.S. Foreign Policy.* Wilmington, DE: Scholarly Resources, 1999.

Marks, Frederick W. III. *Power and Peace: The Diplomacy of John Foster Dulles.* Westport, CT: Greenwood Press, 1993.

Spiegel, Steven. *The Other Arab-Israeli Conflict: Making America's Middle East Policy, from Truman to Reagan.* Chicago: University of Chicago Press, 1985.

ZACHARY KARABELL
UPDATED BY NEIL CAPLAN

DUNUM

See GLOSSARY

DURAND LINE

Afghanistan-Pakistan border.

The present border of approximately 1,500 miles between Afghanistan and Pakistan was agreed upon in a treaty signed on 12 November 1893, in Kabul by Sir Mortimer Durand, representing British India, and Abd al-Rahman, amir of Afghanistan.

Durand, the Indian foreign secretary, had been sent by Lord Landsdowne, the viceroy of British India, to pursue Britain's "Forward Policy" designed to control tribal activity along the northwest border of British India. Afghanistan has never accepted the legitimacy of this border, however, arguing that it was intended to demarcate spheres of influence rather than international frontiers. In addition, the Afghans contend that this border bisects the Pushtun tribal area, leaving more than half the Pushtun tribes in Pakistan. Afghans believe that Pushtuns are true Afghans and therefore the Pushtun area, sometimes called Pushtunistan, should be part of Afghanistan. The "Pushtunistan question" has remained an obstacle to good relations between Pakistan and Afghanistan.

After the communist takeover of Afghanistan in 1978, the government of Nur Mohammed Taraki and Hafizullah Amin actively challenged the legitimacy of the Durand line, largely because of their strong Pushtun sentiments. For this reason, the Afghan government formally repudiated the Durand Agreement in 1979. In 1993, 100 years since the signing of the agreement, the Durand Agreement formally lapsed. Afghanistan refused to renew the treaty, leaving Afghanistan and Pakistan with no official border.

Bibliography

Dupree, Louis. *Afghanistan.* Princeton, NJ: Princeton University Press, 1980.

Ewans, Martin. *Afghanistan: A Short History of Its People and Politics.* New York: HarperCollins, 2002.

GRANT FARR

DURRANI DYNASTY

Rulers of Afghanistan.

The Durrani dynasty (1747–1842) was founded in Kandahar, Afghanistan, in 1747, when a group of Pakhtun (Pushtun) elders elected Ahmad Durrani to lead them. Members of the house of Ahmad Shah ruled over the empire he created until its collapse in 1818. A branch of the family maintained control over Herat and the northwestern region until 1842. A grandson of Ahmad Shah regained the Afghan throne in 1838 but was overthrown in 1842, in the course of a popular uprising against British forces.

The province of Kandahar had changed hands repeatedly between the Moghul and Safavid empires when, in 1708, a coalition of Pakhtun and non-Pakhtun elements under the leadership of Mir Wais Hotak freed the province from the Safavids. In 1722, the Pakhtuns conquered Isfahan, establishing a short-lived Ghilzai empire. By 1737, their capital in Kandahar was taken over by the Persian conqueror, Nadir Shah Afshar, whose death in 1747 provided Ahmad Shah with the opportunity to establish the Durrani empire.

Ahmad Shah belonged to the Saddozai lineage, which had provided the Abdali clan with its leaders for several centuries. On assuming power, Ahmad Shah changed the name of the clan from Abdali to Durrani (Pearl of Pearls). He be stowed special privileges on the Saddozai lineage but confined the kingship to his own house. The crown was hereditary in the house of Ahmad Shah. But in the absence of clear rules, every succession gave rise to an intense struggle for the throne. When Ahmad Shah died, two of his four sons emerged as contenders, but their conflict was quickly resolved in favor of the eldest, Timur Shah (ruled 1772–1793). When he died, the continuous struggle among his numerous sons became a permanent feature of the politics of the dynasty, ultimately leading to its collapse. Three of his sons became rulers, Shah Zaman (ruled 1793–1800), Shah Mahmud (ruled 1800–1803; 1809–1818), and Shah Shuja (ruled 1803–1809; 1838–1842).

Under Ahmad Shah, foreign conquest was the main goal of the dynasty. To build himself a base of support at home and provide a force for conquest abroad, Ahmad Shah showered the Durrani clans with privileges, investing their leaders with the main offices of the empire. Most of the ministers and generals belonged to various branches of the Durrani clan, though rarely to the Saddozai lineage to which Ahmad Shah's house belonged. But near the end of his rule, changed regional conditions had rendered further conquests unprofitable. Timur Shah, who fought only defensive wars, rarely called the Durrani clans to action. To reduce the power of his ministers, he moved the capital from Kandahar, the heartland of Pakhtuns, to Kabul, a predominantly Persian- (Farsi-) speaking city. He also created new offices, to which he appointed non-Durranis owing loyalty to his person.

The warring princes, however, not only had to reconfirm Durrani nobles in their privileges but had to concede to them new powers as well. The cumulative effect of these concessions resulted in the weakening of the crown to the point that ministers were in a position to depose rulers at will. Most of the rulers, however, managed to prevent members of a single lineage from monopolizing all official positions. But under Shah Mahmud, members of the Barakzai clan managed to gain control of the most important offices. When, in 1818, the crown prince blinded the powerful Barakzai chief minister, the latter's brothers, seeking revenge, overthrew the house of Ahmad Shah and brought about the collapse of the Durrani empire.

A civil war ensued. The Indian provinces of the Durrani empire gained their independence, and Afghanistan was divided into a number of independent principalities. A great-grandson of Ahmad Shah, Prince Kamran, gained control of the province of Herat, which he ruled until 1842. Shah Shuja, a grandson of Ahmad Shah and former ruler, mounted a number of expeditions from his exile in India to regain power but without success. Fearing the rising influence of Russia in Persia and Central Asia, British officials in India decided to extend their support to Shah Shuja. To help restore him to power, they sent forces simultaneously against the rulers of Kabul and Kandahar in 1838, thereby initiating the first Anglo–Afghan War. The house of Ahmad Shah still retained enough legitimacy, and Shah Shuja was welcomed by the people. Soon, however, he revealed himself to be no more than a stooge of British power. In 1841, anxious about their own loss of influence, Afghan notables led a popular revolt against the British forces. The British army was destroyed, and Shah Shuja was assassinated in 1842. His descendants fled to India, and from then on, no member of the house of Ahmad Shah ever played a prominent role in the politics of Afghanistan.

The advent of the Durrani dynasty transformed the Pakhtuns in general, and the Durrani clans in particular, into the dominant political force in Afghanistan. The dynasty, however, derived its model of power from the ancient Persian and Islamic theories of government. Persian was the language of bureaucracy, and it gradually became the language of the court.

See also AHMAD DURRANI; BARAKZAI DYNASTY; KABUL; PUSHTUN.

Bibliography

Dupree, Louis. *Afghanistan.* Oxford and New York: Oxford University Press, 1997.

Leech, R. "An Account of Early Abdalees." *Journal of the Asiatic Society of Bengal* 14 (1845): 445–470.

ASHRAF GHANI

DUSTUR, AL-

See NEWSPAPERS AND PRINT MEDIA: ARAB COUNTRIES

EASTERN DESERT

Also called the Arabian Desert; it makes up almost a quarter of Egypt's land surface, covering an area of 85,690 square miles (221,937 sq km).

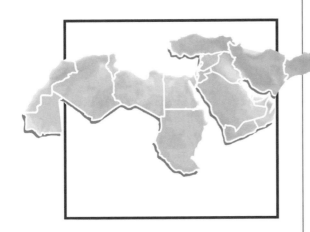

The northern sector, from the Mediterranean coast to the latitude of Qena, is a limestone plateau marked by rolling hills. At Qena the Eastern Desert is marked by cliffs, some as high as 6,500 feet (2,000 m), and scored by deep *wadis* (dry streambeds or valleys) that are difficult to cross. Farther south the desert becomes a sandstone plateau broken by ravines, but some can be traversed easily, such as the ancient trade route from the Nile River to al-Qusayr. In the eastern section of the desert, a chain of hills, more like a series of interlocking systems than a continuous range, runs from near Suez south to the border of the Sudan. At the foot of these hills lies the Red Sea coastal plain, which gradually widens as one moves south.

The sedentary population lives in towns and villages on the Red Sea coast; their main occupations are fishing, transport, and serving the growing Red Sea tourist trade. Nomadic pastoralists make up about 10 percent of the Eastern Desert's population. Pasturelands and water suffice to support small herds of sheep, goats, and camels. Arab tribes include the Huwaytat, Maʿaza, and Ababda. In the south are the Bisharin, part of the Beja, a Hamitic ethnic group.

See also BEJA.

Bibliography

Hobbs, Joseph J. *Bedouin Life in the Egyptian Wilderness.* Austin: University of Texas Press, 1989.

Metz, Helen Chapin, ed. *Egypt: A Country Study,* 5th edition. Washington, DC: U.S. Government Printing Office, 1991.

Tregenza, L. A. *Egyptian Years.* London and New York: Oxford University Press, 1958.

ARTHUR GOLDSCHMIDT

EASTERN ORTHODOX CHURCH

Direct descendant of the Byzantine State Church; also includes a group of independent national Christian churches.

The Eastern Orthodox Church comprises a group of autonomous Christian churches united by doctrine, liturgy, and internal hierarchical organizations. The heads are patriarchs or metropolitans, with the patriarch of Constantinople only the first among equals. Orthodox churches represented in the Middle East include the Russian, the Balkan, the Greek; the churches of Antioch (now based in Damascus), Alexandria, Jerusalem, and the See of Constantinople (now Istanbul); and the old churches that date to the fifth century C.E., which emancipated themselves from the Byzantine State Church—the Nestorian Church in the Middle East and India (with a half million members) and the Monophysite churches (with some 17 million, including the Coptic of Egypt, the Ethiopian, the Syrian, the Armenian, and the Mar Thoma of India). There are also the Uniate churches, which, properly speaking, are not Orthodox churches because, though they retain traditional eastern liturgies, they acknowledge the primacy and authority of the pope in Rome. Orthodox Christians today number some 150 million or more worldwide—with 125 million in Europe, 25 million in Africa, 3.5 million in Asia, and about 1 million in North America.

Eastern Christianity, with its decentralized organization, diverged from the Western hierarchically organized Roman (Catholic) Church after the fourth century C.E., when Constantinople became the capital of the Roman Empire. The theological split between the Western and Eastern churches was formalized in the Schism of 1054. Rivalry between Rome and Constantinople, aided by longstanding differences and misunderstandings, led to the schism: The Eastern Orthodox churches recognize only the canons of the seven ecumenical councils (325–787 C.E.) as binding for faith, and they reject doctrines that have subsequently been added in the West.

After the fall of the Byzantine Empire in 1453 to the Ottoman Turks, the Orthodox patriarch was entrusted with full civil administration over all Orthodox Christians in the Ottoman Empire. This centralized administration contrasted with the Eastern church's traditional localist organization. Although the Ottomans granted Christians freedom of worship, the restrictions they imposed on the public profile of the church bred resentment and stagnation in theological scholarship.

In the nineteenth and twentieth centuries, the Ottoman Empire's Orthodox community once again splintered under the impact of European Catholics and Protestants and of emerging nationalism. The Russian Empire assumed a pan-Slavic stance in its attempts to expand south and east into warm-water ports during the nineteenth and early twentieth centuries; the affinity of Russian Orthodoxy with other Eastern Orthodox communities was stressed. World War I, the Russian Revolution, and the breakup of the Ottoman Empire ended that gambit, although Russian and Soviet interests in the Middle East never diminished.

Today in the Arab East, the Antioch (Melkite) church represents the largest Arab Christian group, with dioceses in Syria, Lebanon, and Iraq. The Alexandria church has become the center of emerging African Orthodox communities.

Bibliography

Braude, Benjamin, and Lewis, Bernard, eds. *Christians and Jews in the Ottoman Empire: The Functioning of a Plural Society.* New York: Holmes and Meier, 1982.

Haddad, Robert M. *Syrian Christians in Muslim Society.* Princeton, NJ: Princeton University Press, 1970.

Shaw, Stanford. *History of the Ottoman Empire and Modern Turkey,* Vol. 1: *Empire of the Gazis: The Rise and Decline of the Ottoman Empire, 1280–1808.* Cambridge, U.K., and New York: Cambridge University Press, 1976.

ELIZABETH THOMPSON

EASTERN QUESTION

A concept coined in the initial stage of the Greek War of Independence (1821–1829) to describe the territorial effect of the political decline of the Ottoman Empire on great-power diplomacy in Europe.

In the seventeenth century the Ottoman Empire, at its greatest extent, sprawled across southeast Europe (Hungary included), southwest Asia, and northern Africa (Morocco excluded). The weakening of the sultan's power began in the last decade of the reign of Sultan Süleyman (1520–1566). Europe, however, remained paralyzed by religious wars until the Peace of Westphalia (1648), and the Sublime Porte (the Ottoman imperial government) did not admit its growing frailty vis-à-vis Europe until the end of the seventeenth century. Only then did it negotiate treaties and other international acts, chiefly with the great powers of Europe. In the Treaty of Karlowitz (1699), for the first time, the sultan ceded large tracts in Christian Europe—in this instance to Austria and Poland—which were never recovered.

For a century longer, Ottoman military might was still respected on the Continent. Tsar Peter I (1682–1725), the first European monarch to send troops into Ottoman Asia, occupied the Sea of Azov and its Crimean rim in 1696, only to lose the short-lived conquest along with a claim to power over the Black Sea after a disastrous defeat (1711) at the Prut River (later in Romania). The Ottoman recapture of the Crimea's Tatar khanates was ratified in 1713, in the Treaty of Edirne (Adrianople). That delayed for six decades—until Catherine II (1762–1796), after a six-year war with Turkey—Russia's taking the first solid step toward establishing itself as a Black Sea power through the treaty of Kuçuk Kaynarca (1774), which detached the khanates from the sultan's realm by declaring them independent. Russia did not annex them until nine years later. Finally in 1792, after four more years of war, the Sublime Porte, in the treaty of peace at Jassy, the capital of the Ottoman province of Moldavia (later part of Romania), at last acknowledged this segment of the Black Sea coast as Russian. The victories set in motion Ottoman territorial attrition in southwest Asia; it spread to North Africa in 1830, when France began its conquest of Algeria.

Europe's expansion into the Ottoman Empire at times appeared to consist of predators rushing as far and as fast as they could, paying no heed to the risks of collision. Such a judgment, however, belies the realities. Contenders for the same or overlapping districts were sensitive to one another's interests. Avoidance of conflict became the name of the game as early as the Congress of Vienna (1814–1815). At the end of the Congress the conveners—Austria, Great Britain, Prussia, and Russia—styled themselves the Concert of Europe to act as a permanent executive for settling all their disputes by conference or consensual diplomacy.

In 1818, at Aachen, the four powers admitted France to their ranks and promptly instructed the restored Bourbon monarchy to join Britain, as the Concert's sole maritime powers, in suppressing the institutionalized piracy in the western Mediter-ranean, carried out by the sultan's autonomous *ocaklar* (garrisons) or provinces of Tripoli (Libya), Tunis, and Algiers. A dozen years elapsed before the Barbary garrisons of the Ottoman Maghrib were finally put out of the piracy business.

Only once between 1815 and 1914 did the great powers resort to war over a dispute arising from the Eastern Question. In that case Britain, France, and Russia were the Concert's belligerents in the Crimean War (1854–1856); Austria served as mediator, and Prussia stayed aloof. The entry of the Kingdom of Sardinia, alongside Britain and France, as allies of the Sublime Porte against Russia served, in effect, as its application for membership in the Concert. Having led the Risorgimento for the political unification of the city-states in the Italian peninsula after 1848, Sardinia provided the monarchs following the emergence in 1861 of the kingdom of Italy, which was promptly made a member of the Concert.

The great-power contest for ownership or denial of the sultan's strategic realm reflects the pace and the modes of Europe's expansion into Asia and Africa. The Ottoman Empire spanned the heart of the eastern hemisphere by joining its three continents. The desire to control the Turkish Straits, which separate Asia and Europe while linking the Black and Mediterranean Seas, became a fixed, if also thwarted, aim of Russia after 1774. The Black Sea remained closed to Russia's naval power while the tsardom was exposed to possible attack by hostile maritime powers, as occurred in the Crimean War.

Similarly, on occupying Egypt in 1798, Napoléon declared, in the name of France, his intention to construct and own a manmade waterway from the Mediterranean's landlocked southeast corner to the Red Sea. By cutting across Asia and Africa, such a canal would reduce the distance (and the time) of uninterrupted travel from western Europe, notably from Britain and France, to India by two-thirds, and by lesser amounts to all points along the African and Asian shores of the Indian Ocean.

Given the challenge of two rivals, the cautious shaping by Britain, as the world's foremost maritime and naval power, of its own strategy to deny Russia and France a naval presence on the Mediterranean's eastern littorals was remarkable.

A portrait of Ismet Pasha, chief Turkish negotiator at the Lausanne Conference, which began in November 1922. The present-day territory of Turkey was essentially recognized by the Treaty of Lausanne. © BETTMANN/CORBIS. REPRODUCED BY PERMISSION.

As the decades passed, Saint Petersburg's aspiration became an obsession. In preparation for the expected takeover of the Turkish Straits, Russia continued swallowing Ottoman property that circled the Black Sea in both Europe and Asia, in the latter from the Crimea through the Caucasus; the last bit was the adjacent corner of Anatolia in 1878. To support the quest for the Turkish Straits even before the Crimean War, Russia established precedents to assert its right to protect the sultan's Orthodox subjects in Anatolia and Syria (including Lebanon and Palestine). In 1856, the Islahat Fermani (Reform Edict) of Sultan Abdülmecit I (1839–1861), reinforced by Article 9 of the Treaty of Paris ending the Crimean War, briefly interrupted, but did not end, the Russian practice.

Meanwhile, over Britain's resolute opposition, French investors in the late 1850s launched the Suez Canal Company, which in 1869 completed the waterway. Backed by the government of France, these entrepreneurs also preempted Britain's moves to take control of the company's policy-framing executive before and after Britain's occupation of Ottoman Egypt in 1882. By 1914 Algeria and Tunisia were part of France's empire, although the Sublime Porte withheld formal recognition of the protectorate in Tunisia. Of the surviving Ottoman provinces in Asia, France's interest centered on Lebanon and Syria from 1860 on. After a lapse of about a century, France in the 1840s had revived earlier treaty rights to custody of papal institutions and their members, covering affiliated eastern Uniate churches as well as Roman Catholicism. Finally, the financial community of France bankrolled railway, harbor, and other concessions in Syria, Lebanon, and Palestine and became the dominant shareholder in the Ottoman Imperial Bank, the Ottoman Empire's official agent.

But above all, the overseers of Britain's empire saw the shrinking Islamic state as both a continuing barrier and an unfolding passage to India. In both functions, the Ottoman Empire had grown into a major asset for Britain. Little wonder that, under Britain's persistent lead, the Concert of Europe in 1840 began nearly four decades as guarantor of the integrity of Ottoman Asia and Africa. The chosen formula was that of a self-denying protocol, first used in the Concert's convention of 1840 for "the Pacification of the Levant," which stated that "in the execution of the engagements resulting to the Contracting Powers from the . . . Convention, those Powers will seek no augmentation of territory, no exclusive influence, no commercial advantage for their subjects, which those of every other nation may not equally obtain." Even France, which had upheld Egypt in the crisis, rejoined the Concert in 1841.

Foreign Secretary Lord Palmerston, the strategy's author, saw in Egypt's threats to the Osmanli dynasty's survival (1831–1833, 1839) a threat to the British Empire. With the appearance of the steamship in the 1820s, Britain belatedly discovered what the East India Company had begun learning under sail more than half a century earlier: that through the sultan's realm there ran developing routes of communication and transportation between the métropole and the empire in India. In the regional contest of the 1830s, Russia backed the sultan, and France, the viceroy. The main problem, in Palmerston's diagnosis, was to keep Russia and France apart, for if they joined forces, Britain would suffer along with the Osmanli dynasty. Palmerston preferred a weak Ottoman Empire to a powerful Egypt. He thus responded favorably in 1839 and 1840 to the tsar's proposal for joint military intervention, with the cooperation of the Sublime Porte, to contain an ominous threat to the survival of the Ottoman Empire posed by Muhammad Ali, the viceroy of Egypt, backed by France. Austria and Prussia adhered to this plan of action.

France returned to the fold in 1841, as part of the settlement of the regional crisis. It reduced Muhammad Ali from quasi independence to Ottoman vassalage, but only upon his being recognized as the founder of a hereditary provincial dynasty with full domestic autonomy (though subject to Ottoman control of Egypt's foreign policy). "[A]ll the Treaties concluded and to be concluded between my Sublime Porte and the friendly Powers," read the Sultan's *ferman,* "shall be completely executed in the Province of Egypt likewise." This clause immediately imposed on Egypt the Porte's obligations to Britain, France, and the Netherlands to change the basis of Ottoman foreign commerce from protection to free trade. That deprived Muhammad Ali of the assured revenues from his commercial and industrial monopolies and put an early end to his integrated program of economic and military modernization. Those steps reduced the innovative, self-made, ambitious governor to manageable size. Later they enabled Palmerston, as foreign minister and prime minister, to delay for a dozen years execution of Egypt's grant of a ninety-nine year concession to a national of France to build and operate the Suez Canal.

In 1840 and 1841 the Concert had thus created a subsidiary system expressly to defuse crises in Europe arising from the rivalry over the Middle East (and North Africa) portions of the sultan's realm. For nearly forty years the great powers, with the Sublime Porte taking part and Britain playing the balancer in alternating alliances with Russia against France or the reverse, met five times—in London (1840–1841, 1871), Paris (1856, 1860–1861), and Berlin (1878)—and framed obligatory guidelines on policies toward the Ottoman Empire. Military occupation without time limit, commonly unilateral, was denied legitimacy; formal protectorates were le-

Ismet Pasha of Turkey, his assistants, and detective Colonel Tafik at the Allied Conference with the Turks at Lausanne. The Treaty of Lausanne was signed in 1922–1923. © HULTON/ ARCHIVE BY GETTY IMAGES. REPRODUCED BY PERMISSION.

gitimated by the powers, not by the Sublime Porte (in the end by the Turkish Republic); direct annexation was invariably solemnized by formal agreement with Constantinople. All three practices rested on general usage under (Western) international law.

Other styles of Europe's imperialism were particular to the Eastern Question. In the economic sphere the practices derived from the capitulations (nonreciprocal commercial treaties that the Porte had concluded with Europe's governments from the fifteenth to the mid-nineteenth centuries), assured Western residents unilateral extraterritorial privileges. They and their enterprises—banks, railroads, harbors, the Suez Canal—were immune from sultanic and provincial laws and taxes, and subject only to those of home governments. To such built-in dominance by Europe over key developmental aspects of the Ottoman economy was added guardianship of selected religious communities, with Russia and France the leading practitioners. The prevalence in the same districts of resident missionaries and their many charitable, medical, and educational, as well as religious, institutions attested to this.

Strategy apart, Britain's most valuable interest was commerce. As the sole industrializing nation from the last third of the eighteenth century through the Napoleonic wars, Britain speedily moved into first place in the foreign trade of the Ottoman Empire. By 1850, the Porte had become Britain's third-best customer. Britain clung to its commercial lead up to the outbreak of World War I. Financial investment by British nationals lagged far behind. The quest for oil in Ottoman Arab Asia quickened only when the Anglo–Persian Oil Company discovered commercial quantities in Persia in 1908, too late for the find to become practicable before the outbreak of war six years later. Still, the oil potential of the *vilayet* (province) of Mosul riveted the attention, during World War I and afterward, of Britain's companies and their bureaucratic supporters on the Sublime Porte's promise of a concession, in June 1914, to the Turkish Petroleum Company, a nonoperating international consortium of British, Dutch, and German interests registered in London.

Meanwhile, Italy, upon its unification in 1861, promptly entered the fray. After losing a bid for Tunisia in Berlin in 1878, Italy finally occupied Libya and the Dodecanese Islands in a lackluster war with the Ottoman Empire (1911–1912). One of Italy's primary aims in entering the war in 1915 was to legalize the titles to both and, if possible, enlarge its imperial holdings.

Upon replacing Continent-centered Prussia in 1871, unified Germany was the final entrant into the competition. Otto von Bismarck moved into the role vacated by Benjamin Disraeli. Germany centered its regional activity after 1882 on serving as military and naval adviser and supplier to Sultan Abdülhamit II (1876–1909). And from 1903, German entrepreneurs, with their government's encouragement and protection, sponsored the building of the Baghdad Railroad to link Europe, across Anatolia through the *vilayets* of Mosul, Baghdad, and Basra, to the head of the Persian Gulf, with Ottoman assurances of privileged investment rights along the way.

Britain's occupation of Egypt in 1882 helped draw Russia and France together, binding them twelve years later in a formal alliance. In all this time and for a decade longer, France kept urging Britain to fix a date for leaving Egypt, while Britain refused to ratify the 1888 Suez Canal Convention until France accepted, for the duration of the occupation, Britain's exercise of the supervisory powers of the projected international commission. Finally the two quarrelers signed an entente cordiale in 1904 that rested on a trade: Britain's responsibility for the canal's security by occupation in return for France's creating a protectorate in Morocco. Before the year's end, the Concert ratified the amended convention that implied approval of Britain's military presence in Egypt. Finally, Britain and Russia reduced irritants in their relations in the Ottoman Empire by reaching an accord on Iran, Afghanistan, and Tibet in 1907.

The three bilateral instruments underlay the formation of the Triple Entente (Britain, France, and Russia) on the outbreak of war in 1914 against the Central Powers (Germany and Austria). For the first time, the Sublime Porte, which entered World War I in November 1914 as an ally of the Central Powers, placed itself simultaneously at war with the three countries that had territorial scores to settle with the sultan—Britain in Egypt (and Sudan), France in Tunisia, and Russia at the Turkish Straits. The secret accords of the Entente powers (the Constantinople Agreement of 1915 and the Sykes–Picot Agreement of 1916) proposed assigning the Turkish Straits and eastern Anatolia to Russia, parceling the Fertile Crescent (later Iraq, Lebanon, Palestine, Syria, and Transjordan) under variable terms among the three allies, and declaring the Arabian Peninsula a British sphere of influence.

In April 1915, Italy associated itself with the Entente for the express aim of legitimizing its occupation of Libya and the Dodecanese Islands. Two years later, after the overthrow of the tsarist regime, Italy concluded a separate agreement (treaty of Saint-Jean de Maurienne) with Britain and France, to become a party to the Entente plans for sharing in the Ottoman spoils; to the Sykes–Picot arrangement were added zones for Italy's administration and influence in southern and western Anatolia. But the instrument never won the requisite assent from the Bolshevik regime, which seized power in the fall of 1917. After the war the unratified draft did not deter Italy from trying—but failing—to anchor itself in Anatolia.

Meanwhile, the secret correspondence of Sir Henry McMahon (Britain's high commissioner for

Egypt) with Sharif Husayn ibn Ali of Mecca (the Ottoman governor of the province of Hijaz) served as the basis for mounting an Arab rebellion against the sultan. Clearly, Britain perceived McMahon's exchanges with Husayn, which were started and finished (July 1915–March 1916) before the Sykes–Picot negotiations (December 1915–April 1916), as a solidifying step in the Arabian Peninsula. They agreed on mutual military commitments but left unsettled their political differences that gave rise to bitter Anglo–Arab quarrels. The later conflicting Anglo–French–Arab claims in the Fertile Crescent were compounded by the Balfour Declaration: Britain's secret understanding with the Zionists and public declaration of sympathy for the formation in Palestine of a Jewish national home. This was the price that Britain's government had to pay for finally acquiring an exclusive mandatory presence in Palestine in defense of the Suez Canal.

The Eastern Question thus was not resolved until the defeat of the Ottoman Empire in World War I, the empire's formal dissolution in 1922, and the peace treaty of Lausanne—the only such settlement negotiated but not imposed after that war—that the Entente and associated powers signed with the Republic of Turkey in 1923 and ratified a year later. Even then, Turkey's nationalist regime at Ankara contested the proposed transfer of two territorial slivers, losing one (the *vilayet* of Mosul to Iraq) in 1926 but winning the other (the return to Turkey by France, as mandatory of Syria, of the *sanjak* [provincial district] of Alexandretta) in 1939. In between, at Turkey's insistence, in the Montreux Convention of 1936, the naval signatories of the Treaty of Lausanne restored to the Republic of Turkey full sovereignty over the Turkish Straits by dissolving the International Straits Commission.

See also Abdülhamit II; Abdülmecit I; Balfour Declaration (1917); Capitulations; Crimean War; Fertile Crescent; Greek War of Independence; Husayn ibn Ali; Husayn–McMahon Correspondence (1915–1916); Lausanne, Treaty of (1923); McMahon, Henry; Montreux Convention (1936); Muhammad Ali; Palmerston, Lord Henry John Temple; Paris, Treaty of (1857); Sublime Porte; Sykes–Picot Agreement (1916).

Bibliography

Anderson, M. S. *The Eastern Question, 1774–1923: A Study in International Relations.* London: Macmillan; New York: St. Martin's, 1966.

Hurewitz, J. C. *The Middle East and North Africa in World Politics: A Documentary Record,* 2d edition. 2 vols. New Haven, CT: Yale University Press, 1975–1979.

Marriott, J. A. R. *The Eastern Question: An Historical Study in European Diplomacy,* 4th edition. Oxford: Clarendon Press, 1940.

J. C. Hurewitz

EAST INDIA COMPANY

British trading firm doing business in the Middle East during the nineteenth and early twentieth centuries.

The East India Company was active on behalf of Britain in the Persian Gulf, from 1820 until World War I, to ensure the security of Britain's merchant vessels heading toward ports in southern Iraq and Iran. This was achieved by signing peace treaties with the shaykhs of the lower Gulf, the first in 1820 and two more in 1835 and 1853. The main objectives of these treaties were to put an end to piracy, to prevent traffic in slaves, to curb widespread smuggling of arms and other goods, and to promote peaceful trade. By 1869, Britain was able to conclude a treaty in which the Gulf rulers pledged to refrain from conducting foreign relations with powers other than Britain, in effect providing Britain with protectorate powers over those territories.

Britain's interests were represented in the Gulf by the government of India through the local political resident, headquartered in the coastal township of Bushehr in Iran (moved after World War II to Bahrain). The political resident had representatives, called political agents, posted in Kuwait, Qatar, and Bahrain, and political officers in the Trucial Coast.

See also Trucial Coast.

Jenab Tutunji

EBADI, SHIRIN

[1947–]

Iranian attorney and human rights advocate.

Shirin Ebadi was born in 1947 and graduated in 1969 from the Law Faculty, Tehran University. Ebadi became one of the first female judges in Iran. After the 1979 Iranian Revolution, when women judges were dismissed, she lost her position but remained an employee of the Ministry of Justice until 1984, when she took early retirement. In 1992 Ebadi obtained a license to practice as an attorney, and she soon emerged as the leading figure in the Iranian human rights movement. In 1994, along with other women, Ebadi founded the Society for Protecting the Rights of the Child, which has lobbied parliament to introduce legal reforms in line with the United Nations Convention on the Rights of the Child. She has defended many victims of human rights violations. In 1998 she was defense lawyer for the families of the victims of the political assassinations of writers and intellectuals by rogue elements of the Ministry of Intelligence. Ebadi's vocal defense of human rights has antagonized the Iranian judiciary, who arrested her in June 2000. She was accused of producing and distributing a videocassette that allegedly "disturbs public opinion" and implicates certain senior officials in atrocities against reformist personalities and organizations. She was tried in closed court, sentenced to a suspended sentence, and banned from practicing law, but this sentence was overturned in a court of appeal. Ebadi has published many books in Persian and has received many awards, including the 1996 Human Rights Watch Award and the Rafto Prize for Human Rights 2001, in recognition of her sustained fight for human rights and democracy in Iran. In October 2003 the Norwegian Nobel Committee awarded Ebadi the Nobel Peace Prize for 2003, citing her efforts for democracy, human rights, and the rights of women and children.

Bibliography

Ebadi, Shirin. *The Rights of the Child: A Study of Legal Aspects of Children's Rights in Iran,* translated by M. Zaimaran. Tehran: UNICEF, 1994.

Kim, Uichol; Aasen, Henriette Sinding; and Ebadi, Shirin, eds. *Democracy, Human Rights and Islam in Modern Iran: Psychological, Social and Cultural Perspectives.* Bergen, Norway: Fagbokforlaget, 2003.

ZIBA MIR-HOSSEINI

EBAN, ABBA (AUBREY)

[1915–2002]

Israeli politician; foreign minister, 1966–1974.

Born in Capetown, South Africa, Aubrey Eban was educated at Queens' College, Cambridge, where he specialized in Middle Eastern languages and literature. He received a master's degree in this field in 1938 and stayed on at Cambridge as a lecturer in Arabic, Persian, and Hebrew literature. After Cambridge, Eban joined the British army, and in 1941 he served as a British army major in Cairo. In the British army, he helped train Jewish volunteers to fight against a German invasion of Palestine.

Eban worked for the Jewish Agency in 1946, and in 1947 he was made a liaison officer to the United Nations Special Committee on Palestine. He also served as a member of the Jewish Agency's delegation to the General Assembly of the United Nations (UN). After the creation of the State of Israel in 1948, Eban was appointed Israel's representative at the UN; he held that position from 1950 to 1959, during which time he also was Israel's ambassador to the United States.

In 1959, Eban was elected to the Knesset for the first time. From 1960 to 1963, he served in David Ben-Gurion's cabinet as minister of education and culture, and, from 1964 to 1965, he was deputy prime minister in the government of Levi Eshkol. During this time, from 1959 to 1966, Eban also was president of Israel's prestigious Weizmann Institute of Science. He was foreign minister from 1966 to 1974, and it was during this period in 1967 that he achieved his greatest international visibility, when he presented the case for Israel's war policy before the UN Security Council.

While a member of the Israeli cabinet, Eban argued against the idea of Arab migrant labor, which Moshe Dayan and other cabinet members supported. Eban thought that Israel should not become dependent upon Arab labor, both for economic reasons and for more philosophical reasons relating to the pioneering character of Israel. He was in the minority on this question, however, and Arab day labor increased over time.

In 1974, when Golda Meir resigned, primarily because of political criticism of her government's handling of the Arab–Israel War (1973), Eban was mentioned by some as a possible successor to the prime minister, but his candidacy did not generate much excitement or support from either the public or from members of the MAPAI Party. In many respects, Eban subsequently had a bigger following overseas than in Israel. To the surprise of many, he failed to win reelection to the Labor Party's list of nominees for the Knesset. He thereafter retired from politics and devoted himself to educational pursuits and to writing. He died on 17 November 2002 in Israel.

See also ARAB–ISRAEL WAR (1973); BEN-GURION, DAVID; DAYAN, MOSHE; ESHKOL, LEVI; ISRAEL: POLITICAL PARTIES IN; JEWISH AGENCY FOR PALESTINE; KNESSET; MEIR, GOLDA; UNITED NATIONS SPECIAL COMMITTEE ON PALESTINE, 1947 (UNSCOP); WEIZMANN INSTITUTE OF SCIENCE.

Bibliography

Eban, Abba. *Abba Eban: An Autobiography.* New York: Random House, 1977.

Eban, Abba. *Personal Witness: Israel through My Eyes.* New York: Putnam, 1992.

Sachar, Howard M. *A History of Israel: From the Rise of Zionism to Our Time,* 2d edition. New York: Knopf, 1996.

GREGORY S. MAHLER

EBTEKAR, MA'SUMEH
[1960–]

Iranian feminist and politician.

Ma'sumeh Ebtekar was born in 1960 in Tehran. She spent part of her childhood, from age three to nine, in the United States, but received most of her education in Iran: a B.S. in medical technology from Shahid Beheshti University, in Tehran, in 1985; an M.S. in 1989; and a Ph.D. in immunology from Tarbiat Modarres University, in Tehran, in 1995.

As one of the students who participated in the takeover of the U.S. embassy in Tehran in 1979, Ebtekar came to be known as Mary, the spokesperson for the student militants to the U.S. media. She appeared on almost every U.S. television program that was aired during the 444 days of the hostage crisis. Twenty-one years later, she wrote a book, *Takeover in Tehran: The Inside Story of the 1979 U.S. Embassy Capture,* in order "to set the record straight."

Aside from a few articles on immunology, most of Ebtekar's writings and professional activities have been in the area of women's studies, particularly on issues related to the integration of women into the processes of socioeconomic development. She was a member of the official Iranian delegation to the 1985 Third World Conference on Women, in Nairobi, and vice chair of the national committee for the 1995 Fourth World Conference on Women, in Beijing. She was a founding member and has been a member of the board of directors of the Center for Women's Studies and Research since 1986; a faculty member of the Tarbiat Modarres University School of Medical Science from 1989 to 1995; editorial director and license holder of *Farzaneh: Journal of Women's Studies* since 1994; and director of the Women's NGOs (nongovernmental organizations) Coordination Office since 1994. Appointed by President Mohammad Khatami in 1997 as vice president and head of the Department of Environment, Ebtekar became the first woman in the cabinet since the Iranian Revolution and the first female vice president in Iran's history.

See also IRANIAN REVOLUTION (1979); KHATAMI, MOHAMMAD.

Bibliography

Ebtekar, Massoumeh. *Takeover in Tehran: The Inside Story of the 1979 U.S. Embassy Capture.* Burnaby, BC, Canada: Talonbooks, 2000.

Zangeneh, Hamid. "Massoumeh Ebtekar, Takeover in Tehran: The Inside Story of the 1979 U.S. Embassy Capture." In *Journal of Iranian Research and Analysis* 17, 1 (April 2001).

NAREYEH TOHIDI

ECEVIT, BÜLENT
[1925–]

Turkish politician and prime minister.

Born in Istanbul, Bülent Ecevit graduated from Robert College, in Istanbul, in 1944 and then studied English literature at Ankara University. Following his appointment to the Press General Directorate, he was sent as an assistant to the press attaché at the Turkish Embassy in London. After his return to Turkey, he worked for the daily *Ulus.* In 1957, he received a Rockefeller scholarship and spent a year at Harvard University. In the same year, he was elected to parliament on a ticket of the Republican People's Party (CHP). After the 1960 military coup, Ecevit

Prime Minister Bülent Ecevit at a polling station during the 2002 national elections. Dogged by ill health and fresh political crises throughout the year, Ecevit lost the election, and his government was supplanted by members of the Justice and Development Party. © AP/WIDE WORLD PHOTOS. REPRODUCED BY PERMISSION.

served as the minister of labor until 1965 and was elected secretary general of the CHP in 1966. During this period, he also wrote a daily commentary in *Milliyet,* where he developed his political philosophy, which he called "left of center." His ideas found a large audience within the CHP, which elected him chairman in 1972.

In the general elections of 1973, the CHP gained the highest number of seats, and after long negotiations Ecevit established a coalition government with the pro-religious National Salvation Party. His government intervened in Cyprus in 1974 to protect the ethnic Turkish minority. Nevertheless, insurmountable conflicts between Ecevit and his coalition partner, Necmeddin Erbakan, led to the resignation of the government on 17 September 1974.

Ecevit became prime minister again in 1978, but he had to resign after the CHP's defeat in the 1979 by-elections. Following the 1980 military coup, Ecevit was detained, together with other party leaders, at Hamzaköy for "safety" reasons and was deprived of his political rights for ten years.

Ecevit was arrested twice in 1982 for declaring, in statements to the foreign press, that the new constitution was undemocratic. During this period, his wife, Rahşan Ecevit, founded the Democratic Left Party (DSP) and became its first chairperson. In 1987, after his political ban was lifted, Ecevit assumed leadership of the DSP. When the DSP failed to receive 10 percent of the national vote in the 1987 elections, he resigned from his party post with the intention of withdrawing from politics. Two years later, however, he resumed his party duties and in the general elections of 1991 his party gained seven seats in the National Assembly.

In the 1995 elections, the DSP gained 14.64 percent of the votes and won 76 parliamentary seats. In 1997, Ecevit joined a coalition with Mesut Yılmaz's Anavatan (Motherland) Party and became deputy prime minister. The government, however, stepped down in 1998 after allowing a parliamentary investigation into Yılmaz's financial affairs. Ecevit formed and led a minority government until the 1999 general elections, in which his party won the highest percentage of votes and 136 parliamentary seats. In 1999, he formed a coalition with the Motherland Party and the ultranationalist National Action Party.

This coalition lived through two economic crises and two devastating earthquakes, but the most serious challenges to its survival came from the insurmountable differences among the coalition partners, primarily between the DSP and the National Action Party, and from Ecevit's deteriorating health. Ecevit remained prime minister until the 2002 general elections, when his party received only 1.22 percent of the votes and no parliamentary seats.

See also CYPRUS; ECEVIT, RAHŞAN; ERBAKAN, NECMEDDIN; MOTHERLAND PARTY; REPUBLICAN PEOPLE'S PARTY (RPP).

Bibliography

Goindi, Farrukh Suhail, ed. *Dynamics of Democracy in Developing Countries: Bülent Ecevit.* Lahore, Pakistan: Jumhoori Publications, 1996.

Tachau, Frank. "Bülent Ecevit: From Idealist to Pragmatist." In *Political Leaders and Democracy in Turkey,* edited by Metin Heper and Sabri Sayarı. Lanham, MD: Lexington Books, 2002.

NERMIN ABADAN-UNAT
UPDATED BY BURÇAK KESKIN-KOZAT

ECEVIT, RAHŞAN

[1923–]

Founder of Turkey's Democratic Left Party and wife of the former prime minister, Bülent Ecevit.

Rahşan Ecevit was born into a middle-class family in Bursa. She graduated from Robert College in Istanbul, where she met her husband, Bülent Ecevit. Although she was interested in the arts, she did not pursue a career in the field.

Ecevit always supported her husband's political activities. When he was banned from politics after the 1980 military intervention, she founded the Democratic Left Party (DSP) in 1985 and served as its chairperson. When the ban was lifted in 1987, she left her post to Bülent Ecevit and became the party's general secretary. Although she retained that position, she never participated in general or local elections.

Ecevit is widely believed to advise her husband on political matters, especially his pardoning of prisoners during his two separate terms as prime minister. The Ecevits frequently have been criticized for imposing absolute authority and eliminating any opposition within the DSP. Rahşan Ecevit particularly has been accused of isolating the upper cadres so that they would resign rather than challenge her husband. During her husband's last term in government, especially from 2000 to 2002, she was strongly criticized for failing to care for his deteriorating health.

See also GENDER: GENDER AND POLITICS; TURKEY.

Bibliography

Tachau, Frank. "Bülent Ecevit: From Idealist to Pragmatist." In *Political Leaders and Democracy in Turkey*, edited by Metin Heper and Sabri Sayarı. Lanham, MD: Lexington Books, 2002.

BURÇAK KESKIN-KOZAT

ECONOMIC AND MILITARY AID

Countries of the Middle East are prominent both as recipients and donors of foreign assistance.

Israel, Egypt, Jordan, Syria, and Turkey are major long-term recipients of economic aid, but nearly every country in the region has, at one time or another, received economic and development aid as well as military assistance. These transfers have come in the form of grants and concessional loans for goods and services, for projects and programs, and for direct budgetary support. From the mid-1950s until 1991 the United States and the Soviet Union divided and sometimes shared the region's aid clients, providing most of the assistance to the region. France and Britain, along with other countries in the European community, have also been major benefactors, and in recent years Japan has provided direct assistance. Bilateral aid aside, many Middle East states have looked to regional and international lending institutions for financing.

In spite of suspicions about foreign interference, most governments in the region actively seek foreign aid in order to strengthen economies, improve technologies, and bolster military capabilities. The loans and grants are intended to overcome the constraints of insufficient capital investment resulting from limited savings and foreign exchange. Chronic domestic budget deficits—often traceable to generous consumer subsidies and heavy outlays for arms—help to create and perpetuate a dependence on foreign aid. Some governments in the region have become chronically dependent on these and other rental incomes.

Politics of Bilateral Aid

In the 1980s and 1990s major donors, especially the International Monetary Fund (IMF), the World Bank, and the United States government, pushed for liberal economic reforms in recipient countries, stressing export-led growth and expansion of the private sector at the expense of state-owned enterprises. Support for market-oriented economies is thought to enhance political pluralism and strengthen civil societies in the region. Increasingly, the United States and others have said that the promotion of democratic institutions and human rights is an objective in giving aid. Environmental and population concerns are also reflected in programs, and humanitarian assistance remains available in times of acute need. But strategic political objectives overshadow other motives. Donors seek to reward political friends or woo others by improving the ability of governments to realize the demands and fulfill the expectations of their elites and wider publics. Political expediency can lead to minimizing developmental objectives, waiving economic reforms,

On 18 January 1957, Arab leaders met in Cairo, Egypt, to sign an agreement providing aid to Jordan, giving that country the capability of cutting its final ties to Great Britain. Jordan continues to receive economic and military aid from oil-rich nations in the region. © BETTMANN/CORBIS. REPRODUCED BY PERMISSION.

and ignoring democratic-rights violations. Emphasis on political criteria by the more important donors has, moreover, resulted in the lion's share of foreign aid going to middle-income countries rather than to the poorest, most needy ones.

U.S. economic aid obligated through the Economic Support Fund (ESF) is deemed specifically to be in the foreign-policy interests of the United States. Over the history of the program, aid to Israel and Egypt has dominated expenditures. With strategic concerns uppermost, regimes in Turkey, Jordan, and Morocco have also been amply rewarded. Proponents argue that U.S. economic and military aid to the Middle East contributes to cooperation and stability, and that it helped to thwart communist penetration into the region. Thus, U.S. policymakers have at various times actively discour-

aged direct or indirect assistance to Libya, South Yemen, Syria, Afghanistan, and Iraq, all of which have been at one time beholden for aid to the Soviet Union. More recently, efforts to prevent technological assistance to Iran have figured strongly in U.S. policy.

U.S. assistance to the Middle East advanced dramatically with the Arab–Israel War of 1973 and its aftermath. Israel was first resupplied militarily, and then helped to recover economically from the war. Egypt, which had been heavily dependent on the Soviet Union for aid, was supported in its decision to join the Western camp with promises of development, commodity, and military assistance. U.S. aid subsequently provided critical incentives for signing the Camp David Accords and a peace treaty. Since 1977, Israel and Egypt have received nearly 40 percent of all U.S. aid—more than $75 billion in total.

Egypt, with annual aid at roughly $2.1 billion, had by 2000 received more than $40 billion from the United States—in the last decade, mainly in the form of grants rather than repayable loans. As a reward for Egypt's helpful role in the 1991 Gulf War, the United States agreed to the cancellation of $7 billion of military debts. Jordan, after concluding a peace agreement with Israel in October 1994, also came in line for debt relief and a major increase in weapons aid from the United States.

Creditors to the region also include the wealthier, oil-exporting states of the Persian Gulf, most notably Saudi Arabia, Kuwait, and the United Arab Emirates. They have assisted the Yemen Arab Republic, Jordan, Sudan, Egypt, and Syria, among others, in filling their investment-resource gap and relieving budgetary pressures. Arab aid has also been designed to buy off potential enemies.

Economic Reform and Multilateral Aid

Politically motivated bilateral aid is less bound by stringent economic requirements than that set by the IMF and the World Bank. Middle East countries receiving aid from these multilateral-aid sources have been obliged to agree to comprehensive structural reforms of their economies in order to attain loans and to reschedule previous debts. These reforms may include the elimination of state subsidies and removal of other price distortions, reform of tax collection, reduction in imports, devaluation of currency, and unification of exchange rates—essentially deflationary policies aimed at greater adherence to free-market principles.

Demands for fiscal and monetary changes and revised development strategies have been widely resented and often resisted. Under pressure from the IMF and World Bank, governments that have accepted the conditions for aid have been forced to introduce economic reforms that bear down hardest on the least well-off in their societies. As a consequence, several countries in the region have had to contend with popular demonstrations against mandated changes. IMF austerity programs over the years have led to street violence in Egypt, Jordan, Tunisia, and Morocco, and contributed to antigovernment activities in Algeria and Sudan.

Israel in May 2000 unconditionally withdrew most of its forces from the southernmost part of Lebanon, which it had invaded and occupied in June 1982. Days later, Martin Indyk, the U.S. ambassador to Israel, visited the northern Israeli village of Metulla and announced the release of $50 million in U.S. military aid for improvements to Israeli security along its border with Lebanon. © AP/WIDE WORLD PHOTOS. REPRODUCED BY PERMISSION.

Among the regional multilateral-aid givers, the Arab Monetary Fund, the Islamic Development Bank, and the OPEC Fund for International Development are the most prominent. The Arab Monetary Fund assists members in balance-of-payments difficulties. Between 1978 and 2002 it lent $4.3 billion to Arab countries. The Islamic Development Bank offers interest-free loans (with a service fee), mainly for infrastructural financing, agricultural projects, and technical assistance, all of which are expected to have an impact on long-term social and economic development. Priority is given to the import of goods from other member countries of the bank. Major contributors to the bank are Saudi Arabia, Kuwait, and Libya. Loans have been made to several countries outside the region in Africa and Asia. The OPEC fund is a multilateral agency that seeks to reinforce financial cooperation between OPEC member countries and other developing countries. It provides concessional loans for balance-of-payments support, the implementation of development projects and programs, and technical assistance and research financing through grants. The OPEC fund, which has had recipients

General Hugh Shelton of the U.S. Joint Chiefs of Staff, followed by Israeli Chief of Staff Shaul Mofaz, passes an honor guard in Tel Aviv after arriving in Israel in August 1999 to discuss military cooperation between Israel and the United States. Israel has long been a major recipient of U.S. economic and military aid, followed by Egypt and other countries in the Middle East. © AP/WIDE WORLD PHOTOS. REPRODUCED BY PERMISSION.

in Africa, Asia, and Latin America, gives priority to countries with the lowest income. Yet, with heavy debts of their own owing to the Gulf War and low oil prices, the bilateral and multilateral generosity of the once-cash-rich Arab states declined in the 1990s.

Foreign Military Aid

Foreign military credits and grants have greatly eased the burden of defense spending for many Middle East countries. The region is the largest arms market in developing countries, accounting for 56 percent of all agreements from 1990 to 1993. With an average of some 30 percent of government expenditures for the military, the Middle East ranked ahead of any other region. In terms of the percentage of gross domestic product devoted to arms expenditures over the last two decades, nine of the top twelve countries—Iraq, Israel, Jordan, Oman, Syria, Egypt, Libya, the Yemen Arab Republic, and the Yemen People's Democratic Republic—have been in the Middle East. Among the leading recipients of

major conventional weapons in the last decade are Saudi Arabia, Turkey, Afghanistan, Syria, Israel, and Iran. The major suppliers of arms to the region were the United States, the Soviet Union, France, Britain, and China.

U.S. military sales have been based in large part on a loan program set up in 1975 under which the U.S. Treasury, bypassing the U.S. Congress, provides credits from a special fund at prevailing commercial interest rates. Since most commercial lenders are reluctant to finance weapons purchases, these credits represent a form of foreign assistance. Several countries in the Middle East also received some or all of their arms from the United States on concessionary-loan terms or as outright grants. Beneficiaries include Turkey, Morocco, and Jordan, but Egypt and Israel virtually monopolize the most favorable military-assistance programs. From 2001 to 2003 the United States extended to Middle East countries foreign military assistance worth $10.2 billion, nearly all of which went to Egypt and Israel. The annual value of Russian arms to the Middle East, having fallen to only $400 to $500 million in 1997 to 2001, had been running at more than $15 billion annually during the 1980s.

Effects of Foreign Aid

It is difficult to assess whether foreign aid has improved the lives and increased the security of most people in the Middle East. Bilateral- and multilateral-aid programs have brought visible infrastructural improvements throughout the region. They have also addressed humanitarian needs, especially in areas of armed conflict, and induced estimable health and social gains. In recent years, foreign advisers have succeeded in forcing national planners to rationalize strategies of economic growth and have promoted integration within the global economy. But foreign aid also has disappointed both recipient countries and their donors. Aid-giving countries and agencies have complained about the inefficiencies and domestic corruption that often accompany sponsored programs, and they doubt the will of national leaders to implement reforms fully. Critics point out that much foreign assistance never actually reaches those it was intended to help. The region has lagged behind most of the world in economic liberalization. Recipient-country industries and trade continue to be highly protected, and although donors applaud evidence of growing democratization in several Arab states, they are concerned about the likely political beneficiaries of free elections. Bilateral donors are also frequently left unsatisfied with the diplomatic cooperation they have extracted from policymakers in Middle East countries.

Aside from the political resentments it provokes, foreign aid is criticized by recipients for its failure to put development on a self-sustaining basis and for possible disincentive effects on domestic production. Although donors have made industrial growth and higher agricultural output high priorities, unemployment remains a serious problem, and appropriate technologies and training are sometimes withheld. Considerable foreign assistance for agriculture that began in the 1980s has neither paid off in terms of impressive export earnings nor greatly improved the capacity for food self-sufficiency in the region's less well-off countries. With the mandating of difficult economic reforms, foreign assistance is also seen as increasing inequities and exacerbating domestic class conflicts.

Most controversial is whether, by selling arms to the Middle East, the United States and other suppliers are reducing conflict by allowing countries to better protect themselves, or stimulating defense spending and a regional arms race. Investment of borrowed money and domestic savings in weapons programs may also come at the expense of efforts to deal with severe economic problems and address the welfare of citizens. Accumulated loans have created considerable national debt and a long-term drain on national treasuries. Even so, although the end of the Cold War and the outcomes of recent regional wars have changed some of the sources and character of military and economic assistance, the quest for and dependence on foreign aid is unlikely to diminish any time soon.

Some of the poorer states in the region have received large flows of finance from abroad that have been essential for their survival. These have come from oil-rich countries in the region and from outside the region. The classic "rentier state" state is Jordan; other significant recipients have been Egypt and Syria. Aid has been bilateral and multilateral, civilian and military. It has taken the form of loans, grants, and debt write-offs. Between 1973 and 1989, poorer states in the Arab world received $55 billion

of interregional aid. This was made possible by the huge rise in oil income in the region. Political rents have been paid to help maintain the state and the regime. Often the two were the same, but with the rise of fundamentalism within Arab states, aid has been provided to governments in order to maintain them in power.

Foreign aid has fallen in value since the 1980s for several reasons. First, Arab oil wealth has declined, and so there was less to give. Second, it did not result in economic improvements in the recipient countries (or at least not on a scale that satisfied the donors) and was thus considered as wasted. Third, the decline of pan-Arabism led countries to go their own ways and be less interested in inter-Arab relations. Fourth, Western countries and multilateral bodies have tied aid to economic reforms, the success of which reduced the need for external assistance.

The share of aid given on a concessional basis to countries in the Middle East and North Africa was higher than anywhere else in the developing world. In 1999, 38 percent of long-term debt in the region was concessional, compared to 19 percent on average for developing countries. In Egypt it came to 86 percent; in Jordan, 54 percent; in Syria, 93 percent; and in Yemen, 92 percent. This was an indication of political favor.

See also INTERNATIONAL DEBT COMMISSION; INTERNATIONAL MONETARY FUND; RUSSIA AND THE MIDDLE EAST; UNITED STATES OF AMERICA AND THE MIDDLE EAST; WORLD BANK.

Bibliography

Boogaerde, Pierre van den. *Financial Assistance from Arab Countries and Arab Regional Institutions.* Washington, DC: International Monetary Fund, 1991.

Easterly, William. *The Elusive Quest for Growth.* Cambridge, MA: Harvard University Press, 2001.

Global Development Finance2003. Washington, DC: World Bank, 2003.

Lavy, Victor, and Sheffer, Eliezer. *Foreign Aid and Economic Development in the Middle East.* New York: Praeger Publishers, 1991.

Richards, Alan, and Waterbury, John. *A Political Economy of the Middle East.* Boulder, CO: Westview Press, 1996.

Rivlin, Paul. *Economic Policy and Performance in the Arab World.* Boulder, CO: Lynne Rienner, 2001.

Sadowsky, Yahya. "The Political Economy of Arms Control in the Arab World." *Middle East Report* (July–August 1992): 3–13.

Sullivan, Denis J. "Extra-State Actors and Privatization in Egypt." In *Privatization and Liberalization in the Middle East,* edited by Ilya Harik and Denis J. Sullivan. Bloomington: Indiana University Press, 1992.

Tendler, Judith. *Inside Foreign Aid.* Baltimore, MD: Johns Hopkins University Press, 1975.

Weinbaum, Marvin G. *Egypt and the Politics of U.S. Aid.* Boulder, CO: Westview Press, 1986.

MARVIN G. WEINBAUM
UPDATED BY PAUL RIVLIN

Traders at the Baghdad Stock Exchange (BSE). The self-financed, nonprofit BSE began operation in March of 1992; by 2000, it was holding three trading sessions a week, with approximately ninety companies listed. © MICHAEL S. YAMASHITA/CORBIS. REPRODUCED BY PERMISSION.

ECONOMICS

The economics of the Middle East can be divided into oil producers and nonproducers.

The main oil producers in the Middle East include Saudi Arabia, Iran, Kuwait, Iraq, Qatar, the United

Oil is a major resource commodity of the Middle East, with its top producing countries containing over 65 percent of the world's oil reserves. Additionally, the total number of oil reserves in the world has doubled in the last two decades, almost entirely due to exploration in the Middle East. © GEORGINA BOWATER/CORBIS. REPRODUCED BY PERMISSION.

Arab Emirates (U.A.E.), Oman, Algeria, and Libya. There are three marginal producers: Bahrain, Yemen, and Syria. The nonproducers or minimal producers are Egypt, Turkey, Jordan, Sudan, Tunisia, and Morocco.

Another taxonomic variable is population. The Middle East has countries with large populations—Iran, Egypt, Turkey, Morocco, and Algeria. Others, such as Qatar and the U.A.E., have minimal indigenous populations.

The production of oil per capita tends to define the type of economy to which each Middle Eastern country belongs. Countries with oil production of more than 0.25 barrels per day per capita tend to emphasize the development of low-labor, high-capital industries. Saudi Arabia, U.A.E., and Qatar have sought to develop alternatives to their dependence on crude oil by investing heavily in industry, mainly in petrochemicals, which require large amounts of natural gas or crude oil, energy, and capital, but minimum labor. Until 1995 most of the development in oil and petrochemicals was spearheaded by the governments, with some support from the private sector. Due to lessening income streams from lower oil prices, efforts are being made to include private industry more fully.

The non-oil economy in the countries with high per capita oil output tends to be liberal, except in Libya. None of the countries in this group has any foreign-exchange controls, restriction on import or export of capital by nationals, or limits on imports and exports of products (except pork products and alcohol). Most prices are set by supply and demand, although some food staples are subsidized by the governments.

The countries with production between zero and 0.10 barrels per day per capita mostly have large populations. Some are minor oil producers, but major producers like Iran, Iraq, and Algeria have a low production per capita. These low per capita producers tend to emphasize centrally planned industrial growth with more labor content. They have very stringent regulations on investments and on foreign-exchange and capital export by residents. Large segments of their economy tend to be nationalized, including banks, mining, and large manufacturing plants. Their economic growth has been minimal, and most are attempting to deregulate their economies.

The final group (Turkey, Egypt, Morocco, Jordan, etc.), with very limited earnings from oil,

Agricultural products are a primary export for some Middle Eastern countries, including Israel, Egypt, and Morocco. However, due to limited water supplies, poor land quality, and a reluctance to adopt newer, more mechanized farming techniques, the majority of Arab countries produce less than half of their food requirements and must import heavily from other regions. © ATTAL SERGE/CORBIS SYGMA. REPRODUCED BY PERMISSION.

Country	Oil Production Average 2002 in thousands of b/d	Population in thousands	Bbls/Capita	Reserves in billions of barrels 2001	GDP in billions of $
Kuwait	1,853	1,970	0.94	96.5	30.9
Qatar	640	700	0.91	15.2	16.3
United Arab Emirates	1,952	2,650	0.74	97.8	51
Oman	950	2,620	0.36	5.5	21.5
Saudi Arabia	7,551	21,030	0.36	261.8	248
Libya	1,317	5,410	0.24	29.5	40
Iraq	2,014	23,580	0.09	112.5	28.6
Iran	3,470	64,530	0.05	89.7	456
Bahrain	27	650	0.04		8.4
Syria	530	16,720	0.03	2.5	54.2
Algeria	883	31,840	0.03	9.2	177
Yemen	470	19,110	0.02	4	14.8
Egypt	630	67,890	0.01	2.9	258
Turkey	48	68,610	0		468
Tunisia		9,670	0	0.3	24.9
Jordan		6,850	0		22.8
Lebanon		6,560	0		22.8
Israel		6,450	0		122
Morocco		650	0		112
Total	**22,335**	**357,490**	**0.06**	**727.4**	

SOURCE: This table compiles information from *Middle East Economic Survey*, vol. XLV, 2002; the EIA country analysis briefs (available from <http://www.eia.doe.gov/emeu/cabs/contents.html>); and the U.S. State Department Country Background Notes (available from <http://www_state.gov>)

TABLE BY GGS INFORMATION SERVICES, THE GALE GROUP.

relies on private local and foreign investment as well as foreign aid to fund their development.

A large segment of the population in the Middle East is active in agriculture (35.35%). However, this average is skewed by the large numbers of people employed in that sector in Egypt (43%) and Morocco (50%). Mining, manufacturing, and construction employs about 20.57 percent; public administration and services employs 23.54 percent; and trade, transport, and communication employs 9.27 percent.

Oil producers tend to have a much larger percentage of their population in public administration and services, suggesting that oil resources are downstreamed to the population through the creation of jobs in the civil service (34% in Saudi Arabia, 40% in Qatar, 39% in Iraq, 53% in Kuwait).

See also PETROLEUM, OIL, AND NATURAL GAS.

Bibliography

Gause, Gregory. *Oil Monarchies: Domestic and Security Challenges in the Arabian Gulf States.* New York: Council on Foreign Affairs, 1994.

Seznec, Jean-François. *The Financial Markets of the Arabian Gulf.* London: Croon Helm, 1988.

JEAN-FRANÇOIS SEZNEC

EDDÉ, EMILE

[1884–1949]

Prime minister (1929–1930) and president (1936–1941) of Lebanon.

Emile Eddé, a Lebanese lawyer and politician, was a strong supporter of French policies in Lebanon and the Middle East. He was a devoted Francophile who came from a family that was well connected to French interests. Eddé was prime minister in 1929 and 1930 and president from 1936 to 1941 under the French mandate over Lebanon (1920–1943). He also initiated and headed during the mandate the Parliamentary National Bloc, which became a party in 1946 after independence. Eddé was highly controversial due to his conservative views, anti-Arab sentiments, and zealous adherence to French colonialism. Raymond Eddé, Emile's son, headed the party in 1949 and directed it

toward more liberalism and less dependency on France.

See also EDDÉ, RAYMOND; LEBANON.

SAMI A. OFEISH

EDDÉ, RAYMOND

[1913–2000]

Lebanese politician and leader of the National Bloc party since 1949; minister of the interior, social affairs, and communications (1958–1959); minister of public works, hydraulic and electric resources, agriculture, and planning (1968–1969).

The eldest son of former president of Lebanon Emile Eddé, Raymond Eddé was trained as a lawyer at St. Joseph University in Beirut. Following his father's death in 1949, he took over the leadership of the National Bloc party. A leader of the opposition to President Bishara al-Khuri, he was elected to parliament in 1953 from the Jubayl district. He was reelected in 1960, 1968, and 1972. Appointed minister following the 1958 civil war, Eddé soon broke with President Fu'ad Chehab over the latter's reliance on the Deuxième Bureau (military intelligence) to implement his policies. In 1967, arguing that the growing influence of the military posed a threat to the open and democratic nature of Lebanon's society, he joined the Tripartite Alliance (with Pierre Jumayyil and Camille Chamoun), thus ensuring the defeat of the Chehabist candidate Ilyas Sarkis in the 1970 presidential elections.

By the time civil hostilities broke out in 1975, Eddé had become the most outspoken and prominent Christian opponent of the Phalange, which he described as a fascist organization. A representative of the more moderate Maronites, he warned about the potentially disastrous consequences of the growth of paramilitary organizations in Lebanon and strove to prevent the growing polarization in the country by reaching out to like-minded Muslim leaders. However, because he never was a grassroots organizer, lacked mass support within the Maronite community, and refused to organize a militia of his own, he was rapidly marginalized. In January 1977, after three attempts on his life, he went into exile in Paris. In 1989 he opposed the Ta'if Accord on the grounds that it institutionalized Syria's power in Lebanon, and expressed support for General Michel Aoun. Following the 1992 legislative elections, he refused to recognize the legitimacy of the new Parliament. Although he was widely respected as a man of principle and was often described as "the moral conscience of Lebanon," his long exile cut him off from the realities in Lebanon, and his influence over politics there became very limited. He died in Paris in May 2000.

See also AOUN, MICHEL; CHAMOUN, CAMILLE; CHEHAB, FU'AD; JUMAYYIL, PIERRE; PHALANGE.

Bibliography

Goria, Wade R. *Sovereignty and Leadership in Lebanon, 1943–1976.* London: Ithaca Press, 1986.

Rabinovich, Itamar. *The War for Lebanon, 1970–1985.* Ithaca, NY: Cornell University Press, 1985.

GUILAIN P. DENOEUX
UPDATED BY MICHAEL R. FISCHBACH

EDEN, ANTHONY

[1897–1977]

British statesman; prime minister, 1955–1957.

Richard Anthony Eden, first earl of Avon, was elected a Tory member of Parliament between 1923 and 1957. As minister without portfolio for League of Nations affairs (1935) and as secretary of state for foreign affairs (1935–1938), he concluded the "gentlemen's agreement" with Italy's Count Ciano in 1937 concerning the Mediterranean, after negotiating the 1936 Anglo–Egyptian treaty and the Montreux Convention with Turkey. He resigned in disagreement with the policy of Sir Neville Chamberlain concerning Hitler's ambitions for Nazi Germany and the Munich conference but returned as foreign secretary in the World War II governments of Prime Minister Winston S. Churchill.

After the war, he objected to the Labour Party's conciliatory policy toward Iran's Prime Minister Mohammad Mossadegh. When he resumed office in 1951, he opposed Mossadegh's nationalization of the Anglo–Iranian Oil Company and worked with the United States to bring him down. In 1954, he negotiated an agreement with Egypt for the withdrawal of Britain's troops from the Suez Canal zone and, in the years following, hardened against Egypt's President Gamal Abdel Nasser.

As prime minister from 1955 to 1957, Eden was determined to maintain Britain's prestige in the Middle East. Convinced that Nasser was dangerous, Eden reacted quickly after Nasser nationalized the Suez Canal on 26 July 1956. With France and Israel as allies, Eden orchestrated the October attack on Suez—the Arab–Israel War of 1956—without informing his main ally, the United States. Furious, President Dwight D. Eisenhower and U.S. Secretary of State John Foster Dulles refused to support Eden in the United Nations, insisting on a withdrawal. Humiliated and ill, Eden resigned in January 1957 and was replaced by Harold Macmillan. Eden was made first earl of Avon and Viscount Eden in 1961. He is the author of *Full Circle* (1960), *Facing the Dictators* (1972), and *The Reckoning* (1965).

See also ARAB–ISRAEL WAR (1956); CHURCHILL, WINSTON S.; DULLES, JOHN FOSTER; EISENHOWER, DWIGHT DAVID; MONTREUX CONVENTION (1936); MOSSADEGH, MOHAMMAD; NASSER, GAMAL ABDEL.

Bibliography

Louis, William Roger, and Owen, Roger, eds. *Suez 1956: The Crisis and Its Consequences.* Oxford: Clarendon; New York: Oxford University Press, 1989.

ZACHARY KARABELL

EDIRNE

Turkish province in Europe and city on the Bulgarian border, 209 kilometers (130 miles) northwest of Istanbul.

The city of Edirne (in English, Adrianople) was founded by the Roman emperor Hadrian in 125 C.E.. It was conquered by the Ottoman Turks in the fourteenth century and served as their capital between 1361 and 1453. Between 1829 and 1923, the city was occupied by foreign forces several times: by Russia in 1829 and 1879; by Bulgarian forces in 1913; and by Greece from 1919 to 1922. The modern city is a manufacturing center and a commercial center for western Thrace (European Turkey). It has notable tourist sites, including ruins of its ancient and medieval walls, and three mosques and a covered bazaar that date from the fifteenth century. According to the 2000 census, the population of

Edirne city was 230,908; that of Edirne province was 402,606.

Bibliography

Shaw, Stanford. *History of the Ottoman Empire and Modern Turkey.* New York and Cambridge, U.K.: Cambridge University Press, 1976–1977.

ERIC HOOGLUND

EDOT HA-MIZRAH

See ADOT HA-MIZRAH

EDUCATION

Education and social transformation in the Middle East.

Institutions of formal education have undergone marked transformations in societies of the Middle East since 1800. Education refers to processes in which knowledge, skills, moral behavior, values, tastes, loyalties, and a range of cultural competencies and dispositions get transmitted, learned, and negotiated in various settings. Schooling, on the other hand, refers to a set of practices and behaviors that occur in the bounded institutional universe of the school and is referred to as "formal education."

Institutions of learning in the Middle East once held a position of global preeminence. During the height of the Islamic civilization from the ninth to possibly as late as the sixteenth century, they contributed to staggering advances in fields as diverse as optics, mathematics, medicine, physics, astronomy, philosophy, geometry, translation, architecture, and music. Similarly, the *madrasa* (plural, *madaris*), the Islamic college of law, produced the dual intellectual movements of humanism and scholasticism which, as George Makdisi methodically documents, were borrowed in the medieval period by the Christian West and incorporated into their institutions of higher learning (Makdisi 1981, 1990). Despite the primacy of formal learning in the Muslim Middle East for many centuries, by the eighteenth century the region began looking elsewhere for educational models. In the wake of the European Renaissance, Industrial Revolution, and rise of Europe as a global economic and imperial force, and also within the context of Russian impe-

rial expansion, there rose an urgency among the leaders of Ottoman, Egyptian, and Iranian states to modernize their armies and supporting institutions, including scientific and humanistic educational institutions. The educational model from Europe and to some extent Russia was considered to contain the formula for achieving power, economic success, and scientific advancement in the new world order.

The type of schooling that became increasingly important for projects of military, social, political economic, scientific, and cultural reform throughout the last two centuries has been variously termed "modern," "Western," "civil," "foreign," "secular," "new order," "new method," or simply "new"; what is clear is that this new schooling was intended to transform the organization of knowledge transmission by utilizing new disciplining techniques of power, as Timothy Mitchell and Brinkley Messick elaborate in their discussions of new schooling in Egypt and Yemen respectively (Mitchell; Messick). In their ideal configurations the new schools differed in content, organization, and culture in certain fundamental ways from the existent Islamic indigenous *madaris* and schools for elementary learning, the *kuttab* (plural, *katatib*) or *maktab* (plural, *makatib*), in which students learned the Qur'an by rote and might acquire basic writing and reading skills. Among the more distinguishing features of the new schooling were that students were separated into classes by age groups; knowledge—including religious knowledge—was codified and fixed into textbooks and curricula, thus contributing to secularization; the school day was organized according to a regimented timetable; school grounds, classrooms, and equipment were spatially arranged to instill discipline and order in students; a new professional class of teachers competent in new pedagogies and located to a large degree outside the Muslim scholarly class (*ulama*) was trained to staff the new schools; and the planning and administration of formal schooling over time became more centralized in state bureaucratic apparatuses.

In actuality, however, the new schools often overlapped with and contained elements of the pre-existing indigenous schools in areas such as staff, disciplinary codes, and texts, testifying to their syncretic nature. As Benjamin Fortna demonstrates in his outstanding social history of new schooling in the late Ottoman period, members of the *ulama* often served as teachers in the new schools, in which (Islamic) morality played a central role. Furthermore, even with the rise of new schooling as a dominant educational paradigm, Islamic institutions of learning in countries such as Iran and Morocco maintained a position of eminence, as Roy Mottahedeh and Dale Eickelman show in their portrayals of religious education in the contemporary period in the two countries respectively (Mottahedeh; Eickelman).

Although the appearance of "Western"-looking and -organized schools in the Middle East from the nineteenth century has sometimes been interpreted as reflecting a kind of cultural Westernization of those societies, or at least of their institutions, the reality has been much more complex. The new schools have embodied the tensions, aspirations, and negotiations inherent in processes of institutional and cultural adaptation.

Pre-1800 to 1877: The Incipient New School Movement between the State and Private Sphere

As early as the 1720s official state delegations from the Ottoman Empire traveled to Europe to visit and study their institutions of learning. As Ekmeleddin Ihsanoğlu notes, one of the first attempts to "set up an Ottoman intellectual institution without an organic structure" occurred during the reign of Ottoman Sultan Ahmet III when scholars were assembled in 1720 for the purpose of translating works of history and philosophy from European languages into Turkish and Arabic (Ihsanoğlu, p. 165). By the first decades of the nineteenth century, states more systematically supported the use of nonorganic education for modernizing reforms.

The figure most often credited with utilizing new schooling for military and accompanying scientific and technological reform was the viceroy of Egypt, Muhammed Ali Pasha (r. 1805–1849). In 1809 he sent the first group of students on an educational mission to Europe, and over the next decades he established numerous schools in Egypt—roughly equivalent to vocational high schools and technical colleges—that specialized in military sciences, medicine, agriculture, veterinarian medicine, midwifery, pharmaceutics, chemistry, engineering, and translation (Heyworth-Dunne). With the exception of the

School of Midwives, all schools were exclusively for male students. In 1825 the first state preparatory (postprimary) school for boys, Qasr al-Ayni, was established to supply students for the new specialized schools. The new schools, many of which did not endure beyond his reign, were administered by the Ministry of War *(Diwan al-Jihadiyya)* and depended largely on foreign staff. The education policies under his grandson Khedive Ismael (1864–1879), in which the famous teacher-education college, Dar al-Ulum (est. 1872), and the first state school for girls, al-Saniyya School (est. 1873), were established, had more lasting impact.

Parallel developments occurred throughout the Ottoman Empire under the reigns of Sultan Selim III (r. 1789–1807) with his "New Order" *(Nizam al-Jadid)* program; Mahmud II (1808–1839); Abdülmecit (r. 1839–1861), the Tanzimat sultan; and Abdülhamit II (1876–1909). Similar to Egypt, students were sent on educational missions abroad, state schools for higher technical and vocational training were established, and primary *(rüşdiye)* and preparatory *(idadi)* schools were developed. Among the more famous Ottoman state schools for secondary and higher learning were the School of Military Medicine (est. 1827), the War College *(Mekteb-i Harbiye,* est. 1846), Mülkiye School (est. 1859), and Galatasaray Lycée *(Mekteb-I Sultanî,* est. 1868). The *ulama* in Iran, who were politically stronger than *ulama* in Egypt and the Ottoman Empire, maintained a near monopoly on formal education, and very few new schools were founded. During the reign of Qajar Shah Nasir al-Din (r. 1848–1896), however, Crown Prince Abbas Mirza initiated a New Order reform program and established the renowned *Dar al-Funun* (est. 1851), an elite military institution in which French was the language of instruction.

As it became increasingly evident in the early decades of the nineteenth century that the new education was to become an enduring part of state apparatuses of power and reform, legislation was issued and new administrative bodies formed to manage it. Among the early landmark education legislation from Istanbul was an 1824 decree mandating compulsory elementary education for boys. In Egypt the Primary School Regulation of 1836 led to the establishment of the first education ministry, the Department of Schools *(Diwan al-Madaris).*

Tanzimat era (1839–1876) reforms included the Education Regulation of 1869 (*Maarif Nizamnamesi*), which was the blueprint for the empire's first centrally organized and controlled network of schools, and the 1876 Iranian Constitution stipulated that elementary education was to be compulsory and provided by the state free of charge. Such ambitious far-reaching plans would not begin to be effectively implemented until the middle of the twentieth century, but they indicated the hopes the Muslim majority government placed on new schooling for societal change.

States also pursued policies of school expansion with the aim of cultivating a Muslim middle class that would be able to compete with the prosperous segments of foreign and minority communities in matters of trade and other commercial endeavors. The economic success of non-Muslim groups in Egypt and the Ottoman territories was attributed in part to the legal privileges afforded them by the capitulations, but also to the skills, languages, and other competencies they acquired through their participation in the new schooling.

New education had been spreading among minority *millet* and foreign communities since the eighteenth century. By the 1860s, a period of precarious European economic investment and colonial encroachment in the region, there arose a vast proliferation of schools established by religious missions, foreign governments, local communities, and private associations from France, Britain, Austria, Greece, England, Germany, the United States, and Italy. They served ethnic minority and religious communities such as the Armenians, Jews, and Christians, and also progressively higher numbers of elite Muslim children who were attracted to the prestigious foreign schools. Among the organizations with notable quantitative and qualitative educational impact were the Church Missionary Society of Great Britain (CMS) (est. 1799), the American Board of Commissioners for Foreign Missions (est. 1810), and the French-based *Alliance Israélite Universelle* (est. 1860). Collectively these organizations founded hundreds of schools throughout the region, serving tens of thousands of students. Foreign schools played pioneering roles in, among other areas, girls' and women's education, and higher education (Thompson). The institutions of higher education founded by foreign missions and organizations included the

Syrian Protestant College, later named the American University of Beirut (est. 1866); Saint Joseph University, also located in Beirut and founded by French jesuits (est. 1874); Robert College, Istanbul, which became the location for Bogazici University in 1971 (est. 1863); the Istanbul-based American College for Girls (est. 1890); and the American University in Cairo (est. 1920).

The proliferation of foreign educational institutions in the region did not occur without a great deal of tension, and schooling became an ever more hotly debated issue as the century progressed.

1878 to 1913: Colonialism, Nascent Nationalist Movements, and Fragmented Schooling

The new schooling was involved in forging a different kind of society, and its role in societal transformation was widely debated by government officials, foreign missionaries, social reformers, public intellectuals, ordinary citizens, Muslim clerics, and colonial government representatives. They raised pressing questions relating to what populations should participate in the new schooling, who should fund and regulate it, and what its content, methods, and objectives should be. Whereas the British Mandate government in Egypt (1882–1922), for example, advocated limited educational development to maintain the local population in a subordinate position, the French considered the spread of schooling as part of their *mission civilatrice*. Members of emerging reform and nationalist movements, engaged citizens, local notables, and officials, on the other hand, perceived new schooling as a requisite for much-needed social reform; however, they largely frowned upon foreign control over it. Foreign schooling was criticized for contributing to a climate of intensified sectarianism and for threatening local religious, cultural, and national sovereignty. Local groups and individuals spearheaded educational alternatives for the moral, scientific, and political socialization of their youth.

A notable experiment that took place in the Levant and Egypt was the Benevolent Society school movement. Benevolent societies were locally funded Muslim, Christian, and intersectarian associations that provided social services by way of support for widows and the poor, hospitals, libraries, student hostels, and, most prominently, schools for boys and girls. These schools were modeled on the government and foreign schools but placed more emphasis on Arabic studies, regional history, vocational training, religion, and morals. The first school of this type was the Maqasid School of the Maqasid Benevolent Society (*Jamʿiyat al-Maqasid al-Khayriyya)*, established in Beirut in 1878 by Abd al-Qadir al-Qabbani. The following year the Benevolent Society School of Alexandria, which later added the word *Islamic* to its name (*Madrasat al-Jamʿiyya al-Khayriyya al-Islamiyya bi al-Iskandariyya)*, was opened in Egypt by Abdullah al-Nadim. Within two decades a growing network of benevolent-society schools spread in the region, the most famous among them the *al-Maqasid* schools of Egypt started by Muhammad Abduh in 1892. Similar examples of local alternative schooling in later periods include the Moroccan Free Schools, which proliferated in the 1920s as an alternative to French colonial schools, and the extensive network of Muslim Brotherhood schools in Egypt from the 1920s until the organization was outlawed in the 1940s.

It is no coincidence that the founders and advocates of benevolent-society schools were in many instances prominent figures in the emerging press, which constituted, with the schools, a powerful component of the new education. With the growth of the press (including a vibrant women's press), an active and engaged public sphere was in the making. As with schools, governments increasingly regarded with trepidation the press because it could be a means of fomenting popular unrest and political opposition. The new education ministries in Egypt and the Ottoman Empire, for example, took on the task of not only supervising schools, but also of censoring the press. School texts, journals, pamphlets, plays, and books of all sorts were subject to censorship. Education ministries have also been closely linked with state security apparatuses. During the Hamidian period, for example, the secret police monitored classes in the Ottoman University (est. 1890), where potentially subversive subjects such as politics, sociology, history, and philosophy were excluded from the curriculum. Censorship and surveillance policies were ultimately unsuccessful, for the secret revolutionary society that eventually aided in the overthrow of the Ottoman sultan, the Committee of Union and Progress or "Young Turks," was begun by four cadets in the Military Medical College in 1889, and their literature spread largely

through the growing networks of schools and school inspectors.

Throughout the period leading up to World War I, schooling, including religious schooling, was gradually taken out of the jurisdiction of the ministries of religious endowments (*awqaf*) and put under the legal authority of new state education ministries. The process of centralization of formal schooling would continue with a vengeance in the period following World War I.

1913 to 1960s: Nationalization and Centralization of Mass Education

In the post–World War I era the Ottoman Empire was dismantled and the political configuration of the region altered substantially. Turkey became an independent republic, and the Arab territories of the Gulf, Maghreb, Levant, Transjordan, and Egypt were carved up and divided between England and France. In 1948 the Jewish State of Israel was established by British mandate. The age of direct European colonialism came to an end as sovereign nation states were born. The new governments, influenced by modernist ideologies that advocated mass education as the panacea for economic, social, and political development, pursued policies of vigorous educational expansion. Education also figured prominently in the new and revised constitutions, which, with the exception of Saudi Arabia's and Bahrain's, made stipulations for compulsory schooling for boys and girls. This period also witnessed the development of national universities, to which women eventually gained full access.

Two major features characterized national education at the preuniversity level in the Arab states and Iran: Education was centrally administered, one consequence being that foreign schools to a large degree were incorporated into national systems; and education was organically linked to upbringing (*tarbiya* in Arabic, and *parvaresh* in Persian). Schools are socializing institutions par excellence, but in Muslim majority states the upbringing aspect of schooling is expressed in explicit terms. As Gregory Starrett notes, "Muslim states have followed a different course to modernity, insisting explicitly that progress requires a centrally administered emphasis upon moral as well as economic development" (Starrett, p. 10). Most of the education ministries in the region contain the word *upbringing* in their official designations, as in the Ministry of Upbringing and Education (*Wizarat al-Tarbiya wa al-Taʿlim*) in Egypt, Jordan, and the United Arab Emirates; the Ministry of National Upbringing (*Wizarat al-Tarbiya al-Wataniyya*) in Algeria and Morocco; and the Ministry of Education and Upbringing (*Vezarat-e Amuzesh va Parvaresh*) in Iran.

The upbringing component of state-monitored formal schooling serves as a way of ensuring that indigenous, usually Islamic cultural tenets get incorporated into national, and tacitly "secular," education programs. Through school policies that include mandatory religion classes and a host of formal and informal cultural policies such as sex segregation, dress and grooming codes, and supervision of youth behavior in and outside school grounds, educators attempt to guide youth toward socially acceptable conduct. Yet the contours of what is "acceptable" shift and differ according to the historic moment and individual interpretation, social class, region, life stage, and gender. Similar to the Muslim majority states, in the Jewish state of Israel religion is a required subject in state schools from the first grade through high school. The state also supports Jewish religious state schools in which moral conduct and behavior based on Jewish principles play a central role.

Education has long been regarded as a means of national-identity building. Schools are infused with ideological and nationalist content that gets transmitted through curricula, rituals, celebrations, and symbols. In the Arab states, particularly in the post-1950s when pan-Arabism was at its peak, education was seen as a means of solidifying the "Arab nation." In Israel, schools and kibbutzim were intended to generate allegiance to the Jewish state, a process that the non-Jewish Arab minority remained outside of. In secular republican Turkey, education was a means of forging a secular citizenry, and in Iran under the Pahlavi Dynasty, education was geared toward cultural secularization. However, national-identity building does not always evolve according to state policy. The decline of Arab nationalism, the onset of the Iranian revolution, the rise of Islamism throughout much of the region (including "secular" Turkey), and the appearance of an increasingly fragmented polity in Israel have all posed challenges to national education systems. National educational policies would undergo further challenges and

changes in the succeeding period characterized by a new globalization.

1970s to the Present: Education between the Local and the Global

The Middle East has undergone dramatic economic, political, and ideological changes since 1970, all of which have had a major impact on development and practice of formal education. The 1970s oil boom in Persian Gulf countries and subsequent massive interregional labor migrations; the 1979 Iranian Revolution, which gave way to the establishment of the Islamic Republic of Iran; the Iran–Iraq War; the 1967 Arab–Israeli War and ensuing Israeli occupation of Arab lands; the first and second (al-Aqsa) Palestinian intifadas; the ongoing civil war in Sudan; the 1990 Gulf War; the U.S. war on and occupation of Iraq; the rise of Islamism as a political and sociocultural movement; and the rise of Middle Eastern states as major debtor nations are all some of the major factors that have contributed to profound changes in the realm of education.

Education has long developed as a result of transnational, regional, and global exchanges, borrowings, and adaptations, but certain unique characteristics underpin education in the current period of globalization. To a growing extent supranational, nonlocally accountable organizations such as the World Bank, International Monetary Fund (I.M.F.), and United Nations (UN) determine policies and measurements of education as Robert Arnove and Carlos Torres put forward in their tome on comparative education (2003). The "success" or "failure" of national education sectors tend to be measured in quantitative terms and based on factors such as enrollments rates and test scores, with scant attention to "quality." The Arab world has not fared well in these global assessments with illiteracy rates in the mid-1990s as high as roughly 55 percent for females and 30 percent for males. Debtor states of the Middle East and elsewhere have also been compelled to follow certain austerity measures that have included increased privatization and decentralization of national education. Studies on the Middle East region and other regions of the south have repeatedly shown that such policies unequivocally disadvantage the poor, rural populations, and women, and accentuate social inequality. Indeed, these "global" policies are often in direct contravention of national and community interests, indicating a lack of real autonomy and sovereignty among postcolonial states and in educational policy design.

Yet, with growing homogenization of education policies a host of local responses have emerged. In the Middle East there has been an unmistakable revitalization of religious-oriented education. In "secular" Turkey, for example, there was a prodigious growth of the Islamic-oriented *Imam Hatip* schools until they were curbed by legislative intervention from the end of the 1990s. There has also been a rise in religious Jewish schools in Israel. Various types of Islamic schools, including *katatib* and new hybrid private Islamic schools, have been on the rise in Egypt, Jordan, Yemen, and Palestine. With the growing privatization and subsequent commercialization of education (with its lucrative financial possibilities), new manifestations of religious schooling have appeared, such as the "five-star" Islamic school, which incorporates up-to-date computer labs, swimming pools, and other signs of prestige and desires being produced in a globalized world in their programs (Herrera, p. 185). In keeping with the privatization pattern, the decade of the 1990s also witnessed prodigious growth in the private university sector, with the opening of twelve new private universities and higher education institutions in Jordan, fifteen in Turkey, seven in Lebanon, and six in Egypt, with plans in all countries for more. Much of the privatized higher education discourse has focused on issues of accreditation, competitiveness, professional degrees, financing, profit, and the needs of the global economic markets, largely removing the new private universities from humanistic endeavors.

The record of national regional universities in social science, humanities, and sciences, however, has been mixed at best. The scientific quality of universities and individual faculties varies substantially. In the Arab countries and Iran, national universities have reflected authoritarian political systems and been characterized by especially cumbersome bureaucratic structures and severe restrictions on academic freedom, both of which have contributed to the problem of "brain drain." In the Persian Gulf countries, for example, scholarly research is allowed except where the "general social system . . . religious precepts, social traditions, cultural and ethical considerations are concerned" (Morsi, p. 44). National

universities in Egypt, Jordan, and Syria are heavily monitored and censored by state security apparatuses that interfere in aspects of research, student conduct, travel of faculty, and topics of conferences. In Iran during the "cultural revolution" under Ayatollah Ruhollah Khomeini (r. 1979–1989), faculty and students were purged from universities on ideological grounds and materials censored. Under the previous regime of Mohammed Reza Pahlavi, censorship and surveillance were also widespread. Lack of freedom in academia, however, is not necessarily indicative of the absolute power of political regimes, for state policies have often been subverted and resisted at the sites of schools and universities. Students movements, as Ahmad Abdallah documents in the case of Egypt from the 1920s to the 1970s, have been a powerful social and political force.

Early in the twentieth century women struggled for the right to join universities as full participating members. In the 2000s the participation of women in universities throughout the region is proportionally high. In Persian Gulf states such as Saudi Arabia, Qatar, and Kuwait, women make up more than half of the undergraduate population. In 2001 Iranian women overtook men in university entrance. In Egypt women make up more than half of the students in some of the prestigious medical faculties. Although women have made tremendous strides in higher education, at present the attainment of university degrees does not translate into comparable participation in the political arena and the labor force. However, as history has repeatedly demonstrated, the outcomes of mass education are unpredictable at best, and the trend toward increased female attainment of higher education could very well translate into far-reaching social changes.

Conclusion

The "new" education of the past two centuries has developed alongside movements of modernism, nationalism, pan-Arabism, Islamism, and globalism. As with other forms of institutional borrowing and adaptation, education has been characterized by "intertwined and overlapping histories" (Said, p. 18). It has served as a force in cultural and political reproduction and in social transformation, with often unintended and unpredictable consequences.

Bibliography

Abdallah, Ahmed. *The Student Movement and National Politics in Egypt, 1923–1973.* London: Al Saqi Books, 1985.

Arnove, Robert F., and Torres, Carlos Alberto, eds. *Comparative Education: The Dialective of the Global and the Local,* 2d edition. Lanham, MD: Rowman and Littlefield, 2003.

Eickelman, Dale. *Knowledge and Power in Morocco: The Education of a Twentieth-Century Notable.* Princeton, NJ: Princeton University Press, 1985.

Herrera, Linda. "Islamization and Education in Egypt: Between Politics, Culture, and the Market." In *Modernizing Islam: Religion in the Public Sphere in Europe and the Middle East,* edited by John L. Esposito and François Burgat. London: Hurst and Company, 2003.

Heyworth-Dunne, J. *An Introduction to the History of Education in Modern Egypt,* 2d edition. London and Edinburgh: Frank Cass, 1968 [1939].

Ihsanoğlu, Ekmeleddin. "Genesis of Learned Societies and Professional Associations in Ottoman Turkey." *Archiuum Ottomanicum* 14 (1995/1996): 160–190.

Makdisi, George. *The Rise of Colleges: Institutions of Learning in Islam and the West.* Edinburgh, U.K.: Edinburgh University Press, 1981.

Makdisi, George. *The Rise of Humanism in Classical Islam and the Christian West.* Edinburgh, U.K.: Edinburgh University Press, 1990.

Messick, Brinkley. *The Calligraphic State: Textual Domination and History in an Islamic Society.* Berkeley: University of California Press, 1993.

Mitchell, Timothy. *Colonising Egypt.* Cambridge, U.K.: Cambridge University Press, 1988.

Morsi, Monir Mohamed. *Education in the Arab Gulf States.* Doha: Educational Research Center, University of Qatar, 1990.

Mottahedeh, Roy. *The Mantle of the Prophet: Religion and Politics in Iran.* New York: Pantheon Books, 1985.

Said, Edward. *Culture and Imperialism.* New York: Vintage Books, 1993.

Starrett, Gregory. *Putting Islam to Work: Education, Politics, and Religious Transformation in Egypt.* Berkeley: University of California Press, 1998.

Thompson, Elizabeth. *Colonial Citizens.* New York: Columbia University Press, 2000.

LINDA HERRERA

EFFENDI

See GLOSSARY

EFFLATOUN, INJI
[1924–1989]

A painter, activist, and pioneer of modern Egyptian art.

Inji Efflatoun was an instrumental part of the women's movement in Egypt. She is known for her leftist activities, including her involvement in forming a student group dedicated to women's rights, and for her writing on the relationships among class difference, women's oppression, and colonial imperialism. These activities eventually resulted in her imprisonment under Gamal Abdel Nasser in the postindependence period. Noted for her Van Gogh-esque paintings, filled with lively brushstrokes of intense color, Efflatoun's art explored political and social subjects throughout her lifetime. Much of her work was in the nationalist vein, including early spirited depictions of nationalist activities and icons such as peasant women.

Although like many Egyptian artists she continued to turn to the countryside and peasant life to express her cultural identity, her paintings during and after her imprisonment took on a significantly more emotional and tragic character. Important works from this period include dark portrayals of the women's prison and the violent struggles on the battlefield in the Egyptian/Arab wars with Israel. A significant portion of her paintings deal with women's and feminist issues, and much of her work reflects her Marxist politics. Efflatoun also wrote a number of books dealing with social issues, including *We Egyptian Women* and *Eighty Million Women with Us.*

See also GENDER: GENDER AND EDUCATION.

Bibliography

Efflatoun, Inji. "We Egyptian Women." In *Opening the Gates: A Century of Arab Feminist Writing,* edited by Margot Badran and Miriam Cooke. Bloomington: Indiana University Press, 1990.

Karnouk, Liliane. *Contemporary Egyptian Art.* Cairo: The American University in Cairo Press, 1995.

JESSICA WINEGAR

EGE UNIVERSITY

Public university in İzmir, Turkey.

Ege (Aegean) University was founded in 1955. In 1982, its academic body was divided into two separate universities, Ege and Dokuz Eylül, for administrative reasons. Ege University has eleven faculties (administrative and social sciences; agriculture; communication; dentistry; education; engineering; letters; medicine; natural sciences; pharmacology; and water products), a conservatory of Turkish music, eight vocational schools, and seven research institutes. Some of its establishments are located in the neighboring provinces: Manisa, Aydın, and Uşak. Instruction is in both English and Turkish. During the 2001–2002 academic year, the university had more than 2,800 faculty members and 30, 887 students, 2,807 of whom were graduate students. Its budget in 2003 amounted to 128,029 billion Turkish liras, 99 percent of which came directly from state funds.

Turkey's third-oldest university, Ege was established in response to a growing demand for higher education in the region around İzmir, whose traditional agricultural and commercial potential led to rapid industrial development during the early 1950s. As befits its name, the university has tried to establish programs emphasizing its relationship with the Aegean Sea and the rest of the Mediterranean area as a cultural and ecological region.

See also İZMIR.

Bibliography

Ege University. Available from <http://www.ege.edu.tr>.

Turkish Council of Higher Education. Available from <http://www.yok.gov.tr./duyuru/butce/imi_butce _kontrol.htm>.

I. METIN KUNT
UPDATED BY BURÇAK KESKIN-KOZAT

EGYPT

Arab country controlling northeastern Africa and the Sinai Peninsula.

Egypt is bordered by the Mediterranean Sea on the north, Sudan on the south, the Red Sea on the east, and Libya on the west. It consists of three regions: (1) the Nile Valley and Delta (less than 4% of the total area), extending from Sudan north to the Mediterranean; (2) the Eastern Desert–Sinai Peninsula (28%), extending from the Nile Valley to the Gulf of Aqaba and the border with Israel; and (3)

the Western Desert (68%), stretching from the Nile Valley west to Libya.

Egypt's geographic position makes the country easy to control and rule. Its society and polity are characterized by central rule and the absence of long-standing regional allegiances. Dependence on the Nile River for irrigation has called for central administration and enabled the government to extend its authority to the distant parts of the land. Because most of the territory is desert, 96 percent of the Egyptian people live on less than 5 percent of the country's total land area, despite a massive land reclamation project that is starting to irrigate parts of the Western Desert.

Population and Social Structure

Egypt is one of the oldest continuously settled lands in the world. Egyptians, except for a few Nubians, speak Arabic. About 90 percent of the people are Muslim, and Islam is the state religion. The Copts are the largest non-Muslim religious group. Estimates of their numbers vary between six million and nine million. In 2003, the total population of Egypt was seventy million and was increasing by one million every ten months. The birth rate in 2002 was 24.4 per thousand and the death rate was 7.6 per thousand; the natural rate of population increase was 16.8 (the world average for the period in question was 13.5).

Half of the Egyptian people are under twenty years of age; two-thirds are under thirty. The number of dependent children supported by working adults is high, a situation that severely strains the economy. Egypt's government and economy are increasingly unable to meet the demands for food, shelter, education, and jobs. Some three million Egyptians have migrated to other Arab countries, particularly the oil-producing states, in search of work. Their remittances to their families constitute a major source of Egypt's hard currency and help to offset the difference between the country's imports and exports.

In contrast to many developing countries, Egypt has a high degree of social and national integration. Presidents Gamal Abdel Nasser (1954–1970), Anwar al-Sadat (1970–1981), and Husni Mubarak (1981–) have all spoken proudly about Egypt's national unity, by which they mean the peaceful coexistence

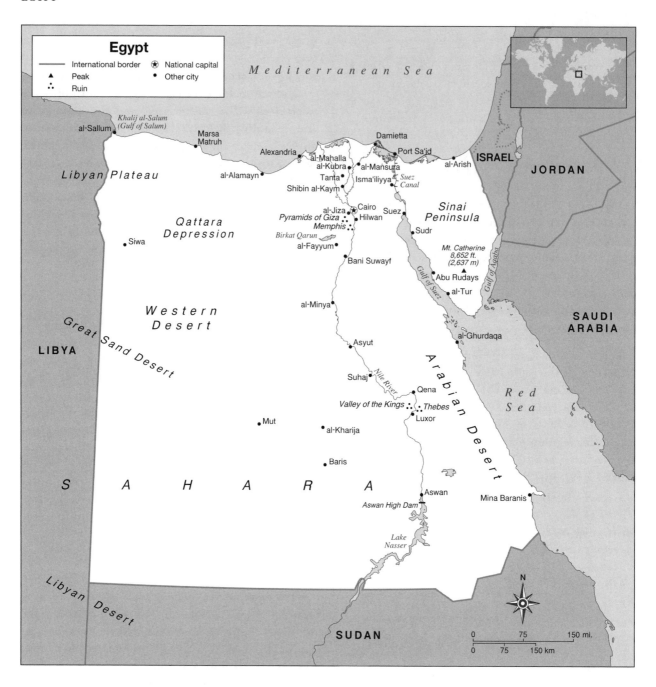

MAP BY XNR PRODUCTIONS, INC. THE GALE GROUP.

between the country's Muslims and Copts. This unity has been tested when Muslim extremists attacked, robbed, and occasionally murdered Copts. The Copts also began to fear growing pressure to apply Islamic law in Egypt, which could weaken their position relative to the Muslim majority.

Population growth has limited Egypt's development efforts by aggravating unemployment, increas-

ing the ratio of mouths eating to hands working, spurring rural migration to urban centers, and diverting resources from investment to consumption. Population rises by almost 2 percent annually, a rate that exceeds the increase of arable land and is far beyond Egypt's educational and industrial development. Although the cropped area almost doubled between 1882 and 1970, the population growth absorbed and exceeded the increase. Once the bread-

In Egypt, school enrollment is compulsory for children between the ages of six and fourteen, and primary and intermediate education is free. Despite the irregular attendance of children who must work to support their families, classrooms tend to be overcrowded, and many Egyptian schools lack up-to-date equipment and texts. © Thomas Hartwell/Corbis Saba. Reproduced by permission.

basket of the ancient world, modern Egypt has had to import cereal grains, making it more dependent on the outside world and vulnerable to the fluctuations of food prices.

Economy

Economic factors have played a crucial role in Egypt's politics. In 1991, inflation was nearly 21.3 percent a year, the national debt was US$25 billion, the gross national product (GNP) per capita was US$600, and the country agreed to a major restructuring program. Indeed, since World War II, Egypt has had a balance-of-payments deficit that has had to be made up from other sources. From 1945 to 1958 it simply drew down existing reserves, which had accumulated during World War II. From 1958 to 1964, Egypt received foreign aid from Eastern and Western sources; from 1965 to 1971, the former Soviet Union paid for most of the deficit; from 1971 to 1977, the aid was primarily from Arab states;

and since 1978, support has come from the United States and other Western nations. The rate of inflation in 2001 was 2.3 percent, the national debt was US$29 billion, and the GNP per capita reached US$3,600. The economy declined slightly during the period from 2001 to 2003 and the Egyptian pound has been allowed to float against the U.S. dollar; it lost half its value between 1997 and 2003.

In 1974 Sadat inaugurated his *Infitah,* or open-door economic policy, to attract foreign investment. He justified it on the following grounds: (1) the failure of Nasser's socialist policies; (2) the availability of capital from Arab oil-producing countries; and (3) the superpowers' détente. From an economic standpoint, the *Infitah*'s main purposes were twofold: to attract export-oriented foreign enterprises by setting up duty-free zones and to attract foreign capital through a liberal investment policy. Its ultimate goal was to develop Egypt's economy through joint ventures and projects, combining Egyptian labor, Arab capital, and Western technology and entrepreneurship.

Egypt's policy of liberal reform led to a restructuring of its economy. In 1991 the government implemented financial stabilization (unifying the rate of exchange, reducing subsidies) and started a program of structural adjustment (privatization and trade liberalization). The economy grew rapidly during the 1990s but stagnated in the early twenty-first century. Per capita GDP skyrocketed, and imports exceeded exports in value by a factor of three to one, but the deficit was made up by remittances, Suez Canal tolls, pipeline fees, and tourism. After the terrorist attack on New York's World Trade Center in September 2001, most of these sources diminished. The trade deficit in the first quarter of 2002 was US$1.6 billion. In addition, the gap between rich and poor Egyptians widened perceptibly as a result of both Sadat's *Infitah* policy and the economic restructuring. In 2000 it was estimated that the top tenth of Egyptians enjoyed 25 percent of the national income, while the bottom tenth earned only 4.4 percent.

History and Politics

On 1 July 1798 the people of Alexandria watched some 400 French ships in the Mediterranean bring 34,000 soldiers and 16,000 sailors to Egypt. Led by Napoléon Bonaparte, this expedition subjected Egypt, then a part of the Ottoman Empire, to direct confrontation with European expansionism. The occupation was harsh and stirred up popular resistance in Cairo, but it took a joint Anglo-Ottoman expeditionary force to expel the French in 1801. Following France's withdrawal, a popular uprising in Cairo forced the Ottoman government to name Muhammad Ali as governor of Egypt. Ruling from 1805 to 1848, Muhammad Ali modernized Egypt's administrative, economic, and military structures by introducing Western methods and technologies on a large scale.

In 1854, during the reign of his son, Saʿid Pasha, a French diplomat secured permission to build a maritime canal across the Isthmus of Suez. The opening of the Suez Canal in 1869 greatly increased Egypt's strategic importance to the European powers and helped attract large numbers of Europeans to settle in Egypt's main cities. The Egyptian government also borrowed large sums of money from European banks at ruinous rates of interest, resulting in a state debt of 100 million Egyptian pounds by the end of the reign of Muhammad Ali's grandson, Ismaʿil ibn Ibrahim, in 1879. Egypt's European creditors established the Caisse de la Dette Publique (Fund for the Public Debt) to supervise the collection and disbursement of government revenues in 1876, followed later in that same year by the Office of Dual Financial Control. By 1881, the government was frantically cutting its expenditures to avert bankruptcy, contributing to the rise of a reformist movement led by Ahmad Urabi. The British intervened to suppress the revolt, bombarding Alexandria on 11 July 1882 and occupying Cairo nine weeks later, marking the start of an occupation that would last for seventy-four years. Initially British rule took the form of a veiled protectorate, honoring Ottoman suzerainty and the authority of the khedive (Egyptian ruler) and his ministers, although in reality Egypt was governed by Sir Evelyn Baring (later Lord Cromer) and his successors. In December 1914, following the Ottoman entry into World War I on the German side, the British government proclaimed a formal protectorate over Egypt.

Following the war, a nationwide revolution, led by Saʿd Zaghlul, broke out. His movement, known as the Wafd, achieved success on 28 February 1922, when Britain formally terminated the protectorate, proclaimed Egypt a sovereign, independent kingdom, and reserved four issues for future negotiations: (1) imperial communications, (2) defense, (3) minorities, and (4) the Sudan. On 15 March 1922 Ahmad Fuʾad was proclaimed king, and a constitution was issued on 9 April 1923. Free elections were held in two stages, resulting in a large parliamentary majority for the Wafd, which reconstituted itself as a political party.

From 1923 to 1936, negotiations took place on the four reserved points. The 1936 Anglo-Egyptian Treaty settled most of the issues between the two countries. Britain's troops remained in Alexandria, Cairo, and the Suez Canal Zone. The treaty was opposed, however, by a number of political forces, including the popular Muslim Brotherhood. On 15 October 1951, Egypt's government unilaterally abrogated the treaty and Egyptian commandos attacked British soldiers and installations in the Canal Zone. Egypt's military defeat in the Arab-Israel War of 1948 coincided with social and political instability that had begun in the early 1940s as a result of increasing class disparities, uncontrolled urbanization, and labor unrest.

Egypt's government failed to respond to these conditions, nor did it respect the will of the people. The monarchy violated or suspended the 1923 constitution and dissolved parliaments whenever its power was threatened. The Wafd, the political party that won every election that was not rigged, held power less than eight years altogether and was dismissed from office on four separate occasions. Between 1923 and 1952, no popularly elected Egyptian parliament ever completed its term, and the average life of a cabinet was less than eighteen months.

These tensions led to frequent demonstrations, widespread political alienation, and the growth of revolutionary movements, such as the Muslim Brotherhood, the Young Egypt Party, Communist organizations, and the Free Officers. The insistence of the palace on absolute rule, the opposition of the ruling class to reform, and Britain's rigid refusal to withdraw from the Suez Canal Zone led the Egyptians to believe that only revolution could bring about reform. On 23 July 1952, the army seized control; three days later King Farouk abdicated in favor of his infant son. In June 1953, the monarchy was terminated and a republic was declared. All political parties, including the Wafd and the Muslim Brotherhood, were abolished.

From 1952 to 1970, the basic characteristics of Egypt's government under Muhammad Naguib and Gamal Abdel Nasser were military dictatorship, concentration of power, emphasis on mobilization rather than participation, and the supremacy of the executive branch. In the absence of political parties, three successive organizations became vehicles for political mobilization: the Liberation Rally (1953–1956), the National Union (1956–1962), and the Arab Socialist Union (1962–1977). An imbalance clearly existed between politics and administration. The bureaucracy, police, and army far eclipsed interest groups and political organizations. Whenever possible, the government attempted to penetrate and dominate groups such as trade unions, professional societies, and religious institutions. During the same period, the state took control of the economy in order to achieve rapid development and social justice, a policy known as Arab Socialism.

Gamal Abdel Nasser (left) took power in 1954 and in 1956 declared Egypt a socialist state with a single-party system. Nasser ruled Egypt for eighteen years, garnering a reputation for being a champion of Arab interests, but turning the country into a veritable police state in the process. © HULTON-DEUTSCH COLLECTION/CORBIS. REPRODUCED BY PERMISSION.

After Nasser's death in 1970, Egypt's political system began to change. The ruling elite became increasingly civilianized, and a pluralistic political culture began to emerge. Anwar al-Sadat professionalized the army, disengaged it from politics, and appointed more civilians to high posts. For the first time since 1952, civilians held the posts of vice president and prime minister. The gradual democratization of the political structure led in 1977 to the formation of a controlled multiparty system. Domestically, Sadat was eager to establish his legitimacy apart from Nasser's. Most Egyptians acknowledged that the Arab Socialist Union had failed as an instrument of popular mobilization, and intellectuals and professional associations came to advocate political pluralism. Sadat often called for popular plebiscites to ratify his policies, such as the peace treaty with Israel. Externally, Sadat's rapprochement with the United States and his desire to make Egypt seem more democratic reinforced these

Husni Mubarak, a former military pilot, became president of Egypt following the assassination of Anwar al-Sadat in 1981. Mubarak is a skilled mediator who has worked hard to nurture and strengthen diplomatic relations with the United States and Russia, as well as with the other Arab countries. © AP/WIDE WORLD PHOTOS. REPRODUCED BY PERMISSION.

trends. Although Sadat was assassinated by Islamist militants in 1981, his successor, Husni Mubarak, has cautiously allowed the democratization process to continue by holding multiparty parliamentary elections at regular intervals.

The judiciary, an independent and respected institution, referees many issues, including the formation of new political parties. Applications for new parties must be submitted to a government committee whose decisions are subject to judicial review. Since the committee was established in 1977, it has never approved any applications, but its rejections have been reversed by court verdicts, thus allowing new parties to form.

In 2002, Egypt had fourteen political parties. The most important were the ruling National Democratic Party (NDP), headed by President Husni Mubarak and claiming 85 percent of all parliamentary seats; the Socialist Labor Party, led by Ibrahim Shukri, which adheres to Islamist ideology and formerly had a coalition with the Muslim Brotherhood; and the leftist National Progressive Unionist Party, also called Tajammu, led by Khalid Muhyi al-Din. The other parties are the New Wafd, Socialist Labor, Umma, Socialists, Greens, Social Justice, Democratic Union, Nasserist Arab Democrats, Misr al-Fatat (Young Egypt), Democratic Peoples, and Takaful (Solidarity). Few of these parties play any meaningful role in parliament, and only the NDP actually takes part in Egypt's government. Islamist movements, no matter how many Egyptians support them, are not recognized as political parties.

Since 1977, Egypt's political life has been dominated by the NDP, which has not become a credible political force. All of Egypt's political parties suffer from lack of a strong organization and a coherent ideology. Opposition parties have been reluctant to compromise and have failed to master coalition politics. Ideological cleavages, historical legacies, and leadership rivalries have kept them from working together to challenge the NDP. In the 2000 elections, the ruling party won 388 of the 444 seats in Egypt's parliament.

Egypt has not succeeded in integrating Islamist groups into the political process. The Muslim Brotherhood, which wants to make the shari'a the law for the country, had approximately fifty members in parliament in 1987–1990. Their boycott of the 1990 parliamentary elections and their opposition to the government during the Gulf War weakened their position, yet they remain the most influential Islamist group. Members of the parliament elected in 2000 who were listed as independent were mainly Muslim Brothers. Smaller but more militant Islamist groups, such as al-Jihad and al-Jami'a al-Islamiyya, have resorted to violence against government officials, foreign tourists, and Copts, especially between 1992 and 1997. By 1992, Islamist groups controlled most university student unions and professors' associations, as well as a number of professional societies (e.g., of engineers, physicians, pharmacists, and lawyers), and the state passed laws in 1995 to limit their influence. The Egyptian government's efforts to weaken the militant groups have curbed terrorism, but at grave cost to human rights and its own legitimacy. Thousands of Islamists languish in Egyptian prisons, often without having been tried and convicted of any crime. The Islamist newspapers and magazines were closed after Sadat's assassination and have not been allowed to reopen. Mosque sermons are monitored, and any expression of Islamist militancy is suppressed. It is noteworthy that four of the nineteen men implicated in the 11 September 2001 attack against the United States were Egyptians.

Both Islamists and the Egyptian government have stifled the growth of a civil society. For publishing scholarly articles critiquing early Arabic literature, Nasr Abu Zayd, a Cairo University professor, was obliged to leave Egypt after a secular court, inspired by Islamists, asked his wife to divorce him for allegedly renouncing Islam. Saʿd al-Din Ibrahim, a respected sociologist, was tried and condemned to hard labor by a military court for defaming Egypt, accepting foreign money for his research center without government authorization, embezzlement, and bribing public officials. After a widespread public outcry, he was released, retried by a civilian court, and set free. Neither case speaks well for the independence of Egypt's judiciary.

What is the balance sheet for the democratization process in Egypt? On the positive side are a liberal tradition, a strong sense of national identity, and a complex civil society. Another positive element is a middle class that has organized itself into a growing network of business associations, trade unions, and professional syndicates, thus helping to form a civil society outside the political process. On the negative side, Egypt has a tradition of authoritarianism. The ruling elite has grown up with and worked within a single-party system. The ruling and opposition parties have little internal democracy. Many parties espouse ideologies that are incompatible with democratic institutions. The government uses the armed forces and the police to stifle dissent, creating an atmosphere of fear and leading to either apathy or conspiracies against public order. Ultimately, Egypt's democracy and political stability will rest on its ability to increase economic production and to narrow the yawning gap between the few rich and the many poor.

See also ALEXANDRIA; ARAB–ISRAEL WAR (1948); ARAB SOCIALIST UNION; BARING, EVELYN; BONAPARTE, NAPOLÉON; CAIRO; COMMUNISM IN THE MIDDLE EAST; COPTS; FAROUK; FREE OFFICERS, EGYPT; FUʾAD; INFITAH; ISLAM; ISMAʿIL IBN IBRAHIM; JAMIʿA AL-ISLAMIYYA, AL-; LIBERATION RALLY; OTTOMAN EMPIRE; MOHAMMAD ALI SHAH QAJAR; MUBARAK, HUSNI; MUHYI AL-DIN, KHALID; MUSLIM BROTHERHOOD; NAGUIB, MUHAMMAD; NASSER, GAMAL ABDEL; NATIONAL PROGRESSIVE UNIONIST PARTY; NATIONAL UNION (EGYPT); NEW WAFD; NILE RIVER; SADAT, ANWAR AL-; SHARIʿA; SUEZ CANAL; WAFD; WORLD WAR I; WORLD WAR II; YOUNG EGYPT; ZAGHLUL, SAʿD.

Bibliography

Amin, Galal. *Whatever Happened to the Egyptians?: Changes in Egyptian Society from 1950 to the Present.* New York; Cairo: American University in Cairo Press, 2000.

Fahmy, Ninette. *The Politics of Egypt: State-Society Relationship.* New York: Routledge, 2002.

Goldschmidt, Arthur, Jr. *Modern Egypt: The Formation of a Nation-State.* Boulder, CO: Westview, 1988.

Hopwood, Derek. *Egypt: Politics and Society, 1945–1990,* 3d edition. New York; London: HarperCollins, 1991.

Kienle, Eberhard. *A Grand Delusion: Democracy and Economic Reform in Egypt.* New York; London: I.B. Tauris, 2001.

Vatikiotis, P. J. *The History of Modern Egypt from Muhammad Ali to Mubarak,* 4th edition. Baltimore: Johns Hopkins University Press, 1991.

Waterbury, John. *The Egypt of Nasser and Sadat: The Political Economy of Two Regimes.* Princeton, NJ: Princeton University Press, 1983.

Weaver, Mary Anne. *A Portrait of Egypt: A Journey through the World of Militant Islam.* New York: Farrar, Straus, and Giroux, 1999.

ALI E. HILLAL DESSOUKI
UPDATED BY ARTHUR GOLDSCHMIDT

EGYPTIAN FEMINIST UNION

The first formal, self-consciously feminist organization in Egypt, al-Ittihad al-nisaʾi al-misri (in English, the Egyptian Feminist Union, or EFU).

The Egyptian Feminist Union was founded in Cairo on 16 March 1923 by a small group of women from elite families who had been active in the struggle for independence from British occupation. The group originally had aligned itself with the Wafd movement and was called the Wafdist Women's Central Committee (founded 1919). Bringing together a larger group of women, the EFU worked for Egyptian nationalist aims while opposing women's subordinate status in the Wafd Party and focusing on women's objectives for their own lives. From the start, its leader, Huda al-Sha'rawi, made connections with international feminist organizations, notably the International Woman Suffrage Alliance (IWSA); in May 1923, the EFU sent a delegation to the IWSA's Rome meeting, and the presence of Egyptian feminists received notice in Egypt's press—as did a public act of unveiling by Sha'rawi and fellow delegate Sayza Nabarawi in the Cairo train station upon their return from Rome.

The EFU's agenda ranged from demands for political rights—the EFU picketed the opening session of the Egyptian parliament in 1924 after the new constitution had failed to grant women the right to vote—to social activism, carrying on the philanthropic work of earlier generations of women. In its second year of existence, the EFU started a dispensary for women and a program to train girls in handicraft production; when new headquarters on Cairo's Qasr al-Ayni street were ready in 1932, these became part of a professional and domestic school, and throughout the decade other dispensaries and training programs were founded outside the capital. The EFU founded two journals, the French-language *L'Egyptienne* (1925–1940) and the Arabic-language *Al-Misriyya* (1937–1940), through which it outlined its demands for legal reform in personal status law, equal education for girls, and the right for women to enter university and have access to professional training and positions. Careful to emphasize Egypt's Islamic character and pharaonic past, Sha'rawi, the EFU's leader until her death in 1947, steered a careful path between her European contacts and the nationalists, both liberal and conservative, at home, while increasingly turning to regional Arab concerns. Although the EFU encompassed a range of feminist perspectives, it was not the only Egyptian organization of the time working to advance women's rights.

See also ARAB FEMINIST UNION; GENDER: GENDER AND EDUCATION; GENDER: GENDER AND LAW; GENDER: GENDER AND POLITICS; WAFD; WAFDIST WOMEN'S CENTRAL COMMITTEE.

Bibliography

Al-Ali, Nadje. *Secularism, Gender, and the State in the Middle East: The Egyptian Women's Movement.* Cambridge, U.K.: Cambridge University Press, 2000.

Badran, Margot. *Feminists, Islam, and Nation: Gender and the Making of Modern Egypt.* Princeton, NJ: Princeton University Press, 1995.

MARILYN BOOTH

EGYPTIAN GEOGRAPHICAL SOCIETY

Group of geographers in Egypt.

Khedive Isma'il founded the Khedivial (later Royal, now Egyptian) Geographical Society in 1875 to promote and legitimize his empire in the Sudan and the Horn of Africa. The society later shifted its concentration to Egypt itself and evolved from a foreign-dominated layman's society into the professional society of Egyptian geographers.

See also ISMA'IL IBN IBRAHIM.

Bibliography

Reid, Donald Malcolm. "The Egyptian Geographical Society: From Foreign Layman's Society to Indigenous Professional Association." *Poetics Today* (1993).

DONALD MALCOLM REID

EGYPTIAN–ISRAELI PEACE TREATY (1979)

Treaty signed by Egypt and Israel on 26 March 1979.

The Egyptian–Israeli Peace Treaty derives from the Camp David Accords signed by Egypt, Israel, and the United States on 17 September 1978. The 1978 agreements included two documents, "A Framework for Peace in the Middle East" and "A Framework for the Conclusion of a Peace Treaty between Egypt and Israel." The other Arab states and the Palestinians rejected the Camp David Accords and declined to pursue talks with Israel toward a comprehensive peace. Although they required many more rounds of negotiations, U.S. mediation, and a Middle East visit by U.S. president Jimmy Carter, Egypt and Israel successfully brought the framework for a bilateral peace to fruition.

The Egyptian–Israeli Peace Treaty signed by Egyptian president Anwar al-Sadat and Israeli prime minister Menachem Begin and witnessed by Carter is a relatively short document: nine articles, three annexes, and a series of side letters among and between the three signatories. In a classic land-for-peace swap, the treaty explicitly terminates the state of war between Egypt and Israel and establishes a full and formal peace, including an exchange of ambassadors; in return, the parties accept the international boundary between Egypt and the former Palestine Mandate as the permanent border between them, allowing for the phased return of the entire Sinai Peninsula, captured by Israel in the 1967 war, to Egypt. The treaty called for demilitarized zones and United Nations' forces to monitor the border and, clearly bearing in mind the catalysts which led to war in 1956 and 1967, both sides agreed that neither could unilaterally request the withdrawal of UN personnel. The treaty also affirmed Israel's right of free passage through the Suez Canal, the Strait of Tiran, and the Gulfs of Aqaba and Suez. The normalization of Egyptian–Israeli relations included full recognition; diplomatic, economic, and cultural relations; and the termination of economic boycotts and barriers to the free movement of goods and people.

Although the preamble to the treaty references UN Security Council Resolutions 242 and 338 and calls repeatedly for Israel's other Arab neighbors to join this peace process, the Arab world reacted angrily to Sadat's separate peace with Israel and refused to endorse or participate in it. The Arab League moved its headquarters from Cairo and most of its members broke ties with Egypt, ushering in nearly a decade of Egyptian isolation. Within Egypt, opposition elements protested the peace with Israel, and Islamic radicals, already at odds with Sadat over his economic and social programs, assassinated him on 6 October 1981. Israelis generally welcomed the treaty, although some on the right opposed establishing the precedent of Israeli territorial concessions and Israeli soldiers had to bodily remove protestors from homes in the Sinai town of Yamit.

Husni Mubarak succeeded Sadat and managed to reap the benefits of the treaty, especially massive U.S. foreign aid, without the stigma of having negotiated it. Under his stewardship, Egypt regained its leadership role in the Arab world while preserving the peace with Israel. Despite Israel's initial en-thusiasm, Egyptian wariness has made it a cold peace, however, with low-level trade exchanges, few cross-border visitors, and correct but frosty relations at the top. The treaty has withstood numerous regional crises, but genuinely warm relations would seem to hinge on the resolution of the Palestinian-Israeli conflict.

See also BEGIN, MENACHEM; CAMP DAVID ACCORDS (1978); CARTER, JIMMY; LEAGUE OF ARAB STATES; MUBARAK, HUSNI; SADAT, ANWAR AL-.

Bibliography

Bar-Siman-Tov, Yaacov. *Israel and the Peace Process, 1977–1982: In Search of Legitimacy for Peace.* Albany: State University of New York Press, 1994.

Carter, Jimmy. *Keeping Faith: Memoirs of a President.* New York: Bantam, 1982.

Dayan, Moshe. *Breakthrough: A Personal Account of the Egypt–Israel Peace Negotiations.* London: Weidenfeld and Nicolson, 1981.

Eisenberg, Laura Zittrain, and Caplan, Neil. *Negotiating Arab-Israeli Peace: Patterns, Problems, and Possibilities.* Bloomington: Indiana University Press, 1998.

Kamel, Mohammed Ibrahim. *The Camp David Accords: A Testimony.* London: Kegan Paul, 1986.

Quandt, William B. *Camp David: Peace Making and Politics.* Washington, DC: Brookings Institution, 1986.

Telhami, Shibley. *Power and Leadership in International Bargaining: The Path to the Camp David Accords.* New York: Columbia University Press, 1990.

LAURA Z. EISENBERG

EGYPTIAN MUSEUM

Museum containing the world's finest collection of pharaonic antiquities.

In 1858 the Ottoman Empire's viceroy of Egypt, Saʿid Pasha, commissioned French Egyptologist Auguste Mariette to create an antiquities service and a museum. In 1863 Saʿid's successor, Ismaʿil Pasha, inaugurated the Egyptian Museum in the Bulaq district of Cairo. The museum was moved to Giza in 1891, then to its present building in Tahrir Square in Cairo in 1902. Gaston Maspéro succeeded Mariette as director of the museum and the antiquities service in 1881. For ninety-four years, until the 1952 revolution, all directors of the service were French. In 1954 Mustafa Amir took over as the first Egyptian director. The museum gradually relegated subsidiary collections to the Greco-Roman, Arab (later called Islamic), and Coptic museums. Since the 1920s, the Tutankhamen collection has been the museum's greatest treasure. The present building has been overcrowded almost since it opened. A 1925 proposal by U.S. Egyptologist James Henry Breasted and John D. Rockefeller, Jr. to fund a more spacious new museum foundered on political grounds. In 2001 an international competition was announced for the design of a UNESCO-sponsored Grand Egyptian Museum on a site just north of the Giza pyramids plateau.

See also ARCHAEOLOGY IN THE MIDDLE EAST; MARIETTE, AUGUSTE; MASPÉRO, GASTON.

Bibliography

Bongioanni, A., and Croce, M. S., eds. *The Illustrated Guide to the Egyptian Museum.* Cairo: American University in Cairo Press, 2001.

Al-Misri, Mathaf; De Luca, Araldo; Tiradritti, Francesco; and Mubarak, Suzanne. *Egyptian Treasures from the Egyptian Museum in Cairo.* New York: Harry N. Abrams, 1999.

Reid, Donald Malcolm. *Whose Pharaohs? Archaeology, Museums, and Egyptian National Identity from Napoleon to World War I.* Berkeley: University of California Press, 2002.

DONALD MALCOLM REID

EGYPTIAN WOMEN'S UNION

Women's rights organization.

Often called the Egyptian Feminist Union, the Egyptian Women's Union was founded by Huda al-Shaʿrawi in 1923 to demand voting rights for women in Egypt. It also spearheaded the rejection of the veil by Egyptian women as a step toward their emancipation. After opening a women's clubhouse in Cairo, the group published monthly journals in both French and Arabic, ran a clinic and a dispensary for poor women and children, and established child-care centers for working mothers. As a result of their actions, the government set a minimum marriage age and opened its first secondary school for girls. As the Palestine conflict intensified, the Egyptian Women's Union convened an Arab

women's conference in 1938 and another in 1944; it thus laid the groundwork for the Arab Feminist Union, which elected Huda al-Shaʿrawi as its first president. Following her death in 1947, the Egyptian Women's Union was eclipsed by other feminist groups that attracted younger women. After the 1952 revolution, the union's functions were taken over by government ministries, and it faded away.

See also SHAʿRAWI, HUDA AL-.

Bibliography

Keddie, Nikki R., and Baron, Beth, eds. *Women in Middle Eastern History: Shifting Boundaries in Sex and Gender.* New Haven, CT: Yale University Press, 1992.

Shaarawi, Huda. *Harem Years: The Memoirs of an Egyptian Feminist (1879–1924),* translated by Margot Badran. New York: Feminist Press at the City University of New York, 1987.

ARTHUR GOLDSCHMIDT

8 *MARS* NEWSPAPER

Newspaper of the grassroots Moroccan women's organization Union de l'Action Féminin (Feminist Action Union).

8 Mars (8 March) was launched in the mid-1980s. Its title is the date of International Women's Day. Published in Arabic by women, for women, *8 Mars* has a monthly circulation of over 20,000. Featuring articles on and analyses of legal and political issues that affect women's lives, as well as reports on educational and cultural issues, the publication's proceeds fund the activities of the Union de l'Action Féminin, which was founded in 1983 and as of 2003 had twenty-five branch offices in Morocco and one in Cairo. *8 Mars* advocates women's full exercise of all citizenship rights and features articles and editorials on gender equality in law, everyday life, and culture; it encourages women's integration into decision-making positions at all levels and in all sectors of Moroccan society. Union de l'Action Féminin undertakes projects such as literacy classes, income-generating projects, and public advocacy on women's rights, as well as projects involving women in the political process and all levels of government and advocacy on legal issues, particularly a campaign to change Morocco's *mudawwana* (family law) to give women more legal and economic rights and enhanced personal independence. Partly through grassroots networking and partly through *8 Mars,* the Union de l'Action Féminin gathered over 1 million signatures for a petition to change the *mudawwana* laws in the mid 1990s.

See also JABABDI, LATIFA.

Bibliography

Fernea, Elizabeth Warnock. *In Search of Islamic Feminism: One Woman's Global Journey.* New York: Doubleday, 1998.

Union de l'Action Féminin. Available from <http://www.mtds.com/uaf/FAU%20%20PROFILE.htm>.

LAURIE KING-IRANI

EISENHOWER, DWIGHT DAVID
[1890–1969]

U.S. Army officer; president of the United States, 1953–1961.

Born in Denison, Texas, Dwight David Eisenhower was graduated from the U.S. Military Academy at West Point, New York, in 1915. During World War II, he was chief of the war plans division, U.S. general staff, before becoming commander in chief of U.S. forces, European theater, and commander of allied forces in Northwest Africa. In 1943, he was appointed general, supreme commander in North Africa and the western Mediterranean, and he planned the invasions of North Africa, Sicily, and Italy. He was made general of the army in 1944 and planned and commanded the European invasion at Normandy, France, called D-Day (6 June 1944). After conquering Nazi Germany, Eisenhower remained in Europe as the U.S. member of the Allied Control Commission for Germany and chief of staff of the U.S. Army (1945–1948).

In 1948, Eisenhower returned to the United States and became the president of Columbia University (1948–1953) while remaining supreme commander of the North Atlantic Treaty Organization (NATO) forces in Europe (1951–1952). He was then persuaded to run for president of the United States on the Republican ticket, won, and served two terms (1953–1961). Along with his secretary of state, John Foster Dulles, he was concerned about preventing Soviet incursions in the Middle East, whether economic, political, or ideological. Careful to maintain good relations with the Arab states,

he showed no undue favoritism to the new State of Israel. At first he was interested in funding the Aswan High Dam in Egypt, but President Gamal Abdel Nasser's 1955 arms deal with Czechoslovakia, a Soviet satellite country, led Eisenhower, on the advice of Dulles, to deny the loan. In the 1956 Arab–Israel War, when France, Britain, and Israel attempted to take back the Suez Canal from Nasser's nationalization of it, Eisenhower angrily brought the matter to the United Nations, calling for a cease-fire and a withdrawal. This stance won him few friends in the Middle East—only Hashimite-ruled Iraq and Reza Pahlavi's Iran.

On 5 January 1957, Eisenhower proposed the policy that became known as the Eisenhower Doctrine, calling on Congress to provide military and economic aid to any Middle Eastern nation that believed itself under risk from "armed aggression from any country controlled by international communism." In July 1958, in the wake of the revolution in Iraq, President Camille Chamoun of Lebanon appealed to the United States for help. Believing that the security of Lebanon was endangered by Nasser and by communism, Eisenhower dispatched a contingent of U.S. Marines from the Sixth Fleet; they landed on 15 July to be greeted by astonished sunbathers but stayed for almost four months. Order was restored to Lebanon, and power passed from Chamoun to General Fu'ad Chehab.

See also ARAB–ISRAEL WAR (1956); CHAMOUN, CAMILLE; CHEHAB, FU'AD; DULLES, JOHN FOSTER; NASSER, GAMAL ABDEL; NORTH ATLANTIC TREATY ORGANIZATION (NATO); PAHLAVI, REZA; SUEZ CANAL.

Bibliography

Alteras, Isaac. *Eisenhower and Israel: U.S.–Israeli Relations, 1953–1960.* Gainesville: University of Florida Press, 1993.

Ambrose, Stephen. *Eisenhower: The President.* New York: Simon and Schuster, 1984.

Schoenebaum, Eleanora, ed. *Political Profiles: The Eisenhower Years.* New York: Facts On File, 1977.

Spiegel, Steven. *The Other Arab–Israeli Conflict: Making America's Middle East Policy, from Truman to Reagan.* Chicago: University of Chicago Press, 1985.

ZACHARY KARABELL

EITAN, RAFAEL
[1929–]

Chief of staff of the Israeli military; member of Israel's Knesset.

Rafael ("Raful") Eitan was born in Mandatory Palestine, at Moshav Tel Adashim. He attended Tel Aviv University and Israel's National Security College. He joined the Palmah in 1946 and fought in the Arab–Israel War of 1948. After serving in a number of high posts in the Israeli military, he became chief of staff in 1978, serving until 1983. As chief of staff, he worked with Defense Minister Ariel Sharon to plan and execute the invasion of Lebanon in the Arab–Israel War of 1982. In the aftermath of that war, he was criticized by the Kahan Commission, which investigated Israel's conduct in the war, for failing to prevent the mass killing of Palestinian civilians by Lebanese militiamen in the Sabra and Shatila refugee camps.

In 1983, Eitan entered politics, founding the right-wing nationalist Tzomet Party, which united with the Tehiya Party before the 1984 elections. Eitan has been a member of the Knesset (Israel's parliament) representing the Tzomet and Tehiya parties since 1984 and advocating annexation of the West Bank and Gaza Strip. He served as minister of agriculture and the environment and deputy prime minister from 1996 to 1999.

See also ARAB–ISRAEL WAR (1948); ARAB–ISRAEL WAR (1982); GAZA STRIP; ISRAEL: POLITICAL PARTIES IN; KNESSET; PALMAH; SHARON, ARIEL; WEST BANK.

Bibliography

Rolef, Susan Hattis, ed. *Political Dictionary of the State of Israel.* New York: Macmillan, 1987.

MARTIN MALIN

ELDEM, SEDAD HAKKI
[1908–1988]

Turkish architect.

Sedad Hakki Eldem was born into an artistic Istanbul family. His uncle was Osman Hamdi Bey, founder of the Istanbul Fine Arts Academy. Eldem went to school in Switzerland and Germany before studying architecture at his uncle's academy from 1924 to 1928; he remained a teacher at the academy until 1962. By age thirty-one, he had designed some of the major buildings in the new Republic of Turkey: the Yalova Termal Hotel (1937), the office building for the prime ministry (1938), and the Turkish pavilion at the New York World's Fair (1939). He became the most influential architect in mid-twentieth-century Turkey.

Eldem wrote articles defending local architectural styles over international styles and, in a nationalist vein, argued that foreign architects should never be allowed to build in Turkey. Nonetheless, because of German influence and a shortage of materials in the 1940s, Eldem built the faculties of arts at Ankara and Istanbul universities in a modern, monumental, streamlined style. His only gesture toward Turkish roots was ornamental detail. In 1954, he built the modern-style Istanbul Hilton Hotel. Eldem also served as president of Turkey's antiquities committee and wrote a book on Turkish domestic architecture.

See also ARCHITECTURE.

Bibliography

Yavuz, Yildirim. "Turkish Architecture during the Republican Period (1923–1980)." In *The Transformation of Turkish Culture: The Ataturk Legacy,* edited by Günsel Renda and C. Max Kortepeter. Princeton, NJ: Kingston Press, 1986.

ELIZABETH THOMPSON

ELITES

Small but powerful minorities with a disproportionate influence in human affairs.

Both tribal society and Islam have a strong egalitarian component, but early Islamic writers assumed a distinction between the few (*khassa*) and the many (*amma*) not unlike that in modern Western elite theory between the elite and the masses. Like the term *elite*, *khassa* had vague and various meanings. It was applied on occasion to the following: the early (661–750) Arab aristocracy under the Umayyads; the whole ruling class; the inner entourage of a ruler; educated people generally; and philosophers who pursued a rational (and sometimes a mystical) road to truth.

In the 1960s and 1970s, elite analysis—pioneered by V. Pareto and G. Mosca early in the twentieth century, partly as an alternative to Marxist class analysis—attracted many Western scholars of the Middle East. National political elites received much of the attention, although anthropologists continued their special interest in local elites. Economic, social, and cultural elites attracted notice particularly when they overlapped with political elites. Elite studies examine the background, recruitment, socialization, values, and cohesiveness of elites. They probe elite-mass linkages, circulation into and out of the elite, the effects of elite leadership on society, and the evolution of all these factors over time.

The Ottoman Empire, which ruled loosely over most of the Middle East in the late eighteenth century, conceived of society as divided into a ruling class of *askaris* (literally, "soldiers" but also including "men of the pen"—*ulama* [Islamic scholars] and scribal bureaucrats) and a ruled class of *re'aya* (subjects). "Ottomans" were the core elite among the *askaris,* presumed to be Muslim, available for high state service, and familiar with the manners and language (Ottoman Turkish, which also entailed a knowledge of Arabic and Persian) of court. The recruitment of slaves into the elite was one mechanism that made for extreme upward social mobility.

Ever shifting social realities rarely match prescriptive theories. Although theoretically excluded from the *askari* elite, merchants, Coptic scribes, Jewish financiers, and Greek Orthodox patriarchs wielded considerable power in some times and places. Women attained such great informal power during one seventeenth-century period that the Ottomans called it "the sultanate of women." When central control weakened—as in the Fertile Crescent provinces in the eighteenth and early nineteenth centuries, a "politics of notables" mediated between the center and the provincial masses. Notable status often ran in families; the notables could include *ulama,* tribal shaykhs, merchants, large landowners, and local military forces.

Since 1800, the Middle East and its elites have greatly changed under the impact of the Industrial Revolution, European conquest and rule, the breakup of the Ottoman Empire, nationalism and independence struggles, the Arab–Israel conflict, the petroleum and oil bonanza, secularist and Islamic ideologies, and the frustrations of continuing military, cultural, and economic dependency. Yet there has been continuity too.

Sunni *ulama,* or Islamic scholars at such sites as Yildiz Mosque, were among the elites of the Ottoman Empire at the height of its power in the Middle East. In the past two centuries, however, the influence of *ulama* declined in what eventually became Turkey and much of the rest of the Sunni-dominated countries of the region, even as the military elite generally remained powerful. © CORBIS. REPRODUCED BY PERMISSION.

In the countries where colonialism prevailed, foreign elites forced the partially displaced indigenous elites to make the painful choice of collaboration or resistance. Collaboration was particularly tempting to some religious and ethnic minorities. In the Fertile Crescent, tribal shaykhs and large landowners functioned as notables mediating between the colonial power and the people, as they had once done with the Ottomans. Whether one collaborated or not, knowledge of the West and Western language became a career asset for officials and the emerging professional class. In the milieu of mandates and of party and parliamentary politics between the two world wars, lawyers flourished in both government and opposition. After World War II, as most Middle Eastern countries regained control of their affairs, landed elites and reactionary politicians in many cases still frustrated serious social reform. Pressure built, and army officers of lower-middle-class origin overthrew one regime after another. Was it a return to the praetorian politics of the Ottoman Janissaries and the Mamluks—the

The shah of Iran and Empress Farah used oil wealth and authoritarian rule to withstand the socialist challenge that spread elsewhere in and around the Middle East. However, the monarchs and their elite associates in Iran eventually fell before determined opposition by a revolutionary counterelite under the leadership of Islamic clerics. © Bettmann/Corbis. Reproduced by permission.

armed forces that early nineteenth-century rulers had destroyed to clear the way for Western-style armies? The new armies remained on the political sidelines for most of the nineteenth century, reemerging briefly in Egypt during Ahmad Urabi's vain attempt to resist colonial control.

After 1900, armies reentered politics first in countries that had escaped colonial rule—Turkey with the Young Turks and Mustafa Kemal Atatürk and Iran with Reza Shah Pahlavi. Military coups in the Arab countries began later, following independence from colonial rule: Iraq in the 1930s and again in 1958, Syria in 1949, and Egypt in 1952. The regime of Gamal Abdel Nasser—with its Soviet alliance, single-party authoritarianism, and Arab socialism—became a prototype for many others. Hopes that the new military elites and their civilian technocratic allies—economists, engineers, scientists—represented the progressive vanguard of a new middle class soon proved to be overblown.

Patrilineal monarchies in Morocco, Jordan, Saudi Arabia, and elsewhere in the Arabian Peninsula weathered the revolutionary Arab socialist challenge. Oil wealth helped rulers purchase political acquiescence, but it did not save the monarchs of Iraq, Libya, or Iran. In both the monarchies and their revolutionary challengers, patterns of authoritarian rule persisted. Family connections, old-boy networks, and patron-client relations still figure prominently in elite recruitment and perpetuation

despite the widespread longing for a fair and open system.

Unlike the military, the *ulama* have lost much of the influence they had in 1800. During the nineteenth century, reforming rulers appropriated revenues from religious endowments, tried to turn the *ulama* into bureaucrats, and bypassed them with Western-style courts and state-school systems. In the *ulama*'s willingness to provide legitimization for almost any regime in power, they have jeopardized their moral authority. Engineers and others associated with the state schools, not the *ulama,* have been in the forefront of Islamic and Islamist protest since the late 1960s. Yet in contrast to the turbulent 1950s and 1960s, most Middle Eastern regimes proved remarkably durable in the 1970s and 1980s. In Iran, however, the distinctive tradition of Shiʿism enabled a counterelite of *ulama* to lead a revolution against the shah and to consolidate its power as the core of a new ruling elite. Attempts to export the revolution to Sunni-dominated countries have met little success.

See also Atatürk, Mustafa Kemal; Colonialism in the Middle East; Fertile Crescent; Janissaries; Mamluks; Nasser, Gamal Abdel; Nationalism; Pahlavi, Reza; Shiʿism; *Ulama*; Urabi, Ahmad; Young Turks.

Bibliography

Binder, Leonard. *In a Moment of Enthusiasm: Political Power and the Second Stratum in Egypt.* Chicago: University of Chicago Press, 1978.

Findley, Carter Vaughn. *Ottoman Civil Officialdom: A Social History.* Princeton, NJ: Princeton University Press, 1989.

Hourani, Albert. "Ottoman Reform and the Politics of Notables," In *The Emergence of the Modern Middle East.* Berkeley: University of California Press, 1981.

Hunter, F. Robert. *Egypt under the Khedives 1805–1879.* Pittsburgh, PA: University of Pittsburgh Press, 1984.

Zartman, I. William, et al. *Political Elites in Arab North Africa.* New York: Longman, 1982.

Donald Malcolm Reid

EMERGENCY REGULATIONS

During the British mandate of Palestine and as adopted by Israel, rules allowing the restriction of civil rights in emergencies.

On 22 September 1945, Britain's high commissioner in Palestine issued Defense Emergency Regulations that in turn were based on the 1937 Palestine (Defense) Order in Council. That order gave the commissioner broad powers to adopt measures needed in defense of "public safety" and to suppress mutiny. The regulations were originally enacted to subdue the Palestine Arab Revolt of 1936–1939. They were later used against Zionism's guerrilla organizations fighting to remove British rule from Palestine.

The regulations were carried over after the State of Israel was established (15 May 1948), under the 1948 Law and Administration Ordinance. On 21 May 1948, the Provisional State Council proclaimed a state of emergency that has never been revoked, although various sections have been amended or adapted. The regulations, consisting of 170 articles divided into fifteen sections, allow the government and the military to introduce extreme measures and abolish the most elementary rights, such as freedom of movement, travel, and work. Thus, between 1948 and 1966, approximately 90 percent of Israeli Arabs were placed under military administration, with military governors appointed directly by the defense minister. The governors drew their virtually unlimited powers from the Emergency Regulations. The regulations have also been widely used to detain Israeli Arabs and Palestinian refugees without trial, without formal charges, and without judicial or legislative review.

See also PALESTINE ARAB REVOLT (1936–1939).

Bibliography

Lustick, Ian. *Arabs in the Jewish State: Israel's Control of a National Minority.* Austin: University of Texas Press, 1980.

Rolef, Susan Hattis, ed. *Political Dictionary of the State of Israel,* 2d edition. New York: Macmillan, 1993.

BENJAMIN JOSEPH

ENTEBBE OPERATION

Israeli hostage rescue operation, code-named Kadur ha-Ra'am (Thunderbolt).

On 27 June 1976, two German nationals and two Palestinians boarded Air France Flight 139 en route from Tel Aviv to Paris during a stopover in Athens,

and hijacked it first to Benghazi, Libya, then on to Entebbe Airport in Uganda. Following a plan masterminded by Dr. Wadi Haddad, renegade figure associated with the Popular Front for the Liberation of Palestine (PFLP), and Ilyich Sanchez Ramirez, which involved terrorists of varied affiliations (including the notorious "Carlos") the hijackers were there joined by a second team, the passengers divided into Jews and non-Jews, and the latter released. While feigning negotiation with the hijackers and with their host, President Idi Amin of Uganda, Israel made preparations for a military rescue mission. On the night of 3 July four Hercules transport jets carrying 150 Israeli commandos took off from Sharm al-Shaykh and flew 2,484 miles (4,000 km) to Entebbe, evading detection throughout. Accompanied by diversionary measures, the paratroopers stormed the terminal where the 101 hostages were kept, killing all eight captors and numerous Ugandan soldiers. The Israeli commander, Lieutenant Colonel Yonatan Netanyahu, and three hostages were killed during the operation, which lasted some forty-five minutes from landing to takeoff. (An elderly Jewish woman who had been hospitalized in Kampala and was not present during the rescue was later murdered.) The jets refueled at Nairobi and returned to a tumultuous welcome the following morning in Israel. Arab and African countries and the Communist bloc condemned the Israeli action, while in the West reaction was largely positive.

See also HADDAD, WADI; POPULAR FRONT FOR THE LIBERATION OF PALESTINE; SHARM AL-SHAYKH.

Bibliography

Ben-Porat, Yeshayahu; Haber, Eitan; and Schiff, Zeev. *Entebbe Rescue,* translated by Louis Williams. New York: Dell, 1977.

ZEV MAGHEN

ENTE NAZIONALE IDROCARBONI (ENI)

Italian oil company that sought access to Algeria's oil industry.

Ente Nazionale Idrocarboni, a multistate petroleum company, was headed by Enrico Mattei. Mattei promised both arms and money to Algeria's Front de Libération Nationale (FLN; National Liberation

Front) during the Algerian War of Independence (1954–1962) in return for unspecified future access to the oil and natural gas supplies discovered in Algeria's Saharan region. Mattei's private plane crashed under mysterious circumstances in October 1962, and Algeria nationalized its oil and gas industry after independence.

See also ALGERIAN WAR OF INDEPENDENCE; FRONT DE LIBÉRATION NATIONALE (FLN).

DIRK VANDEWALLE

ENVER PAŞA
[1881–1922]

Ottoman general and strongman of the Committee for Union and Progress.

Enver Paşa was born in Constantinople (now Istanbul) 23 November 1881. When his father, a railway employee, was transferred to Macedonia, Enver attended the Monastir military junior high school. He was graduated from the War Academy (Mekteb-i Harbiye) as staff corporal in 1902 and was posted to the Third Army in Macedonia.

In 1906 Enver joined the Ottoman Liberty Society in Salonika, a constituent group of the reorganized Committee for Union and Progress (CUP). He led one of a series of revolts in Macedonia in 1908 that triggered the Young Turk Revolution of 23 July 1908. In Constantinople he was hailed as a revolutionary hero. His appointment to Berlin as military attaché at the end of 1908 failed to remove him from the political changes taking place in the capital. During the counterrevolutionary uprising of April 1909, he joined the Army of Deliverance, which marched to Constantinople to restore order, then returned to his post in Berlin. In 1911, after a brief assignment in Scutari at the time of the Albanian uprising, he transferred to Libya, where he commanded Ottoman forces in Benghazi against the Italians. His betrothal to the granddaughter of Sultan Abdülmecit II, Naciye Sultan, was concluded in his absence, presaging a more prominent public role for him in Constantinople.

Enver led the armed CUP coup against the Kamil government in January 1913. He fought for the recapture of Edirne from the Bulgarians during the Balkan War. Enver received multiple pro-

Enver Paşa was a general and a leader of the Young Turks, a reformist movement in the last years of the Ottoman Empire. Although the group's revolution restored a liberal constitution in 1908, he soon assumed dictatorial power and made an alliance with Germany, leading the empire into World War I and its final defeat. © HULTON-DEUTSCH COLLECTION/CORBIS. REPRODUCED BY PERMISSION.

motions and became minister of war in January 1914 and proceeded to reorganize the army by purging the senior officers. He set up a paramilitary intelligence and propaganda organ.

Enver Paşa was responsible for authorizing the passage of German dreadnoughts into the Black Sea in November 1914, effectively committing the Ottoman Empire to war on the side of Germany. As deputy commander in chief of Ottoman forces, he personally led the Russian campaign in Eastern Anatolia that resulted in the earliest and most devastating setback of the entire war for the empire. After Russia withdrew from the war, however, Enver delegated his uncle Halil and brother Nuri to lead the Ottoman armies into the Caucasus, seeking a pan-Turkish union. This strategy was aborted by Ottoman defeats on other fronts.

Following the Ottoman surrender at Mudros, Enver fled abroad with other prominent CUP leaders. In November 1918, he first went to Odessa and was arrested attempting to travel to the Caucasus, possibly to establish a resistance against Allied armies in occupation of Ottoman territories. He managed to flee to Germany. In August 1920, he returned to the Soviet Union. After an audience with the Bolshevik leaders in Moscow, Enver went to Baku and participated in the Congress of Eastern Nations. The Turkish nationalist government in Ankara prevented his entering Anatolia. The Bolsheviks allowed him to go to Turkistan to form an Islamic army to liberate India. Instead, in September 1921, Enver joined the Turkistan resistance movement in Bukhura, which he coordinated signing communiqués as "the son-in-law of the caliph." He was killed near Dushanbe, 4 August 1922, as he personally led attacks against the Bolshevik forces.

Enver's reputation as the "hero of liberty" and his notoriety as the dictator of the CUP, though both exaggerated, cast him in history as a controversial figure. A similar hyperbole is the occasional German reference to the Ottoman Empire as "Enverland." Enver personified the eclectic currents prevalent among the Ottoman political elite after 1908. He was sympathetic to the Turkish, and following the Ottoman loss of the Arab provinces, to pan-Turkish ideas. As a member of the royal household and a pious man, Enver was also deeply committed to Ottomanism and the Islamic principles that sustained the Ottomanist ideology.

See also ABDÜLMECIT II; COMMITTEE FOR UNION AND PROGRESS.

Bibliography

Swanson, Glen W. "Enver Pasha: The Formative Years." *Middle Eastern Studies* 16 (1980): 193–199.

Yamauchi, Masayuki, comp. *The Green Crescent under the Red Star: Enver Pasha in Soviet Russia, 1919–1922.* Tokyo: Institute for the Study of Languages and Cultures of Asia and Africa, 1991.

HASAN KAYALI

EQBAL, MANOUCHEHR
[1908–1977]

Iranian politician and prime minister.

Born in Mashhad to a prominent Khorasani family, Manouchehr Eqbal pursued his medical studies in France and returned to Iran in 1933. In 1939, he joined the Faculty of Medicine at Tehran University and was promoted to full professor in 1941. He began his political career in 1942 as deputy minister of health in the cabinet of Ahmad Qavam, when the authority of Reza Shah Pahlavi was challenged by the *majles* (parliament). In 1949, after an attempt on the life of the shah, it was Eqbal who announced the government's decision to outlaw the Tudeh Party. In that same year, he was appointed minister of interior. In 1950, he was made governor of Azerbaijan and chancellor of Tabriz University but he was forced to resign in 1951, a few months after the nationalist government of Mohammad Mossadegh assumed power. After the Central Intelligence Agency-sponsored coup, which brought back the shah from exile, Eqbal's political career flourished. He was appointed a senator in 1954, chancellor of Tehran University in 1954, and minister of the royal court in 1956. In 1957, he was made prime minister.

In that same year, as part of the shah's plans to effect U.S.-supported reform of Iran's political system, a two-party system was implemented and Eqbal was charged with founding the government majority party, Hezb-e melliyun (Nationalist Party). Eqbal's long-time rival and another member of the shah's inner circle, Amir Asadollah Alam, established the loyal opposition party, Hezb-e mardom (People's Party). During Eqbal's tenure as prime minister, the SAVAK (the domestic intelligence service) was created in 1957, and an abortive land reform law promulgated in 1960. In 1961, under U.S. pressure and faced with increasing domestic criticism, the shah reluctantly removed Eqbal from the premiership. In 1961, he was made Iran's representative to United Nations Educational, Scientific, and Cultural Organization (UNESCO), and in 1963 chairman of the National Iranian Oil Company. With the rise to prominence of Alam during the 1960s and the 1970s, Eqbal gradually fell from favor. He was also a grand master of several Freemason lodges, including Homayun and Mowlavi, from the 1950s to the 1970s.

See also MOSSADEGH, MOHAMMAD; PAHLAVI,
REZA; TUDEH PARTY.

Bibliography

Ashraf, Ahmad. "Eqbal, Manuchehr." In *Encyclopaedia
Iranica*, vol. 7, edited by Ehsan Yarshater. Costa
Mesa, CA: Mazda Publishers, 1998.

Gasiorowski, Mark J. *U.S. Foreign Policy and the Shah: Building a
Client State in Iran*. Ithaca, NY: Cornell University
Press, 1991.

NEGUIN YAVARI

ERBAKAN, NECMEDDIN

[1926–]

*Turkey's most prominent Islamist politician, 1970–1998;
prime minister, 1996–1997.*

Necmeddin Erbakan was born in Sinop on the Black
Sea. He graduated from Istanbul Technical University as a mechanical engineer in 1948 and then
went to Germany for further study. Beginning in
1962 he taught in Istanbul Technical University,
and he became full professor in 1965. With the support of Turkey's small merchants and artisans, he
was elected chairman of the Union of Chambers of
Commerce. His opposition to state-led economic
policies, which favored large-scale industrialists, led
to his removal from office. Thereafter he became
the spokesman of the "little man" in Turkey, and in
1969 he was elected to parliament as an Independent from Konya. In 1970, with the support of
Naqshbandi Shaykh Mehmet Zahid Kotku, Erbakan
formed the National Order Party (Milli Nizam
Partisi), which had an Islamic, anti-Western, anticapitalist agenda. The Turkish Constitutional
Court closed down the party in 1971 because of
its antisecularist activities. It re-merged as the National Salvation Party (Milli Selamet Partisi) in
1973. The party stressed "heavy industrialization"
and "moral and spiritual development" as the two
principles of its political agenda. Erbakan became
the vice-premier and minister of state in 1973, when
his party formed a coalition government with
Bülent Ecevit's RPP. Erbakan also served in the
National Front cabinets of Süleyman Demirel
(1977). The leaders of the 1980 military coup
banned all parties, including the National Salvation
Party. Erbakan was arrested, and after a long trial
in military court, he was acquitted. He returned to

national politics in 1987 as head of the Refah Party,
which won major mayoral offices in the 1994 municipal elections and dominated Turkish politics in
the 1990s. Refah won the largest number of seats,
but not a majority, in the 1995 parliamentary elections, and Erbakan became prime minister in a
coalition government formed in 1996. He was
forced out of office following the military's "soft
coup" of 28 February 1997. Subsequently, the Constitutional Court banned Refah for antisecular activities (1998). Erbakan and other party leaders then
organized the Virtue Party, which was banned in
2000. The younger and more reformist members
challenged Erbakan's domination of the party beginning in 1998; they eventually split and formed
the Justice and Development Party (AKP) under the
leadership of Tayyip Erdoğan.

See also BLACK SEA; DEMIREL, SÜLEYMAN;
ECEVIT, BÜLENT; ERDOĞAN, TAYYIP; NAQSH-
BANDI; NATIONAL SALVATION PARTY; REFAH
PARTISI.

Bibliography

Yavuz, M. Hakan. *Islamic Political Identity in Turkey*. Oxford,
U.K.: Oxford University Press, 2003.

FRANK TACHAU
UPDATED BY M. HAKAN YAVUZ

ERBIL, LEYLA

[1931–]

Turkish novelist and short-story writer.

Born in Istanbul, Turkey, Erbil studied at the
Kadiköy Girls School and the Faculty of Literature.
She began writing stories while working as a secretary and translator. Her first poetry was published
in 1945, but she is known for her stories, which began to appear in various journals in the 1950s.
Breaking away from the traditional techniques of
Turkish literature and the syntax of the Turkish language, Erbil searched for a new narrative voice to
depict the existential struggles of the modern individual who clashes with society. Erbil is noted for
her ability to observe individuals using different societal perspectives, and her stories are characterized
by efforts to depict the multiple dimensions of reality. Among her books are *The Wool Carder* (1960),
At Night (1968), *A Strange Woman* (1971), *The Old Lover*

(1977), and *The Day of Darkness* (1985). She was a founding member of the Turkish Union of Writers in 1974.

See also LITERATURE: TURKISH.

Bibliography

Reddy, Nilufer Mizanoğlu, ed. *Twenty Stories by Turkish Women Writers.* Bloomington: Indiana University, 1988.

DAVID WALDNER

ERDOĞAN, TAYYIP
[1954–]

Turkish politician and leader of the Justice and Development Party who became prime minister in 2003.

Tayyip Erdoğan was born in the Black Sea town of Rize. He moved to Istanbul in 1967 and subsequently graduated from the business school at Marmara University. As a candidate of the Refah Party (Refah Partisi), he was elected to a four-year term as mayor of Istanbul in 1994. During his tenure as mayor of Turkey's largest city, he achieved a reputation for improving public services and for making the city greener and cleaner. After the Constitutional Court banned the Refah Party in 1998, Erdoğan joined its successor, the Virtue Party. In that same year the State Security Court charged him with inciting religious hatred for reciting a poem by Ziya Gökalp at a public gathering; he was convicted and sentenced to ten months in prison, of which he served four months. In 2001, after the Constitutional Court, under military pressure, banned the Virtue Party, Erdoğan joined with a group of former Virtue parliamentarians to form the Justice and Development Party (AKP), and he led it to victory in the November 2002 elections. However, because of his previous conviction, he could not become prime minister until March 2003, after the Turkish Grand National Assembly had amended the constitution so that he could be a candidate in a by-election for Siirt. Erdoğan has disavowed some of the extreme Islamic views of his past and is trying to recast himself as a pro-Western conservative. For example, he does not insist on Turkey leaving the North Atlantic Treaty Organization (NATO) and he says that the country's membership in the European Union is a necessary and useful step. He has avoided the issue of Islamic dress for women by saying he will not bring his own wife—who wears a headscarf—to official functions.

See also AKP (JUSTICE AND DEVELOPMENT PARTY); BLACK SEA; GÖKALP, ZIYA; ISTANBUL; REFAH PARTISI; TURKISH GRAND NATIONAL ASSEMBLY.

Bibliography

Yavuz, M. Hakan. *Islamic Political Identity in Turkey.* Oxford, U.K.: Oxford University Press, 2003.

M. HAKAN YAVUZ

ERETZ YISRAEL

The Hebrew phrase meaning Land of Israel.

The name *Eretz Yisrael* is biblical in origin, where it refers, variously, to parts of the region that were under Jewish sovereignty at different times. Since the dispersion of the Jews in 70 C.E., it has been used to designate Zion and "the Promised Land." Its actual borders are defined variously in the Talmud. It was also the Hebrew name for Palestine under the British Mandate. Indeed, when the first Palestine stamps were being issued, strong albeit unsuccessful pressures were exerted on the British authorities to have the designation be *Eretz Yisrael* rather than Palestine, the latter being a Roman designation.

After 1948, David Ben-Gurion insisted on the term *State of Israel (Medinat Yisrael),* because of his statist emphasis. By contrast, Menachem Begin frequently spoke of *"Eretz Yisrael,"* reflecting his allegiance to the historic Israel, the "Greater Israel." Likewise, *haredi* (ultra-Orthodox) Jews, whose attachments are much more religious than political—even if they accept the political legitimacy of the state—are apt to refer to *Eretz Yisrael* rather than *Medinat Yisrael.*

After the 1967 war, the Greater Land of Israel movement *(Eretz Yisrael ha-Shelema)* developed. Sparked by an enhanced attachment to the biblical Promised Land, its adherents—predominantly religious but comprising secular nationalists as well—opposed ceding sovereignty over the newly conquered territories and embarked on a settlement campaign.

See also BEGIN, MENACHEM; BEN-GURION, DAVID.

Bibliography

Liebman, Charles S., and Don-Yehiya, Eliezer. *Civil Religion in Israel: Traditional Judaism and Political Culture in the Jewish State.* Berkeley: University of California Press, 1983.

Storrs, Ronald, *The Memoirs of Sir Ronald Storrs.* New York: Putnam, 1937.

CHAIM I. WAXMAN

ERSOY, MEHMET AKIF
[c. 1870–1936]

Turkish poet and Islamist.

Mehmet Akif Ersoy was born in Istanbul to a religious Muslim family; his father was a teacher at Fatih Medrese, and his mother's ancestors were from the Uzbek city of Bukhara. He learned Arabic, Persian, and French privately and studied veterinary medicine at the Halkali Baytar high school, which he finished in 1893. He held various posts as a veterinarian and teacher. In 1908, he began writing and became editor of the monthly Islamist journal *The Straight Path* (which proclaimed the cause of Islam), later called *Fountain of Orthodoxy,* to which he contributed poetry and essays. During the Turkish war of independence, he preached the cause of nationalism in the mosques and local newspapers of the Anatolian provinces.

Later in life, Ersoy would become known as one of the greatest poets in modern Turkish and the leader of the most intellectual of the Islamist movements in Turkey. He opposed nationalist reformers who argued that Turkey must import the West's civilization as well as its technology. He contended that the two were not necessarily linked and that importing the ethics and institutions of another culture would widen the cultural gap between elites and common people. Ersoy advocated an Islamic (not a secular) democracy, with a parliament based on consultative councils, as used by the prophet Muhammad's followers.

Bibliography

Toprak, Binnaz. "The Religious Right." In *Turkey in Transition: New Perspectives,* edited by Irvin C. Schick and Ertugrul Ahmet Tonak. New York: Oxford University Press, 1987.

ELIZABETH THOMPSON

ERTUĞRUL, MUHSIN
[1892–1979]

Turkish actor and director in cinema and theater.

Muhsin Ertuğrul was born in Istanbul, where he attended state-run schools. He began acting in 1909, and in 1911 and 1913 he went to Paris to study theater. Known as the pioneer in all areas of modern Turkish drama, Ertuğrul was the principal man of the stage in Turkey between 1908 and 1923 and the sole movie director in the country until 1939. He received personal support from Atatürk in the development of the theater arts.

Ertuğrul turned the Istanbul Municipal Theater into an influential institution when he was appointed its director in 1927, substituting for the usual vaudeville shows and melodramas foreign classics and innovative new scripts in the Turkish language. When he was appointed director of the state theater and opera in Ankara in 1947, he produced *Kerem,* the first opera composed by a Turk. As director from 1947 to 1958, he opened local theaters in other cities, such as İzmir, Adana, and Bursa.

Meanwhile, Ertuğrul began making films in 1922; his 1935 *Aysel, Daughter of the Marshy Village* is now considered his masterpiece.

See also ATATÜRK, MUSTAFA KEMAL.

Bibliography

Dorsay, Atilla. "An Overview of Turkish Cinema from Its Origins." In *The Transformation of Turkish Culture: The Ataturk Legacy,* edited by Günsel Renda and C. Max Kortepeter. Princeton, NJ: Kingston Press, 1986.

Nutku, Özdemir. "A Panorama of the Turkish Theater under the Leadership of Atatürk." In *The Transformation of Turkish Culture: The Ataturk Legacy,* edited by Günsel Renda and C. Max Kortepeter. Princeton, NJ: Kingston Press, 1986.

ELIZABETH THOMPSON

ERZURUM

The most important city in eastern Turkey and the capital of Erzurum province.

Erzurum is an ancient frontier town that historically was a site of contestation between Byzantium and Persia, Byzantium and the Arabs, and the Ottoman and Safavi empires. Erzurum is located in a high valley 2078 yards (1,900 meters) of the Kara

Su and Aras rivers. During the Ottoman period, the town had a large Armenian population, but the community was forcibly deported during the Armenian genocide of 1915. Later, Erzurum was the site of the first nationalist congress in 1919, which was attended by Mustafa Kemal (Atatürk) and issued the declaration of the Turkish war of independence from Allied occupation. Modern Erzurum has grown into the major urban center of eastern Turkey, with a population of 565,516 (census of 2000). It is the site of a large military base and Atatürk University, and is a trade center, especially for local products such as iron, copper, sugar, grain, cattle, and leather.

See also ARMENIAN GENOCIDE; ATATÜRK, MUSTAFA KEMAL; ERZURUM CONGRESS (1919).

Bibliography

"Erzurum." Available at <http://www.allaboutturkey .com/erzurum.htm>.

ELIZABETH THOMPSON
UPDATED BY ERIC HOOGLUND

ERZURUM CONGRESS (1919)

Congress called to assert the integrity of the Ottoman state, 1919.

Named for the city in which it was held, the congress was called immediately after the Ottoman Empire had been on the losing side of World War I; the empire was to be dismembered. It was feared that the local area around Erzurum would become part of an Armenian state. The congress declared the nationalists' intention of defending the sultanate/caliphate against foreign occupiers and appealed to U.S. President Woodrow Wilson's principles of national self-determination. Mustafa Kemal (Atatürk) was elected chairman of the congress, and although the Istanbul government declared the congress illegal, ordering his arrest, he escaped. It was here that he made his first declaration of principles that would guide his war to unite Turkey as an independent nation.

See also ATATÜRK, MUSTAFA KEMAL; WILSON, WOODROW.

Bibliography

Lewis, Bernard. *The Emergence of Modern Turkey,* 3d edition. New York: Oxford University Press, 2002.

ELIZABETH THOMPSON

ERZURUM, TREATY OF (1823)

Two treaties, 1823 and 1847, that settled boundary disputes between the Ottoman Empire and Iran.

Although the Treaty of Zuhab in 1639 had established the boundary between Ottoman Turkey and Iran, the border in the mountainous Zuhab region remained a site of intermittent conflict in the subsequent two centuries. Attacks from Iran into Ottoman territory prompted Sultan Mahmud II in 1821 to declare war on Iran. Fath Ali Shah Qajar's army had initial success and marched east as far as Diyarbekir in the south and Erzurum in the north. The first Treaty of Erzurum was signed in July 1823, but it essentially confirmed the 1639 border and thus failed to resolve the disputes that had led to conflict. A series of border incidents in the 1830s again brought Iran and Turkey to the brink of war. Britain and Russia offered to mediate, and a second Treaty of Erzurum was signed in May 1847. This treaty divided the disputed region between Iran and Turkey and provided for a boundary commission to delimit the entire border. The boundary commission's work encountered several political setbacks but finally completed its task in 1914.

See also FATH ALI SHAH QAJAR; MAHMUD II.

Bibilography

Lambton, Ann K. S. "The Qajar Dynasty." In *Qājār Persia: Eleven Studies,* edited by Ann K. S. Lambton. Austin: University of Texas Press, 1987.

ZACHARY KARABELL
UPDATED BY ERIC HOOGLUND

ESENDAL, MEMDUH ŞEVKET
[1883–1952]

Turkish novelist, short story writer, and politician.

Memduh Şevket Esendal was born in Çorlu to the Karakahyaoğullari family, which had migrated there from Rumelia. After attending elementary school in Istanbul and high school in Edirne, he returned to Çorlu to tend the family farm. He joined the Committee for Union and Progress party in 1906, and during the Balkan War fled to Istanbul, where he held several government jobs. He was Turkey's representative to Azerbaijan in 1920, ambassador to Iran from 1925 to 1930, and ambassador to Afghanistan and the Soviet Union in the early 1930s. Esendal was in the Turkish Grand National Assembly from 1939 to 1950 and was general secretary of the Republican People's Party from 1941 to 1945.

Esendal is perhaps best known for his many short stories, which he wrote in a distinctively direct and realistic style, with careful depictions of daily life. He evoked daily life in Turkey often in a humorous way and with kindliness. With Sait Faik Abasiyanik, he is associated with the emergence of the modern Turkish short story form. Esendal also wrote several novels, which resembled his short stories in style.

See also COMMITTEE FOR UNION AND PROGRESS; REPUBLICAN PEOPLE'S PARTY; TURKISH GRAND NATIONAL ASSEMBLY.

ELIZABETH THOMPSON

ESFANDIARY, FEREYDUN
[1930–2000]

An Iranian essayist and novelist.

Fereydun Esfandiary was born in Belgium to Iranian parents. His father was a diplomat, and as a child Fereydun Esfandiary lived in several foreign countries, including Afghanistan, India, and Lebanon, although he also spent long periods with family in Iran. In 1948 he was a member of Iran's national team at the Olympics in London. He then studied at the University of California, first in Berkeley and later in Los Angeles. In the early 1950s, he worked at the United Nations on the Conciliation Commission for Palestine and subsequently taught at the New School for Social Research in New York. In the 1960s, he moved to Los Angeles, where he lectured at the University of California.

In the late 1950s, Esfandiary turned to writing. Three of his novels dealt with his perception of Iran's ills: *Day of Sacrifice* (1959), *The Beggar* (1965), and *Identity Card* (1966). By the early 1970s, he was writing mostly essays. He embraced futurist ideas and legally changed his name to FM2030. His better-known futurist books include *Optimism One, Up-Wingers, Telespheres,* and *Are You a Transhumanist?* In these books he depicted modern technology as dehumanizing and school as obsolete. Esfandiary died of pancreatic cancer in July 2000; in accordance with his wishes, his body was frozen and stored in a special vault where it can be retrieved and revived once science has perfected a way to increase human longevity.

Bibliography

Esfandiary, F. M. *Identity Card: A Novel.* New York: Grove Press, 1966.

MICHAEL C. HILLMANN
UPDATED BY ERIC HOOGLUND

ESHKOL, LEVI
[1895–1969]

Israel's Labor Party leader; prime minister, 1963–1969.

Born in Kiev, Ukraine, as Levi Shkolnik Eshkol immigrated to Palestine in 1914, where he was a founder of Kibbutz Degania Bet and served in the Jewish Legion from 1918 to 1920. He was active in labor politics and Zionism throughout the period of British mandate (1922–1948). For three years, Eshkol headed the settlement department of the Palestine office in Berlin during the period of Nazi rule. He organized immigration and transfers of funds from Germany to Palestine, using the money to establish new settlement projects and the Mekorot Water Company, of which he was both the founder and the first president. In the same period, he was active in the High Command of the Haganah as the chief financial administrator, organizing arms procurement for the defense organization.

After the establishment of the State of Israel in 1948, Eshkol served in numerous government, Jewish Agency, and cabinet positions including director general of the ministry of defense (1948), where he was instrumental in establishing the Israeli weapons industry; head of the land settlement department of the Jewish Agency (1949), where he coordinated the settlement of the masses of new immigrants arriving in Israel; treasurer for the Jewish Agency (1950–1952); minister of agriculture (1951); and minister of finance (1952), where he was responsible for the implementation of the reparations agreement with Germany from World War II.

In 1963, upon the retirement of David Ben-Gurion as prime minister, Eshkol took his post and that of defense minister (with Ben-Gurion's recommendation)—Ben-Gurion, however, soon accused him of mishandling state business, especially the government scandal called the Lavon Affair (in which Israeli spies were caught in Egypt but no one in the Israeli cabinet admitted to knowing about the mission). Consequently, Ben-Gurion left the MAPAI Party and formed Rafi.

Eshkol continued as prime minister during the period leading to the Arab–Israel War of 1967 and was faced with a divided cabinet over the question of war with Egypt. Because of public pressure, he ceded the defense portfolio to Moshe Dayan. Eshkol also enlarged the cabinet and brought in members of the right-wing Gahal bloc, establishing a National Unity government, which was retained in the 1969 elections to the sixth Knesset but ended when Gahal broke away in 1970.

See also ARAB–ISRAEL WAR (1967); BEN-GURION, DAVID; DAYAN, MOSHE; HAGANAH; ISRAEL: POLITICAL PARTIES IN; JEWISH AGENCY FOR PALESTINE; LAVON AFFAIR.

Bibliography

Oren, Michael. *Six Days of War: June 1967 and the Making of the Modern Middle East.* London and New York: Oxford University Press, 2002.

Rolef, Susan Hattis, ed. *Political Dictionary of the State of Israel,* 2d edition. New York: Macmillan, 1993.

MARTIN MALIN

ESKINAZI, ROZA
[c. 1895–1980]

Popular Greek singer.

Roza Eskinazi was the most celebrated Greek café singer of the twentieth century. Born Sarah Skinazi in Constantinople to Sephardic Jewish parents, Avram and Flora Skinazis, Eskinazi dominated Greek popular music during the late 1920s and 1930s, just as sound recording technology was enabling the dissemination of Levantine musical forms to a large and growing diaspora. Possessing a sweet and lilting soprano, Eskinazi sang in Greek, Turkish, Arabic, Ladino (Djudezmo), Italian, and Armenian. Her recordings in Athens for both Columbia and Orthophonic Records assured Eskinazi's international popularity. Her recordings were

marketed to a worldwide network of Greek, Armenian, and Sephardic Jewish diaspora communities uprooted by the fall of the Ottoman Empire and the population transfers of the early 1920s. Several notable records, such as *To Neo Hanoumaki,* included multilingual songs of the Greek and Balkan café scene. By the 1920s, vibrant Greek emigrant communities were found not only in North America but in the Congo, Abyssinia, and especially in the Egyptian cities of Alexandria and Suez. As a consequence of the targeted marketing of Eskinazi's recordings, several ethnic groups claim her as a part of their musical heritage.

Although Eskinazi's popularity waned after World War II, she toured in Turkey and the United States during the 1950s. In 1952, she recorded some forty songs for the Balkan Record Company of New York City. During the 1960s and 1970s, she still commanded considerable interest in Greece and continued to appear in limited public performances. Throughout the 1980s, a growing resurgence in Greek café music placed the genre firmly in the world music scene. At the same time, scholars of ethnomusicology and social history argued for a conflation of various Balkan and Middle Eastern musical genres into one: *rebetika.* Eskinazi was soon recognized as one of the most prominent *rebetika* performers of all time. The enduring power and beauty of her performances is evidenced by the fact that, even when removed from her original cultural setting and musical traditions, her work continues to attract new listeners with every passing year.

Roza Eskinazi died on 2 December 1980 and is buried in an unmarked grave at Stomio, near the Gulf of Corinth.

See also DIASPORA; MUSIC; OTTOMAN EMPIRE.

Bibliography

Chianis, Sotirios (Sam). "Survival of Greek Folk Music in New York." *New York Folklore* 24, no. 3–4 (1988).

Conway-Morris, Roderick. "Greek Cafe Music with a List of Recordings." *Recorded Sound* 80 (July).

Frangos, Steve. "Portraits in Modern Greek Music: Rosa Eskenazi." *Resound* 12, no. 1 (January/April 1993).

Gauntlett, Stathis. "*Rebetiko Tragoudi* As a Generic Term." *Byzantine and Modern Greek Studies* 8 (1982–1983).

STAVROS FRANGOS

ESMATI-WARDAK, MASUMA
[1930–]

Afghan woman writer and politician.

Masuma Esmati-Wardak was born in 1930 in Kabul. She graduated from Malalai High School in 1949 and from Kabul Women's College in 1953. In 1958 she received a degree in business administration in the United States. Upon her return to Afghanistan, she became principal of Zarghuna High School in Kabul, and then in 1959, the director-general of secondary education. She was a member of the Constitutional Advisory Commission and a participant in the *Loya-Jirga* (National Assembly) that endorsed the 1964 Afghan Constitution. In 1965 she was elected from Kandahar to the *Wulosi Jirga* (the lower house of parliament) and became a voice for women's rights. In 1976 she was recognized by the Women's Coordination Committee of India for her contribution to the cause of women. She served as president of *Shura-i-Zanan-i-Afghanistan* (Afghanistan's Women's Council) and then as minister of education during the government of Najibullah (1986–1992). She has written extensively on issues pertaining to women, including a book in Dari (the Persian dialect of Afghanistan) on the history of Afghan women, and a book in Pashtu titled *Women's Contributions to Pashtu Oral Tradition* that was translated into English.

Bibliography

Dupree, Nancy, and Rahimi, Fahima. *Women in Afghanistan/Frauen in Afghanistan.* Liestal, Switzerland: Stiftung Bibliotheca Afghanica, 1986.

SENZIL NAWID

ETEMADI, SALEHA FARUQ
[1928–]

Afghan activist for women's rights, 1962–1974.

Saleha Faruq Etemadi, an important public figure in Afghanistan in the 1960s and early 1970s, was born in 1928 in Kabul. She was among the first graduates of Malalai High School, a French lycée for girls in Kabul. After graduation from the college of literature for women in 1951, she became a teacher and then was appointed vice principal and later principal of Malalai High School. In 1962 she became president of the government-sponsored Women's Association (*De Mirmono Tolena*). She was

also editor of the association's monthly magazine, *Mirmon* (Woman). Under her leadership, the Women's Association became an important force for the promotion of women's rights in Afghanistan in the 1960s and the early 1970s. Etemadi was out of office during the presidency of Muhammad Daud (1974–1978) and the Marxist regimes of the Khalqis and Parchamis, the two divisions of the People's Democratic Party of Afghanistan. However, during the government of Najibullah (1987–1992), she once again gained prominence as a public figure when she was appointed minister of social security (*Amniyyat-i-Ijtema'i*) in 1990. After the fall of Najibullah in 1992, Etemadi left Afghanistan to live in exile in Switzerland.

See also AFGHANISTAN: OVERVIEW; GENDER: GENDER AND LAW.

Bibliography

Knabe, Erika. "Afghan Women: Does Their Role Change." In *Afghanistan in the 1970s,* edited by Louis Dupree and Linette Albert. New York: Praeger Publishers, 1974.

SENZIL NAWID

ETHIOPIAN JEWS

Jews of Ethiopia, many of whom have emigrated to Israel.

In Ethiopia, the Jews referred to themselves as Beta Israel (the House of Israel) but were most commonly known as Falashas (wanderers, outsiders). In Israel, these same people call themselves Ethiopian Jews, symbolically expressing their equality with other Jews and rejecting the stigma they once held in Ethiopia.

There were 85,000 Ethiopian Jews living in Israel in 2002, 23,000 of whom were Israeli born. Their mass emigration from Ethiopia began during the early 1970s, encouraged by a decree issued by Israel's chief rabbis that the Jews from Ethiopia were "full" Jews (although they still required symbolic conversion to Judaism). In Operation Moses (which took place during 1984–1985), 7,700 Jews were airlifted to Israel from refugee camps in Sudan. A second large-scale airlift known as Operation Solomon took place in 1991. As the Mengistu Haile Mariam regime was collapsing in Addis Ababa, 14,400 Ethiopian Jews were transferred to Israel.

The majority of the early immigrants to Israel from Ethiopia hailed from the northern province of Tigre and are Tigranian speaking. More than 80 percent of Ethiopian Jewry in Israel originate from Gonder, Semien (or Simyen), Woggera, and other areas. They speak Ethiopia's official language, Amharic, which is a Semitic language. The younger immigrants in Israel speak Hebrew. Beta Israel holy books, including the Bible, are written in Geez, the script of Ethiopian scholarship.

In Ethiopia, the Beta Israel community observed a unique form of Judaism that was based on biblical commandments and was influenced by Ethiopian Orthodox Christianity (which in turn displays remarkable similarities to aspects of Judaism). The Beta Israel did not know the Oral Law; nor were they aware of rabbinic interpretations. They strictly observed rules of purity and pollution. The cornerstone of their religion until this century was monasticism, with the monks passing down liturgy, literature, and religious edicts.

During the twentieth century, urged on by visiting Jews such as Dr. Jacques Faitlovitch from Paris, some Beta Israel were exposed to mainstream Judaism. Faitlovitch's pupils, who studied in Europe and other countries, included Taamrat Emmanuel (1888–1962), aide to the Emperor Haile Selassie; Tadesse Yacob (1913–), deputy minister of finance in Ethiopia; and Yona Bogale (1908–1987), who acted as teacher and intermediary between Jews in Ethiopia and Israel.

The Ethiopian Jews are in the process of coming in line with Israeli Judaism, although some *kessoth* (priests) and members of the community do not wish to accept the authority of Israel's chief rabbinate. In 1985 the Ethiopian Jews demonstrated in front of the rabbinate's offices, objecting to the ritual immersion they had to undergo for acceptance as "full" Jews. To date, Ethiopian Jews are referred to one particular rabbi for marriage purposes.

In 1992 some Ethiopian Jews organized demonstrations to demand that the Feresmura, Jews who had converted to Christianity in Ethiopia from the nineteenth century on, should be allowed to immigrate to Israel under the Law of Return (1950). In 2003 the Ariel Sharon government gave 19,000 Feresmura the right to immigrate to Israel.

A group of Ethiopian Jews from the Quara region arrive in Israel in 1999. Ariel Sharon, at the time Israel's outgoing foreign minister, led the effort to implement the relocation. © AP/WIDE WORLD PHOTOS. REPRODUCED BY PERMISSION.

In Ethiopia, the Beta Israel were primarily agriculturists and tenant farmers. They also engaged in petty trading and seasonal occupations, such as metalwork and sewing. In Israel, they have been settled almost exclusively in seven concentrations in a few localities (Netanya, Rehovot, Haifa, Hadera, Ashdod, Ashkelon, Beersheba) where they are largely employed in manufacturing and public services. In 1999 53 percent were in the labor force. Most Ethiopian Israelis own their homes. There is still a difficult situation regarding the housing of singles who live in mobile-home sites.

All Ethiopian Jewish children study in regular Israeli schools. Teens attend residential schools. Large numbers of young people have undergone occupational retraining courses. Several hundred Ethiopian Jews study in institutes for higher learning in Israel; many more have graduated from colleges and universities, majoring in technological and social sciences and in paramedical fields.

See also LAW OF RETURN.

Bibliography

Parfitt, Tudor, and Trevisan Semi, Emanuela, eds. *The Beta Israel in Ethiopia and Israel: Studies on Ethiopian Jews.* Surrey, U.K.: Curzon Press, 1999.

Quirin, James. *The Evolution of the Ethiopian Jews: A History of the Beta Israel (Falasha) to 1920.* Philadelphia: University of Pennsylvania Press, 1992.

Swerski, Shlomo, and Swerski, Barbara. "Ethiopian Housing, Employment, Education." *Israel Equality Monitor,* 11 June 2002.

Weil, Shalvah. "Ethiopian Jews in Israel: A Survey of Research and Documentation." *Jewish Folklore and Ethnology Review* 2 (1989): 28–32.

SHALVAH WEIL
UPDATED BY EMANUELA TREVISAN SEMI

EUPHRATES DAM

The Keban, Tabaqa, and Atatürk dams on the Euphrates river.

Since 1970, Turkey and Syria have built three major dams on the Euphrates, which as a group will severely limit the river's flow into Iraq. The Keban dam, near Elaziğ, was the first to be completed. It supplies electricity to large cities in western Turkey. The Tabaqa Dam in Syria is both a major power and irrigation project. The Atatürk (Karababa) Dam, near Urfa, is the most ambitious of the three. It is intended to spur development in the Turkish southeast (something the Keban project failed to do) by irrigating nearly 4.5 million acres (1.7 ha), almost three times the area to be irrigated by the Tabaqa.

When all dams are in operation, of the 30 billion cubic meters of water that once reached Iraq, only 11 billion cubic meters will remain. Since Iraq claims that its minimum requirement is 13 billion cubic meters, there will be a shortfall. Since no treaty exists to allocate the water, Iraq has no recourse; in its weakened political position (since the Gulf Crisis of 1990/91) it will be in a poor position to bargain.

See also TABAQA DAM.

Bibliography

Drysdale, Alasdair, and Blake, Gerald H. *The Middle East and North Africa: A Political Geography.* New York: Oxford University Press, 1985.

JOHN R. CLARK

EVIAN ACCORDS (1962)

March 1962 agreements between the French government and the Gouvernement Provisoire de la République Algérienne.

The Evian Accords—reached between the French government and the Algerian Front de Libération Nationale's (FLN) Gouvernement Provisoire de la République Algérienne (GPRA)—were very difficult to conclude. Their negotiation took place in a climate roiling with rebellion and revolution. Belkacem Krim presided over the Algerian delegation, ably assisted by Saad Dahlab. Louis Joxe headed the French team.

Negotiations began in May 1961 in Evian, France, one month after President Charles de Gaulle suppressed a military rebellion by recalcitrant generals who opposed Algerian decolonization. The talks soon broke down over the future status of the Sahara (with Joxe suggesting the possibility of its partition) and the option of double citizenship in a future Algerian state for the *pieds-noirs,* or European settlers. Secret discussions in late 1961 resulted in a resumption of full negotiations in February 1962 at Les Rousses, a hideaway in the Jura Mountains. By that time, the Organisation de l'Armée Secrète (OAS) was wreaking havoc in an increasingly anarchic, uncontrollable Algeria. Furthermore, ideological fissures in the FLN widened. There were intense pressures on both sides to arrive at a settlement. De Gaulle had already ruled out partitioning the Sahara. The FLN, in turn, allowed France to preserve its petroleum and natural gas concessions and its military and nuclear testing bases. The *pieds-noirs* also received numerous guarantees on the assumption that most of them would remain in Algeria. After settling these arduous issues, negotiations adjourned briefly. Krim and Dahlab successfully defended their actions and compromises before the GPRA and the increasingly hostile general staff of the Armée de Libération Nationale (ALN). The negotiators returned to Evian to complete the accords, which were signed on 19 March 1962.

A joint cease-fire introduced the accords. This was followed by five "chapters." Chapter I addressed the formation of an interim, provisional government whose chief task was to prepare a self-determination referendum. Chapter II stipulated the *pieds-noirs'* future role in independent Algeria, and it framed the future French-Algerian relationship of "cooperation." Chapter III considered "military questions." Chapter IV stated that disputes would be negotiated with "recourse" to the international court of justice. Chapter V asserted that if self-determination (i.e., Algerian independence with cooperation) was affirmed by the referendum, France pledged to recognize immediately the new nation. The meticulous guarantees to protect the settler minority ensued, followed by detailed "declarations of principles" particularly regarding post-colonial cooperation.

Given the neocolonial implications of the accords, alienated FLN members and the general staff officers condemned the loss of sovereignty symbolized by the perpetuated French economic and military presence. The Tripoli Program of June 1962 displayed the nationalists' discontent. Differences over the accords contributed to an intra-FLN fratricide in the summer of 1962 that overthrew the GPRA. Succeeding Algerian governments subsequently aimed to revise the accords and pursue "postcolonial decolonization" in moves such as the nationalization of French Saharan concessions in February 1971. In addition, changing historical realities vitiated the guarantees meant to secure the *pieds-noirs*. The violent nihilism of the OAS and the general insecurity forced hundreds of thousands of settlers—almost the entire community—to flee Algeria for France, thereby making the protective stipulations anachronistic. Despite their controversial shortcomings, the accords liberated Algeria and freed France from a destructive colonial relationship.

See also FRONT DE LIBÉRATION NATIONALE (FLN); KRIM, BELKACEM; ORGANISATION ARMÉE SECRÈTE (OAS).

Bibliography

Ambassade de France, Service de Presse et d'Information. *Texts of Declarations Drawn up in Common Agreement at Evian, March 18, 1962 by the Delegations of the Government of the French Republic and the Algerian National Liberation Front.* New York: Ambassade de France, Service de Presse et d'Information, 1962.

Naylor, Phillip C. *France and Algeria: A History of Decolonization and Transformation.* Gainesville: University of Florida Press, 2000.

PHILLIP C. NAYLOR

EVIN PRISON

See HUMAN RIGHTS

EVREN, KENAN

[1918–]

Seventh president of the Republic of Turkey; architect of 1982 constitution.

Kenan Evren graduated from military college in 1938 and the military academy in 1948. He rose to the rank of general in 1964. He served as Turkey's commander of land forces from 1977 to 1978 and the chief of the general staff from 1978 to 1980. He was the leader of the September 1980 military coup against the government of Süleyman Demirel, and afterwards he ruled the country as the head of the National Security Council, which had full powers of the legislature and executive. In 1981 Evren and the National Security Council formed a Constitutional Assembly to prepare a new constitution, which was approved in a national referendum in November 1982. The constitution included a temporary article that automatically conferred on the head of the National Security Council the office of president for a seven-year term; subsequently the president would be elected by the parliament. Thus, with the ratification of the constitution, Evren became the seventh president since the establishment of the republic in 1923. Upon becoming president, he gave up his military duties and served as a civilian president until November 1989.

See also DEMIREL SÜLEYMAN; NATIONAL SECURITY COUNCIL (TURKEY).

Bibliography

Zürcher, Erik J. *Turkey: A Modern History,* revised edition. London: I. B. Tauris, 1997.

DAVID WALDNER
UPDATED BY M. HAKAN YAVUZ

EXODUS (1947)

An illegal immigration ship carrying Holocaust survivors to British-ruled Palestine in 1947, which became a symbol of the Zionist struggle for a Jewish state.

The *Exodus* was purchased in the United States by the Mossad le-Aliyah Bet, a Zionist agency that organized the illegal immigration of Jews to Palestine. It set sail from France in July 1947 carrying 4,500 refugees from the displaced persons (DP) camps in occupied Germany. When the ship approached Palestine, the British attacked it. In the ensuing battle, three were killed and dozens were wounded. The damaged vessel, escorted by British warships, sailed to Haifa, Israel (then Palestine), where the passengers were transferred to three ships that deported them to France. Following their resistance to landing in France, culminating in a hunger strike, the British expelled them to Germany. From Germany they emigrated to Palestine within a year.

The "Exodus Affair" played a part in the propaganda war against the British. The arrival of the ship at Haifa during the widely publicized visit of the United Nations Special Committee on Palestine (UNSCOP) spread the story worldwide, and the ship's symbolic name drew attention, too: Originally named *President Warfield,* the ship was renamed after the second book of the Bible, which tells the story of the ancient exodus of the Jews from Egypt.

Since the 1990s, a post-Zionist trend in Israel has elicited a debate as to whether the Zionist leadership exploited the illegal immigrants in order to win points in the struggle for the foundation of a Jewish state or whether they acted in true partnership in the interests of the refugees and in pursuit of a common national goal.

Bibliography

Exodus. Directed by Otto Preminger. United Artists, 1960.

Halamish, Aviva. *The Exodus Affair: Holocaust Survivors and the Struggle for Palestine,* translated by Ora Cummings. Syracuse, NY: Syracuse University Press, 1998.

Uris, Leon. *Exodus* (1958). New York: Gramercy Books, 2000.

Zertal, Idith. *From Catastrophe to Power: Holocaust Survivors and the Emergence of Israel.* Berkeley: University of California Press, 1998.

RACHEL WEISSBROD

EYÜBOĞLU, BEDRI RAHMI
[1911–1974]

Turkish painter and poet.

Bedri Rahmi Eyüboğlu was born in Giresun-Görele, the son of a *kaimmakam* (local ruler). He attended the Istanbul Fine Arts Academy in 1927 and studied in Paris in 1931 and 1932. From 1937 to his death, he was a teacher at the Fine Arts Academy, while producing paintings, drawings, mosaics, and three books of poetry. His works are most notable for their motifs drawn from Anatolian popular culture.

Eyüboğlu was associated with two important art movements of the mid-twentieth century. While painting in a fauvist style in the 1930s he joined the D-Group, which eschewed academicism in art and promoted the latest Western trends. In the 1940s, he and his students formed the Group of Ten, which sought a synthesis between Western technique and Eastern decorative motifs.

See also ART.

Bibliography

Renda, Günsel. "Modern Trends in Turkish Painting." In *The Transformation of Turkish Culture: The Ataturk Legacy,* edited by Günsel Renda and C. Max Kortepeter. Princeton, NJ: Kingston Press, 1986.

ELIZABETH THOMPSON

EZRA AND NEHEMIAH OPERATIONS

Massive airborne transfer in 1950–1951 of the overwhelming majority of the Jews of Iraq to Israel.

The mass emigration, invoking names of the two organizers of the return of Jews from the Babylonian Exile to the Holy Land some 2,500 years earlier, was made possible by a draft law introduced into Iraq's Parliament on 2 March 1950, permitting Jews to leave the country provided they surrendered their Iraqi nationality. The measure came in the wake of a massive wave of illegal emigration of Jews via Iran, organized by the Zionist underground. Prime Minister Salih Jabr told Parliament, "It is not in the public interest to force people to stay in the country if they have no desire to do so."

The number of emigrants far exceeded original estimates. Whereas immigration authorities in Israel had planned to receive about 300 persons a day—and this with difficulty—the daily influx at its peak reached an average of 1,400. By the end of 1951, Iraqi Jews airlifted to Israel totaled 107,603; some 16,000 others had departed the country by other means—some illegally to Palestine, some legally to countries in the West. By the beginning of 1952, it was estimated that no more than 6,000 (out of a total of some 130,000) Jews remained in Iraq.

See also JABR, SALIH.

Bibliography

Rejwan, Nissim. *The Jews of Iraq: 3000 Years of History and Culture.* Boulder, CO: Westview Press, 1985.

NISSIM REJWAN

FADAN KHARASA

See Tribes and Tribalism: Fadan Kharasa Tribe

FADLALLAH, SHAYKH HUSAYN
[1935–]

Shi'ite scholar and teacher in Lebanon.

Shaykh Husayn Fadlallah was born in 1935 in al-Najaf, Iraq, where his father Abd al-Ra'uf served as religious scholar and teacher in the famed Shi'ite religious seminaries. Fadlallah attend religious schools very early, and studied under some of the most famous Shi'ite Grand Ayatullahs of the twentieth century such as Muhsin al-Hakim, Abu al-Qasim al-Khu'i, Husayn al-Hilli, and Mahmud Al-Sharawadi. Fadlallah started teaching in al-Najaf, entering into the polemical debates between the Marxists and their rivals, which were common in Iraqi politics at the time. He returned to Beirut in 1966 and settled in the Eastern suburbs of Nab'a, where he founded the society of Usrat at-Ta'akhi, a cultural Islamic organization. He also founded a religious seminary, which he continues to head, and teaches weekly seminars in the Shi'ite religious seminary in Damascus. He believes that Islamic jurisprudence should be freed from its abstract formulations and expressed in a language that can be understood by lay people. His literary taste is also evident in his poetic language.

Fadlallah came to international prominence after 1982 and the rise of Hizbullah. He was blamed by the United States for serving as its "spiritual guide" and for religiously sanctioning the suicide attacks against Israeli, French, and U.S. targets in Lebanon in 1980s. Fadlallah had close ties to the Iraqi al-Da'wa Party and to Hizbullah, but he has denied occupying an official position in the partys' hierarches. In 1985 Fadlallah miraculously survived a car bomb that reportedly was planted by the CIA in the neighborhood of Bir al-Abd, where he had settled after the eviction of Shi'a from the eastern suburbs of Beirut after 1975. Fadlallah was an advocate of Ayatollah Ruhollah Khomeini's doctrine of *Wilayat al-Faqih* (Persian: *velayat-e faqih*) in the 1980s, but seems to have moved away from it in the

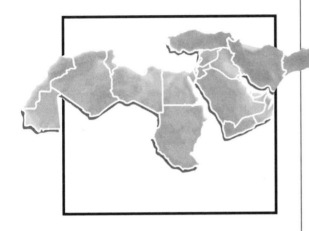

F

1990s. His views have moderated in recent years—he now stands for multiculturalism and does not call for an Islamic republic in Lebanon. His relations with Iran and Hizbullah have been strained in recent years. Fadlallah is now referred to as *Ayatullah*, a sign of his emergence as a Shi'ite senior *marji*.

See also DA'WA AL-ISLAMIYYA, AL-; HIZBUL-LAH; MARJA AL-TAQLID; NAJAF, AL-.

Bibliography

Ranstorp, Magnus. *Hizb'allah in Lebanon: The Politics of the Western Hostage Crisis.* New York: Palgrave Macmillan, 1997.

AS'AD ABUKHALIL

FAHD IBN ABD AL-AZIZ AL SA'UD
[1921–]

King of Saudi Arabia, in power since 1982 but unable to rule since the late 1990s because of failing health.

King Fahd of the Al Sa'ud dynasty took power in Saudi Arabia after his brother, Khalid, died of a heart attack in 1982. Until he was sidelined by failing health in the mid-1990s, Fahd played a significant role in mediating inter-Arab conflicts and attempted to strengthen his country's ties with the United States. © AP/WIDE WORLD PHOTOS. REPRODUCED BY PERMISSION.

Fahd ibn Abd al-Aziz Al Sa'ud was born in 1921 in Riyadh, the eleventh son of Abd al-Aziz ibn Abd al-Rahman Al Sa'ud, the founder of Saudi Arabia. Like other Saudi princes, he received an education in the royal court, where the emphasis was on Islam, but also included a grounding in history and political affairs. As the eldest of seven sons of Abd al-Aziz's favorite wife, Hassa bint Ahmad al Sudayri, Fahd and his full brothers form the largest and most cohesive grouping within the Al Sa'ud (House of Sa'ud), the Al Fahd or, in popular Western (not Saudi) usage, the Sudayri Seven. They are thus the dominant faction in a system of government in which political power is held mainly by the Al Sa'ud ruling family. Fahd is the first Saudi king to attain power after rising through the bureaucracy. In 1953 he became the country's first minister of education, and he has been instrumental since then in developing the country's education system. In 1958 he helped lead the attempt to force the abdication of his half brother, King Sa'ud. When the older half-brother Faisal assumed executive powers as prime minister in 1962, he named Fahd interior minister, confirming a close partnership that would continue until King Faisal's death. Fahd was effective in implementing Faisal's reforms and by the early 1970s had emerged as the most influential prince, already a key voice in foreign-policy issues.

In 1965 the royal family had agreed on Fahd's designation as second deputy prime minister, shortly after it had prevailed on the reluctant Prince Khalid ibn Abd al-Aziz to become crown prince. (Thus a smooth succession was assured when an unbalanced nephew assassinated King Faisal on 25 March 1975.) Khalid and Fahd had formed an effective partnership, with contrasting personalities and qualities. Fahd was, in the Saudi context, a progressive and had made his mark as an able administrator. He enjoyed the exercise of power and worked effectively with bureaucrats and technocrats.

Though King Khalid suffered from heart disease, undergoing open-heart surgery both before and after his accession, he played an active role in all major decisions, and Fahd was always careful to defer to the king in his presence. Together they guided the kingdom through a period of great perils—the U.S.-brokered Camp David Accords between Egypt and Israel, which estranged Saudi Arabia from its principal Arab ally; the Iranian

King Fahd of Saudi Arabia (right) with Egyptian president Husni Mubarak. Relations between the two countries became strained after Egypt signed a peace treaty with Israel in 1979, but Fahd reestablished diplomatic relations with Mubarak in 1987, ushering in Egypt's return to the Arab fold. © REUTERS NEWMEDIA INC./CORBIS. REPRODUCED BY PERMISSION.

Revolution of 1979 that fomented Shi'ite unrest in Saudi Arabia's Eastern Province (al-Hasa) and helped to trigger a profoundly unsettling attempt at a neoconservative Islamic uprising when militants seized the Great Mosque at Mecca; and the outbreak of the Iran–Iraq War, which threatened to spill over into Saudi Arabia. In 1981 he put forward a proposal for settling the Arab–Israeli dispute, which came to be known as the Fahd Plan.

When Khalid succumbed to a heart attack on 13 June 1982, Fahd's accession was smooth, with his next eldest half-brother Abdullah immediately confirmed as crown prince and Sultan ibn Abd al-Aziz Al Sa'ud, his next eldest full brother, designated as second deputy prime minister and effectively the next in succession.

Serious challenges have marked Fahd's rule. He became king just as petroleum prices were beginning a downward plunge that reduced the kingdom's oil revenues more than fivefold. This forced the king to cut back on implementing development plans and increased pressure to wean the country from its overreliance on foreign labor. The country's economic woes made it easier for voices of dissent to gain credibility among segments of the population. Fahd responded to some expressions of dissent with arrests and suppression. However, by the early 1990s he had put together a series of government reforms meant to signal his willingness to open up new channels of consultation. On the regional stage, Fahd was successful in asserting the kingdom's role as an important actor, mediating political conflict in Lebanon, nurturing Egypt's return to the Arab League, and laying the ground-work for greater cooperation among the Arab states of the Persian Gulf, in the form of the Gulf Cooperation Council. Fahd's attempts to expand his country's good relations with the United States in the area of military cooperation ran into difficulties when a planned sale of advanced warning and air control aircraft (AWACS) ran afoul of congressional opposition in 1986, and the revelation of the purchase of Chinese missiles brought similar criticism from some U.S. quarters two years later. Finally, the Iran–Iraq War presented Saudi Arabia with a constant menace.

In 1986, in order to make a statement about his importance in the Islamic world, he adopted the title custodian of the two holy mosques. He personally supervised an aggressive Saudi oil policy to protect the kingdom's long-term interests. In the Gulf Crisis, his decision to invite U.S. and other non-Muslim forces to enter Saudi Arabia in August 1990, over Crown Prince Abdullah's objections, to defend the kingdom against possible invasion by Iraq and then to liberate Kuwait from Iraqi occupation fatally upset the calculations of Iraq's President Saddam Hussein that Fahd would remain passive. The decision also has been one of the principal points of contention between the ruler and segments of the Islamist opposition, some of whom sent petitions, others engaged in protests, and still others carried out violent attacks against Saudi and U.S. targets. On 1 March 1992 Fahd issued a new basic law that included provision for a long-discussed consultative council (Majlis al-Shura) but going beyond what had been anticipated in the scope of proposed governmental changes, including the opening of the royal succession to the grandsons of Ibn Sa'ud. Reforms of this period also included a restructuring of the regional government system. One of the last significant accomplishments of Fahd was a reshuffling of the Council of Ministers, the most extensive in twenty years. In 1995 Fahd suffered a stroke, and his deteriorating medical condition prevented him from carrying out his responsibilities as ruler. As a result, during the late 1990s and early 2000s, Abdullah gradually has taken over leadership of the country, acting as de facto ruler.

See also AL SA'UD FAMILY; CAMP DAVID ACCORDS (1978); FAHD PLAN (1981); GULF CRISIS (1990–1991); IRANIAN REVOLUTION (1979); IRAN–IRAQ WAR (1980–1988); KHALID IBN ABD AL-AZIZ AL SA'UD.

Bibliography

Al-Farsy, Fouad. *Custodian of the Two Holy Mosques: King Fahd bin Abdul Aziz.* Guernsey, Channel Islands: Knight Communications, 2001.

Kechichian, Joseph A. *Succession in Saudi Arabia.* New York: Palgrave, 2001.

Al Kilani, Kamal. *Progress of a Nation: A Biography of King Fahd bin Abdul-Aziz.* London: Namara, 1985.

Long, David E. "Fahd bin Abd al-Aziz Sa'ud." In *Political Leaders of the Contemporary Middle East and North Africa: A Biographical Dictionary,* edited by Bernard Reich. Westport, CT: Greenwood Press, 1990.

Metz, Helen Chapin, ed. *Saudi Arabia: A Country Study.* Washington, DC: Library of Congress, 1993.

Al-Rasheed, Madawi. *A History of Saudi Arabia.* New York; Cambridge, U.K.: Cambridge University Press, 2002.

MALCOLM C. PECK
UPDATED BY ANTHONY B. TOTH

FAHD PLAN (1981)

Arab–Israel peace plan proposed by Crown Prince Fahd in 1981.

Because the Camp David Accords had failed to address several central issues of the Arab–Israel conflict, Crown Prince Fahd of Saudi Arabia unveiled an eight-point peace proposal on 7 August 1981. The plan called for Israel's withdrawal from Arab territories occupied in 1967, including East Jerusalem, and the dismantling of Israel's settlements in those territories; guarantees of freedom of worship for all in the holy places; the Palestinian people's right to self-determination; indemnity for Palestinian refugees not exercising the right of return; West Bank and Gaza placed under UN control for a transitional period (a few months), leading to an independent Palestinian state with East Jerusalem as its capital; subsequent Security Council guarantee of peace among all states in the area, including the new Palestinian state; and the Security Council guarantee of the above principles. The plan was adopted in a modified form, at the Arab summit in Fez, Morocco, on 9 September 1982, and remained the Arab position until the Madrid conference in 1991.

JENAB TUTUNJI

FAHMI, MAHMUD PASHA
[1839–]

Egyptian officer and politician associated with the Urabi revolution.

Born in the small village of Shantur to a poor family, Mahmud Pasha Fahmi benefited from a governmental decree requiring villages to send one of their children to the new schools set up by Muhammad Ali Pasha. He later studied at the engineering college at Bulaq and after graduation joined the Engineers corps of the Egyptian army. He was assigned to teach at the new military academy created by Muhammad Sa'id Pasha and later was given the task of overseeing the building of military fortifications in the northern districts. He participated in the Ottoman war against Serbia and returned after it ended to public service. As one of the few Arab officers in an army dominated by Circassians, he was called to serve in 1881 in the ministry of war under Mahmud Sami, who had replaced Circassian Uthman Rifqi Pasha after the army's revolt at the latter's arrest of Colonel Ahmad Urabi. Urabi was reinstated but the Khedive's policies of containing the army led to a new revolt with demands for parliamentary representation and new army regulations.

The attempts by France and Britain to limit constitutionalism caused the new cabinet to fall and Mahmud Sami was called to form a new cabinet in which Urabi and his friends dominated, and Mahmud Fahmi was given the ministry for public works. But the 1882 riots of Alexandria, caused in part by the increased impoverishment of Egyptians as a result of the Capitulations, and the threats to European economic interests and lives, led England to send in its navy and to order the Egyptian army out of the city. The Khedive initially ordered the army to fight back, but later cooperated with the British and fled to Alexandria. In Cairo, a hastily convened council with broad popular support declared the Khedive a traitor and directed Urabi to fight back. The resistance was organized by Urabi, Mahmud Fahmi, and fellow officers at Kafr al Duwwar. The Egyptian army was not able to resist the British who invaded Egypt in due form and restored the Khedive to power. However, Britain prevailed over the latter's attempts at having his former officers executed. Instead, Urabi, Fahmi, and five other officers were exiled to Ceylon. Embittered by the way he was treated by his fellow officers and by what he saw as a defeat caused by their mistakes and arrogant demands, Mahmud Fahmi distanced himself from them and refused to return to Egypt. He died in exile in Ceylon.

MAYSAM J. AL-FARUQI

FAISAL IBN ABD AL-AZIZ AL SA'UD
[c. 1904–1975]

King of Saudi Arabia, 1964–1975.

Faisal ibn Abd al-Aziz Al Sa'ud was the third son of Abd al-Aziz ibn Sa'ud Al Sa'ud (known in the West as Ibn Sa'ud), born in Riyadh, Saudi Arabia, probably in 1904 or 1905, though some accounts place his birth on 9 April 1906, to coincide with one of his father's important early victories. With no full brothers and no half brothers close to him in age, Faisal grew up in relative isolation. He left the royal court at an early age to study under his maternal grandfather, a prominent religious scholar, which served to reinforce that isolation.

Faisal assumed military, political, and diplomatic responsibilities at a young age. He led Saudi forces in the Asir campaign of 1920 and by 1926 was his father's viceroy in charge of the recently conquered province of Hijaz. This included responsibility for the Muslim holy cities of Mecca and Medina and the annual *hajj* (pilgrimage). He early developed a special, broadly informed expertise in the area of foreign affairs; this began in 1919 when he represented his father on a diplomatic mission to Europe, the first of the Al Sa'ud family to do so. In 1930, Faisal officially became foreign minister, retaining that position until his death in 1975, with only a brief interruption, thus making him the longest serving foreign minister in the twentieth century.

Faisal's natural intelligence and his success on important state assignments, such as representing Saudi Arabia at the creation of the United Nations in San Francisco in 1945, clearly marked him as the ablest of the sons of Ibn Sa'ud. Yet in 1933, Ibn Sa'ud had the family recognize Faisal's elder brother Sa'ud, the crown prince, as successor despite Sa'ud's obvious lack of intellectual gifts or meaningful preparation for rule. Faisal had doubtless hoped, perhaps expected, that his demonstrated abilities would have secured him the succession, consistent with the well-established Arabian custom of choosing the ablest near relative of the deceased as the new shaykh or amir. Ibn Saᶜud evidently sought to avoid intrafamily rivalries that had fatally weakened the Al Saᶜud during his own father's generation. Though Faisal came to feel contempt for his incompetent elder brother, he insisted in family councils on a scrupulous adherence to the oath of allegiance (bayᶜa) to Saᶜud that he had led the family in swearing. To do otherwise would, in his view, have established a dangerous precedent in undermining the family's rule.

King Saᶜud's reign, 1953–1964, brought nearly constant crisis, with a pattern of events in which the Al Saᶜud called Faisal to assume responsibility for the government, although Saᶜud subsequently reasserted his claim to power. In early 1958, the kingdom was financially bankrupt from Saᶜud's profligacy and at risk because of his ill-conceived challenge to Egypt's President Gamal Abdel Nasser and radical Arab nationalism. Faisal then assumed executive powers, imposing for the first time fiscal austerity with real limits on princes' pensions and a true budget. He came to a *modus vivendi* with Nasser, with whom he had earlier been careful to cultivate tolerable relations, though ideologically they were poles apart. By 1959, Saᶜud had forced Faisal out of the government and allied himself with a group of reformist half brothers, the Free Princes, whose embarrassing public split with the rest of the Al Saᶜud and declaration of solidarity with Nasser helped to place the kingdom in real peril.

In 1962, Faisal once again assumed executive powers as prime minister, doing so as a republican coup was about to overthrow the traditional imamate in Yemen and Saudi Air Force officers were preparing to defect to Cairo (Egypt). Faisal revamped the Council of Ministers and established the team of princes that continues to lead Saudi Arabia in the early 1990s. This included the progressive and ambitious Fahd and Sultan ibn Abd al-Aziz Al Saᶜud. They comprise part of the largest and most powerful grouping of full brothers in the family, those born to the favorite wife of Ibn Saᶜud, Hassa bint Ahmad Al Sudayri. Fahd at forty-one was both interior minister and, in a new departure, was designated second deputy prime minister behind Prince Khalid, while thirty-eight-year-old Sultan ibn Abd al-Aziz Al Saᶜud became defense minister,

the position he holds today. To counterbalance them, Faisal selected the traditionalist Abdullah who, in contrast both to the king and the Al Sudayri family enjoyed close ties with the Arab tribes, a constituency whose support was critical to the monarchy. Faisal himself, with his genuine piety and austere morality well established (after sowing a few youthful wild oats), secured the support of the crucial religious establishment. Faisal's care in creating and maintaining balance in the government was key to preserving stability. Thus, when Saᶜud's final attempt to recover his powers led the senior princes, backed by a *fatwa* (ruling) from the *ulama* (religious establishment), to force his abdication in 1964, the government had been put in place that would endure with few changes through King Faisal's own eleven-year rule and then Khalid's seven years as king, with its core still intact in the early 1990s.

The creation of an efficient, stable government in place of the circle of cronies or inexperienced sons on which Saᶜud had heavily relied was typical of the reforms that Faisal enacted. They were meant not to open up the political system in a modern, democratic sense but to enable it to confront the challenges of the twentieth century, so as to preserve the kingdom's traditional values. Thus, Sultan, Fahd, and King Faisal's brother-in-law Kamal Adham, head of the state intelligence service, were given full rein to build up the military and internal security establishments. Bright young technocrat commoners—such as Ahmad Zaki Yamani, who long served as petroleum minister, and Ghazi al-Qusaybi, for many years minister of industry and electricity—began to play significant roles, though without political power, as the bureaucracy began a rapid expansion. Modern public instruction at all levels underwent massive expansion, with girls admitted for the first time, reflecting the king's realization of the necessity of an educated population. The press and radio broadcasting experienced rapid expansion and, against strong conservative opposition, Faisal introduced television—he saw the need to diffuse information rapidly in a modern state and viewed the print and broadcast media as means of promoting national unification.

Faisal met external dangers to the kingdom with reliance on restored prestige and stability at home and on bold initiatives when required. Financial assistance to Yemeni royalists helped to checkmate the radical threat in that quarter, and Nasser's defeat in the Arab–Israel War of 1967 greatly strengthened Faisal's hand in dealing with the Arab nationalist challenge. As oil revenues mounted toward the end of his reign, "riyal diplomacy" helped to moderate the behavior of radical recipients of largesse and to strengthen conservative regimes. The new wealth gave substance to Faisal's attempt to promote an international policy based on the conservative values of Islam. In 1970, he took the lead in establishing the Organization of the Islamic Conference as an intended alternative to the Arab League (the League of Arab States). Ultimately, however, Faisal knew that Saudi Arabia's security against external threats—principally the Soviet Union, its regional allies, and proxies—could come only from the United States. This dependence placed Saudi Arabia in the painful dilemma of being intimately linked to the principal supporter of Israel. The dilemma became an acute crisis in U.S.–Saudi relations when Faisal led the imposition of the 1973–1974 Organization of Petroleum Exporting Countries (OPEC) embargo after President Richard M. Nixon's decision to resupply massively Israel's armed forces during the Arab–Israel War of 1973. It was typical of Faisal's pragmatic realism that, within months of that crisis, the U.S. and Saudi governments had signed agreements, especially the Joint Commission on Economic Cooperation, that created unprecedented links between the two countries.

In his statecraft, Faisal balanced a fundamental commitment to traditional values with an informed acceptance of the means of creating a strong modern state. He combined a rigorous Islamic view of the world with a sophisticated realpolitik, and he devoted himself unswervingly to the survival of Saudi Arabia. It is likely that, next to his father, Faisal will be remembered as the greatest of the twentieth-century Saudi rulers.

See also ABD AL-AZIZ IBN SAʿUD AL SAʿUD; AL SAʿUD FAMILY; AL SUDAYRI, HASSA BINT AHMAD; ARAB–ISRAEL WAR (1967); ARAB–ISRAEL WAR (1973); FAHD IBN ABD AL-AZIZ AL SAʿUD; KHALID IBN ABD AL-AZIZ AL SAʿUD; LEAGUE OF ARAB STATES; NASSER, GAMAL ABDEL; NIXON, RICHARD MILHOUS; ORGANIZATION OF PETROLEUM EXPORTING COUNTRIES (OPEC); ORGANIZATION OF THE ISLAMIC CONFERENCE; YAMANI, AHMAD ZAKI.

Bibliography

Beling, Willard A., ed. *King Faisal and the Modernisation of Saudi Arabia.* London: Croom Helm; Boulder, CO: Westview, 1980.

Bligh, Alexander. *From Prince to King: Royal Succession in the House of Saud in the Twentieth Century.* New York: New York University Press, 1984.

Holden, David, and Johns, Richard. *The House of Saud: The Rise and Rule of the Most Powerful Dynasty in the Arab World.* New York: Holt, Rinehart, and Winston, 1981.

Lacey, Robert. *The Kingdom.* New York: Harcourt Brace Jovanovich, 1981.

MALCOLM C. PECK

FAISAL I IBN HUSSEIN
[1889–1933]

King of Iraq, 1921–1933; also known as Amir Faisal, leader of the Arab Revolt against the Ottoman Turks, 1916; king of Syria for a brief period in 1920.

The third son of Sharif Husayn of the Hijaz, Faisal was from a prestigious, wealthy family (Hashimite) that traced its lineage back to the Prophet Muhammad. He spent his early boyhood among the bedouin in Arabia, educated by private tutors, and, at age six, moved to Istanbul, capital of the Ottoman Empire, where he lived during his father's exile until 1908. Faisal completed his education in Istanbul, becoming multilingual and well versed in court etiquette and politics. Life in cosmopolitan Istanbul and his later service as representative from Jidda in the Ottoman parliament, where he was an early spokesman for Arab interests, provided valuable political experience that served Faisal well in his later negotiations with the European powers.

In January 1915, Faisal was sent by his father to Istanbul to determine the political situation of the Hijaz and to contact secret Arab societies in Damascus, Syria, to ascertain if there was support for an Arab uprising against the Ottoman Turks. At first, signs were positive; but at a second meeting in Damascus in January 1916, after these groups had been disbanded by Cemal Paşa, the few remaining nationalists indicated via the Damascus Protocol that Hussein should initiate a revolt for Arab independence. Hussein incorporated these ideas in his correspondence with the British. Faisal was less sanguine about British support than was his brother,

A portrait of Faisal I ibn Hussein (1889–1933), king of Iraq from 1921 to 1933. Faisal died of a heart attack in Geneva, Switzerland, on 7 September 1933. He was succeeded by his son, Ghazi ibn Faisal. © HULTON-DEUTSCH COLLECTION/ CORBIS. REPRODUCED BY PERMISSION.

Abdullah I ibn Hussein, but Ottoman Turkish moves to strengthen their hold on Medina made action more imminent. (The Turks were fighting on the side of the Central powers—Austria-Hungary and Germany—and against the Allies, including Britain and France, in World War I.)

Faisal's note to Cemal Paşa advocated an Arab *umma* (community). His statement and the cutting of the railroad lines between Damascus and Medina launched the Arab Revolt on 10 June 1916. Concern in Cairo that the Arab troops in Arabia needed military training led to the dispatch of the British Colonel T. E. Lawrence, who by December 1916 had joined Faisal and suggested to the British that the amir become the field commander of the Hijaz.

The suggestion was taken, and, though unable to take Medina, Faisal's troops later occupied Aqaba on 6 July 1917, a victory that provided the Arabs credibility with the British. Faisal was deputized a British general under the command of General Edmund Allenby, commander in chief of the Egyptian Expeditionary Force. Faisal's troops, some 1,000 bedouin supplemented by approximately 2,500 Ottoman ex-prisoners of war, proceeded to harass the Ottoman Turkish army as the British moved to take Gaza, Beersheba, and Jerusalem.

On 25 September 1918, Allenby ordered the advance on Damascus. As party to the Sykes–Picot Agreement, Britain attempted to assign organized administration of the city both to the French and to the Arabs, but in the confusion of the British advance and the Ottoman retreat, the Damascus Arabs hoisted their own flag before Faisal and his army had time to reach Damascus. With the aid of Faisal's supporter, Nuri al-Saʿid, pro-Faisal officials controlled the city and were later confirmed by the French. Lawrence asserted that Faisal's men had slipped into the city on 30 September to 1 October and had liberated it in advance of the British and Australian troops.

At the Versailles conference in 1919, Faisal was caught between British–French international diplomacy and events in the Middle East that were taking their own course. As the Arab representative to Versailles, Faisal pressed claims for Syrian independence, but under British sponsorship. Discussions with American proponents of Zionism and with Zionist leader Chaim Weizmann elicited Faisal's support for Jewish immigration to Palestine, culminating in the Faisal–Weizmann Agreements signed on 3 January 1919. To the published document, Faisal added a handwritten addendum that Arab support for Jewish aspirations would be conditional upon the achievement of Arab independence. Faisal continued to support Jewish immigration within the context of his later pan-Arab federation programs.

In May, Faisal called for a general congress to be held in Damascus to endorse his position at Versailles. Convened in June, the meeting was dominated by the prewar Arab nationalist clubs—the primarily Iraqi al-Ahd, the Palestinian Arab Club (al-Nadi al-Arabi), which tried to persuade Faisal to relinquish his support for Zionism, and the al-Fatat (youth) dominated Istiqlal Party. The congress called for an independent Syria that also would include Lebanon, Jordan, and Palestine. Backed by the British, who wished to exclude the French from the Middle East, Faisal received a grudging acquiescence for an Arab regime from the politically weakened French president, Georges Clemenceau.

Still in session in March 1920, the congress declared Syria (including Lebanon and Palestine) an independent kingdom ruled by Faisal as constitutional monarch. Some Arabs in Palestine proclaimed Palestine a part of Syria, and Basra and Baghdad were declared independent by a group of Arabs in Iraq who wished to be ruled by Faisal's brother, Abdullah. In spite of the international repercussions, Faisal accepted the Syrian draft and allowed Arab nationalists to harass French troops in Syria while he began to negotiate with the forces of Kemalism in Anatolia who had proclaimed an independent Turkey. As the British withdrew their support from the Arabs in Syria, and a new government in Paris followed a more vigorous policy in Syria, the French ordered their high commissioner in Syria, General Henri-Joseph-Eugène Gouraud, to confront Faisal. Occupying Damascus on 26 July 1920, the French forced Faisal into exile the following day and proclaimed Syria to be under French rule.

A shift in British priorities affected policy after 1920, influenced by an Arab revolt in Iraq against the British occupation and the policies of Winston Churchill, newly appointed colonial secretary, which included leaving Syria to the French and installing Hashimites elsewhere as local rulers who would "reign but not govern" in order to save the expense of full-scale occupation. At the Cairo Conference in March 1921, Churchill and his aides proceeded to redraw the map of the Middle East and to plan the installation of Faisal as king of a newly created Iraq.

The British looked to Faisal as a malleable vehicle for their Mesopotamian/Iraqi policy, which was to secure the area and its oil for themselves. He was deemed suitable to both the Sunni and Shiʿite Iraqis because of his Hashimite lineage and his Arab nationalist credentials as leader of the Arab Revolt. Any local candidates, such as Sayyid Talib of Basra, were duly eliminated. The British contrived a plebiscite in July 1921 to authorize Faisal's candidacy. In August 1921, Faisal arrived in Iraq to a lukewarm reception and was proclaimed king.

The leader of the Arab Revolt brought with him to Iraq a coterie of Iraqi (former Ottoman) Arab nationalist army officers who had supported him in Syria and who now took top positions in the new Iraqi administration. Jaʿfar al-Askari became minister of defense; perennial cabinet minister Nuri al-Saʿid became chief of staff of the new Iraqi army; and Ottoman educator Sati al-Husari instituted an Arab nationalist curriculum in Iraqi schools. Faisal's tenure in Iraq was a tightrope walk between nationalism and cordial relations with Britain, without whose financial and military support and advisers he could not rule. Always maintaining his own goals, while remembering the bitter Syrian experience, Faisal worked from 1921 until his death in 1933 to create a modernized, unified country with a centralized infrastructure, to achieve immediate political independence from Britain, and to continue his dream of uniting Arab areas of the Middle East into a pan-Arab union under Hashimite aegis. From the beginning, the British regretted their choice, as Faisal proved to be less docile than they had anticipated.

Throughout the 1920s, Faisal was preoccupied with the fact that Iraq was a British mandate and not an independent state. Faced with local nationalist opposition to himself and to the British presence in the country, he used his considerable personal charisma to garner the support of urban nationalists and tribal leaders in Shiʿite areas. Comfortable both in traditional dress meeting with bedouin and in Western-style clothes playing bridge with British officials in Baghdad, Faisal negotiated for independence. He also understood the necessity for British political and military support to ensure the territorial integrity of the new state until Iraq was able to build up its own army and defend its interests against the Persians, Saudis, and Turks, from whom Britain managed to secure Mosul for Iraq.

During treaty negotiations in 1922, delayed by his appendicitis attack, and again in 1927, the king encouraged the anti-British nationalist opposition, all the while advocating moderation by both sides. The result was an agreement signed in 1930 that gave Britain control of Iraqi foreign policy and finances but also resulted, in 1932, in Iraq's nominal independence and admission to the League of Nations.

The Iraqi constitution gave Faisal the power to suspend parliament, call for new elections, and confirm all laws. During his tenure, the king attempted to forge a united Iraq with a nationalist focus instead of the patchwork of disparate religious and ethnic groups. Once independence was assured, Faisal used his prestige and his position as king of an independent Arab state to engage in foreign policy.

Faisal never abandoned his interest in Syria. In contact with the French in Syria over the possibility that a Hashimite such as Abdullah or Ali (especially after the latter lost his throne in Arabia to the Saudis) might be installed there as he was in Iraq, Faisal was also active in local Syrian politics. In 1928 he organized a monarchist party aimed at making him ruler both in Iraq and in Syria. To Faisal, Iraqi independence in 1932 would be but the first step toward an Arab union to include not only Syria and Palestine, but possibly Arabia as well. From 1929 until Syrian elections in 1932, Faisal sent emissaries to lobby Syrian politicians, conducted an intense propaganda campaign to promote his interests, and used the Islamic Congress that met in Jerusalem in 1931 to advance his cause. Plans were made for another congress to meet in Baghdad in 1933, despite British opposition to Faisal's pan-Arab plans. The defeat of his cause in the Syrian elections, anti-Saudi revolts in the Hijaz, and his untimely death put Hashimite unity attempts on hold.

In June 1933, Faisal left for London on a prearranged state visit, leaving an anti-British government in power in Baghdad. He then spent the summer in Switzerland for reasons of health. When word reached him of the crisis with the Assyrian minority in Iraq, Faisal pleaded for moderation. But the exploits of the new Iraqi army that resulted in hundreds of Assyrian civilian deaths were popular in Baghdad, where there were demands for Faisal's resignation. On 7 September 1933, Faisal died of a heart attack in Geneva. He was succeeded by his son, Ghazi ibn Faisal.

See also ABDULLAH I IBN HUSSEIN; ALLENBY, EDMUND HENRY; ARAB REVOLT (1916); ASKARI, JAʿFAR AL-; CAIRO CONFERENCE (1921); CEMAL PAŞA; FAISAL–WEIZMANN AGREEMENTS; GHAZI IBN FAISAL; HASHIMITE HOUSE (HOUSE OF HASHIM); KEMALISM; LAWRENCE, T. E.; SYKES–PICOT AGREEMENT (1916).

Bibliography

Kedourie, Elie. *England and the Middle East: 1914–1921.* Hassocks, U.K.: Harvester Press, 1978.

Muslih, Muhammad Y. *The Origins of Palestinian Nationalism.* New York: Columbia University Press, 1988.

Nevakivi, J. *Britain, France, and the Arab Middle East, 1914–1920.* London: Athlone, 1969.

Simon, Reeva S. *Iraq between the Two World Wars.* New York: Columbia University Press, 1986.

Sluglett, Peter. *Britain in Iraq, 1914–1921.* London: Ithaca Press for the Middle East Centre, St. Antony's College, Oxford, 1976.

REEVA S. SIMON

FAISAL II IBN GHAZI
[1935–1958]

King of Iraq, 1953–1958.

Born in May 1935, Faisal II ibn Ghazi was killed, along with his uncle Abd al-Ilah ibn Ali and other members of the royal family, on 14 July 1958, in the course of the Iraqi revolution. Faisal's father Ghazi ibn Faisal had died in an accident in April 1939 when Faisal himself was only three years old. For most of his life, he was overshadowed by his uncle, who acted as regent until he came of age in 1953.

Faisal was educated in the palace in Baghdad and then at Harrow School near London between 1949 and 1952. Although personally popular, he could not escape the stigma that attached to his uncle and the other *éminence grise* of Iraqi politics, Nuri al-Saʿid—both of whom were stout defenders and major beneficiaries of the close connection with Britain that characterized Iraqi politics in the 1940s and 1950s.

See also ABD AL-ILAH IBN ALI; GHAZI IBN FAISAL; HASHIMITE HOUSE (HOUSE OF HASHIM).

PETER SLUGLETT

FAISAL–WEIZMANN AGREEMENTS

Signed in London, 3 January 1919, between Amir Faisal I ibn Hussein ("representing and acting on behalf of the Arab Kingdom of Hedjaz") and Dr. Chaim Weizmann ("representing and acting on behalf of the Zionist Organisation").

The agreement between Faisal ibn Hussein and Chaim Weizmann was worked out with Colonel T. E. Lawrence, who acted as both midwife and translator in an arrangement whose immediate purpose was to harmonize the positions of all three parties before the Paris Peace Conference that followed World War I. Its preamble contained remarks about "the racial kinship and ancient bonds existing between the Arabs and the Jewish people," and called for "the closest possible collaboration" between the signatories as "the surest means of working out the consummation of their national aspirations." In its nine articles, the agreement spelled out methods and areas of cooperation between two mutually recognized entities: "the Arab State" and Palestine. The latter was to be governed in a way that would "afford the fullest guarantee for carrying into effect" Britain's Balfour Declaration. This meant the promotion of large-scale immigration and settlement of Jews and the protection of the rights of "the Arab peasant and tenant farmers," who would also be "assisted in forwarding their economic development." Separate articles assured the free exercise of religion and the keeping of "Mohammedan Holy Places . . . under Mohammedan control." The World Zionist Organization promised to "use its best efforts to assist the Arab State [i.e., the independent Greater Syria to which Faisal was aspiring] in providing the means for developing the natural resources and economic possibilities thereof." In an important proviso, Faisal linked his signature on this agreement to the complete fulfillment of Arab demands as submitted in a memorandum to the British Foreign Office.

The agreement, which remained secret for several years, quickly became inoperative, as neither signatory proved to be in a position to "deliver the goods" to the other. The authenticity of the agreement was challenged by some Arabs during the 1930s when Zionist leaders sought to gain propaganda advantage by publishing the text. Recent historical research has established that the document is genuine enough; thus, only Faisal's motives remain the subject of some debate.

See also BALFOUR DECLARATION (1917); FAISAL I IBN HUSSEIN; GREATER SYRIA; LAWRENCE, T. E.; WEIZMANN, CHAIM; WORLD ZIONIST ORGANIZATION (WZO).

Bibliography

Caplan, Neil. "Faisal ibn Husain and the Zionists: A Re-examination with Documents." *International History Review* 5, no. 4 (November 1983): 561–614.

Caplan, Neil. *Futile Diplomacy*, Vol. 1: *Early Arab–Zionist Negotiation Attempts, 1913–1931*. London and Totowa, NJ: F. Cass, 1983.

Perlmann, M. "Chapters of Arab–Jewish Diplomacy, 1918–1922." *Jewish Social Studies* 6 (1944): 132–147.

Tibawi, A. L. "T. E. Lawrence, Faisal and Weizmann: The 1919 Attempt to Secure an Arab Balfour Declaration." *Royal Central Asian Journal* 56 (1969): 156–163.

NEIL CAPLAN

FALCONRY

The art of training falcons, hawks, and other game birds to hunt.

Rooted in pre-Islamic Arabia, falconry became a fashionable courtly pastime from the time of Caliph Yazid ibn Mu'awiya (680–683 C.E.) to that of the Ottoman Empire sultans. Also practiced by commoners, falconry's popularity spread from Persia to Morocco. Most prized were the gyrfalcons of Siberia. These Siberian birds were often exchanged as ceremonial gifts among ambassadors. Many treatises were written on the art of training, and the hawk became a common motif in the Islamic arts. Hunting with falcons remains a popular pastime of the wealthy today on the Arabian Peninsula.

ELIZABETH THOMPSON

FAMILY PLANNING

See BIRTH CONTROL

FANON, FRANTZ

[1925–1961]

French West Indian psychiatrist, author, and ideologue of the Algerian Revolution.

A black man born in 1925 on the French Antilles island of Martinique, Frantz Fanon became the best-known theoretician of the Algerian revolution and, through it, one of the best-known theoreticians of African liberation in general. The child of middle-class parents, Fanon spent the early years of his life attempting to be French. During World War II, however, humiliating experiences of racism in the Antilles and in North Africa and Europe, where he served in the French armed forces, made him increasingly aware of the anomalies confronted by a black man in a world dominated by whites.

After the war Fanon went home to Martinique, but in 1947 he returned to France and entered medical school. He received a degree from the University of Lyons in 1951. In July 1953 he passed his *Médicat de hôpitaux psychiatrique* and, in November 1953, he accepted a position as chief of staff (*chef de service*) in the Blida-Joinville Hospital, the largest psychiatric hospital in Algeria.

While serving at Blida, Fanon treated many patients suffering from the pressures of their colonized status and from the trauma of the revolutionary situation. He came to the conclusion that the resentment that had brought about the Algerian revolution was of the same order as the resentment he had come to feel as a black man in a white world. In 1956, Fanon resigned his medical post and secretly joined the Front de Libération Nationale (FLN; National Liberation Front). Receiving in January 1957 a "letter of expulsion" from the colonial authorities, he fled to Tunis, where the FLN was beginning to establish its headquarters. There he became an editor of *al Moudjahid*, the official organ of the FLN, served in FLN medical centers, and became a roving ambassador to solicit support for Algeria in African countries. In December 1960, Fanon was diagnosed with leukemia. He died of that illness a year later in Bethesda, Maryland.

Fanon wrote three books. The earliest, *Peau Noire, Masques Blancs* (Black skin, white masks), appeared in 1952. It diagnoses the psychologically dependent status of Caribbean blacks and suggests ways for them to transcend that dependency and discover self-possession and authenticity. The second, *L'an V de la Révolution Algérienne* (Year 5 of the Algerian revolution), was written in great haste in 1959 and is essentially a sociology of the revolution. In it, Fanon describes

the transformation of Algerian society brought about by individuals' decisions to revolt. In revolting against colonial oppression, militants also revolt against patriarchal and other oppressions. Out of these individual decisions, a nation of free men and women is born, a process that cannot be reversed. Fanon's last book, *Les Damnés de la Terre* (Wretched of the Earth), was published in 1961. It takes up many of the themes of the preceding works, but with greater urgency. Fanon insists that it is only through violence that colonialism can be defeated and the native overcome his dependency complex. Native bourgeoisies must also be overturned, because they are in a state of permanent dependence upon the West. The Algerian revolution is the model for global revolution, because it represents a peasant revolution led by a genuinely popular party. A fourth book, *Pour la Révolution Africaine* (For the African revolution), a collection of articles written during Fanon's *Moudjahid* period, was published after his death.

See also FRONT DE LIBÉRATION NATIONALE (FLN).

Bibliography

Bulhan, Hussein Abdilahi. *Frantz Fanon and the Psychology of Oppression.* New York: Plenum, 1985.

Geisner, Peter. *Fanon.* New York: Dial, 1971.

Gendzier, Irene L. *Frantz Fanon: A Critical Study.* New York: Pantheon Books, 1973.

JOHN RUEDY

FAO PENINSULA

The southernmost tip of Iraq.

The Fao Peninsula lies between the Shatt al-Arab and Bubiyan Island. It became the site of the landing place of the submarine cable to India in 1964, of an oil port in 1951, of an offshore oil rig, and of heavy fighting (February 1986 to April 1987) during the Iran–Iraq War.

See also BUBIYAN ISLAND; IRAN–IRAQ WAR (1980–1988); SHATT AL-ARAB.

ALBERTINE JWAIDEH

FAQIR, FADIA

[1956–]

A Jordanian novelist.

Fadia (also Fadiya) Faqir was born in Amman, Jordan. She earned her Ph.D. in England and teaches Middle Eastern politics, Arabic literature, and women's studies at Durham University. She is one of a number of Arab novelists writing in English. Her first novel, *Nisanit* (1990), is a grim account of Palestinian life under Israeli occupation. Torture, hate, love, and sacrifice are intertwined in this bleak and powerful text. Her second novel, *Pillars of Salt* (1996), is the story of two women confined to a mental hospital in Jordan during and after the British Mandate. The novel contains a strong homoerotic subtext. Her narrative techniques undermine the centrality of Islamic religious texts. Faqir has been recognized as a new kind of storyteller and one who, because of the accessibility of her English texts, is being discovered in the West.

Faqir also gained visibility as a critic with the collection she edited, *In the House of Silence: Autobiographical Essays by Arab Women Writers* (1999), and because of her leadership in the Arab Women Writers series, published by Garnet in London. To date, five novels by Arab women have been published in the series.

See also GENDER: GENDER AND EDUCATION; JORDAN; LITERATURE: ARABIC.

ELISE SALEM

FARAJ, MAYSALOUN
[1955–]

Iraqi artist and curator.

Maysaloun Faraj was born in the United States to an Iraqi family. After a childhood there, she moved to Iraq, where she received a degree in architecture from Baghdad University. She later received training in England, where she has lived and worked since 1982. She is a noted ceramicist and mixed media painter, as well as the curator of a major exhibition, *Strokes of Genius: Contemporary Iraqi Art,* which traveled through England and the United States between 2000 and 2002. Faraj also edited a volume of the same title to accompany the show. The exhibition was the first major presentation of contemporary Iraqi art in the West and reflects Faraj's concern with challenging stereotypes that perpetuate political conflicts involving her native country. Many of her paintings and ceramics make innovative use of Arabic calligraphy in a manner that links her contemporary, often political, concerns with her heritage. Some of her work also contains symbols reminiscent of Iraqi folk art and ancient Assyrian art. Faraj has described her work as an attempt to recover all that is being destroyed in her homeland, from its ancient civilization to its people and their spirit. She is inspired by her Muslim faith. Her work is included in the public collections of the British Museum as well as in Washington, D.C.'s National Museum for Women in the Arts.

See also ANI, JANNANE AL-; ART; ATTAR, SUAD AL-; GENDER: GENDER AND EDUCATION; IRAQ.

Bibliography

Faraj, Maysaloun, ed. *Strokes of Genius: Contemporary Iraqi Art.* London: Saqi Books, 2002.

Lloyd, Fran, ed. *Displacement and Difference: Contemporary Arab Visual Culture in the Diaspora.* London: Saffron Books, 2001.

JESSICA WINEGAR

FARAJ, MURAD
[1866–1956]

Egyptian Jewish-Karaite author and theologian; Egyptian nationalist and Zionist.

Murad Faraj was born in Cairo and trained as a lawyer; he became a government official during the reign of Khedive Abbas Hilmi I (1892–1914) and wrote articles and poems for the two epoch-making newspapers of the pre-1914 era, *al-Jarida* and *al-Mu'ayyad.* He wrote books on Jewish-Karaite topics, theology and law, biblical exegeses, Hebrew and Arabic philology, medieval Jewish poets who wrote in Arabic, and current legal issues. He also translated Hebrew works into Arabic.

By the mid-1920s, as a noted author in the field of modern Arabic culture, he advocated Egyptian national unity and interreligious dialogue. His essays, notably *Harb al-Watan* (The national battle), appealed to Muslim Egyptians to treat their Christian and Jewish compatriots as equals. By the mid-to-late 1920s, Faraj advocated Jewish nationalism, hoping that Zionism would be seen as similar to Egypt's national aspiration. His poetry, the *Diwan Faraj,* collected in four volumes (1912–1935), stresses Zionist themes.

See also ABBAS HILMI II.

Bibliography

Nemoy, Leon. "A Modern Karaite-Arabic Poet: Mourad Faraj." *Jewish Quarterly Review* 70 (1979/1980): 195–209.

Nemoy, Leon. "Murad Faraj and His Book, *The Karaites and the Rabbanites.*" *Revue des Etudes Juives* 135, nos. 1–3 (1976): 87–112.

Somekh, Sasson. "Participation of Egyptian Jews in Modern Arabic Culture, and the Case of Murad Faraj." In *The Jews of Egypt: A Mediterranean Society in Modern Times,* edited by Shimon Shamir. Boulder, CO: Westview, 1987.

MICHAEL M. LASKIER

FAR'A, WAHIBA
[1954–]

First Yemeni minister for human rights.

Wahiba Far'a, born in 1954 in Ta'iz, Yemen, was the first woman as full cabinet member in the Yemeni government. She acted as the minister of state for human rights during 2001–2003. She was the first minister in this new ministry, which was established in 2001. She is a prominent women's rights activist and scholar. Far'a received her B.A. in English literature from San'a University, continued her studies at Cairo University with a specialization in women's education, and earned her Ph.D. in Cairo (philosophy). She worked as a lecturer at San'a University while conducting research on women and development, women in higher education, child labor, and polygamy in migration. Far'a is the founder and rector of Queen Arwa University in San'a (established in 1996) and dean of Yemen International Language Institute (established in 1989, and now a department of the university). She is a member of the Supreme National Committee for Human Rights and the ruling People's General Congress Party. As a minister, Far'a made women's rights, prison reform, and the rights of children and people with disabilities key priorities. The minister was confronted with challenges: a record of human rights abuses, an independent judiciary that limits freedom of the press, and a civil society proposing a large number of human rights initiatives.

See also GENDER: GENDER AND LAW; GENDER: GENDER AND POLITICS; YEMEN.

SUSANNE DAHLGREN

FARÈS, NABILE
[1940–]

Algerian novelist and poet.

A key figure in post-colonial Maghrebi literature and literary experimentation, Nabile Farès is known for a unique, dreamlike style of writing that blurs the boundaries between the novel and poetry, the two genres in which he works.

Often identified primarily as a Berber writer, Farès has sought a new language to make sense of new, post-colonial, transnational experiences; likewise, he has attempted to find a voice and a place for indigenous people in contemporary literature. Like most of his contemporaries, he writes in French, and very few of his works have been translated into English. His key themes are displacement, migration, exile, and the cultural, psychological, and historical ruptures implied by these phenomena, so familiar to North Africans.

Born on 25 September 1940 in Collo, Algeria, Nabile Farès was influenced by his grandfather, a well-read and contemplative man, and his father, a well-known politician who later became president of the provisional executive committee during the transition to independence. Farès was educated at the college of Ben Aknoun of Algiers, where he developed an interest in philosophy, anthropology, and literature. In France, he received a *doctor d'état* in literature, and he taught literature in Paris and in Algiers.

His first novel, published in 1970, was *Yahia, pas de chance* (Yahia, No Chance). In it, he introduced themes that have preoccupied him ever since: ruptures on all levels—linguistic, psychological, physical, and cultural. His novels also reveal the important role Berber women have played in sustaining and enlivening cultural and literary oral traditions, whether in post-independence Algeria or in France. Much of his work is autobiographical and is conveyed in a semi-confessional tone, exploring the impact of dramatic sociopolitical change on Berber and Algerian subjectivity. Farès is currently a professor of literature at the University of Grenoble.

Bibliography

Bensmaia, Reda. *Experimental Nations, or the Invention of the Maghreb*. Princeton, NJ: Princeton University Press, 2003.

Gikandi, Simon, ed. *Encyclopedia of African Literature*. London: Routledge, 2002.

LAURIE KING-IRANI

FARHAD, GHULAM MUHAMMAD

[1917–1984]

Mayor of Kabul, 1948–1954.

Born in Kabul in 1917, Ghulam Muhammad Farhad was educated in Kabul and Germany and trained as an engineer. Twenty years after being elected mayor of Kabul, he was elected to the Afghan parliament (1968). He was an active member of the Afghan socialist party Afghan Nation and was the publisher of a newspaper of the same name (1966–1967).

Bibliography

Adamec, Ludwig. *Historical Dictionary of Afghanistan*, 2d edition. Lanham, MD: Scarecrow Press, 1997.

GRANT FARR

FARHAT AL-ZAWI

Muslim judge and politician from Tripolitania.

Farhat al-Zawi studied in Tripoli, Tunis, and Paris and was a judge in Zawiya, Tripolitania, as well as a member of the Ottoman parliament from 1908 to 1912. A leader of the Tripolitanian resistance to Italian rule in Libya (1911–1912), he negotiated with the Italians for the region's future (December 1912) and became their adviser, helping to consolidate Italian rule.

See also TRIPOLITANIA.

Bibliography

Anderson, Lisa. *The State and Social Transformation in Tunisia and Libya, 1830–1980*. Princeton, NJ: Princeton University Press, 1986.

Simon, Rachel. *Libya between Ottomanism and Nationalism: The Ottoman Involvement in Libya during the War with Italy (1911–1919)*. Berlin: K. Schwarz, 1987.

RACHEL SIMON

FARHI FAMILY

Dynasty of Jewish financiers in Ottoman-controlled Damascus during the eighteenth and nineteenth centuries.

The Farhis were granted the status of *sarrafs* (bankers) by the authorities in the Ottoman provinces of Damascus and Sidon; they subsequently emerged as the chief financial administrators of these provinces' treasuries.

The most illustrious member of this family was Hayyim Farhi, who in the 1790s entered the service of Ahmad al-Jazzar Pasha, the governor of Sidon. There he became responsible for al-Jazzar's financial affairs until the latter's death in 1804. The following year Farhi was involved in the political succession struggle that led to Sulayman Pasha's ascendance to the governorship of Sidon. Given Farhi's assistance to this development, Suleiman allowed him to manage Sidon's financial administration as al-Jazzar had done previously. It was only during the second decade of the nineteenth century under Abdullah Pasha, Suleiman's successor, that Farhi's position declined, eventually resulting in his execution.

Their financial power in Sidon eliminated, the Farhis nonetheless continued to exercise considerable financial influence in Damascus until the early 1830s. In the wake of the Egyptian occupation of Syria and Palestine (1831–1840), the family's status declined temporarily in Damascus. Yet once the Ottomans regained authority in the province, the Farhis once again were partially responsible for running its financial affairs.

See also AHMAD AL-JAZZAR.

Bibliography

Holt, P. M. *Egypt and the Fertile Crescent, 1516–1922: A Political History*. Ithaca, NY: Cornell University Press, 1966.

MICHAEL M. LASKIER

FARHUD

Persian word, commonly used in Iraq to refer to the anti-Jewish rioting of June 1941.

After the defeat of Rashid Ali al-Kaylani's pro-Nazi coup and his flight from Baghdad on 1 and 2 June

1941, Jewish life and property were attacked in what came to be called in Baghdad the Farhud. The looting was started by Iraqi soldiers who had been allowed to roam the streets of Baghdad carrying their weapons. On the second day, when bedouin started pouring into the city across the unguarded bridges, authorities began to worry that the attacks would spread beyond the Jewish community; order, however, was finally restored.

The looting and killing had continued for two days while the British army sat on the outskirts of the city, prevented from intervening by order of the British ambassador, Sir Kinahan Cornwallis. Hundreds of houses and businesses were looted. Accounts vary from 120 Jews killed to more than 600; 2,118 injured; and more than 12,000 who lost part or all of their property. An official committee of inquiry reported the lowest figure; but the text of the secret report was published by the chronicler Abd al-Razzaq al-Hasani, who said that a member of the committee reported the largest figures, and orders were given to reduce this figure.

No attempt was made by Iraq to seek out and punish the perpetrators, but some token compensation to the victims was promised.

See also KAYLANI, RASHID ALI AL-.

Bibliography

Kedourie, Elie. "The Sack of Basra and the Farhud in Baghdad." In *Arabic Political Memoirs and Other Studies.* London: Cass, 1974.

Twena, Abraham. *Jewry of Iraq: Dispersion and Liberation.* Ramla, Israel, 1977, 1979.

Udovitch, A. L., and Cohen, Mark R. *Jews among Arabs: Contacts and Boundaries.* Princeton, NJ: Darwin Press, 1988.

SYLVIA G. HAIM

FARID, NAGWA KAMAL
[c. 1950–]

The first woman appointed to the shari'a *court system in Sudan and perhaps, in the modern era, in Islamic Africa.*

Nagwa Kamal Farid's appointment was a rare step in the Muslim world, since some religious scholars believe that women should be precluded from po-
sitions where they exert power and authority over men. The Qur'anic verse "men are in charge of women, because they spend of their property" (Sura 4:34) has been interpreted by some as precluding women from holding public office ranging from judge to president or prime minister in predominantly Muslim states. For example, a female judge was not appointed in Egypt until 2003; however women judges have been appointed in Tunisia, Iraq, and Indonesia, and women have been heads of state in Pakistan, Bangladesh, Turkey, and Indonesia. In Islamic Africa, women judges in the Islamic (shari'a) courts are virtually nonexistent. In Sudan, shari'a female judges did not act as sitting judges in public courts—where their personal honor and dignity might be compromised—but they worked in offices in the judiciary, protected from public view.

Nagwa Kamal Farid was appointed in 1970 by the last grand *qadi al-quda* (chief justice) of the *shari'a* courts, Shaykh Muhammad al-Gizuli. A liberal in his interpretations and in practice, Chief Justice al-Gizouli had been Sayeda Nagwa's *shari'a* law professor at the University of Khartoum. (*Sayyida* is the respectful term of address for a married woman, and is the customary honorific used when referring to a female jurist.) She was appointed shortly after her graduation in 1970 and was quickly promoted to first-class judge assigned to the High Court, where she heard cases on appeal from the lower district and provincial courts. After her appointment, other women were appointed in 1974 and 1975, including justices Amal Muhammad Hassan, Rabab Muhammad Mustafa Abu Gusaysa, and Fatima Makki al-Sayyid Ali.

Avoiding political activism, Justice Farid survived the political turmoil of the Muhammad Ja'far Numeiri presidency (1969–1985). When Islamic law was made state law in 1983, the *shari'a* and civil courts were combined into a single system of judges, courts, and appeals. When the National Islamic Front (NIF) seized power in 1989, many judges were purged for their politics, not necessarily their gender. The NIF saw itself as an Islamic modernist movement and therefore did not oppose women holding positions of power and influence; however some non-NIF women were removed. Justice Farid survived this purge and retains her position within the High Court of the Sudan Judiciary.

See also NUMEIRI, MUHAMMAD JAʿFAR; SHARIʿA; SUDAN.

Bibliography

Fluehr-Lobban, Carolyn. *Islamic Law and Society in the Sudan.* Totowa, NJ; London: Frank Cass, 1987.

CAROLYN FLUEHR-LOBBAN

FARMANFARMA, ABD AL-HOSEYN MIRZA
[1857–1939]

Persian prince and prominent politician. His other titles were Nosrat al-Dowleh and Salar Lashkar.

Abd al-Hoseyn Mirza Farmanfarma was the son of Firuz Mirza and the grandson of Abbas Mirza, who had been heir to the throne of Fath Ali Shah, the second monarch of the Qajar dynasty. His mother was Homa Khanum, daughter of Bahman Mirza Baha al-Dowleh, another son of Abbas Mirza.

Abd al-Hoseyn Mirza was educated in the military school in Tehran, run by Austrian officers. He married the daughter of the crown prince and, by his proximity to the throne, gained great influence and wealth. He was an astute and ambitious politician of great resilience in the face of adversity, which was not lacking, as Persia underwent revolution, civil war, foreign invasion, and a change of dynasty in his lifetime.

Farmanfarma first served at the court of the crown prince until he became shah in 1896. He was then made governor of Tehran and minister of war in that year. He was exiled to Iraq when the shah was said to fear him, but he was recalled in 1906 and appointed governor of Kerman, just as the first stirrings of the Constitutional Revolution were beginning. He became minister of justice, then governor of Azerbaijan. In 1909, he became minister of the interior, then of war, and, later, governor of Kermanshah.

During World War I, his sympathies were with the British in the complicated relations that developed between the government and the belligerents on the one hand and, on the other, between the government and the nationalists. In 1915, he was made minister of the interior, then prime minis-

ter. He remained in this post only a few months, then was appointed governor of Fars, which was under British control. This was his last government post. His son, Nosrat al-Dowleh, however, served the new shah, Reza Shah Pahlavi, and was executed in 1937 by a monarch grown suspicious and tyrannical. Abd al-Hoseyn Mirza died in 1939.

See also ABBAS MIRZA, NAʾEB AL-SALTANEH; PAHLAVI, REZA; QAJAR DYNASTY.

Bibliography

Sykes, Ella C. *Through Persia on a Side-Saddle.* London: A.D. Innes, 1898.

Sykes, Percy Molesworth. *Ten Thousand Miles in Persia; or, Eight Years in Iran.* London: J. Murray; New York: Scribners, 1902.

MANSOUREH ETTEHADIEH

FARMANFARMIAN, SETTAREH

Advocate for social services in Iran.

Settareh Farmanfarmian, the daughter of a wealthy *shahzade* (prince), spent her childhood during the 1920s and 1930s in a Persian harem compound in Tehran. She began her education at home, and as a young woman she traveled across Iran, India, and the Pacific to attend the University of Southern California in the United States, where she earned an advanced degree in social work.

Farmanfarmanian returned to Iran in the 1950s and in 1958 founded the Tehran School of Social Work, which she directed until 1979. It was the only independent, private school of social work in Iran. As director, she was responsible for creating social welfare agencies for fieldwork placement of the school's graduates and for supervising their work in private clinics, schools, and health centers throughout Iran. From 1954 to 1958 she served as a United Nations expert for the Middle East, in Baghdad, Iraq. She also founded the Family Planning Association of Iran.

Farmanfarmanian introduced the concept of the community welfare center and provided motivation for various laws, including juvenile court laws and the legislation on the status of women. From 1980 to 1992 she worked for the County of Los

Angeles Department of Social Services, Children's Services. She published her autobiography in 1992.

See also GENDER: GENDER AND HEALTH.

Bibliography

Farmanfarmanian, Settareh, with Munker, Mona. *Daughter of Persia: A Woman's Journey from Her Father's Harem through to the Islamic Republic.* New York: Anchor Books, 1993.

CHERIE TARAGHI

FAROUK

[1920–1965]

Egypt's last king, 1936–1952.

Farouk, the son of King Fuʾad (reigned 1922–1936) and Queen Nazli, and the grandson of Khedive Ismaʿil ibn Ibrahim (reigned 1863–1879), was born in Cairo, on 11 February 1920. Privately tutored until the age of fifteen, Farouk intended to enter a British public school. He was, however, unable to gain admission to Eton and the Royal Military College at Woolwich, but he went to England anyway to pursue his studies. At the Royal Military College he took afternoon classes as an unenrolled student. His formal education was cut short by the death of his father, King Fuʾad, on 28 April 1936. Returning to Egypt, he ascended the throne as a minor and ruled with the assistance of a Regency Council until July 1937.

Upon first coming to power, he enjoyed much local popularity. Young, handsome, and seemingly progressive, he was thought to be an ideal person to foster parliamentary democracy in Egypt. In truth, however, he engaged in the same anticonstitutional practices that had so marked his father's tenure of power. During his reign he constantly plotted against the Wafd, Egypt's majority political party, contended with Britain over monarchical privilege, and intrigued to enhance the sway of the monarchy over the Egyptian parliament. In 1937, shortly after coming to the throne, he removed the Wafd from office. The Wafd had just concluded the Anglo–Egyptian Treaty of 1936, which increased Egypt's autonomy but fell far short of realizing the long-cherished goal of complete independence.

With the onset of World War II, Farouk's clashes with the British intensified. The monarch supported a series of minority ministries, many of which were, in British eyes, insufficiently committed to the Allied war cause. Political tensions came to a head in early 1942 while Germany military forces under the command of General Erwin Rommel were advancing in the western desert toward Alexandria. The British demanded a pro-British Wafdist ministry. When Farouk delayed, the British ambassador, Miles Lampson, on 4 February 1942 surrounded Abdin Palace with tanks and compelled the monarch, under threat of forced abdication, to install the Wafd in office. That day was a defining moment in Egypt's twentieth-century history. It undermined the legitimacy of parliamentary democracy and prepared the way for the military coup of 1952.

The immediate postwar years in Egypt were full of political violence and official corruption. In 1948 the Egyptian army suffered a humiliating defeat in the Arab–Israel War as the state of Israel came into being. During this period, groups opposed to parliamentary government increased their following throughout the country, most notably the Muslim Brotherhood, the Communists, and the Socialists. Within the army an elite of idealistic, young officers organized themselves in the Free Officers movement. Increasingly, King Farouk came to symbolize all that was wrong with the old order. Outrageously wealthy, he flaunted his wealth in a country wracked by poverty. His penchant for gambling and carousing with women offended many. Learning of the growing opposition to his rule inside the military, he tried to move on his enemies before they turned on him. He did not succeed. On 23 July 1952 the Free Officers, led by Gamal Abdel Nasser, seized power. Three days later, on 26 July 1952, the new rulers exiled the king. Sailing from Alexandria harbor on the royal yacht *Mahrussa*, he was accompanied into exile by his family, gold ingots, and more than two hundred pieces of luggage. His deposition in 1952 effectively brought an end to the rule over Egypt of the family of Muhammad Ali, who had come to Egypt as a military leader in the midst of Napoléon Bonaparte's invasion and had installed himself as Egypt's ruler in 1805. Farouk's infant son, Ahmad Fuʾad, succeeded briefly to the throne, but in June 1953 Egypt abolished the monarchy and became a republic. Farouk continued to lead a dissolute life while residing in Rome. On 18 March 1965 he succumbed to a heart attack in a nightclub.

See also ARAB–ISRAEL WAR (1948); FREE OFFICERS, EGYPT; FUʾAD; ISMAʿIL IBN IBRAHIM; MUHAMMAD ALI; MUSLIM BROTHERHOOD; NASSER, GAMAL ABDEL; ROMMEL, ERWIN; WAFD.

Bibliography

Gordon, Joel. *Nasser's Blessed Movement: Egypt's Free Officers and the July Revolution.* New York: Oxford University Press, 1992.

Vatikiotis, P. J. *The History of Modern Egypt: From Muhammad Ali to Mubarak,* 4th edition. Baltimore, MD: Johns Hopkins University Press, 1991.

ROBERT L. TIGNOR

FARROKHZAD, FORUGH
[c. 1934–1967]

A leading modernist female Iranian poet.

Forugh Farrokhzad was the first woman poet in over a thousand years of Persian literature to present feminine perspectives with recognizably female speakers in lyric verse. In her 150 or so mostly short poems, composed from the mid-1950s onward, she established the female gender and voice in the Persian language.

Farrokhzad is controversial and the most translated twentieth-century Iranian poet. Frank and personal representations of feelings and views in everyday situations, both palpably Iranian and emotionally universal, characterize her verse, for which faith in art and love constitute the spiritual underpinnings.

See also LITERATURE: PERSIAN.

Bibliography

Farrokhzad, Forugh. *Bride of Acacias: Selected Poems of Forugh Farrokhzad,* translated by Jascha Kessler with Amin Banani. Delmar, NY: Caravan Books, 1982.

Hillmann, Michael C. *A Lonely Woman: Forugh Farrokhzad and Her Poetry.* Washington, DC: Three Continents Press, 1987.

MICHAEL C. HILLMANN

FASHODA INCIDENT (1898)

Crisis in which both France and Britain, vying for territory in Africa, claimed control over a Sudanese outpost.

At the end of the nineteenth century, the European powers were competing for control of Africa. As the French extended eastward from the Congo, the British expanded south from Egypt. In July 1898, a French expedition commanded by Captain Jean-Baptiste Marchand arrived at the Sudanese outpost of Fashoda on the Nile, some 400 miles (644 km) south of Khartoum. After British General Herbert Kitchener's victory at Omdurman on 2 September, he proceeded to Fashoda on orders from the British prime minister, Lord Salisbury. He arrived on 19 September and met with Marchand. Kitchener claimed the entire Nile valley for Great Britain, and, after several days, both parties withdrew peacefully. The solution to the conflicting claims was later worked out by diplomats in Britain and France, and it reflected the fact that Britain had an army in Khartoum while France had no appreciable forces in the vicinity. France renounced all rights to the Nile basin and the Sudan in return for a guarantee of its position in West Africa. The Fashoda incident is seen as the high point of Anglo–French tension in Africa.

See also KITCHENER, HORATIO HERBERT.

Bibliography

Eldridge, C. C. *Victorian Imperialism.* London: Hodder and Staughton, 1978.

Porter, Bernard. *The Lion's Share: A Short History of British Imperialism, 1850–1983,* 2d edition. London and New York: Longman, 1984.

ZACHARY KARABELL

FASI, ALLAL AL-
[1906–1973]

Moroccan nationalist politician and writer.

From a prominent Fez family of scholars of Andalusian (Spanish) origin, Allal al-Fasi was an early Moroccan nationalist, involved with the Salafiyya Movement during his education at the Qarawiyin University. In the 1920s he helped organize the Free School Movement, which established schools to educate Moroccan youths in a modernist Islam tradition rather than according to French colonial ideas, and in 1930 he led protests against the Berber Dahir. In 1934 he helped draw up the "Plan of Reforms," a manifesto that demanded radical reforms of the administration and economy of the French protectorate so that Moroccans might benefit from French rule. After his 1937 exile to Gabon, he maintained contact with the founders of the Istiqlal Party and at independence in 1956 returned to lead the party, remaining its leader after the split with the Union Nationale des Forces Populaires (UNFP; National Union of Popular Forces) in 1959. The party adopted a strongly nationalist program but was committed to a constitutional monarchical system.

After being minister of state for Islamic affairs (1961–1963), al-Fasi resigned and led the Istiqlal Party into opposition, while remaining loyal to the monarchy. He was secretary-general of the party until his death in May 1973. Al-Fasi wrote *al-Haraka al-Wataniyya fi al-Maghrib al-Arabi*, translated by Ahuzen Zaki Nuseibeh as *Independence Movements in Arab North Africa* (1954), and *al-Naqd al-Dhati* (Self criticism; 1966).

See also BERBER DAHIR; ISTIQLAL PARTY: MOROCCO; SALAFIYYA MOVEMENT; UNION NATIONALE DES FORCES POPULAIRES (UNFP).

Bibliography

Pennell, C. R. *Morocco since 1830: A History.* New York: New York University Press, 2000.

C. R. PENNELL

FASI, MUHAMMAD AL-
[1908–1991]

Moroccan academic and political leader.

Muhammad al-Fasi was educated at Qarawiyyin University in Fez and at the Sorbonne and École des Langues Orientales (School of Oriental Languages) in Paris. He taught at the Institut des Hautes Études Marocaines (Moroccan Institute of Higher Studies; 1935–1940); tutored the crown prince, later King Hassan II; and modernized the Qarawiyyin when he served as its president (1942–1944, 1947–1952). A founding member (1944) of the nationalist Hizb al-Istiqlal Party, he was held under restriction by the French authorities (1944–1947, 1952–1954). Fasi was minister of national education during the transition to independence (1955–1958). He wrote *Contes Fassis* (Tales of Fasi; 1926), *L'evolution politique et*

culturelle au Maroc (The political and cultural evolution of Morocco; 1958), and *Chants anciens des femmes au Maroc* (Ancient songs of Moroccan women; 1967).

See also HASSAN II; QARAWIYYIN, AL-.

Bibliography

Halstead, John P. *Rebirth of a Nation: The Origins and Rise of Moroccan Nationalism, 1912–1914.* Cambridge, MA: Harvard University Press, 1967.

Pennell, C. R. *Morocco since 1830: A History.* New York: New York University Press, 2000.

Waterbury, John. *Commander of the Faithful: The Moroccan Political Elite.* New York: Columbia University Press, 1970.

C. R. PENNELL

FASSIH, ISMAIL
[1935–]

Persian novelist and translator.

Ismail Fassih was born in Tehran and left Iran in 1956 to study English literature in the United States. Upon his return, he became an employee at the National Iranian Oil Company and taught at the Abadan Institute of Technology. His first novel, *Sharab-e kham* (The unripe wine; 1968), treats the life of an employee of the National Iranian Oil Company, Jalal Aryan, who is unwittingly involved in a crime mystery. Fassih's later novels continue the life of this fictitious character and his family in Tehran. In addition to his popular novels, Fassih has published a collection of short stories titled *Namadha-ye dasht-e moshavvash* (Symbols of the shimmering desert; 1990). Fassih is now retired and lives in Tehran.

See also LITERATURE: PERSIAN.

Bibliography

Moayyad, Heshmat, ed. *Stories from Iran: A Chicago Anthology, 1921–1991.* Washington, DC: Mage Publishers, 1991.

PARDIS MINUCHEHR

FATAH, AL-

Palestinian nationalist movement headed by Yasir Arafat.

The name *Fatah* has a double meaning: It is both the Arabic word for *conquest* (literally, "opening up"), used to denote the seventh-century Muslim Arab conquests of the Middle East and North Africa, and

a reversed acronym of *Harakat al-Tahrir al-Filastini* (Palestinian Liberation Movement). The full name of the group is Harakat al-Tahrir al-Watani al-Filastini (Palestinian National Liberation Movement). Although it was identified for nearly three decades with the leadership of the Palestine Liberation Organization (PLO), al-Fatah (also al-Fateh, al-Fath) existed separately and before the foundation of the PLO. It was established by a group of Palestinian exiles working in the Persian (Arabian) Gulf countries, many of whom would be its principal leaders for many years. Most important were the engineer Yasir Arafat; his friend and colleague Salah Khalaf; Khalil al-Wazir; Khalid al-Hasan, an employee of the Kuwaiti government, and his brother Hani al-Hasan; and others working in Kuwait, Qatar, Saudi Arabia, and Europe. The founders sometimes date al-Fatah's beginning to 1959, when the Kuwait group was working together and took over a magazine, *Filastinuna* (Our Palestine).

The movement has been led from the beginning by a central committee, and occasionally holds general conferences. A revolutionary council was formed early on, but gradually its power was overshadowed by the central committee. (It should not be confused with al-Fath—Revolutionary Council, the name adopted by the dissident organization of Sabri al-Banna.) It also created a military wing that operated under the name *al-Asifa* (the storm), which began military action against Israel at the end of 1964. During 1965 it continued to claim guerrilla operations, though these had little effect upon Israel. Meanwhile, in 1964, the League of Arab States, with Egyptian prodding, had created the PLO under Ahmad Shuqayri, to some extent preempting al-Fatah's constituency. After the June 1967 Arab–Israel War, Arafat and other al-Fatah leaders slipped into the West Bank (from which al-Fatah had previously launched operations) to organize resistance. Failing to successfully pull together a revolt in the newly occupied territories, Arafat and other al-Fatah leaders withdrew and established new training camps in Jordan and Syria. Al-Fatah and other Palestinian guerrilla groups were able to increase their military capabilities and training in the camps.

Al-Fatah's ideology was ill defined and not highly theoretical. Its main principles were armed struggle, "Palestine first," and noninterference in

Yasir Arafat (left), seen here with Palestine Liberation Organization (PLO) spokesman Kamal Nasser in Cairo, Egypt, in 1971, has led al-Fatah ever since about 1959, when he and other Palestinian exiles founded the movement for armed struggle against Israel. A decade later, Arafat and his al-Fatah colleagues won control of the PLO, an interconnected but distinct coalition of resistance groups. © AP/WIDE WORLD PHOTOS. REPRODUCED BY PERMISSION.

the affairs of the Arab states. Al-Fatah cadres insisted upon liberating Palestine themselves rather than waiting for the Arab states to do it, and through armed struggle rather than negotiation. This "people's war" would also give the Palestinian people an identity and a sense of empowerment. Instead of viewing the liberation of Palestine as a derivative of pan-Arab unity, al-Fatah stressed "Palestine first": The Palestinian cause could not wait any longer for Arab unity. Finally, al-Fatah sought to avoid the radical sociopolitical agendas advocated by some leftist Arab parties that sought to bring about revolution in the Arab world. Al-Fatah pledged to cooperate with both radical and conservative Arab states. All considered, this vague bourgeois nationalist agenda reflects the conservative background of al-Fatah's founders: Most were middle-class Muslims whose vision of national liberation did not include sweeping socioeconomic change in Palestinian society.

Meanwhile, al-Fatah began to undermine Shuqayri's leadership of the PLO. In December 1967 Shuqayri, who had close ties to Egypt's Gamal Abdel Nasser and therefore to Egypt's massive defeat in June 1967, resigned. In January 1968 al-Fatah convened a meeting in Cairo of most of the guerrilla groups and set up a coordinating bureau among them. On 21 March 1968, Israeli forces raided al-Fatah base at Karama in Jordan. Forewarned, the guerrillas were able to inflict relatively heavy losses on the Israeli attackers with considerable support from Jordanian troops, and Karama became a rallying cry for the Palestinian resistance. Al-Fatah's numbers and reputation swelled. During the fourth and fifth Palestine National Council (PNC) sessions in 1968 and 1969, the various guerrilla groups, including al-Fatah, won larger and roles in addition to an amendment to the Palestine National Charter to support armed struggle. At the fifth PNC in February 1969 in Cairo, al-Fatah elected Yasir Arafat the new chairman of the Executive Committee of the PLO. The following year, he was given the title commander in chief as well. Thereafter, al-Fatah gained greater control of senior PLO positions, with Arafat's close aides Salah Khalaf (known by the nom de guerre Abu Iyad), Khalil al-Wazir (Abu Jihad), Faruq Qaddumi (Abu Lutf), Khalid al-Hasan, and others taking key posts.

Since 1969 the history of al-Fatah has been intertwined with that of the PLO, though the other guerrilla movements have often been able to limit al-Fatah's freedom of action. Until after the PLO's withdrawal from Beirut in 1982, al-Fatah's positions were sometimes hard to distinguish from the PLO's, but with each successive split within the PLO (or withdrawal of various rejectionist groups from the PLO leadership), al-Fatah's role as the main pro-negotiation faction became more pronounced. Starting in the late 1970s, al-Fatah merged its al-Asifa forces within the PLO's Palestine Liberation Army.

With the outbreak of the Palestinian Intifada in Gaza and the West Bank in 1987, al-Fatah leaders inside the occupied territories became prominent in the Unified National Leadership of the Intifada. At the same time, Arafat and his al-Fatah colleagues in exile were the main force in pushing the PLO toward recognition of Israel's right to exist. Despite many predictions over the years that al-Fatah would lose control of the PLO or that Arafat, at least, would be replaced as its head, and despite the assassinations of Khalaf and al-Wazir, Arafat and the al-Fatah leadership moved the PLO toward a negotiated peace with Israel in the September 1993 Oslo Accord.

The Oslo Accord led to the emergence of the Palestinian Authority (PA), an autonomous government under the PLO's leadership. Al-Fatah-dominated leadership cadre became the leaders of the PA, as factions opposing the Oslo Accord either broke from the PLO or were unable to reverse the new course. Yet the former al-Fatah exiles, some of whom built luxurious homes in the West Bank and were involved in cronyism and corruption, were resented by West Bank al-Fatah veterans who had lived through years of Israeli occupation. The outbreak of the al-Aqsa Intifada in October 2000 led to the emergence of armed al-Fatah groups in the West Bank, the Tanzim militia and the al-Aqsa Martyrs Brigade. The latter was involved in suicide bombings and other attacks on Israelis. The divisions within al-Fatah were most acrimonious during the summer of 2003, when Arafat was locked in a bitter power struggle with his former colleague and PA prime minister, Mahmud Abbas, which he eventually won. Abbas was replaced by another veteran al-Fatah member, Ahmad Qurai (Abu Ala), who also faced a power struggle with Arafat. In February 2004, the revolutionary council met for the first time in three years to deal with al-Fatah's mounting internal strife, which included mass resignations over alleged misrule by the group's veteran leadership.

See also ABBAS, MAHMUD; ARAFAT, YASIR; BANNA, SABRI AL-; HASAN, HANI AL-; HASAN, KHALID AL-; KHALAF, SALAH; LEAGUE OF ARAB STATES; OSLO ACCORD (1993); PALESTINE NATIONAL CHARTER (1968); PALESTINE NATIONAL COUNCIL; PALESTINIAN AUTHORITY; QADDUMI, FARUQ; QURAI, AHMAD SULAYMAN; SHUQAYRI, AHMAD; WAZIR, KHALIL AL-.

Bibliography

Aburish, Said. *Arafat: From Defender to Dictator.* New York: Bloomsbury, 1999.

Cobban, Helena. *The Palestinian Liberation Organization: People, Power, and Politics.* New York: Cambridge University Press, 1984.

Iyad, Abou, with Rouleau, Eric. *My Home, My Land: A Narrative of the Palestinian Struggle.* New York: Times Books, 1981.

Khalidi, Rashid. *Under Siege: PLO Decisionmaking During the 1982 War.* New York: Columbia University Press, 1986.

MICHAEL DUNN
UPDATED BY MICHAEL R. FISCHBACH

FATAT, AL-

A clandestine Arab organization that made a significant impact on the development of Arab nationalism.

Al-Fatat was founded in 1911 by a small group of Arabs from Syria, Lebanon, and Palestine in the course of their higher studies in Paris. Initially called Jam'iyyat al-Natiqin bi al-Dhad (literally, the "society of those who speak the letter Dad," i.e., Arabic), its name was later changed to al-Jami'a al-Arabiyya al-Fatat (The Young Arab Society). The original aim of al-Fatat was the administrative independence of the Arab lands from Ottoman rule. This meant that the Arab and Turkish nationalities should remain united within the Ottoman framework, but that each should have equal rights and obligations and administer its own educational institutions. Al-Fatat moved its offices from Paris to Beirut late in 1913 and set up a branch in Damascus.

The new environment created by World War I, particularly the Turkish government's execution of prominent Arab nationalists in 1915 and 1916, made al-Fatat amend its political program and opt for the complete independence and unity of Arab lands. By enlisting Amir Faisal (Faisal I ibn Hussein) in 1915, al-Fatat put itself in direct contact with the family of Sharif Husayn ibn Ali and, through them, with the British. In 1915, al-Fatat and the Iraqi-dominated al-Ahd drew up the Damascus protocol, which expressed the Arab nationalists' readiness to join the British war effort against the Ottoman state if Britain pledged to support complete Arab independence and unity. After the war, al-Fatat shifted its attention to the principle of pan-Syrian unity. It reached the height of its political influence during

Faisal's short-lived Arab government in Damascus (1918–1920). Although al-Fatat was the backbone of Faisal's government, its founding members preferred to operate clandestinely. They used Hizb al-Istiqlal al-Arabi (Arab Independence party) as a public front for their organization. Differences over Faisal's controversial dealings with the Zionists and the French, as well as the different political priorities of the Iraqi, Palestinian, and Syrian elements that constituted al-Fatat, created serious schisms within the organization. The collapse of Faisal's government in Damascus in the summer of 1920 sealed al-Fatat's fate as a structured political organization. Many of its members, however, continued to be active in the politics of Arab nationalism in the generation after World War I.

See also AHD, AL-; ARAB NATIONALISM; FAISAL I IBN HUSSEIN; HUSAYN IBN ALI.

Bibliography

Antonius, George. *The Arab Awakening: The Story of the Arab National Movement.* London: H. Hamilton, 1938.

Khoury, Philip S. *Urban Notables and Arab Nationalism: The Politics of Damascus 1860–1920.* Cambridge, U.K., and New York: Cambridge University Press, 1983.

Muslih, Muhammad Y. *The Origins of Palestinian Nationalism.* New York: Columbia University Press, 1988.

MUHAMMAD MUSLIH

FATH ALI SHAH QAJAR
[1771–1834]

Second monarch of Persia's Qajar dynasty, 1797–1834.

Born Baba Khan, Fath Ali Shah Qajar took the name Fath Ali Shah upon his accession to the throne. He was the nephew of the first shah, Agha Mohammad Qajar, and had been designated heir apparent. In 1796, when Agha Mohammad was on his second military campaign to Georgia, Baba Khan was governor of Isfahan; news reached him that his uncle had been assassinated. His right to the throne was immediately challenged by several pretenders who had to be eliminated before he could be crowned in 1797. Fath Ali Shah's reign was marked by wars with Russia—attacks on the Caucasus principalities that had passed out of Persian suzerainty during the several years of turmoil and civil war.

The war with Russia began in 1804 and drew Persia into the European rivalries that are called the Napoleonic Wars. On one side was Britain, nervous of Russian and French designs on India; on the other was France's Napoléon Bonaparte, who was at war with Britain and Russia. The Persian forces were led by Crown Prince Abbas Mirza, who was then also governor of Azerbaijan.

Fath Ali Shah needed European aid in his war against Russia, so first he allied himself with the French, then with the British—but each time was abandoned when they changed their policies. Persia suffered a disastrous defeat in 1813 and signed the Treaty of Golestan. This treaty did not prove final, since the borders between Persia and Russia were not well defined and neither country was satisfied. War resumed in 1824, despite the unwillingness of the shah—who would not send sufficient financial help. Persia was defeated and signed the Treaty of Turkmanchai in 1828. According to this treaty, Persia ceded to Russia all the areas north of the Aras River, paid an indemnity of 5 million *tuman,* accepted other indemnity and capitulatory conditions that weakened the economy, and gave to Russian consuls judicial powers in disputes involving Russian subjects. The Treaty of Turkmanchai, in spirit if not in actuality, became the model for all the future treaties Persia (or Iran) was to conclude with other European nations.

The first premier (*sadr-e azam*) of Fath Ali Shah was Mirza Ebrahim Khan E'temad al-Dowleh, who had helped Agha Mohammad Shah gain the throne; he subsequently grew so powerful that he was feared by the shah, who put him and his family to death. The next premier was Mirza Shafi, a man of modest background. During his ministry, the bureaucracy of the Qajar dynasty and the administration of the country were developed. Iran, disrupted after the fall of the Safavids, was once again strongly centralized and expanded. The capital, Tehran, was developed and endowed with new palaces, mosques, and pleasure gardens.

During the reign of Fath Ali Shah, some attempts at modernizing the army were made to meet any foreign challenge, but none was successful. Modernization was attached to European rivalries and lost ground each time policy shifted. Because of the interest of the European nations, the shah's court was visited by many envoys who have left their accounts of its splendor and extravagance. Nevertheless, the reign of Fath Ali Shah left Persia impoverished and with less territory than he had inherited.

See also ABBAS MIRZA, NA'EB AL-SALTANEH; QAJAR, AGHA MOHAMMAD; QAJAR DYNASTY; TURKMANCHAI, TREATY OF (1828).

Bibliography

Avery, Peter. *Modern Iran.* New York: Praeger, 1965.

Curzon, George Nathaniel. *Persia and the Persian Question.* 1892. Reprint, London: Cass, 1966.

Sykes, Percy Molesworth. *A History of Persia.* 1915. London: Routledge and K. Paul, 1969.

Watson, Robert G. *A History of Persia from the Beginning of the Nineteenth Century to the Year 1858.* London: Smith, Elder, 1866.

MANSOUREH ETTEHADIEH

FATWA

Technical term for the legal judgment or learned interpretation that a qualified jurist (mufti) can give on issues pertaining to the shari'a *(Islamic law).*

Originally only a *mujtahid,* that is, a jurist satisfying a number of qualifications and trained in the techniques of *ijtihad* ("personal reasoning," the fourth source of Islamic law after the Qur'an, the Prophet Muhammad's *sunna,* and *ijma,* or consensus), was allowed to issue a legal opinion or interpretation of an established law. Later, all trained jurists were allowed to be muftis. Fatwas are nonbinding, contrary to the laws deriving from the first three sources, and the Muslim may seek another legal opinion. The fatwas of famous jurists are usually collected in books and can be used as precedents in courts of law.

Because most Muslim countries stopped following the *shari'a* during the twentieth century and adopted secular legal systems, fatwas are issued mostly on a personal basis or for political reasons. The practice of having a government-appointed mufti issue fatwas justifying government policy has been a major criticism by reformist contemporary Muslim movements. However, many of the latter often allow individuals without the requisite legal training to issue fatwas. Such edicts may be considered by their followers as binding but they are not recognized by the jurists or the rest of the Muslim community as legitimate juristic opinions.

Bibliography

Masud, Muhammad Khalid; Messick, Brinkley; and Powers, David S., eds. *Islamic Legal Interpretation: Muftis and Their Fatwas.* Cambridge, MA: Harvard University Press, 1996.

WAEL B. HALLAQ
UPDATED BY MAYSAM J. AL FARUQI

FAWWAZ, ZAYNAB
[c. 1850–1914]

Lebanese essayist, novelist, poet, and dramatist.

Zaynab Fawwaz immigrated from south Lebanon to Egypt as a young woman and became a prominent writer on gender issues in the nationalist press. Much remains mysterious about her early life: She was the daughter of a Shi'ite family of modest means from Tibnin, Jabal Amil, and as a young girl she apparently was employed or taken into the local ruling household of Ali Bey al-As'ad. She caught the attention of Ali Bey's consort, Fatima bint As'ad al-Khalil, a literate woman who taught her the rudiments of reading and writing, and perhaps more. Sources provide divergent narratives on Fawwaz's first marriage(s) and her move to Egypt. She became the protégée of newspaper publisher and litterateur Hasan Husni Pasha al-Tuwayrani, in whose newspaper, *al-Nil,* she published essays in the early 1890s while also publishing in women's journals and other periodicals. Her essays and poetry were published in *al-Rasa'il al-Zaynabiyya* (The Zaynab epistles, c. 1906); like other intellectuals of her time, she wrote across genres, publishing a massive biographical dictionary of famous women, *al-Durr al-manthur fi tabaqat rabbat al-khudur* (Scattered pearls on the generations of the mistresses of seclusion, 1894), as well as two novels, *Husn al-awaqib aw Ghada al-zahira* (Good consequences, or Ghada the radiant, 1899) and *al-Malik Kurush awwal muluk al-Fars* (King Kurush, first sovereign of the Persians, 1905), and one play, *al-Hawa wa al-wafa* (Passion and fidelity, 1893). She is considered an Arab feminist pioneer; her work is notable for emphasizing the importance of women's access to income-generating employment.

See also GENDER: GENDER AND EDUCATION.

Bibliography

Booth, Marilyn. *May Her Likes Be Multiplied: Biography and Gender Politics in Egypt.* Berkeley: University of California Press, 2001.

Fawwaz, Zaynab. "Fair and Equal Treatment," translated by Marilyn Booth. In *Opening the Gates: A Century of Arab Feminist Writing,* edited by Margot Badran and Miriam Cooke. Bloomington: Indiana University Press, 1990.

Zeidan, Joseph. *Arab Women Novelists: The Formative Years and Beyond.* Albany: State University of New York Press, 1995.

MARILYN BOOTH

FAYRUZ
[c. 1933 –]

One of the Arab world's most popular modern singers.

Fayruz (also Fairouz) was born Nuhad Haddad in Lebanon in approximately 1933. In the early 1950s, after several years of singing in Radio Lebanon's choir, she began to collaborate artistically with the brothers Asi (1923–1986) and Mansur al-Rahbani (1925–). She married the latter in 1954. The vast majority of the hundreds of songs that she sang during the first thirty years of her career were written and composed by the al-Rahbani brothers. Most of them were written for her, and the al-Rahbani brothers' folkloric musical theater extravaganzas—works such as *Jisr al-Qamar* (The moon's bridge, 1962) and *Bayya al-Khawatim* (The ring seller, 1964)—were staged at the Ba'albak Festival beginning in 1959 and eventually at a variety of venues throughout Lebanon and the Arab world.

The annual Ba'albak Festival evolved into a mixture of local and international avant-garde and folkloric acts. The al-Rahbanis' plays, which became more extravagant and operatic as the 1960s progressed, were in large part vehicles for Fayruz's talent. In light of the civil violence of 1958, these works, performed in the site's spectacular ancient Roman ruins, contributed to the effort by the country's Christian political elite to unify a diverse population cobbled together after the breakup of the Ottoman Empire at the end of World War I.

All of Fayruz and the al-Rahbani Brothers' plays were broadcast repeatedly on local television and radio. Three were made into feature films, including one by the Egyptian director Yusuf Shahin. In addition to songs from the plays, Fayruz's numerous recordings also contain tunes from her pre-theater career on radio and from her live concerts, as well as Christmas carols and liturgical hymns. In addition to songs by the al-Rahbani brothers, she also sang songs written or composed by Muhammad Abd al-Wahhab, Sa'id Aql, Tawfiq al-Basha, al-Sayyid Darwish, Juzif Harb, Jubran Khalil Jubran (also Kahlil Gibran), Zaki Nasif, Nizar Qabbani, al-Akhtal al-Saghir, and Filmun Wahba.

In an age when songs in the Egyptian dialect dominated regional markets, Fayruz and the al-Rahbani brothers were credited with popularizing a distinctly Lebanese idiom. However, at the beginning of their collaboration they often performed Latin-style dance tunes and waltzes, and much of their music depended on nonindigenous instruments, such as the piano, and non-Eastern techniques, such as harmonization.

Due to radio and to recording technologies, increased emigration, and her and her composers' use of diverse musical styles, Fayruz's fan base rapidly transcended Lebanon's borders. In addition to working for Radio Lebanon, Fayruz and the al-Rahbani brothers sang and recorded for the British Near East Radio, Radio Damascus, and Gamal Abdel Nasser's influential Voice of the Arabs. It was at the latter organization's behest in 1955 that the al-Rahbanis and Fayruz recorded the Palestinian resistance song "Raji'un" (We shall return).

After the Arab defeat in the war of June 1967, Fayruz and the al-Rahbanis's songs and musical theater works became more urban in theme and setting. What remained consistent, however, was the contrast between their theatrical representations of a unified Lebanon—usually embodied in miraculous solutions to conflict offered by Fayruz's character—and the increasing sectarian tension, which culminated in the outbreak of a protracted Lebanese civil and regional war in 1975.

Shortly after the outbreak of war, the artistic trinity fell apart with the divorce of Asi and Fayruz. During the war and since its end, Fayruz has worked extensively, albeit not exclusively, with her son Ziyad al-Rahbani (1956–). Although this collaborative effort resists simple categorization, it has been

characterized—for example, on records such as *Kifak inta?* (How are you? 1991)—by jazzy orchestration and relatively sensual lyrics. This shift has not prevented Fayruz from continuing to sing old al-Rahbani standards, many of which have been re-orchestrated, sometimes ironically, by Ziyad, such as those on the record *Ila Asi* (To Asi, 1995). Whatever the style, period, or medium, Fayruz and her voice have consistently been considered symbols of freedom and unity, not just for the Lebanese, but for all Arabs.

See also ABD AL-WAHHAB, MUHAMMAD IBN; AQL, SA'ID; ART; GENDER: GENDER AND EDUCATION; LEBANESE CIVIL WAR (1958); LEBANESE CIVIL WAR (1975–1990); LEBANON; MUSIC; QABBANI, NIZAR; THEATER.

Bibliography

Fairouz and the Rahbani Brothers. Available at <http://www.Fairouz.com>.

Fayrouz: Legend and Woman. Available at <www.fayrouz.org>.

Racy, Ali Jihad. "Legacy of a Star." In *Fayruz, Legend and Legacy*, edited by Kamal Boullata. Washington, DC: Forum for International Art and Culture, 1981.

CHRISTOPHER REED STONE

FAYSAL IBN TURKI AL SA'UD
[c. 1785–1865]

Ruler of central Arabia for more than a quarter century (1834–1838, 1843–1865).

Faysal ibn Turki Al Sa'ud was the eldest son of Turki ibn Abdullah, who was murdered in 1834. Faysal succeeded his father and soon consolidated his rule over most of the original Al Sa'ud domain. He acknowledged Abdullah ibn Rashid as overlord of the dependent emirate of Jabal Shammar in northern Najd, thus laying the foundation for the Al Rashid dynasty that would briefly eclipse the Al Sa'ud. In 1837, Egypt, which had crushed the Saudi state in 1811–1818 while acting in the name of the Ottoman sultan, again invaded central Arabia, this time to further Muhammad Ali's ambition of a Middle East empire. The next year the defeated Faysal was imprisoned in Cairo, and Khalid, son of "Sa'ud the Great" (1803–1814), ruled as an Egyptian puppet. Faysal's dramatic escape from Egypt in 1843 (probably with the connivance of Muhammad Ali's son, Abbas) led to the rapid reassertion of his rule. He overthrew Abdullah Thunayyan, who had supplanted Khalid in 1841. Faysal soon took control of Najd, the Saudi state's core, and of al-Hasa on the Persian/Arabian Gulf. To the southeast he once again asserted Saudi authority in the Buraymi Oasis area and other parts of northern Oman, but the Hijaz and its holy cities of Mecca and Medina remained beyond his reach. Throughout the second phase of his rule, Faysal was preoccupied with the rebellious Qasim area of north-central Najd and with recalcitrant tribes, especially the Ajman.

A follower of the puritanical Wahhabi Islamic reform movement, Faysal ruled in accordance with its austere dictates. His regime, however, lacked the proselytizing thrust of both the eighteenth-century creation and the twentieth-century re-creation of the Saudi realm. In a state with only a rudimentary administrative apparatus he served as imam, leader of the community of the faithful, as well as chief executive of the state and commander in chief of its military forces. At the same time, he allotted considerable power to his three eldest sons. Abdullah was administrator for the capital of Riyadh and central Najd, Sa'ud and Muhammad governed the southern and northern districts, respectively. In the rebellious Qasim district, Faysal installed his brother, Jiluwi.

Agricultural produce and livestock were taxed, as were Muslim pilgrims crossing Saudi territory. Tribute from Musqat and other territories supplemented tax revenues. Towns and tribes throughout the realm were obligated to provide quotas of men and animals when military emergencies required them. Soldiers were paid largely in the form of booty. Faysal's external relations established patterns for the future, especially in the three-way diplomatic game played with the Sublime Porte and Great Britain. Britain thwarted Faysal's designs on Muscat and Bahrain, but he and they generally cooperated on maritime issues, roughly prefiguring relations between Britain and Saudi Arabia on the Gulf littoral in the twentieth century.

At his death Faysal had regained and consolidated authority over the principal part of the Al Sa'ud patrimony. Although his sons squandered their patrimony, Faysal's long reign reestablished the rule of the Al Sa'ud in central Arabia and thus made possible the restoration under his grandson, Abd al-Aziz ibn Abd al-Rahman (Ibn Sa'ud), in the next century.

See also Abd al-Aziz ibn Sa'ud Al Sa'ud; Ajman; Hasa, al-; Hijaz; Jabal Shammar; Muhammad Ali; Najd; Sublime Porte.

Bibliography

Safran, Nadav. *Saudi Arabia: The Ceaseless Quest for Security.* Cambridge, MA: Harvard University Press, 1985.

Troeller, Gary. *The Birth of Saudi Arabia: Britain and the Rise of the House of Sa'ud.* London: F. Cass, 1976.

MALCOLM C. PECK

FAYSAL, TUJAN
[1948–]

Jordanian feminist, democracy activist, and former member of parliament.

In 1993, Tujan Faysal became the first woman ever elected to the Jordanian parliament. Born in Amman, Jordan, in 1948, Faysal grew up in the capital, attended the University of Jordan, and earned bachelor's and master's degrees in English. Although Jordanian society features a relatively small gender gap in terms of education levels and literacy, this has not translated into a similar degree of equality in political representation. Women in Jordan received the right to vote and to run for office in 1974, but no new national elections were held until the kingdom's liberalization program began in 1989.

Faysal, by then a well-known television commentator and talk-show host, registered her candidacy, running for one of the three seats reserved for the kingdom's minority Circassian community. She became the victim of a smear campaign engineered by Islamists opposed to any participation of women in Jordanian public life. These activists were especially hostile to Faysal, who was an outspoken feminist and had published a newspaper article refuting Islamist interpretations of women's rights in Islam. A mufti of the Jordanian army declared Faysal apostate, despite her devout Muslim beliefs, and Islamist activists tried to have her marriage rescinded. She was forced to stand trial, but the case was ultimately dismissed just before election day. However, the character assassination had been effective and Faysal lost the election. When she again ran for parliament in 1993, similar levels of Islamist opposition emerged, but this time Faysal was successful. From 1993 to 1997, she was the only female deputy in the lower house of parliament, the Majlis al-Nuwwab. Faysal served on the parliamentary committees on education, health, and environmental protection—important but nonetheless gendered assignments familiar to female parliamentarians and cabinet ministers in many parts of the world. She promoted the rights and opportunities of women, regardless of religion, ethnicity, or social class.

Faysal narrowly lost her reelection bid, and the 1997–2001 parliament included no women. With the exceptions of Layla Sharaf and Rima Khalaf, few women have been included in the royally appointed upper house, or in roles as cabinet ministers. But in 2003 King Abdullah II ibn Hussein issued a decree reserving a minimum of 6 seats (out of 110) in the lower house for women.

In 1997 Faysal had intended to run for office, but instead found herself on trial again. She had been arrested for sending an e-mail to the king accusing the prime minister, Ali Abu al-Raghib, of having personally benefited from a new government policy that doubled the costs of car insurance. She was sentenced to eighteen months in prison but was pardoned and released by the king after serving one month. She was banned from running in the 2003 elections for having been sentenced to prison. Nonetheless, from outside the walls of parliament, Faysal continued to campaign for women's rights and democracy in Jordan.

See also ABDULLAH II IBN HUSSEIN; CIRCASSIANS; GENDER: GENDER AND LAW; GENDER: GENDER AND POLITICS; JORDAN.

Bibliography

Amawi, Abla. "Gender and Citizenship in Jordan." In *Gender and Citizenship in the Middle East,* edited by Suad Joseph. Syracuse, NY: Syracuse University Press, 2000.

Brand, Laurie A. "Women and the State in Jordan: Inclusion or Exclusion?" In *Islam, Gender, and Social Change,* edited by Yvonne Yazbeck Haddad and John L. Esposito. New York: Oxford University Press, 1998.

Brand, Laurie A. *Women, the State, and Political Liberalization: Middle Eastern and North African Experiences.* New York: Columbia University Press, 1998.

CURTIS R. RYAN

FEDA'IYAN-E ISLAM

A small religious terrorist group active in Iran between 1945 and 1955.

Feda'iyan-e Islam (Devotees of Islam) was founded by Sayyed Mujtaba Mirlavhi, a theology student, who adopted the name Navab Safavi. His followers were mostly youngsters employed in the lower levels of the Tehran bazaar. The group interpreted the Qur'an literally, demanded a strict application of the *shari*ᶜa (Islamic law), and called for the physical elimination of the "enemies of Islam." Despite ideological affinity with the Muslim Brotherhood in Egypt, the two groups had no organizational links. The Feda'iyan-e Islam's victims included Ahmad Kasravi, the iconoclastic writer, and General Ali Razmara, Iran's prime minister in 1951. It also tried to assassinate Husayn Fatemi, Mohammad Mossadegh's foreign minister, and Hoseyn Ala, the prime minister in 1955. After the last attempt, the government destroyed the organization by executing Safavi and his three closest colleagues. Immediately after the Iranian Revolution of 1979, some members tried to revive the Feda'iyan-e Islam, but others sabotaged the attempt, arguing that there was no need to resurrect the organization. Other members, however, channeled their activities into an influential right-wing group named the Coalition of Islamic Societies. Consequently, some surviving members of the Feda'iyan can now be found in the majles, in the cabinet, in the Council of Guardians, and, most noticeably, in the Tehran Chamber of Commerce.

See also MUSLIM BROTHERHOOD.

Bibliography

Kazemi, Farhad. "The Feda'iyan-e Islam: Fanaticism, Politics, and Terror." In *From Nationalism to Revolutionary Islam,* edited by Said Amir Arjomand. Albany; State University of New York Press; London: Macmillan, 1984.

ERVAND ABRAHAMIAN

FEDA'IYAN-E KHALQ

The main Marxist guerrilla movement in contemporary Iran.

Feda'iyan-e Khalq (The People's Devotees) was created during the early 1970s by young dissidents from both the Tudeh Party and Mohammad Mossadegh's National Front who felt that their parent organizations, with their conventional political strategies, would never succeed in overthrowing the Pahlavi regime. These young activists were inspired by Mao Zedong, Ho Chi Minh, and, most important of all, Che Guevara. A few of them received guerrilla training from the Palestinians in Lebanon. Their first military exploit was to assault a gendarmerie station in the Caspian village of Siyahkal in February 1971. This attack, famous later as the Siyahkal incident, acted as a catalyst for the whole revolutionary movement in Iran. It prompted others, especially religious radicals such as the Mojahedin-e Khalq, to follow their example. Even Ayatollah Ruhollah Khomeini's disciples have admitted that Siyahkal left a "deep impression" on the Iranian population.

In the years following Siyahkal, the Feda'iyan lost all its original leaders and most of its rank and file—either in shoot-outs, under torture, or by firing squads. Most of these martyrs came from the ranks of the intelligentsia—they were teachers, engineers, and university students. By the time of the Iranian revolution, the Feda'iyan enjoyed a widespread mystique of revolutionary heroism and martyrdom, but little remained of its armed organization. This little, however, did play a part in delivering the old regime its coup de grace in the dramatic days of February 1979.

After the revolution, the Feda'iyan grew quickly to become the main Marxist organization in Iran, far outshadowing the older Tudeh Party. By early 1981, it had a nationwide structure, its Tehran rallies attracted over 100,000 participants and, with the Mojahedin, its armed cells posed a serious threat to the clerical Islamic Republic. After 1981, however, the Feda'iyan went into sharp decline in part because of a massive government repression and in part because of constant internal fragmentation. Government repression took more than 600 Feda'iyan lives. The backgrounds of these martyrs were similar to those before the revolution, with one minor variation—the new ones included many more high school students.

The main split came over how to deal with the clerical state. One faction, known as the Aksariyat (Majority), viewed the Khomeini regime as intrinsically anti-imperialist and, therefore, potentially progressive. In this respect, it followed a policy similar to the Tudeh. But the other faction, labeled the Aqalliyat (Minority), saw the regime as the executive committee of the petty bourgeoisie, and, therefore, inherently conservative and even reactionary. The two factions published newspapers with the same title of *Kar* (Work). Both, however, soon experienced their own splits over such issues as the Tudeh Party, the Mojahedin, the Iraqi war, the Kurdish revolt, and the fall of the Soviet Union. By the early 1990s, there were at least six groups in exile, each with its own newspaper, each tracing its origins to Siyahkal, and each incorporating into its formal name a variation of the term *Feda'yi*. By the early 2000s, these had withered down to two—both based in Germany.

See also MOJAHEDIN; NATIONAL FRONT, IRAN; TUDEH PARTY.

Bibliography

Behrooz, Maziar. *Rebels with a Cause: The Failure of the Left in Iran.* New York and London: I. B. Tauris, 1999.

Matin-Asgari, Afshin. *Iranian Student Opposition to the Shah.* Costa Mesa, CA: Mazda, 2002.

ERVAND ABRAHAMIAN

FEDDAN

See GLOSSARY

FELAFEL

See FOOD

FELLAGHA

See GLOSSARY

FELLAH

See GLOSSARY

FEMALE GENITAL MUTILATION

Surgical operation performed on girls in the Nile Valley, northeast Africa, and parts of West Africa

Female circumcision has been the subject of fascination, horror, and feminist agitation in the West. There is little doubt that circumcising women is linked to control of female sexuality. In the feminist literature, the term *female genital mutilation* (FGM) has tended to replace *female circumcision* as a more accurate description of the operation performed upon young African girls in the Nile Valley, northeast Africa, and parts of West Africa.

There is no reference to female circumcision in the Qurʾan, and it is only mentioned in the *hadith* where Muhammad is said to have advised the use of the *sunna* (customary) method, not to destroy or mutilate, for this is better for the man and would make the woman's face glow. The right of a woman to sexual satisfaction in marriage is upheld in Muslim interpretations. There is general agreement that female circumcision was already customary in societies where Islam spread, and that since it was not prohibited by Islam its continued practice was permitted.

The greatest prevalence of female circumcision is in the African continent—especially in northeast and eastern Africa and across the Sahel to West Africa—where it is also practiced by some Christian groups in Ethiopia and Egypt. The Islamic faith enjoins modesty and proper sexual conduct for both males and females, but as is true for other faiths originating in the Middle East, the sexual double standard demands more protection and greater monitoring of women to guard their chastity. Female circumcision is a powerful ally, but it is neither the only approach nor is it commanded by Islam. The religious scholars (*ulama*) in different Muslim countries have at different times interpreted the *shariʿa* as either being neutral to the practice (Sudan during colonial times) or in favor of female circumcision (Egypt under recent Islamist pressure). The grand shaykh of Al-Azhar University, Gad al-Haq Ali Gad al-Haq, ruled in a 1995 *fatwa* that "female circumcision is a noble practice that does honor to a woman," and that medieval scholars had ruled that both male and female circumcision is mandated by Islamic law. However, Egypt's grand mufti Sayyid Tantawi argued that circumcising women is not part of Islamic teaching and is a matter best evaluated by medical professionals.

Three different forms of circumcision are recognized: (1) clitoridectomy, or the excision of the tip of the clitoris only; (2) modified excision, or the removal of the clitoris and parts of the *labia majora* and *minora;* (3) infibulation, or excision of the clitoris and all of the *labia majora* and *minora,* leaving a smooth vulva and a small opening for the common flow of urine and menses. The latter (called Pharaonic circumcision in Sudan) is most widely practiced in Somalia and parts of East Africa. The less severe forms of the operation are more commonly found in West Africa. Female circumcision is not practiced in some of the most patriarchal of Muslim countries, such as Saudi Arabia or Afghanistan, or in Jordan, where killings of allegedly unchaste women are believed to protect family honor.

The global women's rights movement has asserted that female circumcision is in a category with other human rights violations, such as domestic abuse and honor killings. An international human rights campaign against FGM has advocated banning it, or at least some amelioration of the practice, as a violation of girls' and women's rights. The Vienna Human Rights Conference in 1993 and the Beijing International Women's Conference in 1995 passed resolutions against FGM and called for state-supported and international educational and public health campaigns to end or ameliorate the various practices associated with it.

See also CIRCUMCISION; HADITH; *SHARIʿA.*

Bibliography

Gruenbaum, Ellen. *The Female Circumcision Controversy.* Philadelphia: University of Pennsylvania Press, 2000.

Sanderson, Lilian Passmore. *Against the Mutilation of Women.* London: Ithaca Press, 1981.

Toubia, Nahid. *Female Genital Mutiliation: A Call for Global Action.* New York: Women Ink, 1995.

CAROLYN FLUEHR-LOBBAN

FERAOUN, MOULOUD
[1913–1962]

Algerian writer.

Mouloud Feraoun was born to an impoverished Kabyle family. He received a French education and a teaching degree. Feraoun's publications dealt with Kabyle life as viewed in the novels *Le fils du pauvre* (1950); *La terre et le sang* (1953); *Les chemins qui montent* (1957); and the essays, *Jours de Kabyle* (1954). Feraoun also translated the poetry of the renown Kabyle, Si Mohand. Feraoun's posthumous *Journal, 1955–1962* (1962) chronicled the Algerian war of independence. He was murdered by the colonialist Secret Army Organization (Organisation de l'Armée Secrète; OAS). Feraoun belonged to the famous "Generation of 1954" literary figures (composed also of Mohammed Dib, Yacine Kateb, Moulaoud Mammeri, and Malek Haddad).

See also ALGERIAN WAR OF INDEPENDENCE; DIB, MOHAMMED; HADDAD, MALEK; KATEB, YACINE; ORGANISATION ARMÉE SECRÈTE (OAS).

Bibliography

Feraoun, Mouloud. *Journal, 1955–1962: Reflections on the French–Algerian War*. Lincoln: University of Nebraska Press, 2000.

PHILLIP C. NAYLOR

FERIT, DAMAT MEHMET

[1853–1923]

Ottoman politician and grand vizier.

Damat Mehmet Ferit Paşa rose to prominence first by marrying the sister of future sultan Vahideddin and then by founding the Freedom and Accord Party in November 1911. As a revival of the Liberal Union Party, the Freedom and Accord Party opposed the Committee for Union and Progress government and demanded an investigation of the Ottoman defeat at Tripoli the same year.

In two terms as grand vizier in 1919 and 1920, Damat Ferit Paşa allied with Sultan Vahideddin and Allied occupiers against the emerging Kemalist national movement, obtaining *fatwas* condemning nationalist leaders to death and inciting the Kurds against Kemalist forces in eastern Anatolia. On 17 October 1920, he resigned under Allied pressure and fled to Yugoslavia. In 1921, the Ankara national assembly condemned him to death in absentia for treason. He died of natural causes on 6 October 1923, the same day the Allies evacuated Istanbul under the Treaty of Lausanne.

See also COMMITTEE FOR UNION AND PROGRESS; LAUSANNE, TREATY OF (1923).

Bibliography

Lewis, Bernard. *The Emergence of Modern Turkey*, 3d edition. New York: Oxford University Press, 2002.

Shaw, Stanford, and Shaw, Ezel Kural. *History of the Ottoman Empire and Modern Turkey*, Vol. 2: *Reform, Revolution, and Republic: The Rise of Modern Turkey, 1808–1975*. Cambridge, U.K., and New York: Cambridge University Press, 1977.

ELIZABETH THOMPSON

FERMAN

An imperial edict carrying the Ottoman sultan's tughra, *or signature.*

Fermans were regulations or communiqués issued on a wide variety of topics in response to appeals from government officials and subjects throughout the empire. They were issued after discussion by top officials at the sultan's palace, or Sublime Porte, often but not necessarily including the sultan himself. The grand vizier handled appeals of a general administrative nature, while the *defterdar* considered fiscal matters and the *kadi-asker* matters of *shariʿa*, or religious law. The sultan's *tughra* would be affixed near the top of the document, which would then be placed in a small bag and sent by courier to the appellant.

With the expansion of government and the increasingly autonomous responsibility of the grand vizier in the nineteenth century, *fermans* were replaced by *irade*, which means "the sultan's will." The *irade* was an inscription expressing the sultan's approval that was affixed at the bottom of a document drawn up by the grand vizier. Documents originating personally with the sultan were then called *hatt-i hümayun*, literally "imperial documents."

See also SUBLIME PORTE.

Bibliography

Shaw, Stanford, and Shaw, Ezel Kural. *History of the Ottoman Empire and Modern Turkey*, Vol. 2: *Reform, Revolution, and Republic: The Rise of Modern Turkey, 1808–1975*. Cambridge, U.K., and New York: Cambridge University Press, 1977.

ELIZABETH THOMPSON

FERTILE CRESCENT

Term used by historians and prehistorians to describe the ancient Near East's agricultural heartland, which produced the Neolithic revolution and the rise of the world's first civilizations.

The Fertile Crescent stretches from the Mediterranean coast north across the Syrian Desert to Mesopotamia and then south to the Persian/Arabian Gulf. Parts of Egypt, Israel, Lebanon, Syria, Iraq, and Iran are within it.

The first civilization of Sumer and the civilizations of the Bible—Assyria, Akkad, Persia, and ancient Egypt, as well as the Jewish kingdoms of Judah and Israel—all developed in the Fertile Crescent, with cities, agricultural towns and villages, and herders of domesticated sheep and goats. Both ancient Greece and Rome invaded to control the richness of the region, and the Roman Empire continued through the Islamic conquests of the 700s, its Byzantine emperors ruling from Constantinople until the Ottoman Turks conquered the capital in 1453, making it their own capital of Istanbul.

Under the Ottoman Empire, the crescent had districts or provinces *(vilayets)* and subdistricts *(sanjaks)*. After World War I, with the defeat of the Ottomans, Britain and France administered most of it under League of Nations mandates. Beginning in the 1920s, Arab leaders developed various plans for unifying it, and the Hashimites were especially eager to see it ruled by one of their amirs. After World War II, the concept of pan-Arabism was championed by Egypt's President Gamal Abdel Nasser and by the Ba'thist political parties of Iraq, Syria, and elsewhere. Today, Fertile Crescent unity is little talked about, but the Islamist political resurgence and the Organization of Petroleum Exporting Countries (OPEC) remind many that common interests and common heritage may yet serve to unite the Arab world, much of which now exists in the Fertile Crescent.

See also Hashimite House (House of Hashim); Istanbul; Nasser, Gamal Abdel; Organization of Petroleum Exporting Countries (OPEC); Pan-Arabism; Persian (Arabian) Gulf.

Bibliography

Braver, M., ed. *Atlas of the Middle East.* New York: Macmillan, 1988.

Zachary Karabell

FERTILE CRESCENT UNITY PLANS

Post–World War I plans to unify the Arab lands in Asia of the former Ottoman Empire.

After World War I, various plans, differing in source and motivation, were advanced for the unification of that area of Arab Asia known as the Fertile Crescent. This followed the dismemberment of the Ottoman Empire and the sanctioning by the League of Nations of mandates for France and Britain in 1922, to become effective in 1923, covering Mesopotamia and geohistorical or Greater Syria (which included Lebanon, Palestine, and Transjordan). The Fertile Crescent was a conceptual broad arc from Basra to Beersheba, embracing all the mandated territory; it was moderately fertile and, in addition to Arabs, included Kurds, the Druze people, Alawites, and other ethnic minorities.

Well before the collapse of the Ottoman Empire, its Arab provinces in Asia had been edging toward regional autonomy. Such separatist aspirations were submerged in the expectation of a single independent Arab state, ostensibly promised during the World War I undertakings of Britain and France. By 1919, however, the Syrian national congress urged upon the investigating U.S. King–Crane Commission the reunification of geohistorical Syria as a separate entity. (In March 1920, Faisal, eldest son of Sharif Husayn of Hijaz—who had cooperated with T. E. Lawrence [of Arabia] and British General E. H. Allenby in uniting Arab forces to take Jerusalem and Damascus—was proclaimed king of Syria by the Syrian national congress; he was deposed by the French in July 1920.) The Anglo–French repudiation of the congress's resolution and Britain's granting of the throne of Iraq to Faisal after his brief rule in Syria set in motion the first major effort—promoted by Faisal—for the unification of the crescent. Faisal recognized, however, that the sanction of Britain and France was essential. From neither was it forthcoming. France suspected the project of being inspired by Britain to undermine French influence; for Britain, maintaining the Entente Cordiale outweighed other considerations. Later, the French were to give Faisal momentary encouragement on his visit to Paris in 1931, since, following the signing of the Anglo–Iraqi Treaty of 1930, which looked forward to the termination of Britain's mandate, the French saw possible advantage in Fertile Crescent unity. The project also drew support from the Aleppine People's Party and the Syrian monarchists; but the dominant National Bloc in Damascus favored the unification of Greater Syria on its own as a republic. One permanent obstacle to Northern Arab unification, whether under Hashimite auspices or not, was the rooted objection of Ibn Saʿud, king of Saudi Arabia (1932–1953).

Faisal's final plea for British support in 1933 had received no answer before he died three months later; Nuri al-Saʿid, his prime minister, pursued the cause, but in Iraq and elsewhere, Arab nationalism, which sought the union of all Arabs, exerted a more potent appeal for political theorists, such as the Iraqi Sati al-Husari. Amir Abdullah of Transjordan, Faisal's brother, was meanwhile brooding on his grand design for the unification of Greater Syria with himself as king, while in Syria itself a quite different movement for the cohesion of the "Syrian" people, on a wider interpretation, was being canvassed by the charismatic Antun Saʿada, a Lebanese-born Christian convinced that "natural" Syria, embracing in his view the whole crescent (if not more), enjoyed a particularism owed neither to Islam nor to the Arabs but to the ethnic mix within the region's distinctive environment. The aim of the Syrian Social Nationalist Party (SSNP), which he founded, was to unify this Syrian people and defend its separatism. His appeal expectedly attracted non-Muslims; more remarkable was the number of influential Syrian Muslims who gravitated into his orbit. In 1938, after arrests by the French for inciting disorder, he fled to South America, returning to the fray in 1947. Before his departure, membership of the SSNP was alleged (improbably) to have reached 50,000. All these movements for Arab Federation, as the British authorities called it, were regarded in 1939 by London as subject to insurmountable obstacles—internal rivalries as well as French, Saudi, and Zionist opposition. London's conclusion was to let natural forces take their course.

In July 1940, Amir Abdullah formally launched his Greater Syria plan, finding some support from Syrian ethnic minorities and even from Arab tribal and army factions; but the response of the British government, preoccupied with World War II, was unfavorable. In 1941, the emergence in Iraq of the anti-British Rashid Ali al-Kayani, with the exiled mufti of Jerusalem at his side, and the encouragement of the Axis powers, led to a new call for Fertile Crescent unity; but his briefly successful coup d'état in April was suppressed by British army intervention with Jordanian support. The expected military backing of the Axis had failed to materialize.

Britain's search for a posture that might strengthen its wartime position in the Middle East led in May 1941 to British Foreign Secretary Anthony Eden declaring his nation's "full support for any scheme of [Arab] unity which commanded general approval." Britain's high commissioner in Jerusalem, Lord Samuel, prompted by his Arab adviser, George Antonius, urged active support for Fertile Crescent unity and the abolition of the artificial frontiers imposed on Greater Syria after World War I. The authorities in London remained unmoved.

In December 1942, Amir Abdullah presented a new version of his Greater Syria scheme, in which "cultural union" with Iraq would lead to confederation of the two. The response of the rival Hashimite court in Baghdad was the launching by Prime Minister Nuri al-Saʿid of his so-called Blue Book, an elaborate scheme for solving all Middle East problems, in which a reunified historic Syria would join with Iraq to form the core of an Arab league open to all—the whole scheme resting on an international guarantee. Opposition from Ibn Saʿud and Amir Abdullah was instant; and Nuri's bid for wider Arab unity was trumped in Cairo where Prime Minister Mustafa al-Nahhas announced in March 1943 his intention of consulting all Arab governments with the object of reconciling ideas on Arab unity—a ploy that gathered strength and led eighteen months later to the foundation of the Arab League on Egyptian terms. This was to forebode an end to all Fertile Crescent models, although their proponents by no means yet admitted defeat. Both Amir Abdullah and Nuri continued to propagate their respective schemes, Nuri now toying with a plan for Iraq's merger with Syria, where a number of old-guard politicians and transient strongmen gave him encouragement. Antun Sa'ada, too, returning from exile in 1947, relaunched his own Fertile Crescent vision by organizing from Syria, with undercover support from its President Husni al-Za'im, a coup in Lebanon as a starting point. Za'im betrayed him, and Sa'ada was executed in Lebanon. The zealotry of his SSNP partisans was to survive unabated and lead to a final futile coup attempt in Lebanon in 1963.

Further efforts by Iraq to revive its Fertile Crescent project in other modes were made in 1954 by Fadhil al-Jamali, the then prime minister, and again the following year by Nuri al-Sa'id on the basis of the ill-fated Baghdad Pact of 1955. Both were resisted by Syria; and the emergence of Gamal Abdel Nasser as the potent manipulator of Arab resistance to what he saw as continuing British imperialism ended any general Arab acceptance of Iraqi aspirations in the crescent. In response to Nasser's unification of Egypt and Syria in February 1958, the two Hashimite monarchies laid their jealousies aside and declared the Federal Union of Iraq and Jordan, seeking at the same time to revive the Fertile Crescent concept by detaching Syria from Nasser's embrace. Both initiatives failed, Hashimite rule in Iraq being violently overthrown in the July revolution.

Whether there was ever serious popular enthusiasm anywhere for the Fertile Crescent maneuvers of political leaders is questionable. What mostly animated vocal commoners was independence from the West; political configuration took second place. By the time independence was finally vouchsafed, national particularisms had begun to entrench themselves, as the provisions of the Arab League wisely recognized. Nonetheless, and despite the self-seeking ambitions of rival leaders, Fertile Crescent unity may be seen as a genuine cause, even if the facts made it a lost one. Its revival in the 1990s cannot be excluded in the light of such possible developments as a reconciliation between Syria and Iraq, the disintegration of Lebanon, the weakening of Hashimite control in Jordan, and the ending of superpower confrontation with its divisive effects. Nevertheless, many of the original obstacles remain.

See also Abd al-Aziz ibn Sa'ud Al Sa'ud; Abdullah I ibn Hussein; Allenby, Edmund Henry; Anglo–Iraqi Treaties; Antonius, George; Eden, Anthony; Faisal I ibn Hussein; Fertile Crescent; Hashimite House (House of Hashim); Husari, Sati al-; Jamali, Muhammad Fadhil al-; Kaylani, Rashid Ali al-; Lawrence, T. E.; League of Arab States; Nahhas, Mustafa al-; Ottoman Empire: Overview; Sa'ada, Antun; Syrian Social Nationalist Party; Za'im, Husni al-.

Bibliography

Dawn, C. E. *The Project of Greater Syria.* Ph.D. diss., Princeton University, 1948.

Hourani, Albert. *Syria and Lebanon: A Political Essay.* London: Oxford University Press, 1946.

Hussein, Abdullah ibn. *The Memoirs of King Abdullah of Transjordan,* edited by Philip P. Graves. London, 1950.

Khadduri, Majid. *Independent Iraq, 1932–58.* London: Cape, 1960.

Longrigg, Stephen Hemsley. *Iraq, 1900–1950: A Political, Social, and Economic History.* London and New York: Oxford University Press, 1953.

Longrigg, Stephen Hemsley. *Syria and Lebanon under French Mandate.* London and New York: Oxford University Press, 1958.

Said, Nuri al-. *Arab Independence and Unity.* Baghdad, 1943.

Seale, Patrick. *The Struggle for Syria: A Study of Post-war Arab Politics, 1945–1958.* New Haven, CT: Yale University Press, 1987.

Zuwiyya Yamak, Labib. *The Syrian Social Nationalist Party: An Ideological Analysis.* Cambridge, MA: Harvard University Press, 1966.

H. G. Balfour-Paul

FES, TREATY OF (1912)

Document providing for the establishment of the French protectorate over Morocco, initialed in Fez, 30 March 1912.

The signers to the Treaty of Fes (also known as the Treaty of Fez) met in Morocco—Eugene Regnault, France's representative in Tangier had negotiated the treaty with the sultan, Mulay Abd al-Hafid. In addition to clauses that accorded Spain control over the Atlantic coastal zone plus the enclaves of Melilla, Ceuta, and Ifni and that established Tangier as an international city, the treaty spoke of "a new regime" in Morocco based on those "administrative, judicial, educational, financial and military reforms which the French Government judged were necessary to introduce into the territory of Morocco." The treaty also provided for the safeguarding of the "traditional prestige of the sultan [and] the exercise of the Muslim faith."

Only a few weeks later, Abd al-Hafid was forced to abdicate by the new French colonial governor Louis-Hubert Gonzalve Lyautey—in favor of his more malleable brother Mulay Yusuf.

The signing of the treaty was the culmination of at least a half century of diplomatic maneuvering to take over Morocco by France, Britain, Spain, and Germany, with other nations including the United States standing by. Since the eighteenth century, systematic piracy and kidnapping had occurred in the Mediterranean, sponsored by corsairs and rulers of the so-called Barbary coast; European and American ships and cargoes were taken and Christian sailors and passengers sold into slavery in the Ottoman Empire and Africa. In the early nineteenth century, the almost unassailable Barbary States were subdued and opened to European concessions. The lure in Morocco became important mineral resources (mainly phosphates). Within Morocco, decades of political fragmentation had left the Alawi sultanate all the more vulnerable to European pressures. By the late nineteenth century, in fact, the rivalry between the Western nations was probably all that allowed Morocco to remain independent.

The first of several crises leading to the Treaty of Fes erupted with the signing of the Franco–British agreement of 1904 in which, in effect, France was given free rein in Morocco in exchange for its support of British imperialism in Egypt. The agreement met with opposition from Germany, which had important commercial interests in Morocco. Tensions between the three nations led to the convening of the Algeciras Conference in January 1906 and the Act of Algeciras in April of that year. The act provided for international supervision over Morocco and, specifically, for French and Spanish control over Moroccan ports, police, and commercial affairs; it sparked off acts of protest and

Representatives of France and Spain sign the Treaty of Fes, which established Morocco as a protectorate of Spain. The treaty ended many years of contention among European countries over the territory. © HULTON-DEUTSCH COLLECTION/CORBIS. REPRODUCED BY PERMISSION.

violence against Europeans and European interests within Morocco. French and Spanish troops were sent in on the pretext of preserving order, and through 1907 the French gradually extended their military presence. The reigning Moroccan ruler Abd al-Aziz was forced out of office by his brother Abd al-Hafid, who was recognized in 1909 by the French after his acceptance of the Act of Algeciras.

From 1909 to 1911, French forces in the center and west of Morocco and the Spanish in the north expanded their areas of control. In protest, Moroccan tribal forces marched on the city of Fez against Abd al-Hafid, giving the French an excuse to seize both Meknes and Fez following their defeat of the tribes. German opposition, which peaked in a symbolic show of force off the Moroccan Atlantic coast in 1911, was defused with an agreement to cede portions of French-controlled Congo to German authority. The signing of the Treaty of Fes followed shortly thereafter. Insofar as French control over Morocco was concerned, however, the treaty was only the first step in a long and difficult campaign for consolidation and colonialism. Moroccan nationalism eventually prevailed, however, when independence was declared in 1956.

See also ALAWITE DYNASTY; ALGECIRAS CONFERENCE (1906); BARBARY STATES; CORSAIRS; FEZ, MOROCCO; LYAUTEY, LOUIS-HUBERT GONZALVE; PHOSPHATES.

Bibliography

Hahn, Lorna. *North Africa: Nationalism to Nationhood.* Washington, DC: Public Affairs Press, 1960.

Pennell, C. R. *Morocco since 1830: A History.* New York: New York University Press, 2000.

MATTHEW S. GORDON

FEZ

See CLOTHING

FEZ ARAB SUMMIT

See ARAB LEAGUE SUMMITS

FEZ, MOROCCO

Historical capital of Morocco.

Fez (Arabic, *Fas*), one of four Moroccan imperial cities, was a historical capital and the economic and cultural center. It declined under the French protectorate of 1912, when Rabat became the administrative capital; after World War II, French economic interests were shifted to Casablanca. Fez's prominence is partially due to its location at the juncture of two geographical axes—an East–West route from the Atlantic coast toward Algeria and points east; and the North–South route from the Mediterranean to the Sahara. The plenitude of water from the Fez River as well as numerous nearby springs, rich resources, and productive surrounding plains has encouraged settlement.

Fez was founded in 789 (172 A.H.) on the right bank of the Fez River by Idris ibn Abdallah, who died before his town could be developed. Twenty years later, Idris's son, Idris II, founded another town, al-Aliya, on the left bank of the river. The Berber and Arab population of Fez received a vital population infusion in the early ninth century when refugees from Andalusia (now Spain) arrived in 818 and settled the right bank. Families from Kairouan (Tunisia) settled the left bank around 825. The two rival sides of the city were united under the Almoravid dynasty, which, however, made Marrakech its capital. When the Marinids (c. 1258–1465) took power, Fez became their capital and remained the center of Moroccan political life even when Mulay Isma'il made Meknes his capital and then under the French protectorate. The post–World War II shift from traditional products, leather, textiles, and handicrafts to the mining of phosphates and the export of agricultural produce lessened Fez's economic importance. It must be noted that the transshipment and trade city of Casablanca was developed by Fassi entrepreneurs who moved there with the shift of economic emphasis.

The modern city of Fez had two predecessors: Fas al-Bali, the old Arab city *(madina)* in the river valley; and Fas al-Jadid, the administrative complex built by the Marinids, which encompassed the royal palace, a military complex, the Jewish quarter *(mellah)*, and a commercial district located on hills outside the ramparts to the west. The third city, modern Fez (Nouvelle Ville), was built in European style to the southwest of Fas al-Jadid, and its suburbs stretch out into the surrounding farmland. Fez traditionally housed an array of social and ethnic forces—Berbers, Arabs, Jews, *shurafa, murabits,* artisans, merchants, notables, and the poor. These groups often disputed among themselves and with the governments in power, which often made the city of Fez an independent political entity.

The historical monuments of Fez include the shrine of Idris I, the tomb complex of Idris II, the Qarawiyyin mosque, the Andalusian mosque, the Madrasa of the Attarin, Bou Inaniya Madrasa, and the monumental gates and city ramparts. The Qarawiyyin mosque and university, established in the tenth century by the Fatimids and enlarged by the Alamoravid Sultan Ali ibn Yusuf, became a center of Islamic science and one of the earliest universities ever established. Fez also houses the Sidi Muhammad ibn Abdullah University, established in 1974. Fez's narrow streets forced builders to accent vertical facades of public structures and private dwellings. The result in Fas al-Bali is a unique pub-

The Green Mosque sits centered in the city of Fez (Fes), in North Morocco. An important center for business and industry, Fez is located on the commercial roads, which join the Atlantic Ocean and the Mediterranean Sea with the South of Sahara. Fez, the famous felt hat, is named after this native city. © KAREN HUNTT MASON/CORBIS. REPRODUCED BY PERMISSION.

lic architecture. Time and neglect have, however, taken a predictable toll. UNESCO has developed a project to renovate the rapidly decaying Fas al-Bali as an international historic site, but the project has, to date, been halted through lack of funds. Morocco's rapid population growth and the rural migration to urban centers has forced Fez's expansion into suburban residential areas and bidonvilles. According to 2002 figures, the province of Fez had a population of 1.5 million people.

Bibliography

Boulanger, Robert. *Morocco.* Paris: Hachette, 1966.

Cigar, Norman, ed. *Muhammad al-Qadiri's Nashr al Mathani: The Chronicles.* London: Oxford University Press for the British Academy, 1981.

Julien, Charles-André. *History of North Africa: Tunisia, Algeria, Morocco,* translated by John Petrie. New York: Praeger, 1970.

Le Tourneau, Roger. *Fez in the Age of the Marinides,* translated by Besse Alberta Clement. Norman: University of Oklahoma Press, 1961.

Terasse, Henri. *History of Morocco.* Casablanca, 1952.

DONNA LEE BOWEN

FEZZAN

Former province of southwest Libya, with an area of about 213,000 square miles (340,800 sq km).

Fezzan was located south of the former province of Tripolitania, which bordered it approximately along the 30th parallel. The southern part of the former province of Cyrenaica lay to the east. Fezzan had international frontiers with Algeria to the west and with Chad and Niger to the south. The region's chief town and administrative center is Sebha, largely a twentieth-century creation; most other settlements have developed around small but long-established

---

Neolithic cave paintings of giraffes found on walls in Fezzan, Libya. Paintings resembling animal life that once lived in the Sahara can still be found in this area. © ARCHIVO ICONOGRAFICO, S.A./CORBIS. REPRODUCED BY PERMISSION.

oasis villages. Fezzan is now divided into Sebha, al-Shati, Awbari, Murzuq, Ghat, and al-Jufrah; combined population (1984 census) is some 214,000.

Fezzan is characterized by a series of east-west depressions over artesian waters and oases, some extensive. Widely scattered in the surrounding desert, these oases are the only settled areas. Along the southern and southwestern borders, the land rises toward the Ahaggar and Tibesti massifs of the central Sahara.

Fezzan is approximately one-third the distance from Tripoli to Lake Chad and, historically, has been a main artery for caravans between the Mediterranean Sea and central Africa. It has always had a certain Sudanic ethnic and cultural character. Its oases have traditionally provided shade, water, camels, and dates for caravans and, in the past—despite intermittent domination by Tripoli—derived modest prosperity as transshipment centers of the northbound slave trade and the southbound traffic in manufactured goods. In the mid-nineteenth century, the Ottoman Empire imposed direct rule from

Tripoli, and the Saharan trade prospered intermittently until its terminal decline at the century's end. In the second half of the nineteenth century, Fezzan became one of several centers of the Sanusi order.

Italy invaded Libya in 1911 and in 1914 briefly occupied Fezzan's main oases. The province was reconquered by Italy in 1929 and 1930 and was designated Territorio Militare del Sud (Southern Military Territory), administered from Hon. It had by then become a social and economic backwater, cut off from most traditional trade contacts. During World War II, Free French forces advancing from Chad in 1942 and 1943 expelled the Italians and set up a military administration closely linked with Algeria and Tunisia. Fezzan became one of the three constituent provinces of the United Kingdom of Libya declared independent in December 1951.

Although the poorest and least populous of Libya's three regions, Fezzan gained a certain cachet after the 1969 revolution, because the Libyan leader, Colonel Muammar al-Qaddafi, had been educated and conceived his revolution there. Since 1969, the infrastructure has been developed and attempts made to promote agriculture with abundant newly discovered water reserves, which are also being piped to northwest Libya. Crude oil has been found in the Murzuq Basin and large quantities of iron ore in the Wadi Shati, but commercial exploitation has been slow. The region still relies on northern Libya for most of its economic and social needs.

See also QADDAFI, MUAMMAR AL-; SANUSI ORDER.

Bibliography

Ahmida, Ali Abdullatif. *The Making of Modern Libya: State Formation, Colonization, and Resistance, 1830–1932.* Albany: State University of New York Press, 1994.

Wright, John. *Libya, Chad and the Central Sahara.* Totowa, NJ: Barnes and Noble Books, 1989.

JOHN L. WRIGHT

FIDA'IYYUN

Guerrillas or commandos.

Although the Arabic term *fida'iyyun* or *fida'iyyin* ("those who sacrifice themselves") is usually associated with modern military operations, it has its roots in medieval Islamic concepts. The Hashashiyyun (Assassin) sects of Isma'ili Shi'ism, a branch of Islam, were early fighters who conducted guerrilla warfare and developed a clandestine organizational structure. More recently, various groups have referred to themselves as fida'iyyun. Examples include the Young Turk revolutionaries of the early twentieth century and Iranian groups such as the Feda'iyan-e Islam.

Since the 1960s, the term has come to refer to Palestinian guerrillas conducting sabotage, terrorism, and other military operations against Israeli, and sometimes Arab, targets. After the Arabs' defeat in the Arab–Israel War of 1967, the Palestinian commando groups took charge of the movement to liberate Palestine. The fida'iyyun first came to prominence after their participation in the defeat of Israel's troops at the battle of Karama in Jordan in 1968, despite the fact that they were vastly outnumbered. Other events, such as Jordan's civil war (1970–1971), dubbed Black September by the Palestinians, along with a series of Palestinian attacks in Israel, the Arab world, and Europe, established the fida'iyyun as actors on the international political stage.

Although most factions in the Palestine Liberation Organization (PLO) have moved away from commando activities, the term fida'iyyun is still used. Radical followers of Islamic groups such as the Islamic Resistance Movement, HAMAS, and Islamic Jihad, operating in the West Bank and the Gaza Strip, consider themselves fida'iyyun. HAMAS's military components are called the Sheikh Izz al-Din al-Qassam brigades, named after the man whom many Palestinians consider the first Palestinian guerrilla. Qassam was killed in 1935, during a battle with British forces in Palestine. In the 1990s and early 2000s, both groups conducted guerrilla operations and terrorism (including suicide bombings) against Israeli military targets and civilians in the West Bank, Gaza, and Israel, killing hundreds of Israelis.

See also BLACK SEPTEMBER; FEDA'IYAN-E ISLAM; FEDA'IYAN-E KHALQ; HAMAS; ISLAMIC JIHAD; PALESTINE LIBERATION ORGANIZATION (PLO).

Bibliography

Abu-Amr, Ziad. *Islamic Fundamentalism in the West Bank and Gaza: The Muslim Brotherhood and Islamic Jihad.* Bloomington: Indiana University Press, 1994.

Cobban, Helena. *The Palestinian Liberation Organization.* New York: Cambridge University Press, 1984.

Smith, Pamela Ann. *Palestine and the Palestinians, 1876–1983.* London: St. Martin's Press, 1984.

LAWRENCE TAL
UPDATED BY PHILIP MATTAR

FILASTIN

See NEWSPAPERS AND PRINT MEDIA: ARAB COUNTRIES

FILM

Film industry of the Middle East.

The film industry of the Middle East has flourished and prospered over the past century, producing a number of world-renowned auteurs despite internal opposition, political strife, strong government control of the industry in various Middle Eastern countries, and often a lack of decent equipment. Middle Eastern films have become some of the leading artistic influences in world cinema.

The ruling classes in Iran and Turkey early on were curious about the moving image. Moving pictures were viewed in the Turkish sultan's court soon

Iranian director Abbas Kiarostami and actress Mania Akbari attend a film screening at the Cannes Film Festival in 2002. Kiarostami, one of the country's most well-known directors, first garnered notice in the 1970s as he battled political censorship to produce skillful, thought-provoking films. © AP/WIDE WORLD PHOTOS. REPRODUCED BY PERMISSION.

A movie theatre in Baghdad. Iraq's film industry, which flourished until the country's 1958 revolution, was severely inhibited under the Baʿth Party. © PETER TURNLEY/CORBIS. REPRODUCED BY PERMISSION.

after the Lumière brothers' first public showing of a film in France, in 1895, followed by a public screening in 1897. Iran followed suit in 1900 when Mirza Ebrahim Akkas-Bashi, a photographer in the court of Mozaffar al-Din Qajar, the fifth Qajar ruler, purchased film equipment in France, shot footage, and projected it for the Iranian royal court. Film was introduced to the public shortly after with the opening of the first public cinema, only to be met with disfavor by the religious clergy. In 1931 the first Iranian feature film, *Abi o Rabi* (Abi and Rabi), was shot. In 1933 the first Persian talkie, *Dokhtar-e Lor* (The Lor girl), was also the first non-Western commercial success.

Meanwhile, in Turkey, film production was introduced during World War I and was the near-exclusive domain of the Turkish army from that period until just before the founding of the Turkish republic in 1923. The country's first features, *Pene* (The claw) and *Casus* (The spy), were made under the aegis of the Association for National Defense. In 1932 the government sought some control over the medium with the issuance of "Instructions Con-cerning the Control of Cinema." Censorship was thus institutionalized and has survived in various degrees since.

The first Arab film, *Gazelle Eye,* was shot in Tunis by a Tunisian, Shemama Chicly. In 1927 the stage actress Aziza Amir and the writer Wadad Orfy set up the first Arab Film Company in Cairo. Their first film, *Layla* (1927), made with an Egyptian producer, director, and cast, is the first Egyptian film. By the 1950s the Egyptian film industry was the most prolific in the region. The director Yusef Chahine, an innovator working in Cairo, began making films as early as 1953 and continues to this day.

By the 1950s the Middle East had many well-established film centers creating both entertainment films—especially musicals, such as Chahine's popular *Cairo Station* and others produced by Film Farsi in Iran—and more artistic, sociopolitical films highly influenced by the work of the Italian Neo-realists (such as Vittorio DeSica). The first real foray into social realism in Turkey was signaled by *Strike the Whore* (1949). In 1969 the Iranian director Daryush Mehrjui's *The Cow* critiqued the shah's modernization project through the tale of a villager and his only cow. The film was banned and not released in Iran until it won international recognition in foreign film festivals. Despite increased political censorship in Iran during the 1970s, a number of highly critical documentaries like Furugh Farokhzad's *The House Is Black,* and the works of Kamran Shirdel, Bahram Bayzai, Sohrab Shahid Saless, Parviz Kimiavi, Parviz Sayyad, Abbas Kiarostami, Amir Naderi, and Bahman Farmanara arrived on the scene.

In Turkey the military coup of May 1960 resulted in a new constitution and an era of free political and artistic expression that revitalized the film industry. Directors began to tackle the issues of women's rights, labor rights, and social injustice, and respected writers began to be drawn to script-writing. In 1974 Turkey entered the international award circuit with *The Bus.* Most recently Turkish directors, both those living in Turkey and in other countries, have been pioneers in the exploration of gender and sexuality with films like Ferzan Ozpetek's *Steam: The Turkish Bath* and Kutlug Ataman's film *Lola and Billy the Kid.*

The post-Revolutionary Iranian government placed a strong emphasis on film, initially to promote Islamic values and lifestyle. Today Iran has become one of the leading world cinemas. Despite censorship, Iran's most famous directors—Mohsen Makhmalbaf, Abbas Kiarostami, Rakshan Bani-Etemad, and Jafr Panahi—have created artistically beautiful and intellectually challenging films. They work mainly in a social realist vein, adapting elements of the French New Wave (as in the films of François Truffaut and Jean-Luc Godard) and Italian Neorealism. Collectively, they have created a genre known as the Iranian New Wave.

Arab cinema continues to gain international success. In the 1990s many Arab films reached world audiences, such as Moufida Tlatli's *Silences of the Palace,* Mohamed Khan's *The Dreams of Hind and Camilla* and *Supermarket,* Ziad Dowaitir's *West Beirut,* and Yusef Chahine's *Destiny.*

The first Israeli feature films were made in 1932–1933. After statehood in 1948, Israeli directors worked mainly in the genre of documentary films, dealing with the challenges faced by the new state. Baruch Dienar's *Tent City* dealt with the absorption of the massive number of immigrants from Europe and the Arab countries. Others examined the establishment of an army, reclamation of the desert, and kibbutz life; they depended on financing by the government, public institutions, and organizations. The earliest Israeli feature films accentuated the values of Zionism. Since the 1980s, many Israeli films have penetratingly faced the dilemmas raised by the Arab–Israel conflict.

Since the 1990s the work of a number of Palestinian directors has become internationally known. These films include Hany Abu-Assad's *Rana's Wedding,* Elia Suleiman's *Chronicle of a Disappearance* and *Divine Intervention,* and Michel Khleifi's *Wedding in Galilee.*

Bibliography

Akrami, J. "The Blighted Spring: Iranian Cinema and Politics in the 1970s." In *Film and Politics in the Third World,* edited by John D. H. Downing. New York: Praeger, 1987.

Armes, Roy. *Third World Film Making and the West.* Berkeley: University of California Press, 1987.

Dorsay, Atilla. "An Overview of Turkish Cinema from Its Origins to the Present Day." In *The Transformation of Turkish Culture: The Ataturk Legacy,* edited by Gunsel Renda and C. Max Kortepeter. Princeton, NJ: Kingston Press, 1986.

Nafcy, H. "The Development of an Islamic Cinema in Iran." In *Third World Affairs,* edited by Alta Gruahar. London: Third World Foundation for Social and Economic Studies, 1987.

Ozgucedil, Agah. "A Chronological History of the Turkish Cinema." *Turkish Review* (Winter 1988).

Schorr, Renen. "Forty Years of Film-Making." *Ariel* (1988).

Skylar, Robert. *Film: An International History of the Medium,* 2d edition. Upper Saddle River, NJ: Prentice Hall; and New York: Harry N. Abrams, 2002.

Tapper, Richard, ed. *The New Iranian Cinema: Politics, Representation, and Identity.* London and New York: I. B. Tauris, 2002.

STEPHANIE CAPPARELL
GEOFFREY WIGODER
JAMSHEED AKRAMI
HIND RASSAM CULHANE
UPDATED BY ROXANNE VARZI

FILS

See GLOSSARY

FIQH

Islamic jurisprudence.

Literally, *fiqh* means understanding; it refers to the study of the law in Islam and is usually defined in jurisprudence textbooks as the knowledge of the rights and duties whereby human beings are enabled to observe right conduct in this life and to prepare themselves for the world to come. Whereas *shariʿa* refers to the divine law itself, *fiqh* denotes the human interpretation of the divine commands; it constitutes the discipline of deriving and formulating positive law in a number of branches (*furu*), including worship (*ibadat*), contractual law (*muʿamalat*), criminal law (*taʿzir* and *hudud*), and family and personal law (*ahwal shakhsiyya*).

The discipline of *fiqh* relies on the process of interpreting positive law within a systematic body of rules and principles elaborated by the discipline of *usul al-fiqh* (principles of *fiqh*), which constitutes as such the methodology of the law. *Usul al-fiqh* identifies the legal indicators or sources from which the law can be derived: the *nass* (textual sources; the Qur'an and Sunna); *aql* or reason (expressed in *ijtihad,* individual reasoning); and *ijma,* (consensus.) The hierarchy and rules governing each of these are developed by *usul al-fiqh* along with the linguistic principles applicable in the legal criticism of the textual sources. *Usul al-fiqh* also categorizes the applicable legal norms (obligatory, recommended, permissible, reprehensible, and prohibited) and the declarative rules, as well as the principles regulating these. It defines the general legal principles that govern the goals and intent of the law *(maqasid al-shari'a),* globally referred to as *maslaha* and defined as the promotion of public interest and exclusion of harm.

Although there is general agreement among the schools of law on the main principles of *usul al-fiqh,* differences exist on the legitimacy of some legal methods or sources, as for instance *istislah,* or *maslaha mursala,* in which law can be derived without reference to textual sources. Eventually, however, restrictions were introduced to reduce the possibility of arbitrariness and to legitimize these legal procedures.

The reform movements of the eighteenth century emphasized textual sources and turned away from consensus, which was considered to be the cause for the eventual lack of development in the law. The call by some contemporary jurists for the use of unrestricted *ijtihad* to resolve modern issues has caused tension and stalled attempts at reforming Islamic law. With the adoption of secular constitutions, most Muslim countries have stopped using *fiqh* except in the matter of family law.

See also SHARI'A; SUNNA.

Bibliography

Kamali, Mohammad Hashim. *Principles of Islamic Jurisprudence.* Cambridge, U.K.: Islamic Texts Society, 1991.

MAYSAM J. AL-FARUQI

FISH AND FISHING

Fishing and fish consumption is found throughout the Middle East.

Fish is consumed locally throughout the Middle East in those areas that border bodies of water. The primary fishing sources are the Aegean Sea, the Atlantic Ocean, the Black Sea, the Caspian Sea, the Indian Ocean and the Arabian Sea, the Mediterranean Sea, the Persian Gulf and Gulf of Oman, and the Red Sea, as well as the Nile and other major rivers. Most fishing is done near the coasts or shore using small boats, although several governments have supported programs since the late 1980s to upgrade local fisheries. The only Middle East country with a major commercial fishing industry is Morocco, whose fishermen landed an average of 400,000 to 500,000 metric tons of fish annually during the 1990s. At least one-half of this catch is sardines, a fish that is canned, mainly for export. In fact, canned sardines constitute 50 percent of Morocco's food exports (primarily to the European Union) and up to 11 percent of its total overall exports in years when fish stocks are good and the annual catch high. But overfishing is a problem, as well as competition from foreign fishing vessels, especially those of Spain.

Iran and Tunisia also export small quantities of fish. Iran's main fish product export is the roe of the Caspian sturgeon, or caviar. Throughout the 1990s, the sturgeon catch annually declined due to overfishing by poachers in the Republic of Azerbaijan and Russia who were taking advantage of the lax enforcement of quotas in the aftermath of the collapse of the Soviet Union. Better sea patrols since 2000 have halted much of the poaching and helped fish stocks recover. In countries such as Oman, Turkey, and the United Arab Emirates, marine fishing contributes significantly to the local diet. In Egypt, the Nile River, rather than the nearby Mediterranean, is the major source of fish, providing two-thirds of the average annual 300,000 metric tons of fish caught in that country.

Bibliography

Food and Agriculture Organization. *The State of World Fisheries and Aquaculture.* Rome: Author, annually.

Food and Agriculture Organization. *Yearbook of Fishing Statistics.* Rome: Author, annually.

ERIC HOOGLUND

FLAPAN, SIMHA
[1911–1987]

Israeli writer and peace activist.

Simha Flapan was a writer and peace activist who emigrated from Poland during the 1930s and became national secretary of the leftist MAPAM Party and the director of its Arab Affairs department. MAPAM was the second largest party in the Knesset after the 1949 election. Flapan was one of a few Israeli writers who challenged the accepted interpretation of Israel's past. In books such as *Zionism and the Palestinians* (1979) and *The Birth of Israel: Myths and Realities* (1987), Flapan sought to challenge what he perceived to be historical myths, including that the Palestinian Arabs left their homes in 1948 on the urging of Arab leaders. In *The Birth of Israel,* Flapan wrote: "like most Israelis, I had always been under the influence of certain myths that had become accepted as historical truth" (p. 8). He concluded that it was Israeli policy in 1948 to force the Palestinians to flee. Israel saw itself as a victim of inhumane enemies, justifying unacceptable policies as policies of self-defense. Flapan was a critic of Israel's treatment of the Palestinians in the West Bank and Gaza, and he served as editor of *New Outlook,* an Israeli publication that explored paths to peace in the Middle East.

Bibliography

Flapan, Simha. *The Birth of Israel: Myths and Realities.* New York: Pantheon, 1987.

Flapan, Simha. *Zionism and the Palestinians.* New York: Barnes & Noble Books; London: Croom Helm, 1979.

ZACHARY KARABELL
UPDATED BY GREGORY MAHLER

FLY WHISK INCIDENT (1827)

Diplomatic cause célèbre of 1827 in which the Algerian ruler, Husayn Dey, struck the French consul, Pierre Deval, with a fly whisk.

The Fly Whisk Incident was caused by friction over Franco–Algerian business transactions dating from the late eighteenth century. In the 1790s, the French government customarily purchased Algerian wheat, most of it through two Jewish commercial families by the names of Busnach and Baqri. By the turn of the century, France owed these Algerian suppliers several million francs.

This debt remained outstanding at the time of Husayn's accession in 1818. It attracted his attention because both the Busnachs and the Baqris owed money to the Algerian government but insisted they could not afford to pay until they had recovered what

was owed to them by France. When the French government arranged a financial settlement in 1820 that ignored the claims put forward by successive deys since 1802, Husayn concluded that France and his Jewish debtors had colluded to keep the money from him. In a further irritant to Franco–Algerian relations, the vice-consul at Bône fortified several French trading posts in eastern Algeria in 1825, in direct contravention of existing treaties. Despite Husayn's complaints, the French government took no steps to reprimand its officials.

These tensions exploded in a meeting between Deval and Husayn on 29 April 1827. In the consul's version of the event, the session rapidly degenerated into an exchange of insults culminating with the dey striking Deval three times with his fly whisk and ordering him from the room—an accusation Husayn did not refute but justified on the basis of crude comments made by the consul about Islam and Muslims. Enraged by Deval's behavior, the dey rejected the French government's demand for an apology.

In retaliation, French warships instituted a blockade of Algiers, which Husayn countered by ordering the destruction of French trading posts in the country. The confrontation dragged on for more than two years, but the dey, backed by the Ottoman sultan and encouraged by Great Britain's consul in Algiers, refused to yield. His own corsair captains proved adept at running the blockade, which proved far more damaging to the Marseilles merchants engaged in trans-Mediterranean commerce than to Algerians. By 1828, businessmen from the south of France had begun urging the government to undertake a campaign against Algiers that would restore trade to its previous level. When the dey responded to a French invitation to send a negotiating delegation to Paris in the summer of 1829 by firing on a French vessel, the pressures on the French government to mount an expedition to Algiers peaked. With liberal deputies challenging his power, King Charles X viewed such an undertaking as a means of reasserting royal prerogatives and providing a distraction from domestic issues. The decision to invade Algeria was announced in March; the fleet sailed in May; and Algiers fell in July.

Although the need to avenge the dey's insult gave the monarchy a dramatic issue upon which it seized to rally popular support for an attack against Algeria, this contretemps was not as crucial a cause of the French invasion of Algeria as it has sometimes been portrayed. French commercial interests in North Africa and a last-ditch effort to shore up the monarchy by diverting public attention to an overseas adventure suggest that the encounter between Deval and Husayn was an excuse for, rather than the cause of, the events that followed.

See also ALGERIA: OVERVIEW; BAQRI FAMILY; BUSNACH FAMILY; CORSAIRS.

KENNETH J. PERKINS

FOOD

This entry consists of the following articles:

ASH
BAKLAVA
BOREK
BULGUR
CHELOW
COFFEE
COUSCOUS
DOLMA
FELAFEL
FUL
HUMMUS
KUFTA
MANSAF
MAZZA
MUHAMMARA
MUJADDARA
MULUKHIYYA
OLIVES
PILAF
SHASHILIK
SHAWARMA
SHISH KEBAB
TABBULA
TAHINA
TAJIN

ASH

Term for a traditional Persian stew.

Ash (thick soup) is made from different combinations of noodles, rice, vegetables, meat, and fruits,

as well as yogurt and vinegar. Usually served hot, each specific ash derives its name from its main ingredient. Persian tradition has ascribed a specific ash for different occasions; for example, ash-e posht-e pa, which marks farewell ceremonies, is cooked to shorten the duration of the sojourn. According to Islamic ritual, acts of charity alleviate illness, and these acts are also accompanied by the preparation of some type of ash for distribution among the needy.

Bibliography

Dabirsiyaqi, Mohammad. *Persian Lexicon*, Vol. 4. Tehran: 1984.

NEGUIN YAVARI

BAKLAVA

A sweet pastry found throughout the Middle East.

Baklava is made with a filling of ground almond, pistachio, or walnut mixture bound with an egg white and sugar. The nut stuffing is layered with butter and wrapped in phyllo pastry. It is soaked in sugar syrup or honey flavored with rose water. Baklava is baked in several rows on large baking trays, then cut into triangles, quadrangles, or rhomboids. Baklava comes from the Turkish word for lozenge, originally a diamond shape.

CLIFFORD A. WRIGHT

BOREK

The name of a specialty pastry of Turkish or Balkan origin, served fried or baked.

The paper-thin pastry is rolled, then filled with savory flavored meat or cheese. The most popular boreks are usually thin and long, shaped like a cigarette, or square, resembling a cushion. Boreks are best taken with cocktails or as an appetizer.

CYRUS MOSHAVER

BULGUR

Cracked hard-wheat.

Bulgur is a parched and cracked hard-wheat (Triticum durum) food product, high in nutritional value. The wheat kernels are boiled until soft and about to crack, then drained, sun-dried, and finally ground into fine or coarse particles. This process dissolves some of the vitamins and minerals in the bran; the water soaks into the endosperm, bringing the dissolved nutrients with it to the inside of the grain. Coarse bulgur is used in stews and pilaf, while fine bulgur is used in kibbeh and tabbouleh.

CLIFFORD A. WRIGHT

CHELOW

Chelow is a Persian-style steamed rice preparation.

Long-grain rice is soaked in cold water and drained. The rice is poured into boiling water and cooked for a few minutes, drained, and rinsed. The rice is then sauteed in butter and steamed in small amounts of water until done. Some cooks add saffron and yogurt.

CLIFFORD A. WRIGHT

COFFEE

A drink popular in the Middle East and worldwide.

The first mention of coffee appears to be from a tenth-century pharmacological work by the Persian physician Rhazes (Muhammad ibn Zakariyya al-Razi). The coffee bean (the seed from pods of the Coffea arabica tree) is believed to have originated in Ethiopia, traveling to Yemen by way of Arab trade routes. The Yemeni town of Maqha gave its name to a type of coffee, mocha. It had arrived in Mecca by 1511 when it was forbidden by the authorities, and by 1615 it had reached Venice. The popularity of coffee spread throughout the Islamic world, where it gave rise to the coffee houses that have enduring popularity in the Middle East and elsewhere.

Arabic or Turkish-style coffee is always prepared to order. The coffee beans are roasted in large frying pans and ground very fine. The ground coffee and water are brought to a gentle boil in small long-handled pots called rakweh. The coffee is poured into demitasse cups without handles. After the grounds have settled, the coffee is drunk without being stirred. Sugar, cardamom, orange-blossom water, rose water, or saffron may be added to the coffee

A young boy sells olives and canned goods in the market. Green and black olives are present in many Middle Eastern dishes, and olive oil is most frequently used in food preparation. © OWEN FRANKEN/CORBIS. REPRODUCED BY PERMISSION.

during the brewing process. Coffee is always served as part of social interactions in the Middle East.

CLIFFORD A. WRIGHT

COUSCOUS

A staple food of North Africa.

Couscous is the husked and crushed, but unground, semolina of hard wheat (Triticum durum), although the preparation of the same name can be made with barley, millet, sorghum, or corn. Semolina is the hard part of the grain of hard-wheat, which resists the grinding of the millstone. The word "couscous" derives from the Arabic word kaskasa, to pound small, but the word is also thought to derive from the Arabic name for the perforated earthenware steamer pot used in steaming the couscous, called a keskes in Arabic (couscousière in French). Another theory is based on onomatopoeia—from the sound of the steam rising in the couscousière. In any case, the Arabic word derives from a non-Arabic, probably Berber, word. Couscous is also the general name for all prepared dishes made from hard-wheat

Middle Eastern women prepare rice for their families. Some form of wheat or rice usually accompanies each meal. © DAVID TURNLEY/CORBIS. REPRODUCED BY PERMISSION.

grains, usually used for sweet couscous dishes, are called mesfouf.

Couscous is processed from a fine and coarse grade of semolina. The fine grain affixes to the coarse grain by sprinkling water and salt by hand (although mechanization is used for mass production). The grains are rolled and rubbed with the palms and fingers until the desired size is formed. The couscous may be dried and stored, or it may be steamed over water or broth in a couscousière. Couscous is served in a pile on a large platter with meat, chicken, or fish and vegetables and spices. It is also served in bowls as a loose stew with similar ingredients included.

CLIFFORD A. WRIGHT

DOLMA

Stuffed vegetables.

Dolma are rice, meat, herb, and spice-stuffed vegetables found especially in Turkish cuisine but common to many Middle Eastern cuisines. The most popular vegetables for stuffing are zucchini, eggplant, peppers, tomatoes, and grape leaves.

CLIFFORD A. WRIGHT

FELAFEL

Ground beans with spices, fried.

Originally an Egyptian dish, felafel is today popular in Syria, Lebanon, and Israel as well. Traditionally, it is prepared with chickpeas ground into a paste and fried in oil, which is then served in pita bread with salad. Local variations include the use of other beans. In Egypt, felafel is also known as tamiyya.

Bibliography

Der Haroutunian, Arto. *Middle Eastern Cookery.* London: 1983.

ZACHARY KARABELL

FUL

Fava-bean mash.

Ful mudammis, a mash of fava beans (the broad bean, a vetch, Vicia faba) is considered the Egypt-

or other cereals. In fact, it would not be incorrect to call couscous a kind of pasta.

Couscous is a staple food in the Maghrib (North Africa). Hard-wheat couscous was probably invented by Arabs or Berbers in the twelfth century based on techniques possibly learned from Saharan Africans. This is suggested by Ibn Battuta's description of a millet couscous he ate in Mali in 1352. One of the first written references to couscous is in an anonymous thirteenth-century Hispano-Muslim cookery book, *Kitab al-Tabikh fi al-Maghrib wa al-Andalus.*

The Berbers call this food sekrou (or seksou), while it is known as maftul or mughrabiyya in the countries of the eastern Mediterranean and suk-sukaniyya in the Sudan. In Algeria it is called tha'am or keksou. In Tunisia it is called keskesi. Very large couscous grains are called m'hammas, and very fine

ian national dish. There, it is often eaten with bread for breakfast. The peeled fava beans are soaked in water for a day, then covered with fresh water and simmered overnight with onion, some tomatoes, and red lentils, to control the color. Once the ful is cooked, it is salted and eaten plain or accompanied by olive oil, corn oil, butter, smen (clarified butter), buffalo milk, béchamel sauce, basturma (dried beef), fried eggs, tomato sauce, tahini (sesame-seed paste), or other ingredients.

CLIFFORD A. WRIGHT

HUMMUS

Middle Eastern dish of chickpeas, sesame seeds, and spices.

A staple food of Syria, hummus has become popular in Jordan and Israel as well as throughout America and Europe. It is a pureé of tahini, chickpeas, garlic, cumin, and lemon, often garnished with parsley and paprika. It is served with pita bread as an appetizer or a course unto itself.

Bibliography

Der Haroutunian, Arto. *Vegetarian Dishes from the Middle East.* London: 1983.

ZACHARY KARABELL

KUFTA

A meatball.

Kufta (also Kifta) is a ground meat, onion, parsley, and spice mixture popular in Turkey, Syria, Lebanon, Jordan, and among Palestinians. The meat is molded around a skewer and then grilled. Kufta can also be baked or braised.

CLIFFORD A. WRIGHT

MANSAF

Popular Middle Eastern lamb dish.

A bedouin dish particularly popular in Jordan and Saudi Arabia. It is a combination of lamb and yogurt served with rice. Mansaf is often prepared at festivals or in honor of guests.

Spices, dried fruits, nuts, and seeds fill the bowls in Misir Carsisi (Egyptian, or Spice Market) in Istanbul. © ROYALTY-FREE/CORBIS. REPRODUCED BY PERMISSION.

Bibliography

Der Haroutunian, Arto. *Middle Eastern Cookery.* London: 1983.

ZACHARY KARABELL

MAZZA

An assortment of foods served as appetizers, accompaniments to main dishes, or a complete meal.

A feature of Middle Eastern cuisine from Morocco to Persia, mazza is usually served with a beverage, and may be simple or elaborate. Typically, it consists of nuts, fresh vegetables and herbs, cheeses, salads and dips, savory pastries, and "miniature foods" (smaller versions of main dishes, including grilled meats, vegetable dishes, and beans).

JENAB TUTUNJI

MUHAMMARA

A Middle Eastern dip.

Made with walnuts and concentrated pomegranate juice, muhammara is seasoned with hot red pepper and cumin. It is a Syrian specialty commonly associated with the cuisine of Aleppo. It is served as an appetizer, as part of a mazza, or as a condiment with a meat dish.

JENAB TUTUNJI

MUJADDARA

A lentil and rice dish.

Mujaddara, which traces its origins to medieval times, is considered the food of the poor because the ingredients are cheap and plentiful, and it does not contain meat. It is nevertheless a great favorite and occurs in many variations throughout the Middle East.

JENAB TUTUNJI

MULUKHIYYA

Arabic name for the plant called jew's mallow, the main ingredient of a popular Arab dish by the same name.

Mulukhiyya is prepared in two ways: the Lebanese, where the leaves are left whole and are cooked with stew meat, garlic, and dried coriander; and the Egyptian style, in which the finely chopped leaves are cooked with chicken, rice, vinegar, and finely chopped onion. Eating mulukhiyya is prohibited within the Druze community.

TAYEB EL-HIBRI

OLIVES

A staple of Middle Eastern cuisine.

Olives have been cultivated since ancient times, and both olives and olive oil constitute an important part of the diet in the Middle East. Olive trees grow in nonirrigated, rain-fed areas and bear fruit for generations. Green olives are cured in brine to extract the bitter taste, whereas black olives are cured by packing them in sea salt. Olive oil, pressed from green olives, is a staple in the Mediterranean area. In Arab cuisines, it is favored for frying vegetables and fish.

JENAB TUTUNJI

PILAF

A seasoned rice preparation.

Pilaf is a Persian and Turkish word denoting a rice dish boiled with meat and vegetables, seasoned with spices. But pilaf also means a way of cooking rice—knowing exactly the water-absorption capacity of the rice. In Turkish cuisine, pilaf is usually a side dish. In Persian cuisine, pilaf (pilow) is a main dish with other ingredients added to it. Pilaf is also made with bulgur in Turkey.

CLIFFORD A. WRIGHT

SHASHLIK

Grilled lamb on a skewer.

Shashlik is a Turkish dish of marinated lamb. The marinade usually consists of onions, olive oil, and paprika. The lamb is skewered and grilled and served with scallions.

CLIFFORD A. WRIGHT

SHAWARMA

A lamb-based meatloaf sold by street vendors and in restaurants.

Shawarma is a popular Levantine Arab specialty. A combination of lean and fatty sliced or ground lamb is seasoned with onion, garlic, allspice, cinnamon, coriander, or other ingredients and molded in conical form around a large skewer that is adjusted to a vertical rotisserie. The outside becomes crusty brown as it cooks, is sliced off and wrapped in flat bread and served with chopped onions, tomatoes, and cucumber-yogurt sauce. Shawarma is also popular in Greece and Turkey where it is called gyro and döner kebab, respectively. Shawarma is sold by street vendors and restaurants but rarely made at home.

CLIFFORD A. WRIGHT

SHISH KEBAB

Meat roasted over open fires on skewers.

The origin of shish kebab is lost in antiquity, but given the swordlike skewers so common in the Middle East, it probably originated with Turkish horsemen cooking wild game over open fires. In Turkish, shish kebab means "gobbets of meat roasted on a spit or skewer"; the Arabs call it lahm mishwi, grilled lamb.

The threading of vegetables—onions, mushrooms, tomatoes, and peppers—onto the skewer, interspersed with meat, appears to be a modern restaurant introduction.

CLIFFORD A. WRIGHT

TABBULA

Salad made with bulgur (cracked wheat), chopped fresh parsley, scallions, mint, and tomatoes, and dressed with salt, pepper, olive oil, and lemon.

Since tabbula is always made with fresh, in-season vegetables, it is commonly served as part of mazza during the summer or is eaten with fresh lettuce, cabbage, or vine leaves. Although the Lebanese are credited with perfecting the most popular version of tabbula, the idea for incorporating bulgur in a salad may have originated with the Turks.

JENAB TUTUNJI

TAHINA

Sesame seed paste.

One of the basic ingredients of Middle Eastern food, tahina is an oily paste made from crushed sesame seeds. It is used in a variety of foods such as hummus and babaghanush as well as on its own as a condiment. Tahina is also popular in Israel.

Bibliography

Der Haroutunian, Arto. *Vegetarian Dishes from the Middle East.* London, 1983.

ZACHARY KARABELL

TAJIN

Moroccan earthenware casserole pot; Tunisian stuffed omelette.

Tajin is the name of an earthenware casserole with a conical top lid used in Morocco to make a variety of stews known by the same name. Meat and vegetables are simmered for a long time until the meat is soft and the stew aromatic. Touajen (plural of

A young boy balances a tray of simit bread on his head. This delicious bagel-like bread is coated with sesame seeds. © OWEN FRANKEN/CORBIS. REPRODUCED BY PERMISSION.

tajin) are flavored with cumin, harissa, coriander, caraway, paprika, and other spices.

In Tunisia, a tajin is an entirely different dish, a variety of stuffed omelette similar to the Spanish (but not the Mexican) tortilla.

CLIFFORD A. WRIGHT

FOREIGN OFFICE, GREAT BRITAIN

The Foreign Office leads the conduct of British international relations.

Occupying a palatial building in London since the mid-nineteenth century, the Foreign Office is linked with the world by modern communications technologies. The Foreign Office is led by a British politician whose power depends on the prime minister, cabinet, and party. The foreign secretary relies on the information and advice he receives from the permanent undersecretary and his staff. The foreign secretary must sell British policy to parliament and the media at home as well as to diverse regimes and public opinions abroad.

Foreign policy has pivoted less upon events and relations in the Middle East and North Africa than upon maintaining Britain's ties to the great powers of Europe and, since World War II, the United States. As foreign secretary and prime minister for over two decades, from the 1830s to the 1860s, Lord Palmerston (Henry John Temple) saw the Ottoman and Qajar Empires as buffers against the Asiatic expansion of Russia, while the defense of India concerned him less than maintaining the balance of power in Europe. Benjamin Disraeli backed the "good ol' Turk" but increased the British presence in the eastern Mediterranean, particularly at the Suez Canal. To counter Germany, Edward Grey's concessions to France in North Africa and Russia in Persia alienated the Young Turks, who joined Germany in World War I. A. J. Balfour's declaration to the Zionists late in 1917 put the Jews of America, Europe, and Russia before the Arabs of the Middle East. George Nathaniel Curzon limited his Middle Eastern ambitions because of diplomatic pressures and Turkish nationalism. Anthony Eden, the only foreign secretary trained as an Orientalist, relied on Arab collaborative regimes before and during World War II, after which Ernest Bevin tried to put people before pashas. Since the Suez Crisis in 1956, when Britain's secret alliance with France and Israel against Egypt's Gamal Abdel Nasser infuriated the United States, the British Foreign Office has mostly followed the U.S. lead in the Middle East and North Africa.

See also BALFOUR DECLARATION (1917); BEVIN, ERNEST; EDEN, ANTHONY; PALMERSTON, LORD HENRY JOHN TEMPLE.

Bibliography

Yapp, M. E. *The Making of the Modern Near East, 1792–1923.* New York; London: Longman, 1987.

Yapp, M. E. *The Near East since the First World War: A History to 1995.* New York; London: Longman, 1996.

ROGER ADELSON

FORQAN

A secret religious group responsible for the deaths in early 1979 of a number of prominent figures in the Islamic Republic of Iran.

This group took its name from its journal *Forqan* (Sacred Book), published intermittently from 1977 until 1979. Describing itself as the "true followers" of the Qurʾan and Ali Shariʿati, Forqan called for an "Islam without mollahs" and denounced the regime of Ayatollah Ruhollah Khomeini as a reactionary and clerical dictatorship that had betrayed the principles of egalitarian Islam. The group's leaders, former seminary students, also denounced liberals, such as Premier Mahdi Bazargan, as "bazaar intellectuals." In addition to being a radical and anticlerical group, Forqan was also highly antileftist, denouncing Marxism as an international atheistic conspiracy that was engaged in scheming to dominate the Muslim world. A series of executions in mid-1979 decimated the group.

ERVAND ABRAHAMIAN

FORUGHI, MIRZA MOHAMMAD ALI KHAN ZAKA AL-MOLK
[1877–1942]

Iranian politician.

Mirza Mohammad Ali Khan Zaka al-Molk Forughi was the son of Mirza Mohammad Hoseyn Khan Zaka al-Molk. Mirza Mohammad Ali Khan inherited the title Zaka al-Molk from his father upon the latter's death in 1908. Originally Iraqi Jews, his family had migrated to Iran and settled in the old quarter of Isfahan. He was elected to the parliament several times, and in 1911 was appointed minister of finance, then head of the supreme court. In 1915, he was named minister of justice and after that served four times as prime minister, finally resigning in 1935. His last appointment as minister of court came in 1942, the same year that he died.

See also ISFAHAN.

NEGUIN YAVARI

FORUM

See NEWSPAPERS AND PRINT MEDIA: TURKEY

FOUCAULD, CHARLES EUGÈNE DE
[1858–1916]

French soldier, explorer, and ascetic.

Born in Strasbourg, France, to a famous aristocratic family, Charles Eugène de Foucauld was a graduate of Saint-Cyr (1876) who led a frivolous life until his assignment to North Africa. Fascinated by the Maghrib (North Africa), Foucauld left his army career and explored Morocco and the Sahara disguised as the servant of a rabbi. This resulted in his book titled *Reconnaissance au Maroc, 1883–84.* Foucauld gained a deep appreciation of Islam, asceticism, and spirituality, which led to his entering a Trappist monastery (Christian) to begin a life of contemplation. He later left the Trappists but was ordained a priest in 1901.

Returning to North Africa, Foucauld set up a hermitage in Béni Abbès, Algeria, and in 1905 moved to what became his famous retreat at Assekrem in the desolate Ahaggar (Hoggar) mountains near Tamanrasset. While he failed to convert Twareg tribesmen to Christianity, he produced a significant ethnographic contribution—a dictionary of their language, Tamahak. Although respected by neighboring Twareg, marauders murdered the priest who had pursued an inspiring spiritual mission while symbolizing a French presence in the deep Sahara.

See also TWAREG.

Bibliography

Porch, Douglas. *The Conquest of the Sahara.* New York: Knopf, 1984.

PHILLIP C. NAYLOR

FOURTH SHORE, THE

Italy's Fourth Shore (Quarta Sponda) became a key element in the propaganda of Italy's colonialist opinion formers at the start of twentieth century.

The term *Fourth Shore* implied that Italy needed an overseas colonial extension along the North African Mediterranean that would partner its other three—the Adriatic, Tyrrhenian, and Sicilian. It also reflected the growing concern in Italy, in the wake of the Risorgimento of the 1860s, to re-create the splendor of the classical Roman Empire, with Libya as its jewel (after Italy was prevented from annexing Tunisia by France's occupation of that country in 1881).

Once Libya had been conquered—officially by January 1932—Mussolini's Fascist policy toward Libya put the concepts of the Fourth Shore into practice. Libya's supposed agricultural potential was to be realized by the immigration of Italy's excess peasant population from the *mezzogiorno* (the South). After an effective infrastructure would be created, Libya was to become an extension of the Italian mainland itself. This would guarantee Italy's strategic security and make it into a power in North Africa, alongside France and Spain.

Fascist ideology promoted individual family farm units through state-sponsored schemes. Libyans were to become economic collaborators and coparticipants in this process; they were to be transformed into Muslim Italians, as Italy, after 1937, sought to become "Protector of Islam," in Mussolini's words.

See also ITALY IN THE MIDDLE EAST.

Bibliography

Segrè, Claudio G. *Fourth Shore: The Italian Colonization of Libya.* Chicago: University of Chicago Press, 1974.

GEORGE JOFFE

FRANCE AND THE MIDDLE EAST

The centuries-old relations between the French and the peoples of the Middle East have been replete with confrontations and contradictions.

Constituents of a Mediterranean world encompassing the Mashriq and the Maghrib, the geographic proximity of the French and the peoples of the Middle East has helped sustain both their affinities and their animosities. In war as in peace, they have had to deal with the problems, as well as the opportunities, of economic life. Some of the ambiguous features of their relationship have derived from their collective links to frequently discordant Greco-Roman, biblical, and Islamic traditions and to no less problematic modern ideologies of social change and nation building. In whatever combination of identities—whether religious, as, for example, Roman Catholic on the one hand, and Muslim, Eastern Christian, or Jewish on the other, or secular, as, for example, French on the one hand, and

French soldiers on a ship set for Gallipoli (ca. 1914) to participate in the Allies' disastrous military campaign—the battle between Allied and Turkish forces for access to the Sea of Marmora at the Gallipoli Peninsula. © HULTON-DEUTSCH COLLECTION/CORBIS. REPRODUCED BY PERMISSION.

Ottoman, Turkish, Arab, or Israeli on the other—their encounters have been marked by a bittersweet interaction of words and deeds. Negative images of the "other" have been more often in evidence, particularly on the part of the French, than mutual displays of consideration or acknowledgements of collective achievement.

France's contentious presence in the modern Middle East was shaped in part by distinctive percolations of change among the Western powers. The forces of modernity, which advantaged the West before other parts of the world, enabled the French, as one of Europe's great powers, to exercise an intrusive, frequently aggressive imperialist presence in various parts of the Middle East from Syria to Morocco. France itself, however, suffered from constraining imbalances in the modern reconfigurations of power that left it at a disadvantage when confronting rival intrusive presences in the region—Britain's for much of the period, Germany's before and during the two world wars, and that of the United States during and after World War II.

The history of France's involvement with the peoples of the Middle East was also determined by

the different ways in which they responded to the challenges of modernization. In some cases, the peoples of the Middle East sought to remove the intrusive features of French influence, as was the case with the Ottoman Empire and Turkey by 1923 and with Egypt by 1956; in others, they sought to secure their independence from French occupation, as in Syria and Lebanon by 1945–1946, in the North African states of Tunisia and Morocco by 1956, and in Algeria by 1962. Their national movements and modernizing administrative polities were shaped by internally developed and externally induced changes. The character of French relations with the relatively unconstrained nineteenth-century Ottoman reformers and their twentieth-century Turkish successors thus differed significantly from their relations with the more dependent mid-nineteenth-century viceroys of Egypt. These, in turn, differed from France's relations with the disfranchised Arab politicians of French-mandated Syria during the 1920s and 1930s and with Algeria's revolutionary leaders struggling for independence in the 1950s and early 1960s.

French Entry into the Middle East

Antithetical undercurrents were never far below the surface in the modern history of Franco–Middle Eastern relations. While the Franks of the Middle Ages had vigorously embraced Europe's Roman Catholic Crusades against the Muslims, sixteenth-century France recognized the strategic usefulness of friendly relations with the Ottomans as a counterweight to the Hapsburgs. The French subsequently developed a commercial preeminence in the Mediterranean over much of the seventeenth and eighteenth centuries as the Ottomans were increasingly drawn into the European-dominated world economy. Expatriate French merchant communities in the Mashriq, the region they called the Levant, traded under the umbrella of the capitulations, France having been among the first to enjoy this Ottoman assignment of extraterritorial juridical status to resident foreigners. Yet, the French offset the Muslim policy that had brought them closer to former enemies with a preclusive Roman Catholic policy that harnessed their good relations with the Ottomans to the development of a religious protectorate in the empire, favoring the work of proselytizing Roman Catholic missionaries. By the nineteenth century, the most important corollary to this policy

A French military convoy moves through a street in Algiers, the capital of Algeria. © MARC GARANGER/CORBIS. REPRODUCED BY PERMISSION.

had become their informal, but nevertheless real, support for the political autonomy of the Roman Catholic community of Maronites in Ottoman Lebanon.

The Ottomans, for their part, had assigned less importance to these contacts with France until the eighteenth century when modernizing changes began to attract the interest of reformers concerned with the fate of the receding empire. Sultan Selim III, the beginning of whose reign in 1789 coincided with the outbreak of the French Revolution, did not allow the problem of regicide in Europe to distract him unduly from applying, with the help of French advisers, the lessons of the French military sciences to some of the reforms he attempted to introduce. The sultan's friendship with the French, however, failed to prevent Napoléon Bonaparte from trying in 1798 to gain an advantage in Europe's revolutionary wars by means of a grandiose and abortive scheme pegged to the occupation of the Ottoman

province of Egypt, which came to be considered a strategic key to hegemony in the East. In the same vein, by the time the occupation ended in 1802, France had alienated the Egyptians. Their experience was such that French administration, development projects, and scientific advances did not outweigh the adverse effects of the military invasion, or of the political opportunism, cultural arrogance, and colonial aims underlying the occupation. This proved to be an early example of the kind of power relationship that undermined French claims to the exercise of a civilizing mission.

The antithetical features of French interaction with the peoples of the Middle East remained generally pervasive. On the one hand, the history of France's contribution to the betterment of the human condition ensured that accounts of its progressive ideas and sociopolitical experiences received frequent and attentive hearings in the debates on reform that engaged the leading Middle Eastern advocates of change, to many of whom French became a second language. On the other hand, France's imperial interests frequently ran counter to reforms based on the very principles to which the French so eloquently laid claim. The French were not above combining sound investments in Middle Eastern economies with political support for speculative cupidity. As self-interested players in the so-called nineteenth-century Eastern Question, they not only helped to petrify the extraterritorial privileges they enjoyed, and to encourage continued foreign administration of the public debts in which they had invested, but they also participated in the consolidation of imperial spheres of influence in the Middle East.

British Influence on French Policy

The history of French influence in the Middle East was further complicated by unrelenting Anglo–French rivalries. Britain's industrial advantages, combined with the naval superiority it had acquired in the Mediterranean during the Revolutionary and Napoleonic wars, limited France's strategic options and commercial opportunities. Overtaken by Britain at the Sublime Porte, the French tried to refocus their interest during the 1820s and 1830s on links with Muhammad Ali Pasha, the independent-minded and expansionist Ottoman governor of Egypt. They were unwilling, however, to risk a European conflagration by coming to the pasha's assistance in 1840, when Britain and the concert of Europe curtailed his power during the second Syrian war. They reconciled themselves instead to falling back for influence in the Levant on their links with the Maronites of Mount Lebanon, who continued to respond best, though to a narrowly focused Roman Catholic policy. During the nearly two decades of Napoléon III's second empire, and in the aftermath of France's participation in the Crimean War on the side of the Ottomans, French influence among the Maronites equaled that of Britain. During this period the two powers cooperated in an imaginative resolution to the civil strife that had broken out in Lebanon in 1860. In Egypt, France even won an advantage at this time by working for the construction of the Suez Canal. Thereafter, however, three debilitating wars with Germany between 1870 and 1945 left the French at a lasting disadvantage. They had their eyes firmly fixed across the Rhine in 1882 when they failed to act with the British in Egypt, thereby forfeiting to Britain the base from which it was better able to develop its lead.

The French, having once more returned to reinforcing their links with the Maronites after 1870, were subsequently able to use Mount Lebanon as a stepping-stone to a sphere of influence in the Ottoman Empire's Syrian regions. Nevertheless, they secured only a Pyrrhic victory there in the aftermath of World War I and the defeat of the Ottoman Empire. For one thing, partitioning the empire ran counter to the not inconsiderable capital investments they had made during the later part of the nineteenth century in its overall development. For another, their Roman Catholic policy limited the influence they were able to exercise in Syria and Lebanon over Muslim and non-Roman Catholic Christian constituencies upon whose acquiescence they were dependent. Franco–British alliances in the two world wars did not substantially affect this unfavorable equation. After World War I, Britain limited the imperial expansion of the French to the Lebanese and Syrian mandates, denying them the role in Palestine and the Mosul region that they had been led to expect from the Sykes–Picot Agreement of 1916. By the end of World War II, Britain, backed by the United States, which was even less tolerant of French imperial claims, helped the Lebanese and the Syrians to exclude France altogether from the Levant.

Waning French Influence in the Twentieth Century

In the aftermath of the war, the French were peripherally involved in the question of Palestine and the Zionists as this problem developed into the Arab–Israel conflict that more directly affected Britain and the United States. Frequently criticized for their failings in the Middle East, the French rarely denied themselves the opportunity to embarrass their "allies" by taking the high ground in their assessments of the problem. French involvement with Zionism, however, reflected their ambiguous relationship to the Jew as "other." This relationship had traversed the spectrum from the offer of assimilation and French citizenship at the time of the French Revolution, to threats of rejection in the turn-of-the-century Dreyfus Affair, to denial of protection against Nazi Germany by Vichy France during World War II. French opportunism, how-

Napoleon Bonaparte (1769–1821) offers pardon to the leaders of the resisting Arabs in Cairo, Egypt, during the Egyptian Campaign. © BETTMANN/CORBIS. REPRODUCED BY PERMISSION.

ever, was such that France secretly armed and courted Israel for assistance when, for the last time, it joined Britain as a principal actor in the Middle East in the ill-conceived Suez expedition of 1956, a century after the two had concluded the Crimean War as equal partners. Together they made a futile attempt not only to turn the clock back and humiliate Egypt's president Gamal Abdel Nasser, the symbol of changes in an Arab world they could no longer control, but also to belie the lesser roles assigned them in the new global superpower rivalries of the cold war.

The French had embraced the Suez adventure primarily in the hope of stemming the tide of Arab independence, which had surfaced with revolutionary ardor in 1954 in Algeria, their only remaining North African possession. Their occupation of that

region of the Maghrib had begun in 1830 when an opportunist French government swept away the autonomous Ottoman administration of the city of Algiers, whose tradition of privateering had alienated what was then international opinion, and with whom commercial cupidity had brought the French in dispute. Sometime after they completed the conquest of Algeria, a combination of imperialist pressures and the nineteenth-century scramble for African territories encouraged the French to flank it with a protectorate over Tunisia in 1881 and another over Morocco in 1912.

Collapse of French Imperialism and Its Aftermath

France's more pervasive domination of North Africa, and the colonization that accompanied it, particularly in Algeria, meant that the French encounter with the peoples of the Middle East was more deeply experienced in the Maghrib than in the Levant. The conquest of the Algerian interior spanned four decades of intermittent campaigning against the resistance of its Muslim Arab and Berber inhabitants. They underwent a more painful and less rewarding experience than that of the Egyptians earlier in the century. The extensive destabilization of their traditional societies eased the way for colonists who were as repressive of the rights of the indigenous majority as they were determined to safeguard their own exclusive rights as French citizens by attaching the most productive region of Algeria to metropolitan France. Always active in French politics, the colons resisted a number of imaginative projects that might have helped them build up a working relationship with their Arab and Berber neighbors. Not surprisingly, after Charles de Gaulle's Fifth Republic wound up the Algerian War in 1962, the whole colon community beat a headlong retreat to France.

The idea of carrying on a bilingual cultural dialogue to find ways of accommodating Islamic and French sociopolitical conduct was more welcome to Tunisian and Moroccan reformers, both before and after the French occupation. They were attracted to accommodation as a way of both assimilating modernizing changes on their own terms and equipping themselves to deal with the French in their midst. The antithetical features of French influence were such, though, that the latter, belittling the validity of compromises with the "other," were generally reluctant to make the necessary concessions in terms of either association or assimilation. The differences between what the French imperialists practiced and what France's social conscience preached did little to smooth the way for modernizing changes in the Maghrib and France; rather, they overburdened the process. In order to move forward and to overcome the impeding French presence, the North Africans pursued costly struggles for independence, while France only recognized their independence in the 1950s and early 1960s after suffering the consequences of its own failures, first in the Indo–Chinese War and then in the Algerian War.

French influence and the problems of working out an accommodation with the "other" did not disappear with the demise of the French empire in the Middle East and North Africa. France and the peoples of these regions continue as long-standing neighbors in the coalescing global village of the twenty-first century, where the management of changes has become an even greater challenge, and where socioeconomic and political developments have a more immediate ripple effect. France's cultural and socioeconomic experiences have been directed toward European union, while those of the Middle East and North Africa have been directed toward revolution, dictatorship, reexamination of fundamental beliefs, and, in the case of Lebanon, which has been overcome by the magnitude of the problems facing it, civil war. In a world of permeable frontiers, differences in the felicity of these two experiences have resulted in the reverse flow of a substantial number of Middle Eastern and North African immigrants to France. Their communal presence there—the result of France's encounter with the people of those regions—has brought home to French society, as never before, the problem of accommodating the "other," a challenge that has been carried over to twenty-first-century France, as much as the problem of reconciling French-inspired changes to their own traditions has been carried over to the twenty-first-century Middle East and North Africa.

See also ALGERIAN WAR OF INDEPENDENCE; BONAPARTE, NAPOLÉON; CAPITULATIONS; COLONS; CRIMEAN WAR; DE GAULLE, CHARLES; DREYFUS AFFAIR; EASTERN QUESTION; MAGHRIB; MARONITES; MUHAMMAD ALI; NASSER, GAMAL ABDEL; SELIM III; SUBLIME PORTE; SYKES–PICOT AGREEMENT (1916).

Bibliography

Horne, Alistair. *A Savage War of Peace: Algeria 1954–1962,* revised edition. New York: Penguin, 1987.

Khoury, Philip S. *Syria and the French Mandate: The Politics of Arab Nationalism, 1920–1945.* Princeton, NJ: Princeton University Press, 1987.

Landes, David. *Bankers and Pashas: International Finance and Economic Imperialism in Egypt.* London: Heinemann, 1958.

Moreh, Shmuel, tr. *Napoléon in Egypt: Al-Jabarti's Chronicle of the First Seven Months of the French Occupation, 1798.* Princeton, NJ: M. Wiener, 1993.

Ruedy, John. *Modern Algeria: The Origins and Development of a Nation.* Bloomington: Indiana University Press, 1992.

Spagnolo, John P. *France and Ottoman Lebanon, 1861–1914.* London: Ithaca Press for the Middle East Centre, St. Antony's College Oxford, 1977.

JOHN P. SPAGNOLO

FRANCO–TUNISIAN CONVENTIONS

Agreements in which France stipulated the nature of autonomy it was granting Tunisia.

Spurred by the Neo-Destour Party of Habib Bourguiba, the Tunisian independence movement gathered steam in the early 1950s. After initial resistance, the French finally conceded Tunisia's right to autonomy in July 1954 when Premier Pierre Mendès-France made a historic announcement to that effect in Carthage, Tunisia. Toward the end of that year, Bourguiba was released from prison and entered into negotiations with the French. On 3 June 1955 the Franco–Tunisian Conventions were signed between Bourguiba and the French, stipulating the nature of Tunisian autonomy. Bourguiba's opponents, however, most notably Salah Ben Yousouf, denounced the conventions for not granting independence to Tunisia. Though the Neo-Destour-controlled Congress endorsed the conventions, when France announced its intent to allow Morocco to become independent in the November 1955 Declaration of La Celle St. Cloud, the conventions came under renewed fire in Tunisia. After considerable pressure, France conceded, and Tunisia became independent in March 1956.

See also BEN YOUSOUF, SALAH; BOURGUIBA, HABIB; DECLARATION OF LA CELLE ST. CLOUD.

Bibliography

Barbour, Neville, ed. *A Survey of North-West Africa (the Maghrib).* London: Oxford University Press, 1959.

Mansfield, Peter. *The Arabs,* 3d edition. New York: Penguin, 1985.

ZACHARY KARABELL

FRANJIYYA FAMILY

Prominent political family of Lebanon.

The Franjiyyas (also Frangiehs) are Maronite Christians from Zgharta, in northern Lebanon, who have dominated the region politically. Several of their members became important politicians in the twentieth century. Hamid (1907/1908?–1981), the elder brother of Sulayman Franjiyya, was the family's initial political leader who became a longtime parliamentarian and government minister, beginning in the late 1930s, until he suffered a stroke in 1957. Tony (Antoine; 1942–1978) was the only son and heir apparent of Sulayman. He headed the family's al-Marada militia and served as a government minister from 1973 to 1975. The Franjiyyas opposed the Phalange party's Bashir Jumayyil and his attempt to control all Christian militias in Lebanon. As a result, Jumayyil's forces attacked Tony's home in Ihdin in May 1978, killing him, his wife, his infant daughter, and over two dozen other people. Sulayman (1964–). Tony's son first expressed political ambitions as a youth in the mid-1980s. In 1990, he took control of the al-Marada from his uncle Robert. He became the family's political patriarch upon his grandfather's death in 1992. Sulayman first served in the parliament in 1991 and has served in several cabinet positions beginning in 1990.

See also FRANJIYYA, SULAYMAN; JUMAYYIL, BASHIR; PHALANGE.

Bibliography

Hudson, Michael C. *The Precarious Republic: Political Modernization in Lebanon.* New York: Random House, 1968.

Salibi, Kamal S. *Crossroads to Civil War: Lebanon, 1958–1976.* Delmar, NY: Caravan Books, 1976.

MICHAEL R. FISCHBACH

FRANJIYYA, SULAYMAN
[1910–1992]

President of Lebanon, 1970–1976.

Sulayman Franjiyya (also Frangieh), born in 1910, was the political leader of to the Franjiyyas, an influential Maronite family of northern Lebanon. His presidential term is associated with the outbreak of the Lebanese civil war of 1975. He was not initially slated to represent the Franjiyya family in politics. His brother, Hamid Franjiyya, was the political leader of the family; after Hamid suffered a stroke in 1957, Sulayman was chosen as his successor. Unlike his brother, Sulayman was an uneducated "tough guy" who resorted to violence when it served his family's political interests. He was associated with bloodshed in northern Lebanon that targeted supporters of rival families. To avoid arrest, he fled to Syria where he established contacts with the Asad family that he later utilized.

Franjiyya served in Parliament throughout the 1960s and was active in the centrist (Wasat) bloc, which comprised opponents of the Chehab era. He also held various ministerial positions. He was elected president in 1970 by a one-vote margin. During his administration the Middle East was radicalized, and the Palestine Liberation Organization (PLO) relocated from Jordan to Lebanon after the 1970 Black September clash between Jordanian troops and PLO forces. Franjiyya strongly opposed the presence of armed Palestinians in Lebanon and authorized Lebanon's army to train and give weapons to members of right-wing militias. He aligned himself with the government of Syria for the duration of the Lebanese civil war. He broke off his alliance with Maronite-oriented parties and groups in 1978, when his son, Tony Franjiyya, was killed by gunmen loyal to the Lebanese Forces.

See also FRANJIYYA FAMILY; LEBANESE CIVIL WAR (1975–1990); LEBANESE FORCES.

Bibliography

Hudson, Michael C. *The Precarious Republic: Political Modernization in Lebanon.* New York: Random House, 1968.

Salibi, Kamal S. *Crossroads to Civil War: Lebanon, 1958–1976.* Delmar, NY: Caravan Books, 1976.

AS'AD ABUKHALIL
UPDATED BY MICHAEL R. FISCHBACH

FREEDOM MOVEMENT (NEZHAT-E AZADI IRAN)

Islamic nationalist party.

The Freedom Movement of Iran, a splinter group of the Second National Front, was formed in 1961 by Ayatollah Mahmud Taleqani, Mehdi Bazargan, and Yadollah Sahabi. The new group's primary appeal was to religious technocrats and modernists, and it had strong ties to the bazaar. The founders had been active in the National Front since the late 1940s, but they sought a plausible Islamic alternative to that movement's secular nationalism. After the June 1963 uprisings in Qom and other cities in response to the arrest of Ayatollah Ruhollah Khomeini, Freedom Movement leaders were imprisoned by the government of Mohammad Reza Shah Pahlavi. However, their cooperation with Khomeini continued even after the shah sent the ayatollah into foreign exile. This history of working together contributed to the effectiveness with which the Freedom Movement and Khomeini's network of former seminary students jointly organized mass anti-shah demonstrations during the Iranian Revolution of 1978 through 1979. Even before the final victory of the revolution, Khomeini used his authority as its leader to designate the Freedom Movement's head, Bazargan, to lead a provisional government, which assumed office when the shah's regime collapsed in February 1979.

The Freedom Movement espoused a philosophy that can be termed Islamic modernism. Members were pious Muslims who felt comfortable with modern education; they disliked political extremism and policies of economic and social engineering. Thus they soon fell out with the radical clerics with whom they had to share power. The November 1979 takeover of the American embassy by Students in the Line of the Imam was the last straw for Bazargan; he resigned with his entire cabinet after Khomeini endorsed the embassy seizure. Thereafter, the Freedom Movement became part of the loyal opposition to the government of the nascent Islamic Republic. However, the party's relations with officials became increasingly tense, and by 1981 its newspaper had been banned; subsequently, its members were disqualified from running in elections for the Majles al-Shura or for the presidency. Although the Freedom Movement continued to act as a conscience for the Islamic government, and throughout the 1980s and 1990s periodically circulated pamphlets and issued press statements critical of government policies, lack of access to the government-controlled media effectively silenced its voice. The greater tolerance for dissenting views that prevailed after Mohammad Khatami was elected president in 1997 provided the Freedom Movement an opportunity to publicize its views. However, its greater visibility proved a liability when the judiciary cracked down on reformers and dissidents beginning in April 2000. Subsequently, most Freedom Movement activists were arrested and charged with attempting to overthrow the government. Trials in 2001 and 2002 resulted in prison sentences for many; the trial for Freedom Movement leader Ibrahim Yazdi (who became head of the party in 1995, after Bazargan's death) continued sporadically throughout 2003.

See also BAZARGAN, MEHDI; IRANIAN REVOLUTION (1979); KHATAMI, MOHAMMAD; KHOMEINI, RUHOLLAH; MAJLES AL-SHURA; NATIONAL FRONT, IRAN; PAHLAVI, MOHAMMAD REZA; STUDENTS IN THE LINE OF THE IMAM; YAZDI, IBRAHIM.

Bibliography

Chehabi, Houchang E. *Iranian Politics and Religious Modernism: The Liberation Movement of Iran under the Shah and Khomeini.* Ithaca, NY: Cornell University Press, 1990.

NEGUIN YAVARI
UPDATED BY ERIC HOOGLUND

FREEDOM PARTY

Turkish political party, 1955–1958.

Established late in 1955 by a group of dissident members of the ruling Democrat Party, the Freedom Party signified rising opposition to the undisciplined economic policies and authoritarian tendencies of the regime of Adnan Menderes. Prime Minister Menderes reacted to intensifying criticism in the aftermath of destructive riots in Istanbul and other cities in September 1955 by forcing the resignation of the entire government while retaining office himself, thus violating the cardinal principle of collective cabinet responsibility. Composed of some of the most cosmopolitan and intellectual elements of the dominant party, the Freedom Party called for effective constitutional guarantees against arbitrary government and greater freedom of association and expression. Ironically, the departure of the dissidents from the Democrat Party strengthened Menderes and paved the way for even more dictatorial policies. The Freedom Party garnered only 4 out of a total of 610 seats in the election of 1957, while the main opposition Republican People's Party (RPP) polled 40 percent of the vote and gained 178 seats. Consequently, the Freedom Party merged with the RPP in November 1958.

See also MENDERES, ADNAN; REPUBLICAN PEOPLE'S PARTY (RPP).

Bibliography

Ahmad, Feroz. *The Turkish Experiment in Democracy, 1950–1975.* Boulder, CO: Westview Press, 1977.

Frey, Frederick W. *The Turkish Political Elite.* Cambridge, MA: MIT Press, 1965.

FRANK TACHAU

FREE FRENCH MANDATE

Attempt by France to control Lebanon and Syria.

In June 1941, Free French troops joined British imperial forces in overthrowing the Vichy administration in Damascus. General Charles de Gaulle's envoy to Cairo, General Georges Catroux, initially offered Syria and Lebanon independence if they would accept Free French rule. But de Gaulle then made independence conditional upon the conclusion of treaties ensuring continued French predominance over the two countries' economic, military, and cultural affairs. Catroux became delegate-general for Syria and Lebanon, a post virtually identical to the earlier office of high commissioner.

Free French officials could not block the integration of Syria and Lebanon into either the sterling area or the Anglo–American Middle East Supply Center. In addition, London pressured the Free French to meet local nationalists' demands, resulting in the restoration of the two countries' prewar constitutions. Elections in July 1943 gave the National Bloc control of Syria's national assembly; nationalists captured Lebanon's parliament two months later and immediately took steps to dismantle the mandate. Free French authorities responded by arresting the Lebanese leadership, but massive popular demonstrations forced the prisoners' release. When the government in Damascus adopted a similar program, the Free French first tried to suppress the Syrian nationalist movement but then agreed to a series of negotiations, which culminated in the dual evacuations of April and August 1946.

See also CATROUX, GEORGES; DE GAULLE, CHARLES.

FRED H. LAWSON

FREEMASONS

A secret fraternal order.

Drawing on guild practices of the masons and deriving its "oriental" origins from the period of Solomon's temple in Jerusalem, the order of Free and Accepted Masons recognizes some six million members worldwide. The order's first Grand Lodge was organized in London in 1717. Incorporating a complex system of secret rituals, rites, and decrees, the society admits members who profess a belief in God, but keep the particulars of their faith private. Members include Muslims, Christians, and Jews. There is no central authority. Freemasonry advocates religious toleration, fellowship, and political compromise, and members work for peace and harmony between peoples.

Freemasonry in the Middle East is traced initially to individuals, most notably Iranians who, serving as diplomats, were invited to join lodges by Europeans and upon their return disseminated the ideology. Masonic lodges in the region were established by Europeans in areas they influenced and were used by the French and the British to cultivate local individuals. Lodges in Calcutta (founded in 1730) attracted Hindus and Muslims, and the philosophy probably entered Iran at this time with Iranian merchants who lived in India.

The establishment in the Middle East of masonic lodges affiliated with the European movement, however, dates from Napoléon's invasion of Egypt, when French soldiers established chapters in Cairo (1798) and in Alexandria (1802). Italian émigrés, after their abortive revolution in Italy (1830), set up Italian lodges, and the British and the Germans became active in the 1860s. In Iran, the first lodge (a nonaffiliated one) was set up in 1858 by an Armenian convert to Islam, Mirza Malkom Khan, and was short lived. The French masonic lodge in Istanbul, L'Union d'Orient, dates from 1865. During the Ottoman period, there were lodges in Beirut and Jerusalem, and the society flourished under the Palestine mandate. Jewish, Christian, and Muslim members support a mutual insurance fund, an old-age home, a library, and masonic temples in Israel. There have been lodges in most Middle Eastern countries at one time or another, depending upon the regime in power.

Although it never attracted many members on the popular level, freemasonry in the Middle East was a significant component of Middle Eastern reform politics during the latter part of the nineteenth century until World War I. Because it incorporated unique rites, a clandestine apparatus, and a select membership—features familiar in Sufi, *futuwwa*, and other Islamic movements—and was a convenient vehicle for the dissemination of European ideas, it drew Islamic modernists and political activists such as the Egyptian Muhammad Abduh, the Iranian Jamal al-din al-Afghani, and the Algerian Abd al-Qadir.

Masonic lodges were convenient covers for clandestine activities. Because they were, by and large, Western institutions protected under the capitulations, governments could not penetrate them or monitor their activities. Members were also able to draw upon the support of European masons in defense of local members. During the 1870s, the movement was used as a tool by Prince Halim of Egypt who was denied succession and conspired to rule. Khedive Isma'il and his successor, Tawfiq, banished a number of prominent members who were also active in reformist political activities—Ya'qub Sanu and Afghani, among others. Ottoman modernists of the Tanzimat period were responsible for Ottoman Sultan Murat V's brief rule in 1876. In Iran, lodges existed sporadically in the nineteenth century and were allowed under Mohammad Ali Shah until 1911 and the end of the constitutional movement. Iranians, Egyptians, and Ottomans met at lodges throughout the Middle East when they traveled, but there is no evidence that any unified political actions emerged.

For the Young Turks, exposed to freemasonry largely in the Balkans and Constantinople (now Istanbul), the lodges were convenient meeting places to bring together Christians and Muslims, and to plan the overthrow of the regime of Sultan Abdülhamit II. The existence of so many Freemasons in the large secular leadership of the Committee for Union and Progress generated polemical literature of a conspiratorial nature against the regime just before Turkey's entry into World War I on the side of Germany.

See also ABD AL-QADIR; ABDUH, MUHAMMAD; ABDÜLHAMIT II; AFGHANI, JAMAL AL-DIN al-; Capitulations; Committee for Union and Progress; Malkom Khan, Mirza; Sanu, Ya'qub; Tanzimat; Young Turks.

Bibliography

Algar, Hamid. "An Introduction to the History of Freemasonry in Iran." *Middle Eastern Studies* 6 (1970).

Hanioğlu, M. Sükrü. "Notes on the Young Turks and Freemasons, 1875–1908." *Middle Eastern Studies* 25 (1989).

Kedourie, Elie. "Young Turks, Freemasons, and Jews." *Middle Eastern Studies* 7 (1971).

Landau, Jacob M. "Prolegomena to a Study of Secret Societies in Modern Egypt." *Middle Eastern Studies* 1 (1964).

REEVA S. SIMON

FREE OFFICERS, EGYPT

Clandestine military organization that engineered and executed the coup of 23 July 1952, which began a new chapter in the history of modern Egypt.

The genesis of the Free Officers is much disputed among historians and specialists. Some argue that the group was formed in 1942 after the British ultimatum to King Farouk. Others take the Arab–Israel War (1948) as the starting point. Notwithstanding these differences, general agreement exists on four major points. First, Gamal Abdel Nasser was the undisputed leader of the group from its inception, and his position was never challenged. This fact laid down the foundation of his prominence as the strongman and president of Egypt until his death in 1970. Second, the group did not have an organized file or registry of its membership. It was organized into cells and sections, each with a specific function. The overall command and supervision was provided by a revolutionary committee headed by Nasser.

The organization of the Free Officers reflected a high degree of flexibility that was demonstrated in the frequent movements of individuals into and outside the group. Actually, the first attempt to develop a form of registry was under President Anwar al-Sadat (1970–1981) when he decided to provide a special pension for the Free Officers. Third, the group did not represent an ideologically homoge-

neous group. Among its members were officers with Islamist inclinations, such as Kamal al-Din Husayn and Abd al-Mun'im Amin; others were more or less leftists, such as Khalid Muhyi al-Din and Yusuf Sadiq. Lacking a clear ideology, all that the group had was the "six principles," which were their guiding directives after assuming power. The existence of ideological differences within the group was one of the factors that explains the power struggle among the Free Officers after 1952. Fourth, the group, under Nasser, was conscious of retaining its organizational autonomy, resolving not to be absorbed in any other political movement.

As individuals, the Free Officers had contacts with the Young Egypt party, the Muslim Brotherhood, the Democratic Movement for National Liberation, and other communist groups; while, as a group, they maintained a high degree of independence. Nasser believed that they could succeed only if they established a firm independent base within the army. One of the distinct features of the Free Officers is that they were purely military; the group had no civilian members and this has come to affect the nature of the post-1952 political ruling elite.

In the mid-1940s, the voice of the Free Officers was heard for the first time. They began to distribute leaflets, the first of them in 1945 was titled "The Army Gives Warning." The first open clash with the king took place in the early summer of

Members of the Revolutionary Council on 4 January 1955 in Cairo, Egypt. © Bettmann/Corbis. Reproduced by permission.

1952, when the officers' club in Cairo elected as president General Muhammad Naguib, who was the Free Officers' nominee, turning down the king's own candidate.

Between 1949 and July 1952, the Free Officers worked to recruit other sympathetic officers and strengthened their ties with civilians and politicians opposed to the monarchy. During this period too, because most of them were in their early thirties, they looked for a senior officer who could be presented to the public as their leading figure. Finally, they chose Naguib, who was a well-known infantry division commander and had been popular, especially since the Arab–Israel War, among the troops and young officers.

The actual seizure of power took place in the early hours of 23 July 1952, when troops commanded by Free Officers and their supporters occupied and controlled army headquarters, airports, the broadcasting station, telecommunication center, and major roads and bridges in Cairo. The details of what happened on that day show that the plan for seizing power was neither well thought out nor were its parts tightly integrated. Indeed, a combination of coincidence and luck made the operation successful. Within three days, the king abdicated the throne to his infant son and left the country. From then on, the Free Officers became the new rulers of Egypt.

See also ARAB–ISRAEL WAR (1948); FAROUK; MUHYI AL-DIN, KHALID; MUSLIM BROTHERHOOD; NAGUIB, MUHAMMAD; NASSER, GAMAL ABDEL; SADAT, ANWAR AL-; YOUNG EGYPT.

Bibliography

Gordon, Joel. *Nasser's Blessed Movement: Egypt's Free Officers and the July Revolution.* New York: Oxford University Press, 1992.

Vatikiotis, P. J. *The Egyptian Army in Politics: Pattern for New Nations?* Bloomington: Indiana University Press, 1961.

ALI E. HILLAL DESSOUKI

FREE OFFICERS, YEMEN

Junior officers who led North Yemen's 1962 revolution.

These fifteen or so junior officers were at the center of the planning and execution of the 1962 rev-olution that overthrew the Zaydi imamate in North Yemen. Inspired by the Egyptian revolution and the revolutionary Arab nationalism of Gamal Abdel Nasser, they recruited the more prominent senior officers who participated in the successful revolt, only to be upstaged or shunted aside by some of these older figures in the sharp political struggles that followed.

See also NASSER, GAMAL ABDEL; ZAYDISM.

ROBERT D. BURROWES

FREE REPUBLICAN PARTY

Turkish political party, 1930.

This short-lived party was founded in August 1930 by associates of Turkey's president, Mustafa Kemal Atatürk, at his behest, possibly to siphon off discontent spawned by economic problems and the government's radical reform program. Fethi Okyar, former prime minister and close associate of Kemal, returned from his post of ambassador to France to assume the leadership of the party. It opposed the government's *dirigiste* (paternalistic, state directed) economic policy and emphasized individual rights and freedoms, including freedom of (religious) conscience. It rapidly gained enthusiastic support, especially in the Aegean region. Among its adherents was Adnan Menderes, leader of the Democrat Party of the 1950s, indicating that the Free Republican Party was a harbinger of things to come. Contrary to Kemal's image of gentlemanly debates between parties, relations between the new party and the governing People's Party were bitter. The latter feared that it might in fact lose power in a free election and accused the Free Republican Party of stirring up reaction against Kemal's nationalist reform program. Consequently, the Free Republican Party voluntarily dissolved itself after only ninety-nine days, in November 1930.

See also ATATÜRK, MUSTAFA KEMAL; MENDERES, ADNAN.

Bibliography

Frey, Frederick W. *The Turkish Political Elite.* Cambridge, MA: MIT Press, 1965.

Karpat, Kemal H. *Turkey's Politics: The Transition to a Multi-Party System.* Princeton, NJ: Princeton University Press, 1959.

Weiker, Walter F. *Political Tutelage and Democracy in Turkey: The Free Party and Its Aftermath.* Leiden, Netherlands: Brill, 1975.

FRANK TACHAU

FREE YEMENIS

Political party of North Yemen in the 1940s.

Founded in Aden in 1944 by such fathers of the modern Yemeni nation-state as Qaʾid Muhammad Mahmud al-Zubayri and Shaykh Ahmad Muhammad Nuʿman, the Free Yemeni party (al-Ahrar) was the first major modern expression of constitutional reform and political opposition to the Hamid al-Din imamate in North Yemen. Although their party existed only for a few years, the Free Yemenis led the way from reformism and a constitutional imamate to new, more advanced political ideas (republicanism and revolution), organization (such as the Yemeni Unionists), and action. It could be said that a Free Yemeni movement, more than the party itself, traces an unbroken line from 1944 to the 1962 revolution. The Free Yemenis, however, far from being radical political modernists, were initially the mid-twentieth-century equivalents of the Turkish reformers of the Ottoman Empire during the Tanzimat period in the nineteenth century. This did not prevent them from playing a major role in the failed 1948 revolution and in laying a big part of the foundation for the successful 1962 revolution.

See also TANZIMAT; ZUBAYRI, QAʾID MUHAMMAD MAHMUD AL-.

Bibliography

Douglas, Leigh J. *The Free Yemeni Movement, 1935–1962,* edited by Giovanni Chimienti. Beirut, Lebanon: American University of Beirut, 1987.

ROBERT D. BURROWES

FREIER, RECHA
[1892–1984]

Founder of Youth Aliyah, writer, musician.

Born in Norden, Ostfriesland (Germany), Recha Freier studied philology at Breslau and Munich universities, worked as a teacher and pianist, and began research on children's tales, moving with her rabbi-husband to Sofia (Bulgaria) and then Berlin.

In 1932 Freier, disturbed by discrimination against Jewish jobseekers in Germany, conceived the idea of settling groups of young Jews on kibbutzim in Palestine. The head of the Jewish Agency's Social Welfare Department, Henrietta Szold, initially rejected the idea, so, in 1933, Freier raised funds to establish Youth Aliyah, sent a first group to Bet Shemen, and established an office in Berlin. That year she persuaded Szold, the Zionist Organization, and the main representative body of German Jews, to take on the program, and she spent the next eight years helping young Jews across Europe to emigrate. In 1941 she fled Germany and settled in Palestine, remaining active in children's welfare activities and founding an agricultural training school. After the establishment of the state of Israel, she founded the Israel Composers Fund (1958) and Testimonium (1966), a fund sponsoring accounts of events in Jewish history set to music. Freier published one such composition, a book of poetry (*On the Steps,* 1976), and a novel (*Shutters,* 1979). In 1954 Albert Einstein nominated her for a Nobel Peace Prize, and in 1981 she was awarded the Israel Prize. Freier saved more than 5,600 children—some say 10,000—and Youth Aliyah has to date given support to more than 300,000 impoverished refugee and Israeli children.

See also KIBBUTZ; SZOLD, HENRIETTA; YISHUV; YOUTH ALIYAH; ZIONISM.

Bibliography

Freier, Recha. *Let the Children Come: The Early History of Youth Aliyah.* London: Weidenfeld and Nicolson, 1961.

GEORGE R. WILKES

FRENCH FOREIGN LEGION

French military unit created by Louis Philippe in 1831 and made up of foreign volunteers.

Deployed only outside metropolitan France, the French foreign legion saw combat first in Algeria. It played a decisive role in the capture of Constantine in 1837 and fought in numerous engagements as the conquest proceeded. Although the legion served in the Crimea, Italy, and Mexico in the 1850s and 1860s, and throughout the French Empire later in the century, an encampment established in 1843 at Sidi-bel-Abbès, southwest of Oran, remained its headquarters.

The legion helped check the insurrection of the Walad Sidi Shaykh in western Algeria in 1881 and 1882, but much of its work in that country in the last quarter of the nineteenth century involved efforts to expand French influence into the Sahara as a prelude to linking North Africa with France's possessions south of the desert.

Legionnaires participated in many of the military operations that resulted in the establishment of a French protectorate over Morocco. They formed part of the forces that consolidated French power along the ill-defined southern Morocco–Algeria border during the first several years of the twentieth century and were involved in occupations of the Moroccan cities of Oujda and Casablanca in 1907. Thereafter, they helped maintain security in the areas around both cities. In 1911, a company of the legion was among the troops that lifted a rebel siege of Fez, the sultan's capital, thus paving the way for the inauguration of the protectorate the following year. During the pacification of Morocco's mountainous and desert regions in the 1920s and 1930s, French commanders relied heavily on the legion. Its men also took part in the fighting that ended the rebellion of Muhammad ibn Abd al-Karim al-Khattabi in 1925 and 1926.

During World War I, a battalion of legionnaires landed with other Allied soldiers at Gallipoli. After the war, legionnaires were dispatched to the French mandates of Syria and Lebanon. They saw action in the Druze uprising of 1925 and remained on garrison duty in the Levant in the 1930s.

In World War II, units of the legion made up part of the Free French contingent that seized Syria and Lebanon from the Vichy government in 1941. Subsequently attached to the British army in Egypt's Western Desert, they fought in the battle of Bir Hakeim in 1942 and advanced westward with the British following the battle of al-Alamayn. Other legionnaires from Sidi-bel-Abbès worked with American and British forces upon their arrival in Morocco and Algeria late in 1942 until the defeat of the Axis in Tunisia the following spring.

After 1954, the legion was heavily involved in French efforts to end the Algerian rebellion. Paratroopers, who had been added to the legion in the late 1940s, were instrumental in breaking up Front de Libération Nationale (FLN) cells during the 1957 Battle of Algiers. A legion paratroop battalion also formed part of the French expeditionary at Suez in 1956. When Algeria acquired independence in 1962, the headquarters of the legion were transferred from Sidi-bel-Abbès to France.

See also ALGIERS, BATTLE OF (1956–1957); FRONT DE LIBÉRATION NATIONALE; KHATTABI, MUHAMMAD IBN ABD AL-KARIM AL-.

Bibliography

O–Ballance, Edgar. *The Story of the French Foreign Legion.* London: Faber and Faber, 1961.

Porch, Douglas. *The French Foreign Legion: A Complete History of the Legendary Fighting Force.* New York: HarperCollins, 1991.

KENNETH J. PERKINS

FRENCH REPORT (1931)

See PALESTINE

FRISCHMANN, DAVID
[1859–1922]

Pioneer of modern Hebrew literature.

David Frischmann was born in Poland and died in Berlin. As a writer he was versatile and created an enormous body of work—short stories, essays, literary criticism, poetry, translations, and news stories. He was also an editor and publisher. An innovative writer, he is credited with introducing Western standards of aesthetics into Hebrew literature—which he considered provincial at that time.

His stories manifest a sympathy for and portray European Jewish characters who are in conflict with tradition; they often abandon it. His poems express the futility of adapting Judaism to modern European life. He shunned public office and remained apolitical to retain artistic and literary integrity; as a result, he was accused of being against Zionism. Deeply affected by a visit to Palestine in 1911 and 1912, however, he recorded his impressions in a book, *Ba-Aretz* (1913). His collected works appear in the seventeen-volume *Kol Kitvei David Frischmann u-Mivhar Tirgumav* (Warsaw, 1922).

See also LITERATURE: HEBREW.

ANN KAHN

FRONT DE LIBÉRATION NATIONALE (FLN)

The organizing group behind the Algerian War of Independence; later became the dominant single party of independent Algeria.

The instigators of the Algerian revolution created the Front de Libération Nationale (FLN; National Liberation Front) in October 1954 as a vehicle for mobilizing Algerians behind the war of independence. As the war went on, the movement spun off various deliberative, executive, and military institutions, creating by September 1958 a Provisional Government of the Algerian Republic. By January 1960 the revolutionary parliament—Conseil National de la Revolution Algerienne (CNRA)—declared the FLN a single party responsible for carrying out a deeper social and economic revolution.

The Algerian constitutions of 1963 and 1976 confirmed this decision, declaring the FLN the people's monitor of government and the avantgarde of the revolution. By the late 1970s, however, it had grown into a bureaucratized organization of more than 300,000 members, whose principal function was the recruitment and indoctrination of members for support of the government it ostensibly monitored.

The constitution of February 1989 ended the FLN's single-party status, but before newer parties could unseat it, the army seized control of the government.

See also ALGERIAN WAR OF INDEPENDENCE; CONSEIL NATIONAL DE LA RÉVOLUTION ALGÉRIENNE (CNRA).

Bibliography

Entelis, John. *Algeria: The Revolution Institutionalized.* Boulder, CO: Westview Press, 1986.

JOHN RUEDY

FRONT FOR THE LIBERATION OF SOUTH YEMEN

South Yemeni independence movement.

The Front for the Liberation of South Yemen (FLOSY) was a political party established in January 1966 in Britain's Aden Crown Colony and the Protectorate States. The party was forged under heavy Egyptian pressure from a combination of the National Liberation Front (NLF) and the Organization for the Liberation of the Occupied South (OLOS) in an effort by Egypt to sustain its influence over the course of the campaign against the continued British presence in southern Arabia. When the NLF quickly backed out, FLOSY became nothing more than a renamed OLOS and the political property of Abdullah Ali Asnaj and Abd al-Qawi Makawi. The NLF successfully fought FLOSY to succeed the British in an independent South Yemen in 1967. FLOSY then became a vehicle for opposition from abroad to the regime, and it remained so with decreasing relevance from the late 1960s through the 1970s.

See also ORGANIZATION FOR THE LIBERATION OF THE OCCUPIED SOUTH.

Bibliography

Dresch, Paul. *A History of Modern Yemen.* Cambridge, U.K., and New York: Cambridge University Press, 2000.

Halliday, Fred. *Revolution and Foreign Policy: The Case of South Yemen, 1967–1987.* Cambridge, U.K.: Cambridge University Press, 2002.

ROBERT D. BURROWES

FRONT ISLAMIQUE DU SALUT (FIS)

Algerian Islamic political party.

The Front Islamique du Salut (FIS, Islamic Salvation Front) is Algeria's largest Islamic political party. Founded in February 1989 by a large group of Algerian religious leaders, the FIS calls for the establishment of an Islamic state based on the Sunna and the Qur'an. It is headed by Abassi al-Madani, a university professor, and Ali Belhadj, a radical imam. Since their imprisonment in June 1991, Abdelkader Hachani has served as the provisional leader. The principle structures of the party are the Majlis al-Shura, a consultative body of some forty religious leaders, and the National Executive Bureau.

The FIS has been Algeria's most highly mobilized party. It has gained substantial financing from local businessmen and Saudi Arabian sources. With solid support from the young, urban unemployed, it won the most votes in Algeria's last two elections. In the June 1990 elections for regional and municipal assemblies, it garnered 55 percent of the vote and an absolute majority of the seats. In the first round of National Assembly elections in December 1991, the FIS won 188 of the 430 seats and was poised to win an absolute majority in the second round. The Algerian army staged a coup d'état in January 1992, arrested thousands of FIS members, and declared the party illegal. Since then, the party has been in a state of disarray, its entire leadership imprisoned, and its activities repressed.

See also BELHADJ, ALI; MADANI, ABASSI AL-; QUR'AN; SUNNA.

Bibliography

Quandt, William B. *Between Ballots and Bullets: Algeria's Transition from Authoritarianism.* Washington, DC: Brookings Institution Press, 1998.

Shahin, Emad Eldin. *Political Ascent: Contemporary Islamic Movements in North Africa.* Boulder, CO: Westview Press, 1997.

BRADFORD DILLMAN

FRONT POUR LA DÉFENSE DES INSTITUTIONS CONSTITUTIONELLES (FDIC)

Moroccan political group.

Founded in 1963 by Ahmad Rida Gudeira, a close confidant of King Hassan, the Front pour la Défense des Institutions Constitutionelles (FDIC) attempted to unite pro-monarchy groups in parliament against Istiqlal and the Union Nationale des Forces Populaires (UNFP) during a time of social and economic tensions. Having failed to win a majority in the 1963 parliamentary elections, it split in 1964 into Gudeira's Parti Socialiste Démocratique and the Mouvement Populaire (MP)—the latter had been part of the original FDIC. The failure of the FDIC led the king to assume emergency governing powers in June 1965.

See also ISTIQLAL PARTY: MOROCCO; MOROCCO: POLITICAL PARTIES IN; MOUVEMENT POPULAIRE (MP); UNION NATIONALE DES FORCES POPULAIRES (UNFP).

BRUCE MADDY-WEITZMAN

FU'AD
[1868–1936]

Sultan of Egypt, 1917–1922; king, 1922–1936.

Fu'ad was born in Giza, Egypt, on 26 March 1868, the youngest child of Khedive Isma'il Pasha, who ruled Egypt from 1863 until 1879. Fu'ad left Egypt for Constantinople (now Istanbul) in 1879 at the time of his father's exile. Subsequently, he studied at Geneva, Turin, and the Italian Military Academy, returning to Egypt in 1892. His eligibility for the Egyptian throne was enhanced when the British deposed Abbas Hilmi II as khedive of Egypt in 1914 at the beginning of World War I. At the time of Abbas's removal, Britain severed the juridical ties that bound Egypt to the Ottoman Empire, proclaimed a protectorate over the country, and named Fu'ad's elder brother, Husayn Kamil, as the first sultan of Egypt. When Husayn Kamil died on 9 October 1917, Fu'ad succeeded him to the throne.

Fu'ad reigned in Egypt from 1917 until his death in 1936. He aspired to be a powerful ruler and did much to enlarge the powers of the monarchy. Following the conclusion of the war, Egypt's elite, including Sultan Fu'ad, pressed the British to end the protectorate and to increase the political autonomy of their country. Britain's failure to respond to these overtures set off a powerful protest movement, led by Sa'd Zaghlul and his new political party, the Wafd. The political turmoil led to Britain's unilateral proclamation of Egypt's independence on 28 February 1922, subject to the exclusion of a wide range of powers reserved to the British. In the wake of the altered political status of the country, Fu'ad became king of Egypt on 15 March 1922. In 1923 an appointed committee drafted a new constitution for the country. Through the intervention of Fu'ad and the British, the constitution gave far-reaching authority to the monarch. Under its provisions, the crown had the power to designate the prime minister, dissolve the parliament, and postpone sessions of parliament. Additionally, the king controlled charitable and educational institutions and decided upon diplomatic appointments and military commissions.

Armed with its formal, albeit restricted, political independence and a new, sophisticated constitution, Egypt embarked upon an experiment in liberal democracy. Unfortunately, civilian parliamentary government, which lasted until the military ousted the politicians from office in 1952, tended to degenerate into a three-cornered struggle among Egypt's most popular party, the Wafd, the palace, and the British. During these years, the Wafd invariably won any fair electoral contest, but was kept from office through the political manipulations of the palace and the British. Monarchical power reached its apex between 1930 and 1935, after Fuʾad removed the Wafd from office and appointed Ismaʿil Sidqi as prime minister. Immediately upon assuming power, Sidqi replaced the 1923 constitution with a new one and enacted a new, more restrictive electoral law. Both changes enhanced royal authority. Jealous of the power that Sidqi wielded, Fuʾad removed him from office in 1933 and ruled Egypt through a set of palace appointees. In 1935, under pressure from the British and responding to fears of an impending world war, Fuʾad agreed to restore the 1923 constitution and to hold new elections. Predictably, the Wafd won the 1936 elections. Fuʾad died on 28 April 1936, just months before the signing of the Anglo–Egyptian Treaty, which gave greater political autonomy to Egypt.

Although he was an autocrat and did much to impede the development of parliamentary democracy, Fuʾad was a noteworthy patron of Egyptian education. He played a role in reviving the Egyptian University, which had been founded in 1908 but languished until Fuʾad and others gave it their support. It was named Fuʾad I University in 1940 and became today's Cairo University in 1954.

See also ABBAS HILMI II; CAIRO UNIVERSITY; SIDQI, ISMAʿIL; WAFD; ZAGHLUL, SAʿD.

Bibliography

Sayyid-Marsot, Afaf Lutfi al-. *Egypt's Liberal Experiment, 1922–1936.* Berkeley: University of California Press, 1977.

Vatikiotis, P. J. *The History of Modern Egypt: From Muhammad Ali to Mubarak,* 4th edition. Baltimore, MD: Johns Hopkins University Press, 1991.

ROBERT L. TIGNOR

FUJAYRA

One of the seven emirates making up the United Arab Emirates; also the city of the same name.

Occupying a slender strip of land along the Gulf of Oman side of the Musandam Peninsula, Fujayra was under the sovereignty of the al-Qawasim rulers of Sharjah and Raʾs al-Khayma for most of the modern era. Lingering ill feelings between Fujayra and its former overlords have manifested themselves in minor border disputes. Fujayra was only recognized as a distinct emirate by the British in 1952. It is ruled by Hamad ibn Muhammad al-Sharqi, and because it has no oil reserves or other significant resources, it must rely financially on Abu Dhabi. Some extractive industries exploit materials from the Hajar Mountains, including cement and asbestos. Like Dubai, Fujayra has a port and free zone for industry and trade, but on a much smaller scale. However, the port's petrochemicals storage and loading facilities are among the region's most heavily used. In 1997 the emirate's population was estimated to be 83,000, on an area of 715 square miles.

See also SHARQI FAMILY, AL-; UMM AL-QAYWAYN; UNITED ARAB EMIRATES.

Bibliography

Hoogland, Eric, and Toth, Anthony B. "United Arab Emirates." In *Persian Gulf States: Country Studies,* edited by Helen Chapin Metz. Washington, DC: U.S. Government Printing Office, 1994.

Vine, Peter, and Casey, Paula. *United Arab Emirates: A Profile of a Country's Heritage and Modern Development.* London: Immel Publishing, 1992.

MALCOLM C. PECK
UPDATED BY ANTHONY B. TOTH

FUJAYRA–SHARJAH CONFLICT

Clash over land ownership in the United Arab Emirates (1972).

A few months after establishment of the United Arab Emirates, these two members of the federation clashed over ownership of a tiny parcel of land with a well that had traditionally been used by tribesmen from both. Some twenty lives were lost before federal intervention ended the conflict. The incident underscored the disruptive potential of numerous unresolved border disputes, and the federal government's response reflected its determination to keep them in check.

See also UNITED ARAB EMIRATES.

Bibliography

Anthony, John Duke. *Arab States of the Lower Gulf: People, Politics, Petroleum.* Washington, DC: Middle East Institute, 1975.

MALCOLM C. PECK

FUL

See FOOD

FUNDAMENTAL PACT

An 1857 Tunisian law that increased freedoms for non-Tunisians.

The law was issued by Muhammad Bey (1855–1859) of Tunisia on 10 September 1857. Entitled Ahd al-Aman (Pledge of Security), the Fundamental Pact resulted from an incident involving a Tunisian Jew, Batto (Samuel) Sfez, who was executed on orders of the bey for having blasphemed Islam. The French and British consuls saw in the episode an opportunity to intervene in Tunisian affairs. The two men—Richard Wood of Britain and Leon Roches of France—pressed for the promulgation of reforms that would ensure the security of both Tunisians and foreigners; that would establish mixed courts to handle matters concerning Europeans; and, importantly, that would allow non-Tunisians to conduct business and own property in Tunisia more easily. On the one hand, the law opened the way to greater European economic activity and, on the other, spurred a group of Tunisian notables, led by Khayr al-Din Pasha, to pressure the bey to enact structural reforms that would, in part, place limits upon the powers of the bey's office. The campaign of these notables, backed by the foreign consuls who continued to press for enforcement of the new laws, led Muhammad Bey and his successor Muhammad al-Sadiq Bey (1859–1882) to draw up a formal constitution.

See also KHAYR AL-DIN; MIXED COURTS; MUHAMMAD AL-SADIQ.

Bibliography

Abun-Nasr, Jamil M. *A History of the Maghrib in the Islamic Period.* Cambridge, U.K., and New York: Cambridge University Press, 1987.

Nelson, Harold D., ed. *Tunisia: A Country Study.* Washington, DC: U.S. Government Printing Office, 1988.

MATTHEW S. GORDON

FUTUWWA

Associations of young men who claimed to embody certain virtues and who tried to maintain the distinct identities of their quarters in Cairo. Also, paramilitary youth organizations in Iraq.

In medieval times, the term *futuwwa* (plural, *futuwwat*) referred to either a specific body of virtues—courage, manliness, chivalry, generosity, truth, honor, self-reliance, altruism—or to informal urban associations of young men who claimed to promote these values. By the early nineteenth century, the word was used in Cairo (Egypt) to refer to a few influential men who acted as informal leaders of their quarters. Their primary function was to protect their quarters against outside threats, other *futuwwat*, and the government. While they performed good deeds, they also quarreled and were violent among themselves and with police. Some were thugs who preyed on the local populace instead of furthering its welfare.

In Egypt, between Muhammad Ali Pasha's accession to power in 1805 and World War II, their influence declined, mainly as a result of government efforts to centralize authority. After the war, their number and role diminished further, under the combined effects of rapid urbanization, industrialization, expansion of the role of the bureaucracy in the daily life of the people, and the increasing religious and socioeconomic heterogeneity of neighborhoods. The few remaining *futuwwat* in the older, medieval quarters of Cairo now include a large proportion of toughs engaged in various semilegal and illegal activities.

In another context, the term has been used in Iraq, first in the 1930s and again since the Ba'th party takeover in 1968, to refer to paramilitary youth groups strongly reminiscent of the Hitler Youth of Nazi Germany. In Ba'thist Iraq, the *futuwwa* is one of three paramilitary youth organizations that belong to the state-run General Federation of Iraqi Youth. It brings together Iraqis aged fifteen to twenty, is strongly hierarchical, and is patterned after the Ba'th party itself. Its members wear uniforms, undergo military training, and participate in various activities and rituals aimed at strengthening the new generation's loyalty to the regime.

See also BA'TH, AL-; MUHAMMAD ALI; YOUTH MOVEMENTS.

Bibliography

Makiya, Kanan. *Republic of Fear: The Politics of Modern Iraq,* revised edition. Berkeley: University of California Press, 1998.

Messiri, Sawsan el-. "The Changing Role of the *Futuwwa* in the Social Structure of Cairo." In *Patrons and Clients in Mediterranean Societies,* edited by Ernest Gellner and John Waterbury. London: Duckworth, 1977.

GUILAIN P. DENOEUX

GAFSA INCIDENT (1980)

Confrontation between Tunisia and Libya.

In January 1980, during a period of heightened tension between Libya under Muammar al-Qaddafi and Tunisia under Habib Bourguiba, Tunisian guerrillas (trained by the Libyan military) crossed into Tunisia and attacked the south-central city of Gafsa. Tunisia responded by severing ties with Libya; in turn, Libya ordered some 10,000 Tunisian workers in Libya to return home.

See also BOURGUIBA, HABIB; QADDAFI, MUAMMAR AL-.

Bibliography

Perkins, Kenneth. *Tunisia: Crossroads of the Islamic and European Worlds.* Boulder, CO: Westview Press, 1986.

MATTHEW S. GORDON

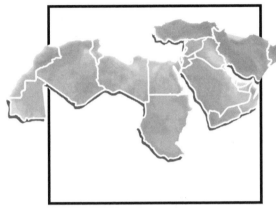

G

GAILANI, AHMAD
[1932–]

Afghan resistance leader; Sufi pir (spiritual leader).

Ahmad Gailani played an important role in Afghan resistance politics of the 1980s and in the political events of the early 1990s. Gailani is the spiritual leader of the Qadiriyya Sufi order in Afghanistan and well connected to the former royal family through marriage. Gailani assumed the leadership of the Qadiriyya order upon the death of his older brother Sayyid Ali in 1964. He was educated at Abu Hanifa College.

A member of the Kabul elite before 1978, Gailani fled Kabul after the Marxist revolution in April 1978 and founded the resistance group Mahaz-e Milli-e Islami-e Afghanistan (National Islamic Front) in Peshawar, Pakistan, in 1979. This group had a strong following among Gilzai Pushtun tribes and among supporters of the ex-king Zahir Shah. After the collapse of the communist government in 1992 Gailani returned to Kabul and participated in the transitional government of Sabghatullah Mujaddidi. He was first offered the position of foreign minister, but refused to serve. Later he accepted the post of supreme justice.

When the Taliban captured Kabul in 1996 Gailani was forced from his leadership role and again fled to Pakistan. After the events of 11 September 2001 Gailani returned to Kabul to play a role in the formation of the government of Hamid Karzai and to support Zahir Shah, although he held no official position in the Afghan government.

Bibliography

Roy, Olivier. *Islam and Resistance in Afghanistan.* New York; Cambridge, U.K.: Cambridge University Press, 1986.

Rubin, Barnett R. *The Fragmentation of Afghanistan: State Formation and Collapse in the International System.* New Haven, CT: Yale University Press, 2002.

GRANT FARR

GALATA

District of Istanbul on the north bank of the Golden Horn.

A Genoese settlement in the Byzantine era, Galata was officially incorporated into the city of Constantinople (now Istanbul) only in 1840. It continued through the nineteenth century to be the section of Constantinople where Europeans resided. Long the center of international trade and banking in the capital, the district's population and business activity boomed beginning in the Crimean War (1853–1856). Galata and its neighboring district Beyoğlu (formerly Pera) became the modernized center of the city, with many theaters and hotels and the city's first tramway and telephone lines. The famous Galatasaray Lycée, established in 1868, was actually located in Beyoğlu.

See also CRIMEAN WAR; GALATASARAY LYCÉE.

Bibliography

Shaw, Stanford, and Shaw, Ezel Kural. *History of the Ottoman Empire and Modern Turkey,* Vol. 2: *Reform, Revolution, and Republic: The Rise of Modern Turkey, 1808–1975.* Cambridge, U.K., and New York: Cambridge University Press, 1977.

ELIZABETH THOMPSON

GALATASARAY LYCÉE

One of the oldest and most prestigious educational institutions in Turkey.

The Galatasaray Lycée opened in 1481 as a palace school to train young men for service in the Ottoman court or in cavalry regiments. The most accomplished students were selected to continue their education and service at the emperor's Topkapi Palace. As a result of educational reforms on a Western model during the nineteenth century, the Galatasaray buildings were first converted to a medical school, then to a military preparatory school. In 1868, the institution began its modern incarnation as the Imperial Lycée (Mekteb-i Sultani), with support from the French government. Modeled after the grand French *lycées* (schools), it was designed to offer a European-style secondary education using French as the primary language of instruction. While similar schools in the empire catered to non-Muslim subjects, Galatasaray was open to both Muslim and non-Muslim boys. The school continued to function after the Ottoman Empire became the Turkish Republic, and many of its graduates went on to study at the School of Government (Mekteb-i Mülkiye) and then took up positions in government.

During the 1960s, a primary school was opened on a separate campus to prepare students for the *lycée.* The admission of girls began in 1965, and by the late 1990s the student body was approximately 40 percent female. English language instruction was offered starting in 1990, bringing to three the number of languages used in the school. In 1992, during a visit by French president François Mitterrand to Turkey, it was announced that the school would be reorganized as the Galatasaray Educational Institution and that it would also become an institution of higher education. Accordingly, Galatasaray University was founded in 1994, with faculties of law, engineering and technology, administration, communication, and arts and sciences. Because the institution historically has attracted an ambitious and able body of students, the Galatasaray has been an important factor in the history of the Ottoman Empire, its successor states, and modern Turkey. Galatasaray graduates include many prominent political leaders, diplomats, government officials, artists, writers, and educators.

See also OTTOMAN EMPIRE.

Bibliography

Galatasaray Alumni Association of U.S.A. "The History of Galatasaray." Available at <http://www .galatasaray-usa.com/history.html>

Kuran, E. "Ghalata-Sarayi," In *Encyclopedia of Islam,* new edition, edited by B. Lewis, C. Pellat, and J. Schacht. Leiden: Brill, 1965.

I. METIN KUNT
UPDATED BY ANTHONY B. TOTH

GALILEE

In Hebrew, ha-Galil, *probably meaning "the circle"; in Arabic,* al-Jalil; *mountainous and comparatively fertile region of northern Israel.*

The Galilee region is bounded by the Mediterranean Sea on the west, the river Jordan on the east, the Lebanese border in the north, and the Jezreel Valley to the south. A line running from Acre on the coast to the northwest shore of the Kinneret (Sea of Galilee or Lake Tiberias) divides Lower Galilee, reaching an elevation of 1,500 feet (458 m) above sea level, from Upper Galilee, which attains altitudes of 4,000 feet (1,220 m).

Joshua and Deborah conquered the entirety of this area, which in biblical times was allotted to four Israelite tribes and later to the northern kingdom of Israel. Controlled by a series of empires, Galilee became a preeminent Judaic stronghold for some five centuries after the destruction of the Second Temple, and a center of Christianity especially after the sixth century C.E. The region became part of the province of al-Urdunn (Jordan) following the Arab conquest (c. 640), then formed a crusader principality, and was later ruled successively by Ayyubids, Mamluks, Ottomans, and intermittently by local potentates such as Zahir al-Umar, Ahmad al-Jazzar, and Muhammad Ali of Egypt. Zionist settlement activity, both before and after Britain's General Edmund Allenby's conquest of the area from the Ottoman Turks in September 1918, was slow in penetrating Galilee itself, whose overwhelming Arab majority caused it to be apportioned to the Arab state under partition. Conquered in its entirety by Israel in the 1948 Arab–Israel War, Galilee witnessed a smaller scale Arab displacement than other parts of the country, most of those leaving being Muslim. Since the 1960s the area has been the target of many government settlement and development projects.

See also AHMAD AL-JAZZAR; ALLENBY, EDMUND HENRY; ARAB–ISRAEL WAR (1948); GALILEE, SEA OF; JEZREEL VALLEY; MUHAMMAD ALI.

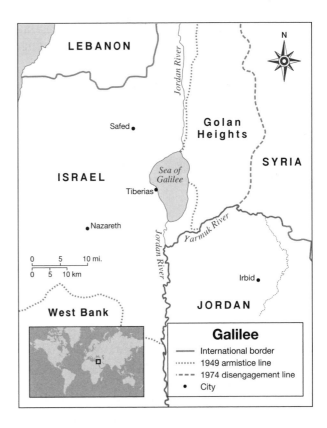

MAP BY XNR PRODUCTIONS, INC. THE GALE GROUP.

Bibliography

Horsley, Richard A. *Galilee: History, Politics, People.* Valley Forge, PA: Trinity Press International, 1995.

Meyers, Eric M., ed. *Galilee through the Centuries: Confluence of Cultures.* Duke Judaic Studies Series, vol. 1. Winona Lake, IN: Eisenbrauns, 1999,

ZEV MAGHEN

GALILEE, SEA OF

Freshwater lake located in northeast Israel.

Measuring 64 square miles (166 sq km) in area, the Sea of Galilee (also Lake Tiberias or Kinneret) is located 680 feet (207 m) below sea level and is formed by waters flowing down from the Jordan River. The lake was the source of a thriving fishing industry in the time of Christ, but today only small numbers of fish (called "St. Peter's fish") are caught for local consumption. Deganya, the first Israeli kibbutz, is located on the shore. From the beginning of the British mandate in 1920, the Sea of Galilee was located within the borders of Palestine and, after 1948, the state of Israel. It acts as the principal freshwater source for Israel and supplies the National Water System.

See also NATIONAL WATER SYSTEM (ISRAEL); WATER.

Bibliography

Atlas of Israel: Cartography, Physical and Human Geography, 3d edition. New York: Macmillan, 1985.

BRYAN DAVES

GALLEI TZAHAL

Israel's army radio station, created in 1951 to entertain the troops and to bring information on army life to civilians.

The range and level of Gallei Tzahal's programs expanded markedly following the Arab–Israel War of 1967. The nonmilitary programs are controlled by the Israel Broadcasting Authority. Many productions have been aimed at young people who are approaching National Service age in the Israel Defense Force.

See also ARAB–ISRAEL WAR (1967).

ANN KAHN

GALLIPOLI

Peninsula between the Dardanelles and the Aegean Sea on the European side of the Turkish Straits.

Gallipoli was the site of an unsuccessful World War I Allied campaign (1915 and 1916) aimed at defeating the Ottoman Empire, opening up a second front against Austria–Hungary and Germany, and opening a supply route to Russia. Britain's First Lord of the Admiralty Winston Churchill proposed this plan, expecting secretary of war Lord Kitchener to supply the necessary land troops, but Kitchener did not fully support Churchill's plan.

An Anglo–French force (mostly ANZAC [Australia and New Zealand Army Corps]) landed at Gallipoli in April 1915, after four unsuccessful naval attacks; they met a stubborn land defense by the Ottoman Turks. Although suffering enormous losses, the Allies—including Italy by August—nearly succeeded in a breakthrough. Lack of Russian cooperation, faulty intelligence, and skillful tactics on the part of the Ottomans and Germans, however, led to a stalemate, then to Allied withdrawal in January 1916. Churchill became the scapegoat and lost his position.

See also AUSTRIA-HUNGARY AND THE MIDDLE EAST; CHURCHILL, WINSTON S.; KITCHENER, HORATIO HERBERT; OTTOMAN EMPIRE; WORLD WAR I.

Bibliography

Moorehead, Alan. Gallipoli. New York: Harper, 1956.

SARA REGUER

GAMAL, SAMIYAH
[1924–1994]

Egyptian dancer and actress on stage and screen.

Born Zaynab Khalil Ibrahim Mahfuz, Samiyah Gamal (also Samiyya Jamal) changed her name to conceal her identity from her family after becoming a dancer at Badiʿa Masabni's famous Cairo casino. At her debut in the late 1930s, she was paralyzed by stage fright until she thought of kicking off her brand-new high-heeled shoes. She danced in comfort and earned the nickname "the barefoot dancer." Among her fellow dancers at the Casino was Tahiya Kariyuka, another accomplished dancer and actress. The two women remained rivals until Gamal's death.

Gamal's dancing and acting led to appearances in some fifty-five films. After bit parts in the early 1940s, her first starring role was with actor Najib al-Rihani, "the Molière of Egypt," in *Ahmar shafayif* in 1946. She is best known for a series of charming musical films she made with costar Farid al-Atrash between 1947 and 1952. Her hopes for marriage to al-Atrash were disappointed and their extremely successful artistic partnership came to an end; her husbands included Sheppard W. King, a Texas cotton and oil baron, and Rushdi Abaza, an Egyptian actor. Gamal retired in 1972 but returned to the stage briefly in the early 1990s.

See also ART; KARIYUKA, TAHIYA.

Bibliography

Ahmar shafayif (Lipstick). Directed by Wali al-Din Samih. 1946.

Ali Baba et les quarantes voleurs (Ali Baba and the forty thieves). Directed by Jacques Becker. 1954.

Al-Wahsh (The beast). Directed by Salah Abu Sayf. 1953.

Habib al-umr (Love of my life). Directed by Henry Barakat. 1947.

Ma-tqulsh il-hadd (Don't tell anyone). Directed by Henry Barakat. 1952.

Zuqaq al-Midaqq (Midaq Alley). Directed by Hasan al-Imam. 1963.

ROBERTA L. DOUGHERTY

GANIM, HALIL

Ottoman opposition politician and newspaper publisher.

A Lebanese Maronite by birth, Halil Ganim (also Khalil Ghanim) served in the Ottoman parliament in 1877 and 1878. When the parliament was closed, he took up exile in Paris, where his prominent opposition newsletter, *La jeune Turquie*, soon gave its name to the emerging Young Turk movement. In 1895, Ganim collaborated with Young Turk leader Ahmet Riza, also in Paris, in publishing the first major organ of the cause, *Meşveret*. In 1901, he published a book against despotism, *Les sultans ottomans* (The Ottoman sultans). Ganim was one of a very few Arabs prominent in the Young Turk movement. He lived in Paris for the remainder of his life.

See also AHMET RIZA; YOUNG TURKS.

Bibliography

Hourani, Albert. *Arabic Thought in the Liberal Age, 1798–1939.* Cambridge, U.K., and New York: Cambridge University Press, 1983.

Lewis, Bernard. *The Emergence of Modern Turkey*, 3d edition. New York: Oxford University Press, 2002.

Shaw, Stanford, and Shaw, Ezel Kural. *History of the Ottoman Empire and Modern Turkey*, Vol. 2: *Reform, Revolution, and Republic: The Rise of Modern Turkey, 1808–1975.* Cambridge, U.K., and New York: Cambridge University Press, 1977.

ELIZABETH THOMPSON

GANJI, AKBAR
[1959–]

Iranian journalist, and writer.

Akbar Ganji was born and raised in Tehran, where he became a leading investigative journalist and the editor of the journal *Rah-e Now* (The new path), and newspaper *Sobhe Emruz* (Today's morning), and one of the most prominent and outspoken figures of the 23 May movement after the election of Mohammad Khatami in 1997. Ganji actively participated in the Iranian Revolution of 1979. After the revolution, he joined the Islamic Revolutionary Guard and from 1985 to 1989 he served as a cultural staff member of the Islamic Republic at the Iranian embassy in Turkey. In 1989 he was appointed to the media department of the publicity and press affairs of the Ministry of Culture and Islamic Guidance. He published a collection of newspaper articles in early 2000, *Dungeon of Ghosts*, in which he described a secret group affiliated with powerful, high-level officials whom he claimed had masterminded the serial killings of writers and political figures in 1998. He cited murders as part of a policy of state terror designed to subdue dissidents, and identified Ali Akbar Hashemi Rafsanjani as the chief architect of the serial assassinations. The book was sensational and made a major contribution to the defeat of conservative candidates in the parliamentary elections of February 2000. In April 2000 Ganji was arrested for his participation in an international conference in Berlin on the future of democracy in Iran. At the subsequent trial he was convicted of antistate activities and sentenced to ten years of imprisonment.

Bibliography

Ansari, Ali M. *Iran, Islam and Democracy: The Politics of Managing Change.* London: Royal Institute of International Affairs, 2000.

Nabavi, Negin, ed. *Intellectual Trends in Twentieth-Century Iran: A Critical Survey.* Tallahassee: Florida University Press, 2003.

BABAK RAHIMI

GARANG, JOHN
[1945–]

Sudanese advocate for the Bor Dinka people.

Born in Wagkulei, John Garang is from the Bor Dinka people in the southern Sudan and the most influential advocate on their behalf in the face of the Khartoum government. He was educated at Catholic mission schools in southern Sudan and graduated from high school in Tanzania. In 1970 he joined the southern resistance movement, Any-Nya, which was later incorporated into the Sudanese

Dr. John Garang (left), chairman of the Sudan People's Liberation Movement, shakes hands with Sudanese president Umar al-Bashir during April 2003 negotiations to end the Sudanese civil war. The negotiations continued throughout the year, and an agreement was hammered out that provided some degree of self-rule in Sudan's southern regions. © AP/WIDE WORLD PHOTOS. REPRODUCED BY PERMISSION.

armed forces (after the Addis Ababa negotiated peace in 1972). He rose to the rank of colonel in the Sudanese army.

Garang received his bachelor of science degree from Grinnell College in Iowa in 1971 and later returned to the United States for military training at Fort Benning, Georgia. In 1981 he earned a Ph.D. in economics from Iowa State University, focusing on economic development of the southern Sudan. Garang taught at the University of Khartoum and the Khartoum military academy.

The Addis Ababa peace accords broke down after Islamic law was made state law in Sudan. Garang was sent to the south in 1983 to put down the mutinies of southern officers led by Kerubino Kwanyin and William Bany. Instead he joined the revolt and he and a group of other officers and civilians founded the Sudan People's Liberation Movement (SPLM), of which he became chairman, and the Sudan People's Liberation Army (SPLA), of which he became commander. Garang was responding to attempts by the Sudanese government under Muhammad Ja'far Numeiri to eliminate local autonomy in southern Sudan, which had been agreed to in Addis Ababa in 1972. Garang favored a federal relationship between the southern regions and the

government in Khartoum, and also objected to Khartoum's decision to divide the previously united southern region along ethnic lines. He opposed the imposition in September 1983 of *shari'a,* or Islamic law, on the non-Muslim south. Garang wrote later that in founding the SPLM his aim was "to create a socialist system that affords democratic and human rights to all nationalities and guarantees freedom of religion, beliefs and outlooks." His movement was quickly categorized as being communist and secessionist, although he denied the validity of both labels.

At various times Garang received support from Libya (until 1985), from Ethiopia (until the fall of Mengistu Haile Mariam in 1991), and newly independent Eritrea on Sudan's eastern border, especially under the rule of Isaias Afwerki. Garang found it difficult to attain political unity among his followers because of their diverse ethnic loyalties; for example, he sought to divide the Nuer from the Dinka but in doing so intensified the war. He has also had personal conflicts with his commanders. In the protracted civil war against the Sudan government in Khartoum, neither side has been able to win in this war of attrition, nor has peace been successfully negotiated.

In 1989 an Islamist military regime backed by the National Islamic Front and its leader, Hasan al-Turabi, became intransigent on the issue of removing *shari'a* as state law. Still not seeking secession, Garang tried to make southern Sudan a world political issue. In this effort he was helped by U.S. Congressperson Mickey Leland, who welcomed him to congressional hearings on Sudan in July 1989. But Leland died in a plane accident shortly afterward. During the 1990s southern Sudan was in the international limelight because of severe food shortages and famine; displacement of humans and loss of life estimated at one to two million persons; the "lost boys," young refugees resettled in the United States; and allegations about the revival of slavery. Since 1995 Garang has been military commander of the opposition National Democratic Alliance forces in Ethiopia and Eritrea, as well as remaining head of the SPLM.

See also NUER; NUMEIRI, MUHAMMAD JA'FAR; SUDAN; SUDANESE CIVIL WARS; TURABI, HASAN AL-.

Bibliography

Garang, John. *The Call for Democracy in Sudan,* 2d revised edition, edited by Mansour Khalid. New York; London: Kegan Paul, 1992.

"John De Mabior Garang." In *Historical Dictionary of the Sudan,* 3d edition, edited by Richard A. Lobban, Jr., Robert S. Kramer, and Carolyn Fluehr-Lobban. Lanham, MD, and London: Scarecrow Press, 2002.

PAUL MARTIN
UPDATED BY CAROLYN FLUEHR-LOBBAN

GARDANNE MISSION

French military mission to Persia, 1807–1808.

The Gardanne Mission's purpose was to train the Persian army along European lines. It consisted of seventy officers and sergeants, led by General Claude-Matthew Gardanne. The mission was a result of the Finkenstein Treaty of May 1807, in which Iran sought help from France against Russia—while France had visions of using Iran as a stepping stone to British India. The Treaty of Tilsit in July 1807 temporarily ended hostilities between France and Russia, so support of Persia against Russia was no longer a French priority. Persia then negotiated with Britain, agreed to dismiss Gardanne, and signed a preliminary treaty in March 1809 that provided British officers to train the Persian army.

Bibliography

Daniel, Norman. *Islam, Europe and Empire.* Edinburgh: Edinburgh University Press, 1966.

DANIEL E. SPECTOR

GASPIRALI, ISMAIL BEY

[1851–1914]

Turkish journalist, educator, and reformer.

Born in the Crimea into a noble family (the Russian form of his name was Gasprinskii), Ismail Bey Gaspirali was a reformer who introduced a new educational method *(usul-i cedid).* He also advocated a single shared identity for all Muslim Turkic peoples of Imperial Russia, hoping to unite them with the motto "unity in language, thought, and action." In 1883, he founded the newspaper *Tercüman,* which was influential throughout the Turkic world; it ceased publication in 1918. Gaspirali intended the language of this newspaper, based on Ottoman Turkish, to serve as a common literary language for all Muslim Turkic speakers.

See also TURKISH LANGUAGE.

Bibliography

Kirimli, Sirri Hakan. "National Movements and National Identity among the Crimean Tatars (1905–1916)." Ph.D. diss., University of Wisconsin, 1990.

ULI SCHAMILOGLU

GAZA (CITY)

Principal city of the Gaza Strip.

Gaza City is located in the northern part of the Gaza Strip, on the coast of the Mediterranean Sea. Along with the rest of the Gaza Strip, it was inhabited by Philistines in ancient times and subsequently conquered by many peoples due to its strategic location As part of the British Mandate, it came under Egyptian administration after the 1948 Arab–Israel War. The city contains a small port that serves local fisherman. Gaza's population consists of 400,000 mostly Muslim Palestinians. After the 1948 war, Gaza experienced an influx of refugees (approximately 190,000) and was six times larger by 1967. Today, about half the city's population are refugees.

Since the 1967 Arab–Israeli War, Gaza has been occupied by Israel. At the beginning of the first Palestinian uprising (intifada) in 1987, Gaza became a center for political unrest. In May 1994 the city became the first provincial headquarters for the Palestinian National Authority, which administers Palestinian areas in the Gaza Strip and West Bank.

Gaza is the economic center for citrus fruits and other crops and contains small industries, such as textiles. Gaza's economy has been weakened due to closures by the Israeli military, implemented in the wake of the first intifada, and its dependency on wage labor in Israel. As a result of the al-Aqsa intifada (which began in 2000), more than half of the city's population are unemployed and living below the poverty line.

Bibliography

"Gaza City." Palestine: Home of History. Available from <http://www.palestinehistory.com/gazacity.htm>.

Municipality of Gaza. Available from <http://www .mogaza.org/gaza_city.htm>.

Roy, Sara. *The Gaza Strip: The Political Economy of De–Development,* 2d edition. Washington, DC: Institute for Palestine Studies, 2001.

MALLIKA GOOD

GAZA STRIP

Region bordering Israel and Egypt on the Mediterranean Sea.

The inhabitants of the Gaza Strip are almost all Palestinians with a population estimated at 1,100,000 (2003). Some 65 percent of these are refugees, descendants of the 250,000 refugees who flooded into the territory in 1948 during the first Arab–Israel War. Few carry passports and everyone is stateless. Arabic is the primary language; Islam is the primary religion, but Christians are also in residence. Eight UN-sponsored Palestinian refugee camps are located in the Gaza Strip.

The boundaries of the Gaza Strip have not changed since 1948; with only one-fifteenth the area of the West Bank, it has one of the highest population densities in the world. The Strip is almost rectangular, bordered by Israel on the north and east and by Egypt on the south. It has no capital, but its largest cities are Gaza City, Khan Yunis, and Rafah. It measures some 28 miles (45 km) by about 5 miles (8 km).

The northern third belongs to the red sands of the Philistian plain; the southern two-thirds (south of the main watercourse, the Wadi Gaza) belong to the more fertile sandy loess of the northern Negev Desert coast. It is hot and humid in the summer, cooler and humid in the winter, with limited rainfall.

Gaza's economy is small, underdeveloped, and weak, historically generating close to 50 percent of its national product from external sources. Under Israeli control, its economy became heavily dependent on wage labor in Israel, where over half of Gaza's labor force was traditionally employed. Israeli military law undermined local economic development, and the combined impact of the first (1987–1993) and second (2000–) Palestinian uprisings and the Israeli government's harsh response has seriously weakened the local economy. Natural resources, notably land and water, are very limited and diminishing, and no mineral resources exist. Agriculture historically played a large role in the local economy, with citrus the primary agricultural export. Industry is largely traditional and rudimentary. Small factories manufacture beverages, tobacco, textiles, clothing, wood products, and plastics.

In ancient times the area was inhabited by the Philistines. It is mentioned in the Bible as the place of Samson's death and as the burial place of one of the great-grandfathers of the Prophet Muhammad. The Gaza area was conquered by many peoples, including the Jews (Hebrews), Romans, and Arabs, before it became part of the Ottoman Empire. After World War I, when the Ottoman Empire was dismembered, the Gaza region became part of the British mandate over Palestine. In 1947 the mandate disintegrated and resulted in a call for the partition of Palestine into an Arab and a Jewish state. Following the Arab–Israel War of 1948, the Egypt–Israel General Armistice Agreement of February 1949 left Egypt ruling the Gaza Strip under a mil-

MAP BY XNR PRODUCTIONS, INC. THE GALE GROUP.

itary administration. During the Arab–Israel War of 1956, Israel controlled the Gaza Strip from November until March of 1957, when it reverted to Egypt.

Since the Arab–Israel War of 1967, Gaza has been under Israeli military rule. The Palestinian uprising (or intifada) started in Gaza in 1987. In 1993 the Oslo peace process began with an agreement between the Israeli government and the Palestine Liberation Organization (PLO) to implement limited autonomy in the Gaza Strip and in the West Bank town of Jericho. The failure of the Camp David Summit (July 2000) effectively ended this process. The second Palestinian uprising, known as the al-Aqsa Intifada, has created unprecedented hardship for Palestinians, especially those living in the more impoverished Gaza Strip.

See also AQSA INTIFADA, AL-; ARAB–ISRAEL WAR (1948); CAMP DAVID SUMMIT (2000); GAZA (CITY); INTIFADA (1987–1991); MUHAMMAD; NEGEV; PALESTINE LIBERATION ORGANIZATION (PLO); PALESTINIANS; WEST BANK.

Bibliography

Roy, Sara. *The Gaza Strip: The Political Economy of De-Development,* 2d edition. Washington, DC: Institute for Palestine Studies, 2001.

SARA M. ROY

GEAGEA, SAMIR

[1952–]

Lebanese politician and leader of the Lebanese Forces.

A Maronite from Bsharra in northern Lebanon, Samir Geagea studied medicine at the American University of Beirut, but did not complete his studies due to his early participation in the Lebanese Civil War. He fought during the 1975 to 1976 phase of the war in the militia of the Lebanese Phalange Party. By the late 1970s, he had become a senior commander of the Lebanese Forces (LF) and was committed to using force to restore Christian hegemony over Lebanon. He was very loyal to Bashir Jumayyil, who used him for the most vicious and brutal operations. Thus, he was dispatched by Bashir in 1978 to aid in the attack on the home of

Tony Franjiyya that resulted in the deaths of Franjiyya and several members of his family. When LF leader Elie Hubeika signed the Tripartite Accord on behalf of the Christian community in December 1985, Geagea denounced it as a surrender to Syria. In January 1986, as chairman of the executive committee of the LF, he challenged President Amin Jumayyil and the Phalangist leadership and consolidated his ties with Israel.

After Jumayyil stepped down, Geagea clashed with General Michel Aoun when he attempted to curb the militias. Tensions between them culminated in devastating fighting for control of East Beirut's Christian enclave in the first half of 1990. In April 1990 Geagea endorsed the Ta'if Accord, largely to neutralize Aoun. After the defeat of Aoun in October 1990 and the normalization of political and security conditions in the country, Geagea became one of the most vocal critics of Syria's power in Lebanon.

By late 1993, Geagea had become a marginal figure in Lebanon's politics because of his past association with Israel, Syria's animosity toward him, and the de facto political neutralization of his militia. More fundamentally, he was the target of deep popular resentment against the warlords. Even among Christians, he was blamed for the loss of lives and property in East Beirut, and his reputation was tainted by his participation in the mass killing of Christian rivals, including Tony Franjiyya. Geagea was put on trial for the killing of Dany Chamoun and Rashid Karame, and was found guilty of dispatching a car bomb to a rival church. He has been in jail since 1994; right-wing forces continue to demand his release.

See also AMERICAN UNIVERSITY OF BEIRUT (AUB); AOUN, MICHEL; CHAMOUN, DANY; FRANJIYYA FAMILY; JUMAYYIL, AMIN; JUMAYYIL, BASHIR; KARAME, RASHID; LEBANESE CIVIL WAR (1975–1990); LEBANESE FORCES; PHALANGE; TA'IF ACCORD.

Bibliography

Petran, Tabitha. *The Struggle over Lebanon.* New York: Monthly Review Press, 1987.

GUILAIN P. DENOEUX
UPDATED BY AS'AD ABUKHALIL

GEBEYLI, CLAIRE
[1935–]

Greek/Lebanese writer.

Of Greek origin, Claire Gebeyli was born and raised in Alexandria, Egypt, where she studied the humanities and social sciences. Steeped in ethics and philosophy, she is fluent in classical and modern Greek, French, English, and Arabic. She left Egypt under Gamal Abdel Nasser's rule and came to Lebanon, where she presently resides and which she has fully adopted as her own. Poet, novelist, journalist, professor of francophone literature at the Jesuit University of Beirut, national officer of the United Nation Program for Development throughout the Lebanese war (1975–1990), and member of the prestigious Academy of Science in New York, Gebeyli also has contributed articles in medicine, culture, fashion, literature, and women's profiles to the daily francophone newspaper *L'Orient–Le jour* since 1967. A pioneer in journalism, her *Billets* (Notes) on the dramatic events of the Lebanese war were collected in a volume of prose poems. She is the author of several other volumes of poetry in French and a novel titled *Cantate pour l'oiseau mort* (Cantata for a dead bird), which was awarded the Albert Camus Prize in 1996.

See also GENDER: GENDER AND EDUCATION; LEBANON; NEWSPAPERS AND PRINT MEDIA: ARAB COUNTRIES.

MONA TAKIEDDINE AMYUNI

GECEKONDU

Literally, homes "built up at night" without permits in slum areas of Turkish cities.

The low-income neighborhoods lacking many urban amenities that surround Turkey's large cities are known as *gecekondu*s because the houses are built during the night on vacant land and without construction permits. Once the exterior walls and roof are in place, owners of the land—often the government—are not permitted to tear the houses down without going through a lengthy court process. Thus, for the squatters who build these homes, their overnight construction work becomes a fait accompli. In this way, extensive *gecekondu*s have been established on the outskirts of Adana, Ankara, Bursa, Diyarbakir, Istanbul, and İzmir. Houses in *gecekondu* neighborhoods often make illegal connections to urban water and electricity lines. Long-established *gecekondu*s have been successful in pressuring municipalities to provide legal urban services such as piped water, sewers, electricity, and transportation.

Bibliography

Gursoy-Tezcan, Akile. "Mosque or Health Centre? A Dispute in a Gecekondu." In *Islam in Modern Turkey: Religion, Politics, and Literature in a Secular State*, edited by Richard Tapper. London: I.B. Tauris, 1991.

Karpat, Kemal H. *The Gecekondu: Rural Migration and Urbanization*. Cambridge, U.K.: Cambridge University Press, 1979.

ERIC HOOGLUND

GENCER, LEYLA
[1928–]

Turkish operatic soprano.

Leyla Gencer is revered by fans all over the world as the "regina" of the Donizetti operas. Her timing and perfection of theatrical gesture onstage, her deep chest tones, and perfectly pitched and executed coloratura are legendary.

Gencer was born in Istanbul on 10 October 1928. Her Polish Catholic mother, Alexandra Angela Minakovska—who later converted to Islam—was from Adampol, a village on the outskirts of Istanbul that was a colony for Polish refugees fleeing from the invading Russians during the mid-nineteenth century. Her father, Hasanzade Ibrahim Ceyrekgil, was from a prominent Safranbolu family with lucrative business interests in Istanbul. While attending the Italian High School in Istanbul, Leyla met and married a young banker, Ibrahim Gencer. She persuaded her husband and his family to allow her to attend the Istanbul Conservatory where she began pursuing voice lessons.

During the summer of 1949 she met Giannina Arangi Lombardi and followed her to Ankara, where Lombardi had an engagement as a voice coach at the Ankara State Opera. Lombardi died a year later, and Gencer continued her voice studies with Apollo Granforte; Italian repertoire with Di Ferdinando, Adolfo Camozzo, and Domenico Trizzio; and German opera with Georg Reinwald. She debuted at the Ankara State Opera in 1950 as Santuzza in

Mascagni's *Cavalleria rusticana,* followed by *Tosca* in 1952 and *Cosi fan tutte* in 1953. Her Italian debut was in 1954 at the Teatro San Carlo in Naples, where she performed *Madama Butterfly* and *Eugene Onegin.* In September 1956 she was invited to the San Francisco Opera to perform *Francesca da Rimini* by Zandonai, but her breakthrough came when Francis Poulenc chose her as his Madame Lidoine in his opera *Dialogues des Carmélites,* which was produced at the Teatro La Scala in Milan on 26 January 1957. Her career took flight from 1957 to 1980 with a great variety of roles. She had an immense repertoire which included all of Verdi, Puccini, Donizetti, and Bellini operas and a great variety of works by other major composers.

Gencer retired from the stage in 1987, but continued giving concerts. She is the director of La Scala Singing School in Milan and received the Puccini Honorary Award from the Licia Albanese Puccini Foundation at the New York City Lincoln Center on 2 November 2002.

See also GENDER: GENDER AND EDUCATION; MUSIC; THEATER.

FILIZ ALI

GENÇ KALEMLER

A Turkish nationalist group and its journal.

Genç Kalemler was founded in 1910–1911 in Salonika, bringing together a group of writers and poets under the leadership of famous nationalists Ömer Sayfettin and Ziya Gökalp. Theirs was the first organized attempt at Turkish language reform, born of reaction to the ornate linguistic excesses of the Servet-i Fünun group of the 1890s. They sought to bring written Turkish closer to its spoken form, without the Arabic and Persian grammar and vocabulary of the elite of the Ottoman Empire.

The group also sought to bring realism to what they felt was artificial Ottoman literature—by producing numerous critical essays in its journal and by publishing new stories and poems. Genç Kalemler's pursuit of simple direct language also had a political aim, because it was felt that to rescue the empire, a language understandable to the common people was needed. Genç Kalemler had close ties to the Turkish nationalist Committee for Union and Progress. The journal was published until the Turkish war of independence after World War I.

See also COMMITTEE FOR UNION AND PROGRESS; GÖKALP, ZIYA; SALONIKA; TURKISH LANGUAGE.

Bibliography

Arai, Masami. *Turkish Nationalism in the Young Turk Era.* Leiden, Netherlands, and New York: Brill, 1992.

ELIZABETH THOMPSON

GENDER

This entry consists of the following articles:

GENDER AND THE ECONOMY
GENDER AND EDUCATION
GENDER AND LAW
GENDER AND POLITICS
GENDER: STUDY OF

GENDER AND THE ECONOMY

Women's economic participation in developing countries includes issues such as the invisibility of women's economic activities and their concentration mainly in low-wage and menial jobs in farming activities due to the lack of equal education and training, as well as limited access to productive assets, land and property, and credit.

Despite variations in woman's status in the Middle East and North Africa, gender bias in this region remains the highest in the world, thereby obstructing social and political development. Gender bias therefore limits the economic potential of half of the society. In contrast with other parts of the world, Middle Eastern women's economic participation in the labor force and in decision-making sectors is notably among the lowest in the world. Historically, a wide range of cultural, ideological, legislative, and political constraints have hindered women's economic roles and advancement. Moreover, political and economic instability caused by weak states, ongoing conflicts, and the repercussions of chronic war have had a negative impact on women's opportunities for economic advancement.

Restrictive Environment

Ideologically, the inferior status of women in Middle Eastern and North African societies stems from patriarchal interpretations of the religious rulings of Islam, Christianity, and Judaism. Such interpretations have stressed women's family roles as wives, daughters, and mothers. Therefore, women remained "jural minors," economically, legally, and socially dependent on fathers, brothers, and, after marriage, husbands. Given this historical and ideological context, an autonomous public life for a woman was outside the norm and was often perceived as a threat to her family's honor and reputation.

Following the end of the colonial era, the attaining of independence, and the creation of national governments in the region, gender-biased regulations have been institutionalized in legislation, with the result that women are often deprived of basic rights and privileges enjoyed elsewhere. Personal status laws and other legal codes have limited women's full integration into society. For example, women in countries such as Saudi Arabia, Iran, and Egypt must obtain the permission of their fathers, brothers, or husbands to attain a passport or travel outside of their country. In certain cases this authorization is required to open a business, receive a bank loan, or get married. A Saudi newspaper reported in November 2002 that Saudi women's bank accounts contained more than $26 billion in unutilized funds because of the laws that prevent women from conducting business autonomously.

Furthermore, women who marry foreigners are denied the right to extend their citizenship to their husbands or any children they may bear, unlike men married to foreign wives. The combination of these new codes and regulations affects the economic rights of women negatively and systematically.

Low female participation in the work force is also the result of limited industrialization in the region. Middle Eastern and North African economies are mainly dependent on oil exports. Therefore, governments chose development strategies that relied on oil and finance. In return, this strategy minimized the use of labor and offered scant employment opportunities for women. In fact, the reliance of Gulf economies on oil and the associated economic boom has affected labor market trends throughout the region, not just women's participation. The oil boom has contributed to the preservation of a patriarchal family structure, according

to which men act as breadwinners and women as homemakers, the former having a public role, the latter a private one. High income in oil-producing countries and associated increased remittance to labor-exporting countries in the region make it unnecessary for women to seek paid employment outside the home.

In non–oil exporting economies that adopted import-substitution industrial strategies, such as Egypt, both private and public sectors established industrial projects and opened work opportunities that favored male workers but also created new spaces for female workers. In other countries, such as Morocco and Tunisia, export-led development strategies and associated flows of foreign capital into both countries has enabled active female participation in the work force. Nevertheless, reports revealed that female workers in garment subcontracting workshops in Morocco are exploited, and owners will not hire married women.

Lagging female integration in the region's economy also has political dimensions. During the Cold War, Western countries, mainly the United States, supported the rise of political Islam, including Islamic armed groups, thus limiting women's chances for emancipation. Many of the oppressive governments in the region survived only because of Western military or economic support. In Afghanistan, Taliban rule, originally stemming from the *mojahedin* movements supported by the United States in its proxy war against the Soviet Union, confined Afghan women to their homes and banned them from education and work for years. Furthermore, the concept no less than the practice of gender equality is opposed by many groups in the region, who view the idea as a manifestation of colonization, since colonial authorities supported women's rights primarily to denigrate and thereby dominate the cultures of the region.

Gender and Socioeconomic Transformation

Until recently, rural women comprised the majority of women in the region. Thus women's traditional economic roles included household labor, farming, and livestock breeding. However, exposure to Western culture in the nineteenth century through increased integration of the region into the world economy, colonization, missionary activities,

Moroccan girls embroider a tapestry. Women in Morocco comprise 35 percent of a labor force that totals 11 million and have an unemployment rate of 27.6 percent. © SCHEUFLER COLLECTION/CORBIS. REPRODUCED BY PERMISSION.

and male students' scholarships to study in Europe generated forces within Middle Eastern and North African societies that favored changes in the conditions of women. Egpyt's Qasim Amin, considered the father of feminism in the region, published his influential book *The Liberation of Women* in 1889.

Unlike Egypt and Turkey, where elites and upper classes partook early in modernity, and where women's status improved notably, in Lebanon, the emigration of peasants to the United States engaged entire, far-reaching networks of Lebanese in modernization processes at home and abroad. According to Khater, this early contact with American society and economy created a new "mobile middle class" that put considerable pressures on the prevailing social and economic arrangements in communities of origin, resulting in changed patterns of marriage and other gender relations.

In the early twentieth century, modernization and urbanization further improved the conditions of women, including access to education and health care. Education has enabled women with skills to enter the non-agricultural work force and to practice extra-domestic income-generating activities. Thanks to accelerated modernization, combined with widespread gender advocacy led by women's organizations, many societies in the region have witnessed an unprecedented rise in woman's literacy rates. This has resulted in women's increasing engagement in public life. In countries such as Israel, Pakistan, Bangladesh, and Turkey, women have become heads of government. Furthermore, groups of highly educated and professional women have become significant agents of reform and change, such as Hanan Ashrawi of Palestine, Nawwal as-Saʿdawi of Egypt, and Shirin Ebadi of Iran.

Women in North Africa learn to weave rugs. The Arab world has one of the lowest proportions of women in the work force due to numerous factors, including cultural emphases stressing women's place in the home, lack of training and education for women in some professions, low levels of industrialization throughout the region, and economic instability, as well as the reliance on migrant laborers in wealthy states in the region. © SCHEUFLER COLLECTION/CORBIS. REPRODUCED BY PERMISSION.

Increased rates of urbanization, literacy, and employment have changed attitudes, practices, and perceptions. Women in the region are trying to move toward egalitarian ideas and the reconstruction of modern life, especially the family structure and its associated gender roles and relations. Growing access to the Internet and other communication technologies in recent years is expected to enhance such reforms.

Women's Economic Status

Official statistics for the region indicate that women's empowerment policies have effectively targeted female education and health services, which have improved significantly over the last few decades. These improvements are essentially due to increased public spending on education and health care and the spread of mass media. In the year 2000, average spending on education reached 5.3 percent of gross domestic product (GDP)—the highest in the world—and 2.9 percent on health care. As a result, the welfare of women has improved significantly. Female life expectancy has increased by ten years since 1980 and the female literacy rate increased from less than 17 percent in 1970 to more than 52 percent in 2000.

Yet, as the UN's Human Development Report for 2003 has noted, the region has the lowest gender empowerment ratings, which reflects the participation of women in economic, professional, and political activities using indicators of per capita income, women's percentage share for professional and technical positions, and women's percentage share of parliamentary seats. More specifically, Israel is rated highest at 61.2 percent, followed by the

United Arab Emirates (31.5%), Turkey (29%), and Egypt (25.3%). Yemen is the lowest on the list, with a rate of 12.7 percent. By contrast, the measure for countries in Latin America exceeded 50 percent and 75 percent of rates for specific European and North American countries. No data was available for Sub-Saharan Africa and other Middle Eastern and North African countries. The Arab Human Development Report (2002) explained that the lack of such data is an index of official disregard for women's empowerment in the region.

The report also reveals that women's economic participation remains lower than prevailing rates elsewhere. Similarly, female participation in the labor market remains among the lowest rates in the world, despite an evident increase over the last three decades from less than 23 percent in 1970 to 32 percent in 2000. Official statistics suggests that female participation in work force rates varies significantly among individual countries in the region. In Israel, female participation is around 41 percent compared with only 16 percent in Saudi Arabia (see table 1). International comparisons suggest that the highest recorded rate was in East Asia and the Pacific (76%), followed by Europe and Central Africa (67%), and sub-Saharan Africa (62%). Thus, the gender gap in labor force participation remains profound in the Middle East and North Africa.

In addition to the lower work force participation rate, the distribution of men and women workers among economic sectors presents a continuation of traditional trends. In countries such as Turkey and Yemen, the largest share of women is employed in agriculture as unpaid family workers. Women's employment in other countries has increased mainly in the traditionally accepted public services such as health and education, which channels traditional female skills into paid forms of care giving. In contrast, female employment remains low in manufacturing and minimal in communication, trade, and tourism activities. In Israel, the most dynamic and diversified economy in the region, women's work is also mostly concentrated in lower-paying jobs, services, education, health, welfare, and clerical positions. Israeli women are significantly less represented in prestigious occupations such as technology, management, government, the military, and engineering.

In 2002 a study conducted by the United Nation Development Fund on women's participation in the Information and Communication Technologies (ICT) in Jordan found that women make up only 28 percent of the ICT labor force. The larger proportion of Jordanian women is employed in the low-skilled jobs, such as data entry and support jobs. The findings also suggested that only 7 percent of the female ICT workers are decision

Gender and the economy

Country	Population (in millions)	Female population (% total)	Total labor force (in millions)	Female labor force (% total)	Unemployment rate Total	Unemployment rate Female
Algeria	30.4	49.4	10	28	n.a.	n.a.
Egypt	64	49.1	24	30	8.2	19.9
Iran	63.7	49.8	20	27	n.a.	n.a.
Iraq	23.3	49.2	6	20	n.a.	n.a.
Israel	6.2	50.4	3	41	8.2	8.1
Jordan	4.9	48.3	1	25	13.2	20.7
Kuwait	2	46.8	1	31	n.a.	n.a.
Lebanon*	4.3	50.8	2	30	8.6	7.2
Morocco	28.7	50	11	35	22	27.6
Saudi Arabia	20.7	45.7	7	16	n.a.	n.a.
Syria	16.2	49.5	5	27	n.a.	n.a.
Tunisia	9.6	49.5	4	32	n.a.	n.a.
Turkey	67.4	49.5	31	38	8.3	6.6
Yemen	17.5	49	6	28	11.5	8.2

*unemployment data for Lebanon refers to 1995. n.a.: not available.

SOURCE: World Bank online Database of Gender Statistics

TABLE BY GGS INFORMATION SERVICES, THE GALE GROUP.

makers and only 2 percent are project mangers and team leaders. Equivalent estimates for other Arab countries in the region are expected to be much lower, since Jordan is considered one of the ICT hubs of the Arab *mashriq* region.

Clearly, the public sector is the preferred employment venue for female workers throughout the region. Government jobs assure women of more equal treatment and benefits. Conversely, women employed in private enterprises suffer gender discrimination, including lower wages and limited professional prospects. In the case of Egypt, an employed woman in the private sector receives only 50 percent of a male coworker's wage despite having equal qualifications. This phenomenon might be attributed to non-wage benefits, including shorter working hours, lengthy maternity leaves, and early access to pension.

However, ongoing economic restructuring strategies in the region have a significant impact on women and have reduced female job opportunities in public institutions. This trend has pushed women workers into the informal employment sector, with low remuneration and no social protection, as suggested by the Moroccan case.

Women's low participation in the labor market has serious economic implications. At the individual level, it is costly for women and their families. The welfare of the family—including consumption of food, housing, healthcare, and other goods and services—is determined by the available income for the entire family. Logically, two workers in the household earn more income. During the oil boom in the 1970s and early 1980s, higher real wages made it possible for the small number of workers to support large number of dependents within their families while still enjoying high standards of living. Since the mid-1980s, real wages stagnated or declined. Consequently, fewer workers were able to support their families and maintain the same living standards. Nationally, lower participation rates for women in Middle Eastern and North African economies mean that almost half of the available human resources remain unutilized. Research has revealed that lower female participation in the labor market in the region has negatively affected successful structural adjustment reforms and competitiveness in the context of the global economy.

No Access to Assets

In addition to the significant gap in the labor market, limited access to assets and opportunities further restrict overall female economic participation in the region. For example, women's entitlement to land is minimal. Traditionally, sons are entitled to inherit the father's properties while women are discouraged to claim inheritance rights. In Egypt, the overall share of female landholders is less than 6 percent of all holders, although female labor is concentrated in agriculture activities.

Women's access to credit services is also restricted because formal credit institutions offer loans to those who have collateral such as land. Hence, women are almost excluded from such services since they do not have the required collateral. Moreover, females' access to new information and communication technologies is minimal.

Despite the quantitative improvement in female education, a closer look at female enrollment rates by subject suggests significant difference relative to males. For example, in the academic year 1995/1996 around 64.4 percent of female students in Jordan were enrolled in humanities and only 17.7 percent in engineering and physical and technical sciences. The United Nations Economic and Social Commission for Western Asia (ESCWA) estimates this gap is more severe in other Arab countries. In the Arab world, the number of male students enrolled in fields of study such as engineering, commercial studies, and law is four times higher than that of female students. As a result, male students will have better career prospects and greater economic potential compared to that of their female colleagues.

Living in Poverty

The overall economic imbalance is also reflected in income and wages earned by female workers compared to those of their male counterparts. Wage discrimination against female workers is significant in the region compared to other countries. On average, a woman is paid only 73 percent of a man holding similar qualifications. According to the World Bank, if women in the region were paid for their qualifications in a manner equivalent to men, women's earnings would increase by an average of 32 percent, so they would earn 93 cents for every dollar earned by men, instead of 73 cents. Wage and income discrimination have increased the vulnerability of women and of female-headed households.

Based on the patriarchal notions according to which the man is the income earner, family benefits and non-wage allowances are usually channeled only through men. This practice increases discrimination against female workers and hinders female participation in general. Women's vulnerability also increased in recent years because of rising unemployment and poverty rates in the region due to increased political instability and associated economic decline. At the same time, war and conflicts have increased the number of households headed by women in the region.

Addressing the Imbalance

In order to reduce gender imbalance and empower women in the region, various initiatives are currently being implemented in the region by civil organizations, governments, and international organizations, including the United Nations and the World Bank. In 2002 the first Arab Human Development Report urged enhancing women's roles in Arab society and economy.

This approach implies legal education as well as training and infrastructure components. The legal component requires the review of legislative regulations to amend legal provisions that fail to recognize gender equality and women's rights. The legal component also requires the reform of the labor market law to reflect the emerging development model based mainly on the private sector in job creation.

The report also calls for continued attention to education to provide women with better market skills through vocational and lifelong learning opportunities. Female supportive infrastructure is needed to allow women to combine work and family roles easily and with minimum sacrifice. Nevertheless, the successful implementation of this approach requires a profound change at all levels of society, from top-level government to local communities and individual households.

Bibliography

Center of Arab Women for Training and Research (CAWTAR). *Globalization and Gender: Economic Participation of Arab Women.* Tunis: Author, 2001.

Kandiyoti, Deniz, ed. *Gendering the Middle East: Emerging Perspectives.* New York: Syracuse University Press, 1996.

Khater, Akram. *Inventing Home: Emigration, Gender, and the Middle Class in Lebanon, 1879–1920.* Berkeley: University of California Press, 2001.

Khoury, Nabil, and Moghadam, Valentine, eds. *Gender and Development in the Arab World: Women's Economic Participation, Patterns and Policies.* London: Zed Books, 1995.

United Nations Development Programme and Arab Fund for Economic and Social Development. *Arab Development Report 2002: Creating Opportunities for Future Generations.* New York: Author, 2002.

United Nations Development Programme and Arab Fund for Economic and Social Development. *Arab Development Report 2003: Building Knowledge Societies in Arab Countries.* New York: Author, 2003.

United Nations Economic and Social Commission for Western Asia (ESCWA). *Women and Men in the Arab World.* Amman: Author, 2002.

World Bank. *Gender and Development in the Middle East and North Africa: Women in the Public Sphere.* Washington DC: Author, 2003.

World Bank. *Turkey: Women in Development.* Washington, DC: Author, 1992.

KHALED ISLAIH

GENDER AND EDUCATION

Formal schooling, informal education, and gender socialization have historically been strong factors in the development of women, societies, and states in the Middle East, reflecting social, political, and religious trends and tensions within the region.

The education of girls and women in the Middle East is a complex and contentious subject. What knowledge women should acquire, relative to that of men, and how they should use that knowledge are matters of great debate, both among educators and among the public throughout the region and beyond. Indeed, discussions of gender and education often serve as markers of political or religious dissent and have become a key factor in the debate around women's status in the region. These debates reveal the complexity of gender socialization for Middle Eastern women and men, and the ways in which formal and informal educational structures and opportunities have variously, and often simultaneously, served as sources of empowerment and control. This complexity is best understood through a historical analysis of the role of education in the development of gender role identity among different populations in the modern Middle East.

Participation and Content

Formal schooling for women and girls in the Middle East is characterized by both progress and regression. The region's states have accepted education as a basic right and, when compared to developing countries generally, over the last fifty years have made significant quantitative gains in female schooling. The enrollment of girls has increased notably, particularly following the introduction of nondiscriminatory compulsory public education laws in most states, and in many Middle Eastern countries girls and boys now have equal access to schooling and similar levels of participation. In the Middle East as a whole, girls are more likely to be attending school than their counterparts in West Africa or South Asia, and academically they usually outperform their male peers, both on assessments and in terms of grade repetition.

However, there are indications that these gains may be slowing, if not reversing. Nearly one girl in four of primary school age in the Arab states is not in school, and the ratio is far higher in Afghanistan. In addition, enrollment rates for girls drop noticeably beginning in middle school and continue to decline through secondary and tertiary schooling. Although Turkey, Iran, and Israel all boast high levels of both primary and secondary enrollment for girls, in the Arab states slightly less than 47 percent of the 60 percent of all students in the secondary age group enrolled in school are girls. High dropout rates among girls and high numbers of girls who never enroll contribute to the high overall levels of female illiteracy in the region (an average of 50% for women in the Arab states).

Gender bias in curricula varies from country to country within the region, but instructional programs and texts generally reinforce subordinate or domestic roles for women. However, the effects of these messages on student choices and participation are unpredictable. Secondary schools across the region, which typically track students into arts and humanities or sciences, generally sort females into the arts and humanities tracks and, in vocational programs, into such fields as nursing, typing, home economics, and simple bookkeeping. Tertiary programs reflect similar imbalances of women in social sciences, humanities, and education, as opposed to more technical fields. However, an increasing proportion of Middle Eastern women (indeed, a larger proportion than their Western counterparts) are choosing science and mathematics as specializations, and (as noted above), their performance has outpaced that of male students in these fields, even in more traditional societies.

Social Context

Such contradictory data indicate a need to view education within a broader framework than that of simple formal schooling. Social forces affect academic performance and gendered life choices. For Middle Eastern girls and women, as for women elsewhere, informal training and upbringing, popular discourses, and media engagement are as important to their overall education as any formal schooling they receive. Gender roles are conveyed, modeled, and reinforced in these venues in ways that interact with schooling to shape students' expectations, desires, and performance, thus exerting a profound influence on the future of the region's women and girls.

Historically, this interaction has been part of a larger tension between Middle Eastern cultures and educational reforms largely developed in or modeled on those of Western Europe and North America. Although traditional forms of education, including the *kuttab* and *madrasa* (Islamic schools focusing on religious instruction), have remained important throughout the region, colonialism, modernization campaigns, and now globalization have layered external influences over indigenous institutions and concerns. State school systems in the contemporary Middle East are heavily dependent on funding from international sources to maintain their capacity, and thus typically reflect an understanding of education that is based on external models (although content and pedagogy are typically at least one step behind efforts in the countries on which they are based). This dependence on the West has resulted both in greater Middle Eastern interest in and acceptance of Western norms and in rejection of those norms in favor of local or regional efforts grounded in religion and culture.

Islamic Influence

Religion has played a central role in the education of Middle Eastern girls and boys, and in the shap-

Students learn the art of embroidery during vocational training. © Hulton-Deutsch Collection/Corbis. Reproduced by permission.

ing of their gender identity. Islam, the dominant religion for most of the region's countries, strongly emphasizes learning as an obligation of faith, and has in most cases been used historically as a support for education, including that of girls and women. Muslim women across the region have studied and continue to study in traditional Islamic schools and colleges; in schools operated by Christian missionaries; in public, state-sponsored schools; and in overseas institutions of higher learning. Local custom and beliefs, however, have affected the enrollment of girls and women and have strongly influenced both men's and women's fields of study. Formal secular education for women, as opposed to religious instruction, is seen across the region on a continuum ranging from necessity to nuisance, and there are notable differences of opinion about where the

line between benefit and drawback occurs. Some extreme interpretations, such as that of Afghanistan's Taliban, have opposed women's education altogether, but these represent the exception rather than the rule. Most stances value female schooling's contribution to family and social development.

The influence of Islam has not been limited only to the formal schools. Family norms, social and political projects, and economic activities in the Middle East are all shaped by understandings of religious text and practice (even aggressively secular Turkey's rejection of Islam in the public sphere indicates the importance of the faith's influence). Islamic understandings of appropriate roles and activities for girls and women, and the training required for them to achieve those roles, are important subjects for

Two female students study in Iran. The segregation of the sexes in Iran has had a major effect on medical education. Iran will begin training female doctors to ensure that there are enough female physicians to treat the country's female population. © PAUL ALMASY/CORBIS. REPRODUCED BY PERMISSION.

debate across the region's states and are prominently argued in the media, in public discourse, and in law. Interpretations range from liberal to conservative extremes, but have in general favored domestic roles for women, or public service roles (such as teaching and nursing) that parallel and do not overwhelm their domestic responsibilities, with related limitations on the necessity of advanced formal training. Correspondingly, men are expected to provide income and support for families and to serve in public positions with parallel powers of provision and oversight that in theory benefit from more advanced education. Arguments in favor of extending women's service role to government and other forms of public leadership (with greater education as a prerequisite) are varyingly received: Highly educated women hold positions as government officials and are important religious figures in countries as varied as Palestine, Egypt, Iran, and Qatar but their formal participation in political life is much more limited in other states in the region.

Christian Influence

Islam is not the only religious tradition exerting influence on schooling and gendered identity in the Middle East, however. Christian missionaries have

also contributed, largely through the establishment, beginning in the late nineteenth century, of formal schools for girls and of universities. Both in areas with larger indigenous Christian populations, such as Palestine, Lebanon, and Egypt, and in areas where Christian minority presence is nearly negligible, missionary schools provided an educational option for Middle Eastern students before the establishment of public education, and they continue to offer an alternative educational venue today. Some of these schools are indigenously governed and run and are closely connected to local Christian communities; others remain service arms of foreign missionary organizations. The latter, in particular, have tended to hold an outsider's perspective on the appropriate forms and functions of education for their students, and in many cases these closely paralleled the positions of the colonial regimes of Britain and France.

Many of the Christian schools and universities catered to an elite population (both Muslim and Christian) that has been at the center of political and cultural debates across the region, both in support of increased Westernization and in opposition to foreign influence. Together with institutions sponsored by colonial governments to train local administrators, these schools produced a new class of Middle Eastern intellectuals and political actors in the late nineteenth century and throughout the twentieth century. Their graduates, fluent in the languages and cultures of their educational hosts, were intended to serve as bridges between societies, or facilitators of external influence, but their exposure to Western norms often had unintended consequences. Although many have been key to the processes of internationalization that have occurred in Middle Eastern states through their roles in government, cultural institutions, and social leadership, others—well informed and critical of Western approaches to and interests in the developing world—have formed a base of intellectual and material support for nationalist and regionalist movements and opposition to globalization.

Women graduates of these institutions have often taken positions on women's roles and rights that lean toward the liberal end of the political and cultural continuum, although not all would welcome being classified as feminists. These women have contributed to debates about women's roles and identity locally and internationally and challenge both internal and external stereotypes of Middle Eastern women as unquestioning, submissive, or oppressed. Some do this from positions of comparative Westernization, others from a nationalist or Islamist stance, but all argue the importance of women's active contributions to the health of their respective societies.

Women's Role in Society

Whether such contributions should be instrumental, strategic, or intrinsically valuable is, however, a matter of debate. In throwing off colonial regimes and pursuing development agendas, many Middle Eastern states have framed women as important but temporary contributors to efforts at liberation and nation-building, only to relegate them to subordinate status once the national struggle has been resolved. Others have viewed women only as economic drivers whose contributions as physical laborers, wage earners, or child-rearers are essential to modernization and development. Both perspectives necessitate a rethinking of gender roles, and both support the increased education of women across the region, but neither values women for themselves, viewing them instead as instruments for achieving national goals that are determined mostly by men.

Modernization and related human capital models of development, which draw on an understanding of individual and population-group contributions to the economy as a form of investment capital, have emerged as the dominant framework across the Middle East, largely through pressure from institutions such as the World Bank, the United Nations Development Program, and other Euro-American development agencies determined to bring the region into line with international market norms. Research in this tradition argues that higher levels of education increase women's direct and indirect contribution to the market by increasing their productive skills, delaying marriage, increasing their average number of years in the formal labor pool, and reducing their fertility rates, thus increasing the health and education (and therefore the future productivity) of those children that they do bear.

Adopting this approach has led to broad public campaigns for girls' education in the Middle East and corresponding efforts to increase the quality of schooling for girls, particularly in those fields believed to most directly support technical and scientific development. Arguments for educated women's participation in public economic roles have created opportunities for many, but these positions tend to add to rather than replace women's unpaid labor in reproduction, and they have not been paralleled by legal changes to reduce their generally subordinate status.

Linking education first and foremost to economic development relegates learning to an instrumental role in the lives of women (and men) across the region and implies that it has no meaning or value apart from its connection to marketable skills or services. The intrinsic benefits and less measurable outcomes of education are devalued in an approach to development that many in the Middle East argue impoverishes culture and community. Recent regional attempts to articulate strategies for education drawing on the rich culture and history of the Middle East focus on humanistic and critical strains in early Islam and on socio-cultural structures that support socially engaged educational practice. Both approaches offer opportunities for the exploration of gender roles and expectations in ways that do not simply mimic Western feminist or neoliberal arguments for the improvement of women's status. Rather, they challenge societies to reexamine the roots of the social and moral order governing their lives and to develop indigenous strategies through which all members are able to flourish without sacrificing cultural heritage and communal dignity.

See also BAʿTH, AL-; KUTTAB; MADRASA; TALIBAN; WORLD BANK.

Bibliography

Abu-Lughod, Lila, ed. *Remaking Women: Feminism and Modernity in the Middle East.* Princeton, NJ: Princeton University Press, 1998.

Christina, Rachel, with Mehran, Golnar, and Mir, Shabana. "Education in the Middle East: Challenges and Opportunities." In *Comparative Education: The Dialectic of the Global and the Local,* 2d edition, edited by Robert F. Arnove and Carlos Alberto Torres. Lanham, MD: Rowman and Littlefield, 2003.

Joseph, Souad, and Slymovics, Susan, eds. *Women and Power in the Middle East.* Philadelphia: University of Pennsylvania Press, 2000.

Moghadam, Valentine. *Modernizing Women: Gender and Social Change in the Middle East,* 2d edition. Boulder, CO: Lynne Reinner, 2003.

Rihani, May. *Learning for the Twenty-first Century: Strategies for Female Education in the Middle East and North Africa.* Amman, Jordan: UNICEF, 1993.

El-Sanabary, Nagat. "Middle East and North Africa." In *Women's Education in Developing Countries: Barriers, Benefits, and Policies,* edited by Elizabeth M. King and M. Anne Hill. Baltimore, MD: Johns Hopkins University Press, 1993.

Stromquist, Nelly. "Women's Education in the Twenty-first Century: Balance and Prospects." In *Comparative Education: The Dialectic of the Global and the Local,* 2d edition, edited by Robert F. Arnove and Carlos Alberto Torres. Lanham, MD: Rowman and Littlefield, 2003.

UNESCO Institute for Statistics. *Arab States Regional Report, 1999/2000.* Quebec: Author, 2003. Available from <http://www.uis.unesco.org/>.

UNESCO Institute for Statistics. *Education Statistics 2003.* Quebec, Canada: Author, 2003. Available from <http://www.uis.unesco.org/>.

United Nations Development Programme. *The Arab Human Development Report.* New York: Author, 2002.

World Bank. *Education in MENA: A Strategy towards Learning for Development.* Washington, DC: Author, 2000.

RACHEL CHRISTINA

GENDER AND LAW

The modern Middle East and North Africa contain diverse political structures and a variety of legal regimes, yet the way that law constructs and shapes gender roles, hierarchies, and relationships evidences more similarities than differences throughout the region.

Among the most significant transformations of modernity to have influenced Middle Eastern societies over the last 200 years were far-reaching reforms of administrative structures, processes, and practices. Institutions of governance changed dramatically throughout the region, especially after the mid-nineteenth century, eventually giving rise to the different political entities and the diversity of legal regimes embodied by the present-day states of the contemporary Middle East. The region today is home to monarchies, constitutional democracies, secular republics, religiously based states, and, in the case of Lebanon's eighteen different legally recognized ethnoconfessional sects, a living remnant of the Ottoman millet system. Yet despite the diversity of politicolegal institutions, gendered aspects of the law are more alike than different throughout the region today.

Factors and forces catalyzing the political and legal transformations in the Middle East were indigenous as well as external. From within the region, the Qajar and Ottoman states decided to introduce parliamentary systems while also improving and centralizing their administrative structures. From outside, particularly after the Ottoman defeat in 1918, European colonial powers and private institutions such as missionary aid societies and Western educational institutions left a profound mark on the legal regimes of the Middle East. Throughout the nineteenth and twentieth centuries, whether Ottoman, Qajar, colonial, or postcolonial, there were limited progressive transformations or advances in women's rights and duties under the law. Middle Eastern women's participation in the labor force as well as in decision-making bodies remains among the lowest in the world. Women cannot vote or stand for election in Kuwait; neither men nor women can vote or be elected in Saudi Arabia and the United Arab Emirates. In most of the Persian Gulf countries, women still cannot travel alone. Women in Saudi Arabia are forbidden by law to drive, and, until the early 1990s, Lebanese laws prevented women from owning their own businesses without obtaining permission from a male relative.

A leading issue of feminist legal activism in many countries is that of women's equal citizenship rights: Women who marry foreigners usually do not enjoy the legal right to extend their citizenship to their husbands or their children, unlike men, who can extend their citizenship to foreign wives and any children they bear. Lebanon and Israel have witnessed very similar public debates and political reactions concerning civil marriage between individuals of differing religions. Both states forbid secular marriage ceremonies but do recognize civil marriage certificates from other states. As a result, Israelis and Lebanese who wish to marry outside their faith traditions must either convert to the religion of their intended spouse or travel outside their countries (usually to Cyprus or Europe) to be married in a civil ceremony.

Despite legislation that in theory protects women and girls from harm and ensures respect for their rights, customary practices continue in many countries of the modern Middle East that violate international laws and conventions safeguarding the rights of women, girls, and sexual minorities: female genital mutilation, early marriage, denial of schooling, crimes of "honor," domestic violence, and the arrest, imprisonment, and torture of lesbians, gays, and transgendered persons. Many of these problems are present in other regions of the world as well, but a particular combination of historical, ideological, and geopolitical factors has rendered issues related to gender and the law particularly sensitive in the contemporary Middle East. Legal and educational responses to violations of the rights of women, children, and sexual minorities in the Middle East are complicated by some Western attempts to demonize or pillory the peoples and cultures of the Middle East by highlighting these very practices as evidence of the inferiority or barbarity of the region in comparison with the West. A notable repercussion of the tense geopolitical confrontation between the Arab-Islamic world and the West over the last two centuries has been the depiction of Arab and Islamic woman either as icons of cultural purity, moral righteousness, authenticity, and inviolability, or as symbols of Middle Eastern backwardness and a general failure to modernize. Hence, issues related to gender, the law, and women's rights and duties in the region are among the most controversial topics of public discussion, media coverage, and academic inquiry.

Nineteenth-Century Reform: The Gendered Repercussions of State-Building and Colonialism

The Ottoman *Tanzimat* (reorganization or reordering) reforms of the mid-nineteenth century encompassed civil, legal, educational, economic, and political decrees. Though designed to stave off European influences in the region, attempts at reorganizing the Empire were also responses to growing internal pressures for legal reform and greater respect for human rights, particularly in large multiethnic cities. The Gühane Imperial Edict of 1839 guaranteed equal rights before the law for all persons regardless of ethnicity or religious confession (though not, however, gender). By establishing principles that enabled executive and legislative powers to pass from monarchs to representative bodies, the Gühane Edict echoed U.S. and French revolutionary political discourses

and ideals, and revealed indigenous attempts to reconceptualize and modernize the theory and practice of citizenship in the Ottoman Empire.

One of the aims of the Tanzimat was to create a nondenominational, secular judicial system. The Hatt-i hümayun (Imperial Edict) of 1956, often referred to as the "Ottoman Bill of Rights," reiterated the Gühane Edict's legal designation and political embrace of non-Muslim groups as full citizens. With this declaration, Christians as well as Jews could serve on the Ottoman Council of State and act as judges in the Supreme Court. These and other reforms of the Tanzimat helped to lay the groundwork for the introduction into the region of the quintessentially Western political institution of modernity: the nation-state.

Some of the Tanzimat's economic reforms resulted, unintentionally, in the undermining of traditional communal support systems that had protected women, widows, orphans, the poor, and the disabled. Without the benefit of legally codified frameworks to safeguard their needs and interests during a period of rapid change, such vulnerable groups were among the hardest hit as the Ottoman Empire began to disintegrate. In particular, the Land Reform Law of 1858 attempted to secure and clarify land-tenure systems by reaffirming state ownership of land, and granted deeds of usufruct in the names of individuals to those in occupation and possession of productive tracts of land. The aim was to encourage settled and productive agriculture and thus to produce state revenues. Land reforms led, in effect, to an institution similar to private property, thereby transforming traditional tribal and village social structures into more formally institutionalized and legally codified landed feudal structures. Tribal shaykhs (leaders) and rural nobles became wealthy landlords, while their kinsmen and followers became tenant farmers. The prohibition on collective rights to land resulted in a new, profoundly hierarchical and asymmetrical social structure that created a new elite class of wealthy land-owners and a new—and much larger—class of impoverished farming families and landless individuals. Traditional moral structures emphasizing rights and responsibilities rooted in a pastoral nomadic or a rural agricultural lifestyle based on solidarity, honor, mutual assistance, and dignity began to break down as populations throughout the region became increasingly integrated into legally codified relations with centralized administrative authorities (usually major cities such as Baghdad, Damascus, and Istanbul), as well as increasingly integrated into an international capitalist order.

Socioeconomic transformations of modernity generated new social roles and relationships, altered age-old solidarities, and created new hierarchies and inequities. The Ottoman legal system could not meet these rapidly emerging challenges by codifying new rights, duties, and requirements. It was left primarily to the European colonial powers to reconfigure Middle Eastern societies and to address pressing needs for legislation in fields as diverse as commercial, property, and criminal law. In so doing, they usually introduced versions of British or French legal systems, complete with their underlying frames of meaning and values. As a result, states throughout the contemporary Middle East have hybrid legal systems and constitutional structures that reflect the colonial era's legacy. Syria and Lebanon have French-influenced systems, whereas Jordanian and Iraqi laws were influenced by the British. Palestine, never having achieved sovereignty as a state, has a particularly hybrid legal legacy: Palestinians in the West Bank and Gaza Strip live under an overlapping mélange of Ottoman, British Mandatory, and Jordanian law, all of which are framed and affected by the current decisive legal system: Israeli military law.

Throughout the region, and regardless of the European power that had been in place in each country after the end of World War I, family law and laws related to "personal-status affairs" (i.e., laws related to birth, marriage, inheritance, burial, adoption, child custody, alimony, and divorce) remained largely beyond the reach of colonial powers. With the exception of Turkey, which under Atatürk had secularized its legal system, and Tunisia, which under Bourguiba had modernized personal-status laws, family law and laws related to gender issues throughout most of the remaining states of the Middle East remain conservative.

Gender and the Law in the Contemporary Middle East

Whereas the basic political unit in the Western liberal state was the individual citizen, the basic unit of society and politics throughout much of the Ottoman Empire remained the extended family, the faith community, or the confessional sect (millet). Hence, the subject of legal rights and duties was not always or primarily the abstract, free-agent individual, but rather the individual as embedded in and tied to family, community, or sect. This relational conception of the subject of the law has had a profound impact on the interplay between gender and the law throughout the Middle East, because the family, community, and sect in the region are profoundly hierarchical and patriarchal structures in which males and seniors are accorded more privileges than females and juniors. Patriarchy, not Islam, Christianity, or Judaism, accounts for the differential legal status and political roles of women and men throughout the Middle East.

Regardless of laws ensuring equal treatment in theory, patriarchal roles, ideologies, and practices continue to hold sway not only in formal institutions of governance, but even more so through informal, daily structures of resource allocation, decision making and power brokering. One such structure is the informal social network, which can link neighborhoods, families, villages, and cities, and can even transcend state borders through the manipulation or invocation of kin and ethnic ties. Much of everyday life, public and private, is shaped by the dynamics of informal networks that operate according to custom, not codified laws. Given the challenges of administrative centralization and national integration that have confronted the largely artificial and externally imposed states of the region, monitoring, legislating, and policing gender-related practices in these informal social networks has been difficult.

Personal Status Laws

Given that the Middle East is comprised of new states founded on ancient informal civilizational structures, national identity in most countries of the region is fraught with competing tensions. In most cases citizenship, citizens' rights and their sense of national and supra-local identities, collective membership, and political belonging are not as clear or as compelling as are local kinship, religious or ethnic modes of identification, and political action. This has far-reaching implications for women's legal rights and their participation in national politics, given that the cultural construction of kinship and the social and political organization of local-level confessional communities in most countries of the Middle East are profoundly patriarchal. Following the end of the colonial era, the attaining of independence, and the creation of national governments throughout the region, gender-biased customs and procedures attained a more formal status in legislation. As a result, women in many countries of the Middle East do not enjoy all of the basic rights and privileges enjoyed elsewhere. In theory, women in most countries in the region are allowed to vote and to run for any office in the land. The constitutions of most countries uphold the equality of women and men. However, actual practices do not reflect constitutional writ, largely because of the maintenance of personal status laws.

Personal-status laws not only give religious authorities and conservative political actors extensive powers over women's lives in situations of marriage, divorce, child custody, and inheritance, but they also emphasize women's roles as wives, mothers, and daughters at the expense of their roles as citizens. Personal-status laws can and do reduce women to the status of "legal minors" requiring the agency of male relatives or male religious specialists to maneuver in society outside the domains of family and home. This is a primary hindrance to women's ability to initiate legal or political action as agents on their own. Considerable grassroots political and legal activism has been focused on this problem for several years, particularly by transnational organizations such as Women Living Under Muslim Laws and Equality Now (neither of which is based in the Middle East). Personal status laws limit women's legal recourse in the event of divorce to the archaic rulings of religious authorities. In Lebanon, home to eighteen legally recognized confessional sects, this is a particularly complex and vexing issue. Orthodox Jewish women in Israel and Christian women in Arab countries have a much more difficult time obtaining a divorce than do their Muslim counterparts in the Arab world or in Iran.

Throughout the Arab-Islamic world, regardless of confessional membership, child custody in the event of divorce always favors the father. Patriarchal values and institutions dictate, in practice and in law, that the father's family has ultimate custody of all children because they are legally defined as members of his patriline under personal status laws. While they are young, children may stay with their mother following a divorce, but by adolescence, children of

both genders are expected to live with their father's family. Inheritance presents a variety of legal rulings depending on one's confessional membership. Sunni religious courts grant daughters less than sons: In the event that a Sunni man has fathered only daughters, they usually will inherit less from their father than will their male paternal cousins and uncles. Shiʿite religious rulings on daughters' inheritance are much more equitable. In Lebanon more than a few Sunni men having only daughters, no sons, have become Shiʿite in order to pass their wealth and property directly to their daughters. Having a confessional membership is part and parcel of being a Lebanese citizen and profoundly shapes one's legal identity, status, and role. Atheism and secularism are not, legally and administratively speaking, options for anyone, male or female.

Although most countries in the region have signed the Convention on the Elimination of All Forms of Discrimination Against Women (CEDAW), most have also entered strong reservations concerning issues related to personal-status laws. For example, in Lebanon (having had a French colonial influence) and Jordan (which had a British colonial influence), women married to non-nationals cannot pass their citizenship on to their children. Soon after the cessation of the war in Lebanon in 1990, Lebanese women won the right to travel abroad without the permission of their male relatives. Jordanian women are still pressing for this same right more than a decade later. A primary demand of Jordanian feminists, the rescinding of Article 340 of the Penal Code, which effectively permits men to kill female relatives to avenge "crimes of honor," has yet to be realized. A Jordanian forensic doctor recently estimated that a quarter of all murders committed annually in Jordan are "honor killings" (U.S. Department of State Annual Human Rights Report–Jordan 2000). Yet, to appease a political opposition that utilizes the rhetorical discourses of Islamic authenticity and family inviolability, the Jordanian government has not been able to halt such killings.

Although "honor crimes" have yet to be criminalized in Lebanon either, avid public discussions and debates about these crimes (as well as other controversial issues such as domestic violence, homosexuality, mixed marriages, civil marriage, and abortion) are standard fare on Lebanese public television and in Lebanese magazines. Though laws may be slow to change, public debate over legal and gender issues is hastening thanks to the mass media.

Gay, Lesbian, and Transgendered Rights

In recent years, public debates concerning sexuality, gender, and sexual preference have become more common in most major cities of the Middle East. Although calls for gay, lesbian, and transgendered rights are still more controversial in the Middle East than they are in Europe or North America, annual gay-pride events take place publicly in Tel Aviv and in semipublic clubs in Beirut. Films, magazines, and web sites that address the special concerns and interests of gay, lesbian, and transgendered communities in the Middle East also allow members of the Jewish, Arab, Iranian, and Turkish diasporas to share information and build alliances that transcend national as well as confessional dividing lines in the region. Key among the concerns of gays, lesbians, and transgendered persons in the Middle East have been the invocations of religious discourse and religious teachings to criminalize homosexual activities. Activism in opposition to such human-rights abuses has included efforts by Amnesty International and Human Rights Watch, whose spokespersons have decried the targeting of gay men in Egypt and lesbians in Lebanon as part of wider repressions of human-rights activists, religious minority groups, political opponents, journalists, and many others who question the legal and political status quo in the region. Defending the rights of gays, lesbians, and transgendered persons also affords opportunities to address wider human-rights abuses and legal deficiencies related to gender issues, enabling activists to reiterate and redefine the spaces and subjects of the law, as seen in this 26 August 2002 communiqué by the director of a Lebanese legal rights institute protesting the arrest, imprisonment, and mistreatment of two lesbians in Lebanon: "We are aware of the conservative social settings of Lebanon and the negative societal attitude toward the homosexual community. However, this does not entitle the Lebanese government to deprive the liberty of homosexuals, nor does it warrant the torture and abuse sanctioned by the Lebanese police. Through this system of human rights abuses, Lebanon is breaching many international covenants and human rights conventions of which it is a member, not to mention basic human integrity" (Mouhrab, Arz).

Gender and the Law in the Middle East: Regional and International Perspectives

Regional and international developments, particularly the 1995 Beijing International Woman's Conference, Jordan's participation in the Euro-Med partnership, and the Reform Movement in Iran, have already had a noticeable impact on the official framing and treatment of women's issues and concerns not only within, but also beyond, the Middle East. International laws, movements, discourses, and conventions have had a growing impact on the way gender and the law are perceived and discussed, and how they interact and develop in the region.

One example of Middle Eastern women coming together to voice concerns about laws and rights in order to build political alliances was the Women's Tribunal, first held in Beirut in 1995. The Women's Tribunal was an international event, not a strictly Lebanese affair, but its convening in Beirut caused a public stir and generated fruitful and lively discussions about the psychological dynamics, legal consequences, and ideological underpinnings of women's domination in patriarchal societies. The tribunal, the first event of its kind ever to be held in the Middle East, dramatically broke through the silences that isolate women behind walls of shame, fear, and despair. It provided a rare opportunity for Arab women from different countries and various backgrounds to join together, share experiences, and form networks to confront the issue of violence against women in all of its forms: domestic, political, economic, and military.

Throughout the region, the primary obstacles to the attainment of full legal and political rights by women and sexual minorities are: cultural and psychological obstacles that hinder the transformation of personal experiences, attitudes, and stances into political agenda; women's continuing pronounced economic dependence on men; and legal and political structures that do not respect the human rights of either men or women, as well as the continuing enforcement of personal-status laws. Regional and international activists cite a crucial need for broad social movements based on grassroots networks that transcend class, ethnic, confessional, ideological, and gender divisions to surmount these obstacles, which are interrelated and interlocking. The past decade has witnessed increasing attempts to link national, regional, and international human-rights monitoring agencies in order to advance women's rights as well as the rights of gays and lesbians. Largely through the medium of the internet, groups and individuals have been able to join forces in new ways to expose violations of women's rights and to protest the draconian treatment of gays and lesbians.

Yet, given the overall poor socioeconomic and human-rights situation throughout the region, a focus solely on women's rights or gay rights strikes some as narrow. One of the best-known human-rights activists in the region, the late Laure Mughaizel, a Lebanese human-rights activist, feminist, and lawyer, noted shortly before her death: "What will it serve us to fight for women to have rights equal to those of men if men's rights are also deficient?" (Mughaizel, public speech in 1996 in Lebanon). Ultimately, any analysis of gender and law in the Middle East must take into consideration the political economy of the region, as well as ongoing debates over universal human rights and their definition in the evolving body of international laws and conventions.

See also CRIMES OF HONOR; FEMALE GENITAL MUTILATION; GÜLHANE IMPERIAL EDICT (1839); TANZIMAT; TUNISIA: PERSONAL STATUS CODE.

Bibliography

AbuKhalil, As'ad. "Gender Boundaries and Sexual Categories in the Arab World." *Feminist Issues* 15/1–2 (1997), pp. 91–104.

Accad, Evelyne. "Sexuality and Sexual Politics: Conflicts and Contradictions for Contemporary Women in the Middle East." In *Third World Women and the Politics of Feminism,* edited by Chandra T. Mohanty, Ann Russo, and Lourdes Torres. Bloomington: Indiana University Press, 1991.

Afary, Janet. "The War Against Feminism in the Name of the Almighty: Making Sense of Gender and Muslim Fundamentalism." *New Left Review* 224 (July/August 1997), pp. 89–110.

Ahmed, Laila. *Women and Gender in Islam, Historical Roots of a Modern Debate.* New Haven, CT: Yale University Press, 1992.

Amnesty International. *Breaking the Silence: Human Rights Violations Based on Sexual Orientation.* London: Amnesty International U.K., 1997.

Asdar Ali, Kamran. "Notes on Rethinking Masculinities: An Egyptian Case." *Learning About Sexuality: A Practical Beginning.* New York: The Population Council and the International Women's Health Coalition, 1995, pp. 98–109.

Baron, Beth. "Mothers, Morality and Nationalism in Pre-1919 Egypt." In *The Origins of Egyptian Nationalism,* edited by Rashid Khalidi, Lisa Anderson, Muhammad Muslih and Reeva S. Simon. New York: Columbia University Press, 1991.

Dunne, Bruce W. "French Regulation of Prostitution in Nineteenth-Century Colonial Algeria." *Arab Studies Journal* 2/1 (1994), pp. 24–30.

Dunne, Bruce W. "Power and Sexuality in the Middle East." *Middle East Report* 28/1 (1998), pp. 6–9.

Equality Now! Available from <http://www.equalitynow.org/english/navigation/hub_en.html>.

Esposito, John L., and DeLong-Bas, Natana J. *Women in Muslim Family Law.* Syracuse, NY: Syracuse University Press, 2001.

Gay and Lesbian Arab Society. Available from <http://www.glas.org/ahbab/>.

Hatem, Mervat. "The Politics of Sexuality and Gender in Segregated Patriarchal Systems: The Case of 18th- and 19th-Century Egypt." *Feminist Studies* 12 (1986), pp. 251–274.

Joseph, Suad, ed. *Gender and Citizenship in the Middle East.* Syracuse, NY: Syracuse University Press, 2000.

Kandiyoti, Deniz. "The Paradoxes of Masculinity: Some Thoughts on Segregated Societies." In *Dislocating Masculinity: Comparative Ethnographies,* edited by Andrea Cornwall and Nancy Lindisfarne. London and New York: Routledge, 1994.

King-Irani, Laurie. "From Program to Practice: Towards Women's Meaningful and Effective Political Participation in Jordan and Lebanon." In *Middle Eastern Women on the Move,* edited by Haleh Esfandiari. Washington, DC: Woodrow Wilson International Center for Scholars, 2003.

MERIP. "Sexuality, Suppression, and the State in the Middle East." Special issue of *Middle East Report,* Spring 2004, No. 230.

Moghadam, Valentine M. "Revolution, Islam and Women: Sexual Politics in Iran and Afghanistan." In *Nationalisms and Sexualities,* edited by Andrew Parker, et al. New York and London: Routledge, 1992.

Mouhrab, Arz, director. *Lebanese Equality for Gays and Lesbians.* Available from <http://legal.20m.com>.

Plummer, Kenneth, ed. *Modern Homosexualities: Fragments of Lesbian and Gay Experience.* London and New York: Routledge, 1992.

Swirski, Barbara, and Safir, Marilyn, eds. *Calling the Equality Bluff: Women in Israel.* New York: Teachers College Press, 1991.

Tucker, Judith, ed. *Arab Women: Old Boundaries, New Frontiers.* Bloomington: Indiana University Press, 1993.

U.S. Department of State. *Annual Human Rights Report—Jordan.* Washington, DC: author, 2000.

Wikan, Unni. "Man Becomes Woman: Transsexualism in Oman as a Key to Gender Roles." *MAN* 12 (1977), pp. 304–319.

Women Living under Muslim Laws. Available from <http://www.wluml.org/english/index.shtml>.

LAURIE KING-IRANI

GENDER AND POLITICS

Gender consciousness, feminist goals, and gender itself have all affected citizenship politics throughout the history of the Middle East.

Formal, or institutional, politics in the Middle East has been dominated by men. An awareness of gender—the identification and comparison of continuously changing men's and women's roles and differences—is essential to an understanding of women's political experiences in the region. By focusing on women, one sees the struggles of the sex that is otherwise invisible in Middle Eastern politics and the challenges women face in attaining full citizenship.

Female voters cast their ballots in an Iranian election. Voting restrictions were lifted for Iranian women in 1980. © WEBISTAN/CORBIS. REPRODUCED BY PERMISSION.

While literature on the Middle East often tends to relate women as a broad category, women in fact belong to diverse groups and pursue various interests. Women have habitually formed alliances across the lines of class, ethnicity, race, religion, family, or nation in their struggles against the oppressions they faced. Moreover, women live in a context of national, religious, state-sponsored, and consciously feminist political struggles. The following sections will outline the roots of gender consciousness, forms of feminist goals typical to the Middle East, and challenges to gender imbalance in their historical context.

The Roots of Gender Consciousness

Around the 1900s, the figures who facilitated the participation of women in the public sphere were mainly male Islamic scholars in Egypt, Iran, and Turkey. In Egypt, reformist thought traces back to Rifaʿa al-Rafi al-Tahtawi (1801–1873), an Azhari scholar educated in France who became the first major figure to call for the liberation and education of Egyptian women.

Qasim Amin (1863–1908) is considered the father of women's reform in the Muslim Middle East. His book *Liberation of Women* (1899) initiated women's liberation literature in the Arab world. He raised the issues of patriarchal oppression, polygamy, and the *hijab,* calling for an end to veiling and arguing for the education of women. The sections of his book that were based on Islamic law are believed to have been authored anonymously by Muhammad Abduh (1849–1905), the *mufti* of Egypt at that time. Muhammad Abduh, a disciple of the father of the modern Islamic reform, Jamal al-Din al-Afghani (1838–1897), called for the elevation of women as a way to end foreign domination. Abdu's ideas significantly influenced the Muslim world.

Some Egyptian women had publicly challenged gender biases before these male figures appeared, including Maryam al-Nahhas (1856–1886), Zaynab Fawwaz (1860–1894), and Aʾisha al-Taymuriyya (1840–1902). Women feminists had campaigned for education, done charitable work, and challenged colonialism. Huda al-Shaʿrawi became the acknowledged leader of Egyptian feminism, playing an essential role against British occupation through the women's wing of the Wafd Party and forming the Egyptian Feminist Union in 1923. Doria Shafik led the struggle for voting rights, which were granted in 1956.

Reformers emerged in Iran in the late nineteenth century, starting with Mirza Agha Khan Kirmani and Shaykh Ahmad Ruhi, who wrote about women's equality with men in pleasure, benefits, marriage rights, and education. Historically, however, women's education did not receive full attention in Iran until Amin's book was translated into Persian in 1900. Ahmad Kasravi, a historian, reformer, and jurist, argued for women's education in the 1940s but opposed women's involvement in politics. He emphasized, however, that women could participate for national causes.

Reza Shah Pahlavi and his son, Mohammad Reza Shah Pahlavi, combined enforced modernization with the crushing of any opposition. Acknowledging Mustafa Kemal Atatürk's influence, Reza Shah Pahlavi banned the veil *(chador)* in 1936, in an enforced program for emancipating women, and set about improving education. The veil was later chosen as a symbol of revolutionary protest by women who marched against the Pahlavi regime during the 1979 Islamic Revolution.

Several prominent women helped shape Iranian history. Writer, poet, teacher, and religious rebel Qurrat al-Ayn (born in 1814, executed in 1852) preached Babism (a religious sect founded in 1844 by the Bab out of Shi'i Islam and which gave birth to the Baha'i faith) for women's emancipation. The doctrines forbid polygamy, concubinage, and trading in slaves, among many things. In the second half of the nineteenth century, Taj Saltaneh and Bibi Khanoum Astarabadi publicly criticized the status of women in Iran. Siddiqeh Dowlatabadi started the first girls' school, in Isfahan in 1917, and the first major woman's magazine, *Zaban-i Zanan* (Women's tongue), which was both feminist and nationalist, in 1919.

By the time of the Islamic Revolution, Iranian women had already experienced nearly a century of political success unparalleled in the Middle East, including participation in the Tobacco Revolt of 1890. Iranian women were active in the Constitutional Revolution in 1906 and by 1963 had gained the right to vote. Iranian women held high political positions and had gained laws that gave them priority in child custody and equal rights to divorce.

Princess A'isha Bint al-Hussein (center) on a visit to Israel to learn about the women's service in the army, 1 June 1997. © AP/WIDE WORLD PHOTOS. REPRODUCED BY PERMISSION.

In Turkey, after the collapse of the autocratic regime in 1908, women formed organizations, participated in political demonstrations, and wrote for the press. Atatürk abrogated *shari'a* (Islamic law) and secularized personal status law, which he modeled on the Swiss legal code. Turkish new-wave feminists entered the political arena in the 1980s, waging campaigns against domestic violence and sexual harassment and petitioning the government to sign the 1985 UN Convention on the Elimination of All Forms of Discrimination against Women. Turkey is one of two Middle Eastern countries to have had a female head of state, Prime Minister Tansu Çiller, who took office in 1993 (Israel is the other; Golda Meir was prime minister from 1969 through 1974).

Islamic Feminism

Feminism is political action against the oppression of women. In the Middle East, both secular feminism (invoking the UN Declaration of Human Rights) and religious feminism (invoking Islamic or Jewish

A member of the women's army demonstrates the handling of a Sten gun on 15 June 1948 at the Hen women's corps camp near Tel Aviv. © AP/WIDE WORLD PHOTOS. REPRODUCED BY PERMISSION.

scripture) are active. Both categories include a wide range of ideas, beliefs, and actions.

Egypt is the epicenter of Islamist feminist activism, which has rested on the involvement of middle-class professional women. Nazira Zayn ad-Din in the 1930s and A'isha Abd al-Rahman (Bint al-Shatti) in the 1980s called for *ijtihad* (Islamic legal deliberation) to solve gender problems such as polygamy and the assumption of male superiority. In the 1930s, following the Institute for the Mothers of the Believers model established by Hasan al-Banna (founder of the Muslim Brotherhood), Zaynab al-Ghazali formed the Muslim Women's Association. In 1964, when Gamal Abdel Nasser banned the Brotherhood and al-Ghazali was arrested, it had over a hundred branches in Egypt. Heba Rauf Ezzat (also Hiba Ra'uf Izzat), a political science professor, invoked al-Ghazali's discourse on women and politics through alternative interpretations of the Islamic scripture. Similarly, beginning

the 1990s, Iranian women began to press for equality using the argument that religious literature is tainted by misogynist interpretations.

Islamist groups have recognized women's potential to serve Islamist interests. In Algeria, for example, the Front Islamique du Salut (FIS) did not object to women voting but sought to limit their employment. These groups generally encourage women activists to undertake community work through which Islamist political ideologies may infiltrate into society. Most contemporary Islamic scholars view feminism as something that originated in the West and that is a form of cultural imperialism. Islamists seek to counter by preaching veiling as a symbol of morality, authenticity, and cultural independence. Some Middle Eastern feminists also assert that much of the feminist discourse originated with and mirrors the concerns of white, middle-class Western women.

Nationalism and State Feminism

Since the 1800s, the development of women's political and social movements was intertwined with broader movements for national independence and state-building. Many Middle Eastern regimes have practiced state feminism in order to secure their legitimacy, creating programs designed to raise the levels of education, literacy, or employment; revive imagined or real traditional practices; modify personal status laws; and establish state-sponsored women's organizations.

Under regimes as diverse as those of Atatürk, Reza Shah Pahlavi, the Iraqi Ba'thists, and Nasser, women were mobilized in order to achieve national consolidation and an appearance of modernization. Any call for women's rights outside those on the state's agenda was perceived as antinationalist and thus divisive. After the Islamic Revolution, Ayatollah Ruhollah Khomeini crushed all women's protests and nullified the Family Protection Law. In North Africa, many women lost their lives fighting for independence, but once independence was gained women were told to return to their proper place in the home. Tunisian and Moroccan women have experienced some state-directed expansion of their freedoms, but the freedom of Algerian women has been severely constrained, particularly since the early 1990s.

The Israeli women's organizations that formed in the 1950s, such as Naʿamat (the women's branch of the labor union and the women's division of the Labor Party), the Women's International Zionist Organization or WIZO (the women's division of the Likud Party), and Emunah (affiliated with the National Religious Party), did not have a feminist mission and still do not. The General Union of Palestinian Women (GUPW), formed in 1965, is the chief women's organization in Palestinian communities and legitimized by the Palestine Liberation Organization (PLO). However, it has never challenged the male-dominated leadership of the PLO or its attitudes toward women. Held up as symbols of cultural integrity, women in both Israel and the Palestinian Authority are often valorized as biological reproducers of the nation.

Women have taken advantage of their abilities as mobilizers to advance women's activism and increase their decision-making roles. Samiha al-Khalil (c. 1940–1999) was a member of the Palestine National Council starting in 1965; president of the Women's Federation Society, al-Bira, the Union for Voluntary Women's societies, and the GUPW; and the founder of the Inʿash al-Usra Society beginning in 1967. Hanan al-Ashrawi (1946–), a human rights activist and professor of literature, became a minister in the Palestinian Authority government and since the 1990s has served as an articulate, internationally renowned spokesperson for the Palestinians.

Nationalist issues have created openings for other shared interests. After the first intifada (Palestinian uprising), many Israeli and Palestinian women demanded peace. The international movement Women in Black began in Jerusalem in 1988 when Israeli women dressed in black spoke out publicly for peace. This organization and others have included Palestinians. Shulamit Aloni (1929–), a teacher and attorney, was a Knesset member for many years and headed the Meretz Party; she has spoken on behalf of peace and justice, particularly criticizing policies that endanger Israelis and Palestinians.

Governments in the rapidly developing Persian Gulf consider the integration of women into the labor force a necessity if they are to reduce their dependence on foreign labor, which they see as a security threat. This has led to the formation of state-sponsored organizations with state appoint-

Hanan Ashrawi, Palestinian Legislative Council member, is removed by Israeli police from a site in Jerusalem, 27 May 1999. The police charged into the crowd of protesters, preventing them from entering the Jewish neighborhood of Ras al-Amud in east Jerusalem under construction. © AP/WIDE WORLD PHOTOS. REPRODUCED BY PERMISSION.

ment of members. The Arab Women's Development Society, a feminist organization campaigning for the vote in Kuwait, was disbanded after members refused to cooperate with a government-imposed director. Unlike the Princess Basma Center for Women and Development in Jordan, which is also state sponsored, AWDS does not address violence against women, such as honor killings. Even though the Women's Union of Syria operates under a republic, it follows preset national strategies.

In the Persian Gulf, women have been struggling for basic rights, as North African women were at the beginning of the twentieth century. Kuwaiti women are still fighting for their voting rights while Bahraini women won their voting rights in 2002 predominantly through informal Shiʿite Maʾtam/ Husayniyya religious-social gatherings. Yet, Saudi women are demanding more civic freedoms. However, some Gulf leaders are supporting the participation of women within the framework of the development process, specifically Shaykh Zayid of United Arab Emirates and Sultan Qabus of Oman.

Challenges to the Gender Imbalance

Women have sought to improve their status through numerous campaigns. These include strategies to respond to extremist Islamist movements. In 1990, when the FIS was gaining political clout, Algerian feminists led by Khalida Toumi (Messaoudi), a founding member of the Independent Association for the Triumph of Women's Rights, were notably outspoken. Sudanese writer and speaker Fatima Ahmed Ibrahim, president of the Sudanese Women's Union, has risked her life speaking out against National Islamic Front extremists in southern Sudan. Mehrangiz Kar, a former political prisoner and human rights lawyer, has published widely on the status of women in pre- and postrevolutionary Iran; her publications include a work coauthored with Shahla Lahiji, Iran's first woman publisher, who was also detained. In 2003, Shirin Ebadi received a Nobel Prize for her human rights activism. These women, along with Islamic feminist Shahla Sherkat, editor of *Zanan,* lead the debate on women's rights in Iran.

Tojan Faysal, the first woman to be elected to the Jordanian parliament (1993–1997), has been a staunch critic of human rights abuses and was detained in 2001. Asma Khader (also Khadir), a Jordanian lawyer, led the campaign to outlaw honor killings and received the 2003 Poverty Eradication Award from the UN Development Program. Laure Moghaizel, a founding member of numerous Lebanese women's organizations, worked locally, regionally, and internationally for the advancement of women's rights.

Nawwal al-Saʿdawi, an Egyptian doctor and writer and a particularly prominent feminist, formed and headed the Arab Women's Solidarity Association in 1985. Even though fervently secular, she attributes her awareness of women's rights to the teachings of Muhammad Abduh, who taught her father in al-Azhar. Moroccan sociologist Fatima Mernissi, another leading feminist in the Arab world, critiques and analyzes Islamic law from a secular perspective.

In Turkey, Women for Women's Human Rights has worked since 1993 to raise feminist consciousness and confront domestic violence, as have the Purple Roof Foundation and Altindag Women's Solidarity Foundation. In Afghanistan under the Taliban, women and girls were banished to seclusion in the home and thousands were raped, tortured, killed, or forced into prostitution. Since 1977, the Revolutionary Association of the Women

of Afghanistan has struggled for women's human rights as an independent political and social organization, also undertaking social and relief work.

Numerous research centers have developed across the Middle East. These include the New Woman Research and Study Centre in Egypt, the Women's Library and Information Centre in Istanbul, the Lebanese American University's Institute for Women's Studies in the Arab World, and the Association des Femmes Tunisiennes pour la Recherche et le Développement. Although some are purely research oriented, some also engage in advocacy for gender equity.

Regional organizations include the Arab Women's Federation, the Women's Committee of the Arab League, the Center for Arab Women for Training and Research, and the Arab Women's Forum (AISHA), a regional nongovernmental organization made up of fourteen Arab women's organizations. International organizations include the World Federation for Women, Development Alternatives with Women for a New Era, and the United Nations Development Fund for Women (UNIFEM). Conferences, such as UN conferences on women, are important forms of global support for Middle Eastern women.

Conclusion

Middle Eastern women have proven resourceful and dynamic participants in the political processes that shaped recent Middle Eastern history. Feminism in the Middle East cannot be separated from nationalist and anticolonial movements, or from issues such as poverty and illiteracy that Middle Eastern women have faced. However, the interventionist measures of postindependence states have been primarily geared toward national development, treating women's rights as a secondary concern.

See also ABDUH, MUHAMMAD; AFGHANI, JAMAL AL-DIN AL-; AMIN, QASIM; ASSOCIATION DES FEMMES TUNISIENNES POUR LA RECHERCHE ET LE DÉVELOPPEMENT (AFTURD); ÇILLER, TANSU; FRONT ISLAMIQUE DU SALUT (FIS); IBRAHIM, FATIMA AHMED; IRANIAN REVOLUTION (1979); KAR, MEHRANGIZ; KHALIL, SAMIHA SALAMA; MEIR, GOLDA; MERNISSI, FATEMA; MUSLIM BROTHERHOOD; REVOLUTIONARY ASSOCIATION OF THE WOMEN OF AFGHANISTAN (RAWA); SAADAWI, NAWAL AL-;

Sha'rawi, Huda al-; Tahtawi, Rifa'a al-Rafi al-; Tobacco Revolt; Toumi, Khalida; Women and Family Affairs Center; Women in Black; Women's Affairs Center (Gaza); Women's Centre for Legal Aid and Counseling; Women's Forum for Research and Training (Yemen).

Bibliography

Afsaruddin, Asma, ed. *Hermeneutics and Honor: Negotiating Female "Public" Space in Islamic/ate Societies.* Cambridge, MA: Harvard Center for Middle Eastern Studies, 1999.

Afshar, Haleh. *Women in the Middle East: Perception, Realities, and Struggles for Liberation.* London: Macmillan, 1993.

Ahmed, Leila. *Women and Gender in Islam.* New Haven, CT: Yale University Press, 1992.

Baron, Beth. *The Women's Awakening in Egypt: Culture, Society, and the Press.* New Haven, CT: Yale University Press, 1994.

Brand, Laurie A. *Women, the State, and Political Liberation: Middle Eastern and North African Experiences.* New York: Columbia University Press, 1998.

Chatty, Dawn, and Rabo, Annika, eds. *Organizing Women: Formal and Informal Women's Groups in the Middle East.* Oxford, U.K.: Berg, 1997.

Joseph, Suad. *Gender and Citizenship in the Middle East.* Syracuse, NY: Syracuse University Press, 2000.

Joseph, Suad, and Slymovics, Susan. *Women and Power in the Middle East.* Philadelphia: University of Pennsylvania Press, 2001.

Kandiyoti, Deniz. *Women, Islam, and the State.* London: Macmillan, 1991.

Karam, Azza. *Women, Islamisms, and the State: Contemporary Feminisms in Egypt.* London: Macmillan, 1998.

Keddie, Nikki, and Baron, Beth, eds. *Women in Middle Eastern History: Shifting Boundaries in Sex and Gender.* New Haven, CT: Yale University Press, 1992.

Magno, Cathryn S. *New Pythian Voices: Women Building Political Capital in NGOs in the Middle East.* New York: Routledge, 2002.

Moghissi, Haideh. *Feminism and Islamic Fundamentalism: The Limits of Postmodern Analysis.* London: Zed, 1999.

Mughni, Haya al-. *Women in Kuwait: The Politics of Gender.* London: Saqi, 1993.

Paidar, Parvin. *Women and the Political Process in Twentieth-Century Iran.* Cambridge, U.K.: Cambridge University Press, 1995.

Wanda C. Krause

Gender: Study of

A theoretical approach to Middle Eastern issues that considers assumptions made about sex roles and the impact of those assumptions.

Contemporary scholars see gender as the social, cultural, politico-legal, and ideological construction of male and female roles, relations, and rights on the basis of perceived gender differences. Scholars also view gender as a system of social relations and ideologies that influences other social relations, institutions, and processes. The common, overarching frameworks within which gender has been studied, interpreted, and taught in the context of the modern Middle East are Islam, patriarchy, and the construction of the nation-state. Scholars often divide the evolution of women's struggles for social, economic, and political rights in the Middle East and North Africa into three historical periods: the period of anticolonial struggles from the mid-nineteenth century through the early twentieth century; the era of nationalist movements of the mid-twentieth century; and the era of globalization from the 1980s into the twenty-first century. Academic approaches to the study of gender shifted from the study of texts, interpretations, and structures to the analysis of social practices, identity construction, and the language and rules concerning gender in various fields. In the process, the binary divisions that defined gender studies in the earlier periods (male/female, public/private, state/civil society, global/local, East/West) became problematic. The understanding of gender turned away from such categories and descriptions and focused instead on the dynamics of the construction, change, and transformation of social roles. Gender studies became institutionalized through the creation of women's studies departments, institutes, and transnational organizations and Web sites. Simultaneously, international conferences and international conventions concerning women's civil and human rights made women's status a global issue. In these contexts, Western discourses concerning identity formation, citizenship, and human rights began to be challenged.

Development of Gender Studies

Although the global nature of ideas is now generally accepted, systematic attempts to analyze areas of dialogue and confrontation between approaches from distinct socio-historical settings have been rare until recently. Scholarship on gender in the Middle East did not escape interpretations that tended to trap women between the grand narratives of the West and local narratives of resistance, be they modernist-nationalist or fundamentalist, in which real women are replaced by woman-as-symbol. In the West, feminists have often enough looked through the lens of a universalized Western concept in which citizen-subjects were seen as autonomous individuals who owned themselves and entered into social contracts with other autonomous individuals. Feminists grounded in this perspective strove to illuminate the ways in which these social contracts were not gender blind; they argued for equality based on gender-neutral categories. In the Middle East, the viewpoints generally envisioned subject-citizens as deeply embedded in communities, families, ethnic, racial, or other social groupings. Their members were seen as relational selves whose identities were developed interdependently rather than independently from one another. Men's and women's roles and identities were seen as complementary. As in the West, patriarchy has been universal, but the particular ways that gender is altered and affected by inequalities of power is site specific. In the Middle East and North Africa, both liberal modernist-nationalists and conservative fundamentalists put the defense of Islamic/Arab culture in the foreground, rendering women's rights secondary to women's symbolic value as the embodiment of the nation or the image of the moral community. Contemporary women's studies challenges this tendency to reduce the richness and complexities of women's actual lives to one-dimensional symbols or stereotypes.

Contemporary Debates

At least three common paradigms have obstructed more complex understandings of women's lives in the Middle East and North Africa. One is the religious paradigm, in which the existence of gender inequality is attributed to Islam's influence upon the lives of women and men in North Africa and the Middle East. The unstated assumption here is that religion is at once the cause of and the solution to gender inequality: If the religion is done away with, equality between men and women will ensue. The second is what Cooke calls the rescue paradigm—or, "white men saving brown women from brown men." This gendered logic of empire not only provides a

pretext for global superpower interventions but may at times reveal the neocolonial underpinnings of international sisterhood. The third is the passivity paradigm, in which women are seen as objects rather than agents, living apolitically, in the private sphere. Recent scholarship has revealed how porous the boundary is between the public and private spheres in societies where kinship, family, and community have primacy over individuals. To understand women's roles in society, it helps to examine what counts as political in a given place and time, how individuals are encouraged to become agents (to act rather than merely be acted upon), and what forums and institutions give access to power. These questions are crucial to current academic and policy debates concerning civil society, political reform, and economic development.

Institutionalization of the Study of Gender

In recent decades, women's and gender studies have become institutionalized on a number of levels. Meetings such as the UN-sponsored International Women's Conferences, held periodically since 1975, and the signing of international conventions such as the Convention on the Elimination of All Forms of Discrimination against Women have brought women's status into the international arena, putting pressure on nation-states to safeguard women's human rights. On a national level, the spread of nongovernmental organizations focusing on women's status in countries across the Middle East and North Africa is linked to the fact that development projects which include grass-roots gender perspectives are more likely to succeed. On a local level, the spread of women's and gender studies centers, programs in academic institutions such as Birzeit University or the American University in Cairo, and women's social service centers in areas plagued by violence and war have made visible the gendered nature of social decision-making. On a virtual level, the creation of Web sites such as the Machreq/Maghreb Gender Linking and Information Project, sponsored by Oxfam GB and the European Union; the International Women's Tribune Center, associated with the UN-sponsored conferences; the Web site of the Women's Environment and Development Organization; and the newer H-Gender-Mideast have provided forums for ongoing international discussion of the centrality of gender to all areas of social life.

The discipline of gender studies is not merely an addition to the other disciplines that make up Middle Eastern area studies. Gender studies has reconstituted the field itself. Its perspective from the margin has revealed the ways in which power—gender privilege among males and Western constructions of the Middle East (orientalism)—shaped the approach to the object of study. Putting women in the center, valorizing their experiences and contributions as half the population in any society, meant reexamining areas of social practice that had previously been rendered secondary, misrepresented, or silenced. These include oral literature, domesticity, complex communication patterns based on indirection, informal work, the intersection of public and private worlds. As Lila Abu-Lughod has pointed out, the most important contribution of this theorizing has been the way it has revealed that analytical categories often conceal Western cultural notions. The study of gender in the Middle East, framed as it has been by the violence of colonization and of postcolonial wars, the struggle for women's rights as human rights, and the responsibility to address global injustice and inequality, has challenged scholarly inquiry to move beyond ethnocentric, binary categories that have reduced, objectified, and stereotyped the subjects in question.

See also ORIENTALISM.

Bibliography

Abu-Lughod, Lila. "Anthropology's Orient: The Boundaries of Theory on the Arab World." In *Theory, Politics, and the Arab World: Critical Responses*, edited by Hisham Sharabi. New York: Routledge, 1990: 81–131.

Ahmed, Leila. *Women and Gender in Islam: Historical Roots of a Modern Debate.* New Haven, CT: Yale University Press, 1992.

Badran, Margot, and Cooke, Miriam, eds. *Opening the Gates: A Century of Arab Feminist Writing.* Bloomington: Indiana University Press, 1990.

Cooke, Miriam. "Islamic Feminism before and after September 11." *Journal of Gender Law & Policy* 9 (2000): 227–235.

Hatem, Mervat. "Toward the Development of Post-Islamist and Post-Nationalist Feminist Discourses in the Middle East." In *Arab Women: Old Boundaries, New Frontiers*, edited by Judith E. Tucker. Bloomington: Indiana University Press, 1993.

Joseph, Suad, and Slyomovics, Susan, eds. *Women and Power in the Middle East.* Philadelphia: University of Pennsylvania Press, 2001.

Kandiyoti, Deniz, ed. *Gendering the Middle East: Emerging Perspectives.* Syracuse, NY: Syracuse University Press, 1996.

Keddie, Nikki R. "Women in the Limelight: Some Recent Books on Middle Eastern Women's History." *International Journal of Middle East Studies* 34 (2002): 553–573.

Lazreg, Marnia. "Feminism and Difference: The Perils of Writing as a Woman on Women in Algeria." *Feminist Studies* 14, no. 1 (spring 1988): 81–107.

Meriwether, Margaret L., and Tucker, Judith E., eds. *Social History of Women and Gender in the Modern Middle East.* Boulder, CO: Westview Press, 1999.

Moghadam, Valentine M. "Gender, National Identity, and Citizenship: Reflections on the Middle East and North Africa." *Comparative Studies of South Asia, Africa, and the Middle East* 19, no. 1 (1999): 137–157.

Tucker, Judith E., ed. *Arab Women: Old Boundaries, New Frontiers.* Bloomington: Indiana University Press, 1993.

LAURA RICE

GENERAL DIRECTORATE ON THE STATUS AND PROBLEMS OF WOMEN

An institution that serves as a liaison between the Turkish state and society on the issue of women's rights and problems.

The General Directorate on the Status and Problems of Women was founded in 1990 in line with the requirements of the United Nations Convention on Elimination of All Kinds of Discrimination against Women. Attached to the Turkish Prime Ministry, its activities are supervised by the State Ministry responsible for women and the family. The directorate is comprised of four main departments: Educational and Social Affairs; Economic Affairs; Documentation, Publications, and Statistics; and Foreign Affairs.

Its major objectives are to protect and to promote women's rights; to improve women's social, economic, cultural, and political status; and to ensure that women enjoy equal rights and opportunities in all walks of life. To these ends, it conducts and finances research projects with a policy orientation; collaborates with other public institutions, local administrations, and women's associations; and raises consciousness through the mass media about women's issues.

During its first years, the directorate raised serious suspicions among nongovernmental women's organizations, most of which believed that its aim was to control and co-opt women's independent activism. These perceptions greatly diminished with the appointment of a former nongovernmental leader as its director and with the success of its collaborative projects and campaigns.

See also GENDER: GENDER AND LAW; TURKEY.

Bibliography

Berik, Günseli. "State Policy in the 1980s and the Future of Women's Rights in Turkey." *New Perspectives on Turkey* 4 (1990): 81–96.

General Directorate on the Status and Problems of Women. Available from <http://www.kssgm.gov.tr>.

Kardam-Monterey, Nüket, and Ertürk, Yakin. "Expanding Gender Accountability?: Women's Organizations and the State in Turkey." *International Journal of Organization Theory and Behavior* 2, no. 1–2 (1999): 167–197.

BURÇAK KESKIN-KOZAT

GENERAL FEDERATION OF IRAQI WOMEN

The strongest women's organization in Iraq during the Baʿthist regime, and an effective arm of the Baʿthist Party.

The General Federation of Iraqi Women was established in the early 1970s, after Saddam Hussein and the Baʿthist Party assumed political power. Its stated goals were to improve the situation of Iraqi women and to marshal their skills in the task of building an Arab socialist state. Campaigns were launched to promote literacy, better childcare, maternity leave, improve wages, and promote women within the economic sector and in politics. An arts committee was established later. By all accounts, the federation was responsible, at least in part, for the many gains made by Iraq's women in the last quarter of the twentieth century and for Iraq's record on women's rights, which, before the U.S. invasion in 2003, were often cited as the best in the Arab world. As of 2004, literacy rates for women are close to 50 percent but were much higher before the 1991 Gulf

War. According to federation officials, before the Gulf War all women received one full year of maternity leave: six months with full pay and six months with half pay, plus six weeks at the time of the baby's birth. (This was independently confirmed by the author in 1996 interviews in Iraq.)

As of 1996, the federation had 1,500,000 members in twenty-two branches throughout the country. Each branch had a clubhouse, where women gathered freely. Women who were interviewed by the author in both city and countryside in Iraq stated that the federation's greatest contributions were its record in family law and its campaign for equal pay for women. Officials stated that secular law had replaced Islamic family law (*shariʿa*) The secular code guaranteed women their rights to inheritance and prohibited polygamy unless the first wife was ill and could not bear children; even then, the first wife had to agree. (These claims were confirmed in author interviews.) The federation was involved in the creation of a Women's Museum in Baghdad, financed by the Baʿthist Party, the only such museum in the Arab world.

Since the 2003 U.S. invasion, and the fall of Saddam Hussein, little or no mention has been made of the federation. As it was an official arm of the Baʿthist party, its future remains in doubt.

See also BAʿTH, AL-; IRAQ; *SHARIʿA*.

Bibliography

Fernea, Elizabet Warnock. "Iraq." In *In Search of Islamic Feminism*. New York: Anchor/Doubleday, 1998.

The General Federation of Iraqi Women in 20 Years. Baghdad: Al Hurriya Press, 1989.

Suad, Joseph. "The Mobilization of Iraqi Women into the Wage Labor Force." *Studies in Third World Societies,* no. 16, 1982, pp. 69–90.

ELIZABETH FERNEA

GENERAL PEOPLE'S COMMITTEES

Libya's ruling cabinet.

The General People's Committees were established in March 1978 in Libya when Muammar al-Qaddafi and the other members of the ruling Revolutionary Command Council formally renounced their government positions. Exercising executive powers, the General People's Committees have a function equivalent to ministerial cabinets.

See also QADDAFI, MUAMMAR AL-; REVOLU-TIONARY COMMAND COUNCIL (LIBYA).

LISA ANDERSON

GENERAL PEOPLE'S CONGRESS (GPC)

Ostensibly, Libya's governing body.

Formally the preeminent governing body of Libya, the General People's Congress (GPC) was formed after the March 1977 declaration of the era of the *jamahiriyya.* Delegates are selected from among district-level basic people's congresses, people's committees, and professional associations. Charged with debating reports from government agencies, the GPC meets infrequently and serves primarily as a sounding board for the head of state, Muammar al-Qaddafi.

See also JAMAHIRIYYA; QADDAFI, MUAMMAR AL.

LISA ANDERSON

GENERAL TUNISIAN UNION OF STUDENTS (UGTE)

Tunisian student union.

The Union Générale Tunisienne des Etudiants (UGTE) was Tunisia's major student group until the government banned it in early 1991 because of its association with the Islamist movement. Beginning in the 1980s, the Islamic Tendency Movement (Mouvement de Tendance Islamique; MTI) actively sought to take over the UGTE. It charged its University Bureau's Mokhtar Bedri with securing Islamist domination at the University of Tunis and provincial colleges through control of the UGTE.

The UGTE Islamist leadership was decimated by numerous arrests, trials, and imprisonments from 1991 to 1992. The government then infiltrated cadres of RCD (government party) candidates into leadership positions in the UGTE. As a result, the UGTE is more nonactivist and pro-government.

Bibliography

Dunn, Michael Collins. *Renaissance or Radicalism? Political Islam: The Case of Tunisia's al-Nahda.* Washington, DC, 1992.

LARRY A. BARRIE

GENERAL UNION OF PALESTINIAN WOMEN'S COMMITTEES (GUPWC)

Organization that provides opportunities for women, undertakes family assistance, and organizes kindergartens.

The General Union of Palestinian Women's Committees (GUPWC) was established in 1965 under the framework of the Palestine Liberation Organization. As such, it is the official representative body for Palestinian women around the world and encompasses all Palestinian women's organizations. The main goal of the union is to mobilize women to participate in social, economic, and political processes that will contribute to their development. The union is also politically active, supporting women in all aspects of the struggle for a Palestinian state, and at the nationalistic and social levels by providing leadership programs.

The GUPWC maintains a number of activities for women in order to integrate them into the labor force and raise cultural and health standards. Branches of the union are active throughout the Middle East and also in the United States, the Netherlands, and England. It has established vocational training centers and educational institutions in Palestinian refugee camps and holds classes to eradicate illiteracy. It also maintains nurseries and kindergartens so that women are able to partake in the union's activities and programs. Local specialized committees handle various activities and programs sponsored by the union.

See also PALESTINE; PALESTINE LIBERATION ORGANIZATION (PLO).

Bibliography

General Union of Palestinian Women. Available from <http://www.gupw.net>.

MALLIKA GOOD

GENERAL WOMEN'S UNION OF SYRIA

Also called the GWU, the General Women's Union is the major women's political organization in Syria.

The GWU was founded in 1967 by a consortium of women's groups. The organization is funded by the government and has developed projects focusing on children and education. The union is divided into fourteen branches throughout Syria, which assist associations and centers that deal with women's and children's issues and promote the active participation of women working in and outside the home.

The main focus of the GWU is to promote women's rights, to involve women effectively in the public sphere, and to end the exclusion of women and their marginalization in Syrian society. It has established child care centers, kindergartens, and vocational training and income-generating centers that train adult women in various skills and then sell the resulting products.

Internationally, the union has forged close ties with women's organizations throughout the Arab world. These groups meet, exchange ideas, share experiences, and prepare new strategies to improve women's lives in the region and allow them fuller participation. The union also works closely with the United Nations and international nongovernmental organizations. The GWU put together the National Syrian Women's Strategy, whose guidelines are based on the platform of the 1995 Beijing Conference for Women. The program is a plan of action, dealing with the implementation of various proposals from 1995 to 2005, when the next international conference on women is scheduled to convene.

Members of the union also participate in political debates about the Israeli occupation, the Palestinian situation, and the war in South Lebanon. Some of the GWU's strategies include: researching laws and legislation that deal with women, their citizenship rights and responsibilities, and any discrepancies between the ideals of equality and the current realities; working to ensure that laws are in place to protect and promote women and their human rights, and that they are enforced at all levels of government; helping women understand their rights and responsibilities and providing them with the knowledge and support they need to make the most of their opportunities; addressing social issues as poverty, health care, education, and family planning and their effect on women; enhancing women's ability to participate in decision-making at the national level and at home; and eradicating gender-related stereotypes that place women at a disadvantage.

See also GENDER: GENDER AND LAW; GENDER: GENDER AND POLITICS; SYRIA.

Bibliography

Al-Ahram Weekly On-line no. 508 (16–22 November 2000). Available from <http://weekly.ahram.org.eg>.

Machreq/Maghreb Gender Linking and Information Project. Available from <http://www.macmag-glip.org>.

"Syrian National Committee of Women's Affairs Post-Beijing." *Arab Women Connect.* Available from <http://arabwomenconnect.org>.

"Syria: Women in Public Life." United Nations Development Programme, Arab Region. Available from <http://www.pogar.org/countries/syria/gender.html>.

MIRNA LATTOUF

GENEVA PEACE CONFERENCE (1973)

Conference called by the United Nations after the Arab–Israel War of 1973.

The 22 December 1973 conference was convened in Geneva, Switzerland, in accordance with United Nations Security Council resolution 338. Its purpose was to settle issues that led to or arose from the Arab–Israel War of 1973. Of the Arab states, Egypt and Jordan participated, but Syria did not. Palestinian representatives were not invited to the opening session. After the opening speeches and ceremony, the conference adjourned and never reconvened. Israel had been reluctant to participate in multiparty conferences where pressures might be exerted for withdrawal from occupied territories and other steps it opposes. Disengagement agreements were signed in 1974 ending the war between Israel and Egypt and between Israel and Syria.

See also ARAB–ISRAEL WAR (1973).

Bibliography

Rolef, Susan Hattis, ed. *Political Dictionary of the State of Israel,* 2d edition. New York: Macmillan, 1993.

BENJAMIN JOSEPH

GEOGRAPHY

The topography and geography of the Middle East are closely related to the geology and climate of the region.

A zone of mountainous terrain in the north in combination with higher latitudes, lower temperatures, and increased precipitation gives a distinctive character to Turkey, Iran, and parts of the Levantine (eastern Mediterranean) coast. To the south, in North Africa and the Arabian Peninsula, tilted fault-block mountains and volcanoes provide intermittent physical relief to an area largely consisting of plateaus and plains. Unremitting aridity and high temperatures typify the desert that dominates this southern part of the region.

The geology of the Middle East is determined by the movement of continental plates in a northwesterly direction. This movement, in turn, deforms masses of sedimentary strata deposited in Paleozoic times in the ancient Tethyan Sea, which once separated Eurasia and Africa. The African plate is the largest and consists of ancient igneous materials overlain, in part, by a relatively thin layer of more recent sedimentary rocks. With the exception of the folded strata that make up the Atlas and Anti-Atlas Mountains in the west of the Maghrib (North Africa), the Ahaggar and Tibesti Mountains of Algeria and Libya, as well as the highlands of the Ethiopian plateau, are volcanic in nature. The Arabian plate to the east consists of tilted Mesozoic sedimentary strata dipping beneath the Persian/Arabian Gulf: These strata overlie pre-Cambrian igneous basement rock exposed by erosion in the Asir Mountains along the western shores of the peninsula. The Red Sea, which the uptilted edge of the Asir overlooks, is a continuation of the East African rift valley system and is formed by the moving apart of the African and Arabian blocks. This rift system continues north through the Gulf of Aqaba and forms the valley of the Dead Sea and the Jordan River. It eventually disappears in the down-folded strata of the Biqa (Bekaa) Valley of Lebanon.

The heavily folded Zagros Mountains bordering the Gulf on its eastern side result from the collision and subduction of the Arabian plate under the Iranian plate. The Persian/Arabian Gulf, which is an inlet of the Indian Ocean along the axis of the subduction zone, has accumulated huge quantities of sediments from the Tigris and Euphrates rivers, the Karun River, and numerous intermittent streams draining the lands on either side. Within these Tertiary sedimentary strata are found the largest petroleum fields in the world, with deposits in Saudi Arabia, Kuwait, Iran, Iraq, the United Arab Emirates, Qatar, and Oman, in descending order of importance. To the northwest, the Turk-

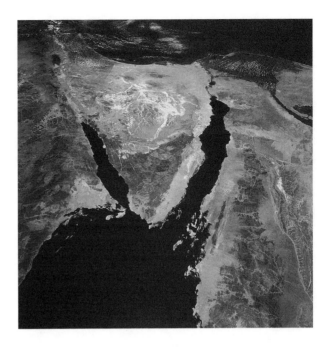

Aerial view of the Gulf of Aqaba (also known as the Gulf of Elat) on the Red Sea. It stretches 120 miles north from the Straits of Tiran, ending where the southern border of Israel meets the borders of Egypt and Jordan. © CORBIS. REPRODUCED BY PERMISSION.

ish plate is sliding westward along a transform fault and colliding with the Aegean plate. These areas of movement create major fault zones subject to severe earthquakes. In Turkey, the Erzincan earthquake of 1992 was typical. Faulting and recent volcanism terminate the northward extension of the rich petroleum fields of the Gulf beyond a few poor deposits near Batman, Turkey.

The northern part of the Middle East is a mountainous extension of the Alpine orogeny. The Pontic Mountains paralleling Turkey's Black Sea coast merge with the eastern highlands notable for volcanic Mount Ararat of biblical fame. The Taurus Mountains along Turkey's south shore extend eastward as the Anti-Taurus Mountains, joining the Zagros Mountains running southeast between Iran and Iraq. Another extension forms the Elburz Mountains bordering the Caspian Sea in Iran. Mount Damavand (18,934 ft [5775 m]), the highest peak in the Middle East and North Africa, is part of this range. Still farther east, the Kopet Mountains merge with those in Afghanistan and the Hindu Kush.

Great rivers have played their part in the history and development of the Middle East. The White

Most of Iraq consists of mountains surrounding a central plain. Iraq is located in western Asia, between the Middle and the Far East. © PAUL ALMASY/CORBIS. REPRODUCED BY PERMISSION.

eled through the Bosporus to bring grain from the shores of the Black Sea, and Roman triremes linked Italy and Africa. During the Middle Ages, some Arab navigational skills were conveyed to Europeans as Islam was spread. In the nineteenth century, the Mediterranean route was enhanced when the French and Egyptians completed the Suez Canal, joining the Mediterranean Sea to the Red Sea and thus reducing the trip from Europe to India (originally by way of the Cape of Good Hope) by thousands of miles.

The Middle East is composed of four environments, expressed by climate, vegetation, and traditional lifestyle. Well-watered humid and subhumid lands border the Black Sea in Turkey and extend along the Caspian shore of Iran. In these well-populated places, maize (corn), tea, hazelnuts, and rice are important crops.

Mountainous terrain, with remnant forests of pine, cedar, and juniper, rims the Anatolian plateau of Turkey and extends southward into coastal Syria and Lebanon. Similar but drier environments are found in the Zagros and Elburz Mountains of Iran. These areas once supported dense growths of mature trees, but with the exception of more remote places in the Taurus Mountains, the logger's ax and the charcoal burners' ovens have depleted the forests while nomads' goats have prevented regrowth through overgrazing. The result is either disturbed and impoverished woodlands (French, *maquis*) or barren and rocky ground supporting low herbaceous shrubs (French, *garrigue*).

The interior plateau of Turkey, the foothills of the Anti-Taurus and Zagros Mountains, and the northern portions of Jordan and Israel are semiarid, with grazing or grain production depending on the amount of each year's precipitation. The variance of rainfall on the drier margins of these areas makes permanent rain-fed agriculture difficult. As a result, ancient peoples developed pastoral nomadism as a lifestyle that met this challenge. Herds and flocks were moved seasonally to new pastures to avoid overgrazing of sparse vegetation as well as to seek out water sources. Once an important means of livelihood, nomadism has largely been abandoned.

Nile, which rises in equatorial Africa, is joined at Khartoum in Sudan by the Blue Nile, flowing from the highlands of Ethiopia. No precipitation sufficient for human survival occurs from that juncture north to the Mediterranean Sea, and all life in Egypt depends on the use of the combined waters of the two Niles. The Euphrates River and its companion the Tigris both rise in Turkey and join in southern Iraq to form the Shatt al-Arab, which empties into the Persian/Arabian Gulf. The area between the two streams, ancient Mesopotamia, was the site of the earliest civilization, Sumer (3500 B.C.E.), and other ancient civilizations based on irrigation farming.

The Mediterranean Sea also has influenced many of the cultural and geographical characteristics of the Middle East. It has served as a major link between Europe, Africa, and southwest Asia since ancient times. The Turkish Straits, composed from north to south of the Bosporus, the Sea of Marmara, and the Dardanelles, are an important waterway joining the Black Sea to the Aegean Sea and the Mediterranean. Bronze Age ships plied these straits and sailed along the coast of Turkey as well as among the Aegean Islands. Early Phoenician traders established sea routes leading to the Straits of Gibraltar and beyond. Ancient Greek ships trav-

The semiarid steppes merge gradually into true deserts, which dominate southern Israel, Jordan, and Iraq as well as the Arabian Peninsula and North

Africa west to the Atlas Mountains. Saharan conditions extend to the Mediterranean shore of North Africa from Gaza to Sfax in Tunisia, the only exception being a small outlier of Mediterranean climate on the Jabal al-Akhdar (Green Mountain) of Libya. Under desert conditions, agriculture is possible only in scattered oases and along the banks of rivers like the Euphrates in Iraq and the Nile in Egypt.

The narrow rim of Mediterranean climate, which extends north from Gaza through Israel, along the coasts of Lebanon, Syria, and Turkey, is the fourth environment. This same climate is also found from Tunis west to the Atlantic shores of Morocco. The Mediterranean environment is typified by winter rains and hot dry summers, which allow for the production of irrigated vegetables and citrus fruits, as well as various winter grains.

> See also AEGEAN SEA; AQABA, GULF OF; ARABIAN PENINSULA; ARARAT, MOUNT; ATLAS MOUNTAINS; BIQA VALLEY; BLACK SEA; CLIMATE; DEAD SEA; HINDU KUSH MOUNTAINS; LEVANTINE; MAGHRIB; MEDITERRANEAN SEA; NILE RIVER; PERSIAN (ARABIAN) GULF; PETROLEUM, OIL, AND NATURAL GAS; SHATT AL-ARAB; STRAITS, TURKISH; SUEZ CANAL; TAURUS MOUNTAINS; TIGRIS AND EUPHRATES RIVERS.

Bibliography

Beaumont, Peter; Blake, Gerald H.; and Wagstaff, J. Malcolm. *The Middle East: A Geographical Study,* 2d edition. New York: Halsted Press, 1988.

Blake, Gerald; Dewdney, John; and Mitchell, Jonathan. *The Cambridge Atlas of the Middle East and North Africa.* Cambridge, U.K., and New York: Cambridge University Press, 1987.

Held, Colbert C. *Middle East Patterns: Places, Peoples, and Politics,* 3d edition. Boulder, CO: Westview Press, 2000.

Longrigg, Stephen H. *The Middle East: A Social Geography,* 2d edition. Chicago: Aldine, 1970.

JOHN F. KOLARS

GERMANY AND THE MIDDLE EAST

German involvement in the Middle East in the nineteenth and twentieth centuries.

Brief contacts between Prussia and the Ottoman Empire occurred before the 1880s. In 1760 Frederick the Great sought an alliance with the Ottomans during the Seven Years' War; and in the 1830s Helmuth von Moltke, later chief of the Prussian General Staff, served as adviser to the Ottoman military in Constantinople (now Istanbul).

Nineteenth Century

After 1870, the new Germany was not concerned with the Eastern Question. German prime minister Otto von Bismarck, acting as the "honest broker" at the Berlin Congress in 1878, wished to avoid conflict with Austria, Hungary, Britain, and Russia—countries that already had imperialist stakes in the area. German intellectual interest in Iranian culture, language, and poetry had led to a treaty of friendship and commerce between Prussia and Persia (Iran) that was renewed in 1873; the relationship was cautious, however, because Bismarck understood that the area was under the domination of Russia and Britain. He agreed to open a German legation at Tehran in 1885 but would not meet with Naser al-Din Shah when the Iranian ruler visited Berlin in 1889. Similarly, in 1882 Bismarck reluctantly agreed to send military officers to the Sublime Porte after Abdülhamit II decided to replace France's military advisers with military personnel from Germany.

In this case, Germany's military mission inaugurated a more active political and economic policy toward Turkey that was advocated by Kaiser Wilhelm II, who ascended the throne in 1888 and replaced Bismarck in 1890. Germany's "drive to the East" (*Drang nach Osten*) was the means by which it would achieve imperialist parity with France and Britain through cultural and economic penetration of the declining Ottoman Empire. Advocated by Baron Hatzfeld, Germany's ambassador to Turkey from 1879 to 1881, the policy took into account the possibilities for Germany that resulted from the vacuum created by Britain's loss of prestige in the area after they assumed control of Cyprus (1878), occupied Egypt (1882), and became involved in Ottoman affairs because of the Ottoman public debt. Wilhelm II's visit to the Middle East in 1898, during which he advocated friendship with Islamic peoples, solidified ties between Germany and Abdülhamit II (called by some the Bloody Sultan because of his treatment of the Armenians). Acquiescence to Ottoman sensibilities resulted in lack of official

Emperor Wilhelm II of Germany (1859–1941) boards a ship in Turkey with Enver Paşa (1881–1922). Enver Paşa, War Minister during World War I, was instrumental in bringing Turkey into the war on the side of the Central Powers. © HULTON/ARCHIVE BY GETTY IMAGES.

support by Germany for Zionism, in spite of an initial favorable reaction to discussions with Theodor Herzl, and for the German Templars, Protestants from southern Germany who were seeking to establish ideal communities, began settling in Palestine in 1868.

From 1885, Germany's military mission, now under the command of Kolmar Freiherr von der Goltz, was responsible for instituting a network of military preparatory schools and reorganizing the Ottoman officer corps on the Prussian model. German advisers worked with Ottoman troops throughout the crises that beset the Sublime Porte before World War I. By that time, despite Germany's diplomatic failures in the Moroccan crises (1905–1906, 1911) and Ottoman defeats in the Balkan Wars (1912–1913), German officers were teaching and working in Turkey, and Turkish officers were sent to Berlin for advanced training.

Germany's ambassadors to Turkey, Marschall von Bieberstein (1897–1912) and Hans von Wangenheim (1912–1915), worked assiduously to open markets for their nation's products. Concessions were granted to a German bank (Deutsche Bank) and an arms merchant (Mauser) to build the Berlin-Baghdad Railway and the Hijaz Railroad; and in 1906 the Hamburg Amerika steamship line sailed the Persian Gulf in competition with ships from Britain. By 1914, Germany's share in the Ottoman public debt reached 22 percent (it had been 4.7% in 1888), and it had a 67.5 percent share in Ottoman railway investment. The Deutsche Bank played a major role in the Turkish economy, as did the Deutsche Palästina Bank in Palestine.

World War I

Despite Britain's presence in Turkey, Germany's influence, especially in the army, increased throughout the Young Turk period. Disunity in the approach of the Committee of Union and Progress to foreign policy led some to seek different allies as Europe headed toward war. The negotiations of Enver Paşa and Mehmet Talat with Germany resulted in a secret alliance on 1 August 1914. The Ottoman Empire entered World War I in November 1914.

Once the lines of communication between Germany and Turkey were secure, hundreds of German military officers were transferred to Turkey, some in command of Turkish troops, but not as decision-makers regarding policy and strategy. As head of the military mission since 1913, General Otto Liman von Sanders advised the Turks to invade the Ukraine from Odessa; Enver, however, insisted upon the ill-fated Caucasus campaign. Liman von Sanders commanded the defense of Gallipoli in 1915 and intervened successfully in the Armenian deportations at İzmir. Lieutenant Colonel (later Major General) Friedrich Kress von Kressenstein, a restraining influence on Cemal Paşa, served in Palestine. Field Marshal Kolmar Freiherr von der Goltz was called back to defend Baghdad in 1915; Lieutenant General Hans von Seeckt (chief of the Turkish General Staff in 1917), General Erich von Falkenhayn, and Franz von Papen (who was ambassador to Turkey during World War II) also fought with the Turkish army.

German Middle East academic specialists were utilized in the war effort. Influenced by predecessors who had been engaged in philological and archaeological research in the Middle East since the latter part of the nineteenth century, some claimed German-Turkish racial affinities. Orientalist Max

Kaiser Wilhelm II and the Sultan of Constantinople riding in a carriage through a cobbled street during World War I. © HULTON-DEUTSCH COLLECTION/CORBIS.

von Oppenheim directed an information service for the East that advocated fomenting Islamic uprisings in Persia, Afghanistan, and Egypt in order to dislodge the British.

In Iran, Germany had no coordinated policy, and as Russia's army moved toward Tehran in 1915, only Wilhelm Wassmuss fought against the British in the south. Germany's competition with Britain in support of Zionist aspirations in order to gain Jewish support became inactive after the United States entered the war.

The defeat of Germany in 1918 and the provisions of the Treaty of Versailles altered Germany's approach to the Middle East. From the Weimar Republic through the early 1930s, official German policy was inherently cautious, more concerned with revising the Treaty of Versailles and not alienating Britain than with taking an active role abroad. Although sympathetic to Zionism, once Germany became a member of the League of Nations (1926), it supported Britain's policy in Palestine and did not take a position on local Arab-Zionist issues. The low-key diplomatic approach, however, did not lessen Germany's economic interest in Turkey, Egypt, and Iran; Iran, due to Reza Shah Pahlavi's pro-German sympathies, was supplied by German companies with arms, machinery, and regular air service through the 1920s.

Third Reich and World War II

Germany's official policy toward the Middle East remained inconsistent through the Third Reich because it was predicated upon ideological, diplomatic, and economic factors that contradicted one another. The Nazi doctrine of racial purity and the search for markets in the Middle East lent themselves to support of the Zionist movement through the ha-Avarah (transfer) agreements as useful tools to rid Germany of Jews. When, after 1937, it was understood that Jewish sovereignty was possible, and that a large population of Jews (a circumstance noted after the war in eastern Europe began) might be a base for activity against Germany, Hitler opposed Jewish immigration to Palestine.

Also opposed to Jewish Palestinian immigration were German nationals, including archaeologists, scholars, members of the Palestine Templars, and diplomatic personnel who worked in the area. Both German nationalists looking back to imperial glory and Nazis became disseminators of German propaganda, finding allies in some pan-Arab groups and the military in Egypt, Syria, and Iraq. Max von Oppenheim and German Ambassador to Iraq Fritz Grobba advocated financial and military support for local anti-British pan-Arab movements as early as 1937. Meetings between pan-Arab nationalists such as Shakib Arslan, Muhammad Amin al-Husayni, and Aziz Ali al-Misri and German diplomatic officials took place, resulting in a declaration of support in December 1940 but no real aid.

Officially, Germany remained uninvolved in the Middle East, initially leaving the area to Britain. After 1939 and the outbreak of World War II, Germany left the area to Italy, which sought hegemony in North Africa and in the eastern Mediterranean. Italy's losses to the Allies in Greece and in Libya in 1941 sparked a belated interest by Germany, which had planned to turn to the Middle East only after anticipated successes in Russia (Operation Barbarossa).

Last-minute German arms deliveries to the pro-Axis Rashid Ali al-Kaylani government did not prevent Britain's victories in Iraq in June 1941 and in Vichy-ruled Syria in July. Fear that Iran was a potential fifth column because of its economic dependence on Germany—because of the large numbers of German nationals working there, and because it offered a haven for those fleeing the British in Iraq—resulted in Pahlavi's abdication and control of Iran by Russia and Britain. A planned pro-Axis Free Officers' revolt involving Aziz Ali al-Misri and Anwar al-Sadat, among others, together with Abwehr (German military intelligence) agents infiltrated into Cairo, failed to coordinate with Erwin Rommel's advance toward Egypt in the summer of 1942. Berlin provided sanctuary for some pro-Axis Arabs, among them the Jerusalem *mufti*, who left the Middle East during the war and worked for the German propaganda machine in return for Germany's promise to support Arab independence. After the war, a number of Nazis immigrated to the Arab world.

Two Germanys emerged from the war: East Germany, the German Democratric Republic (GDR); and West Germany, the Federal Republic of Germany (they united in 1991). The GDR followed the policy of the Soviet Union and never established diplomatic relations with Israel.

1950 to the Present

From the early 1950s, the Cold War and political obligations to the United States dominated German foreign policy. While blocking international, especially developing nations', recognition of the GDR, the Federal Republic strove to balance its economic interests in the Arab world with a commitment to Israel and the Jewish people forged in reaction to Germany's Nazi past and the Holocaust. Restitution and reparations agreements were signed in 1952, clandestine arms deals were negotiated throughout the 1960s, and diplomatic relations were established in 1965. All Arab states except Morocco, Tunisia, and Libya severed diplomatic ties with Germany, but had restored them by 1974.

Germany's economic ties in the Persian Gulf grew dramatically in the 1970s through the export of manufactured goods, the recycling of petrodollars through German banks, and the import of almost 50 percent of its oil needs from the region. As the price of oil fell in the 1980s, so did German dependence on Gulf markets. Germany's share in the arms market during the Iran-Iraq War represented only 1 percent of the total market (by comparison, France's participation amounted to some 15 percent). German companies' significant but illegal involvement in technology transfers contributed to the development of weapons of mass destruction in Libya and Iraq.

West Germany expressed support for the Palestinians' right to self-determination and, although its relations with Israel remained intact, it increasingly became critical of the Israeli occupation of the West Bank and Gaza Strip. Working through the European Union, Germany supported the 2003 U.S.-led peace plan, Road Map, that called for an independent state in Palestine within three years.

After Iraq invaded Kuwait in 1990, Germany supported United Nations (UN) Security Council Resolution 660, which condemned the Iraqi occupation, and Resolution 678, which authorized military measures to expel Iraq from Kuwait. It joined the U.S.-led coalition of twenty-eight states by sending air units to Turkey, contributed mine sweepers,

and pledged $5.5 billion to the war effort. But Germany offered no such support to the United States as it planned with Britain in 2003 to invade Iraq. The United States and Britain claimed that Iraq had weapons of mass destruction (WMD) and was an imminent danger to world security. Together with France and Russia, Germany—now a nonpermanent member of the UN Security Council—opposed a draft resolution supported by the United States, Britain, and Spain that authorized the use of force. Instead, it sought the return of UN weapons inspectors to Iraq to investigate whether Iraq had WMD. Although Germany helped defeat the resolution, it was unable to deter the invasion of Iraq by mainly the United States and Britain. The Gulf crises and war that followed damaged Germany's generally friendly relations with the United States and Britain.

See also ABDÜLHAMIT II; ARSLAN, SHAKIB; BALKAN WARS (1912–1913); BANKING; BERLIN–BAGHDAD RAILWAY; EASTERN QUESTION; ENVER PAŞA; FREE OFFICERS, EGYPT; GALLIPOLI; GROBBA, FRITZ KONRAD FERDINAND; HA-AVARAH AGREEMENT; HERZL, THEODOR; HIJAZ RAILROAD; HUSAYNI, MUHAMMAD AMIN AL-; ISTANBUL; KAYLANI, RASHID ALI AL-; MISRI, AZIZ ALI AL-; OTTOMAN EMPIRE: OVERVIEW; ROMMEL, ERWIN; SADAT, ANWAR AL-; SUBLIME PORTE; TALAT, MEHMET; TEMPLARS; WEST GERMAN REPARATIONS AGREEMENT; YOUNG TURKS; ZIONISM.

Bibliography

Chubin, Shahram. *Germany and the Middle East: Patterns and Prospects.* New York: Palgrave Macmillan, 1992.

Hirszowicz, Lukasz. *The Third Reich and the Arab East.* London: Routledge and Kegan Paul, 1966.

Nicosia, Francis R. *The Third Reich and the Palestine Question.* Austin: University of Texas Press, 1985.

Simon, Reeva S. *Iraq Between the Two World Wars: The Creation and Implementation of a Nationalist Ideology.* New York: Columbia University Press, 1986.

Trumpener, Ulrich. *Germany and the Ottoman Empire, 1914–1918.* Princeton, NJ: Princeton University Press, 1968.

Wallach, Yehuda L., ed. *Germany and the Middle East, 1835–1939.* Tel Aviv: Tel Aviv University, 1975.

REEVA S. SIMON
UPDATED BY PHILIP MATTAR

GEZIRA SCHEME

A Sudanese agricultural project established by the British.

The Gezira Scheme, located in the plains between the Blue Nile and White Nile of the central Sudan, was the first large-scale irrigated agricultural project established by the British government under the Anglo–Egyptian condominium. When it opened in 1926, it covered 300,000 *feddans* (ca. 300,000 acres), of which a third grew cotton. In the 1950s, Sudanese managers replaced the British officials, and the Gezira Board invested a greater share of the profits for social development projects among the tenants. Later extensions quadrupled the area of the scheme, but costs escalated, cotton prices dropped in the world markets, and the tenants and Gezira Board became increasingly indebted. International loans have helped, but they have also increased the country's overall debt burden.

Bibliography

Barnett, Tony. *The Gezira Scheme: An Illusion of Development.* London: F. Cass, 1977.

ANN M. LESCH

Two women jog along the running path at the Gezira Sporting Club. The athletic club in Zamalek, Cairo, is exclusive to members only. © PETER TURNLEY/CORBIS. REPRODUCED BY PERMISSION.

GEZIRA SPORTING CLUB

Country club in Cairo.

Long a symbol of British imperialism and insularity in Egypt, the Gezira, as it is usually called, was founded in 1882 and originally limited its membership to high-ranking British civil servants in the Egyptian government and officers of the army of occupation. Between the two world wars, the club's rosters also listed the names of titled European aristocrats wintering in Cairo, members of the diplomatic corps, prominent Levantine Jews and Christians, and Egyptian Muslims and Copts, many of whom were close to the palace. The flavor of the club during its British heyday has been admirably transmitted in memoirs written by former foreign residents of the city, in travel literature, and in such works of fiction as Olivia Manning's *Levant Trilogy,* which is set in Egypt's capital.

The exclusive and exclusionary character of the club was maintained until after World War II, when the tide of nationalism and a rising indigenous bourgeoisie forced its Egyptianization in January 1952. The ethos and structure of the club were further altered during the anti-Western years of the Nasser regime. In the early 1960s, the Gezira was both figuratively and literally truncated when the government, in a tactic calculated as a humiliation, forced it to permanently yield half of its grounds to a politicized athletic institution established to promote sports among the masses called the Ahli, or National Sports Club. Insult was added to injury when the Sadat regime built a suspended highway over the remaining nine-hole golf course and six-furlong racetrack to commemorate its performance in the 1973 Arab-Israel War.

Despite its contraction and urbanization, the Gezira still offers most of the sports and games practiced by its founders: golf, squash, bowls, croquet, riding, and even cricket. The last is played almost exclusively by Indian and Pakistani residents of Cairo. Horse racing, one of the club's original *raisons d'être,* takes place during the winter season. Polo, however, which led to the founding of the Gezira as a gift from Egypt's viceroy to the officers of the British army of occupation, is no longer played for lack of grounds, players, and schooled ponies.

With the passing of Nasserism, the Gezira regained a small measure of its colonial grandeur, catering mostly to nouveau-riche Egyptians and a few foreign technocrats.

See also NASSER, GAMAL ABDEL; SADAT, ANWAR AL-.

Bibliography

Grafftey-Smith, Lawrence. *Bright Levant.* London: J. Murray, 1970.

Oppenheim, Jean-Marc R. "Twilight of a Colonial Ethos: The Alexandria Sporting Club, 1890–1956." Ph.D. diss., Columbia University, 1990.

JEAN-MARC R. OPPENHEIM

GHAB, AL-

In Syria, the largest plain of a large trough which also includes the low plains of al-Asharina, al-Ruj, and al-Amq.

Al-Ghab is located between the mountains Jabal al-Ansariyya (al-Alawiyyin) in the west and Jabal al-Zawiya in the east. Its length from south to north is about 56 miles (90 km), its width between 5 and 7.5 miles (8 to 12 km), and its elevation above sea level is between 558 and 656 feet (170 and 200 m). It slightly slopes toward the north like the Orontes River that traverses it to the northeast of Hama. Its yearly rainfall averages 19.5 to 27 inches (500 to 700 mm), but it receives other sources of water, notably from the Orontes River, which is rejected back into it by the basaltic bedrock of Qarqar in the north. Before 1954, al-Ghab was intersected by swampland, infested by malaria, and covered by reeds used for catching its celebrated catfish.

Within two decades after 1954, the landscape of al-Ghab changed dramatically as a result of the drainage of its swamps, the building of dams, such as the ones at al-Rastan, Maharda, and notably al-Asharina, to regulate its irrigation, and the creation by the Syrian government of a number of projects in it. Of its total area of 136,000 acres (55,000 ha), 42,000 acres (17,000 ha) are irrigated by river flooding and dam water, 74,000 acres (30,000 ha) depend on rainfall, and the remaining parts are turned into farms. In 1969, land in al-Ghab was distributed by the government to 11,000 beneficiaries according to the decrees of agricultural reform. To encourage the cultivation of land, fifty-two cooperatives were established there. Other projects include a cattle farm, fisheries, and a sugar factory at the village of Salhab.

ABDUL-KARIM RAFEQ

GHALI, BOUTROS

[1846–1910]

Egyptian diplomat and cabinet minister.

Born in a village near Bani Suwayf in Egypt, Boutros Ghali went to the reformist Coptic school at Harat al-Saqqayin and the princes' school of Mustafa Fadil. He later studied at the School of Languages, learning Arabic, French, English, Turkish, and Persian, but never earned a *license* or any other degree. He became a clerk for the Alexandria Chamber of Commerce and in 1873 was appointed by the sharif to the head clerkship of the justice ministry. At this time he also helped to organize the Coptic (Lay) Council. When the mixed courts were being established, Ghali helped the justice minister write an Arabic translation of their (mainly French) law code, even though he lacked any legal training.

His work brought him to the attention of Prime Minister Boghos Nubar Pasha, who made him Egypt's representative to the Caisse de la Dette Publique, thus mediating frequently between the Egyptian government and its European creditors. Named deputy justice minister in 1879, he held various responsible posts during the Urabi revolution. Afterward, he mediated between Khedive Tawfiq and the nationalists, saving many from execution.

Ghali received his first ministerial appointment in 1893 when Khedive Abbas Hilmi II challenged the British occupation by appointing his own cabinet under Husayn Fakhri (without consulting Lord Cromer). He remained finance minister under the compromise cabinet of Mustafa al-Riyad. He served as foreign minister from 1894 to 1910 and continued to mediate between power centers, signing the 1899 Sudan Convention that set up the Anglo–Egyptian Condominium Agreement. He represented the cabinet on the bench at the 1906 trial in the Dinshaway Incident, concurring in the death sentences on four of the accused peasants and angering Egypt's nationalists.

Khedive Abbas and Sir Eldon Gorst concurred in naming him prime minister in 1908, despite misgivings about having a Copt as the head of Egypt's government. He further angered the nationalists by reviving the 1881 press law and publicly advocating the extension of the Suez Canal Company's concession, policies that he reportedly opposed privately. His assassination by Ibrahim Nasif al-Wardani, a nationalist, in February 1910, set off a wave of Coptic–Muslim confrontations and led to a more repressive government policy against the nationalists.

See also ABBAS HILMI II; BARING, EVELYN; CONDOMINIUM AGREEMENT (1899); DINSHAWAY INCIDENT (1906); GORST, JOHN ELDON; MIXED COURTS; NUBAR PASHA; RIYAD, MUSTAFA AL-; URABI, AHMAD.

Bibliography

Seikaly, Samir. "Coptic Communal Reform (1860–1914)." *Middle Eastern Studies* 6 (1970):4.

Seikaly, Samir. "Prime Minister and Assassin: Butrus Ghali and Wardani." *Middle Eastern Studies* 13 (1977):1.

ARTHUR GOLDSCHMIDT

GHALLAB, ABD AL-KARIM
[1919–]

Moroccan novelist, short-story writer, and journalist.

Abd al-Karim Ghallab was born in Fez. He studied at the mosque college of al-Qarawiyyin in Fez, then obtained his B.A. in Arabic literature from Cairo University. He is editor in chief and director of the daily *Al-Alam*.

Ghallab is a prolific writer whose publications cover a wide range of topics and interests, some purely literary and others dealing with political and cultural issues. Through his writings he seeks to promote nationalist feelings and a deep attachment to Arabic-Islamic culture, counteracting the French education that was particularly threatening to Moroccans during the years of French colonialism.

Some of Ghallab's short stories in the collection *Wa Akhrajaha min al-Janna* (1977; He led her out

of paradise) criticize the tendency of the upper middle class to communicate in French. Similar concerns are expressed in his novel *Sabahun wa Yazhafu al-Layl* (1984; Morning, then the night creeps in). Ghallab's fiction works illustrate and defend his beliefs and values. An active nationalist, he was often at odds with the French colonial power and was imprisoned, an experience depicted in his novel *Sab'at Abwab* (1965; Seven gates). Some of his other fiction works, such as *Dafanna al-Madi* (1966; We buried the past), reveal his patriotic feelings. Ghallab fervently preaches attachment to the land and its safeguard by Moroccan farmers, as illustrated in his collection of short stories *Al-Ard Habibati* (1971; The land, my beloved), his novel *Al-Mu'allim Ali* (1971; Master Ali), and his essay "Fi al-Islah al-Qarawi" (1961; Of rural reform).

Ghallab's nationalist positions date back to his student years in Egypt, where he agitated for the independence of the three Maghribi countries, Algeria, Tunisia, and Morocco. Back in Morocco, he joined the Istiqlal Party and became deeply involved in politics. He was appointed a minister plenipotentiary for the Middle East (1956–1959) and a minister in the Moroccan government (1983–1985). His nonfiction writings also reflect his political views, ranging from his preoccupation with political governance to Arab unity. These works include *Hadha Huwa al-Dustur* (1962; This is the constitution), *Al-Tatawwur al-Dusturi wa al-Niyabi bi al-Maghrib min sanat 1908 ila sanat 1978* (1988; The Constitutional and the legal development in the Maghrib from 1908 to 1978, 2 vols.), *Ma'rakatuna al-Arabiyya fi Muwajahat al-Isti'mar wa al-Sahyuniyya* (coauthor, 1967; Our Arab battle with colonialism and Zionism), *Nabadat Fikr* (1961; The beat of a thinking mind), *Thaqafa wa al-Fikr fi Muwajahat al-Tahaddi* (1976; Culture and thought in the face of challenge), and *Risalatu Fikr* (1968; The message of a thinking mind).

Religious feelings and a pious way of life are also of concern to Ghallab; they are implicit in his fiction and explicitly expressed in his book *Sira al-Madhhab wa al-Aqida fi al-Qur'an* (1973; The struggle of ideology and faith in the Qur'an). In his collection of short stories, *Hadha al-Wajh A'rafuhu!* (1997; I know this face) he sheds some of the didactic tone of his fiction writings.

See also LITERATURE: ARABIC, NORTH AFRICAN; MAGHRIB.

Bibliography

Allen, Roger. *Encyclopedia of Arabic Literature,* edited by Julie Meisami and Paul Starkey. London and New York: Routledge, 1998.

Bamia, Aida A. "Ghallab, Abd al-Karim." In *Encyclopedia of World Literature in the Twentieth Century,* vol. 5, edited by Leonard S. Klein. New York: Ungar, 1993.

AIDA A. BAMIA

GHANIM, AL-

Merchant family in Kuwait.

The al-Ghanim family, together with the Al Sabah, the Al Saqr, and the al-Qatami, were among the original Anaza settlers in Kuwait in the eighteenth century. The family made money first in shipping and trade, but a disaster at sea in 1925 encouraged them to diversify their interests. Ahmad al-Ghanim became an agent of the Anglo-Persian Oil Company (APOC) during its negotiations for the Kuwait oil concession and the family did business with both APOC and the concessionaire, the Kuwait Oil Company. During the 1930s, al-Ghanim family income provided the government of Kuwait with two-thirds of its revenues. Ahmad's son Yusuf, along with other family members, fled Kuwait after the failure of the 1938 Majlis movement, returning in 1944 under a general amnesty. By the end of World War II the al-Ghanim employed 7,000 men, about half the workforce of Kuwait. The family became the top labor and supply contractor for the Kuwait Oil Company and Faysal al-Ghanim served as one of its managing directors. The al-Ghanim also acquired agencies and distributorships, including a lucrative arrangement with General Motors. Thunayan Faysal al-Ghanim served with the small contingent of Kuwaiti troops among the forces liberating Kuwait from Iraqi occupation in 1991. The family owns al-Ghanim Industries, a holding company that ranks among the top companies in the world.

See also PETROLEUM, OIL, AND NATURAL GAS.

Bibliography

Carter, J. R. L. *Merchant Families of Kuwait.* London: Scorpion Books, 1984.

Crystal, Jill. *Oil and Politics in the Gulf: Rulers and Merchants in Kuwait and Qatar.* Cambridge, U.K.: Cambridge University Press, 1990.

MARY ANN TÉTREAULT

GHANIM, FATHI
[1924–1999]

Egyptian novelist and political writer.

Born in Cairo to middle-class background, Fathi Ghanim studied law at the Cairo University. After serving until the early 1950s at the ministry of education, he devoted himself to political and fictional writing. He served as the editor for Rose al-Yusif and a number of Egyptian newspapers and other periodicals, including *Akhar Sa'a* (The last hour) and *Sabah al-Khayr* (Good morning). In 1966 the government made *al-Jumhuriyya* (The republic) the sole official organ of the Arab Socialist Union, and Ghanim was appointed editor in chief. A strong partisan of pan-Arab socialist and nationalist ideology, in "The Crisis between Islam and Politics" (1998) he denounced the political involvement of Muslim movements and blamed the Islamic regime of Iran for invading Iraq in the 1980s. He portrayed Islam as a religion of reason that in his view calls for secularism, and he saw the Islamic state as an expression of fanaticism and backwardness.

In 1959 he published *al-Jabal* (The mountain), a satirical portrayal of the Egyptian government's attempts to resettle peasants. His most famous literary work, *The Man Who Lost His Shadow* (1966), describes the social and political evolution of Egypt from the 1920s to the 1950s through the lives of four main characters. This theme was continued in *Zaynab and the Throne* (1976). Both novels were made into television series. He also wrote *The Story of Tou* in 1987, which described in fictional terms the political oppression and torture carried out by the government. His fluid style and dynamic plots allowed him to write engaging novels that served as realistic portrayals and criticisms of Egyptian society while exploring the wider themes of oppression, fanaticism, violence, and injustice. Ghanim received the State Merit Award for Literature in 1994.

See also LITERATURE: ARABIC.

Bibliography

Ghanem, Fathy. *The Man Who Lost His Shadow: A Novel in Four Books,* translated by Desmond Stewart. London: Chapman and Hall, 1966.

Ghanem, Fathy. *The Right Man and Other Stories,* translated by Nayla Naguib. Cairo: General Egyptian Book Organization, 1994.

MAYSAM J. AL-FARUQI

GHANMI, AZZA

Tunisian feminist activist.

In 1978–1979, Azza Ghanmi joined other feminist activists to found the Club d'Etude de la Condition de la Femme at the Club Tahar Haddad. Restricted to women only, the group debated the condition of women in Tunisian society. The institution of the Tunisian Code of Personal Status, promulgated in 1956 as part of Habib Bourguiba's modernization program, had granted women a number of rights making them equal citizens (for example, the stipulation of minimum marriage ages, requirement of personal consent to marriage, prohibition of polygamy, the right to vote, women's full legal capacity to enter contracts, and women's right to education and work). However, everyday social practices remained patriarchal.

In the early 1980s Ghanmi, along with other activists, participated in the group Femmes Démocrates, which emerged in response to political events such as the Israeli invasion of Lebanon and the massacres at Sabra and Shatila. She contributed to its feminist journal *Nissa,* and eventually became the secretary general of the Association Tunisienne des Femmes Démocrates (AFTD), instituted in1989. Ghanmi has been an outspoken advocate of the rights of the child and of women's human rights, especially in the context of compliance with the international Convention for the Elimination of Discrimination Against Women (CEDAW) to which Tunisia is a signatory.

See also GENDER: GENDER AND LAW; GENDER: GENDER AND POLITICS; HUMAN RIGHTS; NEWSPAPERS AND PRINT MEDIA: ARAB COUNTRIES; TUNISIA; TUNISIA: POLITICAL PARTIES IN.

Bibliography

Dwyer, Kevin. *Arab Voices: The Human Rights Debate in the Middle East.* Berkeley: University of California Press, 1991.

LAURA RICE

GHANNOUCHI, RACHED

[1941–]

Islamist politician; founding member and head of the Islamic Tendency Movement, an offshoot of the Islamic Revival Movement formed in Tunisia in 1979.

Rached Ghannouchi entered politics in the 1970s as a member of the Society for the Preservation of the Qur'an. Along with other leaders of the Islamist movement in Tunisia, he argues for a reintegration of Islam and Islamic law (*shariʿa*) in all aspects of national life, including politics. He has been fiercely critical of Westernizing trends in Tunisia and of the secular character of the ruling party, the Destour Socialist Party (PSD). To him, the decline of Islamic values and the reliance on Western ideologies and economic-development models have led to social corruption and economic decline in Tunisia and throughout the Islamic world.

In June 1981, his Islamic Tendency Movement (Mouvement de Tendance Islamique; MTI) filed, without success, for formal recognition. Ghannouchi and his party, renamed al-Nahda (Reawakening) in 1989, attracted a growing number of, in particular, young followers during the 1980s. For his antigovernment activism, he was arrested in 1981 and remained in prison until 1984; he was rearrested in 1987. The issue of his trial and execution, sought by Tunisia's President Habib Bourguiba in the fall of 1987, precipitated Bourguiba's overthrow by Zayn al-Abidine Ben Ali. Pardoned by Ben Ali in May 1988, Ghannouchi left Tunisia in April 1989 to begin what he described as a self-imposed exile.

See also BEN ALI, ZAYN AL-ABIDINE; BOURGUIBA, HABIB; NAHDA, AL-; QUR'AN; SHARIʿA.

Bibliography

Nelson, Harold D., ed. *Tunisia: A Country Study.* Washington, DC: U.S. Government Printing Office, 1988.

MATTHEW S. GORDON

GHARB

Moroccan plain.

The Gharb, inhabited by Arab tribes (Banu Malik, Sufiyan, Khlut, and Tliq), is located between Wadi Lukkus, Wadi Sabu, and the Middle Atlas Mountains in Morocco. Before colonization, the tribes lived by limited agriculture and pastoralism. Under the French protectorate, the Gharb became a rich region where colons settled and developed different types of agriculture for export.

After independence, the Gharb was subject to intensive development through allocation of irrigated plots of land to peasants and the creation of small exploitation units of industrial agriculture. During this period, the Gharb witnessed an intensive intervention by state agencies, such as national offices of rural modernization and of irrigation and the division of water and forests.

The cities of the Gharb are Mechra Bel Ksiri, Sidi Sliman, Sidi Yahya, and Kenitra. Except for Kenitra, which is located on the margin of the region, the Gharb has not experienced the development of any major urban agglomeration because of its closeness to big cities such as Rabat, Casablanca, and Meknes.

See also COLONS.

RAHMA BOURQIA

GHARBZADEGI

Persian term meaning "Weststruck."

Coined in the late 1940s and made a household term in Iran's intellectual circles by writer and social critic Jalal Al-e Ahmad (1923–1969) in a clandestinely published book by the same name (1962, 1964), *gharbzadegi* signals a chief sociological notion and concern among many Iranians in the post–World War II era.

As Al-e Ahmad describes it, throughout the twentieth century Iran has resorted to "Weststruck" behavior—adopting and imitating Western models and using Western criteria in education, the arts, and culture in general—while serving passively as a market for Western goods and also as a pawn in Western geopolitics. Consequently threatened with loss of cultural, if not Iranian, identity, Al-e Ahmad argues that Iran must gain control over machines and become a producer rather than a consumer, even though once having overcome Weststruckness it will still face that desperate situation, he argues, that remains in the West—that of "machinestruckness."

See also AL-E AHMAD, JALAL; IRAN.

Bibliography

Al-e Ahmad, Jalal. *Occidentosis: A Plague from the West (Gharbzadegi)*, translated by R. Campbell. Berkeley, CA: Mizan Press, 1983.

Al-e Ahmad, Jalal. *Plagued by the West (Gharbzadegi)*, translated by Paul Sprachman. Delmor, NY: Center for Iranian Studies, Columbia University, 1982.

Al-e Ahmad, Jalal. *Weststruckness (Gharbzadegi)*, translated by John Green and Ahmad Alizadeh. Costa Mesa, CA: Mazda Publishers, 1997.

MICHAEL C. HILLMANN

GHASHMI, AHMAD HUSAYN
[c. 1923–1978]

Yemeni president and soldier.

Ahmad Husayn Ghashmi was a career soldier of limited education and of deeply rooted tribal origins. Born in Dhula, an area just northwest of San'a, he came from a family of tribal leaders, his brother being the paramount shaykh of the strategically located, but otherwise not very important or powerful, Hamdan tribe. As a commander of armored forces, he provided crucial support to President Ibrahim al-Hamdi in his struggle to consolidate his power against strong opposition in the Yemen Arab Republic (YAR) after the 1974 coup. Despite occupying the number-two post of armed forces chief-of-staff for three years, Ghashmi was directly involved in the assassination of al-Hamdi and his brother in 1977; he then became YAR president, only to be assassinated himself (blown up by a bomb carried in a briefcase of an emissary from South Yemen) in June 1978 after only eight months in office. The fears of his modernist critics notwithstanding, Ghashmi as president seemed inclined to protect the weak Yemeni state from its tribal challengers and Saudi Arabia. His assassination had less to do with North Yemeni politics than with a power struggle in South Yemen; he was succeeded by the much younger, much longer serving Ali Abdullah Salih.

See also HAMDI, IBRAHIM AL-; HATIM SULTANS OF HAMDAN; SALIH, ALI ABDULLAH; YEMEN ARAB REPUBLIC.

Bibliography

Burrowes, Robert D. *The Yemen Arab Republic: The Politics of Development, 1962–1986*. Boulder, CO: Westview Press; London: Croom Helm, 1987.

Dresch, Paul. *Tribes, Government, and History in Yemen*. New York: Oxford University Press; Oxford, U.K.: Clarendon, 1989.

ROBERT D. BURROWES

GHASSEMLOU, ABDUL RAHMAN
[1930–1989]

Leader of the Kurdish Democratic Party of Iran.

Abdul Rahman Ghassemlou was born in Urumia, West Azerbaijan province, Iran, and became engaged in Kurdish nationalist struggles in the mid-1940s. He left his native city in 1947 and continued his education and political activism in both the Kurdish Democratic Party of Iran (KDPI) and the Tudeh Party in Tehran. In 1948 he moved to Paris, and then went to Prague, Czechoslovakia, where he lived until his return to Iran in 1952. Forced into exile in Czechoslovakia in 1958, he earned a doctoral degree there in 1962 and taught at the Prague School of Economics. In 1973 he reorganized the KDPI in its third congress, held clandestinely in Baghdad, Iraq. He returned to Iran on the verge of the fall of Pahlavi monarchy in early 1979 and pursued a policy of negotiating Kurdish autonomy within the evolving Islamic regime. However, the government mobilized the army against the autonomist movement in August 1979. The KDPI and other opposition groups were forced out of Kurdistan in the mid-1980s. In July 1989 Islamic government officials assassinated Ghassemlou in Vienna, Austria, where he was negotiating with them a peaceful settlement of the Kurdish question.

See also IRAN; KURDISH REVOLTS.

Bibliography

"Dr. A. R. Ghassemlou, Man of Peace and Dialogue." Democratic Party of Iranian Kurdistan. Available from <http://www.pdki.org/ghassemlou.htm>.

Ghassemlou, Abdul Rahman. *Kurdistan and the Kurds,* translated by Miriam Jeliinková. Prague: Publishing Hours of the Czechoslovak Academy of Sciences, 1965.

AMIR HASSANPOUR

GHAZALI, MUHAMMAD AL-
[1917–1996]

Leading proponent of a centrist Islamism, renowned for opposition to secularism and anti-intellectual extremism.

Muhammad al-Ghazali graduated from al-Azhar in 1941 and became a leading political radical in the Egyptian Muslim Brotherhood before his dismissal from the Brotherhood's constituent body in December 1953, reportedly after involvement in an attempt to oust the movement's leader. His subsequent rise in the Egyptian Muslim jurisprudential system was accompanied by the publication of more than fifty books, ensuring popularity for his approaches to Qur'anic exegesis and Islamic responses to modernity across the Muslim world. In 1989 he won the King Faisal International Prize for Islamic Studies, but his subsequent books, *The Sunna of the Prophet* and the influential *Journey through the Qur'an,* drew fierce attacks from Saudis for his outspoken attack on the simplistic methods of antimodernist extremists. In the 1980s he headed Islamic university academies in Mecca, Qatar, and Constantine (Algeria), where President Chadli Bendjedid sought to use him as a mediator with more radical Islamists. After publicly debating leading secularists in Egypt, Ghazali drew fire for justifying the killing of Farag Foda as an apostate in 1992. In favor of taking ideas from the non-Muslim world, Ghazali was moderate in supporting women's rights and a gradualist approach to Islamic democracy.

See also AZHAR, AL-; BENDJEDID, CHADLI; MUSLIM BROTHERHOOD.

Bibliography

Esposito, John. *Islam and Politics.* Syracuse NY: Syracuse University Press, 1998.

Meijer, Roel. *From al-Da'wa to al-Hizbiyya: Mainstream Islamic Movements in Egypt, Jordan, and Palestine in the 1990s.* Amsterdam, 1997.

GEORGE R. WILKES

GHAZALI, ZAYNAB AL-
[1917–]

Egyptian Islamist writer and activist.

Zaynab al-Ghazali al-Jabili was born in the Egyptian Delta and educated in religious schools. She is a Muslim activist associated with the Muslim Brotherhood and was the founding president of the Jam'iyyat al-Sayyidat al-Muslimat (Muslim Women's Association, 1936), with which al-Ghazali sought to counter the secularist Egyptian Feminist Union. Al-Ghazali refused to subsume her association into the Muslim Brotherhood, as its leader Hasan al-Banna suggested, and she led the association in its charity and educational activities until the Nasser regime closed it down in 1964. In 1950, she founded the

Majallat al-Sayyidat al-Muslimat (Muslim women's journal) while also writing regular columns in the Muslim Brotherhood's journal. Active in Islamic politics and associated with the Brotherhood at least since 1949, she is famous for having put *al-da'wa* (the call to propagate the faith) before conjugal demands in her own life while admonishing Muslim women that in an ideal Muslim society women's energies would center on home and family.

Al-Ghazali's best-known work is her prison memoir, *Ayyam min hayati* (Days of my life), first published in 1972 and republished many times. Incarcerated along with many other Islamist activists in 1965, she was transferred in 1967 to the women's prison and released in 1971. The memoir prefaces its account of solitary confinement, torture, and ultimate triumph with a narrative of her earlier work; the text operates not only as an individual memoir but also as a collective autobiography of Brotherhood activists and as a testimony to spiritual struggle under extreme conditions and thus serves as an exemplary text for other contemporary Muslims. Prison becomes a microcosm of society, exemplifying "the swamps, brackish with depravities" that Muslim activism is to tackle. Although the book shows the gender-specific treatment of imprisoned women and although al-Ghazali's biographies of early Muslim women, published in *al-Da'wa* from 1979 until it was banned late in 1981, claim female exemplars for contemporary activism, to characterize her as a feminist, as some have done, is a debatable move.

See also GENDER: GENDER AND EDUCATION; GENDER: GENDER AND LAW; GENDER: GENDER AND POLITICS; MUSLIM BROTHERHOOD; SHARI'A.

Bibliography

Booth, Marilyn. "Prison, Gender, Praxis: Women's Prison Memoirs in Egypt and Elsewhere." *MERIP Middle East Report* 149 (1987): 35–41.

Cooke, Miriam. "*Ayyam min Hayati*: The Prison Memoirs of a Muslim Sister." *Journal of Arabic Literature* 26, no. 1–2 (1995): 147–64.

Hoffman, Valerie. "An Islamic Activist: Zaynab al-Ghazali." In *Women and the Family in the Middle East*, edited by Elizabeth W. Fernea. Austin: University of Texas Press, 1985.

MARILYN BOOTH

GHAZEL

See GLOSSARY

GHAZI IBN FAISAL
[1912–1939]

King of Iraq from 1933 to 1939.

The son of King Faisal I, Ghazi ibn Faisal inherited little of his father's sophistication and political understanding. As his father's popularity began to wane at the end of the 1920s, Ghazi began to court a following of his own by identifying himself more or less openly with the opposition politicians and associating with the leaders of the Iraqi army. This continued after his accession, and as the army high command began to exert an increasing influence on the country's political life (especially after the coup organized by Bakr Sidqi in 1936). Ghazi's relations with the British Embassy, and with Britain's protégé Nuri al-Sa'id, became increasingly strained. While there was no direct evidence linking Nuri to the car accident in which Ghazi was killed, the circumstances surrounding his death always remained obscure. Nuri, Ghazi's cousin Abd al-Ilah, and Ghazi's estranged wife, Abd al-Ilah's sister Aliya, were long suspected of some form of involvement in it.

See also ABD AL-ILAH IBN ALI; FAISAL I IBN HUSSEIN; HASHIMITE HOUSE (HOUSE OF HASHIM); SIDQI, BAKR.

PETER SLUGLETT

GHORBAL, ASHRAF
[1925–]

Egyptian diplomat.

Educated at universities in the United States, Ashraf Ghorbal (also Ghurbal) was the first secretary to the United Nations in Geneva from 1958 to 1962, and an adviser to the Egyptian delegation in New York from 1962 to 1964. When Egypt's embassy in Washington, D.C., was closed following the 1967 Arab–Israel War, Ghorbal became head of the Egyptian/United Arab Republic interests section of the Indian embassy, where he served until 1973.

During the October 1973 war—after having served nearly a year as assistant security adviser to President Anwar al-Sadat—he was placed in charge of Egypt's information and public relations. In November 1973 Ghorbal was appointed ambassador to the reopened Egyptian embassy. He earned the gratitude of many Americans after playing a key role in negotiating the release of hostages held by a terrorist in the B'nai B'rith building in Washington, D.C., in 1977. Ghorbal took part in the Camp David meetings of 1978, and the subsequent isolation of Egypt from the Arab League in the years that followed meant that he was excluded from meetings of the Arab ambassadors in Washington. Nevertheless, he maintained relations with individual ambassadors privately, ultimately also working with key Arab states as dean of the African diplomatic corps. He reached compulsory retirement age in 1985.

See also ARAB–ISRAEL WAR (1967); CAMP DAVID ACCORDS (1978); SADAT, ANWAR AL-.

Bibliography

Findley, Paul. *They Dare to Speak Out: People and Institutions Confront Israel's Lobby.* Chicago: Lawrence Hill Books, 1989.

DAVID WALDNER
UPDATED BY GEORGE R. WILKES

GHORFA

See GLOSSARY

GHOUSSOUB, MAI
[1952–]

A London-based multimedia artist, writer, and publisher of Lebanese descent.

Born in Lebanon, Mai Ghoussoub (also Ghussup) is a sculptor, installation and performance artist, writer, editor, and publisher who has lived in Britain since she moved there from Lebanon in 1979. She was educated at the American University of Beirut and at Morley College in London. Ghoussoub is the founder of the Saqi Books, a London publishing house known for its translations of contemporary Arabic writing. Like other artists of Arab descent living in exile, she has explored issues of the body in Orientalist images and paintings as well as in advertisements from the Arab world. She has also written extensively on diasporic identities, masculinity and politics, and feminism as it relates to the Arab world. Ghoussoub is the author of a short-story collection,

Leaving Beirut: Women and the Wars Within (1998). She also co-edits *Abwab,* an Arabic cultural magazine.

In her visual art, Ghoussoub has worked in clay, metals, and resin. Her work from the late 1990s focuses on female divas, whom she finds inspiring because of their ability to connect with everyday people and the unreachability that comes from their iconic status. She has made metal sculptures that deconstruct divas to show this contradictory aspect of their presence in popular culture. For example, her sculptures based on the Egyptian singer Umm Kulthum and the African-American performer Josephine Baker both highlight the outline of their figures and their famous accoutrements (e.g., the handkerchief of Umm Kulthum) as iconic symbols of their work. This focus on musicians reflects her interest in remembering the vitality of her native Lebanon, in contrast to the overwhelming focus in much art and media on its destruction. Like other artists living in exile, her Arab background serves as a source for her art, but she resists strict categorization of her work as Middle Eastern.

See also ART; GENDER: GENDER AND EDUCATION; LEBANESE CIVIL WAR (1958); LEBANESE CIVIL WAR (1975–1990); LEBANON; LITERATURE, ARABIC; UMM KULTHUM.

Bibliography

Ghoussoub, Mai. "Chewing Gum, Insatiable Women, and Foreign Enemies: Male Fears and the Arab Media." In *Imagined Masculinities: Male Identity and Culture in the Modern Middle East,* edited by Mai Ghoussoub and Emma Sinclair-Webb. London: Saqi Books, 2000.

Ghoussoub, Mai. "Our Bodies: Our Orient and Art." In *Displacement and Difference: Contemporary Arab Visual Culture in the Diaspora,* edited by Fran Lloyd. London: Saffron Books, 2001.

Lloyd, Fran, ed. *Contemporary Arab Women's Art: Dialogues of the Present.* London: Women's Art Library, 1999.

JESSICA WINEGAR

GHOZALI, AHMED
[1937–]

Algerian prime minister; ambassador; technocrat.

Ahmed Ghozali studied at the prestigious Ecole des Ponts et Chausées, in Paris. From 1966 to 1977 he was the director-general of SONATRACH, Algeria's national hydrocarbons enterprise, and then minister of energy from 1977 to 1979. Charged with mismanagement, he quietly returned to prominence as ambassador to Belgium and to the European Community (EC) from 1984 to 1988. After the October 1988 riots, he served as finance minister in the Kasdi Merbah government and concluded Algeria's first agreement with the International Monetary Fund (IMF). Prime Minister Mouloud Hamrouche then selected Ghozali as foreign minister in 1989. President Chadli Bendjedid replaced Hamrouche with Ghozali in June 1991 as violent protests wracked the country as it prepared for parliamentary elections. Ghozali rescheduled the elections, which resulted in the stunning first-round success of the Front Islamique du Salut (FIS) in December. With the second round inevitably ensuring a new Islamist FIS government, alarmed civilian and military elites deposed President Bendjedid and set up the Haut Comité d'Etat (HCE). Ghozali kept his position, which strongly suggested his complicity with the coup. The assassination in June 1992 of Mohamed Boudiaf, the HCE president, was a severe blow to the country and to Ghozali personally. Belaid Abdesselam replaced Ghozali as prime minister in July. Ghozali then briefly served as ambassador to France. In 1999 he founded the Front Démocratique Algérien (FDA). He supported Khaled Nezzar and the army's reputation at the libel trial in Paris in 2002. Nevertheless, Ghozali is critical of the Pouvoir—the dominant governing power establishment—for its lack of attention to social affairs. Ghozali may run for the presidency in 2004.

See also ALGERIA: POLITICAL PARTIES IN; SONATRACH.

Bibliography

Ghiles, Francis. "Precocious Talent of Algeria's Premier." *Financial Times.* 7 June 1991.

Naylor, Phillip C. *Historical Dictionary of Algeria,* 3d edition. Lanham, MD: Scarecrow Press, 2005.

PHILLIP C. NAYLOR

GHURI, EMILE AL-
[1907–1984]

Greek Orthodox Palestinian activist.

Emile al-Ghuri was born in Jerusalem and studied at Saint George's School. He went to the United States in 1929 to study at the University of Cincin-

nati, where he received his M.A. in political science in 1933. Upon his return to Jerusalem, he published the *Arab Federation,* an English-language weekly which was later closed down by the British authorities in Palestine because of the political line it had adopted. In 1933, he was elected a member of the Arab Executive. Al-Ghuri published the weekly *al-Shabab* (Youth) in 1934 and was later on the staff of the pro-Hajj Amin al-Husayni, mufti of Jerusalem, English-language weekly *Palestine and Transjordan.* Between 1936 and 1939, he was sent on propaganda and fundraising missions to England, the United States, and the Balkans. He quickly joined the ranks of his country's political elite, becoming in 1935 the secretary-general of the Husayni-led Palestine Arab Party. He later joined al-Husayni in Iraq after the outbreak of World War II. As an active mufti supporter, al-Ghuri was pursued and captured by the British in Iran in September 1941 but was allowed to return to Palestine the next year. Until 1944, the British authorities in Palestine prohibited him from engaging in politics. In 1944, he reorganized the Palestine Arab Party, which was replaced two years later by a reconstituted Arab Higher Committee. He joined this body of Palestinian politicians and represented it at the London Conference on Palestine (1946–1947) and at several United Nations conferences between 1948 and 1950. Throughout his political career, al-Ghuri enjoyed the support of the mufti and some of his closest associates. He served for many years on the Arab Higher Committee and after 1948 represented it in various Arab and international forums. He also occupied a number of senior positions in the Jordanian government between 1966 and 1971 and wrote several books on the Palestinian cause, including *Filastin,* and on Arab nationalism, including *Harakat al-Qawmiyya al-Arabiyya.* He also wrote a memoir, *Filastin Ibr Sittin Aman.*

See also ARAB HIGHER COMMITTEE (PALESTINE).

MUHAMMAD MUSLIH
UPDATED BY PHILIP MATTAR

GIA (ARMED ISLAMIC GROUPS)

Algerian terrorist group.

Among the many terrorist groups in the Algerian civil war, the Armed Islamic Groups (Groupes islamiques armés, or GIA) were the most radical and

The Groupes Islamiques Armés, or GIA, is an Algerian terrorist organization formed in 1991 in response to the government's repression of a strike protesting electoral laws that favored the National Liberation Front. Although in the early 1990s the GIA contained as many as seventy groups, by 1997 its numbers had fallen considerably. © AFP/Corbis. Reproduced by permission.

destructive. According to a report of French secret services in 1993, the GIA was comprised of seventy groups leading noncoordinated actions in northern Algeria. The appearance of these autonomous groups goes back to the Algerian government's repression of the unlimited general strike announced by the FIS (Islamic Salvation Front) in May–June 1991 to protest against the enactment of an uninominal electoral law with two rounds and an electoral redistricting putatively designed to favor the FLN (National Liberation Front). The most active and publicized group of the GIA was led by Mohamed Allel; it became famous in the working-class districts of Algiers for attacking police and regime representatives.

After the cancellation of the 1991 elections and the arrest of at least 4,000 Islamist activists, the radicalization of the movement became irreversible.

An important leader was Mansouri Miliani, former brother-in-arms of Mustapha Bouyali, the founder of the Armed Islamic Movement (Mouvement islamique armé, or MIA) in 1982 who was killed in 1987. According to the testimony of a former Algerian fighter in Afghanistan, Slimane Rahmani, the armed movement was launched in military training camps in Pishawar, Pakistan, by two Algerian mercenaries in the Afghanistan war against the Soviets, Nourredine Seddiki and Sid Ahmed Lahrani. Miliani, the head of this group of about 100 fighters, was assisted by Abdelhak Layada, Moh Leveilly, and Omar Chikhi.

Upon the arrest of Miliani in July 1992, Moh Leveilly became for a short time amir (leader) of the GIA, which by that time was composed of several cells of ten to twenty terrorists each. He was neutralized quickly by the Algerian army during a secret meeting with Abdelkader Chabouti, chief of the Islamic State Movement (MEI), who wanted to federate all armed groups under the banner of a united Islamic army. Leveilly's first lieutenant, Abdelhak Layada, proclaimed himself national chief of the GIA in September 1992. He gave the movement greater structure and led it to spread its fighting beyond the Algiers region. According to the investigation led by the journalist Hassane Zerrouky, Layada divided the Algerian territory into nine military areas under the authority of a national amir who presided over a consultative assembly of lieutenants and regional chiefs. At the head of every area, he named a regional amir who commanded several operational units (katibate) and was assisted by an officer legislator (thabit char'i). To assist himself, Layada named two lieutenants, Mourad Sid Ahmed and Cherif Gousmi, and two spiritual guides (mounther) empowered to enact fatwas to legitimize their actions, Omar Eulmi and Ikhlef Cherati. According to the Algerian authorities, the Islamic Armed Groups remained in contact with one another by means of "links agents" living abroad, particularly in London, and by communicating via satellite telephones.

With this new organization in place, the GIA began broadcasting every Wednesday via clandestine radio (Wafa) information on their groups' activities. In addition to attacking regime representatives and the security forces, it formulated new aims: the elimination of the French-speaking elite by the murder of intellectuals and journalists; the destabilization of the economic potential of Algeria by attacks against infrastructure; and the diplomatic isolation of the country by the murder of foreign workers and attacks against foreign interests. In response, the Algerian army intensively targeted Islamist bases, killing many activists including Mourad Sid Ahmed, and struck hard blows against urban guerrilla warfare. Thereafter, the GIA chiefs announced the union of Islamic Armed Groups and published a bulletin in which they presented the new program of the unified GIA: institution of a caliphate in Algeria and the creation of a government which would include some influential members of the FIS. At the same time, the group intensified its campaign against civilians and foreigners, killing several Algerian intellectuals and attacking the residential neighborhoods of Aïn Allah, where five employees of the French consulate at Algiers were killed. In retaliation, the French government ar-

rested and expelled twenty Islamist activists who had been living in France since 1992.

Jamel Zitouni, amir from October 1994 to July 1996, spread the Algerian civil war to France, where several bombings were perpetrated in August 1995 by his sleeping terrorists cells in Europe. He also organized an attempt on the life of Shaykh Sahraoui, a historic member of the FIS, the hijacking of an Air France plane on 24 December 1994, and, three days later, the murder of four Catholic clerics at Tizi Ouzou. From January 1995 the GIA multiplied their attacks against security forces and set up road blocks to kill car and bus passengers, and the number of their victims reached 200 per week. In March 1996 they killed seven monks at Tibéhirine. Djamel Zitouni, among the most bloodthirsty of the GIA chiefs, took credit for this action, but according to some sources he may have been a double agent controlled and manipulated by the Algerian security forces. He reigned as a king in the Islamist bases of Algiers, Sidi-Bel-Abbes, Bejaïa, and Djijel, and he commanded 4,000 men (600, according to the Algerian authorities). His brutal methods earned him the nickname "Green Pol Pot." When he died in July 1996, Antar Zouabri became head of the GIA. Zouabri, who was as violent as his predecessor, organized collective massacres in Mitidja villages that caused more than 1,500 civilian deaths. These crimes were denounced by most Islamist groups throughout the world and and damaged the cohesion of the GIA, which fell apart into small autonomous groups. Most of these groups rallied around the cease-fire initiated by the Islamic Salvation Army (AIS) in October 1997. After Zoubri's death in September 1997, Ouakali Rachid proclaimed himself amir of what remained of the GIA, but it progressively weakened. During their decline from 1998 onward, the Islamic Armed Groups, weakened greatly by the vigorous campaign of the Algerian army and deprived of their support network in Europe and in the Arab world, took refuge in mountain area, from which they launched raids and depredations against travelers and isolated villages.

See also FRONT ISLAMIQUE DU SALUT (FIS); ISLAMIC SALVATION ARMY (AIS).

Bibliography

Ciment, James. *Algeria: The Fundamentalist Challenge.* New York: Facts on File, 1997.

Cooley, John K. *Unholy Wars: Afghanistan, America, and International Terrorism.* Sterling, VA: Pluto Press, 1999.

Malley, Robert. *The Call from Algeria: Third Worldism, Revolution, and the Turn to Islam.* Berkeley: University of California Press, 1996.

Martinez, Luis. *The Algerian Civil War, 1990–1998.* New York: Columbia University Press, 2000.

Rich, Paul B. "Insurgency, Revolution and the Crises of the Algerian State." In *The Counter-Insurgent State: Guerrilla Warfare and State Building in the Twentieth Century,* edited by Paul B. Rich and Richard Stubbs. New York: St. Martin's Press, 1997.

Willis, Michael. *The Islamist Challenge in Algeria: A Political History.* New York: New York University Press, 1996.

ALGERIA: G. MANSOUR

GIADO CONCENTRATION CAMP

An internment camp for Libyan Jews.

During World War II, Giado was built by the Italian fascist authorities on the Tripolitanian plateau, about 150 miles (240 km) south of Tripoli. It was established after the second British occupation of Cyrenaica, which ended 27 January 1942. The Italians, who had colonized Libya, decided on a "cleaning out" (*sfollamento*) of all Jews from the province. Over 3,000 Jews were taken to internment and labor camps in Tripolitania between May and October. About 75 percent of these were sent to Giado. The camp was administered by Italian officers. The guards included both Italians and Arabs. Rations and sanitary conditions in Giado were very poor, and a typhus epidemic broke out in December 1942.

By the time the British liberated the camp during the North Africa campaign, in late January 1943, 526 of the inmates had died. Others had been shot trying to escape as the Axis forces retreated westward.

Bibliography

Stillman, Norman A. *The Jews of Arab Lands in Modern Times.* Philadelphia: Jewish Publication Society, 1991.

NORMAN STILLMAN

GIBRAN, KHALIL

[1883–1931]

Lebanese author of prose and poetry.

Gibran (Jubran Khalil Jubran) was born at Bshirri in northern Lebanon and in the late 1880s moved to the United States with his sisters. He is known in the West for his book *The Prophet,* and in the Arab world for his contributions to the reformation of the modern usage of the Arabic language. He wrote in prose and poetry, and excelled in both. He ignored the rigid, traditional forms and called for free artistic expressions. Gibran was nonconformist: He opposed the dominance of the clerical establishment and called for the modernization of the Middle East without copying Western models.

Gibran's works in Arabic and in English celebrate individual freedoms and warn against sectarianism and class oppression. His attacks on the religious establishment made him enemies among leaders of the Lebanese church. After his death, however, Lebanese revered his memory and treated him as a cultural icon. Gibran never viewed himself as a Lebanese nationalist, however, but wrote as a Syrian Arab. His experience in the United States led him and other Arab writers and poets to form a literary society, Al-Rabita al-Qalamiyya (Pen's League), which played an important role in the cultural revival in the Middle East in the first two decades of the twentieth century.

See also FILM; LITERATURE: ARABIC.

AS'AD ABUKHALIL

GILBOA, AMIR

[1917–1984]

Israeli poet.

Amir Gilboa was born in the Ukraine and arrived in Palestine in 1937 as an illegal immigrant. Until 1942, when he joined the Jewish brigade of the British army, he worked in agricultural settlements, stone quarries, and orange groves. As a member of the Eighth Army, he participated in its activities in Egypt, North Africa, Malta, and Italy. At the end of World War II he was active in the transfer of Jewish Holocaust survivors from Europe to Palestine. Gilboa fought in the Israeli War of Independence of 1948 and his experiences play a major role in his poetry. He served as the editor of Massada Publishing in Tel Aviv, published nine volumes of his own poetry and received numerous literary awards, including the Israel Prize for Poetry and the New York

University Newman Prize. A collection of his poetry in English translation, *The Light of Lost Suns,* was published in 1979.

Gilboa's early poetry is marked for its figurative expressionism, its prophetic voice, and intense tonality. Repetition, imagination, and colorful carnivalism are characteristic devices. His later poetry combines lyrical expression with nationalistic statements through references to biblical personae and events. The narrative voice often speaks from the excited and naive viewpoint of a child, creating poetic irony and ambiguity.

See also ARAB–ISRAEL WAR (1948); HOLOCAUST; LITERATURE: HEBREW.

ZVIA GINOR

GIRGIR

See NEWSPAPERS AND PRINT MEDIA: TURKEY

GIZA

A middle Egyptian province (governorate).

West of Cairo, Giza (also Jiza) has an area of 32,878 square miles (85,153 sq km) and a 1986 population estimated at 3.7 million. Famous for its three large pyramids and Sphinx, Giza lagged behind other parts of Egypt in converting to Christianity and then in embracing Islam. Its capital and main city, also called Giza, had some 1.9 million inhabitants, according to the 1986 census estimate. Several of the other towns and villages of Giza province—Duqqi and Imbaba—are suburbs of Cairo, and it has grown rapidly since World War II.

See also PYRAMIDS; SPHINX.

ARTHUR GOLDSCHMIDT

GLAWI FAMILY, AL-

Powerful Moroccan family of the late nineteenth century.

Originating from the Glawa tribe in the High Atlas mountains in Morocco, the al-Glawi family played an important role in the nineteenth century in linking the tribes of the High Atlas to the Makhzen. Two members of the family contributed to Morocco's recent history.

Madani Glawi (1863?–1918) inherited the chiefdom of Tlwat from his father Mohamed Ibabat, who was an *amghar* (tribal leader). He built a close relationship with the sultan Mulay Hassan, whom he received in Tlwat in 1893 in the High Atlas. After the sultan gave him the title of caliph (Islamic leader) of Tafilalt, he became a *qaʾid* (chief) of the Atlas. His power grew and his authority became widespread when he supported Mulay Hafid against his brother Mulay Abd al-Aziz and became the prime minister of the Cherifian government. Glawi ultimately built a powerful chiefdom in the High Atlas after 1913, when the sultan Mulay Youssef came to the throne under the French protectorate of Morocco.

Thami Glawi (?–1957), Madani's youngest brother, became pasha of Marrakech in 1909. With French intervention in Morocco, his authority grew even more. After the death of his brother, he inherited his power over the surrounding tribes of Marrakech. He stayed faithful to the French. When Sultan Sidi Muhammad Ben Yussef (later King Muhammad V) returned from exile in 1956, he gave him the *aman* (forgiveness). He died 23 January 1957.

See also MUHAMMAD V; YOUSSEF, MULAY.

RAHMA BOURQIA

GLUBB, JOHN BAGOT
[1897–1986]

British officer who served the Arabs in Iraq and Transjordan during the British mandate, and later in Jordan.

Known as Glubb Pasha, chief of staff of the Arab Legion (1939–1956), John Bagot Glubb belonged to a West Country British family with a long tradition of service to the crown. He followed his father, Major General Sir Frederick Glubb, into the military. Educated at Cheltenham and the Royal Military Academy, Woolwich, Glubb served in France during World War I. He was sent to Iraq in 1920 and served there during Faisal's monarchy for ten years, first in the army and, after resigning his commission in 1926, as a member of the administration of the British mandated territory.

As administrative inspector in Iraq's southern desert, Glubb's main task was to organize the defenses of the bedouin tribes against raids by the Wahabi troops of King Ibn Saʿud of Saudi Arabia. During this assignment, Glubb acquired his excel-

Sir John Bagot Glubb (1897–1986), or Glubb Pasha, rides through the deserts of Jordan with his young son Godfrey Faris on 20 October 1951. © HULTON/ARCHIVE BY GETTY IMAGES. REPRODUCED BY PERMISSION.

lent command of Arabic, an intimate knowledge of the bedouin tribes, and a profound understanding of Arab history, culture, and traditions.

In 1930, as Captain Glubb, he was sent to Transjordan to pacify the bedouin tribes, who were also being attacked by the Wahhabi raiders from Saudi Arabia and here, too, he achieved remarkable success. When Glubb joined the Arab Legion—Transjordan's army—it was a tiny force with almost no bedouin in its ranks and was under the command of another Englishman, Frederick Peake, called Peake Pasha by the legion. As Peake's second-in-command and from 1939 as commander, Glubb developed the Arab Legion from little more than a gendarmerie into the best-trained, most disciplined, and most efficient of all the Arab armies. His most distinctive contribution, however, was the recruitment of bedouins and their transformation from unruly nomads into disciplined soldiers and loyal citizens. Although recruits from the settled areas of Transjordan continued to predominate, the bedouin became the hard core of the Arab Legion and infused it with the fighting spirit for which it became renowned.

A good soldier and organizer, Glubb was also a very subtle politician. As chief of staff of the Arab Legion he needed to be a good politician, because

the legion was the mainstay of the Hashimite regime in Amman. Unlike the officers who were posted to the Arab Legion by the British army, Glubb served under contract to the Transjordan government and therefore owed his allegiance to Amir Abdullah. The British government, however, continued to finance the Arab Legion even after Transjordan became independent in 1946; so Glubb had to serve two very different masters; because of his skill as a politician, he managed to sustain this dual loyalty.

In 1948, Glubb commanded the Arab Legion against the new State of Israel, alongside the other regular and irregular Arab armies. Although the Arab Legion was the only Arab army to distinguish itself on the battlefield, Glubb was blamed for the fall of the cities of Lydda and Ramla and for the failure to capture West Jerusalem. Arab nationalists accused him of deliberately curtailing the operations of the Arab Legion in line with a British plan to partition Palestine between Transjordan and the Jews.

Sir John Bagot Glubb, British soldier and commander in chief of the Arab Legion (1939–1956) sits in a chair, feeling his *mesbah*, or Muslim prayer beads. © HULTON/ARCHIVE BY GETTY IMAGES. REPRODUCED BY PERMISSION.

After the Arab–Israel War of 1948 and the incorporation of the West Bank into the Hashimite Kingdom of Jordan, Glubb prepared the plans for the defense of the enlarged kingdom. He also played a key role in curbing Palestinian infiltration into Israel, because it generated perpetual tension along the border and provoked military reprisals from Israel. Glubb's aim was to keep the border quiet and avoid clashes with Israel's powerful army.

Arab nationalists, inside and outside Jordan, continued to view Glubb as both the symbol and instrument of British imperial domination over the Middle East. Therefore, having a British chief of staff became an increasing liability for the Hashimite rulers of Jordan as the tides of nationalism swept through the Middle East. In March 1956, Jordan's King Hussein abruptly dismissed Glubb and replaced him with a Jordanian chief of staff. Glubb's dismissal temporarily strained the relations between Britain and Jordan, but it also constituted a turning point on Jordan's path to real independence.

Upon his dismissal, Glubb returned to Britain and became a political writer. Of his many books, the most important is his 1957 autobiography, *A Soldier with the Arabs*. A British officer who had served under Glubb in the Arab Legion, James Lunt, wrote a biography of Glubb.

See also ABD AL-AZIZ IBN SAʿUD AL SAʿUD; ABDULLAH I IBN HUSSEIN; ARAB–ISRAEL WAR (1948); FAISAL I IBN HUSSEIN; HUSSEIN IBN TALAL; PEAKE, FREDERICK GERARD.

Bibliography

Glubb, John Bagot. *Arabian Adventures: Ten Years of Joyful Service.* London: Cassell, 1978.

Glubb, John Bagot. *Britain and the Arabs: A Study of Fifty Years, 1908–1958.* London: Hodder and Staughton, 1959.

Glubb, John Bagot. *The Changing Scenes of Life: An Autobiography.* London: Quartet, 1983.

Glubb, John Bagot. *The Course of Empire: The Arabs and Their Successors.* Englewood Cliffs, NJ: Prentice-Hall, 1965.

Glubb, John Bagot. *The Empire of the Arabs.* Englewood Cliffs, NJ: Prentice-Hall, 1963.

Glubb, John Bagot. *The Great Arab Conquests.* Englewood Cliffs, NJ: Prentice-Hall, 1963.

Glubb, John Bagot. *Haroon al-Rasheed and the Great Abbasids.* London: Hodder and Staughton, 1976.

Glubb, John Bagot. *Into Battle: A Soldier's Diary of the Great War.* London: Cassell, 1978.

Glubb, John Bagot. *The Life and Times of Muhammad.* London: Hodder and Staughton, 1970.

Glubb, John Bagot. *The Lost Centuries: From the Muslim Empires to the Renaissance of Europe, 1145–1453.* London: Hodder and Staughton, 1967.

Glubb, John Bagot. *The Middle East Crisis: A Personal Interpretation.* London: Hodder and Staughton, 1969.

Glubb, John Bagot. *Peace in the Holy Land: An Historical Analysis of the Palestine Problem.* London: Hodder and Staughton, 1971.

Glubb, John Bagot. *A Purpose for Living.* London: S.C.P.K., 1979.

Glubb, John Bagot. *A Short History of the Arab Peoples.* London: Hodder and Staughton, 1969.

Glubb, John Bagot. *A Soldier with the Arabs.* New York: Hodder and Staughton, 1957.

Glubb, John Bagot. *Soldiers of Fortune: The Story of the Mamlukes.* London: Hodder and Staughton, 1973.

Glubb, John Bagot. *The Story of the Arab Legion.* London: Hodder and Staughton, 1948.

Glubb, John Bagot. *Syria, Lebanon, Jordan.* New York: Walker, 1967.

Glubb, John Bagot. *War in the Desert: An RAF Frontier Campaign.* London: Hodder and Staughton, 1960.

Glubb, John Bagot. *The Way of Love: Lessons from a Long Life.* London: Hodder and Staughton, 1974.

Lunt, James. *Glubb Pasha: A Biography.* London: Harvill, 1984.

Massad, Joseph Andoni. *Colonial Effects: The Making of National Identity in Jordan.* New York: Columbia University Press, 2001.

AVI SHLAIM

GÖKALP, ZIYA
[1876–1924]

Turkish social and political thinker.

Ziya Gökalp was born in the province of Diyarbekir. At the time of his birth, Diyarbekir contained ethnic groups of Kurdish origin, leading some of Gökalp's political opponents to assert that he was of Kurdish lineage. His father, Tevfik, was director of the provincial archives and editor of the official gazette. Gökalp's education incorporated both Western and Islamic values. Along with religious instruction by family elders, he received a secular education in a military junior high school and a state senior high school in Diyarbekir. He then entered the veterinary college in Constantinople (now Istanbul), but was expelled in his second year for his membership in the secret Society for Union and Progress. After a brief imprisonment he was exiled to Diyarbekir, where he continued his avid reading in the natural sciences, philosophy, sociology, politics, and pedagogy, and resumed his study of Islamic philosophy, especially Sufism.

Gökalp became secretary of the Chamber of Commerce (1902) and the assistant secretary general of the Provincial Council (1904) of Diyarbekir. In 1908 the Committee for Union and Progress (CUP) appointed Gökalp inspector of its organizations in Diyarbekir, Van, and Bitlis while he continued to serve as inspector of elementary education for the provincial government. In 1910, he became a member of the Central Committee (CC) of the Union and Progress Party and went to Salonika, where he taught sociology at the party school, directed the party's youth department, and continued writing and lecturing. In 1912, after the removal of the CC headquarters to Constantinople, Gökalp was named the first professor of sociology at Darülfünün (now Istanbul University). He was exiled to Malta following dissolution of the last Ottoman parliament in 1919. There he conducted a "one-man university" for the distinguished exiles, many of whom joined the Kemalist nationalist resistance in Anatolia. Upon his release from Malta in 1921, Gökalp returned to Diyarbekir, taught at the secondary school and the teachers' seminary, and continued to publish. He was elected to the Second Grand National Assembly (1923–1927) as a deputy from Diyarbekir, served on the parliamentary committee on national education, and participated in the preparation of the 1924 constitution.

Gökalp did not participate in practical politics in the narrow sense. He was a thinker and writer with a profound sense of responsibility for the public good. He was foremost a social and political theoretician, a public educator, and a formulator of Unionist and Kemalist modernizing reforms. Gökalp was the intellectual leader of modern Turkish nationalism in the transition from the multiethnic Ottoman Empire to the nation-state of the Turkish republic, despite the distance between his thinking and that of the Ottomanist Unionists and the Republican Kemalists. He was the acknowledged mentor of these two movements, although both developed into authoritarian, one-party regimes.

Gökalp's "social idealism" was an attempt at a reconciliation of cultural Turkism, ethical Islam, and European corporatism. His nationalism was based on language, subjective self-identification, socialization, and acculturation in a distinct Turkish culture that was to interact peacefully with other Western cultures. Gökalp called for modernizing reforms in Islamic thought and institutions, the essence of which was a reduction of Islam—for centuries the state religion of the Ottoman Turkish society—into a body of moral norms and codes of social behavior based on the nonorthodox Sufi (mystic) form of Islam. As a follower of Auguste Comte and Emile Durkheim, Gökalp took a lay attitude toward Islam, both in the narrow sense of separation of state and religion and in the wider sense of primacy of rational, scientific thought over nonsecular thought.

Perhaps the more important influence of European corporatist thought on Gökalp's own thinking was the rejection of the individualism of liberal capitalism (without rejecting capitalism in general) and of the Marxist categories of class struggle and classless society. Gökalp followed Durkheim in believing that society is composed not of egoistic individuals or warring classes, but of interdependent occupational groups working harmoniously for the public good. This approach enabled him to take both a sociological view of society and an ideological stand against liberal and socialist politics. His form of "populism" viewed society as an organic whole and called for political representation of interests through occupational corporations, in which capital and labor were integrated and the social being of the individual was realized.

The racist-fascist Kemalist movement of the 1940s, the fascist Nationalist Action Party (1960s–1980), and the Nationalist Work Party tried to interpret Gökalp's thought in a fascist manner. Meanwhile, mainstream Kemalism remained within the confines of Gökalp's corporatism, and his thought continues to dominate Turkish social and political thinking via Kemalism, which remains the official ideology and hegemonic public philosophy of contemporary Turkey.

See also COMMITTEE FOR UNION AND PROGRESS; KEMALISM; SUFISM AND THE SUFI ORDERS.

Bibliography

Gökalp, Ziya. *The Principles of Turkism,* translated by Robert Devereux. Leiden, Netherlands: E.J. Brill, 1968.

Gökalp, Ziya. *Turkish Nationalism and Western Civilization: Selected Essays of Ziya Gökalp,* translated by Niyazi Berkes. Westport, CT: Greenwood Press, 1981.

Heyd, Uriel. *Foundations of Turkish Nationalism: The Life and Teachings of Ziya Gökalp.* Westport, CT: Hyperion, 1979.

Parla, Taha. *The Social and Political Thought of Ziya Gökalp.* Leiden, Netherlands: E.J. Brill, 1985.

TAHA PARLA

GOLAN HEIGHTS

A mountainous plateau important militarily as well as for its water resources.

Situated between south Lebanon, south Syria, and northern Israel, the Golan Heights (in Arabic, *al Jawlan*) have an average altitude of 3,300 feet (1,000 m) and they cover an area of approximately 700 square miles (1,800 sq km). Their north–south length is 40 miles (65 km) and their east–west dimension varies between 7 to 15 miles (12 to 25 km). Elevations range from 6,500 feet (2,000 m) in the north, to below sea level along the Sea of Galilee (Lake Tiberias) and the Yarmuk River in the south.

The word *Golan* seems to be related to the Arabic verb *jala* (to circulate or wander about) and to the word *ajwal,* meaning an area that is exposed to dusty winds. After the death of Herod the Great in 4 B.C.E., the Golan must have been given to his son Herod Antipas (died after 39 C.E.), governor of Galilee and Peraea (land east of the Jordan River). The Golan flourished during this period. A large number of towns emerged, including Seleucia, Sogane, and Gamla.

After the defeat of the Byzantine Empire, at the Yarmuk River, all of Syria, including the Golan, ultimately fell into the hands of Muslim Arabs (633–640). After the Umayyads (661–750), the area fell to the Seljuk Turks, Saladin, the Mongols, the Mamluks, and the Crusaders. It was part of the Ottoman Empire from 1516 until the end of World War I, and, in 1920, France received a League of Nations mandate over modern Syria including the Golan.

Between 1948 and 1967, the struggle between Israel and Syria over their demilitarized border zone

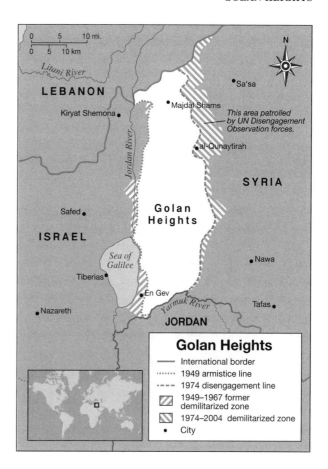

MAP BY XNR PRODUCTIONS, INC. THE GALE GROUP.

was a principal reason behind the Arab–Israel (Six-Day) War of 1967, which ended in Israel capturing the Golan Heights. At the end of the war, the Israeli army was stationed about 22 miles (35 km) from Damascus, while the Syrian army was stationed about 150 miles (250 km) from Tel Aviv. As a result of the Israel–Syria disengagement agreement of the following year, Israel returned to Syria about 40 square miles (100 sq km) of the Golan.

In December 1981, the Likud-led government of Israel's Prime Minister Menachem Begin extended Israeli law, jurisdiction, and administration to the Golan, an action criticized by the Reagan administration and considered "null and void" by resolution 497, unanimously adopted by the United Nations Security Council on 17 December 1981.

Prior to its seizure by Israel, the Golan had a population of approximately 130,000 Syrians living in 139 villages and on 61 farms. By 2003 about 16,000 people remained in five Arab villages. The

The Golan Heights region is a hilly plateau with a predominately rocky terrain located in southwestern Syria. It possesses elevations as high as 6,500 feet and commanding views of Lebanon and Syria to the south and Israel to the west, making it an area of great military importance. © DAVID RUBINGER/CORBIS. REPRODUCED BY PERMISSION.

Druze constitute the overwhelming majority of the remaining Syrian population. According to some observers, one reason that the Druze community was allowed to remain was the initial assumption by the Israeli government that the Syrian Druze would cooperate with Israel, along with their coreligionists in the Galilee. Efforts were made to encourage the Golanis to acquire Israeli-citizenship identification cards. By 2003 there were more than thirty-five Jewish settlements, with an estimated population of 15,000, in the Golan. Many of these settlements are on the southern approaches above the Sea of Galilee.

In terms of military significance, the Mount Hermon massif (7,300 ft; 2,224 m) in the north is of exceptional geostrategic value because it offers a commanding position overlooking southern Lebanon, the Golan plateau, and much of southern Syria and northern Israel. To the east, a range of volcanic hills offers downhill access to Galilee in the west and

to Damascus in the east. To the west, the Golan plateau overlooks Israeli metropolitan centers.

The Golan is also important for its regional water sources. This is particularly true of the area of Mount Hermon, where the headwaters of the Jordan River lie. Additionally, the Baniyas spring, a major Jordan River source, is located on the lower slopes of the Golan, thus enhancing the latter's importance. To the south, the Sea of Galilee and the Yarmuk River constitute two more important regional water sources.

Peace-negotiations, in which the Golan Heights were a crucial component, have been ongoing intermittently between Israel and the regime of the late Syrian president Hafiz al-Asad beginning in 1991 (with representatives of the Likud government in Israel) and later, in 1992, when the late Yitzhak Rabin assumed the Israeli premiership. In 1994 negotiations were held between the Israeli ambassador to the United States, Itamar Rabinovitch, and Walid Mualem, his Syrian counterpart in Washington. In 1994 and in 1995 meetings took place in the United States between General Ehud Barak, the Israeli chief of staff and General Hikmat Shihabi, his Syrian counterpart. The assassination of Prime Minister Rabin created a vacuum, which interrupted any further discussions for some time. Subsequent attempts at renewing the negotiations remained futile.

Bibliography

Cobban, Helena. *The Israeli–Syrian Peace Talks, 1991–1996 and Beyond.* Washington, DC: Institute of Peace Press, 1999.

Rabinovich, Itamar. *The Brink of Peace: Israel and Syria, 1992–1996.* Princeton, NJ: Princeton University Press, 1998.

Schumacher, Gottlieb. *The Golan: Survey, Description and Mapping.* Jerusalem, 1998.

MUHAMMAD MUSLIH
UPDATED BY YEHUDA GRADUS

GOLDBERG, LEAH
[1911–1970]

Hebrew poet, literary critic, translator, educator, and children's author.

Born in Kovno (now Kaunas, Lithuania), Leah Goldberg studied at the universities of Kovno, Berlin, and Bonn. In 1933, she received a doctorate in philosophy and Semitic languages. In 1935, she arrived in Tel Aviv, in British-mandated Palestine, where she published her first volume of poetry, *Tabbe ot Ashan* (1935, Smokerings).

She served on the editorial boards of *Davar* and *ha-Mishmar* and, from 1952, taught literature at the Hebrew University of Jerusalem. In 1963, she became chair of its department of comparative literature, a position she held until her death.

Goldberg wrote numerous volumes of poetry—unpretentious, delicate, and lyric. Except for the Holocaust, her themes are universal rather than Jewish: childhood, love (especially unrequited), aging, and death. She excelled as a translator into Hebrew of classical European authors—Tolstoy, Gorky, Chekhov, Mann, and Ibsen. She was also a successful children's author of twenty books; in later years she took up art and illustrated her own works.

See also HOLOCAUST; LITERATURE: HEBREW; NEWSPAPERS AND PRINT MEDIA: ISRAEL.

Bibliography

Goldberg, Leah. *On the Blossoming*, translated by Miriam Billig Sivan. New York: Garland, 1992.

Negev, Eilat. *Close Encounters with Twenty Israeli Writers.* London and Portland, OR: Vallentine Mitchell, 2003.

ANN KAHN

GOLDEN SQUARE

Name given to the four ex-sharifian, pan-Arab Iraqi army officers whose anti-British, pro-Axis politics led to the Rashid Ali coup of 1941 and the war with Britain that followed.

The original "Four" included the leader, Salah al-Din al-Sabbagh, and Kamil Shabib, Fahmi Sa'id, and Mahmud Salman. They organized after the 1936 Bakr Sidqi coup and then joined with three other officers, Aziz Yamulki, Husayn Fawzi, and Amin al-Umari, to form a military opposition bloc to the government. Jamil al-Midfa'i's government in 1938 tried to transfer the officers out of Baghdad, but succeeded only in making them more politically active.

The officers supported the goals of the Jerusalem *mufti* (chief Muslim jurist), Hajj Amin al-

Husayni, who arrived in Baghdad and solicited Germany's help to achieve total Iraqi independence from Britain and the pan-Arab goal of Arab unity of the Fertile Crescent. They opposed Prime Minister Nuri al-Sa'id's severance of relations with Germany in 1939. In 1940 and 1941, the officers and the mufti were in contact with the Japanese and the Italians through their missions in Baghdad and supported Rashid Ali al-Kaylani's government (31 March 1940 to 31 January 1941) as the British pressured Iraq to declare war on Germany. When Rashid Ali resigned, the pro-British regent, Abd al-Ilah, asked General Taha al-Hashimi, who had worked with the Four, to form a government, thinking that he could control the generals. But Taha's weakness and the attempt by the regent to transfer Kamil Shabib out of the capital led them, in collusion with the mufti, to take control of the government in April 1941, with Rashid Ali again as the prime minister.

At the end of the abortive war against Britain in May 1941, the Four fled but were later caught and executed.

See also ABD AL-ILAH IBN ALI; FERTILE CRESCENT; HASHIMI, TAHA AL-; KAYLANI, RASHID ALI AL-; MIDFA'I, JAMIL AL-; SABBAGH, SALAH AL-DIN AL-.

Bibliography

Tarbush, Mohammad A. *The Role of the Military in Politics: A Case Study of Iraq to 1941.* London and Boston: Kegan Paul, 1982.

REEVA S. SIMON

GOLDMANN, NAHUM

[1895–1982]

Zionist leader.

Born in Lithuania, Nahum Goldmann spent most of his formative years in Germany, where he obtained a Ph.D. from Heidelberg University and was active in the Radical Zionist faction—a student group on campus at the time. During World War I, he worked at the propaganda division of the German Foreign Ministry and in the 1920s was one of the originators of the German-language *Encyclopedia Judaica,* and later of its English-language edition.

In 1934, Goldmann was appointed the Jewish Agency's representative to the League of Nations in

Geneva. He was a cofounder in 1936 of the World Jewish Congress, of which h e was president from 1949 to 1977. From 1956 to 1968, he was also president of the World Zionist Organization.

In 1940, he moved to New York. During 1947 and 1948, Goldmann was active in London and Washington, soliciting international support for the plan to partition Palestine. He was offered a seat in Israel's provisional government in 1948 but declined. During the early 1950s, he played a key role in negotiating the reparations agreement involving West German payments to Israel. In 1962, he became a citizen of Israel, living his remaining years alternately there and in Switzerland.

After the Arab–Israel War of 1967, Goldmann became increasingly critical of the Israeli government and advocated mutual recognition between Israel and the Palestine Liberation Organization, which most Jewish and Israeli leaders reviled at the time as a terrorist organization. In early 1970, he offered to visit Cairo on a mission of peace in response to an invitation from Egypt's President Gamal Abdel Nasser, but the Israeli government vetoed the idea.

Goldmann was instrumental in the planning of Bet ha-Tefutsot (Museum of the Jewish diaspora) in Tel Aviv, which bears his name in its official title.

See also ARAB–ISRAEL WAR (1967); NASSER, GAMAL ABDEL; PALESTINE; PARTITION PLANS (PALESTINE); WORLD ZIONIST ORGANIZATION (WZO); ZIONISM.

Bibliography

Goldmann, Nahum. *The Autobiography of Nahum Goldmann: Sixty Years of Jewish Life.* New York: Holt, Rinehart, and Winston, 1969.

"Nahum Goldmann." Beit ha-Tefutsot. Available from <http://www.bh.org.il/Names/POW/Goldmann.asp>.

Patai Raphael. *Nahum Goldmann, His Missions to the Gentiles.* University: University of Alabama Press, 1987.

GREGORY S. MAHLER
NEIL CAPLAN

GOLESTAN, EBRAHIM
[1922–]

Iranian writer, photographer, translator, publisher, and filmmaker.

Ebrahim Golestan was born in Shiraz. He went to Tehran to attend the University of Tehran, then the only secular college in Iran. He studied law at the university but was attracted to socialist ideas. In 1944 he joined the Tudeh, Iran's most important Marxist political party. In the ideological debates that splintered the party following the Azerbaijan Crisis, Golestan sided with the reformists led by Khalil Maleki and joined him and other dissidents in resigning from the Tudeh in early 1948. That same year his first collection of short stories, *Azar, mah-e akhar-e payiz* (Azar, the last month of autumn), was published. Although he continued to write stories, in the early 1950s his main occupation became filmmaking. During a twenty-year period, Golestan wrote the scripts for, directed, and produced several films. His movie *A Fire* was the first Iranian film to receive an international award, winning a bronze medal at the 1961 Venice Film Festival.

In 1958 Golestan met and hired for his film studio the poet Forugh Farrokhzad. Because he was married and a father, his eight-year relationship with her was controversial. In the mid-1970s Golestan moved to Britain, where he resettled permanently. He continued to write short stories in the 1980s and 1990s. In 2003 his son, photojournalist Kaveh Golestan, was killed by a land mine while covering the U.S. war in Iraq.

See also AZERBAIJAN CRISIS; FARROKHZAD, FORUGH; TUDEH PARTY.

Bibliography

Moayyad, Heshmat, ed. *Stories from Iran: A Chicago Anthology, 1921–1991.* Washington, DC: Mage, 1991.

Sprachman, Paul. "Ebrahim Golestan's *The Treasure*: A Parable of Cliché and Consumption." *Iranian Studies* 15, no. 1–4 (1982): 155–180.

ERIC HOOGLUND

GOLESTAN PALACE

A museum built in Tehran, Iran, in 1894, for the Peacock Throne and other royal jewels.

Built in the last years of Naser al-Din Shah Qajar's reign (1831–1896), the Golestan palace, or Rose Garden palace, was a museum for the royal jewels, including the famous Peacock Throne brought by Nadir Shah Afshar (1688–1747) from his expeditions to India. The construction of the palace took five years, with the personal supervision of the shah. In the upheavals of the tobacco revolt (1891–1892) people resorted to the Golestan Palace demanding justice. Subsequently, fearing for the safety of the jewels, the shah moved them to the royal palace, donating, instead, other precious items to the Golestan. The Golestan Palace also includes other chambers, collectively known as Talar-i Berelian (or Diamond Chamber). The Golestan is still a museum.

See also NASER AL-DIN SHAH; TOBACCO REVOLT.

PARVANEH POURSHARIATI

GOLPAYAGANI, MOHAMMAD REZA
[1899–1993]

Iranian religious scholar; the most senior in Qom.

Mohammad Reza Golpayagani began his religious studies in his birthplace of Golpayagan, in central Iran, where his father, Seyyed Mohammad Baqer, was a highly respected cleric of Islam. In 1917, he moved to Arak to join the circle of Shaykh Abd al-Karim Ha'eri, one of the most prominent legal authorities of his day within Shi'ism. When Ha'eri left for Qom in 1922, to reestablish the religious institution in that city, Golpayagani followed him at his invitation and was entrusted by him with the teaching of elementary courses. After the death of Ha'eri in 1937, he graduated to the teaching of jurisprudence, and his lectures, held in the Masjed-e A'zam, would often attract as many as 800 students. He attained still greater influence after the death in 1962 of Hosayn Borujerdi, Ha'eri's successor, and assumed the major responsibility for administering the complex of colleges and mosques that make up the religious institution in Qom. By then, he had also attained the position of *marja al-taqlid* (source of imitation), an authoritative guide in matters of religious law.

Unbending and rigorous in his understanding of Shi'ite law, he entered the political arena in 1962 with a denunciation of the redistribution of land by the state as contrary to Islam. Despite the conservatism that this implied, he was supportive of the movement inaugurated in 1963 by Ayatollah Ruhollah Khomeini, and in 1978, when the Iranian Revolution erupted, numerous proclamations condemning the regime of Mohammad Reza Shah Pahlavi were

issued over his signature. He consistently refrained from taking a position on the controversies that plagued postrevolutionary Iran, both because of advancing years and because of a fundamentally apolitical disposition. He died on 2 December 1993 and was eulogized by all the leading figures of the Islamic republic.

See also BORUJERDI, HOSAYN; IRANIAN REVOLUTION (1979); KHOMEINI, RUHOLLAH; MARJA AL-TAQLID; PAHLAVI, MOHAMMAD REZA; SHI'ISM.

HAMID ALGAR

GOLSHIRI, HOUSHANG
[1937–2000]

Iranian fiction writer, poet, essayist, and editor.

Houshang Golshiri was born in Isfahan to a working-class family. When he still was a child, the family moved to Abadan, where his father had found work in the oil industry. The family moved back to Isfahan when Golshiri was in high school, and he completed his secondary education in his native city. He attended college and earned B.A. and M.A. degrees while working to help support his family. His first essays, poems, and short stories were published in literary journals in the early 1960s. In 1965, he and two other Isfahan writers founded *Jong-e Isfahan* (Isfahan anthology), a semiannual short-story magazine that brought Golshiri national attention. In 1969, his novella *Shazdeh Ehtejab* (Prince Ehtejab) was published. It was made into a popular Iranian movie and was translated into English and other languages.

Golshiri wrote against political oppression and censorship, and his efforts on behalf of freedom of expression resulted in his arrest by the SAVAK on three occasions during the reign of Mohammad Reza Shah Pahlavi. After the Iranian Revolution, the government forbade the publication of many of his works. In 1989, one collection of short stories was published in Persian in Sweden. His novel about repression under the Islamic Republic, *Shah-e siyah pushan*, was published in 1990 in English translation as *King of the Benighted*. In 1999, Germany awarded him the prestigious Erich Maria Remarque Peace Prize.

See also IRANIAN REVOLUTION (1979); ISFAHAN; LITERATURE: PERSIAN; PAHLAVI, MOHAMMAD REZA.

Bibliography

Golshiri, Houshang. *Black Parrot, Green Crow: A Collection of Short Fiction,* edited by Heshmat Moayyad. Washington, DC: Mage Publishers, 2003.

PARDIS MINUCHEHR
UPDATED BY ERIC HOOGLUND

GOLSORKHI, KHOSROW
[1943–1972]

Leftist Iranian poet and advocate of revolutionary commitment in literature, who was executed after a political show trial.

Born in Rasht, Khosrow Golsorkhi became a journalist by profession. In 1972 he was arrested and accused of plotting against the royal family. In fact, the plot was concocted by SAVAK, which used agents provocateurs to string together a dozen leftist intellectuals, some of whom had discussed plans to kidnap members of the royal family and swap them for political prisoners.

Contrary to the usual procedure for closed political tribunals, highlights of the so-called Golsorkhi group's trial were broadcast on Iran's network television. The defendants were expected to recant publicly and appeal to the shah, who would then commute the court's harsh sentences. Tortured and facing the gallows, most recanted and received lesser punishments. However, Golsorkhi, along with the filmmaker Karamat Daneshian, denounced the regime. They were both executed and immediately became heroes to the opposition as well as to the general public. University and high school students went on strike and the defiant duo's names (especially Golsorkhi's, evoking the leftist symbol of the red flower) were commemorated in numerous literary references and popular songs.

See also LITERATURE, PERSIAN.

Bibliography

Matin-asgari, Afshin. *Iranian Student Opposition to the Shah.* Costa Mesa, CA: Mazda, 2002.

AFSHIN MATIN-ASGARI

GORDON, AARON DAVID
[1856–1922]

Jewish pioneer in Palestine; philosopher of Labor Zionism.

A. D. Gordon was born in Tryano, Russia, and died in Palestine. He was educated in both Jewish studies and Russian secular subjects and spent his early adult life as financial manager of the Guenzburg estate. In 1904, when the estate was sold, he went to Palestine. He had been influenced by the secular Hebrew language and literary movement, particularly by the essays of Ahad Ha-Am. In Palestine he worked as a farm laborer, and then he and his family participated in a model cooperative agricultural community, Degania, forerunner of the kibbutz.

Although Gordon never affiliated with any of the political parties of Labor Zionism, he published essays that influenced their activities and ideologies. Extolling the virtues of working on the land, Gordon reflected on the distortions in Jewish society caused by the Diaspora. Jews had not simply been dispersed to many lands but had been denied the opportunities to work in all occupations, especially those that might sustain communal vitality. Gordon argued that only through the ideal of physical farm labor, cooperation, and mutual aid, in a return to the soil on their own land in their own country, would Jews individually and collectively be revitalized.

He was opposed to socialism in its Marxist form and was uninterested in politics, but he viewed humanity as part of the cosmos, with national communities forming and embodying a living cosmic relationship. He rejected urban culture as alienated from nature and from creativity. Just as the exile could be ended by bringing Jews to Palestine, so could the exile be banished from the Jewish soul through agricultural labor. The establishment of an agricultural base would provide the possibility for the creation of a just, humane Jewish society, especially with respect to the Arabs. He has said: "Their hostility is all the more reason for our humanity."

See also AHAD HA-AM; DIASPORA; LABOR ZIONISM.

Bibliography

Avineri, Shlomo. *The Making of Modern Zionism: Intellectual Origins of the Jewish State.* New York: Basic Books, 1981.

Elon, Amos. *The Israelis: Founders and Sons.* New York: Penguin, 1983.

Hertzberg, Arthur, ed. *The Zionist Idea: A Historical Analysis and Reader.* Philadelphia: Jewish Publication Society, 1997.

Laqueur, Walter. *A History of Zionism.* New York: Holt Rinehart Winston, 1972.

Shimoni, Gideon. *The Zionist Ideology.* Hanover, NH: University Press of New England, 1995.

DONNA ROBINSON DIVINE

GORDON, CHARLES
[1833–1885]

British army engineer, explorer, and empire builder active in the Crimea, China, and Africa.

Born into a military family on 28 January 1833, Charles Gordon was commissioned in the Royal Engineers in 1852 and two years later fought in the Crimean War. In 1863 he became commander of the Ever Victorious Army, a Chinese ragtag mercenary outfit, which defeated the Taiping rebellion against the Manchu emperor. The popularity he subsequently won in the British press earned him the nickname Chinese Gordon.

It is, however, through his service in Africa that Gordon attained both lasting fame and martyrdom. In 1874 the viceroy of Egypt sent him to the Sudan and equatorial Africa to suppress the slave trade and extend, through exploration, the southern boundaries of Egypt's African dominions. In 1877 he continued his antislavery crusade as governor general of the Sudan; frustrated in his efforts, he resigned three years later.

When Muhammad Ahmad, claiming to be the Mahdi (the Muslim messiah), led a revolt in the Sudan that threatened Egypt's and Britain's African interests, Gordon was appointed to lead the evacuation of Khartoum's garrison. Disobeying his instructions, he tried to crush the rebellion but failed in the face of overwhelming odds. Besieged in Khartoum, he chose to make a suicidal stand. The Mahdi's troops stormed the city on 26 January 1885, killing Gordon and most of his soldiers.

See also AHMAD, MUHAMMAD; CRIMEAN WAR.

Bibliography

Nutting, Anthony. *Gordon of Khartoum: Martyr and Misfit.* New York: C.N. Potter, 1966.

JEAN-MARC R. OPPENHEIM

GORST, JOHN ELDON
[1861–1911]

Anglo–Egyptian and Foreign Office official, 1886–1907; British agent and consul-general in Egypt, 1907–1911.

The family of John Eldon Gorst was mainly from Lancashire, England; it had prospered under Queen Victoria's reign. Gorst (known as Jack to his friends) was born in New Zealand but was raised in London. His father and namesake, Sir John, returned to England from New Zealand after the last Maori War, where he embarked on an erratic career in Conservative Party politics. Gorst suffered a painful and unhappy childhood, because an abscess in his pelvis kept him bedridden or wearing a brace for almost seven years. Educated in day schools, at home by tutors, then at Eton and at Trinity College, Cambridge, he earned a degree in mathematics in 1882 and was called to the bar in 1885. Rather than face exclusion, like his father, from the largely aristocratic Tory Party inner circle, Gorst entered the diplomatic service in 1885; he was sent to Egypt.

Egypt was still formally under the sovereignty of the Ottoman Empire, but Muhammad Ali Pasha had managed to make it a virtually independent state from 1805 until 1842, when the Ottoman sultan recognized his right to pass the control of Egypt on to his descendants. Because of the building of the Suez Canal and European greed, Egypt became burdened with financial debts. Both France and Britain intervened and, in 1882, British troops occupied Egypt. By 1886, when Gorst arrived, Sir Evelyn Baring, later the Earl of Cromer, was consolidating his power as Egypt's de facto ruler. Gorst learned Arabic well enough to bypass an interpreter and cultivate friendships among the Egyptian Ottoman elite, including Khedive Abbas Hilmi II. Between 1890 and 1904, Gorst distinguished himself at Egypt's ministries of finance and interior. He helped organize and recruit Englishmen to extend British control in Egypt and the Sudan. In 1898 he succeeded Sir Elwin Palmer as financial adviser in Egypt—the most influential post after Cromer's. In 1904, Gorst, now Cromer's heir-apparent, returned to the Foreign Office, especially to act as Cromer's agent there.

In 1907, the Liberal cabinet sent Gorst back to Egypt to reduce Cromer's autocracy and to give selected Egyptians limited responsibility for their internal affairs. This "new policy" of "conciliation" and "moderation" would, the cabinet hoped, diminish Egyptian nationalism and appease hostile critics in Britain and Egypt. By working with the Egyptian ministers and the khedive, Gorst quickly and successfully undermined the nationalists. Unlike Cromer, he did not usually bully the Egyptian Ottoman elite.

Gorst, however, made three major mistakes. First, he alienated the Anglo–Egyptian officials and influential circles in Britain by reducing their influence on the veiled protectorate over Egypt. Second, in 1908, he appointed Boutros Ghali, a Coptic Christian, as prime minister to replace the elderly time server, Mustafa Fahmi. Ghali was able but hated by the nationalists for his record and distrusted by many Muslims for his faith. Third, Gorst sought in 1909 and 1910 to extend the Suez Canal Company's concession, mainly to provide development funds for the Sudan. He lost Ghali and the experiment in limited self-rule to a nationalist assassin, and a defiant Egyptian General Assembly rejected the concession extension.

Gorst's last year as British agent had an element of anticlimax. Despite alarmists who predicted further trouble for the British in Egypt, little or nothing occurred. Although his health deteriorated rapidly, Gorst's control and British influence in Egypt did not. It was enough for the agency to warn, bribe, or deport certain nationalists, suppress so-called seditious periodicals, and indulge in a limited amount of counterpropaganda.

Gorst died of cancer in July 1911, in Castle Combe, England. The khedive, whom he had befriended, rushed to comfort him on his deathbed.

See also ABBAS HILMI II; BARING, EVELYN; GHALI, BOUTROS; MUHAMMAD ALI.

Bibliography

Mellini, Peter. *Sir Eldon Gorst: The Overshadowed Proconsul.* Stanford, CA: Hoover Institution Press, 1977.

Sayyid-Marsot, Afaf Lutfi. *Egypt and Cromer: A Study in Anglo–Egyptian Relations.* New York: Praeger, 1969.

Tignor, Robert L. *Modernization and British Colonial Rule in Egypt, 1881–1914.* Princeton, NJ: Princeton University Press, 1966.

PETER MELLINI

GOVERNMENT

Exercise of authority over and the performance of functions for a political unit; usually classified by the distribution of power within it.

The modern Middle East is a large and diverse region, the differences well illustrated by the structures and dynamics of governments in the area. There are nearly as many types of government as there are states, and many of the systems undergo almost constant change as the need to accommodate domestic and international pressures emerges. Since the terrorist attacks of 11 September 2001 some states are seen by the United States and other nations as failed or rogue states that pose an imminent threat to world security, and international forces have compelled "regime changes" in the region (Afghanistan, Iraq).

Constitutional government is not deeply rooted or widespread in the Middle East. Israel's democracy rests in part on a series of basic laws that provide a framework for governmental action rather than on a formal written constitution, but this does not affect its role as a parliamentary democracy. Syria has a constitution with the trappings of constitutional government, yet hardly qualifies as a democratic regime. Other states have written constitutions, but these rarely provide a clear guide to governmental action. The Republic of Turkey, however, is a significant exception.

The legislative institutions of Middle East states generally are limited in number and power. In much of the Middle East, the legislatures are rarely representative bodies, although when present they often perform useful functions. In some of the Persian Gulf states, such as Saudi Arabia, Oman, and the United Arab Emirates, there exist consultative bodies that generally serve at the pleasure of the ruler but also tend to legitimate the ruler's actions. This function has proven particularly critical in times of crisis and challenge to the regime. In some instances elected (although not in wholly unfettered processes) legislatures are involved in lawmaking and engage in criticism of the regime despite regime-imposing limitations. Such legislatures have existed in Egypt, Iran, Iraq, Jordan, Tunisia, Morocco, Algeria, Syria, and Yemen. Qatar, Bahrain, and Kuwait experiment with such systems, whereby the democratization process in Kuwait after the liberation from Iraqi occupation was slow. The form of legislative dynamic most familiar to Western observers exists in Israel and Turkey (and did exist in Lebanon until the 1975 civil war). In Israel the parliament has antecedents in the British model. The Turkish government has been subjected to periodic military interference, but parliament has been empowered to bolster Turkey's membership plea for the European Union. In both countries legislatures are freely elected, real political opposition exists, and multiparty competition is the norm.

Throughout most countries of the Middle East, political opposition is still controlled, as are elections. Morocco is undergoing a constitutional reform since the coming into power of King Mohammed VI in 1999. The recent dramatic change in the foreign policy of Libya has not yet changed the autocratic regime within. Algeria is still in a process of reconstruction of civil society, and the reform process in Tunisia is still slow as of early 2004. As in Morocco the key to democratization in all these countries is an approach to give human rights (not at least the rights of women) a prominent place on the reform agenda.

The politics of the Middle East are dominated mostly by the individuals of the executive branches of government who control a country's system and its decisions. More often than not, this is a single authoritarian individual, whether his title is king, prince, general, or president. Most Middle Eastern governments can be classified as authoritarian; the autonomy of their political institutions is limited, and there are serious constraints on personal political freedoms. Individuals' political rights and personal freedoms are not accorded considerable attention in most of the region's systems, and are rarely guaranteed. Nevertheless, despite the range and extent of government control over the public sector and formal governmental activity, totalitarian regimes are not a conspicuous regional feature, as there is often a clear separation between the public and private sectors, with the private sector insulated from governmental interference.

Forms of Government

Authoritarian systems include several major forms of government, including monarchy (absolute or constitutional) with a king, prince, or sultan at its head.

The monarchic principle is firmly rooted in Middle Eastern tradition and history. Such leaders—caliphs, sultans, shahs, khedives, shaykhs, and amirs—have held the reins of government in some areas for centuries, often sustaining control through hereditary succession. Monarchies have been seen as legitimate forms of government, even if individual monarchs were given to excesses in the assumption or exercise of power. Monarchies were established by the British, or at least with their acquiescence, in Iraq and in Transjordan during their respective mandates. The coup in Iran after World War I shifted dynasties, but monarchy was retained until the Islamic Revolution in 1979. Egypt retained its monarchy until 1952 and Libya until 1969; Morocco, Jordan, and the Persian Gulf states still maintain the tradition of monarchical rule. Turkey's caliphate-sultanate was terminated after World War I; the imamate of Yemen survived until the 1950s. The formal change from monarchy to republic does not, however, assure an end to personal control of the affairs of state. On the contrary, often the deposed monarch has been succeeded by a popular leader or dictator, such as Mustafa Kemal Atatürk in Turkey, Gamal Abdel Nasser in Egypt, or Saddam Hussein in Iraq.

A republican form of government was formally established during the French mandate over Syria and Lebanon, and these two states emerged from French control after World War II as republics. Nevertheless, they soon moved in very different directions, with Lebanon retaining at least the form of a republic and Syria establishing a single-person system, which has been dominated by the al-Asad family since the early 1970s.

Political pluralism is a rare feature in the Middle East, restricted to Israel and Turkey and, arguably, Lebanon and some minor Gulf states. In Israel, the tradition of proportional representation and coalition government, which originated in the British model for the prestate Zionist structures in Palestine, has helped to generate party pluralism. In Lebanon, the National Pact of 1943 divided elected and appointive government positions proportionately among the various religious denominational groups. Although it has survived since the French mandate and has been modified various times since, its premise of proportional ethnic and religious representation remains a central feature of Lebanese politics, albeit buffeted by civil war. Turkey is a prominent example of a state that has moved from a one-party to a multiparty system since 1945.

Periodically, suggestions have been advanced for political change and reform as well as for further democratization of the states in the region, but these have rarely advanced beyond the stage of pronouncement, thereby allowing the retention of existing structures and types of government. As part of its "War on Terror," the administration of U.S. president George W. Bush has argued for a democratization of the region, whereby the use of foreign force for such regime changes is seen as a legitimate tool. The transitional constitution in Iraq may pave the way for such approaches, as it is a consensus of major ethnic and religious factions under U.S. guidance.

Islamic governments (theocracies) have been the exception, not the rule, in the Arab world—Israel is a Jewish state but not a theocracy, and Turkey abolished the caliphate in the 1920s and proclaimed itself a secular state. An Islamic government was installed in Iran only after the Iranian Revolution and the ouster of the shah in 1979. The role of Islam in government has varied. Most Islamic states are so described because the majority of their populations are Muslims and they utilize elements of Islam to guide their activities. Many of their constitutions include provisions that the state is Islamic, that Islam is the established religion, or that certain officials (generally, the head of state) must be Muslim, but in most states some of the elements of Islam coexist with extensive borrowings from Western and secular conceptions of government and political life. In some states, Islam has been used as a mechanism for achieving and sustaining the legitimacy of the regime; in others it has been a mobilizing force to generate popular opposition to government policies. The Iranian revolution (1979) established a regime in which Ayatollah Ruhollah Khomeini and the clerics who supported him dominated the executive, legislative, and judicial branches of government as well as the military, the media, and the Revolutionary Guards, and traditional Islamic law was enshrined as the law of the land. The structure of government was one peculiar to the Shi'ite system of Iran as molded and guided by Khomeini; it achieved its form only after significant internal discord among varying interpreters of the legacy of Shi'ism. The Iranian model has not been emulated

in other states, and it is under pressure in Iran itself. No Arab country has yet formally established an Islamic government, although Saudi Arabia has many of the trappings, including a shari'a-based legal system and the Custodian of the Two Holy Mosques (king) as head of state (king).

Bibliography

Bill, James A., and Springborg, Robert. *Politics in the Middle East,* 5th edition. Glenview, IL, and London: Longman Publishing Group, 1999.

Black, Antony. *The History of Islamic Political Thought: From the Prophet to the Present.* Edinburgh, U.K.: Edinburgh University Press, 2001.

Hudson, Michael C. *Arab Politics: The Search for Legitimacy.* New Haven, CT, and London: Yale University Press, 1979.

Long, David E., and Reich, Bernard, eds. *The Government and Politics of the Middle East and North Africa,* 4th edition. Boulder, CO, and London: Westview Press, 2002.

BERNARD REICH
UPDATED BY OLIVER BENJAMIN HEMMERLE

GOZANSKI, TAMAR
[1940–]

Knesset member; leading figure in the Israeli Communist Party.

Born in Petah Tikvah, Israel, Tamar Gozanski received her master of science in economics at the State University of Leningrad. She served in the twelfth through fifteenth Knessets (during most of the 1980s and 1990s) as a member of RAKAH (the Israeli Communist Party). While a member of the Knesset, she played key roles on the following committees: Labor and Welfare, Early Childhood, Advancement of the Status of Women, Foreign Workers, Special Committee for School Dropout Rates, and Parliamentary Inquiry Committee on Trafficking in Women.

Gozanski's public activities include membership on the Political Bureau of the Israeli Communist Party and serving as deputy chairperson of the Council of the Democratic Front for Peace and Equality, the membership of which is predominantly Arab. Her publications include *Economic Independence: How?* (1969) and *The Development of Capitalism in Palestine* (1988). She is a frequent contributor to the newspapers *Ha'aretz, Yediot Aharanot,* and *Zu Haderekh.*

Gozanski has been a consistent supporter of Arab civil liberties and has long advocated full Israeli withdrawal from all Palestinian territories. She sponsored numerous bills in the Knesset to assist workers, the poor, and those living below the poverty line—Jews and well as Arabs—in Israeli society. She is fluent in Hebrew, Russian, and English. Gozansky, a veteran member of RAKAH as well as HADASH/DFPE, the Jewish-Arab Democratic Front for Peace and Equality, was the last Communist to hold a Knesset seat.

See also COMMUNISM IN THE MIDDLE EAST; ISRAEL: POLITICAL PARTIES IN; PALESTINIAN CITIZENS OF ISRAEL.

Bibliography

"Tamar Gozansky." Knesset. Available from <http:www.knesset.gov.il/mk/eng/exmk_eng.asp?ID=31>.

LAURIE KING-IRANI

GRADY–MORRISON PLAN (1946)

See MORRISON–GRADY PLAN (1946)

GRAND MOSQUE

The most important mosque in Islam and destination for Muslim pilgrims from around the world.

The Grand Mosque is located in Mecca and known in Arabic as *al-Masjid al-Haram* (the Mosque of the Holy Sanctuary). Around the year 622 (the year 8 hijri in the Muslim calendar) the prophet Muhammad made into a mosque the sacred precinct around the Ka'ba, the well of Zamzam, and the Maqam of Abraham. In keeping with the needs of the growing community of worshipers, the mosque was enlarged and embellished with collonades and minarets. In its large courtyard with the Ka'ba in the center were constructed four shelters *(maqams),* to be used during prayer times by the prayer leader (imam) for each of the main schools in Sunni Islam (Hanbali, Maliki, Shafi'i, and Hanafi). It was probably the first monumental mosque in Islam, constructed before the Al-Aqsa Mosque in Jerusalem.

Major modifications were made from 1572 to 1577, including the construction of a series of small domes to replace the flat roof covering the mosque's interior spaces. The most recent extensions and improvements were begun in 1991. The Grand Mosque is the devotional focal point for Muslims around the world, who face in its direction whenever they pray. Historically a center for intellectual life, the mosque is still used for teaching and research.

See also KA'BA; UTAYBI, JUHAYMAN AL-.

Bibliography

Rutter, Eldon. *The Holy Cities of Arabia.* New York; London: Putnam, 1928.

Wensinck, A. J. "Al-Masjid Al-Haram." *Encyclopedia of Islam, New Edition,* vol. 6, edited by C. E. Bosworth, E. van Donzel, and C. Pellat. Leiden: Brill, 1989.

MALCOLM C. PECK
UPDATED BY ANTHONY B. TOTH

GRAZIANI, RODOLFO
[1882–1955]

Italian military officer.

Rodolfo Graziani first came to prominence as the conqueror of Tripolitania in 1925, during the second Italo–Sanusi War. In 1929, under the direction of the new governor of Tripolitania and Cyrenaica, Marshal Pietro Badoglio, he completed the conquest of the Fezzan. In 1930, General Graziani was made vice-governor of Libya and military governor of Cyrenaica, and during the next year, he completed its pacification using brutal and ruthless tactics. The nomadic population of northern Cyrenaica was herded into detention camps; a wire fence was constructed along the northern Cyrenaican–Egyptian border and the Sanusi *zawiyas* (Islamic religious centers) were destroyed. Graziani's tactics reached their peak with the public execution of the veteran resistance leader, Umar al-Mukhtar, at Soluk on 16 September 1930. Graziani went on to succeed Marshal Balbo as governor of Libya on the latter's death in action in Tobruk in June 1940.

See also BALBO, ITALO; FEZZAN; ITALY IN THE MIDDLE EAST; MUKHTAR, UMAR AL-.

Bibliography

Evans-Pritchard, E. E. *The Sanusi of Cyrenaica.* Oxford: Clarendon Press, 1947.

GEORGE JOFFE

GREATER ISRAEL

See ERETZ YISRAEL

GREATER SYRIA

Pre-1914 name for present-day Syria, Lebanon, Israel, and Jordan.

Until World War I the name Syria generally referred to Greater or geographical Syria, which extends from the Taurus Mountains in the north to the Sinai in the south, and between the Mediterranean in the west and the desert in the east. The name was first given by the Greeks to the city of Tyrus (now Tyre)—Sur in Arabic—and then applied by them to the whole of the province.

The early Arabs referred to Greater Syria as Bilad al-Sham; in Arabic *al-Sham* means left or north. Bilad al-Sham is so called because it lies to the left of the holy Kaʿba in Mecca, and also because those who journey thither from the Hijaz bear to the left or north. Another explanation is that Syria has many beauty spots—fields and gardens—held to resemble the moles (*shamat*) on a beauty's face.

The term *Syria*, referring to greater or geographical Syria, began to be used again in the political and administrative literature of the nineteenth century. The Ottoman Empire then established a province of Syria, and more than one newspaper using the term *Suriyya* in its name was published at the time. In 1920, Greater Syria was partitioned by the Allies of World War I into present-day Syria, Greater Lebanon, Palestine, and Transjordan.

See also SINAI PENINSULA; TAURUS MOUNTAINS; TYRE.

Bibliography

Hourani, Albert. *Arabic Thought in the Liberal Age, 1798–1939.* Cambridge, U.K., and New York: Cambridge University Press, 1983.

Le Strange, Guy. *Palestine under the Moslems: A Description of Syria and the Holy Land from A.D. 650 to 1500 (Translated from the Works of the Mediaeval Arab Geographers).* New York: AMS Press, 1975.

ABDUL-KARIM RAFEQ

GREATER SYRIA PLAN

Plan for unification of the central regions of the Middle East.

Championed by King Abdullah of Transjordan, the Greater Syria plan was the expression of an old dream to unify Syria, Lebanon, Palestine, and Jordan. After Faisal's kingdom in Syria collapsed in 1920, Abdullah tried to unite Transjordan and Syria under his rule, and throughout the 1930s, he kept the dream alive for the Hashimites. Although he received little encouragement from British officials, his ideas revived after World War II and met with the approval of Nuri al-Saʿid of Iraq; certain aspects of the program were incorporated into the Arab League charter in 1945. Most Syrian leaders, however, not to mention those of Lebanon and Palestine, were against a Hashimite-led Greater Syria and distrusted Abdullah accordingly. Although the Syrian Social Nationalist Party of Antun Saʿada supported the scheme, the rest of the Syrian leadership rejected it, including the first president of independent Syria, Shukri al-Quwatli, and his successor, Husni al-Zaʿim. With the assassination of Abdullah in 1951, the Greater Syria plan lay in ruins, though it was kept alive by Nuri al-Saʿid until his untimely death in 1958.

See also ABDULLAH I IBN HUSSEIN; FAISAL I IBN HUSSEIN; FERTILE CRESCENT UNITY PLANS; HASHIMITE HOUSE (HOUSE OF HASHIM); LEAGUE OF ARAB STATES; QUWATLI, SHUKRI AL-; SAʿADA, ANTUN; SYRIAN SOCIAL NATIONALIST PARTY; ZAʿIM, HUSNI AL-.

Bibliography

Lenczowski, George. *The Middle East in World Affairs,* 4th edition. Ithaca, NY: Cornell University Press, 1980.

Seale, Patrick. *The Struggle for Syria: A Study of Post-War Arab Politics, 1945–1958.* London: I.B. Tauris, 1986.

ZACHARY KARABELL

GREAT GAME, THE

Phrase coined at the beginning of the nineteenth century, referring to the imperial competition between Britain and Russia over control of southern central Asia.

Thanks in part to Rudyard Kipling, mention of "The Great Game" conjured up images of dashing heroism in the wilds of the Afghanistan mountains. While this romanticism was certainly a part of the game, it was more often played by politicians in London and St. Petersburg than by adventurers in the steppe.

Bibliography

Fromkin, David. *A Peace to End All Peace.* New York: H.
  Holt, 1989.

ZACHARY KARABELL

GRECO–TURKISH WAR (1897)

*Brief war won by Turkey but also benefiting Greece due
to the intervention of major European powers.*

The Greco–Turkish War of 1897 ended in an easy victory for Turkey. It began in April 1897 with clashes
across the Greco–Turkish border, which at the time
ran between Thessaly and Ottoman-held Macedonia.
The hostilities ended in May 1897 when the Turkish
army drove the Greeks back deep into Greek territory.

The war grew out of tension between Greece and
Turkey that was fueled by a Greek uprising on the
Ottoman-controlled island of Crete. Calling for a
more dynamic stance by Greece toward Turkey, the
Greek nationalist organization Ethniké Hetairia
(National Association) orchestrated an incursion
into Turkish territory by Greek irregular troops
(March 1897), apparently with the knowledge of the
Greek government. Although Turkish forces re-
pulsed the irregulars, the incident led to a break in
diplomatic relations between Greece and Turkey
and a massing of their respective armies on the
mountainous frontier between Greek Thessaly and
Ottoman Epirus and Macedonia.

The Greek army, consisting of two divisions,
was unable to capitalize on its early incursions across
the Macedonia–Thessaly border and suffered defeats in several battles around the mountain passes
between Macedonia and Thessaly south of Mount
Olympus. The Greek front collapsed on 12 April
1897, and the Greek forces began to retreat into the
Thessalian plain. Within two weeks and with little
resistance, the Turkish army controlled all of Thessaly, including its major towns of Larissa and Vo-
los. There was relatively little activity on the western
front in Epirus, where the Turkish army successfully repulsed the Greek offensive.

The war came to an end when the advancing
Turkish army scored another two victories in battles on the mountains that divide the Thessalian
plain from the rest of Greece, thus consolidating its
control over Thessaly. The danger that further Greek

Greek troops in Thessaly. The inadequately prepared Greek
combat forces numbered around 100,000 men, of which
approximately 500 were lost. In comparison, Turkish forces
numbered around 400,000, with 1,500 losses. © CORBIS.
REPRODUCED BY PERMISSION.

territories would fall to the Ottomans prompted
Russia's Czar Nicholas II, with the support of other
European governments, to intervene and persuade
Sultan Abdülhamit to agree to a cease-fire; it was
signed by the combatants on 7 May 1897, although
the end of the war was not formally agreed upon by
the Greek and Turkish governments until November 1897. Because of the involvement of Russia and
the other European powers in the resolution of
the conflict, the Ottoman Empire gained very little
from its victory except monetary compensation and
slight changes to its borderline that it considered
strategically advantageous. In an important gesture
that served to acknowledge Greece's original grievances, the European powers prevailed upon Ab-
dühamit to accept previously Ottoman-ruled Crete
as an autonomous region.

Bibliography

Dakin, Douglas. *The Greek Struggle in Macedonia, 1897–1913.*
  Thessaloniki, Greece: Institute for Balkan Studies,
  1993.

ALEXANDER KITROEFF
UPDATED BY ERIC HOOGLUND

GREEKS IN THE MIDDLE EAST

Greek communities in the Middle East, especially in Egypt, once played a vital economic role.

Once significant, the Greek presence in the Middle East is currently limited to about 6,000 persons in Egypt (primarily in Cairo and Alexandria), and it is much smaller in the Sudan, the Arabian Peninsula, and elsewhere in the region. (No official statistics are available to provide reliable figures.)

The geographical proximity of the Middle East to the Greek islands and mainland, the development of Greek maritime trade in the seventeenth century, and the existence of Greek Orthodox patriarchates in Alexandria, Antioch, and Jerusalem ensured that there would be small numbers of Greek merchants and clerics in the Middle East around 1800. Their numbers began increasing substantially in the nineteenth century, after Muhammad Ali, Egypt's ruler, invited foreign entrepreneurs, including Greeks, to Alexandria to help modernize Egypt. The greatest number of resident Greeks in Egypt's history—99,793 persons, of whom 76,264 were Greek citizens—was recorded in Egypt's annual census of 1927. Constituting the largest of the numerous foreign communities inhabiting Egypt from the mid-nineteenth

Greek Orthodox clergy perform the annual Holy Week reenactment of Christ's "Washing of the Feet" of His apostles. A priest humbly washes the feet of twelve church members. © HANAN ISACHAR/CORBIS. REPRODUCED BY PERMISSION.

through the mid-twentieth century, the Greeks were a socially diverse group that ranged in occupation from wealthy bankers and exporters to employees in the service sector and even factory workers. Smaller Greek communities of a few thousand also could be found in Sudan, Palestine, and in cities along the North African coast. The end of the capitulations in Egypt (1937) signaled the onset of the decline in numbers of Greeks in Egypt, and the Egyptian Revolution of 1952 accelerated this decrease. The Suez Crisis of 1956 reinforced the trend, although a large part of the Greek community supported Egypt in its claim on the canal. The nationalization measures taken by the Egyptian government in 1963 caused the numbers of Greeks remaining in Egypt to fall to a few thousand.

Spread out across the country, the Greeks in Egypt were formerly to be found even in small towns in the Nile delta and in upper Egypt, and they formed the largest foreign communities in Alexandria, Cairo, Port Saʿid, and Suez. In 1927, out of 99,605 foreign citizens residing in Alexandria, over a third (37,106) were Greek citizens, and the same proportion held for the other major cities. As they had been in Greece, the Greeks in Egypt were Greek Orthodox, and they continued to use their native tongue. With a number of important Greek journals and literary societies based there, Alexandria became a very important Greek literary center in the first three decades of the twentieth century. The Alexandrian Greek poet C. P. Cavafy (1863–1933) gained an international reputation and Alexandrian writer Stratis Tsirkas (d. 1979) enjoys a good reputation in Greece. Like most of the foreigners in Egypt, the Greeks were noted for their cosmopolitanism. Many Greeks were fluent in either French or English, and the wealthier strata of Greek society in Egypt had very close ties with Europe. Several Greeks sat on company boards whose members came from mixed European backgrounds. In the 1930s, more and more Greeks began to acquire a knowledge of Arabic.

As did all the foreign residents, the Greeks benefited from the broad-ranging privileges Egypt provided to the citizens of other countries. Capitulation rights were extended to the Greeks the year after Greece signed a capitulations treaty with the Ottoman Empire (1855); previously, some Greeks had been under the protection of European consuls. Greece agreed to participate in the mixed courts system in 1876. The Egyptian uprising and the British occupation of 1882 that followed it did not affect the status of the Greeks, nor did the outbreak signaling the beginning of the Egyptian nationalist movement (1919), with which many Greeks sympathized. The Greek government was unable to offer the Greeks in Egypt any help in the diplomatic negotiations preceding the end of the capitulations (1937) or the abolition of the mixed courts (1949); the Greeks had hoped that in regard to these arrangements their traditionally close relationship with the Egyptians would have earned them more favorable treatment than they received.

The Greeks made their greatest impact in Egypt via their role in the banking and cotton sectors. The first group of Greeks brought to Alexandria by Muhammad Ali in the early 1800s were merchants, shipbuilders, and sailors whose activities helped increase commerce and building of the merchant marine in Egypt. The Greek community in Alexandria was unaffected by Egypt's involvement on the side of the Ottomans during the Greek War of Independence (1821–1830), and the number of Greeks in Egypt gradually increased in the following decades, as did their economic strength. The boom in Egyptian cotton production and export in the 1860s, which catapulted the Egyptian economy to new levels and integrated it into the world economy, also further increased the role and economic power of the Greek merchants and financiers, who remained central to the financing, production, and exporting of cotton in Egypt until the eve of World War II. In the 1920s, Greek exporting houses were responsible for 25 percent of all Egyptian cotton exports. The largest of the Greek exporting companies of that period was Choremi, Benachi & Co.; in the banking sector, Greeks such as the Salvago family were well known and influential.

The Greeks in Egypt remained closely identified with issues of Greek nationalism and with Greek party politics. The early settlers had supported the Greek War of Independence and subsequent efforts to incorporate Greek-populated areas within the Greek state. With time, increasing numbers of Greeks returned to Greece to fight as volunteers in the Greek army, especially during the 1912–1913 Balkan War. The wealthiest financed the building of schools or philanthropical institutions in their hometowns or villages, and others made contributions that went toward developing the Greek state. For example, the donations of George Averoff helped complete the marble stadium in Athens where the first Olympic games were held in 1896 and made it possible to purchase the battleship *Averoff,* which proved a factor in Greece's victories in the Balkan War.

The Greeks in Egypt created a broad network of communal institutions: schools, hospitals, churches, orphanages, nursing homes, and a variety of leisure and athletic societies, most of them run by the city-based Greek community organizations, which were themselves administered by prominent Greeks in the community. A small and weak institution in the 1800s, the Greek Orthodox patriarchate of Alexandria gradually grew in stature and importance as the numbers of Greeks in Egypt increased.

See also BALKAN WARS (1912–1913); CAPITULATIONS; GREEK WAR OF INDEPENDENCE; LEVANTINE; MIXED COURTS; MUHAMMAD ALI; SUEZ CRISIS (1956–1957).

Bibliography

Kitroeff, Alexander. *The Greeks in Egypt, 1919–1937: Ethnicity and Class.* St. Anthony's Middle East Monographs no. 20. London: Ithaca Press, 1989.

Politis, A. *Hellenism and Modern Egypt.* 2 vols. Alexandria, 1931. In Greek.

ALEXANDER KITROEFF

GREEK WAR OF INDEPENDENCE

Aided by the great powers, Greece broke away from the Ottoman Empire to establish a modern state.

The Greek War of Independence began with two uprisings in March 1821. The first was led by Alexander Ipsilanti, a Greek officer in the Russian army, who led an ill-fated attack of Greek rebels into Moldavia from Russian territory. The second uprising took place in southern Greece, in the Peloponnese, and was to lead eventually to the establishment of the modern Greek state. The uprising in the Peloponnese, launched by Greek military chieftains, spread northward to parts of Rumelia and to the maritime islands off the eastern coast of the Peloponnese. In their clashes with the local Ottoman garrisons, the Greek rebels' object was to capture the fortified towns of the region; Greek vessels proved important in assisting the rebels to lay siege to the coastal forts. By the end of 1821, the Greeks controlled enough territory to be able to convene a meeting of representatives that proclaimed Greece's independence.

The rebels could not, however, sustain the successes they had scored in the first year of the revolt and were soon facing serious military, financial, and political difficulties. Ottoman army units stationed farther north marched southward into Rumelia and the Peloponnese and eventually recaptured some of the forts the Greeks had taken. The presence of European philhellenes fighting for the Greek cause did not serve to make less urgent the Greeks' need for more funds and equipment. Although the Greek leaders were able to obtain two loans in London for the purpose of acquiring armaments and equipment, they did so under unfavorable terms. By late 1924, the Greeks had managed to contain the Ottoman counterattack and controlled about half the Peloponnese and parts of Rumelia, but they encountered political dissent within their own ranks. Long-standing regional and personal ties stood in the way of forming an effective, centralized leadership, and the vision of a liberal, democratic constitution was not shared by all the diverse elements who made up the Greek leadership—that is, the military chieftains, the notables, and the Greeks of the diaspora.

The landing of an Egyptian army in the Peloponnese (1925) in response to the sultan's request for help in suppressing the Greek uprising threatened to put an end to the Greek War of Independence. After two more years of hostilities, in which the Greeks had to deal with the Egyptian army's attempt to sweep the Peloponnese and with an Ottoman offensive on the Greek strongholds in Rumelia, the areas under Greek control were considerably contracted, especially after the fall of Athens to the Ottomans in May 1927. At the same time, Britain, France, and Russia had agreed upon a plan to end the war and to grant independence to Greece (i.e., the Peloponnese, Rumelia, and the islands involved in the war, which were to be ruled by a governor appointed by the great powers and acceptable to the Greek leadership). The agreement, formalized by the signing of the Treaty of London (1827), was rejected by the Sublime Porte and by Ibrahim ibn Muhammad Ali Pasha, the leader of the

Egyptian army and navy. As diplomatic initiatives were being examined, a combined British, French, and Russian fleet that had sailed to the Peloponnese to blockade the Egyptian and Turkish navies engaged them in the Battle of Navarino (October 1927) and destroyed them completely. This development cleared the way for the implementation of the Treaty of London, and Count Ioannes Kapodistrias, a Greek in the Russian diplomatic service, became Greece's first governor.

Kapodistrias set about building a modern state and dealing with the devastation the war had inflicted. The formerly privileged class of military chieftains and notables resisted the centralization inherent in state building, however, and this resistance was to culminate in Kapodistrias's assassination by one of the military chieftains (1832). The work of establishing the modern Greek state had nevertheless progressed, both domestically and diplomatically. The Treaty of Adrianople (1829) ending the Russian–Ottoman War (1828–1829) included an article that proclaimed Greece to be an independent state, and the ambassadors of the great powers delineated the Greek state's boundaries in a document communicated to the Porte in the same year (1829). After the Porte had recognized both the Treaty of Adrianople and the Treaty of London as well as the Greek boundaries, the great powers formally proclaimed Greece to be an independent state in 1830.

See also Ibrahim ibn Muhammad Ali; Rumelia; Russian–Ottoman Wars; Sublime Porte.

Bibliography

Petropoulos, John. *Politics and Statecraft in the Kingdom of Greece, 1833–1843*. Princeton, NJ: Princeton University Press, 1968.

Alexander Kitroeff

GREENBERG, URI ZVI
[1894–1981]

Hebrew poet.

Born in Bialykamien in eastern Galicia, Poland, Uri Zvi Greenberg was a descendant of prominent Hasidic families both from his mother's and father's side. While he was still very young, his parents moved to Lvov where he received a traditional Hasidic education.

Greenberg's earliest poems, written in Yiddish and Hebrew, were published in 1912. Drafted into the Austrian army in 1915, he served on the Serbian front, which he deserted in 1917. The Polish pogroms against the Jews in 1918 made a lasting impression on him. Following World War I, he continued to publish in the same two languages as before; upon his emigration to Eretz Yisrael (Palestine), however, in 1924, he wrote exclusively in Hebrew. For a number of years after his arrival, Greenberg was a dedicated Laborite and became a regular contributor to the Labor daily, *Davar*, when it was founded in 1925.

Subsequent to the Arab riots in 1929, he abandoned the Labor Party and joined the ultranationalist Zionist Revisionist Party, which he represented as a delegate to several Zionist Congresses. From 1931 to 1934 Greenberg served as emissary of the Revisionist movement in Warsaw where he edited its Yiddish weekly, *Di Velt*. He returned to Eretz Yisrael in 1936. In his poetry and articles of the period, he harshly criticized moderate Zionists and warned of the impending doom destined for European Jewry.

During Israel's struggle for independence, Greenberg was a sympathizer of the Irgun Zva'i Le'umi, pre-Israel's underground resistance movement. Following the establishment of the State of Israel, he was elected to the Knesset as a representative of the Herut Party. He served from 1949 to 1951.

Unlike secularist writers, Greenberg viewed Zionism from a religio-mystical perspective. He saw Jewish existence as outside the pale of history and the Jews' return to Zion as nothing less than the fulfillment of their destiny. In his pre-Eretz Yisrael poetry, Greenberg manifests an inordinate preoccupation with what he correctly foresaw as the horrors of the Holocaust, which he interpreted as the culmination of the struggle between Christians and Jews. His poetry is strongly ideological and his sources are almost exclusively Jewish and rooted in the Jewish past.

Among Greenberg's works in Yiddish are: *In Malkhus fun Tselem* (In the kingdom of the cross, 1922)

which deals with the Holocaust and *Krig oyf der Erd* (War in the land, 1921). His Hebrew works include *Eimah Gedolah ve-Yare'ah* (1925); *Sefer ha-Kitrug ve-ha-Emunah* (1937); *Min ha-Hakhlil ve-el ha-Kakhol* (1949); *Rehovot ha-Nahar—Sefer ha-Ilyot ve-ha-Ko'ah* (1951); and *Be-Fisat ha-Ariq u-ve-Helkat ha-Hevel* (1965). Greenberg was awarded the Israel Prize for Hebrew Literature in 1957.

See also IRGUN ZVA'I LE'UMI (IZL); KNESSET; LITERATURE: HEBREW.

Bibliography

Negev, Eilat. *Close Encounters with Twenty Israeli Writers.* London and Portland, OR: Vallentine Mitchell, 2003.

ANN KAHN

GREEN BOOK

The governing philosophy of Libya's ruler, Muammar al-Qaddafi.

The Green Book contains the brief, three-part statement of the Third International Theory, the governing philosophy of Muammar al-Qaddafi, ruler of Libya. Designed to be an alternative to both capitalism and communism, the Third International Theory is the theoretical basis for the institutions and policies of the Jamahiriyya. The first part, issued in 1976 and titled, "The Solution of the Problem of Democracy: The Authority of the People," discusses the dilemmas of just and wise government and declares the solution to be the rule of the people through popular congresses and committees. Part 2, "The Solution of the Economic Problem: Socialism," which appeared in 1978, calls for the end of exploitation implied by wages and rent, in favor of economic partnership and self-employment. Part 3, "The Social Basis of the Third International Theory," treats social issues, including the importance of family and tribe and the status of women and minorities.

See also JAMAHIRIYYA; QADDAFI, MUAMMAR AL-.

Bibliography

Deeb, Mary Jane, and Deeb, Marius K. *Libya since the Revolution.* New York: Praeger, 1982.

LISA ANDERSON

GREEN LINE

The 1949 armistice lines between Israel and Egypt, Jordan, Syria, and Lebanon.

The Green Line designates Israel's borders as demarcated during the 1949 armistice negotiations following the establishment of the state of Israel and the first Arab–Israeli war. Among other things, the creation of this boundary brought into being the separate territory known as the West Bank. Following the Arab–Israeli war in June 1967, the Green Line boundary remained *in situ* as an administrative line of separation between the sovereign state of Israel and the Occupied Territories. The line was removed from all official Israeli maps in the post-1967 era and was opened up to movement of Palestinian workers who commuted into Israel for work. Following the onset of the first intifada in 1987, the Green Line was again closed, by road blocks and curfews, reverting to its former role as a boundary between the two peoples and their respective territories. In 2002 the Israeli government began to construct a wall along, or close to, parts of the Green Line, arguing that this was a necessary security measure. All negotiations aimed at bringing about the establishment of a Palestinian state have considered the Green Line to be the default boundary, to which only minor territorial changes could be made.

Bibliography

Alpher, Y., and Brawer, M. "The Making of an Israeli-Palestinian Boundary." In *The Razor's Edge: International Boundaries and Political Geography,* edited by Clive Schofield, et al. New York: Kluwer Law International, 2002.

Newman, D. "Boundaries in Flux: The Green Line Boundary between Israel and the West Bank." *Boundary and Territory Briefing* 1, no. 7 (1995).

Newman, D. "The Functional Presence of an Erased Boundary: The Re-Emergence of the Green Line." In *World Boundaries,* Vol 2: *The Middle East and North Africa,* edited by C. Schofield and R. Schofield. New York: Routledge, 1984.

BRYAN DAVES
UPDATED BY DAVID NEWMAN

Map showing the Green Line, West Bank, Israel, Jordan, and surrounding region, with cities including Nazareth, Jenin, Netanya, Tulkarm, Nablus, Tel Aviv, Ramallah, Jericho, Jerusalem, Bethlehem, Hebron, and Amman. Legend: Green Line — International border, "Green line," City.

MAP BY XNR PRODUCTIONS, INC. THE GALE GROUP.

GREEN MARCH

March of 350,000 volunteers to demonstrate Morocco's claim on Western Sahara.

The background to the Green March was a twofold struggle in the mid-1970s: (1) the sophisticated POLISARIO Front movement for nationalism by the Sahrawi people in the former Spanish colony of Western Sahara, and (2) a series of challenges against King Hassan II of Morocco, which culminated in two attempted coups in 1971 and 1972. Seeking to claim Western Sahara's mineral resources (mainly phosphates) and spurred by the ideology of a "Greater Morocco," Hassan succeeded in signing the Madrid Accords of 14 November 1975, which ceded the territory from Spain to Mauritania and Morocco.

A month earlier, however, a United Nations report had rejected Morocco's claims. In response, Hassan announced that he would seek volunteers to march into Western Sahara, in what his state-run press described as a demonstration of the will of the Moroccan people to reclaim its territory. By early November, some 350,000 volunteers had signed up—mostly poor and unemployed, rural and urban, they were organized by regional quota. An enormous effort was launched to provide food and medical care for them. Amid intense diplomatic efforts over Western Sahara's future, and just after initial clashes between Moroccan and POLISARIO troops, the marchers crossed the border at Tarfaya. Tens of thousands reached Umm Deboa, where they halted.

On 14 November the Madrid Accords were signed. The march was recalled on 18 November; it had been a successful gamble by Hassan to pressure Spain into reaching an accord with him—and to rally support within Morocco for his claim.

See also HASSAN II; POLISARIO.

Bibliography

Hodges, Tony. *Western Sahara: The Roots of a Desert War.* Westport, CT: L. Hill, 1983.

MATTHEW S. GORDON

GRIBOYEDOV INCIDENT

One of the first major anti-Western incidents that was religiously inspired.

The Griboyedov Incident took place when a Russian mission led by the well-known author Aleksandr Sergeyevich Griboyedov was sent to Iran in 1829. The purpose of the mission was to force the Iranian government to pay the indemnity for its defeat in the recent Russian–Iranian war and abide by the humiliating provisions of the Treaty of Turkmanchai. The mission heard that two or more Georgian or Armenian women had been forcibly converted to Islam and brought to the harems of Iranian nobility. In flagrant opposition to Iranian norms, the mission forced its way into the harems and took all the women away, allegedly keeping some overnight. The Iranian *ulama* (religious leaders) reacted by issuing a *fatwa* (legal decree) allowing people to rescue the Muslim women from the unbelievers. The crowd of people then entered the mission and became uncontrollable. When the Russian Cossacks shot an Iranian boy, the crowd retaliated by killing the whole mission, including Griboyedov, with one exception.

See also TURKMANCHAI, TREATY OF (1828).

Bibliography

Keddie, Nikki R. *Roots of Revolution: An Interpretive History of Modern Iran.* New Haven, CT: Yale University Press, 1981.

PARVANEH POURSHARIATI

GRIVAS, GEORGIOS THEODOROS
[1898–1974]

Greek Cypriot political and military leader.

Born in Greece, Georgios Theodoros Grivas served in the Greek army from 1920; he was the organizer of the Greek resistance to the Nazi occupation of Athens in 1944 and 1945. In 1951, he went to Cyprus at the invitation of Archbishop Makarios II to help in the fight for Cypriot independence from Britain.

In 1954, Grivas founded EOKA (Ethniki Organosis Kipriakou Agonos), a covert nationalist group that used political violence to combat the British. In 1959, he was the general, then commander (1964–1967) of the Greek Cypriot National Guard. After the independence of Cyprus in 1960, Grivas broke with Makarios and supported *enosis* (union) with Greece, founding EOKA B in 1971 toward that end.

See also CYPRUS.

Bibliography

Lenczowski, George. *The Middle East in World Affairs.* Ithaca, NY: Cornell University Press, 1980.

Shimoni, Yaacov, and Levine, Evyatar, eds. *Political Dictionary of the Middle East in the Twentieth Century,* revised edition. New York: Quadrangle/New York Times, 1974.

ZACHARY KARABELL

GROBBA, FRITZ KONRAD FERDINAND
[1886–1973]

German diplomat, orientalist, and specialist in Middle Eastern affairs during the Weimar Republic and the Third Reich; one of the more important and most controversial European diplomats in the Middle East between the two world wars.

Fritz Konrad Ferdinand Grobba was born in Gartz/Oder, Germany, where he attended elementary and high school. He studied law, economics, and Oriental languages at the University of Berlin, from which he received his doctorate in law in 1913. Before World War I, he worked briefly as a dragoman trainee in the German consulate in Jerusalem; during the war, he served as a lieutenant in the German army in France and in Palestine.

Grobba joined the legal affairs department of the German foreign ministry in September 1922.

In January 1923, he was transferred to Abteilung III, the department responsible for the Middle East. When diplomatic relations were established between Germany and Afghanistan in October 1923, Grobba was named Germany's representative in Kabul with the rank of consul. In 1925, the Afghan government accused him of attempting to help a visiting German geographer escape from Afghanistan shortly after the geographer had shot and killed an Afghan citizen near Kabul. Grobba denied the charge. A diplomatic crisis between Germany and Afghanistan over Grobba's role ensued, and he was recalled to Berlin in April 1926. From 1926 to 1932, he served again in Abteilung III, where he was in charge of the section for Persia, Afghanistan, and India.

In February 1932, Grobba was named German ambassador to Iraq, a post he held until September 1939, when war caused the break in diplomatic relations between Germany and Iraq. He was also Germany's ambassador to Saudi Arabia from November 1938 until September 1939. From October 1939 until May 1941, Grobba served in the German foreign ministry in Berlin. In May 1941, the foreign ministry dispatched him to Baghdad as German special representative to the pro-Axis government of Rashid Ali al-Kaylani; but he left Baghdad later that month, since the Rashid Ali coup collapsed. In February 1942, Grobba was named foreign ministry plenipotentiary for the Arab States, a job that entailed liaison between the German government and Arab exiles in Berlin, such as Rashid Ali and the mufti of Jerusalem, Hajj Amin al-Husayni. In December 1942, Grobba was named to the Paris branch of the German archives commission, a post he held until his brief return to the foreign ministry in April 1944. He was officially retired from the foreign ministry in June 1944, although he continued to work there until the end of the year. In 1945, he worked briefly in the economics department of the government of Saxony, in Dresden.

Grobba published the following books: *Die Getreidewirtschaft Syriens und Palästinas seit Beginn des Weltkrieges* (Hanover, 1923); *Irak* (Berlin, 1941); and *Männer und Mächte im Orient: 25 Jahre diplomatischer Tätigkeit im Orient* (Göttingen, 1967). The latter constitutes his memoirs of his work and experience in Middle Eastern affairs.

Grobba was the most influential German diplomat in the Middle East after World War I. He worked for the restoration of Germany's pre–World War I economic and political position in the region, within the context of peaceful coexistence with England. The governments of the Weimar Republic and the Third Reich did not, however, entirely share his ambition for the region. Moreover, lingering wartime animosity coupled with bitter and violent Middle East opposition to Anglo–French imperialism, against the backdrop of Nazi expansionism during the 1930s, created Anglo–French distrust of Grobba. This made him one of the more controversial figures in Middle East diplomacy between the world wars.

See also GERMANY AND THE MIDDLE EAST; HUSAYNI, MUHAMMAD AMIN AL-; KAYLANI, RASHID ALI AL-.

Bibliography

Hirszowicz, Lukasz. *The Third Reich and the Arab East.* London: Routledge and K. Paul, 1966.

Nicosia, Francis R. "Fritz Grobba and the Middle East Policy of the Third Reich." In *National and International Politics in the Middle East: Essays in Honour of Elie Kedourie,* edited by Edward Ingram. London: Frank Cass, 1986.

Nicosia, Francis R. *The Third Reich and the Palestine Question,* 2d edition. New Brunswick, NJ: Transaction, 1999.

FRANCIS R. NICOSIA

GROSSMAN, HAIKA

[1919–1993]

Leading resistance fighter during the Holocaust; senior politician in the Israeli Knesset.

Born in Bialystok (Poland), Haika Grossman joined the Zionist youth movement ha-Shomer ha-Tzaʿir and became a member of its central committee. The Nazis invaded in 1941, and Grossman moved secretly between ghettos across Poland, smuggling weapons, organizing hiding places, and liaising with the Polish resistance groups and Soviet partisans. After the war, she was awarded the Gruenwald Cross for valor, and moved to Warsaw, where she was elected to the Central Committee of Polish Jews.

At the beginning of the Arab–Israeli War of 1948, Grossman emigrated to a kibbutz in Israel and became head of the Gaʾaton Regional Council, concentrating on refugee relief. Elected four times to the Knesset, she served first for the Maʿarach Party and later chaired the MAPAM faction. Grossman turned the Public Services Committee into one of the most important Knesset committees, introducing legislation across a spectrum of social issues, and was a forthright critic of Israeli government policy towards the Palestinians. She supported cooperation between Arabs and Jews in Israel throughout her career, and in the 1980s she founded the dialogue and education center Givʿat Haviva. Grossman was also a member of the unofficial international war crimes tribunal established in protest against the Vietnam War in 1967.

See also ALONI, SHULAMIT; GENDER: GENDER AND LAW; GENDER: GENDER AND POLITICS; HA-SHOMER HA-TZAʿIR; ISRAEL: MILITARY AND POLITICS; ISRAEL: POLITICAL PARTIES IN; NAMIR, ORAH.

Bibliography

Grossman, Haika. *The Underground Army: Fighters of the Bialystok Ghetto.* New York: Holocaust Library, 1987.

"Haika Grossman: A Mirror of Our History." Available from <http://www.haika.org.il>.

GEORGE R. WILKES

GRUENBAUM, YIZHAK
[1879–1970]

Polish Zionist.

Active in the early Zionism movement at the start of the twentieth century, Yizhak Gruenbaum participated in several Zionist congresses before World War I. He was elected to the Polish Sejm (parliament) from 1919 to 1932, when he immigrated to Palestine. He soon became a leader of the Jewish Agency, but he resigned after Lord Moyne's assassination in November 1944. He was Israel's minister of interior in the 1948–1949 provisional government, but he failed to win a Knesset (parliament) seat in the 1949 election. He was a MAPAI (labor party) supporter and an ardent champion of a secular Israeli state.

See also GUINNESS, WALTER EDWARD; ISRAEL: POLITICAL PARTIES IN; JEWISH AGENCY FOR PALESTINE; KNESSET; ZIONISM.

ZACHARY KARABELL

GUEST WORKERS

Term used in Germany and other European countries for migrant workers from Mediterranean countries, especially Turkey.

The migration of Turks to Europe in search of work started in the late 1950s and accelerated after the first bilateral agreement was signed between Turkey and West Germany in October 1961. A series of treaties widened the field of host countries—Austria (May 1964), France (April 1966), Sweden (March 1967), and Australia (October 1967). Between 1961 and 1973, almost a million workers went from Turkey to Western Europe. The program was phased out following the oil crisis and economic recession

In 1955, as its economy began booming, West Germany signed treaties with several countries suffering from underemployment and brought foreign workers under limited-term contracts to its cities. When the boom subsided in the 1970s, many of these workers chose to stay in the country instead of returning to their homelands, causing the population to swell. © REUTERS NEWMEDIA INC./CORBIS. REPRODUCED BY PERMISSION.

A clothing shop in Berlin's "Little Istanbul" section. A flood of Turkish immigrants poured into West Germany in the 1960s as its expanding economy demanded a larger labor force. Some 2.5 million Turks still live in Germany today, making them the largest ethnic minority in the country. © REUTERS NEWMEDIA INC./CORBIS. REPRODUCED BY PERMISSION.

In the Middle East, the oil-producing monarchies of the Arabian Peninsula hosted more than four million foreign workers throughout the 1990s. Prior to 1990, the majority of these guest workers were Arabs from Egypt and Yemen and Palestinians. During the 1990s, the majority of foreign workers gradually became non-Arab Asians such as Afghans, Pakistanis, Indians, Filipinos, and Thais.

Through the years, migrant workers have sent substantial remittances home to their native countries, and for Egypt and Turkey in particular, these remittances have helped to ease balance of trade deficits. The foreign migrants, especially Turks in Germany and Arabs in France, generally are not well integrated into their host countries, a situation that has affected their children more keenly than the parents. By the early 2000s, a generation of migrant worker children had matured to adulthood in Europe; a majority of these young adults have cited their experiences with various subtle and overt forms of discrimination.

Bibliography

Abadan-Unat, Nermin. *Turkish Workers in Europe, 1960–1975: A Socio-economic Reappraisal.* Leiden: Brill, 1976.

ERIC HOOGLUND

that hit Europe beginning in late 1973. The majority of guest workers, however, resisted repatriation programs and remained in Germany and other countries. By 2000, the guest workers and their dependents from Turkey constituted Germany's largest ethnic minority community, numbering about 2 million Turks, with about one-third under age 18. They owned over 30,000 small businesses, providing more than 100,000 jobs.

In France, the majority of foreign workers—the term *guest workers* is not used in France—are Arab migrants from Algeria, Morocco, and Tunisia. They constitute France's largest ethnic minority, numbering with dependents over 2 million in 2000. During the 1990s, several thousand people, mostly young men, began to enter the European Union countries illegally from Afghanistan, Iran, Iraq, and Lebanon in hopes to finding jobs; some "disappeared" in the wide community of foreign workers while others claimed political refugee status.

GUILDS

Organizations of skilled workers or artisans.

The earliest evidence for workers in Middle Eastern urban trades and crafts associating in guilds for their common economic and social benefit dates from the fourteenth century, though there are hints of looser groupings before that time. The Ottoman and Safavid Empires and the kingdom of Morocco developed extensive guild systems with each guild being self-governing through a hierarchy of ranks. Government approval or oversight, variously expressed, kept them from being totally independent, however. The goal of the guilds was to ensure a stable level of production and an equitable distribution of work among guild members. The guilds thus constituted a generally conservative force disinclined to change with evolving economic conditions. Nevertheless, they were often important foci of communal and religious life for their members, as in annual guild-organized commemorations of the martyrdom of Imam Husayn by Shiʿites in Iran. The terms used for guilds include *sinf* (category), *taʾifa* (group), *jamaʿa* (society), and *hirfa* (craft). Guilds were commonly subjected to collective taxation administered by the market inspector *(muhtasib)* or other government official. Jews and Christians were members of guilds in some cities, but exclusively Christian or Jewish guilds, like that of the kosher butchers of Aleppo, were rare.

Records of the city of Aleppo mention 157 guilds in the middle of the eighteenth century. Cairo had 106 in 1814. The survival of guilds in the nineteenth and twentieth centuries varied according to country and rate of Westernization. In northern Egypt, for example, guilds had virtually disappeared by the end of the nineteenth century because of the influx of mass-produced European goods and the growing market for labor created by European investment. By contrast, the guilds of Fez in Morocco escaped severe crisis until the worldwide depression of the 1930s. Even so, municipal statistics of 1938 show the continued domination of small-scale craftwork. The largest guild, that of the slipper-makers, counted 7,100 members, 2,840 of them employers. There were also 800 tanners, 280 of them employers; and 1,700 weavers, of whom 520 were employers. Altogether the guilds numbered 11,000 members.

The potential for guild political activity had manifested itself from time to time over the centuries, as in occasional revolts by workers in the food trades in Cairo at the end of the eighteenth century. By the time modern political life focused on constitutions and participatory government developed, however, economic forces had diminished the importance of guilds in most areas. Iran, where guilds survive to the present day, provides an exception because of its comparatively late exposure to economic and political influences from Europe. The guilds formed the most cohesive group in the Constitutional Revolution of 1906. In Tehran, separate guilds formed seventy political societies *(anjoman)*. The guild leaders lacked a sophisticated understanding of politics, however, so the guilds found themselves barred from political power by the electoral law of 1909. With the advent of the Pahlavi regime in 1926, 230 guilds lost government recognition as corporate entities in an effort to dissipate the coalescence of popular feeling around them; but

Potters handcraft items in a Fez workshop. Production of traditional ceramic tiles and pottery continue to thrive as a craft industry in Morocco. © CARMEN REDONDO/CORBIS. REPRODUCED BY PERMISSION.

because the new system of individual taxation proved unworkable, they regained their status in 1948. Many guild members were drawn to the communist Tudeh Party or to the movements led by Mohammad Mossadegh, Ayatollah Ruhollah Khomeini, and other critics of the monarchy. In 1969 the 110 guilds of Tehran had a membership of about 120,000. Guild members played an important role in the demonstrations that led to the Iranian Revolution of 1979.

See also ANJOMAN; CONSTITUTIONAL REVOLUTION; KHOMEINI, RUHOLLAH; MOSSADEGH, MOHAMMAD; PAHLAVI, REZA; TUDEH PARTY.

Bibliography

Lawson, Fred H. *The Social Origins of Egyptian Expansionism during the Muhammad Ali Period.* New York: Columbia University Press, 1992.

Marcus, Abraham. *The Middle East on the Eve of Modernity: Aleppo in the Eighteenth Century.* New York: Columbia University Press, 1989.

RICHARD W. BULLIET

GUINNESS, WALTER EDWARD
[1880–1944]

British deputy minister of state for the Middle East (1942–1944) and minister resident in the Middle East (1944).

Walter Edward Guinness was known as Lord Moyne. In Cairo, while deputy minister of state, he argued that a partition plan for Palestine would not succeed unless both the Jewish and Arab areas were made part of Greater Syria. He proposed creating four states: Greater Syria (comprising Syria, Muslim Lebanon, Transjordan, and the Arab part of Palestine after partition), Christian Lebanon, a Jewish state, and a "Jerusalem state" that would remain under British control. He urged postponement of plans for a Jewish army, favored by Chaim Weizmann and Winston Churchill, but agreed to enlarge Jewish settlement police and give them military training.

Lord Moyne presided over a conference of Britain's representatives in the Middle East in the fall of 1944 that did not favor his four-state plan, recommending instead that a southern Syria be created out of Transjordan and the Arab part of Palestine. He was assassinated at Cairo by Jewish terrorists, members of the Lohamei Herut Yisrael (Stern Gang), on 6 November 1944.

> *See also* CHURCHILL, WINSTON S.; GREATER SYRIA; LOHAMEI HERUT YISRAEL; WEIZMANN, CHAIM.

> **JENAB TUTUNJI**

GUISH TRIBES

> *See* TRIBES AND TRIBALISM: GUISH TRIBES

GÜLBENKIAN, CALOUSTE
[1869–1955]

Armenian businessman and philanthropist.

Born in Istanbul, Calouste Gülbenkian was educated in France and England. In 1902, he acquired British citizenship, to be eligible for the concession for petroleum fields in Mosul. Later, he transferred this concession to the Iraq Consortium established in 1920 by the United States, France, Britain, and the Netherlands. Because he retained a 5 percent stake in the property and profits of the consortium, he was given the nickname "Mr. Five Percent." Gülbenkian, an enthusiastic art collector, bequeathed his valuable collection to the Gülbenkian Foundation in Lisbon, Portugal, the city in which he died.

> *See also* RED LINE AGREEMENT.

> **DAVID WALDNER**

GÜLEN, FETULLAH
[1938–]

Founder of Turkey's largest Islamic movement and an important Muslim thinker.

Fetullah Gülen was born in the village of Korucuk near Erzurum in eastern Anatolia. He was educated in religious schools and in 1958 was appointed as a mosque preacher in Edirne. He moved to İzmir in 1966 to become an official preacher for the Directorate of Religious Affairs. During the next seventeen years, he developed study circles, or *dershanes,* and summer camps in which students were trained in Islam and encouraged to engage in purposeful civic action. The writings of Said Nursi, especially his ideas about the reconciliation of Islam and modern science, had a deep influence on Gülen. In 1983 Gülen moved to Istanbul, where he expanded his network of *dershanes* into a nationwide movement. His goal is the construction of a Turkified Islam, and he also stresses dialogue and knowledge as core Muslim precepts. His thinking is very much informed by his understanding of the classical period of the Ottoman state. His hundreds of thousands of followers constitute the Gülen movement, and its presence is organized in media, education, and finance. The educational goal of the Gülen movement is to raise up the "golden generation" imbued with the ethical values of Islam and capable of leading Turks to a restoration of "greater Turkey" (i.e., Turkey plus the Turkic-speaking republics of Central Asia). The Gülen movement consists of loosely organized horizontal networks for the realization of its goals. During the early 2000s it controlled more than two hundred educational institutions, both inside and outside Turkey.

> *See also* ANATOLIA; EDIRNE; ISTANBUL; İZMIR; NURSI, SAID.

Bibliography

Yavuz, M. Hakan, ed. *Turkish Islam and the Secular State: The Gülen Movement.* Syracuse, NY: Syracuse University Press, 2003.

> **M. HAKAN YAVUZ**

GULF COOPERATION COUNCIL

An organization of six Arab states in the Persian Gulf region, formed to promote joint military, economic, and political endeavors.

The Iranian Revolution, the Soviet invasion of Afghanistan, and the outbreak of the Iran–Iraq War were among the major reasons that the leaders of Bahrain, Kuwait, Oman, Qatar, Saudi Arabia, and the United Arab Emirates decided to establish the Gulf Cooperation Council (GCC). Because the member countries had at the outset much in common regarding economic matters, these could be agreed upon and implemented more easily than matters of defense. Thus, six months after its founding in May 1981, the GCC announced a Unified Economic Agreement that provided for the free movement of people and capital among member states, abolished customs duties, made banking and financial systems more compatible, and improved technical cooperation among the states. During the 1980s and 1990s many of the provisions of the agreement were implemented, and the GCC moved slowly forward in dealing with security matters. In 1984 members agreed to establish a rapid deployment unit called the Peninsula Shield Force. In 2000 the member states formally committed to a policy of mutual defense against foreign attack, and expansion of the Peninsula Shield Force from 5,000 to 22,000. The GCC also has been involved in mediating territorial disputes between members (for example, Qatar and Saudi Arabia, Qatar, and Bahrain) and between member states and other countries (such as the United Arab Emirates and Iran).

Bibliography

Peterson, Erik R. *The Gulf Cooperation Council: Search for Unity in a Dynamic Region.* Boulder, CO: Westview Press, 1988.

EMILE A. NAKHLEH
UPDATED BY ANTHONY B. TOTH

GULF CRISIS (1990–1991)

A critical international situation that began on 2 August 1990, when Iraq invaded Kuwait, and that officially ended on 28 February 1991, after a U.S.-led military coalition defeated Iraq and liberated Kuwait.

The reasons for Iraq's invasion of Kuwait were primarily financial and geopolitical. Iraq emerged from the 1980–1988 Iran–Iraq War financially exhausted, with a debt of about $80 billion. Its president, Saddam Hussein, tried to service the debt—and fund Iraq's high-technology defense industry, reconstruction, and food imports—with oil revenue. But oil prices fell between January and June 1990 from $20 to $14 a barrel. Saddam Hussein charged, with merit, that Kuwait and the United Arab Emirates had exceeded their Organization of Petroleum Exporting Countries (OPEC) quotas, therefore keeping the price of oil low. He claimed that overproduction was encouraged by the United States in order to weaken Iraq, and he considered the Kuwaiti action an act of war. He demanded that the price of a barrel of oil be raised to US$25, that Kuwait "forgive" $10 billion in debt incurred during his war with Iran and pay $2.4 billion for Iraqi oil it "illegally" pumped from the Rumayla oil field (the southern tip of which is under Kuwait), and that the Gulf states give Iraq financial aid amounting to $30 billion. Saddam Hussein based these demands on the claim that Iraq's war with Iran and sacrifice of hundreds of thousands of lives protected the Gulf states from revolutionary Iran.

Saddam Hussein also wanted to lease two uninhabited islands, Warba and Bubiyan, to provide Iraq secure access to the Persian/Arabian Gulf and as possible bases for a blue-water navy. Kuwait was reluctant to negotiate with Iraq, a country of seventeen million with vast potential, because Bubiyan was very close to Kuwait City and because of concerns that the demand was a precursor to Iraqi claims to disputed border territories and, indeed, to all of Kuwait, which Iraq historically considered a part of itself. Kuwait's reluctance to negotiate and its continuing demand for loan repayment were seen as arrogant by Saddam Hussein and shortsighted by others in the region.

Paradoxically, the end of the Iran–Iraq War had left Iraq militarily strong, strong enough to aspire to leadership of the Arab world. Iraq had 1 million experienced soldiers, 500 planes and 5,500 tanks, and was developing chemical, biological, and nuclear weapons of mass destruction. Officials in the West and Israel voiced alarm, and Western media criticism of human rights violations, especially against the Kurds in Iraq, made Saddam Hussein suspicious. Fearing an action similar to Israel's destruction of Iraq's nuclear reactor in 1981, he issued a sensational threat on 2 April 1990 to burn half of Israel with chemical weapons if it should

U.S. warplanes hit targets in the Iraqi capital of Baghdad, early on the morning of 18 January 1991. The Gulf War (1990–1991), also known as Desert Storm, was fought to expel Iraq from Kuwait and restore Kuwait's independence. © AP/WIDE WORLD PHOTOS. REPRODUCED BY PERMISSION.

attack Iraq. The threat produced an outpouring of support throughout the Arab world, where he was viewed as a blood-and-guts Arab Bismarck ready to take on Israel, which had annexed Jerusalem and the Golan, had invaded Lebanon, had bombed the Palestine Liberation Organization (PLO) head-quarters in Tunis, and since 1987, had been sup-pressing a civilian uprising in the West Bank and Gaza, all without an Arab response. By August Saddam Hussein had used a potent mixture of themes—Western imperialism, Arab impotence, the Palestinian cause, and Islam (later, the poor against the rich)—to tap Arab anger and alienation and to rally the Arab masses.

On the eve of the invasion, the United States gave Saddam Hussein mixed signals. On 25 July, U.S. Ambassador April Glaspie assured him that U.S. President George H. W. Bush wanted better relations with Iraq and that the United States had

no opinion on "Arab–Arab conflicts, like your bor-der disagreement with Kuwait," but she cautioned him against the use of force. There is no evidence that the United States deliberately misled him, but Saddam Hussein ignored a fundamental element of U.S. foreign policy: Oil is a vital U.S. interest, one for which it would go to war.

Saddam Hussein invaded Kuwait on 2 August 1990, to the surprise of most observers. His army occupied the country in a few hours with little re-sistance, killing hundreds of Kuwaitis and jailing and torturing hundreds more. Soldiers looted schools and hospitals of their equipment and banks of their deposits and bullion.

At the government level, Arab reaction split into two camps. The anti-Iraq group consisted of the Gulf countries (Saudi Arabia, Kuwait, Bahrain, Qatar, the United Arab Emirates, and Oman), as well as Egypt, Syria, Morocco, Lebanon, Djibouti, and Somalia. The neutral or pro-Iraq group included Jordan, the PLO, Yemen, Sudan, Libya, Tunisia, Algeria, and Mauritania. The split was reflected in the first voting at a 3 August Arab League meeting of foreign ministers, the majority of whom voted to condemn both Iraqi aggression and foreign intervention. With each passing day, the crisis slipped from Arab League hands, becoming an international confrontation between Iraq and a U.S.-led coalition of twenty-eight countries.

President Bush moved swiftly to galvanize opposition to Iraq. The United Nations (UN) Security Council condemned the invasion on 2 August—the day it occurred—and demanded Iraq's immediate and unconditional withdrawal. During the following few days, the Soviet Union and the Islamic Conference Organization joined in the condemnation, and the UN placed economic sanctions on Iraq. Most significant was Saudi Arabia's agreement on 6 August to allow U.S. troops and aircraft on its soil, under the code name Operation Desert Shield, after being shown U.S. satellite photographs of Iraqi troops close to Saudi borders. On 8 August Saddam Hussein formally annexed Kuwait, and the UN reacted by declaring the annexation "null and void." On 10 August the Arab League summit passed resolutions authorizing the use of foreign troops to reverse the annexation. Thus, most nations, willingly or under U.S. pressure, condemned the invasion and demanded Iraq's withdrawal.

Saddam Hussein's response on 12 August was to link the withdrawal of Iraq from Kuwait to Israel's withdrawal from Gaza and the West Bank (including Jerusalem) and Syria's withdrawal from Lebanon. The linkage idea generated support in the Arab world, particularly among Palestinians and their organization, the PLO.

The United States rejected linkage, insisting on unconditional withdrawal and on denying Saddam Hussein any fruits of his invasion. Nevertheless, Bush declared on 1 October at the UN that an Iraqi withdrawal from Kuwait might provide an opportunity "to settle the conflicts that divide the Arabs from Israel." Despite numerous diplomatic missions by world leaders, Saddam Hussein remained intransigent. In November the United States declared that it would double its troop strength in the Gulf from about 200,000 to 400,000—an action that guaranteed an offensive military option—and the UN authorized the use of force to liberate Kuwait. Bush gave Saddam Hussein until 15 January 1991 to vacate Kuwait. When he did not, U.S. and allied forces began air attacks on 16 January on Iraq and on Iraqi positions in Kuwait under the code name Operation Desert Storm. Some of the air strikes were conducted from Turkey, which had supported the coalition, even though most Turks were against a military confrontation with Iraq. Iraq in turn fired Scud missiles at Tel Aviv, damaging hundreds of buildings and killing several people. Israel uncharacteristically did not retaliate, in deference to U.S. concerns that Israeli involvement in the war would risk the continued cooperation of the Arab partners in the coalition. Instead, the United States sent the Patriot antimissile system to Israel to intercept the Scuds, and a number of nations compensated Israel for the damage. Iraq also fired missiles at Saudi Arabia, and Iraqi troops crossed its borders in late January. In an attempt to break out of its isolation, Iraq offered Iran major concessions regarding the Shatt al-Arab waterway, but fearing Saddam Hussein's ambition, Iran stayed neutral throughout the crisis, even though it exchanged prisoners with Iraq and gave sanctuary to 122 Iraqi combat aircraft.

After another ultimatum from Bush and a number of unsuccessful diplomatic attempts, the coalition launched ground forces into Iraq on 23 February, led by U.S. General Norman Schwarzkopf. Kuwait was liberated four days later, and Iraq, after accepting the relevant UN Security Council resolutions, agreed to a cease-fire on 28 February, but not before setting fire to some 600 or 700 Kuwaiti oil wells.

The Gulf crisis, including the war, had enormous consequences for the region. Iraq's infrastructure was destroyed. Middle East Watch charged that the United States and its allies may have deliberately targeted the infrastructure, costing $200 billion according to an Iraqi estimate, and, in addition, may have bombed civilian residences to encourage Saddam's overthrow, even though such actions are in violation of international law. Neither the United States nor Iraq have been forthcoming about Iraq's casualties, which numbered in the tens of thousands.

Kuwait, of course, suffered the ravages of invasion, occupation, and war. Hundreds of Kuwaitis were killed and tortured. The looting, destruction, sabotage, and liberation cost $65 billion, with another $25 billion earmarked for reconstruction. Kuwaitis exacted revenge on the thriving community of about 350,000 Palestinians in Kuwait, some of whom had publicly supported the Iraq army. (Others, however, had fought with the Kuwaiti resistance, while most had gone about their daily life.) After liberation, hundreds of Palestinians were tortured and killed. The community lost $8 billion and was reduced to about 30,000, most of the remainder having resettled in Jordan.

The Gulf crisis produced political divisions—especially involving Kuwait and Saudi Arabia, on the one hand, and Iraq, Jordan, and the PLO, on the other—between not just the governments but also the peoples of the Arab world. These divisions will take a long time to heal.

See also Bubiyan Island; Bush, George Herbert Walker; Hussein, Saddam; Iran–Iraq War (1980–1988); Iraq; Kuwait; League of Arab States; Organization of Petroleum Exporting Countries (OPEC); Palestine Liberation Organization; Persian (Arabian) Gulf; Shatt al-Arab.

Bibliography

Freedman, Lawrence, and Karsh, Efraim. *The Gulf Conflict, 1990–1991: Diplomacy and War in the New World Order.* Princeton, NJ: Princeton University Press, 1993.

Ibrahim, Ibrahim, ed. *The Gulf Crisis: Background and Consequences.* Washington, DC: Center for Contemporary Arab Studies, Georgetown University, 1992.

Khalidi, Walid. *The Gulf Crisis: Origins and Consequences.* Washington, DC: Institute for Palestine Studies, 1991.

Marr, Phebe. "Iraq's Uncertain Future." *Current History* 90, no. 552 (January 1991): 1–4, 39–42.

Mattar, Philip. "The PLO and the Gulf Crisis." *Middle East Journal* 48, no. 1 (Winter 1994): 31–46.

Salinger, Pierre, and Laurent, Eric. *Secret Dossier: The Hidden Agenda behind the Gulf War,* translated by Howard Curtis. New York: Penguin, 1991.

Sifry, Micah L., and Cerf, Christopher, eds. *The Gulf War Reader: History, Documents, Opinions.* New York: Times Books, 1991.

PHILIP MATTAR

GULF OF OMAN

The northwest arm of the Arabian Sea, measuring 350 miles (560 km) in length.

The Gulf of Oman forms the only entrance to the Persian Gulf from the Indian Ocean. It is bounded by Iran on the north, Oman on the south, and the United Arab Emirates on the west. The gulf is relatively shallow because of its origin as a fissure in the mountain spine now divided between Iran and Oman. Two hundred miles (320 km) wide at its outer limit, it narrows to 35 miles (56 km) at the Strait of Hormuz. Roughly one-third of the world's oil is exported via the Strait of Hormuz and the Gulf of Oman. Iran's Revolutionary Guards attacked oil tankers in the waterway during the Iran–Iraq War but were never able to disrupt shipping. Environmental concerns have grown in recent years because of an increase in oil spills and the emptying of ballast by oil tankers in the Gulf of Oman before entering the strait.

See also Persian (Arabian) Gulf; Revolutionary Guards.

Bibliography

Lorimer, J. G. "Oman (Promontory and Gulf of)." In *Gazetteer of the Persian Gulf, Oman, and Central Arabia,* Vol. 2B: *Geographical and Statistical.* Calcutta, 1908–1915. Reprint, Farnsborough: Gregg, 1970.

U.S. Central Intelligence Agency. *Indian Ocean Atlas.* Washington, DC, 1976.

J. E. PETERSON

GULF OF SUEZ

Maritime inlet that connects the Isthmus of Suez to the Red Sea and, with the Suez Canal, separates the Sinai Peninsula from the rest of Egypt.

Almost 200 miles (320 km) long and 12 to 20 miles (20–32 km) wide, the Gulf of Suez is 210 feet (65 m) deep at its deepest point. It is an important passageway for shipping between Egypt and the lands of the Red Sea, the Arabian Sea, and the Indian Ocean, and for ships using the Suez Canal. It contains rich petroleum deposits, which have been used on a large scale since the 1960s.

See also Sinai Peninsula; Suez Canal.

ARTHUR GOLDSCHMIDT

GULF WAR (1991)

The military expulsion of Iraq from Kuwait after the August 1990 invasion.

The Iraqi invasion of Kuwait on 2 August 1990 evoked a quick response from the United States. Within hours, two U.S. Navy carrier groups were steaming towards the Persian Gulf. Military planners began reviewing U.S. Central Command plans for operations in the Persian Gulf, while other officials consulted with Saudi Arabia about defense of that nation. Thus began a two-phase operation to counter the Iraqi moves. The first phase was Operation Desert Shield, designed to shield Gulf states. The second was Operation Desert Storm, the United Nations–sanctioned action to drive Iraq from Kuwait.

Military actions for Desert Shield proceeded rapidly. By 7 August, elements of the Eighty-second Airborne Division and U.S. Air Force fighter planes were en route to the Gulf. Britain, France, Egypt, and Syria launched parallel actions, while other nations sent small forces to the area.

Original plans envisioned a force of 200,000 to defend Saudi Arabia. Within less than ninety days the U.S. had 184,000 troops in the Gulf, backed by thousands of armored vehicles, helicopters, heavy artillery, and aircraft, as well as a substantial naval force. The scope of the effort was demonstrated by the fact that it took a year to reach such numbers in the Vietnam War.

Although sufficient for the defense of Saudi Arabia, U.S. and allied forces were not sufficient to expel Iraq from Kuwait, which soon became the objective of the United Nations. The U.S. response was to order additional forces to the Gulf. In effect, the U.S. commitment was doubled in just over two months. The result was a U.S. force of over 500,000 in the theater, plus substantial allied forces, by the time Desert Shield gave way to Desert Storm. The U.S. commitment was two Army corps, two Marine divisions, six Navy carrier groups, two battleships (the last time World War II Iowa Class battleships were deployed), and over a thousand airplanes. Included were substantial numbers of National Guard and Reserve personnel.

The transition from Desert Shield to Desert Storm began with a spectacular air offensive on 17 January 1991, viewed worldwide on television. Air operations continued until 24 February, when a massive ground offensive succeeded in driving Iraqi forces out of Kuwait in one hundred hours. The temporary cease-fire on 28 February led to Iraqi acceptance of UN resolutions on April 7.

At the time, Iraq had one of the world's largest military forces—over one million, half of whom were in Kuwait—plus 4,300 tanks. Iraq, however, did not have much of a navy. Its air arm was 660 aircraft. Allied strength was 800,000, 1,800 combat aircraft, and 3,000-plus tanks, in addition to a formidable naval force. Moreover, Iraq had to defend the entire nation. The allies could focus on evicting Iraq from Kuwait.

The five-week air offensive destroyed the Iraqi ability to use its air forces, neutralized air defense and command and control capabilities, struck at transportation systems, and attacked war production facilities, especially those suspected of being related to weapons of mass destruction. The allies attacked Scud missile sites and effectively isolated Iraqi forces in Kuwait. The air offensive weakened Iraqi ground forces for a successful ground offensive.

The plan for the ground attack envisioned fixing Iraqi attention on an amphibious attack on the coast of Kuwait coupled with a direct assault across the Saudi-Kuwait border. The real attack, however, would be from the west, across the Saudi-Iraqi border. That attack would aim toward the Euphrates River to cut off the Iraqi forces in Kuwait.

The hundred-hour ground campaign was a total success. Iraqi forces retreated in disarray from Kuwait. The allies also gained control of 30,000 square miles of Iraq. Allied losses were about 240 killed and 775 wounded. Original estimates of Iraqi losses were as high as 100,000, but later estimates varied from 10,000 to 50,000. They were probably closer to the lower end. The media images of Iraqi soldiers surrendering to helicopters in the air and to reporters suggests the totality of the defeat.

It was the subject of considerable concern that Iraq might use chemical weapons, as it had in the war with Iran. The allies also feared that Iraq might have biological weapons as well. Neither fear was realized.

See also GULF CRISIS (1990–1991); IRAN–IRAQ WAR (1980–1988); IRAQ; KUWAIT.

Bibliography

Finlan, Alistair. *The Gulf War 1991*. New York: Routledge, 2003.

Freedman, Lawrence, and Karsh, Efraim. *The Gulf Conflict, 1990–1991: Diplomacy and War in the New World Order.* Princeton, NJ: Princeton University Press, 1993.

Friedman, Norman. *Desert Victory: The U.S. Army in the Gulf War.* Annapolis, MD: 1991.

Grossman, Mark. *Encyclopedia of the Persian Gulf War.* Santa Barbara, CA: ABC-CLIO, 1995.

Scales, Robert H. *Certain Victory: The U.S. Army in the Gulf War.* Washington, DC: Office of the Chief of Staff, U.S. Army, 1993.

Schubert, Frank N., and Kraus, Theresa L., eds. *The Whirlwind War: The United States Army in Operations Desert Shield and Desert Storm.* Washington, DC: Center of Military History, U.S. Army, 1995.

Watson, Bruce W., ed. *Military Lessons of the Gulf War.* Novato, CA: Presidio Press, 1991.

DANIEL E. SPECTOR

GÜLHANE IMPERIAL EDICT (1839)

Ottoman edict initiating an era of diplomacy and Western-inspired reforms.

The Gülhane Imperial Edict (Gülhane Hatt-ı Hümayunu) of 1839 declared a set of legal, administrative, and fiscal reforms in order to strengthen the Ottoman state and make it a member of the new European diplomatic order. The edict was proclaimed on the accession of the new sultan, Abdülmecit I (1839–1861), on 3 November 1839. It was read by Prime Minister Mustafa Reşid Paşa to an audience that included the sultan, ministers, top civilian and military administrators, religious leaders of the Greek, Armenian, and Jewish communities, and the ambassadors of foreign countries. After its proclamation, the edict was published in the official state newspaper and its French translation was sent to various European states and the embassies in Istanbul.

The ideas in the edict originated in the tradition of Ottoman reform during the second half of the eighteenth century, when Ottoman bureaucrats were already experiencing a paradigm shift in their vision of the ideal political order and their relations with the European states. Mahmud II implemented an intense series of reforms during the two decades before the Gülhane Imperial Edict, centralizing the government, restructuring the military and administration, establishing new educational institutions, and introducing European-style dress and head coverings. Thus there is a strong line of continuity of reform before and after the Gülhane Imperial Edict. The rupture, however, lies in the way the edict was designed to enhance the central government's control by empowering the bureaucracy while changing and reshaping the relationship between the sultan and his subjects. The promised new legal system of the edict was intended to gradually reduce the arbitrary powers of the sultan and assure full rights and equality to non-Muslims under the reinterpreted rule of *shariʿa* (Islamic law plus customary and useful law endorsed by *shariʿa*).

The content of the Gülhane Imperial Edict reflects the agenda of the reformist bureaucrats led by Sadik Rifat Paşa and Mustafa Reşit Paşa, both of whom had experience as ambassadors in European capitals. The bureaucrats wanted to institutionalize and rationalize the reforms, strengthening the scope and legality of their powers. They believed in the necessity of declaring a long-term commitment to "self-civilizing" reforms in harmony with the standards of Europe as a basis for peaceful relations with the European powers. Diplomatically, the image of the Ottoman state as a reformed and civilized polity would allow the Ottomans to receive the support of England and France against external and internal challenges exemplified by Russian pressures on behalf of Christian subjects of the Ottoman Empire and the Egyptian province's demands for autonomy.

In the Imperial Edict of Gülhane, the Abdülmecit I guaranteed the rule of law and an end to arbitrary decisions as well as safety of life, property, and honor for all of his subjects, regardless of religious affiliation. He also pledged himself to a just system of tax collection and military conscription. The edict's persistent reference to *shariʿa* is commonly interpreted as a tool for preventing negative reactions from conservative elements. It could, however, be read as an indication that, in the mind of the Ottoman reformist group, certain aspects of the European standard, such as the rule of law, equality of religious minorities, and protection of property, did not contradict the traditions of Islamic legal thinking. Although the edict's emphasis on *shariʿa* might imply a notion that the basic rights guaranteed in the edict were natural rights, an instrumental state-interest rationale is also provided in the edict, since if the people are happy and safe, they will work better for the welfare and the power of the state. Moreover, implicitly, if the Ottoman state carried out "civilizing" reforms, it would benefit from becoming a part of the European state system.

Although the Gülhane Imperial Edict gave full legitimacy to the reformist bureaucrats and inspired further acts of reform, its implementation involved a gradual process during which the old institutions and customs were allowed to reach extinction naturally rather than immediately being eradicated. Thus, though legal equality of all subjects was declared, different religious communities continued to have separate religious laws and privileges. Traditional Islamic courts or educational institutions were not abolished but left to become the weaker part of the dichotomous Ottoman legal and social structure. More importantly, interventions by the European powers to protect the privileges of the Christian minorities prevented the process of their full equality, since they became more privileged than the empire's Muslim subjects. Hence, the edict's implementation for the next three decades fell short of its intended goals. However, as a foundational text, the Gülhane Imperial Edict continued to provide inspiration and legitimacy to the Ottoman reforms throughout the rest of the nineteenth century.

See also ABDÜLMECIT I; MAHMUD II; OTTOMAN EMPIRE: OVERVIEW; *SHARI'A.*

Bibliography

Davison, Roderic. *Reform in the Ottoman Empire, 1856–1876.* Princeton, NJ: Princeton University Press, 1963.

Shaw, Stanford J. *History of the Ottoman Empire and Modern Turkey,* Vol. 2. Cambridge, U.K.: Cambridge University Press, 1977.

CEMIL AYDIN

GÜNEY, YILMAZ
[1931–1984]

Turkish film actor, writer, and director.

Born the son of a peasant in Siverek, a village near Adana, Yilmaz Güney earned his keep as a boy toting water, caring for horses, and selling *simits* (pretzels) and soda. He attended law school at Ankara University and returned to Adana, where he got a

job with Dar Film. He began scriptwriting and acting in 1958, and moved to Istanbul, becoming a popular star by the mid-1960s. Güney directed his first film in 1966, and went on to become the preeminent filmmaker of the era, with more than a dozen more films. His 1970 film *Hope*, about the mystical adventures of a poor carriage driver from Adana, was a turning point in Turkish film, marking the beginning of an era of neorealism. His 1982 *Yol* (The road) shared the Palme d'Or award at Cannes with Costa-Gavras's *Missing.*

Güney wrote the script for *Yol* while serving a nineteen-year prison sentence for killing a judge in 1974, over a question of honor. The film was directed by Şerif Gören, but Güney escaped from prison in time to finish editing it in France. The film, about five prisoners on hometown leaves, has never been shown publicly in Turkey. Since his death, numerous books have been written about him, and the scripts for all his important films have been published. His films, short stories, and novels reflect his own outspoken Marxism and his preference for outlawed figures on the fringes of society.

Bibliography

Dorsay, Atilla. "An Overview of Turkish Cinema from Its Origins." In *The Transformation of Turkish Culture,* edited by Günsel Renda and C. Max Kortepeter. Princeton, NJ: Kingston Press, 1986.

Özgüç, Agâh. "A Chronological History of the Turkish Cinema." *Turkish Review* (Winter 1989): 53–115.

ELIZABETH THOMPSON

GURI, CHAIM
[1923–]

Israeli poet, writer, and journalist.

Guri was born in Tel Aviv and educated at the Hebrew University of Jerusalem and the Sorbonne in Paris. A principal representative of Dor ha-Palmah (the Palmah generation), he fought against the British in Mandatory Palestine and in the Arab–Israel Wars of 1948, 1967, and 1973. As a Haganah member sent to rescue survivors of the Holocaust, Guri had his first encounter with diaspora Jews, which profoundly affected him and his identity as a Jew. From that time on, the question of "who is a Jew" has significantly influenced his works.

Guri's songs and poems, written during the 1948 Arab–Israel War, portray the experiences of the Palmah fighters and the battlefield. From 1953 to 1970, Guri was a reporter and an essayist for the paper *la-Merhav*, for which he covered the trial of Nazi war criminal Adolph Eichmann (1961–1962). His notes of the trial were published in the book *Mul Ta ha-Zekhukhit* (Facing the glass booth). After the June 1967 Arab–Israel War, Guri, along with other members of Israel's literary elite such as Natan Alterman, Moshe Shamir, S. Y. Agnon, Yitzhak Tabenkin, and Naomi Shemer, was among the founders of the Movement for Greater Israel.

From 1970 to 1980, Guri was on the editorial staff of the *Davar*. From 1972 to 1984, he made several documentaries dealing with the Holocaust (*The 81st Blow*), Jewish resistance against the Nazis (*Flame in the Ashes*), and the illegal immigration to Palestine (*The Last Sea*). An anthology of his poems, *Heshbon Over* (1988), won him the Israel prize for literature. His novella, *Iskat ha-Shokolada* (1965; The chocolate deal, 1968), takes place in an anonymous European city with a flourishing black market and deals with the state of anarchy among the refugees of the Holocaust after World War II. In 2002 he published (in Hebrew) a compilation of poems entitled *Me'uharim* (Late poems). As of 2003, Guri has published nineteen books, nine of them poetry.

Bibliography

Guri, Haim. *The Chocolate Deal: A Novel,* translated by Seymour Simckes. New York: Holt Rinehart, 1968.

Guri, Haim. *Words in My Lovesick Blood: Milim be-dami ha-holeh ahavah,* translated and edited by Stanley F. Chyet. Detroit, MI: Wayne State University Press, 1996.

ANN KAHN
UPDATED BY ADINA FRIEDMAN

GUR, MORDECHAI
[1930–1995]

Israeli general and politician.

Mordechai (also Mordekhai) Gur completed his undergraduate education in political science and Middle East studies at Hebrew University of Jerusalem and went on to a more specialized program at the École Militaire–École de Guerre in Paris.

Gur served in the Haganah forces after 1943 and was a hero of the 1967 Arab–Israel War (commanding a division that took Jerusalem). He served with the Northern Command from 1970 to 1972 and then as the Israel Defense Force (IDF) chief of staff from 1974 to 1978. He coordinated the rescue at Entebbe (1976) and the Litani Operation in southern Lebanon (1978). During his tenure, he tried to reshape the general staff to be more responsive to field conditions. Following his discharge from the IDF in 1978, he attended Harvard Business School. From 1979 to 1984 he held a position with Koor Mechanics.

Gur was elected as a Labor member of Knesset in the Tenth Knesset in 1981; after being re-elected to the Eleventh Knesset he served as minister of health (1984–1986). In the Twelfth Knesset he served as minister without portfolio. In 1992 he was appointed acting defense minister by Prime Minister Yitzhak Rabin; he held that position until his death in 1995.

See also ENTEBBE OPERATION.

Bibliography

Government of Israel, Knesset. "Knesset Members." Available from <http://www.knesset.gov.il/mk>.

Government of Israel, Ministry of Foreign Affairs. "Mordechai Gur." Available from <http://www.mfa.gov.il>.

Rolef, Susan Hattis, ed. *Political Dictionary of the State of Israel,* 2d edition. New York: Macmillan, 1993.

ZACHARY KARABELL
UPDATED BY GREGORY S. MAHLER

GÜRPINAR, HÜSEYIN RAHMI
[1864–1944]

Turkish novelist, journalist, and translator.

Born in Istanbul, Hüseyin Rahmi Gürpinar studied political science and worked as a freelance journalist and translator in a government office of the Ottoman Empire, until he turned to writing in his forties. During World War I, he became famous for his entertaining and realistic novels and short stories. After the war, he moved to an island near Istanbul, where he lived alone with his dog, Kahraman Findik (Hazelnut Hero). He emerged from seclusion to be elected to the Turkish Grand National Assembly, serving between 1936 and 1943.

Although Gürpinar was associated with Turkey's elitist Servet-i Fünun (Wealth of Knowledge) literary movement, he eschewed their ornate style and wrote popular novels influenced by French naturalism. He often wrote about the contradictions between tradition and modernity, modern sexuality, adventures, and current events, such as the 1910 panic at Halley's comet and the devastating 1918 worldwide influenza epidemic. Gürpinar often employed humor and caricature, portraying fanatics, charlatans, and gossiping women with wit and psychological insight.

See also TURKISH GRAND NATIONAL ASSEMBLY.

Bibliography

Mitler, Louis. *Ottoman Turkish Writers: A Bibliographical Dictionary of Significant Figures in Pre-Republican Turkish Literature.* New York: P. Lang, 1988.

ELIZABETH THOMPSON

GÜRSEL, CEMAL
[1895–1966]

Turkish military officer, fourth president of the Turkish republic.

Cemal Gürsel was born in Erzurum, the son of a police officer. World War I broke out while he was studying at the military college in Constantinople (now Istanbul), and he was sent to the front at Çanakkale. After the war, he joined the independence movement led by Mustafa Kemal Atatürk. In 1959 Gürsel was appointed commander of the Turkish land forces. In May 1960, he wrote a letter to the minister of defense protesting Prime Minister Adnan Menderes's use of the army to suppress dissent; in response, he was stripped of his command and placed under house arrest in İzmir. At this point, a group of junior officers invited Gürsel to lead their movement. Gürsel accepted, and on 27 May 1960 he headed a group of thirty-eight officers in a coup that overthrew the civilian government. Gürsel became head of the newly established National Unity Committee, as well as prime minister, president, and commander of the armed forces. An advocate of returning to civilian rule as quickly as possible, Gürsel expelled from the country fourteen younger officers, led by Colonel Alparslan Türkeş, who called for continued military rule. In 1961, following the promulgation of a new constitution and election of a new parliament, Gürsel was elected fourth president of the Turkish republic. In 1966, his failing health forced him to resign his office, and he died shortly thereafter.

See also ATATÜRK, MUSTAFA KEMAL; MENDERES, ADNAN; NATIONAL UNITY COMMITTEE (TURKEY); TÜRKEŞ, ALPARSLAN.

DAVID WALDNER

GUSH EMUNIM

Movement dedicated to the establishment and strengthening of Jewish settlements throughout the West Bank (Judea and Samaria) and the Gaza Strip.

Gush Emunim (Bloc of the Faithful) has played a significant role in Israeli political life since its inception in the mid-1970s. The movement is concerned with establishing and strengthening Jewish settlement throughout the West Bank and Gaza Strip, which its members believe belong to the Jewish people and the State of Israel by divine promise. Gush members are opposed to any territorial compromise or Israeli withdrawal from these regions, even as part of a peace agreement between Israel and the Palestinians.

The movement was formed in 1974 by a group of national religious activists associated with the Young Guard of the National Religious Party (now Mafdal). They opposed the minimalist policies of the Allon settlement plan and, in the light of the limited withdrawal on the Golan Heights after the October 1973 war, set out to create the conditions that would prevent any similar withdrawals taking place in the West Bank and Gaza.

Opposed by the Labor Party governments of the time, Gush Emunim underwent a process of legitimization following the election of the right-wing Likud Party of Menachem Begin in 1977. It created a settlement movement, known as Amanah, that undertook the logistics of establishing settlements throughout the region. Its settlement blueprint envisaged no less than 2 million Jews throughout the West Bank and Gaza by the year 2000, but this translated into a more realistic policy aimed at creating twelve new settlements in the first year of the Begin administration, thus laying the foundations for future settlement activities.

Armed Jews clash with Palestinians in the West Bank in December 1993. The Gush Emunim movement advocates the Jewish settlement of the West Bank and the Gaza Strip, and its members react to any encroachment on what they consider their territory with sometimes violent opposition. © AP/WIDE WORLD PHOTOS. REPRODUCED BY PERMISSION.

The ideology of the movement stems from its belief that God promised Abraham the whole of the land of Israel (from the Mediterranean to the Jordan River and even further east) for the Jewish people as their exclusive territory, as stated in the Old Testament. Gush Emunim draws much of its support from the ranks of the Bnei Akiva youth movement, whose slogan is, "The land of Israel, for the people of Israel, according to the Torah of Israel." They view Eretz Yisrael (the land of Israel) as holy territory, parts of which were liberated (not occupied) by divine intervention in the June 1967 war and which is never to be relinquished by any human decision, not even by a democratically elected government of the state of Israel.

In the early 1980s, Gush activists were implicated in the Jewish underground movement Terror-Neged-Terror (Terror against Terror), which undertook attacks against Palestinians in revenge for Palestinian killings of Jewish settlers. Its targets included mayors Bassam Shak'a (Nablus), Karim Khalif (Ramallah), and Ibrahim Tawil (al-Bira), and the Islamic College in Hebron. Plots to blow up Arab buses in Jerusalem and, more sensationally, the Dome of the Rock, were thwarted by Israeli intelligence.

During its first almost twenty-eight years of existence, Gush Emunim transformed itself from a grassroots extra-parliamentary movement to one that provided the ideological underpinnings for a number of political parties, municipal organizations, and settlements (villages and townships) throughout the West Bank and Gaza Strip. Its representatives have been active in right-wing political parties in successive Israeli governments since 1977, in some cases achieving cabinet positions. Two leading ministers in Ariel Sharon's government of January 2003, Infrastructure Minister Rafael Eitan (National Religious Party) and Tourism Minister Benny Elon (National Israel Party), were staunch supporters of the Gush and the West Bank settlements.

Gush Emunim does not have any formal membership; it is difficult to estimate its size or support, but it has become the most visible ideological force for active and, in some cases violent, opposition to all attempts to reach a peace agreement with the Palestinians involving any form of territorial withdrawal.

Leading Gush Emunim activists have also become administrators of the regional and local councils set up to administer the settlement network and provide a conduit for the transfer of public resources from the central government to the settlements. The major political lobby for the West Bank settlement network, the Yesha (an acronym for Yehuda ve-Shomron, Judaea, and Samaria) Council, is made up of leading Gush personalities. This organization also serves as an umbrella group for West Bank municipal councils in the face of political threats to remove any settlements.

The original leaders of the Gush Emunim movement, notably Rabbis Moshe Levinger of Hebron and Hanan Porat from Gush Etzion, have stepped aside to make way for a younger generation of leaders, although none of the new generation has achieved their prominence. Some of the younger activists have attempted to set up new settlement outposts not approved by the government and have been called "the hilltop youth." They are perceived by many as constituting the contemporary equivalent of the earlier Gush activists of the mid-1970s, who attempted to establish the first settlements despite government opposition of the time.

Gush Emunim's Greater Israel and prosettlement ideology has had a major impact on Israeli society in general and on the peace process in particular. Its opposition to any form of territorial withdrawal or settlement evacuation added to the obstacles that faced the post-Oslo negotiation process.

See also ARAB–ISRAEL WAR (1967); ARAB–ISRAEL WAR (1973); BEGIN, MENACHEM; GAZA STRIP; LEVINGER, MOSHE; OSLO ACCORD (1993); SHARON, ARIEL; WEST BANK.

Bibliography

Friedman, Robert I. *Zealots for Zion: Inside Israel's West Bank Settlement Movement.* New York: Random House, 1992; New Brunswick, NJ: Rutgers University Press, 1994.

Lustick, Ian S. *For the Land and the Lord: Jewish Fundamentalism in Israel.* New York: Council on Foreign Relations, 1988.

Newman, David, ed. *The Impact of Gush Emunim: Politics and Settlement in the West Bank.* New York: St. Martin's Press, 1985.

Newman, David, and Hermann, Tamar. "Extra-Parliamentarism in Israel: A Comparative Study of Peace Now and Gush Emunim." *Middle Eastern Studies* 28, no. 3, (1992): 509–530.

Segal, Haggai. *Dear Brothers: The West Bank Jewish Underground.* Woodmere, NY: Beit Shamai Publications, 1988.

DAVID NEWMAN

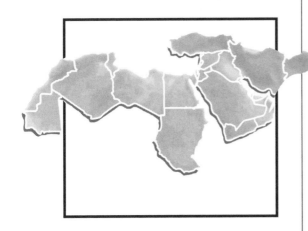

H

HA-AVARAH AGREEMENT

Agreement that allowed Jews to transfer limited assets from Nazi Germany to Palestine.

In August 1933 the German Ministry of the Economy concluded the so-called Ha-avarah (transfer) Agreement with Jewish officials in Palestine and representatives of the German Zionist Federation. Violently antisemitic and eager to rid Germany of its Jews, the new government of Adolf Hitler shared with Zionists the goal of facilitating Jewish departures to Palestine. The Ha-avarah Agreement permitted Jews whose assets were held in blocked accounts in Germany to transfer part of their savings to Palestine, where the money was to be used to purchase German products. For the new Nazi government, Ha-avarah had the advantage of promoting both Jewish emigration and German exports; for beleaguered German Jews, the agreement was a way of salvaging some Jewish assets and escaping persecution. Although pleased at the way in which Ha-avarah undercut those Jews championing a boycott of Germany, Nazi policymakers also came to oppose an independent Jewish state in Palestine, believing that this would strengthen the Jews' hand against Germany internationally. Nevertheless, Hitler himself refused to reject Ha-avarah, and so his subordinates maintained the policy until shortly after the outbreak of war in 1939. In the end, about 60,000 Jews may have benefited from its provisions, and some 100 million reichsmarks were transferred from Germany to Palestine.

See also HOLOCAUST.

Bibliography

Nicosia, Francis. *The Third Reich and the Palestine Question.* Austin: University of Texas Press, 1985.

MICHAEL R. MARRUS

HABASH, GEORGE

[1925–]

Leading Palestinian activist; former secretary-general of the Popular Front for the Liberation of Palestine.

George Habash (also known as al-Hakim, the sage) was born into a prosperous Greek Orthodox Palestinian family in Lydda in Mandate Palestine. After completing his education in Jerusalem, he worked as a teacher and then attended the Faculty of Medicine at the American University of Beirut (AUB), graduating with distinction in 1951.

Habash witnessed the expulsion of Lydda's population on 13 July 1948 and saw his sister die through lack of medical care. Although some sources indicate that he immediately volunteered with Arab forces active in Palestine, all agree that in 1949 he helped establish the Partisans of Arab Sacrifice (Kata'ib al-Fida al-Arabi), which attacked Western targets in Beirut and Damascus until it was dissolved by the Syrian authorities in mid-1950. Back at the AUB, Habash joined the Society of the Firm Tie (Jam'iyyat al-Urwa al-Wuthqa), a student literary club inspired by Arab nationalist writers such as Constantine Zurayk and Sati al-Husari. An eloquent and forceful personality, in 1950 he was elected president of the group's executive committee. In 1951, this committee became the nucleus of a new, clandestine pan-Arab movement, the Arab Nationalist Movement (ANM; Harakat al-Qawmiyyin al-Arab). Habash emerged as ANM's leader.

In 1952, Habash left for Amman to develop ANM's Jordanian branch. He opened a clinic for the poor and established the Arab Club to combat illiteracy and serve as a discussion and recruitment center. He was forced underground in 1954, remained in Jordan until the nationalist Nabulsi government fell in 1958, then fled to Damascus, and again to Beirut when the B'ath Party took over in Syria in 1961.

At this stage, the ANM viewed Egyptian president Gamal Abdel Nasser as the best hope for Arab unity and the restoration of Palestinian rights. When specifically Palestinian nationalist organizations began to emerge in the 1960s, Habash condemned them as regionalists who had abandoned general Arab interests and whose guerrilla activities would provide an excuse for Israel to attack the Arab states before they were ready for the challenge. However, in 1964, confronted with the establishment of the Palestine Liberation Organization (PLO), Habash established the National Front for the Liberation of Palestine within the ANM, and in 1967 Nasser's stunning defeat prompted him to dissolve the ANM and create the Popular Front for the Liberation of Palestine, of which he became secretary general. The Popular Front adopted a radical Marxist-Leninism, an approach Habash had fought against in the ANM when pressed by a Marxist-Leninist faction led by Nayif Hawatma and Muhsin Ibrahim.

The Popular Front nearly disintegrated in 1968 while Habash was imprisoned in Syria for sabotaging the Trans-Arabian Pipeline, although after his escape to Amman and later to Beirut it developed into the most important Palestinian rival to al-Fatah. Its uncompromising stance toward Israel, the West, and conservative Arab regimes was based on an insistence that the Palestinian revolution could succeed only as part of a regional and international struggle committed to radical social and political change. During the 1970s and 1980s, the Popular Front's willingness to pursue its agenda through military strikes—and until 1973 through the hijacking of civilian airliners—won it wide support among frustrated Palestinian refugees but unleashed harsh responses from Jordan (notably in Black September); from Lebanese opponents, provoking the civil war of 1975 through 1976; and from Israel until the 1980s, when Habash fled to Damascus.

Habash called a halt to many of the Popular Front's military and terrorist tactics at the behest of the Palestinian National Council in 1973, but he remained convinced that such actions were both legitimate and necessary. Believing Israel to be unprepared to reciprocate Palestinian concessions, the Popular Front has launched armed and terrorist attacks on Israelis during both intifadas.

Once the leading radical rival to PLO chairman Yasir Arafat, Habash appeared poised at several critical junctures to displace him. Habash has suffered from heart trouble since the 1970s and was increasingly marginalized by both the rise of Islamist movements and the Oslo peace process, of which he has been a consistent critic. In the late 1990s, he appeared prepared to consider flexibility toward the Western powers, but brief hopes of a reconciliation with Arafat in 1999, which were supported by the Popular Front majority, proved illusory, and he resigned from the declining organization to establish a research center.

See also AQSA INTIFADA, AL-; ARAFAT, YASIR; BLACK SEPTEMBER; FATAH, AL-; HAWATMA,

NAYIF; HUSARI, SATI AL-; INTIFADA (1987–1991); NASSER, GAMAL ABDEL; OSLO ACCORD (1993); PALESTINE LIBERATION ORGANIZATION (PLO); POPULAR FRONT FOR THE LIBERATION OF PALESTINE; REFUGEES: PALESTINIAN; ZURAYK, CONSTANTINE.

Bibliography

Abukhalil, As'ad. "Internal Contradictions in the PFLP: Decision Making and Policy Orientation." *Middle East Journal* 41 (1987): 361–378.

Cubert, Harold. *The PFLP's Changing Role in the Middle East.* London: Frank Cass, 1997.

Gresh, Alain. *The PLO: The Struggle Within: Towards an Independent Palestinian State*, revised edition, translated by A. M. Berrett. London: Zed, 1988.

Ismael, Tareq Y. *The Arab Left.* Syracuse, NY: Syracuse University Press, 1976.

Kazziha, Walid W. *Revolutionary Transformation in the Arab World: Habash and His Comrades from Nationalism to Marxism.* New York: St. Martin's, 1975.

Moois, Nadim. "The Ideology and Role of the Palestinian Left in the Resistance Movement." Ph.D. dissertation, Oxford University, 1991.

Smith, Charles D. *Palestine and the Arab–Israeli Conflict*, 4th edition. Boston: Bedford-St. Martin's, 2001.

MOUIN RABBANI
UPDATED BY GEORGE R. WILKES

HABIBI, EMILE
[1922–1996]

Noted Palestinian writer and politician.

Born in Haifa to a Protestant family, Emile Habibi worked in an oil refinery and later as a radio announcer. In 1940, he joined the Palestine Communist Party and helped form the Israeli Communist Party (ICP) in 1948. Habibi became one of leading Arab communists in Israel. He represented first the ICP in the Knesset (Israeli legislature) from 1952 to 1965 and later the New Communist List (also called RAKAH) from 1965 to 1972. He was also the longtime editor of the communist newspaper *al-Ittihad*. He left RAKAH in 1991 in the wake of disagreements about how the party should deal with the reforms of Soviet leader Mikhail Gorbachev. Throughout his career, he was one of most important leaders of the Arab community that remained in Israel in 1948, after the first Arab–Israeli war displaced over 725,000 Palestinians.

Habibi was also a leading Arabic-language writer whose works, which included plays, novels, and short stories, were read throughout the Arab world even though he was an Israeli citizen. His 1974 novel, translated as *The Secret Life of Saeed, the Ill-Fated Pessoptimist: A Palestinian Who Became a Citizen of Israel*, rose to become a classic work of modern Arabic fiction and provided political insight into the challenges of being a Palestinian Arab citizen of a Jewish state. He was awarded the Jerusalem Medal of the Palestine Liberation Organization in 1990 and the Israel Prize in 1992.

Habibi died in May 1996 and was buried in Haifa. He instructed that his epitaph simply read, "Emile Habibi—Remained in Haifa."

See also COMMUNISM IN THE MIDDLE EAST; LITERATURE: ARABIC; PALESTINE LIBERATION ORGANIZATION (PLO).

Bibliography

Fischbach, Michael R. "Emile Habibi." In *Encyclopedia of the Palestinians*, edited by Philip Mattar. New York: Facts On File, 2000.

Habibi, Emile. *The Secret Life of Saeed, the Ill-Fated Pessoptimist: A Palestinian Who Became a Citizen of Israel*, translated by Salma Khadra Jayyusi and Trevor Le Gassick. New York: Vantage, 1982.

Jayyusi, Salma, ed. *Anthology of Modern Palestinian Literature.* New York: Columbia University Press, 1995.

MICHAEL R. FISCHBACH

HABIBOLLAH KHAN
[1871–1919]

Amir of Afghanistan, 1901–1919.

Born in Samarkand, Habibollah Khan was the son of Amir Abd al-Rahman and an Uzbek woman. After being active in his father's administration (1880–1901), he succeeded him to the throne in 1901. He was a successful and well-liked monarch, especially in comparison to his autocratic father. He released prisoners, increased the pay of the army, and invited back political exiles his father had forced out of the country.

His reign has been credited with two accomplishments. A great modernizer who was attracted to Western ideas and technology, he traveled to Europe, brought the first automobiles into Afghanistan, and introduced Western secular education there. He also drew Afghanistan away from British control; for example, he kept Afghanistan neutral during World War I.

He was assassinated on 20 February 1919 while hunting at Kala Gosh in Laghman.

See also ABD AL-RAHMAN KHAN.

Bibliography

Adamec, Ludwig. *Historical Dictionary of Afghanistan,* 2d edition. Lanham, MD: Scarecrow Press, 1997.

GRANT FARR

HABIB, PHILIP CHARLES
[1920–1994]

U.S. diplomat.

Philip Charles Habib was U.S. president Ronald Reagan's special envoy to the Middle East, 1981–1983. In the summer of 1981, he negotiated with Syria for the removal of ground-to-air missiles in Lebanon; in August, he brokered a cease-fire agreement between the Palestine Liberation Organization (PLO) and Israel that lasted until June 1982.

After Israel invaded Lebanon on 6 June (the 1982 Arab–Israel War), Habib negotiated another series of cease-fires but none lasted. In late 1982, Habib, ignoring Syria, supervised formal negotiations between Israel and the Lebanese government of President Amin Jumayyil, which resulted in the May 1983 agreement ending the war. Implementation of the agreement was contingent on Syrian withdrawal from Lebanon, however, and following Syrian President Hafiz al-Asad's refusal to withdraw, Habib lost favor with President Reagan and, in July 1983, was replaced by Robert McFarlane.

See also ARAB–ISRAEL WAR (1982); ASAD, HAFIZ AL-; JUMAYYIL, AMIN; PALESTINE LIBERATION ORGANIZATION (PLO); REAGAN, RONALD.

Bibliography

Hof, Frederic C. *Galilee Divided: The Israel–Lebanon Frontier, 1916–1984,* foreword by Philip C. Habib. Boulder, CO: Westview, 1985.

Spiegel, Steven. *The Other Arab–Israeli Conflict.* Chicago: University of Chicago Press, 1985.

ZACHARY KARABELL

HABL AL-MATIN

See NEWSPAPERS AND PRINT MEDIA: IRAN

HABOUS

In North Africa, a family endowment whose usufruct is destined for charitable purposes.

According to Maliki jurisprudence, a family endowment, or *habous,* can be established over property "whose utilization will not result in its dissipation or consumption" (Powers, p. 382). The terms under which the endowment will work must be stipulated in an endowment deed. Public *habous* were created for the benefit of religious organizations or public institutions such as schools, mosques, hospitals, the shrines of *marabouts,* orphanages, or public foundations. Private or family *habous* were created for the benefit of the constituent's descendants. *Habous* properties—known as *waqf,* or *awqaf* outside the Maghrib—are inalienable. Traditionally, the *nadhir* (administrator) who controlled the collection and distribution of the revenues was under the supervision of the chief *qadi* (judge). The French colonial administration nationalized public *habous* during the mid-nineteenth century.

After independence, Morocco and Tunisia enacted legislation transforming the role of the *habous.* With the introduction of national welfare policies, the *habous* lost its importance as a guarantor of social services. During the nineteenth century, one-third of Tunisia's land was *habous.* Tunisian urban aristocrats (known as *baldi,* who were closely related to prominent religious families) administered most of the *habous* land and were severely affected by its nationalization after the Habib Bourguiba government instituted a sweeping agrarian reform. Public *habous* was abolished in 1956; family *habous* was abolished a year later. In 1971, a new program of economic liberalization scheduled the redistribution of 300,000 hectares of collectivized farmland, and *habous* land that had been appropriated by the state was returned to the original benefactors. The simultaneous dismemberment of the *habous* system and collective land has partially contributed to an increase in the number of farmers. A law promulgated in 2000 reactivated the *habous* liquidation procedure, but auditing of *habous* lands remains incomplete.

In Morocco, the administration of *habous* land depends on the Islamic Affairs and *Habous* Ministry (Ministère des *Habous* et des Affaires Islamiques). Although technically inalienable, during the protectorate period *habous* land could be exchanged or sold. After independence, the state has consistently encouraged the registration of *habous* land. A royal edict *(dahir)* in 1977 allowed for the liquidation of family *habous* by the authorities in charge of its administration for reasons of public interest.

See also MARABOUT.

Bibliography

Islamic Affairs and Habous Ministry of the Kingdom of Morocco. Available from <http://www.habous.gov.ma/ministere/fr/index.htm>.

Nelson, Harold D., ed. *Tunisia: A Country Study,* 3d edition. Washington, DC: American University, 1988.

Powers, Davis S. "The Maliki Family Endowment: Legal Norms and Social Practices." *International Journal of Middle East Studies* 25, no. 3 (1993): 379–406.

VANESA CASANOVA-FERNANDEZ

HACENE, FAROUK ZEHAR
[1939–]

Algerian novelist and short-story writer.

Farouk Zehar Hacene, born in Ksar el-Boukhari, Algeria, left for Europe in 1956 and studied in Switzerland while working at various odd jobs. He considers himself to be the one who ended the trend of committed literature among Algerian writers, freeing himself from the stronghold of tradition without denying his national identity. He published a collection of short stories, *Peloton de tête* (Paris, 1965; The winning regiment) and a novel, *Le miroir d'un fou* (Paris, 1979; The crazy man's mirror), that deal with subjects totally removed from the events of the Algerian war of independence. Hacene's short stories are preoccupied with the psychological condition of humans and the search for an aim and a meaning to life.

Bibliography

Qader, Nasrine. *Encyclopedia of African Literature.* London: Routledge, 2003.

AIDA A. BAMIA

HACETTEPE UNIVERSITY

Public university in Ankara.

Hacettepe University was founded in 1954, when an academic unit on children's health was established under the supervision of Ankara University. In 1957, it was transformed into a research institute with an affiliated hospital dedicated to instruction and public service. The institute grew gradually in the following years, with the establishment of academic units on dentistry, medical technology, nursing, physiotherapy-rehabilitation, and home economics. It was eventually accredited as a university in 1967.

Hacettepe University comprises nine faculties (dentistry; economics and administrative sciences; education; engineering; fine arts; letters; natural sciences; medicine; and pharmacology), fourteen vocational schools, twelve institutes, and twenty-seven research centers. It also administers the Ankara State Conservatory of Turkish Music. It has five major campuses in Ankara (Sihhiye, Beytepe, Beşevler, Keçiören, Polatli, and Kaman), and one of its vocational schools is located in neighboring Zonguldak province. Turkish constitutes the main medium of instruction, but half of the medical school classes are conducted in English. Some of the vocational programs are conducted in German and French. In the 2002–2003 academic year, the university had about 3,148 faculty members and 24,415 students. Its budget for that year amounted to 187,332 billion Turkish liras, 99 percent of which came directly from state funds.

Hacettepe's origins as a medical school explain the variety of health-related programs that are administered by the university. Its founder, Prof. Ihsan Doğramaci, is a medical doctor. His innovative approach to medical education and research has been a major contributor to the prestige that Hacettepe currently enjoys among other Turkish universities with a medical concentration. With Ankara University, Hacettepe has promoted research and development in nuclear physics, computer engineering, and electronics.

See also ANKARA; ANKARA UNIVERSITY.

Bibliography

Hacettepe University. Available from <http://www .hacettepe.edu.tr>.

Turkish Council of Higher Education. Available from <http://www.yok.gov.tr/duyuru/butce/imi_butce _kontrol.htm>.

I. METIN KUNT
UPDATED BY BURÇAK KESKIN-KOZAT

HA-COHEN, MORDECHAI

[1856–1929]

Zionist activist in Tripoli, Libya; teacher, author, educational reformer, and rabbinical court judge.

Although Mordechai Ha-Cohen was born in Tripoli, his family had come from Genoa, Italy. His father, Rabbi Yehuda Ha-Cohen, died in 1861. His mother worked as a seamstress, supported her children, and had Mordechai assist by giving instruction in Bible and Talmud. On his own, he studied arithmetic and the literature of the Hebrew Enlightenment (Haskalah). He married in 1883, worked as a Hebrew teacher, and when his income was insufficient, taught himself to repair clocks. As his family grew (four boys and nine girls), he studied rabbinic law and worked as a clerk in the court. His major work was a manuscript titled *Highid Mordechai,* in which he describes the history, customs, and institutions of Tripolitanian Jewry.

As a reformer, he advocated changes in the educational system that were eventually adopted against the will of the establishment. He supported young Zionists and joined the Zionist club, Circolo Sion, when the community leaders opposed it. He contributed news items to the Italian Jewish paper *Israel* and to Hebrew papers in Warsaw, London, and Palestine.

As a jurist in Tripoli, Ha-Cohen was in conflict with lay and religious leaders on matters of rabbinic law. In 1920, he was appointed magistrate in the rabbinic court of Benghazi, Libya, where he served until his death on 22 August 1929.

See also HASKALAH.

Bibliography

De Felice, Renzo. *Jews in an Arab Land: Libya, 1835–1970,* translated by Judith Roumani. Austin: University of Texas Press, 1985.

Goldberg, H. E. *Cave Dwellers and Citrus Growers: A Jewish Community in Libya and Israel.* Cambridge, U.K.: University Press, 1972.

Ha-Cohen, Mordechai. *The Book of Mordechai: A Study of the Jews of Libya,* edited and translated by Harvey E. Goldberg. Philadelphia: Institute for the Study of Human Issues, 1980.

MAURICE M. ROUMANI

HADASSAH

Jewish women's philanthropic organization.

The largest Jewish women's organization in the United States, Hadassah was founded by Henrietta Szold and fifteen other women on 24 February 1912. Its stated purpose was to foster Zionist ideals through education in America and to begin public-health and nursing training in Palestine. In Hebrew, the word *hadassah* means myrtle, a hardy plant used to bind and enrich the soil.

In 1913, Hadassah sent two nurses to Jerusalem to set up a maternity and eye clinic. This was the beginning of its continuing involvement in the medical care of the people of Palestine. In 1939, the Rothschild–Hadassah University Hospital, the first teaching hospital in Palestine, opened atop Mount Scopus in Jerusalem. During the Arab–Israel War of 1948, Mount Scopus was designated a demilitarized zone. The hospital was evacuated, and a new center was built in Jewish Jerusalem. After the Arab–Israel War of 1967, the Mount Scopus center reverted to Jewish control.

Hadassah has more than 1,500 chapters, with over 385,000 members and 22,000 associates (male members). Its activities support the Hadassah medical center in Jerusalem and other philanthropic activities in Israel.

See also ARAB–ISRAEL WAR (1948); ARAB–ISRAEL WAR (1967); SZOLD, HENRIETTA.

Bibliography

Baum, Charlotte; Hyman, Paula; and Michel, Sonya. *The Jewish Woman in America.* New York: Dial, 1976.

MIA BLOOM

HADDAD, MALEK

[1927–1978]

Algerian novelist, poet, and journalist.

Malek Haddad was born in Constantine and later attended the University of Aix-en-Provence in France. After working as a journalist, he began a literary career that merited inclusion in the distinguished "Generation of 1954" (with Mohammed Dib, Yacine Kateb, Moulaoud Mammeri, and Mouloud Feraoun). Themes of exile and engagement characterized his works. He wrote four novels (*La dernière impression*, 1958; *Je t'offrirai une gazelle*, 1959; *L'elève et la leçon*, 1960; *Le quai aux fleurs ne répond plus*, 1961) and published two collections of poetry (*Le malheur en danger*, 1956; *Ecoute et je t'appelle*, 1961). He regretted his inability to compose in Arabic and reflected: "The French language is my exile." During the war of independence, he served on diplomatic missions for the Front de Libération Nationale (FLN; National Liberation Front). He edited the newspaper, *al-Nasr* in Constantine from 1965 to 1968 and became secretary of the reorganized Union of Algerian Writers in 1974.

See also DIB, MOHAMMED; FERAOUN, MOULOUD; FRONT DE LIBÉRATION NATIONALE (FLN); KATEB, YACINE.

PHILLIP C. NAYLOR

HADDAD, SA'D

[1937–1984]

Lebanese military officer and militia leader.

Sa'd Haddad was born in the town of Marj'ayun to a Maronite Christian mother and a Greek Orthodox father. His father was a farmer and a corporal in the Troupes Speciales du Levant during the French mandate (1920–1941). Haddad was graduated from the Patriarchal College in Beirut in 1957, and the military academy at Fayadiyya. After the outbreak of the Lebanese civil war in 1975, Major Haddad assumed command of the southern sectors of Lebanon, ostensibly on the orders of the army command in Beirut, though in fact, Haddad's fifteen hundred–strong, predominantly Christian, militia was financed by and under the orders of Israel. In February 1979, Haddad openly broke with the Lebanese government and declared the land under his control "Free Lebanon."

See also LEBANESE CIVIL WAR (1975–1990); SOUTH LEBANON ARMY.

Bibliography

Hamizrachi, Beate. *The Emergence of the South Lebanon Security Belt: Major Saad Haddad and the Ties with Israel, 1975–1978.* New York: Praeger, 1988.

DAVID WALDNER

HADDAD, WADI

[1927–1978]

Palestinian militant.

A member of a prosperous Greek Orthodox family from Safed, Wadi Haddad joined George Habash in establishing a medical clinic for Palestinian refugees in Jordan after completing medical studies at the American University of Beirut in 1952. He later worked in United Nations–administered refugee clinics in 1956.

Haddad and Habash also helped establish both the influential Arab National Movement in Beirut after 1948, as well as the Popular Front for the Liberation of Palestine (PFLP) later in 1967. Haddad became the main figure behind the airplane hijackings and other spectacular terrorist acts during the late 1960s and early 1970s that made the PFLP, and the Palestinian national movement generally, infamous. He planned the July 1968 hijacking of an Israeli passenger jet, the first instance of Palestinians seizing a plane. He was also involved in the September 1970 hijacking of four aircraft that were flown to Jordan and blown up after the passengers had been evacuated. That incident triggered the bloody Black September crisis (the Jordanian civil war) between Palestinian guerrillas and the Jordanian army. When the PFLP decided to cease such actions in 1971, Haddad split from the group to form the PFLP–External Operations and continued terrorist activities. That group was noted for the June 1976 hijacking of a French plane carrying Israeli passengers that was flown to Entebbe, Uganda, where Israeli forces staged a dramatic rescue operation.

Haddad died in East Germany in March 1978 and was buried in Baghdad.

See also ARAB NATIONAL MOVEMENT; BLACK SEPTEMBER; ENTEBBE OPERATION; HABASH,

George; Jordanian Civil War (1970–1971); Popular Front for the Liberation of Palestine.

Bibliography

Cooley, John K. *Green March, Black September: The Story of the Palestinian Arabs.* London: Frank Cass, 1973.

Fischbach, Michael R. "Wadi Haddad." In *Encyclopedia of the Palestinians,* edited by Philip Mattar. New York: Facts On File, 2000.

Sayigh, Yezid. *Armed Struggle and the Search for State: The Palestinian National Movement, 1949–1993.* New York: Oxford University Press; Oxford, U.K.: Clarendon Press, 1997.

LAWRENCE TAL
UPDATED BY MICHAEL R. FISCHBACH

HADITH

Reports (also known as khabar, *pl.* akhbar*) transmitting the sayings and actions of the prophet Muhammad.*

Hadith (sing. and pl.) consists of a body (the report) and the *isnad* (chain of reporters). It can be *qawli* (reporting the sayings of the Prophet), *fiʿli* (reporting his deeds), or *qudsi* (reporting divinely inspired sayings). Because the Qurʾan explicitly mandates Muslim obedience to the Prophet in legal and ritual matters, the *hadith* became in Islamic law *(shariʿa)* a source of legislation second only to the Qurʾan.

The classification and authentication of the *hadith* is then of crucial importance to the *shariʿa.* As most reports were collected about 150 years after the death of the Prophet, a number of disciplines collectively known as the sciences of the *hadith* were developed, specializing in external criticism (investigation of the *isnad,* biographical studies of the reporters and of their characters, historical context of each report and each subsequent transmission) and internal criticism (consistency with the Qurʾan, consistency with other *hadith,* historical consistency). Depending on the findings of these various studies, a *hadith* would be classified as *sahih* (authentic), *hasan* (good), *daʿif* (weak), and *mawdu* or *batil* (forged). Six main collections of the *hadith* gained wide acceptance, and of these the *Sahih* of Muhammad ibn Ismaʿil al-Bukhari (d. 869) and the *Sahih* of Abu al-Husayn Muslim (d. 875) are the most authoritative.

If the *hadith* is authentic or good, it is admissible as legal proof in the *shariʿa.* It will constitute a definite legal basis if it is *mutawatir* (one following after another). However, if *ahad* (solitary *hadith,* with only one transmission chain), it will not constitute, according to most jurists, legal proof without further qualification from other legal indicators. Most controversial issues and conflicts with the Qurʾanic text arise from *hadith ahad.*

Though much effort went into the collection of the *hadith,* the sheer volume of circulating reports (al-Bukhari is said to have accepted 7,275 out of more than 600,000 reports) and the fact that the Shiʿite and the Sufi schools have their own distinct collections indicate that the field could greatly benefit from the use of newly refined methods in textual and historical criticism as used for instance in biblical studies. But while the *shariʿa* admits of analytical methods to evaluate the *hadith,* the traditionally accepted collections are seen in popular religion and by some jurists and theologians almost as "sacred" sources that may not suffer any scrutiny. This defensive position is in part due to the controversial rejection by some Muslim reformers and modernists, such as Sayyid Ahmad Khan (d. 1898), of *hadith* as a source of law and has so far precluded new studies and evaluations of the historicity of the *hadith.*

See also SHARIʿA.

Bibliography

Kamali, Mohammad Hashim. *Principles of Islamic Jurisprudence,* revised edition. Cambridge, U.K.: Islamic Texts Society, 1991.

WAEL B. HALLAQ
UPDATED BY MAYSAM J. AL FARUQI

HADJ, MESSALI AL-
[1898–1974]

Renowned Algerian nationalist.

Messali al-Hadj was born in Tlemcen and was the son of a cobbler. He received a religious education influenced by the Darqawa sect of Islam and later, in France, enrolled in Arabic language university courses. While serving in the French army from 1918 to 1921, Messali was disturbed by discrimination within the ranks and distressed by the demise of the Ottoman Empire during the post–World War I years. He was attracted by labor politics, which drew him to a French Communist party–affiliated movement known as the Etoile Nord-Africaine (ENA; Star of North Africa). He became its leader in 1926, but the ENA disbanded in 1929. Messali reorganized it in 1933 and distanced it from the French Communists as a new Algerian nationalist organization called the Glorieuse Etoile (Glorious Star—then renamed the Union Nationale des Musulmans Nord-Africans [National Union of North African Muslims] in 1935). It was dedicated to achieving an Arab Muslim independent state of Algeria. After a sojourn in Geneva, Switzerland, in 1935 with the cultural and political nationalist Chekib Arslan (a Druze leader), Messali placed greater emphasis on Arabism within his movement.

Messali supported the Popular Front (France) but did not endorse its proposed assimilationist Blum–Viollette legislation (which, anyway, never passed in Parliament in 1936). His criticism of France's colonial policy and his agitation in Algeria led to the official dissolution of his movement in January 1937, although Messali responded quickly by forming the Parti du Peuple Algérien (PPA; Algerian People's Party) in March. He was arrested several months later, freed in August 1939, only to be incarcerated again in November. Messali was tried by a Vichy (pro-German French government during World War II) court in March 1941 and sentenced to sixteen years of hard labor. He remained under arrest after the Allied forces landed in North Africa during World War II (late 1942). Messali did not concur with Ferhat Abbas's "Manifesto of the Algerian People" of 1943 but in 1944 agreed to head the Amis du Manifeste et de la Liberté (AML; Friends of the Manifesto and Liberty), an organization that briefly (1944–1945) united nationalist movements and called for Algerian autonomy. The announcement in April 1945 of Messali's impending deportation to exile in France heightened tensions but, by that time, Messali's PPA had infiltrated the AML, directing it toward a confrontation with the French colonialists. This was dramatically disclosed in the Sétif Revolt in May when, during the parade celebrating victory in Europe, nationalist placards provoked violence that resulted in 103 European deaths and thousands of retributive Muslim fatalities. The AML disintegrated and the nationalists resumed their separate paths.

In 1946, Messali organized the Mouvement pour le Triomphe des Libertés Démocratiques (MTLD; Movement for the Triumph of Democratic Liberties). The younger elite, tempered by the Sétif riots, wanted direct action and formed the Organisation Spéciale (OS; Special Organization), which was still linked to the MTLD. The OS paramilitary operations (1947–1950) led to the arrest of its leaders and its demise. The MTLD concurrently faced a Berber crisis, as the Berbers (or Kabylia) believed that the organization was too Arabized, and they questioned Messali's authoritarianism. In 1953, the MTLD split between the centralists and the Messalists over the role of immediate and violent attacks against French colonialism. At first, Messali rejected the centralist position, which soon transmuted into the Front de Libération Nationale (FLN; National Liberation Front). The FLN's attacks, from 31 October to 1 November 1954, convinced Messali that he had to organize his own military group; it appeared in December as the Mouvement National Algérien (MNA; Algerian National Movement).

During the Algerian War of Independence, the MNA and the FLN's Armée de Libération Nationale (National Liberation Army) campaigned against each other. This fratricide was underscored by the MNA's highly publicized and grievous losses at Mélouza (south of Kabylia) in 1957. Messali's movement lost its credibility (i.e., the Bellounis affair) and its predominant influence over the emigrant community. France intimated a willingness to initiate discussions with the MNA before the Evian negotiations in 1961, but this was generally viewed as a stratagem challenging the FLN's legitimacy.

Even after the war of independence was won by Algeria, Messali remained in exile in France until his death in 1974. He was returned for burial in Tlemcen, the place of his birth. He and his ideas were always viewed as a threat—even after the October 1988 riots and the political liberalization they inspired, a regenerated PPA was denied legal status. Nevertheless, the extensive historical section of Algeria's revised National Charter (1986) could not ignore Messali's commitment and contribution to Algeria's independence.

See also ABBAS, FERHAT; ALGERIAN WAR OF INDEPENDENCE; AMIS DU MANIFESTE ET DE LA LIBERTÉ; ARMÉE DE LIBÉRATION NATIONALE (ALN); ARSLAN, SHAKIB; BELLOUNIS,

MUHAMMAD; BLUM–VIOLLETTE PLAN; FRONT DE LIBÉRATION NATIONALE (FLN); MOUVEMENT NATIONAL ALGÉRIEN; MOUVEMENT POUR LE TRIOMPHE DES LIBERTÉS DÉMOCRATIQUES; PARTI DU PEUPLE ALGÉRIEN (PPA); POPULAR FRONT; SETIF REVOLT (1945); STAR OF NORTH AFRICA.

Bibliography

Naylor, Phillip C., and Heggoy, Alf A. *Historical Dictionary of Algeria,* 2d edition. Metuchen, NJ: Scarecrow Press, 1994.

PHILLIP C. NAYLOR

HADRAMAWT

Region of the Arabian Peninsula bordered by the Rub al-Khali desert on the north and the Arabian Sea on the south.

The Hadramawt is a mountainous land traversed by a valley and a narrow coastal strip with a hot, arid climate. In 1986 there were 686,000 people living in an area of 62,150 square miles (155,376 sq km). Mukalla is the capital, and Shabwa, Hurayda, Shibam, Saywun, Tarim, Inat, and Kabr Hud are important towns.

Agriculture is largely confined to the upper valley, where there is alluvial soil and water from intermittent flooding; the lower valley that runs to the ocean on the east is largely uninhabited. Newly introduced irrigation and flood control methods are increasing agricultural production. Although dates have typically formed the main crop because of their hardiness, cotton has become an important commodity in recent times. Corn, wheat, and oats are the local grain crops, and tobacco is grown along the coast.

The inhabitants of the Hadramawt have sought their fortunes abroad for centuries. In the modern period, they have been economic middlemen in the European colonial domains spanning littoral East Africa, India, and Southeast Asia—so much so that the economy of the Hadramawt has been heavily dependent on foreign remittances. Indonesia had the most important Hadrami colony until World War II; now it is in the Hadramawt's oil-rich neighbors. The discovery of gold deposits in the 1980s was an important development.

The language of the Hadramawt is Arabic. Outside of literate circles, where modern standard or classical Arabic is the norm, a Hadrami dialect that is close to the former is in general usage. The languages and cultures of the Hadrami diaspora have influenced life in the Hadramawt. Besides its fame as a center for Islamic scholarship, the Hadramawt is noted for its social structure, in which descendants of the Prophet (known as *sayyids*) have occupied a position of politico-religious and economic paramountcy.

Although the Ottoman government historically claimed the Hadramawt as part of its empire, it did not maintain garrisons or levy taxes in the area. The imam of Yemen exerted some authority, but it is the Kuwaiti and Kathiri ruling houses that have competed for political control over the area in its modern history. The Hadramawt was a British protectorate from the late nineteenth century until 1967, when it became independent under the leadership of the National Liberation Front. It was one of the six governorates of the People's Democratic Republic of Yemen until 1991, when it became part of the Republic of Yemen.

See also RUB AL-KHALI.

Bibliography

Bujra, Abdalla S. *The Politics of Stratification: A Study of Political Change in a South Arabian Town.* Oxford: Clarendon Press, 1971.

SUMIT MANDAL

HAFID, MULAY

See ABD AL-HAFID IBN AL-HASSAN

HAFIZ, ABD AL-HALIM
[1929–1977]

Egyptian singer and film actor.

Abd al-Halim Hafiz was a singer known for his work in romantic films. He appeared in more than a dozen films, including *Lahn al-Wafa, Dalila, Banat al-Yawm* (which included Muhammad Abd al-Wahhab's famous song "Ahwak"), the autobiographical *Hikayat al-Hubb,* and *Ma'budat al-Jamahir.*

He was born Abd al-Halim Ali Isma'il Shabana on 21 June 1929 to Ali Shabana and Zaynab Amasha in a village near Zaqaziq in the Egyptian delta province of Sharqiyya. Upon the deaths of his parents shortly thereafter, his maternal uncle took him and his three siblings into his home in Zaqaziq, where Abd al-Halim attended *kuttab* (Qur'an school) and later primary school.

At the age of eighteen, Abd al-Halim followed his brother Isma'il to Cairo and enrolled in the Institute of Arabic Music. He wanted to study voice and *ud* (oud; a short-necked lute); he soon moved, however, to the Higher Institute for Theater Music where he took up the oboe. Upon leaving the institute, he worked as a music teacher in several primary schools for girls and played oboe in the Egyptian Radio orchestra. The oboe, however, was considered a Western instrument and not part of Arabic tradition. Disenchanted, Abd al-Halim returned to his previous ambition of becoming a professional singer.

Among his colleagues at the institute were two young composers, Kamal al-Tawil and Muhammad al-Muji, and the conductor Ahmad Fu'ad Hasan who later established an accomplished and prestigious instrumental ensemble. All three became lifelong colleagues. In 1951, Abd al-Halim performed his first successful song, "Liqa" by Kamal al-Tawil; he also began singing for radio. Shortly thereafter, he signed a two-year contract with Muhammad Abd al-Wahhab to record Abd al-Wahhab's songs and appear in his films.

Along with works by numerous popular lyricists, Abd al-Halim sang the poetry of Abd al-Rahman al-Abnudi, beginning in the early 1960s. At this time, Abd al-Halim sought to change his style from that of ordinary love songs (*al-aghani al-atifiyya*) to one closer to that of popular folk song. He sought colloquial poetry more colorful and meaningful than the common romantic song lyric. Together, Abd al-Halim and al-Abnudi produced "al-Hawa Hawaya," "Ahdan al-Habayib," and other works that had significant impact on popular song.

Like many other commercial performers, Abd al-Halim was eager for artistic and financial control over his work. In 1959, he and cinematographer Wahid Farid formed their own film company, Aflam al-Alam al-Arabi, and produced, among other works, *Al-Banat wa al-Sayf*, based on three short stories by the well-known writer Ihsan Abd al-Quddus. In 1961, Abd al-Halim and Abd al-Wahhab formed the record company Sawt al-Fann and, in 1963, Aflam al-Alam al-Arabi became Aflam Sawt al-Fann, with Abd al-Wahhab as the third partner.

The beginning of Abd al-Halim's singing career coincided with Muhammad Abd al-Wahhab's shift away from singing to composition. Abd al-Halim's voice differed considerably from that of his famous predecessor: It was mellow and resonant, and his distinctive vocal style was characterized as subtle, with meticulous intonation. He left the impression of extended, almost endless musical phrases. He sang the songs of numerous composers, such as Abd al-Wahhab, Baligh Hamdi, Kamal al-Tawil, and Muhammad al-Muji, all in his own style, in his "confined and fertile vocal space" (al-Najmi, 142). Among his most famous songs are "Safini Marra" (by al-Muji), "Ala qadd al-Shuq" (by al-Tawil), "Ahwak" (by Abd al-Wahhab), and "Qari'at al-Finjan" (by al-Muji, with poetry by Nizar Qabbani).

Abd al-Halim was diagnosed as having schistosomiasis (bilharzia, a parasitic disease of the tropics) in 1939. Debilitating attacks resulting from the disease began in 1955 and ended with his death in 1977.

See also ABD AL-QUDDUS, IHSAN; ABD AL-WAHHAB, MUHAMMAD IBN; QABBANI, NIZAR.

VIRGINIA DANIELSON

HAFIZ, AMIN AL-

[1920–]

Syrian politician and veteran member of the Ba'th party.

When the Ba'th started to consolidate its hold on power in the coup of March 1963, al-Hafiz emerged as a prominent Syrian politician. After serving as deputy prime minister and minister of the interior in the government of Salah al-Din al-Bitar, al-Hafiz became chairman of the Revolutionary Command Council in July 1963, after which he served as prime minister from November 1963 to May 1964. He also held the post of president of Syria from 1963 to 1966. In the internal political fighting that became the hallmark of Syrian domestic politics in the 1960s, al-Hafiz took the side of the rural-based regionalist group led by General Salah

Jadid and Dr. Yusuf Zuʿayyin. As early as January 1965, the regionalists launched a sweeping nationalization program that attacked the entrenched interests of the urban bourgeoisie and put nearly all industry in the hands of the Syrian state. This left-wing group of regionalists was far from being united. In the summer and fall of 1965, internal party strife was brewing. The strife ended with the ouster of al-Hafiz's wing of the Baʿth Party in February 1966, and the ascendance of the neo-leftist Salah al-Jadid faction. Having lost out to al-Jadid, al-Hafiz went into exile in Lebanon in June 1967. From there he moved with Michel Aflaq and other Syrian politicians to Iraq and aligned himself with the orthodox Baʿthists who seized power in Baghdad in July 1968. His embrace of the pro-Iraqi Baʿth wing made his return to Syria a virtual impossibility. In August 1971, he was sentenced to death in absentia. The sentence was commuted to life imprisonment in November of the same year. Al-Hafiz and his Syrian associates formed a loose coalition of politicians who opposed Syrian president Hafiz al-Asad and who were involved in anti-Syrian activities on behalf of the rival Baʿth wing in Iraq.

See also AFLAQ, MICHEL; ASAD, HAFIZ AL-; BAʿTH, AL-; JADID, SALAH.

Bibliography

Batatu, Hanna. *Syria's Peasantry, the Descendants of Its Lesser Rural Notables, and Their Politics.* Princeton, NJ: Princeton University Press, 1999.

MUHAMMAD MUSLIH
UPDATED BY MICHAEL R. FISCHBACH

HAGANAH

Underground military defense organization for Jewish community in Palestine, 1920–1948.

The Haganah ("defense") was founded in June 1920 by the Labor Zionist Party Ahdut ha-Avodah in response to Arab riots in April. Its military and organizational complexity increased as the conflict with the Palestinian Arabs intensified during the Mandate era. By the time full scale Arab–Jewish warfare erupted in Palestine following the November 1947 United Nations partition resolution, the Haganah was well positioned to serve as the Yishuv's main armed force and to become the core element of the Israel Defense Force (IDF).

In December 1920 the Haganah was placed under the direct control of the newly created Histadrut, headed by David Ben-Gurion. After the 1929 riots, the Haganah expanded into a Yishuv-wide defense force, and a six-member civilian National Command council was established, led by Eliyahu Golomb. The 1936–1939 Arab Revolt was a watershed event in the development of the Haganah. In the process of responding to the rebellion it developed new doctrines and structures and became an army capable of taking offensive military actions. The Haganah mobilized Jewish youth for military training, established officers' courses, and set up arms depots and underground small arms factories. Elite units were formed under the command of Yitzhak Sadeh, who would also become a major figure in the Palmah and the IDF.

The military doctrine of the Haganah during the 1920s and 1930s was based on self-restraint (*havlagah*). As the Arab Revolt intensified, those most opposed to *havlagah* split off and in 1937 formed the Irgun Zvaʾi Leʾumi, which committed retaliatory acts of terrorism against Arab civilians. In 1940 some Irgun members, led by Abraham Stern, rejected the Irgun's wartime truce with Britain and founded the "Stern Gang," also known as LEHI.

In 1938 the British created a Jewish military unit for counterinsurgency missions against the Arabs, the Special Night Squads. They were trained and commanded by Orde Wingate and drew volunteers from the Haganah, even though the Haganah was technically illegal according to the Mandatory government. Wingate's commando tactics greatly influenced the Haganah and later the IDF. Yigal Allon (Palmah commander) and Moshe Dayan were Wingate protégés.

In 1939 control over the Haganah was transferred to the MAPAI-dominated Jewish Agency, which was headed by Ben-Gurion. A professional Military General Staff was established and Yaʿakov Dori became the Haganah's first chief of staff. The Haganah ran illegal immigration operations (Aliyah Bet) during and after World War II to circumvent the 1939 White Paper restrictions. At the same time, Britain supported the creation of an elite strike force, the Palmah (Plugot Mahatz, or "shock companies") in May 1941, and Haganah members enlisted in the British Army's Jewish Brigade. When Britain refused to lift the White Paper restrictions after the war, the Haganah and Palmah joined with the Irgun and LEHI to form the Hebrew Resistance Movement (1945–1946). The undergrounds coordinated military operations against British targets in Palestine. The harsh British crackdown on the Yishuv in June 1946 convinced Ben-Gurion to end the Haganah's participation.

By 1947 the Haganah had evolved into a cohesive military organization with British Army professionalism and combat experience. The original Palmah battalions had expanded to three full brigades, and the Haganah grew to twelve brigades. On the eve of the first Arab–Israel war, the Haganah had a nascent air force, medical and signal corps, and intelligence units, with membership totaling 60,000. The bulk of Jewish fighters during the Arab–Israel War of 1948 came from Haganah ranks.

On 28 May 1948 Order Number 4 of the Provisional Government declared the establishment of a single national army with a unified national command, to be called the Israel Defense Force (Zva Haganah le-Yisrael, or ZAHAL). All independent military organizations were to be dismantled and absorbed into the IDF. The Haganah's personnel and command structure became the main elements of the new Israeli army and Dori became the IDF's first chief of staff. Many Haganah veterans would later become generals in the IDF, including Dayan, Yigael Yadin, Mordechai Gur, and Ariel Sharon.

See also IRGUN ZVA'I LE'UMI (IZL); LOHAMEI HERUT YISRAEL; WHITE PAPERS ON PALESTINE; YISHUV.

Bibliography

Ben-Eliezer, Uri. *The Making of Israeli Militarism.* Bloomington: Indiana University Press, 1998.

Herzog, Chaim. *The Arab–Israeli Wars: War and Peace in the Middle East from the War of Independence through Lebanon,* revised and updated. New York: Vintage Books, 1982.

Jewish Agency for Israel. "Israel and Zionism: The Haganah." Available from <http://www.jafi.org.il/education/>.

Peri, Yoram. *Between Battles and Ballots: Israel Military in Politics.* New York and Cambridge, U.K.: Cambridge University Press, 1983.

Van Creveld, Martin. *The Sword and the Olive: A Critical History of the Israeli Defense Force.* New York: Public Affairs, 1998.

PIERRE M. ATLAS

HAGGIAG FAMILY

Prominent North African Jewish family.

The Haggiag family name has several probable origins. According to Mordechai Ha-Cohen, the family originated in Oran, Algeria. In 1555, the family fled to Gharian in south Tripolitania. Others claim the family to be of Berber origin, cave dwellers who inhabited the area of Jabal Nafusa and Gharian. The name may have derived from their pilgrimage to Jerusalem, Safed, and Tiberias, hence the Arabic *haj,* plural *hujjaj,* related to *hajjaj* or *haggiag,* meaning pilgrims. Once the Haggiag settled on the coast of Tripoli, they maintained the name as it is but added surnames, such as Pagani and Liluf: One finds, for example, Isacco and David Haggiag Liluf and Abramo Haggiag Pagani.

Hmani (Rahmin) Haggiag was head of the Jewish community of Gharian in 1837 and was a physician. Better known was Rabbi Khalifa Haggiag (died c. 1915). He presided over the Jewish community of Gharian in 1880, served as its spiritual leader, and was a poet and physician-surgeon. He is known to have written poems that appeared in the books of Nahum Slouschz.

Another branch may have come from Tunisia, where they lived as subjects of the bey of Tunis and held French citizenship. Notable were Rabbi Nessim and his son Simeone (born 1882). After the Italian occupation, Simeone's life became intertwined with the destiny of the Jewish community and the economic development of Tripoli. He acquired his education at the Italian school of the Franciscans, in addition to his Jewish studies. He went to the Italian advanced business school and upon graduation joined the company Vadala, which specialized in import/export and banking. He remained until 1911, when the company liquidated assets in Libya.

Simeone assumed the presidency of the Jewish community of Tripoli in the by-elections of 1924, replacing Halfallah Nahum. He was by then a prominent private banker. His tenure lasted until 1926, when disagreements among the council members brought about his resignation. He was then appointed by Italian authorities as commissioner; when in 1929 elections were called and the Haggiags' faction was defeated amid irregularities of voting procedure, the community grew tense and incidents erupted. This led the governor of Libya, Pietro Badoglio, to appoint a non-Jewish Italian, Dr. Alberto Monastero, as administrator of the community in 1929. Until 1938, the eve of World War II, the community was left leaderless.

See also NAHUM, HALFALLAH.

Bibliography

Arbib, Lillo. "Unedited Studies of Surnames of Jews in Libya." Courtesy of the author, Tel Aviv, 1991.

De Felice, Renzo. *Jews in an Arab Land: Libya, 1835–1970,* translated by Judith Roumani. Austin: University of Texas Press, 1985.

Ha-Cohen, Mordechai. *The Book of Mordechai: A Study of the Jews of Libya,* edited and translated by Harvey E. Goldberg. Philadelphia: Institute for the Study of Human Issues, 1980.

Roumani, Maurice M. "Zionism and Social Change in Libya at the Turn of the Century." *Studies in Zionism* 8, no. 1 (1987).

MAURICE M. ROUMANI

HA-HALUTZ

Umbrella group for various Zionist youth movements throughout Europe and the United States.

Beginning in the 1880s in Eastern Europe, various groups of young Jews began to prepare themselves for eventual resettlement in Palestine to create a Jewish community. They stressed manual labor, agricultural proficiency, self-defense, and the speaking of modern Hebrew; they called themselves *halutzim* (pioneers). Branches differed over political issues, but all encouraged physical fitness and horticultural studies. Nurtured by Yosef Trumpeldor and Menahem Ussishkin, ha-Halutz became the organizational framework for preparing young men and women for pioneering work in Palestine, particularly on the land. The organization's many branches also emphasized the role of Jewish youth in transforming and secularizing Jewish society. The movement reached its high point in 1935 with some 90,000 members, but the Holocaust virtually annihilated it. During World War II the group assisted in the illegal settlement of Jews in Palestine.

Bibliography

Oppenheim, Israel. *The Struggle of Jewish Youth for Productivization: The Zionist Youth Movement in Poland.* New York: Columbia University Press, 1989.

DONNA ROBINSON DIVINE

HAIFA

Major city in northwestern historic Palestine and, after May 1948, Israel.

Established in the late Bronze Age on the edge of the Bay of Haifa on the Mediterranean coast, Haifa was part of the Ottoman Empire, which ruled Palestine from 1516 until the winter of 1917/18. Haifa's population was predominantly made up of Muslim and Christian Palestinians until Jews began to settle in the city in the late nineteenth century. A number of factors contributed to its economic revival: the Egyptian conquest and reforms of the mid-nineteenth century, which inaugurated modernization in Palestine; the arrival of European steamboats, which began to visit Haifa as their port of call; the immigration in 1868 of German Templars and, after 1880, of European Jews, both of whom introduced modern economic practices and machinery; and the extension of the Hejaz Railway to Haifa in 1905.

The British ruled Palestine from 1917 to 1948. During these thirty years, Haifa experienced expansion and population growth, especially after a deepwater port was opened in 1933. The 1922 census recorded 25,000 people, of whom 6,000 were Jews and 18,000 were Palestinians. As a result of growth and increased Jewish immigration, by 1944 Haifa had about 66,000 Jews and 62,000 Palestinians. It also had a small community of Bahais, who established their religious center at Mount Carmel. During the Arab–Israel War of 1948, Arab and Jewish forces fought for control of Haifa. Of the city's Palestinian population, only 3,000 remained after the war; the rest were expelled by Jewish forces or fled to Lebanon.

Haifa is now Israel's third largest city as well as its principal port and industrial and commercial center. The city's industries include oil refining, cement, chemicals, electronics, and steel. The city is composed of three sections: port facilities and warehouses at the bottom of Mount Carmel; the business district at the slopes of the mountain; and houses, apartment buildings, and parks on top of the mountain. It also has a maritime museum and two universities. Its 2001 population was over 270,000, of whom 10 percent were Palestinian.

See also ARAB–ISRAEL WAR (1948); HAIFA UNIVERSITY; ISRAEL; MANDATE SYSTEM; OTTOMAN EMPIRE; PALESTINE; PALESTINIAN CITIZENS OF ISRAEL.

Bibliography

Herbert, Gilbert, and Sosnovsky, Silvina. *Bauhaus on the Carmel and the Crossroads of Empire: Architecture and Planning in Haifa during the British Mandate.* Jerusalem: Yad Izhaq Ben-Zvi, 1993.

Seikaly, May. *Haifa: Transformation of an Arab Society, 1918–1939.* New York: St. Martin's Press, 1995.

PHILIP MATTAR

HAIFA UNIVERSITY

Public university in Haifa, Israel.

Opened in 1963, Haifa University did not become firmly established until the 1970s. With help from the Hebrew University in Jerusalem, Haifa University solidified its place as one of the top institutions of higher learning in Israel. It has nurtured a disproportionate number of original and often controversial figures, particularly in the humanities and the social sciences. In general, the faculty tends toward the left, and the university has been the seat of innovative studies on such topics as the attitudes of Arabs toward Israelis and of Israelis toward Arabs. A total of 13,000 students are enrolled in the university's undergraduate and graduate divisions.

See also HEBREW UNIVERSITY OF JERUSALEM.

Bibliography

Sachar, Howard M. *A History of Israel: From the Rise of Zionism to Our Time,* 2d edition. New York: Knopf, 1996.

ZACHARY KARABELL

HAIGAZIAN COLLEGE

Armenian academic institution established in Lebanon in 1955 by the Union of Evangelical Armenian Churches and the Armenian Mission Delegation.

Haigazian is a liberal arts college catering mostly to the needs of the Armenian community in Lebanon. Arabic, English, and Armenian literature are taught, as well as political science, economics, sociology, psychology, computer science, and business administration. There are also professors who teach chemistry, physics, and religious studies.

In 1975, Haigazian College had an enrollment of 650 students; by the mid-1990s there were 312 students and 50 faculty. All courses are taught in English and students are required to take a course on religion. Most of Haigazian's faculty also teach at the American University of Beirut and Beirut University College.

GEORGE E. IRANI

HAIK

Woman's draped, concealing garment.

A *haik* (pl. *hiyak*) is a simple, traditional outdoor costume of Moroccan townswomen, worn at the turn of the twentieth century, made of either fine white or coarse lumpy wool, a mixture of silk and wool, or simply cotton. *Hiyak* are white, with the exception of the black *haik* of Taroudant, and measure about 5 by 1.6 meters. The *haik* drapes the woman from head to foot with only the eyes showing.

See also CLOTHING.

Bibliography

Besancenot, Jean. *Costumes of Morocco,* translated by Caroline Stone. London and New York: Kegan Paul, 1990.

RHIMOU BERNIKHO-CANIN

HAJIR, ABD AL-HOSEYN
[1900–1949]

Iranian politician.

Abd al-Hoseyn Hajir began his political career in the ministry of foreign affairs and then became a clerk at the Russian embassy in Tehran. After holding several ministerial positions, he was appointed prime minister in 1947. In 1949, he was elected to the parliament and also acted as minister of court. Opposed by the popular National Front, his appointments caused mass demonstrations. Hajir was assassinated in Tehran as he was praying in the Sep-ahsalar Mosque (1949). The murder was attributed to Sayyid Hoseyn Emami of the Feda'iyan-e Islam, a militant Islamic group that accused Hajir of being an Anglophile and having Baha'i affiliations.

See also BAHA'I FAITH; FEDA'IYAN-E ISLAM; NATIONAL FRONT, IRAN.

NEGUIN YAVARI

HAJJI BABA OF ISPAHAN

Title of the first and most famous of four travel novels about Persia by an Englishman who had spent time there in the British diplomatic corps.

Hajji Baba of Ispahan (1824) by James Justinian Morier (c. 1780–1849) appealed to contemporary interest in things oriental and gave readers a satirical look into Persian society of the early Qajar period (the Qajar dynasty, ruled 1795–1925). Its title character and picaresque narrator is a barber whose desire to get ahead, and cleverness in so doing, leads him from his hometown of Ispahan (now Isfahan) to Mashhad, to life with a band of Torkamans (Turk-men), Tehran, Qom, Karbala, Baghdad, Constantinople (Istanbul), and finally back to Ispahan as a wealthy representative of the shah. In these places and situations—in the bazaar and the royal court and among dervishes and clerics—Hajji Baba satirically depicts Iranian ways and offers entertaining observations on human nature.

Hajji Baba of Ispahan has played a role in modern Persian literature insofar as its Persian translation in 1905 became a popular model for a type of narrative for which indigenous precedents did not exist. Readers in Iran have even given Morier the ultimate tribute, by alleging that the Persian version was the original and Morier's the translation. They thought the book was so accurate and detailed in its depiction of culture-specific situations and behavior that only an Iranian could have written it.

See also LITERATURE: PERSIAN; QAJAR DY-NASTY.

Bibliography

Johnston, Henry McKensie. *Ottoman and Persian Odysseys: James Morier, Creator of Hajji Baba of Ispahan, and His Brothers.* London and New York: British Academic Press, 1998.

Morier, James. *The Adventures of Hajji Baba of Ispahan.* London: Cresset Press, 1949.

MICHAEL C. HILLMANN

HAJRI, ABDULLAH AL-
[?–1977]

Yemeni judge and government official.

A religious, traditional *qadi* or judge, Abdullah al-Hajri sided with the royalists in the Yemen civil war in the 1960s. He then helped pave the way for the republican-royalist reconciliation by switching sides and working to give the republican regime a more conservative cast. As prime minister in 1973, he both secured from his Saudi friends large amounts of state-to-state aid on a regular, annual basis and cracked down harshly on Yemeni leftists. Adviser to the younger, much less conservative President Ibrahim al-Hamdi in the mid-1970s, he was assassinated in 1977.

See also HAMDI, IBRAHIM AL-; YEMEN CIVIL WAR.

ROBERT D. BURROWES

HAKIM, ADNAN AL-
[?–1991]

Lebanese politician.

A Sunni Muslim from Beirut who played a leading role in the Lebanese Civil War of 1958, Adnan al-Hakim won a parliamentary seat from Beirut in 1960 and 1968. He is considered an extremist who mobilized the masses following sectarian lines and did not get along with other Sunni politicians, whom he accused of compromising Muslim demands in dealing with the Maronite (Christian) political establishment.

His political career is closely tied to that of the al-Najjada party, which was founded as a paramilitary organization in 1946. It emerged from the structure of the Muslim Scouts in Syria and Lebanon. Hakim served as the commander of the Beirut section and a vice-president. In the wake of the dissolution of paramilitary organizations in 1949, he revived the organization and became its head in 1951.

The party sought the "propagation of the Islamic heritage" and called for the union of the Arab lands. It cooperated closely with Egypt's President Gamal Abdel Nasser in the 1960s and led a campaign against the pro-Western foreign policies of Lebanon's President Camille Chamoun. The motto of the party is "the Lands of the Arabs are for the Arabs," and it called for the elimination of Western influence and interests from the Middle East.

Al-Najjada's role in the Lebanese civil war of 1975–1976 was insignificant because most Muslims were attracted to parties with a more revolutionary agenda. The party was seen as belonging to the past, and Hakim was too old to energize party recruitment as he had done in the late 1950s. His political role in the 1970s and 1980s was limited to his ownership of the Beirut daily *Sawt al-Uruba.*

> *See also* CHAMOUN, CAMILLE; LEBANESE
> CIVIL WAR (1958); LEBANESE CIVIL WAR
> (1975–1990); NAJJADA, AL-; NASSER, GAMAL
> ABDEL; SCOUTS.

AS'AD ABUKHALIL

HAKIM FAMILY

Prominent Iraqi family of Shi'ite religious scholars.

The Najaf-based Hakim family of *ulama* call themselves Tabataba'i Sayyids, or "descendants of the Prophet." In the family were Ali ibn Abi Talib and his elder son, al-Husayn, the second imam of Shi'ism. In the twentieth century the most prominent scholar in the family was Ayatullah al-Uzma Muhsin ibn Mahdi (1889–1970). He was educated at the *hawza* of Najaf by some of the greatest *mujtahids* of his time—Akhund Khurasani, Muhammad Kazim Yazdi, Muhammad Husayn Na'ini, and others.

Following the death in 1962 of Marja al-Taqlid Husayn ibn Ali Tabataba'i Burujirdi in Iran, Muhsin al-Hakim became the most widely followed *marja* in the world, but he never managed to acquire sufficient influence in Qom and thus never became supreme *marja al-taqlid.* Under the monarchy Hakim was regarded as a political quietist, but under the revolutionary regime of general Abd al-Karim Qasim (1958–1963) he became very active against the rising influence of the Communist Party, which was felt in the Shi'ite south as well as in Baghdad. This brought about a number of clashes between the Iraqi Communist Party and Hakim's followers. He

Ayatollah Mohammad Bager al-Hakim, a Shi'ite leader, is shown praying with other Muslims. © REUTERS NEWMEDIA INC./CORBIS. REPRODUCED BY PERMISSION.

also openly criticized Qasim for introducing a secular law of personal status and called upon him to abolish it. At the same time, however, he maintained cordial personal relations with Qasim himself. This is also when he started to sponsor a young and ingenious activist mujtahid, Muhammad Baqir al-Sadr (1933–1980) who, in 1957, established the clandestine Da'wa Party. Its purpose was to fight atheism and bring people, and in particular the Shi'a masses, back to Islam. As a result of strong criticism leveled by conservative Shi'ite *ulama* against this Western innovation, however, in 1962 Hakim forced Sadr to distance himself from the Da'wa, at least in appearance. But Hakim continued to sponsor similar activities performed through traditional channels. He sent some of his and Sadr's disciples as agents (*wukala*) to various parts of Iraq, as well as to Lebanon, to spread the message, and he dedicated great resources to the establishment of libraries, schools, mosques, and other educational activities in and outside of Iraq. Under the first Ba'th rule (1963) of the Arif brothers (1963–1968) relations with the regimes were frosty. The Arifs were regarded by the Shi'ites as extreme Sunni bigots, and Hakim considered their Arab Socialism a deviation from Islam's social teachings. Finally, he had strong reservations about their Nasserist pan-Arabism.

In June 1969, less than a year after it came to power for the second time in Baghdad, the Ba'th regime initiated an unprecedented confrontation with the Shi'ite religious establishment. This came as reprisal for Hakim's reluctance to support the regime against the shah of Iran. The Ba'th decided to draft the students of religion, to eliminate the educational autonomy of the *hawzat* (the Shi'ite religious universities), and to control the huge funds donated to the Shi'ite holy shrines. They also accused Hakim's son Mahdi of espionage and forced him to flee the country. Hundreds of students and teachers had to escape to Iran, and the religious centers of Najaf, Karbala, and Kazimayn quickly deteriorated. Hakim led the doomed struggle and died brokenhearted in June 1970.

Mahdi al-Hakim eventually settled down in London, where he established a Shi'ite European political movement, Harakat al-Afwaj al-Islamiyya, and a cultural center, Markaz Ahl al-Bayt. In January 1988 he was assassinated by Saddam Hussein's agents at an Islamic conference in Sudan. His brother, Hujjat al-Islam (later Ayatullah) Muhammad Baqir, established in Iran in November 1981 the Supreme Assembly of the Islamic Revolution in Iraq (SAIRI), the largest Iraqi Shi'ite opposition movement to the Ba'th regime. Supported by Iran, his movement's 4,000-strong military wing, the Badr Forces, participated in operations against the Iraqi armed forces during the Iran–Iraq War. Following the August 1988 cease-fire SAIRI's position in Iran became more precarious, but as long as there is no Iranian–Iraqi peace Hakim can still rely on his hosts for some support. In May 1983 Saddam Hussein imprisoned many members of the al-Hakim family, threatening that unless Muhammad Baqir stopped his opposition activities from Tehran his relatives would be executed. Between 1983 and March 1985 at least eight *ulama* members of the family, including sons, grandsons, and nephews of the late *marja*, as well as many other Shi'ite *ulama*, were executed by Iraq.

See also ARIF, ABD AL-RAHMAN; ARIF, ABD AL-SALAM; BA'TH, AL-; MARJA AL-TAQLID; QASIM, ABD AL-KARIM; SADR, MUHAMMAD BAQIR AL-.

Bibliography

Momen, Moojan. *An Introduction to Shi'i Islam: The History and Doctrines of Twelver Shi'ism.* New Haven, CT: Yale University Press, 1985.

AMATZIA BARAM

HAKIM, TAWFIQ AL-
[1898–1987]

Egyptian dramatist, novelist, and man of letters.

Tawfiq al-Hakim was born in Alexandria, and his early life was shaped by his father's frequent moves from job to job and by his ambition that his son should become a lawyer. Al-Hakim's real interests, however, lay elsewhere; while still a student at the School of Law in Cairo, he wrote some plays (published under a pseudonym) for the Ukasha troupe. When he failed in his legal studies, his father sent him to France to study for a doctorate. Al-Hakim traveled to Paris in 1925, an event that was to be a turning point in his life. Instead of studying law, he immersed himself in European culture, particularly drama, and was strongly influenced by the works of Shaw, Pirandello, Ibsen, and Maeterlinck. Upon returning to Egypt in 1928, he prepared for publication a number of literary projects begun in Paris but also worked for a time as a deputy public prosecutor (*na'ib*) in the Nile delta area and, later, as an official in the ministry of social affairs. In 1943 he resigned his position as a civil servant to devote himself to his writing. Later in life, and particularly during the presidency of Anwar al-Sadat, he became somewhat controversial, partly because of his book *Awdat al-Wa'y* (1974; published in 1985 in English as *The Return of Consciousness*), in which the course of the Egyptian revolution and the status of Egypt's former president Gamal Abdel Nasser was critically reexamined. Only a short time before his death in 1987, he published a series of articles under the title "Hiwar ma' Allah" (Conversation with God), which aroused the ire of the religious establishment.

The inspiration that al-Hakim had found in France bore fruit when two of his works were published in 1933 to immediate critical acclaim: the play *Ahl al-Kahf* (People of the cave) and the novel *Awdat al-Ruh* (Return of the spirit). The latter was to be the first of a series of partially autobiographical contributions to fiction to be published in the 1930s. While it deals with the life of an Egyptian family during the turbulent years surrounding the revolution of 1919, *Yawmiyyat Na'ib fi al-Aryaf* (Diary of a provincial public prosecutor, 1937; published in English as *The Maze of Justice*, 1989) is a most successful portrait of the dilemma faced by Egyptian rural society in its confrontation with the laws and imported values of Europe, and *Usfur min al-Sharq* (1938;

published in English as *A Bird from the East,* 1966) takes Muhsin, the main character in *Awdat al-Ruh,* to Paris.

Ahl al-Kahf was to mark the official beginning of the most notable career in Arabic drama to date. Along with several other plays written in the 1930s and 1940s (such as *Shahrazad* [1934; in English, 1981], *Pygmalion* [1942], and *Al-Malik Udib* [1949; in English, *King Oedipus,* 1981]), it dealt with historical and philosophical themes culled from a wide variety of sources and thus was seen as providing the dramatic genre with a cultural status that it had not enjoyed previously. Al-Hakim's dramatic output is vast and extends over five decades. It includes other plays with philosophical themes, two collections of shorter plays addressing social issues, and a number of works that experiment with dramatic technique (such as *Ya Tali al-Shajara* [Oh, tree climber, 1962; in English, *The Tree Climber,* 1966] and varying levels of language (such as *Al-Safqa* [The deal, 1956]).

Tawfiq al-Hakim is the major pioneer figure in the development of a dramatic tradition in modern Arabic literature, and he has attained the status of one of the greatest Arab litterateurs of the twentieth century.

See also LITERATURE: ARABIC; NASSER, GAMAL ABDEL; SADAT, ANWAR AL-; THEATER.

Bibliography

Long, Richard. *Tawfiq al-Hakim: Playwright of Egypt.* London: Ithaca, 1979.

Starkey, Paul. *From the Ivory Tower: A Critical Study of Tawfiq al-Hakim.* London: Ithaca for the Middle East Centre, St. Antony's College, Oxford, 1987.

ROGER ALLEN

HALAKHAH

The Jewish religious system indicating the "path" that Jews are to follow.

Biblically derived and elaborated upon by oral tradition (especially in the Mishna, from 50 C.E. and Talmud, from 220 C.E.), Halakhah regulates a wide range of personal and communal behavior, from dress codes, dietary rules, and daily religious prayers and rituals to requirements concerning life cycle events, such as marriage and divorce, and the de-

termination of Jewish identity and procedures for conversion. An orderly, topical presentation of the rabbinic tradition appears in *Mishne Torah* (Repetition of the law) by Maimonides (also known as Rabbi Moshe ben Maimon, or Rambam, 1135–1204). The essential guide for the commandments to be followed in daily life is the *Shulkhan Arukh* (Prepared table) by Joseph Karo (1488–1575).

The attitude toward Halakhah is a major determinant affecting Jewish denominationalism. Orthodox Judaism basically accepts Halakhah as an unchanging corpus of law. Minor differences of interpretation are tolerated in accordance with the historical customs that have evolved in local communities. Noteworthy are Ashkenazic and Sephardic customs that inadvertently perpetuate Jewish ethnicity. Conservative Judaism is more flexible in introducing religious change, while the Reform and Reconstructionist movements reject Halakhah as a mandatory system dictating contemporary behavior.

Only a minority of world Jews adheres strictly to Halakhah, with Israel having the highest percentage— between 20 and 25 percent. But the institutionalization of some aspects of Halakhah in Israel's state rabbinate and in the political sphere (inter alia, defining who is Jewish according to Halakhic standards) affects the entire Israeli population. This has resulted, in Israel, in tension between religiously observant Jews, nonobservant Jews, and persons who are not considered Jews by Halakhah (for example, patrilineal descendants of Jews who are accepted as such by the North American Reform movement, or persons converted to Judaism by non-Orthodox rabbis).

The conflict over the acceptance of Halakhic Judaism as the sole legitimate manifestation of contemporary Judaism and the consequent implications for the acceptance of other denominations' rabbis and religious rulings carries over to world Jewry, in part because of the central role of Israel in world Jewish life.

Bibliography

Heger, Paul. *The Pluralistic Halakhah: Legal Innovations in the Late Second Commonwealth and Rabbinic Periods.* Berlin: W. de Gruyter, 2003.

Lewittes, Mendell. *The Nature and History of Jewish Law.* New York: Yeshiva University, 1966.

Schimmel, Harry C. *The Oral Law: A Study of the Rabbinic Contribution to the Torah She-be-al-peh.* New York; Jerusalem: Feldheim, 1971.

Urbach, Efraim E. *Halakhah: Its Sources and Development,* translated by Raphael Posner. Ramat Gan, Israel: Massada, 1986.

SAMUEL C. HEILMAN
UPDATED BY EPHRAIM TABORY

HALAL

See GLOSSARY

HALUKKA

Financial support of Palestinian Jews by Jews living outside Palestine.

Halukka is the Hebrew term for "distribution." The system, which dates back to the Second Temple period (536 B.C.E.–70 C.E.), enabled those not living in the Holy Land, Eretz Yisrael, to assist those who were. Throughout the centuries, emissaries from Palestine travelled to diaspora nations to solicit donations. Periodically, Ashkenazi and Sephardic communities in Eretz Yisrael clashed over the proportion of funds to be distributed in their respective communities. The system became a source of contention between the traditional Orthodox, who wished to preserve it and their communal autonomy, and the Zionists, who viewed it as parasitical—claiming it hindered incentive—and a barrier to national regeneration and growth. As the "New Yishuv" grew, the segment of Palestine Jewry supported by halukka contributions steadily shrank and became a very small minority.

Bibliography

Barual, Jacob. *The Jews in Palestine in the Eighteenth Century: Under the Patronage of the Istanbul Committee of Officials for Palestine,* translated by Naomi Goldblum. Tuscaloosa: University of Alabama Press, 1992.

Ruppin, Arthur. *Building Israel: Selected Essays.* New York: Schocken, 1949.

CHAIM I. WAXMAN

HALUTZ

See HA-HALUTZ

HAMA

Ancient town built on the banks of the Orontes River in central Syria (Sem., Hamath; Gk. Epiphania).

Hama, located on the main road between Damascus and Aleppo, is about 130 miles (210 km) north of Damascus, the capital of Syria, and about 94 miles (152 km) south of Aleppo. Like Homs, Hama lies close to the frontier of settlement facing the Syrian Desert, making it a flourishing market for the nomadic people and villagers in the countryside.

Agriculture in the Hama region profits from the water of the Orontes River. Water wheels (*nawriyas*), which raise the river water up into canals, help irrigate large stretches of land. Of the 100 water wheels in Hama province, only twenty are in use. Grains and fruits abound in the countryside.

The U.S. Department of State estimated the city's population in 2002 at 1.6 million. In the 1980 census, the inhabitants of the city of Hama numbered 177,208 out of a total of 475,582 inhabitants for the whole province. In the 1922 census, the inhabitants of Hama numbered 40,437 out of a total of 69,745 inhabitants for the whole province. The bedouin in the countryside of Hama are not accounted for.

The city of Hama prides itself on a number of ancient monuments. It has many mosques (the most important of which is the Umayyad Mosque), khans (caravansaries), and luxurious palaces belonging to the Azm family, which governed in Syria in the eighteenth century. Important archaeological sites in the countryside include Crusader castles and those built by Saladin, such as those of Shayzar, al-Madiq, and Misyaf.

Hama was a center of resistance to the French during the 1925–1927 Syrian rebellion and to Col. Adib Shishakli's government in 1954. After the Ba'th seizure of power in 1963, the city remained resistant to Damascus's edicts, driven largely by the popularity of the Islamist movement among the Sunni majority and by the merchant community's antagonism to the Ba'th's socialist strictures.

This opposition was first expressed in the spring 1964 rebellion in Hama, led by the Muslim Brotherhood (Ikhwan), but reached its peak during the countrywide Ikhwan-led underground movement (1976–1982), sparked in part by the government's Alawi sectarian composition and by its intervention in the Lebanese civil war. In April 1981 government forces, responding to an Ikhwan-led ambush of an Alawi village on Hama's outskirts, entered the city, killing hundreds. The next year, a government attempt to suppress the Ikhwan led to a month-long rebellion in Hama (2 February–5 March 1982). In putting down the revolt the government massacred an estimated 5,000 to 10,000 civilians and destroyed large parts of the city.

See also ALAWI; ALEPPO; DAMASCUS; HAMA MASSACRE; HOMS; MUSLIM BROTHERHOOD.

Bibliography

Batatu, Hannah. "Syria's Muslim Brethren." *MERIP Reports* 110 (Nov.–Dec. 1982): 12–20, 34, 36. Washington, DC: Middle East Research and Information Project, 1971–1985.

Lawson, Fred H. "Social Bases for the Hamah Revolt." *MERIP Reports* 110 (Nov.–Dec. 1982): 24–28. Washington, DC: Middle East Research and Information Project, 1971–1985.

Middle East Watch. *Syria Unmasked: The Suppression of Human Rights by the Asad Regime.* New Haven, CT: Yale University Press, 1991.

U.S. Department of State. *Background Note: Syria.* February 2002. Available at <http://www.state.gov>.

ABDUL-KARIM RAFEQ
UPDATED BY GEOFFREY D. SCHAD

HAMADAN

An ancient and important city in western Iran.

Hamadan, located at an elevation of 5,732 feet, occupies a fertile agricultural plain. It is associated with the ancient Median city of Ecbatana, built in the seventh century B.C.E., and it was an important capital of successive pre-Islamic dynasties, being situated on the trade route that linked Mesopotamia with the East. In the seventeenth and early eighteenth centuries, the city was occupied by the Ottoman Empire several times, but in 1732 it finally reverted to Iran.

Hamadan retained its role as a large commercial city in the modern period. In the nineteenth century it functioned as a transshipment center for the trade of southwestern Iran with the West. Goods destined for Tabriz, Trebizond (now Trabzon), and the Black Sea were brought to Hamadan. After the development of the Anglo-Indian trade, Hamadan prospered as a result of its location on the trade route via Basra and Baghdad to the east. During the twentieth century the city continued to serve as a regional transshipment center and also developed diverse manufacturing industries. A shrine popularly believed to contain the remains of the biblical Esther is a major Jewish pilgrimage site in the city. There is also a monument for Ibn Sina (Avicenna). The population of Hamadan in 1996 was 401,281.

Bibliography

Bosworth, C. E., ed. *An Historical Geography of Iran.* Princeton, NJ: Princeton University Press, 1984.

PARVANEH POURSHARIATI

HAMADI, SABRI

Lebanese politician.

Sabri Hamadi, a member of one of the most influential Shi'ite families in Lebanon, was born in Hirmil. He received no formal education beyond some elementary schooling in Juniya. He was first elected to parliament in 1925 and was its speaker for much of the 1960s. With Bishara al-Khuri, Hamadi was one of the founders of the Constitutional Bloc. He was a shrewd politician who knew how to exploit the differences among his enemies.

Under Hamadi, the parliament was chaotically structured; appointments within it were made on the basis of total loyalty to him. His cronies from Ba'labak-Hirmil, including some who rarely came to Beirut, where the parliament is located, were on the payroll in key administrative positions. His rule was closely associated with the ascendancy of Chehabism in Lebanon; Hamadi believed that Fu'ad Chehab was the best leader in the Arab world.

As a speaker of parliament in the summer of 1970, Hamadi played a crucial role in the presidential election of that year. When Sulayman Franjiyya defeated the Chehabi candidate, Ilyas Sarkis, Hamadi initially refused to accept the results. He changed his mind after his advisers and Fu'ad Chehab personally warned him of the dire consequences if Franjiyya's election was not ratified. Franjiyya's armed gunmen were waiting outside the parliamentary hall. Hamadi lost the speakership position that year but served as minister of agriculture under Franjiyya.

See also CHEHAB, FUʾAD; CONSTITUTIONAL BLOC; FRANJIYYA, SULAYMAN; KHURI, BISHARA AL-; SARKIS, ILYAS.

AS'AD ABUKHALIL

HAMAMA, FATEN
[1931–]

Egyptian film actress.

Born in Cairo in 1931, Faten (also Fatin) Hamama made her film debut as a young girl in *A Happy Day* (1940), directed by industry pioneer Muhammad Karim. By the 1950s, Hamama was considered to be the leading star of the Egyptian cinema. Her marriage to Omar Sharif in 1953 increased his popularity, and they made several films together. Best known for her melodramatic roles, she played in more than one hundred movies over five decades. Notable films featuring Hamama include some of director Henri Barakat's best work, such as *Call of the Curlew* (1959), *The Open Door* (1963), *The Sin* (1965), and *The Thin Thread* (1971).

See also SHARIF, OMAR.

Bibliography
Darwish, Mustafa. *Dream Makers on the Nile: A Portrait of Egyptian Cinema.* Cairo: American University in Cairo Press, 1998.

Farid, Samir. *Fatin Hamama.* Cairo: Cultural Development Fund, 1995.

DAVID WALDNER
UPDATED BY ANDREW FLIBBERT

HAMA MASSACRE

Islamist uprising against Syrian regime.

In February 1982, Syrian security forces entered the densely populated old city of Hama, situated on the Orontes River south of Aleppo, to search for weapons hidden by Islamist militants. Local residents, urged on by alarms from neighborhood mosques, attacked the troops and pushed them out of the central city. Armed militants then seized control of the provincial headquarters of the ruling Baʿth Party and other key government installations. Elite military and security units commanded by the president's brother, Colonel Rifʿat al-Asad, rushed to the area and, from the heights of the nearby citadel, rained artillery and tank fire into the town, leveling its major commercial and residential districts. Estimates of the dead range from 10,000 to 30,000.

Although Hama had long been a center of Islamist political activism and the location of frequent outbreaks of popular challenge to successive Baʿthist regimes after the 1963 revolution, the 1982 uprising was notable for its massive scale, the broad range of social forces that took part, the high degree of organization evidenced by its leaders, and the ruthlessness with which it was crushed. The most militant Islamist organization in north-central Syria, the Fighting Vanguard, led by Adnan Uqla, never recovered. Even more moderate Islamists scaled back their activities sharply, while some prominent figures, to avoid being harassed, tortured, and killed, initiated overtures to the authorities. For almost a decade the government refused to allocate funds to rebuild the city, whose ruins stood as a stark warning to other dissidents.

See also HAMA.

Bibliography
Abd-Allah, Umar F. *The Islamic Struggle in Syria.* Berkeley, CA: Mizan Press, 1983.

Seale, Patrick. *Asad of Syria: The Struggle for the Middle East.* Berkeley: University of California Press; London: I. B. Taurus, 1988.

FRED H. LAWSON

HAMAS

Palestinian Islamic resistance movement.

HAMAS was created in Israeli-occupied Gaza in December 1987 as the resistance wing of the Islamic revivalist organization, the Association of the Muslim Brotherhood. *HAMAS* (zeal, in Arabic) is an acronym for Harakat al-Muqawama al-Islamiyya (Islamic resistance movement).

Prior to the outbreak of the anti-Israeli uprising in the West Bank and Gaza known as the Intifada in December 1987, the Brotherhood's agenda focused on proselytizing and social purification as the basis for Palestinian socio-spiritual renewal. Hostile to secular nationalist groups within the Palestine Liberation Organization (PLO), the Brotherhood shunned overt acts of anti-Israeli resistance. Israeli authorities quietly assisted the Brotherhood in hopes that it might provide a quieter political alternative to the PLO. The leading figure in the Brotherhood was Shaykh Ahmad Yasin.

Massive popular participation in the intifada prompted the Brotherhood to change tactics and establish HAMAS; its August 1988 charter clearly noted the group's connection with the Brotherhood. Brotherhood leaders argued that the time for vigorous jihad (holy war) had arrived. The move was political as well as religious—secular groups and another militant religious group, Islamic Jihad, were already resisting the Israeli occupation.

The charter called for the total liberation of Palestine from Israeli rule, declaring that Palestine is Islamic *waqf* (religious trust) land that must never be surrendered to non-Muslim rule. HAMAS supported the establishment of an Islamic Palestinian state in all of Palestine, in contrast to the PLO's vision of a secular state in the occupied territories. Israeli authorities struck hard at the HAMAS leadership during the intifada. Shaykh Yasin was arrested in May 1989 and sentenced two years later to life imprisonment. Other important HAMAS figures, such as Shaykh Ibrahim Qawqa, were deported. In December 1992 Israel deported 418 members from HAMAS and Islamic Jihad to Lebanon, including HAMAS leader Abd al-Aziz Rantisi.

HAMAS has maintained a difficult relationship with the PLO. It refused to join the PLO-led Unified National Command of the Uprising (UNCU) that emerged to coordinate resistance activity during the intifada. According to an October 1988 agreement between HAMAS and the UNCU, HAMAS operated alongside of but separate from the UNCU. By 1991 HAMAS was pushing for elections to the Palestine National Council, the PLO's parliament-in-exile, which would be held both in exile and in the territories, where its own strength lay. HAMAS also resolutely opposed the Arab-Israeli peace talks that began in late 1991, and HAMAS ac-

tivists from its armed wing, the Martyr Izz al-Din al-Qassam Brigades, increased the number of attacks against Israeli targets. HAMAS joined nine other Palestinian groups opposed to the talks in the National Democratic and Islamic Front and denounced the resulting Oslo Accord (September 1993).

HAMAS accelerated its resistance to the accords after establishment of the Palestinian Authority (PA) in 1994. In 1995, as serious intra-Palestinian disputes continued, the al-Qassam Brigades carried out a number of deadly suicide bombings against Jewish civilians in Israel proper, not against troops in the West Bank and Gaza; this prompted the PA to crack down on HAMAS. The following year, HAMAS bus bombings directly led to the election of hardliner Benjamin Netanyahu as Israeli prime minister and the virtual collapse of the peace process. King Hussein ibn Talal demanded Shaykh Yasin's release in October 1997 in return for the release of two Israeli intelligence operatives who had been captured after their failed attempt to assassinate HAMAS leader Khalid Mash'al in Amman. HAMAS maintains offices in several countries, including Syria, the current home of exiled senior leader Musa Abu Marzuq.

The al-Aqsa Intifada, which started in 2000, saw the al-Qassam Brigades increase their suicide attacks against Israeli civilian targets. In addition, HAMAS and Islamic Jihad put aside their rivalry and began working in tandem. Israel, in return, assassinated more than 100 militants from the al-Qassam Brigades, Islamic Jihad, and al-Fatah's al-Aqsa Martyrs Brigade. Among them was senior HAMAS spokesman Isma'il Abu Shanab. Israel tried but failed to assassinate several other senior figures, such as Abd al-Aziz Rantisi (who returned to Gaza in 1993), in June 2003, and Shaykh Yasin, in September 2003. Israel repeated its assassination attempt on Shaykh Yasin on 22 March 2004, this time killing him.

Polls consistently show that Palestinians approve of HAMAS's suicide bombings, although that public support began to wane because of their deleterious effect on global support for the Palestinian cause. By late 2003 the future of the peace process seemed to depend upon the PA's ability to halt attacks by HAMAS.

See also AQSA INTIFADA, AL-; FATAH, AL-;
GAZA (CITY); HUSSEIN IBN TALAL; INTIFADA
(1987–1991); ISLAMIC JIHAD; JIHAD; MUSLIM
BROTHERHOOD; NETANYAHU, BENJAMIN;
OSLO ACCORD (1993); PALESTINE LIBERA-
TION ORGANIZATION (PLO); PALESTINE NA-
TIONAL COUNCIL; PALESTINIAN AUTHORITY;
WEST BANK; YASIN, AHMAD ISMAʿIL.

Bibliography

Hroub, Khaled. *Hamas: Political Thought and Practice.* Washington, DC: Institute for Palestine Studies, 2000.

Mishal, Shaul, and Sela, Avraham. *The Palestinian Hamas:
Vision, Violence, and Coexistence.* New York: Columbia
University Press, 2000.

MICHAEL R. FISCHBACH

HAMAS (MOVEMENT FOR A PEACEFUL SOCIETY)

A moderate Islamic party in Algeria.

Hamas is Algeria's second most popular Islamic
party, after the Islamic Salvation Front. It was established in 1990 by Shaykh Mahfoud Nahnah
(1942–2003), after constitutional amendments allowed for political pluralism, as the Movement of
the Islamic Society, with the Arabic acronym HAMAS.
To conform to a law requiring that the name make
no reference to Islam, in 1991 the party changed its
name to the Movement for a Peaceful Society. Influenced by the teachings and methods of the Egyptian Muslim Brotherhood, the party's origins go back
to the 1970s, when Shaykh Nahnah was arrested for
opposing the state's socialist orientation. In 1989,
he formed a social and cultural society, Jamʿiyyat al-
Irshad wa al-Islah (Association of Guidance and Reform), which became Hamas in 1990 and drew its
following from among students, teachers, and professionals. In the 1991 legislative elections, the party
garnered over 450,000 votes. Since the cancellation of these elections, Hamas has maintained a
moderate and nonviolent stance and advocated national reconciliation and the preservation of the republic and the institutions of the state. It has been
criticized by some for taking a conciliatory position
toward the military-backed regime. Others see its
program as realistic and pragmatic. Shaykh Nahnah

ran as a candidate during the presidential elections
of 1995 and came in second, winning over three
million votes. In the 1999 presidential elections, the
party supported the candidacy of Abdelaziz Bouteflika. Since the 1997 legislative elections, Hamas has
participated in several ministerial cabinets and
placed representatives in the Algerian parliament.
It has advocated a moderate Islamic position; adherence to the country's fundamental cultural components (Islamic, Arab, and Amazegh [the indigenous
population]); the restoration of order and national
peace; pluralism; the peaceful transfer of power;
women's participation in society; and respect for
human rights. In 2003 Shaykh Nahnah died of
leukemia, leaving behind a movement that is expected to survive its founder.

See also ALGERIA: POLITICAL PARTIES IN;
FRONT ISLAMIQUE DU SALUT (FIS); NAHNAH,
MAHFOUD.

Bibliography

Harakat Mujtama al-Silm. Available from <www
.hmsalgeria.net>.

Shahin, Emad Eldin. *Political Ascent: Contemporary Islamic
Movements in North Africa.* Boulder, CO: Westview
Press, 1998.

EMAD ELDIN SHAHIN

HAMDI, IBRAHIM AL-
[1943–1977]

President of Yemen Arab Republic (1973–1977).

Ibrahim al-Hamdi was born to a *qadi* family in North
Yemen. After the revolution that overthrew Imam
Yahya in 1962, he entered the army of the newly
formed Yemen Arab Republic. He rose rapidly
through the ranks, and during the civil war, he became increasingly involved in politics. In the early
1970s al-Hamdi became commander of the Reserves, an elite army unit; in 1972 he was appointed
deputy prime minister, and in 1973, deputy commander in chief of the armed forces.

In 1973, al-Hamdi led a military coup against
the civilian government of Abd al-Rahman al-
Iryani, which was widely perceived as ineffective. His
first government included technocrats and was supported by some of the more conservative tribal elements, including leaders of the Hashid and Bakil
confederations.

Upon assuming office, al-Hamdi consolidated his power by methodically reducing the independence of other forces in the country through his "Correction Movement," a nationwide effort to reform the administration, staffing, and operations of all government institutions.

Eventually, the tribal leaders and the more progressive elements (the latter organized into the National Democratic Front) began to oppose al-Hamdi's modernization programs. Political unrest increased in early 1977, amid signs that al-Hamdi desired closer relations with the People's Democratic Republic of Yemen. In October, despite signs that his political situation was improving, he was assassinated.

Al-Hamdi is regarded today as one of the most dynamic and progressive of Yemen's leaders after the civil war of the 1960s, and his role is compared, in meaning and importance, with that of John F. Kennedy in American political history.

See also BAKIL TRIBAL CONFEDERATION; IRYANI, ABD AL-RAHMAN AL-; NATIONAL DEMOCRATIC FRONT (NDF); YEMEN CIVIL WAR.

Bibliography

Dresch, Paul. *A History of Modern Yemen.* Cambridge, U.K., and New York: Cambridge University Press, 2000.

MANFRED W. WENNER

HAMID AL-DIN FAMILY

A ruling dynasty of North Yemen.

This Sayyid family provided the last dynasty of Zaydi imams in North Yemen and produced a late, brilliant flowering of the traditional authoritarian political system that had been an important part of Yemeni politics for over one thousand years. Founded by Imam Muhammad ibn Yahya Hamid al-Din in 1891, the dynasty was consolidated and reached its zenith during the long reign of his son, Imam Yahya ibn Muhammad Hamid al-Din (1867–1948), a reign that began in 1904 and ended with his assassination in 1948. Imam Yahya's son, Imam Ahmad ibn Yahya, long the crown prince, quickly overturned the 1948 revolution and went on to restore and develop further the institutions and practices of his father until his death in 1962. Imam

Ahmad, however, was less successful than his father in insulating traditional Yemen from the outside world and modernity. Imam Muhammad al-Badr succeeded his father, only to be overthrown a week later by the 1962 revolution that created the Yemen Arab Republic. More than a generation later, the Hamid al-Din family remains officially banned from Yemen.

See also AHMAD IBN YAHYA HAMID AL-DIN; BADR, MUHAMMAD AL-; YAHYA IBN MUHAMMAD HAMID AL-DIN; ZAYDISM.

Bibliography

Dresch, Paul. *A History of Modern Yemen.* Cambridge, U.K.: Cambridge University Press, 2000.

ROBERT D. BURROWES

HAMINA, MOHAMMED LAKHDAR
[1934–]

Algerian filmmaker.

Mohammed Lakhdar Hamina is one of the world's most distinguished directors. Three of his motion pictures have been honored at the Cannes Film Festival: *Le vent des Aurès* (The Wind from the Aurès, 1966); winner of the grand award, Palme d'Or, *Chronique des années de braise* (Chronicle of the years of embers, 1975); and *Vent de sable* (Desert wind, 1982). Like other postcolonial Algerian directors, Hamina's films explore the promise and paradox resulting from the revolution (1954–1962) and independence.

Bibliography

Naylor, Phillip C., and Heggoy, Alf A. *The Historical Dictionary of Algeria,* 2d edition. Metuchen, NJ: Scarecrow Press, 1994.

PHILLIP C. NAYLOR

HAMMARSKJÖLD, DAG
[1905–1961]

United Nations secretary-general, 1953–1961.

Born in Uppsala, Sweden, Dag Hammarskjöld was successively a professor of economics, permanent under-secretary of the Finance Ministry and chairman of the board of the Swedish National Bank, Swedish representative in negotiations on the Marshall Plan and on European institutions, and minister in the Swedish Foreign Office. Elected United Nations secretary-general in 1953, he revitalized the world organization.

Hammarskjöld's brilliant personal diplomacy was a new factor in international affairs. In 1955, in talks with Chou En-Lai, he secured the release of seventeen U.S. airmen imprisoned in China, resolving a serious potential threat to international peace. In 1956 he shored up the crumbling Arab–Israeli armistice agreements. In talks in New York he tried to resolve the crisis that followed Gamal Abdel Nasser's 1956 nationalization of the Suez Canal Company, an effort aborted by the Anglo-French-Israeli invasion of Egypt.

Hammarskjöld persuaded the invaders to accept a cease-fire on the condition that a UN force arrive in the area immediately. The first UN peacekeeping force (UNEF I) arrived in the Suez Canal area eight days later. Early in 1957 UNEF replaced the Israelis in Sinai and Gaza.

Hammarskjöld's friendship with both Israeli prime minister David Ben-Gurion and Mahmud Fawzi, Nasser's foreign minister, facilitated his efforts. He failed however, to get Egypt to agree to navigation for Israeli ships or Israel-bound cargoes in the Suez Canal. In 1958 Hammarskjöld played a crucial role in containing, negotiating, and finally resolving the Lebanese crisis, during which, under mistaken premises, U.S. Marines landed in Beirut and British troops in Jordan.

In 1960 Hammarskjöld organized the UN's largest and most difficult peacekeeping operation in the newly independent and chaotic Congo. In the absence of directives from a paralyzed Security Council, his independent actions led to his rejection by both Nikita S. Khrushchev and Charles de Gaulle, who also furiously resented Hammarskjöld's visit to Tunisia when French forces violently reoccupied Bizerte in the summer of 1961.

Hammarskjöld died on 17 September 1961 while on a mission to end fighting in Katanga, when his aircraft crashed at Ndola, Northern Rhodesia.

Bibliography

Hammarskjöld, Dag. *Markings*, translated by Leif Sjöberg and W. H. Auden. New York: Alfred A. Knopf, 1964

Lash, Joseph P. *Dag Hammarskjöld: Custodian of the Brushfire Peace.* Garden City, NY: Doubleday, 1961.

Urquhart, Brian. *Hammarskjöld.* New York: Knopf, 1972.

BRIAN URQUHART

HAMMER, ZEVULUN
[1936–1998]

Member of Israel's Knesset and cabinet minister.

Zevulun Hammer was born in Haifa and was educated in the Israeli national religious school system, concentrating on biblical and Judaic studies at Bar-Ilan University. He did his military service working on a kibbutz. He was a leader of the National Religious Party and was instrumental in getting the party involved in security issues and foreign policy and supporting the Gush Emunim program to settle the Occupied Territories. During the 1980s Hammer moderated his views on the West Bank, arguing that domestic unity was more important than holding onto a vision of Greater Israel.

First elected to the Knesset in 1969, he served as minister of welfare in 1975 and 1976 and was minister of education and culture from 1977 to 1984. He served as minister of religious affairs from 1986 until 1990. In 1990 he again became minister of education, and served until 1992. From 1992 to 1996, he served on the Knesset Foreign Affairs and Defense Committee but did not hold ministerial position. In June of 1996 he was again appointed minister of education and culture as well as deputy prime minister. In August of 1997 he also became minister of religious affairs.

Bibliography

Government of Israel, Knesset. "Zevulun Hammer." Available from <http://www.knesset.gov.il/mk>.

Rolef, Susan Hattis, ed. *Political Dictionary of the State of Israel,* 2d edition. New York: Macmillan, 1993.

MARTIN MALIN
UPDATED BY GREGORY S. MAHLER

HAMRA RIOTS

Muslim–Christian riots in Egypt.

In June 1981 continuing intercommunal tensions between Muslims and Coptic Christians in Egypt erupted into violence in Zawiyat al-Hamra, in the Shurabiyya district of Cairo. Seventeen people died and fifty-four were injured. The violence contributed to the government's September 1981 dismissal of the Coptic pope, Shenouda III, and banning of the Muslim Brotherhood movement.

See also MUSLIM BROTHERHOOD; SHENOUDA III.

MICHAEL R. FISCHBACH

HAMROUCHE, MOULOUD
[1943–]

Prime minister of Algeria, 1989–1992.

Mouloud Hamrouche was born into a family imbued with Algerian nationalism; his father was killed during the War of Independence. At the age of fifteen Hamrouche joined the the Armée de Libération Nationale (ALN). He rose within the Front de Libération Nationale (FLN) to serve in the protocol service under Colonel Houari Boumédienne, who encouraged him to return to his studies. Hamrouche holds a law degree and a master's degree obtained in the United Kingdom. He was appointed chief of protocol in President Chadli Bendjedid's government and served until 1984. He then served as secretary-general of the government and then of the presidency. He replaced Kasdi Merbah as prime minister in September 1989 and was charged with accelerarating political, economic, and social reforms. This required reimagining the FLN, but Hamrouche's efforts were stymied by party factions, and he also confronted emerging populist Islamism, exemplified by the Front Islamique du Salut (FIS). Although Hamrouche is credited with liberalizing Algeria and creating a more open society, regional and local elections in June 1990 resulted in the stunning success of the FIS. Hamrouche permitted gerrymandering by the FLN-controlled Assemblée Populaire Nationale (APN) before the scheduled June 1992 parliamentary elections, provoking FIS protests. Subsequent violence forced President Bendjedid to sack Hamrouche, whom he replaced with Sid Ahmed Ghozali. Hamrouche led the reformist bloc of the FLN until he was forced out of the party. He ran as an independent for president in 1999 but withdrew, along with six other candidates, because of irregularities. Hamrouche remains an independent appealing for political and economic transparency. He hopes to see the Pouvoir—the ruling civilian and military elite that has dominated Algerian politics since independence—replaced in order to have genuine democratic reform. Hamrouche appears poised for another presidential campaign in 2004.

See also ALGERIA: POLITICAL PARTIES IN; BENDJEDID, CHADLI; BOUMÉDIENNE, HOUARI; FRONT DE LIBÉRATION NATIONALE (FLN); FRONT ISLAMIQUE DU SALUT (FIS).

Bibliography

Mouloud Hamrouche web site. Available from <http://www.hamrouche.8m.com>.

Naylor, Phillip C. *The Historical Dictionary of Algeria,* 3d edition. Lanham, MD: Scarecrow Press, 2005.

PHILLIP C. NAYLOR

HAMZAWI, RASHID AL-
[1934–]

Tunisian novelist, playwright, and linguist.

Rashid al-Hamzawi was born in Thala, Tunisia. He received his doctorate from the University of Paris and wrote his dissertation on the Arabic language academy in Cairo. He worked in the Office of Arabization and Translation in Rabat and is presently a professor at the University of Tunis. In addition to his novels, al-Hamzawi has published works on language and translation, particularly in relation to the efforts of the Arab academies to unify Arabic terminology.

Hamzawi's novel *Bududa mat* (Tunis, 1962; Boudouda died), which won the Ali al-Bahlawan Prize, relates the hardships experienced by Tunisians after World War II. Boudouda symbolizes the suffering Tunisian people. The novel also describes rural emigration and the resulting social changes in the cities. Whereas a feeling of optimism pervades the novel, Hamzawi's collection of short stories, *Tarnannu* (Tunis, 1975), is pessimistic; the poor and socially disadvantaged seem trapped by their problems. Hamzawi's plays deal with the corrupt world of politics. In *al-Shayatin fi al-qariya* and *al-Sarikhun fi al-sahra* (Tunis, 1976; The devils in the village; Those who shout in the desert) he searches for the most suitable ideology for developing countries but refrains from choosing one, preferring to leave the doors open. A recent publication is a novel titled *Safar wa Hadhar* (1998; Travel and prattle), which is concerned with the issue of freedom of expression.

See also LITERATURE: ARABIC, NORTH AFRICAN.

AIDA A. BAMIA

HANAFI, HASAN
[1935–]

Egyptian scholar of the Islamic left.

Hasan Hanafi, a prolific professor of philosophy at Cairo University, is identified with his project for the creation of an Islamic left within the context of the Islamic reform movement of al-Afghani and Abduh (although he faults that old movement for confining its message to the elite). Hanafi calls for the recognition of class differences, and believes that the Islamic left should always side with the poor against the rich, the powerless against the powerful, and the downtrodden against the elite. He has also called for the unity of Muslims, especially among Persians and Arabs. Although he is not a secular, the moderateness of his views has earned him the enmity of Islamic fundamentalists, and some militants called him an "apostate" in 1997, prompting him to ask for police protection. Hanafi has published widely in the field of Islamic philosophy and jurisprudence, and has a book on Western political philosophy.

Bibliography

Esposito, John L., and Voll, John Obert. *Makers of Contemporary Islam.* New York: Oxford University Press, 1997.

AS'AD ABUKHALIL

HANAFI SCHOOL OF LAW

One of the four approaches to Sunni Muslim law, often called schools.

Though it bears the name of Abu Hanifa al-Nuʿman ibn Thabit (died 767), the Hanafi School of Law in fact owes its doctrine to his two disciples Abu Yusuf (died 798) and Muhammad ibn al-Hasan al-Shaybani (died 805). They laid down the systematic foundations for the work of later Hanafis. In the eighth and ninth centuries, the law school (*madhhab*) was as-

sociated with the rationalists (*ahl al-raʾy*), who advocated free legal reasoning not strictly bound by the revealed texts. Although by the eighth century *raʾy*, a form of free reasoning, was largely abandoned in favor of a more disciplined and text-bound reasoning, the Hanafis continued to resort to similar methods of legal argument, notably *istihsan* (juristic preference). After the ninth century, and certainly by the beginning of the eleventh, even *istihsan* was restructured so as to render it subsidiary to the imperatives of the religious texts.

Though the Hanafi school finally came to adopt the mainstream legal methodology and philosophy, it did maintain peculiar characteristics such as its emphasis on the practical aspects of the law. Particularly in the first three centuries of Islam, its followers, more than any other school, were the chief authors and experts on formularies (*shurut*), notarial documents, and the profession and conduct of judgeship (*adab al-qada*).

Among the most important Hanafi authors on positive law after Abu Yusuf and Shaybani are Abu al-Hasan al-Karkhi (died 951), Abu al-Layth al-Samarqandi (died 985), al-Quduri (died 1036), Shams al-Aʾimma al-Sarakhsi (died 1096), al-Kasani (died 1191), al-Marghinani (died 1196), Abu al-Barakat al-Nasafi (died 1310), and Ibn Nujaym (died 1563). For these authors, the works of Shaybani, known collectively as *zahir al-riwaya*, remained authoritative; they are *al-Mabsut, al-Jami al-Kabir, al-Jami al-Saghir, al-Siyar al-Kabir, al-Siyar al-Saghir,* and *al-Ziyadat.* The most prominent legal theorists (*usuliyyun*) of the school are Pazdawi (died 1089), Sarakhsi, Nasafi, Sadr al-Shariʿa al-Thani al-Mahbubi (died 1346), and Mulla Khusraw (died 1480).

In 1876, the Hanafi law of contracts, obligations, and procedure was codified in the Ottoman law code of Mecelle, in an effort to modernize the law and to achieve uniformity in its application. The primary source on which the Committee of the Mecelle based its work was Shaybani's collected works, *zahir al-riwaya*, with the commentary on it by Sarakhsi, an eleventh-century Hanafi. In the first few decades of the twentieth century, however, the Mecelle was superseded by civil codes in all the countries that fell previously under Ottoman jurisdiction, with the notable exception of Jordan.

In medieval times, the school had a large following in its birthplace, Iraq, as well as in Syria, Transoxania (now Uzbekistan, a former Soviet Republic), the Indian subcontinent, the Mediterranean island of Sicily, and to a lesser extent in North Africa. Later on, the Ottoman Empire declared Hanafism the official doctrine of the state, thus rendering it dominant in all areas that fell under its sway. In modern times, Hanafism still prevails in these regions as well as in Afghanistan, the Balkans, Pakistan, Turkistan, the Caucasus (between the Black and Caspian Seas), India, and China.

Bibliography

Mahmassani, Subhi. *The Philosophy of Jurisprudence in Islam*, translated by Farhat J. Ziadeh. Leiden, Netherlands: Brill, 1961.

Schacht, Joseph. *The Origins of Muhammadan Jurisprudence.* Oxford: Clarendon Press, 1975.

WAEL B. HALLAQ

HANANU, IBRAHIM
[1869–1935]

Syrian nationalist.

Ibrahim Hananu was born in Kafr Takharim, a fertile olive-growing area west of Aleppo, to a wealthy rural family of Kurdish extraction. He studied at the prestigious Mülkiye school of public administration in Istanbul. Later he joined the bureaucracy of the Ottoman Empire, only to retire and manage his estates. Having embraced nationalism when the Arab Revolt broke out in 1916, Hananu joined the Arab army of Faisal I ibn Hussein and entered Aleppo with the Allies in 1918. He also joined the secret nationalist society al-Fatat and, with the support of prominent merchants in Aleppo, he founded the League of National Defense and the Arab Club of Aleppo.

Under the influence of Hananu, the Muslim elite of Aleppo gradually assumed an Arab national identity, which was reinforced by the Hananu revolt. Breaking out in the autumn of 1919 in the countryside surrounding Aleppo, the months before French forces occupied the city, the Hananu revolt received aid from the Turkish nationalist movement of Mustafa Kemal Atatürk, which was

battling the French army of the Levant for control of Cilicia and southern Anatolia. With the withdrawal of Turkish military assistance following the signing of the Franklin-Bouillon Agreement in October 1921, Hananu and his men could no longer sustain a revolt, and their struggle collapsed.

Hananu continued to play an active role in the Syrian national movement. He was one of the founding fathers of the National Bloc, which emerged from the Beirut conference of October 1927, and which steered the course of the independence struggle in Syria until its completion nineteen years later. After his death, Hananu's house in Aleppo was used by Syrian nationalists as a "house of the nation."

See also ALEPPO; ARAB REVOLT (1916); FATAT, AL-; NATIONAL BLOC.

Bibliography

Khoury, Philip S. *Syria and the French Mandate: The Politics of Arab Nationalism, 1920–1945.* Princeton, NJ: Princeton University Press, 1987.

MUHAMMAD MUSLIH
UPDATED BY MICHAEL R. FISCHBACH

HANBALI SCHOOL OF LAW

One of the four approaches to Sunni Muslim law, called schools.

The Hanbali School of Law takes its name from Ahmad ibn Hanbal (died 854), a major theologian of the ninth century. He was a fierce opponent of the Mu'tazila, a school of religious thought that flourished under the Abbasids. Ibn Hanbal emerged victorious in the *mihna* (inquisition), led by the Abbasid caliph al-Ma'mun and the rationalist theologians against the traditionalists who upheld the doctrine that the Qur'an is not the created but the eternal word of God. Ibn Hanbal's career as a dogmatic theologian, coupled with the fact that he did not elaborate a complete system of law, gave him and his immediate followers the reputation of being a theological rather than a legal school *(madhhab).* Indeed, the school's first complete work on positive law, *al-Mukhtasar,* appeared as late as the beginning of the tenth century, at the hands of Abu Qasim al-Khiraqi (died 946).

Being strict traditionalists, the Hanbalis of the ninth century rejected the rationalist elements of what had by the end of the century become the mainstream legal theory *(usul al-fiqh)*. Later Hanbalis, however, gradually adopted the main elements of this theory, and by the eleventh century, their legal theory finally came to accept *usul al-fiqh* as elaborated by the Shafi'i School of Law and Hanafi School of Law. Thus, it took the Hanbali school nearly two centuries after ibn Hanbal's demise to develop into a full-fledged school of law.

Two centuries later, the celebrated Hanbali jurist and theologian Taqi al-Din ibn Taymiyya (died 1328) even subscribed to a theory of *istihsan* (juristic preference), advocated by later Hanafis and vehemently opposed by early traditionalist Shafi'is and Hanbalis.

There were several figures who dominated the history of Hanbalism. Among the prominent names are al-Khiraqi, Ibn al-Farra, Ibn Aqil, Abd al-Qadir al-Jili (died 1166), Abu al-Faraj ibn al-Jawzi (died 1200), Ibn Taymiyya, and his disciple Ibn Qayyim al-Jawziyya (died 1351), to name only a few. Distinguished as a major figure in Islamic religious history, Ibn Taymiyya was involved in the study of law, theology, philosophy, and mysticism and was engaged in the politics of the Mamluk state. He wrote at length against the Shi'a, the philosophers, the logicians, and the pantheistic Sufis, though he himself belonged to the mystical school of Abd al-Qadir al-Jili.

Ibn Taymiyya's thought exercised significant influence on Muhammad ibn Abd al-Wahhab (died 1792), who, with the assistance of Ibn Sa'ud, founded Wahhabism, an ideology that has sustained the Saudi state during the last two centuries. Saudi Arabia remains the principal country that applies Hanbali law. Nevertheless, the writings of ibn Taymiyya and ibn Abd al-Wahhab still continue to influence the Muslim reform and religious movements in the Middle East, from Rashid Rida (died 1935) to the Muslim Brotherhood.

See also ABD AL-AZIZ IBN SA'UD AL SA'UD; ABD AL-WAHHAB, MUHAMMAD IBN; HANAFI SCHOOL OF LAW; MUSLIM BROTHERHOOD; RIDA, RASHID; SHAFI'I SCHOOL OF LAW.

Bibliography

Makdisi, George. "Hanbalite Islam." In *Studies on Islam,* translated and edited by Merlin L. Swartz. New York: Oxford University Press, 1981.

WAEL B. HALLAQ

HAND OF FATIMA

A folk motif.

European name for the *khamsa* (from Arabic, "five"), the hand with five fingers extended. It can be found today throughout the Middle East in women's jewelry, flat-weaving, embroidery, door-knockers, automobile ornamentation, and so on. Precursors include the Punic "Hand of Baal" and the Roman V-shaped amulets (possibly representing the Roman numeral five), all for protection from the evil eye.

LAURENCE MICHALAK

HANOUNE, LOUISA
[1954–]

Leader of the radical Workers Party, deputy in the national assembly, and women's and human rights advocate in Algeria.

Born to a poor peasant family, Louisa Hanoune was the first girl in her family to go to school. Overcoming considerable hardship, she earned a law degree at the University of Annaba in 1979. She entered politics by joining the clandestine Socialist Workers Organization (Organisation Socialiste des Travailleurs; OST), a Trotskyist party. Arrested in December 1983 for her political activities, she was released in May 1984 and became the first secretary-general of the Association for Equality before the Law of Men and Women as well as a founding member of the Algerian Human Rights League.

Once a multiparty system was instituted, OST became the Workers Party (PT) with Hanoune serving as its spokesperson. She opposed the army's cancellation of the 1991 elections, and in 1995 signed the Platform of Rome, urging negotiations with the Islamist movement as a way to end the civil war. An outspoken advocate of democracy in Algeria, Hanoune won election to parliament in 1997, one of four PT deputies. In 2002, she led her party to a stronger showing, winning twenty-one seats while continuing her vehement criticism of the Bouteflika government. Her political ideas are spelled out in her book *Une autre voix pour l'Algérie* (1996). A feminist and social critic, she is the first woman to lead an Algerian political party.

See also ALGERIA; ARAB SOCIALISM; GIA (ARMED ISLAMIC GROUPS).

ROBERT MORTIMER

HAQ, AL-

A Palestinian human rights organization.

Al-Haq was established in 1979 in Ramallah, the West Bank, by two prominent lawyers, Raja Shehadeh and Jonathan Kuttab. Initially it was known as Law in the Service of Man. For at least a decade, it became the leading human rights and legal services organization in the Occupied Territories, on which many in the Western media and human rights organizations relied on for information—found in its numerous publications—on Israeli violations of international law and human rights during Israel's occupation of the West Bank and Gaza. In addition, through its staff and library, al-Haq is a legal resource center for the Palestinian community. It is affiliated with the International Commission of Jurists in Geneva, Switzerland.

See also HUMAN RIGHTS.

MICHAEL R. FISCHBACH

HARAM

See GLOSSARY

HARAM AL-SHARIF

Third holiest site in Islam.

Al-Haram al-Sharif (the noble sanctuary), also known as the Temple Mount, is the third holiest site in Islam. It is located in the southeastern part of the Old City of Jerusalem. Built between 685 and 709 C.E., it is an enclosure on a raised platform that includes two renowned holy sites: the Qubbat al-Sakhra (the Dome of the Rock) and al-Aqsa mosque. The Dome of the Rock is where Jews believe that Abraham attempted to sacrifice his son, Isaac, to God, and where Muslims believe that the prophet Muhammad ascended to heaven. He is believed to have tethered his "fabulous steed," al-Buraq, in an area located in the interior portion of the Western Wall of the Temple Mount. Close by is al-Aqsa mosque, which is regarded as the place in the Qurʾan where Muhammad prayed following his "night journey," and it was the direction for prayer *(qibla)* for Muslims before it was changed to Mecca. The subterranean areas of the Haram include a large vault, known as Solomon's Stables, now a mosque. Al-

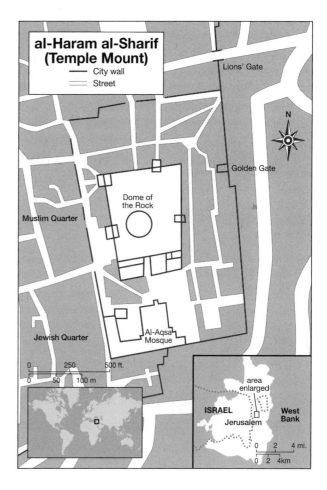

MAP BY XNR PRODUCTIONS, INC. THE GALE GROUP.

though much repaired and restored by the Romans and in the Middle Ages, the vault is a Herodian creation and is thought to be part of the original Jewish Temple, built in 970 B.C.E. The exterior wall of the enclosure to the west, the Western or Wailing Wall (in Hebrew, *ha-Kotel ha-Maʿaravi*), is the holiest site in Judaism.

The Haram played a significant role in the history of Jerusalem. As a site of veneration it attracted pilgrims, scholars, and benefactors from all parts of the Islamic world. Much real estate and arable land was endowed for the upkeep of schools, orphanages, mosques, prayer-rooms, and hostels, either inside the enclosure itself or nearby, creating an Islamic center for learning, ritual devotions, and good works. During the early twentieth century, tensions in the city between the predominantly Muslim and growing Jewish populations erupted into rioting over access and use of these holy places; the most notorious were the Western Wall Disturbances in 1929. Since the Israeli occupation of East Jerusalem in 1967, activities emanating from the Haram have played a pivotal role in preserving an Islamic and Palestinian presence in the Old City in the face of attempts by Israeli settler groups and government agencies to transfer ownership of the site to Israel. During the negotiations that followed the 1993 Oslo Accords, the future of the Haram was left unresolved. In September 2000 a visit to the Haram by the Likud Party leader, Ariel Sharon, provoked a violent clash that led to an uprising, since dubbed the al-Aqsa Intifada, that contributed to the collapse of negotiations.

See also AQSA INTIFADA, AL-; JERUSALEM; WESTERN WALL; WESTERN WALL DISTURBANCES.

Bibliography

Arif, Arif al-. *A Brief Guide to the Dome of the Rock and al-Haram al-Sharif.* Jerusalem: Industrial Islamic Orphanage Press, 1964.

Dumper, Michael. *The Politics of Sacred Space: The Old City of Jerusalem in the Middle East Conflict.* Boulder, CO: Lynne Rienner Publishers, 2002.

Duncan, Alistair. *The Noble Sanctuary: Portrait of a Holy Place in Arab Jerusalem.* London: Middle East Archive, 1981.

Peters, Francis. *Jerusalem.* Princeton, NJ: Princeton University Press, 1985.

Wasserstein, Bernard. *The British in Palestine: The Mandatory Government and the Arab–Jewish Conflict, 1917–1929.* Oxford, U.K.: Basil Blackwell, 1991.

MICHAEL DUMPER

HAREL, ISSER
[1912–2003]

"Little Isser," the second and most powerful head of Israeli Mossad, considered to be the founder of the country's intelligence community.

Born Isser Halperin in Russia, Harel emigrated in 1931 with his family to Palestine, where he was among the founders of Kibbutz Shefayim. He served in the Haganah and with the British coast guard during World War II. In 1944 Harel was appointed secretary of the "Jewish Department" of the Haganah's intelligence service (Shai), and was responsible for counterespionage and for operations against "dissident" Jewish underground groups, the

Irgun Zvaʾi Leʾumi and LEHI. His ruthless successes endeared Harel to Prime Minister David Ben-Gurion, and he rose from Tel Aviv district commander of the Shai (1947) to head the newly formed General Security Service (Shin Bet, or Shabak, 1948–1952), replacing Reuven Shiloah as head of the Mossad and becoming *memuneh* ("the one in charge") of all Israeli intelligence agencies (1953–1963).

While maintaining extensive (and often criticized) internal surveillance, primarily of the pro-Soviet left, the fiercely anticommunist Harel also developed a powerful international intelligence operations network. He was credited with the exposure of several Soviet spies, including Yisrael Beer. He orchestrated the capture of Adolf Eichmann in Argentina in 1960, and he oversaw the beginnings of Israel's "periphery doctrine," forging ties with non-Arab Middle Eastern regimes such Turkey, Iran, and Ethiopia.

Harel left office in April 1963 following a bitter dispute with Ben-Gurion and the Israel Defense Force (IDF) and with military intelligence chief Meir Amit over operations against the German rocket scientists in Egypt and elsewhere. He briefly coordinated Levi Eshkol's intelligence apparatus in 1965 and 1966, when he was accused of working to undermine Amit, his successor as Mossad chief. He later won a seat in the eighth Knesset (parliament) on the Rafi Party list. He authored several books on episodes of his career and Israeli security.

See also BEN-GURION, DAVID; MOSSAD; SHILOAH, REUVEN.

Bibliography

Black, Ian, and Morris, Benny. *Israel's Secret Wars: A History of Israel's Intelligence Services.* New York: Grove Press, 1991.

Harel, Isser. *The House on Garibaldi Street,* 2d edition. London: Frank Cass, 1997.

ZEV MAGHEN
UPDATED BY IAN BLACK

HAREM

The women's section of a home.

In Arabic, the word *haram* refers to that which is forbidden, and *harim,* or *harem,* means the women's section of a home, which is forbidden to males who are not unrelated to the household. This prohibition is maintained in order to protect female kin and family honor. Veiling and the seclusion of women are part of an ancient Middle Eastern social pattern that predates Islam and originated in antiquity with the rise of classes, cities, and states. The wives of the prophet Muhammad were secluded, yet played important public roles during and after his life. In Muslim societies where sexual segregation is practiced, women may form their closest bonds in the harem. Women who are relatives, friends, or neighbors visit in the secluded section of each other's homes. The streets in the traditional Arab-Muslim city are generally the province of men.

It is within the social setting of the harem where important family-related decisions are made informally. For example, marriages may be arranged first among women before they are negotiated by male kin. Within the harem, it would be determined whether a young woman is interested in and consents to a suggested marriage before any public announcement would occur.

See also CLOTHING; GENDER: GENDER AND LAW; GENDER: GENDER AND POLITICS; *HIJAB.*

Bibliography

Ahmed, Leila. *Women and Gender in Islam.* New Haven, CT: Yale University Press, 1992.

Fluehr-Lobban, Carolyn. *Islamic Society in Practice.* Gainesville: University Press of Florida, 1994.

CAROLYN FLUEHR-LOBBAN

HAREVEN, SHULAMIT
[c. 1931–]

Hebrew novelist, poet, essayist, journalist, and activist.

Shulamit Hareven was born in Warsaw, Poland. When World War II broke out, her family was smuggled through Europe and in 1940 settled in Jerusalem, where Hareven still lived in 2004. The memory of this escape was responsible for Hareven's belief in self-defense. She served in the Haganah underground and was a combat medic during the siege of Jerusalem in Israel's War of Independence; later she took part in founding the Israel Defense Force radio. In the fifties, she became an officer and worked in the Jewish refugee camps, especially those with Jews from Arab countries. She was a military correspondent before and during the Yom Kippur War. Hareven was the first woman member of the Academy of the Hebrew Language. She was also a longtime member of the spokesteam of the Peace Now movement, and during the first Palestinian Intifada entered Arab refugee camps and reported to the Israeli press. She worked as a columnist on current social, cultural, and political events.

Hareven published seventeen books of poetry, fiction, and essays, in addition to her latest autobiography, *Yamim Rabim* (Many days), published in Hebrew in 2002. Her first novel, *City of Many Days* (1972), depicts Jerusalem of the British mandate with great compassion, intimate understanding, and poetic richness. Hareven's Jerusalem is a detailed, colorful, and intricate tapestry woven of Arab, British, Sephardic, and European Jewish characters. The novel is also a "coming of age" story of a strong, autonomous woman. Its feminist sensibilities, although ambivalent, represent a first in Israeli literature. The novel, largely dismissed when it first appeared, was ahead of its time in terms of both its feminism and its implicit critique of Zionist ideology. Hareven wrote two novellas set in biblical times, *The Miracle Hater* (1983) and *Prophet* (1989), employing a concise, laconic, biblical style. An avid advocate of human rights, she writes in her essays and articles about Jews and Arabs, new immigrants and Israelis, and declares herself a "selective feminist." In 1995, the French magazine *L'express* elected Hareven as one of the one hundred women "who move the world."

See also INTIFADA (1987–1991); PEACE NOW.

Bibliography

Feldman, Yael. "Feminism under Siege: The Vicarious Selves of Israeli Women Writers." *Prooftexts* 10 (1990).

Hareven, Shulamit. *Thirst: The Desert Trilogy,* translated by Hillel Halkin with the author. San Francisco, CA: Mercury House, 1996.

Hareven, Shulamit. *The Vocabulary of Peace: Life, Culture, and Politics in the Middle East.* San Francisco, CA: Mercury House, 1995.

NILI GOLD
UPDATED BY ADINA FRIEDMAN

Lebanon's wealthy prime minister, Rafiq Baha'uddin al Hariri, built his financial empire from scratch, founding a small construction company in the 1970s that frequently garnered work from the Saudi royal family. Hariri served as prime minister from 1989–1998 and was selected for the post again in the 2000 parliamentary elections. © AP/WIDE WORLD PHOTOS. REPRODUCED BY PERMISSION.

HARIRI, RAFIQ BAHA'UDDIN AL-
[1945–]

Saudi businessman, philanthropist, and prime minister of Lebanon from 1989 to 1998.

Rafiq Baha'uddin al-Hariri was born in Sidon, Lebanon. At an early age, he helped support his family by working in the orchards. He graduated from the Arab University of Beirut in 1965 and found work as a mathematics teacher in Jidda, Saudi Arabia. He soon joined a Saudi engineering firm as an accountant and in 1970 founded a small construction company.

His relationship with the Saudi royal family began in 1977, when he completed a palace project in al-Ta'if for King Khalid ibn Abd al-Aziz Al Sa'ud within the low bid originally proposed and in record

time. Henceforth, Hariri was sought for most of the Ministry of Finance's contracting bids. He became a naturalized Saudi citizen and expanded his global business to include ownership of Paris's Entreprise Oger and the Luxembourg-based Mediterranée Investors Group.

From the early days of his financial success, Hariri assisted his native Sidon by offering educational grants and building a hospital and university in nearby Kafr Falus, although his critics have always believed that his philanthropy was politically motivated as it helped propel him to the highest post occupied by Sunnis in the government. After the Israeli invasion of Lebanon in 1982, he provided some aid for reconstruction while also providing financial support for divergent militias in the country. He also enjoyed direct Saudi political backing and established a close relationship with the Syrian political and military elite. He played an active political role in Lebanon, helping to bring about the 1989 Ta'if Accord under Saudi auspices, after which he became prime minister. His foundation, which had supplied loans and grants to needy students, ceased to exist after his election. He continued as prime minister until 1998, when the new president, Emile Lahhud, selected Salim al-Hoss for the post. Hariri stayed out of office for two years but won a landslide election to the Lebanese parliament in 2000, after which he was again named prime minister. He is associated with Lebanon's burgeoning foreign debt, which reached $32 billion on his watch, and with the privatization efforts he championed.

See also ARAB–ISRAEL WAR (1982); HOSS, SALIM AL-; KHALID IBN ABD AL-AZIZ AL SA'UD; LEBANON.

Bibliography

Dagher, Carole H. *Bring Down the Walls: Lebanon's Post-War Challenge*. New York: St. Martin's Press, 2000.

BASSAM NAMANI
UPDATED BY AS'AD ABUKHALIL

HARKABI, YEHOSHAFAT
[1921–1994]

Senior Israeli intelligence officer; professor.

Harkabi Yehoshafat was born in Haifa in 1921. He studied philosophy, history, and Arabic at the Hebrew University of Jerusalem, interrupting his studies to volunteer in the British Army. After demobilization in 1946, he attended a school to prepare future diplomats for the Jewish state. During the 1948 war, Harkabi fought in Jerusalem as commander of a students' company. In 1949, he participated in the negotiations that led to the signing of armistice agreements with Egypt and Jordan, and twice met personally with King Abdullah. After a short stint in the ministry of foreign affairs, he returned to military service and spent a year studying in Paris. In 1955, he was named chief of the intelligence division of the Israel Defense Force General Staff with the rank of major general. During this period, Fati, as he was nicknamed, enjoyed the confidence of important personalities like David Ben-Gurion, Moshe Sharett, and Moshe Dayan. He was instrumental in weaving secret relations with the French military and intelligence services during the 1956 Suez War. In 1959, he was forced to retire from active service in the wake of an ill-advised public reserve call-up exercise.

Harkabi then spent several years in the United States and earned a Ph.D. from Harvard University. As a professor at the Hebrew University in Jerusalem, he became a renowned expert in Middle Eastern studies, strategic studies, and international relations theory. His first book, written before the June 1967 Arab–Israel War and published shortly afterwards (in Hebrew and English), was titled *Arab Attitudes to Israel.* In it, he analyzed the growing hatred in the Arab world of Israel and of Jews, and presented a pessimistic view of the intractability of the conflict because of those hostile attitudes.

Soon after the June 1967 war, Harkabi changed his views and considered the situation created by the war as an opportunity for peace. In numerous publications, he advocated a dovish stance, recommending a full withdrawal from territories occupied in 1967. He became a sort of a guru for the Israeli peace movement but nevertheless remained on good terms with the Labor Party elite and especially with Yitzhak Rabin, who sought his advice on many occasions. Harkabi died of cancer on 26 August 1994.

See also ABDULLAH I IBN HUSSEIN; ARAB–ISRAEL WAR (1967); BEN-GURION, DAVID; DAYAN, MOSHE; RABIN, YITZHAK; SHARETT, MOSHE; SUEZ CRISIS (1956–1957).

Bibliography

Harkabi, Yehoshafat. *Arab Attitudes to Israel,* translated by Misha Louvish. New York: Hart, 1972.

Harkabi, Yehoshafat. *Arab Strategies and Israel's Response.* New York: Free Press, 1977.

Harkabi, Yehoshafat. *The Bar Kokhba Syndrome: Risk and Realism in International Politics,* translated by Max D. Ticktin. Chappaqua, NY: Rossel, 1982.

Harkabi, Yehoshafat. *Israel's Fateful Hour,* translated by Lenn Schramm. New York: Harper and Row, 1988.

MORDECHAI BAR-ON

HARKIS

Pro-French Algerians during the war of independence (1954–1962); also known as French Muslims.

Harkis is derived from the Arabic *harakat,* meaning "military movement" or "operation." Since the beginning of French colonialism in Algeria in July 1830, local people served as military auxiliaries. During the Algerian War of Independence (1954–1962), approximately 100,000 *harkis* served France in various capacities (e.g., regular French army, militia self-defense units, police, and paramilitary self-defense units). Their most prominent leader was the Benaïssa Boulam. After the war, many *harkis* left for France, but the majority remained in Algeria and faced brutal retributions.

Those in France found inadequate housing conditions (often in isolated relocation camps) and a lack of educational and economic opportunities. This provoked a variety of protests by these forgotten French citizens, ranging from hunger strikes and kidnappings in the 1970s to violence in the 1990s. The French government issued a stamp in 1990 to honor the *harkis'* contribution, which elicited official protest from Algeria. The population of the French–Muslim community is about 475,000. In France, they remain second-class citizens, are victims of discrimination, and are often confused with the emigrant worker community. It is still unsafe for *harki* veterans to visit Algeria, but their children and descendants are welcome.

See also ALGERIAN WAR OF INDEPENDENCE.

PHILLIP C. NAYLOR

HARRATIN

*A group of people in northwest Africa generally of low
social status.*

In Arabic, *hartani* (singular); in Berber, *ahardan* (singular) and *ihardanan* (plural); in the Twareg dialect,
ashardan. The *harratin* inhabit the oases of the Saharan regions. Ethnically, this population is a mixture
of people originating from sub-Saharan Africa and
North Africa; they were formerly slaves before being freed. Although they are no longer slaves, they
constitute a sort of caste considered by other populations as inferior, below the status of *bidan* and
shorfa groups in Mauritania. Because of their low status, the *harratin* seek protection among powerful
families for which they work and show respect.

Since land and water are owned by white *shorfa*
and because *harratin* occupy the lowest position on
the social scale, the *harratin* do not witness any social
mobility. They work in less prestigious occupations:
When they are sedentaries, they work in agriculture;
when they emigrate to the cities, they work as carriers of water, diggers of wells, and ironworkers; and
among the nomads they work as shepherds.

In Morocco, the Sultan Mulay Isma'il (eighteenth century) recruited his famous army of *bukhari*
from the *harratin* population of Mauritania. This
group had also provided the traditional Moroccan
state (Makhzen) with secretaries and functionaries.
Families in imperial cities in Morocco such as Fez,
Marrakech, and Meknes used to have *hartani* women
under their protection working as servants.

In vernacular language, after the progressive
disappearance of slavery, the words *harratin* and *hartani* have replaced the word *abd* (slave) to mean
"black" and have acquired a pejorative meaning.

See also SHORFA.

RAHMA BOURQIA

HARRIMAN, W. AVERELL
[1891–1986]

U.S. diplomat.

While ambassador in Moscow (1943–1946) during
World War II (1939–1945), W. Averell Harriman
became concerned with the USSR's involvement in
Iran and advocated U.S. support for Iran's shah,

Mohammad Reza Pahlavi. In July 1951, Harriman
was U.S. President Harry S. Truman's special envoy to Iran's Prime Minister Mohammad Mossadegh,
and Harriman tried unsuccessfully to persuade
Mossadegh to compromise with Britain over nationalization of the Anglo–Iranian Oil Company.
Harriman respected Mossadegh as a genuine nationalist and counseled against intervention by
Britain or the United States to remove him.

Harriman was elected governor of New York
(1955–1958) but returned to national politics in the
Kennedy and Johnson administrations. In 1965, as
undersecretary of state, he was sent to Jerusalem to
inform the government of Israel that the United
States intended to sell arms to Jordan. Harriman
was later one of the chief negotiators in ending the
Vietnam War.

See also ANGLO–IRANIAN OIL COMPANY;
MOSSADEGH, MOHAMMAD; PAHLAVI, MO-
HAMMAD REZA.

Bibliography

Bill, James, and Louis, William Roger, eds. *Musaddiq,
Iranian Nationalism, and Oil*. Austin: University of Texas
Press, 1988.

Findling, John, ed. *Dictionary of American Diplomatic History*,
2d edition. New York: Greenwood Press, 1989.

Spiegel, Steven L. *The Other Arab–Israeli Conflict: Making America's Middle East Policy, from Truman to Reagan*. Chicago:
University of Chicago Press, 1985.

ZACHARY KARABELL

HASA, AL-

*An area in Saudi Arabia's Eastern Province noted for
agriculture and oil resources.*

Originally, al-Hasa was the name given to a series
of oases about 40 miles inland from the Persian
Gulf in eastern Arabia; its largest town and capital
was al-Hufuf. It later denoted a province of Saudi
Arabia stretching from Kuwait in the north to Qatar
in the south, separated from Najd by the al-Dahna
sand belt, and including the other important oasis
region on the coast around Qatif. Today the region
is called the Eastern Province.

As the largest groundwater-fed oasis in the
world, al-Hasa historically has been an important
agricultural region, noted for dates, grains, fruits,

vegetables, and its famous white donkeys. It also has been a center for administration and trade, with a population divided evenly between Sunnis and Shi'a. One of the region's few strategic and economic prizes even before the oil era, al-Hasa has been controlled from al-Hufuf in the past two centuries by Ottomans, Egyptians, the Bani Khalid tribe, and the Al Sa'ud family.

With the discovery of massive oil fields in the region, large-scale economic development and dislocations followed, sometimes resulting in labor unrest. Although agriculture suffered when field workers left to work in the oil industry, new revenues eventually were used to improve irrigation systems, prevent sand encroachment, and improve technology.

See also AL SA'UD FAMILY; ARABIAN AMERICAN OIL COMPANY (ARAMCO).

Bibliography

Vidal, F. S. "Al-Hasa." In *Encyclopedia of Islam, New Edition*, vol. 3, edited by B. Lewis, V. L. Ménage, C. Pellat, and J. Schacht. Leiden: Brill, 1971.

Vidal, F. S. *The Oasis of al-Hasa.* Dhahran, Saudi Arabia: Aramco, 1955.

MALCOLM C. PECK
UPDATED BY ANTHONY B. TOTH

HASAN, FA'IQ
[1919–]

Iraqi artist.

One of Iraq's leading and most influential visual artists during the second half of the twentieth century, Fa'iq Hasan was born in Baghdad and educated in its Institute of Fine Art (which, after 1939, added painting and sculpture to music). He later spent a few years studying art in Paris. In 1950 he established Jama'at al-Ruwwad (the avant-garde group), also called Société Primitive. This was the first art circle in Iraq to be inspired by ancient Mesopotamian and Iraqi themes and that adopted modern styles. Hasan started off with impressionist landscapes but since the 1950s has changed both subject matter and style. While the subject matter of his paintings is local, describing bedouin and other country life, or still life, the style is cubist with strong French influences. Some of his paintings are in the primitive style. He and his group experi-

mented with color planes, and many of his later works are abstract.

AMATZIA BARAM

HASAN, HANI AL-
[1937–2003]

Palestinian politician.

Born in Haifa like his brother Khalid, Hani al-Hasan was educated at the University of Darmstadt, West Germany, after the family fled as refugees in 1948. He graduated with a degree in construction engineering. While studying, he led the General Union of Palestine Students. He joined al-Fatah in 1963, became a member of its central committee, and rose to become one of its leading figures. By 1967 he was Fatah's leader in Europe, and he became the group's chief contact with China. Al-Hasan also was appointed deputy to Salah Khalaf (Abu Iyad) in Fatah's powerful intelligence service.

Although he became a senior advisor to Yasir Arafat, head of both Fatah and the Palestine Liberation Organization, al-Hasan criticized both Arafat's handling of the Gulf Crisis of 1990–1991 and the 1993 Oslo Accord. He moved to the Palestinian Authority (PA) in 1995 and continued his dissent, although he later served in the PA cabinet and became embroiled in the rivalry between Arafat and PA Prime Minister Mahmud Abbas during the spring and summer of 2003.

Bibliography

Cobban, Helena. *The Palestinian Liberation Organisation: People, Power, and Politics.* New York and Cambridge, U.K.: Cambridge University Press, 1984.

Fischbach, Michael R. "Hani al-Hasan." In *Encyclopedia of the Palestinians,* edited by Philip Mattar. New York: Facts On File, 2000.

Sayigh, Yezid. *Armed Struggle and the Search for State: The Palestinian National Movement, 1949–1993.* New York: Oxford University Press; Oxford: Clarendon Press, 1997.

LAWRENCE TAL
UPDATED BY MICHAEL R. FISCHBACH

HASANI, TAJ AL-DIN AL-
[1890–1943]

President of Syria under French mandate.

Taj al-Din al-Hasani was born in Damascus to a North African family. In 1912, he was appointed instructor of religion at the Sultaniyya school in Damascus. Al-Hasani was a member of the Council for School Reform and the General Assembly for the *vilayet* of Syria. He was also an owner of the newspaper *al-Sharq*, which was first published in 1916 with support from the Fourth Ottoman Army. Under the rule of King Faisal I, he was appointed member of the council of state *(majlis shura)*, the court of appeal, and then judge in Damascus. Al-Hasani taught principles of Islamic jurisprudence *(fiqh)* at the Institute of Arab Law in Damascus. Under the French mandate, al-Hasani was prime minister from 1928 to 1931 and from 1934 to 1936. He then resigned and traveled to France where he remained until the French appointed him head of the Syrian republic in 1941. He stayed in power until his death in 1943.

See also FAISAL I IBN HUSSEIN; FIQH.

GEORGE E. IRANI

HASAN, KHALID AL-
[1928–1994]

Palestinian politician.

The brother of Hani al-Hasan, Khalid al-Hasan was born in Haifa and fled with his family as refugees in 1948. Thereafter he was active in the Islamic political party Hizb al-Tahrir in Syria, but he moved to Kuwait in 1952 and remained there most of his life. He helped Yasir Arafat and others found al-Fatah during the late 1950s and served in the group's leadership bodies for the rest of his life. Al-Hasan also sat on the Palestine Liberation Organization (PLO) Executive Committee and its Political Department from 1969 to 1973. A noted diplomat, he later directed the Palestine National Council's foreign relations committee until 1994.

Al-Hasan was often at odds with Arafat during their long association and definitively parted company with him in 1990 in opposition to the PLO's support of Iraqi President Saddam Hussein. His opposition to Arafat, and to the latter's handling of the 1993 Oslo Accord, was cut short by his death in October 1994.

Bibliography

Cobban, Helena. *The Palestinian Liberation Organisation: People, Power, and Politics.* New York and Cambridge, U.K.: Cambridge University Press, 1984.

Rabbani, Mouin. "Khalid al-Hasan." In *Encyclopedia of the Palestinians,* edited by Philip Mattar. New York: Facts On File, 2000.

LAWRENCE TAL
UPDATED BY MICHAEL R. FISCHBACH

HASAN SALIM

See SALIM HASAN

HASHEMI, FAEZEH
[1962–]

Iranian advocate for women's rights.

Faezeh Hashemi, the younger daughter of former Iranian president Ali Akbar Hashemi Rafsanjani, was born in 1962. She has a B.A. in political science and physical science and is the founder and president of the Islamic Countries' Solidarity Sport Council, vice president of Iran's National Olympic Committee, and a member of the Islamic Republic's High Council for Women's Sport. Because of her advocacy of women's sports, especially outdoor cycling, against condemnation by traditionalists, Hashemi became tremendously popular with women and young people, and she received the second highest number of votes in Tehran's 1996 legislative elections for the Fifth Majles (parliament). During the electoral campaign she criticized discriminatory laws, which she argued hinder women's progress, but did not advocate a quota system for women. In 1997 she played an important role in Mohammad Khatami's electoral campaign. In the summer of 1998 she launched a newspaper called *Zan* (Woman) that paid particular attention to women's and youths' issues and grievances. It was closed down in March 1999 by the Revolutionary Court for publishing a message from Iran's former empress, Farah Diba, on the occasion of the Iranian New Year, and for printing a cartoon that ridiculed the law on blood money. (The law on blood money permits one who has caused loss of life to avoid capital punishment by providing monetary compensation to the family of the victim. The blood money for women is half of that of men.) She was a candidate for the 2000 legislative elections, but because she sided with her father against the reformers, she lost popular support and was not elected.

See also GENDER: GENDER AND POLITICS; RAFSANJANI, ALI AKBAR HASHEMI.

Bibliography

Kian, Azadeh. "Women and Politics in Post-Islamist Iran: The Gender Conscious Drive to Change," *British Journal of Middle Eastern Studies* 24, no. 1, (1997): 75–96.

AZADEH KIAN-THIÉBAUT

HASHIM, IBRAHIM
[1888–1958]

Head of the Executive Council and prime minister of Jordan several times, starting in 1933.

Ibrahim Hashim accompanied Amir Abdullah I ibn Hussein to the 1946 negotiations in London to abolish the mandate and renegotiate the Anglo–Jordanian treaty. Thus he was the first prime minister of the newly independent kingdom when the Legislative Assembly (precursor to the parliament) proclaimed King Abdullah a constitutional monarch on 25 May 1946. Hashim was also a leading member of the three-man Crown Council, then the Regency Council, which ruled Jordan briefly between May and August 1952 following the abdication of King Talal. He was in Baghdad as the deputy prime minister of the joint Jordanian–Iraqi cabinet of the newly formed Arab Federation—a short-lived union between Jordan and Iraq that was formed on 14 February 1958 in response to rising pan-Arab sentiment and to forestall pressures on the conservative monarchies that were likely to result after the planned merger of Egypt and Syria. Hashim was killed during mob violence in Baghdad at the outbreak of the Iraqi revolution in May 1958.

See also ABDULLAH I IBN HUSSEIN; TALAL IBN ABDULLAH.

JENAB TUTUNJI

HASHIMI, TAHA AL-
[1888–1961]

Iraqi officer, politician, teacher, and author.

Taha al-Hashimi was born into a Sunni Arab Muslim family of limited means. He attended school in

Baghdad and was graduated from military college in Constantinople (now Istanbul). He served in the Ottoman army in various capacities and reached the rank of lieutenant colonel. He joined the al-Ahd society, formed in 1913 by Aziz al-Misri. Although the members of Ahd were mostly Ottoman officers of Iraqi origin, Hashimi remained loyal to the Ottomans and did not undertake any activities against them during World War I. He worked with the Faisal government in Syria (1919–1920) as director of defense, then returned to Iraq at the urging of his brother, Yasin al-Hashimi, who played a leading role in Iraq's politics in the 1920s and 1930s. Hashimi held various civilian posts in the newly established government, including director of the Census Bureau, director of education, and tutor to Prince Ghazi ibn Faisal. In 1930, he returned to the army, was appointed commander in chief, and then promoted to the rank of general. In 1936 the acting chief of staff, General Bakr Sidqi, executed a military coup against Prime Minister Yasin al-Hashimi. This marked the first military interference in Iraq's modern history.

Hashimi returned to Iraq following a coup launched in 1937. As minister of defense in 1938 and 1939, he acted as an intermediary among the nationalist elements of the army, in particular among the four colonels known as the Golden Square, who played an important role in Iraq's army politics from 1937 to 1941. They espoused the ideas of Arab nationalism, objected to Britain's constant interference in Iraq's affairs, and wanted to expand and modernize the army. In February 1941, Hashimi became prime minister of Iraq, this time for two months. Having been a compromise candidate, he hoped to resolve the dispute between the regent, who wanted to implement the British government's desire for Iraq to break off diplomatic relations with Italy, and Rashid Ali and the nationalist Golden Square officers, who wanted to pursue a course of absolute neutrality toward the Axis powers and the Allies. On 1 April 1941, Hashimi was forced to resign under pressure from the Golden Square.

In 1941 Iraq experienced its seventh coup since 1936, which led to Rashid Ali's uprising against the British. The failed uprising led to what the Iraqis called the second British occupation of Iraq (the first was during World War I). Hashimi fled to Turkey after the failure of the coup and remained there until the end of World War II. He was permitted to return to Iraq in 1946. In 1951, with a group of politicians, he formed the Nationalist Bloc Party, which did not last long because of intense differences among its members. In 1953, Hashimi was appointed vice chair of the Board of Development. He held this position until the board was dissolved after the revolution of 14 July 1958. The board was responsible for preparing and executing general economic and financial plans for the development of Iraq's resources. Among its many accomplishments was the Tharthar Project, which was primarily designed as a flood control system. Hashimi died in London.

Hashimi is considered a centrist and nationalist in Iraq's politics. He was well liked by young military officers disgruntled with Britain's constant interference in Iraq's affairs; they saw him as defender and protector of their interests. Hashimi taught courses at the military college and at al-Bayt University in Baghdad. He wrote books on such subjects as ancient history, Muslim military leaders, Iraq's geography (including an atlas of Iraq), war in Iraq, and the rebirth of Japan. His two-volume memoirs, published posthumously, are filled with insight, opinions, and information about his role in Iraq's history, as well as the roles of other Iraqi politicians during the monarchy.

See also AHD, AL-; ARAB NATIONALISM; GHAZI IBN FAISAL; GOLDEN SQUARE; HASHIMI, YASIN AL-; KAYLANI, RASHID ALI AL-; MISRI, AZIZ ALI AL-; SIDQI, BAKR; THARTHAR PROJECT.

Bibliography

Khaddari, Majid. *Independent Iraq 1932–1958: A Study in Iraqi Politics.* London and New York: Oxford University Press, 1960.

AYAD AL-QAZZAZ

HASHIMITE HOUSE (HOUSE OF HASHIM)

Notable family from Hijaz whose members are Sharifs (descendants of the prophet Muhammad through his grandson Hasan) and who have occupied leadership positions in the twentieth-century Arab world.

The Hashimites are a family whose origins lie in Quraysh family in the Hijaz. Husayn ibn Ali (1852–1931) was appointed Ottoman governor of Hijaz in 1908, later breaking with the Ottomans and leading the Arab Revolt in coordination with the British and with urban Arab nationalists in Syria. Members of the Hashimite family went on to establish three monarchical lines after World War I. The first was the short-lived Kingdom of Hijaz. Husayn was proclaimed king of Hijaz in 1924. He abdicated in favor of his eldest son, Ali (1879–1935), but Hashimite rule in their native Hijaz ended when Ali was defeated in 1925 by their archrival, Abd al-Aziz ibn Sa'ud Al Sa'ud.

The other two Hashimite dynasties were creations of British imperial policies. The British established Husayn's second son, Abdullah I ibn Hussein (1882–1951), as amir (prince) of Transjordan in 1920. He headed an autonomous government within the rubric of the Palestine Mandate. Transjordan was renamed the Hashimite Kingdom of Jordan in 1946. Abdullah was succeeded by his son, Talal ibn Abdullah (1909–1972), his grandson, Hussein ibn Talal (1935–1999), and his great-grandson, Abdullah II ibn Hussein (1962–).

Husayn ibn Ali's third son, Faisal I ibn Hussein (1889–1933), was proclaimed king of Syria by a gathering of Arab nationalists in 1920, but saw his rule end with a French occupation that same year. The British then installed him as king of Iraq in 1921. He was succeeded by his son, Ghazi ibn Faisal (1912–1939). Upon Ghazi's death, Abd al-Ilah (son of Ali ibn Husayn) served as regent until Ghazi's son Faisal II ibn Ghazi (1935–1958) was old enough to serve as king. The Hashimite monarchy in Iraq was violently overthrown in a military coup in July 1958. Husayn ibn Ali's fourth and youngest son, Zayd (1898–1970), occupied no leadership positions.

The family always has stressed its Arab nationalist credentials, as well as its sharifian lineage, attempting to turn these into important sources of legitimacy.

See also ABDULLAH I IBN HUSSEIN; ABDULLAH II IBN HUSSEIN; FAISAL I IBN HUSSEIN; HUSAYN IBN ALI; HUSSEIN IBN TALAL; JORDAN.

MICHAEL R. FISCHBACH

HASHIMI, YASIN AL-
[1884–1937]

Iraqi politician.

Born in Baghdad in the Barudiyya district, Yasin al-Hashimi began life with the name Yasin Hilmi Salman. His father was Sayyid Salman Mukhtar of the Barudiyya district. After graduating from the Military Academy of Istanbul and attaining the rank of major general, he joined the al-Ahd organization along with other young officers who sought to serve the interest of the Arabs with the Ottoman Empire. He acquired the name al-Hashimi to emphasize his relation with the royal Hashimite family and as an indication of his loyalty to King Faisal I ibn Hussein. He became chief of staff of Faisal's army in 1919. Profoundly influenced by Kemal Atatürk, he established the National Brotherhood party. He started his political career as minister of transportation and became a deputy of Baghdad in the Constitutional Assembly in 1924. He held numerous cabinet positions and was prime minister several times. During his tenure as prime minister in 1936, General Bakr Sidqi's militant activities caused the government to fall, and Yasin al-Hashimi was deported to Damascus, where he died in 1937.

Bibliography

Batatu, Hanna. *The Old Social Classes and the Revolutionary Movements of Iraq. A Study of Iraq's Old Landed and Commercial Classes and of its Communists, Ba'thists, and Free Officers.* Princeton, NJ: Princeton University Press, 1978.

MAMOON A. ZAKI
UPDATED BY MICHAEL R. FISCHBACH

HA-SHOMER

Early Jewish defense organization in Palestine.

Ha-Shomer ("the watchman") was established in 1909 in Jaffa, Palestine, by Russian immigrants including Yizhak Ben-Zvi to replace Arab guards hired by Jewish landowners. Imitating Arab dress and horsemanship, Ha-Shomer in 1914 grew to 40 official members employing up to 300 guards. During World War I, many joined the Jewish Legion. Ha-Shomer established the linkage of soldier and settler identities that has persisted in later Jewish defense forces and military organizations. It disbanded when the Haganah was formed in 1920.

See also BEN-ZVI, YIZHAK; HAGANAH; JEWISH LEGION.

Bibliography

Schiff, Ze'ev. *A History of the Israeli Army, 1874 to the Present.* New York: Macmillan, 1985.

Shafir, Gershon. *Land, Labor, and the Origins of the Israeli–Palestinian Conflict, 1882–1914,* updated edition. Berkeley: University of California Press, 1996.

ELIZABETH THOMPSON

HA-SHOMER HA-TZA'IR

Socialist-Zionist youth movement.

This movement was founded in 1913, when Zionist youth organizations in Poland and Galicia united under the name ha-Shomer ha-Tza'ir, meaning "Young Guardian" or "Young Watchman." "Ha-Shomer" was both the name of the largest of the youth organizations that made up the new group and the name of a Jewish self-defense militia organization in Palestine. Ha-Shomer ha-Tza'ir was heavily influenced by both. It emphasized the values of nature, pioneering, and settlement on kibbutzim in Palestine, and in 1919 it sent its first group of settlers to Eretz Yisrael. Ha-Shomer ha-Tza'ir did not have a very unique ideological stance; indeed, most, if not all of its ideology could be found in existing groups and was rooted in such philosophies as that of Aaron David Gordon (1856–1922) and Martin Buber (1878–1965). It apparently had an esprit-de-corps that enabled it to survive and grow even though it did not espouse anything altogether unique. The movement grew to more than 10,000 members by 1924, when it held its first international conference in Danzig. During the late 1920s and early 1930s ha-Shomer ha-Tza'ir developed a strong Marxist-Zionist ideology and many of its leaders referred to the Soviet Union as their "second homeland." They envisioned a socialist Palestine working in conjunction with the Union of Soviet Socialist Republics to bring about a global workers' revolution. By the eve of World War II, ha-Shomer ha-Tza'ir had more than 70,000 members worldwide and thirty-nine kibbutzim in Palestine.

Some of the members who were trapped in Europe when WWII erupted played prominent roles in Jewish armed rebellions against the Nazis, including the Warsaw Ghetto uprising. One of the most famous among these was Mordecai Anielewicz (c. 1919–1943), who commanded the Warsaw Ghetto uprising.

As a result of its stance in favor of the creation of a binational Arab-Jewish state in Palestine prior to 1948, ha-Shomer ha-Tza'ir was somewhat marginalized and exercised little influence on the political decision-making of the yishuv and the Zionist movement. Early in 1948, when a group of socialist factions united to found MAPAM, a socialist-Zionist party to the left of the Labor Party, ha-Shomer ha-Tza'ir became its youth movement. With the decline of the Labor alignment as well as the decline of the kibbutz movement, it remains active primarily as an educational movement.

See also LABOR ZIONISM.

Bibliography

Avineri, Shlomo. *The Making of Modern Zionism: The Intellectual Origins of the Jewish State.* New York: Basic Books, 1981.

Laqueur, Walter. *A History of Zionism.* New York: Holt, Rinehart, and Winston, 1972.

Shimoni, Gideon. *The Zionist Ideology.* Hanover, NH: Brandeis University Press/University Press of New England, 1995.

CHAIM I. WAXMAN

HASIDIM

Followers of an ultra-Orthodox Jewish movement.

In the modern era, *Hasidim* (literally, "pious ones") has come to mean those who identify with a movement founded by Rabbi Israel ben Eliezer (c. 1700–1760), the "Ba'al Shem Tov" or "Besht" (the acronym). Originally, it was a mass movement that emphasized mysticism and personal piety rather than the legalistic learning of elite Judaism. Contemporary Hasidim are generally viewed as ultra-Orthodox, and are composed of hundreds of groups, the most widely known of which are the Lubavitcher (Habad) and Satmar Hasidim. The Lubavitcher is the largest group, and their organizational world center is in Brooklyn, New York, to which they immigrated from the Soviet Union after World War II. In Israel the movement's center is in Kfar Habad, a community of Lubavitcher Hasidim approximately eight miles southeast of Tel Aviv. Kfar Habad has several schools, including a higher yeshiva, and a replica of the red brick building that is the home of the world headquarters in Brooklyn. Although Habad-Lubavitch Hasidim officially reject secular Zionism, they are a highly nationalistic group and exert great effort in outreach to nonobservant Jews. By contrast, Satmar Hasidim have traditionally been adamantly anti-Zionist and antinationalist, and they eschew all but purely formal contacts with outsiders.

In recent decades there have been significant shifts in the activities of both groups. The Satmar group has toned down its anti-Zionism and now avoids overt anti-Zionist activity. The Lubavitcher Hasidim, on the other hand, have become highly active in Israeli politics and were staunch supporters of Benjamin Netanyahu in his successful bid for the office of prime minister in 1996. Since the death of the movement's leader, Rabbi Menachem Mendel Schneersohn, in 1994, the movement has struggled, internally as well as with some other Orthodox groups, because of its increasing proclamations of Rabbi Schneersohn as the Messiah, a notion that others view as antithetical to Judaism.

Although there are no official figures on the number of Hasidim either in Israel or in the United States, a rough estimate suggests that there are approximately 125,000 Hasidim in Israel and a similar number in the United States.

Bibliography

Berger, David. *The Rebbe, the Messiah, and the Scandal of Orthodox Indifference.* London: Littman Library of Jewish Civilization, 2001.

Mintz, Jerome R. *Hasidic People: A Place in the New World.* Cambridge, MA: Harvard University Press, 1992.

CHAIM I. WAXMAN

HASKALAH

Hebrew term for enlightenment.

Haskalah is the name of the movement for the dissemination of modern European culture among the Jews. The movement began in the mid-1700s in Berlin with the work of the German Jewish philosopher Moses Mendelssohn (1729–1786). Advocates argued that to achieve emancipation, the Jews must adopt the modern values and social customs of the countries in which they lived. In the mid-1800s, modern European culture for the Jews generally meant German and French culture and secular education, although efforts were made in this period by groups of Jews throughout Europe.

One consequence of this process was the secular use of the Hebrew language to spread the new ideas, leading to an eventual revitalization of the language. Another effect was the creation of a stratum of Jews versed in both the intellectual traditions of modern Europe and traditional Judaism. It was from subsequent generations of these Jews that the ideas of modern Zionism originated. Finally, for many Jews, acquiring modern European culture meant the abandonment of traditional Jewish customs, resulting in assimilation.

See also HEBREW; ZIONISM.

Bibliography

Ackerman, Walter. *Out of Our People's Past: Sources for the Study of Jewish History.* New York: United Synagogue Commission on Jewish Education, 1977.

MARTIN MALIN

HASS, AMIRA
[1956–]

Israeli Journalist.

Hass was born in 1956 in Jerusalem to European-Jewish parents who had survived the Holocaust. She studied history at the Hebrew and Tel Aviv universities. Hass joined Israel's most respected daily, *Haaretz,* as staff editor after the outbreak of the first uprising (Intifada) of 1987. In addition to her editing position, she started to write daily reports on and from Gaza in 1991.

Hass subsequently decided to move to Gaza Strip and lived there for four years, becoming the only Israeli journalist who lived in the occupied territories in order to cover Palestinian life under Israeli occupation. In Gaza, she wrote her book *Drinking the Sea at Gaza: Days and Nights in a Land under Siege.* The book contains a detailed description of Israeli occupation policies toward the Palestinians, and also includes a thorough analysis of the Israeli closure regime implemented since 1991 to restrict Palestinians' freedom of movement on the grounds of Israeli security concerns.

In January 1997, Hass moved to the West Bank to continue her coverage of occupation and the Oslo process from the city of Ramallah. In late 2002, she stopped writing daily news to focus on writing features and op-eds. In 2003, she published her second book, *Reporting from Ramallah: An Israeli Journalist in an Occupied Land.* The book is a collection of articles and features focused on Israel's repressive measure against Palestinians in the second intifada.

Hass's engaged and courageous reporting has won her numerous awards, including the UNESCO/Guillermo Cano World Press Freedom Prize in 2003.

See also GENDER: GENDER AND EDUCATION; HUMAN RIGHTS; ISRAEL; ISRAELI SETTLEMENTS; NEWSPAPERS AND PRINT MEDIA: ISRAEL.

Bibliography

Hass, Amira. *Drinking the Sea at Gaza: Days and Nights in a Land under Siege,* translated by Elana Wesley and Maxine Kaufman-Lacusta. New York: Metropolitan Books, 1999.

Hass, Amira. *Reporting from Ramallah: An Israeli Journalist in an Occupied Land,* edited and translated by Rachel Leah Jones. Los Angeles, CA, and New York: Semiotext (e); Cambridge, MA: Distributed by MIT Press, 2003.

KHALED ISLAIH

HASSANA TRIBE

See TRIBES AND TRIBALISM: HASSANA TRIBE

HASSAN I
[?–1894]

Sultan of Morocco, 1873–1894.

The favorite son of Sultan Sidi Muhammad, Hassan I was regarded as the last great ruler of precolonial Morocco. As ruler, he resisted foreign influence through control of the local tribes, using both the permanent military units trained by British and French forces and his own status as a political leader of Islam. Through military interventions in the mountains and in the south, he was able to collect taxes and, above all, to prevent the establishment of any potential rival. To reinforce his military power, he created the first military equipment industry in Marrakech and Fez. He was interested in the reforms (Tanzimat) launched by the Ottoman Empire as long as they were not forced on him.

In 1880, he sought to limit the rights of protection and jurisdiction exerted by foreigners on Moroccan nationals. With British support, he held out against both the French and the Spanish, although neither was pleased that he might remain outside their control. That year he convened the Madrid Conference, but the meeting failed to resolve diplomatic tensions. Throughout his reign, Hassan I resisted all external pressure, well aware that his forces were not equal to the European forces, and he gave no pretext for military intervention by limiting his contacts with foreigners. His military reforms and his strategy of defending Morocco by playing one tribe against the other while similarly using existing rivalries between the Europeans did not survive long after his death in 1894.

See also TANZIMAT.

RÉMY LEVEAU

HASSAN II
[1929–2000]

King of Morocco, 1961–2000.

Hassan II was the son of Muhammad V, king of Morocco. As Crown Prince Mulay Hassan, he graduated from the University of Bordeaux in France. In 1961, when his father died unexpectedly, the thirty-two-year-old playboy prince came to power. The heir of the Alawite Dynasty, which has governed Morocco since the sixteenth century, Mulay Hassan had been well prepared by his father—as early as World War II—to assume the throne. He had also attended the 1942 meeting between Muhammad V and U.S. president Franklin D. Roosevelt.

When the French entered North Africa in the nineteenth century they established a policy of colonization and protectorates. Hassan had therefore been trained in both Arabic and French and had studied law and economics at the university; he was at ease in both cultures. He was also acutely aware of the ideas and changes that might come to Morocco from outside. Since his adolescence he was known to favor nationalism, as did many Moroccans of his age. He was said to have some influence on his father, who was more cautious and less brilliant than Hassan. When in 1948 there was a conflict with

France's resident general that had to do with the signing of legal texts presented by French colonial authorities, Hassan was among those who favored a break with France. The consequence was Muhammad V's exile to the French-controlled island of Madagascar. Supporting his father, Hassan participated in the negotiations through intermediaries to reestablish links with the French government and effect Muhammad V's return, which was accomplished in 1955.

In contrast with Muhammad V, who was careful not to offend the parties who had joined the struggle for independence—especially the Istiqlal Party—Hassan wanted to preserve the autonomy of the monarchy. Designated chief of staff of the Royal Armed Forces, Hassan II appeared as the main guarantor of his peoples' destiny. He gathered around himself the former Moroccan officers who had served in the French army, and he ended rebellions in al-Rif, Tafilalt, and Beni-Mellal that had been provoked by various dissident movements. He also reduced the size of the Liberation Army, born of the Moroccan resistance, because it was almost autonomous in the south; it pretended to be fighting the French and Spanish colonial powers, but could easily have offered armed and organized support to any given opposition.

France and Spain recognized Morocco's independence in 1956; by 1958, Hassan II's forces prevailed throughout the country and dissidents were no longer a threat to the monarchy. Thus Muhammad V was able to incorporate the various splinter groups of the former nationalist movement within the government. Hassan was sometimes irritated by his father's caution and he tried to convince him to take back direct control. A change began in May 1960, when Hassan was appointed prime minister. When his father died in March 1961 Hassan II had both the experience and the means to put his theories into practice.

The independence of Algeria (5 July 1962) appeared to be a potential threat to Hassan II's monarchy. Algeria bordered Morocco to the east and south, and Algeria's National Liberation Front (Front de Libération Nationale) was known to support the Moroccan left (socialists) against the monarchy. Hassan sought a new legitimacy by mobilizing universal suffrage, which was largely supported by the rural populace. The December 1962 referendum guaranteed Hassan's success with 80 percent approval of his new constitution.

The results of the March 1963 election did not give him similar support. The old Istiqlal had lost its governmental majority and the king's followers were not able to form a political coalition quickly enough. Most of the ministers were defeated, and it seemed that the parliament could not easily be governed despite a promonarchy majority. In the meantime, the danger posed by Algeria had faded. The October 1963 border war and rivalry related to Tindouf had revived in Morocco a strong nationalist feeling that produced support for the monarchy.

Hassan II dismissed the parliament in 1965 and relied mainly on his army for legitimacy. He protected those in the military who had served French and Spanish colonialism, although some of the young officers were not as loyal or as committed as he had expected. Tempted by populist idealism, some succeeded in convincing former officers of the French colonial army (who controlled the military organization) to join their project. In July 1971 and September 1972 General Medboh and General Muhammad Oufkir, among others, faced death after their rebellion failed.

Paradoxically, Hassan succeeded in restoring faith in his monarchy in 1975 when a dispute with Spain (at the time of Spanish dictator Francisco Franco's death) led to the defense of Morocco's position in the former Spanish colony of Western Sahara. A local nationalistic movement, POLISARIO, which was supported mainly by Algeria and Libya, emerged to challenge Morocco. Both Algeria and Libya saw opportunities in the situation; Algeria, especially, under President Houari Boumédienne, wanted to demonstrate its control over the Maghrib before the new European Community. Bolstered by petroleum revenues, the growing power of Algeria had the effect of reuniting Morocco under Hassan.

Although Hassan had plans for political pluralism (albeit pluralism controlled by the monarchy), his army had been reequipped for possible conflict with Algeria. Many officers disagreed with that policy, and they attempted another coup. General Ahmed Dlimi was to be their leader, but the plot was discovered by the home secretary and Dlimi disap-

Shown speaking at the United Nations in New York on 27 September 1983 is King Hassan II of Morocco. © AP/WIDE WORLD PHOTOS. REPRODUCED BY PERMISSION.

peared in an accident. In the long run, Morocco benefited from its tactical building of the wall (fortified sand barriers in Western Sahara), and Algeria succeeded in having seventy-five countries recognize POLISARIO and make it a member of the Organization of African Unity (OAU).

Hassan managed Moroccan nationalism cautiously to establish national unity. He found external financial resources by getting Western countries as well as the Arab oil monarchies to support his military efforts and to launch economic development based on a private sector far larger than those of neighboring countries. For that reason, as the Pahlavi dynasty in Iran did before the Islamist Iranian Revolution of 1979, Hassan's monarchy became a major economic actor through the All North Africa association (Omnium Nord-Africain; ONA), not only to find resources, but also to prevent other entrepreneurs from obtaining power and becoming politically influential. Because Morocco had no oil, Hassan encouraged and often provided an example of an economic-development policy based on modern agriculture, launching a program to irrigate 2.47 million acres. He also encouraged small and medium-sized manufacturing industries.

In 1984 Hassan signed a treaty of unity with Libya after Libya withdrew its support for POLISARIO in the Western Sahara and Morocco agreed to refrain from sending troops to aid the French in Chad. In 1986, Libya abrogated the treaty when Hassan became the second North African leader to meet with an Israeli leader during Prime Minister Shimon Peres's visit to Morocco.

In 1988 international factors continued to prevail over those within Morocco. After Tunisian president Habib Bourguiba was replaced by General Zayn al-Abidine Ben Ali in November 1987, a process of realignment occurred among the North African countries. A consequence was the reintegration of Morocco, first at a meeting in Algiers (August 1988), then when the Union of the Maghrib (Union du Maghreb; UMA) treaty was signed in Marrakech, Morocco (March 1989). The treaty marked the end of the Algerian/Moroccan rivalry related to the Western Sahara, but at the same time, it deprived Morocco of a compelling reason for internal unity.

The UMA had another, hidden agenda: to constitute a united front against strengthening political movements in North Africa that aimed to establish Islamic religious regimes. Tunisia appeared to be the weak link at the time, and it needed support. Political changes in Algeria, too, had ramifications for Morocco. After the October 1988 riots in Algiers, President Chadli Bendjedid controlled the situation by creating a pluralistic political system open to Islamists; this led to competitive elections. Algerian pluralism looked attractive in comparison to the established Moroccan political system, where the same actors repeated their opposition to the existing power year after year. At a time when the annexation of Kuwait by Iraq (1990) became a military crisis and thus reduced the possibilities of action, Algeria was seen as a model rather than a threat by Moroccans.

In Morocco, the riots that took place in provincial cities by the end of 1990, the important demonstrations in the capital city at the beginning of 1991, and the reports of deserters leaving the Moroccan army to go to Iraq (by way of Algeria) indicated the public's disapproval of Hassan's cautious move in sending a limited contingent to help the United Nations coalition forces to defend the oil monarchy of Kuwait. Moroccan public opinion favored Iraq's President Saddam Hussein, and the Gulf War made visible the differing factions in Morocco.

In the last ten years of his reign Hassan's main preoccupation was to build a national consensus that would support the monarchy for the next century. He incorporated opposition parties into his government, but he was not ready to give up his power to rule directly public affairs without sharing decisions. In 1997 he compromised with socialist leader Alederrhamane Youssouf, dividing government departments into sovereign departments (Interior, Foreign Affairs, Army) that were under the control of the king and the members of the royal house, and ordinary ministries (Education, Finances, Social Affairs, Agriculture, etc.) that were under the direct control of the prime minister. But the minister of the interior, Driss Basri, appeared as a deputy prime minister exercising a global control of public activities on behalf of the king. More attention was given to human rights, and political prisoners were released, but sometimes they were expelled from the country for fallacious reasons. In spite of the limited scope of the changes, they helped to produce a political climate that progressively excluded violence from the functioning of Moroccan political life. The illness of the king and the presumed frailty of the heir apparent, Prince Mohamed, increased public desire for a broad national consensus that would include even moderate Islamist parties to build a more liberal political system after the king's death. Hassan II died in July 2000.

See also ALAWITE DYNASTY; ALGERIA: OVERVIEW; ALGERIAN WAR OF INDEPENDENCE; BEN ALI, ZAYN AL-ABIDINE; DLIMI, AHMED; ISTIQLAL PARTY: MOROCCO; MAGHRIB; MOROCCAN–ALGERIAN WAR; MOROCCO: OVERVIEW; MUHAMMAD V; ORGANIZATION OF AFRICAN UNITY (OAU); OUFKIR, MUHAMMAD; POLISARIO; TINDOUF; WESTERN SAHARA.

Bibliography

Waterbury, John. *The Commander of the Faithful: The Moroccan Political Elite, a Study in Segmented Politics.* New York: Columbia University Press, 1970.

RÉMY LEVEAU

"HA-TIKVA"

The Zionist anthem, unofficial national anthem of the State of Israel.

"Ha-Tikva"—based on a poem written in Jassy, Romania, by Naphtali Herz Imber (1856–1909)—was formally declared the Zionist anthem at the Eighteenth Zionist Congress in 1933, and it was sung at the opening and closing of the ceremonial Declaration of the State of Israel in 1948. It is sung at communal events across the Jewish diaspora, generally alongside the local national anthem. By contrast, its status in Israel has been more debated, particularly with the increasing recognition that Arab citizens do not necessarily identify with the hope of "the Jewish soul" referred to in the words.

The original poem, entitled "Our Hope" (Tikvatenu), was inspired by the founding of the Petah Tikvah settlement in 1878. Closely echoing Psalm 126 (a feature of the Sabbath liturgy expressing the Jewish desire to return to Zion), the words were revised, set to music, and then adapted by the Zionist movement. In 1882 Samuel Cohen, a settler of Rishon le-Zion originally from Moldavia, composed the melody, based on a Moldavian-Romanian folk song—"Carul cu Boi" (Cart and oxen)—also used in Bedrich Smetana's opera *Moldau*.

Bibliography

Edelman, Marsha Bryan. *Discovering Jewish Music.* Philadelphia: Jewish Publication Society, 2003.

Ginor, Zvia. "Is There Hope for Hatikvah? Text, Context, Pretext." *Yakar Le'Mordecai* (1999): 167–185.

GEORGE R. WILKES

HATIM SULTANS OF HAMDAN

Early tribal leaders of North Yemen.

The Hatim sultans were leaders of the Yam tribe, a section of the Hamdan tribal grouping. Control of San'a and much of the north passed into their hands with the loosening of the grip of Queen Arwa and the Sulayhids on that area at the end of the eleventh century. The twelfth century witnessed much competition, from intrigue to warfare, as well as truces and alliances, between the Hatim sultans in San'a and the relatively new Zaydi imams based to the north in Sa'da. Previously loyal to the Isma'ili faith

of the Sulayhids, the Hatim sultans and their followers gradually shifted from opposition to Zaydism to accepting the suzerainty of the Zaydi imams. Despite the ebb and flow of the power, and at times even the absence, of Zaydi imams over subsequent centuries, Zaydism from this time forward was firmly established in the San'a region and the northern highlands of Yemen. However, the legacy of the Isma'ili period explains how the family of President Ahmad Husayn Ghashmi could be and is Isma'ili.

See also GHASHMI, AHMAD HUSAYN; SAN'A; YEMEN ARAB REPUBLIC.

Bibliography

Stookey, Robert W. *Yemen: The Politics of the Yemen Arab Republic.* Boulder, CO: Westview Press, 1978.

ROBERT D. BURROWES

HATM (MOVEMENT FOR REFORM AND RENEWAL IN MOROCCO)

See MOVEMENT FOR UNITY AND REFORM (MUR)

HATOUM, MONA
[1952–]

London-based Palestinian multimedia artist.

Mona Hatoum (also Muna Hatum) is arguably the best-known female artist of Arab descent living and working in the West. Born in Beirut to Palestinian parents, she left Lebanon in the 1970s, trained at the Byam Shaw and Slade schools of art in London, and has resided there ever since. Widely regarded for her conceptual art, which is primarily executed in performance, video, objects, and installation, Hatoum has worked primarily with the issue of power relationships—especially as they are manifested, manipulated, and subverted in class, gender, and race relationships, and in processes of cultural difference and displacement. Her early works were direct political statements about the body, feminism, and surveillance. Her performances challenged audiences to engage with issues of power and difference. Beginning in the 1990s, her work became more conceptual and subtle, containing implied, complex, and multilayered explorations of these same issues. Her work is increasingly minimalist, and Hatoum is keen to explore the sensuous properties of materials in eliciting contradictory responses—attraction and repulsion, for example, or welcoming and danger—thus creating works that are more complicated than her earlier, more direct, political statements. Although her experience of exile shapes some of her work and she has done pieces critical of Israel's treatment of the Palestinians, she resists interpretations of her art as stemming only from her Middle Eastern background. She insists that her works do not have fixed meanings that relate solely to her background but rather have multiple interpretations that are often paradoxical. Hatoum has exhibited widely in major venues around the world and is the recipient of numerous awards.

See also ART; PALESTINE.

Bibliography

Archer, Michael; Brett, Guy; and de Zegher, Catherine. *Mona Hatoum.* London: Phaidon, 1997.

Dimitrakaki, Angela. "Mona Hatoum: A Shock of a Different Kind." *Third Text,* 43 (1998): 92–95.

Mona Hatoum: The Entire World as a Foreign Land. London: Tate Gallery, 2000.

JESSICA WINEGAR

HATT-I HÜMAYUN

See TANZIMAT

HATT-I SERIF OF GÜLHANE

See TANZIMAT

HAWATMA, NAYIF
[1935–]

Jordanian activist and leader in the Palestinian resistance movement.

Born into a Greek Catholic family in al-Salt, Jordan, Nayif Hawatma (also Nayef Hawatmeh, Hawatima) obtained degrees in both politics and economics from Zarqa College and Hussein College in Jordan, from Cairo University, and from the Beirut Arab University. He joined the pan-Arab Arab Nationalists Movement (ANM) while in Beirut in 1954, and he fled Jordan in 1957 following King Hussein ibn Talal's crackdown on leftist activism. His activ-

ities on behalf of the ANM in Iraq landed him in prison between 1959 and 1963. Back in Lebanon in the mid-1960s, Hawatma was one of several ANM activists who began pushing for a more rigidly Marxist-Leninist line within the movement. Hawatma also formed a group dedicated to armed action in the service of Palestinian liberation, the Vengeance Youth. Although this group was one of several that merged to form the Popular Front for the Liberation of Palestine under the leadership of George Habash in early 1968, ideological disputes between Habash and Hawatma's leftist faction led the latter to break away and form his own new group in February 1969. He named the new organization the Popular Democratic Front for the Liberation of Palestine (later shortened to the Democratic Front for the Liberation of Palestine [DFLP]) and brought the group within the rubric of the Palestine Liberation Organization (PLO).

Hawatma's historical imprint on the PLO has been strong despite the DFLP's small numbers. He has been one of the most ideologically sophisticated leaders in the Palestinian movement, carefully analyzing both the relationship between the Palestinian resistance movement and Israel (and Israeli Jews) and, given his Jordanian nationality and pan-Arab and Marxist internationalist background, the relationship between the resistance movement and the wider Arab world. Hawatma was one of the first leaders of the Palestinian resistance to call for dialogue with certain leftist elements in Israel and to deal ideologically with a Jewish presence in Palestine. He and the DFLP also advanced a series of precisely argued theories about the goals of the Palestinian resistance movement. Initially, Hawatma argued that when Palestine was liberated from Israeli control it should become not a separate state, but a part of a larger, federated socialist Arab state. In particular, Hawatma believed that the struggle of the Palestinian people against Israeli rule and that of the Jordanian people against the pro-Western regime of King Hussein were inseparable. The DFLP's provocative actions in Hawatma's homeland helped to precipitate a disastrous confrontation between the PLO and the Jordanian army in September 1970 that resulted in Hawatma becoming persona non grata in his homeland until 1990.

Always a champion of ideological flexibility, by 1973 Hawatma began was calling for a phased approach to Palestinian liberation. Although he was still opposed to a separate Palestinian state, he argued for establishing a "national authority" in the West Bank and Gaza in the event of an Israeli withdrawal. The PLO committed itself to this idea in 1974. Hawatma later spoke of the establishment of a Palestinian state in the occupied territories, once again before this became official PLO policy. Hawatma has also stood out because of his steadfast rejection of violence directed against targets outside of Israeli-controlled territory. Although committed to armed struggle against Israel, the DFLP eschewed the spectacular airline hijackings and similar acts of international violence carried out by other Palestinian groups. The DFLP did carry out actions, including terrorist attacks inside Israel, however. Among them was the terrorist attack at the Israeli town of Ma'alot in 1974, when DFLP fighters invaded a school and held the students hostage; twenty-two were killed and dozens injured during the incident, which ended when Israeli forces stormed the school.

Hawatma long served as a voice of loyal opposition to Yasir Arafat's leadership of the PLO. This has been particularly true since the early 1980s, when Arafat began to pursue diplomatic ventures that Hawatma and others felt compromised cherished Palestinian goals and subsumed them to U.S.-led imperialist domination of the region. Hawatma opposed the 1991 Madrid Conference and subsequent talks. This helped to precipitate a crisis with Yasir Abd Rabbo and others in the DFLP who supported the peace process, and Abd Rabbo left the organization in 1991. By 1993 the split was institutionalized when Abd Rabbo created the Palestinian Democratic Union (FIDA). Hawatma later played an important role in the "Damascus Ten," a group of Palestinian organizations formed in 1992 in opposition to the peace talks, which began calling itself the National Democratic and Islamic Front the following year. He also criticized the 1993 Israeli–PLO Oslo Accord. However, he always upheld the goal of PLO unity and, despite his opposition to the peace accords, never broke with the PLO. In the late 1990s he softened his stance and engaged in dialogue with Arafat in August 1999 about ways to involve the DFLP in the negotiations.

Hawatma made headlines in February 1999 when he shook the hand of Israeli president Ezer Weiz-

man in Amman during the funeral of Jordan's King Hussein. Israel agreed to allow Hawatma to enter the territory of the Palestinian Authority later that year, but soon reneged on its decision. He operates from Damascus, where he has lived for years.

See also ARAB NATIONALIST MOVEMENT (ANM); ARAFAT, YASIR; HABASH, GEORGE; HUSSEIN IBN TALAL; MADRID CONFERENCE (1991); OSLO ACCORD (1993); PALESTINE LIBERATION ORGANIZATION (PLO); PALESTINIAN AUTHORITY; POPULAR FRONT FOR THE LIBERATION OF PALESTINE; WEIZMAN, EZER; WEST BANK.

Bibliography

Nassar, Jamal R. *The Palestine Liberation Organization: From Armed Struggle to the Declaration of Independence.* New York: Praeger Publishers, 1991.

Sayigh, Yezid. *Armed Struggle and the Search for State: The Palestinian National Movement, 1949–1993.* Oxford, U.K.: Oxford University Press, 1997.

MICHAEL R. FISCHBACH

HAWI, GEORGE
[1938–]

Former general secretary of the Lebanese Communist Party, 1979–1992.

A Greek Orthodox, George Hawi has been a leading figure in the Lebanese Communist Party since the early 1970s. He became its general secretary in 1979 and retained that position until 1992. Calls for Hawi's resignation grew from the mid-1980s onward, as a result of personal rivalries, rising confessional tensions between Greek Orthodox and Shi'a members of the party, and criticism of his pro-Syrian policies and lavish lifestyle. Strong Syrian support nevertheless enabled him to withstand several challenges to his leadership. His position became increasingly precarious following the collapse of communism in eastern Europe in 1989, when the party was split between reformers and backers of Hawi's traditional policies. In June 1992, during the Lebanese Communist Party's Seventh Party Congress, Hawi failed to win reelection as general secretary and was replaced by Faruq Dahruj.

See also COMMUNISM IN THE MIDDLE EAST.

Bibliography

Hiro, Dilip. *Lebanon: Fire and Embers: A History of the Lebanese Civil War.* New York: St. Martin's, 1993.

GUILAIN P. DENOEUX

HAWI, KHALIL
[1919–1982]

One of Lebanon's best-known twentieth-century poets.

Born in Huwaya, Syria, where his Greek Orthodox Lebanese father was working, Khalil Hawi grew up in Shwayr, Lebanon. He studied philosophy and Arabic at the American University of Beirut, where he received a bachelor of arts in 1951 and a master of arts in 1955. After teaching for a few years, he obtained a scholarship to enroll at Cambridge University, in England, where he was awarded his Ph.D. in 1959. He then became a professor of Arabic literature at the American University in Beirut. Within a few years, he established himself as one of the leading avant-garde poets in the Arab world. His poetry relies heavily on symbols and metaphors and images, and it frequently has political and social overtones.

An Arab nationalist at heart, he repeatedly expressed his sense of shame and rage at the loss of Palestine in 1948 and at subsequent Arab defeats at the hands of Israel. He was very critical of Arab regimes for their demonstrated lack of pan-Arab solidarity, and he denounced the hedonism, materialism, and corruption that prevailed in Beirut before the civil war broke out. More generally, he lamented what he saw as the Arab world's political and cultural decay, and he expressed deep pessimism about the possibility of a true Arab cultural and political revival. His deeply felt feelings of frustration and powerlessness at the decline of Arab society and culture and at the Arab world's impotence on the international scene are shared by an entire generation of Arab intellectuals confronted with political authoritarianism and the failure of attempts at Arab unity, as well as persistent and costly inter-Arab rivalries.

After 1975, Khalil Hawi experienced the desperation felt by all Lebanese who had to watch their country's slow descent into chaos, internal disintegration, and manipulation by outside powers. He was outraged by Lebanon's inability to stand up to the Israeli army when the latter invaded on 3 June 1982, and he deeply resented the other Arab governments' silence about the Israeli invasion. He committed suicide on 6 June 1982.

Bibliography

Allen, Roger, ed. *Modern Arabic Literature.* New York: Ungar, 1987.

Boullata, Issa J., ed. and trans. *Modern Arab Poets, 1950–1975.* Washington, DC: Three Continents Press, 1976.

Haddad, Fuad S., ed. and trans. *From the Vineyards of Lebanon: Poems by Khalil Hawi and Nadeem Naimy.* Beirut: American University of Beirut, 1991.

GUILAIN P. DENOEUX

HAWRANI, AKRAM AL-
[1914–]

Syrian politician and political activist.

Akram al-Hawrani was born in Hama, an ancient city in the central plain of Syria and a citadel of landed power and rural oppression. In the 1930s, during the French mandate, he tried to mobilize the landless peasants against their feudal lords. When World War II broke out, he went to Iraq, where he joined Rashid Ali al-Kaylani's 1941 revolt against the British. Having established himself as a champion of agrarian reform, Hawrani was elected to the parliament in 1943, 1947, and 1949. In 1945 he and his *shabiba* (young men) group seized Hama's garrison from the French, and in early 1948 he fought in the Palestine war on the side of Fawzi al-Qawuqji's Army of Deliverance (*jaysh al-inqadh*). Hawrani held ministerial portfolios in the governments of Hashim al-Atasi and Adib Shishakli. In 1950 he mobilized his followers in the Arab Socialist party, with headquarters in Hama and branches in other centers. Three years later, Hawrani's party merged with Ba'th to form the Arab Socialist Ba'th party, a coalition of the urban middle class (mainly schoolteachers and government employees) and politicized peasants.

Shishakli's heavy-handedness sent Hawrani into exile in Lebanon. In 1954, after Shishakli's fall, Hawrani returned to Syria, and in 1957 he became president of the parliament. He was a strong advocate of the United Arab Republic (1958–1961); in the central cabinet that Gamal Abdel Nasser created for the union government, Hawrani served as vice president and minister of justice. In 1959 he resigned his cabinet posts, disenchanted with the authoritarianism of Nasser and the unstable structure that he created in Syria. After Syria's secession from the union in 1961, Hawrani opposed subsequent Ba'th efforts to re-create the union and tried to reestablish his Arab Socialist party. The Ba'th officers who engineered the coup of March 1963 (Hafiz al-Asad, Salah Jadid, and others) ordered the arrest of Hawrani. When he was released, he went to Lebanon, where he tried to mobilize Syrians opposed to the Asad regime in the National Progressive Front. In many respects, Hawrani was an agent of social change, an energetic activist who roused the peasants, politicized the army, and shook the foundations of the old order.

See also ARAB–ISRAEL WAR (1948); ASAD, HAFIZ AL-; ATASI, HASHIM AL-; BA'TH, AL-; JADID, SALAH; KAYLANI, RASHID ALI AL-; NASSER, GAMAL ABDEL; NATIONAL PROGRESSIVE FRONT (SYRIA); QAWUQJI, FAWZI AL-; UNITED ARAB REPUBLIC (UAR).

Bibliography

Batatu, Hanna. *Syria's Peasantry, the Descendants of Its Lesser Rural Notables, and Their Politics.* Princeton, NJ: Princeton University Press, 1999.

Seale, Patrick. *The Struggle for Syria: A Study of Post-War Arab Politics, 1945–1958.* New Haven, CT: Yale University Press, 1987.

MUHAMMAD MUSLIH

HAYAT

See NEWSPAPERS AND PRINT MEDIA: ARAB COUNTRIES

HAYCRAFT COMMISSION (1921)

A British commission that investigated Palestinian anti-Zionist violence in May 1921.

Palestinians attacked the Jewish inhabitants of Jaffa and five Jewish colonies on 1 May 1921, resulting in 47 Jewish deaths and 146 injured, mostly by Palestinians, and 48 Palestinian deaths and 73 wounded, mostly by the military and police. The British high commissioner for Palestine, Sir Herbert Samuel, appointed a commission, headed by the chief justice of Palestine, Sir Thomas Haycraft, to determine the causes of the Arab violence. The commission reported in October 1921 that what triggered the violence was a May Day clash between rival Jewish Communists and Jewish Socialists in nearby Tel Aviv. The fundamental cause, however, was Palestinian "discontent with, and hostility to, the Jews, due to political and economic causes, and connected with Jewish immigration, and with their conception of Zionist policy as derived from Jewish exponents." The report stated that the Palestinians feared that Jewish immigration would lead to unemployment in the short run and to political and economic subjugation in the long run.

After the report was issued, the British took some steps to meet Palestinian demands. In December, Samuel established the Supreme Muslim Council to administer the *awqaf* (religious endowments) and to appoint and dismiss officials and judges of the *shari'a* courts. In January 1922, he allowed the election of Muhammad Amin al-Husayni, a popular Palestinian nationalist, as president of the council. In June 1922, Sir Winston Churchill, secretary of state for the colonies, issued a white paper which, while reconfirming continued British support for the Zionists, reassured the Palestinians that they need not fear the "imposition of Jewish nationality" on them, rejected the idea that Palestine would become "as Jewish as England is English," limited Jewish immigration to the "economic capacity of the country," and proposed a legislative council with limited powers. The Palestinians rejected the new policy because it was based on the Balfour Declaration. The Zionists accepted it but criticized the British for backing away from the Balfour Declaration.

See also BALFOUR DECLARATION (1917); CHURCHILL WHITE PAPER (1922); CHURCHILL, WINSTON S.; HUSAYNI, MUHAMMAD AMIN AL-; SAMUEL, HERBERT LOUIS; SUPREME MUSLIM COUNCIL.

Bibliography

Caplan, Neil. *Palestine Jewry and the Arab Question, 1917–1925.* London: Frank Cass, 1978.

A *Survey of Palestine*, 3 vols. Jerusalem: Government Printer, 1946–1947; Washington DC: Institute for Palestine Studies, 1991.

PHILIP MATTAR

HAYIM, YUSEF
[c. 1833–1909]

Rabbi of Baghdad.

Born in Baghdad during the Ottoman Empire, Yusef Hayim attended the Midrash Bet Zilkha from 1848 to 1853. He became the student of Hakham Abdullah Somikh and his most promising disciple; he married the daughter of Yehuda Somikh, Rahel, and they had children. Hayim belonged to a family of wealthy merchants, which came to be known as Bet al-Hakham. As he became well known to the world of Jewish scholars, especially those in the Middle East, his opinions on religious matters were routinely sought. He left a large number of writings (*responsa*), some of which have been published.

When Hayim's father died in 1859, he inherited the place of chief preacher (*darshan*), which he maintained throughout his life. He also wrote poems (*piyyutim*) and hymns (*pizmonim*), some of which are included in the Baghdad prayer book. His principal work, known as *Ben Ish Hai* (a name by which he came to be known) had the status for Baghdad Jewry as the *Shulhan Arukh* had for all Judaism. Philosophically and practically, he was a moderate traditionalist who assumed that modern Western teachings entering the Middle East by way of the Alliance Israélite Universelle might be adapted and accommodated.

See also ALLIANCE ISRAÉLITE UNIVERSELLE (AIU); SOMIKH, ABDULLAH.

SYLVIA G. HAIM

HAYKAL, MUHAMMAD HASANAYN
[1923–]

Egyptian journalist, author, and politician.

Born to a middle-class Cairo family, Muhammad Hasanayn Haykal (also Heikal) went to government schools and attended both Cairo University and the American University in Cairo. He began working as an unpaid reporter for the *Egyptian Gazette* and *Rose al-Yusuf*, covering the battle of al-Alamayn and the debates in Egypt's parliament. He then became a reporter for *Akhir Sa'a*, winning the King Farouk Prize for investigative journalism for his coverage of the 1947 cholera epidemic. Between 1946 and 1949 he covered the Palestine struggle, interviewing David Ben-Gurion (head of Israel's provisional government and then prime minister) and Jordan's King Abdullah, and also meeting Gamal Abdel Nasser, an Egyptian army major who later led a coup and became Egypt's leader. Haykal's assignments were wide-ranging; he also covered the civil war in Greece, the Mossaddegh crisis in Iran, and (supported by a U.S. State Department "Leader Grant") the 1952 U.S. presidential campaign.

Haykal claims to have been on intimate terms with Egypt's Free Officers before the 1952 revolution; certainly he became closer to Nasser while he was in power than did any other journalist. Editor of *Akhir Sa'a* in the early 1950s, he became editor in chief of *al-Akhbar* in 1956 and of the prestigious but fading *al-Ahram* in 1957, rebuilding it into the most influential newspaper in the Arab world. He became Nasser's adviser, confidant, and spokesman, and is widely credited with ghostwriting Nasser's *Falsafat al-thawra*. A strong believer in press freedom and scientific management, Haykal made *al-Ahram*'s facilities among the most modern in the world and founded periodicals ranging from the Marxist *al-Tali'a* to the business-oriented *al-Ahram al-Iqtisadi*. He also founded a Center for Strategic Studies and a well-stocked research library. His weekly column, "Bi al-saraha" (Speaking frankly), was widely assumed to indicate the direction of Nasser's thinking.

After serving briefly as minister of culture and national guidance in 1970, Haykal broke with Anwar al-Sadat, who succeeded Nasser as Egypt's president, because of Sadat's willingness to seek peace with Israel. Dismissed as editor of *al-Ahram* in 1974, Haykal was barred from publishing articles in the Egyptian press. He went on writing for Lebanese Arabic newspapers and published books in English. Interrogated by the Egyptian police and state prosecutor in 1977 and 1978, he was forbidden to travel abroad, then imprisoned during Sadat's 1981 purge. Although under President Husni Mubarak Haykal has not regained his former influence on policy decisions, he is respected as an intellectual, writer, and possible mediator with other Arab states, such as Libya. He asked President Mubarak to launch a new project for the revival of Arab civilization based on enlightenment, modernization, free expression, rule of law, and social justice. Haykal divides the achievements of Egypt during the twentieth century into four generations: the first generation, which ended in 1919, achieved intellectual enlightenment and cultural structure; the second generation, which ended in 1949, developed the constitutional and national movement, and its best symbol was the revolution of 1952; the third generation, which ended in 1979, achieved Arab nationalism and socialism; and the fourth generation, which will end in 2009, is achieving compromise, peace, capitalist companies, and pluralism.

Haykal's memoirs of events in which he took part should be read with caution. They include *Cairo Documents* (1973), *Road to Ramadan* (1975), *The Sphinx and the Commissar* (1978), *Autumn of Fury: The Assassination of Sadat* (1983), *Cutting the Lion's Tail: Suez through Egyptian Eyes* (1986), and *1967: The Explosion* (1990).

Haykal today is still a very controversial figure, especially since the 1990s, after the publication of numerous books on hot topics. Many books have attempted to analyze his life and to ascertain the claims he made about historical figures and events during the twentieth century. His latest books, which have focused mostly on historical events and biographies, include *The Spring of Anger* (1990), *The Gulf War* (1993), *October 73* (1993), *Power Game* (1995), *Egypt's Gate to the Twenty-First Century* (1995), *The Secret Negotiations between Arabs and Israel* (1996), *Arabs' Crisis and the Future* (1997), *Japanese Articles* (1998), *Crowns and Armies* (1998), and *The Arabian Gulf* (1998). His latest book is *From New York to Kabul* (2001). In 1995 the Egyptian government demanded that Haykal surrender the documents that he has been using in his writings about Nasser's period or face imprisonment. He has kept the secret documents at European banks. In the last three decades Haykal has refused any award to honor his work or life.

See also FREE OFFICERS, EGYPT; MOSSADDEGH, MOHAMMAD; NASSER, GAMAL ABDEL; NEWSPAPERS AND MEDIA: ARAB COUNTRIES.

Bibliography

Nasir, Munir. *Press, Politics, and Power: Egypt's Haykal and Al-Ahram.* Ames: Iowa State University Press, 1978.

ARTHUR GOLDSCHMIDT
UPDATED BY AHMAD S. MOUSSALLI

HAYKAL, MUHAMMAD HUSAYN
[1888–1956]

Egyptian author, political leader, and lawyer.

Born to a landowning family in Daqahliyya, Muhammad Husayn Haykal was educated at the Cairo School of Law and at the University of Paris, where he wrote his doctoral thesis on the Egyptian public debt (1912). Homesick for his native village, he also wrote a bucolic fiction, called *Zaynab* (Cairo, 1914), which is usually described as the first modern Arabic novel.

Upon returning to Egypt, he practiced law, wrote for *al-Jarida* of Ahmad Lutfi al-Sayyid (with whom he remained close throughout his life), published a magazine called *al-Sufur* during World War I, and taught at the School of Law. Egypt had become a British protectorate in 1914, and when the nationwide revolution for independence broke out in 1919, he backed the Wafd and Sa'd Zaghlul, one of its leaders, but broke with them in 1921 over negotiations with Britain. At this time, Prime Minister Adli Yakan, Haykal, and other educated Egyptians formed the Constitutional Liberal Party (Hizb al-Ahrar al-Dusturiyyin), calling for parliamentary democracy. In 1922, Haykal became editor of its newspaper, *al-Siyasa*, and he later founded an influential weekly edition, *al-Siyasa al-Usbu'iyya*. He continued his literary production with the books *Fi awqat al-faragh* (Cairo, 1925), *Tarajim misriyya wa gharbiyya* (Cairo, 1929), and a touching eulogy of his son who died in childhood, called *Waladi* (Cairo, 1931).

In 1934, when the Constitutional Liberals were competing for popular favor with the Wafd, the palace, and rising Muslim groups, he published *Hayat Muhammad* (Cairo, 1934), an attempt to apply modern scholarship to the biography of the prophet Muhammad and to reconcile the principles of personal freedom with the teachings of Islam. Increasingly pious, he made the pilgrimage to Mecca (hajj) in 1936, and published *Fi manzal al-wahy* (Cairo, 1937), relating his experience as a pilgrim. He served as Egypt's minister in seven cabinets in the late 1930s and the 1940s and as president of the Senate from 1945 to 1950. He published his last novel *Hakadha khuliqat* (Cairo, 1955) and also his memoirs, *Mudhakkirat fi al-siyasa al-misriyya* (Cairo, 1951–1978, 3 vols.), of which two volumes appeared in his lifetime and the third posthumously. An ambitious man with many talents, he often felt a conflict between secularism and Islam and between the democratic principles of his party and his belief that Egypt should be governed by its most educated citizens.

See also LITERATURE: ARABIC; NEWSPAPERS AND PRINT MEDIA: ARAB COUNTRIES; WAFD; ZAGHLUL, SAʿD.

Bibliography

Smith, Charles D. *Islam and the Search for Social Order in Modern Egypt: A Biography of Muhammad Husayn Haykal.* Albany: State University of New York Press, 1983.

Wessels, Antonie. *A Modern Arabic Biography of Muhammad.* Leiden, Netherlands: E.J. Brill, 1972.

ARTHUR GOLDSCHMIDT

HAZA, OFRA

[1957–2000]

Israeli singer who revitalized and popularized traditional Yemeni songs for a world audience.

Ofra Haza's singing style was characterized by powerful, artistically rendered emotionality, whether she was interpreting traditional or popular songs. She personified Israeli popular music from the early 1980s until the late 1990s. A nominee for a Grammy Award, she took second place in the 1983 Eurovision Song Contest with "Chai," launching a singing career that would earn her sixteen gold and platinum records.

The ninth and final child born to Yemenite immigrants in the impoverished ha-Tikva neighborhood of south Tel Aviv, Haza joined the ha-Tikva Theater group at the age of twelve and began a rags-to-riches ascent in the Israeli popular imagination. With the encouragement of ha-Tikva Theater founder Bezalel Aloni, who later became her manager, Haza took leading roles within the ha-Tikva group, and by the time she was nineteen, her solo career was launched.

In 1985, Haza released her first internationally acclaimed album, *Yemenite Songs,* a collection of interpretations of devotional poetry written by Shalom Shabazi, a seventeenth-century rabbi. Haza's music appealed to Ashkenazic as well as Mizrahi audiences, and her performances bridged ethnic, class, and generational dividing lines in Israeli society. She was

chosen to sing in Oslo when Yitzhak Rabin, Yasir Arafat, and Shimon Peres received the Nobel Prize, and was chosen again to sing at the memorial concert following Rabin's assassination.

Shaday (1988) was Haza's second international album. It contained "Im Nin'alu," Haza's signature song, which was featured on MTV, a first for an Israeli singer. A striking beauty, she attempted, unsuccessfully, to pursue a film career in California before returning to Israel in the mid-1990s. Religiously devout and noted for remaining humble despite her fame, Haza married in 1998. She died in 2000 from complications resulting from AIDS, possibly contracted from her husband, who committed suicide a year later. The medical panel investigating Haza's death said in a published report that, had Haza admitted herself to hospital earlier, her life could have been saved. Fearful of the negative publicity that could result if her condition were to become known, Haza refused to seek proper medical care until it was too late. Former Prime Minister Shimon Peres delivered a eulogy at her graveside, and Israeli attitudes about AIDS came under critical discussion following her death.

See also ADOT HA-MIZRAH; ASHKENAZIM; MUSIC.

Bibliography

Jerusalem Post Staff. "Ofra Haza: An Appreciation." Available from <http://info.jpost.com/2000/Supplements/OfraHaza/>.

Silver, Eric. "Remembering Ofra Haza." *The Jewish Journal of Greater Los Angeles.* Available from <www.jewishjournal.com/old/silver.3.3.0.htm>.

LAURIE KING-IRANI

HAZARA

Ethnolinguistic group in Afghanistan.

The Hazara live in the high central mountains of Afghanistan in a region called the Hazarajat, and they number between one and two million. The Hazara are racially distinct from the rest of the Afghans, with Mongoloid physical features, including the epicanthic fold of the upper eyelid commonly seen in the people of central Asia. Although Hazara legend has it that they are the descendants of the army of the great Mongol conqueror Genghis Khan, scholars now believe them to be descendants of Chaghatai from Transoxiana, who entered the area as soldiers under Timur and his son Shah Rukh in the fifteenth century. Originally Sunni Moslems, the Hazara were converted to Shi'ism during the time of the Safavid King Abbas I (1588–1692), when this part of Afghanistan was controlled by Iran. The Hazara speak a dialect of Persian known as *Hazaragi*, which contains some Turkic and Mongol words.

The Hazara lived a relatively independent existence in Afghanistan until the 1890s, when they were brought under the control of Kabul in a series of wars during the reign of Abd al-Rahman (1880–1901). Looked down upon by other Afghans, the Hazara are the poorest of the Afghan ethnolinguistic groups. Some have migrated to Kabul and the other major cities, where they work in menial jobs. During the Afghan war of resistance, the Hazara were able to expel the government representatives from the Hazarajat, and in 1979 they established a quasi-independent government under a council led by Sayyid Ali Beheshti. By the mid-1980s, however, the Hazarajat came under the control of the Iranian-backed Shi'ite groups of Nasr and Pasdaran. In the early 1990s the Hazara political groups united in an organization called *Hezb-e Wahadat* (Unity Party), led by Mohammed Karim Khalili. This group played a major role in the formation of the Mojahedin government in 1992.

The Hazara, through Hezb-e Wahadat, fought against the Taliban movement, which captured Kabul in 1996, and joined the United Front in the fight against the Taliban government. As a result, the Taliban government carried out a number of massacres against Hazara civilians, both in the Hazarajat and in the northern city of Mazar-e Sharif, between 1998 and 2000. When the Taliban government was driven from Kabul in December of 2001 the Hazara played an active role in the formation of the interim government of Hamid Karzai, and held several important seats in the interim government.

See also AFGHANISTAN; BAMYAN; SHI'ISM.

Bibliography

Adamec, Ludwig. *Historical Dictionary of Afghanistan*. Metuchen, NJ: Scarecrow Press, 1991.

Farr, Grant. "The Rise and Fall of an Indigenous Resistance Group: The Shura of the Hazarajat." *Afghanistan Studies Journal* 1 (1988): 48–61.

Rubin, Barnett R. *The Fragmentation of Afghanistan: State Formation and Collapse in the International System*. New Haven, CT: Yale University Press, 2002.

GRANT FARR

HAZAZ, HAYYIM
[1898–1973]

Hebrew writer.

Hazaz was born in Sidorvichi, a province of Kiev. His secular and religious education included the study of Russian and Hebrew literature. Hazaz left home at sixteen, and for seven years traveled from one Russian city to another. While in Moscow, during and after the Russian Revolution, he worked at the Hebrew daily *Ha'am*. In 1921, Hazaz settled in Constantinople (now Istanbul) for a year and a half, and subsequently moved to Western Europe. He spent nine years in Paris and Berlin, which replaced pre-Revolutionary Russia as the capital of Hebrew literary activity.

In early 1931, Hazaz left for Palestine and settled in Jerusalem. A political activist, he was president of the Israel–Africa Friendship Association from 1965 to 1969. After the Six-Day War (1967), he became an advocate for the Land of Israel Movement, which called for settling the lands captured during the war and permanently incorporating them into the state of Israel.

Hazaz began his writing career while still in Russia publishing a sketch, *Ke-Vo ha-Shemesh* (1918), in *Ha-Shilo'ah* under a pseudonym. Thereafter he published under his own name. The dominant theme of his Russian-period stories is the fate of the shtetl in the aftermath of the Russian Revolution. The old world had been turned on its head and its generation became disoriented. Among these stories are *Mi-Zeh u-mi-Zeh* (From this and that, 1924) and *Pirke Mahpekhah* (Chapters of the revolution, 1924). Another Hazaz story of the revolution is *Shemu'el Frankfurter* (1925), which has as its protagonist the title character, a revolutionary, whose idealism and integrity doom him. Hazaz's first novel, *Be-Yishuv Shel Ya'ar* (In a forest settlement, 1930), is set during the Russian–Japanese War and depicts a Jewish family among gentiles. As the story evolves, it becomes clear that while the latter are firmly anchored in their land, the former are manifestly rootless.

His Eretz Yisrael (Hebrew: "The Land of Israel," i.e., Palestine) phase began with *Rehayim Shevurim* (Broken millstones, 1942). While some of his stories continue to recount shtetl life, others are located in Palestine. One of his major works, *Ha-Yoshevet ba-Gannim* (Thou that dwellest in the gardens, 1944), recounts the story of three generations of Yemenite Jews in Eretz Ysrael. *Harat Olam* and *Havit Akhurah* describe the life of German-Jewish immigrants. *Esh Boʿeret* and *Drabkin* are studies of immigrants from Eastern Europe. The first describes the idealism of the *halutzim* (pioneers) who fled Russia and suffered immeasurable hardships to reach Palestine; while the second narrative tells of its title hero's disillusionment with Zionism when it fails to fulfill his dreams. Several of Hazaz's protagonists struggle to narrow the gap between their ideals and reality. In *Ha-Derashah* (The lesson) Yudke, the story's hero, questions the commonly accepted premises of Zionism.

Yaʾish, Hazaz's most elaborate work (4 vols., 1947–1952), recounts the life of Yaʾish, a young Yemenite Jew who abandons his mystical beliefs upon arriving in Eretz Yisrael while experiencing external and internal conflicts. In this four-volume opus, Hazaz evinces intimate familiarity with Yemenite culture. *Be-Kolar Ehad* (In the one collar, 1963) deals with the struggle against the British in Palestine. The heroes, young resistance fighters condemned to death by the British, opt to commit suicide. The story is based on historical fact and raises issues of the Diaspora such as redemption and *Kiddush ha-Shem,* Sanctification of the name, i.e., sacrificing one's life for the sake of God.

Since Hazaz's linguistic style is rooted in ancient Jewish texts, reflecting a profound knowledge of the Talmud and Midrash, he is not easily understood by the modern Hebrew reader. To overcome this obstacle, a revised edition of all his works was published in 1968, in which Hazaz deleted many archaic words and allusions.

Hazaz was awarded the Israel Prize for Literature in 1953.

See also LITERATURE: HEBREW.

ANN KAHN

HAZZAN, ELIJAH BEKHOR
[1847–1908]

An important Sephardic scholar, intellectual, and communal leader.

Born in İzmir and raised in Jerusalem, Elijah Bekhor Hazzan traveled to Europe and French North Africa in the early 1870s. He published a philosophical dialogue, *Zikhron Yerushalayim* (Livorno, Italy, 1874), on questions of modernity and Jewish identity.

Appointed Hakham Bashi (chief rabbi) of Tripolitania in 1874, he was a leading, but controversial advocate of reforms. He was more successful as the modernizing chief rabbi of Alexandria, where he served from 1888 until his death. He published four volumes of *responsa* (interpretations), *Taʿalumot Lev* (Livorno/Alexandria, 1879–1902), and a work on Alexandrian Jewish customs, *Neveh Shalom* (Alexandria, 1894).

See also ADOT HA-MIZRAH.

Bibliography

Stillman, Norman A. *The Jews of Arab Lands in Modern Times.* Philadelphia: Jewish Publication Society, 1991.

NORMAN STILLMAN

HEBREW

Major official language of the State of Israel.

Hebrew is the national language of the Jewish population of Israel (about 5 million) and the mother tongue of Jews born in the country. For world Jewry (about 14 million) it is the traditional liturgical language and a link to daily life in contemporary Israel.

Hebrew is the original language of the Bible. It has played a central role in the cultural history of the Jewish people for the past three millennia, and has had an important impact on Western culture. Ancient Hebrew names such as Jacob, Joseph, Sarah, and Mary, and old Hebrew words or concepts such as "amen," "hallelujah," "hosanna," "Sabbath," and "Messiah" have survived, resisting translation in many languages and cultures.

Hebrew belongs to the Canaanite group of the Northwestern Semitic or Afro–Asiatic family of languages. During its long history (which follows the historical course of the Jewish people), it has undergone diverse changes and has developed several different layers, from biblical Hebrew to modern Israeli Hebrew.

Biblical Hebrew (BH) is believed to have crystallized over 3,000 years ago, when the Israelite tribes coalesced into a homogeneous political unit under the monarchy in Jerusalem (eleventh–tenth centuries B.C.E.). It emerged as a fully formed literary language whose poetic grandeur is attested by the oldest portions of the Bible, written about that time.

In its early, classical form BH functioned as a living language until the end of the First Temple Period (586 B.C.E.). Due to its prestigious status as the language of the early books of the Bible, it survived as a literary language until the second century B.C.E., as seen in the late books of the Bible, in the Apocrypha, and in the Dead Sea Scrolls. BH was employed centuries later, mainly by the Hebrew poets of medieval Spain (eleventh to thirteenth centuries) and the writers of the Jewish Enlightenment movement in Eastern Europe (late eighteenth and nineteenth centuries). Most important, because praying and reciting the Bible in the original Hebrew have always been central to synagogue worship, contact with BH has never ceased. The preservation throughout the ages of the morphological structure of BH accounts for the relative uniformity in the various historical layers of the language.

The Second Temple Period (516 B.C.E.–70 C.E.) saw the beginning of Jewish bilingualism. Aramaic, another Northwestern Semitic language, closely akin to Hebrew and a lingua franca in the ancient Middle East, became the second language of the Jewish people. The contact between BH and Aramaic (and, to a certain degree, Greek and Latin) gradually resulted in an enriched and quite different kind of spoken Hebrew with a literary counterpart, known as Rabbinic Hebrew (RH). A change in script occurred at that time, the ancient Canaanite alphabet of BH being replaced by the Assyrian square script used in Aramaic.

Well adapted to deal with everyday practical matters, RH was employed in writing down the Mishna (the oral law, 220 C.E.), and for several hundred years it continued to be used together with Aramaic in the Rabbinic literature (the Talmud and the

Hebrew Alphabet

Name	Letter
alef	א
bet/vet	ב/ב
gimel	ג and ג
dalet	ד and ד
hey	ה
vav	ו
zayin	ז
chet	ח
tet	ט
yud	י
kaf/khaf	כ (final ך)
kaf sofit/khaf sofit	כ (final ך or ך)
lamed	ל
mem	מ (final ם)
nun	נ (final ן)
samekh	ס
ayin	ע
pey/fey	פ/פ (final ף)
tzade	צ (final ץ)
kof	ק
resh	ר
sin/shin	ש/ש
tav	ת and ת

Midrash). Its role as a spoken language, however, declined at the end of the second century C.E., following the destruction of Jerusalem and the Judaean state by the Romans (70 C.E.).

For the following 1,700 years, Hebrew fell into disuse as a spoken language in daily use because the diaspora Jews used the vernaculars of their host countries for communication. Nevertheless, Hebrew was by no means a dead language. In their dispersed communities the Jewish people continued to use it as their written language in their liturgical, scholarly, literary, and even practical activities. Writing and copying were greatly aided in the Middle Ages by the introduction of the Rashi script (which survives among Middle Eastern Jews). In addition to the vast, multifaceted religious and secular literature written in Hebrew at that period, hundreds of books were translated into Hebrew, primarily from Arabic and Latin. Each of these literary activities contributed to the growth of the language by enriching its vocabulary and by introducing new syntactic patterns. At the same time, many Hebrew words and expressions were incorporated into the Jewish languages that developed alongside the vernaculars, such as Judeo–Arabic, Judeo–Spanish, and Yiddish.

The search for a new Hebrew idiom, suitable for a realistic literary expression in the modern era, followed the revival of Hebrew culture by the Jewish Enlightenment Movement. Mendele Mokher Seforim (1835–1917) is considered the first modern writer who integrated in his style varied elements from all the periods of Hebrew as well as from Yiddish. His work contributed to the transformation of Hebrew into a flexible modern literary vehicle and helped pave the way for the rise of modern Hebrew literature.

The renaissance of Hebrew as a spoken language in the twentieth century was closely linked to the national revival of the Jewish people in their forefathers' land. Hebrew was revived thanks to the efforts of a small group of devoted people, led by Eliezer Ben-Yehuda (1857–1922), who in 1881 settled in Jerusalem and pioneered Hebrew usage at home and in school. He published a Hebrew periodical, promoted the coining of new words, and cofounded the Language Committee (1890–1953), which began dealing with language planning issues and set normative measures. Above all, Ben-Yehuda compiled several volumes of the first modern dictionary of ancient and modern Hebrew.

Ben-Yehuda's work gained increasing support from the waves of Jewish immigrants and refugees returning to Zion. When the state of Israel was proclaimed in 1948, Hebrew was a functioning modern language, fully established as the living language of the growing Jewish community in the country. Supervision of its continuous growth was assigned in 1953 to the Academy of the Hebrew Language in Jerusalem.

Since the first days of its rebirth, thousands of new words have been created in Hebrew from its own roots and many of its ancient words have been given new meanings. Influence from other languages on vocabulary and syntax may be discerned as well. Encompassing all areas of life and gaining ever greater flexibility, Hebrew has become the dynamic, vibrant language of modern Israel.

See also BEN-YEHUDA, ELIEZER; DEAD SEA SCROLLS.

Bibliography

Saenz-Badillos, Angel. *The History of the Hebrew Language*, translated by John Elwolde. Cambridge, U.K., and New York: Cambridge University Press, 1993.

Waldman, Nahum. *The Recent Study of Hebrew.* Cincinnati, OH: Hebrew Union College Press, 1989.

RUTH RAPHAELI

HEBREW UNIVERSITY OF JERUSALEM

Israeli university.

The creation of a Jewish university in Jerusalem that would teach subjects in Hebrew was a major cultural goal of Zionism. In 1914 land was purchased on Mount Scopus, and the cornerstone for the university was laid in 1918 by Chaim Weizmann. The Hebrew University of Jerusalem opened on 1 April 1925 in a ceremony attended by major Jewish figures and British officials. Chaim Weizmann is considered its founding father; the first chancellor was Judah Magnes. By 1947 the campus had more than 1,000 students and 200 faculty.

The 1948 Arab–Israel War left the Mount Scopus campus on the Jordanian side of divided Jerusalem. A new campus was established at Givʿat Ram in western Jerusalem. Additional campuses include the Hadassah medical school at Ein Kerem in southwest Jerusalem and an agricultural school in Rehovot. After the 1967 Arab–Israel War the Mount Scopus campus was rebuilt and expanded as the university's main campus. A full range of advanced degree programs is offered, and in 2003 nearly 23,000 students—including Jewish and Arab citizens of Israel as well as international students—attended the four campuses, taught by 1,200 tenured faculty. The multicultural makeup of the Mount Scopus campus was evidenced in the casualties from the bombing of the student cafeteria on 31 July 2002, which killed nine and wounded several dozen. Approximately 40 percent of all civilian scientific research in Israel is conducted at Hebrew University.

See also MAGNES, JUDAH; WEIZMANN, CHAIM.

Bibliography

Gilbert, Martin. *Israel: A History.* New York: Morrow, 1998.

Hebrew University of Jerusalem. "About the University: History." Available from <http://www.huji.ac.il/huji/eng>.

PIERRE M. ATLAS

HEBRON

West Bank city, south of Jerusalem.

Hebron (in Arabic, *al-Khalil*; in Hebrew, *Hevron*) is an ancient city, holy to both Judaism and Islam, because it is the site of the Machpelah burial cave of the Biblical and Qur'anic figures Abraham, Isaac, and Jacob, and their respective wives Sarah, Rebekah, and Leah. Later, in the tenth century B.C.E., David was proclaimed king in Hebron when Saul died, and it became his first capital. Above the Machpelah cave is a mosque complex known as the al-Haram al-Ibrahimi.

Although predominantly a town inhabited by Palestinian Arab Muslims, a small Jewish community lived in Hebron throughout the centuries. During British rule, the Jews left after the Arab-Jewish disturbances of August 1929 when sixty-four Jews were massacred. Hebron was annexed by Jordan in 1950 in the aftermath of the Arab-Israel War of 1948, and it was occupied by Israel during the Arab–Israel War of 1967. As a result, Jews were allowed to pray in the al-Haram, something formerly forbidden to them. A civilian Jewish settlement called Kiryat Arba was established nearby in 1968, and militant nationalist settlers also began moving into the heart of Hebron itself. Formation of the Gush Emunim movement furthered this development. Long a flashpoint for Israeli-Palestinian violence, Hebron's worst violence in decades occurred in February 1994 when Baruch Goldstein, a U.S.-born Jewish settler, entered the al-Haram al-Ibrahimi mosque and massacred twenty-nine Palestinian worshippers before he himself was killed.

Because of the presence of approximately 400 Jewish settlers in Hebron, it was the only major West Bank town (besides Jerusalem) from which Israeli forces did not withdraw in 1994 as a result of the Oslo Accord. The troops later withdrew from 80 percent of Hebron in January 1997 in accordance with the Protocol Concerning the Redeployment in Hebron, leaving the 120,000 Palestinian residents under Palestinian rule. Yet, Israel retained control of the remaining 20 percent of the city, which included the downtown Palestinian market and the al-Haram al-Ibrahimi, to protect the remaining Jewish settlers.

See also ARAB–ISRAEL WAR (1948); ARAB–ISRAEL WAR (1967); GUSH EMUNIM; KIRYAT ARBA; OSLO ACCORD (1993).

BENJAMIN JOSEPH
UPDATED BY MICHAEL R. FISCHBACH

HEDAYAT, SADEGH

[1903–1951]

Iran's most famous and controversial writer.

Sadegh Hedayat was born into a prominent Tehran family. Having received a European-style education in Iran, he traveled to Europe in 1926 to begin his university studies. He returned to Tehran in 1930 without a degree and proceeded to write four collections of short stories and a novella, along with other books and essays on Persian culture and history, in a remarkably productive period that lasted until 1942. He became the most famous and controversial writer in Persian literature and the only Iranian writer of fiction with an appreciable audience outside Iran.

Hedayat wrote story after story about alienated, maladjusted protagonists, all with tragic endings. His writings exude nostalgia for an Indo-European Iranian past; they are filled with nationalism, strident anti-Arab sentiments, antipathy toward his fellow countrymen, disgust with the local social and political milieu, and familiarity with contemporary European literature. His masterwork is the novella *Buf-e Kur* (1937; The blind owl); it is Iran's most famous piece of fiction, a much translated, enigmatic, surrealistic narrative of a character out of tune with his times and perhaps deranged.

See also LITERATURE: PERSIAN.

Bibliography

Hillmann, Michael C., ed. *Hedāyat's "The Blind Owl" Forty Years After*. Austin: University of Texas Press, 1978.

Katouzian, Homa. *Sadeq Hedayat: The Life and Literature of an Iranian Writer*. New York; London: I.B. Tauris, 1991.

MICHAEL C. HILLMANN
UPDATED BY ERIC HOOGLUND

HEKMATYAR, GOLBUDDIN
[1940–]

Afghan resistance leader; prime minister of Afghanistan from 1993–1994.

Born in 1940 in the city of Baghlan in northern Afghanistan to a Kharoti Gilzai Pushtun family, Hekmatyar attended college at Kabul University's faculty of engineering in the 1960s and became active in campus politics. In 1970 he joined the Muslim Youth movement and was imprisoned in Kabul (1972–1973) because of his political activities. He was released after the Daud coup (1973) and fled to Pakistan, where he began his antigovernment activities. In Pakistan, he became a leader in the Jami'at-e Islami (1975) but left this group to form his own party, Hezb-e Islami (1978). After gaining the support of Pakistan and other Islamic countries, he turned his party into an effective force in Afghanistan, and by the 1980s Hekmatyar's guerrilla fighters controlled large parts of Afghanistan.

In 1992, after the collapse of the Najibullah government, he returned to Afghanistan to take part in the Islamic government in Kabul. He attempted unsuccessfully to seize control of the government by forming a coalition with Dustom, an Uzbek warlord. The effort was eventually defeated by the troops of Ahmad Shah Mas'ud. He later accepted the post of prime minister in the government of Burhanuddin Rabbani (1993), but never fully occupied that position; instead, he joined other leaders in the attempt to form an alternative government and continued to attack Mas'ud's troops in Kabul. When the Taliban drove the Rabbani government from Kabul in 1996, Hekmatyar fled to Tehran, where he continued his activities in exile. In 2002, after the Taliban had been driven from Kabul, Hekmatyar was expelled by Iran and was thought to have returned to Jabal Saraj, his former stronghold. He has been strongly anti-American and hostile to the interim government of Hamid Karzai.

See also Hezb-e Islami; Karzai, Hamid; Rabbani, Burhanuddin; Taliban.

Bibliography
Ewans, Martin. *Afghanistan: A Short History of Its History and Politics.* New York: HarperCollins, 2002.

Roy, Olivier. *Islam and Resistance in Afghanistan.* New York; Cambridge, U.K.: Cambridge University Press, 1986.

GRANT FARR

HELMAND RIVER

Major river system in Afghanistan.

The Helmand River originates in the high mountains of the Hindu Kush range in central Afghanistan and flows to the Hamun-e Helmand (Lake Helmand) in Iran. The longest river in Afghanistan (more than 2,000 miles), the Helmand River drains 40 percent of the Afghan watershed. In the 1940s and 1950s, the Helmand Valley Project was initiated as a cooperative venture between the United States and Afghanistan. A series of dams and canals was constructed to irrigate the arid Helmand valley. Despite problems of salination and poor drainage in some areas, as well as massive corruption, the project produced beneficial effects, since thousands of farmers were relocated from other areas of Afghanistan and given land in this area.

Since 1979, war and drought have had an impact on the Helmand River. The drought that lasted from 1997 through 2002 dramatically reduced stream flow and led to increased desertification in much of the Helmand basin. Twenty years of war diverted attention and manpower, so canals and equipment vital to maintaining the irrigation were not maintained. In addition, with no governmental control, the cultivation of opium poppies replaced many of the traditional crops and has led to warlordism and lawlessness.

See also AFGHANISTAN.

Bibibliography
Dupree, Louis. *Afghanistan.* Princeton, NJ: Princeton University Press, 1980.

Rubin, Barnett R. *The Fragmentation of Afghanistan: State Formation and Collapse in the International System.* New Haven, CT: Yale University Press, 2002.

GRANT FARR

HERAT

Province and city in western Afghanistan.

Herat is both a province in northwestern Afghanistan and the name of the provincial capital of that province. In 2003 the population of the city of Herat was generally held to number about 180,000, although some estimates have the population much higher. Even using the lower figure, Herat is the third largest city in Afghanistan and the major city in the country's western region. Close to the Iranian border, the people in the province are largely Persian speakers, although some Turkomans live in the northern area.

Because of its strategic location, Herat has been a fortified town for several thousand years. Mention of it first appears in the Avesta, the holy book of the Zoroastrians (1500 B.C.E.), and scholars have conjectured that the name *Herat* may be a derivative of Aria, a province in the ancient Persian empire. Alexander the Great built Alexandria Ariorum on the site (330 B.C.E.). During the Afghan war of resistance (1978–1992), the city of Herat saw considerable fighting and suffered significant destruction. When the Najibullah government fell in 1992, Isma'il Khan, a commander in the Jami'at-e Islami, took control of the area.

The Taliban captured Herat in 1995, and Ismail Khan and his fighters fled to Iran. The Taliban installed an administration imposing strict Islamic rule. When the Taliban fell in 2001, Isma'il Khan returned to Herat and was appointed governor of the province by the Hamid Karzai government. Herat now serves as a major smuggling route for foreign goods coming into Afghanistan, and for the export of Afghan opium.

See also AFGHANISTAN.

Bibliography

Adamec, Ludwig. *Historical Dictionary of Afghanistan.* Metuchen, NJ: Scarecrow Press, 1991.

Ewans, Martin. *Afghanistan: A Short History of Its People and Politics.* New York: HarperCollins, 2002.

GRANT FARR

HERUT PARTY

See ISRAEL: POLITICAL PARTIES IN

HERZL, THEODOR

[1860–1904]

Herzl is considered the founder of political Zionism.

A secular Jew, Theodor Herzl earned a doctorate in law in 1884, and worked in the courts of Vienna and Salzburg. After only a year he left the legal profession and began a successful career as a writer and journalist.

As Paris correspondent for the liberal Vienna newspaper *Neue Freie Presse,* Herzl observed and reported on emerging French antisemitism. He was court correspondent at the court-martial of Captain Alfred Dreyfus and witnessed the anti-Jewish disturbances by Parisian mobs during the ceremony expelling Dreyfus from the military. Herzl's interest in Jewish affairs was roused by these firsthand observations of French antisemitism. Herzl articulated his beliefs in his book, *Der Judenstaat* (The Jews' State), which was published in Vienna in 1896.

In order to translate his vision into reality, Herzl had to convince both the international Jewish community and leaders of the great powers. In June 1896, he submitted a proposal to the Grand Vizier whereby the Jews would manage the empire's deteriorating financial affairs. When this proposal was rejected, Herzl requested permission to establish a Jewish state in Palestine that would remain under the suzerainty of the sultan. This too was rejected.

Initial Jewish responses to *Der Judenstaat* were mixed. The Baron Edmond de Rothschild of London rejected Herzl's appeals for support because of his belief that the Jewish masses could not be organized to implement Herzl's scheme of mass resettlement. In 1897, Herzl established news a weekly, *Die Welt,* in which he lobbied for the convening of a congress of Jewish representatives from around the world. At the First Zionist Congress in Basle, Switzerland, on 29 to 31 August 1897, the Zionist program was adopted by the representatives of world Jewry. The Basle Program, as it came to be known, called for the establishment of "a home for the Jewish people in Palestine secured under public law." It proposed the promotion of Jewish settlement in Palestine, the organization of world Jewry by appropriate institutions, the strengthening and fostering of Jewish national sentiment, and preparatory steps toward gaining the consent of the relevant governments. The World Zionist Organization was established as the institutional framework for the

Zionist program, and Herzl served as its president until his death.

See also DREYFUS AFFAIR; ROTHSCHILD, EDMOND DE; WORLD ZIONIST ORGANIZATION (WZO); ZIONISM.

Bibliography

Bein, Alex. *Theodor Herzl: A Biography,* translated by Maurice Samuel. Cleveland, OH: World, 1962.

Chouraqui, Andre. *A Man Alone: The Life of Theodor Herzl,* translated by Yael Guiladi. Jerusalem: Keter, 1970.

Elon, Amos. *Herzl.* New York: Holt, Rinehart, 1975.

SHIMON AVISH

HERZOG, CHAIM
[1918–1997]

Israeli statesman and general.

Chaim Herzog was born in Dublin, the son of Izhak Halevi Herzog, who was chief rabbi of Ireland and, from 1936 to 1959, of Palestine and later Israel. Chaim studied in Hebron Yeshiva in Israel (1935), at Wesley College in Dublin, and at Cambridge University in England. In World War II he served with the British army, attaining the rank of major. From 1945 to 1947 he was with the British army of occupation in Germany. During the Arab–Israel War of 1948 he served as an intelligence officer in Jerusalem and was promoted to head the Israel Defense Force (IDF) Intelligence Corps (1948–1950). From 1950 to 1954 he was the defense attaché at the Israeli Embassy in Washington. Upon his return to Israel, he once again commanded the Intelligence Branch (1959–1962). After retiring from the IDF, he practiced law in Tel Aviv. On the eve of the Arab–Israel War of 1967, his reputation was enhanced when, in a series of broadcasts to an anxious Israeli populace, he lifted the national morale. He was the first military governor of Jerusalem and the West Bank after that war.

From 1968 to 1975 he practiced law, wrote books on history, and contributed many articles to publictions in Israel and abroad. From 1975 to 1978 he was Israel's ambassador to the United Nations. He will be remembered as the Israeli who on the podium of the General Assembly tore up UN Resolution 3379 (10 November 1975), which equated Zionism with racism. Elected to the Knesset on Labor's ticket in 1981, two years later he was chosen as Israel's sixth president and served two terms until 1993.

See also HERZOG, IZHAK HALEVI.

Bibliography

Herzog, Chaim. *The Arab–Israeli Wars: War and Peace in the Middle East.* New York: Vintage, 1984.

Herzog, Chaim. *Living History: A Memoir.* London: Weidenfeld and Nicolson, 1997.

Herzog, Chaim. *Who Stands Accused: Israel Answers Its Critics.* New York: Random House, 1978.

MERON MEDZINI

HERZOG, IZHAK HALEVI
[1888–1959]

First Ashkenazic chief rabbi of Israel.

Izhak Halevi Herzog was born in Lomza, Poland. His family moved to England, where his father served as a rabbi in Leeds. In addition to his religious learning, the younger Herzog studied at the University of Paris and University of London, where he completed his doctorate. After serving as a congregational rabbi in Belfast and Dublin for nine years, Herzog became chief rabbi of Ireland in 1925. He helped found the religious Zionist Mizrahi movement in England and testified before the Anglo–American Committee of Inquiry and the United Nations Special Committee on Palestine. Following the death of Rabbi Abraham Isaac Hacohen Kook, Herzog was elected Ashkenazic chief rabbi of Palestine in 1936. He continued as Ashkenazic chief rabbi after the establishment of the State of Israel until his death. As Israel's first Ashkenazic chief rabbi, he handled many new and delicate issues in Halakhah, Jewish religious law. He was the father of Chaim Herzog and Ya'acov David Herzog.

See also HALAKHAH; HERZOG, CHAIM; HERZOG, YA'ACOV DAVID; KOOK, ABRAHAM ISAAC HACOHEN.

Bibliography

Herzog, Isaac Halevi. *The Main Institutions of Jewish Law.* 2 vols. London: Soncino Press, 1936–1939.

CHAIM I. WAXMAN

HERZOG, YA'ACOV DAVID
[1921–1972]

Israeli scholar and diplomat.

Born in Dublin, Ya'acov Herzog was the son of Rabbi Izhak Halevi Herzog, who was chief rabbi of Ireland and, from 1936 to 1959, of Palestine and later Israel. Herzog grew up in a home imbued with learning and tradition. From an early age he excelled in his studies in yeshivot in Jerusalem and fulfilled a number of official missions aiding his father. In 1949 his scholarship and erudition attracted the attention of both Foreign Minister Moshe Sharett and Premier David Ben-Gurion. Herzog joined the Foreign Ministry in 1949 and headed the Jerusalem and Christian Affairs Department, later heading the North America Division. During the 1956 Arab–Israel War he served as Ben-Gurion's principal political adviser. From 1957 to 1960 he was minister plenipotentiary at the Israeli Embassy in Washington and from 1960 to 1963 ambassador to Canada. His reputation was enhanced due to a much-publicized public debate with British scholar Arnold Toynbee, who had argued that Jews were fossils with no right to a national homeland. Herzog's soaring reputation brought an offer to serve as chief rabbi of Great Britain and the Commonwealth, which he declined. From 1965 until his premature death he was director general of the Prime Minister's Office under Premiers Levi Eshkol and Golda Meir. As their key political adviser, he was the first senior Israeli official to meet King Hussein ibn Talal of Jordan in 1963 and establish this diplomatic channel. Many other secret meetings, mainly in London, followed.

See also HERZOG, IZHAK HALEVI.

Bibliography

Eban, Abba. *Abba Ebban: An Autobiography.* New York: Random House, 1977.

Herzog, Chaim. *Living History: A Memoir.* London: Weidenfeld and Nicolson, 1997.

Louvish, Misha, ed. *A People That Dwells Alone: Speeches and Writings of Yaacov Herzog.* London: Weidenfeld and Nicolson, 1975.

MERON MEDZINI

HESKAYL, SASSON
[1860–1932]

Iraqi Jewish statesman and economist.

Sasson Heskayl was born in Baghdad where his father, Hakam Heskayl, was the leading rabbinical authority. After graduating from the Alliance Israélite Universelle, he went to Vienna to study economics and law. His knowledge of foreign languages (French, German, English, Turkish, Persian, Arabic, and Hebrew) enabled him to become chief translator for the *vilayet* of Baghdad upon his return from Europe. In 1908, Heskayl was elected a representative of Baghdad to the Chamber of Deputies in Constantinople (now Istanbul). He spent several years there and was adviser to the ministry of commerce and agriculture. Upon returning to Baghdad in 1920, he was appointed minister of finance in the first government headed by Abd al-Rahman al-Naqib, retaining that post (with a short interruption) for the next five years. In 1925 he was elected to parliament and was chairman of its finance committee. He died in Paris while undergoing medical treatment.

At the 1921 Cairo Conference, which was convened by Winston Churchill, the British colonial secretary, and decided upon the election of Amir Faisal I as king of Iraq, Heskayl was one of two representatives of the government of Iraq, the other one being Ja'far al-Askari. Heskayl was knighted in 1923.

During negotiations with the British Petroleum Company, Heskayl demanded that oil revenue be calculated on the basis of gold. His demand was reluctantly accepted. This concession benefited Iraq's treasury during World War II, when the pound sterling plummeted. Some historians maintain that Heskayl's confrontation with the British eventually caused his removal as minister of finance.

See also ASKARI, JA'FAR AL-; CAIRO CONFERENCE (1921); CHURCHILL, WINSTON S.; FAISAL I IBN HUSSEIN; JEWS IN THE MIDDLE EAST.

Bibliography

Rejwan, Nissim. *The Jews of Iraq: 3000 Years of History and Culture.* London: Weidenfeld and Nicolson, 1986.

SASSON SOMEKH

HESS, MOSES
[1812–1875]

German Zionist writer.

A committed German Jewish Socialist and a contemporary of Karl Marx and Friedrich Engels, Moses Hess spent much of his life in Paris and is sometimes thought of as the first Zionist Communist. He collaborated with Marx and Engels in 1830s and the 1840s, but he rejected their economic determinism and broke with them after 1848. In 1862 Hess wrote *Rome and Jerusalem,* in which he argued that the Jews, like the Italians, should establish their own state. This book later influenced such proponents of Zionism as Theodor Herzl. Hess believed that antisemitism and German nationalism went hand in hand and that with the growth of the latter, a Jewish state was imperative. A firm adherent of peaceful change rather than violent revolution, in *Rome and Jerusalem* Hess extolled the ethics of love, harmony, and cooperation. Once in their own country, Hess claimed, the duty of the Jews was to prepare themselves for a Socialist "Sabbath of History," which would mark the liberation not just of the Jews but of all mankind.

See also HERZL, THEODOR; LABOR ZIONISM.

Bibliography

Elon, Amos. *The Israelis: Founders and Sons.* New York: Penguin, 1983.

Hertzberg, Arthur, ed. *The Zionist Idea: A Historical Analysis and Reader.* Philadelphia: Jewish Publication Society, 1997.

Laqueur, Walter. *A History of Zionism.* New York: Schocken, 1989.

ZACHARY KARABELL

HEZB-E ISLAMI

Afghan Islamist political party.

The Hezb-e Islami, or Party of Islam, formed as an Afghan paramilitary resistance organization in Pakistan in 1977, splitting from the Islamist Jami'at-e Islami. The organization evolved into two branches, the larger led by Golbuddin Hekmatyar and the smaller by Maulawi Yunis Khalis. The party follows fundamentalist Islamic principles and is strongly anti-Western and anti-American.

Hezb-e Islami was one the best organized, most successful organizations in the Afghan war of resistance (1978–1992). In 1992 the Hezb-e Islami and its leader Hekmatyar returned to Kabul to participate in the government formed by the resistance groups after the fall of the Najibullah government. Hezb-e Islami soon turned against that government and was driven from Kabul when the Taliban came to power in 1996. Exiled to Iran, the party had little role in the formation in 2002 of the interim government of Hamid Karzai. Remnants of the party still exist in some parts of Afghanistan.

See also HEKMATYAR, GOLBUDDIN; JAMI'AT-E ISLAMI.

Bibliography

Roy, Olivier. *Islam and Resistance in Afghanistan.* New York; Cambridge, U.K.: Cambridge University Press, 1986.

Rubin, Barnett R. *The Fragmentation of Afghanistan: State Formation and Collapse in the International System.* New Haven, CT: Yale University Press, 2002.

GRANT FARR

HEZBOLLAHI

See GLOSSARY

HIBBAT ZION

First international Zionist organization to be founded; established in the aftermath of the Russian pogroms of 1881 and 1882.

Hibbat Zion was formed in 1884 by Dr. Leo Pinsker, a Russian physician who practiced in Odessa. Its membership combined European Jewish traditionalists—long committed to support the growing scholarly Jewish community in Palestine—with newly recruited secular nationalists from Eastern Europe. Dr. Pinsker had been appalled by the pogroms and realized that even assimilated Jews could not consider themselves safe in their adopted lands. In his pamphlet *Auto-Emancipation,* Pinsker argued that Jews in the diaspora could not afford to remain passive in the hopes of either divine redemption or some voluntary ending of antisemitism. Instead Jews had to liberate themselves by reconstituting themselves as a nation in a land of their own.

Orthodox rabbis joined Hibbat Zion assuming that secular nationalists could be won back to piety.

These assumptions were translated into policies: Those who wished to settle as farmers in Palestine and who received financial aid from Hibbat Zion had to observe Judaism and its traditions. For secular nationalists, like Dr. Pinsker, this was a troublesome policy. The enthusiasm initially engendered by the creation of Hibbat Zion waned as the uneasy alliance experienced financial crises and internal disputes. Nevertheless, a few colonies were established and aided in Palestine, such as Petah Tikvah (founded in 1878), and the educational aspect of the movement resulted in the Zionist thought and actions of other individuals and groups in Eastern Europe.

See also ANTISEMITISM; DIASPORA; PETAH TIKVAH; PINSKER, LEO; POGROM.

Bibliography

Hertzberg, Arthur, ed. *The Zionist Idea: A Historical Analysis and Reader.* Philadelphia: Jewish Publication Society, 1997.

Luz, Ehud. *Parallels Meet: Religion and Nationalism in the Early Zionist Movement (1882–1904).* Philadelphia: Jewish Publication Society, 1988.

DONNA ROBINSON DIVINE

HIGH COMMISSIONERS (PALESTINE)

Heads of the Palestine government during British civilian rule (1 July 1920–14 May 1948).

Except for a short period (December 1917–June 1920) of British military government, Palestine under the British mandate was run by a civilian administration headed by a high commissioner, who reported directly to London. Though entrusted by the League of Nations to Great Britain as a mandate, which entailed the "development of self-governing institutions," Palestine was governed as a British crown colony; that is, full power and authority were vested in the high commissioner. His powers included censorship, deportation, detention without trial, demolition of the homes of suspects, and collective punishment—powers that were used against both Palestinian and Jewish communities.

The high commissioner was assisted by an executive council consisting of a chief secretary, attorney general, and treasurer and by an advisory council consisting, from 1920 to 1922, of British officials and prominent Arab and Jewish appointees; after 1922 its members were all British officials. In 1922 and 1923, the high commissioner proposed to the Arab and Jewish communities the establishment of self-governing institutions for Palestine, in particular a legislative council, but due to the conflicting political goals of the two communities and to Britain's Balfour Declaration, which favored a Jewish national home in Palestine, such institutions were never agreed to or established and the high commissioner continued to exercise sole authority over Palestine until the end of the mandate.

The Palestine government was headed by seven high commissioners, whose names and dates of appointments were as follows:

Sir Herbert Samuel, 1 July 1920

Lord Herbert Plumer, 14 August 1925

Sir John Chancellor, 1 November 1928

Sir Arthur Wauchope, 20 November 1931

Sir Harold MacMichael, March 3, 1938

Viscount John Gort, 31 October 1944

Sir Alan Gordan Cunningham, 21 November 1945

See also BALFOUR DECLARATION (1917); LEGISLATIVE COUNCIL (PALESTINE); MANDATE SYSTEM; PALESTINE; PLUMER, HERBERT CHARLES ONSLOW.

Bibliography

Jones, Philip. *Britain and Palestine, 1914–1948.* Oxford: Oxford University, 1979.

Palestine Government. *A Survey of Palestine*, 2 vols. (1946). Washington, DC: Institute for Palestine Studies, 1991.

Patai, Raphael, ed. *Encyclopedia of Zionism and Israel*, 2 vols. New York: Herzl Press, 1971.

PHILIP MATTAR

HIGH STATE COUNCIL (ALGERIA)

Algerian interim executive, 1992–1994.

When the first round of parliamentary elections on 26 December 1991 made it clear that the Islamist

FIS (Front Islamique du Salut) would gain majority control of the Algerian parliament if the second round of elections were to proceed as scheduled on 16 January 1992, a bitter dispute broke out within the government of President Chadli Bendjedid. The president favored continuing the electoral process whereas the military and other ardent secularists wanted the process terminated. The military forced Chadli to dissolve the sitting parliament, where the speaker—his constitutional successor—sat, and then forced the president himself to resign on 11 January, leaving the Algerian state without an executive branch. Three days later a five-man Haut Comité d'État (High State Council; HCE) was appointed to serve as a collective transitional executive until the end of 1993 when Chadli's term would officially expire. The most powerful member of the council was Defense Minister Khaled Nezzar. Others included Ali Kafi, the influential head of the Moudjahidine organization, Tedjini Haddam, Mohamed Ali Haroun, and Mohamed Boudiaf. Boudiaf, one of the few surviving *chefs historiques* of the War of Independence, was invited to return from twenty-eight years of exile to chair the council.

From the outset the HCE moved aggressively to dismantle the FIS and other Islamist organizations, rounding up and imprisoning many of their leaders and members. The result was escalating violence against security forces and governmental institutions. Boudiaf, an ardent secularist, announced a program for authentic democratization, major economic reform, and thorough investigation of alleged corruption within the ruling establishment. On 29 June 1991, while giving a speech at Annaba, he was assassinated. Many assume the murder was orchestrated by the military because of its unease with Boudiaf's priorities, though some in the establishment blame Islamists offended by Boudiaf's secularism.

Ali Kafi was named chair of the HCE after Boudiaf's assassination. He appointed as prime minister Belaïd Abdessalam who, because of dissent over economic policies, was subsequently replaced by Redha Malek in August 1993. While Kafi in May 1993 announced a forthcoming constitutional referendum to determine what institution was to succeed the HCE when its mandate expired, security and political considerations prohibited such a solution. Ultimately the military, coming together in January 1994 as the High Security Commission, appointed Liamine Zeroual head of state. He had succeeded the ailing Nezzar as defense minister the preceding summer. The Haut Comité d'État was dissolved.

Bibliography

Martinez, Luis. *The Algerian Civil War, 1990–1998.* London: Hurst, 2000.

Quandt, William B. *Between Ballots and Bullets. Algeria's Transition from Authoritarianism.* Washington, DC: Brookings Institution Press, 1998.

JOHN RUEDY

HIJAB

The practice of veiling, covering either the entire face and body or only the hair and neck.

Islam—a religion of balance, moderation, and modesty—places a strong emphasis on the maintenance of proper boundaries, whether social or moral. The practice of *hijab* among Muslim women is grounded in religious doctrine, yet the Qur'an does not require it. Support for veiling is found in the *hadith* of Sahih Bukhari: "My Lord agreed with me (Umar) in three things. . . . (2) And as regards the veiling of women, I said 'O Allah's Apostle! I wish you ordered your wives to cover themselves from men because good and bad ones talk to them.' So the verse of the veiling of the women was revealed" (Bukhari, volume 1, book 8, *sunnah* 395).

Display of the self in public, for men as well as women, is a subject of considerable concern in Islamic teachings and practices. The care, treatment, and presentation of the human body are influenced by Qur'anic teachings, as well as by *hadith,* and codified in the *shariʿa.* In examining Islamic teachings about bodily presentation, the issue of boundaries (*hudud,* in Arabic) is of primary importance, particularly gender boundaries and spatial boundaries, which usually overlap in daily practice. Islam draws a clear distinction between the public and the private. Men's and women's roles in these domains are complementary, not equal. Since Islam views the family as central to and crucial for the survival of society and the continuation of proper human life, boundaries that specify men's and women's roles, and boundaries that mark off the private realm of familial space from wider public spaces are elaborated and crucial for the preservation of an Islamic social order. Concerns with literal and figurative boundaries are evident in everyday practices, including dress, bodily ornamentation, architecture, and contact between men and women.

The practice of veiling is a visible recognition of the maintenance of proper boundaries. It is a way of keeping proper distance and ensuring respect and moral behavior between men and women in public space. In private, women do not veil, and in public women may well be wearing attractive clothing and elaborate jewelry under their *abayas* or *chadors*. The Qur'an and *hadith* stipulate that a woman should not display her personal adornments or physical charms to anyone but her husband (Sura 24:31 and Sura 33:59). There are, however, a wide variety of views on how much of a woman's body should be covered from public view. Islam is not an ascetic religion preaching the negation of the flesh. The veils and headscarves worn by observant Muslim women in public are often used to aesthetic effect to accentuate the eyes or the curve of the face, emphasizing, though modestly, a woman's best features. Scarves and veils are often embroidered and edged with subtle lace designs for added aesthetic impact within the bounds of Islamic propriety.

Veiling as a social practice predates Islam. Depending on the wider social and political contexts, *hijab*'s meanings, for Muslims as well as non-Muslims, have changed, sometimes dramatically. In the nineteenth century, upper-class urban women were more likely to veil than were working-class or peasant women. By the 1960s, the reverse was the case. The veil has been a charged political, cultural, and moral issue, as well as a site of misunderstanding and conflict between Muslims and non-Muslims, or even between observant and nonobservant Muslims. Turkey, an overwhelmingly Muslim country, has witnessed some of the fiercest debates on the meaning of *hijab*; veiling is perceived as a threat to the secular political order established by Atatürk in the 1920s.

In the early twentieth century, many leading Arab women activists and intellectuals displayed their modernity by removing the veil, as did Huda al-Sha'rawi upon her return to Egypt from a women's conference in Europe. Yet the veil is also a potent symbol of resistance to the West and its political and economic agenda in the Middle East and North Africa. From the late 1970s until today, many young women throughout the Arab and Islamic world have voluntarily adopted *hijab* and conservative dress in general in order to make a political as much as a religious statement of identity and ideological commitment. Many women assert that the veil guarantees them freedom, dignity, and greater scope for movement in a world that sexualizes women. According to this argument, the *hijab* deflects and neutralizes the objectifying male gaze, enabling women to emerge as autonomous subjects in the public realm. In Iran, the *hijab* became obligatory for all adolescent girls and women shortly after the Islamic revolution (1979). The changing balance of forces between conservatives and reformists in Iran is often read in the degree to which women comply with *hijab* and how much hair they reveal.

See also CLOTHING; HADITH; QUR'AN; SHA'RAWI, HUDA AL-.

Bibliography

Ahmed, Leila. *Women and Gender in Islam: Historical Roots of a Modern Debate.* New Haven, CT: Yale University Press, 1992.

Fernea, Elizabeth Warnock, and Bezirgan, Basima Qattan, eds. *Middle Eastern Muslim Women Speak.* Austin: University of Texas Press, 1977.

Mernissi, Fatima. *Beyond the Veil: Male-Female Dynamics in a Modern Muslim Society.* New York: John Wiley, 1975.

Mernissi, Fatima. *The Veil and the Male Elite: A Feminist Interpretation of Women's Rights in Islam.* Reading, MA: Addison-Wesley, 1991.

Moruzzi, Norma. "Women's Space/Cinema Space: Representations of Public and Private in Iranian Films." *Middle East Report* 212 (Fall 1999): 52–55.

Sabbagh, Suha, ed. *Arab Women: Between Defiance and Restraint.* New York: Olive Branch Press, 1996.

Sha'rawi, Huda. *Harem Years: The Memoirs of an Egyptian Feminist 1879–1924*, edited and translated by Margot Badran. New York: Feminist Press, 1987.

Zuhur, Sherifa. *Revealing, Reveiling: Islamist Gender Ideology in Contemporary Egypt.* Albany: State University of New York Press, 1992.

LAURIE KING-IRANI

HIJAZ

An arid, mountainous region in western Saudi Arabia, and site of Mecca and Medina.

The Hijaz region is the cradle of Islam and home to the faith's two Holy Cities. Hijaz reached the peak of its political importance after the rise of Islam, when Mecca was the seat of the first four caliphs (rulers) of the Muslim community. Since that time, the ebb and flow of the annual Muslim pilgrimage (*hajj*) has dictated the region's economic viability. Lack of water and arable land severely limited human settlement before the oil era. Dates were cultivated in several oases, such as al-Ula and Tayma, and other crops were grown where conditions permitted, most notably in the elevated regions around al-Taʾif. Nomadism was also important, but declined after the creation of the Saudi state. Fishing and trade permitted the growth of settlement on the Red Sea coast, with the port city of Jidda serving as way station for pilgrims to the Holy Cities as well as for commercial traffic. Hijaz regained a degree of political prominence after it became an Ottoman province in 1517, ruled by sharifs, descendents of the prophet Muhammad. After World War I the region attained brief independence, but was conquered by the forces of the Al Saʿud in 1926 and subsequently incorporated into Saudi Arabia.

Bibliography

Ochsenwald, William. *Religion, Society, and the State in Arabia: The Hijaz under Ottoman Control, 1840–1908.* Columbus: Ohio State University Press, 1984.

Rentz, G. "Al-Hidjaz." In *Encyclopedia of Islam, New Edition,* Vol. 3, edited by B. Lewis, V. L. Ménage, C. Pellat, and J. Schacht. Leiden, Netherlands: Brill, 1971.

KHALID Y. BLANKINSHIP
UPDATED BY ANTHONY B. TOTH

HIJAZ RAILROAD

Railroad connecting Damascus and Medina.

Built during the reign of Sultan Abdülhamit II, the Hijaz Railroad is 811 miles (1,308 km) long. It is so named because Medina, its eastern terminus, is located in a western region of the Arabian Peninsula called the Hijaz. Abdülhamit built the railroad to facilitate the movement of the Ottoman army, thus allowing for closer Ottoman control of southern Syria and the Hijaz. In addition, easier movement of religious pilgrims to Mecca would buttress his claim to be caliph of the Muslims. Additional branches were built connecting the main line to

The Hijaz Railway was built in the early 1900s to transport pilgrims from Damascus to Medina and Mecca, a trip that had previously been undertaken by camel. The railway was heavily damaged during World War I and, despite sporadic attempts at revival, remains abandoned. © JAMES SPARSHATT/CORBIS.

Haifa, Basra, Lydda, and Ajwa, bringing total trackage to 1,023 miles (1,650 km) in 1918.

The railroad, which cost 4 million Turkish liras (equivalent to about 15 percent of the Ottoman budget), was financed without foreign loans. Arguing that the railroad was essential to the protection of Mecca and Medina, and that it should be financed and operated by Muslims, the Ottoman government raised between one-third and one-fourth of the total cost through contributions from its subjects and donations from Muslims around the world. The remainder was financed by the state.

As the Ottomans began to design and construct the railroad in 1900, they wanted to build the railroad without foreign assistance. Yet because all previous railroads and public utilities had been built and managed by foreigners, their experience was limited. Thus, the goals of speeding construction and limiting costs dictated the use of foreign assistance. Ottoman military officers, led by Mehmet Ali Paşa, supervised the initial engineering and construction, assisted by an Italian engineer, La Bella. But incompetent surveying, maltreatment of workers, and financial problems limited progress in the first six months of construction to the preparation of 12.5 miles (20 km) of earthwork for tracks. As pressure from Constantinople (now Istanbul) to speed up construction increased, Mehmet Ali Paşa was removed and court-martialed.

His successor, Kazim Paşa, de facto ceded Ottoman control over the technical aspects of construction to a German engineer, Heinrich Meissner. Meissner supplemented his largely foreign staff with Ottoman engineers trained in Europe. Ottoman soldiers pressed into service provided most of the labor force, though foreign workmen also were employed. The railroad reached Medina in August 1908. Over the next six years, facilities including storehouses, switching yards, and repair facilities were constructed.

Passenger service for the pilgrimage began in 1908. In 1914, operations included three weekly passenger trains from Damascus to Medina, and seven weekly trips from Damascus to Haifa. The run to Medina was scheduled to take fifty-six hours, although three days was average; the shorter run to Haifa was scheduled for eleven and a half hours.

During World War I, the Hijaz Railroad was central to the strategy of both the Ottoman army and the Arab army of Sharif Husayn ibn Ali that launched the Arab Revolt in 1916. For the Ottomans, a planned invasion of Egypt, defense of the Hijaz, and defense of southern Syria depended on control and extension of the railroad. Unable to confront 25,000 Ottoman troops directly, the Arab army directed raids against the railroad, disrupting service and wresting control of sections from the Ottomans. On 1 October 1918 the Ottoman Hijaz Railroad administration was replaced by an Arab general directorate.

See also ABDÜLHAMIT II; ARAB REVOLT (1916); HUSAYN IBN ALI.

Bibliography

Issawi, Charles. *An Economic History of the Middle East and North Africa.* New York: Columbia University Press, 1982.

Ochsenwald, William. *The Hijaz Railroad.* Charlottesville: University Press of Virginia, 1980.

Owen, Roger. *The Middle East in the World Economy, 1800–1914.* London: Methuen, 1981.

Shaw, Stanford, and Shaw, Ezel Kural. *History of the Ottoman Empire and Modern Turkey,* Vol. 2: *Reform, Revolution, and Republic: The Rise of Modern Turkey, 1808–1975.* Cam-

bridge, U.K., and New York: Cambridge University Press, 1977.

DAVID WALDNER

HIKMA UNIVERSITY, AL-

University founded by American Jesuits in Iraq in 1956.

Al-Hikma University was built in Za'franiyya, on the southern edge of Baghdad, by American Jesuits. They have been engaged in education in that city since 1932, when they were invited by the Christian hierarchy to open a secondary school—Baghdad College.

Al-Hikma offered degrees in business administration, civil engineering, and literature; instruction was mainly in English. The student body was coeducational, with 95 percent Iraqis; the faculty was about 50 percent Iraqi. Enrollment grew slowly and was approaching 1,000 when the Ba'thist government seized the university and expelled the Jesuits in 1968. The students enrolled at the time of nationalization continued their studies until graduation, then the university ceased to exist. The site was transformed into a technical institute.

In 1969, the Jesuits were also expelled from Baghdad College, which continued in existence as a secondary school attached to the Iraqi ministry of education.

JOHN J. DONOHUE

HILAL, AL-

Monthly magazine founded in 1892 in Cairo by Jurji Zaydan.

Probably the oldest magazine in Arabic, until World War I *al-Hilal* was the most important journalistic forum of the Arab Nahda (Renaissance) in all its aspects. Later it became a platform for progressive Egyptian literature; after nationalization under Gamal Abdel Nasser, it adapted, increasingly, the *Reader's Digest* model in format and content.

See also LITERATURE: ARABIC; NAHDA, AL-; NASSER, GAMAL ABDEL; ZAYDAN, JURJI.

Bibliography

Philipp, Thomas. *Gurgi Zaidan: His Life and Thought.* Wiesbaden, Germany: Steiner, 1979.

Philipp, Thomas. *The Syrians in Egypt, 1725–1975.* Stuttgart, Germany: Steiner, 1985.

THOMAS PHILIPP

HILLEL, SHLOMO
[1923–]

Israeli politician.

Born in Baghdad, Shlomo Hillel immigrated to Palestine in 1930 and graduated from the prestigious Herzliyya High School in Tel Aviv. A member of the Haganah underground from his teens, he was a founder of Kibbutz Ma'agan Mikha'el in 1945 and managed the Ayalon Institute, a clandestine Haganah munitions factory. In 1947 he was recruited by Mossad le-Aliyah Bet (the clandestine Haganah immigration arm) and brought a planeload of Iraqi Jews to Palestine. From 1948 to 1951 he ran immigration operations in Lebanon, Syria, Egypt, and Iran and masterminded Operation Ezra and Nehemia, which airlifted 124,000 Iraqi Jews to Israel in 1950 and 1951. His best-selling book *Operation Babylon,* which appeared in 1987, recounts his experiences in immigration operations.

Elected to the Knesset on the Labor Party ticket in 1951, Hillel resigned in 1959 to join the foreign service. He was Israel's first ambassador to the Ivory Coast and Guinea. Later he headed the Africa Department of the Foreign Ministry and until 1967 served on the Israel Delegation to the United Nations. From 1967 to 1969 he was assistant director general of the Foreign Ministry, dealing with contacts with Palestinian Arab leadership in the occupied territories. Hillel was minister of police in the Golda Meir cabinet (1969–1974) and in the first Yitzhak Rabin cabinet (1974–1977). He also served briefly as minister of the interior. Re-elected to the Knesset in 1977, he served as its speaker from 1984 to 1988.

From 1989 to 1998 Hillel served as world chairman of Keren ha-Yesod–United Israel Appeal, responsible for fund-raising worldwide, with the exception of the United States. He was awarded the Israel prize in 1998 for lifetime achievement. He heads the Shazar Center for the Study of History and the Association for the Preservation of Historic Sites in Israel.

Bibliography

Hillel, Shlomo. *Operation Babylon,* translated by Ina Friedman. Garden City, NY: Doubleday, 1987.

MERON MEDZINI

HILMI, AHMAD
[1882–1963]

Palestinian politician during British mandate.

Born Ahmad Hilmi Abd al-Baqi in Palestine, Hilmi was active in banking and used his financial leverage for nationalist ends, founding the Arab National Bank in 1930 and later purchasing the newspaper *Filastin.* He used wartime profits from deposits held in the Arab National Bank to invest in Palestine's industry and commerce. Ownership of *Filastin* provided him with a platform from which to air his anti-Zionist, Palestinian nationalist views.

Throughout his life, Hilmi was associated with the Istiqlal (Independence) Party. This strongly nationalist party was ideologically rooted in Arab nationalism of the World War I era. In April 1936, the general strike in Palestine led to the formation of the Arab Higher Committee (AHC), of which Hilmi became an independent member. In October 1938, the AHC was outlawed, and Hilmi was arrested and deported to the Seychelles. In 1939, he and Awni Abd al-Hadi urged the AHC to accept the British white paper, which signaled a change in British policy by restricting the levels of Jewish immigration to Palestine. This display of moderation caused the mandate authorities to allow Hilmi to return to Palestine.

In July 1948, the Administrative Council for Palestine was founded in Gaza under the auspices of the Arab League. It was replaced by the All-Palestine government claiming authority over the newly founded state of Israel, the Gaza Strip, and the Jordanian-held West Bank. Hilmi was appointed to head the all-Palestine government, which included Jamal al-Husayni as foreign minister. Although this government was recognized by all the Arab states except Jordan, Hilmi had no authority, and the government was weak and powerless. It was officially laid to rest with Hilmi's death.

See also ABD AL-HADI FAMILY; ALL-PALESTINE GOVERNMENT; ARAB HIGHER COMMITTEE

(PALESTINE); HUSAYNI, JAMAL AL-; ISTIQLAL PARTY: PALESTINE; LEAGUE OF ARAB STATES; MANDATE SYSTEM; NEWSPAPERS AND PRINT MEDIA: ARAB COUNTRIES; WHITE PAPERS ON PALESTINE.

Bibliography

Brand, Laurie A. *Palestinians in the Arab World: Institution Building and the Search for State.* New York: Columbia University Press, 1988.

Porath, Yehoshua. *The Palestinian Arab National Movement: From Riots to Rebellion, 1929–1939.* London and Totowa, NJ: F. Cass, 1977.

LAWRENCE TAL

HILU, CHARLES
[1911–2001]

President of Lebanon, 1964–1969.

Charles Hilu was born in Beirut to a Maronite (Christian) family. He received a French education, earning law degrees from the Jesuit St. Joseph University and the French School of Law in Beirut. He founded the newspaper *L'eclair du nord* in Aleppo (1932) and *Le jour* in Beirut (1934). In the 1930s, Hilu was sympathetic to the ideology of the Phalange party and was one of its founding members. He later realized that despite his reluctance to cooperate with the Arab world, the narrow sectarian base of the party would thwart his political ambitions. He later presented himself as a moderate Maronite politician who did not oppose good ties with the Arab world.

Hilu was Lebanese minister to the Vatican in 1947 and headed Catholic Action of Lebanon. He held several ministerial positions in the 1950s and 1960s, and he was serving as minister of education in 1964 when he was elected president. His election was made possible because of his close association with Chehabism; when Fu'ad Chehab could not be persuaded to run for another term, Hilu emerged as a candidate who could carry forward the legacy of Chehabism. Chehab later said that his selection of Hilu was one of his biggest mistakes.

Hilu's administration is remembered for allowing the military-intelligence apparatus to control the affairs of the state. Some army officers in the military intelligence bureau had more power than some elected representatives. Hilu is blamed for the increasingly dangerous situation in Lebanon caused by the unwillingness of the state to respond to Israel's attacks and to Palestine Liberation Organization (PLO) activities. Many Lebanese, particularly those living in south Lebanon, thought that he forfeited the sovereignty of southern Lebanese territory. To protect himself against Maronite critics, he solidified his alliance with such conservative Maronite organizations as the Phalange party and the National Liberal Party of Camille Chamoun.

The worst crisis of Hilu's administration occurred in 1969, when Lebanese army troops fought with the PLO and its Lebanese allies (in the wake of attacks on them by Israel within Lebanon). Hilu wanted to use heavy-handed methods in dealing with the PLO, but his Sunni prime minister, Rashid Karame, refused to deal with the PLO, which at the time was the best hope for the restoration of Palestinian rights after the Arabs' humiliating defeat in the Arab–Israel War of 1967. The failures of Hilu's administration discredited Chehabism, thereby causing the Chehabi candidate, Ilyas Sarkis, to lose the presidential election of 1970.

After his retirement, Hilu lived a quiet life. He continued to make political statements but refrained from taking provocative or extremist stands. He was respected within the Maronite community.

See also ARAB–ISRAEL WAR (1967); CHAMOUN, CAMILLE; CHEHAB, FU'AD; KARAME, RASHID; MARONITES; NATIONAL LIBERAL PARTY; PALESTINE LIBERATION ORGANIZATION (PLO); PHALANGE; SARKIS, ILYAS.

AS'AD ABUKHALIL

HILU, PIERRE
[1928–2003]

Maronite politician in Lebanon.

Pierre Hilu, a wealthy industrialist born in Beirut, was a deputy representing the district of Alay. He was first elected in 1972, and became a cabinet minister for the first time in 1973. He was mentioned as a possible presidential candidate in 1988, but he refused to succeed Amin Jumayyil without Muslim support. Hilu was still considered a potential pres-

identical candidate, especially because his ties with Syria were good over the years, although he was not seen as a pawn. He was one of the few credible Maronite deputies to seek reelection in 1992 when many right-wing Christians boycotted the election. He was also again elected in the election in 2000, and had served as head of the Maronite League. In 2003, Hilu suffered a heart attack while participating in a television talk show, and was succeeded in his parliamentary seat by his eldest son Henri in the same year.

See also JUMAYYIL, AMIN; LEBANON.

AS'AD ABUKHALIL

HINDU KUSH MOUNTAINS

Main mountain chain in Afghanistan, extending to China; part of the great chain of central Asian mountains.

Beginning west of Kabul, the capital of Afghanistan, the Hindu Kush Mountains stretch some 600 miles (965 km) east across the northern tip of Pakistan and Jammu and Kashmir to the Pamir and Karakoram Mountains on the border of China. The highest peak is Tirich Mir at 25,260 feet (7,700 m). Both the Indus and Amu Darya Rivers spring from the Hindu Kush. It is the main mountain chain in Afghanistan, and during the nineteenth century, it marked the limits of British expansion north of India and the unofficial and often-contested boundary between Russia and Britain in their struggle for hegemony in Central Asia. After World War II, the Hindu Kush divided American from Russian influence in Afghanistan, with the bulk of U.S. aid flowing south and the bulk of Russian aid going to the north. After the 1979 Soviet intervention and invasion of Afghanistan, the Hindu Kush became one of the main refuges of Afghan guerrillas in their struggle to force the Soviets out of the country. The mountains were a major battle area during the United States's 2001 campaign to oust the Taliban government and break the al-Qa'ida terrorist network.

See also AMU DARYA.

Bibliography

Ewans, Martin. *Afghanistan: A Short History of Its People and Politics.* New York: HarperCollins, 2002.

Tanner, Stephen. *Afghanistan: A Military History from Alexander the Great to the Fall of the Taliban.* New York: Da Capo, 2002.

ZACHARY KARABELL

HINNAWI, SAMI AL-
[1898–1950]

A Syrian colonel who, on 14 August 1949, overthrew his predecessor, Husni al-Za'im, as military dictator of Syria and had him shot.

Sami al-Hinnawi's coup came barely four and a half months after Za'im had staged his military coup, the first in Syria's modern history. Hinnawi collaborated with the People's Party, which was disposed toward Iraq. He invited Hashim al-Atasi to form a government. A constituent assembly to draw a new constitution was elected, women voted for the first time, and all the political parties were legalized, with the exception of the Communist Party and the rightist Socialist Cooperative Party. Atasi then became president of the republic. Discussions with Iraqi officials to bring about a union between Syria and royalist Iraq were then in full sway. But Syrian republicanists and the army were not happy with the proposed union. On 19 December 1949, Colonel Adib Shishakli overthrew Hinnawi, whom he charged with treason and conspiracy with a foreign power, a reference to the proposed union with Iraq.

See also ATASI, HASHIM AL-; ZA'IM, HUSNI AL-.

Bibliography

Petran, Tabitha. *Syria.* London: Ernest Benn; New York: Praeger, 1972.

Seale, Patrick. *The Struggle for Syria: A Study of Post-War Arab Politics, 1945–1958.* New Haven, CT: Yale University Press, 1987.

ABDUL-KARIM RAFEQ

HIRAWI, ILYAS AL-
[1926–]

President of Lebanon, 1989–1998.

Born in Hawsh al-Umara near Zahla, al-Hirawi was born to a politically active Maronite family and attended Saint Joseph University. He was in charge of the family's agricultural estates while his brothers served in government. Ilyas was elected to parliament in 1972, and he established a reputation of moderation and blunt talk. He was not part of the right-wing Maronite militia establishment during the war; he was a founding member of the Independent Maronite Bloc in the Lebanese parliament, which tried to promote moderation but became famous for comprising presidential candidates among its members. Al-Hirawi maintained good relations with the Syrian government and with the right-wing Phalange militia of Bashir Jumayyil during the war, which allowed him to play a mediating role between the two sides, especially during the Zahla crisis of 1981. He served as minister in the administration of Ilyas Sarkis (1976–1982) and was elected president in 1989, after the assassination of president-elect René Muʿawwad. Al-Hirawi's administration witnessed the rise of billionaire prime minister Rafiq Hariri, who first became prime minister in 1992. His relationship with Hariri was close, although al-Hirawi and his sons were accused of corruption during his administration. Al-Hirawi established the juridically based "distinctive relations" with the Syrian government, and he was one of the closest allies of Syria in Lebanon. After leaving office, al-Hirawi published his memoirs, in which he attacked most of his political rivals and former political allies. During his administration, he promoted civil marriage, but clerics on all sides objected. Al-Hirawi retired from politics after leaving the presidency.

See also HARIRI, RAFIQ BAHAʾUDDIN AL-; JUMAYYIL, BASHIR; PHALANGE; SARKIS, ILYAS; ZAHLA.

AS'AD ABUKHALIL

HISTADRUT

Israeli federation of labor.

The Histadrut—full name in Hebrew, ha-Histadrut ha-Kelalit shel ha-Oevdim ha-Ivriʾim be-Eretz-Yisrael (The General Organization of the Jewish Workers in Eretz-Yisrael)—was founded in 1920, with a membership of 5,000. In 1930 it had 28,000 members; in 1940, 112,000; in 1950, 352,000; in 1960, 689,000; in 1970, 1,038,000; and in 1980, 1,417,000. By 1992 it had approximately 1.6 million members.

Politician Golda Meir (1898–1978) (center standing) speaks at the Histradrut headquarters. Founded in 1920 at the Haifa Technion, the Histadrut was started as a trade union to organize economic activities of Jewish workers. © PHOTOGRAPH BY ZOLTAN KLUGER. GOVERNMENT PRESS OFFICE (GPO) OF ISRAEL. REPRODUCED BY PERMISSION.

The Histadrut, which has often been called a state within the state, acts as an umbrella organization for trade unions. It has also played an important role in the development of agriculture, wholesale and retail marketing of food and other products, rural settlement, industry, construction and housing, industry, banking, insurance, transportation, water, health, and social services.

Following the creation of the State of Israel in 1948, the Histadrut handed some of its educational functions as well as its employment exchanges to the government. In recent years, it has sold a number of commercial concerns to the private sector.

In the 1920s, under the British mandate, the Histadrut's role was to help develop the Jewish economy in Palestine. To this end, in 1921 it set up Bank Hapoalim (The Workers' Bank), and in 1923, Hevrat Ovdim (The Workers' Company or Cooperative Federation) was founded. This was to become a holding company for most of the Histadrut's wide range of economic enterprises.

By 1927, when the Solel Boneh construction and industrial group first went bankrupt, the importance of reinvesting profits and maintaining an independent capital base was understood. From the late 1920s onward, economic enterprises were directed toward capital accumulation so as to avoid reliance on outside sources of finance. Solel Boneh, as well as being the largest construction company in the pre-independence period, had investments in industry. Its subsidiary, Koor, owned the Phoenicia glass works, the Vulcan foundry, and other industrial companies. The policy of financial independence was successful until the 1980s, when a number of Histadrut bodies got into serious financial difficulties.

By 1930 the retail cooperative, Hamashbir; the insurance company, Hasneh; and other groups were incorporated into Hevrat Ovdim. The Histadrut had become both a large employer as well as a trade union body. The basic structure has remained unchanged since the 1920s, but attitudes toward profits and dismissing workers have become more pragmatic and less socialist since the late 1980s.

Although about three-quarters of all wage earners in Israel are members of the Histadrut, this includes many who do no more than pay dues to its health fund, Kupat Holim Kelalit, the largest fund in the country. A share of the membership fee is passed on to the Histadrut by the health fund. Members of kibbutzim and other cooperatives are also automatically enrolled, as are those working in Histadrut enterprises. Although far fewer are, therefore, voluntary members, about 85 percent of the labor force is covered by collective labor agreements negotiated by the Histadrut. About forty trade unions, representing a wide range of blue- and white-collar workers in the public and private sectors, are affiliated. While the Histadrut is highly centralized, professional workers' unions have a high degree of autonomy.

Elections are held every four years on a political party base, and the Labor Party and its allies have had a majority since the Histadrut's foundation. Each party, in proportion to its share of the votes cast, nominates delegates to a forum that elects the central committee. The latter consists of members of the ruling coalition alone. Workers' committees at plant level are elected annually or biannually.

The Histadrut and its affiliated organizations (such as the kibbutzim) in 1991 were responsible for about 16 percent of industrial output, and 14 percent of industrial investment in Israel. Exports of these industries came to US$1.4 billion.

In that year, it was also responsible for 80 percent of agricultural output and exports, about 38 percent of the assets of the banking system (through Bank Hapoalim), 9 percent of insurance companies' assets (through Hasneh), the construction of 8 percent of homes being built, as well as large shares of retailing and wholesaling through its producer cooperatives and marketing organizations. It operated most of the country's buses through two large cooperatives and, both directly and through the kibbutzim, had a range of hotels and guest houses. About 70 percent of the population were members of Kupat Holim Kelalit, which provides medical insurance and services through clinics and hospitals. The Histadrut owns the *Davar* daily newspaper and a publishing company and has interests in the shipping and airline industries. Finally through Bank Hapoalim, it has large shareholdings in joint ventures with private sector industry.

During the 1980s, many of the Histadrut's companies and affiliates ran into serious financial difficulties. These included Koor, the kibbutzim, Kupat Holim Kelalit, and Bank Hapoalim. In all these cases, the government provided financial assistance and forced management changes. It remains to be seen if the Histadrut can regain control of these groups by buying shares back from the government or by other means.

The Histadrut's position in Israel has weakened both politically and economically. It has been weakened by grassroots alienation, by the dominance of right-wing parties in the Knesset between 1977 and 1992, and by its own lack of a clear socioeconomic message. It has faced serious financial difficulties in many of its economic enterprises and has had to be bailed out by Likud and Labor governments. The Labor Party has distanced itself from the bureaucracy of the Histadrut, which it considers an electoral hindrance. This would have been inconceivable in the first half of the twentieth century.

See also ISRAEL: POLITICAL PARTIES IN; KNES-
SET; KOOR INDUSTRIES; LABOR ZIONISM;
LIKUD.

Bibliography

Broido, Ephraim. "Jewish Palestine: The Social Fabric."
In *Palestine's Economic Future,* edited by Joseph Burton
Hobman. London: P.L. Humphries, 1946.

Preuss, Walter. *The Labour Movement in Israel: Past and Present,*
3d edition. Jerusalem: R. Mass, 1965.

Rivlin, Paul. *The Israeli Economy.* Boulder, CO: Westview,
1992.

Shalev, Michael. *Labour and the Political Economy in Israel.* New
York: Oxford University Press, 1992.

Sternhell, Zeev. *The Founding Myths of Israel: Nationalism, Socialism, and the Making of the Jewish State.* Princeton, NJ:
Princeton University Press, 1998.

PAUL RIVLIN

HISTORIOGRAPHY

Trends in historical writing about the Middle East.

Academic history-writing about the Middle East
took shape during the first half of the twentieth
century. European-style universities were founded
in the early 1900s in Istanbul and Cairo, and state
education, museums, historical associations, and
journals expanded between the wars, alongside
state-building. History-writing became a profession. Long-established forms—dynastic chronicles,
political biographies, and historical topographies—
were slowly displaced. History (ta'rikh) took on its
ambivalent, modern meaning, referring not just to
a form of knowledge, but also to the actual course
of past events. In Europe, scholars working in Oriental Studies and trained in language, philology,
and the study of Islam increasingly produced work
recognizable as modern historiography. The amateur histories of colonial officials and travelers became much-trawled primary source material to
complement chronicles and literary texts.

Civilization and Nationalism

Before 1945, historians from Europe and the Middle East formulated the past in terms of the flowering of an Islamic civilization that achieved its zenith
at some point during the Middle Ages and subsequently entered a lengthy decline. The last centuries

of Ottoman rule in particular were depicted as years
of decay and oppression. Exemplary historians in
this period were the prolific and popular Ottoman-
Syrian Christian Jurji Zaydan (1861–1914), who
wrote *Ta'rikh al-Tamaddun al-Islami* (1902–1906; History of Islamic civilization), and the British Orientalists Hamilton Gibb and Harold Bowen, who did
more than anyone else in English to set afoot the
historical study of the modern Middle East, particularly in *Islamic Society and the West* (1950). Such work
measured civilization by great men and their battles, politics, and high cultural production. Nationalist historians such as the Egyptian Abd al-Rahman
al-Rafi'i (1889–1966) and Palestinian George Antonius, author of *The Arab Awakening* (1938), chronicled the recent past in terms of the triumphant rise
of the new nation, led by a new elite, who disseminated enlightened ideas in a backward land, and
thus drew their fellow citizens toward freedom.

Modernization

With the beginning of the Cold War, national independence in the region, and the emergence of
Area Studies, academics trained as historians started
to multiply in and outside the region. They added
to the older sources colonial reports, state correspondence and statistics, and the tracts of modernizing elites. Borrowing from conventional currents
in Europe, the field divided into political, intellectual, economic, and social history. Bernard Lewis,
Stanford Shaw, and others wrote political histories
of the Ottoman Empire, European colonial rule,
and the high politics of nationalism. Albert Hourani
wrote a seminal work of intellectual history, *Arabic
Thought in the Liberal Age, 1798–1939* (1962). Charles
Issawi did most to chart what he saw as the decline
and rise of Middle Eastern economies. Influenced
by the Annales School, Ömer Lutfi Barkan and
Halil Inalcik pioneered Ottoman socioeconomic
history, which was taken up also at Cairo University
by students of Muhammad Anis. Gabriel Baer studied guilds, town and country, and André Raymond
transformed historians' understanding of socioeconomic change in eighteenth-century Egypt.

The achievements of these decades were very
real, but assumptions left over from Oriental Studies, entrenched by bourgeois-nationalism and introduced by modernization theory, were pervasive.
The object of study was often Islamic society, which

was still often assumed to be in long-term decay. Many judged the region according to a linear and idealized notion of European modernization, seeing the Middle East as laggard mainly as a result of local failings that were often linked to psychology. Europe's impact, typically marked off as commencing with Napoléon Bonaparte's brief occupation of Egypt (1798–1801), still signified the beginnings of progress in the region.

The drastically limited success of state-led projects of modernization and development, underlined by the Arab defeat in the Arab–Israel War of 1967 and the rise of more radical currents in Third World socialism and nationalism, gave increasing currency—inside and outside the region—to more critical scholarship. Rigid boundaries dividing politics, economics, and society started to blur, and history drew increasingly on other disciplines.

Marxism

Particularly influential during the 1970s was the broad current of Marxism: dependencia, world systems theory, and analysis based on social class. These ideas gave rise to numerous groundbreaking studies. Samir Amin, Resat Kasaba, and Roger Owen situated the Ottoman Empire and the Middle East within the world economy. Hanna Batatu's monumental study, *The Old Social Classes and the Revolutionary Movements of Iraq,* remains without peer. Ervand Abrahamian's seminal history of twentieth-century Iran, *Iran Between Two Revolutions,* owed much to notions of uneven development and social class. Anwar Abd al-Malik, Mahmud Hussein, and Eric Davis understood Egyptian history in terms of different fractions within the bourgeoisie in interaction with the state. Amin Izz al-Din, Ra'uf Abbas, Joel Beinin, and Zachary Lockman chronicled the rise of the working class in Egypt from the late nineteenth century until the 1960s.

Instead of depicting an Islamic society in decline, these scholars detailed the incorporation of a part of the periphery into a world economy with its core in Europe. Instead of seeing backwardness as the result of local cultural and political failings, backwardness was seen as the systemic result of a process of world capitalist development. Instead of viewing transformation as a process of elite-driven, ideas-based modernization that remained laggard,

society and change were freshly understood as internally structured by state and class.

Social History

Critiques of Marxist determinism, not least from Edward Said, who depicted Karl Marx as an Orientalist in *Orientalism* (1978), formed the background to increased interest in more grounded social history, which took a critical distance from grand meta-narratives of modernity. Social history particularly benefited from increasingly accessible national archives, especially the use of Islamic court records. Kenneth Cuno, Beshara Doumani, Suraiya Faroqhi, André Raymond, and others transformed understandings of the period 1600 to 1800, showing dynamism, market forms, urban change, social stratification, and changing patterns of social reproduction instead of backwardness and decline. Their work, along with that of Juan Cole, Zachary Lockman, Donald Quataert, and others has greatly diversified understandings of socioeconomic change and popular protest in the nineteenth and twentieth centuries: The deindustrialization thesis has been challenged; the end of the guilds appears to be far more complicated than it did; and the rise of the working class is no longer seen econometrically, and workers outside the factory, from artisans to migrants, are also seen as playing active roles in popular politics and world economic incorporation. F. Robert Hunter, Eugene Rogan, and others have given a far more embedded sense of state formation in Egypt and Jordan, respectively. Edmund Burke's *Struggle and Survival in the Middle East* (1993) made groundbreaking use of popular social biography.

Such work has opened the door to new forms of cultural history, in which culture is no longer an elite preserve, and constitutes (rather than simply reflects) the social process. Exemplary here are Abbas Amanat on the beginnings of the Baha'i movement in Iran, Ussama Makdisi on the modernity of sectarianism in Lebanon, and Ella Shohat on Israeli cinema. Work by historically minded anthropologists such as Michael Gilsenan, who studies violence and narrative in rural Lebanon, is highly suggestive for new directions.

Nationalism

Another important body of work has challenged the verities of idealist, elite-centered, and teleological nationalism. Rashid Khalidi, C. Ernest Dawn, James Gelvin, and others have given more heterogeneous and less emancipatory histories of the rise of Arab and regional nationalism, and have pointed to the agency of previously ignored social groups. Avi Shlaim, Ilan Pappé, Benny Morris, and others, working with newly released archival material, have presented a dramatic and far-reaching challenge to the conventional Zionist account of the events of 1948.

Women and Gender

Feminist historiographical influence, and growing criticism of male-centered history, gave impetus from the 1970s onward to research on women and gender. Leila Ahmed, Lila Abu-Lughod, Judith Tucker, and others have paid systematic attention to the place of women in society and to constructions of gender, and they write the social, cultural, and political histories of women. Patriarchy, seclusion, and veiling are no longer understood as simply vestigial backwardness or as the expression of some essential Islamic essence, but as cultural practices grounded in processes of political and cultural contestation. The hypocrisy of colonial feminism has been exposed, as well as the pitfalls of simple nationalist assertion as an unwitting defense of patriarchy. After 1990 scholars successfully made the social construction of gender—masculinity as well as femininity—an integral part of larger accounts of social change. Elizabeth Thompson's work on Mandate Syria, for example, has argued that forms of colonial citizenship were forged in part from an interwar crisis of paternity, which had much to do with changing gender practices and norms.

Foucault

A number of historians have been inspired by the work of the French philosopher Michel Foucault, whose oeuvre suggests a radically critical genealogy of modernity. Timothy Mitchell's groundbreaking work sees Egypt's nineteenth-century history in terms of the inscription of modern disciplinary practices, which gave rise to and were ordered by a new metaphysics of modern representation—the "world-as-exhibition." Khaled Fahmy on nineteenth-century Egyptian state-building and Joseph Massad on Jordanian national identity have undertaken rich archival research to pursue such insights in productive ways.

Overall, the historiography of the region has become less vulnerable to the charge of being outmoded. It presents a diversity of approaches, a more developed theoretical awareness than before, and an increasingly rich resource for those trying to understand the past, present, and future of the region.

See also ANTONIUS, GEORGE; BARKAN, ÖMER LUTFI; BONAPARTE, NAPOLÉON; HOURANI, ALBERT; ZAYDAN, JURJI.

Bibliography

Ahmed, Leila. *Women and Gender in Islam: Historical Roots of a Modern Debate*. New Haven, CT, and London: Yale University Press, 1992.

Antonius, George. *The Arab Awakening*. London: Hamish Hamilton, 1938.

Batatu, Hanna. *The Old Social Classes and the Revolutionary Movements of Iraq*. Princeton, NJ: Princeton University Press, 1978.

Beinin, Joel. *Workers and Peasants in the Modern Middle East*. Cambridge: Cambridge University Press, 2001.

Burke, Edmund III, ed. *Struggle and Survival in the Modern Middle East*. Berkeley: University of California Press, 1993.

Gibb, Hamilton A. R., and Bowen, Harold. *Islamic Society and the West*. Oxford: Oxford University Press, 1950.

Hodgson, Marshall G. S. *The Venture of Islam: Conscience and History in a World Civilization*, Vols. 1–3. Chicago: University of Chicago Press, 1974.

Mitchell, Timothy. *Colonising Egypt*. Cambridge: Cambridge University Press, 1988.

Said, Edward. *Orientalism*. London: Penguin Books, 1978.

JOHN T. CHALCRAFT

HIZBULLAH

Shi'ite political party in Lebanon.

Hizbullah (also known as Party of God) was established in 1982 at the initiative of a group of Shi'ite clerics and former AMAL movement supporters, some of whom were adherents of Shaykh Husayn Fadlallah. By 1987 the party was the second most important Shi'ite organization in Lebanon, after AMAL. It was a reaction to the perceived moderation of the AMAL movement under the leadership of Nabi Berri, and partly a reaction to the Israeli invasion of Lebanon in 1982. It has consistently followed the political and theological lines of the government of Iran and called

Iranian president Mohammad Khatami (left) with Secretary
General Shaykh Hasan Nasrallah of Hizbullah. Born in Beirut,
Nasrallah joined Hizbullah shortly after its conception in 1982
and was chosen to be its secretary general by the Consultative
Council in 1992 after Abbas al-Musawi was killed by Israeli
troops. © AFP/CORBIS. REPRODUCED BY PERMISSION.

(with various degrees of explicitness) for the creation
of an Islamic republic in Lebanon. In pursuit of this
goal, Hizbullah has coordinated its activities closely
with the government of Iran and its representatives in
the region. For years the party rejected any compromise with the Christians of Lebanon, Israel, and the
United States. This hard-line approach appealed to
many Shi'a, who abandoned the AMAL movement to
join the Party of God. Those who left AMAL tended
to be young, radical, and poor.

Hizbullah is headed by the Consultative Council (Majles al-Shura), which consists of the highest-
ranking party officials, some of whom are clerics. Its
members' responsibilities include financial, military,
judicial, social, and political affairs. The party's operations were geographically organized, with branches
in the Biqa Valley, the South, and the southern suburbs of Beirut. In the late 1980s the Politburo was
created to handle day-to-day operations.

Hizbullah gained international attention in 1983
when press reports linked it to attacks against U.S.,
French, and Israeli targets in Lebanon, and to the
abduction of Western hostages in Lebanon. The party
continues to deny responsibility for some of those
acts. Syria let Hizbullah keep its arms because it considered the party to be pursuing a legitimate struggle
against Israel's occupation of South Lebanon. The
party's armed opposition to Israel's presence resulted
in significant confrontations, and Israel's forces
killed the party's leader, Abbas al-Musawi, in 1992.
In the 1992 election, Hizbullah won eight seats in the
parliament; it now participates in the legitimate political arena after years of underground existence.
The party has been trying to change its image since
1992 and has entered into dialogue with many of its
former enemies, both leftists and Christians. It is
now headed by Shaykh Hasan Nasrallah, who has become one of the most popular leaders in Lebanon
and in the larger Arab world. The party's standing
was dramatically boosted after the withdrawal of Israeli troops from most of South Lebanon in 2000,
for the party had led the resistance movement against
the Israeli occupation. The party has been identified
as "the A-team of terrorism" by the deputy secretary
of state in the administration of U.S. president
George W. Bush. The party insists that although it
supports armed struggle against Israeli occupation, it
opposes the terrorism of Osama bin Ladin.

See also AMAL; BERRI, NABI; BIN LADIN,
OSAMA; BIQA VALLEY; BUSH, GEORGE W.;
FADLALLAH, HUSAYN; MAJLES AL-SHURA;
NASRALLAH, HASAN.

Bibliography

Kramer, Martin. *The Moral Logic of Hizbullah.* Tel Aviv:
Shiloah Institute, Tel Aviv University, 1987.

AS'AD ABUKHALIL

HOBEIKA, ELIE
[1956–2002]

A leader of the Lebanese Forces.

Elie Hobeika (also Hubayqa) was a close aide to
Bashir Jumayyil, leader of the Maronite Catholic-
dominated militias the Lebanese Forces. Hobeika
became prominent following Israel's siege of West
Beirut in 1982. On 16 September 1982, with other

militiamen, Hobeika is known to have entered the Sabra and Shatila refugee camps, where he participated in the massacre of at least one thousand Palestinians. In 1984, internecine battles erupted between the followers of President Amin Jumayyil, who was also head of the Phalange party, and the Lebanese Forces led by Hobeika. In December 1985, Hobeika and the heads of two other militias, Walid Jumblatt of the Druze-dominated Progressive Socialist party and Nabi Berri of the Shiʿite militia AMAL, signed the Damascus Tripartite Agreement. The agreement, engineered by Syria, established strategic, educational, economic, and political cooperation between Lebanon and Syria. This accord placed Lebanon virtually under a Syrian protectorate.

Heavy opposition faced the Damascus agreement, especially in the Maronite and Sunni Muslim communities of Lebanon. President Jumayyil called for the support of Samir Geagea, who had replaced Hobeika as head of the Lebanese Forces in the course of their internal conflicts. Early in January 1986, Hobeika and his followers were defeated and Hobeika escaped to Paris. He then went to Damascus. Hobeika became a favored ally of Damascus and was elected to parliament in the 1992, 1996, and 2000 elections. He formed the Promise Party but failed to attract a popular following beyond a small band of followers from his militia days. He served as minister in the 1990s; accusations of rampant corruption accompanied his service. He was killed in a massive car bomb in January 2002. It was widely believed that Israel was behind his assassination, since he was about to travel to Belgium to testify in a case against Ariel Sharon for his role in the Sabra and Shatila massacres. Hobeika's wife succeeded him as leader of the Promise Party.

See also AMAL; BERRI, NABI; DRUZE; GEAGEA, SAMIR; JUMAYYIL, AMIN; JUMAYYIL, BASHIR; JUMBLATT, WALID; LEBANESE FORCES; MARONITES; PHALANGE; SABRA AND SHATILA MASSACRES; SHARON, ARIEL.

Bibliography

Collelo, Thomas, ed. *Lebanon: A Country Study,* 3d edition. Washington, DC: Federal Research Division, Library of Congress, 1989.

GEORGE E. IRANI
UPDATED BY ASʿAD ABUKHALIL

HOCA

See GLOSSARY

HODEIDA

The major Red Sea port of Yemen since about 1849.

In 1849, the Ottoman Empire, during its second occupation of Yemen, selected Hodeida (also Hudayda) as its major base and point of entry from the Red Sea. In fact, Hodeida is not a natural deep-water port, and years of ballast dumping have made it incapable of accepting anything but small local ships. The major port activity now takes place at Raʾs Khatib, a short distance north of Hodeida; this is a modern facility with wharves, unloading equipment, warehouses, and a transportation infrastructure that can accommodate modern freighters.

Raʾs Khatib was constructed by the Soviet Union as part of its foreign aid program during the 1960s. It remained the key access point to Yemen until 1990, when the Yemen Arab Republic merged with the People's Democratic Republic of Yemen. Then, Aden, one of the world's best natural harbors, became the primary port and economic capital of the new republic.

See also ADEN; OTTOMAN EMPIRE; PEOPLE'S DEMOCRATIC REPUBLIC OF YEMEN; YEMEN; YEMEN ARAB REPUBLIC.

MANFRED W. WENNER

HOFFMAN, YOEL
[1937–]

Israeli writer and scholar.

Yoel Hoffman was brought to Palestine as an infant by his Austro-Hungarian Jewish parents. His mother died a couple of years later and his father entrusted him to a day-care home, whose owner became Hoffman's beloved stepmother when he was seven.

As a college student, Hoffman studied Hebrew literature and Western philosophy but wrote his thesis on Far Eastern philosophy. He had lived in a Japanese Buddhist temple where he studied Chinese and Japanese texts with Zen monks. His academic work ranged from comparative philosophy to interpretations of haiku and Zen koans. A professor at

Haifa University, Hoffman began to write fiction in his late forties. Although chronologically a member of the sixties "generation of the State," his writing is in the forefront of the Israeli avant-garde of the nineties.

With his first collection of stories, *The Book of Joseph* (1988), Hoffman began his lyrical, experimental literary journey. But only with *Bernhardt* (1989) and *Christ of Fishes* (1991) did his mature creative voice emerge. In atomistic texts of unusual typography and poetic rhythms, Hoffman blended Far Eastern with Western philosophy, minimalist aesthetics with unbridled imagination, murmuring of the heart with rationalism, and educated awareness with Nirvana-like trance. Hoffmann's personae—middle-aged widowers, orphaned children, lonely aunts—often speak or remember in their German mother tongue, transliterated phonetically into Hebrew and glossed in the margins. Reconstructing a culturally and psychologically complex metabolism of loss, Hoffman's work negates boundaries between life and death, self and other, man and woman, human and animal.

Bibliography

Gold, Nili. "Bernhardt's Journey: The Challenges of Yoel Hoffmann's Writing." *Jewish Studies Quarterly* 1, no. 3 (1993/1994).

Hoffman, Yoel. *Katschen and the Book of Joseph,* translated by David Kriss et al. New York: New Directions, 1998.

Hoffman, Yoel, compiler. *Japanese Death Poems: Written by Zen Monks and Haiku Poets on the Verge of Death.* Boston, MA: Charles E. Tuttle, 1998.

NILI GOLD
UPDATED BY ADINA FRIEDMAN

HOLOCAUST

Term commonly used in English (Hebrew, Shoah) *to denote anti-Jewish policies conducted by the Third Reich (Nazi Germany, 1933–1945), resulting in the systematic and bureaucratically organized genocide of approximately 6 million Jews.*

Exploiting anti-Jewish themes present in Christian theology and culture, but going far beyond them by incorporating them onto a racist worldview, Nazi ideology presented the Jews as a satanic and corrupting element and demanded their "total removal" (the formulation of Germany's dictator, Adolf Hitler: *"Entfernung der Juden überhaupt"*) from human society. They held a special place among a variety of undesirable elements (Gypsies, homosexuals, people deemed genetically defective or incurable) that had to be eliminated.

History

During the 1930s, Nazi policies gradually crystallized: German Jews were legally defined, humiliated through propaganda and education, and disenfranchised. Many were deprived of their livelihoods and property and openly encouraged to emigrate. These policies became harsher and more brutal after Nazi Germany's annexations and conquests of 1938 and 1939. After September 1939, the more than 2 million Jews living in Nazi-occupied Poland were herded into ghettos, where they were exposed to death by hunger and disease on a massive scale. The occupation of western, central, and southern Europe resulted in the legal, political, economic, and social disempowerment of the Jews, causing harsh living conditions, followed by their deportation to camps in eastern Europe beginning in 1942.

In January 1939, Hitler foreshadowed a more radical policy when announcing that, if the nations would be plunged "once more into a world war, then the result will not be the bolshevization of the earth, and thus the victory of Jewry, but the annihilation *(Vernichtung)* of the Jewish race in Europe." It took, however, more than two years for this vision to begin to be implemented. Germany's mass murder of Jews began in mid-1941 with mass executions, led by special death squads (Einsatzgruppen) accompanying the advancing troops that invaded the Soviet Union; it was supported and aided by other German units, including the German army; by local collaborators; as well as by Germany's ally, Romania. During the summer and fall of 1941, the shape of a Europe-wide "Final Solution" crystallized both in theory and practice, and in November and December Hitler's final decision became known to his entourage. On 20 January 1942, a meeting of senior Nazi bureaucrats in Berlin (the Wannsee Conference) coordinated plans for the systematic murder of the rest of European Jewry, stage by stage. The method of choice was gassing, administered in specially designed or adapted annihilation camps in Poland: Chelmno, Belzec, Majdanek, Sobibor, and Treblinka. By far the greatest number of Jews and Gypsies perished at a sixth location: the Auschwitz-Birkenau complex, to which Jews from all over Europe were shipped aboard freight trains for immediate death in gas chambers. Many Jews also died while on the way to the annihilation camps or as a result of being worked to death in forced labor camps.

The Holocaust cast its shadow over the Middle East and North Africa as well as over Europe. For several months during 1942, the Jews of Palestine feared the prospect of annihilation at the hands of the German armies under the command of General Field Marshal Erwin Rommel, which threatened to overrun Palestine. The threat was lifted following the Allied victory at the battle of al-Alamayn (23 October–2 November 1942) in Egypt. Jews in German-occupied Tunisia and Libya were not so fortunate. They suffered humiliation and persecution—some were deported to Italy and others were brought to the Bergen-Belsen camp—but they were spared the full force of the Final Solution.

From the end of 1944, when the Allied advance moved toward Germany and Poland, hundreds of thousands of Jewish and non-Jewish inmates of concentration camps were marched away from the front lines; more than half of the evacuated inmates died in these death marches. Some 200,000 European Jews probably survived the camps; a smaller number survived in hiding or as partisan fighters against the Germans.

The Jews of Europe received little help from the Allied powers or from the local population of the countries where they lived. Yet a small number of non-Jews, subsequently honored as "righteous Gentiles," endangered their lives to hide or help rescue Jews. The most significant example of Jewish armed resistance, lasting several weeks, took place in the Warsaw Ghetto in 1943. Elsewhere, there were instances of Jewish escape, rebellion, and participation in underground and partisan resistance, but with little tangible result against overwhelming odds and in inauspicious conditions. Prominent among the resisters were Jewish youth who had been members of various Zionist and non-Zionist youth movements.

Repercussions for the Middle East

The impact of the Holocaust on the Middle East has been felt in several ways. German-Jewish emigra-

Holocaust survivors and refugees arrive at Haifa Port. Haifa is one of the deepest and best-protected ports in the Mediterranean. © Photograph by Zoltan Kluger. Government Press Office (GPO) of Israel. Reproduced by permission.

tion to Palestine increased shortly after the Nazi rise to power, aided by the August 1933 ha-Avara (property transfer) agreement between the Jewish Agency for Palestine and the German government. The desperation of European Jews also contributed to illegal immigration to Palestine (Aliyah Bet) in the late 1930s, during World War II, and in the wake of the Holocaust (1945–1948).

The responses of the Yishuv (the organized Jewish community in Palestine) and Zionist leadership toward Nazi policies were the cause of much controversy within Jewish circles. Did the leadership emphasize the building up of a Jewish national home in Palestine at the expense of wider international efforts to rescue European Jewry? After the outbreak of World War II, the plight of the European Jews was used, unsuccessfully, as a major argument against the 1939 White Paper's limitations on Jewish immigration. Arab and Palestinian spokesmen countered that the two issues should not be linked. Later on, the Holocaust served as a motive for establishing the Jewish Brigade within, and the recruitment of Jews from Palestine into, the British army.

The real extent of the mass murder campaign in Europe penetrated only in November 1942. Afterwards, Zionist and Yishuv organizations contributed moral and financial aid to European Jews, some of it via a delegation based in Istanbul. In a few cases, missions were sent out (e.g., the dropping of some Palestine Jewish paratroopers into Slovakia and Hungary in 1944, in cooperation with the Royal Air Force) in attempts to rescue and support European Jews.

On the Palestinian side, the mufti of Jerusalem, Amin al-Husayni, tried to establish contacts with the Italians and the Germans in the mid-1930s, viewing them as potential allies for his goal of removing British and Zionist influence from Palestine. Cooperation on several issues lasted until the downfall of Nazi Germany. The peak was on 28 November 1941, when the mufti met with Adolf Hitler; Hitler alluded to the Nazi Final Solution, while al-Husayni emphasized common German-Arab interests. There is no evidence to support claims that it was the mufti who inspired Hitler to initiate the Final Solution.

The extent to which the Holocaust was a factor in the establishment of the state of Israel remains a question in both historiography and nonacademic polemics. One stream of Zionist historiographers and religious Zionist thinkers, along with many Arab and post-Zionist commentators, view the Holocaust as the single decisive factor in the creation of Israel. Careful historical research, however, undermines such a simple causal connection.

On the other hand, it is undeniable that the Holocaust helped Zionism become the dominant political stream within world Jewry. The immediate post-Holocaust trauma and disillusion of Jews everywhere were so extreme that many Jews in the United States and Western Europe became committed to promoting a Jewish state. Yet the Holocaust had decimated European Jewry so drastically that the very foundations of the Zionist solution for the so-called Jewish problem in Europe were undermined.

From 1944 onwards, many Holocaust survivors made their way to Palestine on their own initiative, even before Yishuv emissaries came to convince them to do so. The Zionist movement became active in directing people to Palestine, and the struggle of the ha Apala (overcrowded illegal immigration boats crossing the Mediterranean Sea) served as a major tool in Zionist propaganda for open immigration and an end to British restrictions. The link between the plight of the Holocaust survivors in the Displaced Persons (DP) camps in Germany and the creation of a Jewish state was accepted by the United Nations Special Committee on Palestine (1947), thereby strengthening the Zionist case.

Recent research suggests that guilt about the Holocaust had little effect on the UN decision to partition Palestine. Britain wanted the Jews to stay in Europe, and the United States considered the direction of DPs to Palestine a humanitarian issue and did not at first see it leading to adverse political consequences. Latin American states supported the 1947 partition plan because of Christian pro-Zionist feelings, while communist states cast their vote with the intention of weakening Britain and advancing the decolonization process.

After the establishment of Israel, the Holocaust became a central issue in the building of national identity. An annual Holocaust Remembrance Day, memorials, the trial of Rudolph Kasztner (1954) and its repercussions, the kidnapping and trial of Adolf Eichmann (1960–1961), literature and theater, and more recently journeys of youngsters to extermination sites in Europe all contributed to keeping this topic center stage. Holocaust imagery also deeply penetrates Israeli discourse. On several occasions, it has been politically linked to the Israeli–Arab conflict. For example, Prime Minister Menachem Begin justified the Israeli bombing of Iraq's Osirak nuclear facility in 1981 by vowing that Israel would not allow anyone to prepare a "second Holocaust" in his lifetime.

The Arab world has done little or nothing to deal directly with the issue of the Holocaust dissociated from the conflict with Israel. Arabs often claim that the establishment of Israel would not have occurred without the Holocaust to justify it; they accuse Jews and Israelis of manipulating the Holocaust to bolster Zionist claims to Palestine. Since the mid-1990s a few Arab and Palestinian intellectuals have displayed greater awareness of the gravity of the Holocaust, partially disconnecting it from the polemics of the Arab–Israel conflict. Reconciliation groups among Israeli Arabs (and Jews) have created courses and activities to sensitize Arab educators to the impact of the Holocaust on Jewish and Israeli thinking; one such activity was a joint Arab–Jewish pilgrimage to Auschwitz in summer 2003, led by a Palestinian priest from Nazareth. Yet, hardened by their own feelings of victimization and defeat at the hands of Israel's army, many Arabs find it difficult to empathize with Jewish suffering. A number of Arab authors and politicians have gone so far as to openly associate themselves with Holocaust deniers, while others downplay the extent of the Nazi genocide.

See also ALAMAYN, AL-; JEWISH AGENCY FOR PALESTINE; KASZTNER AFFAIR; ROMMEL, ERWIN; UNITED NATIONS SPECIAL COMMITTEE ON PALESTINE, 1947 (UNSCOP); WORLD WAR II; YISHUV.

Bibliography

Arnow, David. "The Holocaust and the Birth of Israel: Reassessing the Causal Relationship." *Journal of Israeli History* 15, no. 3 (autumn 1994): 257–281.

Caplan, Neil. "The Holocaust and the Arab-Israeli Conflict." In *So Others Will Remember: Holocaust History and Survivor Testimony,* edited by Ronald Headland. Montreal: Véhicule Press, 1999.

Laqueur, Walter, and Tydor Baumel, Judith, eds. *The Holocaust Encyclopedia.* New Haven, CT: Yale University Press, 2001.

Michman, Dan. *Holocaust Historiography: A Jewish Perspective: Conceptualizations, Terminology, Approaches, and Fundamental Issues.* London: Vallentine Mitchell, 2003.

Nicosia, Francis R. *The Third Reich and the Palestine Question.* London: I.B. Tauris, 1985.

Yahil, Leni. *The Holocaust: The Fate of European Jewry, 1932–1945.* New York: Oxford University Press, 1990.

DAN MICHMAN

HOLY LAND

An overall characterization of the area in the Middle East connected with biblical and New Testament narratives.

References to the Holy Land are found in Jewish biblical and rabbinic literature and later in Christian tradition. The area is centered at Jerusalem, and it extends from modern Israel to Egypt, which is associated with Jesus' family in the Gospels, and to Asia Minor, which is associated with the Virgin Mary and Saint John. As the dwelling place of the divine presence, the Holy Land has been the location of pilgrimage sites since the era of the Roman emperor Constantine in the fourth century. It began to take on distinct borders with the resurgence of Christian interest in the holy sites and the development of archaeology during the nineteenth century. The area is also holy to Muslims because it is home to important shrines associated with the prophet Muhammad and the early days of Islam, including Islam's third holiest mosque, in Jerusalem.

See also JERUSALEM.

Bibliography

Ben-Arieh, Yehoshua. "Perceptions and Images of the Holy Land." In *The Land That Became Israel: Studies in Historical Geography,* edited by Ruth Kark. New Haven, CT: Yale University Press, 1990.

Long, Burke O. *Imagining the Holy Land: Maps, Models, and Fantasy Travels.* Bloomington: Indiana University Press, 2002.

Peters, F. E. *Jerusalem and Mecca: The Typology of the Holy City in the Near East.* New York: New York University Press, 1986.

Wilkin, Robert. *The Land Called Holy: Palestine in Christian History and Thought.* New Haven, CT: Yale University Press, 1994.

REEVA S. SIMON
UPDATED BY MICHAEL R. FISCHBACH

HOLY SEPULCHRE, CHURCH OF THE

Christian church in Jerusalem said to contain the tomb of Jesus.

The Church of the Holy Sepulchre is in the Old City of Jerusalem. Originally a group of separate churches in a single enclosure, in the fourth century (starting in 325 C.E.), Emperor Constantine sought to turn it into an architectural monument. The Crusaders gave it its present form in 1149, combining its structures into one Romanesque church with a two-story facade. The interior has two principal sections: the rotunda—modeled on the Pantheon—which contains a shrine covering the tomb of Christ, and an Orthodox cathedral. Several Christian sects have appointed chapels and zealously guard their rights within the structure according to the Ottoman-era "Status Quo" agreement of 1852. The keys to the church have been kept by the Muslim Nusayba family for generations, so that no one Christian sect might control it.

Bibliography

Irani, George E. "Holy Places." In *Encyclopedia of the Palestinians,* edited by Philip Mattar. New York: Facts On File, 2000.

JENAB TUTUNJI
UPDATED BY MICHAEL R. FISCHBACH

HOMS

Syrian city and religious center.

Homs, strategically situated on the Orontes River at the eastern gateway of a pass connecting Syria's central plains to the Mediterranean coast, traces its history back to at least Greco–Roman times. Along with Baʿalbak, it was a center of sun worship from the first to the third century C.E. Arab Muslim armies led by Khalid ibn al-Walid captured the city in 637 and converted its massive church of St. John into a mosque. Homs was designated headquarters of one of five Syrian military districts under Muʿawiya. Its inhabitants repeatedly rebelled against the Abbasids before falling under the control of the Tulunids of Egypt (878–944) and Hamdanids of Aleppo (944–1016). Byzantine commanders raided the city throughout the tenth and eleventh centuries, but by the late eleventh century rivalry among competing Saljuq client states shaped politics in the region. Duqaq ibn Tutush turned Homs into a major base of operations against the Crusaders at the beginning of the twelfth century, bringing the city under the direct control of Damascus for the first time. It suffered a series of ferocious attacks from the Zangids of Aleppo in the early twelfth century and provided the linchpin for Nur al-Din Mahmud's defense of Damascus against the Second Crusade.

Salah al-Din ibn Ayyubi captured Homs in 1175, retaining the local Asadi dynasty to block incursions into central Syria from the Crusader strongholds of Tripoli and Krak de Chevaliers (Qalʿat al-Husn). After siding with the Mongols at Ayn Jalut, the Asadi ruler al-Ashraf Musa was pardoned by Qutuz, the Mamluk sultan whose successor, Baybars, rebuilt the city's citadel. In 1260,

al-Ashraf Musa joined the rulers of Aleppo and Hama to defeat a second Mongol invasion force on the outskirts of the city. With the death of al-Ashraf Musa two years later, Homs vanished under the shadow of the rulers of Hamah and Damascus and continued to be dominated by the Mamluks of Egypt, by Timur, and by a succession of bedouin chieftains before becoming a subdivision (*pashalik*) of the Ottoman governorate of Damascus. The city's inhabitants revolted against the 1831 Egyptian occupation of Syria, prompting Ibrahim Pasha to raze the citadel.

Contemporary Homs is known for being the site of Syria's main oil refinery, as well as of the country's military academy. Several important public sector industrial enterprises, including a massive sugar factory, are located in and around the city. Syria's newest university, al-Baʿth, opened in the southern suburbs in 1979.

See also BAʿALBAK; IBRAHIM IBN MUHAMMAD ALI.

FRED H. LAWSON

HOPE-SIMPSON COMMISSION (1930)

British commission of inquiry into economic conditions in Palestine.

The Hope-Simpson Commission was established in the wake of the August 1929 Western (Wailing) Wall disturbances. A previous commission, the Shaw Commission, had concluded in March 1930 that the causes for the 1929 disturbances were Palestinian fear of Jewish immigration and land purchases. Because the commission recommended the curtailment of both, the Labor government of Prime Minister Ramsay MacDonald appointed a commission of inquiry under Sir John Hope-Simpson to investigate land settlement, immigration, and development. The Hope-Simpson Report (Command 3686), issued on 30 August 1930, found that almost 30 percent of Palestinians were landless, presumably because of Jewish land purchases, and that Palestinian unemployment was exacerbated by a Jewish boycott of Arab labor.

The assumptions and recommendations of Hope-Simpson were incorporated in a policy paper called the Passfield White Paper of 1930 (Command 3692), which recommended restrictions on Jewish immigration and land purchases consistent with the economic absorptive capacity of Palestine. The recommendations caused a political furor in Great Britain. Under pressure from the Zionists and their supporters, MacDonald issued a February 1931 letter, known as the MacDonald Letter, or to Arabs as the Black Letter, which in effect reversed the policy of the White Paper of 1930. Consequently, the Hope-Simpson Commission resulted in no permanent change in British policy toward Palestine.

See also MacDonald, Ramsay; Shaw Commission; Western Wall Disturbances; White Papers on Palestine.

Bibliography

Palestine Government. *A Survey of Palestine* (1946), 2 vols. Washington, DC: Institute for Palestine Studies, 1991.

Porath, Y. *The Palestinian Arab National Movement, 1929–1939.* London: Frank Cass, 1977.

Philip Mattar

HOSAYNIYEH

See Glossary

HOSS, SALIM AL-
[1929–]

The most important Sunni politician in Lebanon.

Salim al-Hoss was born in Beirut. He attended the International College and the American University of Beirut, where he excelled in economics. He earned a Ph.D. in economics from Indiana University. Hoss taught at the American University of Beirut for years and did consulting work for the government of Kuwait during the 1960s. Although he was aloof from the political scene in Lebanon, in 1967 he was appointed chair of the state council that monitors banking activities. As a result he became a friend of Ilyas Sarkis, then governor of the Central Bank.

When Sarkis was elected president in 1976, he appointed Hoss prime minister. Hoss held that position in the next two administrations, under Amin Jumayyil and briefly under Ilyas al-Hirawi. Although he was considered a political moderate, he was criticized by some Maronite leaders for opposing the president of the republic. In general, however, Hoss remains one of the most widely respected figures in Lebanon; he is seen as one of the few politicians who resisted the temptations of corruption and unprincipled compromises. His views tend to conform to the moderate views of the Sunni political establishment, although he is far less prone to sectarian agitation and mobilization. Hoss ran for parliament in the 1992 election on a platform of "salvation and reform." He was critical of Israel's occupation of Lebanon and maintained close ties with Syria, although he is regarded as less deferential to the latter's wishes than most political leaders in Lebanon.

Hoss has published two books on his experience in government and remains active on the political scene. His integrity and relative independence allow him a degree of political power that other politicians can only envy. Although his power base has been centered in Beirut, he has been popular in most parts of Lebanon. Although committed to a free economic system, in the early years of the twenty-first century Hoss was critical of Western governmental policies toward the Arab-Israel conflict and the situation in Lebanon. In 1988, Hoss served as de facto president in a large part of Lebanon when Jumayyil decided to name the commander in chief of Lebanon's army as president. Hoss, supported by many Lebanese and by Syria, served as acting president until the election of René Muʿawwad. In 1998, after the election of President Emile Lahhud, Hoss served as prime minister for two years, and he was seen as the key rival to powerful Sunni billionaire Rafiq Bahaʾuddin al-Hariri. To the surprise of many, and thanks to lavish campaign spending and sectarian mobilization by Hariri, Hoss lost his parliamentary seat in 2000. He remains active in politics, although as an outside critic of the Hariri government. Hoss is known for his independent views, and in 2003, despite his staunch support for the Palestinian cause, spoke out against Palestinian suicide bombings and urged a struggle of civil disobedience.

See also American University of Beirut (AUB); Hariri, Rafiq Bahaʾuddin al-; Hirawi, Ilyas al-; Jumayyil, Amin; Lahhud, Emile; Sarkis, Ilyas.

Asʿad AbuKhalil

HOSTAGE CRISES

International crises intertwined with domestic politics in Iran and Lebanon.

In Tehran on 4 November 1979, a mob led by radical college students overran the U.S. embassy and took its personnel hostage. They announced that they would not free the diplomats until the United States agreed to extradite the country's former ruler, Mohammad Reza Shah Pahlavi (1941–1979). The shah, overthrown nine months earlier, had been admitted to the United States for cancer treatment two weeks before seizure of the embassy. Within days of the incident, Iran's revolutionary leaders endorsed the demands of the students and supported their claim that the U.S. embassy was a "den of espionage." U.S. efforts to exert pressure on Iran through diplomatic means (UN resolutions), economic sanctions (freezing Iran's assets in U.S. banks), and military actions (an abortive helicopter rescue attempt) proved unsuccessful in getting the hostages freed. Even the death of the shah, in July 1980, had no apparent effect. Only after Iraq invaded Iran in the fall of 1980 did Tehran indicate a serious interest in resolving the hostage issue. Iran and the United States subsequently accepted Algerian mediation, an accord that freed the hostages and established a tribunal to settle outstanding claims was signed in January 1981.

The kidnapping of Europeans and Americans in Lebanon that began in 1984 created a new, albeit less dramatic, hostage crisis. The militias that carried out the kidnappings wanted the governments of the hostages to pressure Israel to release Lebanese nationals that were detained in a special prison for those suspected of organizing resistance to Israel's occupation of south Lebanon. Because Iran supported these same militias, the United States was convinced that Iran could exert influence to get the hostages released. Some U.S. officials undertook secret negotiations with Iran that included covert arrangements to sell Iran weapons in exchange for the release of hostages in Lebanon. The weapons sales led to the freeing of only two hostages over the course of a year during which more Westerners in Lebanon were abducted. In October 1986, revelations of the arms-for-hostages deals caused grave embarrassment to the administration of U.S. president Ronald Reagan and resulted in the resignation of several senior aides. The scandal was compounded by revelations that profits from the secret arms sales to Iran had been diverted to secret accounts used to buy weapons for U.S.-backed forces (contras) trying to overthrow the government of Nicaragua. The fallout from the scandal put hostage negotiations on hold for several months. The last U.S. and other Western hostages in Lebanon were not released until 1991.

See also IRAN–CONTRA AFFAIR; PAHLAVI, MOHAMMAD REZA; REAGAN, RONALD.

Bibliography

Picco, Giandomenico. *Man without a Gun: One Diplomat's Secret Struggle to Free the Hostages, Fight Terrorism, and End a War.* New York: Times Books/Random House, 1999.

Sick, Gary. *All Fall Down: America's Tragic Encounter with Iran.* New York: Random House, 1985.

ERIC HOOGLUND

HOURANI, ALBERT
[1915–1993]

Leading twentieth-century historian of the modern Middle East.

Albert Habib Hourani was born in Manchester of Lebanese parents. From 1933 to 1936 he studied politics, philosophy, and economics at Magdalen College, Oxford. He then taught for two years at the American University of Beirut, and then held a position at the Royal Institute of International Affairs (RIIA) in London until 1943. From 1943 to 1945 he was attached to the office of the British minister of state in Cairo. From 1945 to 1947 he was a researcher for the Arab Office in Jerusalem and London, during which time he gave evidence to the Anglo-American committee of inquiry on Palestine. In 1946 the RIIA published his *Syria and Lebanon: A Political Essay* and in 1947 *Minorities in the Arab World,* two works that have stood the test of time.

In 1948 Hourani returned permanently to Oxford, where he became the first director of the Middle East Centre at St. Antony's College in 1953. In 1962 he published *Arabic Thought in the Liberal Age, 1798–1939,* which deals with the reception of European political philosophy, particularly the ideas of the Enlightenment and of liberalism, in the Arab world during the nineteenth and twentieth centuries, and the various intellectual movements (the

Arab literary revival, national self-consciousness, Islamic modernism, Arab nationalism) of the period. Hourani published three volumes of collected essays, *Europe and the Middle East* (1980), *The Emergence of the Modern Middle East* (1981), and *Islam in European Thought* (1991). In 1991 he published his last and best-known work, *A History of the Arab Peoples,* which became a runaway success. The book emphasizes the variety and heterogeneity at the heart of Arab and Islamic civilization; it is beautifully written, with a finely modulated appreciation and mastery of an enormous range of subject matter. It is especially notable for its nuanced and intuitive understanding both of historical processes and of the intricate and complex relationships within Arab society.

PETER SLUGLETT

HOVEYDA, AMIR ABBAS

Iranian politician, and prime minister continuously from 1965 to 1977.

Amir Abbas Hoveyda was born in Tehran in 1919 and attended high school in Beirut. With a bachelor's degree in political science from Brussels, he returned to Iran in 1942 and was hired at the ministry of foreign affairs. In the 1950s he became a high administrator in the National Iranian Oil Company. In the early 1960s Hoveyda joined Hasan-Ali Mansur's Iran-e Novin Party, a new political grouping charged with implementing the shah's reform program known as the White Revolution. When Mansur was assassinated in 1965, Hoveyda replaced him as prime minister. As Iran's second most powerful man during the two prerevolutionary decades, he presided over a crucial period marked by rising oil income and various development projects, as well as widespread corruption and repression. In 1977, facing mounting economic and political problems, the shah demoted Hoveyda to court minister and later placed him under house arrest, as a scapegoat, when revolution loomed on the horizon in 1978. Left behind after the shah's January 1979 departure from Iran, Hoveyda was captured by Ayatollah Khomeini's provisional revolutionary government and executed quickly following a show trial in April 1979.

Bibliography

Hoveyda, Fereydoun. *The Fall of the Shah.* New York: Simon and Schuster, 1980.

Milani, Abbas. *The Persian Sphinx: Amir Abbas Hoveyda and the Riddle of the Iranian Revolution: A Biography.* Washington, DC: Mage Publishers, 2000.

Pakravan, Saïdeh. *The Arrest of Hoveyda: Stories of the Iranian Revolution.* Costa Mesa, CA: Blind Owl Press, 1998.

NEGUIN YAVARI
UPDATED BY AFSHIN MATIN-ASGARI

HULA SWAMPS

Valley and former lake in the upper eastern Galilee region of Israel, known for its marshlands.

The Hula swamps, once a breeding ground for malaria mosquitoes, became the site for displaying Zionism's determination to transform marshes into fertile soil by marshaling economic resources and deploying technological forces. Earlier attempts to drain the swamps and develop the land, initiated by the Ottoman Empire, were never implemented. In 1934 the Palestine Land Development Company acquired the Hula concession and began to drain the land, a project completed in the 1950s by the state of Israel. As the number of Jewish settlements in the reclaimed region increased, the new fertile lands were stripped of their natural foliage, compromising the quality of the water in Lake Kinneret (Sea of Galilee), the country's only natural reservoir, and disrupting the flow of water in the Jordan River. To restore water quality and currents, the Jewish National Fund reintroduced the wetlands by constructing an artificial lake and digging a network of canals, creating a new and important nature reserve and tourist site in Israel.

See also JEWISH NATIONAL FUND; PALESTINE LAND DEVELOPMENT COMPANY.

Bibliography

Lowi, Miriam R. *Water and Power: The Politics of a Scarce Resource in the Jordan River Basin.* New York and Cambridge, U.K.: Cambridge University Press, 1993.

Orni, Efraim, and Efrat, Elisha. *Geography of Israel.* Jerusalem: Israel Universities Press, 1966.

DONNA ROBINSON DIVINE

HUMAN RIGHTS

Middle East states and international human rights conventions.

Special envoy of the President of the Palestinian National Authority, Hanan Ashrawi speaks to the 58th session of the Commission on Human rights in 2002. © AP/WIDE WORLD PHOTOS. REPRODUCED BY PERMISSION.

The term *human rights* refers herein to the human rights norms established in the international system in and following from the Universal Declaration of Human Rights 1948 (UDHR). The poor (indeed, often critical) state of the protection of these rights is one of the major features of the human rights debate in the region, which continues to challenge the regional human rights movement, despite recent progress toward reform in certain states; the contestation of the universality of certain of these rights is another feature.

All states in the region are party to two or more of the United Nations human rights treaties. A number are not yet parties (as of 2004) to either the International Covenant on Civil and Political Rights or the International Covenant on Economic, Social, and Cultural Rights which, together with the Universal Declaration of Human Rights (UDHR), make up the International Bill of Human Rights; these include Bahrain, Oman, Qatar, Saudi Arabia, and the United Arab Emirates (U.A.E.). All are parties to the Convention on the Rights of the Child (CRC), but Iran, Iraq, Oman, Syria, and the U.A.E. have yet to sign the Convention Against Torture. A similar number of states (Iran, Oman, Qatar, Somalia, Sudan, and the U.A.E.) have not yet become parties to the Con-

vention on the Elimination of All Forms of Discrimination Against Women (CEDAW). Many Middle Eastern states that have signed CEDAW, along with many states elsewhere in the world, have attached reservations to their ratification of this treaty. Certain of these reservations have attracted attention because of their broad nature; they purport to subject compliance with the Convention to the principles of Islamic *shariʿa;*. Arguments continue at the UN over the compatibility of such reservations with the intentions of CEDAW, and arguments continue in the region as to the universality of the norms provided in this particular treaty. There have been a few ratifications of the Optional Protocols to the ICCPR, CEDAW, and the CRC, enabling the appropriate monitoring committee to hear complaints from individual citizens against the state party.

Domestically, it is rare that individuals realize human rights protections through directly invoking international human rights instruments in the national courts, even though there may be constitutional provision for the incorporation in national legislation of international instruments to which the state is party. Furthermore, in many states in the region, weak and unempowered national judiciaries are unable to assert their independent will against the executive to secure effective judicial protection of human rights, even though the rights enshrined in the international instruments are also guaranteed in the texts of most of the constitutions of the region.

A number of states in the region are also party to the African Charter on Human and Peoples' Rights, and Turkey has ratified the European Convention on Human Rights. There is also the Arab Charter on Human Rights, which was adopted in 1994 by the members of the League of Arab States. The original text has been criticized by the Geneva-based International Commission of Jurists as "a fatally flawed instrument, containing significant gaps and elements which run contrary to fundamental human rights principles." In the years following its adoption, no member state ratified the charter, and in 2003 a process of review for the "modernization" of its contents was initiated.

Another set of standards proclaimed by all states in the region (except for Israel) is contained in the

Cairo Declaration of Human Rights in Islam. The declaration was adopted in 1990 by member states of the Organization of the Islamic Conference (OIC) to serve "as a general guidance for member states in the field of human rights." The rights elucidated in the declaration differ in certain significant respects from those set out in the international human rights treaties to which many of the states in the region are parties, and resolutions from OIC summits have consistently asserted the significance of cultural relativity in response to the demands of the international human rights norm of universality. Thus, a 2003 resolution from the OIC foreign ministers recognizes "the obligations and endeavours of the member states to promote and protect the internationally recognized human rights while taking into account the significance of their religious, national, and regional specificities and various historical and cultural backgrounds, and with due regard to the 'Cairo Declaration on Human Rights in Islam.'" The arguments over universality versus cultural relativity of human rights norms revolve particularly around the rights of women and minorities, and freedom of religion.

Concern is articulated by many states and citizens in the region over the exploitation of the international human rights discourse for political ends. There are evocations of a larger context of colonial and neocolonial agendas, cultural imperialism, and hostility to Islam. Although these states have political interests in seeking to divert and undermine criticism of their human rights records in international forums (as, in a different discourse, does Israel), among civil society these evocations have a popular resonance, and there is widespread criticism of selectivity in the application of human rights discourse and principles by powerful Western states. This criticism has traditionally centered on the question of Palestine in light of the absence of enforcement action against Israel for its violations of the human rights of Palestinians. It has expanded to include a perception of a lack of attention to the human rights of all Muslims by the major Western powers. These issues have been heightened in the aftermath of the attacks in the United States on 11 September 2001.

These real political issues have immediate impact on the work of nongovernmental domestic, regional, and diasporic human rights organizations (NGOs) established since the late 1970s to challenge widespread, egregious, and systemic human rights violations. These organizations have had critical influence in establishing and maintaining the human rights debate and discourse in the region. Regional networking has increased significantly over the last ten years, with a number of formal regional programs and less formal networks established. The NGO human rights movement in the region is also critical of selectivity in the approach of powerful Western states (and in some cases, international human rights organizations), and of Western influence over the agenda of the international human rights movement. Activists may find themselves caught between hostility at home and indifference to regional concerns in the international arena. Regionally, there is general consensus on the need to increase the popular resonance of universal human rights norms and discourse, as well as focusing on national and international state law and policy in order to increase the prospects for implementation of international human rights.

See also ORGANIZATION OF THE ISLAMIC CONFERENCE.

Bibliography

An-Naʿim, Abdullahi. "Human Rights in the Arab World: A Regional Perspective." *Human Rights Quarterly* 23 (2001): 701–732.

Azzam, Fateh. *Arab Constitutional Guarantees of Civil and Political Rights.* Cairo, Egypt: Centre for International Human Rights Studies, 1996.

Bowen, Steven. *Human Rights, Self-Determination, and Political Change in the Occupied Palestinian Territories.* The Hague, Netherlands: Martinus Nijhoff Publishers, 1997.

Cotran, Eugene, and Yamani, Mai, eds. *The Rule of Law in the Middle East and the Islamic World: Human Rights and the Judicial Process.* London: I. B. Tauris, 2000.

Dwyer, Kevin. *Arab Voices: The Human Rights Debate in the Middle East.* London: Routledge, 1991.

Rishmawi, Mona. "The Arab Charter on Human Rights: A Comment." *INTERIGHTS Bulletin* 10 (1996): 8–10.

PAUL MARTIN
UPDATED BY LYNN WELCHMAN

HUMMUS

See FOOD: HUMMUS

HUMPHREYS, FRANCIS
[1879–1971]

British diplomat.

Francis Humphreys was the last British high commissioner in Iraq (1929–1932) before Iraqi independence in 1932. In that capacity, he played a central role in negotiating the Anglo–Iraqi Treaty of 1930, which paved the way for independence. Humphreys then served as the first British ambassador to Iraq (1932–1935).

See also ANGLO–IRAQI TREATIES.

ZACHARY KARABELL

HUNCHAK PARTY

Armenian-oriented Lebanese political party.

The Hunchak Party, organized in Geneva, Switzerland, in 1887, has promoted the dual objective of liberating Turkish Armenia and establishing a socialist regime in a unified Armenian homeland. In Lebanon, the party has advocated a planned economy and a just distribution of national income. In 1972, for the first time in its history, the party fielded a joint slate of candidates for parliament with the Dashnak Party. In the world of Armenian politics in Lebanon, ties of Armenian national solidarity supersede ideological considerations that might divide Armenians. During the Lebanese Civil War, the differences between the Hunchak and the Dashnak became insignificant.

The Hunchak Party achieved a victory in the 1992 election when Yeghya Djerijian, an Armenian (Greek Orthodox, born in 1957) was elected to parliament. He chairs the executive committee of the party.

See also ARMENIANS IN THE MIDDLE EAST; DASHNAK PARTY; LEBANESE CIVIL WAR (1975–1990).

AS'AD ABUKHALIL

HUNKAR-ISKELESI, TREATY OF (1833)

Mutual defense agreement between Russia and the Ottoman Empire.

In February 1833, the Egyptian army of Ibrahim Pasha reached Kutahya in Ottoman Turkey, less than 200 miles (322 km) from Constantinople (now Istanbul), seat of the Ottoman Empire. With few options short of capitulation, the Ottoman sultan Mahmud II sought help from his former enemy, Czar Nicholas I of Russia. Nicholas complied, and Russian troops and ships were dispatched to the Bosporus (Turkish straits). Though the Russian presence did not save the sultan from severe concessions to Ibrahim and his father Muhammad Ali, viceroy of Egypt, it did force Ibrahim to temper his demands and depart from Kutahya. Having helped the sultan, Nicholas demanded payment in the form of a defensive alliance. The Treaty of Hunkar-Iskelesi, named after the Russian camp, was concluded on 8 July 1833. Concluded for eight years, it bound the sultan to close the Turkish straits to warships in times of war, and it provided for Russian aid if the Ottoman Empire was attacked. Though defensive, the treaty greatly alarmed the other European powers, who believed that it gave the Russians preponderant influence in Constantinople. Britain protested against the treaty and over the next years worked assiduously to reverse this setback to British interests in the Ottoman Empire.

See also IBRAHIM IBN MUHAMMAD ALI; MAHMUD II; MUHAMMAD ALI; STRAITS, TURKISH.

Bibliography

Anderson, M. S. *The Eastern Question, 1774–1923: A Study in International Relations.* London: Macmillan; New York: St. Martin's, 1966.

Hurewitz, J. C., trans. and ed. *The Middle East and North Africa in World Politics,* 2d edition. New Haven, CT: Yale University Press, 1975.

Shaw, Stanford, and Shaw, Ezel Kural. *History of the Ottoman Empire and Modern Turkey.* 2 vols. Cambridge, U.K., and New York: Cambridge University Press, 1976–1977.

ZACHARY KARABELL

HÜRRIYET

Daily newspaper in Turkey.

Hürriyet (Freedom) is a politically centrist newspaper known for its ardent antifundamentalist stand. In 1990, its managing editor, Cetin Emeç, was allegedly assassinated by Muslim fundamentalist terrorists.

Hürriyet has a circulation of 600,000, with 150,000 copies distributed in Western Europe, making it the most widely read Turkish newspaper outside the country. In Turkey, *Hürriyet*'s readers are typically middle class and high school educated.

Hürriyet was founded in 1948 by journalist and publisher Sedat Simavi, in the early years of Turkey's multiparty politics. It quickly became the top-selling daily in Turkey and remained in that position for about forty years, making it the country's most influential newspaper. Once a gossip paper, it gradually improved its serious news coverage. By the end of the 1970s, the paper maintained an extensive network of domestic bureaus and about a dozen international ones. For three years, until 1991, *Hürriyet* copublished with Bağimsiz Basin Ajansi an English-language weekly, *Dateline Turkey*.

Hürriyet remained in the Simavi family following the death of the founder in 1953, with his son, Erol, eventually taking sole control. In 1994, the Dogan Group, owner of *Milliyet*, took a controlling share of the newspaper with the purchase of 70 percent of Hürriyet Holding. Of the remaining stake, 15 percent stayed in the Simavi family and another 15 percent was held by various investors.

See also NEWSPAPERS AND PRINT MEDIA: TURKEY; SIMAVI, SEDAT.

STEPHANIE CAPPARELL

HUSARI, SATI AL-

[1880–1968]

Social philosopher, political activist, and pioneer theorist of Arab nationalism.

Sati al-Husari (also spelled Sate al-Husri) was born in Aleppo, Syria, in 1880 and moved to the Balkans in his early youth. He joined the Committee for Union and Progress formed by Young Turks and Young Ottomans in 1907. After the collapse of the Ottoman Empire, Husari left Istanbul and joined the movement for Arab nationalism. He assumed the position of minister of education in the reign of King Faisal I Ibn Hussein. When Faisal was ousted from Syria by the French in 1920, Husari followed him to Iraq, where he became the most important theoretician of modern Arab nationalism.

Al-Husari was fluent in many languages and had learned nationalist conceptions from nineteenth-century European thinkers such as Ernst Moritz Arndt, Johann Gottfried Herder, Georg W. F. Hegel, and Johann Gottlieb Fichte. He developed a theory of nationalism that identified the nation not as a voluntary association but as a living organism that develops through common language and history. He pinned all his hopes on the educated youth, to whom he hoped to teach the proper nationalist values by establishing schools, training teachers, and delivering lectures. He considered every person who spoke Arabic or who was affiliated with those who did to be an Arab. Hence, his conception of pan-Arabism was founded on secular values like language and history, but nonetheless integrated Islam as an important component of Arab cultural identity. He believed in Ibn Khaldun's concept of *asabiyya* (solidarity based on blood ties) as well as the notions of *le lien social* (social bonds) and *esprit de corps* (common feeling of purpose). To him, unity had spiritual and physical depths.

For al-Husari, freedom did not mean democracy or constitutionalism; it meant national unity. A nation (*umma*) denoted a secular group of people bound together by mutually recognized ties of language and history. This was distinct in his mind from state (*dawla*), a sovereign and independent people living on common land within fixed borders. He identified several challenges to nationalism, including imperialism, regionalism, communist internationalism, and the pursuit of Islamic political unity. He argued that the Muslim nations possessed many linguistic and cultural differences, which prevented their unity. Instead, he campaigned for an Arab unity based on the Arabic language, because Arabic preceded Islam and possessed many cultural traits that Islam did not have.

Even though al-Husari was willing to borrow from Western civilizations, he distinguished between civilization and culture. The former included sciences, technologies, and the means of production, and by its very nature it was internationalist. The latter included literatures and languages, and by nature it was nationalist. Thus, al-Husari instituted "the rule of separation" in the nationalist reasoning. His writings include: *Abhath Mukhtara fi al-Qawmiyya al-Arabiyya* (Selected studies in Arabic nationalism), *Thawrat 14 Tammuz* (The July 14 revolution), *Ara wa*

Ahadith fi al-Wataniyya wa al-Qawmiyya (Opinions and conversations in Arab nationalism), and *al-Amal al-Qawmiyya* (National aspirations).

See also COMMITTEE FOR UNION AND PROGRESS; FAISAL I IBN HUSSEIN; YOUNG TURKS.

Bibliography

Cleveland, William L. *The Making of an Arab Nationalist: Ottomanism and Arabism in the Life and Thought of Sati al-Husri.* Princeton, NJ: Princeton University Press, 1971.

"From Reformism to Independence." Institut du Monde Arabe. Available from <http://www.imarabe.org/ang/perm/mondearabe/theme/docs/9.html>.

Thornton, Ted. "Sati al-Husri." History of the Middle East Database. Available from <http://www.nmhschool.org/tthornton/mehistorydatabase/sati_alhusri.htm>.

Tibi, Bassam. *Arab Nationalism: A Critical Enquiry,* edited and translated by Marion Farouk-Sluglett and Peter Sluglett. London: Palgrave Macmillan, 1981.

Tibi, Bassam. *Arab Nationalism: Between Islam and the Nation-State.* London: Palgrave Macmillan, 1997.

RITA STEPHAN

HUSAYNI, ABD AL-QADIR AL-
[1908–1948]

Palestinian nationalist and military leader.

Abd al-Qadir al-Husayni was born in Jerusalem to a notable family. He was the son of Musa Kazim, a major leader of the Palestinian struggle against Zionism. Abd al-Qadir saw military service during the Palestinian rebellion between 1936 and 1939. During World War II, he took part in the Iraqi revolt of Rashid Ali al-Kaylani, a pro-Axis Iraqi politician who replaced Nuri al-Saʿid as prime minister of Iraq in March 1940. After the British crushed al-Kaylani's revolt in 1941, Abd al-Qadir was imprisoned; following his release he went to Egypt.

In 1947, Abd al-Qadir managed to return to Palestine where he commanded, together with Fawzi al-Qawuqji, the Arab Liberation Army, a poorly equipped force of some 2,000 volunteers who crossed the Israeli border from Syria in January 1948, under the sponsorship of the Arab League.

At the battle of Jabal al-Qastl (April 1948) on the Jaffa–Jerusalem highway, the better-trained and better-armed Haganah forces dealt the Arab forces a decisive blow, reopening the Jerusalem highway, killing Abd al-Qadir, and routing al-Qawuqji's troops. Soon thereafter, the Jewish forces took possession of most of the important Palestinian towns, including the major part of Jerusalem. For the Palestinians, their resistance at al-Qastil remains one of the proudest moments in their modern history, and Abd al-Qadir one of their most honored national heroes.

See also ARAB LIBERATION ARMY; HAGANAH; HUSAYNI FAMILY, AL-; HUSAYNI, MUSA KAZIM AL-; KAYLANI, RASHID ALI AL-; LEAGUE OF ARAB STATES; QAWUQJI, FAWZI AL-.

MUHAMMAD MUSLIH

HUSAYN IBN ALI
[1852–1931]

Arab leader from the Hashimite family.

Descended from the Hashimite family of Mecca, Husayn was the amir of Mecca (1908–1916), king of the Hijaz (1916–1924), and the father of Ali, Zayd, and of King Faisal I ibn Hussein of Iraq and Amir Abdullah I ibn Hussein of Transjordan, later king of Jordan.

In 1893, Husayn moved to Constantinople (Istanbul), seat of the Ottoman Empire, at the bidding of Sultan Abdülhamit II, and remained there for the next fifteen years. During these years of "gilded captivity," Husayn established himself as the leading candidate for the Meccan emirate, and in 1908, the sultan appointed him to that position. Once in Mecca, Husayn found himself at odds with the Young Turk government in Istanbul. While he sought autonomy for himself and the hereditary office of amir for his sons, the Young Turks and the Committee for Union and Progress attempted to extend their control over the Hijaz through the construction of the Hijaz Railroad.

Husayn's attitude toward Arab nationalism before World War I has been the subject of some dispute. In 1911, he was approached by Arab deputies in the Ottoman parliament as a possible leader of a pan-Arab independence movement. He declined to take active part in their movement. Yet, by 1914, his sons Faisal and Abdullah were actively involved in various secret societies, and in the spring and summer of 1914, Abdullah met with British officials in Cairo. After the outbreak of World War I, Husayn entered into discussions with Britain about the possibility of an Arab revolt led by him against the Ottomans, but he continued to assure the Young Turks of his loyalty. In 1915, he began a correspondence with Sir Henry McMahon, the British high commissioner in Cairo. The Husayn–McMahon Correspondence established the terms for a British-sponsored Arab revolt, with several critical ambiguities surrounding the status of Palestine.

In June 1916, Husayn launched the Arab Revolt, during which active military leadership passed to his four sons and the British. After the war, he refused to endorse the Versailles Treaty on the grounds that the British had reneged on the Husayn–McMahon correspondence and other wartime promises. At the same time, he came under increasing pressure from Abd al-Aziz ibn Saʿud Al Saʿud of the Najd in central Arabia. Estranged from the British, who terminated aid to Husayn after 1920, and bitter about the mandate system, Husayn declared himself caliph (head of Islam) after Turkey abolished the caliphate in 1924. This ill-advised move alienated Husayn from many of his remaining supporters, and in August 1924, Abd al-Aziz ibn Saʿud Al Saʿud launched a major assault on the Hijaz. Husayn abdicated, went into exile on Cyprus, and died in 1931 in Amman. He was buried in the al-Haram al-Sharif in Jerusalem.

See also ARAB REVOLT (1916); COMMITTEE FOR UNION AND PROGRESS; HASHIMITE HOUSE (HOUSE OF HASHIM); HUSAYN–MCMAHON CORRESPONDENCE; YOUNG TURKS.

Bibliography

Fromkin, David. *A Peace to End All Peace.* New York: Holt, 1990.

Morris, James. *The Hashemite Kings.* New York: Pantheon, 1959.

Paris, Timothy J. *Britain, the Hashemites, and Arab Rule, 1920–1925: The Sherifian Solution.* London: Cass, 2003.

ZACHARY KARABELL
UPDATED BY MICHAEL R. FISCHBACH

HUSAYNI FAMILY, AL-

Prominent Palestinian Arab family in Jerusalem.

By the late nineteenth century, the Husayni family had become extremely wealthy. They owned vast tracts of land amounting to about 50,000 *dunums,* including extensive areas and plantations in Jericho district. The social and political influence of members of the Husayni family was rooted in their ancient status as descendants of the prophet Muhammad, landowners, delegates to the Ottoman parliament, mayors and district governors, religious leaders, jurists, and educators. The family's influence also grew from a style of politics based on a delicate balance between the central authority of the Ottoman state and dominance in local Palestinian society. This balancing created a partnership between the central government in Constantinople (now Istanbul) and the urban upper class of the Arab provinces from the mid-nineteenth century until the demise of the Ottoman state in 1917 and 1918. Such partnership contributed to the further ascendance of the Husayni family since it enabled senior members of the family to act as intermediaries between the Ottoman government and local Palestinian society. The British, like the Ottomans before them, had to depend on the Husaynis and other locally influential notables to administer the local affairs of Palestine.

The senior members of the family include the following: Musa Kazim al-Husayni (1853–1934) was president of the Arab Executive from 1920 to 1934. Muhammad Amin al-Husayni (1895–1974) was a founder of Palestinian nationalism and the leader of the Palestine national movement until the *nakba* of 1948. Munif al-Husayni (1899–1983) was a close associate of al-Hajj Amin and editor of the Husayni camp's newspaper, *al-Jamiʿa al-Arabiyya.* Jamal al-Husayni (1892–1982), born in Jerusalem, served as secretary of the Arab Executive and the Supreme Muslim Council, as well as foreign minister for the All-Palestine government. Rajaʾi al-Husayni (1902–?) was active from 1945 in the Arab Information Offices, which were organized by Musa al-Alami under the auspices of the League of Arab States, served as minister in the All-Palestine government, and later went to Saudi Arabia to work as a senior official in the government. Ishaq Musa al-Husayni (1904–1990), a writer who at-

A portrait taken in 1938 of the mufti of Jerusalem and president of the Supreme Muslim Council of Palestine (1921–1936), Al-Haji Amin al-Husayni (1893–1974). Husayni opposed British rule and the establishment of a Jewish state in Palestine. © BETTMANN/CORBIS. REPRODUCED BY PERMISSION.

tained literary prominence on a pan-Arab level, studied Arabic language and literature at the American University in Cairo (1923–1926), Cairo University (1927–1930), and the University of London (1930–1934) where he received a doctoral degree in Semitic languages and literature under the guidance of H. A. R. Gibb, an English expert on Arab culture and literature. Ishaq taught Arabic literature at the American University of Beirut, McGill University in Canada, the American University in Cairo, and the Arab League's Institute for Arab Studies in Cairo. He wrote numerous articles and books, the most widely acclaimed being *Memoirs of a Hen* (1943), which won the prize of Dar al-Maʿarif, one of Egypt's most prestigious publishing houses.

Dr. Daʾud al-Husayni (1903–1994), political activist, played an active role in the Palestine Arab Revolt, 1936–1939. He was captured by the British in Iraq in 1941 and detained in Rhodesia. Allegedly a coconspirator in the assassination of King Abdullah ibn Hussein (July 1951) he then served as a member of the Jordanian Parliament (1956, 1962), reportedly as a member of the Executive Committee of the Palestine Liberation Organization (PLO). He stayed in East Jerusalem after the Arab–Israel

War of 1967 but was expelled to Jordan by the Israeli authorities in 1968 on charges of hostile political activities. Abd al-Qadir al-Husayni (1908–1948) was a son of Musa Kazim. Unlike most politicians who hailed from notable families, he actually joined the Palestinian commando groups both in the revolt of 1936–1939 and in the Arab–Israel War of 1948. He died in action (April 1948) at al-Qastal, a mountain along the Jerusalem–Jaffa highway. His son Faysal (1940–2001) established the Arab Studies Center in East Jerusalem in the 1980s. A senior figure in Fatah, he emerged as a local leader of the Palestinian Arabs in the territories occupied by Israel in 1967 and served on the advisory committee of the Palestinian delegation to the Middle East Peace Conference. Faysal was a pragmatist who advocated coexistence between Israel and a Palestinian state in the West Bank and Gaza.

After 1948, the Husayni family was no longer able to retain its dominance over the field of Palestinian politics. This was due to a combination of changes: the dispersal of the Palestinians, the loosening of family ties, the spread of new ideologies, the emergence of new political elites in many parts of the Arab world, as well as the orientation of Palestinian politics and the general weakening of the landowning, scholarly, and mercantile families that constituted a fairly cohesive social class from the second half of the nineteenth century until the end of the British mandate in 1948.

See also ABDULLAH I IBN HUSSEIN; ALAMI FAMILY, AL-; ALL-PALESTINE GOVERNMENT; ARAB–ISRAEL WAR (1948); ARAB–ISRAEL WAR (1967); FATAH, AL-; HUSAYNI, ABD AL-QADIR AL-; HUSAYNI, JAMAL AL-; HUSAYNI, MUHAMMAD AMIN AL-; HUSAYNI, MUSA KAZIM AL-; LEAGUE OF ARAB STATES; PALESTINE ARAB REVOLT (1936–1939); PALESTINE LIBERATION ORGANIZATION (PLO); SUPREME MUSLIM COUNCIL.

Bibliography

Mattar, Philip. *The Mufti of Jerusalem: Al-Hajj Amin al-Husayni and the Palestinian National Movement,* revised edition. New York: Columbia University Press, 1992.

Muslih, Muhammad Y. *The Origins of Palestinian Nationalism.* New York: Columbia University Press, 1988.

MUHAMMAD MUSLIH

HUSAYNI, HIND AL-
[1916–1994]

Palestinian philanthropist.

Hind al-Husayni was the daughter of Tahir Shuqri al-Husayni, a member of the prominent Jerusalem family that has dominated the city's politics and society for centuries. He died in 1918, leaving a family of six. Hind attended the Jerusalem Girls College (JGC) in the 1930s and was a member of a private girls' school strike committee during the 1936–1939 Strike and Revolt. Husayni became interested in social work through her studies with Victoria and Elizabeth Nasir, aunts of Palestinian academic Hanna Nasir. After finishing her training at the JGC, she taught at the Islamic Girls School in Jerusalem until 1946. During the 1940s Husayni was president of the Women's Solidarity Society, whose work focused on child care for the children of working mothers. On 14 April 1948, after the massacre of Palestinians by the Irgun in the village of Dayr Yasin, many orphaned children were deposited in Jerusalem, where Husseini found them. In order to care for them, she founded an orphanage named Dar al-Tifl al-Arabi (House of the Arab Child), which was located in her family home in Jerusalem. From then until the present, the institution developed and expanded its philanthropic activities, which included a nursery, kindergarten, and school; vocational and computer training; and a farm. Hind al-Husayni died in 1994.

See also DAYR YASIN; HUSAYNI FAMILY, AL-.

Bibliography

Okkenhaug, Inger Marie. *The Quality of Heroic Living, of High Endeavour and Adventure: Anglican Mission, Women, and Education in Palestine, 1888–1948.* (Studies in Christian Mission 27.) Boston and Leiden, Neth.: Brill, 2002.

ELLEN L. FLEISCHMANN

HUSAYNI, HUSAYN AL-
[1937–]

Shiʿite politician in Lebanon.

Husayn al-Husayni was born to a prominent family in Shmistar, near Baʿalbak. He first ran for public office in 1964 and was elected to parliament in 1972, when his close association with Imam Musa al-Sadr paid off. His political role in the political life of Lebanon was minimal until 1978, when Musa al-Sadr "disappeared" and Husayni assumed the leadership of the AMAL movement. His conflict with other militant factions within the movement began in 1980, when Nabih Berri (his archrival) took control of AMAL.

With strong backing from Syria, Husayni was elected speaker of parliament in 1984, and he held the position until 1992, when Berri succeeded him. Husayni's showing in the 1992 election was poor, and the candidates of the Hizbullah (Party of God) in his district of Baʿalbak achieved great success. The election results weakened his ties with the government of Lebanon, and he became one of the most bitter opposition figures. He directs his attacks against Prime Minister Rafiq Bahaʾuddin al-Hariri, whom he accuses of corrupting Lebanon and of profiting from his high office. Husayni has been marginalized in the Shiʿite community by Berri and by Hizbullah. In 2003 Husayni joined deputies Naʾila Muʿawwad and Umar Karami to form an opposition front. He has been criticized for refusing to release the minutes of the parliamentary deliberations in Taʾif that produced the Taʾif Accord.

See also AMAL; BERRI, NABI; HARIRI, RAFIQ BAHAʾUDDIN AL-; TAʾIF ACCORD.

AS'AD ABUKHALIL

HUSAYNI, JAMAL AL-
[1892–1982]

Palestinian nationalist leader.

Jerusalem-born Jamal al-Husayni was secretary of the Arab Executive and the Supreme Muslim Council. In 1935 he was elected president of the Palestine Arab Party, and one year later he became a member of the Arab Higher Committee (AHC). A firm believer in public relations and political lobbying as well as a relative and close aide to al-Hajj Muhammad Amin al-Husayni, the *mufti* of Jerusalem, he participated as member (1930) and as president (1939) of the Palestinian delegations dispatched to London to discuss Palestinian demands with the British government. He also served on the AHC's delegations to the League of Arab States and the United Nations. He was briefly detained by the British authorities in Palestine for his role in the Jerusalem and Jaffa demonstrations of October

1933. Following the *mufti*'s escape to Beirut in 1937, Jamal secretly joined him and from there he fled to Iraq, then to Iran where he was arrested by the British in 1942 and deported to Rhodesia, now Zimbabwe. Four years later, he returned to Palestine and, after 1947, he served as foreign minister for the All-Palestine Government and later settled in Saudi Arabia where he was adviser to King Saʿud (1953–1964). Jamal died in Beirut and was buried there.

On behalf of the political bodies on which he served during the mandate period, Jamal submitted compromise ideas to the Palestine government and to Jewish representatives concerning a new basis for relations between the government and the Jewish community on the one hand and the Palestinian Arabs on the other hand. The unpublished autobiography of Jamal reveals a feeling of apathy toward the *mufti*, partly because of the rift between the *mufti* and Musa al-Alami, whose sister Jamal had married.

See also ALAMI FAMILY, AL-; AL SAʿUD, SAʿUD IBN ABD AL-AZIZ; LEAGUE OF ARAB STATES; SUPREME MUSLIM COUNCIL.

Bibliography

Lesch, Ann M. *Arab Politics in Palestine, 1917–1939: The Frustration of a Nationalist Movement.* Ithaca, NY: Cornell University Press, 1979.

Porath, Yehoshua. *The Emergence of the Palestinian-Arab National Movement, 1918–1929.* London: Cass, 1974.

Porath, Yehoshua. *The Palestinian-Arab National Movement, 1929–1939: From Riots to Rebellion.* London: Cass, 1977.

MUHAMMAD MUSLIH

HUSAYNI, MUHAMMAD AMIN AL-
[1895–1974]

Palestinian leader during the British mandate.

Born in Jerusalem, Amin al-Husayni (later often referred to as Hajj Amin) was the scion of a prominent Palestinian Muslim family, which included landed notables and religious officeholders such as the mufti (Islamic legal expert). He studied in Cairo briefly at al-Azhar University and at the Dar al-Daʿwa wa al-Irshad of Rashid Rida, the Muslim reformer and precursor of Arab nationalism, and at the military academy in Istanbul. He served in the Ottoman army in 1916, but his loyalty to the Ottoman Empire was shaken by Turkish attempts to impose their language and culture on their Arab subjects. Upon returning to Palestine in 1916, he participated in the British-supported Arab Revolt of 1916 against the Turks and worked for the establishment of an independent Arab nation. In 1918, he was elected president of al-Nadi al-Arabi (the Arab Club), a literary and nationalist organization opposed to Zionist claims on Palestine. After participating in a violent anti-Zionist demonstration in 1920, he escaped to Damascus, Syria, where he worked for the short-lived Arab nationalist government of Amir (later King) Faisal. The first high commissioner of Palestine, Sir Herbert Samuel, pardoned him from a ten-year sentence in absentia for his role in the 1920 demonstration, and appointed him to succeed his brother as mufti of Jerusalem in 1921.

Al-Husayni's political career can be divided into two distinct phases: the Palestine years of 1917 to 1936, when he cooperated with the British while opposing Zionism, and the exile period after 1936, when he became intransigent and cooperated with Nazi Germany.

Palestinian Phase

The fundamental explanation for al-Husayni's co-operation with the British can be traced to the politics of the class from which he emerged. The notables were defenders of the status quo and worked with the imperial government to guarantee or enforce stability while representing their society's interests and demands to the ruling power—first the Ottomans, then after 1917 the British. Before being appointed mufti, al-Husayni assured Samuel that he and his family would maintain tranquility in Jerusalem. In early 1922, he was appointed president of the Supreme Muslim Council, which gave him control over Muslim courts, schools, and mosques, and an annual budget. During the 1920s al-Husayni used his office to extend his influence in religious and political affairs within and beyond Palestine. His rise to power coincided with the decline of the Palestine Arab Executive, which led the Palestinian national struggle from 1920 to 1934, and with the perception that he had stood up to the Zionists during the 1928 through 1929 Western (Wailing) Wall controversy and riots. In fact, he neither organized nor led the riots, according to the

British Shaw Commission, which investigated the disturbances.

From 1929 to 1936, al-Husayni cooperated with the British while attempting to change British policy. He opposed militant activities against British rule and sent his secretary to London to propose a representative government. For their part, the British proposed, in the Passfield White Papers of 1931, restrictions on Jewish immigration and land purchase but withdrew the proposal because of Zionist pressure. The mufti convened a general Islamic Congress in December 1931 to galvanize Arab and Muslim opposition to Zionism and to caution Britain that support for Zionism would jeopardize her interests in the Arab and Muslim world.

British policy did not change, however. Jewish immigration rose in 1935 to a record annual high of 61,854, which helped radicalize the Palestinian community. The British killing of an insurgent, Izz al-Din al-Qassam, further embittered Palestinians, who began to challenge the mufti's ineffective methods. Until 1936, al-Husayni was able to serve two masters: his British employers and his people. But in April 1936, a general strike was declared and violence spread. The public urged him to assume the leadership of the strike, which protested Jewish immigration and land purchase and demanded a national government. His acceptance put him on a collision course with the British.

Exile Phase

Over the next few years, several events radicalized al-Husayni. When the British proposed, in the 1937 Peel Commission Report, to partition Palestine, he rejected the proposal because the Jews, who owned 5.6 percent of the land, would receive many times that area and in the most fertile region, from which most Palestinians would be expelled; the British would remain in control of the third holiest city of Islam, Jerusalem; and the rest would be attached to Amir Abdullah's Transjordan. Faced with the mufti's refusal to cooperate, the British stripped him of his offices and sought to arrest him.

He escaped to Lebanon in 1937, continued to lead the revolt, and most likely acquiesced in the assassination of his Palestinian opponents. The revolt was finally suppressed in 1939, after more than three thousand Palestinians had been killed, their lead-ers exiled, and the Palestinian economy shattered. Al-Husayni became bitter and uncompromising, rejecting the 1939 White Paper even though its terms were favorable to the Palestinians: It proposed a limitation on Jewish immigration and land purchases and a Palestine state with a representative government based on ratio of two Arabs to one Jew. He again escaped, this time from Lebanon to Iraq, where he encouraged a pan-Arab revolt against British rule in 1941. British prime minister Winston Churchill approved his assassination, but a British and Zionist mission to assassinate him in Baghdad failed.

Al-Husayni fled to the Axis countries, where he conferred with Mussolini and Hitler. He cooperated with the Nazis in exchange for German promises that the Arab nations would be liberated and given their independence after the war, and he assisted in anti-British and antisemitic propaganda campaigns and in recruiting Muslims for the war effort. The mufti, fearing that Jewish immigration to Palestine would lead to the domination or dispossession of his people, tried unsuccessfully to persuade Nazi officials not to allow Jews to leave Axis countries for Palestine. By doing so, he endangered the lives of thousands of Jews, mostly children, who probably would have been sent to concentration camps. Israeli writers and their supporters were so eager to indict him as a war criminal who participated in the Holocaust that they exaggerated his activities, whereas Arab writers, especially Palestinians, were so intent on justifying his actions in Axis countries that they ignored his cooperation with a barbaric regime. What is certain is that his association with the Nazis tainted his career and his cause and limited his effectiveness during the critical period from 1946 to 1948.

In 1946, al-Husayni returned to the Arab world with the aim of continuing his struggle against the Zionists and establishing an Arab Palestine. But he misjudged the balance of forces. He rejected the UN General Assembly's partition resolution (181) of November 1947 largely because it gave the Jews 55 percent of Palestine when they owned only 7 percent of the land. In the civil strife and war that followed, about 725,000 Palestinians fled or were expelled by Israel forces. After the Arab–Israel War of 1948, al-Husayni gradually lost political influence and became a religious leader, settling first in Cairo and then in Beirut.

Assessment

Although astute, incorruptible, and dedicated to the welfare of his people, al-Husayni's policies during both phases of his career were a failure. From 1917 to 1936, despite his rhetoric about the ominous threat of Zionism to Palestinian national existence, he cooperated with the British and rejected an overt struggle, preferring petitions, delegations, and personal appeals. In the meantime, the Zionists' numbers increased from 50,000 in 1917 to 384,000 in 1936. It was only after 1936 that al-Husayni participated in active measures to stop Jewish immigration, which if unchecked, the Palestinians felt, would result in their expulsion or domination. But by then it was too late: The Zionists had become too powerful, and the British had lost their discretionary authority in the country. Conversely, the Palestinians, especially after the suppression of the Arab Revolt, were too weak.

Al-Husayni did not adjust his demands to the realities and made little effort to reach an accommodation with the British and the Zionists. His rejection of the 1947 UN resolution was a missed opportunity that contributed to Palestinian dispossession. However, even had he accepted the resolution, it is uncertain that a Palestinian state would have been established because of a 1946 and 1947 agreement, supported by the British, between Amir Abdullah ibn Hussein and the Jewish Agency to divide Palestine between them.

The overriding factors that frustrated Palestinian nationalists have as much to do with al-Husayni's intransigence as with the balance of forces. The 1897 Basel Zionist program and the 1917 Balfour Declaration policy, backed by the British military and by Western support, gave Palestine's Jewish community time to grow through immigration and land purchases and to establish modern quasigovernmental and military institutions. The Palestinians were a weak, divided, and traditional society and never a match for the British and the Zionists.

See also ARAB CLUB; ARAB–ISRAEL WAR (1948); ARAB REVOLT (1916); BALFOUR DECLARATION (1917); HAYCRAFT COMMISSION (1921); ISLAMIC CONGRESSES; JEWISH AGENCY FOR PALESTINE; PEEL COMMISSION REPORT (1937); QASSAM, IZZ AL-DIN AL-; RIDA, RASHID; SAMUEL, HERBERT LOUIS; SHAW COMMISSION; SUPREME MUSLIM COUNCIL; UNITED NATIONS AND THE MIDDLE EAST; WESTERN WALL DISTURBANCES; WHITE PAPERS ON PALESTINE.

Bibliography

Elpeleg, Zvi. *The Grand Mufti of Jerusalem: Haj Amin al-Husayni, Founder of the Palestinian National Movement.* London: Frank Cass, 1993.

Khadduri, Majid. "The Traditional (Idealist) School—the Extremist: Al-Hajj Amin al-Husayni." In *Arab Contemporaries: The Role of Personalities in Politics.* Baltimore, MD: Johns Hopkins University Press, 1973.

Mattar, Philip. *The Mufti of Jerusalem: Al-Hajj Amin al-Husayni and the Palestinian National Movement,* revised edition. New York: Columbia University Press, 1992.

Porath, Yehoshua. "Al-Hajj Amin al-Husayni, Mufti of Jerusalem: His Rise to Power and Consolidation of His Position." *Asian and African Studies* 7 (1971): 212–256.

Schechtman, Joseph B. *The Mufti and the Fuehrer: The Rise and Fall of Haj Amin el-Husseini.* New York: Thomas Yoseloff, 1965.

PHILIP MATTAR

HUSAYNI, MUSA KAZIM AL-
[1853–1934]

Palestinian nationalist leader.

Musa Kazim al-Husayni played a major role in the early phase of the Palestinian national movement. Born in Jerusalem to a socially and politically prominent family, he acquired senior positions in the Ottoman imperial bureaucracy in Palestine, Transjordan, Syria, Yemen, and Iraq. After the British occupied Palestine, he was appointed mayor of Jerusalem in March 1918, succeeding his deceased predecessor and brother, Husayn al-Husayni. Throughout his political career, Musa Kazim followed a policy of cautious engagement in politics and discreet opposition to the British, who sponsored and supported the Zionist movement. In 1918 he refrained from demonstrating against Zionism after the Jerusalem governor, Ronald Storrs, told him that he must make a choice between political activism and the mayoralty. His circumspect behavior, which was typical of a generation of Palestinian politicians whose political style was shaped by their experience in the Ottoman system of government, did not stop him from fighting for Palestinian nationalism. In 1920 he was removed from his post as mayor of Jerusalem by the British for participating in a demonstration against the Jewish National Home policy of the British government.

Husayni was elected president of the third Palestinian Arab Congress (held in Haifa in December 1920) and the Arab Executive, a loosely-structured political body formed in 1920 to coordinate the Palestinian national struggle. Husayni led the Palestinian Arab delegations that were dispatched to London to present the Palestinian point of view to the British authorities. During the 1929 Western (Wailing) Wall Disturbances, Husayni signed a manifesto urging his fellow Palestinians not to engage in violence and to arm themselves instead with mercy, wisdom, and patience.

Partly as a result of his disappointment with the British pro-Zionist policy, and partly because of the pressure of the action-oriented Palestinian groups that emerged during the late 1920s, he led the October 1933 Palestinian demonstrations against Zionist immigration in Jerusalem. A product of Ottoman times with a penchant for discretion and a love for senior political posts, Husayni was unable to devise a strategy that would alter the British pro-Zionist policy. The balance of power, which was overwhelmingly in favor of the Zionists and their British supporters, together with internal Palestinian bickering—epitomized by the Husayni-Nashashibi rivalry—put Husayni and his generation of Palestinian nationalists at a decisive disadvantage.

Beaten by British security forces during the October 1933 demonstration, he never fully recovered. He died the "venerable father" (al-ab al-jalil) of the Palestine national movement.

See also HUSAYNI FAMILY, AL-; ZIONISM.

Bibliography

Porath, Y. *The Emergence of the Palestinian-Arab National Movement, 1918–1929.* London: Frank Cass, 1974.

Porath, Y. *The Palestinian–Arab National Movement: From Riots to Rebellion,* volume 2, *1929–1939.* London: Frank Cass, 1977.

MUHAMMAD MUSLIH
UPDATED BY MICHAEL R. FISCHBACH

HUSAYN–MCMAHON CORRESPONDENCE (1915–1916)

Correspondence between Sharif Husayn ibn Ali of Mecca and the British high commissioner in Egypt, who promised independence to Arab countries.

Ten letters, written between 14 July 1915 and 30 March 1916 but unpublished until 1939, constitute an understanding of the terms by which the sharif would ally himself to Britain and revolt against the Ottoman Turks in return for Britain's support of Arab independence. Sharif Husayn ibn Ali of Mecca asked Sir Henry McMahon, the British high commissioner in Egypt, to support independence of the Arab countries in an area that included the Arabian Peninsula (except Aden), and all of Iraq, Palestine, Transjordan, and Syria up to Turkey in the north and Persia in the east. He also asked Britain to support the restoration of the caliphate.

McMahon's reply on 24 October 1915 accepted these principles but excluded certain areas in the sharif's proposed boundaries: coastal regions along the Perisan Gulf area of Arabia; the Iraqi province of Baghdad, which would be placed under British supervision; areas "where Britain is free to act without detriment to the interests of her ally France"; and, in Syria, "the districts of Mersina and Alexandretta and portions of Syria lying to the west of the districts of Damascus, Homs, Hama, and Aleppo." The Arabs assumed that at least Arabia, northern Iraq, central Syria, and Palestine—which was regarded as southern, not western, Syria—were part of the area that was to be independent. They started the Arab Revolt of 1916, which helped the British to defeat the Turks and to occupy the region. After the war, Arabs felt betrayed because Britain conceded Syria to France and promised to help in the establishment of the Jewish national home in Palestine. The British claimed that they intended to exclude Palestine from McMahon's pledges.

The interpretations of the letters have been disputed ever since, in part because of official oversight, and because of deliberate vagueness by the British who—to obtain French, Arab, and Jewish support during the war—made conflicting promises they could not keep. Contributing to the confusion are partisan scholars who read into the correspondence interpretations that fit their ideological positions.

See also ARAB REVOLT (1916); HUSAYN IBN ALI; MCMAHON, HENRY.

Bibliography

Antonius, George. *The Arab Awakening*. New York: Capricorn Books, 1946.

Hurewitz, J. C. *The Middle East and North Africa in World Politics: A Documentary Record*, Vol. 2: *British-French Supremacy, 1914–1945*. New Haven, CT: Yale University Press, 1979.

Kedourie, Elie. *In the Anglo-Arab Labyrinth: The McMahon-Husayn Correspondence and Its Interpretations, 1914–1939*. Cambridge, U.K.: Cambridge University Press, 1976.

Monroe, Elizabeth. *Britain's Moment in the Middle East, 1914–1956*. Baltimore, MD: Johns Hopkins University Press, 1963.

Smith, Charles D. "The Invention of a Tradition: The Question of Arab Acceptance of the Zionist Right to Palestine during World War I." *Journal of Palestine Studies* 22, no. 2 (1993): 48–63.

PHILIP MATTAR

HUSAYN, TAHA
[1889–1973]

Egyptian critic and writer of fiction; Egypt's minister of education, 1950–1952.

Taha Husayn was born in an Egyptian village in the Nile delta. His life was transformed at the age of two, when he was blinded by the village barber's attempt to treat ophthalmia. The course of his early education, with its many frustrations and occasional triumphs, is recorded in one of the major monuments of modern Arabic literature, *Al-Ayyam* (1925; published in English as *An Egyptian Childhood*, 1932). In two later volumes under the same title, Taha Husayn traces his transition from the village Qur'an school to the Azhar mosque-university in Cairo (*Al-Ayyam*, 1939; *The Stream of Days*, 1948) and his sense of acute frustration at the kind of education being offered there. The third volume (*Al-Ayyam*, 1967; *A Passage to France*, 1976) describes his transfer to the new secular Egyptian University (now the University of Cairo) from which he obtained the first Ph.D., with a dissertation on the renowned classical Arabic poet, Abu al-Ala al-Ma'arri, whose blindness clearly led to feelings of close affinity between author and subject. In 1915, Taha Husayn traveled to France. Arriving at the University of Montpelier, he hired a young French woman to read to him. The two fell in love and were married in 1917. Husayn moved to Paris in 1915 where he became a student at the Sorbonne and, in 1918, completed a second doctoral dissertation, this one on the famous historian Ibn Khaldun (1332–1406).

Upon his return home, Husayn set himself, both as author and teacher, the task of introducing to his fellow countrymen and, by extension, to the Arab world as a whole, many of the ideas and ideals he had encountered in Europe. Appointed professor of ancient history immediately following his return from France, he assumed the chair of Arabic literature in 1925. It was at this time that he contributed to the newspaper *al-Siyasa* a series of articles on early Arabic poetry, which were to be published later in three volumes as *Hadith al-Arba'a* (1954, n.d., 1957). His lecture references on the debt of Islam to Hellenistic ideas were already controversial, but when in 1926 he published in book form *Fi al-Shi'r al-Jahili*, his views on the authenticity of pre-Islamic poetry, and suggested that certain stories recorded in the text of the Qur'an might be fables, he was accused of heresy. He offered to resign but was vigorously defended by the president of the university, Ahmad Lutfi al-Sayyid (1872–1963). Eventually a compromise was reached whereby the work was withdrawn. A revised version, *Fi al-Adab al-Jahili*, was published in 1927, with the offending passages removed but the remainder of his argument expanded.

Taha Husayn was not afraid to provoke and confront controversy during the remainder of his career. Appointed dean of the faculty of arts in 1929, he soon clashed with governmental authorities and was dismissed from that position in 1932 amid strikes and resignations. He now became more active in both journalism and politics while continuing his career as a university teacher, administrator, and writer. In 1938 he published another controversial work, *Mustaqbal al-Thaqafa fi Misr*, laying out a broad and ambitious program of educational reform that involved a process of modernization on the model of Europe. During the 1940s he was accorded increasing recognition as a scholar and writer both in Egypt and abroad; in 1950 he was appointed minister of education in the Wafd government. He was in the process of implementing his reforms when a series of events began that were to culminate in the Egyptian revolution of July 1952.

During the final decades of his life, as the pace of development in the literary tradition that he loved began to accelerate, he became a more conservative figure, bent on preserving the great heritage from what he came to regard as the wilder excesses of some of its contemporary inheritors—not least in the call for literature of commitment that so predominated in the critical environment of the 1950s.

Taha Husayn made several contributions to modern Arabic fiction, of which the novels *Du'a al-Karawan* (1932) and *Shajarat al-Bu's* (1944) and the short-story collection *Al-Mu'adhdhibun fi al-Ard* (1949) are the most notable. It is, however, in the realm of literary criticism that his contribution to modern Arabic cultural life is most significant. He played a major role in the formulation of a modern approach to the issues of Arabic literary history; he applied critical methods to the canon of both poetry and artistic prose through a series of studies on genres and various writers. From his early study of al-Ma'arri, mentioned above, via his work on Abu al-Tayyib al-Mutanabbi (died 965), generally acknowledged as the greatest of the classical poets, to contemporary poets such as Ahmad Shawqi (1868–1932) and Hafiz Ibrahim (1871–1932), it is possible to detect a determined effort to introduce into the world of Arabic literature a critical approach based on a recognizable methodology. In so doing, he laid the groundwork for subsequent generations of critics, most notably his own student, Muhammad Mandur (1907–1965).

Taha Husayn was known during his lifetime as the dean of Arabic literature—the title is appropriate. Not only did he write creative works and critical studies, but his sense of mission led him to play a major role in the difficult process of cultural adjustment and change that the Arab world had to face during the course of the twentieth century.

See also IBRAHIM, MUHAMMAD HAFIZ; ISLAM; LITERATURE: ARABIC; QUR'AN; SHAWQI, AHMAD; WAFD.

Bibliography

Brugman, J. *An Introduction to the History of Modern Arabic Literature in Egypt.* Leiden, Netherlands: E.J. Brill, 1984.

Cachia, Pierre. *Taha Husayn: His Place in the Egyptian Literary Renaissance.* London: Luzac, 1956.

Malti-Douglas, Fedwa. *Blindness and Autobiography: "Al-Ayyam" of Taha Husayn.* Princeton, NJ: Princeton University Press, 1988.

Semah, David. *Four Egyptian Literary Critics.* Leiden, Netherlands: E.J. Brill, 1974.

ROGER ALLEN

HUSSEIN IBN TALAL
[1935–1999]

King of Jordan, 1952–1999.

Hussein's rule indelibly stamped the fabric of socio-economic and political life in Jordan, to the point that in some people's eyes Hussein and Jordan were inseparable and almost synonymous for over four decades. Hussein ibn Talal was born in Amman on 14 November 1935, to Prince Talal ibn Abdullah and his wife, Zayn al-Sharaf. Talal was the son of Amir (Prince) Abdullah I ibn Hussein of Transjordan, and grandson of Husayn ibn Ali (Sharif) of the Hashimite family of Mecca. Hussein was a direct descendant of the Prophet Muhammad, representing the forty-second generation after the Prophet. His grandfather Abdullah started instructing the young prince in statecraft at an early age. Following then-King Abdullah's assassination in July 1951, Talal, who suffered from schizophrenia, reigned only thirteen months before being replaced by seventeen-year-old Hussein in August 1952. Only after reaching his eighteenth year (according to the Islamic calendar) in 1953 did Hussein formally begin his rule.

Despite the family's lack of worldly goods—they could not even buy him a bicycle—Hussein enjoyed a broad but abbreviated education. In Amman, he successively attended a religious school and Kulliyat al-Matran (the Bishop's School); this instruction was supplemented by special tutorials in Arabic and Islam. For his middle preparatory years, he was enrolled in the prestigious Victoria College in Alexandria, Egypt, where he broadened his world view. During this period, the Middle East and Jordan were experiencing momentous events. In 1948, when Prince Hussein was thirteen, Israel was created, and the Arab armies attacked, fighting until 1949. They were defeated, but Transjordan gained possession of the West Bank and absorbed a major

King Hussein (center) with his wife, Queen Noor (second row, second from left) and their twelve children. Hussein, a direct descendent of the prophet Muhammad, the founder of Islam, became king at the age of seventeen when his father, Talal ibn Abdullah, was declared mentally unfit to rule. © AP/WIDE WORLD PHOTOS. REPRODUCED BY PERMISSION.

wave of Palestinian refugees. In 1950, when Prince Hussein was fifteen, the West Bank was formally joined to the Hashimite Kingdom of Jordan.

In 1951, this succession of events began to directly affect the young prince; on 20 July, King Abdullah was assassinated by a disgruntled Palestinian. While his father, Talal, temporarily ascended the throne, Prince Hussein was moved to England to join his cousin, Crown Prince Faisal II ibn Ghazi of Iraq, at Harrow, an elite school for future leaders of Britain and the British Empire. On 11 August 1952, King Talal was constitutionally removed from the Jordanian throne due to illness, and the crown was passed to his eldest son, Prince Hussein. Since he had not yet reached his majority, the young King Hussein was transferred to Sandhurst, the British military academy, while a regent ruled in

Amman. In May 1953, King Hussein returned to Jordan and assumed the throne. Despite dire predictions for his political survival—the young king ruled a small country in the midst of a turbulent Middle East—he ended up ruling far longer than any other king of Jordan. By the time of his death in 1999, he had come to symbolize modern Jordan.

Hussein was married four times during his long reign. His first wife was Dina bint Abd al-Hamid (1929–), a distant and older cousin from Cairo. They married in April 1955 but divorced eighteen months later. In May 1961, Hussein married the daughter of a British military attaché, Antoinette Avril Gardiner (1943–), who assumed the name Princess Muna. This union too ended in divorce in 1972. In the following year, the king married a third time, this time to a Palestinian named Alia Baha al-Din Tuqan (1948–1977), from the prominent Tuqan family of Nablus. In February 1977, Queen Alia (also Aliya) died in a helicopter crash. In June 1978, the king married Elizabeth Najeeb Halaby (1951–), an Arab-American who became Queen Noor (also Nur). He had a number of children by his marriages. His marriage to Dina produced a daughter, Aliya (1956–). His two sons by Princess Muna are Abdullah (1962–) and Faysal (1963–), along with two girls, Ayisha (1968–) and Zayn (1968–). Hussein and Queen Alia produced a girl, Haya (1974–), and a son, Ali (1975–). Finally, his children with Queen Noor were two boys, Hamza (1980–) and Hashim (1981–), and two girls, Iman (1983–) and Rayya (1986–). In 1976 he also adopted a daughter with Queen Alia, Abir (1972–).

Hussein's rule may be divided into three major historical periods. The first twenty years were marked by crises and threats to the throne originating from inside and outside the country: street riots stimulated by radical Arab nationalism; challenges from his own prime minister in 1956 and 1957; destabilization by larger and stronger Arab states; and the devastating loss of the West Bank to Israel in the Arab–Israel War of June 1967. Soon after, in 1970, the Palestinian guerrilla organizations challenged Jordan in a bloody civil war known as Black September. Nonetheless, while relying on his loyal military to survive, the king helped put in place the bases for development.

The second phase, starting after the Arab–Israel War of October 1973, is distinguished by quieter internal political conditions, more rapid development fueled by funds (direct grants, loans, individual remittances) derived from the petroleum boom in neighboring states, and improved relations with most of Jordan's Arab neighbors. It was a relatively less radical, regional atmosphere. Despite his problems with the Palestinians and his frequently strained relations with the Palestine Liberation Organization (PLO) and its leader, Yasir Arafat, the king came to be a respected leader in most Arab capitals. Indeed, he hosted two Arab summits—1980 and 1987—in Jordan.

The third phase is dominated by the end of the Cold War and the alteration of regional relationships. In a sense, Hussein's historical July 1988 decision to disengage Jordan politically and admin-

Israeli prime minister Yitzak Rabin (left) with King Hussein of Jordan. The two men signed a peace treaty in 1994 that ended forty-six years of hostile relations between their countries. Major points of the agreement included the resolution of disputes over land and water rights and a pledge of cooperation regarding trade and tourism. © PHOTOGRAPH BY SA'AR YA'ACOV. GOVERNMENT PRESS OFFICE (GPO) OF ISRAEL. REPRODUCED BY PERMISSION.

istratively from the West Bank, in response to the pressures from the first Palestinian Intifada (uprising) that started in 1987 and the clear lack of Palestinian support for continued Jordanian rule, was a precursor to these changes. More important was the withdrawal of the Soviet Union as an active player in the region (1989–1990), and the United States's dominance in areas of its perceived interests. The resulting polarization of the Arab world and the Gulf Crisis of 1990 and 1991 and ensuing war left Jordan (at the time allied politically with Saddam Hussein's Iraq) and a few other poor Arab states politically, economically, and regionally isolated. Finally, following significant anti-government protests in April 1989 in areas that comprised the "Hashimite heartland" that were so important to his rule, Hussein initiated a significant democratization process and called for the first general parliamentary elections in the country since 1967. Political parties were legalized, political exiles allowed to return, and press freedoms were expanded. Leaders from all political streams wrote a national charter, which defined the general principles for the country's political life. A special general congress made up of 2,000 representatives ratified the document on 9 June 1991.

A long-term trend in the king's rule was his moderation and centrism. After times of internal threat to the regime, he did not execute the challengers. Some were sent to prison or exiled, but in time many were brought back and given positions of some authority. Nor did Hussein follow radical or overly conservative social, economic, or cultural policies. His relations with the Arab world follow a similar pattern. As the leader of a small state, Hussein followed a strategic policy for the survival of his country by consistently trying to maintain acceptable ties with some of the strong Arab states; this policy has not always met with success as, for example, during the post–Gulf War period, when his Iraq policy was considered ill advised. Throughout his rule, Hussein was resolutely pro-Western, even when that stance cost him dearly. Finally, he was long convinced of the need to reach a diplomatic resolution of the conflict with Israel. Drawing upon a history of good Hashimite relations with Zionist and Israeli leaders, and as a result of the disastrous loss of the West Bank in the 1967 Arab–Israeli war, Hussein tried to keep Jordan out of the ongoing Arab struggle against Israel. Jordan became the second Arab country to sign a peace treaty with Israel, in October 1994. Throughout the mid and late 1990s, Hussein remained involved in the faltering yet ongoing peace process between Israel and the PLO. He even left his cancer treatment in the United States (see below) in October 1998 to participate in the Wye River conference convened by U.S. president Bill Clinton.

Hussein took one of the most dramatic political moves in his long reign literally just two weeks before he died. A heavy smoker, Hussein was diagnosed with renal cell cancer (of the kidney) in August 1992. After successful surgery, he returned to Jordan the following month to a tumultuous hero's welcome. In July 1998, Hussein was again diagnosed with cancer, this time non-Hodgkins lymphoma, a cancer of the lymph glands. After seeking treatment in the United States on 14 July, he returned to Jordan on 19 January 1999, announcing that he had been cured. He then made a decision that stunned his country: He replaced his brother, Prince Hassan (also Hasan), with his eldest son, Abdullah II ibn Hussein, for the post as crown prince and heir apparent. Hassan (1947–) had been the crown prince and close confidant of the king since April 1965, yet he and Hussein eventually disagreed over who Hassan's successor should be: one of his sons, as the constitution states, or one of Hussein's own sons.

This and other problems caused a rift between the two brothers, something magnified (so reports stated) by the political maneuverings of some of the royal wives. Hussein's sudden and dramatic decision was also surprising given that Abdullah was not one of the king's sons who openly had been groomed for leadership. In the early 1990s, Hussein's choice seemed to be Prince Ali, eldest son of the late Queen Alia, whereas by the late 1990s the king's attentions seemed focused on Prince Hamza, the first son born to him and the reigning Queen Noor. The move also carried significant political import both domestically and internationally, given that Abdullah had no practical political or diplomatic experience, whereas Hassan's resumè was extensive.

Hussein suffered a relapse and returned to the United States on 26 January, the day after the dramatic announcement that Abdullah was the new crown prince. When treatment failed, he flew back to Jordan in a critical state, and died on 7 February. Jordanians were devastated. His funeral was a huge diplomatic gathering attended by a host of world leaders and fellow monarchs, including U.S. president Bill Clinton, former presidents Gerald Ford, Jimmy Carter, and George H.W. Bush, Russian president Boris Yeltsin, French president Jacques Chirac, and Prince Charles and Prime Minister Tony Blair of the United Kingdom, among others. The funeral also brought together a host of Middle Eastern leaders, including those from countries not having diplomatic relations with one another. Among these were Israel's Prime Minister Benjamin Netanyahu and President Ezer Weizman of Israel, President Hafiz al-Asad of Syria, President Husni Mubarak of Egypt, and Palestinian leader Yasir Arafat. Hussein was buried at the royal palace cemetery in Amman, next to the tombs of his father and grandfather.

See also ARAB–ISRAEL WAR (1967); GULF CRISIS (1990–1991); GULF WAR (1991); HASHIMITE HOUSE (HOUSE OF HASHIM); INTIFADA (1987–1991); JORDAN; NOOR AL-HUSSEIN (QUEEN NOOR).

Bibliography

Gubser, Peter. "Hussein ibn Talal." In *Political Leaders of the Contemporary Middle East and North Africa: A Bibliographical Dictionary*, edited by Bernard Reich. Westport, CT, and New York: Greenwood Press, 1990.

Hussein, H. R. M. King. *Uneasy Lies the Head: The Autobiography of His Majesty King Hussein I of the Hashemite Kingdom of Jordan.* New York and London: Heinemann, 1962.

Jureidini, Paul A., and McLaurin, R. D. *Jordan: The Impact of Social Change on the Role of the Tribes.* New York: Praeger, 1984.

Lunt, James. *Hussein of Jordan.* New York: Macmillan, 1989.

Massad, Joseph Adoni. *Colonial Effects: The Making of National Identity in Jordan.* New York: Columbia University Press, 2001.

Satloff, Robert B. *The Troubles on the East Bank: Challenges to the Domestic Stability of Jordan.* New York: Praeger, 1986.

PETER GUBSER
UPDATED BY MICHAEL R. FISCHBACH

HUSSEINI, RANA

[1967–]

Jordanian journalist and women's rights activist.

Rana Husseini (also Husayni) was born in Jordan, and she received a bachelor's degree in 1990 in communications and a master's degree in 1993 in liberal arts from Oklahoma City University. She has been working since 1993 as a reporter and photographer for the *Jordan Times.* Her coverage focuses on crime, women's and children's issues, and the role of the media in advancing women's rights. Throughout her pioneering and persistent reporting on "honor crimes" in Jordan, Husseini drew national, regional, and international attention to the issue. She was a founding member of the Jordanian Campaign Committee to Eliminate So-Called Crimes of Honor in Jordan in 1999. Within a period of four months, the committee collected over 15,000 signatures demanding the cancellation of laws that provide leniency for perpetrators of such crimes. The committee was granted the Human Rights Watch Award in 2000. Husseini served in 1998 as a regional coordinator for the United Nation's Development Fund for Women (UNIFEM) campaign to eliminate violence against women. She received the Ida B. Wells Award for Bravery in Journalism in 2003. She also received the Reebok Human Rights Award for reporting on violence against women in Jordan in 1998, and the MEDNEWS (Med-Media Program, European Union) award in 1995 for best article, "Murder in the Name of Honor."

ISIS NUSAIR

HUSSEIN, SADDAM

[1937–]

President of Iraq from 1979 to 2003.

Saddam Hussein (also Husayn, Hussain) al-Tikriti was born on 28 April 1937 to a Sunni Arab family in Tikrit, Iraq, on the northern bank of the Tigris River. His family was from the village of al-Awja, near Tikrit, and was of poor peasant stock; his father reportedly died before his birth. His stepfather denied him permission to go to school, so Saddam ran away, seeking refuge in Tikrit, in his mother's brother's home.

Early History

Saddam Hussein's maternal uncle, Adnan Khayr Allah Talfa, raised him through adolescence; he was a retired army officer and an advocate of Arab nationalism—a sentiment he imparted to Saddam—and he had participated in the short-lived anti-British revolt in 1941, known as the Rashid Ali Coup.

In 1956, Saddam moved to Baghdad, where he was impressed by the nationalism that swept Iraq in the wake of Egypt's nationalization of the Suez Canal and the British-French-Israeli attack on Egypt. In 1957, he joined the Baʿth Arab socialist party, which had been founded in Syria in 1947. Dedicated to Arab unity, the party had been popular among students in Jordan, Syria, Iraq, and Lebanon since the early 1950s. From 1957 on, his life was inextricably bound up with Baʿth.

In 1959, during the presidency of the Iraqi dictator General Abd al-Karim Qasim, Saddam was a member of a Baʿth team assigned to assassinate Qasim. The attempt failed, and Saddam was wounded in the leg during an exchange of gunfire. He fled Baghdad and later staged a daring escape to Syria, and from there to Egypt, where he joined a number of other exiled Iraqis. He is believed to have become a full member of Baʿth while he was in Egypt.

Qasim's regime ended in February 1963, when a group of Iraqi nationalists and Baʿthist officers brought it down in a violent coup. Qasim was killed, and Saddam returned to Iraq with other exiled Iraqis, although he played only a minor role in the

Ba'athist president Saddam Hussein ruled Iraq from 1979 until the U.S.-led invasion into the country unseated him in 2003. Hussein came to power when President Hasan al-Bakr was forced to resign, and he quickly moved to eliminate any possible challengers to his authority. © AP/WIDE WORLD PHOTOS. REPRODUCED BY PERMISSION.

Ba'th government that took power. The new regime did not last.

In November 1963, General Abd al-Salam Arif staged a successful anti-Ba'thist coup and Saddam went underground again. From 1963 to 1968, he worked in clandestine party activities, and he was captured and jailed, although he managed to escape. In 1966, while still underground, he became a member of the regional command of the Iraqi branch of the Ba'th Party and played a major role in reorganizing the party to prepare for a second attempt at seizing power. He worked closely with General Ahmad Hasan al-Bakr, a fellow Tikriti and a distant relative, who had been prime minister under the Ba'th and was respected by the military. In this period, Saddam was known as a tough partisan and a political enforcer, willing to liquidate enemies of the party.

In July 1968, the Ba'th Party returned to power after two successful coups that took place in rapid succession. Saddam played an important part in both. Ahmad Hasan al-Bakr became president of the republic; Saddam became vice president of the Revolutionary Command Council after some maneuvers to eliminate competitors for the position.

Al-Bakr and Saddam

From 1969 through 1979, Iraq was ruled by al-Bakr, the respected army officer, and Saddam, the young, dynamic manipulator and survivor. No major decisions were made without Saddam's consent, and he gradually built the organs of a police state that spread an aura of fear over the country and of invincibility around himself.

In the 1970s, Saddam had helped shepherd Iraq through major social and economic development, made possible by an increase in petroleum revenues. The changes brought by this expansion of social programs included compulsory primary education, a noticeable increase in women's participation in the workforce, the founding of new universities, and the availability of medical services. An ambitious industrial program in petrochemicals, steel, and other heavy industry began. The Ba'th Party also implemented policies that brought all the social and economic sectors under its control, including the foreign-owned Iraq Petroleum Company, which was nationalized in 1972.

Saddam and the Ba'th Party distanced themselves from the West in the 1970s, instead building strong ties with the Soviet Union and the Eastern bloc. In 1972, an important treaty of friendship was signed between Iraq and the Soviet Union. France was the only Western European country with which Iraq maintained good political and economic relations. Iraq took a hard stand against Israel, attempting to isolate Egypt after the 1978 Camp David Accords.

The Ba'th Party inherited a problem with the Iraqi Kurds, who were struggling for self-determination. After a major revolt that lasted two years, the Kurds had been given special status in 1970, allowing self-rule in Kurdish areas. The Kurds revolted again in 1974 and 1975. Unable to put an end to their revolt, mainly because the Kurds had help from Iran, Saddam demonstrated his daring style by signing the 1975 Algiers Agreement with the shah of Iran, putting an end to Iranian support for the Kurds in return for some modifications of the Iran–Iraq border along the Shatt al-Arab in the south.

Saddam married his cousin Sajida Khayr Allah Tulfa and had five children. His two sons, Uday and Qusay, held high security positions in the mid-1990s.

War with Iran

The health of President al-Bakr had been deteriorating, reportedly due to cancer. Saddam felt that the moment had come for him to assume total power. On 16 July 1979, al-Bakr was forced to resign and Saddam was elected president of the Iraqi republic. Followed a ruthless purge of suspected challengers, he executed five members of the Revolutionary Command Council and some twenty Ba'th Party members. This cleared the way for him to establish personal rule and a total monopoly of power.

Also in 1979, the Iranian Revolution established a Shi'ite Islamic republic. Iran's new government soon became a political threat to Iraq, calling for an uprising among Iraq's Shi'ite population and the establishment of a regime similar to Iran's. Soon border clashes and claims of border violations by troops from both sides were weekly events. Some pro-Iranian Shi'ite elements in opposition to Saddam, mainly the al-Da'wa al-Islamiyya (Religious Call) Party, aggravated this situation with internal violence, including two assassination attempts on top Iraqi government members.

Saddam took advantage of Iran's weakness to settle previous scores. In September 1980, he declared that the 1975 Algiers Accord with Iran was null and void. The Iraqi army then crossed the Iranian border and seized Iranian territories, which were evacuated later in the war. The result was a bitter and costly war that lasted eight years.

Islamic, Arab, and international mediation efforts to end the war were unsuccessful. Both countries used long-range missiles against cities, and Iraq used chemical weapons to ward off Iran's human-wave attacks. Casualties—both military and civilian—mounted on both sides. As the war continued, Saddam adopted a pragmatic stance in international affairs, and the oil-rich Gulf states provided funds to finance the Iraqi military effort. Diplomatic relations with the United States—severed since 1967—were reestablished in November 1984.

In July 1988, Iran unexpectedly announced that it had agreed to a cease-fire after repeated attempts to defeat the Iraqi army near Basra. Peace negotiations continued for months; in the fall of 1990 (after Iraq's August invasion of Kuwait), in a dramatic action, Iraq accepted the reinstitution of the 1975 Algiers Accord and a rectification of borders between the two countries, as demanded by Iran. However, no peace treaty was signed.

Kuwait

On 2 August 1990, Iraq invaded Kuwait. The invasion was swift and met little resistance, and the Kuwaiti ruling family fled to Saudi Arabia. Iraq had longstanding claims to Kuwait, which went back to the days of the Ottoman Empire, but Kuwait's independence had been recognized by Iraq's Ba'thist regime, which had come to power in 1963.

Just before the invasion, relations between Iraq and Kuwait had been tense. Differences existed over loan repayments, oil pricing, and the border. Iraq accused Kuwait of stealing oil by slant drilling under the border into Iraqi oil fields, and of economic warfare because of Kuwait's oil policy. Saddam annexed Kuwait a few days after the invasion, declaring that country a province of Iraq. The Kuwaiti government called for help to force Iraq's withdrawal. The UN Security Council repeatedly convened to debate several resolutions asking Iraq to withdraw and restore Kuwait's legitimate government. The United Nations agreed to impose an economic blockade on Iraq and, if that did not succeed, to use military force. The role of the United States, Britain, France, and the Soviet Union was pivotal in passing these measures.

Mediation efforts and economic pressures proved unsuccessful, but an international coalition of military forces, led by the United States (in accord with the newly cooperative Soviet Union), was deployed to eastern Saudia Arabia. After several months of troop buildup in Saudi Arabia and Saddam's failure to accede to a deadline for withdrawal, the attack began, on 16 and 17 January 1991, with a five-week campaign of air strikes on Iraq, followed by a four-day land campaign. Saddam ordered a retreat from Kuwait when coalition forces entered southern Iraq. A cease-fire was declared on 27 February 1991, and anti-Saddam uprisings began in some southern Iraqi cities—mainly Basra, Amara, al-Najaf, and Karbala, spreading throughout the south. Separatist uprisings took place soon after in Iraq's northern Kurdish cities. The United States had called for Saddam's overthrow but did not aid the rebellion.

Saddam used the army to crush these revolts, and he was successful, but only after fierce fighting with insurgents in southern Iraq, which resulted in major destruction in the Shi'ite cities of the south. The Kurds in the north, faced with Saddam's tanks, left the cities they had occupied and retreated to more secure positions in the mountains. Many retreated to Turkey and Iran.

The plight of the Kurds was dramatized by the international media, especially in the United States and Europe. As a result, public opinion allowed Western leaders to order military penetration of northern Iraq to establish secure zones guarded by coalition forces. Safe havens were established to entice Kurdish refugees back. Saddam invited a top-level Kurdish delegation to negotiate with his government in April 1991, but it failed and Saddam pulled his forces back from Kurdish areas and established a trade embargo on the north. Inside the Kurdish zone, under the protection of UN forces (mainly U.S., British, and French), the Kurds began to establish genuine self-rule and in 1992 elected a Kurdish government.

During his presidency, Saddam established an extreme cult of personality. Photos of him were everywhere; his speeches were printed and widely distributed; schools, towns, and the Baghdad airport were named for him. Any criticism of him as head of state was severely punished. Despite a military defeat, destruction of large parts of the Iraqi economy, and the most widespread rebellion Iraq had experienced since 1920, he remained in control. By the end of 1991, although weakened by these events, his presence was ubiquitous in Baghdad.

Sanctions

Between 1991 and 2003, Saddam Hussein adopted a siege mentality, making rare public appearances, and his whereabouts were a state secret. He received few foreign visitors and never left the country.

Under continuing UN sanctions, the population of Iraq suffered enormously. A rationing system provided basic food items and enabled the population to purchase necessities at nominal prices. However, the health and education systems rapidly deteriorated. Many students dropped out of school to work at menial jobs in order to help their needy families. Malnutrition created a dramatic rise in the number of deaths among children under five. Faced not only faced with economic difficulties but also the pressures of a police state, hundreds of thousands of Iraqis fled the country. The number of Iraqis living abroad was estimated to be at least 3 million. As inflation soared, the value of the national currency, the dinar, dropped sharply without any concomitant increase in salaries.

Since Iraq was unable to sell its oil, its economic situation worsened. By the mid-1990s, the deterioration of social and economic conditions had helped generate a religious revival, which received the regime's blessings. The new Islamic movement did not adhere to any internal or external political group or party.

Saddam's complex and difficult relationship with his family affected the political situation. His three half-brothers, Barzan, Watban, and Sabawi, served in key security posts, but their status deteriorated and by the mid-1990s they had disappeared from public view. Both the regime and Saddam's personal prestige suffered a serious shock in August 1995 when two key relatives and aides defected with their wives, who were Saddam's daughters. They went to Jordan, where they received the protection of King Hussein. The two men, however, were convinced by Saddam's emissaries to return to Baghdad and receive a pardon. When they arrived, they were divorced from their wives and three days later it was announced that they had died in a shootout with members of the extended family. The family declared that they were avenging the dishonor brought on their clan by these defectors.

On 12 December 1996, Saddam's elder son, Uday, was wounded in an assassination attempt in Baghdad. His wound left him partially paralyzed, which excluded him from becoming the eventual successor to his father. This position was taken by his younger brother, Qusay (born in 1968), who slowly assumed all the important security responsibilities in the state.

As part of the 1991 cease-fire accord with the UN coalition forces, Iraq accepted the elimination of its chemical, biological, and nuclear weapons programs. The United Nations charged two bodies with overseeing Iraq's disarmament operations, the United Nations Special Commission (UNSCOM) and the International Atomic Energy Agency. When these two agencies started inspections in Iraq, they were expected to disarm Iraq within a few weeks. Instead, the regime challenged the inspectors constantly, refusing to submit documents and materials and withholding information; the inspections dragged on for over a decade.

In the aftermath of the Kurdish revolt against the regime and the flight of Kurds toward neighboring Turkey and Iran, the United States led the coalition countries in imposing a no-fly zone over northern Iraq. This allowed the Kurds to return home. A similar no-fly zone was imposed in 1992 in southern Iraq in order to protect the Shiʿa. It was also used as a punitive measure against a possible attempt to mass Iraqi armed forces on or near the Kuwaiti border. In 1996, this zone was extended to the outskirts of Baghdad.

The imposition of these no-fly zones curtailed the sovereignty of the Iraqi state over its territory. This was particularly true in northern Iraq, where the two main Kurdish parties, the Democratic Party of Kurdistan (Iraq) and the Patriotic Union of Kurdistan, started to build state institutions and rule over northern Iraq.

In April 1995, responding to the deterioration of the economic situation in Iraq, the UN Security Council passed the Oil-for-Food resolution (Resolution 986), which allowed Iraq to sell some of its oil to buy food and medicine for its population. Iraq initially rejected the resolution, but accepted it in December 1996 due to the worsening economic situation.

U.S. and British war planes continued to patrol the no-fly zones, firing missiles on Iraqi military targets when they were challenged. Tensions increased over weapons inspections. On more than one occasion, Iraq threatened to expel the UN inspectors.

The deterioration of relations between UNSCOM and the Iraqis reached its climax in December 1998, when Richard Butler, head of UNSCOM, presented a negative report to the UN Security Council and withdrew his inspectors. Three days later, U.S. and British airplanes staged air raids on Iraq military installations in Operation Desert Fox. The Iraqis responded by declaring that they would never allow UN inspectors to return.

Military Intervention

Since 1997, faced with the difficulties of disarming Iraq, the U.S. government had considered overthrowing the Saddam regime. The U.S. began to openly encourage Iraqi opposition groups abroad (mainly in London) to cooperate and organize their efforts to topple the Iraqi ruler. The war of words between Iraq and the United States rose in tone. When the terrorist attacks of 11 September 2001 occurred in New York and Washington D.C., Saddam's regime was one of the very few to declare its public satisfaction over what had happened.

Internally, Saddam became more oppressive toward his opponents, putting a brutal end to unrest, especially among the Shiʿa, and assassinating well-known Shiʿite clerics. In a State of the Union address delivered after the 11 September attacks, President George W. Bush labeled Iraq a member of the "axis of evil" and called for "regime change." In 2002, after months of UN discussions and U.S. threats, Saddam finally allowed the UN inspectors to return to Iraq. A new inspection agency, the UN Monitoring, Verification, and Inspection Commission, headed by Hans Blix, was created to oversee this operation. On 27 January 2003, after inspecting suspected sites for several weeks, the team handed in a report that was inconclusive on the question of whether illegal arms or arms programs existed. Meanwhile, the United States and Britain continued to demand regime change in Baghdad and undertook a massive military buildup around Iraq, preparing for military intervention, preferably with the blessing of the UN Security Council. Objections to intervention, however, came from countries such as France, Germany, and Russia, which called for continued inspections, and from individual citizens in many countries. The Security Council did not back intervention.

On 17 March 2003, the United States issued an ultimatum demanding that President Saddam Hussein leave the country within twenty-four hours. He rejected it, and UN inspectors left Iraq. On 20 March, the first air attacks on Baghdad began, followed by U.S. and British troops entering Iraq from Kuwait. Despite some resistance, U.S. troops pushed north toward Baghdad and occupied it on 9 April. Saddam Hussein and his top aides went underground. By 18 April, most of the country was under the control of U.S. and British forces.

The United States issued a list of fifty-five of the most wanted persons in the old regime, including Saddam, his two sons, and his half-brothers. Uday and Qusay were killed in Mosul on July 22 during a firefight with U.S. forces. Two of his half-brothers, Barzan and Watban, were captured but the third, Sabawi, was still at large in 2004. Saddam Hussein himself was captured on 13 December 2003, hiding underground in Dur, a small town south of Tikrit.

After Saddam's capture, the United States declared him a prisoner of war. Several suggestions were made by Iraq's transitional authority (put in place by the Americans) and others on how to bring Saddam to justice. Iraqis insisted that he be held in Iraq and tried by an Iraqi court.

After the fall of Saddam Hussein, Iraq became a theater of violence, with widespread looting, attacks on American troops and the newly installed Iraqi police, and suicide bombings of key targets, including UN personnel and Shiʿite leaders and mosques. These acts were blamed on Iraqi groups resisting foreign occupation. The perpetrators were believed to consist of remnants of the old Baʿthist regime in addition to Muslim fundamentalists, some of whom were believed to have ties to al-Qaʿida. Saddam himself was believed to have directed some of the resistance before his capture. Despite efforts by the Americans to discover them, no hidden weapons of mass destructions were found. David Kay, a former weapons inspector appointed by President Bush to investigate the situation, reported in 2004 that none were likely to be found.

See also ALGIERS AGREEMENT (1975); ARAB NATIONALISM; ARIF, ABD AL-SALAM; BAKR, AHMAD HASAN AL-; BAʿTH, AL-; CAMP DAVID ACCORDS (1978); DAʿWA AL-ISLAMIYYA, AL-; GULF CRISIS (1990–1991); IRAQ PETROLEUM COMPANY (IPC); KURDS; PATRIOTIC UNION OF KURDISTAN (PUK); SANCTIONS, IRAQI; SHATT AL-ARAB; TALFAH, ADNAN KHAYR ALLAH; UNITED NATIONS SPECIAL COMMISSION (UNSCOM); WAR IN IRAQ (2003).

Bibliography

Aburish, Said K. *Saddam Hussein: The Politics of Revenge.* New York: Bloomsbury, 2000.

Henderson, Simon. *Instant Empire: Saddam Hussein's Ambition for Iraq.* San Francisco: Mercury, 1991.

Karsh, Efraim, and Rautsi, Inari. *Saddam Hussein: A Political Biography.* New York: Free Press, 1991.

Khadduri, Majid. *Socialist Iraq: A Study in Iraqi Politics since 1968.* Washington, DC: Middle East Institute, 1978.

Marr, Phebe. *The Modern History of Iraq.* Boulder, CO: Westview, 2003.

Matar, Fuad. *Saddam Hussein: The Man, the Cause, and the Future.* London: Third World Centre, 1981.

Miller, Judith, and Mylroie, Laurie. *Saddam Hussein and the Crisis in the Gulf.* New York: Times Books, 1990.

Munthe, Turi, ed. *The Saddam Hussein Reader.* New York: Thunder's Mouth Press, 2002.

LOUAY BAHRY

HUT, SHAFIQ AL-
[1932–]

Palestinian leader, journalist, and intellectual.

The son of a wealthy Sunni landowner and citrus merchant in the Manshiyya quarter of Jaffa in British Mandate Palestine, Shafiq al-Hut graduated from Jaffa's elite al-Amiriyya School in 1948. When war broke out, he fled with his family to Beirut, where his paternal grandfather had emigrated from.

Al-Hut cut his political teeth in the radical pan-Arabist environment of the American University of Beirut, graduating in 1953 with a bachelor's degree in biology. Initially a schoolmaster, he subsequently worked as a correspondent and as editor of the weeklies *al-Hawadith* (Events) and *al-Muharrir* (The editor).

Al-Hut was a leading figure in the Palestinian Liberation Front—Path of Return (PLF–PR), which was established in 1961, and he took part in the 1964 Palestine National Council, which founded the Palestine Liberation Organization (PLO). Appointed PLO representative to Lebanon in 1964 (a position he held until 1993), from 1965 to 1967 al-Hut led the internal opposition to PLO president Ahmad Shuqayri, who attempted to exile al-Hut to New Delhi in May 1967. Al-Hut was also linked to the Heroes of the Return guerrilla group established in 1966.

In 1968, al-Hut renounced the PLF–PR leadership and the group disbanded. He was increasingly associated with the PLO's al-Fatah mainstream, served on the PLO's executive committee, and survived various attempted assassinations by other Palestinian factions, notably by the Syrian-backed al-Saʿiqa force in 1976 in Lebanon, after the outbreak of armed conflict among Palestinian, Christian, and Muslim communities there. In 1978, he supported Arafat's decision to offer a guarantee of Israeli security in return for Palestinian statehood, but in August 1993, mindful of the interests of Palestinians in Lebanon, he left the PLO in protest

against the Oslo Accord. He has since been prominent in the Palestinian opposition to the direction taken by Palestinian, American, and Israeli diplomats and negotiators. A secularist inspired by Gamal Abdel Nasser's pan-Arabism, al-Hut is the author of several books on Palestinian and Arab politics and has written an autobiography. He married the Palestinian writer Bayan Nuwayhid in 1962 and has three children.

See also ARAB–ISRAEL WAR (1948); FATAH, AL-; OSLO ACCORD (1993); PALESTINE LIBERATION ORGANIZATION (PLO); SHUQAYRI, AHMAD.

Bibliography

Sayigh, Yezid. *Armed Struggle and the Search for State: The Palestinian National Movement, 1949–1993.* New York: Oxford University Press, 1997.

MOUIN RABBANI
UPDATED BY GEORGE R. WILKES

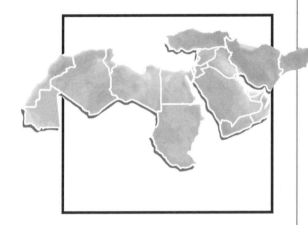

I

IBADIYYA

The only surviving branch today of the Kharijite schismatic rebels of the seventh century.

The Kharijite movement broke with the fourth caliph Ali in 657 after he agreed to submit his conflict with the governor of Syria, Muʿawiya ibn Abi Sufyan, to arbitration. This action, the Kharijites argued, undermined both the religious and political leadership of Ali. Equally hostile to Umayyad rule by hereditary succession, the Kharijites espoused an ideology of absolute egalitarianism, social austerity, and militant puritanism. The two major Kharijite factions were the Azariqa, who waged a relentless war to overthrow the existing social and political order, and the Ibadiyya, who took a politically quiescent position *(kitman)* during the civil wars of the seventh century.

The Ibadiyya, who derive their name from their founder Abdallah ibn Ibad al-Murri al-Tamimi (died c. 720), were originally based in Basra. Under the early Abbasids in the eighth and ninth centuries, the Ibadiyya took an activist missionary approach *(zuhur)* and spread in the desert frontier regions of north Africa (Tahert), and eastern and southern Arabia (Hadramawt) among tribal social segments. The Ibadiyya developed an elaborate political theory that emphasizes the primacy of religious leadership (imamate), but allows the co-existence of various imams (unlike in Shiʿism). Notwithstanding their acceptance of the Muʿtazilite doctrine of the createdness of the Qurʾan, the Ibadiyya largely concur with Sunni Islam, particularly the Maliki school on matters of law. The sect survives today in Oman, eastern Africa (Zanzibar), Libya (Jabal Nafusa and Zuagha), the island of Djerba (Tunisia), and southern Algeria (Wargla and Mzab).

See also MALIKI SCHOOL OF LAW; SUNNI ISLAM.

Bibliography

Watt, W. Montgomery. *Islamic Political Thought: The Basic Concepts.* Edinburgh: Edinburgh University Press, 1968.

TAYEB EL-HIBRI

IBN

See GLOSSARY

IBN MUSA, AHMAD

Regent of Morocco, 1894–1900.

Sultan Mulai Hassan I was succeeded by his youngest son, Abd al-Aziz ibn al-Hassan, aged fourteen. As regent, Ibn Musa (known as Ba Ahmad) maintained stability through the control of dissident tribes and counseled cautious diplomacy toward the European powers. Some scholars believe that this caution undermined the sultanate's legitimacy in the eyes of many Moroccans. Ba Ahmad died during a cholera epidemic, leaving the sultanate ruled by a young, untried sultan.

See also ABD AL-AZIZ IBN AL-HASSAN.

BRUCE MADDY-WEITZMAN

IBN SAʿUD

See ABD AL-AZIZ IBN SAʿUD AL SAʿUD

IBN TULUN MOSQUE

Ancient mosque in Cairo.

Constructed from 876 to 879 C.E. by Ahmad ibn Tulun, semiautonomous governor of Egypt for the Abbasid caliphs, this is not only one of Cairo's best-known monuments but is also the best surviving example of religious architecture from that period of Islam. The mosque was erected along with a palace and a government house in a new district known as al-Qataʿi (the Allotments), to the northeast of the oldest parts of the city.

Built of brick and rendered with a fine and hard layer of plaster, the mosque comprises a courtyard about 300 feet (92 m) square, with a fountain-house in the center. The court is surrounded by hypostyle halls covered with a flat wooden roof supported by arcades resting on piers. The prayer hall, on the southeast, is five aisles deep; those on the other three sides are two aisles deep. The mosque, 400 by 460 feet (122 by 140 m) is enclosed in an outer wall 33 feet (10 m) high, with an elaborate cresting adding some 10 feet (3 m) to its height. Beyond the wall on three sides is an outer court (*ziyada*),

approximately 62 feet (19 m) broad, enclosed in a somewhat lower wall. In this outer court, opposite the prayer hall, stands the minaret (tower), the mosque's most distinctive feature. In its present state this tower consists of a square stone base supporting a cylindrical shaft and an elaborate finial; an external staircase winds around the tower. The interior of the mosque is relatively plain, although the arcades are decorated with nook-shafts at the corners of the piers, carved capitals, and bands of geometricized vegetal ornament around and on the underside of the arches and at the top of the walls. Beneath the roof are long wooden planks carved with verses from the Qurʾan written in an angular script.

Most of the architectural and decorative features of the mosque are foreign to Egyptian architecture in the ninth century, although they were common in the religious architecture of Iraq, the Abbasid heartland, and can be seen there in such buildings as the congregational mosques at Samarra, the Abbasid capital where Ahmad ibn Tulun received his training. It is therefore believed that workmen trained in these techniques came to Egypt in the retinue of Ibn Tulun.

The mosque was repeatedly restored and its functions changed. In 1077, the Fatimid vizier Badr al-Jamali restored the mosque and, in 1094, his son al-Afdal added a beautiful stucco mihrab (a niche indicating the direction of Mecca) to one of the piers. Under the Ayyubids, who believed that Cairo needed only one congregational mosque, the building fell into disrepair and served as a shelter for North African pilgrims to Mecca and also as a bakery. In 1296, the Mamluk sultan Lagin, who had taken refuge in the mosque during one of the struggles that eventually brought him to power, restored it extensively; he added a new mihrab, replaced the fountain-house that had stood in the court with the present domed edifice, and reconstructed the minaret, which had also fallen into disrepair.

By the early nineteenth century, the mosque was again deteriorated and, by the middle of that century, it was used as an insane asylum and poorhouse. In 1884, the newly formed Comité de Conservation des Monuments de l'Art Arabe recommended the restoration of the building, and work was soon begun.

See also MIHRAB; MINARET; MOSQUE; QURʾAN.

Bibliography

Behrens-Abouseif, Doris. *Islamic Architecture in Cairo: An Introduction.* Leiden, Netherlands, and New York: Brill, 1989.

Creswell, K. A. C. *Early Muslim Architecture.* New York: Hacker Art Books, 1979.

JONATHAN M. BLOOM

IBRAHIM, ABDULLAH
[1918–]

Moroccan socialist political leader.

Ibrahim was educated at the Université Ben Youssef in Marrakech and the Sorbonne in Paris. He was a founding member of the Istiqlal party (1944–1959) and served on the editorial committee of *Al-Alam,* the party newspaper, (1950–1952). He was imprisoned for nationalist activities (1952–1954).

After independence from France, Ibrahim served as secretary of state for information (1955–1956); minister of labor and social affairs (1956–1958); and prime minister and minister of foreign affairs (1958–1960). In 1959 he helped form Union Nationale des Forces Populaires (National Union of Popular Forces; UNFP) from the left wing of the Istiqlal and became leader of the UNFP in July 1972 when its Rabat section became the Union Socialiste des Forces Populaires (Socialist Union of Popular Forces; USFP). Since then, the UNFP has reportedly become increasingly subordinated to the Moroccan Labor Union (UMT) and has waned in influence.

See also UNION NATIONALE DES FORCES POPULAIRES (UNFP); UNION SOCIALISTE DES FORCES POPULAIRES (USFP).

Bibliography

Waterbury, John. *The Commander of the Faithful: The Moroccan Political Elite—A Study in Segmented Politics.* New York: Columbia University Press, 1970.

C. R. PENNELL
UPDATED BY ANA TORRES-GARCIA

IBRAHIM, FATIMA AHMED
[early 1930s–]

Sudan's best-known woman politician.

Fatima Ahmed (also Ahmad) Ibrahim was born into a liberal middle-class family in Omdurman in the early 1930s. Upon graduating from Omdurman Girls Secondary School, where she was a student leader and activist, she became a teacher. In the course of her nationalist activities in the 1940s and 1950s in opposition to British rule, she was influenced by Communism and by Abd al-Khaliq Mahjub, secretary-general of the Sudanese Communist Party (SCP), which she joined. She became one of the early leaders of the Sudanese Women's Union (SWU), formed in 1952 under the wing of the SCP, and soon after the editor of the SWU organ, *The Woman's Voice.* In the decades that followed she was arrested and imprisoned many times for her activism. In 1964 she helped to organize the civilian overthrow of the Ibrahim Abbud military regime (1957–1964). In 1965, as the first woman ever elected to parliament, she headed the SWU as it fought for a number of rights for women. Among these were suffrage, equal pay for equal work, and maternity leave. She was active again in the 1985 civilian overthrow of the military regime of Muhammad Ja'far Numeiri (1969–1985). Following the Islamist military coup d'état in 1989, the SWU was banned and Ibrahim was again imprisoned. She went into exile in England in the early 1990s, where she continued her SWU activism. Although her increasing conservatism and stress on religion has alienated some younger feminist and leftist activists, Ibrahim remains a member of the Central Committee of the SCP, president of the SWU, and editor of *The Woman's Voice,* as well as being active in the National Democratic Alliance (an umbrella opposition coalition in exile). In the 1990s, on behalf of the SWU, she accepted human-rights awards from Amnesty International and the United Nations.

See also COMMUNISM IN THE MIDDLE EAST; GENDER: GENDER AND LAW; GENDER: GENDER AND POLITICS; SUDAN; SUDANESE CIVIL WARS.

Bibliography

Hale, Sondra. *Gender Politics in Sudan: Islamism, Socialism, and the State.* Boulder, CO: Westview Press, 1996.

Hall, Marjorie, and Ismail, Bakhita Amin. *Sisters under the Sun: The Story of Sudanese Women.* London: Longman, 1981.

Niblock, Tim. *Class and Power in Sudan.* Albany: State University of New York Press, 1987.

Sanousi, Magda M. el-, and Amin, Nafissa Ahmed el-. "The Women's Movement, Displaced Women, and

Rural Women in Sudan." In *Women and Politics World-wide*, edited by Barbara Nelson and Najma Chowdhury. New Haven, CT: Yale University Press, 1994.

SONDRA HALE

IBRAHIMI, AHMED TALEB
[1932–]

Algerian minister; political party leader.

A medical doctor and son of Bashir Ibrahimi, Ahmed Taleb Ibrahimi was imprisoned during the Algerian War of Independence after serving in the Fédération de France du Front de Libératon Nationale (FFFLN). After being released in 1961, he joined the FLN's Gouvernement Provisoire de la République Algérienne (GPRA) diplomatic team at the United Nations (UN). He opposed the Ahmed Ben Bella government and was detained from June 1964 to January 1965. After Colonel Houari Boumédienne deposed Ben Bella in June 1965, he appointed Taleb Ibrahimi minister of national education. In July 1970 Taleb Ibrahimi became minister of information and culture; in that capacity he supervised the inauguration of Algeria's cultural revolution.

After Boumédienne's death in December 1978, Taleb Ibrahimi served his successor, President Chadli Bendjedid, as a counselor minister and then, after the death of Mohamed Benyahia, as foreign minister from May 1982 until the formation of the Kasdi Merbah cabinet in November 1988. Taleb Ibrahimi became disaffected and associated with the anti-Bendjedid "Islamist" faction within the FLN. After the establishment of the Haut Comité d'Etat (HCE) in January 1992, the Pouvoir—the ruling military and civilian elite—considered Taleb Ibrahimi for the prime ministership before selecting Belaid Abdesselam in July 1992. As the civil war raged, Taleb Ibrahimi became more alienated from the Pouvoir and its attitude toward Islamism. He ran for president in April 1999 but withdrew with the six other candidates because of electoral irregularities. Nevertheless, he still came in second to the expected winner, Abdelaziz Bouteflika. Taleb Ibrahimi organized the Wafa (Trust/Loyalty) Party, but the government refused to recognize it because it had in its ranks former members of the Front Islamique du Salut (FIS). Nevertheless, he is expected to run for president again in 2004. Taleb Ibrahimi is the author of *Lettres de prison* (1966; Letters from prison),

De la décolonisation à la révolution culturelle (1973; From decolonization to the cultural revolution), and *Le drame algérien: La voie de la réconciliation* (1996; The Algerian drama: The way to reconciliation).

See also ALGERIA: POLITICAL PARTIES IN; IBRAHIMI, BASHIR.

Bibliography

Naylor, Phillip C. *Historical Dictionary of Algeria*, 3d edition. Lanham, MD: Scarecrow Press, 2005.

Roberts, Hugh. *The Battlefield Algeria, 1988–2002: Studies in a Broken Polity*. London: Verso, 2003.

PHILLIP C. NAYLOR

IBRAHIMI, BASHIR
[1889–1965]

Islamic religious leader in Algeria.

Born in Béjaïa in northeastern Algeria, Bashir Ibrahimi became a leading companion to Shaykh Abd al-Hamid Ben Badis. Ibrahimi was renowned as an orator for the Association of Algerian Muslim Ulama (Reformist Ulama) and served as its vice president and then its president after the death of Ben Badis. Through his studies in Damascus, he also achieved a great reputation as a scholar of Arabic and Islam while contributing numerous articles to the association's various journals. Ibrahimi was an opponent of French colonialism, as symbolized by the association's support of the Front de Libération Nationale (FLN; National Liberation Front). After the Algerian War of Independence, 1954–1962, he questioned the political leadership's use of foreign ideologies and called for the new nation to identify instead with its Arab Islamic traditions. His son Ahmed Taleb Ibrahimi became a government official under presidents Houari Boumédienne and Chadli Bendjedid.

See also ALGERIAN WAR OF INDEPENDENCE; ASSOCIATION OF ALGERIAN MUSLIM ULAMA (AUMA); BEN BADIS, ABD AL-HAMID; BENDJEDID, CHADLI; BOUMÉDIENNE, HOUARI; FRONT DE LIBÉRATION NATIONALE (FLN); IBRAHIMI, AHMED TALEB.

Bibliography

Gordon, David C. *The Passing of French Algeria*. London and New York: Oxford University Press, 1966.

PHILLIP C. NAYLOR

IBRAHIM IBN MUHAMMAD ALI
[1789–1848]

Nineteenth-century Egyptian general; son of Muhammad Ali Pasha.

Ibrahim ibn Muhammad Ali was the elder son of Muhammad Ali Pasha, the founder of modern Egypt. Born in Kavala, Anatolia, Ibrahim Pasha and his brother Tusun accompanied their father when he assumed power as Egypt's viceroy for the Ottoman Empire in 1805. Ibrahim was assigned various responsibilities that ranged from national finance to the governing of Upper Egypt. Starting his military career in 1816, Ibrahim commanded the expedition sent by Muhammad Ali, at the request of the Ottoman sultan, to Arabia to crush the Wahhabi rebellion. In 1818, Ibrahim Pasha succeeded in what came to be known as the Wahhabi war, destroying their capital (al-Dar'iya, now Riyadh) capturing their leaders, and restoring Ottoman control over Islam's holy cities of Mecca and Medina. Gratified by this success, the Ottoman government (Sublime Porte) named Ibrahim to be *wali* (provincial governor) of the provinces of Hijaz and Abyssinia (today Ethiopia).

In 1822, Ibrahim assisted his brother Isma'il in the invasion of the Sudan and then, in 1824, led the Egyptian army in the name of the Ottoman Empire against a revolt in Greece. By 1826, Ibrahim Pasha was able to capture the Morea (Peloponnesus) and Athens. The European powers, however, despite Muhammad Ali's attempts to reach an agreement with Great Britain, decided to intervene and enforced a blockade on the Morea by the joint naval forces of France, Russia, and Great Britain. In October 1827, the European forces destroyed the whole Egyptian and Ottoman fleet in the battle of Navarino, and Ibrahim Pasha was forced to withdraw.

After the Greek war, Muhammad Ali demanded the governorship of Morea and Syria. Denied by the sultan, he declared war on the Porte in 1831 and sent an Egyptian force to Syria under Ibrahim's command. The troops progressed victoriously through Syria, entered Anatolia, and defeated the Ottoman army in the Battle of Konya in 1832. The Egyptian victory forced the sultan to sign the treaty of Kütahya in which the Porte granted Muhammad Ali the government of Syria and Adana, in what is today southern Turkey. Ibrahim was appointed governor of Syria. During his rule, he attempted to develop the irrigation system and introduced modern industry to the region. His enforcement of military service on the Syrians, however, and his strict discipline, led to the emergence of anti-Egyptian feelings among the population.

In 1839, the war between the Porte and Egypt was renewed and for the second time Ibrahim Pasha achieved a victory over the Ottomans at the battle of Nisib, and the road to Constantinople (now Istanbul) became virtually open. The European powers intervened, however, demanding the withdrawal of Egyptian troops. Muhammad Ali was forced to ask his son to turn back. The European intervention, headed by Britain, was followed by the London Convention of 1840 in which the European powers forced Muhammad Ali to return Syria and Adana to the Porte.

In 1845, Ibrahim Pasha visited France and England. In April 1848, due to the illness of Muhammad Ali and his inability to rule, Ibrahim Pasha proclaimed himself ruler of Egypt and informed the sultan of this change. In October of that year, the Porte conferred on him the government of Egypt. A few weeks later in November, however, Ibrahim Pasha died—even before the death of his father.

See also ISLAM; KONYA, BATTLE OF; KÜTAHYA, PEACE OF; LONDON CONVENTION; MUHAMMAD ALI; OTTOMAN EMPIRE; SUBLIME PORTE.

Bibliography

Dodwell, Henry. *The Founder of Modern Egypt: A Study of Muhammad Ali.* 1931. Reprint, New York: AMS Press, 1977.

Goldschmidt, Arthur, Jr. *Modern Egypt: The Formation of a Nation-State.* Boulder, CO: Westview Press, 1988.

Marsot, Afaf Lutfi al-Sayyid. *Egypt in the Reign of Muhammad Ali.* Cambridge, U.K., and New York: Cambridge University Press, 1984.

ALI E. HILLAL DESSOUKI

IBRAHIMI, LAKHDAR AL-
[1934–]

Algerian diplomat.

Lakhdar al-Ibrahimi studied law and political science in Algiers and in Paris. He was independent

Algeria's first minister of external affairs in 1962 and 1963. He then served as Algeria's ambassador to Egypt, Sudan, and the United Kingdom. From 1963 to 1970 Ibrahimi was Algeria's permanent representative to the Arab League, where he has also acted as assistant secretary-general. In the 1980s Ibrahimi headed the league's efforts to end the Lebanese civil war (1975–1991). From 1991 to 1993 he was Algeria's foreign minister. Between 1994 and 1996, Ibrahimi served as United Nations special representative to countries such as Haiti, South Africa (leading the United Nations observer mission until the 1994 democratic elections of post-apartheid South Africa), Zaire (now the Democratic Republic of the Congo), Yemen, and Liberia. As of 2003, he is the special representative of the United Nations secretary general for Afghanistan (1997–1999; 2001–).

Bibliography

Bustros, Gabriel, ed. *Who's Who in the Arab World 1988–89.* Beirut, 1989.

Middle East Contemporary Survey 1989, Vol. 13. Boulder, CO: 1991.

United Nations. "Lakhdar Brahimi Appointed Special Representative for Afghanistan. Press Release Bio3397." Available from <http://www.un.org>.

ELIZABETH THOMPSON
UPDATED BY ANA TORRES-GARCIA

IBRAHIM, IZZAT
[1942–]

Ba'thist politician in Iraq.

Izzat Ibrahim was born into an Arab Sunni family, rumored to be of Sabean origin, in al-Dur district of Samarra. His father was an ice vendor. Ibrahim joined the Ba'th party in the late 1950s and was in prison during the 1960s for his political activities. He held several important positions following the Ba'th coup of 1968, including: minister of land reform (1969–1974) and minister of the interior (1974–1979). In 1979 he became deputy chairman of the Revolutionary Command Council (RCC). Ibrahim was the constitutional successor to the president of Iraq, Saddam Hussein. His daughter is married to the president's oldest son, Uday.

In 1973, he headed a special court trying the conspirators who were behind an unsuccessful coup.

As deputy chair of the RCC, he was put in charge of several task forces and special commissions in the Ba'th government. Prior to Iraq's invasion of Kuwait, Ibrahim headed the delegation to negotiate the problems between the two countries. Following the 2003 American invasion of Iraq, he went underground, and was rumored to be organizing anti-American resistance activities.

See also BA'TH, AL-; HUSSEIN, SADDAM.

Bibliography

Helms, Christine M. *Iraq: Eastern Flank of the Arab World.* Washington, DC: Brookings Institution, 1984.

AYAD AL-QAZZAZ

IBRAHIM, MUHAMMAD HAFIZ
[1871–1932]

Egyptian poet and writer; one of the best-known Arab neoclassicists.

Whereas Ahmad Shawqi was known as a poet of the court, the "prince of poets," Muhammad Hafiz Ibrahim was the "people's poet." He was also known as the "poet of the Nile"—an appropriate epithet, since he was born on a houseboat on the Nile River near the town of Dayrut.

Hafiz Ibrahim had a somewhat lonely childhood followed by a long struggle to find a vocation. He went to a modern secular school in Cairo, then to a more traditional Qur'anic school in Tanta. Hafiz also served as an apprentice to several lawyers and later was graduated from the Military Academy in Cairo. His military service in the Sudan ended abruptly with a court-martial because of his involvement in an army rebellion. Returning to Cairo, he was unable to find work. This was the beginning of his most difficult years of poverty and unemployment, which lasted until 1911, when he was nominated to head the literary section of the National Library. During these years, Hafiz came into contact with prominent Egyptian nationalists and was popular among them because of his winning balance of earnestness and conversational wit.

Hafiz Ibrahim employed a generally simple, direct, yet fluent poetic diction, adapting traditional forms to speak to new audiences living in a changing world. He reached his audience in two ways:

First, he was a master of "platform poetry," reciting his poetry publicly to large groups of listeners; second, he actively contributed poetry to prominent Egyptian newspapers and periodicals. Hafiz Ibrahim was able to address social and political events in verse, giving voice to common Egyptian opinions. His most successful works were his elegies and his occasional poems.

See also LITERATURE: ARABIC; SHAWQI, AHMAD.

KENNETH S. MAYERS

IBRAHIM, SAʿAD AL-DIN

[1938–]

Renowned human rights activist and professor of sociology at the American University of Cairo.

Saʿd al-Din (also Saʿad Eddih) Ibrahim is an Egyptian American born in Mansura, Egypt, in 1938. He received his bachelor's degree with honors from Cairo University in 1960 and his doctorate in sociology from the University of Washington in 1968. Ibrahim founded in 1988 the Ibn Khaldun Center for Development Studies in Cairo, as an independent research institute for advancing democratization and development. Ibrahim has directed the center's activities in monitoring elections, conducting voter education projects, and training students in social science research methods.

Ibrahim has served as secretary-general of the Independent Commission for Electoral Review, which had monitored the 1990 and 1995 elections in Egypt. He was preparing to monitor the 2000 elections and was producing a documentary film about Egyptian election irregularities when he was arrested. The center's activities came under surveillance; in January 2000 authorities banned its publication *Civil Society* and the center was closed in June. Meanwhile, Ibrahim and twenty-seven of his colleagues were tried and found guilty on charges such as "collecting funds without a permit from the official authorities, misappropriation of funds in a fraudulent manner to prepare forged voting lists and cards, preparing public media containing false phrases and rumors and disseminating provocative propaganda damaging to the public interest, and accepting funds from a foreign country with the purpose of carrying out work harmful to the national interest by producing a film that damages Egypt's reputation abroad." Though Ibrahim was sentenced to seven years of imprisonment with hard labor, three years later, on 18 March 2003, Egypt's highest court acquitted him of all charges brought against him by the Egyptian government in response to international pressure.

Ibrahim teaches at American University of Cairo (AUC) and has taught at several universities in the United States and Egypt. He has published over thirty books in English and Arabic, including *Sociology of the Arab–Israel Conflict, American Presidential Elections and the Middle East, The New Arab Social Order,* and *Society and State in the Arab World.* He has served as the president of Cairo's Union of Social Professions, a board member and head of Arab Affairs of al-Ahram Centre for Political and Strategic Studies, secretary-general of the Arab Organization for Human Rights, the founder and a core member of the Initiative for Peace and Cooperation in the Middle East, the chairman of the Board of Egyptian Enlightenment Association, and the president of the Egyptian Sociologists Association. A champion of democracy and human rights, Ibrahim is considered a leading proponent of democratic reforms and an advocate of minority rights. He has received several awards since his imprisonment, including a nomination for the Nobel Peace Prize for 2002.

Bibliography

Ibn Khaldun Center. Available from <http://www.ibnkhaldun.org/>.

Ibrahim, Saʿad Eddin. *Arab Nonviolent Political Struggle in the Middle East.* Boulder, CO: Lynn Rienner, 1990.

Ibrahim, Saʿad Eddin. *Egypt, Islam and Democracy: Critical Essays, with a New Postscript.* Cairo, Egypt: American University of Cairo Press, 2002.

Norton, Augustus Richard, ed. *Civil Society in the Middle East.* New York: Brill, 1995.

RITA STEPHAN

İDADI SCHOOLS

Ottoman middle or secondary schools.

In the late nineteenth century, İdadi schools provided three years of intermediate and low secondary-level education. Instruction was in Turkish and French. The curriculum included logic, economics, geography, world and Ottoman history, algebra and arithmetic, the physical sciences, and engineering.

In the 1850s the military opened the first provincial İdadi schools in Baghdad, Erzurum, and Sarajevo. The first nonmilitary, state-run İdadi school opened in Constantinople (now Istanbul) in the 1870s. Under the 1869 Regulation for Public Instruction, towns and cities were required to provide one İdadi school for every thousand households. By 1895, about one-third of a total of thirty thousand students attending intermediate school in the Ottoman Empire were enrolled in the fifty-five state and military İdadi schools, the latter being found in every province. The other two-thirds of students attended the seventy millet system–run İdadi schools or the sixty-three foreign ones, such as American-run Robert College in Constantinople. State-run İdadi schools were financed by taxes. The term *İdadi schools* was changed in 1908 to *sultani schools,* and in 1925 in Turkey, to *orta* or middle schools.

See also MILLET SYSTEM; SULTANI SCHOOLS.

Bibliography

Kazamias, Andreas M. *Education and the Quest for Modernity in Turkey.* Chicago: University of Chicago Press, 1966.

Lewis, Bernard. *The Emergence of Modern Turkey,* 3d edition. New York: Oxford University Press, 2002.

ELIZABETH THOMPSON

IDLIBI, ULFAT AL-
[b. 1912 or 1913]

Syrian novelist and short-story writer.

A native of Damascus, Ulfat Idlibi is known for fiction that realistically portrays middle-class urban Syrian women—her own social milieu—during a period of transition when women were becoming visibly active in nationalist politics, were moving into the public workforce, and were earning higher degrees in greater numbers. Idlibi herself, married at 17, participated in nationalist demonstrations and has worked in various areas of national culture. She began writing short stories in 1947; some were published in a Damascus women's cultural journal, and her first collection, *Qisas shamiyya* (Syrian stories, 1954), received the recognition of an introduction by eminent Egyptian writer Mahmoud Taymur. In

addition to four further volumes of stories (the latest published in 1993), three collections of lectures and essays, and a study on Arabic popular literature (*Nazra fi adabina al-sha'bi,* 1974), Idlibi has published two novels, both translated into English by Peter Clark: *Dimashq ya basmat al-huzn* (1980; in English, Sabriya: Damascus Bittersweet, 1995) and *Hikayat jaddi: riwaya* (1991; in English, Grandfather's Tales). Her fictions experiment with techniques of embedded narrative, and while gently portraying Damascene society, they also satirize social usage and constraining expectations. Although the focus is on the domestic site where women's daily lives unfold, she blends coming-of-age narratives (*bildungsroman*) with national stories of liberation from European imperial rule.

Bibliography

Kahf, Mohja. "The Silences of Contemporary Syrian Literature." *World Literature Today* 75, no. 2 (Spring 2001): 225–236.

MARILYN BOOTH

IDLIB PROVINCE

Province in northwest Syria, named after its principal town, Idlib, where the governor resides.

Idlib is north of the mountain Jabal al-Zawiya and east of the al-Ruj plain. There were two Idlib's in the past: Lesser Idlib and Greater Idlib. The last was the most ancient, superseded by Lesser Idlib, the present-day town. The region of Idlib is famed for its olive groves and vineyards. Pistachio and cherry trees have recently proven very productive in its hilly countryside. Cotton of high quality and grains are also among the major crops there. Soap making using olive oil and alkaline burnt herb was the most prosperous industry in Idlib in the past, as evidenced by the presence of three hills in the town made up of accumulating ash from soap furnaces. The soap industry moved to Aleppo, and the hills have been removed.

In the 1952 administrative divisions in Syria, Idlib was part of Aleppo province. Later it became the center of a separate province because of its vast countryside and also because the Aleppo province had become too large. In the administrative divisions of 1982, the province of Idlib had 5 *mintaqas* or *qadas* (sections), 15 *nahiyas* (administrative subdivisions), 6 towns, 16 smaller towns, 411 villages, and 481 farms. The total population of the province, according to the 1980 census, was 352,619 inhabitants, including 51,682 in the town. The province has a number of so-called dead cities dating back to Byzantine times. It also has the well-preserved church of Qalb Lawza and the famous church of Saint Simeon Stylite. The site of historical Ebla has been discovered a few miles from Idlib.

See also ALEPPO.

ABDUL-KARIM RAFEQ

IDRIS AL-SAYYID MUHAMMAD AL-SANUSI

[1890–1983]

Head of the Sanusi order; king of Libya, 1951–1969.

Born in Jaghbub, Cyrenaica, the eastern province of Libya, Idris al-Sayyid Muhammad al-Sanusi was the grandson of Muhammad ibn Ali al-Sanusi, founder of the Sanusi order of Islam, and the son of al-Sayyid al-Mahdi al-Sanusi, the leader of the Sanusis in 1890.

During World War I, while the Sanusis were on the Ottoman side fighting the Italians, Idris was training a Sanusi force to fight with the British. In 1916, the British recognized Idris as the leader of the Sanusi order, and in 1920, Italy recognized him as the amir of Cyrenaica. Despite Italy's wishes, Idris also accepted the title of amir of Tripolitania, offered to him by the people of the province. That same year, however, a Sanusi rebellion forced Idris into exile. He fled to Cairo and remained there for twenty years.

When World War II broke out, Idris called all Libyans to fight on the side of the Allies in order to drive out the Italians. He began a Sanusi unit to fight alongside the Allies in their desert campaign. The British recognized Idris's claim to be the head of an independent Cyrenaica, and later he proclaimed himself the region's amir. When Libya became fully independent in 1951, Idris was offered the crown of a united Libya, and he ascended to the throne on 24 December 1951.

The conservative nature of Idris's rule caused a great deal of friction between him and those in Tripolitania, who were more nationalist. In 1963,

when the province system was abolished, a unitary regime was established. In 1969, while Idris was abroad, the nationalists, led by Muammar al-Qaddafi, took over the country in a military coup. Idris did not challenge their power and lived out the rest of his days in Greece and Egypt.

See also QADDAFI, MUAMMAR AL-; SANUSI, MUHAMMAD IBN ALI AL-; SANUSI ORDER.

Bibliography

Wright, John L. *Libya: A Modern History.* Baltimore, MD: Johns Hopkins University Press, 1982.

JULIE ZUCKERMAN

IDRISIDS

Descendants of Sayyid Muhammad ibn Ali al-Idrisi living in southwestern Arabia.

The principality of Asir has been important in the politics of southwestern Arabia. It was incorporated into the new state of Saudi Arabia in 1926 when Abd al-Aziz ibn Sa'ud Al Sa'ud established a protectorate over the realms of the Idrisi sultanate, as it was known at the time.

In the past, the two major towns of Asir, Abu Arish and Abha, have been the capitals of different families, or clans, accurately reflecting the fact that Asir is really two distinct areas. Geographically, economically, and culturally, much of Asir is a continuation of Yemen and, for most of its history, has been considered a part of Yemen. Nevertheless, when the imams of San'a or of other towns, such as Sa'da, were weak and ineffectual, local Asiri notables declared their independence and carried on their own domestic and foreign policies. The most recent of these independent notables was Sayyid Muhammad ibn Ali al-Idrisi, a grandson of Sayyid Ahmad al-Idrisi, the native of Fez who founded the religious sect to which the founder of the Sanusi belonged. Idrisi immigrated to Arabia and made his base at Abha; he wrested control of most of Asir from the Ottoman authorities in the early years of the twentieth century. He was able to obtain the support of the Italians in their campaigns for influence in the Red Sea region precisely because of his connection to the Sanusi, then established in the Italian areas in North Africa.

Idrisi attempted to expand his influence and territory at the expense of the imams of San'a in the period before World War I. Specifically, he attempted to take Shaykh Saʿid, Luhayya, and Hodeida—Tihama port cities that would have enabled him to add the Yemeni Tihama to his realm. In this effort, he was at times assisted by Italian naval contingents in the Red Sea. During World War I, the British signed an agreement with him in an effort to limit the influence of Yemen, which refused to ally itself against the Ottomans. In return, the British gave him the Yemeni Tihama and other areas, which had to be wrested from Idrisi control by Imam Yahya in the 1920s. After his death, at Sabya, his descendants expanded the influence of the family by taking control of Abu Arish, which had been in the hands of a separate family of sharifs since the eighteenth century. The gradual takeover of Asir by Abd al-Aziz ibn Saʿud, however, ended the separate existence of the Idrisi state, which was reconfirmed in 1930.

Imam Yahya, however, continued to maintain that Asir, and especially its Zaydi and Ismaʿili populations, had been illegitimately removed from Yemeni sovereignty; this led, eventually, to a brief war between Yemen and Saudi Arabia, in which the latter emerged the victor. In the treaty of Taʾif (1934) the Yemenis recognized, albeit grudgingly, Saudi sovereignty over Asir, as well as over the Najran oasis. The treaty was renewed every twenty years until the United Republic of Yemen handed Asir over permanently to Saudi Arabia in 1995.

> See also ABD AL-AZIZ IBN SAʿUD AL SAʿUD; TAʾIF, TREATY OF AL-; YAHYA IBN MUHAMMAD HAMID AL-DIN.

Bibliography

Dresch, Paul. *A History of Modern Yemen*. Cambridge, U.K.: Cambridge University Press, 2000.

Teitelbaum, Joshua. *The Rise and Fall of the Hashimite Kingdom of Arabia*. New York: New York University Press, 2001.

MANFRED W. WENNER

IDRIS, YUSUF
[1927–1991]

Egyptian author of short stories, plays, and novels.

After a childhood spent in the Nile delta region, Yusuf Idris moved to Cairo in 1945 to study medicine at Cairo University. He began writing short stories while a student and published several in newspapers before his graduation in 1951. He began to practice medicine but continued his involvement in both political causes and fiction; his first collection of short stories, *Arkhas Layali* (The cheapest nights), was published to great acclaim in 1954. In the same year he was imprisoned for his involvement in political activities. Following his release in September 1955, he began writing articles for the newspaper *al-Jumhuriyya*. The late 1950s and the 1960s, until the 1967 Arab–Israel War, became Idris's most productive period—in an amazing outpouring of creativity, he published several short-story collections as well as a number of plays and novels. He gave up medical practice in 1967 and assumed an administrative post in the ministry of culture. As was the case with many Arab authors, the Arab–Israel War had a profound effect on his literary career. Until his death in 1991, poor health, depression, and the demands and distractions of a weekly column in the Cairo daily *al-Ahram* combined to reduce his creative output.

Of the literary genres to which Idris made contributions, it is undoubtedly in the development of the Arabic short story that his key role is most obvious. His mastery of the genre was instinctive, and the brilliance of his contributions was recognized by critics from the outset. From the realistic vignettes of provincial and urban life to be found in the earliest collections, such as *Arkhas Layali* and *Hadithat Sharaf* (An affair of honor, 1958), he gradually shifted to more symbolic and surrealistic narratives in such collections as *Akhir al-Dunya* (The world's end, 1961) and *Lughat al-Ay-Ay* (Language of screams, 1965)—many of the stories essentially parables about the alienation of human beings in contemporary society. In these later collections, we still encounter scenes from country life, but the focus has shifted from realistic detail to the symbolic portrait of the inner workings of the mind. Several also show his virtuoso ability to manipulate narrative point-of-view and to incorporate us into the storytelling process. Above all, his command of narrative structure and his use of allusive language has given his contributions to this genre a stature unmatched by any other Egyptian writer—and by very few other Arab litterateurs.

Idris often admitted to writing on impulse, something that may well contribute to his great success in the realm of the short story. This same impulsiveness may explain why his essays in other genres have, for the most part, not met with similar success. While many of Idris's plays have been performed to great popular acclaim, even his most popular and accomplished play, *Al-Farafir* (The Farfoors, 1964), loses cohesion in its lengthy second act. Of his novels, only *Al-Haram* (The taboo, 1959), with its realistic portrayal of migrant communities in the provinces, manages to sustain a narrative focus through the longer fictional mode.

Idris's craft shows the greatest development and made the greatest contribution in the much-discussed area of language. Coupled to a great storyteller's ability in creating scenes and moods with an allusiveness and economy akin to that of poetry, Idris's narrative style co-opted the riches of the colloquial dialect to create a multitextured descriptive instrument of tremendous subtlety and variety. This colloquial level was his natural choice for dialogue in both plays and fiction, but aspects of the colloquial's lexicon and syntax are also to be found in narrative passages of his fiction. This stylistic feature has not endeared him to conservative critics, but it lent his stories an element of spontaneity and authenticity that contributed in no small part to their popularity. Idris's storytelling style, his lively imagination, sardonic sense of humor, and tremendous concern for the plight of modern life, are at their best in his short stories—many of which rival the very best in that most elusive and self-conscious of literary genres.

See also ARAB–ISRAEL WAR (1967); LITERATURE: ARABIC; NEWSPAPERS AND PRINT MEDIA: ARAB COUNTRIES; THEATER.

Bibliography

Allen, Roger, ed. *Modern Arabic Literature.* New York: Ungar, 1987.

Kurpershoek, P. M. *The Short Stories of Yusuf Idris: A Modern Egyptian Author.* Leiden, Netherlands: E.J. Brill, 1981.

ROGER ALLEN

IFNI

Area on Morocco's coast ceded to Morocco by Spain.

Formerly Santa Cruz de Mar Pequena, Ifni was a 675-square-mile Spanish enclave on the coast of southern Morocco. The population of the area was about 40,000, made up mainly of seven predominantly sedentary Berber-speaking tribes. The Span-

ish held a trading post in the area from 1476 to 1524. Under the 1860 treaty of Tetuan, the area was designated as Spanish, and permission was given to build a fishing harbor. However, an exploratory expedition to the area in 1879 ended in failure. The Spanish–French treaty of 1912 recognized Spain's sovereign right to the Ifni enclave, distinct from the protectorate zones, and similar to Spain's rights over Ceuta and Melilla. Spanish general Osvaldo Capaz finally occupied the area in March 1934. In 1946 the coastal town of Sidi Ifni, the capital of the enclave, was made the seat of a single centralized administration for Spanish West Africa. The 1956 Spanish–Moroccan treaty restored to Morocco 15,000 square miles of Spanish Sahara, now known as the province of Tarfaya. But the Ifni enclave remained in Spanish hands, with Spain insisting that Ifni had been ceded in perpetuity by the 1860 treaty. In November 1957 fighting broke out between Morocco's irregular Army for the Liberation of the Sahara and Spanish forces. In December 6,000 Spanish troops took up positions around Sidi Ifni and held on for twelve years. The area was made a Spanish province under the authority of the military commander of the Canary Islands. Morocco first raised the issue of Spain's control of Ifni at the UN General Assembly session in 1957. In 1965 the General Assembly resolved that Ifni should be liberated from colonial domination. On 4 January 1969 Spain and Morocco signed an agreement to turn the area over to Morocco. The actual transfer was made on 30 June. In return, Spain was awarded fishing rights off Morocco's Atlantic coast. Today, Sidi Ifni has a population of 17,000.

See also MOROCCO.

Bibliography

Jones, D. H. "Ifni." In *Encyclopaedia of Islam, New Edition,* edited by B. Lewis, V. L. Ménage, Ch. Pellat, and J. Schacht. Netherlands: Brill, 1991.

BRUCE MADDY-WEITZMAN

IGNATIEV, NIKOLAS PAVLOVICH
[1832–1908]

Russian diplomat.

Born in St. Petersburg, Nikolas Pavlovich Ignatiev entered the diplomatic service in 1856 and served as ambassador to the Ottoman Empire in Constantinople (1864–1878). He was a zealous pan-Slavist, described by one writer as "brilliant and none-too-scrupulous." In contrast to the Russian foreign minister, Aleksandr Gorchakov, Ignatiev worked for the downfall of the Ottoman Empire. He was active in inciting the 1877–1878 Russian–Ottoman War, and is credited with framing the Treaty of San Stefano (1878), which laid the foundation for "Big Bulgaria." In the interest of good relations with Britain and Austria, however, the treaty and Ignatiev's "Big Bulgaria" were jettisoned by Gorchakov at the Congress of Berlin (1878), and with them Ignatiev's career. At the height of his power, Ignatiev influenced the Ottoman government to such an extent that he was referred to as "Sultan Ignatiev."

See also BERLIN, CONGRESS AND TREATY OF; RUSSIAN–OTTOMAN WARS; SAN STEFANO, TREATY OF (1878).

Bibliography

Anderson, M. S. The Eastern Question, 1774–1923: A Study in International Relations. London: Macmillan; New York: St. Martin's, 1966.

Shaw, Stanford, and Shaw, Ezel Kural. History of the Ottoman Empire and Modern Turkey. 2 vols. Cambridge, U.K., and New York: Cambridge University Press, 1976–1977.

ZACHARY KARABELL

IKHA AL-WATANI PARTY

Iraqi political party of the 1930s.

Ikha al-Watani (National Brotherhood) was formed to oppose the Anglo–Iraqi Treaty of 1930. Its principal members were Yasin al-Hashimi, Rashid Ali al-Kaylani, and Hikmat Sulayman. In 1933 some of its members accepted the 1930 treaty and participated in a government under Rashid Ali (March–October 1933). A second Ikha cabinet under Yasin al-Hashimi was formed in March 1935, but the group disbanded itself shortly afterward.

See also ANGLO–IRAQI TREATIES; HASHIMI, YASIN AL-; KAYLANI, RASHID ALI AL-; SULAYMAN, HIKMAT.

PETER SLUGLETT

IKHLASSI, WALID
[1935–]

Syrian novelist, short-story writer, and dramatist.

Walid Ikhlassi was born in Alexandretta. After the cession of Alexandretta to Turkey in 1939, his family moved to Aleppo. He received his education in agricultural engineering at the University of Alexandria in Egypt. He later became a lecturer at the College of Agriculture at the University of Aleppo.

Ikhlassi was raised in a family preoccupied with religious and national issues. Imbued with nationalistic aspirations during the French mandate, Ikhlassi's writings deal mainly with democracy, freedom, responsibility, alienation, the loss of the self, and the failure of human ideals. The Palestinian diaspora is also a significant theme in his work; he tackled it throughout an entire collection of short stories, The Time of Short Migrations, 1970. Although Ikhlassi's first short story, "The Cock," appeared in 1954, his first collection, Stories, had to wait until 1963. Since then, he has published eight more collections. Some stories have been translated into English, French, Russian, and Persian.

Ikhlassi was the first Syrian novelist to experiment with the nouveau roman. While his first novel, A Winter of the Dry Sea, published in 1965, divided the literary critics into conservatives and liberals, his second novel, The Lap of the Beautiful Lady, in 1969, pleased the conservative camp for it adhered to traditional rules and practices of fiction. Ikhlassi has published nine more novels. The latest to date is The Minor Epic of Death in 1993.

Ikhlassi not only feels comfortable manipulating narrative techniques but also alternating among narrative genres. He believes that the subject matter dictates both the form and the genre to be employed in a certain artistic work. Like his novels and short stories, Ikhlassi's plays show innovation in literary devices and a break with the then dominant realistic mode of expression in favor of a more symbolic, surrealistic, and allegorical mode.

See also DIASPORA; THEATER.

Bibliography

Ikhlassi, Walid. "The Path." In Modern Arabic Drama, edited by Salma Khadra Jayysusi and Roger Allen. Bloomington: Indiana University Press, 1995.

SABAH GHANDOUR

IKHWAN

A militant religious movement drawn from Bedouin tribes in northern and central Arabia.

After Abd al-Aziz ibn Abd al-Rahman Al Saʿud reconquered Riyadh from the Al Rashid dynasty in 1901, religious authorities began to spread Wahhabism aggressively. One of the main intellectual forces behind the movement was Abdullah ibn Muhammad ibn Abd al-Latif, a scholar and religious leader in Riyadh. After about 1906, he oversaw the dispersion of his message among the Bedouin by activist-preachers called *mutawwaʿin*. The Bedouin converts and their religious mentors developed a variation on Wahhabism that incorporated the military tendencies of tribal society and the extreme literalist zeal sometimes characteristic of new religious converts. Those Bedouin who espoused this version of Wahhabism were known as *Ikhwan* (brethren, in Arabic). In addition to being called to accept the tenets of Wahhabism, they were encouraged to give up nomadism, obey the amir/imam (Abd al-Aziz), to help other Ikhwan, and to avoid contact with Europeans and other "nonbelievers." Because the movement developed in a society that attempted to retain its tribal prerogatives, the political agenda of its leaders often clashed with those of Abd al-Aziz and his town-oriented allies.

The first Ikhwan settlement, or *hijra* (plural, *hujjar*), was established around 1913 mainly by members of the Mutayr tribe led by Faysal al-Darwish in al-Artawiyya, north of Riyadh. The use of the term *hijra* was a conscious attempt to invoke the first Islamic community under the prophet Muhammad. The *hujar* were located in tribal lands near water sources, and numbered around 120 by 1929.

Abd-al Aziz saw the spread of religion and the sedentarizing imperatives of the Ikhwan movement as a way to "debedouinize" the nomads, to build stronger ties between them and the ruler, and to use their young men as a reliable fighting force. However, from the start, important segments of the Ikhwan movement chafed at the policies of Abd al-Aziz. For example, because by 1914 a *hijra*-versus-town mentality had developed, and victims of Ikhwan intolerance and violence had complained to the ruler of Najd, Abd al-Aziz was forced to issue an edict, backed by his *ulama* allies, that undercut Ikhwan pre-

tensions as arbiters and enforcers of Islamic belief and practice.

Material incentives encouraged some to join the movement. Abd al-Aziz encouraged sedentarization by providing funds, agricultural supplies, and materials to build schools and mosques. In addition, although Abd al-Aziz discouraged intertribal raiding (a major activity of the Bedouin for centuries), he permitted Ikhwan leaders to carry out violent attacks against opponents, which provided a significant source of plunder: animals, tents, weapons, and household items. After World War I, several Ikhwan leaders became strong advocates of military expansion, and beginning around 1919, Ikhwan forces carried out numerous attacks on Muslim populations (some of them Shiʿite) not only in al-Hasa, Najd, and Jabal Shammar, but also in Kuwait, Iraq, and Transjordan.

Among the Ikhwan's most notorious conquests were those in Hijaz, beginning with the sack of al-Taʾif in 1924 and the massacre of hundreds of the town's men, women, and children. Despite repeated efforts by Abd al-Aziz to curb such excesses, the Ikhwan continued to perpetrate acts of untrammeled violence and destruction, including the "purification" of Mecca and Medina through the destruction of many historic religious monuments and shrines, and an attack in 1926 against an Egyptian pilgrimage procession, which resulted in the Ikhwan's banishment from Hijaz. These episodes, as well as the bitter disappointment of al-Darwish and other Ikhwan leaders that their military conquests had not been rewarded by expected political appointments over the newly conquered territories, precipitated a revolt against Abd al-Aziz in 1927. The revolt—and the movement itself—eventually was crushed by the forces of Abd al-Aziz in March 1929 at the battle of Sibila.

The ideology and aims of the Ikhwan movement persisted beneath the surface of official Saudi politics and resurfaced during the attack in November 1979 on the Grand Mosque in Mecca. The leader of the siege, Juhayman al-Utaybi, came from the *hijra* of Sajir, and his followers adopted the dress and violent and doctrinaire methods of the Ikhwan. Like their predecessors, these "neo-Ikhwan" were motivated by a sense that Islam was being perverted, that the Al Saʿud ruling family were corrupt, and that they alone held the key to a pure and true renewal of the Muslim community.

See also UTAYBI, JUHAYMAN AL-

Bibliography

Glubb, John Bagot. *War in the Desert.* London: Hodder and Stoughton, 1960.

Habib, John S. *Ibn Saʿud's Warriors of Islam: The Ikhwan of Najd and Their Role in the Creation of the Saʿudi Kingdom, 1910–1930.* Leiden, Netherlands: Brill, 1978.

Kostiner, Joseph. *The Making of Saudi Arabia, 1916–1936: From Chieftancy to Monarchial State.* New York; Oxford, U.K.: Oxford University Press, 1993.

Rasheed, Madawi al-. *A History of Saudi Arabia.* New York; Cambridge, U.K.: Cambridge University Press, 2002.

Vassiliev, Alexei. *The History of Saudi Arabia.* New York: New York University Press, 2000.

MALCOLM C. PECK
UPDATED BY ANTHONY B. TOTH

ILAYSH, MUHAMMAD
[1802–1882]

Egyptian religious leader and writer.

Muhammad Ilaysh was an important conservative religious figure and a prolific writer of traditional religious texts. He was first a student at al-Azhar University, then a professor there, eventually rising to become the mufti and head shaykh of the Maliki Law School (1854–1882). Of a stern ascetic tendency, Ilaysh also was a shaykh in the sober Shadhili Sufi order, where he upheld the tradition of the earlier Maliki al-Amir al-Kabir (1742–1817). Ilaysh's asceticism extended to his dealings with the government, from which he became increasingly aloof, even though the khedive Ismaʿil provided him with 42 hectares of land as an emolument, apparently to placate him. Ilaysh opposed the introduction of examinations at al-Azhar in 1872, opposed the increasing European influence in the late 1870s, and participated in the Urabi movement of 1881 and 1882. During this time, he supported the removal of the khedive Tawfiq's supporter, Muhammad al-Abbasi al-Mahdi, as the shaykh of al-Azhar; was appointed to advise the new shaykh, Muhammad al-Imbabi; sought to declare a jihad (holy war) to fight the British invasion; and signed a *fatwa* (legal opin-

ion) declaring the khedive an apostate from Islam—an act of open rebellion. As a result, when the British conquered Cairo for the khedive, Ilaysh was arrested and roughly handled, and died in detention.

Ilaysh's writings amount to over 12,000 pages, mostly dealing with fiqh, although some deal with grammar and *aqida*. Some remain unpublished, but others have had an abiding influence. One of the most influential is his enormous commentary on Khalil titled *Minah al-Jalil*, published in 1877, which may be the last work of fiqh composed in Egypt that is free of modern influence and thus represents a final summation of the Maliki school. Another work of lasting influence is his collection of fatwas, *Fath al-Ali al-Malik*, published in 1883, immediately after his death.

See also MALIKI SCHOOL OF LAW; SUFISM AND THE SUFI ORDERS; URABI, AHMAD.

Bibliography

Gesink, Indira Falk. "'Chaos on the Earth': Subjective Truths versus Communal Unity in Islamic Law and the Rise of Militant Islam." *The American Historical Review* 108, no. 3 (2003): 1–59.

KHALID BLANKINSHIP

İLMIYYE

The Learned Institution, or hierarchy of religious officials in the Ottoman Empire.

From the early sixteenth century, the İlmiyye became a distinct hierarchy in the Ottoman government. It was headed by the grand *mufti*, called the Shaykh al-Islam, in Constantinople (now Istanbul) and extended to the lowest provincial *qadi* (judge) and religious schoolteacher. By the seventeenth and eighteenth centuries, the İlmiyye's top posts were dominated by elite families of Constantinople.

In the nineteenth century, Ottoman reforms undermined the İlmiyye's autonomy and influence by organizing the Ministry of Waqfs in 1834 and, in the Tanzimat period, introducing secular courts, law codes, and school systems that competed with religious institutions. While Abdülhamit II increased funding for the İlmiyye, he also furthered its bureaucratization and state control. During World War I, the Young Turks incorporated all religious courts into the secular Ministry of Justice and religious schools into the secular Ministry of Education. The Shaykh al-Islam was reduced to a consultant. The final blow to the İlmiyye institution was the abolition of the Ottoman caliphate in 1924 and the ensuing secularization of public institutions by Mustafa Kemal (Atatürk).

See also ABDÜLHAMIT II; ATATÜRK, MUSTAFA KEMAL; CALIPHATE; SHAYKH AL-ISLAM; TANZIMAT; YOUNG TURKS.

Bibliography

Chambers, Richard L. "The Ottoman Ulema and the Tanzimat." In *Scholars, Saints and Sufis: Muslim Religious Institutions in the Middle East since 1500,* edited by Nikki R. Keddie. Berkeley: University of California Press, 1972.

Repp, Richard. "Some Observations on the Development of the Ottoman Learned Hierarchy." In *Scholars, Saints and Sufis: Muslim Religious Institutions in the Middle East since 1500,* edited by Nikki R. Keddie. Berkeley: University of California Press, 1972.

Shaw, Stanford, and Shaw, Ezel Kural. *History of the Ottoman Empire and Modern Turkey,* Vol. 2: *Reform, Revolution, and Republic: The Rise of Modern Turkey, 1808–1975.* Cambridge, U.K., and New York: Cambridge University Press, 1977.

ELIZABETH THOMPSON

ILTIZAM

See GLOSSARY

IMAM

See GLOSSARY

IMAMZADEH

See GLOSSARY

IMPERIALISM IN THE MIDDLE EAST AND NORTH AFRICA

Direct or indirect control exerted by one nation over the political life or economic life (or both) of other nations.

Imperialism is generally defined as a phenomenon that began with the overseas expansion of Europe in the fifteenth century. That expansion did not seri-

French troops in 1941. The French colonial empire reached its peak in the early 1900s, with its empire extending to 4.5 million square miles. After World War II, France saw widespread revolts in its North African colonies, and was forced to withdraw from them completely by the late 1960s. © BETTMAN/CORBIS. REPRODUCED BY PERMISSION.

ously affect the Maghreb or Egypt, however, until the nineteenth century, and, except economically, it did not affect the most populous areas of southwest Asia until the early twentieth century. The major reason for this delay was the power and durability of the Ottoman Empire.

Originating around 1300, the Ottoman Empire eventually expanded to include most of the Balkans and the Black Sea area, Anatolia, the Fertile Crescent, and northern Africa as far west as the borders of Morocco. It was for centuries the primary empire in the Middle East and North Africa. (An empire is a singular political unit—not necessarily based on territorial contiguity—that incorporates different peoples who were previously self-governing and who retain some institutional autonomy.) In taking over so many regions, the Turkish-speaking armies of the sultans created an empire that included many different linguistic, religious, and ethnic groups, in which Turks were always a minority. The Ottomans engaged in imperial rivalry to expand their territory. Their rivals were the Holy Roman Empire (later Austria-Hungary), the Russian Empire, and the Iranian state of the Safavids and their succes-

Colonial Secretary Winston Churchill (center) with British officials at the 1921 Cairo Conference to discuss the future of the Arab nations. The conference delegates sought to find a way to maintain political control over the areas mandated to Britain in the Sykes–Picot agreement while cutting costs and reducing British overseas military presence. © HULTON-DEUTSCH COLLECTION/CORBIS. REPRODUCED BY PERMISSION.

sors, which was sometimes called an empire despite its much smaller size because it was multilingual, multiethnic, and periodically expansive.

This description of the Ottoman Empire does not differ substantially from the description that could be applied to the Christian European empires established from the sixteenth century onward, except that the Europeans were normally less willing to admit non-Europeans into the ranks of officials. The sultans, like the Russian tsars, were primarily motivated by the desire to acquire land and wealth, whereas the overseas European empire builders sought raw materials and markets. Thus the Europeans had a greater impact on the international division of labor than did the Ottomans, although this analytical distinction was not necessarily reflected in the attitudes of the imperialists and their subjects.

Despite the substantial similarities between European and Middle Eastern empires, the term *imperialism* is rarely used to describe the underlying principles of the Ottoman Empire. More often, imperialism is defined as a peculiarly European phenomenon embodying military or political control of non-European peoples; unrestrained exploitation of their economies for the disproportionate benefit of the European home country; feelings of racial, religious, and cultural superiority over the dominated peoples; and, in some regions, the implantation of European colonies or importation of nonindigenous laborers, often as slaves.

Historians in the Marxist tradition have considered economic exploitation by such means as joint-stock companies, forced labor on plantations, and suppression of indigenous manufactures to be the most important aspect of European imperialism. Imperialism, according to this view, is an inevitable stage of a capitalist system that needs to expand in order to survive. Immanuel Wallerstein, whose theories have been particularly influential, portrays imperialism as the imposition upon the entire world of a system through which capitalist Europe made the rest of the world economically dependent and imposed economic underdevelopment by monopolizing resources, reorienting self-sustaining regions toward extraction of primary goods for European manufacturers, and preventing the emergence of viable mixed economies in non-European areas.

Some clear distinctions between the way the Ottomans and the Europeans ran their empires may be noted. The Islamic religion provided a bond for most people under Ottoman rule, whereas European Christianity remained a culturally elitist, minority faith in the parts of the European empires that did not have large colonies of European settlers or where religions of comparable sophistication, such as Islam, impeded religious conversion. Ottoman lands remained comparatively open to trade by foreigners (though not to land acquisition), and the Ottoman government rarely took action to protect its own merchants, as the Europeans commonly did. Finally, the Ottomans generally administered their territories with a lighter hand than did the Europeans.

In 1800 most subjects of the Ottoman sultan considered it normal to be ruled from a distant capital by means of a rotation of officials and military forces sent from afar and often speaking a foreign language. Napoléon Bonaparte's propaganda effort in 1798 to convince the Egyptians that they were victims of imperial oppression by foreigners fell on deaf ears. Soon thereafter, however, the Christian peoples of the Balkans, stimulated in part by the exposure of community members to European ideas as a consequence of educational or personal contacts outside Ottoman territories, did begin to see themselves as victims of Ottoman domination. Through a series of wars and militant movements—often encouraged by European powers with strategic or ideological agendas—they endeavored to gain their freedom and establish independent states with comparative ethnic and religious homogeneity. The anti-imperialism of the Balkan secessionists even-

Persian, Arab, and Kurd prisoners in a Mesopotamian prison camp in 1916. In that year the Sykes–Picot agreement divided the Arab Middle East between Britain and France, with Russia giving its assent. © HULTON-DEUTSCH COLLECTION/CORBIS. REPRODUCED BY PERMISSION.

tually affected the Armenian Christians of Anatolia and more slowly gained headway in Arab nationalist circles after 1900.

European imperialism took three forms in the early nineteenth century: direct occupation and colonization of Algeria by France from 1830 onward, diplomatic pressure on the Ottoman sultans to grant economic and legal privileges to Europeans and non-Muslim minorities, and treaties with rulers and chiefs controlling seaports in the Persian Gulf and southern Arabia designed to ensure British military control of the sea route to India in return for maintaining the rulers and chiefs in power. In the second half of the century, new forms of European imperialism emerged. Rulers granted concessions to European entrepreneurs for the building of canals, railroads, and telegraph lines; operation of banks; and marketing of primary products. They also sought loans from private European bankers. When Egypt, the Ottoman Empire, Tunisia, and Iran were successively unable to repay these loans, Europeans assumed financial control over customs and other sources of state revenue. In Egypt, fear that Colonel Ahmad Urabi's military rebellion would interrupt these financial controls prompted Britain to suppress the rebellion militarily and commence an occupation in 1882 that would last for seventy years. In 1881 France occupied Tunisia and subsequently imposed a protectorate upon its Husaynid beys. In 1900, primarily for strategic reasons, France began the occupation of the territory that subsequently became Mauritania, and in 1912, in partnership with Spain, it imposed a protectorate on the sultanate of Morocco. France had already recognized Spain's sovereignty over certain "presidios" in the Spanish Sahara.

Growing European imperialism gave rise to anti-imperialist sentiments that were vented in popular opposition to concessions, as in the Tobacco Revolt in Iran in 1891 and in the mobilization of political action around religious symbols and leaders (e.g., in Libya, where the Sanusi Sufi brotherhood spearheaded opposition to Italian occupation after 1911). Anti-imperialism also sparked political movements, most notably the Wafd in Egypt, whose members saw the end of World War I as a possible opportunity to escape British rule. Farther west, the Young Tunisian and Young Algerian movements began demanding reform and greater rights for natives. Armenians and Kurds looked to the peace negotiators to grant them independence from outside control, even if it meant accepting some measure of European protection.

The mandate system established at San Remo in 1920 to resolve the problems caused by the defeat of the Ottoman Empire extended European imperialism by giving France control of Lebanon and Syria and Britain control of Palestine and Iraq. Legally, the mandate from the League of Nations to France and Britain required them to nurture these territories toward total independence, but these countries' motivation to do so (strongest in Iraq and weakest in Lebanon and western Palestine) was often adversely affected by issues of national interest. In Palestine, in particular, Britain was committed in the terms of the Balfour Declaration (1917) to fostering the establishment of a Jewish national home. In the eyes of many Arabs and Muslims, the migration of tens of thousands of Jews from Europe to Palestine represented a form of settler colonialism similar to that in Algeria. Between the two world wars France and Great Britain had to deal with extremely determined and sometimes violent resistance by both Syrians and Palestinians, while nationalist movements in the Maghreb also mobilized increasing support.

Unlike parts of the world rich in raw materials or agricultural products that could not be grown in Europe, most parts of the Middle East and North Africa did not offer great rewards to their imperial masters. Egyptian cotton, Algerian wine, and Iranian oil flowed into international markets, and the Suez Canal was profitable, but the cost of military occupation in the face of rising nationalist hostility, and the cost of infrastructure investment, limited though it was in most areas, brought the economic value of imperialism into question. After World War II, the greatly depleted European powers were no longer able to bear the cost, either in money or manpower. One by one, the countries of the Middle East became free of direct imperial control. Only in the most profitable or politically contested countries was the withdrawal of empire accompanied by significant bloodshed. British withdrawal from Palestine in 1948 brought on Israel's declaration of independence and the first Arab–Israel War. The army coup that terminated British control of Egypt in 1952 was followed by the Suez War in 1956 in which Britain, in alliance with France and Israel, attempted to regain control of the Suez Canal. Through effective political activism that was largely but not totally peaceful, Tunisians and Moroccans were able to terminate the French protectorates by 1956. In 1960, as part of a broader de-colonization process, France's president Charles de Gaulle granted independence to Mauritania. In Algeria, colonists' refusal to permit meaningful reform led the Front de Libération Nationale to launch a revolution in 1954; France's attempt to repress it cost roughly 500,000 Algerian lives and ended in independence for Algeria in July 1962. Francisco Franco granted the Western (formerly Spanish) Sahara independence in 1975, but this led to conflict with Morocco that had not been resolved by the early twenty-first century.

As direct imperial control waned and overt indirect control in the form of military bases and foreign ownership of oil companies diminished in the 1950s and 1960s, cultural imperialism came to be looked upon as a pervasive remnant of the imperialist era. Cultural imperialism was considered to have several components: imposition of Euro-American cultural values and lifestyles through market domination by imported consumer goods, motion pictures, and television shows; ideological subversion in the form of secular nationalist political movements philosophically rooted in Western thought; and intellectual domination through the distorted writings and pejorative imaginative constructions of European Orientalists and their successors in the American academic field of Middle East studies.

Direct imperial domination had evoked a fairly uniform nationalist reaction throughout the region, but the more nebulous concept of cultural imperialism led its proponents in different directions. In Iran, Jalal Al-e Ahmad's concept of *gharbzadegi* or "Westoxication" contributed to the explicitly anti-Western character of the 1979 revolution. Other Islamic activist movements have, to varying degrees, shared hostility or suspicion of the West as an imperialist force. The Islamist insurgency that erupted in Algeria in the 1990s was viewed as principally if not totally cultural in nature. The discourse of al-Qaʿida, which also emerged in the 1990s, is primarily cultural. Secular intellectuals, on the other hand, have refused to accept Islam as the only alternative to cultural domination by the West. Calls for a decolonization of history and exposure of Orientalist fantasies have come mainly from secularists such as Morocco's Abdallah Laroui and the Palestinian Edward Said.

Further stimulus for resistance to Western imperialism came in 1993 from Samuel Huntington's article "The Clash of Civilizations" in the influential journal *Foreign Affairs*. Huntington visualized a future in which an undefined Islamic civilization was destined to conflict with a similarly undefined Western civilization, and he called for the formulation of a strategy that would assure Western victory in such a confrontation. Middle Eastern religious and secular thinkers alike viewed this projection as a portent of continued Western imperial ambition in the post–Cold War era.

See also ALGERIAN WAR OF INDEPENDENCE; ARAB–ISRAEL WAR (1948); BALFOUR DECLARATION (1917); BONAPARTE, NAPOLÉON; GHARBZADEGI; IRANIAN REVOLUTION (1979); MANDATE SYSTEM; OTTOMAN EMPIRE; QAʿIDA, AL-; SAID, EDWARD; TOBACCO REVOLT; URABI, AHMAD; WAFD; YOUNG ALGERIANS; YOUNG TUNISIANS.

Bibliography

Amin, Samir. *The Arab Nation: Nationalism and Class Struggle.* London: Zed Books, 1982.

Berque, Jacques. *French North Africa: The Maghrib between Two World Wars.* New York: Praeger Publishers, 1967.

Huntington, Samuel. "The Clash of Civilizations." *Foreign Affairs* 72, no. 3 (Summer 1993): 22–28.

Hurewitz, J. C. *The Middle East and North Africa in World Politics,* 2d edition. New Haven, CT: Yale University Press, 1975–1979.

Monroe, Elizabeth. *Britain's Moment in the Middle East 1914–1971,* new revised edition. Baltimore, MD: Johns Hopkins University Press, 1981.

Said, Edward. *Orientalism.* New York: Vintage, 1979.

RICHARD W. BULLIET
UPDATED BY JOHN RUEDY

INCENSE

Aromatic gum resins.

Frankincense and myrrh are taken from trees that grow in Dhufar, Oman, and in Hadramawt, Yemen. Recent archaeological discoveries confirm their export from about 3000 B.C.E. through an extensive commercial network. The trade, reaching as far as Rome and India, helped create considerable prosperity and interstate rivalry in southwest Arabia. Exports and prosperity declined when Rome made Christianity its official religion and the use of incense at funerals largely ceased.

See also DHUFAR; HADRAMAWT.

Bibliography

Allen, Calvin H., Jr. *Oman: The Modernization of the Sultanate.* Boulder, CO: Westview Press, 1987.

MALCOLM C. PECK

INDUSTRIALIZATION

Manufacturing in the Middle East, with a legacy of state-led industrialization, remains underdeveloped and ill prepared for the challenges of globalization.

The countries of the Middle East and North Africa have failed to develop viable manufacturing sectors and industrialize in a way comparable to more dynamic countries in Southeast Asia and Latin America. After decades of state-led industrialization efforts, most economies of the region remain dependent on primary produce exports, labor remittances, and foreign aid, while few manufacture

A cotton mill in Egypt. Cotton, Egypt's second largest export, became a major factor in the country's economy after the Alexandria–Cairo railway was completed in the mid-1800s, creating lines to important cotton manufacturing centers such as Samannud and Zaqaziq. © AP/WIDE WORLD PHOTOS. REPRODUCED BY PERMISSION.

goods that are competitive in international markets. Indeed, without tariff and quota protection and subsidies, most of the existing industries that have been established would fail to compete successfully in their own domestic markets. As a result, the economies of the region remain unprepared to meet the challenges posed by economic globalization and will be hard-pressed to provide sufficient employment and wealth generation for the growing populations of the region.

Overview

From the perspective of global economic history, the Middle East would appear to have the necessary prerequisites for successful industrialization given its manufacturing inheritance, artisan skills, and availability of finance. In the early postwar period, expectations for industrial modernization were high, yet half a century later the region's industrial sec-

tors appear to be mismanaged and technologically deficient. Although conditioned by the experience of colonialism, this fate was not predetermined by geography, religion, or culture. For most economies of the region, it has rather been the result of authoritarian regimes failing to overcome the legacies of inward-oriented, state-led industrialization efforts through market reform and technological innovation. Meanwhile, economies across the region have been sustained by oil incomes, labor remittances, and strategic aid flows while suffering the strains of regional insecurity, leading to high spending on imported military equipment and diverting investment away from the region.

The Middle East has a strong preindustrial manufacturing tradition, for the ancient cities of the region served not only as centers of commerce but also as bases for handicraft manufacturing. The skills of Arab and Jewish craftsmen from Andalusia to Baghdad were renowned throughout the medieval world. Later in the sixteenth century, cities such as Isfahan in Iran had more skilled artisans than Paris, with more than half a million workers engaged in manufacturing.

In the eighteenth and nineteenth centuries, European capitalist penetration and various forms of direct and indirect colonialism led to the dislocation of indigenous economic patterns, while defensive modernization efforts, such as that of Muhammad Ali in Egypt, failed to sustain local industrialization. With the inability to protect local markets, European industrialization resulted in the relative deindustrialization of the Middle East. Small-scale artisan and domestic manufacturing for local consumption, however, continued and in some cases expanded in isolated markets. By the early twentieth century intense economic interaction with Europe did bring access to investment and technology, resulting in establishment of mechanized factories often owned by Europeans as well as ethnic and religious minorities.

These possible foundations for industrial development, however, were disrupted by the rise of nationalist movements that led to the evacuation and expropriation of the assets of much of the existing bourgeoisie. Postcolonial states led by a new class of reform-oriented elites took over the drive toward import substitution industrialization (ISI). With a heavy urban bias, these regimes viewed large-scale factory production as a marker of modernity and national independence. These projects, however, were often driven more by an interest in expanding state power and employment generation than long-range development goals. As a result, most industrial sectors remained dominated by state-owned enterprises and/or supported by tariff and quota protection and subsidies that have proved politically difficult to remove ever since.

Although state-led ISI efforts made impressive early gains, their inward-oriented development models soon faced crises. In the 1970s states such as Turkey, Egypt, and Tunisia adopted "open door" policies to attract investment, but only in the 1980s and 1990s did they implement substantial price liberalization and the privatization of state-owned assets. Economic liberalization spurred smaller scale, private sector investments in light manufacturing, textiles, and food processing.

Meanwhile, in the wake of the 1973 oil embargo the region witnessed a massive inflow of capital with the soaring price of oil. This income allowed the oil-rich states of the Persian Gulf to expand their modern infrastructure and oil-related sectors. Many would also later seek to diversify their economies.

Regional oil dependency, however, has resulted in "rentier" economies marked by excessive state expenditures, unproductive investments, and unsustainable import levels. At the same time, investment in turnkey projects rapidly increased industrial capacity but failed to sustain technological advancement or encourage local innovation. Moreover, oil incomes gave these states the ability to provide extensive educational and social welfare benefits for their populations while eliminating the need for taxation, reducing pressures for administrative accountability and political representation. The bulk of the excess capital generated by the oil boom was invested in the advanced industrial economies, and regional investment was mostly limited to tourism, real estate, and construction. The oil boom also produced rentier effects in the oil-poor states by generating flows of aid and private remittances.

Throughout the post-1945 era, some of the greatest negative factors inhibiting industrialization have been the successive wars, continuous political hostilities, and military authoritarian regimes in the region. In many states, more effort and finance has gone into building military might than into developing civilian industry. In fact, the Middle East devotes a greater share of income to arms purchases than any other region.

The wars and political tensions in the Middle East, caused by regional insecurity and external intervention, have also resulted in investors being put off by the risks and uncertainties. As investment flooded the "emerging markets" in the post–Cold War era, there has been little foreign direct investment in the Middle East, and major multinational companies are still reluctant to establish substantial production facilities in the region.

While economic fortunes vary considerably across the region, in general, Arab states have failed to encourage knowledge-intensive fields and make investments in research and development. And in the last two decades of the twentieth century, encompassing both the oil boom and the decline of oil prices in the late 1980s, per capita growth in the Arab states was on average 0.5 percent, which is well below the global average of 1.3 percent. As a result, most states remain ill prepared to face the challenges of economic globalization. In many states, large sections of the population view globalization as an externally driven threat to their well-being and way of life.

Country Experiences

Not surprisingly, Turkey has experienced the most success with industrialization in the region. The regional paradigm for state-led ISI was set by Turkey, which under Mustafa Kemal (Atatürk) established heavy industries in the 1920s and 1930s such as steelmaking and modern textile plants. These were planned on the Soviet model, primarily to serve a protected domestic market. These plants provided the inputs for more consumer-oriented industries such as clothing and household fabrics, and eventually consumer durable manufacturing was developed, including vehicle assembly using domestically produced sheet steel.

Despite the substantial size of the domestic market in Turkey, the import substitution process was running out of steam by the 1960s, and most of the state-owned industries were sustaining heavy losses. Change finally came in 1980, when economic liberalization measures were introduced, liberalizing prices, reducing subsidies, removing import restrictions, and, most importantly, letting the exchange rate find its own level in the market. An export boom resulted, encompassing a range of manufacturing sectors, and Turkey moved into balance of payments surplus as a result of flourishing trade with Europe and exports of manufactured goods to neighboring Middle Eastern countries.

Egypt's state-led industrialization drive under Gamal Abdel Nasser had also faltered by the 1970s, although it was the Arab–Israel War of 1967 that led to the end of development planning and economic policies based on Arab socialism. In the wake of the 1973 Arab–Israel War President Anwar al-Sadat initiated the *infitah* (open door policy) to attract foreign investment. Husni Mubarak followed up by introducing a partial liberalization of the economy, but it was much less sweeping than Turkey's changes.

Egypt's subsidies have been reduced at the behest of the International Monetary Fund (IMF), some price controls removed, and the exchange rate floated.

There has been some privatization, but Egypt's industries are not yet internationally competitive, due as much to lack of quality control as to price. Although the large state-owned firms still provide substantial employment, the most dynamic firms are the privately owned export-oriented ones engaged in light manufacturing for international franchises. Much of Egypt's private capital, however, has been invested in real estate and service-sector businesses such as tourism.

Although oil was discovered in the Middle East before World War II, it was the development of the Organization of Petroleum Exporting Countries (OPEC) and the 1973 oil embargo that led to the rapid rise of oil prices, which in turn led to massive revenue increases in the oil-rich states such as Saudi Arabia, Kuwait, Iraq, and Iran.

In Saudi Arabia, the state-owned Saudi Basic Industries Corporation (SABIC) has become a major petrochemical producer working in collaboration with leading multinational oil and chemical companies. Jabal Ali has risen from the desert sands to become the leading industrial complex in the Persian Gulf and the largest in the Arab world. It produces not only a large variety of petroleum derivatives, but also fertilizers and steel. The petrochemicals are the feedstocks for plastics, and Saudi Arabia already has a range of downstream manufacturing, producing everything from transparent bags and other disposables to heavy durable plastic products.

Apart from Turkey, Saudi Arabia is the only Middle Eastern country to have experienced a considerable degree of industrial success. The Riyadh government took the lead because of the substantial scale of the financing involved, but Saudi Arabia, like Turkey, has a vigorous and growing private manufacturing sector. In Turkey, the comparative advantage lies in its modest labor costs and the adaptability and skills of its people. In Saudi Arabia, where much of the labor is foreign, the advantage is the abundance of energy and a tradition of trade and commerce.

With oil resources, abundant human capital, and an agricultural base, Iraq could have been expected to develop into a regional economic powerhouse. After an emphasis on agricultural development and decentralized food-processing factories in the early republican (post-1958) era, during the oil boom Iraq came to focus on its oil and gas sector. By the late 1970s Iraq had shifted toward heavy industry and armament manufacturing. In the wake of two wars and a decade of sanctions, however, its oil sector and industrial base became dilapidated, and it will be difficult to rebuild it in the wake of the U.S.-led toppling of the Ba'athist regime.

Iran saw its industrial output in steel and petrochemical production decline throughout the 1980s following the disruption of the Islamic Revolution and the Iran–Iraq War. Many industrialists and managers left after the overthrow of the shah, and the war resulted in severe shortages that made it difficult for industries to obtain necessary raw materials and imported inputs. After the war the Tehran government engaged in a "construction jihad" to develop the country's infrastructure and educational system, but political isolation has continued to limit its industrial prospects.

Israel is the most industrialized country in the region and one of the few with a highly skilled workforce and a commitment to supporting research and development. Industrial development, however, has been hampered by isolation and continuing regional conflict. The Oslo peace process of the mid-1990s led to short period of exaggerated hopes in Israel and across the region for economic cooperation in inward investment, but these expectations fell with the decline of the peace process in the late 1990s. As a small state trying to diversify with a limited domestic market, Israel has suffered from its exclusion from regional markets, despite post-Oslo efforts towards regional normalization. Israel's trade with Egypt and Jordan has been minimal, though some low-skilled labor-intensive production has been outsourced to these states, which have peace treaties with Israel. Trade relations with the European Union have been difficult despite a cooperation agreement, and the United States is a somewhat distant market.

Cut diamonds remain a major industrial export for Israel, but earnings are static and the industry provides direct employment for only a few hundred skilled workers. Much of the country's industry is defense related and is dependent on the financial injections from the United States, which sustain the country's high level of military expenditure. Defense equipment, including aircraft, is exported to a number of countries.

In the 1990s Israel made considerable efforts to build up its civilian high technology industries, including electronics and software development. But Israel is a relatively high-cost producer and faces cutthroat international competition. Export growth in its high-technology sector came to a halt in 2000 with the high-tech bust in the United States and with the collapse of the peace process.

The peace treaty between Israel and Jordan failed to generate extensive economic cooperation, but Jordan has sought to diversify and liberalize its economy. With a small domestic market, Jordan had relied on mineral exports and trade with Iraq during its oil-boom phase, but since the mid-1990s has sought to promote tourism development, as well as export-oriented light manufacturing by granting incentives to firms located in qualified industrial zones (QIZ) and through its free trade agreement with the United States. Jordan has also developed a relatively successful pharmaceuticals sector, but its generic drug production might run into trouble with intellectual property rights.

In North Africa, Algeria's industrialization drive, supported by oil and gas revenues, was anchored by heavy-industry plans that failed to act as growth poles. Socialist planning has been disastrous, in particular, for truck and tractor assembly plants. Most consumer durables industries were established to serve the domestic market and have been protected from competition by tariffs and foreign exchange rationing. This also applies to Morocco, which never adopted socialist controls over its economy, as Algeria and Tunisia did. In fact, in Morocco, small-scale craft-based activities such as ceramics, woodcarving, metalworking, and clothing remain a source of strength, providing employment and output possibly equal to that of the country's industrial plants.

Tunisia and Morocco have pursued outward-oriented industrialization policies by promoting tourism development and building private-sector textile plants that carry out subcontracting work for

European garment producers. These firms expanded during the 1980s and early 1990s, but have suffered from lower-cost Asian producers. Despite investment incentives and liberal laws on foreign capital, they have failed to attract considerable industrial investment from overseas. Both states have signed association agreements with the European Union that will gradually reduce tariff barriers on industrial products. In the meantime, Tunisia and Morocco have benefited from preferential access and have sought to promote an innovative industrial modernization program (*mise à niveau*) for small- and medium-sized firms in order to meet the challenges of integration into European and global markets.

See also ALGERIA: OVERVIEW; ECONOMICS; EGYPT; INTERNATIONAL MONETARY FUND; IRAN; IRAQ; ISRAEL: OVERVIEW; JORDAN; MANUFACTURES; MOROCCO: OVERVIEW; ORGANIZATION OF PETROLEUM EXPORTING COUNTRIES (OPEC); PETROLEUM RESERVES AND PRODUCTION; SAUDI ARABIA; TUNISIA: OVERVIEW; TURKEY.

Bibliography

Henry, Clement M., and Springborg, Robert. *Globalization and the Politics of Development in the Middle East.* Cambridge, U.K.: Cambridge University Press, 2001.

Issawi, Charles. *An Economic History of the Middle East and North Africa.* New York: Columbia University Press, 1982.

Richards, Alan, and Waterbury, John. *A Political Economy of the Middle East,* 2d edition. Boulder, CO: Westview Press, 1998.

United Nations Development Programme. *Arab Human Development Report 2003: Building a Knowledge Society.* New York: UNDP, 2003.

RODNEY J. A. WILSON
UPDATED BY WALEED HAZBUN

INFITAH

Anwar al-Sadat's program to encourage private investment in Egypt, often called the Open Door policy.

Officially launched with the 1974 "October Paper," which called for relaxing some of the government controls applied under the Arab Socialism of Gamal Abdel Nasser, this policy actually started in 1971 as an effort to attract investment by other Arab countries to rescue Egypt's faltering economy. This policy was accelerated after the Arab–Israel War of 1973 because Egypt needed foreign exchange to finance the importation of materials and parts that would bring its economy back to full production. Egypt hoped also to convert its short-term debt to longer indebtedness under less onerous terms and to attract private investments to increase future income, jobs, and foreign exchange.

Law 43 (1974) activated *infitah* by giving incentives, such as reduced taxes and import tariffs and guarantees against nationalization, to Arab and foreign investors in Egyptian industry, land reclamation, tourism, and banking. Some of the advisers to Anwar al-Sadat wanted to limit *infitah* to encouraging foreign investment in Egypt's economy; others hoped to apply capitalist norms to all domestic firms, whether owned by the government or by private investors. Sadat adopted the latter view, causing a deterioration of state planning and labor laws.

Corruption increased under a rising entrepreneurial class of *munfatihin* (those who operate the open door), whose profiteering and conspicuous consumption antagonized many poor and middle-class Egyptians. Their strikes and protest demonstrations erupted almost as soon as the policy was implemented. Sadat's attempt, under World Bank urging, to remove exchange controls and reduce government subsidies on basic foodstuffs led to the January 1977 food riots, but *infitah* continued. Under Husni Mubarak, the *munfatihin* have become a distinct interest group that has resisted his efforts to reduce their opportunities for enrichment or to trim their level of consumption. The *infitah* policy has made Egypt economically dependent on richer Arab countries, Europe, and the United States. It has also widened the economic and social gap between rich and poor, with potentially explosive implications for Egypt's future.

See also ARAB–ISRAEL WAR (1973); MUBARAK, HUSNI; NASSER, GAMAL ABDEL; SADAT, ANWAR AL-.

Bibliography

Baker, Raymond William. *Sadat and After: Struggles for Egypt's Political Soul.* Cambridge, MA: Harvard University Press, 1990.

Cooper, Mark N. *The Transformation of Egypt.* Baltimore, MD: Johns Hopkins University Press, 1982.

Heikal, Mohamed. *Autumn of Fury: The Assassination of Sadat.* New York: Random House, 1983.

Henry, Clement Moore. "The Dilemma of the Egyptian Infitah." *Middle East Journal* 38 (Fall 1984): 4.

Hirst, David, and Beeson, Irene. *Sadat.* London: Faber and Faber, 1981.

Ikram, Khalid. *Egypt: Economic Management in a Period of Transition.* Baltimore, MD: Johns Hopkins University Press, for World Bank, 1980.

Waterbury, John. *The Egypt of Nasser and Sadat: The Political Economy of Two Regimes.* Princeton, NJ: Princeton University Press, 1983.

ARTHUR GOLDSCHMIDT

İNÖNÜ, ERDAL
[1926–]

Founder of Turkey's Social Democratic Party.

Erdal İnönü is the oldest son of İsmet İnönü, a hero of the Turkish War of Independence and the second president of the Turkish Republic. He graduated from the physics department of Ankara University in 1947 and received a Ph.D. from the University of California in 1951. He taught at Princeton University, the Oak Ridge Laboratory in Tennessee, and Middle East Technical University in Ankara. By 1983, when he founded the Social Democratic Party (SDP), İnönü was considered to be one of Turkey's leading scientists. In spite of İnönü's prominence, President Kenan Evren banned the SDP (as well as ten other newly formed political parties) from participating in parliamentary elections on the grounds that it was a front for the disbanded Republican People's Party. However, the SDP was allowed to participate in the 1984 local elections, and it won 23 percent of the vote. In the following year İnönü merged his SDP with Necdet Calp's left-of center Populist Party to form the Social Democratic Populist Party (SHP). In 1991 İnönü became deputy prime minister as leader of the junior partner in the coalition government formed by Süleyman Demirel. İnönü is credited with unifying the center-left, but his detractors contend that he lacks vision and is not adept at mass mobilization. After the SHP merged with the Republican People's Party in the early 2000s, İnönü retired from active politics.

See also DEMIREL, SÜLEYMAN; EVREN, KENAN; İNÖNÜ, İSMET; REPUBLICAN PEOPLE'S PARTY; SOCIAL DEMOCRATIC POPULIST PARTY.

Bibliography

Zürcher, Erik J. *Turkey: A Modern History,* revised edition. London: I. B. Tauris, 1997.

DAVID WALDNER
UPDATED BY M. HAKAN YAVUZ

İNÖNÜ, İSMET
[1884–1974]

Turkish politician and statesman; several times prime minister and the second president of Turkey.

İsmet İnönü was born in İzmir, where his father was a judge, and educated in military schools, including the Artillery School in Istanbul and the General Staff College (where he finished first in the class two years behind that of Mustafa Kemal Atatürk). In 1912, he became chief of the Ottoman general staff in Yemen and later held the same position in Istanbul. During World War I, the Ottoman Empire joined the Central Powers to fight the Allies; İnönü was sent to fight the British in Palestine and then to the Russian front in eastern Turkey, as chief of staff to Atatürk. In the Turkish war of independence, he continued working with Atatürk. His most distinguished action was in twice defeating the Greeks near the village of İnönü (from which he later took his surname, in the Western style).

In 1922, Atatürk made İnönü foreign minister, so that he could head the Turkish delegation to the Lausanne peace conference. There he gained recognition for his intense and successful work in winning almost all Turkey's demands. He was then made prime minister, an office he held until 1937. He was one of President Atatürk's closest associates, although his views were generally more moderate with regard to the intensity of projected reforms. He fully supported their direction and their basic philosophy, however, and as head of government he vigorously enforced all the reform laws. For this he acquired a reputation as Atatürk's ruthless henchman, the ideal second man.

İnönü was replaced as prime minister in 1937 by Celal Bayar for reasons not fully clear; a personal rivalry then continued for many years. When Atatürk died in 1938, however, İnönü became his successor, Turkey's second president. After the strains of World War II, İnönü was faced with demands for multiparty politics; until that time

During his long political career, İsmet İnönü (1884–1973) did
much to help Turkey establish itself as an independent republic.
In 1938, he became the country's second president and in 1946
he helped put in place a pluralistic governmental system.
© HULTON-DEUTSCH COLLECTION/CORBIS. REPRODUCED BY
PERMISSION.

Turkey had been a de facto one-party state under
the aegis of the Republican People's Party (RPP).
Based on implicit promises of eventual multiparty
democracy, a second party was formed by four RPP
rebels, the Democrat Party (DP), in 1946. An early
election was called, which the RPP won, partly because the opposition had little time to prepare, but
in İnönü's famous declaration of 12 July 1947, he
took the statesmanlike position that both parties
should have the same privileges. When the Democrats won the 1950 election, rumors surfaced that
they would not be allowed to take power, but İnönü
stayed true to his word and quietly assumed the role
as leader of the opposition, an act for which he won
worldwide acclaim. During the 1950s, İnönü led the
RPP in the Turkish Grand National Assembly,
strongly defending Atatürk's policies of secular
Western-style government in the face of Democrat
policies that many RPP militants saw as a betrayal of
Kemalism.

İnönü's political history made him a target for
many Democrats, particularly his rival Celal Bayar,
who had become Turkey's third president. As a
result of the Democrat government's repressive
measures and political shortcomings, the Bayar–
Menderes regime was ousted by the armed forces on
27 May 1960. The belief that the military coup was
to enable the RPP to return to govern was confirmed
for many people when President Cemal Gürsel invited İnönü to form a government despite the RPP
having won only a small plurality in the assembly
and having run a poor second to the moderate right-
wing Justice Party (JP) in the Senate. He formed a
coalition with the grudging participation of the Justice party, but it fell in May over the issue of amnesty
for the ousted Democrats (which the RPP and the
military opposed but which the JP supported on
behalf of the former Democrats, to whom they considered themselves successors). In June, the commanders again called on İnönü, and his second
coalition was formed, with the New Turkey and Republican Peasants Nation party plus some independents.

İnönü's party had little in common with them
in terms of programs, and he was faced with strong
dissatisfaction within the RPP as well, because of
concessions made to his right-wing coalition partners. He also faced criticism because of the RPP's
poor vote-getting record since the transition to
multiparty politics; this was attributed to a combination of too moderate centrist policies plus his
failure to rejuvenate the party with younger successors and those not as closely identified with
Atatürk's militant methods. The RPP's poor performance in the 1963 election led to his resignation
as prime minister once more, but when other parties could not form cabinets, he was called on a third
time, in December 1963, and he formed his third
coalition. In the 1964 Cyprus crisis, İnönü spoke
out against the letter sent him by U.S. President
Lyndon B. Johnson, which threatened not to defend Turkey from a Soviet attack should Turkey invade Cyprus. Even this did not strengthen his
domestic position, and he resigned for the last time
early in 1965. Nevertheless, he remained as RPP
leader until mid-1972, when the party elected the
younger and more leftist Bülent Ecevit as chairman.

One of İnönü's three children, Erdal, became
a politician—the leader of the Social Democratic

Populist Party, starting in the late 1980s, and deputy prime minister in the coalition government in 1992.

See also ATATÜRK, MUSTAFA KEMAL; BAYAR, CELAL; CYPRUS; DEMOCRAT PARTY; ECEVIT, BÜLENT; GÜRSEL, CEMAL; İNÖNÜ, ERDAL; JOHNSON, LYNDON BAINES; JUSTICE PARTY; KEMALISM; LAUSANNE, TREATY OF (1923); REPUBLICAN PEOPLE'S PARTY (RPP); SOCIAL DEMOCRATIC POPULIST PARTY; TURKISH GRAND NATIONAL ASSEMBLY.

Bibliography

Ahmad, Feroz. *The Turkish Experiment in Democracy 1950–1975.* Boulder, CO: Westview, 1977.

Heper, Metin, and Landau, Jacob M., eds. *Political Parties and Democracy in Turkey.* London and New York: I.B. Tauris, 1991.

Karpat, Kemal H. *Turkey's Politics: The Transition to a Multi-Party System.* Princeton, NJ: Princeton University Press, 1959.

Weiker, Walter F. *Political Tutelage and Democracy in Turkey: The Free Party and Its Aftermath.* Leiden, Netherlands: E.J. Brill, 1973.

WALTER F. WEIKER

INQUILAB

See GLOSSARY

INSTITUT D'ÉGYPTE

Institute in Cairo, Egypt, for study and promotion of Egyptian culture.

Napoléon Bonaparte founded the Institut d'Égypte (al-Majma al-Ilmi al-Misri) in Cairo in 1798. Its members were the elite of the French expedition's Commission des Sciences et Arts, whose massive *Déscription de l'Égypte* (1809–1826) surveyed all aspects of the Egyptian scene. The institute disappeared when the French evacuated Egypt in 1801.

Inspired by the original institute, Europeans founded the Institut Egyptien in Alexandria in 1859 with Saʿid Pasha's approval. Egyptologist Auguste Mariette was among the forty-odd European founders. The Egyptian scholar Rifaʿa al-Rafi al-Tahtawi and Egypt's future prime minister Nubar Pasha were among the seven Middle Eastern founders. The institute maintained a library, sponsored lectures, and published a bulletin and scholarly memoirs. The institute was moved to Cairo in 1880, and resumed the Napoleonic name *Institut d'Égypte* in 1918. When most European residents left Egypt during Gamal Abdel Nasser's tenure in office, the membership became mostly Egyptian. Neglected by the government since 1952 when Nasser's coup took place, the institute struggles to find funds to keep up its publications, its building just off Cairo's central square, and its once impressive library.

See also MARIETTE, AUGUSTE; NUBAR PASHA; TAHTAWI, RIFAʿA AL-RAFI AL-.

Bibliography

Reid, Donald Malcolm. *Whose Pharaohs? Archaeology, Museums, and Egyptian National Identity from Napoleon to World War I.* Berkeley: University of California Press, 2002.

DONALD MALCOLM REID

INSTITUTE FOR PALESTINE STUDIES

Palestinian research and publishing center.

The Institute for Palestine Studies was established in Beirut in December 1963 as the first nonprofit, independent research and publishing center focusing exclusively on the Palestinian problem and the Arab–Israeli conflict. Financed primarily by an endowment, the institute is independent of governments, parties, organizations, and political affiliations. It is not affiliated with the Palestine Liberation Organization in any way.

With branches currently in Beirut, Paris, Washington, D.C., and Jerusalem, the institute has striven to accomplish several academic goals over the decades. These have included collecting documents, manuscripts, maps, photographs, newspapers, and books for its library and archives in Beirut, the largest of its kind in the Arab world. The institute was also the first Arab institution to promote the study of the Hebrew language and to translate important Hebrew-language documents into Arabic. The institute continues to publish books and documents relating to the Palestinians and the Arab–Israeli conflict, as well as research journals such as *al-Dirasat al-Filastiniyya, Revue d'études palestiniennes,* and *Journal of Palestine Studies.*

MICHAEL R. FISCHBACH

INSTITUTE FOR WOMEN'S STUDIES IN THE ARAB WORLD (LEBANON)

Institute in Lebanon that offers innovative activities and outreach programs pertaining to Arab women and children.

In 1973, the newly coeducational Beirut University College (BUC), which later became the Lebanese American University, founded the Institute for Women's Studies in the Arab World (IWSAW) through a grant from the Ford Foundation. The dean of BUC, Riyad Nassar, was one of the founding members of the institute. Julinda Abu Nasr, who was the first director of IWSAW and a faculty member at the university, was another founding member.

The main objectives of the institute are to "engage in academic research aimed at the study and support of women's issues and conditions in the Arab world, serve as a data bank and resource center on such subjects, serve as a catalyst for policy changes regarding the human rights of women in the region, and facilitate networking among individuals, groups, institutions and governments concerned with such topics." The institute has embarked on many projects, including research and publication about education, employment, the legal and social status of women, child rearing, literature, art, history, labor conditions, the environment, and the documentation of published and unpublished material about women's issues.

In addition to hosting an annual lecture series, conferences, and workshops, the institute publishes a quarterly journal, *al-Ra'ida,* meaning 'the female pioneer.' Since 1976, *al-Ra'ida* has focused on recording the social, economic, and legal conditions of women in the Arab world. The journal promotes educational outreach efforts to the community and facilitates dialogue on the issues. The institute also produces books, monographs, and studies in English and Arabic.

IWSAW has several outreach programs dealing with academic activities and advocacy. Academic activities offered by the institute include conferences, research, and targeted courses. The institute also houses a library, with a collection of over 6,000 documents, all in the process of being placed on the Internet. Advocacy and action programs include rural development and income-generating projects, basic living skills programs that target illiterate and semiliterate women, and educational lectures on such topics as family planning, child care, rights, nutrition, health, and civic education.

The Institute for Women's Studies in the Arab World entered the twenty-first century as an active educational center under the direction of Muna Khalaf, who teaches economics at the university. It has established strong relationships with the community, works with the Lebanese Ministry of Social Affairs, and initiates projects with nongovernmental agencies, local and international.

See also BEIRUT COLLEGE FOR WOMEN (BCW); GENDER: GENDER AND EDUCATION; LEBANESE CIVIL WAR (1958); LEBANESE CIVIL WAR (1975–1990); LEBANESE UNIVERSITY; LEBANON.

Bibliography

Institute for Women's Studies in the Arab World. Available from <http://www.lau.edu.lb/centers-institutes/iwsaw>.

Lebanese American University Academic Catalogue 1996. Beirut: Focus Press, 1996.

MIRNA LATTOUF

INSTITUTE OF WOMEN'S STUDIES OF BIR ZEIT UNIVERSITY

Palestinian research center on women and gender.

The Institute of Women's Studies (IWS) at Bir Zeit University was established in 1994 by a group of female academics. The principal researchers affailiated with the institute include: Lamis Abu Nahleh, Rema Hammami, Islah Jad, Penny Johnson, Eileen Kuttab, and Lisa Taraki. Founded initially as the Women's Studies Program in the university's faculty of arts, it became an institute in 1997 with a full-time staff and graduate studies program. Its overall goals are to develop women's studies as an academic discipline, to conduct scholarly research on women and gender relations in Palestinian society, and to facilitate more equitable policies and legislation.

The IWS is involved in teaching, research, training, and advocacy. It offers an undergraduate curriculum of core courses leading to a minor in women's studies. In partnership with the Institute of Law at Bir Zeit, it offers an interdisciplinary master's program in gender, law, and development to increase awareness of the cultural and practical implications of gender divisions and inequalities.

Broad political and economic trends in the West Bank and Gaza Strip influence the institute's research priorities. Between 1994 and 1999 IWS research comprised a series of studies concerning health, education, law, the labor market, and other sectors during a period when institution and capacity-building of governmental and nongovernmental agencies dominated development activities in the West Bank and Gaza Strip. With the collapse of the Oslo Accord, the advent of the second Palestinian uprising of September 2000, and an economic downturn, IWS research began to center on poverty, political violence, and militarism.

IWS faculty members participate in regional research projects contributing to the discourse and scholarship on women and gender in Arab society. Members also engage in consulting and gender training in order to influence policy and increase the institute's sustainability.

See also Aqsa Intifada, al-; Bir Zeit University; Gaza Strip; Gender: Gender and Education; Gender: Study of; Intifada (1987–1991); Oslo Accord (1993); Palestine; Palestinian Authority; West Bank.

Bibliography

Institute of Women's Studies as Birzeit University. Available from <http://home.birzeit.edu/wsi/index .htm>.

Mona Ghali

INTELLIGENCE ORGANIZATIONS

Modern information-gathering techniques, as first effected by European colonial powers in the Middle East, and later, those implemented by the United States and the Soviet Union after World War II.

Intelligence services in the Middle East originated with European imperialism and colonialism during the nineteenth century. Spies and informers were not new to the region—the Ottoman Empire had monitored the activities of their officials—but the systematic collecting, organizing, and evaluating of political and strategic data for decision making from both open (overt) and confidential (covert) sources was an innovation.

By the late nineteenth century, European governments saw political and military intelligence as a more effective means of advancing colonial interests than military force alone. In Algeria, interest in political and ethnographic intelligence peaked during periods of resistance to French colonial rule, but when France perceived no further threat, interest in intelligence waned. In contrast, since 1904, Morocco's political and social institutions—including its tribal and religious leadership—had been systematically cataloged by the Mission Scientifique au Maroc (the Scientific Mission to Morocco), with the explicit goal of facilitating political intervention. After France established its Protectorate regime in Morocco in 1912, the head of the mission became the director of native affairs.

Most Western intelligence services compartmentalize their activities: the clandestine collection of data; the analysis of overt and covert sources; counterintelligence blocking an enemy's sources, deceiving an enemy, and reporting against hostile penetration; and covert action. In both the colonial bureaucracies and their postindependence successors in the region, the lines between these activities are blurred. The collection of intelligence data sometimes becomes confounded with the supervision, control, and intimidation of populations; and the analysis and reporting of domestic and external threats become subordinate to reassuring insecure rulers or manipulating the information they receive to further individual political careers or factional interests.

The framework of intelligence activities in the colonial era often continued into the initial years of independent Middle Eastern states, and former colonial powers established arrangements for the training of local intelligence specialists. Thus military and civilian intelligence personnel in Jordan and the Persian/Arabian Gulf area receive training in Britain, and the French have provided equivalent training for Morocco and Tunisia.

Military and intelligence organizations were profoundly shaped by foreign advice and training,

Career military officer Danny Yatom was appointed to the leadership of the Mossad in 1996 by Israel's prime minister Shimon Peres, marking the first time the identity of the intelligence agency's director was publicly announced. Yatom resigned his position in 1998 after his actions regarding a failed Mossad attempt to assassinate a top HAMAS leader were brought into question. © CORBIS SYGMA. REPRODUCED BY PERMISSION.

even in countries that did not experience colonialism. Iran's SAVAK was created in 1957 with advice from the U.S. Central Intelligence Agency (CIA), whose role was supplemented in the 1960s by Israel's counterpart, Mossad. Following Egypt's 1952 revolution, the CIA assisted in restructuring the intelligence apparatus; and Soviet-bloc technical assistance stepped in after 1956 during Gamal Abdel Nasser's socialist government. By the 1960s, Soviets and East Germans had begun to play important advisory and training roles in Iraq, Syria, the former People's Democratic Republic of Yemen, and Libya. The Cold War's players were right in the midst of the petroleum-rich Middle East.

Formal training from foreign services notwithstanding, subtle changes occur as intelligence methods and techniques are adapted to local circumstances. First, rival and overlapping services are created to check authority and autonomy, and the result is faction-

alism. Some rulers—those of Syria and Iraq provide examples—appoint close relatives to key intelligence posts. For instance, in Syria, Rifʿat al-Asad, brother of President Hafiz al-Asad, was head of the Syrian intelligence service and was linked to the Red Knights.

In contrast to U.S. intelligence, which has traditionally placed more emphasis on international rather than domestic threats, the principal task in the region is the surveillance, control, and frequently the intimidation of their own populations—both domestically and abroad. In some states, such as Iraq and Syria, such surveillance is pervasive and unchecked. Intelligence services in other Middle Eastern countries may be more restrained, although human-rights organizations report abuses in all states of the region, as is the case with Tunisia, whose president Zayn al-Abidine Ben Ali received military training in France and the United States. Governments do little to mitigate people's percep-

The head of Egyptian intelligence, Omar Sulayman (second from right), meets with Palestinian president Yasir Arafat (second from left) in Ramallah in July 2002. Sulayman held discussions with both Israeli and Palestinian officials in an attempt to improve relations between the two. © AFP/CORBIS. REPRODUCED BY PERMISSION.

tion of the power of intelligence organizations because such notions help to suppress public dissent. The secretiveness of such services provides formal (diplomatic) deniability for countries' actions against regional rivals—providing arms or refuge to opponents of a neighboring regime, for example—which, if publicly acknowledged, might lead to a major confrontation. Domestic factions can also receive discreet assistance in the same manner. Regional intelligence services opportunistically cooperate with foreign services; for example, during the Iran–Iraq War in the 1980s, the United States provided both sides with intelligence data from the database it was amassing for its own purposes.

The political intelligence activities of the superpowers in the Middle East have been primarily concerned with their own rivalries, protecting oil supplies, and—for the United States—guaranteeing the security of Israel. For Arab historians, the arch example of foreign intervention is the role of the British, including T. E. Lawrence (of Arabia) during World War I, in instigating the Arab Revolt against Ottoman rule. The British abandoned the Arab cause once their objectives were accomplished. Other examples include U.S.–British cooperation in overthrowing Iran's Prime Minister Mohammad Mossadegh in 1953; and covert U.S. operations against suspected leftist groups in Syria from the late 1940s through 1958. A converse example in 1978 is the Phalange Party and the South Lebanese Army's acceptance of help from Israel during the Lebanese civil war; later, after the head of the party, Bashir Jumayyil, became president of Lebanon, he refused to sign peace accords with Israel. Testimony during the 1987 Iran-Contra hearings in the United States demonstrates how covert intelligence activities can work against formal state control and declared public policy.

Understanding intelligence organizations and their activities is difficult, because information on them is uneven. The history of Israel's intelligence service is better known than those of other Middle

Eastern countries, since many agents have published memoirs and relevant political archives (subject to a thirty-year delay for state papers) are available to scholars. Thus historians can trace the development of Israeli intelligence operations from the early Zionist monitoring of Arab nationalist movements at the beginning of the British mandate in Palestine (1922), to professionalization in the mid-1930s as an element of Haganah (the Zionist military underground), to its bureaucratic separation into military, domestic, and foreign units following the 1948 establishment of the state of Israel. While Israel's security forces are well articulated, so too is its opposition, apparent in the many Palestinian liberation groups. The Palestine Liberation Organization (PLO), once considered little more than a terrorist organization although greatly hindered after the restriction of movement placed on Yasir Arafat during the Intifada in 2000, was viewed by many as the voice of the Palestinian people. One country's terrorists are another's security.

Other intelligence services of the region are known primarily through information provided by defectors (Iraq, Iran, Sudan, Egypt, Libya); deliberate leaks; the release of documents during major domestic crises (the trial in Egypt following Anwar al-Sadat's assassination in 1981) or changes of regime (the release of security files on the Iraqi Communist party following the monarchy's overthrow in 1958); and the capture of documents from foreign security services—such as Israel's publication of Jordanian documents seized during the Arab–Israel War of 1967 or the publication of U.S. intelligence documents and diplomatic reports taken from the U.S. Embassy in Tehran.

Much speculation has emerged after 11 September 2001 as to the changing nature of security in the Middle East. It is apparent that some Middle Eastern governments' security and overall governmental structures will be thoroughly reorganized in line with U.S. security demands. Afghanistan and Iraq are two cases in point. Some governments, like Tunisia, have managed to turn the 11 September attacks into an argument to defend their own internal struggles. Some countries, like Morocco, have adopted profiling techniques similar to those used in the United States after the creation of the Homeland Security Council. Others may argue, however, that there is now a cross-pollination of security

strategies between the United States and other countries, and that in fact the United States is borrowing tactics—from the Middle East and elsewhere—that limit domestic civil liberties. Just as colonial intervention shaped intelligence in the Middle East at the time of the Ottoman Empire and after, so too will the United States and other powerful countries continue to influence the evolution of security measures in the region.

Middle Eastern states have historically been more concerned with their own domestic threats than with those involving their neighbors; this most probably will not change in the future, as their own national security is linked to wider international security priorities. These governments have traditionally placed strict limits on civil liberties and have focused surveillance in domains of the public sphere, such as the press. As domestic public spheres are projected into international spheres via satellite television and the Internet, internal security too will invariably evolve. More than ever, citizens in the Middle East are aware that what may be seen domestically as a legitimate action to defend national sovereignty by limiting civil liberties can very quickly become a case for defending human rights within international headlines.

All countries have intelligence services within either the domestic police at various levels, the armed forces, or in some cases private security companies. This list reflects national security institutions that stand on their own as semi-independent organizations working in collaboration with national governments.

Intelligence organizations:

D4 Israeli Navy Shayetet 13 (maritime countermeasures unit)

IAF Israeli Air Force

IDF Israeli Defense Force

ISI Inter-Services Intelligence (Pakistan)

MOIS Iranian intelligence service (post-Islamic revolution)

OAS Secret Army Organization (France/Algeria)

SANG Saudi Arabian National Guard

SAVAK Iranian secret police (during reign of Mohammad Reza Pahlavi)

SSF Special Security Force (Saudi Arabia)

SSG Special Service Group (Pakistan)

Unit 269 Counter-terrorist unit of Sayeret Matkal (Israel)

The following are some groups that have engaged in movements of reclaiming land, resources, and political sovereignty.

Armed/revolutionary/independence/ antigovernment groups:

ALF Arab Liberation Front

ARGK Military wing of Kurdistan Worker's Party (Turkey)

ASALA Armenian Secret Army for the Liberation of Armenia

DFLP Democratic Front for the Liberation of Palestine

DRMLA Democratic Revolutionary Movement for the Liberation of Arabistan

FIS Islamic Salvation Front (Algeria)

GIA Islamic Armed Group (Algeria)

GIA-CG Islamic Armed Group, General Command

HAMAS Islamic Resistance Movement

MAK Service Office of the Mujahideen (Afghanistan)

MAN Movement of Arab Nationalists

PFLP Popular Front for the Liberation of Palestine

PFLP-GC Popular Front for the Liberation of Palestine, General Command

PFLP-SC Popular Front for the Liberation of Palestine, Special Command

PFLP-SOG Popular Front for the Liberation of Palestine, Special Operations Group

PIJ Palestinian Islamic Jihad

PIO Palestinian Islamic Organization

PKK Kurdistan Worker's Party (Turkey)

PLA Palestine Liberation Army

PLF Palestine Liberation Front

PLO Palestine Liberation Organization

PPSF Palestinian Popular Struggle Front

See also ARAB LIBERATION FRONT; CENTRAL INTELLIGENCE AGENCY (CIA); FRONT ISLAMIQUE DU SALUT (FIS); HAGANAH; KURDISTAN WORKERS PARTY (PKK); MOSSAD; PALESTINE LIBERATION ORGANIZATION (PLO).

Bibliography

Eickelman, Dale F., and Anderson, Jon W., eds. *New Media in the Muslim World: The Emerging Public Sphere.* Bloomington: Indiana University Press, 1999.

Harclerode, Peter. *Secret Soldiers: Special Forces in the War against Terrorism.* London: Cassell, 2000.

Powers, Thomas. *Intelligence Wars: American Secret History from Hitler to Al-Qaeda.* New York: New York Review of Books, 2002.

"Tunisia." In Human Rights Watch: Middle East and North Africa. Available from <http://www.hrw.org/mideast/tunisia.php>.

DALE F. EICKELMAN
UPDATED BY MARIA F. CURTIS

INTERNATIONAL, DANA
[1972–]

Israeli singer.

Born Yaron Cohen to a poor Jewish family of Yemenite descent in Tel Aviv, Dana International became one of Israel's most prominent singers in the late 1990s and the country's first renowned transsexual artist. Her career began in drag shows at Tel Aviv gay clubs, and between her first album in 1993 and the late 1990s, her dance music mixed styles, intermingled languages, and emphasized multiculturalism grounded in the Middle East. Jewish tradition, U.S. music, and Israeli and Arab cultures have inspired her songs. As Israel's representative, she won the 1998 Eurovision song contest. Her records were banned in Egypt, yet her popularity expanded to the Arab world. An advocate of gay and transsexual rights, International offered a positive model of transsexuality and posed in an Amnesty International advertisement captioned "Gay rights are human rights." In 2001 Israel's Foreign Ministry booked her performance at the San Francisco Gay Pride celebration to promote Israeli diversity in the face of increasing criticism of state policies. International's songs became more conventional as the demise of the Oslo peace process and the rise of the second intifada altered the cultural landscape in which she had previously offered a multicultural model of transnational Middle Eastern art.

See also ART; GENDER: GENDER AND EDUCATION; HUMAN RIGHTS; MINORITIES; MUSIC; THEATER.

YAEL BEN-ZVI

INTERNATIONAL DEBT COMMISSION

Established in 1876 to defend the interests of European creditors when Khedive Isma'il's Egypt went bankrupt.

Britain, France, Austria–Hungary, Italy, and later Russia and Germany had seats on the International Debt Commission, which was usually called La Caisse de la Dette Publique. The Caisse's insistence on putting the interests of European creditors first was a major cause of the deposition of Isma'il ibn Ibrahim and of the Urabist resistance of 1881 and 1882. After the British occupied the country in 1882, their administrators came to see the Caisse as an impediment to necessary financial and agricultural reforms. Britain's entente cordiale with France in 1904, however, removed most of the friction. The weight of external debt on the Egyptian economy lightened between the two world wars, with the importance of the Caisse declining accordingly. During World War II, sterling balances accumulated from Allied expenditures in Egypt essentially eliminated the problem of external debt until the 1960s.

See also ISMA'IL IBN IBRAHIM; URABI, AHMAD.

Bibliography

Issawi, Charles. *Egypt at Mid-Century.* London and New York: Oxford University Press, 1954.

DONALD MALCOLM REID

INTERNATIONAL MONETARY FUND

An international institution charged with maintaining international monetary stability.

The International Monetary Fund (IMF) is an international organization that provides temporary financial assistance to any of its 184 member countries in order to correct their payment imbalances. The IMF was established during the conference at Bretton Woods, New Hampshire, in 1944 because the Allies wanted to avoid the competitive currency devaluations, exchange controls, and bilateral agreements that the world had witnessed prior to World War II. The IMF's main goal was to promote stable currencies in order to enhance international commerce.

Originally, the IMF's position was that restoring payments equilibrium could be achieved within a year by eliminating excess demand. It was not until 1974 that the IMF established the external fund facility to provide its members with up to three years of financial assistance and also introduced a long-term approach, termed the enhanced structural adjustment facility. In exchange for this financing, the IMF demands that borrowers make fundamental changes in their economies to prevent future balance of payments problems. These changes range from stabilization of the exchange rate and of government deficits to structural adjustment of the economy through privatization of state enterprises and liberalization of trade.

By article IV of its charter, the IMF was given the right to monitor on a yearly basis the exchange rate, monetary and fiscal policies, structural policies, and financial and banking policies of every member. It has been heavily involved in many Middle Eastern countries. It has been involved in Egypt and other North African countries since the 1970s. It became involved in Lebanon during the 1990s and finally in Sudan and Yemen through its Heavily Indebted Poor Countries Initiative (HIPC). One Middle Eastern country, Saudi Arabia, enjoys a permanent voting position on the IMF board of governors.

See also ECONOMICS.

Bibliography

Spero, Joan. *The Politics of International Economic Relations.* London: Allen and Unwin, 1978.

Vreeland, James. *The IMF and Economic Development.* Cambridge, U.K.: Cambridge University Press, 2003.

DAVID WALDNER
UPDATED BY KHALIL GEBARA

INTIFADA (1987–1991)

Palestinian uprising.

The Intifada erupted in Israeli-occupied Gaza and the West Bank in December 1987. In broad perspective, it was a continuation of the century-old Arab–Israel conflict. The immediate cause was opposition to Israel's twenty-year occupation and military rule of Gaza, the West Bank, and Arab East Jerusalem. Under Israeli military government, there was censorship of school texts and other publications; punitive demolition of Arab homes; and the institution of a permit system for travel outside the territories and for constructing new buildings, opening businesses, digging wells, and conducting other routine daily activities. Civilian courts were replaced by Israeli military tribunals without habeas corpus and the imprisonment of Palestinians for lengthy periods without trial. Often torture was used by Israeli security services.

Israeli plans for integration of the occupied territories included control and allocation of water resources in the West Bank and Gaza and integration of the electricity grid and road network with those in Israel. Approximately half the Palestinian workforce of the territories was employed at the bottom of the Israeli wage scale, in jobs such as construction and agriculture. Many highly educated and

Palestinian refugees in the Gaza Strip in 1989. The 1993 Oslo Accord returned a degree of Palestinian self rule to the Gaza territory, but a comprehensive peace agreement was never reached, and after the second Intifada began in 2000 the Israelis again established dominance in the region. © PETER TURNLEY/CORBIS. REPRODUCED BY PERMISSION.

skilled Palestinians were forced to accept such employment bcause of deteriorating economic conditions.

During the twenty years of occupation prior to the Intifada, about half the land in the West Bank was taken over by Israeli authorities and much of it allocated to Jewish settlers. The substantial increase in the number of Jewish settlers and settlements aroused growing apprehension among Palestinians who feared that Israel would absorb or annex the territories.

By December 1987 Palestinian dissatisfaction reached a crisis. The spark that ignited the Intifada was a road accident on 8 December, in which an Israeli-driven vehicle killed or seriously wounded several Palestinians returning to Gaza from work in Israel. Reports of the incident spread quickly, resulting in protest demonstrations, first throughout Gaza and, within a few days, throughout the West Bank. When Israeli troops arrived to quell the unrest, they were pelted with stones and iron bars by hundreds of demonstrators. Children throwing stones at Israeli soldiers soon became a global symbol of the Intifada.

Israeli soldiers with a Palestinian POW during the first Intifada. When it began, the first Intifada was loosely organized and generally comprised of acts of civil disobedience. As it continued, however, the violence increased, and popular participation decreased. © PETER TURNLEY/CORBIS. REPRODUCED BY PERMISSION.

A man in the West Bank gathers stones to throw at Israeli soldiers during the first Intifada. Not all of the resistance was violent, however, and many Palestinians instead showed their displeasure at Israeli occupation by demonstrating, organizing strikes, boycotting Israeli goods, and creating independent schools and political institutions. © PETER TURNLEY/CORBIS. REPRODUCED BY PERMISSION.

The extent and intensity of the uprising caught Israeli, Palestinian, and Arab leaders by surprise. Shortly after the first spontaneous demonstrations in December, the uprising began to be organized by young representatives of several Palestinian factions in the territories, many of them from the refugee camps and the working class. The Unified National Leadership of the Uprising (UNLU) was an underground organization with delegates representing al-Fatah, the Popular Front for the Liberation of Palestine (PFLP), Democratic Popular Front for the Liberation of Palestine (DPFLP), and the Palestine Communist Organization, all banned by Israeli authorities. Representatives of Islamic Jihad at times cooperated with the UNLU, although Islamic fundamentalist factions maintained their freedom of action. Membership in the UNLU frequently rotated, making it difficult for the occupation authorities to apprehend the leaders.

Because of the overwhelming power of the Israeli military, the Intifada avoided the use of firearms. Instead, tactics included strikes and demonstrations; extensive posting of illegal slogans, flags, and symbols; boycotting Israeli-made products; resigning from posts in the military government; withholding labor from Israel; and refusing to use Israeli official

documents. The UNLU and the fundamentalist factions issued instructions and political pronouncements to the Palestinian population through posters and leaflets called *bayanat* and through broadcasts from underground radio stations that moved from place to place.

By 1990 more than 600 Palestinians had been killed by Israelis since the beginning of the Intifada, and over 1,000 injured. Arrests and imprisonments associated with the Intifada totaled about 50,000. During this period the uprising resulted in 20 Israeli deaths.

Initial objectives of the Intifada included releasing Palestinian prisoners, ending the policy of expulsion, ceasing Jewish settlement, and removing restrictions on Palestinian political activity and contacts between those in the territories and the leadership of the Palestine Liberation Organization (PLO) abroad. Later demands were the ending of Israeli occupation and Palestinian self-determination.

Whereas the Intifada galvanized Palestinian society, overcoming divisions among regions, religious groups, political factions, sexes, and social classes, it polarized Israel between those who called for a political solution to the Palestine problem and those who demanded greater use of force to suppress the uprising. The Intifada had a detrimental impact on Israel's economy because it required a great increase in military manpower in the territories and entailed the loss of cheap Arab labor in important sectors of the economy.

The Intifada brought the Palestine question to the forefront of international attention, leading to renewed attempts by the United States and Western Europe to find a solution. As a result, the PLO gave greater consideration to the views of Palestinians resident in the territories, and declared in December 1988 that it would accept the coexistence of Israel and a Palestinian state within the West Bank and Gaza. The Intifada and the 1990 Gulf War were catalysts that led to the Middle East peace conference that opened in Madrid in 1991.

See also AQSA INTIFADA, AL-; ARAB–ISRAEL CONFLICT; FATAH, AL-; GULF WAR (1991); ISLAMIC JIHAD; ISRAEL; ISRAELI SETTLEMENTS; PALESTINE; PALESTINE LIBERATION ORGANIZATION (PLO); POPULAR FRONT

FOR THE LIBERATION OF PALESTINE; WEST BANK.

Bibliography

Lockman, Zachary, and Beinin, Joel, eds. *Intifada: The Palestinian Uprising against Israeli Occupation.* Boston: South End Press, 1989.

Nassar, Jamal R., and Heacock, Roger, eds. *Intifada: Palestine at the Crossroads.* New York: Praeger, 1990.

O'Balance, Edgar. *The Palestinian Intifada.* London and New York: Macmillan and St. Martin's Press, 1998.

Peretz, Don. *Intifada: The Palestinian Uprising.* Boulder, CO: Westview Press, 1990.

Schiff, Ze'ev, and Ya'ari, Ehud. *Intifada: The Palestinian Uprising—Israel's Third Front.* New York: Simon and Schuster, 1990.

DON PERETZ

INTIFADA 2000

See AQSA INTIFADA, AL-

İPEKCI, ABDI
[1929–1979]

Turkish newspaper editor.

Born in Istanbul, Abdi İpekci attended Galatasaray High School and studied law at Istanbul University while beginning his journalism career as a sportswriter, cartoonist, and reporter. At twenty-one, he became editor of the daily *Express,* and four years later took the job that gained him nearly universal respect for the next twenty-five years, editor at *Milliyet,* one of Istanbul's leading dailies. İpekci was assassinated in 1979 by Mehmet Ali Ağa, who shot Pope John Paul II two years later.

In İpekci's hands, *Milliyet* became a popular paper that combined slick, attractive presentation with serious news coverage. He was known for maintaining a neutral, but perceptive and reasoned stance in his editorials, although the paper was known to be left-of-center politically. For example, in 1967 İpekci presciently warned against the myth of a communist menace, which he saw as a prelude to a military takeover. As president of the Istanbul Journalists Association (1958–1960) and later, he played a leading role in unionizing journalists and developing a professional code of ethics.

See also NEWSPAPERS AND PRINT MEDIA: TURKEY.

Bibliography

Şahin, Haluk. "Mass Media in Turkey." In *Turkic Culture: Continuity and Change,* edited by Sabri M. Akural. Bloomington: Turkish Studies, Indiana University, 1987.

ELIZABETH THOMPSON

IQBAL, MUHAMMAD
[1877–1938]

Muslim Indian poet, philosopher, and political thinker.

Muhammad Iqbal contributed greatly to Islamic revivalism and to the establishment of Pakistan as an Islamic state. He may be considered the most important Muslim thinker of the twentieth century. His most influential work is *The Reconstruction of Religious Thought in Islam.*

Born in Sialkot, India, under British colonial rule, Iqbal studied literature, law, and philosophy at the Government College at Lahore, Cambridge University, and the University of Munich. He wrote originally in Urdu, then in Farsi in order to reach a wider Muslim audience, and was (and still is) celebrated for his poetry. Iqbal's conceptual goal was to analyze the reasons for the decay of Muslim culture and provide the tools by which Muslims may reclaim their faith. In his view, *taqlid* (imitation) on the part of the theologians and the spread of pantheistic and ascetic Sufism eventually led to the reification of Muslim thought and concealed the dynamism and activism of the Qur'anic vision. He called for the renewal of Muslim thought and Muslim institutions through the exercise of *ijtihad* and the establishment of democratic societies through the process of *ijma* (consensus). The necessity for Muslims to live by Islamic law led him to call for a separate jurisdiction for Muslim Indians, a concept that the Muslim League in India adopted and that eventually led to the creation of Pakistan. Though Iqbal did not live to see the birth of Pakistan, he is considered by the Pakistanis as the father of their country. The purpose of the Islamic state was to allow the Muslims to create the social and political ideals that the true understanding of the Qur'anic spirit would lead them to actualize.

In methodology and content, Iqbal draws in his writings on his encyclopedic knowledge of both Islamic and Western thought. A true humanist, he rebuts the claims of Orientalists on the backwardness of Islam without reverting to similar attacks on Christian and Western thought. As he criticizes the Muslims for failing to live up to the ideals of Islam, he also condemns various aspects of Western thought, especially the secularism of the West and its materialist and nationalist ideology that led to colonialism and racism. He rejects the culturally centered views of Western thinkers such as Georg Wilhelm Friedrich Hegel and Auguste Comte on the basis that they lead to a fatalistic and deterministic understanding of man's evolution, denying human freedom and creativity. Instead, he insists on the unity of a humanity derived from a single creator expressed in the diversity of human societies engaged in similar attempts at actualizing their divine gifts; thus, he regards all cultures as genuine and equal contributors to human civilization when they try to remain in touch with the divine inspiration that lies at their heart.

Although Iqbal strongly condemns the practices of Sufism, he retains a powerful spirituality that cannot be separated from action in his vision of the complete human being. His writings are a modern rendition of Muslim thought but stand in the same line as the great works of classical Muslim thinkers.

Bibliography

Malik, Hafeez, ed. *Iqbal, Poet-Philosopher of Pakistan.* New York: Columbia University Press, 1971.

Vahid, Syed Abdul. *Iqbal: His Art and Thought.* London: Murray, 1959.

MAYSAM J. AL FARUQI

IRADEH-YE MELLI PARTY

Pro-British political party in Iran, formed in 1943 and dismantled in 1946.

Initially called the Fatherland Party, the Iradeh-ye Melli Party was formed in September 1943 in Iran by Sayyed Ziya Tabataba'i. He was a pro-British journalist who had helped Reza Khan's rise to power in his youth and was made premier in 1921 but was subsequently exiled by Reza Shah Pahlavi, the title assumed by Reza Khan as king of Iran. In 1943

Sayyed Ziya revived his old paper *Ra'd* (Thunder) and called on the *bazaaris* (merchants), *ulama* (clerics), and the tribes to revolt against the military dictatorship of the shah, the "atheistic communism" of Iran's communist-leaning party, the Tudeh, and the corruption of the landed aristocracy. Five months later, Sayyed Ziya renamed the party Iradeh-ye Melli (the National Will). The party had a strong reputation for being pro-British. Included in its program were designs for repeal of all anti-constitutional laws, convening of provincial assemblies, protection of handicraft industries, distribution of state land among peasantry, and formation of a volunteer army. In 1946, the party was dismantled and Sayyed Ziya was arrested by premier Ahmad Qavam as part of the premier's plan for dismantling British influence in the country.

See also PAHLAVI, REZA; TABATABA'I, ZIYA.

Bibliography

Abrahamian, E. *Iran between Two Revolutions.* Princeton, NJ: Princeton University Press, 1982.

PARVANEH POURSHARIATI

IRAN

Country in southwestern Asia between the Caspian Sea and the Persian Gulf.

Iran has an area of 636,290 square miles and an estimated population of 67 million (2004). It is bounded on the north by the Caspian Sea and the republics of Armenia, Azerbaijan, and Turkmenistan; on the east by Afghanistan and Pakistan; on the south by the Persian Gulf and the Gulf of Oman; and on the west by Turkey and Iraq.

Land and Climate

Iran lies on a high plateau with an average altitude of around 4,000 feet, surrounded by the Zagros Mountains, running from the Armenian border to the shores of the Gulf of Oman, and in the north by the Elburz Mountains. An extensive salt desert in the interior is separated from a sand desert by two mountain ranges in the east. Temperatures reach a low of -15°F in the harsh winters of the northwest and a high of about 123°F in the south during the summer, with most of the country enjoying a temperate climate. Average rainfall ranges from 80

A mosque in Tehran, capital and largest city of Iran. The Tehran area was first settled as early as the fourth century B.C.E., but for centuries the major city was Ray, which was destroyed by the Mongols in the thirteenth century. Tehran developed after the destruction of Ray, initially as a village and small market town until Agha Muhammad Khan, the founder of the Qajar dynasty, chose it as his capital in 1788. Tehran now covers an area of 240 square miles and boasts a population of approximately 8 million, with over 3 million more in the suburbs. MOSQUE IN TEHRAN, IRAN, PHOTOGRAPH BY CORY LANGLEY. REPRODUCED BY PERMISSION.

inches along the Caspian coast to less than 2 inches in the southeast.

Population

With an estimated population of 67 million in 2004, Iran is one of the most populous countries in the Middle East. It had grown at over 3 percent per annum from the mid-1950s to the mid-1980s. However, the successful family-planning campaign begun in the late 1980s has decreased the rate to about 1.6 percent. Iran's population is comparatively young; 45.5 percent of the population was under 15 years old in 1986, but that percentage fell to 40 percent in 1996 due to the sharp decline in population growth rate. Approximately two-thirds of Iran's people live in the cities: In 1996 the capital, Tehran, accounted for 7 million; Mashhad for more

than 1.9 million; and Tabriz, Isfahan, and Shiraz for more than 1 million each.

About 80 percent of Iran's population is of Iranian origin, of whom the ethnic Persians are predominant. According to the 1986 census 82.7 percent of the population (90.9% in the urban areas and 73.1% in the rural areas) could both comprehend and speak Persian, and another 2.7 percent could understand it. Persians are overwhelmingly Shiʿite Muslims. Azeris, or Azerbaijanis, are Iran's largest linguistic minority. Estimated at 25 percent of the population, they are concentrated in the provinces of East and West Azerbaijan, Ardabil, and Zanjan, as well as in and around the cities of Qazvin, Saveh, Hamadan, and Tehran. Iran's second largest ethnolinguistic minority, the Kurds, make up an estimated 5 percent of the

country's population and reside in the provinces of Kerman and Kurdistan as well as in parts of West Azerbaijan and Ilam. Kurds in Iran are divided along religious lines as Sunni, Shi'ite, or Ahl-e Haqq. The predominantly Sunni Baluchis reside mainly in the Sistan/Baluchistan province and make up 2 percent of Iran's population. Other ethnic minorities include the Shi'ite Arabs (5%) and the Sunni Turkmen (2%). Also residing in Iran are nomadic and tribal groups, including the Qashqa'is, Bakhtiaris, Shahsevans, Afshars, Boyer Ahmadis, and smaller tribes.

According to the 1996 census, 99.5 percent of the population was Muslim. Followers of the other three officially recognized religions included 279,000 Christians, 28,000 Zoroastrians, and 13,000 Jews. An additional 56,000 were listed as followers of other religions, and 90,000 did not state their religion. The majority of the latter two groups are presumed to be Baha'is, followers of a religion that has not been officially recognized by the government and has been subjected to persecution since the 1979 revolution.

Education

The modern national education system emerged in the 1920s and 1930s, when the influence of the religious establishment was repressed and the control

In November 1979 Iranian students stormed the U.S. embassy in Tehran and took sixty-six Americans hostage. Despite a rescue attempt by the military and the freezing of Iranian assets and oil imports, the majority of the hostages remained in captivity until Iran and the United States signed the Algiers Accord in January 1981. © AP/WIDE WORLD PHOTOS. REPRODUCED BY PERMISSION.

of the rising nation-state over the school system was established. The period from 1956 to 2002 saw the rapid expansion of modern education. The number of students at all levels rose from 1.1 million in 1956 to 7.5 million in 1976, 16 million in 1992, and 18.3 million in 2000 (nearly 30% of the total population). The percentage of girls in elementary schools rose from 21 percent of total enrollment in 1926 to 38 percent in 1976 and 47 percent in 1996; girls in secondary schools increased from 6 percent to 35 percent and then to 47 percent in the same years; and the number in universities leaped from almost none in 1926 to 28 percent in 1976, 57 percent in 1996, and more than 61 percent in 2001. As a result of the adult literacy campaign and the expansion of primary education, the literate population age six and over increased from about 15 per-cent in 1956 to approximately 62 percent in 1976 and 80 percent in 1996.

The educational reforms of 1966 to 1978 marked the transformation of Iran's school system from the French model to one similar to that of the United States. The structure and organization remained virtually intact after the 1979 Islamic Revolution, but the focus of educators became shaping pupils' behavior according to Islamic values through curriculum and textbooks. Other measures included converting all coeducational schools into single-sex institutions and imposing Islamic dress codes. In 1992 secondary education was reduced from four years to three years and divided into general educa-tion (including academic and technical-vocational divisions) and professional education (focusing on

Iranian schoolgirls. Education is compulsory in Iran for children of primary and middle school age. Since the Islamic Revolution in 1979, the number of girls attending public schools, incuding non-mandatory high schools, has incresed from less than 50 percent nationwide to more than 80 percent, and girls comprise over 60 percent of undergraduate college students. © Peter Turnley/Corbis. Reproduced by permission.

specific, practical work-related skills). The twelfth year of high school became a college preparatory program accepting only high school graduates who pass the entrance examination.

In May 1980 the government closed all universities and appointed a panel, the Cultural Revolution Headquarters, to provide a program of reform for higher education in accordance with Islamic values. When the universities were reopened in October 1981, the University Jihad and other militant groups took control and purged 8,000 faculty members (about half). Following disputes between these groups and the Ministry of Culture and Higher Education over reform issues, the Supreme Council of the Cultural Revolution was founded in 1984 to supervise the reconstruction of universities. In 2000 government-sponsored colleges and universities accredited by the Ministry of Culture and Higher Education and technical, vocational, and

teacher training schools (primarily two-year junior colleges) administered by the Ministry of Education and other government agencies enrolled 413,000 students. In addition, the Open Islamic University (836,000 enrollment in 2000) is open to any student upon the payment of fairly steep tuition and fees.

The Economy

Iran's economy is a mixture of large state and semi-public enterprises, small-scale private manufacturing, trade and service ventures, and village agriculture. State enterprises have expanded substantially since the revolution, and market-reform plans set in motion in the 1990s have made little progress toward privatization of large public enterprises. As noted by the International Monetary Fund in 2003, the "Iranian economy continues to face important challenges: employment creation has not been sufficient to meet the rapid increase in the labor force; inflation is high and rising again; and price subsidies and control continues to hinder economic efficiency; and structural impediments for private sector development remain" (International Monetary Fund, p. 1).

The Iranian economy is heavily dependent on oil, which accounted for 15 percent of the total value of gross domestic product (GDP), 50 percent of state revenue, and 75 percent of total exports from 1996 to 2001. It is estimated that Iran's oil reserves are about 93 billion barrels, or 10 percent of the world's total. Iran also possesses the second largest natural gas reserve in the world, estimated at about 20 trillion cubic meters, or 15 percent of the world's reserves. Hydropower, coal, and solar energy resources are also significant, and there are substantial deposits of copper, zinc, chromium, iron ore, and gemstones.

From 1963 to 1976, Iran's GDP grew by an average annual rate of around 10.5 percent in real terms, and per capita income leaped from some US$170 to over $2,060. The 1978–1980 period of revolutionary crisis saw the flight of skilled workers and entrepreneurs, the transfer of large sums of capital abroad, and the abandonment of many productive establishments. Under these circumstances, the GDP in constant 1974 prices fell from 3.7 trillion rials in 1977 to 2.5 trillion in 1980, and per capita GDP declined from 108,000 rials to 63,000 rials. Following a short period of increase in oil revenues and financial recovery, the period of 1985 to 1988 saw an annual GDP decline of 4 percent due to the fall in oil revenues, negative fixed capital formation, and the heightening of the "tanker war" in the Persian Gulf. In the postwar period and between 1988 and 1992 the rise of oil revenues led to an average annual growth rate of 8 percent in the GDP. The annual growth rate of the GDP fluctuated considerably for the next eight years, but averaged about 4 percent. In 2001 agriculture accounted for 19 percent of Iran's GDP, industry for 26 percent, and services for 55 percent. The state together with semipublic organizations created after the revolution own all heavy industries, many other large industrial establishments, and all major transportation networks and agroindustries. Nationalization of large enterprises and confiscation by the revolutionary government considerably expanded the public sector. As a result, all banks (and insurance companies) were owned by the state until 2000, when a more liberal interpretation of the revolutionary constitution led to the enactment of a new law permitting the establishment of privately owned banks and, later, insurance companies. Four newly established private banks compete with state-owned banks.

Modern industry made its appearance in Iran in the early twentieth century, but it was not until the late 1950s that the government adopted a clear industrialization policy. By the early 1970s the average annual growth rate of the industrial sector was more than 10 percent. From the early 2000s, Iran has had an industrial base consisting mainly of import-substituting industries that are subsidized and heavily protected, and dependent on imported materials. Steel, petrochemicals, and copper ore remain Iran's three basic industries.

Only about one-fourth of Iran is potentially suitable for agricultural production—the other three-fourths receives less than 10 inches of rainfall per year—and less than half of the crops grown are irrigated. In 2001 wheat production amounted to 9.5 million, sugar beets 4.6, potatoes 3.6, barley 2.4, rice 2, and onions 1.3 million tons. In 1998 livestock and dairy products included 763,000 tons of red meat, 5 million tons of milk, 720 tons of poultry, and 625 tons of eggs.

After the revolution, imports fell from $14.6 billion in 1977 to $10.8 billion in 1980 and $8.2 billion in 1988. In 1991 imports rose to $25 billion, then declined between 1993 and 1995 due to the fall of oil revenues, reaching an annual average of $14 billion in the late 1990s. Non-oil exports rose from $2.9 billion in 1992 to $4.2 billion in 2000. In 1999 Iran's total exports (including oil) amounted to $21 billion and its imports amounted to $14.3 billion. Iran's main export markets for both oil and non-oil goods are Japan and United Kingdom; together they accounted for nearly one-third of Iran's total exports in 1999. Germany, with an annual export of $1 to $2 billion goods in the postrevolution period, is the main exporter to Iran.

Government

Iran is a theocratic republic that combines the absolute authority of the ruling Shi'ite jurist combined with an elected president and parliament and an appointed chief of the judicial branch. The sovereignty of Shi'ite clerical authority (velayat-e faqih), the supreme spiritual guide, is the deputy of the twelfth Shi'ite imam, the Lord of the Age. He appoints the head of the judiciary branch and the theologians of the Council of Guardians of the Constitution, and as commander in chief of the armed forces, he appoints and dismisses all commanders of the armed forces, Revolutionary Guards Corps, and security forces and is empowered to declare war. The president, elected for four years, is the head of the cabinet and the civilian wing of the government's executive branch.

The legislature comprises two institutions: the parliament (Majles) and the Council of Guardians. Under the provisions of the constitution all bills must be approved by the Majles and then be ratified by the Council of Guardians before they are signed into law by the president. The Majles is a body of 290 legislators elected to four-year terms. The twelve members of the Council of Guardians, consisting of six clerics and six lay judges appointed by the supreme guide, review legislation passed by the Majles and are empowered by the constitution to veto laws considered to violate Islamic or constitutional principles. The appointed Expediency Council, created in February 1988 and formally recognized in an amendment to the constitution in July 1989, rules on legal and theological disputes between the Majles and the Council of Guardians. It is charged with ruling in the best interest of the community, even when such rulings go beyond a strict interpretation of the tenets of Islamic law. The elected Assembly of Experts determines succession to the supreme guide.

The judicial branch consists of regular civil and criminal courts, as well as a special clerical court and revolutionary tribunals that hear civil and criminal suits concerning counterrevolutionary offenses. The head of the judiciary is appointed by the supreme guide. The minister of justice functions as a liaison among the judicial, executive, and legislative branches. The Supreme Council of Cultural Revolution has legislative powers over educational matters.

Iran is divided into twenty-eight provinces (ostans) administered by governors (ostandars) who are nominated by the minister of the interior and appointed by the president. The second level of local government consists of 195 counties (shahrestans) under junior governors (farmandars). At the third level, 500 districts (bakhshs) are under executives (bakhshdars), and at the fourth level, 1,581 clusters of villages (dehestans) are under headmen (dehdars). Villages, the base level, are administered by elected councils. Towns and cities have municipal governments with mayors and councils.

The armed forces and Revolutionary Guards Corps are responsible for defending Iran against foreign aggression. The 300,000-man army is organized into ten divisions and six brigades. The air force consists of about 35,000 men, with more than 400 pilots on active duty and 100 combat aircraft. The 15,000-man navy operates in the Persian Gulf, the Indian Ocean, and the Caspian Sea. It includes two fleets, three marine battalions, and two Russian-made submarines. The 180,000-member Revolutionary Guard Corps is organized into eleven regional commands with four armored divisions and twenty-four infantry divisions, as well as air and naval capacities. Iran's police force incorporates revolutionary committees and the rural police force into the urban police force. The suppression of opposition to the regime is the responsibility of the Ministry of Information and a 100,000-man mobilization corps (basij) recruited from veterans of the Iran–Iraq War (1980–1988). Ideological-political bureaus have been established in government agencies and in the armed forces to ensure conformity to the regime's rules of conduct. The armed forces and security organizations are under the command of the supreme spiritual guide.

Since the 1979 revolution various groups, organizations, and factions within the ruling party have fallen into four main political camps. First, those who support the interests of the religious groups (ulama) and the bazaar merchants, and who advocate the traditional Islamic jurisprudence, are referred to as conservatives, traditionalists, or rightists. The conservatives fear the cultural penetration of Western lifestyles and are zealous on cultural issues such as women's rights, Islamic dress codes, music, and the media. In the early post-Khomeini era, a major political shift to the right occurred and the conservative camp prevailed. Second, those who support the cause of the economically deprived (mostaz'afan) and advocate a progressive Islamic jurisprudence, distributive justice, and tighter state control of the private sector are called radicals, leftists, or followers of Imam Ruhollah Khomeini's line. Receptive to Western progressive ideas and more tolerant on cultural issues, the radicals are nevertheless highly suspicious of Western imperialism and Iran's dependency on the world capitalist system. The Bureau for Promotion of Unity (Daftar-e Tahkim-e Vahdat), major student unions, and the young Combatant Clerics (Ruhaniyun-e Mobarez) are among the radical organizations. In much of the 1980s the radicals dominated the regime. Third, those who advocate a pragmatic approach—the new middle-class professional and bureaucratic groups—and are concerned with peaceful coexistence in the modern world under a mixed economy are called pragmatists, centrists, or moderates. Former president Ali Akbar Hashemi Rafsanjani has led the centrist camp since its inception in the late 1980s. In the fourth Majles (1992–1996) conservatives controlled more than two-thirds of the seats, pragmatists around one-fifth, and radicals about one-tenth.

In the mid 1990s a popular, reformist movement emerged when there was a major shift in the ideological orientation of the leftist faction from a radical to a relatively moderate and liberal interpretation of Islam. The roots of this ideological shift can be traced to a series of political developments since the revolution, including various failures of the revolutionary regime to fulfill its populist and egalitarian promises; a considerable erosion in the legitimacy of the ruling clerics; the successful (though largely silent) resistance by youth and women to the culturally restrictive policies of the Islamic Republic; the rise of a distinctly antifundamentalist, liberal-reformist interpretation of Islam by a number of Iranian theologians and religious intellectuals; and the precipitous decline in the popularity of revolutionary ideas in the 1990s.

The main Islamic opposition to the regime inside the country includes the liberal Iran Freedom Movement (Nahzat-e Azadi-ye Iran), established in the early 1960s under the leadership of Mehdi Bazargan, who was prime minister in the provisional revolutionary government of 1979. Also organized by Bazargan to fight against frequent violations of human rights in Iran was the Society for the Defense of Liberty and National Sovereignty of the Iranian Nation. Another organization active in Iran is the nationalist Nation of Iran Party (Hezb-e Mellat-e Iran). These groups have been outlawed and systematically suppressed by the government. Absence of opportunities for genuine political participation, imposition of a strict Islamic code of conduct, and, above all, shrinking opportunities for employment have led to increasing alienation of young intellectuals and students.

There are several opposition groups among the one million Iranian political and cultural exiles in Europe and the United States, including liberal nationalists such as the National Front, whose origin can be traced to the period of Mohammad Mossadegh, and a number of small groups that advocate the establishment of a secular, Western-style parliamentary system in Iran. Also active are monarchists seeking to resurrect Pahlavi rule through the former Crown Prince Reza Pahlavi. A few small leftist groups conduct a propaganda campaign against the regime through newspapers and magazines. The most active, militant opposition force has been the People's Mojahedin of Iran (Mojahedin-e Khalq-e Iran). Between 1987 and 2003 it waged guerrilla operations and a military offensive against Iran from its camps across the border in Iraq.

History since 1800

Iran began the nineteenth century under the Qajar Dynasty (1796–1925) and the political and economic influence of Russia and Great Britain. Two wars with Russia were ended by the treaties of Golestan (1813) and Turkmanchai (1828), and Russia took over the area north of the Araks River. Following a futile attempt by Iran to reclaim Herat, its former territory in western Afghanistan, the British waged war in 1857 and forced Iran to give up all claims to British-controlled Afghanistan. To resist the European expansionist schemes, Crown Prince Abbas Mirza initiated a series of military reforms in the 1820s that were continued by more comprehensive reforms of the grand vizier Mirza Taqi Khan Amir Kabir in the mid-nineteenth century. Mirza Hosayn Khan Sepahsalar continued the reforms of his predecessor in the early 1870s.

In the latter half of the nineteenth century, Russia and Britain increased their economic and political domination over Iran. European companies were granted trade concessions that often were disadvantageous to nascent Iranian industries and local merchants. Meanwhile, new ideas of political freedom were introduced by intellectuals and others who had come in contact with the West. The 1890 grant of a tobacco concession by Naser al-Din Shah to a British citizen provoked the local tobacco merchants and the *ulama* to instigate riots that eventually forced cancellation of the concession. Many intellectuals and popular religious leaders believed that by reforming the government they could improve the country's economic and social conditions and ensure its political independence. Antigovernment protests were led by a broad alliance of Islamic clergymen, intellectuals, and merchants. On 30 December 1906 the ailing monarch, Mozaffar al-Din Qajar, finally yielded to demands for a constitution. In 1907 Great Britain and Russia divided Iran into two spheres of influence and a neutral zone. With the outbreak of World War I in 1914, Iran declared its neutrality; nevertheless, Britain and Russia occupied the country, spying on each other and engaging in hostilities on Iran's territory.

In February 1921 a pro-British journalist, Sayyed Ziya al-Din Tabataba'i, and Brigadier Reza Pahlavi staged a bloodless coup and took control of the government in Tehran. With the army as his power base, Reza became the country's monarch in 1925 and founded the Pahlavi Dynasty. After establishing the authority of the central government throughout the country in the 1920s, he tried to Westernize Iran's economic and social institutions in the 1930s. He replaced the traditional religious schools and courts with a secular system of education and a judicial system based on European legal patterns. He created a modern army and national police force and established a number of state-owned industrial enterprises and a modern transport system. The period of his rule (1925–1941), however, was marked by suppression of individual freedoms and political activities.

In August 1941 troops from the Soviet Union and Britain invaded Iran and forced Pahlavi to abdicate his throne to his son, Mohammad Reza. After the conclusion of World War II, the Soviet Union refused to withdraw its forces from Iran. Through a combination of international pressure and internal maneuverings by Prime Minister Ahmad Qavam, Russia's forces finally left in late 1946, and the pro-Soviet autonomous government of Azerbaijan and the Republic of Kurdistan collapsed. For much of this period, the young shah and his cabinets were forced to conform to the will of the parliament, which was dominated by the old-guard politicians and propertied classes. Following an attempted assassination of the shah on 4 February 1949, the pro-Soviet Tudeh Party was outlawed. The Constitutional Assembly that convened on 21 April granted the shah the right to dissolve the Majles.

At the beginning of the 1950s the National Front, a loose coalition of liberal nationalists under the leadership of Mohammad Mossadegh, demanded greater control over the British-dominated Anglo-Iranian Oil Company. The oil industry was nationalized, and Mossadegh became prime minister in April 1951. The Soviet-backed Tudeh Party strongly opposed the nationalization and the Mossadegh government. In a struggle with the shah over control of the armed forces, Mossadegh resigned, and Ahmad Qavam was appointed premier on 18 July 1952. Three days later, riots broke out in Tehran and major cities; Qavam was forced to resign and Mossadegh was reinstated.

In August 1953 a coup conceived by the British MI6 and delivered by the U.S. CIA ousted Mossadegh; Fazlollah Zahedi became prime minister. The new regime ordered the arrest of supporters of the National Front and the Tudeh Party and placed severe restrictions on all forms of opposition to the government. Between 1953 and 1959 the shah's power gradually increased, and the government signed an agreement with a consortium of major Western oil companies in August 1954, joined the Baghdad Pact in October 1955, and with CIA assistance established an effective intelligence agency (SAVAK) in 1957.

In the early 1960s, under increasing pressure from the U.S. Kennedy administration, the shah appointed Ali Amini as prime minister and Hassan Arsanjani as minister of agriculture, and the government initiated a series of social and economic reforms later called the White Revolution. In January 1963 a national referendum supported six reform measures including land reform, women's suffrage, workers' sharing up to 20 percent of industrial profits, and the nationalization of the forests. Major urban uprisings protested the referendum and the government's arrest of Ayatollah Ruhollah Khomeini in June 1963. After cracking down on rioters, the shah emerged as an autocratic ruler. He allocated oil revenues among state agencies and projects, and he directly supervised the armed forces and security organizations, foreign policy and oil negotiations, nuclear power plants, and huge development projects. The latter half of the 1960s was marked by relative political stability and economic development, and Iran emerged as the regional power in the Persian Gulf after the withdrawal of British forces in 1971. Following border clashes between Iran and Iraq in the early 1970s, an agreement between the two nations was signed in Algeria in 1975. By the mid-1970s Iran had established close ties not only with the United States and Western Europe but also with the Communist Bloc countries, South Africa, and Israel.

Meanwhile, land reform and the rise of a modern bureaucracy eliminated the traditional foundation of the regime—the *ulama,* the bazaar merchants, and the landowning classes. They were replaced by entrepreneurs, young Western-educated bureaucratic elites, and new middle classes discontented with the shah and his policies. The entrepreneurial and bureaucratic elites were unhappy with their lack of political power, the intelligentsia resented violations of human rights, and the *ulama* and the bazaar merchants resented the Western lifestyles, promoted by the state's modernization policies, that contravened Islamic traditions. Under these circumstances, the nucleus of a revolutionary coalition was formed by leaders with ready access to the extensive human, financial, and spatial resources of the bazaar, the mosque, and the school-university networks. They saw an opportunity to challenge the shah after the victory of human-rights champion Jimmy Carter in the U.S. presidential race of November 1976.

In the summer of 1977 a series of open letters written by intellectuals, liberal figures, and professional groups demanded observance of human rights. An article published in the daily *Ettela'at* on 7 January 1978 attacked Khomeini, and violent clashes between religious opposition groups and security forces took place in Qom on 9 January. This conflict marked the beginning of a series of religious commemorations of the fortieth day of mourning (a Shi'ite rite) for those who had been martyred in various cities. In July and August, riots erupted in Mashhad, Isfahan, and Shiraz. September 1978 began with the first mass demonstrations against the shah's regime. Striking government employees brought the oil industry to a standstill on 31 October. Mass strikes continued through early November, when a military government was installed by the shah, and in December hundreds of thousands of people demonstrated in Tehran. In all, approximately 2,500 persons were killed in clashes between demonstrators and the security forces from January 1978 to February 1979. The shah left Iran for Egypt on 16 January 1979, and Khomeini returned to Tehran on 1 February. Four days later, he appointed Mehdi Bazargan prime minister of a provisional government. On 11 February the army's Supreme Council ordered the troops back to their barracks. Military installations were occupied by the people, and major army commanders were arrested.

The April 1979 national referendum sanctioned the declaration of the Islamic Republic of Iran, the December 1979 national referendum approved the constitution, and in January 1980 Abolhasan Bani Sadr was elected the republic's first president. He was impeached by the Majles for opposing the ruling clerical establishment and dismissed from office by Khomeini in June 1981. In July Mohammad Ali Raja'i was elected president; in August a bomb exploded in the prime minister's office, killing the new president and Mohammad Javad Bahonar, the new prime minister. In October Ayatollah Sayyed Ali Khamenehi was elected the third president of the Islamic Republic, and the Majles endorsed the radical prime minister, Mir-Hosain Musavi.

On 4 November 1979 the U.S. embassy in Tehran was occupied by a group of militant students, and sixty-six Americans were taken hostage. The seizure was in response to alleged U.S. interference in Iran's internal affairs and to the U.S. decision in October to admit the shah for medical treatment. President Carter ordered the freezing of some $12 billion of Iran's assets in the United States on 14 November. After 444 days in captivity, the last of the hostages were released on 20 January 1981 as Ronald Reagan was inaugurated U.S. president. Five years later, in September 1986, it was reported that Iran had secretly received 508 U.S.-built missiles in a clandestine "arms-for-hostages" deal with the United States to intercede for the release of American hostages in Lebanon; this episode became known as the Iran–Contra Affair.

Frustrated by an imposed 1975 border agreement and heartened by Iran's military weakness after the 1979 revolution, Iraq invaded Iran on 22 September 1980. After rapidly occupying large areas of southwestern Iran and destroying the oil refinery at Abadan, Iraq's forces became bogged down in siege warfare. In an offensive in May 1982 Iran recaptured the strategic town of Khorramshahr, and its forces entered Iraq. Initiating the "war of the cities," Iraq's forces launched air attacks on Iran's cities in 1984. In May 1987 the United States began direct intervention in Persian Gulf affairs by escorting eleven Kuwaiti oil tankers under the U.S. flag. This action led to increased attacks against oil tankers and merchant ships. After a long pause, the war of the cities resumed in early 1988, when Iraq launched missile attacks against Tehran and other cities, and both Tehran and Baghdad came under fire from ground-to-ground missiles. On 3 July 1988 the U.S. warship *Vincennes,* stationed in the Strait of Hormuz near Bandar Abbas, shot down a civilian Iranian airliner over the Persian Gulf, killing all 290 people aboard. On 18 July Iran accepted UN Security Council cease-fire Resolution 598. The eight-year Iran–Iraq War left about one million casualties and cost several hundred billion dollars in damages and military expenditures.

On 3 June 1989 Ayatollah Khomeini died, and the Assembly of Experts elected President Ali Khamenehi as the supreme spiritual guide of the Islamic Republic; the change of leadership marked the beginning of a major shift of power from the radical left to the conservative right. In July Ali Akbar Hashemi Rafsanjani was elected president, and he was re-elected for a second term in 1993. Rafsanjani's policies for economic, sociocultural, and political reforms were obstructed by the radical faction of the left between 1989 and 1993, and then by the rising conservatives on the right. At this juncture, a new coalition was formed between the moderate, pragmatist group that followed Rafsanjani and the radical, leftist faction within the regime who were excluded from power by the conservative and fundamentalist forces.

Mohammad Khatami's 1997 presidential campaign platform emphasized the rule of law, building a civil society, a moderate foreign policy, and the protection of civil liberties guaranteed by the Islamic constitution. His victory was as much a man-

ifestation of the voters' rejection of the extremist politics of the left in the 1980s and the right in the 1990s as it was an affirmation of Khatami's moderate, well-reasoned, and liberal campaign statements. His 1997 electoral triumph over Ali Akbar Nateq-Nuri would not have been possible, furthermore, without the vast human and financial resources that were contributed to his campaign by members of the pragmatist camp of the incumbent president, Rafsanjani, as well as the many formerly radical elements within the regime. During much of Khatami's first presidential term (1997–2001), his supporters rallied behind the slogans of civil society and the rule of law, but they were besieged by the conservatives, who had gained effective control over key positions within the Islamic state. These included positions in the judiciary and the Council of Guardians, the armed forces and the militia, the intelligence services and vigilante groups working in tandem with them, the broadcast media, and the para-statal foundations. The latter, putatively philanthropic foundations that are not subject to the fiscal and regulatory agencies of the state, form a massive network of patronage and corruption and "an economy within the economy" that effectively controls as much as one-third of the country's domestic production.

Khatami's election victory in 1997 was followed by two other sweeping wins by reformist candidates in the municipal elections of 1999 and the Majles elections of 2000. In the 2000 election the reformists won some 200 of the 290 seats in parliament, thus giving the pro-Khatami candidates a decisive majority in the legislative body, but the conservatives, on the defensive against a formidable majority of the people, resorted to tactics of intimidation and vigilantism against their political rivals. Through their control of the judiciary they started a systematic crackdown of the press, intellectuals, and other outspoken critics of the regime.

In July 1999 *Salam,* a popular pro-reform newspaper, was closed by the order of the Press Court. Following peaceful demonstrations on the campus of Tehran University against the closure, militia forces entered the student dormitories and brutally attacked students, killing one of them in the assault, and injuring and arresting hundreds. The dormitory assault ignited a series of protests over the next several days that escalated into full-scale riots when the demonstrators were attacked by vigilante partisans of the Party of God (Ansar-e Hezbollah). In April 2000 the conservative-dominated judiciary continued the campaign of intimidation against the press. More than forty pro-reform newspapers and magazines were forcibly closed because of their alleged "denigration of Islam and the religious elements of the Islamic revolution." Over the next several months, journalists and editors were the primary targets of the conservatives' attacks against the print media. Iran's best-known investigative journalist and the editor of the newspaper *Fath*, Akbar Ganji, was sentenced to ten years in prison (later reduced to six years) for his writings that implicated several senior officials in the 1998 murders of five intellectuals and political activists. This and the imprisonment of another two dozen well-known journalists prompted the Paris-based Reporters sans Frontiers to dub Iran "the largest prison for journalists in the world."

In April 2000 several prominent Iranian intellectuals, journalists, publishers, and women's rights activists traveled to Berlin to attend an international conference on the future of reform in Iran. Upon their return to Iran many of the participants were brought to trial before the Revolutionary Court in Tehran on charges of conspiring to overthrow the Islamic Republic. In March 2001 the judiciary ordered the closure of the religious-nationalist Iran Freedom Movement (the only tolerated opposition group in the country since the revolution) on charges of attempting to overthrow the Islamic Republic, arresting and detaining twenty-one of its leading members. Khatami's failure to implement his promised political reforms and the lack of any significant improvement in the economy during his first four-year term did not prevent him winning the June 2001 presidential election with 77 percent of the vote. In spite of two mandates for change that he has been given by an overwhelming majority of his countrymen, and even though pro-reform candidates are in control of the Majles as well, Khatami faces the same constitutional constraints and political obstacles from his conservative opponents that stymied his first presidential term.

The catastrophic attacks on the World Trade Center and Pentagon on 11 September 2001 brought a new phase in United States–Iran rela-

tions. Iranian authorities promptly condemned the terrorist attacks, and the mayor of Tehran sent a message of sympathy to the mayor of New York City. The Iranian people showed their sympathy by organizing gatherings in commemoration of the victims of 9/11. In response to the terrorist attacks, the U.S. government put together what it called a coalition against terrorism. As part of this approach, it lent aid to the Northern Alliance, the forces that Iran had supported from their formation in 1996 to fight against the Taliban regime and Osama bin Ladin's forces in Afghanistan. Following 9/11, Iranian and U.S. military advisors worked side by side with Afghan opposition forces to bring down the Taliban. After dismantling the Taliban network and creating a new regime in Afghanistan in Fall 2001, neoconservatives in the Bush administration supported regime change in a number of other countries. This policy unfolded on 29 January 2002 when in his State of the Union address President Bush labeled Iran, Iraq, and North Korea as an "Axis of Evil." On 13 December 2002 the United States accused Iran of launching a secret nuclear weapons program and published satellite images of two sites under construction in the towns of Natanz and Arak. Iran denied any military purpose behind its nuclear activities and agreed to inspections by the Vienna-based International Atomic Energy Agency (IAEA), but refrained from "full cooperation." Despite Iran's insistence that its nuclear program—which included uranium-enrichment activities—was designed to meet its energy needs only, the IAEA gave Iran until 31 October 2003 to provide evidence that it was not trying to build nuclear weapons. Persuaded by the foreign ministers of Great Britain, France, and Germany, Tehran agreed to "total transparency" over its nuclear activities, promising full cooperation with the UN's nuclear agency and agreeing to suspend uranium enrichment, while reserving the right to resume the process if it deemed necessary.

The 2003 Nobel Peace Prize was awarded to the Iranian human-rights activist and ardent reformist Shirin Ebadi, boosting Iranian hopes for the rule of law, justice, and democracy. Yet, in spite of the appeal of liberal-democratic ideas of individual freedom, pluralism, and political tolerance, and the overwhelming endorsement of these ideas in four national elections, the reform movement has had but a limited influence on Iran's political conditions. The willingness of the conservative forces to heed the popular mandate for greater political and cultural freedoms, economic reform, and respect for law—and, above all, for an end to the use of violence—will determine whether a gradualist course of reform will succeed.

See also AHL-E HAQQ; AHVAZ; AZERBAIJAN; AZERBAIJAN CRISIS; BAGHDAD PACT (1955); BAHA'I FAITH; BALUCHIS; BANI SADR, ABOLHASAN; BAZARGAN, MEHDI; EBADI, SHIRIN; GANJI, AKBAR; HAMADAN; IRAN–CONTRA AFFAIR; IRANIAN LANGUAGES; IRANIAN REVOLUTION (1979); IRAN–IRAQ WAR (1980–1988); ISFAHAN; KERMAN; KHAMENEHI, ALI; KHATAMI, MOHAMMAD; KHOMEINI, RUHOLLAH; KURDISTAN; KURDS; MASHHAD; MOJAHEDIN-E KHALQ; MOSSADEGH, MOHAMMAD; MOZAFFAR AL-DIN QAJAR; MUSAVI, MIR-HOSAIN; NASER AL-DIN SHAH; NATEQ-NURI, ALI AKBAR; NATIONAL FRONT, IRAN; PAHLAVI, MOHAMMAD REZA; PAHLAVI, REZA; PERSIAN; QAJAR DYNASTY; QOM; RAFSANJANI, ALI AKBAR HASHEMI; SHI'ISM; SHIRAZ; SISTAN AND BALUCHISTAN; SUNNI ISLAM; TABATABA'I, ZIYA; TABRIZ; TEHRAN; TOBACCO REVOLT; TUDEH PARTY; TURKMANCHAI, TREATY OF (1828); UNITED STATES OF AMERICA AND THE MIDDLE EAST; VELAYAT-E FAQIH; WHITE REVOLUTION (1961–1963); ZAHEDAN.

Bibliography

Abrahamian, Ervand. *Iran between Two Revolutions.* Princeton, NJ: Princeton University Press, 1982.

Akhavi, Shahrough. *Religion and Politics in Contemporary Iran: Clergy–State Relations in the Pahlavi Period.* Albany: State University of New York Press, 1980.

Amuzegar, Jahangir. *Iran's Economy under the Islamic Republic.* London: I. B. Tauris, 1993.

Ashraf, Ahmad. "Charisma, Theocracy, and Men of Power in Postrevolutionary Iran." In *The Politics of Social Transformation in Afghanistan, Iran, and Pakistan,* edited by Myron Weiner and Ali Banuazizi. Syracuse, NY: Syracuse University Press, 1994.

Ashraf, Ahmad. "From the White Revolution to the Islamic Revolution." In *Iran after the Revolution: The Crisis of an Islamic State,* edited by Sohrab Behdad and Said Rahnema. London: I. B. Tauris, 1995.

Ashraf, Ahmad, and Banuazizi, Ali. "Iran's Tortuous Path toward 'Islamic Liberalism.'" *International Journal of Politics, Culture, and Society* 15, no. 2 (Winter 2001): 237–256.

Ashraf, Ahmad, and Banuazizi, Ali. "The State, Classes, and Modes of Stabilization in the Iranian Revolution." *State, Culture, and Society* 1, no. 3 (1985).

Dabashi, Hamid. *Theology of Discontent: The Ideological Foundation of the Islamic Revolution in Iran.* New York: New York University Press, 1993.

Hooglund, Eric, ed. *Twenty Years of Islamic Revolution: Political and Social Transitions in Iran Since 1979.* Syracuse, NY: Syracuse University Press, 2002.

International Monetary Fund. "Islamic Republic of Iran and IMF." *Public Information Notices* (25 August 2003).

Moin, Baqer. *Khomeini: The Life of the Ayatollah.* London and New York: I. B. Tauris, 1999.

Moslem, Mehdi. *Factional Politics in Post-Khomeini Iran.* Syracuse, NY: Syracuse University Press, 2002.

Schirazi, Asghar. *The Constitution of Iran: Politics and the State in the Islamic Republic.* London: I. B. Tauris, 1997.

AHMAD ASHRAF

IRAN-CONTRA AFFAIR

U.S. political scandal involving Iran, Israel, and Nicaragua.

There were no official relations between the United States and Iran after the long U.S. embassy hostage crisis during the Iranian revolution from 1979 to 1981. Beginning in 1984, Shi'ite groups in Lebanon began kidnapping U.S. citizens and other Westerners. The hostage crisis involved the Central Intelligence Agency (CIA) when William Buckley, station chief in Beirut, was seized in March 1984. Out of concern for the release of Buckley, who could potentially reveal U.S. intelligence information, and in the belief that Iran had influence over the kidnappers, the U.S. administration launched an operation whereby missiles and military spare parts were sent to Iran via Israel. This shipment resulted in the release of one U.S. hostage, but not of Buckley, who was already dead. U.S. officials traveled to Iran to establish contacts, and further arms shipments were made.

At the same time and in a completely unrelated effort, the U.S. administration tried to figure out ways to bypass a congressional prohibition of U.S. assistance to the Contra rebels who were attempting to overthrow the leftist Sandinista government in Nicaragua. Lt. Col. Oliver North of the National Security Council devised a plan in which the proceeds from the Iranian sales would fund the Contras. This policy violated both the U.S. commitment not to negotiate with terrorists and the prohibition on aiding the Contra rebels (the two Boland Amendments).

In late 1986 a Beirut-based magazine reported that there were secret negotiations between U.S. officials and Iranians. This led to investigations in the United States and exposure of the operations. U.S. president Ronald Reagan appointed a special commission under the direction of former senator John Tower to investigate. Later, there was a joint congressional committee formed and a special prosecutor appointed. In the end, only some of those involved (North and the two successive National Security Advisers: Robert McFarlane and John Poindexter) were tried and even fewer convicted of any wrongdoing, but it was a political scandal that compromised U.S. credibility with its allies for having violated its pledge not to negotiate with terrorists, and for having sent arms to Iran and having violated a legal ban on providing assistance to the Contras. The actual involvement of President Reagan and of Vice President George H. W. Bush was never clearly established as far as illegal activities were concerned.

See also BUSH, GEORGE HERBERT WALKER; REAGAN, RONALD.

Bibliography

Bill, James A. "The U.S. Overture to Iran, 1985–1986: An Analysis." In *Neither East nor West: Iran, the Soviet Union, and the United States,* edited by Nikki R. Keddie and Mark J. Gasiorowski. New Haven, CT: Yale University Press, 1990.

Woodward, Bob. *Veil: The Secret Wars of the CIA, 1981–1987.* New York: Simon & Schuster, 1987.

BRYAN DAVES
UPDATED BY OLIVER BENJAMIN HEMMERLE

IRANIAN ART

See ART

IRANIAN BUREAU OF WOMEN'S AFFAIRS

A bureau created to improve conditions for women through education, training, and the reform of laws affecting women's status.

The Iranian Bureau of Women's Affairs was created in December 1991. The idea for its founding came from Marziyeh Seddiqi, an American-educated Iranian engineer who later became the bureau's head of planning and research and a member of the Fifth Parliament (1996–2000), and from Shahla Habibi, whom President Hashemi Rafsanjani later appointed director of the bureau and his adviser on women's affairs. These two women had worked closely together, organizing a seminar on the issue, calling for the cooperation of cabinet ministers, and submitting the project of creating the bureau to the president. An offshoot of the presidential office, the bureau's goal was to identify and ameliorate problems in the condition of women and to propose solutions that would elevate women's status and promote their economic, social, cultural, and political participation. Its projects included work on women's education and training, women's managerial skills, reform of the civil code and divorce law, sending female students abroad for higher education, and creating a center for women's employment and a center to provide women with legal advice. Ma'soumeh Ebtekar, a university professor and the editor of a woman's journal, *Farzaneh,* who in 1997 became vice president in charge of the protection of the environment, was in charge of the bureau's education and training program. The bureau worked closely with the High Council of the Cultural Revolution, which determines general policies of the state, with the Social and Cultural Council of Women (created in 1987), with cabinet ministers, and with members of parliament. As a result of this collaboration, women's commissions or bureaus were created in various ministries, cabinet ministers appointed advisers on women's affairs, and several motions were presented by women members of parliament to ameliorate the status of women. Following President Mohammad Khatami's election in 1997, the bureau changed its name and became the Center for Women's Participation, chaired by Zahra Shojaie.

See also GENDER: GENDER AND LAW; GENDER: GENDER AND POLITICS.

AZADEH KIAN-THIÉBAUT

IRANIAN FILM

See FILM

IRANIAN LANGUAGES

Family of languages spoken in Iran and adjacent countries.

The Iranian languages are closely related to those of the Indo–Aryan family, such as Sanskrit, Hindi, and Urdu; both families (the Indo–Iranian and Indo–Aryan languages) are part of the Indo–European language family, which also contains the Germanic, Slavic, Celtic, Romance, and Greek languages. The principal Iranian languages and groups of languages or dialects are discussed below.

The Southern and Southwestern Languages

Modern Persian is the official language of Iran, Afghanistan, and Tajikistan. There are numerous local variants, the most important being the spoken Persian of Afghanistan (Dari) and of Tajikistan (Tajik). The differences between standard Persian and Dari are not great; but the grammar of Tajik, especially the verbal system, has long been influenced by the neighboring Turkic languages and contains constructions that are foreign to standard Persian. Some of the earliest major Modern Persian texts, written by Persian Jews in the Hebrew alphabet, are in several variants of Persian and contain many archaic features.

Modern Persian is descended from Middle Persian, which is known through documents from the late Parthian and Sassanian periods (from c. 200 C.E.). The earliest examples are on coins from the rulers of Fars and inscriptions from the early Sassanian kings that are written in a local variant of the Aramaic alphabet. The Middle Persian Zoroastrian scriptures were written in a more developed variant of the same script, the Pahlavi alphabet, in which many letters are not distinguished. There is also a large Manichaean literature written in a Syriac script, and a few fragments of Christian texts.

Middle Persian is descended from Old Persian, the language of the Achaemenid inscriptions composed by Darius and Xerxes and their successors (c. 520–340 B.C.E.). It is written in a simple cuneiform script invented by the Persians, rather than the complex cuneiform systems of the Babylonians and Elamites in use at the time.

The languages (dialects) spoken in southern and southwestern Iran in the areas of Bakhtiar, Lorestan, and Fars are all more closely related to Persian than to other Iranian languages.

Kurdish is spoken mainly in western Iran, eastern Iraq, Turkey, and in the southern areas of the former Soviet Union. There are several dialect groups: southern (e.g., Kermanshahi), central (e.g., Sorani, Mokri), and northern (e.g., Kurmanji).

West and east-northeast of Tehran, in Mazandaran, and along the southwestern coast of the Caspian Sea a group of related languages is spoken: Tati, Taleshi, Gilaki, Mazandarani, Semnani, and others. Probably also a member of this group is Zaza or Dimili, spoken in eastern Turkey. All of these languages may be ultimately related to the Parthian language, known through documents and Manichaean texts (c. 1st century B.C.E.–3rd century C.E.).

South of the Central Desert, Dasht-e Kavir, a group of languages referred to as the Central Dialects is spoken: Khuri, Naʿini, the dialect of the Zoroastrians of Yazd and Kerman, and others. These may be related to the ancient Median language, the official language of the Median state (c. 700–560 B.C.E.).

In southeastern Iran there are three related languages in several dialects: Larestani and North and South Bashkardi.

Baluchi is spoken mainly in eastern Iran and Pakistan. It has several dialects.

The Northern or Northeastern Languages

North and northeast of Iran, descendants of the various Scythian or Saka languages are still spoken.

Ossetic, in three dialects, is spoken in the Caucasus. It is the descendant of the old Alanic language(s), of which fragments are known.

Pakhtun is spoken in Afghanistan, where it is official language, and in northwest Pakistan.

Numerous languages are spoken in Afghanistan, north of the Afghan border with the central Asian republics, and east of the border with Pakistan; none of them has a written tradition. The most important are the Shughni group (Shughni, Sarikoli,

Yazghulami, Roshani, etc.), Yidgha and Munji (Munjani), Yaghnobi, and Wakhi.

Yaghnobi is descended from a dialect of Sogdian, a Middle Iranian language known from a large corpus of Buddhist, Manichaean, and Christian texts, as well as secular documents (4th–10th centuries, C.E.).

Wakhi is related to the Middle Iranian language Khotanese, spoken in Chinese Turkistan and known from a rich Buddhist literature and secular documents (c. 5th–10th centuries C.E.).

Two other Middle Iranian languages, Bactrian (c. 1st century B.C.E.–c. 4th century C.E.) and Chorasmian (Khwarazmian; c. 3rd–14th centuries C.E.), have no known descendants.

Avestan is the language of the holy scriptures of the Zoroastrians. Old Avestan is very similar to the language of the Indian *Rigveda* and may have been spoken about the middle of the second millennium B.C.E. Young Avestan is similar to Old Persian and may have been spoken throughout the first half of the first millennium B.C.E.

Among the many grammatical features that distinguish the Iranian languages from one another three can be mentioned.

Gender

The distinction between grammatical masculine and feminine has been lost in Modern Persian and Balochi but exists in Kurdish and Pakhtun. For example: Persian, *in mard/zan āmad*; Pakhtun, *dā saṛay rāγay* (this man came) but *dā šəja rāγla* (this woman came).

Cases

In many Iranian languages two or more cases are distinguished (in Ossetic, nine). For example: Mazandarani, *per ume* (my father came), *pére sere* ([my] father's house), Baluchi, *ē ā mardē gis int* (this is that man's house), *gisā int* (it is in the house), Pakhtun, *da de saṛī kitāb* (this man's book).

Ergative Constructions

In many Iranian languages the past tense of transitive verbs is expressed by a construction that resembles the English passive. This construction was originally used for the perfect tenses, corresponding to the English "I have done." For example: Old Persian, *adam akunavam* (I did) but *manā kṛtam* (I have done); Pakhtun *z rasedəm* (I arrived) but *dā saṛṛay me wúlid* (I saw this man).

See also PUSHTUN.

Bibliography

Dehghani, Yavar. *Persian*. Munich, Germany: LINCOM Europa, 2002.

Kent, Roland G. *Old Persian: Grammar, Texts, Lexicon*. New Haven, CT: American Oriental Society, 1953.

Lambton, A. K. S. *Persian Grammar*. Cambridge, U.K.: Cambridge University Press, 1971.

P. OKTOR SKJAERVO

IRANIAN REVOLUTION (1979)

Mass, nationwide uprising lasting several months and culminating in the overthrow of the monarchy.

In February 1979, the regime of Mohammad Reza Shah Pahlavi collapsed in the face of an organized popular revolution. This event marked the end of over 450 years of monarchical rule that had begun with the establishment of the Safavid dynasty in 1501; a republican form of government replaced the deposed monarchy. Some scholars trace the origins of the Iranian Revolution to the 1953 coup d'état against the prime minister and National Front leader Mohammad Mossadegh or to the abortive 1963 uprisings sparked by the arrest of Ayatollah Ruhollah Khomeini. The more immediate cause of the revolution, however, was the failure of the shah's government to address the multifaceted cultural, economic, political, and social grievances that had been building up in Iranian society during the 1970s. The shah not only ignored these grievances but used his secret police agency, the SAVAK, to repress expressions of discontent and both real and suspected opposition activities.

During 1978, Khomeini was the person who succeeded in uniting the diverse currents of discontent into a unified anti-shah movement. He was a senior clergyman of Shi'ism living in exile in Iraq since 1965. Khomeini effectively used popular Shi'ite themes, such as the moral and religious righteousness of struggling against oppression and for justice, to appeal broadly to both religious and secular Iranians. By 1977, his network of former students had begun circulating tapes of his sermons at religious gatherings; these sermons denounced the shah's injustice and called for strict adherence to the 1906 constitution, which had established a constitutional monarchy, with the shah subordinate to the elected Majles, or parliament. (The shah, like his father before him, had asserted his authority over the Majles by controlling parliamentary elections and creating what in practice amounted to a royal dictatorship.) The government tried to counteract Khomeini's growing popularity by placing in a pro-regime newspaper an article that defamed the ayatollah's character. Its publication provoked major protest demonstrations in Qom (January 1978), which resulted in several deaths and the closure of the city's bazaars. The incident galvanized opposition to the shah and set in motion a cycle of protest demonstrations—and brutal repression—every forty days, the fortieth day after a death being a traditional Iranian commemoration of the deceased.

By August 1978, it had become obvious that the repressive tactics that had worked in the past no longer were effective in containing the ever-growing protest movement. The shah sought to defuse the opposition by appointing a new government of royalist politicians who had maintained ties to the clergy, by freeing some political prisoners, and by relaxing press censorship. This led to a major demonstration in Tehran, where more than 100,000 people marched through the city carrying photos of Khomeini and handing out flowers to the soldiers and police; the latter were asked to join the call for free elections. Similar peaceful but smaller-scale demonstrations took place in many other cities. Apparently frightened by the strength of the movement and the evident solidarity among religious and secular groups, the shah declared martial law in Tehran and eleven other cities and ordered the arrest of National Front and Freedom Movement leaders. The first day of martial law, 8 September 1978, became known as Black Friday because several hundred people were killed in Tehran as troops forced thousands of demonstrators to leave the area of the parliament building, where they had gathered to demand free elections.

Black Friday first stunned and then enraged the people. In response to urging from Khomeini,

strikes spread throughout the country, affecting factories, shops, schools, the oil industry, utilities, and the press. By the end of October, Iran's economy was paralyzed. The shah appointed a military government with authority to force oil workers and others back to their jobs. He also freed imprisoned National Front, Freedom Movement, and clerical leaders in hopes that they would go to Paris, where Khomeini had moved, and convince the ayatollah to moderate his views. These tactics failed. Many army conscripts were refusing to shoot at unarmed civilians and even deserting their units, and the strikes continued. Khomeini announced he would accept nothing less than the removal of the shah, and the main secular and religious opposition leaders supported his position. Despite the military government, demonstrations continued throughout November, and each day produced more martyrs as people were killed in cities and towns when the army tried to suppress protest marches. It was clear that the shah's government had lost control of the streets. Fearful of more bloodshed during the Shi'ite religious month of Muharram (the religious calendar is a lunar one, and Muharram began on 1 December in 1978), the government agreed to allow traditional mourning processions if religious leaders promised to keep order. Millions of Iranians participated in peaceful marches throughout the country, but instead of mourning the martyrdom of the saint Imam Hosain, they called for the downfall of the shah. The popular slogan chanted everywhere became "*Azadi, Istiqlal, Jomhuri Islami*" (freedom, independence, Islamic republic). These terms meant political freedom from the oppression of the secret police, independence from the shah's alliance with the United States, and a republican government based on Islamic principles of justice.

The popular message of Muharram was clear, even to the shah, who now sought a dignified way to leave Iran and preserve the throne for his eighteen-year-old son. He persuaded longtime National Front opponent Shapur Bakhtiar to form a government. On 16 January 1979, the shah left Iran on a trip officially described as a medical rest. On 1 February 1979, Khomeini, triumphantly returned from exile, refused to recognize the legitimacy of Bakhtiar's government and appointed a provisional government headed by Freedom Movement leader Mehdi Bazargan. Demonstrations against Bakhtiar and in favor of Bazargan took place throughout the country. On 11 February 1979, military leaders ordered their forces back to their barracks and to remain neutral in the civilian political struggle. This announcement led to the collapse of the Bakhtiar government and the victory of the revolutionary movement.

See also BAKHTIAR, SHAPUR; BAZAARS AND BAZAAR MERCHANTS; BAZARGAN, MEHDI; FREEDOM MOVEMENT (NEZHAT-E AZADI IRAN); KHOMEINI, RUHOLLAH; MOSSADEGH, MOHAMMAD; MUHARRAM; NATIONAL FRONT, IRAN; PAHLAVI, MOHAMMAD REZA; QOM; SHIʿISM; TEHRAN.

Bibliography

Abrahamian, Ervand. *Iran between Two Revolutions.* Princeton, NJ: Princeton University Press, 1982.

Hooglund, Eric. *Land and Revolution in Iran, 1962–1980.* Austin: University of Texas Press, 1982.

Parsa, Misagh. *Social Origins of the Iranian Revolution.* New Brunswick, NJ: Rutgers University Press, 1989.

ERIC HOOGLUND

IRAN–IRAQ WAR (1980–1988)

War between Iran and Iraq, 1980–1988.

On 22 September 1980, Iraq launched a surprise military attack on Iran, thereby igniting a war that would last for eight years, ending only when both countries agreed to accept the terms of a United Nations (UN) cease-fire resolution. Iraq's stated reason for initiating the war was defensive: The government in Baghdad claimed that Iranian forces were staging raids across their common border and that Iran's leaders were using the media to incite Iraqis to revolt. But Iraq had experienced more serious "border incidents" with Iran in the past, most notably in the years 1971–1975, when the regime of Mohammad Reza Shah Pahlavi had provided well-publicized "covert" assistance for a rebellion among Iraq's Kurdish minority. The same Iraqi leaders who were determined to avoid major conflict with Iran in 1975 had become, only five years later, confident of defeating Iran in battle. The Iraqi perception of changes in international, regional, and domestic politics contributed importantly to the decision to invade a larger and more powerful neighbor.

In the fall of 1980, Iran was isolated internationally as a result of the hostage crisis with the United States. Iran's relations with the other superpower, the Soviet Union, also were problematic because Tehran opposed the Soviet role in Afghanistan. In addition, all the Arab neighbors of Iran shared Iraq's apprehensions about the Iranian rhetoric of "exporting Islamic revolution." Within Iraq, Iran's revolution had emboldened an antigovernment movement among some Shiʿite Muslims, although the actual extent of this opposition may have been exaggerated in the minds of officials. Finally, intelligence about Iran supplied by Iranian military officers who had fled their country in the wake of the 1979 revolution was replete with information about serious factional rivalries among the political leaders and disarray and demoralization within the armed forces. The combined weight of all these factors persuaded Iraqi leaders that war against Iran could be undertaken with minimal costs and major potential benefits, such as seriously weakening or even causing the downfall of a much distrusted regime.

Initially the war went well for Iraq. Iranian forces were surprised by and unprepared for the attack. Iraqis captured Iranian border towns in all four provinces adjacent to Iraq, as well as Iran's major port, Khorramshahr. The Iraqis also besieged Abadan, one of Iran's largest cities and the site of its largest oil refinery, and several smaller cities located 12 to 20 miles removed from the border. After several weeks, however, the Iranians recovered from the shock of invasion and mobilized a large volunteer army that stopped the Iraqi advance. Iraq offered a cease-fire in place, which Iran rejected on grounds that part of its territory was under enemy occupation. For the next six months, the two armies fought intermittent battles along the front line in the western part of the Iranian province of Khuzestan, with neither side achieving any significant victory. Beginning in mid-1981, however, the Iranians gradually gained an advantage, breaking the Iraqi siege of several cities, including Abadan in September. A major victory for Iran came in May 1982, when it recaptured Khorramshahr. Several weeks later, in response to Israel's invasion of Lebanon, Iraq announced its forces would withdraw from all Iranian territory.

Iranian soldiers celebrate the taking of Iraqi territory near Basra in 1987. The Iran–Iraq War was one of the more destructive of the twentieth century, and although hostilities ended with a UN-mediated cease-fire agreement in 1988, the countries still have not signed a formal peace treaty. © AP/WIDE WORLD PHOTOS. REPRODUCED BY PERMISSION.

The summer of 1982 seemed an appropriate time to end the war, but Iran's leaders were beginning to feel victorious and wanted revenge. Thus, in July they decided to continue the war by taking it into Iraq. During the next five years, the advantage in the land battles on the Iraqi front remained with Iran, although it was an advantage that gained Iran only a few miles of ground, notably the Majnun Islands in 1984 and the Fao Peninsula in 1986. Strategy in this period may be described as a war of attrition; thousands of men, especially on the Iranian side, which used human wave assaults as a tactic, died in battles that ended as stalemates. In the air, the advantage was on Iraq's side, and the latter used its superiority in aircraft and missiles to strike at Iran's oil installations, industrial plants, shipping, and cities. Iraq also began to use chemical weapons against Iranian forces. Baghdad even authorized the use of chemical weapons against its own Kurdish minority in northeastern Iraq after some of them rebelled and provided logistical support to Iran.

Iraqi missile and aerial bombing of Iranian oil shipping led Iran to retaliate against the shipping of neutral Arab states such as Kuwait, which Iran accused of collaborating with Iraq by providing billions of dollars in loans. The result was the "tanker war" in the Persian Gulf, a phase that added an international dimension to the war when major countries intervened during 1987 to assert the freedom of the seas by sending armed naval ships to escort neutral vessels through Gulf waters. The situation prompted the UN Security Council to pass a cease-fire resolution (1987). Iran initially was reluctant to accept this resolution, but a combination of factors finally secured its acceptance: Iraq's extensive use of chemical weapons in battles during early 1988; a renewed wave of Iraqi missile strikes on Iranian cities, including the capital, Tehran; an increasing war-weariness among the general population; and uncertainty about the intentions of the United States and other countries that had intervened to suppress the tanker war. The UN-mediated cease-fire came into effect in August 1988. By that time, Iran had lost 150,000 men in battle, and about 40,000 more were listed as missing in action; 2,000 Iranian civilians also had been killed in Iraqi bomb and missile strikes. Iraq had lost more than 60,000 men in battle, and at least 6,000 Iraqi Kurdish civilians had been killed by chemical weapons unleashed on them by their own government.

See also HOSTAGE CRISES.

Bibliography

Chubin, Shahram, and Tripp, Charles. *Iran and Iraq at War.* London: I. B. Tauris, 1988.

Hooglund, Eric. "Strategic and Political Objectives in the Gulf War: Iran's View." In *The Persian Gulf War: Lessons for Strategy, Law, and Diplomacy,* edited by Christopher C. Joyner. Westport, CT: Greenwood Press, 1990.

Marr, Phebe. "The Iran–Iraq War: The View from Iraq." In *The Persian Gulf War: Lessons for Strategy, Law, and Diplomacy,* edited by Christopher C. Joyner. Westport, CT: Greenwood Press, 1990.

EFRAIM KARSH
UPDATED BY ERIC HOOGLUND

IRAN NOVIN PARTY

Political party created in Iran in 1963 to support government's reform program.

Iran Novin (New Iran) Party was created as a "majority" or government party in 1963 by Mohammad Reza Shah Pahlavi in place of the Melliyun (National) Party, a royalist party, in order to maintain the semblance of a two-party system. The other was the Mardom or People's Party. The establishment of the Iran Novin Party coincided with the period of a government-sponsored modernization and reform program known as the White Revolution or the "Revolution of the Shah and the People" (1963–1979).

The party platform represented the shah's program of reform, which included land reform, sale of state-owned factories in order to implement the land reform, enfranchisement of women, nationalization of forests and pastures, formation of literacy corps, and implementation of profit-sharing schemes for industry workers. The party chairman, Hasan Ali Mansur, a royalist from a rich landown-

ing family, was at the same time appointed as prime minister. After Mansur's assassination in 1965, the chairmanship, as well as the premiership, was given to Amir Abbas Hoveyda, who served until 1975, the longest tenure in the post. Some of the party leaders, including Hoveyda, were suspected of having Freemasonic ties, often associated with the British in Iran. Hoveyda controlled the party thoroughly.

In the late 1960s, the Women's Party of Iran Novin was created in order to enroll women in the political process. The official organ of the Iran Novin Party was the daily *Neda-ye Iran-e Novin* (Voice of new Iran) with an approximate circulation rate of five thousand in 1970. The New Iran Party was dissolved in March 1975 when the shah decided to create a single-party system with the establishment of the Rastakhiz (or Resurgence) Party, with Hoveyda as secretary-general of the new party.

See also HOVEYDA, AMIR ABBAS; MARDOM PARTY; PAHLAVI, MOHAMMAD REZA; WHITE REVOLUTION (1961–1963).

Bibliography

Arjomand, Said Amir. *The Turban for the Crown: The Islamic Revolution in Iran.* New York: Oxford University Press, 1988.

Keddie, Nikki R. *Roots of Revolution: An Interpretive History of Modern Iran.* New Haven, CT: Yale University Press, 1981.

Lenczowski, George, ed. *Iran under the Pahlavis.* Stanford, CA: Hoover Institution Press, 1978.

PARVANEH POURSHARIATI

IRAQ

Major country of the Middle East.

Iraq, with its current political boundaries, is a new country. It is a product of the twentieth century, formed in the aftermath of World War I. The term *Iraq* was adopted by the government in 1921. Historians disagree about the origin of the word. The most common interpretation is that it is derived from *al-Raq al-Arabi,* a term used in the Middle Ages to designate the southern delta region of the Tigris and Euphrates Rivers from the al-Raq al-Ajami, the Persian Mountains. Before Iraq was established as a state, the Europeans referred to the area as Mesopotamia, a name that was given to the area by the

An Iraqi family gathers for a late evening meal during Ramadan, the holy month of fasting. Fasting, one of the five pillars of Islam, is thought to foster piety, and during Ramadan adult Muslims must abstain from food or drink from sunrise until sunset. © AP/WIDE WORLD PHOTOS. REPRODUCED BY PERMISSION.

ancient Greeks which means the land between two rivers. It corresponds roughly to the Ottomans' provinces of Baghdad, Basra, and Mosul.

Geography and Population

Iraq covers about 169,000 square miles and is surrounded by six countries—Kuwait, Saudi Arabia, Iran, Turkey, Jordan, and Syria. It is essentially a landlocked country. The country's access to the high seas is through two major ports, Umm Qasr on the Persian Gulf and Basra, which is located at the Shatt al-Arab, the confluence of the Tigris and Euphrates Rivers. Geographically, the country is divided into four areas: the Syrian Desert in the west and southwest; the river valleys of the central and southeast areas, which contain the most fertile agricultural soil; the upland between the Upper Tigris and Euphrates Rivers; and the mountains of the north and northeast. The climate is subtropical, with long dry summers and a wide difference in temperatures between summer and winter. Rain falls mostly between the months of October and April, but not heavily.

Iraq's population of about 24 million is a mixture of ethnic and religious communities. About 95 percent is Muslim, of which 60 percent are Shi'ite. Four percent are Christians of various denominations. There are a few other small religious communities of Yazidis, Sabeans, and Jews. About 80 percent of the population is Arab. They live in an area that stretches from Basra to Mosul including the western part of the country. The Kurds represent 18 percent of the population, and they live mainly in the mountains of the northern and eastern areas of the country. The majority of the Kurds are Sunni; a small minority are Kurdish Shi'a called *Fiyliaya.* The Kurds of Iraq speak two different dialects of the Kurdish language—Sorani and Karmanji. Other small ethnic communities include the

Turkomen, Assyrians, Yazidis, and Armenians. Arabic is the official language of Iraq; Kurdish is used in the Kurdish area in addition to Arabic.

Baghdad, the capital of Iraq, is the largest city in the country, with a population of five million. Basra, the second largest city, has a population of more than a million and half, and is the gateway to the Persian Gulf. Mosul, in the north, is the third largest city, and has a population of more than a million. Kirkuk City, also in the north, has more than half a million people. It is situated among major oil reserves. In addition to these cities, Iraq is the site of several Shiʿite holy cities, including al-Najaf, where Imam Ali is buried, and Karbala, where Imam Husayn is buried. Both cities are located on the Euphrates River southwest of Baghdad.

Oil was discovered in large quantities in 1927 near Kirkuk City. The Iraqi Petroleum Company (IPC), a consortium of the British Petroleum Company, Shell, Mobil, Standard Oil of New Jersey (Exxon), and the French Petroleum Company, was formed to manage oil production. IPC and its subsidiaries obtained concessions from the Iraqi government and had total control over oil production. The concessions covered practically the entire land area of Iraq, and they lasted for many decades. For all intents and purposes, Iraq played no role in oil development from the time it was first discovered until the 1950s. Oil production was very limited before 1950, but it began to rise in the 1950s when the Iraqi government slowly but steadily gained control over it. The production increased significantly after Iraq nationalized its oil industry in 1972. Oil production reached its peak in 1979, reaching 3.5 million barrels a day, twice the amount produced in 1971, a year before the nationalization. Since then, the production has decreased as a result of the Iran-Iraq War (1980–1988), the Gulf Crisis and War of 1991, and the invasion of Iraq by U.S. forces in March 2003. Iraq has a proven oil reserve of more than 112 billion barrels, second only to the reserve in Saudi Arabia. Since the 1950s, oil has been the mainstay of the Iraqi economy and the major source of funds for social and economic development.

Pre-Twentieth-Century History

Although Iraq is a new country, it has an extraordinarily rich and complex history. Historians and

The al-Husayn Mosque in the Shiʿite holy city of Karbala. The mosque commemorates the murder of the prophet Muhammad's grandson in 680 C.E., and pilgrims from across the Muslim world travel to worship beneath its golden dome. © CORBIS. REPRODUCED BY PERMISSION.

archaeologists consider Iraq to be the cradle of civilization. It is associated with many ancient civilizations such as the Sumerians, the Akkadians, the Babylonians, the Chaldeans, and the Assyrians. It is the land of the biblical Garden of Eden and of the Hanging Garden of Babylon, the site of the first farming settlements and urban settlements and of the invention of writing and the wheel, and the home of Hammurabi (1800–1760 B.C.E.), the great lawgiver (author of the Code of Hammurabi).

In 637 C.E. Islam poured into Iraq. In 750 C.E. the Abbasids triumphed and the center of the Islamic empire shifted from Damascus to Iraq. In 762 C.E. the second caliph Abu Jaʿfar al-Mansur (754–775 C.E.) founded the new city of Baghdad as the

Statue of Abu Jaʿfar al-Mansur in Baghdad. Al-Mansur, the second caliph of the Abbasid Dynasty, ruled Iraq from 745 to 775 C.E. In 762, after founding Baghdad on the western bank of the Tigris River, he shifted the seat of government to the new city. © AP/WIDE WORLD PHOTOS. REPRODUCED BY PERMISSION.

new capital of the empire. During the reign of Harun al-Rashid (786–810 C.E.) and his son Maʾmun (813–833 C.E.), the Abbasid Empire reached its peak in material splendor and intellectual advances. Baghdad enjoyed grand glory and prosperity as the center of Islamic culture. The city became an international trade center for textiles, leather, paper, and other goods from areas ranging from the Baltic to China. Baghdad also became a magnet for scientific and intellectual achievements. The famous Bayt al-Hikma Academy was established in 830 C.E. by the great patron of scholarship, Caliph al-Maʾmun. The academy included several schools, astrological observatories, libraries, and facilities for the translation of scientific and philosophical works from Greek, Aramaic, and Persian into Arabic.

The empire began to disintegrate gradually, and in 1256 Baghdad and the Abbasid caliphs were destroyed by the Mongols. The Ottoman sultan, Süleiman the Magnificent, incorporated Iraq into his empire in 1534. Thereafter, except for a period of Persian control in the seventeenth century, Iraq remained under Ottoman rule until the Ottoman Empire came to an end at the end of World War I.

Administratively, during the Ottoman rule, Iraq was divided into three provinces: Mosul, where most of the Kurds lived; Baghdad; and Basra, where most of the Arabs lived. During that period, Iraq was totally neglected and the economy was in a state of disarray and confusion. In the second half of the nineteenth century a few Turkish governors, such as the reform-minded Midhat Paşa, introduced a few modern improvements such as the establishment of modern secular schools, reorganization of the army, creation of codes of criminal and commercial law, improvement of provincial administration, and a new system of transportation.

The British occupied Iraq during World War I. After the war, the Treaty of Sèvres placed Iraq under a British mandate. In 1921 the British established a constitutional monarchy headed by Faisal I ibn Hussein, a member of the Hashimite House (House of Hashim) of Arabia and one of the leaders of the anti-Turk Arab Revolt of 1916.

Early Nationhood

On 13 October 1932 Iraq became independent and joined the League of Nations. Between 1932 and 1941 Iraq's political situation was unstable, marked by tribal and ethnic revolts, military coups, and countercoups. In 1941 a nationalistic government assumed power, angering the British and prompting them to reoccupy Iraq and to install a pro-British government.

Between 1941 and 1958 Iraq was basically ruled by two British-oriented rulers: Nuri al-Saʿid, who assumed the office of prime minister several times; and Abd al-Ilah, the regent. From 1932 to 1958, Britain exercised significant influence over the ruling elite. During this time, modern secular education was expanded and became accessible to the general public in a limited way. Economic development was slow but gained some steam in the early 1950s when oil revenue increased. Political life was

MAP BY XNR PRODUCTIONS, INC. THE GALE GROUP.

marred by corruption and manipulation of the election process and domination by a few personalities.

After World War II, Iraq, like many other developing nations, experienced a rise in anti-imperial sentiment that demanded the reduction of British domination and the introduction of social and economic reform. These trends culminated in the nationalistic military coup of 14 July 1958. The coup was executed by the Free Officers, led by General Abd al-Karim al-Qasim, who stayed in power until February 1963. During the coup the king, the regent, and Nuri al-Saʿid were killed. This coup

brought significant changes in Iraq's domestic and foreign policies. The Hashimite monarchy was replaced with a republican regime, and Iraq withdrew from the Baghdad Pact and began a foreign policy of nonalliance. The new regime initiated land reform and expanded education on all levels. It also challenged the existing profit-sharing arrangement with oil companies, and in December 1961 it enacted Public Law No. 80, which resulted in the expropriation of 99.5 percent of the IPC group's concession area that was not in production. This was also a period of political turmoil: There was an attempted coup in Mosul in 1959 and an attempted assassination of Qasim, and the Kurds launched armed rebellion against the government.

The Rise of Saddam Hussein

In February 1963 the Baʿth Party, along with nationalistic officers, seized power in a bloody coup. Nine months later, the Baʿth Party was kicked out of power by a coup led by Abd al-Salam Arif, one of the original Free Officers of the 1958 coup. On 17 July 1968 the Baʿth Party came back to power through a bloodless coup. This marked the ascendance to power of Saddam Hussein, which lasted until the U.S. invasion of Iraq in March 2003. From 1968 to 2003 Hussein dominated the political scene, even when he was vice president from 1968 to 1979. He was the undisputed leader, ruling Iraq with an "iron fist" and discouraging opposition through elimination, imprisonment, and the use of multiple security forces. For all practical purposes, all political activities outside of the Baʿth Party were outlawed.

In the 1970s Iraq nationalized its oil industry. As the price of crude oil went up, the government invested a lot of money in improving the infrastructure of the country, its education system, and social services. The Kurdish revolt reached its peak in the mid-1970s due to the support it had received from Iran, Israel, and the United States. These countries viewed Iraq as a threat. During this period, Iraq advocated Arab nationalism, adopted anti-imperialism policies, and allied itself more with Soviet Union. Also, Iraq adopted a policy against the so-called reactionary regimes of the Gulf who were allies of the United States. Therefore, Iran, Israel, and the United States were interested in destabilizing the regime through the Kurdish revolt. The attempt to quell the Kurdish rebellion in the north was unsuccessful, and in 1975 Saddam signed a treaty with the shah of Iran in which Iraq agreed to share the Shatt al-Arab with Iran in return for the ending of Iran's support of the Kurds. Within a few weeks of concluding the agreement, the Kurdish revolt was quashed, and for more than a decade, the Kurdish region was relatively quiet.

On 16 July 1979 Saddam formally assumed the presidency of Iraq. He began his presidency by eliminating a number of high-ranking members of the Baʿth Party, accusing them of plotting against him. Soon his relationship with Iran began to deteriorate in the aftermath of the Iranian Revolution (1979). A border skirmish between the two countries was used by Saddam to justify the invasion of Iran on 22 September 1980. Saddam erred in his assumption that the war was going to be quick; it lasted for eight years. Iraq was left with hundreds of thousands dead and wounded and a seriously damaged economy. Iranian bombardments of oil facilities in Iraq's south significantly impaired the oil industry, which was the mainstay of the Iraqi economy. The government shifted spending from projects of modern development to spending on the military to meet the requirements of the war. The Kurds resumed their revolt against the Iraqi government with the support of the Iranian government. By the time the Iran-Iraq War ended in July 1988, Iraq was $80 billion in debt to several countries, including Kuwait, Saudi Arabia, France, the Soviet Union, and Japan.

Between 1988 and 1990, Saddam's government struggled to put the country back in order. After the war, Saddam turned against the Kurds. His forces savaged their villages for siding with Iran during the war, forcing many of the Kurds to leave the mountains for detention centers in other parts of the country. The drop in oil prices on the international front led to serious tensions between Iraq and Kuwait. Saddam accused both Kuwait and the United Arab Emirates of conducting an economic war against Iraq by intentionally flooding the oil market by exceeding their export quotas within the Organization of Petroleum Exporting Countries (OPEC). According to Saddam, the high output of these two countries kept prices low, leading to a big reduction in Iraqi oil revenue that was sorely needed to rebuild the country.

The Kuwaiti government stubbornly refused to yield, and the U.S. ambassador to Iraq gave mixed messages—on the one hand declaring that any dispute between Arab countries was not a U.S. matter, and on the other joining Britain in encouraging Kuwait not to accommodate Iraq. Saddam's invasion of Kuwait on 2 August 1990 ultimately led to the first Gulf War, which was executed by the United States and its coalition on 17 January 1991. The war's code name was Operation Desert Storm, and it lasted for forty-three days. The United States and its allies flew more than 110,000 sorties that dropped a total of 99,000 to 140,000 tons of explosives on Iraqi targets—the firepower equivalent of five to seven of the nuclear bombs that were dropped on the Japanese city of Hiroshima during World War II. The war destroyed the infrastructure of Iraq, knocking out electricity grids, roads, bridges, communication systems, sewage and water purification systems, factories, and telephone systems. A United Nations (UN) report written shortly after the war stated that the destruction caused by the war returned Iraq to a preindustrial state.

In the aftermath, both the Kurdish ethnic community in the north and the Shiʿite Muslim community in the south revolted against Saddam's regime. The Kurds hoped to establish an independent state in the north, and the Shiʿa hoped to topple Saddam's regime and replace it with a more sympathetic government. Despite Saddam's recent defeat in the war, he was able to muster enough power to crush both rebellions. He dealt with the rebels harshly, killing thousands of people and wounding many more. Hundreds of thousands of Kurds fled Iraq to the neighboring countries of Turkey and Iran. This massive flight prompted the United States, along with Britain and France, to impose a no-fly zone for Iraqi aircraft in the north. Also, the United States, Britain, and France established a Kurdish Autonomous Zone in Iraq, which Iraqi forces were not allowed to enter, and where Kurds ruled themselves. This new arrangement allowed hundreds of thousand of refugees to return to their homes and villages. The Kurdish zone, for all practical purposes, was independent. It had its own currency, taxes, and educational system. In this area, Kurdish was the primary language and Arabic was waning as the official language.

On 6 August 1990, four days after the Iraqi invasion of Kuwait, the United Nations Security Council passed Resolution 661, imposing on Iraq the most repressive sanctions and embargo in the history of the organization. When the Gulf War ended, the United Nations Security Council passed several new resolutions concerning Iraq. Resolution 687, passed on 3 April 1991, continued the sanctions and the embargo on Iraq until it dismantled its weapons program, including all long- and medium-range missiles, and all chemical, biological, and nuclear facilities. The dismantling was to have been implemented by the Vienna-based Interna-

tional Atomic Energy Agency (IAEA), which had been inspecting Iraq for any possible military use of its nuclear facilities since the 1970s, and the newly established UN Special Commission (UNSCOM) under the chairmanship of Rolf Ekeus, a Swedish diplomat. Resolution 713 established a permanent UN monitoring system for all missile test sites and nuclear installations in the Iraq. Resolution 986, passed in 1992, allowed Iraq to sell $1.6 billion worth of oil every six months, subject to renewal, for the purchase of food and medicine. About one third of the money raised through the sale of oil was designated for war reparations for Kuwait and payments to the UN for its operations in Iraq. Iraq agreed in principle to the first two resolutions, but it rejected the third one on the grounds that it did not allow Iraq to control the funds realized from the sale. But by 1996 the life of the Iraqi people was approaching destitution, and the government was forced to accept the terms of Resolution 986. In 1998 the sale limit was raised to $5.52 billion worth of oil every six months, and in 1999 to $8.3 billion.

Iraq was not happy with UNSCOM's intrusive inspections, and there were confrontations between Iraqis and the inspection teams. The United States, the driving force behind the inspections, used these confrontations as grounds for bombing Iraq in 1993, 1996, and 1998. The last bombardment, codenamed Operation Desert Fox, lasted for four days. Before it began, Richard Butler, the second head of UNSCOM, withdrew the inspections teams without the authorization of the UN Security Council. The bombardment put the future of UNSCOM in doubt, and the inspectors did not return until 2002, and then under a different name. By the time of the 1998 confrontation, the UN had destroyed more than 95 percent of Iraq's weapons of mass destruction (Iraq claimed that it had destroyed the last 5 percent, but could not account for it). There were two reasons for the difficulties that the inspection teams faced: Iraq's concern that the inspection teams violated its sovereignty, and the U.S. government's misuse of some members of the inspection teams as spies.

The sanctions and the embargo begun in 1990 had a dreadful impact on Iraqi society. They hit the sanitation and health-care systems hard, and also led to the breakdown of the electric system, which contributed to chronic problems with sewage and water treatment. The sanctions also contributed to inadequate diets, resulting in malnutrition and a proliferation of diseases, which led to a high mortality rate among children. Furthermore, the sanctions led to many social ills such as homelessness of children, increased crime rates, high divorce rates, a drop in the marriage rate, and the virtual destruction of the educational system. Thousands of schools were left in a state of disrepair. The sanctions weakened the oil industry, the mainstay of the Iraqi economy, because of a lack of spare parts and a lack of investment to update oil facilities. The sanctions lasted for almost thirteen years and contributed to the deaths of more than one million people, many of them children, women, and elderly people. Two UN chief relief coordinators—Denis Halliday in 1998 and Han von Sponeck in 2000—resigned their posts in protest of the continuation of the sanctions.

The terrorist attacks on the World Trade Center and the Pentagon on 11 September 2001 marked a turning point in U.S. policy toward Iraq. The foreign policy of the Republican administration of George W. Bush was controlled by neoconservatives who advocated a regime change in Iraq. Some of the planners of the new policy were behind the passage of the Iraq Liberation Act of 1998, in which the Congress allocated $100 million to help Iraqi opposition groups in their quest to remove Saddam from power. After 11 September, the neoconservatives pushed for the removal of Saddam by military means. The UN adopted Resolution 1441, which demanded that Iraq allow the weapons inspections teams to return. There were two teams—one from the International Atomic Energy Agency, headed by Muhammad El-Baradei from Egypt, and another from the United Nations Monitoring, Verification, and Inspection Commission (UNMOVIC), headed by Hans Blix from Sweden. The new resolution gave the inspectors more freedom to operate and conduct their activities inside Iraq, and it imposed more restrictions on Saddam's regime than previous resolutions had. Iraq agreed to the resolution and emphatically denied having any weapons of mass destruction, stating that it had destroyed all of them. However, the Iraqi government could not give a full accounting of the missing items. Both heads of the inspection teams asked for more time to finish their job.

The United States and Britain refused to wait for UN consensus on the issue. The United States

government continued to claim that Saddam had weapons of mass destruction and that he was a threat to U.S. and world security, and on 17 March 2003 the United States, along with Britain, initiated a military invasion against Iraq, defying world opinion. On 9 April 2003 Baghdad fell, and the occupation of Iraq began. The claims that Iraq possessed weapons of mass destruction, including biological, chemical, and nuclear weapons, turned out to be questionable. In May, under pressure from the United States, the UN Security Council adopted Resolution 1483, which legalized the result of the invasion (though most UN member nations had considered it to be illegal). On 16 October 2003 the UN adopted Resolution 1511, again under U.S. pressure, which authorized a multinational force under U.S. leadership to replace and reduce the burden on the U.S. occupying forces.

See also ARAB REVOLT (1916); ARIF, ABD AL-SALAM; BAGHDAD; BAGHDAD PACT (1955); BASRA; BA'TH, AL-; FAISAL I IBN HUSSEIN; GULF WAR (1991); HASHIMITE HOUSE (HOUSE OF HASHIM); HUSSEIN, SADDAM; IRANIAN REVOLUTION (1979); IRAN–IRAQ WAR (1980–1988); IRAQ PETROLEUM COMPANY (IPC); KARBALA; KIRKUK; KURDISH AUTONOMOUS ZONE; KURDISH REVOLTS; KURDS; MIDHAT PAŞA; MOSUL; NAJAF, AL-; SÈVRES, TREATY OF (1920); SHATT AL-ARAB; TIGRIS AND EUPHRATES RIVERS; UNITED NATIONS SPECIAL COMMISSION (UNSCOM); WAR IN IRAQ (2003).

Bibliography

Graham-Brown, Sarah. *Sanctioning Saddam: The Politics of Intervention in Iraq.* London: I. B. Tauris, 1999.

Mackey, Sandra. *The Reckoning: Iraq and the Legacy of Saddam Hussein.* New York: W. W. Norton, 2002.

Tripp, Charles. *A History of Iraq.* Cambridge, U.K.: Cambridge University Press, 2000.

AYAD AL-QAZZAZ

IRAQI NATIONAL CONGRESS

An Iraqi opposition group.

The Iraqi National Congress (INC) is an umbrella Iraqi opposition group founded in 1992. It was formed with the aid of and under the direction of the United States government following the 1991 Gulf War, for the purpose of fomenting the overthrow of Saddam Hussein. Selected to chair the executive council was Ahmad Chalabi, a secular Iraqi Shi'ite Muslim and mathematician by training. The INC represented the first major attempt by opponents of Hussein to join forces, bringing together not only Sunni and Shi'a Arabs (both Islamic fundamentalist and secular) and Kurds, but also varying political tendencies, including democrats, nationalists, ex-military officers, and others.

In June 1992 nearly 200 delegates from dozens of opposition groups met in Vienna, along with Iraq's two main Kurdish militias, the Democratic Party of Kurdistan (Iraq) and the Patriotic Union of Kurdistan (PUK). In October 1992 the major Shi'ite groups joined the coalition and the INC held a pivotal meeting in Kurdish-controlled northern Iraq, in which it chose a three-person Leadership Council and a twenty-six-member Executive Council. A number of opposition groups continue to belong to the INC, but most have since gone their own ways, leaving the INC primarily a vehicle for Chalabi and his supporters.

The INC's political platform promised human rights and rule of law within a constitutional, democratic, and pluralistic Iraq; preservation of Iraq's territorial integrity; and complete compliance with international law, including United Nations resolutions relating to Iraq. Like the majority of other Iraqi opposition groups, its stated goal was to topple Saddam's regime and its replacement with a democratic form of government with federalism and decentralization at its basis. The INC received $12 million of covert CIA funding between 1992 and 1996. After several years of nonfunding, the administration of George W. Bush agreed to give $8 million of the $25 million that the INC requested in January of 2002.

The INC was subsequently plagued by the dissociation of many of its constituent groups from the INC umbrella, a cutoff of funds from its international backers (including the United States), and continued pressure from Iraqi intelligence services. A major problem the INC faced after the American occupation of Iraq starting in 2003 was the limited degree of support it commands inside the country.

See also BUSH, GEORGE W.; CENTRAL INTELLIGENCE AGENCY (CIA); CHALABI, AHMAD; HUSSEIN, SADDAM; IRAQ.

Bibliography

Marr, Phebe. "Iraq 'The Day After': Internal Dynamics in Post-Saddam Iraq." *Naval War College Review* 56, no.1 (2003): 13–29.

KRISTIAN P. ALEXANDER

IRAQI WOMEN'S FEDERATION

See GENERAL FEDERATION OF IRAQI WOMEN

IRAQI WOMEN'S UNION

Umbrella organization of Iraqi women's groups.

The Iraqi Women's Union was an umbrella organization created in 1945 by progressive, upper-class women to unite all legally sanctioned women's associations and clubs. The union's aims were "to assist women to improve family conditions in the service of society" by raising their "health, social, civil, legal, and economic standards" through civil, constitutional, and peaceful means; and to unify all women's associations in Iraq and initiate cultural, social, and national contacts with Arab and international organizations committed to advancing women's issues. One of their first major social projects in Iraq was the abolition of brothels as degrading to women. In addition, they mobilized women as volunteers during national disasters. In the civil sphere, they campaigned for greater women's rights, particularly in relation to child custody after a divorce, and for an amendment of the legal code in regard to inheritance. In the economic sphere, they campaigned for the improvement of working conditions for nurses, who were mainly women. In addition, they were active in the cultural sphere in promoting awareness of women's issues by organizing a biweekly series of literary, political, and social lectures and debates, which were held at their headquarters in Baghdad. They also sponsored biweekly movies and documentaries of a social and cultural nature. In 1954 the union organized a "Women's Week" in which lectures by legal personalities and political figures were presented in support of women's issues. At the height of its political activities between

1951 and 1958, the union demanded amendments to Iraq's constitution guaranteeing women's equality, right to vote, and right to stand for political office.

See also GENDER: GENDER AND LAW.

JACQUELINE ISMAEL

IRAQ PETROLEUM COMPANY (IPC)

Successor to Turkish Petroleum Company.

The Iraq Petroleum Company (IPC) was organized in 1928 from the remains of the Turkish Petroleum Company (TPC). In 1927, TPC discovered the large Kirkuk field in the Kurdish Mosul region of Iraq. Seven years later, IPC completed a crude oil pipeline with termini in Tripoli, Lebanon, and in Haifa, then in the British mandate of Palestine. Its oil exports reached 1 million tons per year by the end of 1934, but revenues remained modest until the 1950s.

Iraq's militant oil policy can be explained by the country's dependence on pipelines to move crude oil to market, and by its history of bitter conflicts with IPC. The IPC pipeline to Haifa, vulnerable to sabotage, was severed during the Arab–Israel War (1948), and the pipeline through Syria was blown up during the Arab–Israel War (1956). Shipments of crude through the IPC pipeline in Syria were halted for three months in 1966 and 1967 because of a dispute over transit fees between IPC and the government of Syria. This was a preview of the relative ease with which transit countries were able to halt the flow of crude oil through IPC-owned pipelines following the imposition of sanctions by the United Nations in response to Iraq's invasion of Kuwait in August 1990.

Iraq's conflicts with IPC began during the negotiations over the original TPC concession. The government had demanded a 20 percent equity share in the company to give it some influence on management policies, including production levels. The TPC partners resisted giving a share to Iraq and called upon their home governments, then engaged in carving the Ottoman Empire into mandates for themselves, to help them. Needing British support to prevent the Mosul *vilayet* from being lost to Turkey, the government of Iraq reluctantly signed an agreement giving TPC a concession until 2000 and omitting the provision for an equity share for itself.

The most serious dispute between Iraq and IPC was over the laggardly development of Iraq's oil resources. IPC concentrated on developing its fields in Mosul, which depended upon the limited capacity of vulnerable pipelines to transport crude to markets. Development of the southern oil fields, close to the gulf where export via tanker was possible, did not occur until the 1950s. Iraq was convinced that IPC's foreign ownership was responsible for this delay, although other factors, such as the Red Line Agreement, are also likely explanations. IPC's foreign owners agreed to revise their concession agreement in 1952 to conform to the new industry standard of 50–50 profit sharing without the rancor that accompanied these negotiations in Iran. IPC also went along with another industry standard in 1959 and 1960, unilaterally reducing the prices paid to host governments for crude oil. This prompted Iraq to join four other oil-exporting countries to found the Organization of Petroleum Exporting Countries (OPEC) in 1960.

Negotiations between the government of Iraq and IPC in the early 1960s were beset by the inability of each side to understand the reasons behind the positions taken by the other. In December 1962 Iraq's Public Law 80 (PL 80) called for repossession of more than 99 percent of IPC's landholdings, including its share of the southern oil fields. The law also established the Iraq National Oil Company (INOC). PL 80 allowed Iraq to preserve its income stream from IPC, which retained its producing properties in Kirkuk, but also initiated a protracted struggle with IPC over the law's legitimacy. After intensive negotiations, IPC regained control of the southern oil fields in a new agreement initialed in 1965 but lost these rights after passage of Public Law 97 in August 1967, which gave INOC exclusive rights to develop all the territory expropriated under PL 80. IPC threatened to sue purchasers of oil from the disputed fields. INOC developed the disputed fields by itself and disposed of production through barter agreements, in order to circumvent the IPC ban on crude sales.

Following the 1968 coup and the installation of the al-Baʿth party, the government of Iraq moved rapidly toward nationalization. Continued conflicts over IPC's production rates, and company demands to be compensated for losses it had sustained as the result of PL 80, led to Public Law 69 (1 June 1972). This law nationalized IPC and established a state-owned company to take over its operations in Kirkuk. In response, IPC extended its embargo to cover oil from Kirkuk. The immediate impasse between Iraq and IPC was resolved in an agreement reached in February 1973, in which substantial concessions were made by both sides. By the end of the year, however, Iraq had nationalized all foreign oil holdings, including all of the remaining properties of IPC.

See also Arab–Israel War (1948); Arab–Israel War (1956); Ba'th, al-; Kirkuk; Organization of Petroleum Exporting Countries; Red Line Agreement.

Bibliography

Marr, Phebe. *The Modern History of Iraq.* Boulder, CO: Westview Press, 1985.

Penrose, Edith T. *The Large International Firm in Developing Countries: The International Petroleum Industry.* Cambridge, MA: MIT Press, 1969.

Mary Ann Tétreault

IRAQ WAR (2003)

See War in Iraq (2003)

IRBID

Largest city in northern Jordan.

Located 53 miles (85 km) north of the capital city, Amman, Irbid is the third-largest city in Jordan (population 267,200 in 2003) and the traditional administrative capital for the northern province.

Known during the Roman Empire as Arbila, Irbid was counted among the ten towns of the Decapolis—a commercial federation of towns in Judea, Jordan, and Syria during the first century B.C.E.

When reconsolidating their rule over Jordan in the nineteenth century, the Ottoman Empire's representatives in Damascus made Irbid the seat of the subgovernorate of Ajlun, the first district in Jordan

to be ruled directly by the Ottomans. As such, Irbid became the home of some of Jordan's first public institutions. Irbid continued to serve as the capital of Ajlun during the emirate of Transjordan and of today's governorate of Irbid.

As an administrative and commercial center, Irbid has undergone considerable population growth, particularly since the 1950s. Irbid is also home to Yarmuk University, one of Jordan's three public universities.

See also Jordan; Yarmuk University.

Michael R. Fischbach

IRGUN ZVA'I LE'UMI (IZL)

Militant Jewish underground organization in pre-state Israel.

A revisionist group of militants broke from the Haganah in 1931 and formed the Irgun Zva'i Le'umi (Etzel). In 1937, the Irgun signed an agreement with Vladimir Ze'ev Jabotinsky, the president of the Revisionist New Zionist Organization, and became the defense organization of the Revisionist movement. During and after the Arab uprising of 1936–1939 and the British White Paper of May 1939, the Irgun embarked on a series of terrorist attacks on British and Palestinian targets. With the eruption of World War II, however, the Irgun suspended attacks and many members joined the British forces to be trained and to fight against Nazi Germany. Irgun commander in chief David Raziel was killed in Iraq while leading a group of volunteers on behalf of the British army. A small group of dissident Irgun members, led by Abraham Stern, broke with the Irgun, formed LEHI (the "Stern Gang"), and continued to carry out violent actions against the Mandatory forces.

In 1942 Menachem Begin assumed command of the Irgun and, in early 1944, formally embarked on armed revolt against the British in Mandatory Palestine. Though comprised of a small group of poorly equipped Jewish guerrillas, the Irgun inflicted damage on the British forces through a combination of factors, including successful use of the element of surprise, intimate familiarity with the topography and terrain, broad local Jewish sympathy, and a campaign of public relations abroad that built on sympathy for the victims of Nazi genocide.

In 1945, after the British Labour government refused to alter its Palestine policies, the Jewish Agency arranged an alliance of Haganah, Irgun, and LEHI forces, the United Hebrew Resistance Movement, which carried out violent actions against the Mandatory forces. In mid-1946, however, the Jewish Agency reinstituted its policy of self-restraint and disbanded the alliance, but by then the Irgun was sufficiently large to independently escalate attacks on British targets.

The Haganah and mainstream Zionists consistently opposed the Irgun and its terrorist actions. In July 1946, when the Irgun blew up the British army headquarters and the Secretariat of the Mandate government in the King David Hotel in Jerusalem, it was strongly denounced. Less than a month after the British executed four Irgun members in the Acre Prison, in April 1947, an Irgun force of thirty-four men dynamited their way into the prison and freed 250 Jewish and Arab prisoners. The following day, the daring action was widely reported in the world media. On 14 May 1948, with the proclamation of the State of Israel, the Irgun agreed to disband and join the new Israel Defense Force; they continued, however, to carry out a number of independent actions, the most serious of which led to the Altalena affair.

The Irgun did not achieve official recognition until 1968, when President Zalman Shazar formally recognized its efforts, along with those of the Haganah and all groups, including NILI, the Jewish Legion, and LEHI, in the struggle for independence and defense of the State of Israel.

See also AARONSOHN FAMILY; *ALTALENA;* SHAZAR, SHNEOUR ZALMAN.

Bibliography

Begin, Menachem. *The Revolt: Story of the Irgun.* Tel Aviv: Steimatzky, 1951.

Bell, J. Bowyer. *Terror Out of Zion: The Fight for Israeli Independence.* New Brunswick, NJ: Transaction, 1996.

CHAIM I. WAXMAN

IRSHAD AN-NISWAAN

The first Afghan women's journal.

Irshad An-Niswaan (Lady's guide), the first Afghan women's journal, was established in March 1921 as a weekly in Kabul under the direction of three people: Asma Rasmiyya; the famous Afghan journalist Mahmud Tarzi; and the mother of Queen Surraya. Ruhafza, the editor of *Irshad An-Niswaan,* was related to Mahmud Tarzi. In addition to national and international news, *Irshad An-Niswaan* published articles of particular interest to women. Its mission was to inform women of important national and international issues and make them aware of their rights and responsibilities as mothers and citizens. The journal also provided an opportunity for young women writers to contribute articles for publication. *Irshad An-Niswaan* was published in Persian and was intended primarily for upper-class, educated women readers and female students. It ceased publication after the fall of King Amanullah in 1929.

In 1994, during the government of Burhanuddin Rabbani, a short-lived monthly bilingual women's magazine, in Persian and Pashtun, took the same name and was published in Kabul under the editorship of Laila Sarahat Rushani. It focused primarily on the social life and traditional activities of women but included articles on literature and politics as well.

See also AFGHANISTAN: OVERVIEW; GENDER: GENDER AND EDUCATION; NEWSPAPERS AND PRINT MEDIA: ARAB COUNTRIES; QUEEN SURRAYA.

SENZIL NAWID

IRYANI, ABD AL-RAHMAN AL-
[1909–1998]

Second president of the Yemen Arab Republic.

Abd al-Rahman al-Iryani served as head of state of the Yemen Arab Republic from the overthrow of President Abdullah al-Sallal in late 1967 until the bloodless coup led by Ibrahim al-Hamdi in mid-1974. Born in 1909 in the Iryan region of North Yemen, al-Iryani hailed from a famous family of Sunni jurists and teachers; he was the head of that family for five decades. His pre-1962 political activities qualify him as a father of the modern Yemeni republic, and his tenure as head of state was most notable for the republican-royalist reconciliation that ended the Yemen Civil War, for the drafting and adoption of the 1970 constitution, and for holding Yemen's first parliamentary elections in 1971.

A traditionally trained *qadi* (judge) who held to some modern ideas, he bridged the gap between the imamate of the past and the new republic. Indeed, some called him the "republican imam," and claimed that this was the key to the successful transitional role he played; many Yemenis referred to him simply as "the Qadi." After 1974 he spent most of his exile in Damascus, was invited by the regime to return to Yemen in 1982, and made almost annual visits to his native land thereafter. Upon his death in 1998, he was returned to Yemen for a hero's burial.

Bibliography

Burrowes, Robert D. *The Yemen Arab Republic: The Politics of Development, 1962–1986.* Boulder, CO: Westview; London: Croom Helm, 1987.

Dresch, Paul. *A History of Modern Yemen.* New York and Cambridge, U.K.: Cambridge University Press, 2000.

Stookey, Robert W. *Yemen: The Politics of the Yemen Arab Republic.* Boulder, CO: Westview Press, 1978.

ROBERT D. BURROWES

ISA FAMILY, AL-

Prominent Palestinian family from Jaffa.

A Greek Orthodox family of landowners, businessmen, and politicians, the al-Isas became most known in the twentieth century as publishers of the long-lived newspaper *Filastin*. Brothers Yusuf and Isa Da'ud Isa, who both attended the American University of Beirut, Lebanon, founded the newspaper in 1911. Leaders of the Nahda al-Urthuduksiyya (Orthodox Renaissance) before World War I, they were also active in the anti-Zionist movement. Isa's son Raja became editor of *Filastin* in 1951 and of the *Jerusalem Star* in the 1960s. He is now a publisher and owner of the Jordan Distribution Agency in Amman, Jordan. Another member of the family, Michel al-Isa, headed a battalion in defense of Jaffa against the Israelis in the 1948 Arab–Israel War.

A second prominent branch of the al-Isa family is based in Beirut, Lebanon. Elias al-Isa was a wealthy contractor in the early twentieth century from Bsous. His son Emile is a retired banker, and his son Raymond is an architect and engineer.

See also ARAB–ISRAEL WAR (1948); NEWSPAPERS AND PRINT MEDIA: ARAB COUNTRIES.

Bibliography

Khalaf, Issa. *Politics in Palestine: Arab Factionalism and Social Disintegration, 1939–1948.* Albany: State University of New York Press, 1991.

Shafir, Gershon. *Land, Labor and the Origins of the Israeli–Palestinian Conflict, 1882–1914,* revised edition. Berkeley: University of California Press, 1996.

ELIZABETH THOMPSON

ISAWIYYA BROTHERHOOD

Religious brotherhood.

The Isawiyya brotherhood, or Isawa, was founded in Meknes, Morocco, in the sixteenth century by Shaykh Muhammad bin Isa al-Sufyani al-Mukhtari, known as Shaykh al-Kamil (the perfect master). The brotherhood is found all over Morocco and Algeria and has extended its influence to other Muslim countries such as Libya, Syria, and Egypt. Each year during the three days following the Mulud, members hold a celebration in Meknes where music, ecstatic dances, and extravagant rituals are collectively performed. Because it preaches renouncement, Isawa recruit their disciples mostly among poor social categories.

RAHMA BOURQIA

ISFAHAN

Former capital of Iran and major industrial center.

Isfahan is located in west central Iran along both banks of the Zayandeh River. Its origins date back to the Achaemenid era (c. 550–330 B.C.E.), but it did not emerge as an important city until 1150, when Toghril Beg, founder of the Seljuk dynasty, chose it as his capital. The city's golden age coincided with its status as the capital of the Safavi dynasty (1598–1722). Shah Abbas I (r. 1587–1629) and several of his successors embellished the city with bridges, mosques, *madrasehs,* and palaces, many of which are extant and are considered among the finest examples of Islamic architecture. In 1722, an army of invading Afghans besieged Isfahan for several months before finally capturing and looting it and deposing the shah. These events ushered in more than two decades of steady economic and political decline interspersed with several brutal massacres of prominent citizens of the city.

Isfahan at the beginning of the nineteenth century was no longer a major city; it had ceased to be Iran's capital, and its population was only 25 percent of what it had been during the height of Safavi power. Its role as a regional commercial center recovered during the reign of Nasir ed-Din Shah Qajar (1848–1896). In the 1920s entrepreneurs began developing modern factories, especially textile mills, which by the early 1960s employed nearly 20,000 workers and produced one-half of Iran's total output of textiles. The renewed prosperity stimulated greater and more diversified industrialization, and the city became the center of the country's steel industry during the 1970s. Isfahan has experienced considerable immigration, growing at an average annual rate of 4 percent during the last seventy years of the twentieth century. In the 1996 census, its population had reached 1,266,000, making it the third-largest city in Iran. The city also remains the country's premier tourist center, drawing thousands to see such famous Safavi-era architectural landmarks as the Meydan-e Imam, Masjid-e Imam, Masjid-e Shaykh Lotfollah, and the covered bazaar.

Bibliography

Fisher, W. B. "Physical Geography." In *The Cambridge History of Iran*, Vol. 1: *The Land of Iran,* edited by W. B. Fisher. Cambridge, U.K.: Cambridge University Press, 1968.

FARHAD ARSHAD
UPDATED BY ERIC HOOGLUND

ISFAHAN UNIVERSITY

Public university in Isfahan, Iran.

Founded in Isfahan in 1949 as part of an effort to establish public institutions of higher education in the provinces of Iran, Isfahan University had 3,654 students by 1970. It had faculties of administrative sciences and economics, educational sciences, engineering, foreign languages, letters and humanities, and pure sciences, with 450 teachers and 12,000 students, as of 2002. The Isfahan University of Medical Sciences, with faculties of medicine, dentistry, and pharmacy, and a school of nursing, had 300 teachers and 6,321 students as of 2002.

Bibliography

Samii, A.; Vaghefi, M.; and Nowrasteh, D. *Systems of Higher Education: Iran.* New York: International Council for Educational Development, 1978.

PARVANEH POURSHARIATI

ISHAAQ, KAMALA IBRAHIM
[1939–]

Sudanese painter.

Kamala Ibrahim Ishaaq (also Ishaq) was born in Sudan, and trained at the Faculty of Fine Arts in Khartoum and at the Royal College of Art in London. She taught at the Khartoum School of Fine and Applied Art and was a pioneering member of the group known as the Khartoum School, which is widely regarded as responsible for developing the modern art movement in the Sudan. Like many other artists from Arab and African countries, Ishaaq conducted extensive field research on local cultural practices as a basis for her own work. Her early paintings drew on her intensive study of and participation in *zars*, primarily female rituals of spirit possession and purification in northeast Africa. This exploration of local themes was in keeping with the Khartoum School's interest in articulating a distinct Sudanese cultural identity, which they believed consisted of a mixture of African and Islamic traditions. In the 1970s, Ishaaq departed from her earlier work when she joined with two of her students to create the Crystal Manifesto, which some argue was an implicit critique of the Khartoum School. Opposed to the heavy values placed on skill and craftsmanship and an empirical view of the world, the Crystalists argued that humankind was trapped in a crystal-like prism, whose nature looked different depending on the observer's angle, thus providing a source of possibility within the entrapment. This existentialist perspective shaped her later work, which explored women's oppression and possession more broadly, most notably in paintings of grossly distorted female subjects, some imprisoned in crystal cubes.

See also ART; GENDER: GENDER AND EDUCATION.

Bibliography

Hassan, Salah. "Khartoum Connections: The Sudanese Story." In *Seven Stories about Modern Art in Africa.* New York: Flammarion, 1995.

Kennedy, Jean. *New Currents, Ancient Rivers: Contemporary African Artists in a Generation of Change.* Washington, DC: Smithsonian Institution Press, 1992.

JESSICA WINEGAR

ISHAQ, ADIB
[1856–1885]

Arab intellectual.

A Syrian Christian by birth, Adib Ishaq was educated in French schools in Damascus and Beirut. Emigrating to Egypt, Ishaq became the editor of the noted journal *Misr.* While he has been described as an early promoter of Arab nationalism, Ishaq avidly supported the Ottoman Empire as a viable political community. Inspired by liberal thought of France, Ishaq wrote extensively about the nature of freedom and society. In his view, there were several layers of social organization in the Middle East, each of which defined itself differently. There was an "Arab" identity shared by those who spoke Arabic, an "Ottoman" identity shared by those who acknowledged the sultan as sovereign, and even an "Eastern" identity shared by those who felt besieged by the West. These layers were not mutually exclusive; they overlapped, and it was possible for one individual to hold to more than one of these identities.

See also ARAB NATIONALISM; NEWSPAPERS AND PRINT MEDIA: ARAB COUNTRIES.

Bibliography

Hourani, Albert. *Arabic Thought in the Liberal Age, 1798–1939.* Cambridge, U.K., and New York: Cambridge University Press, 1983.

Vatikiotis, P. J. *The History of Modern Egypt: From Muhammad Ali to Mubarak,* 4th edition. Baltimore, MD: Johns Hopkins University Press, 1991.

ZACHARY KARABELL

ISLAH PARTY

Yemeni political party.

The Islah Party (or Reform Grouping) was formed in 1990, soon after the People's Democratic Republic of Yemen and the Yemen Arab Republic united to form the Republic of Yemen (ROY). Although widely characterized as Islamist, Islah is actually a coalition of the Hashid Tribal Confederation, the Muslim Brotherhood, some prominent businesspeople, and a few other small groups; among the latter are militant Islamists, some allegedly with connections with al-Qaʿida. In April 1993 the party won the second-largest bloc in the ROY's first democratic parliamentary elections, gaining about half the seats won by the General People's Congress (GPC) but several more than those won by the Yemeni Socialist Party (YSP), the two parties that unified Yemen in 1990 and then shared power from 1990 to 1993. Although Islah then joined with the GPC and the YSP to form a grand coalition, the party nevertheless remained marginalized until 1994, when civil war brought about the demise of the GPC–YSP partnership and the exile of most YSP leaders. After the war, a new government was formed by the GPC and Islah, providing the latter with key cabinet posts and increased political strength. After the 1997 elections, in which it made a slightly poorer showing than in 1993, Islah declined an invitation to join the government and went into the opposition; after the 2003 elections, it continued to play the role of opposition to the GPC government. Whether in the government or in the opposition, Islah has been an important player in Yemeni politics. For one thing, there are strong tribal ties between President Ali Abdullah Salih, the head of the GPC, and Abdullah ibn Husayn al-Ahmar, the head of Islah. For another, when not in the government, Islah has often acted and been treated as if it were; and, when in the government, it has often behaved as the opposition.

See also MUSLIM BROTHERHOOD; QAʿIDA, AL-; YEMEN.

Bibliography

Carapico, Sheila. *Civil Society in Yemen: The Political Economy of Activism in Modern Arabia.* New York and Cambridge, U.K.: Cambridge University Press, 1998.

Dresch, Paul. *A History of Modern Yemen.* New York and Cambridge, U.K.: Cambridge University Press, 2000.

Dresh, P., and Haykel, B. "Stereotypes and Political Styles: Islamists and Tribesfolk in Yemen." *International Journal of Middle East Studies* 27 (November 1995): 405–431.

JILLIAN SCHWEDLER
UPDATED BY ROBERT D. BURROWES

ISLAH TALEBAN PARTY

A conservative political party in Iran that supported Reza Khan's coming to power as shah and helped support his policies.

An heir to the Moderate Party (or *Firqeh-ye I'tidal*), a conservative party that supported the aristocracy and the traditional middle class, the Islah Taleban (Reformers) Party was established in 1910. Like its predecessor, the Islah Taleban was a conservative party led by prominent clerics, merchants, and landed aristocracy. The party was instrumental in paving the way for Reza Khan's assumption of power as the king of Iran. Almost unanimously, the party supported a bill introduced by the Revival Party that deposed the Qajar dynasty and proclaimed Reza Pahlavi the king (shah) of Iran. With three other political parties, the Reformers formed the alliance system that Reza Shah used for implementing his policies. The leading members of the party were instrumental in passing a new law in the parliament calling for universal adult male suffrage. But in the semifeudal conditions of the country in the early twentieth century, this law extending the vote to the uneducated rural masses helped only to strengthen the elite. The famous Iranian poet Mohammad Taqi Bahar wrote of the law in 1944 that "it continues to plague the country even today."

See also BAHAR, MOHAMMAD TAQI; PAHLAVI, REZA; QAJAR DYNASTY.

Bibliography

Abrahamian, Ervand. *Iran between Two Revolutions.* Princeton, NJ: Princeton University Press, 1982.

PARVANEH POURSHARIATI

ISLAM

A strictly monotheistic faith, Islam is the religion of more than 1.2 billion people, or a fifth of the world population. Muslims can be found mostly in Western and Central Asia, Southeast Asia, and Africa. Only about 350 million live in the Arab world.

Pre-Islamic Arabia and the Rise of Islam

Islam appeared in the seventh century at a time of social and religious decay in the Arabian Peninsula. Arabian society was essentially tribal and the supremacy of tribal law encouraged warfare, raiding, and vendettas. Usurious economic practices led to the impoverishment and enslavement of a number of weaker tribes, and social ills such as alcoholism and prostitution were rampant. Associationism (or *shirk*, as the pre-Islamic religious tradition was referred to at the time) was the main faith, and it acknowledged a number of intercessory gods associated with the Creator, Allah. The representations of these gods were housed in an important shrine (the Ka'ba) in Mecca and attracted most Arabian tribes at the time of the annual pilgrimage (hajj). But Associationism was losing its appeal, as can be seen from the spread of Judaism, Christianity, and especially Hanifism, a local monotheism that took Abraham as its central figure and maintained a simple ethical doctrine and the inevitability of a Day of Judgment.

Islam arose claiming to be the embodiment of Hanifism and the continuation of earlier monotheistic traditions. Muhammad, the Prophet of Islam, started preaching in Mecca in 611 C.E. and quickly gained a strong following. Worried that it might lose its profitable control over the pilgrimage, the leadership of Mecca launched a merciless war on the new faith, forcing the Prophet to seek refuge in 622 C.E. in a neighboring town, Medina, in an event known as *hijra* (migration) that marks the beginning of the lunar calendar of Islam. Having prohibited alcohol, gambling, prostitution, raiding, and usury, and prescribed *zakah* (alms-tax) to restore economic equality, replaced the tribal bond with the bond of faith, and instituted Islamic law as the sole reference in settling disputes, Islam spread rapidly throughout Arabia, despite the continuing hostility of Mecca. But since half of Mecca's population had already converted to the new faith, the surrender of the city was only a matter of time, and when the Prophet died in 632 C.E., most of Arabia was Muslim.

Under the first four *rashidun* (rightly guided) caliphs, the Islamic state spread quickly in the Near East, where it was welcomed by a local Semitic and Arab population that was only too pleased to be rid of the ethnically foreign and abusive rule of the Byzantines, as well as in Persia, where the Sassanid Empire had already started to crumble. Later, the Umayyad dynasty (661–750), which followed the *rashidun* caliphs, spread the frontiers of the new empire from Spain to India.

Theology and Beliefs

Tawhid, the concept of the absolute unity and transcendence of God, forms the cornerstone of Islamic theology as expressed in the Qur'an, the holy book of Islam, which the Muslims believe to be the verbatim word of God, revealed to the Prophet in successive revelations over the span of his prophetic career. *Tawhid* forms the content of the *shahada* (literally, "witnessing," the profession of faith that states that there is no god but God and that Muhammad is His messenger) which therefore constitutes the only requirement for conversion to Islam. The *shahada* and the four main rituals compulsory on the faithful (worshipping *salah* five times a day, fasting from dawn to sunset through the month of Ramadan, performing the pilgrimage to Mecca once in a lifetime, and paying the *zakah,* or alms-tax, annually) eventually became known as the five pillars of Islam.

The Qur'an represents God as an omnipotent, all-powerful Creator, Master of the Day of Judgment. All of creation is created to worship God; humanity, which received lordship over creation when it accepted God's vice-regency (*khilafa*) on earth, is to account on the Day of Judgment for "what [they] did with the boon of life" (Qur'an 102:8). All human beings are under the same obligation to obey the divine law ("Noblest among you is the most righteous" Qur'an 49:13), and this equality is further expressed in the universality of the messages that God sends to His creatures throughout time and place, starting with Adam and concluding with Muhammad ("There is not one community wherein a warner has not been sent" Qur'an 35:24). Other religions are therefore considered to be based on divine revelations that had been somewhat altered by oral transmission over time, but their followers (the People of the Book) can be ensured reward in paradise given belief in God and good deeds: "The Muslims, the Sabeans, the Christians, the Jews, anyone who believes in God . . . and does good deeds shall find their reward with God and will not come to fear or grief" (Qur'an 2:62). Although the Qur'an only mentions Semitic prophets (including Jesus, whom it celebrates as a human messenger of God, and local Arabian prophets), the designation of "the People of the Book" was later extended by the Muslims to all other main religious traditions they encountered, on the basis of the Qur'anic affirmation

Young Egyptian Sunni Muslims attend class in a school affiliated with the famed Islamic al-Azhar University. In the Shubra suburb of Cairo alone, there are thirteen such schools that instruct pupils between the ages of ten and eighteen. Students of al-Azhar are taught a traditional school curriculum focused primarily on Islamic subjects. © AFP/CORBIS. REPRODUCED BY PERMISSION.

of the universality of prophecy. Muslims and followers of other traditions are exhorted to cooperate in establishing a moral society and prohibiting evil and mischief.

Ethics

The Qur'an exhibits a firmly actionalist system of ethics based on individual responsibility in the realization of the optimal social, economic, and political structure of the *umma,* the universal community of believers. Mutual consultation (*shura*) for the ideal political system, just and fair business practices in the economic system, and financial and moral responsibility to one's extended family members in the social system are to be supplemented by various safety nets for the more vulnerable segments of society, such as *zakah* (poor-tax) and *mahr* (the inalien-

The Haram or Great Mosque in Mecca, Saudi Arabia. Mecca is the birthplace of the prophet Muhammad and the most sacred of the Muslim holy cities. Pilgrimage to Mecca is one of the five pillars of Islam, and more than one million Muslims make the journey, or hajj, every year. © AFP/CORBIS. REPRODUCED BY PERMISSION.

able dowry due the bride). Though no self-denial is advocated, the individual is urged to exercise restraint over his and her natural appetites and to show *rahma* (compassion, forgiveness) in all dealings with one's fellow human beings. Pride and greed are especially condemned, as they lead to injustice to others and hence to oneself *(zulm al-nafs)*, ultimately leading to the path of self-destruction. There is no concept of sinful nature, but recurrent sin leads to the hardening of the soul and the eventual silencing of one's conscience. The partial rewards and opportunities provided in this life are considered to be just as much a test to the individual as the difficulties and hardships, and one is exhorted to exercise *sabr* (steadfastness) in the face of life's challenges.

The difficulty of the task is acknowledged by the Qur'an, which expresses faith in humanity's ultimate success in carrying out God's trusteeship. The

individual is urged to remain focused on his or her relationship with God and to never fail to seek Him, for He "hears the prayers of everyone who calls on Him" (Qur'an 2:186). This intensely personal and spiritual relationship, which the Qur'an tries to integrate in the individual's life through the five daily prayers, also expresses the human need for the presence and support of one's Creator and Sustainer, for only "with the remembrance of God do human hearts find peace and come to rest" (Qur'an 13:30). Thus the Qur'an postulates a direct and intimate relationship between the individual and God (hence the absence of clergy in Islam) and God is said to be closer to His creatures than their jugular vein.

Paradise and Hell are in the Qur'anic view the consummation of the individual's life on earth. What is to come is therefore not "another world," but the response to what one has done in this life. This world is to be recreated in a different form at

The Shrine of Hazrat Imam Ali stands in the Iraqi holy city of Najaf. Hazrat Ali, the first imam and a close companion of the prophet Muhammad, was assassinated with a poisoned sword while at prayer and buried in Najaf. © SHEPARD SHERBELL/CORBIS SABA. REPRODUCED BY PERMISSION.

the end of its time span, ushering in the Day of Judgment that will inaugurate punishment and reward; these are set along an absolute scale of justice tempered only by God's infinite mercy, which is assured to all those who genuinely seek it.

Political and Cultural Developments

Islam as a faith spread first in the Near East and Egypt, where in the first few centuries Arab Islamic civilization flourished. The caliphate split after the Abbassid takeover of the Near East and Egypt, while Spain remained under Umayyad rule until 1492. The Abbassid dynasty ruled until 1258, though in the latter part of their rule only nominal allegiance was given to the caliphs in Baghdad by the amirs and sultans who, in effect, governed the various provinces of the empire and fought each other over territory. The internecine war, partly caused by Sunni-Shiʿite conflict, allowed the invading Crusaders (eleventh through thirteenth centuries) to establish a state in

Palestine. It was not until Salah al-Din (Saladin, d. 1193) that Egypt and the Near East were united under Sunni rule, which in turn helped to defeat the Crusaders and later to repulse the Mongols who had sacked Baghdad in 1258. But as the Arab world fell into decline, the Sunni Ottoman Turks swept through Byzantium and extended their rule over the Near East and most of North Africa, ushering in Ottoman Islamic civilization. In the East, the Shiʿite Safavid dynasty took over Iran at the end of the sixteenth century, helping to spread a highly sophisticated Persian culture throughout Central Asia and into Northern India, where a brilliant Indian Islamic civilization climaxed under the Great Moghuls between the sixteenth and eighteenth centuries.

During this period Islamic arts, science, and technology flourished throughout the Muslim world, with contributions in astronomy (al-Biruni, d. 1048; Ibn al-Shatir, d. 1375), algebra and trigonometry (al-Khawarizmi, d. 850; Umar al-Khayyam, d. 1131;

Sharaf al-Din al-Tusi, d. 1213), physics and chemistry (Ibn Hayyan, d. 815; Ibn al-Haytham, d. 1250), and biology and medicine (Abu Bakr al-Razi, d. 925; Ibn Sina, d. 1037, also known as Avicenna, whose *Canon of Medicine* remained the definitive reference book in the field until the seventeenth century in both East and West.)

Islamic Law

The emphasis on submitting to the divine will (the literal meaning of *Islam*) and fulfilling the main Qur'anic injunction, "to enjoin the good and prohibit evil" led to the rapid development of Islamic law *(fiqh)*. In terms of legal sources, the Qur'an was the first and absolute reference; and since it had mandated obedience to the Prophet, his *sunna* (example), which was provided in the reports of his sayings and deeds, naturally came second. Much of the law, however, had to be inferred, and the jurists turned to their own intellectual effort *(ijtihad)* expressed in the methodology of *qiyas* ("analogical reasoning," that is, finding a *ratio legis* parallel to one already identified in the Qur'an or *sunna*). Such individual opinions, however, did not become binding until they submitted to *ijma,* or consensus of the schools of law, though all parties acknowledged to the others the right to dissent *(ikhtilaf).* Eventually, the schools of law coalesced into four main schools. The processes by which laws may be derived became the subject of an extensive and separate discipline, *usul al-fiqh* (literally, the principles of *fiqh*). Islamic law developed rapidly into an extensive field in the first few centuries of Muslim history, but innovation subsided considerably as a result of the reliance on precedents and past consensus.

Religious Schisms

The most important schism in the Muslim community occurred over a political split in the early community. After the Prophet's death, most Muslims supported the election of Abu Bakr and later of Umar ibn al-Khattab, the Prophet's closest companions. However, a small number known as the Shi'at Ali (the party of Ali), insisted on keeping the caliphate within the Prophet's family and championed his cousin Ali. Eventually, the Shi'a became a religious movement, basing their position on the claim that God would not leave His community without guidance, and justifying it through prophetic

sayings and esoteric interpretation of the Qur'an. The belief in the authority of the imams (the leaders who were entitled to rule) was made part of the Islamic creed and gave rise to a clerical structure in Shi'ite Islam. In all other matters of *fiqh* and dogma, the Shi'a are similar to the Sunnis, though this applies only to the Ithna'ashariyya ("Twelvers," who believe in a line of twelve imams), and the Zaydis (who recognize only five imams) and not to the other groups (the Isma'ilis, the Alawis, the Druze, etc.) that split from them and whose beliefs ran contrary to the doctrines of *tawhid* and the finality of Muhammad's prophecy. Thus the main difference between the Sunnis and the Shi'a lies more in the political issue of the community leadership (with the beliefs and practices that the latter entails) than in doctrinal difference of dogma.

Philosophical Developments

The philosophical developments in the Muslim world expressed the tension between the Islamic (Semitic) worldview and the Hellenistic heritage, which to some extent had become part of the Near East's cultural makeup. At one end stood the heirs of Hellenistic thought (called *falasifa*) such as al-Kindi (d. 870), al-Farabi (d. 950), and Ibn Rushd (d. 1198, also known as Averroes) who used Greek logic and incorporated into their works Greek notions such as the eternity of the world, the distinction between essence and existence, and Hellenistic angelology.

At the other end stood the traditionists, staunch defenders of Islamic dogma and method, generally represented by the Hanbalis. Their greatest proponent was Ibn Taymiyya (d. 1328), who delivered devastating blows to the Greek logic used by the *falasifa* in his *al-Radd ala al-Mantiqiyyin.* In between the two groups were two theological Kalam schools; the earlier one, known as the Mu'tazila, was closer to the philosophers and upheld the independence of reason from revelation, the necessity for God to abide by justice, and the creation of the Qur'an; such views prompted the rise of the later school, the Ash'ariyya, which restored the pre-eminence of revelation, the absolute omnipotence of God, and the uncreated nature of the word of God (making use of a somewhat revised Greek logic). Their greatest representative was Abu Hamid al-Ghazzali (d. 1111), who used his incisive analysis of causality to undermine the philosophers.

Mysticism

Mystical thought, which had a basis in the spiritual worldview of the Qur'an and the simple and intense piety of early Muslims, became more formalized through the gradual absorption of Hellenistic, Persian, and Indian thought, and became known as Sufism. The main architect of the Sufi theosophy was Ibn Arabi (d. 1240). Sufi poetical expression of the divine love, articulated by Rabi'a al-Adawiyya (d. 801) and Jalal al-Din al-Rumi (d. 1273), became very popular throughout the Muslim world. But its foreign elements led to opposition by the orthodox jurists and theologians, especially those whose strictly legalistic and ritualistic interpretation of the faith found no place for spiritual expression. Ironically, their opposition encouraged the spread of Sufism as a reaction to their impoverished representation of the personal relationship to God—as did the increase in worldliness and materialism spreading in the Muslim world as the empire expanded. However, most great theologians and jurists (e.g., al-Ghazzali, who silenced the critics of Sufism; Ibn Taymiyya; Muhammad ibn Abd al-Wahhab) defended and indeed practiced the Sufi way, though all of them condemned in strong terms the philosophical expression of Sufism, which advocated a form of pantheism (*wahdat al-wujud*, the unity of being) and extreme asceticism. But Sufism spread widely, and the *tariqas* (Sufi orders, such as the Qadiriyya in the Near East, the Mawlawiyya (Mevlevis and the Naqshbandiyya in Central Asia and Turkey, and the Shadhiliyya in North Africa) were the main impetus behind the spread of Islam in Africa and East Asia.

Reform Movements

The insistence on the importance of spiritualism over and above the law led on one hand to asceticism and withdrawal but also, on the other, to libertarianism, a trend that was accentuated in popular religion by the belief in miracles, superstition, and cultic practices into which the veneration of Sufi saints had slowly degenerated. In North Africa and India, the Sufi movements had also absorbed the cultural and religious heritage of their new converts, a syncretism that included at times non-Islamic beliefs and practices. Meanwhile, the law had become more and more reified as the need for innovation subsided and *taqlid* (imitation or reliance on past tradition) became the norm. The jurists' inability to respond to new needs became a problem as new challenges arose with the industrialization of Europe, which forced the Ottomans to adopt Western laws and institutions. All these problems set the stage for the reform movements of the eighteenth century.

The reform movements rejected consensus as a source of law as it had become a hindrance to change, and they advocated *ijtihad* instead. At the same time, they emphasized a strict interpretation of *tawhid* and repudiated the syncretic beliefs adopted by the Sufi movements as well as the morally lax social practices and the popular beliefs in magic, superstition, and saints' intercession. Building on the philosophical and political thought of Ibn Taymiyya, Muhammad ibn Abd al-Wahhab (d. 1792) started in Arabia the reform movement of Wahhabism, which then spread in the Near East as the Salafiyya movement. At same time, separate but similar movements spread in Africa under the leadership of Ibn Idris (d.1837) and al-Sanusi order (d. 1859), and in India under Sirhindi (d. 1624). These were Sufi masters who criticized the former excesses of the Sufi movements and used the *tariqas* to restore orthodoxy of belief and practice and to purge the movements of syncretic accretions.

However, the colonial ambitions of the European powers quickly changed the Muslim scene from one of reform to one of confrontation with a greater power that soon overcame most of the Muslim world and won from the ailing Ottoman Empire significant concessions. Instead of internal social change, the reform movements turned to armed resistance, and instead of focusing on doctrinal purity and legal tools, the new discourse centered on the necessity of resisting the West and on apologetics for Islam, for the defeat of the Muslims was contemptuously blamed by Western Orientalists on the backwardness and inferiority of Islam.

Islamic Modernist Movements

Islamic modern thought is considered to start with Jamal al-Din al-Afghani (d. 1897), a man with encyclopedic knowledge of both Western and Eastern disciplines who traveled throughout the Muslim world in hope of uniting it in the fight against Western colonization. He advocated reform of education and law and was followed in Egypt by one of his most famous students, Muhammad Abduh (d.1905), a jurist who became the head of the famed al-Azhar *fiqh* university. But few practical solutions were offered, and the problem was compounded by the call by some of his students like Rashid Rida (d. 1935) for compromise with Western institutions, such as interest and the creation of national entities separate from the Islamic Ottoman rule. In India, Muhammad Iqbal (d. 1938) called for a return to the original ethos of Islam and the establishment of the independent state of Pakistan, while Sayyid Ahmad Khan (d. 1898) called for more drastic changes in Islamic thought and cooperation with the British colonial power. The compromises advocated by some led then to an attitude of general rejection of change on the part of most jurists and theologians, and although all had agreed on the necessity of reforming law and education and of adopting Western advances in science and technology, the discourse remained general and did not offer specific and coherent suggestions. In effect, the colonial powers, which by now had also taken over the Near East after the defeat of the Ottoman Empire at the end of World War I, had imposed their legal, political, and educational systems on their colonies. After independence, the local governments maintained the Western institutions they had inherited, leading to the Islamic Revolution in Iran in 1979 and giving rise, throughout the Muslim world, to opposition movements (such as the Muslim Brotherhood in Egypt and Jordan, the Jami'at-e Islami in Pakistan, the Front Islamique du Salut in Algeria and the Rafah Party in Turkey) that called for the restoration of Islamic law and fought the adoption by Muslim elites of the Western ideologies of secularism, socialism, and nationalism. These ideological conflicts, which have led to tensions or all-out civil war in many countries, are exacerbated by the policies of autocratic regimes that do not tolerate opposition or democratic rule and by Western intervention (directly or in support of such regimes) to preserve Western interests in oil and to protect Israel. These interventions have become the focus of Muslim resentment and radicalism throughout the Muslim world.

See also ABDUH, MUHAMMAD; AFGHANI, JAMAL AL-DIN AL-; ALAWI; ALLAH; AZHAR, AL-; DRUZE; FRONT ISLAMIQUE DU SALUT (FIS); HADITH; IQBAL, MUHAMMAD; IRANIAN REV-OLUTION (1979); ISMA'ILI SHI'ISM; JAMI'AT-E ISLAMI; KA'BA; MECCA; MEDINA; MUHAMMAD; MUSLIM BROTHERHOOD; NAQSHBANDI; QADIRIYYA ORDER; QUR'AN; RIDA, RASHID; SALAFIYYA MOVEMENT; SHI'ISM; SUFISM AND THE SUFI ORDERS; SUNNI ISLAM; ZAYDISM.

Bibliography

Arnold, Thomas W. *The Preaching of Islam: A History of the Propagation of the Muslim Faith,* 2d edition. Lahore, Pakistan: Sh. Muhammad Ashraf, 1961.

Al Faruqi, Lois. *Islam and Art.* Islamabad: National Hijra Council, 1985.

Gardet, Louis. *L'Islam.* Paris: Desclée de Brouwer, 1967.

Kamali, Mohammad Hashim. *Principles of Islamic Jurisprudence.* Cambridge, U.K.: Islamic Texts Society, 1991.

Nasr, Seyyed Hossein. *Three Muslim Sages.* Cambridge, MA: Harvard University Press, 1964.

Rahman, Fazlur. *Islam,* 2d edition. Chicago: University of Chicago Press, 1979.

Rahman, Fazlur. *Major Themes of the Qur'an.* Chicago: Bibliotheca Islamic, 1980.

Saliba, George, and King, David A. *From Deferent to Equant: A Volume of Studies in the History of Science in the Ancient and Medieval Near East in Honor of E. S. Kennedy.* New York: New York Academy of Sciences, 1987.

Smith, Wilfred Cantwell. *Islam in Modern History.* Princeton, NJ: Princeton University Press, 1957.

TAYEB EL-HIBRI
UPDATED BY MAYSAM J. AL FARUQI

ISLAMIC ACTION FRONT

Jordanian Islamist political party.

Jabhat al-Amal al-Islami (Islamic Action Front, IAF) grew out of Jordan's Muslim Brotherhood. The two overlap in membership and outlook but are not synonymous. The IAF has maintained a strategy of loyal opposition, emphasizing reformist rather than militant tactics, and is by far the largest and best-organized political party in the kingdom.

The Muslim Brotherhood operated with tacit state approval for decades but was technically registered as a charity. After Jordan's political liberalization process began in 1989, the Brotherhood was the best-organized movement in the country. Its candidates won twenty-two out of a total of eighty seats in the new parliament, with twelve more going to independent Islamists. The IAF was founded in 1992, immediately following the legalization of political parties in Jordan for the first time since the 1950s.

The IAF is known for its regressive social views regarding the rights of women but is also active in charitable work for the poor. The party has been a vocal opponent of U.S. policy in the region, especially regarding Palestine and Iraq, and opposed the Jordanian peace treaty with Israel in 1994. Following the treaty, the IAF organized an ongoing campaign to prevent normalization of relations with Israel at any level.

The IAF has developed increasing levels of support among the lower classes and especially among urban Palestinians of various classes. Hence the IAF sees its electoral strengths in urban, Palestinian-majority communities such as Irbid, al-Zarqa, and most districts of Amman. Yet Jordan's electoral laws favor rural areas and traditional sources of support for Jordan's ruling Hashimite family. To the surprise of the regime, however, Islamists dominated the 1989 elections and Islamist leader Abd al-Latif Arabiyyat even served as the elected speaker of the parliament from 1990 to 1993.

Before the 1993 elections, changes in the elections laws and the unpopular performances of Islamist leaders as cabinet ministers led to a decrease in IAF electoral success. The IAF took sixteen seats and six more went to independent Islamists. IAF secretary general Ishaq Farhan did manage to keep his parliamentary seat, but Arabiyyat lost his reelection bid. In recognition of his importance and influence in the Islamist movement, however, the king appointed Arabiyyat to the upper house of parliament.

The IAF and most opposition parties, from the secular left through the religious right, demanded a revision of the electoral law. When no changes were made, the IAF led a coalition of eleven opposition parties from across the political spectrum in an electoral boycott. As a result, no IAF members were seated in the 1997–2001 parliament, but six independent Islamists did secure seats, including former IAF members Abdullah Akayla and Bassam Ammush. Since IAF figures had been successful within Jordan's professional associations, winning

key leadership posts, these associations took the lead, in the absence of the IAF from the 1997–2001 parliament, in maintaining IAF activism on such issues as the antinormalization campaign.

The IAF returned to full electoral participation in 2003, despite a new electoral law that increased the number of deputies to 110 (including a minimum of six seats for women) and maintained uneven electoral districts. The party negotiated its participation with the palace, fielding only thirty candidates. Secretary General Hamza Mansur and Shura Council president Arabiyyat (president of the party's Shura or consultative council) decided not to run themselves, and also excluded controversial IAF figures such as Abd al-Munʿim Abu Zant. Abu Zant, who shortly thereafter won a seat as an independent, was expelled from the IAF for running anyway. The party gained eighteen seats in the election, including one for Haya al-Musaymi, the only woman candidate in the IAF, who won the largest vote of any woman candidate. An additional six seats went to independent Islamists, many of whom, like Abu Zant, were former IAF members. Having returned to parliament, and with a solid base in the professional associations, the IAF pursued its agenda: abrogating the 1994 peace treaty; preventing normalization of relations with Israel; supporting Palestinian aspirations; countering U.S. dominance in the region; and establishing *shariʿa* and more traditional roles for men and women in Jordanian society.

See also AMMAN; HASHIMITE HOUSE (HOUSE OF HASHIM); IRBID; MUSLIM BROTHERHOOD; SHARIʿA.

Bibliography

Boulby, Marion. *The Muslim Brotherhood and the Kings of Jordan 1945–1993*. Atlanta, GA: Scholars Press, 1999.

Kilani, Saʾeda, ed. and trans. *Islamic Action Front Party*. Amman, Jordan: Al-Urdun Al-Jadid Research Center, 1993.

Schwedler, Jillian, ed. *Islamic Movements in Jordan*, translated by George Musleh. Amman, Jordan: Sindbad Publishing, 1997.

Wiktorowicz, Quintan. *The Management of Islamic Activism: Salafis, the Muslim Brotherhood, and State Power in Jordan*. Albany: State University of New York Press, 2000.

CURTIS R. RYAN

ISLAMIC CONGRESSES

Muslims, either of a certain faction or in general, convening to promote solidarity and interaction among Muslim peoples and states.

Although the concept of Muslim solidarity is intrinsic to the faith of Islam, it took no organized form until modern times. In the course of the twentieth century, Islamic congresses have emerged as the structured expression of that concept. Some of these congresses have evolved into international Islamic organizations that promote political, economic, and cultural interaction among Muslim peoples and states.

The idea of Muslims convening in congresses first gained currency in the late nineteenth century, in the Ottoman Empire. The advent of easy and regular steamer transport accelerated the exchange of ideas among Muslims and made possible the periodic assembling of representatives. The idea also appealed to Muslim reformists, who sought a forum to promote and sanction the internal reform of Islam. Such an assembly, they believed, would strengthen the ability of Muslims to resist the encroachments of Western imperialism.

A number of émigré intellectuals in Cairo first popularized the idea in the Muslim world. In 1900, one of them, the Syrian Abd al-Rahman al-Kawakibi, published an influential book entitled *Umm al-Qura* (that is, Mecca), which purported to be the secret protocol of an Islamic congress convened in Mecca during the pilgrimage of 1899. The fictional congress culminated in a call for a restored Arab caliphate, an idea then in vogue in reformist circles. Support for such a congress also became a staple of the reformist journal *al-Manar,* published in Cairo by Rashid Rida. The Crimean Tatar reformist Ismail Bey Gaspirali (in Russian, Gasprinski) launched the first concrete initiative in Cairo in 1907, when he unsuccessfully worked to convene a general Islamic congress.

Al-Kawakibi's book, Rida's appeals, and Gaspirali's initiative all excited the suspicion of Ottoman authorities. The Ottoman Turks believed that a well-attended Islamic congress would fatally undermine the religious authority claimed by the theocratic Ottoman sultan-caliph and, in particular, it feared the possible transformation of any such congress into an electoral college for choosing an Arab caliph. Steadfast Ottoman opposition thwarted all the early initiatives of the reformers.

With the final dismemberment of the Ottoman Empire after World War I, some Muslim leaders and activists moved to convene general Islamic congresses. In each instance, they sought to mark their causes or their ambitions with the stamp of Islamic consensus. In 1919, Mustafa Kemal Atatürk convened an Islamic congress in Anatolia to mobilize pan-Islamic support for his military campaigns. During the *hajj* (pilgrimage) season of 1924, Sharif Husayn ibn Ali of the Hijaz summoned a pilgrimage congress in Mecca to support his claim to the caliphate—a maneuver that failed to stall the relentless advance of Ibn Saʿud (Abd al-Aziz ibn Saʿud Al Saʿud). Following Ibn Saʿud's occupation of Mecca, he convened his own world congress during the pilgrimage season of 1926. The leading clerics of al-Azhar in Cairo convened a caliphate congress there in 1926 to consider the effects of the abolition of the caliphate by Turkey two years earlier. The congress was supported by King Fuʾad, who reputedly coveted the title of caliph, but no decision issued from the gathering. In 1931, Muhammad Amin al-Husayni, the mufti of Jerusalem, convened a general congress of Muslims in Jerusalem to secure pan-Islamic support for the Arab struggle against the British mandate and Zionism. In 1935, pan-Islamic activist Shakib Arslan convened a congress of Europe's Muslims in Geneva to carry the protest against imperialism and colonialism to the heart of Europe. Each of these congresses resolved to create a permanent organization and convene additional congresses, but all such efforts were foiled by internal rivalries and the intervention of the European powers.

As more and more countries in the Middle East achieved political independence following World War II, Muslim leaders increasingly offered new plans for the creation of a permanent organization of Muslim states. After the partition of India, Pakistan took a number of initiatives in the late 1940s and early 1950s but soon encountered stiff opposition from Egypt, which gave primacy of place to pan-Arabism and the Arab League. When Egypt's President Gamal Abdel Nasser transformed pan-Arabism into a revolutionary doctrine, Saudi Arabia sought to counter him by promoting a rival pan-Islamism, assembling congresses of Muslim activists and *ulama* (Islamic clergy) from abroad. In 1962, the Saudi government sponsored the establishment of the Mecca-based Muslim World League, which built a worldwide network of Muslim clients. Beginning in 1964, Egypt responded by organizing large congresses of Egyptian and foreign *ulama* under the auspices of al-Azhar's Academy of Islamic Research in Cairo. These rival bodies then convened a succession of dueling congresses in Mecca and Cairo, each claiming the sole prerogative of defining Islam. In 1965 and 1966, Saudi Arabia's new king, Faisal (son of Ibn Sa'ud), launched a campaign for an Islamic summit conference that would have balanced the Arab summits dominated by President Nasser, however, had sufficient influence to thwart the initiative, which he denounced as a foreign-inspired Islamic pact, designed to defend the interests of Western imperialism.

Israel's 1967 devastating pre-emptive attack on Egypt, Syria, and Jordan, along with its annexation of Jerusalem, the West Bank, Gaza, the Golan Heights, and the Sinai, eroded faith in the brand of Arabism championed by Nasser, inspiring a return to Islam. This set the scene for a renewed Saudi initiative. In September 1969, following an arsonist's attack against the al-Aqsa Mosque in Jerusalem, Muslim heads of state set aside their differences and met in Rabat, Morocco, in the first Islamic summit conference. King Faisal of Saudi Arabia took this opportunity to press for the creation of a permanent organization of Muslim states. The effort succeeded, and, in May 1971, the participating states established the Organization of the Islamic Conference (OIC; *Munazzamat al-mu'tamar al-Islami*). The new organization, headquartered in Jidda, Saudi Arabia (pending the liberation of Jerusalem), adopted its charter in March 1972.

The OIC eventually earned a place of some prominence in regional diplomacy, principally through the organization of triennial Islamic summit conferences and annual conferences of the foreign ministers of member states. The OIC's activities fell into three broad categories. First, it sought to promote solidarity with Muslim states and peoples that were locked in conflict with non-Muslims. Most of its efforts were devoted to the cause of establishing a state of Palestine and recapturing Jerusalem. Nonetheless, it supported the movement

Abdullah O. Nasseef, the Saudi Arabian president of the World Muslim Congress. An international, nongovernmental organization, the Congress was established in 1926 and is based in Karachi, Pakistan. The organization's motto is "Verily, all Muslims are brethren," and its members strive towards unity between Muslim nations and world peace on the basis of justice. © AP/WIDE WORLD PHOTOS. REPRODUCED BY PERMISSION.

of Muslims from Eritrea—incorporated into Ethiopia in 1962—to the Philippines. Second, the organization offered mediation in disputes and wars among its own members, although its effectiveness was greatly limited by the lack of any force for truce supervision or peacekeeping. Lastly, the OIC sponsored an array of subsidiary and affiliated institutions to promote political, economic, and cultural cooperation among its members. The most influential of these institutions was the Islamic Development Bank, established in December 1973 and formally opened in October 1975. The bank, funded by the wealthier OIC states, financed development projects while adhering to Islamic banking practices.

The OIC represents an ingenious attempt by various Arab governments to organize Muslim states. But it has not put an end to instances of individual states to summoning international congresses of *ulama,* activists, and intellectuals. Saudi Arabia and Egypt, realigned on the conservative end of the Islamic spectrum, have cooperated increasingly in mounting large-scale Islamic congresses. Their rivals—Iran, Libya, and Iraq—have done the same. Divisive events, such as the war between Iran and Iraq (1980–1988), the lethal attack upon several hundred Iranians in Mecca during the pilgrimage season of 1987, and the Iraqi invasion of Kuwait in 1990, produced congresses and counter-congresses, each claiming to express the verdict of a united Islam. Leaders of Muslim opposition movements have also met in periodic congresses, sometimes in Europe. Less than a century after al-Kawakibi's book, a crowded calendar of congresses now bind Muslim states together more than ever before. On the whole, to the extent that healthy and heated discussion of alternatives between friends is salutary, such efforts—however confusing to the outsider—appear most salutary and indicative of a new political awareness among Muslim states and their peoples.

See also ABD AL-AZIZ IBN SAʿUD AL SAʿUD; ARAB LEAGUE; ARSLAN, SHAKIB; ATATÜRK, MUSTAFA KEMAL; AZHAR, AL-; GASPIRALI, ISMAIL BEY; HUSAYN IBN ALI; HUSAYNI, MUHAMMAD AMIN AL-; MUSLIM WORLD LEAGUE; ORGANIZATION OF THE ISLAMIC CONFERENCE; PAN-ARABISM; RIDA, RASHID.

Bibliography

Kramer, Martin. *Islam Assembled: The Advent of the Muslim Congresses.* New York: Columbia University Press, 1986.

Landau, Jacob M. *The Politics of Pan-Islam: Ideology and Organization.* Oxford: Clarendon Press; New York: Oxford University Press, 1990.

Moinuddin, Hasan. *The Charter of the Islamic Conference.* Oxford: Clarendon Press; New York: Oxford University Press, 1987.

MARTIN KRAMER
UPDATED BY CHARLES E. BUTTERWORTH

ISLAMIC COUNTRIES WOMEN SPORT SOLIDARITY GAMES (1992 AND 1997)

International sporting event for women from Islamic countries.

The Islamic Countries Women Sport Solidarity Games, reserved for women from Islamic countries, were held in 1992 and 1997 in Tehran, Iran. Athletes from eleven countries participated in 1992 and from sixteen countries in 1997. Women competed in events including badminton, basketball, volleyball, swimming, archery, and handball. Kyrgyzstan

won in 1992; Iran won in 1997. The games had two aims: to provide a venue for Islamic women to participate in sports in an international arena while remaining faithful to Islamic dress codes; and to strengthen solidarity between Islamic countries and express cultural unity.

Principally sponsored and organized by the Islamic Women Sport Solidarity Council, which was headed by Faezeh Hashemi, former parliamentarian and editor of the journal *Zanan* (Women), the games were also internationally sponsored by the IOC, reinforcing Islamic cultural unity.

The games aroused interest both nationally and internationally due to the focus on women and the idea of an Islamic alternative to international sporting events. The 1992 event marked the first time an Iranian woman participated in an international sporting event. The games were particularly controversial in 1997 because they coincided with the football World Cup qualifier match between Iran and Australia in Tehran, which Iranian women attended in defiance of government orders. The third Islamic Countries Women Sport Solidarity Games were scheduled for December 2004.

See also HASHEMI, FAEZEH.

CHERIE TARAGHI

ISLAMIC JIHAD

Palestinian Islamic fundamentalist resistance movement.

Islamic Jihad emerged from the Islamic revivalist tradition of the association of Muslim Brotherhood in Israeli-occupied Gaza and was formed by Palestinians studying in Egypt. Rather than pursue the Brotherhood's policy of the gradual Islamization of Palestinian society as the basis for future liberation from Israeli occupation, certain militants in the late 1970s began arguing for a more active, armed, Islamic response to the occupation much as secular groups associated with the Palestine Liberation Organization (PLO) had undertaken. Sources of inspiration included such militant historical figures as Shaykh Izz al-Din al-Qassam in Palestine and Sayyid Qutb in Egypt, as well as the revolutionary movements spawned by Muhammad Abd al-Salam Faraj in Egypt (the Jihad Organization) and the Ayatollah Ruhollah Khomeini in Iran. What tied these traditions together was their belief in active struggle (jihad) in the service of Islam as opposed to mere preaching.

It is believed that Islamic Jihad emerged as an actual organization in 1980. Two early leaders were Abd al-Aziz Awda, deported by Israeli authorities in November 1987, and his successor, Fathi Abd al-Aziz Shiqaqi, himself deported in August 1988. Shiqaqi operated in Lebanon thereafter until his assassination in Malta in October 1995. Jihad's new head became Ramadan Abdullah Shallah, who moved to Damascus in the mid-1990s. The group has always maintained close relations with Iran. One of Islamic Jihad's first dramatic acts against the Israeli occupation was an attack on a group of soldiers in Jerusalem in October 1986, followed by a series of well-planned attacks on Israeli targets in late 1987. These helped to precipitate the Palestinian uprising, known as the Infidada, against Israeli rule in the occupied territories, which erupted in December 1987. Islamic Jihad has operated as a small, clandestine group of militants who seek the total liberation of all of Palestine through armed struggle rather than a mass-based organization like the Muslim Brotherhood or HAMAS. Its activities were severely hampered by Israeli repression during the Intifada. Jihad operated alongside but separate from the PLO's Unified National Command of the Uprising during the Intifada. Jihad activists were among the 418 Palestinians from the territories deported by Israel in December 1992.

Jihad opposed the Israeli–Palestinian peace talks, which began in 1991, as well as the subsequent 1993 Oslo Accord. In 1992 it joined the "Damascus Ten," a grouping of Palestinian organizations opposed to the peace talks, which changed its name to the National Democratic and Islamic Front in 1993. Jihad continued to attack Israeli targets even after establishment of a Palestinian Authority (PA) in Gaza and the West Bank in 1994, promoting considerable friction between it and the PA leadership. Jihad figures were arrested; Abdullah al-Shami, the group's spokesman and spiritual leader in Gaza, was arrested by the PA on six different occasions for Friday sermons that criticized the PA and its president, Yasir Arafat. Eschewing any compromise with Israel, Jihad activists have resorted to suicide bombings against Israelis during the 1990s.

Jihad and HAMAS were rivals until the al-Aqsa Intifada tended to bring them together in their activities. Jihad also has undergone some internal problems. Abd al-Aziz Awda eventually left Jihad and returned to the PA from his Israel-imposed exile with Arafat's approval. In 2003 al-Shami was pushed out of his positions and quit the movement as well.

See also AQSA INTIFADA, AL-; HAMAS; INTIFADA (1987–1991); MUSLIM BROTHERHOOD; OSLO ACCORD (1993); PALESTINE LIBERATION ORGANIZATION (PLO).

Bibliography

Abu-Amr, Ziad. *Islamic Fundamentalism in the West Bank and Gaza: Muslim Brotherhood and Islamic Jihad.* Bloomington: University of Indiana Press, 1994.

Hatina, Meir. *Islam and Salvation in Palestine: The Islamic Jihad Movement.* Tel Aviv: Tel Aviv University, 2001.

MICHAEL R. FISCHBACH

ISLAMIC SALVATION ARMY (AIS)

Armed wing of the Islamic Salvation Front, which fought the Algerian regime from 1994 until its disbanding in October 1997.

The Islamic Salvation Army (AIS), or Armée islamique du salut, was founded in Algeria on 18 July 1994 as the "fighting wing" of the Islamic Salvation Front (FIS). Madani Mezrag, who eventually became the national amir (commander) of the organization, and Ahmed Benaïcha (future commander of the western region), were among its founders. The AIS wished to distance itself from the Armed Islamic Group (GIA), which had emerged in 1993 to fight the regime and anyone opposed to the Islamist movement; at the same time, the AIS was fearful of the marginalization of the FIS because many FIS members—including Abderrezak Redjam, Mohamed Saïd, Saïd Makhloufi, and the political refugee Anouar Haddam (all Jaz'arists, the so-called Algerianists as opposed to the *salafists*)— had joined the GIA in May 1994. In their communiqué announcing the creation of the AIS, Mezrag and Benaïcha advocated "recourse to jihad, in the path of God, as a means of establishing an Islamic state in Algeria, prelude to the establishment of the Caliphate." The AIS proclaimed allegiance to imprisoned FIS leaders Abassi al-Madani and Ali Benhadj.

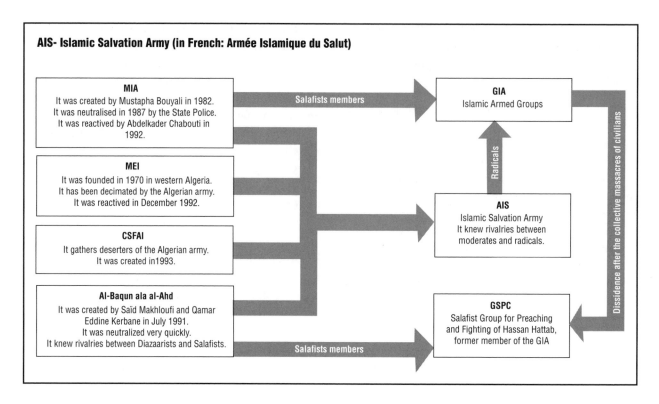

AIS- Islamic Salvation Army (in French: Armée Islamique du Salut)

MIA
It was created by Mustapha Bouyali in 1982. It was neutralised in 1987 by the State Police. It was reactivated by Abdelkader Chabouti in 1992.

MEI
It was founded in 1970 in western Algeria. It has been decimated by the Algerian army. It was reactivated in December 1992.

CSFAI
It gathers deserters of the Algerian army. It was created in 1993.

Al-Baqun ala al-Ahd
It was created by Saïd Makhloufi and Qamar Eddine Kerbane in July 1991. It was neutralized very quickly. It knew rivalries between Diazaarists and Salafists.

Salafists members

GIA
Islamic Armed Groups

Radicals

AIS
Islamic Salvation Army It knew rivalries between moderates and radicals.

Dissidence after the collective massacres of civilians

GSPC
Salafist Group for Preaching and Fighting of Hassan Hattab, former member of the GIA

Salafists members

FIGURE BY GGS INFORMATION SERVICES, THE GALE GROUP.

Unlike the GIA, the AIS conducted, unsuccessfully, classic guerrilla warfare modeled on that which the National Liberation Army (ALN) fought against colonial France from 1954 to 1962. The AIS tried, in vain, to control major portions of the territory, but did garner some support in rural areas. As early as 1995, the AIS sought to negotiate a political solution with the regime. Unlike the GIA, which used horrific methods against its opponents, the AIS, despite recurring alliances with the GIA, advertised its opposition to bombings and indiscriminate massacres of civilians. Its forces were allegedly fighting security forces, not civilians. In 1995 and 1996 the AIS fought gruesome wars against GIA forces. Those wars, which had repercussions on the families of AIS fighters, worked to the advantage of the regime. Negotiations between the Algerian military and the AIS resulted in a unilateral truce proclaimed by Mezrag on 1 October 1997. Thousands of AIS fighters surrendered and handed over their weapons to the authorities. In January 2000 those fighters obtained amnesty under the terms of the "Civil Concord" decreed by President Abdelaziz Bouteflika after his election in April 1999. Both Mezrag and Benaïcha offered their services to the authorities to fight the GIA and the Salafist Group for Preaching and Combat (GSPC), which has links to al-Qaʿida.

See also FRONT ISLAMIQUE DU SALUT; QAʿIDA, AL-.

Bibliography

Zoubir, Yahia H. "Algeria: Islamic Secularism and Political Islam." In *Religion and Politics in the Developing World: Explosive Interactions,* edited by Rolin G. Mainuddin. London: Ashgate, 2002.

Zoubir, Yahia, H. "The Algerian Political Crisis: Origins and Prospects for Democracy." *Journal of North African Studies* 3, no. 1 (spring 1998): 75–100.

YAHIA ZOUBIR

ISLAMIC SALVATION FRONT

See FRONT ISLAMIQUE DU SALUT

ISLAMIC UNIVERSITY OF MEDINA

Institute of religious higher education in Saudi Arabia.

Medina has been a center of religious education in the Islamic world for hundreds of years. The Islamic

University of Medina was founded in 1961, according to Saudi sources, to spread the teachings of Islam in the world; by 1995 it had 3,058 students and 378 staff. About 80 percent of the students are Saudis, and the remainder foreigners. Tuition is paid by the government, and applicants must be Muslims of "good moral character" and be able to read the Qur'an. The university has faculties in *shari'a* (Islamic law), Qur'an, *da'wa* (proselytizing), *hadith* (traditions of the prophet Muhammad), and Arabic. Because the university reflects the influence of the country's powerful and conservative religious establishment, its mission and curriculum reflect the same restrictive view of Islam.

See also MEDINA.

Bibliography

Al Salloom, Hamad I. *Education in Saudi Arabia.* Beltsville, MD: Amana, 1995.

ANTHONY B. TOTH

ISMA'IL, ABD AL-FATTAH
[?–1986]

Yemeni government official.

From North Yemen, Abd al-Fattah Isma'il emigrated to Aden for work as a young man. He became coruler of the People's Democratic Republic of Yemen (PDRY) with his rival Salim Rabiyya Ali from mid-1969 to mid-1978. Isma'il served during this period as head of the regime's evolving political machine. He was an insistent, dogmatic proponent of "scientific socialism" and is regarded as the father of what became a well-developed ruling party, the Yemeni Socialist Party. He ousted Rabiyya Ali in 1978 and led the PDRY until his own ouster in 1980. He returned from his Moscow exile in 1984, only to die in Aden in the intraparty blood bath of January 1986.

See also PEOPLE'S DEMOCRATIC REPUBLIC OF YEMEN; RABIYYA ALI, SALIM; YEMENI SOCIALIST PARTY.

ROBERT D. BURROWES

ISMA'IL IBN IBRAHIM
[1830–1895]

Modernizing viceroy of Egypt, reigning from 1863 until his deposition in July 1879.

Isma'il ibn Ibrahim (1830–1895), pictured with his son, Tewfik, assumed the leadership of Egypt in 1863. Throughout his reign, he spent enormous amounts of money on his dream of a modern Egypt, and borrowed heavily from foreign nations. These debts would lead to British occupation three years after his son replaced him in 1879.

Born in Cairo, Isma'il ibn Ibrahim was educated at the Qasr al-Ayni Princes' School established by his grandfather, Muhammad Ali Pasha, and at the Saint-Cyr Military Academy in France. He served briefly on the council for the sultan of the Ottoman Empire in Istanbul and then chaired the corresponding vice-regal council in Cairo.

Upon succeeding his uncle, Muhammad Sa'id Pasha, in 1863, he started a policy of national modernization in Egypt by ordering the construction of factories, irrigation works, public buildings, and palaces. Many traditional Cairo and Alexandria neighborhoods and buildings were razed to facilitate the Europeanization of these cities. His reign marked the inauguration of many Egyptian cultural institutions, including the Cairo Opera House, the National Library (Dar al-Kutub), the Egyptian Museum, the Geographical Society, and various primary, secondary, and higher schools, such as Dar al-Ulum. The Suez Canal was completed during his reign; its 1869 inauguration occasioned a gala celebration attended by many European leaders.

Isma'il also established Egypt's system of provincial and local administration and convened the Majlis Shura al-Nuwwab, the country's first representative assembly. He reorganized the national and *shari'a* (Islamic law) courts, established the mixed courts, created the postal service, and extended railroads and telegraph lines throughout Egypt. He sent explorers to the African interior and armies to complete Egypt's conquest of the Sudan. Egypt became more independent of the Ottoman Empire. Since Isma'il obtained the title of *khedive* (Persian for "little lord"), he gained permission to pass down his khedivate according to the European rules of succession and the right to contract loans without first obtaining permission from Istanbul. His industrial, military, and construction projects proved costly, and he indulged in other extravagances having no long-term value to Egypt, such as his many palaces and extensive luxuries that he bought for his wives and mistresses or bestowed upon Europeans he wished to impress.

At first, Isma'il paid for his program with revenues derived from the expanded output of Egyptian cotton, for which demand boomed during the American Civil War. Later, when European industrialists could buy cotton from other sources, Isma'il raised taxes and took loans from European bankers at increasingly unfavorable terms. Unable to repay them, he resorted to unorthodox financial measures—such as the 1871 Muqabala loan and the sale of his government's Suez Canal shares in 1875—finally conceding to European control over Egyptian state revenues and disbursements through the 1876 Caisse de la Dette Publique.

In 1878 he surrendered much of his power to the dual control of a "European cabinet" that included English and French ministers. Financial stringencies ensued, leading to an uprising by Egyptian army officers who had been put on half-pay, causing the European cabinet to resign. European creditors and their governments suspected Isma'il of engineering the uprising to regain his absolute rule. In July 1879, their envoys in Constantinople persuaded the sultan to replace him with his eldest son, Tawfiq. Isma'il left Egypt and lived out his life in exile. Although ambitious for Egypt's development and his own reputation, his achievements were eclipsed by his fiscal misrule, which led in 1882 to the British occupation.

See also COTTON; DAR AL-ULUM; DUAL CONTROL; MAJLIS SHURA AL-NUWWAB; MIXED COURTS; MUHAMMAD ALI; *SHARI'A*; SUEZ CANAL.

Bibliography

Hunter, F. Robert. *Egypt under the Khedives, 1805–1879: From Household Government to Modern Bureaucracy.* Pittsburgh, PA: University of Pittsburgh Press, 1984.

Schölch, Alexander. *Egypt for the Egyptians! The Socio-Political Crisis in Egypt, 1878–1882.* London: Ithaca Press, 1981.

ARTHUR GOLDSCHMIDT

ISMA'ILI SHI'ISM

Islamic movement that split from the Twelver Shi'a over the successor of the sixth imam, Ja'far al-Sadiq (d. 765).

Some believed that Ja'far had appointed his son, Isma'il as his successor, but Isma'il predeceased Ja'far, thus making his brother, Musa, their father's successor. Supporters of Isma'il, however, maintained that his son, Muhammad, should become imam.

The Isma'ili movement, whose followers are generally known as seveners of Isma'ilis, spawned several subdivisions, including the Fatimids, the Assassins, the Tayyibis, and the Nizaris. The Fatimids developed from a group of Isma'ilis who had maintained their movement in secret from the time of Ja'far's death until about the mid-ninth century. This group believed that Isma'il had not really died but had gone into occlusion, and that Muhammad, the seventh imam, would reappear as the *Mahdi*. The Fatimids founded Cairo in 969 C.E. and were wiped out in 1021 after their sixth caliph, al-Hakim, died. Al-Hakim's followers consolidated in the mountains of Syria and are known as Druze.

Outside Egypt, the Isma'ili movement was propagated by Hasan-i-Sabbah, from his mountain fortress of Alamut in northern Iran in 1090 C.E. The movement he founded was known as the Assassins because of their use of hashish (users of hashish are called *hashshashin* in Arabic. Hasan's followers were notorious for murdering their enemies as a form of intimidation, from whence *assassin* was coined. After Hasan's death, the followers of the movement came to be known as Nizari Isma'ilis, named for Nizar, an heir to the Fatimid caliphate whose claim was usurped in a palace coup, and whose namesake succeeded Hasan, claiming descent from the Fatimid Nizar. The Nizar Isma'ili rule at Alamut ended with the Mongol conquest of 1256. Survivors kept the movement alive, however, settling in Azerbaijan and India. In 1840, their imam took the title Agha Khan, which continues until today. His followers, known as Khojas, are located mainly in Gujarat, Bombay, and East Africa, with others scattered around the world, including a small group based at Salamiyya, Syria.

See also DRUZE; *MAHDI;* SHI'ISM.

JENAB TUTUNJI

ISRAEL

This entry consists of the following articles:

> OVERVIEW
> MILITARY AND POLITICS
> OVERVIEW OF POLITICAL PARTIES
> POLITICAL PARTIES

OVERVIEW

Officially, the State of Israel, a democratic republic established by proclamation 15 May 1948.

Israel (in Hebrew, Medinat Yisrael) is a small state in both population—estimated at 6.7 million in September 2003—and size—encompassing some 8,019 square miles. It is located on the eastern coast of the Mediterranean Sea, bordered on the north by Lebanon and on the east by Syria and Jordan. In the south, from a short coastline on the Gulf of Aqaba, Israel's border runs northwestward to the Mediterranean along the Sinai Peninsula of Egypt. The West Bank and Gaza Strip territories have been under Israel's administration since the 1967 Arab–Israel

MAP BY XNR PRODUCTIONS, INC. THE GALE GROUP.

Tel Aviv is Israel's second largest city, boasting a population of over 400,000. Founded in 1909, Tel Aviv merged with the much older city of Jaffa in 1950, becoming Tel Aviv–Jaffa. This dynamic city along the Mediterranean Sea is a popular cultural center and tourist destination. © ROYALTY-FREE/CORBIS. REPRODUCED BY PERMISSION.

War. In 1981 Israel extended its law and jurisdiction to the Golan Heights, taken from Syria in 1967.

Israel extends 260 miles south from the northern border with Lebanon and Syria to Elat on the Gulf of Aqaba, and east from the Mediterranean for 60 miles to the Rift Valley, through which the Jordan River flows. The southern half of Israel, mostly desert, is known as the Negev—an area of arid flatlands and mountains. North of the Negev is a highland region with a series of mountain ranges that run from the Sea of Galilee in the north to Judea and Samaria (the West Bank) in the south, divided by the Plain of Esdraelon (some 300 feet below sea level). A narrow but fertile coastal plain 3 to 9 miles wide along the Mediterranean shore is where most Israelis live and most of the industry and agriculture are located, including the citrus crop.

About 90 percent of Israel's people live in urban areas; the three largest cities are Jerusalem, Tel Aviv, and Haifa. Jerusalem is Israel's capital and largest city; it is the spiritual center of Judaism (the Jewish religion) and also a holy city for Christianity and Islam. West Jerusalem, the newer part of the city, is inhabited mainly by Jews. East Jerusalem—captured by Israel from Jordan in 1967—is inhabited mainly by Arabs.

Tel Aviv serves as the country's commercial, financial, and industrial center, and houses some government agencies. Haifa, on the Mediterranean, is a major port city, the administrative and industrial center of northern Israel. Beersheba is considered the capital of the Negev region. In the 1950s Israel's government began creating "development towns," to attract industry to lightly populated areas and to provide homes for new immigrants.

Israel has hot dry summers and cool mild winters, although the climate varies from region to region, partly because of elevation. In August, the

While agriculture is not one of the larger factors in Israel's economy, the country produces almost enough crops to satisfy its yearly domestic need, and also exports significant quantities of citrus fruits, eggs, and processed foods. A sizeable portion of Israel's crops are produced by kibbutzim and moshavim on land leased to them by the Israeli Land Authority. © TED SPIEGEL/CORBIS. REPRODUCED BY PERMISSION.

hottest month, the temperatures may reach 98°F in the hilly regions and as high as 120°F near the Dead Sea. In January, the coldest month, temperatures average 48°F in Jerusalem and 57°F in Tel Aviv. Israel has almost continuous sunshine from May through mid-October. The *khamsin,* a hot dry dusty wind, sometimes blows in from deserts in the east. Almost all the rainfall occurs between November and March, and great regional variations exist. In the driest area, the southern Negev, the average yearly rainfall is only 1 inch. In the wettest area, the hilly parts of upper Galilee, average annual rainfall is 42 inches. Snow also falls sometimes in the hills.

Israel has six administrative districts—Central, Haifa, Jerusalem, Northern, Southern, and Tel Aviv. Elected councils are the units of local government, responsible for such services as education, water, and road maintenance.

Economy

At its independence in 1948 Israel was a poor country with only a little agricultural or industrial production. The economy has grown substantially, and today Israel enjoys a relatively high standard of living, despite limited water and mineral resources. Human resources (large numbers of educated immigrants) plus financial assistance from Western nations (especially the United States and Germany) contribute to Israel's economic well-being. The nation's main trading partners are the United States, Great Britain, Germany, and Italy.

Israel is poor in energy sources, having no coal deposits or hydroelectric power resources and only small amounts of crude oil and natural gas. In 2004 Israel had a technologically advanced market economy with substantial government participation. It imports crude oil, raw materials, and

Beginning in the 1970s, Israel's manufacturing sector began to move away from traditional products such as textiles, chemicals, and metal products into more high-technology fields such as electronics and computer products. Manufacturing employs the second largest percentage of the country's workforce. © RICKI ROSEN/CORBIS SABA. REPRODUCED BY PERMISSION.

military equipment. It has intensively developed its agricultural and industrial sectors. Israel imports significant quantities of grain but is largely self-sufficient in other agricultural products. Cut diamonds, high-technology equipment, and agricultural products (fruit and vegetables) are the leading exports. The influx of Jewish immigrants from the former U.S.S.R. during the period 1989 to 1999, coupled with the opening of new markets at the end of the Cold War, energized Israel's economy, which grew rapidly in the early 1990s; growth slowed in 1996 when Israel imposed tighter fiscal and monetary policies and the immigration bonus declined. Growth was 7.2 percent in 2000, but the outbreak of the al-Aqsa Intifada, difficulties in the high-technology, construction, and tourist sectors, and fiscal austerity in the face of growing inflation, led to small declines in GDP in 2001 and 2002. These rebounded by the end of 2003.

Population

When Israel was established in 1948 it had about 800,000 people. In 2003 Israel's population numbered about 6.7 million; about 81 percent are Jews. Between 1948 and the 1990s more than 2 million Jews migrated to Israel, many to escape persecution in their home countries. In 1950 and 1952 respectively, the Knesset (parliament) passed the Law of Return and the Nationality Law, which together grant the right to every Jew to immigrate to the country and, with minor exceptions, to be granted automatic citizenship. Israel's Jewish population shares a common spiritual heritage but comes from diverse ethnic backgrounds—each group has its own cultural, political, and recent historical roots. The two main groups are the Ashkenazim—who came from the countries of Central and Eastern Europe—and the Mizrahim and Sephardim—who came from the countries of the Middle East and around the Mediterranean. At the time of independence, most of Israel's Jews were Ashkenazim; as a result, the political, educational, and economic systems are primarily Western in orientation. The massive migration of Jews from the former U.S.S.R., which began in the glasnost era of Mikhail S. Gorbachev (late 1980s), brought more than 185,000 in 1990 and hundreds of thousands in subsequent years, and Soviet Jews became the largest ethnic group in Israel in the twenty-first century.

Arabs make up nearly all the remaining 19 percent of Israel's population. Most are Palestinians whose families remained after the independence of Israel and the 1948 Arab–Israel War. Arab and Jewish Israelis generally have limited contact, live in separate areas, attend separate schools, speak different languages, and follow different cultural traditions.

Israel has two official languages—Hebrew and Arabic. Many Israelis also speak English or Russian, and many Ashkenazic Jews speak Yiddish, a Germanic language spoken since the Middle Ages by Jews in Central and Eastern Europe. Because of their diverse diaspora origins, Israelis also speak a great many other languages, reflecting their diverse histories.

Religion

About 20 percent of Israeli Jews observe the religious principles of Judaism and are classified as Orthodox; an additional 50 percent observe some of the principles some of the time, and the rest (30%) tend to be secular. Orthodox Israelis hold that Jewish religious values should play an important role in the shaping of government policy, but secular Israeli Jews seek to limit the role of religion in the state.

Of Israel's non-Jewish population, about 73 percent are Muslims, the largest group of which are Sunni. Another 11 percent of the non-Jews are Christians, mostly Roman Catholic and Eastern Orthodox. Of the remaining 16 percent, the majority are Druze, but there are also some Baha'i and other small religious communities. All faiths are guaranteed religious freedom by law.

Education

Education has a high priority in Israel. One of the first laws passed there established free education and

On 14 May 1948, when the British Mandate over Palestine expired, Israeli prime minister David Ben-Gurion signed the new Jewish state of Israel into being. This action had immediate consequences, as the new nation was promptly invaded by five Arab states, initiating Israel's War of Independence, which lasted until early 1949. © AP/WIDE WORLD PHOTOS. REPRODUCED BY PERMISSION.

required school attendance for all children between the ages of five and fourteen. Attendance is now required to age sixteen. Adult literacy is estimated to be in excess of 97 percent. The Jewish school system instructs in Hebrew, and the Arab/Druze school system in Arabic; both are government-funded systems.

Israel has a number of internationally recognized institutions of higher education—the Technion, Haifa University, Hebrew University of Jerusalem, Tel Aviv University, Ben-Gurion University, Bar-Ilan University, and the Weizmann Institute of Science.

The Arts

With a population drawn from more than one hundred countries, Israel is rich in cultural diversity and artistic creativity. In music, dance, theater, films, literature, painting, and sculpture, many artists work within the traditions of their own ethnic groups. Others have blended various cultural forms

Israel's population, in thousands, by religion

	Druze	Christians[1]	Muslims	Jews	Total
1950	15,000	36,000	116,100	1,203,000	1,370,100
1960	23,300	49,600	166,300	1,911,300	2,150,400
1970	35,900	75,500	328,600	2,582,000	3,022,100
1980	50,700	89,900	498,300	3,282,700	3,921,700
1990	82,600	114,700	677,700	3,946,700	4,821,700
2000	102,500	133,400	952,000	4,914,100	6,102,000[2]

[1]Until 1994, included those not classified by religion by Ministry of Interior.
[2]Does not include Lebanese not classified by religion by Ministry of Interior.

SOURCE: Adapted from *Statistical Abstract of Israel 53*, Jerusalem: Central Bureau of Statistics, 2002, Table 2.1.

TABLE BY GGS INFORMATION SERVICES, THE GALE GROUP.

to create a uniquely Israeli tradition. The arts not only reflect Israel's immigrant diversity, they also draw upon Jewish history and religion and address the social and political problems of modern Israel. The arts are actively encouraged and supported by the government.

Publishing is a major industry—the number of books published per person in Israel is among the highest in the world. Most Israeli authors write in Hebrew, and some have achieved international fame; the novelist and short-story writer Shmuel Yosef Agnon shared the 1966 Nobel Prize for literature. Other renowned authors include Hayyim Nahman Bialik, Saul Tchernichovsky, Amos Oz, and Avraham B. Yehoshua. Israel's newspapers are published daily in Hebrew, with others available in Arabic, Russian, English, French, Polish, Yiddish, Hungarian, and German.

The Israel Philharmonic Orchestra performs throughout the country and on frequent international tours, as does the Jerusalem Symphony, the orchestra of the Israel Broadcasting Authority. Israeli and international artists tour as well, and almost every municipality and small agricultural settlement has a chamber orchestra or jazz ensemble. Folk music and folk dancing, drawing from the cultural heritage of the many immigrant groups, are very popular, as is the theater. Among the museums are the Israel Museum in Jerusalem, which houses the Dead Sea Scrolls and an extensive collection of Jewish religious and folk art; and the Museum of the Diaspora, which is located on the campus of Tel Aviv University. Archaeology is an important pur-

suit, and archaeological remains are on display throughout the country.

Government

Israel has no written constitution; instead, it follows "basic laws" passed by the Knesset (parliament) that deal with subjects such as the president, the Knesset, the judiciary, and other matters generally found in a written constitution. Legislative powers are vested in this unicameral body of 120 members, elected for a term not to exceed four years, in a national, general, equal, secret, direct, and proportional election. The Knesset passes legislation, participates in the formation of national policy, and approves budgets and taxes. All Israeli citizens eighteen years or older may vote. Voters do not cast ballots for individual candidates in Knesset elections, but instead vote for a party list, which includes all the candidates of the political party. The list may range from a single candidate to a full slate of 120 names. A party's seats in parliament are approximately proportional to the share of the votes it receives in the national election.

The prime minister—the head of government—is normally the leader of the party that controls the most seats in the Knesset and must maintain the support of a majority of the Knesset to stay in office. He or she selects, forms, and heads the cabinet, which is Israel's senior policymaking body, composed of the heads of each government ministry as well as other ministers; appointments to the cabinet must be approved by the Knesset. The president—the head of state—is elected by the Knesset to a seven-year term. The powers and functions are primarily formal and ceremonial; actual political power is limited. The president's most important task is selecting a member of the Knesset to form a government, although political composition of the Knesset has, so far, essentially determined this selection.

Since 1948, Israel's governments have been coalitions of several political parties—the result of several factors: the intensity with which political views are held; the proportional representation of the voting system; and the multiplicity of parties. These factors have made it all but impossible for a party to win an absolute majority of seats. Despite the constant need for coalition governments, they have proven remarkably stable. Political life in Israel was dominated during the period of the British Mandate by a small and relatively cohesive elite that held positions in government and other major institutions. The strength of the Israel Labor Party until 1977 helped to stabilize the political situation. Between 1977 and 1983 Prime Minister Menachem Begin's political skills had the same effect. Rigorous party discipline exists in the Knesset.

The judiciary comprises both secular and religious court systems.

Political History

The independence of the State of Israel in 1948 was preceded by more than a half century of efforts by Zionist leaders to establish a sovereign state as a homeland for dispersed Jews. The desire of Jews to return to their biblical home was voiced continuously and repeatedly after the Romans destroyed Jerusalem in 70 C.E. and dispersed the population of Roman Palestine. Attachment to the land of Israel (Eretz Yisrael) became a recurring theme in Jewish scripture and literature. Despite the ancient connection, it was not until the founding of the World Zionist Organization by Theodor Herzl near the end of the nineteenth century that practical steps were taken toward securing international sanction for large-scale Jewish resettlement in Palestine. Small numbers of Jews had remained in the area or had returned to it throughout the centuries, mostly (but not only) Orthodox scribes and scholars residing mainly in the four holy cities of Jerusalem, Hebron, Safed, and Tiberias. Modern Zionism was given added weight by the Balfour Declaration in

1917, which declared the British government's support for the creation of a national home for the Jewish people in Palestine, and Britain was granted a League of Nations mandate for Palestine after World War I that lasted until after World War II.

In November 1947 international support for establishing a Jewish state led to the adoption of the United Nations (UN) partition plan, which called for dividing mandated Palestine into a Jewish and an Arab state and for establishing Jerusalem as an international city under UN administration. Violence between Palestinian Arabs and Jews erupted almost immediately. On 15 May 1948 the State of Israel proclaimed its independence. Armies from neighboring Arab states entered the former Mandate lands to fight Israel in the Arab–Israel War of 1948. In 1949 four armistice agreements were negotiated and signed between Israel and Egypt, Jordan, Lebanon, and Syria. No peace treaties were signed, however, and the new Israeli state maintained a shaky UN-supervised armistice with its Arab neighbors.

After Egypt nationalized the Suez Canal and formed a unified military command with Syria, Israel invaded the Gaza Strip and the Sinai Peninsula in October 1956, in concert with French and British operations against Egyptian forces concentrated near the canal. At the conclusion of the 1956 Arab–Israel War Israel's forces withdrew (March 1957) after the United Nations established an Emergency Force (UNEF) and stationed it along the Egyptian side of the 1949 armistice line and on the Strait of Tiran to ensure passage of Israel-bound ships. In 1966 and 1967 terrorist incidents and retaliatory acts across the armistice demarcation lines increased. In May 1967, after tension had developed between Syria and Israel, Egypt's President Gamal Abdel Nasser moved armaments and troops into the Sinai and ordered withdrawal of UNEF troops from the armistice line and from Sharm al-Shaykh at the Strait of Tiran. Nasser then closed the strait to Israel's ships, blockading the Israeli port of Elat at the northern end of the Gulf of Aqaba. On 30 May Jordan and Egypt signed a mutual-defense treaty.

In response to these and related events, Israel's forces attacked Egypt on 5 June 1967. Subsequently, Jordan and Syria joined in the hostilities of the 1967 Arab–Israel War. After six days of fighting, Israel controlled the Sinai Peninsula, the Gaza Strip, the Golan Heights, the West Bank, and East Jerusalem. At Khartoum on 1 September an Arab summit meeting resolved to have "no peace with Israel, no recognition of Israel, [and] no negotiations with it." On 22 November 1967 the UN Security Council adopted Resolution 242, which called for the establishment of a just and lasting peace; Israel's withdrawal from territories occupied in June 1967; the end of all states of belligerency; respect for the sovereignty of all states in the area; and the right to live in peace within secure recognized boundaries. Swedish ambassador Gunnar Jarring was given the task of implementing the resolution. In the spring of 1969 Nasser initiated the War of Attrition between Egypt and Israel along the Suez Canal. The United States helped to end these hostilities and achieved a cease-fire in August 1970, but subsequent efforts to negotiate an interim agreement to open the Suez Canal, achieve disengagement of forces, and move toward peace were unsuccessful.

On 6 October 1973, Yom Kippur (the holiest day of the Jewish year), Syrian and Egyptian forces attacked Israeli positions along the Suez Canal and in the Golan. Initially, Syria and Egypt made significant advances, but Israel recovered on both fronts, pushing the Syrians back beyond the 1967 cease-fire lines and crossing the Suez Canal to take a position on its west bank. This war was followed by renewed and intensive efforts toward peace. The United States and the Soviet Union helped to achieve a cease-fire based on Security Council Resolution 338, which reaffirmed UN Security Council Resolution 242 as the framework for peace and for the first time called for negotiations between the parties to establish "a just and durable peace in the Middle East."

The United States actively helped Israel and Egypt to reach agreement on cease-fire stabilization and military disengagement. On 5 March 1974 Israel's forces withdrew from the Suez Canal, and Egypt assumed control. Syria and Israel signed a disengagement agreement on 31 May 1974, and the United Nations Disengagement and Observer Force (UNDOF) was established as a peacekeeping force in the Golan. Further U.S. efforts resulted in an interim agreement between Egypt and Israel in September 1975, which provided for another withdrawal by Israel from the Sinai, a limitation of

Egypt's forces therein, and stations staffed by U.S. civilians in a UN-maintained buffer zone between Egypt's and Israel's forces.

In November 1977 Egypt's President Anwar al-Sadat launched an initiative for peace. Sadat recognized Israel's right to exist and established the basis for direct negotiations between Egypt and Israel. This led to meetings at the presidential retreat of Camp David, Maryland, when U.S. president Jimmy Carter helped to negotiate a framework for peace between Israel and Egypt and for a comprehensive peace in the Middle East (known as the Camp David Accords)—with broad principles to guide negotiations between Israel and the Arab states. An Egypt–Israel peace treaty was signed in Washington, D.C., on 26 March 1979 by Prime Minister Menachem Begin and President Sadat, with President Carter signing as witness. This was the first peace treaty between Israel and an Arab state, and it effectively ended the conflict between them. They agreed that negotiations on a transitional regime of autonomy for the West Bank and Gaza would begin one month after ratification. Under the peace treaty, Israel returned the Sinai to Egypt in April 1982. In 1989 the governments of Israel and Egypt concluded an agreement that resolved the status of Taba, a disputed resort area in the Gulf of Aqaba.

Since the 1948 war Israel's border with Lebanon had been quiet compared to its borders with other neighbors. After the Jordanian Civil War (1970–1971), many Palestinians were expelled from Jordan and most eventually went to southern Lebanon, so hostilities against Israel's northern border increased. In March 1978, after a series of terrorist attacks on Israel originating in Lebanon, the Israel Defense Force (IDF) were sent into Lebanon. Israel withdrew its troops after the passage of UN Security Council Resolution 425, which called for the creation of the UN Interim Force in Lebanon (UNIFIL), a peacekeeping force.

In July 1981, after additional fighting between Israel and the Palestinians in Lebanon, U.S. president Ronald Reagan's special envoy, Philip Charles Habib, helped to secure a cease-fire. In June 1982, in response to attacks on Israeli and Jewish targets and the attempted assassination of Israel's ambassador in London, Israel invaded Lebanon with the objective of removing the Palestine Liberation Organization (PLO)'s military and terrorist threat to Israel. In August 1982, after the siege of Beirut and an evacuation plan mediated by several states, the PLO withdrew its headquarters and some forces from Lebanon, relocating in Tunisia. With U.S. assistance in May 1983, Israel and Lebanon reached an accord to withdraw Israeli forces from Lebanon; however, in March 1984, Lebanon, under pressure from Syria, abrogated the agreement. In June 1985 Israel withdrew most of its troops from Lebanon. A small residual Israeli force and an Israeli-supported Lebanese militia remained in southern Lebanon in a "security zone," regarded by Israel as a necessary buffer against attacks on its northern territory.

Until the election of May 1977, Israel had been governed by a coalition led by the Labor alignment or its constituent parties. After the 1977 election, the Likud (Union) bloc came to power, forming a coalition with Menachem Begin as prime minister. Likud retained power in the election in June 1981, and Begin remained prime minister. In 1983 Begin resigned and was succeeded by his foreign minister, Yitzhak Shamir. New elections were held in 1984. The vote was split among numerous parties, and neither Labor nor Likud was able to attract enough small-party support to form a coalition. They agreed to establish a broadly based government of national unity. The agreement provided for the rotation of the office of prime minister and the combined office of deputy prime minister and foreign minister midway through the government's fifty-month term. During the first twenty-five months of the unity government's rule, Labor's Shimon Peres served as prime minister, while Likud's Shamir held the posts of deputy prime minister and foreign minister. Peres and Shamir exchanged positions in October 1986.

The November 1988 elections resulted in a similar coalition government. Likud and Labor formed another national unity government in January 1989, without providing for rotation. Again Shamir became prime minister and Peres deputy prime minister and finance minister. That government fell in March 1990 after a no-confidence vote precipitated by disagreement over the government's response to a U.S. peace initiative. Labor Party leader Peres was unable to attract sufficient support to form a government, and Shamir then formed a Likud-led coalition government, which included members

from religious and right-wing parties; it took office in June 1990. After Iraq's invasion of Kuwait in the summer of 1990 and the Gulf War of 1991, a new peace initiative by the United States led to a major Arab–Israel peace conference, the Madrid Conference (1991).

Soon after Madrid, right-wing parties resigned from Shamir's government over the issue of Palestinian self-rule. Yitzhak Rabin's victory as the new head of the Labor Party in the 1992 Knesset elections brought a clear shift from right to left-of-center, and toward a more pragmatic approach on Arab–Israeli issues. The new government began to alter the nature and direction of Israeli policy, seeking to restore the concepts of Labor Zionism to the center of Israeli politics.

The Madrid Peace Conference was followed by a series of multilateral discussions focusing on functional issues such as refugees, arms control and regional security, water, economic development, and the environment, as well as bilateral negotiations that convened in Washington, D.C. In spring and summer 1993, even as official negotiations continued with little progress in Washington, Israeli and PLO representatives conducted secret negotiations in Norway that led to an exchange of letters and the signing in September 1993 of an historic Declaration of Principles (DOP).

The exchange of letters and DOP, also known as the Oslo Accord, contained the PLO's recognition of Israel's right to exist in peace and security and Israel's recognition of the PLO as the representative of the Palestinian people. The PLO renounced the use of terrorism and other forms of violence, and committed itself to resolve the conflict with Israel through peaceful negotiations. The accord provided for Palestinian autonomy, starting in Jericho (a city of the West Bank) and the Gaza Strip, and for continued negotiations between the two sides to establish the basis for the future relationship between Israel and the Palestinians.

The lengthy and at times acrimonious negotiations known as "the Middle East peace process" saw Israel and the PLO attempting to negotiate interim agreements for a phased Israeli withdrawal from Palestinian population centers and the creation of a Palestine (National) Authority in the West Bank and Gaza Strip. Delays, outbreaks of Palestinian and

Israeli violent opposition, and recriminations about the process soon began to wear down the initial euphoria of the 1993 signing ceremony. The most serious incidents of violence included the massacre of Muslim worshipers in Hebron in February 1994 by Baruch Goldstein; the assassination of Yitzhak Rabin in Tel Aviv in November 1995; and suicide bombings of Israeli buses and terrorist attacks on shopping areas in spring 1996 by members of the Islamic resistance movement HAMAS.

The signing of the DOP allowed Israel and Jordan to publicly continue their decades-long secret negotiations, which culminated in the signing of a peace treaty between the two countries on 26 October 1994. This treaty led to a relatively "warm peace" (compared to its Israeli–Egyptian predecessor) that included a wide range of relationships in numerous sectors.

The assassination of Prime Minister Rabin by Yigal Amir was unexpected and unprecedented, and reflected sharp differences within the Israeli polity on the peace process. Shimon Peres was chosen to lead the government, and he attempted to pursue the Israeli–Syria peace track, but was stymied by the lack of Syrian response and by suicide bombings and Katyusha rocket attacks into northern Israel from southern Lebanon. Peres responded with Operation Grapes of Wrath, directed against Hizbullah bases in Lebanon.

In May 1996 Israelis participated in their first-ever election under a new electoral law requiring them to cast two ballots—one for the Knesset and the other for prime minister. The elections saw the victory of Likud's Benjamin ("Bibi") Netanyahu over Labor's Peres by a margin of less than 1 percent of the votes cast. Netanyahu's victory was attributed to support from the political right and the religious parties, to the failure of the sympathy vote for Rabin to materialize, to Peres's diminished stature among Jewish voters because of his ineffective reactions to terrorism, and to the Arab community's failure to provide Peres with strong support partly because of extensive IDF military operations against the PLO in Lebanon. The election permitted Netanyahu to create a right-of-center coalition government. Netanyahu's tenure was marked by slow progress on the peace process, highlighted by the U.S.-brokered signing of a Hebron redeployment agreement in January 1997 and the Wye Plantation Accord of 1998.

In the May 1999 elections Israelis were again offered two ballots. This time Labor's new leader, Ehud Barak, running as head of the "One Israel" ticket, defeated Netanyahu by a wide margin (56% to 44%) and then formed a broadly based coalition government. Barak was widely seen in Israel and abroad as a true successor to Rabin—an individual with strong security credentials who sought a compromise agreement with the Palestinians. Hope was generated for a reinvigorated peace process, especially because of the substantial involvement of U.S. president Bill Clinton. Barak also moved ahead on other issues. In keeping with a campaign pledge he ordered a unilateral Israeli withdrawal from Lebanon in March 2000. The withdrawal was carried out swiftly, ending Israel's eighteen-year presence in Lebanon and resulting in the United Nations declaring Israel to be in full compliance with UNSC Resolution 425. The withdrawal also seemed to offer a prospect for further negotiations with Syria on outstanding bilateral issues and on the Israel-Lebanon relationship.

The Syrian track became a focal point for Barak's policy, and in January 2000 Clinton, Barak, and Syrian foreign minister Faruk al-Shara joined in an inconclusive meeting in Shepherdstown, West Virginia. Clinton followed up with a summit meeting with Syrian president Hafiz al-Asad in Geneva in March, but the two leaders failed to close the gap between the Israeli and Syrian positions, primarily over the line to which Israel would withdraw from the Golan Heights. Asad's death in June 2000 put an end to Syrian-track negotiations during Barak's tenure.

In summer 2000 President Clinton sought to achieve an Israeli–Palestinian breakthrough with an invitation to Ehud Barak and Yasir Arafat to attend a summit meeting. But the Camp David Summit failed to achieve an agreement, with all parties blaming the others for the failure—especially Barak and Clinton pointing to Arafat's refusal to consider Barak's offer as the basis for future negotiations. This effectively marked the end of the Middle East peace process. In late September 2000 the al-Aqsa Intifada erupted, sending Israelis and Palestinians into a deadly cycle of bloodshed and violence.

Domestic Issues and Electoral Politics since 2000

The decade of the 1990s was marked by a significant immigration of some one million people from the former Soviet Union—the largest single migration to Israel from any one country. This profoundly altered the nature of Israel's society, economics, and politics. At the same time, the economy continued to grow and prosperity became more widespread as Israel's GDP grew beyond the $100 billion level, although there was negative growth when the violence of the al-Aqsa Intifada severely affected the flow of tourism. The economy was also affected by the worldwide economic downturn and by recessions in the United States, Europe, and Japan. Nevertheless, by 2004 the economy began to recoup some of the losses of the previous few years, and positive GDP growth was again recorded.

In January 2003 Israel's first astronaut, Ilan Ramon, was launched into space aboard the U.S. space shuttle *Columbia,* generating pride and elation across Israel and among Jews worldwide. Tragically, Ramon was killed along with his fellow astronauts when the craft disintegrated upon its return to earth in early February after a successful mission in space.

The outbreak of the al-Aqsa Intifada and the protracted failure to achieve a cease-fire and restart the peace process contributed to the disintegration of Ehud Barak's governing coalition. His resignation in December 2000 without the dissolution of the Knesset led to the first-ever election in Israel for prime minister only. That election was marked by the lowest turnout of eligible voters in Israel's history—about 62 percent—and signaled some uncertainty in the body politic. Ariel Sharon's landslide victory (62.6% to Barak's 37.2%) in February 2001 was attributed to Barak's failure to make peace with either Syria or the Palestinians, and to the heightened insecurity and substantial violence caused by the intifada. Sharon was elected as the candidate more likely to bring about the security Israelis were seeking. His election brought Likud back to power, and he formed a government coalition in March 2001 with Labor participation based on the Knesset that was elected in 1999.

Security and the resurrection of the peace process were the dominant themes of Sharon's tenure. Suicide bombings and other violence (such as the as-sassination of Tourism Minister Rehavam Ze'evi) continued to remind Israelis of their vulnerability and of the failure of the peace process. The inability or unwillingness of the Palestinian Authority to put an effective halt to terrorist acts led the Israeli government in December 2001 to declare Yasir Arafat "irrelevant" in the struggle against terrorism and to seek alternative leadership among the Palestinians to foster the moribund peace process. Subsequently, Israel began to isolate Arafat and labeled him "an enemy of the entire free world."

Arms continued to flow to the Palestinians (as evidenced by the January 2002 Israeli interception and capture of the ship *Karine-A,* which was carrying arms from Iranian sources to Gaza) and violence escalated. In response to the March 2002 massacre of mostly elderly Passover celebrants at the Park Hotel in the resort town of Netanya, the IDF launched major raids into the West Bank against terrorist targets in Operations Defensive Shield and Determined Path, in effect reoccupying for several months Jenin, Hebron, Bethlehem, and other population centers it had previously ceded to the Palestinian Authority.

The increasing use of Palestinian suicide bombers claimed hundreds of Israeli civilian lives and led to severe retaliations by the IDF in the form of increased surveillance at checkpoints, destruction of the homes of suicide bombers' families, closures, targeted assassinations of militants, and the building of a security fence. Although it was widely supported by an Israeli population traumatized by suicide bombers infiltrating Jewish population centers and soft targets from the West Bank, the planned 450-mile security barrier (more than 95 percent of which was to be chain-link fence, with the remainder concrete walls) was criticized for being built beyond the Green Line (1949 armistice lines) and for causing hardship by disrupting the daily movements of the Palestinian population. The decision to proceed with this measure despite international criticism and sharp Palestinian denunciation reflected a growing unilateralist tendency among Israel's leaders to consider disengagement and separation from the Palestinians.

The failure of the peace process and the climate of despair and insecurity created a new watershed for Israeli foreign and security policy, and for domestic politics within Israel. It is against this background that the United States and its fellow "Quartet" members (Russia, the UN, and the European Union) pursued their efforts to have the parties agree to halt the violence as a prelude to resuming negotiations. In April 2003 the U.S. State Department made public the Quartet's "Road Map," which incorporated President George W. Bush's June 2002 vision of a two-state solution for the Israel-Palestinian impasse. Diplomatic activity on this front included shuttle diplomacy and high-level meetings, and the selection of two successive Palestinian prime ministers to negotiate with Israel.

In October 2002 Labor quit Sharon's national unity coalition government. Elections were held for the Sixteenth Knesset in January 2003, based on a revised electoral law that abandoned the separate ballot for prime minister used since 1996. The focus of the campaign was peace and security, and Labor's new leader, Amram Mitzna, led his party to its worst electoral defeat, in which its respresentation declined to only nineteen seats in the Knesset, compared to thirty-eight seats for Sharon's Likud. In February 2003 Sharon presented his new coalition government to the Knesset for its approval. The coalition was a narrower one in which Likud was clearly the dominant party, with a reinvigorated militantly secular Shinui Party as the major partner. Sharon's new government seemed poised for domestic changes on religion-society issues and for a continuing tough stand on the matter of security and peace for Israel. In 2004 the peace process was moribund, and a continuing intifada with its climate of insecurity was the main determinant of Israeli foreign and security policy, with strong implications also for domestic politics within Israel.

See also ADOT HA-MIZRAH; AGNON, SHMUEL YOSEF; AQSA INTIFADA, AL-; ARAB–ISRAEL CONFLICT; ARAB–ISRAEL WAR (1948); ARAB–ISRAEL WAR (1956); ARAB–ISRAEL WAR (1967); ARAB–ISRAEL WAR (1973); ARAB–ISRAEL WAR (1982); ARCHAEOLOGY; ASHKENAZIM; BALFOUR DECLARATION (1917); BARAK, EHUD; BEERSHEBA; BEGIN, MENACHEM; BEN-GURION, DAVID; BIALIK, HAYYIM NAHMAN; CAMP DAVID ACCORDS (1978); DAYAN, MOSHE; DEAD SEA; DEAD SEA SCROLLS; DIASPORA; ERETZ YISRAEL; GAZA STRIP; GOLAN HEIGHTS; HABIB, PHILIP CHARLES; HAIFA; HAMAS; HEBRON; HERZL, THEODOR; HIZBULLAH; HOLOCAUST; INTIFADA (1987–1991); ISRAELI SETTLEMENTS; JARRING, GUNNAR; JERICHO; JERUSALEM; JEWS IN THE MIDDLE EAST; LABOR ZIONISM; LAW OF RETURN; LITERATURE: HEBREW; MADRID CONFERENCE (1991); NEGEV; NETANYAHU, BENJAMIN; OSLO ACCORD (1993); OZ, AMOS; PALESTINE LIBERATION ORGANIZATION (PLO); PALESTINIAN CITIZENS OF ISRAEL; PERES, SHIMON; RABIN, YITZHAK; SADAT, ANWAR AL-; SHAMIR, YITZHAK; SHARON, ARIEL; SINAI PENINSULA; TABA; TCHERNICHOVSKY, SAUL; TEL AVIV; TIRAN, STRAIT OF; UNITED NATIONS INTERIM FORCE IN LEBANON; WAR OF ATTRITION (1969–1970); WEST BANK; WORLD ZIONIST ORGANIZATION (WZO); YEHOSHUA, AVRAHAM B.; ZIONISM.

Bibliography

Arian, Asher. *The Second Republic: Politics in Israel.* Chatham, NJ: Chatham House, 1998.

Gilbert, Martin. *Israel: A History.* New York: Morrow, 1998.

Klieman, Aaron S. *Israel and the World after 40 Years.* Washington, DC: Pergamon-Brassey's, 1990.

Liebman, Charles S., and Don-Yehiya, Eliezer. *Civil Religion in Israel: Traditional Judaism and Political Culture in the Jewish State.* Berkeley: University of California Press, 1983.

Reich, Bernard. *A Brief History of Israel.* New York: Facts On File, 2004.

Reich, Bernard, and Goldberg, David H. *Political Dictionary of Israel.* Metuchen, NJ, and London: Scarecrow Press, 2000.

Reich, Bernard, and Kieval, Gershon R. *Israel: Land of Tradition and Conflict,* 2d edition. Boulder, CO: Westview Press, 1993.

Sachar, Howard M. *A History of Israel from the Rise of Zionism to Our Time,* 2d edition, revised and updated. New York: Knopf, 2000.

BERNARD REICH

MILITARY AND POLITICS

The heavy involvement of the Israeli military in Israel's society, economy, and politics and the occasional politicization of the armed forces.

Over the last decade of the twentieth and the beginning of the twenty-first centuries, issues of military-civilian relations and the role the army (Israel Defense Force, IDF) plays in Israeli society have been intensively studied and analyzed by historians, social scientists, journalists, and others in a plethora of published books and articles. The subject is, however, not new to public awareness, having been on the national agenda since Israel's founding and even earlier. The problem is usually addressed on one or more of three levels: the impact of the military on civilian life; the extent of civil control of the military; and the extent of politicization of the military and its involvement in political decision making.

Impact of the Military on Civilian Life

Israeli society has been marked by the central and pervasive role of the military in Israeli politics, daily life, and culture. Three out of eight politicians who served as prime ministers since 1983 were ex-generals (Yitzhak Rabin, Ehud Barak, and Ariel Sharon), one was elected president (Ezer Weizman), and Shimon Peres, although not formally a military person, grew out of the ranks of the Ministry of Defense. During the same period at least a dozen other ex-generals served in the cabinet as ministers. Most of those who served as IDF chiefs of staff ended their careers in politics (Haim Bar-Lev, Mordechai Gur, Rafael Eitan, and Amnon Lipkin-Shahak, for example). In the economic sphere, many ex-generals became corporate heads; others became mayors of large towns. Some generals were nominated as chancellors of universities and others have become headmasters of prestigious high schools.

Almost universal military conscription brings entire cohorts of young men and women to serve in the military for long periods. The large participation of civilians in military reserve duty (*milu'im*) introduces the military experience into almost all Jewish, and many Druze, households. Military affairs are central in every news broadcast from early morning to late at night, and military jargon permeates modern Hebrew vernacular. Many domestic issues are viewed by Israelis as being essentially security issues. Security considerations prevail in the planning and execution of many civilian projects, such as road construction, land tenure, and housing designs. A pledge to give security considerations first priority is a central part of the political plat-

During his tenure as the Israeli prime minister, David Ben-Gurion meshed several existing defense organizations into the single national military known as the Israel Defense Force (IDF), then strove to keep it free from political entanglements. Referring to the IDF as a "nation builder," Ben-Gurion also greatly expanded the role of the military in society, frequently using it to accomplish civilian tasks. © PHOTOGRAPH BY HANS PINN. GOVERNMENT PRESS OFFICE (GPO) OF ISRAEL. REPRODUCED BY PERMISSION.

form of all parties when candidates run for parliament (the Knesset) and when leaders negotiate to form government coalitions. Security considerations are routinely used to stifle criticism raised against harsh measures taken by the authorities.

Obviously, the salience of the military in Israel's political culture is a result of the prolonged conflict between Israel and the Arabs and the recurrent flare-ups of violence engendered since the early 1920s (some count at least a dozen major violent outbreaks). However, critics of Israeli society have in recent years also observed self-propelling dynamics that cannot always be explained away as inevitable outcomes of the contingencies of conflict with the Arabs. Some moderate critics tend to characterize Israel as a "garrison state" or a "nation in uniform." More strident observers speak of the total "militarization" of Israeli society and politics. Most would admit, however, that, despite the dangers brought by such tendencies to the country's sometimes flawed political system, Israel has managed to maintain its essentially democratic, pluralistic, and liberal political system.

Young Palestinians hurl stones at approaching Israeli troops in the Gaza Strip. In 2002 Israeli tanks moved into the village of Beit Lahiya, and soldiers conducted house-to-house searches, arresting three men they claimed were wanted militants. © REUTERS NEWMEDIA INC./CORBIS. REPRODUCED BY PERMISSION.

Civil Control of the Military

Concerns of defense and security preoccupied the Zionist settlers in Palestine from the outset. But only in the early 1920s, when Palestinian resistance to the Zionist project took on more violent and institutionalized forms, was the small, self-appointed secret group ha-Shomer (The Watchman, founded in 1907) replaced by a larger and more popular organization called the Haganah (Defense). From its inception it was clear that the military arm of the movement had to be supervised and directed by the political leadership. After a short period in which it was controlled by the Histadrut (the General Federation of Jewish Labor), it came under the supervision of a broadly based political committee, drawing its power from the elected executives of the Jewish Agency (representing the World Zionist Organization) and the Vaʿad Leʾumi (representing the

Yishuv, i.e., the Jews of Palestine). The establishment in 1937 of the Irgun Zvaʾi Leʾumi (ETZEL, or IZL) and three years later the further secession of Abraham (Yaʿir) Stern to form Lohamei Herut Yisrael (LEHI, or the Stern Gang) challenged the authority of the democratically elected political leadership of the Yishuv and gave rise to ten years of strife. One result of this dissidence was to eventually fortify the principle— to which the majority of the Jews and the much larger Haganah would adhere—that military organizations and movements must yield to their civilian leaders.

The outbreak of the Palestinian Revolt of 1936 to 1939 dispelled earlier Zionist hopes that they might eventually convince the Palestinians of the blessing that Jewish colonization of Palestine would bring them. From this point on, few Jews in Palestine doubted the need for a strong military organization. The Haganah was expanded, weapons were purchased, military training became universal, and units of permanent obligatory service were introduced. Most historians view this period as the turning point at which Zionists recognized the need to resort to force.

David Ben-Gurion was a strong proponent of the principle of civilian supremacy over the military. In the mid-1940s he emerged as the undisputed leader of the Zionist movement and became the first prime minister and minister of defense of the State of Israel in May 1948. With the transformation of Menachem Begin's Irgun into a civilian political party in the summer of 1948, the IDF's showdown with (and attack on) the Irgun ship *Altalena,* and the final crushing of the Stern Gang and the Irgun military squads in Jerusalem following the murder of Count Folke Bernadotte in September, civilian control over the military establishment was assured and was never seriously challenged from the right.

Ben-Gurion was also concerned that most of the command positions in the strongest and most prestigious elite corps of the IDF, the Palmah, were under the ideological influence of MAPAM, a left-wing party that questioned his own authority. Ben-Gurion saw in this situation a dangerous politicization of the military and ordered the disbanding of the Palmah. As soon as the war was over, he dismissed many high-ranking officers affiliated with MAPAM. During the fifteen years of his premiership, he nominated two chiefs of staff who were active members of his own party (Moshe Dayan and Zvi Tzur). But he also nominated to this position three generals who were strictly professional soldiers and did not belong to any party (Yigael Yadin, Mordehai Makleff, and Haim Laskov) and promoted to the rank of general many ex-Palmah battalion commanders. He also assured, before his own resignation, that Yitzhak Rabin, ex-chief of operations of the Palmah, would be nominated as IDF chief of staff in 1964.

Along with his resolve to depoliticize the officer corps, Ben-Gurion never saw a problem in expanding the role of the military in society and using its efficient and disciplined mechanisms to accomplish strictly civilian tasks. Military engineers were often utilized for road and bridge construction.

Army instructors were involved in the establishment of agricultural settlements (NAHAL, an acronym for No'ar Halutzi Lohem, Fighting Pioneer Youth) for new immigrants. When heavy rains or floods threatened to destroy the tent towns used as temporary housing for new immigrants, the military was called in to manage entire civilian communities.

Moreover, Ben-Gurion saw the IDF as the great "nation builder." The compulsory universal service, which included tens of thousands of young immigrants who were inducted soon after their arrival in the country, was designed not only as a security measure but also as an educational endeavor in which Hebrew and elementary schooling were taught and patriotic ideals inculcated. This rationale was also used to justify the establishment of a special military radio station (Galei-Tzahal), a weekly magazine for soldiers (*ba-Mahaneh,* In the camp) and a monthly journal for officers (*Skira Hodshit,* Monthly review). Many of these functions were later discontinued when the IDF became overburdened with military assignments and defense budgets became strained. Nevertheless, the recruitment and army training of young immigrants from the former Soviet Union in the 1990s may well account for the rapid socialization of those young men and women into Israeli society.

Politicization of the Military

In the mid 1950s, during the brief tenure of Moshe Sharett as prime minister (1954–1955), the boundaries between the civilian authority and the military leadership were sharply perforated, especially around the controversial role played by the politically minded chief of staff, Moshe Dayan; the chief of military intelligence, Binyamin Givli; and even the minister of defense, Pinhas Lavon (who replaced Ben-Gurion during 1954). What Sharett wrote in the intimacy of his private diary—that many of the military offensives were either taken without proper cabinet authorization or were expanded beyond the scope authorized—was hardly a secret to the public. Several events gave rise to the widespread impression that the army was acting beyond political control, including the foolhardy activation of a Jewish espionage ring in Egypt in June 1954, the order for which has remained a controversial mystery; the cruel massacre of sixty-five Palestinian civilians in the village of Qibya in October 1953; the unwarranted scope of the attack on Syrian positions on the Sea of Galilee in December 1955; and the murder of five Bedouins in the Judean Desert by a group of paratroopers. The return of Ben-Gurion (toward whom the personal loyalty of Dayan was impeccable) to head the ministry of defense at the end of February 1955 stabilized the situation. After that, the legacy of a strict separation of the military command from active politics remained more or less intact for many years. According to the military norm, soldiers, including career officers, were permitted to sign up as members of a political party, vote in elections, and even attend party meetings as observers; but they were not permitted to be active in party life in any mode or form.

In recent years, however, the likelihood that high-ranking officers may become active politicians after retirement (after a half-year "cooling-off" period) has given rise to recurrent suspicions that those officers may be trying to pave their way into politics well ahead of their retirement, compromising their professionalism by acting and expressing themselves in ways aimed at helping them in their future political careers. During the first two decades of statehood the majority of senior officers tended to sympathize with center and left-of-center parties close to the Labor-Zionist movement. In recent years, however, a right-wing swing may have penetrated IDF's high command. Many retired generals have found their place in the ranks of the Likud and even parties to its right (such as Generals Rehavam Ze'evi and Rafael Eitan).

The nomination of ex-military men to leading political positions has blurred the boundaries between the military and the civil authorities from another perspective as well. Yigal Allon and Moshe Dayan were the first military figures to occupy important ministerial posts, but both were already political figures during their military service and both managed, as ministers, to faithfully uphold civil authority vis-à-vis the military. But later, when officers who spent a large part of their lives as professional soldiers entered the government, a shift in civil-military boundaries could be clearly observed. The 1982 war in Lebanon is a case in point. Ariel Sharon, as minister of defense, prosecuted the war effort primarily out of military considerations, clearly exceeding the goals set for him by Prime Minister Begin and his cabinet. Likewise, responses to the second Palestinian Intifada (September 2000–), which were handled by three generals (Sharon as prime minister, Sha'ul Mofaz as minister of defense, and Moshe Ya'alon as chief of staff), reflected more a military perspective than a civil-political one.

The intensification of Palestinian resistance since the fall of 2000 and the ensuing attempts to defuse tensions and put the peace process back on track have demanded of the IDF higher levels of confrontation with civilians, both Arabs and Jews. The wide diffusion of warfare and the localization of operational management have given to the military command—even to commanders of lower levels—greater autonomy and ability to influence major political outcomes. On the other hand, scenes of Israeli soldiers battling against Jewish settlers, while not unprecedented, have introduced a new dimension in civil-military relations. The resurgence of a refusal to serve in the Occupied Territories, on the one hand, and the repeated guidance that religious leaders of the settlers' movement give their followers to refuse orders to evacuate settlements, on the other, are still marginal phenomena, but they do point to new cracks in Ben-Gurion's legacy of total depoliticization of the military.

See also Irgun Zva'i Le'umi (IZL).

Bibliography

Ben-Eliezer, Uri. *The Making of Israeli Militarism.* Bloomington: Indiana University Press, 1998.

Horowitz, Dan, and Lissak, Moshe. *Trouble in Utopia: The Overburdened Polity of Israel.* Albany: State University of New York Press, 1989.

Luttwak, Edward, and Horowitz, Dan. *The Israeli Army.* New York: Harper & Row, 1975.

Peri, Yoram. *Between Battles and Ballots: Israeli Military in Politics.* Cambridge: Cambridge University Press, 1983.

Peri, Yoram, and Neubach, Ammon. *The Military-Industrial Complex in Israel: A Pilot Study.* Tel Aviv: International Center for Peace in the Middle East, 1985.

Perlmutter, Amos. *Military and Politics in Israel.* London: Cass, 1969.

Perlmutter, Amos. *Politics and the Military in Israel: 1967–1977.* London: Cass, 1977.

Mordechai Bar-On

OVERVIEW OF POLITICAL PARTIES IN

Political parties played an important role in Israel's achieving statehood; many parties operated as organized structures for decades prior to independence.

Among the factors accounting for the central role of political parties in Israeli politics are: (1) the electoral system, (2) the breadth of party influence in all levels of government during much of the early statehood period, (3) the complexity of major political issues, (4) the intensity of Israeli democracy, and (5) social, economic, and political modernization. The combination of these factors has often resulted in considerable political immobility—a governmental inability to take decisive action in specific policy areas for fear of generating a no-confidence vote and losing its political legitimacy.

Electoral System

Israel's electoral system has led to both centralization of control within many parties and frequently to extreme fragmentation of the party system. Structurally, the country is a single constituency, with proportional representation. Voters cast their ballots for a single party list, and parties receive a number of seats in the Knesset in proportion to the votes they receive. A party that receives 10 percent of the vote will receive 12 seats in the Knesset (10 percent of 120 seats); individual winners are determined by their position on the formal electoral lists that parties file with the Central Elections Commission prior to the vote; if a party wins 10 seats, the top ten names on its list are elected, but the eleventh is not. Names lower on the list may move up if vacancies occur in the party's Knesset delegation between elections. The position of candidates on each party's list is determined by the party organization; some parties use primary elections, some use conventions, and some lists are simply determined by party leadership.

Electoral behavior has been affected in recent years by several phenomena. One is the arrival of modern campaign techniques, including television, which have made it possible for charismatic entrants to affect a party's electoral fortunes. Another is the emergence of hitherto underrepresented groups like the Sephardim who have used arenas such as local mayoralty campaigns to challenge a party's central leadership. The two major parties, the Labor Party and the Likud, have responded by broadening their process of selecting party leaders and Knesset candidates through a series of primary elections involving all of their members. Some parties represent very specific constituencies, for example Russian immigrants. Others focus on a single ideological position.

Electoral reform has been an issue in Israel for decades, and after every election proponents of reform have used that election as further proof that reform was necessary. After many years of active debate, in 1992 the Knesset approved a major change in the Israeli electoral system, allowing the prime minister to be elected directly rather than being chosen from among members of the Knesset. Voters would have two ballots, a vote for prime minister and a separate proportional representation vote for a political party for the Knesset. The new electoral system affected three Israeli prime ministerial elections: May 1996, May 1999, and the special election of February 2001. Rather than creating more stable coalition governments—which was the intent of the change—the new system resulted in increased support for small parties in the Knesset and decreased support for the parties of the prime ministerial candidates. In March 2001, the Knesset voted to bring back the electoral system that had operated from independence until 1992, under which voters would cast a single ballot for a political party to represent them in the Knesset and the prime minister would be selected from Knesset members. The first election under the re-established electoral system took place in January 2003.

The fragmented party system is the result of another feature of the electoral system: one of the world's lowest thresholds for winning a legislative seat. Until 1992, a party needed only 1 percent of the vote to win a seat in a Knesset election, which brought many small parties to the Knesset. This meant that no party has ever received a majority in the Knesset, so it has always been necessary for prime minister–designates to form complex and fragile coalitions, making it exceptionally difficult for their governments to survive if they propose bold initiatives. When the threshold was raised to 1.5 percent in the 1992 election, it had some effect: Only

Prime Minister Ariel Sharon (center) at headquarters for the Likud Party. The Likud is a right-wing political party established in 1973 by members of several smaller parties, including the Herut and the Israeli Liberal Party. In 1977, the party was elected to power, ending twenty-nine years of rule by the Israeli Labor Party. © AFP/Corbis. Reproduced by permission.

ten of the twenty-six parties that ran candidates won Knesset seats.

Breadth of Party Influence

Another aspect of party activity is the legacy and breadth of party influence in the early years of statehood. In the prestate period and the early years of statehood, the importance of political parties was enhanced by their role in various quasi-governmental activities, including employment, education, housing, medical care, immigrant absorption, publishing, and even sports. Although many of these functions were later taken over by the government, elections in nongovernmental organizations like the Histadrut (General Confederation of Trade Unions) and the Jewish Agency continue to be contested within the framework of

candidate lists submitted by the major political parties.

Political Issues

The importance of small parties has also been magnified by the complexity of Israeli political issues. The political parties can be divided into five major groups, but the groups are not at all homogeneous, and many parties fit only partially into any group. These groups are (1) the left, which is generally socialist in domestic politics and conciliatory on the Palestinian issue; (2) the center and right, which generally is less sympathetic to socialist ideology, takes a hard line on the Palestinian issue and Greater Israel, and would give up none of the territories won during the Arab–Israel War (1967); (3) the religious parties, which have held the balance of power in every government in Israel's history and some of whose members have made coalitions with both Labor and Likud in exchange for the furtherance of Orthodox religious interests; (4) reform parties, which have pressed for changes beyond those advocated by any of the larger, more entrenched parties; and (5) the far left, Communist, and Arab parties, which provide choices for voters but whose members have traditionally been outside of the mainstream of political decision making.

The proliferation and survival of the many parties is encouraged by the ideological and issue-oriented setting within which Israeli parties operate. Israeli parties cluster around many major issues, including at least one dealing with government activity in the domestic economy, one dealing with policy in relation to Arab states and the Palestinians, one dealing with government and religion, one dealing with government and Zionism (which is distinct from religion), and one dealing with national security (which is distinct from Arab relations). Many issues touch more than one of these dimensions. Given the number of central issues in the polity—and this list of issues does not include the problems of immigrants, gender-related issues, ethnicity and politics, and many other highly contentious issues around which a political party might be created—it is no wonder that literally dozens of political parties compete in each election.

Intensity of Israeli Democracy

Each of the larger groupings of parties is made up of several subgroups, and each of these at one time or another has been a separate political party that ran candidates for the Knesset; many of them still consider themselves to be distinct. The result is what seems a never-ending series of political marriages and divorces, and even though both Labor and Likud have been fairly well established for some time, most of the numerous factions within each insist on keeping their own names.

Modernization

The role of political parties has been diminished by aspects of social, political, and economic modernization. These include an electorate increasingly likely to scrutinize the parties, a large increase in the number of Israelis who consider themselves independents, and dissatisfaction with all of the traditional political parties. The result is that many new parties and movements have frequently received sizable votes, even in their initial ventures into the electoral fray.

Political parties continue to be the vehicle of political activity in Israel, and even with recent structural changes in the political system, no pattern of increased nonpartisan activity has emerged in the polity that would suggest a diminution of the role of political parties in the future.

See also ARAB–ISRAEL WAR (1967); ERETZ YISRAEL; HISTADRUT; LIKUD.

Bibliography

Arian, Alan. *Politics in Israel: The Second Generation.* Chatham, NJ: Chatham House, 1985.

Arian, Alan. *The Second Republic: Politics in Israel.* Chatham, NJ: Chatham House, 1998.

Arian, Alan, and Shamir, Michal. *The Elections in Israel, 1996.* Albany: State University of New York Press, 1999.

Arian, Alan, and Shamir, Michal. *The Elections in Israel, 1999.* Albany: State University of New York Press, 2002.

Aronoff, Myron J. *Power and Ritual in the Israel Labor Party: A Study in Political Anthropology,* revised and expanded edition. Armonk, NY: M. E. Sharpe, 1993.

Diskin, Abraham. *The Last Days in Israel: Understanding the New Israeli Democracy.* London: Frank Cass, 2003.

Elazar, Daniel, and Mollov, M. Benjamin. *Israel at the Polls, 1999.* Portland, OR: Frank Cass, 2001

Elazar, Daniel, and Sandler, Shmuel. *Israel at the Polls, 1996.* Portland, OR: Frank Cass, 1998.

Mahler, Gregory. *Politics and Government in Israel: The Maturation of a Modern State.* Lanham, MD: Rowman and Littlefield, 2004.

Maor, Moshe, and Hazan, Reuven. *Parties, Elections, and Cleavages: Israel in Comparative and Theoretical Perspective.* Portland, OR: Frank Cass, 2000.

Sharkansky, Ira. *The Politics of Religion and the Religion of Politics: Looking at Israel.* Lanham, MD: Lexington Books, 2000.

WALTER F. WEIKER
UPDATED BY GREGORY S. MAHLER

POLITICAL PARTIES IN

Major or significant political parties in Israel, including pre-state forerunners.

Agudat Israel ("Society of Israel")

Agudat Israel is political party founded in Poland in 1912, created by the ultraorthodox Agudat Israel Jewish organization, and established in Palestine in the early 1920s. Agudat Israel moderated its antisecular worldview by indicating its willingness to participate in the 1948 government-in-formation and the initial 1949 to 1951 government coalition by the terms of an agreement known as the "status quo letter," which avoided making key decisions about the relationship of the new state and organized religion. In 1949 the party formed part of the United Religious Front; in the elections of 1955 and 1959 it formed part of the Torah Religious Front with Poʿalei Agudat Israel. The party left the governing coalition in 1951 and remained in opposition until 1977, when it supported Menahem Begin's Likud-led coalition. In 1984 Agudat Israel joined the Begin-Peres national unity government and has since remained part of it, although it has refused a ministry.

Agudat Israel was originally anti-Zionist and messianic, although it has been willing to cooperate with Zionists in areas of immigration, settlement, and defense. In the 1980s this non-Zionist party, directed by a Council of Torah Sages (a panel of rabbis to whom both religious and secular decisions are referred), continued to advocate a theocracy and increased state financial support for its religious institutions. It is generally considered to be pragmatic on foreign-policy issues, including the future of the territories occupied since 1967. It is also concerned with all matters of domestic policy, matters it perceives to affect religion in general, and especially its own educational institutions.

In preparation for the 1984 Knesset elections many of the party's Sephardic members left Agudat Israel and started a new party, SHAS, resulting in a decline in Agudat Israel's Knesset representation from four to two seats.

Ahdut ha-Avodah ("Unity of Labor")

This socialist party was founded in 1919 by veterans of the Jewish Legion and other Palestine pioneers. With strong support in the Kibbutz ha-Meʾuhad

movement, Ahdut ha-Avodah (or Achdut ha-Avodah) worked for the unification of Jewish labor movements and the development of new forms of settlement and labor units. It rejected Marxist doctrines of class warfare in favor of social democracy. In 1930 it joined with others in founding the MAPAI Party. After becoming independent from that party in 1944, Ahdut ha-Avodah joined with ha-Shomer ha-Tzaʾir, a Zionist socialist youth movement, to found the more radical left-wing MAPAM in 1948. It split with MAPAM in 1954, formed an alignment with MAPAI in 1965, and in 1968 merged again with MAPAI and the RAFI parties to form the Israel Labor Party.

Alignment (Maʾarakh)

From 1969 to 1984 the Alignment existed as a combination of the Israel Labor Party, MAPAI, and the United Worker's Party, MAPAM. Although the two parties retained their organizational independence, they shared a common slate in elections to the Knesset, the Histadrut, and local-government offices.

Am Ehad ("One Nation") (Received 2.8% of the vote, 3 seats, in 2003 election)

The Am Ehad Party is a labor-oriented organization with leadership that overlaps with the leadership of the Histadrut, the national labor union. Its focus is on social welfare issues, workers' rights, and collective agreements. The party's goals in the 2003 election were to keep in front of the public the debates over employment, unionization, the right to strike, and the ability to live with dignity; to reduce social gaps in income; and to have the government take an active role against unemployment. It focused its political platform on workers' rights. It also pursued "citizenship issues," ensuring a pension for every citizen and working for salary equality for women, and pressed several social issues, including free education from nursery school to university, equal rights in the health system, and adequate housing for each citizen.

Arab Democratic Party

The Arab Democratic Party was founded in early 1988 by Abdul Wahab Darawshe, a former Labor Party Knesset member. In 1988 it received about 12 percent of the total Arab vote and one seat in the Knesset elections. In a March 1988 interview, Darawshe acknowledged that his resignation from the Labor Party resulted from the Palestinian in-

Election results 1949–2003

	Left/ Socialist	Non-Socialist	Religious	Other
First Knesset (1949)	65 (MAPAI 46) (MAPAM 19)	21 (Herut 14) (Liberals 7)	16 (single-list)	18 (Communist 4) (Arab 2) (Other 12)
Second Knesset (1951)	60 (MAPAI 45) (MAPAM 15)	28 (Herut 8) (Liberals 20)	15 (NRP 10) (Aguda 5)	17 (Communist 5) (Arab 1) (Other 11)
Third Knesset (1955)	59 (MAPAI 40) (MAPAM 9) (Ahdut Ha'Avodah 10)	28 (Herut 15) (Liberals 13)	17 (NRP 11) (Aguda 6)	16 (Communist 6) (Arab 4) (Other 6)
Fourth Knesset (1959)	63 (MAPAI 47) (MAPAM 9) (Ahdut Ha'Avodah 10)	25 (Herut 17) (Liberals 8)	18 (NRP 12) (Aguda 6)	14 (Communist 3) (Arab 5) (Other 6)
Fifth Knesset (1961)	59 (MAPAI 42) (MAPAM 9) (Ahdut Ha'Avodah 8)	34 (Herut 17) (Liberals 17)	18 (NRP 12) (Aguda 6)	9 (Communist 5) (Arab 4)
Sixth Knesset (1965)	63 (MAPAI 45) (MAPAM 8) (Rafi 10)	26 Likud (single-list)	17 (NRP 11) (Aguda 6)	14 (Communist 4) (Arab 4) (Other 6)
Seventh Knesset (1969)	56 Israel Labor party (single-list)	26 Likud (single-list)	18 (NRP 12) (Aguda 6)	20 (Communist 4) (Arab 4) (Other 12)
Eighth Knesset (1973)	51 Israel Labor party (single-list)	39 Likud (single-list)	15 (NRP 10) (Aguda 5)	15 (Communist 5) (Arab 3) (Other 7)
Ninth Knesset (1977)	32 Israel Labor party (single-list)	43 Likud (single-list)	17 (NRP 12) (Aguda 5)	28 (Communist 5) (Arab 1) (DMC 15) (Other 7)
Tenth Knesset (1981)	47 Israel Labor party (single-list)	48 Likud (single-list)	10 (NRP 6) (Aguda 4)	15 (Communist 4) (Tehiya 3) (Tami 3) (Other 5)
Eleventh Knesset (1984)	44 Israel Labor party (single-list)	41 Likud (single-list)	12 (NRP 4) (Shas 4) (Aguda 2) (Morasha 2)	23 (Communist 4) (Arab 2) (Tehiya 2) (Shinui 2) (Civil Rights Movement 3) (Other 6)
Twelfth Knesset (1988	39 Israel Labor party (single-list)	40 Likud (single-list)	18 (Shas 6) (NRP 5) (Aguda 5) (Other 2)	23 (Communist 5) (Arab 3) (Civil Rights Movement 5) (Tehiya 3) (Shinui 2) (Other 5)
Thirteenth Knesset (1992)	56 (Israel Labor party 44)	32 Likud (single-list) (Meretz 12)	16 (Shas 6) (NRP 6) (United Torah Judaism 4)	16 (Communist 3) (Arab 2) (Tzomet 8) (Other 3)

[continued]

TABLE BY GGS INFORMATION SERVICES, THE GALE GROUP.

Election results 1949–2003 [CONTINUED]

	Left/ Socialist	Non-Socialist	Religious	Other
Fourteenth Knesset (1996)	43	45	23	9
	(Labor 34)	(Likud 32)	(Shas 10)	(United Arab List 4)
	(Meretz 9)	(Yisrael B'Aliyah 7)	(National Religious Party 9)	(Hadash 5)
		(Third Way 4)	(Yahdut HaTorah 4)	
		(Moledet 2)		
Fifteenth Knesset (1999)	44	39	27	10
	(One Israel 26)	(Likud 19)	(Shas 17)	(United Arab List 5)
	(Meretz 10)	(Yisrael B'Aliyah 6)	(National Religious Party 5)	(Democratic Front
	(Shinui 6)	(National Unity 4)	(United Torah Judaism 5)	for Peace and
	(One Nation 2)	(Center 6)		Equality 3)
		(Israel Our Home 4)		(Balad 2)
Sixteenth Knesset (2003)	44	46	21	9
	(Labor 19)	(Likud 37)	(Shas 11)	(Arab Parties 9)
	(Shinui 15)	(National Union 7)	(United Torah Judaism 5)	
	(Meretz 6)	(Yisrael B'Aliyah 2)	(National Religious Party 5)	
	(Am Ehad 4)			

tifada in the West Bank and the Gaza Strip and the "diminishing choices" open to Israeli Arab politicians affiliated with the government and yet tied to the Arab community by a sense of shared ethnic identity. Echoing the sentiments of other Israeli Arabs, Darawshe has stated that "the PLO is the sole legitimate representative of the Palestinians" living outside Israel's pre-1967 borders. The party won seats in the twelfth (1988), thirteenth (1992), and fourteenth (1996) Knesset elections, after which its membership merged with other Arab parties.

Balad (See National Democratic Assembly)

Citizens' Rights Movement (CRM, "Ratz")

The Citizens' Rights Movement (CRM) was founded in 1973 by Shulamit Aloni, a former Labor Party Knesset member. The CRM was founded as an expression of dissatisfaction with the conduct of the 1973 Arab–Israel War, and its primary issues involved strengthening civil rights in Israel and greater compromise on Israeli-Palestinian issues; the idea of the separation of religion and government has been particularly important to the party's platform. Its most prominent leader was the leftist, social-liberal activist Aloni. The party won three seats in the Knesset election of 1973 and briefly joined the Labor Party government in 1974, but left when Yitzhak Rabin accepted the National Religious Party as a coalition member. The CRM was reduced to one seat in 1977 by the popularity of the Democratic Movement for Change. At various times it negotiated with

other left-wing groups (such as Shinui) about multiparty mergers, but no mergers resulted. In 1984 the CRM rebounded to win three Knesset seats and grew to five seats in 1988. It refused to join the 1984 National Unity government on matters of principle regarding cooperation with Likud. The CRM's platform centered on freedom of religion and culture; complete equality of all Israelis without regard to religion, nationality, race, or gender; full opposition to religious coercion; and negotiation with representatives of Palestinians and recognition of their right to self-determination. In 1992 many of its members joined the combined left-wing Meretz Party, which became a coalition partner of Labor.

Degel ha-Torah ("Torah Flag") (See United Torah Judaism)

Formed in 1988, the clericalist party is a SHAS-led Ashkenazi spinoff among the ultraorthodox community.

Democratic Front for Peace and Equality (HADASH) (Received 3.0% of the vote, 3 seats in 2003 election)

The Democratic Front for Peace and Equality (DFPE) is considered to be on the "far left" of the political spectrum, and is made up of both Arabs and Jews. It is strongly in favor of the peace process, putting a just, comprehensive, and stable Israeli-Arab peace as a high priority, and it wants to see a Palestinian state established as soon as possible. It supports the State of Israel as a state of all of its citizens rather than simply as a "Jewish state." It also strongly advocates the civil and national rights of Arabs in Israel, including the right of Palestinian refugees of 1948 to either return to their land or to be compensated for property that was abandoned at the time. Related to the issue of Arab rights, it seeks to act on behalf of the Arab working class to raise the standard of living of Israeli Arabs.

Democratic Movement for Change

The Democratic Movement for Change (DMC) was founded in 1976 by several groups, including the Shinui Party, to consolidate movements of dissatisfaction in the aftermath of the Arab–Israel War of 1973. The best-known figures of the DMC were Yigael Yadin, former IDF chief of staff and archaeology professor, and Amnon Rubinstein, Tel Aviv University law professor. Dissidents in the Labor Party helped the DMC to win fifteen seats in the Knesset of 1977. The DMC's program included electoral reform, decentralization of government, reorganization of the educational system, increased emphasis on social integration, and simplification of the bureaucracy. In foreign policy, the DMC stressed the preservation of the Jewish character of the state and territorial compromise on the West Bank, but opposed establishment of an independent Palestinian state there. Divided over the issue of cooperation with the Likud, DMC members decided to join the Likud-led government in 1977 without winning any of the major concessions they had insisted upon. It broke up in 1979 when the Shinui Party left over the issue of the DMC's cooperating with the Likud. The party did not put forward any candidates in the 1981 election.

Free Center

The Free Center was a faction that splintered from the Herut Party in 1967. From 1967 to 1973, through the Seventh Knesset, the Free Center was a party in its own right. It became a faction within Likud from 1973 to 1977, and joined the Democratic Movement for Change in 1977.

GAHAL (Acronym for Gush Herut-Liberalim, "the Freedom-Liberal Bloc," also known as the Herut-Liberal Bloc)

GAHAL is a political coalition list created in 1965 by an electoral combination of the Liberal Party and the Herut Party to compete against the 1965 and 1969 MAPAI-led electoral alignments. In 1967, on the eve of the outbreak of the Arab–Israeli War, GAHAL joined a National Unity Government with Labor; in 1973 GAHAL became part of the Likud Bloc.

General Zionist

A centrist Zionist party during the prestate period, in the 1940s General Zionist split into two factions, A and B, over the issues of attitudes towards the mandatory government and its policies on one hand, and the socialist-dominated Histadrut on the other. In the elections for the First Knesset, group A constituted the Progressive Party; group B, the General Zionists. United for a number of years after 1961 under the name of Liberal Party, they split again when one part (basically former group B) joined Herut in 1965 to form a joint list (GAHAL). The former Progressives continued as Independent Liberals.

Gesher ("Bridge")

Gesher was a splinter party founded in 1996 by a number of former Members of Knesset from the Likud, led by Likud MK David Levy (a former foreign minister known for his support for the Moroccan community in Israel). It was seen by many as a centrist-right party focusing on the social and economic problems of the population in Israel's periphery and development towns, populated initially by immigrants from North Africa.

HADASH (See Democratic Front for Peace and Equality)

Herut Party ("Freedom")

The Herut (Freedom) Party was founded in 1948, and until 1983 was led by Menachem Begin, a protégé of the Revisionist Zionist Vladimir Ze'ev Jabotinsky. Herut was a right-wing party founded by people who had been active in the Irgun in the prestate years, and had an ideology based on Revisionist Zionism. One of the key characteristics of the Revisionist movement was an emphasis on Jewish control of the territory of *Eretz Yisrael*. In 1973 Herut became the senior member of the Likud bloc, which included the Free Center Party, and which Begin led to victory in 1977. Prior to 1977, Herut was identified as a party of opposition, one that would never control a plurality of the national vote (despite a brief appearance in a government of national unity from 1967 to 1970). Since 1977 the Herut, as the major partner of Likud, has been a successful alternative to the Labor Party coalition, and the Herut/Likud bloc has formed the basis of most Israeli governments.

Herut was traditionally associated with the idea of a Greater Israel, which includes the West Bank and Gaza, and many of its leaders favor annexation of those areas. It is committed to a diminution of government regulation in the economy, fewer concessions to the Palestinians, and strong security. It relies heavily on the Sephardic community to stay in power as part of the Likud coalition, which it joined in 1973.

Ihud Le'umi *(See National Union)*

Israel be-Aliyah ("Israel on the Increase") (Received 2.2% of the vote, 2 seats, in 2003 election)

One of the key issues of this party refers to the importance of *aliyah* (immigration) to the state. The party was founded in 1996 by Natan Sharansky, a well-known "refusnik" from the former Soviet Union. It is the only single-issue party that has been successful in recent years. It seeks to advance the rights of all immigrants, not just immigrants from Russia and the former Soviet Union, but Sharansky's background related to the former Soviet Union has made his appeal to that group especially strong.

The party seeks to make progress on the peace process by supporting a democratized Palestinian Authority. It also seeks to support the ingathering of most of the Jewish people in *Eretz Yisrael* (the land of Israel), and to expand the conditions necessary for the absorption of the Jewish people in the land of Israel.

Israel Beiteinu ("Israel Our Home")

Israel Beiteinu is an immigrants' rights party formed in 1999 by former prime minister Benyamin Netanyahu's Russian-born former chief of staff, Avigdor Lieberman. It seeks to curb what Lieberman says are the excessive powers of the police force, justice ministry, and court system. Its platform includes a commitment to work for tolerance, mutual respect, and respect for the rights of the individual; to work in the social and economic fields to assist weak population groups and young couples in the field of subsidized housing; and to work to advance rehabilitation projects for development towns on the basis of land reform.

The party supports the creation of a presidential system of government in Israel, and the entrenching of a fully written constitution and an active constitutional court. It supports a more vigorous separation of government and religion and the adoption of the recommendations of the Neeman Commission on orthodoxy of Judaism in Israel, and wants an expansion of the openness of the civil service. The party also seeks to transfer the authority for dealing with new immigrants from the Ministry of Immigration Absorption to local government.

Israel Communist Party ("Miflagah Komunistit Yisraelit," creating the acronym MAKI)

Under the general name Miflagah Komunistit Yisraelit (MAKI), communist parties in Palestine and Israel date back to at least 1919 and have undergone many metamorphoses. MAKI's membership recognized the new state of Israel and its flag and anthem, but denied linkages between the state and Jews overseas. One of its primary issues involved insisting upon the right of Arabs to establish a state in the territory recommended by the 1947 United Nations Partition Resolution. Ideology of class warfare and affiliation with international communist movements resulted in the party being seen by some Jews as anti-Zionist, and therefore it was excluded from participation in Yishuv affairs. After the establishment of the State of Israel, there were attempts by MAKI, the mainly Jewish communist party, to unify Jewish and Arab communists.

In 1964 an irreconcilable split over policy toward Arab nationalism and pan-Arabism resulted in a split and the formation of an Israeli Arab communist party, which took the name RAKAH (an acronym for Reshima Komunistit Hadashah, "New Communist List") as an alternative to the overwhelmingly Jewish MAKI. In the 1973 election the two communist parties, RAKAH and MAKI, ran together as Moked ("Focus"), but since 1973, only

RAKAH has borne the name *communist*. Jewish communists have carried on their activity in other structures, such as the Democratic Front for Peace and Equality or SHELI (an acronym for Shalom l'Israel, or "Peace for Israel"). One or more communist parties have had seats in every Israeli Knesset, but they have never been included in the coalition governments by which Israel has always been governed.

Israel Labor Party (With Meimad, received 14.5% of the vote, 19 seats, in 2003 election)

The Israel Labor Party (ILP, Mifleget ha-Avodah) has been the major social-democratic party of Israel since its formation in 1968 through a merger of MAPAI, RAFI, and Ahdut ha-Avodah Po'alei Zion. It has never stood for election on its own, but rather has been the major partner in the Alignment, which was formed in 1969 with MAPAM. Labor, in various manifestations, was in power from the foundation of the State of Israel in 1948 until its defeat by the Likud under Menachem Begin in 1977, with the exception of two periods (1967–1969 and 1984–1988), when it shared power with the Likud in a National Unity government. It returned to full power in the election of 1992. As the senior member of the Labor Alignment in each Knesset since the ILP's formation, it received 80 to 85 percent of the Alignment's seats. Its leaders, Israel's most prominent Labor-Zionist figures, were also prime ministers when the Alignment was in power: Levi Eshkol (1968–1969), Golda Meir (1969–1973), Yitzhak Rabin (1974–1977 and 1992–1995), Shimon Peres (1995–96), and Ehud Barak (1999–2001).

The ILP's programs are broadly pragmatic in foreign policy and moderately socialist in domestic policy. In regard to the Palestinians, it has been willing to negotiate with only minimal preconditions, generally preferring a settlement through a Jordanian-Palestinian confederation. It has sought to restart negotiations with the Palestinians based upon a "land for peace" formula, and is willing to consider unilateral withdrawal from certain parts of the West Bank and Gaza Strip—within the framework of the Oslo Accords—if that will bring secure borders. Its public goal has been to "pursue peace as if there were no terror and fight terror as if there were no peace process." But Labor has also joined other Israeli parties in insisting that Israeli security

be the first priority. It rejects the idea of annexation of the West Bank and Gaza but insists that the status of Jerusalem is not negotiable: Jerusalem is the indivisible capital of Israel, under Israeli sovereignty, including eastern neighborhoods, with special status accorded to places holy to Islam and Christianity. The party supports continuing all peace talks with nations of the region. Specifically, it wants to continue talks with Syria, and has indicated that it would be willing to make compromises on the issue of the Golan Heights if sufficient security concerns are met.

Party platforms have also stressed equality for Arab citizens of Israel. On domestic affairs, the ILP stands for a mixed economy, central economic planning, an extensive network of government-run social services, and close cooperation with the Histadrut, but also a large role for the private sector. On the role of religion, it accepts the "status quo agreement," under which religious affairs will be under the jurisdiction of the Orthodox rabbinate and rules about such matters as public transportation on the Sabbath will remain as they were at the time of the founding of the state. However, the party would also like to see Jewish religious pluralism and more rights for the Reform and Conservative movements.

The history of the ILP has often been stormy, providing an arena for conflicts among its strong leading personalities. Among these conflicts was the rivalry between Rabin and Peres, often over questions of who was responsible for ILP election setbacks and for the failures of some government policies. In 1977 Rabin's difficulties over an allegedly illegal bank account belonging to his wife were considered by some to be one of the causes of the Alignment's defeat by the Likud under Begin. In turn, many attribute subsequent electoral defeats to the "colorless" Peres, citing his replacement by Rabin as an important factor in the Alignment's decisive electoral victory in 1992. In an important reform of internal Israeli political party organization in 1968, the ILP broadened the selection process for Knesset candidates through primary elections, a practice that has since then been adopted by some other Israeli parties as well. Following the assassination of Prime Minister Rabin in November 1995, Shimon Peres was elected Labor Party leader.

Kach ("Thus")

Kach, an ultranationalist party, came into being around Rabbi Meir Kahane, a U.S.-born right-wing Orthodox extremist. Kach advocated the forcible expulsion of Arabs from Israel and the Occupied Territories, followed by Israeli sovereignty there. A number of other party leaders have been implicated in Kach-supported terrorist activities. In 1988 the Likud and the Citizens' Rights Movement succeeded in having the Knesset pass a Basic Law empowering the Central Elections Board to prohibit any party advocating racism from contesting parliamentary elections in Israel; Kach, which had gained one seat in the 1984 elections after several earlier unsuccessful attempts to enter the Knesset, was outlawed from participating in the 1988 elections.

Liberal Party

The Liberal Party is a centrist party formed in 1961 by members of the General Zionist and Progressive parties. It is primarily interested in furthering the cause of a strong private sector in the economy with minimal government interference. In 1965 it joined the Herut Party in forming an electoral list called GAHAL, causing one of its wings to split off to become the Independent Liberals. The Liberal Party continues to exist as an independent entity within the Likud. In the Begin cabinet of 1977 one of Liberal's leaders, Simha Ehrlich, served as finance minister; two other Liberals, Yitzhak Moda'i and Moshe Nissim, held the same post in the National Unity government of 1984. Another Liberal leader, Arie Dulzin, served for some time as chairman of the World Zionist Organization (WZO).

Likud ("Union") (Received 29.4% of the vote, 38 seats, in 2003 election)

An Israeli electoral bloc established in 1973, the Likud consisted originally of several independent parties: the Herut Party, the Liberal Party, the Free Center, State List, and part of the Land of Israel Movement. Much of the emphasis of its program has been on extension of Israeli sovereignty to the territories conquered in the Arab–Israel War of 1967. In large part, Likud was the direct ideological descendant of the Revisionist Party, established by Vladimir Jabotinsky in 1925. The Revisionist Party, so named to underscore the urgency of revision in the policies of the WZO's Executive, advo-

cated militancy and ultranationalism as the primary political imperatives of the Zionist struggle for Jewish statehood. The Revisionist Party demanded that the entire mandated territory of historical Palestine on both sides of the Jordan River, including Transjordan, immediately become a Jewish state with a Jewish majority.

Taking advantage of public disenchantment with the Labor Party in 1977, Likud won forty-three Knesset seats and formed a coalition government led by Menachem Begin, which continued until 1984. In that year, neither Likud nor the Labor Alignment bloc won enough to form a coalition without the other. The two joined in a National Unity government in which Likud leader Yitzhak Shamir held the office of prime minister for half of the electoral period, and the blocs divided other government offices. In 1988 Likud and other right-wing and religious parties improved their showing, and Shamir again led the government until the Labor victory of 1992. During its years in power, Likud strongly resisted surrendering sovereignty over the Palestinian territories and made little progress in reducing the role of the government in the economy. One of Likud's problems has been the presence in it of several strong individuals and their factions, including Shamir, former chief of staff Ariel Sharon, and Moroccan leader David Levy, all of whom have tried vigorously to become dominant. In 1993 the Likud chairmanship was won by Benjamin Netanyahu, former ambassador to the United Nations and brother to the hero of the Israeli raid on Entebbe. He defeated his former rivals, Moroccan-born David Levy and Ariel Sharon, as well as younger figures such as Ze'ev Begin, with a spirited campaign based on American-style politics and effective use of the media, even though it was an election confined to party members.

The Likud has indicated that it is willing to negotiate peace with a Palestinian leadership "not compromised by terror," but it has also stated that it is opposed to the dismantling of Israeli settlements in the Occupied Territories. It advocates increasing the population of the settlements in the West Bank, to which it believes Israel has a right, and calls for improvement of the social and economic conditions of Israel's disadvantaged communities, which consisted largely of Jews originating from Middle Eastern and Arabic lands, and the maintaining of the current status quo in government-religious relations. The Likud campaigned heavily against the Oslo Accords. Allthough it claims that it will not "go back" on what has been done, the Likud has been extremely cautious.

MAPAI (Acronym for Mifleget Po'alei Eretz Yisrael, or "Israel Workers' Party")

MAPAI is the principal Zionist and Israeli socialist party (1930–1968). Founded upon the merger of Ahdut Ha-Avodah and Ha-Po'el Ha-Tza'ir in 1930, it constituted the central and dominant political force in the labor movement, in the Yishuv (Jewish community of Palestine under the British Mandate), in the Zionist movement, and later in the State of Israel. Under the spiritual inspiration of Berl Katznelson, the party became the main ideological and political vehicle for the Jewish labor movement during the Yishuv period. Its central program focus was uniting socialist and national goals. To do that, however, it was necessary to work with nonsocialist parties and to accede to some of their premises.

MAPAI's chief political leader from the mid-1930s to 1963 was David Ben-Gurion. A leading pragmatist, he was frequently criticized by party elements who were more ideological. In 1963 Ben-Gurion resigned from MAPAI over the Lavon Affair. In 1965 MAPAI became a partner in the formation of the Labor Alignment, and in 1968 that organization in turn joined with the RAFI Party to form the Israel Labor Party. The 1965 election was the last one in which MAPAI ran candidates under its own name. During its existence, MAPAI's membership supplied all but one of Israel's prime ministers, all but one of the state's presidents and Knesset speakers, and all secretaries-general of the Histadrut.

MAPAM (Acronym of Mifleget Po'alim Me'uhedet, or "United Workers Party")

Founded in 1948, MAPAM was a Marxist-Zionist party that followed a Moscow-led policy until the death of Josef Stalin, when it disavowed that orientation. MAPAM split in 1954; former members of Ha-Shomer Ha-Tza'ir remained with MAPAM, while former members of Ahdut Ha-Avodah-Po'alei-Tziyon left MAPAM to form Ahdut Ha-Avodah. Thereafter, MAPAM concentrated much more on local matters. Combining the goals of La-

bor Zionism with a refusal to dispossess Israeli-Arabs, it received considerable criticism when it accepted Arab members. It advocated greater neutrality in foreign policy and a greater restraint in defense. Immediately after 1967, MAPAM opposed the establishment of Israeli settlements on the West Bank and strongly urged negotiations with the Palestinians. It was also among the quickest and most vigorous objectors to the Arab–Israeli War of 1982.

After 1969 MAPAM became a member of the Labor Alignment with MAPAI and other parties. There were forceful arguments within MAPAM over whether the Alignment's ideology was so mild that MAPAM's very principles were being violated, but those favoring continued membership prevailed until 1984, when the Alignment took part in the formation of the National Unity government in which Likud was a partner. MAPAM broke away from the Alignment and resumed its independent existence in the fall of 1984, when the Labor Party decided to join Likud in forming the National Unity government. In 1992 MAPAM joined with Shinui and the Citizen's Rights Movement to form Meretz, which became Labor's main coalition partner.

MAPAM's socioeconomic program was the most socialist of any Israeli party. It was also one of the strongest proponents of equality for Israeli Arabs. It did not, however, advocate class struggle in orthodox Marxist terms. MAPAM has advocated a strong national security and defense posture, with many of its members playing leading roles in the IDF. At the same time, it has urged continuing peace initiatives and territorial compromise, and has opposed the permanent annexation of the territories occupied in the Arab–Israel War of 1967 beyond minimal border changes designed to provide Israel with secure and defensible boundaries. MAPAM has long believed in Jewish-Arab coexistence and friendship as a means of hastening peace between Israel, the Palestinians, and the Arab states.

Meimad ("Dimensions—Movements of the Religious Center") (With Labor Party, received 14.5% of the vote, 19 seats, in 2003 election)

Meimad was established in 1988 as a religious Zionist alternative to the National Religious Party. Meimad's goal was to represent, to cultivate, to strengthen, and to disseminate the values of religious Zionism in Israel and abroad, and to incorporate Orthodox religious practice in Israeli public life, but it did not want to do so by restrictive legislation. Its platform called for working for the development of the State of Israel and influencing its social, economic, political, and spiritual life on the basis of the Torah. Meimad maintained that peace between Israelis and Arabs was possible and that Israel could negotiate land for peace. In 1999 Meimad joined Ehud Barak's One Israel Party.

Meretz ("Energy") (Received 5.2% of the vote, 6 seats, in 2003 election)

Meretz is seen as a left-wing, social-democratic secular party. Comprising MAPAM, Shinui, and the Citizens' Rights Movement, Meretz won twelve seats in the 1992 Knesset elections and became the most important coalition partner in Israel's Labor Party. Its most widely publicized program includes advocating for more conciliatory policies on negotiations with the Palestinians, supporting an accelerated peace process and a just and comprehensive peace between Israel and its neighbors, and dismantling settlements and withdrawing from the West Bank and Gaza Strip. Many young Israelis are also attracted to its reformist views on education, economic, human rights, and environmental issues. Meretz is a democratic, peace-seeking party in which Jews and Arabs work in complete equality. Meretz is committed to human rights, to equality of citizens of the country, to social justice, to Israel's security, and to the values of humanistic Zionism. Its concern with social justice has led it to take some activist positions in relation to economic policy. It has promoted more state funding for education because since education is the cornerstone of a democratic society. It has also advocated freedom of religion and greater separation between religion and the state, arguing for equal status for all branches of Judaism.

Mizrahi

Mizrahi consists of offshoots of the Orthodox Jewish world Mizrahi movement, established in 1902 with the aim of securing "Eretz Yisrael for the people of Israel according to the Torah of Israel." The Mizrahi and Ha-Po'el Ha-Mizrahi ran as separate political parties in the elections to the first Israeli Knesset (1949), joining together to form the Na-

tional Religious Party (NRP) in 1956. From 1951 to 1977, Mizrahi candidates occupied ten to twelve seats in the Knesset. Although the Mizrahi-Ha-Po'el Ha-Mizrahi movement played a major role in establishing the public religious character of Israel in its initial decades of nationhood, the party's power and prestige had declined by the 1980s. The party continued to struggle to establish mandatory recognition of the Sabbath as the national day of rest and of the practice of *kashrut* (strict observance of dietary laws) in all national institutions, settlements, and organizations, so that the state's constitution would be based on *halakhah* (Jewish religious law). Mizrahi envisages, in the ultimate stage, a Jewish state governed according to *halakhah,* and it considers the present-day secular state to be a precursor of that state.

Since 1981 the number of NRP Knesset seats declined by more than 50 percent. This has been attributed to a number of causes, including the perceived stance of the majority party, Likud, to religious tradition; to ideological confusion, stagnation, and an absence of NRP leadership development; to an empowerment of Sephardic Jews and the creation of parties dominated by Sephardic Jews; and to a move by NRP to the religious right, which led many former Mizrahi loyalists into the more sectarian religious parties, such as Agudat Israel and SHAS.

Moledet ("Homeland")

The Moledet Party ran in 1988 on an extremist platform advocating the forcible "transfer" of Palestinian Arabs from the West Bank to Arab states. It argued that population transfer should be a precondition for peace negotiations with any Arab country. It also advocated the annexation of the West Bank and Gaza into Israel and the continuation of settlements in the areas. The party actively opposed the idea of a binational State of Israel. Led by retired IDF General Rehavam ("Gandhi") Ze'evi, the party won two seats in the 1988 Knesset elections.

Morashah ("Heritage")

Morashah is a nationalist-religious party led by Rabbi Chaim Druckman that broke away from the National Religious Party in 1984. In 1986 it was reincorporated into the National Religious Party.

National Democratic Assembly (Balad) (Received 2.3% of the vote, 3 seats, in 2003 election)

The National Democratic Assembly is an Israeli Arab party that argues that Israel should be a democratic state for all of its citizens. It advocates the right of return for all Arab refugees from the 1948 Arab–Israel War, full Israeli withdrawal from the West Bank, Gaza Strip, and East Jerusalem, and sthe creation of a Palestinian state in the territories conquered in 1967, the capital of which should be eastern Jerusalem. It promotes economic and social advancement of a national Arab minority, and advocates cooperation with Jewish elements that are willing to support its major goals.

National Religious Party (NRP, Mafdal) (Received 4.2% of the vote, 6 seats, in 2003 election)

The National Religious Party, founded in 1956, was the largest and most influential component of the religious bloc, and a member of every Israeli government up to 1992. It had the reputation of being less militant and more pragmatic than some of the others in the religious bloc. At times this image led to its being overshadowed by parties such as TAMI and SHAS, both of which charged that the NRP failed to give adequate representation to Oriental Jews. It advocates a religious Jewish lifestyle as well as full participation in Israeli society for Orthodox Jews, and legislation based on the legal system of the Torah and Jewish tradition. Its central goals are to preserve the religious character of the country, and to ensure the provision of all religious services to the public and to individuals by means of state, local, and other public institutions. It supports the retention of the Occupied Territories based on national security considerations as well as Biblical and Zionistic beliefs, and promotes the expansion of settlements in Judea, Samaria, and the Gaza Strip, as well as in other territories that it sees as the Land of Israel. During the 1950s, 1960s, and 1970s, the NRP always had ten to twelve seats in the Knesset, and usually controlled the Ministry of Religious Affairs as well as the Ministry of the Interior. After 1981 it fell to a consistent level of four to six seats. The losses led it to move further to the right on domestic issues and to a somewhat more moderate position in regard to the territories occupied by Israel.

National Union (Ihud Le'umi, received 5.5% of the vote, 7 seats, in 2003 election)

The National Union is a coalition of three right-wing secular parties—Moledet, Tekumah, and Israel Beiteinu—that came into existence in February 2000. The three parties advocate the voluntary transfer of Arabs from the West Bank and Gaza to other Arab countries, and are against concessions to the Palestinian Authority and the creation of a Palestinian state.

One Nation (See Am Ehad)

Po'alei Agudat Israel ("Agudat Workers' Organization")

Po'alei Agudat Israel was an organization originally established in Poland in 1922 that initiated activities in Palestine in 1925. The PAI identified with Agudat Israel on religious matters, and advocated cooperation with secular workers' organizations and service in the Israel Defense Forces. In most elections the PAI ran on a joint electoral list with Agudat candidates. In 1960 PAI joined the government coalition against the advice of the Agudat Council of Sages.

Po'alei Mizrahi ("Spiritual Center Workers")

An Orthodox religious workers' movement founded in Palestine in 1922 by a left-wing faction of Mizrahi, in 1956 it joined Mizrahi to form the National Religious Party.

Progressive List for Peace

Also known as the Progressive National Movement, this non-Zionist party was one of the strongest challengers to the Israeli Arab community's RAKAH Party. The movement came into being in 1984, advocating recognition of the PLO and the establishment of a Palestinian state in the West Bank and the Gaza Strip alongside Israel. It won two seats in 1984 elections, for Muhammad Mi'ari and Mattityahu Peled, who along with Uri Avnery and Yaacov Arnon met with Yasir Arafat in 1984 and 1984, challenging the Israeli law banning contacts with the PLO.

RAFI (Acronym for Reshimat Po'alei Israel, or "Israel Labor List")

In 1965 MAPAI members who were dissatisfied with the formation of the Labor Alignment split off to form the RAFI Party. Their grievances included resentment over the alleged inflexibility of MAPAI and its failure to give opportunities to young leaders, and their displeasure with the handling of the Lavon Affair (a bitter dispute over government handling of a 1954 espionage and sabotage operation gone awry). The leading dissident was David Ben-Gurion, who was joined by others, including Moshe Dayan, Shimon Peres, and Yizhak Navon. Among the programs that RAFI advocated were regional elections, personal election of mayors, government financing of elections, overhaul of much of the systems of health and unemployment insurance, and free compulsory education between the ages of 1 and 16. RAFI won ten seats in the Knesset in 1965. In 1968 Dayan and most other RAFI leaders, with the exception of Ben-Gurion, rejoined MAPAI and were among those who (along with Ahdut Ha-Avodah) founded the Israel Labor Party.

RAKAH (Acronym for Reshima Komunistit Hadash, or "New Communist List.")

In 1965 a group of former supporters of the Communist Party of Israel—MAKI—broke away from the main group to form RAKAH. RAKAH consisted primarily of Arab communists, and it participated in the 1988 elections. In the 1973 elections RAKAH and MAKI created a joint electoral list called Moked ("Focus").

SHAS (Acronym for Sephardi Torah Guardians) (Received 8.2% of the vote, 11 seats, in 2003 election)

SHAS is an ultraorthodox Sephardic religious movement led by spiritual mentor Rabbi Ovadia Yosef. Due to long-simmering anger over the absence of Sephardic leadership in the party, and specifically over inadequate representation of ultraorthodox Sephardim in the Council of Torah Sages, the Jerusalem Sephardic members of Agudat Israel broke away and established the Sephardi Torah Guardians Party (SHAS) in the early1970s. It was so successful in the October 1983 municipal elections in Jerusalem that it ran a national slate of candidates in 1984 and became an impressive force. SHAS has continued to win seats since 1984, becoming increasingly successful and powerful.

The key issues with which SHAS has been associated all relate to the relationship between govern-

ment and religion. Most fundamentally, SHAS seeks to develop the traditional values of religion and orthodox Judaism in Israel—specifically, Sephardic Jewry. SHAS says that it supports the Talmudic precept of the supreme value of preserving life, and is therefore amenable to territorial compromise if it would bring true peace. It says that it supports autonomy for Palestinians, but it has opposed a Palestinian state. On explicitly religious issues it says that it supports the religious status quo, but would like to see a "Jewish state in every way." The core belief of the party is that governmental policies should be based on strict Jewish law. In the past, the party has been prepared to relinquish land in return for peace, but in recent years has been increasingly uncomfortable with this policy given increased terror.

SHELI (Acronym for Shalom l'Israel, or "Peace for Israel")

SHELI was created in 1977 by MAKI and several other groups. It disbanded before the 1984 elections.

Shinui ("Change") (Received 12.3% of the vote, 15 seats, in the 2003 election)

Shinui was established as a liberal, secular Zionist party in 1973 after splitting from the Democratic Movement for Change in protest against the Arab–Israel War of 1973. It became an ally of the Labor Party and a strong voice for electoral and constitutional reform and for a more flexible policy in the Arab–Israel dispute. It stood for a secular state, and advocated separating religion and the state; it announced that it would not sit in a government coalition with ultraorthodox religious parties. In relation to the Palestinian issue Shinui indicated that it was in favor of a territorial compromise for peace, but that it would be tough on security issues. In economic issues it supported a free-market economy and privatization of government-owned businesses.

In 1992 Shinui, MAPAM, and the Citizens' Rights Movement joined to form Meretz, which won twelve seats and became the main coalition partner of the Labor Party.

State List

In June 1963 Ben-Gurion resigned as Israel's prime minister, citing "personal reasons," and Levi Eshkol took over the posts of prime minister and defense minister. But Ben-Gurion remained active politically, and a rivalry developed between him and Eshkol. In June 1965 the MAPAI Party split, and Ben-Gurion established RAFI ("Israel Labor List"), which won ten Knesset seats in the following election. In 1968 RAFI rejoined MAPAI and Ahdut Ha-Avodah to form the Israel Labor Party, and Ben-Gurion formed a new party, the State List (Ha-Reshima Ha-Mamlachtit), which won four Knesset seats in the 1969 elections.

TAMI (Acronym for Tnu'at Masoret Israel, or "Tradition of Israel Movement")

TAMI was formed from a faction within the National Religious Party in 1981, primarily to increase attention to the problems of Sephardi (Oriental) Jews, especially those from North Africa. It won three seats in the tenth Knesset of 1982 and was part of the second Begin coalition government, but fell to only one seat in 1984. Its program was Zionist and traditional, with emphasis on equality of opportunity for members of all ethnic groups. It was one of only a few essentially ethnic parties in Israeli history. In 1988 it became a faction of the Likud.

Tehiyah ("Renaissance")

Tehiyah, or Ha-Tehiyah, was founded in 1979 by former supporters of the National Religious Party to oppose the return of Sinai land to Egypt as provided by the Camp David Accords. A radical right-wing party, it won three seats in the Knesset of 1981 and five in 1984. It did not join the 1984 National Unity government, in protest against the latter's policy limiting new settlements. In the 1988 election Tehiyah fell back to three seats, and it failed to win any in 1992. Tehiyah advocated the eventual imposition of Israeli sovereignty over the West Bank and supported the transfer of Palestinian Arabs in the West Bank to other Arab countries. It included among its main successes the 1980 Jerusalem Law and the extension of Israeli law to the Golan Heights.

Third Way (Ha-Derekh Ha-Shlishit)

The Third Way was founded in 1995 as a political movement, and it became a party in 1996. The Third Way was founded by Members of Knesset who broke away from the Labor Party, claiming that Labor was making compromises that were dangerous to Israel's security, particularly with regard to withdrawals on or from the Golan Heights. The Third Way saw itself as a centrist party, and claimed to be the only reasonable alternative to Labor and Likud (hence the "third way," if Labor was one choice and Likud the other). It was, essentially, a one-issue party, dealing with concessions to the Arabs over policies governing the Occupied Territories.

Torah Religious Front

The Torah Religious Front was formed by the Agudat Israel and Po'alei Agudat Israel parties to campaign in the 1955 and 1959 elections. The front excluded the two Mizrahi religious parties, claiming that they were insufficiently committed to the concept of a Torah state. The Torah Religious Front was dissolved prior to the 1961 elections.

Tzomet ("Crossroads")

Tzomet, a right-wing party, was formed in 1983 to 1984 as a splinter within the Tehiyah Party, and it won two seats as an independent party in the 1988 Knesset election. In the 1992 election it won eight seats. It joined the Likud in 1996.

Tzomet was designed as a secular party. The basis of its platform was a hard line on the Palestinian issue, but it also advocated populist positions on many quality-of-life issues. It opposed the Oslo Accords, and supported Israel's retention of the West Bank. Although its members called for an active pursuit of peace with the Palestinians and Israel's neighbors, it was opposed to territorial compromise and suggested that Arab refugees in and from the Occupied Territories should be resettled in Arab countries. It promoted Jewish settlements in Judea, Samaria, and Gaza.

United Arab List (Received 2.1% of the vote, 2 seats in the 2003 election)

The United Arab List is a union of three Israeli-Arab parties—the United Arab Party, the Arab National Party, and the Islamic Movement. Under the leadership of, it calls for Israel to have a not overtly Jewish character, saying that Israel should be a state for all of its inhabitants. The party advocates a full Israeli withdrawal from the West Bank, the Gaza Strip, and East Jerusalem, and seeks the establishment of a Palestinian state with Jerusalem as its capital It also calls for the right of return for Palestinian refugees from the 1948 Arab–Israel War.

The party seeks full equality in Israeli society for both Jews and non-Jews, and a just and durable peace between Israel and its neighbors based on the principle of two states for two peoples, the Israeli and the Palestinian.

United Religious Front

The United Religious Front was an electoral alliance created in 1949 composed of the four religious parties: Mizrahi, ha-Poʿel ha-Mizrahi, Poʿalei Agudat Israel, and Agudat Israel. In 1951 the four parties campaigned separately.

United Torah Judaism (Received 4.3% of the vote, 5 seats, in the 2003 election)

United Torah Judaism is a coalition of two ultra-orthodox parties—Agudat Israel and Degel Ha-Torah—representing religious factions in Israel, Europe, and the United States. It is predominantly Ashkenazi. Its basic premise is that governmental policies should be based on Jewish law, and it believes that the Land of Israel was given by God to the Jewish People.

It calls for all domestic and foreign policies to be based in Torah law. Different members of the party support either the religious status quo or the passing of more religious legislation, primarily in the areas of the Law of Return and personal status (the "Who is a Jew?" question). While not active in the political debate over peace, United Torah Judaism is seen as slightly further to the right than SHAS.

The Agudat Israel membership calls for an for and increased role for the Torah in the spiritual, economic, and political life of the Land of Israel. Degel Ha-Torah's concerns focus upon representing the Torah-observant public in Israel in the institutions of government—in the government, the Knesset, and the local authorities—in order to protect and fulfill the special needs of this public in all areas of life, and to prevent discrimination against the Orthodox religious (haredi) public. It also seeks to influence Israeli society to observe a Jewish way of life in accordance with the Torah.

Bibliography

Akzin, Benjamin. "The Role of Parties in Israeli Democracy." Journal of Politics 17 (1955): 507–545.

Arian, Asher. The Second Republic: Politics in Israel. Chatham, NJ: Chatham House Publishers, 1998.

Don-Yehiya, Eliezer. "Origin and Development of the Aguda and Mafdal Parties." Jerusalem Quarterly 20 (1981): 49–64.

Dowty, Alan. The Jewish State: A Century Later. Berkeley, CA: University of California Press, 2001.

Friedman, Menachem. "The NRP in Transition—Behind the Party's Electoral Decline." In Politics and Society in Israel: Theoretical and Comparative Perspectives, edited by Ernest Krausz. New Brunswick, NJ: Transaction Books, 1985.

Greilsammer, Ilan. "The Religious Parties." In Israel's Odd Couple: The 1984 Knesset Elections and the National Unity Government, edited by Daniel J. Elazar and Shmuel Sandler. Detroit, MI: Wayne State University Press, 1990.

Liebman, Charles S., and Eliezer, Don-Yehiya. Civil Religion in Israel: Traditional Judaism and Political Culture in the Jewish State. Berkeley, CA: University of California Press, 1983.

Mahler, Gregory S. Politics and Government in Israel: The Maturation of a Modern State. Boulder, CO: Rowman and Littlefield, 2004.

Sachar, Howard. A History of Israel: From the Rise of Zionism to Our Time. New York: Knopf, 1981.

Sager, Samuel. The Parliamentary System of Israel. Syracuse, NY: Syracuse University Press, 1985.

Schiff, Gary. Tradition and Politics: The Religious Parties of Israel. Detroit, MI: Wayne State University Press, 1977.

Sharkansky, Ira. The Politics of Religion and the Religion of Politics: Looking at Israel. Lanham, MD: Lexington Books, 2000.

Sternhell, Ze'ev. The Founding Myths of Israel: Nationalism, Socialism, and the Making of the Jewish State. Princeton, NJ: Princeton University Press, 1998.

GREGORY S. MAHLER

ISRAEL, ARABS IN

See PALESTINIAN CITIZENS OF ISRAEL

ISRAELI ART

See ART

ISRAELI DANCE

See DANCE

ISRAELI FILM

See FILM

ISRAELI SETTLEMENTS

Towns and villages built since the 1967 Arab–Israel war on lands captured and occupied by Israel.

Since the 1967 Arab–Israel War, successive Israeli governments have promoted the settlement (colonization) of the West Bank and Gaza Strip by Israeli citizens. By 2003, there were in excess of 200,000 settlers residing in a number of villages and townships throughout those areas and at least the same number in the suburbs of east Jerusalem.

The first phase in West Bank settlement activity took place under the Labor governments that remained in power until 1977. Known as the Allon Plan, after its initiator Deputy Prime Minister Yigal Allon, the settlement blueprint was a minimalist one aimed at constructing a line of agricultural settlements along the new eastern border in the Jordan valley. This was part of a concept that assumed that

Israeli soldiers stand guard in the West Bank. The West Bank, which had been annexed by Jordan in 1950, came under the control of the Israeli military after the War of 1967. The area was home to many Palestinians, and clashes arose when Israeli settlers began to move into the territory. © MIKI KRATSMAN/ CORBIS. REPRODUCED BY PERMISSION.

civilian settlements contributed to the defensive posture of the country and that it was necessary to ensure defensible borders between Israel and Jordan. The Allon Plan also proposed the establishment of additional settlements around Jerusalem and in close proximity to the Green Line border as a means of ensuring future territorial changes in favor of Israel. The rest of the West Bank region was deemed unsuitable for settlement because of the dense concentration of Palestinian population, unlike the Jordan valley, which was sparsely populated. Allon envisaged a situation in which the rest of the West Bank would eventually be part of an autonomous area under Jordanian administration and linked to the Kingdom of Jordan by means of a territorial corridor running from Ramallah via Jericho (the only major Palestinian population center in the Jordan Valley) to the border crossings on the Jordan River.

Following the Arab–Israel War of October 1973, a new religious nationalist movement, Gush Emunim ("Bloc of the Faithful"), was established with the objective of promoting settlement throughout the West Bank and Gaza. They saw this as a means of extending Israeli control over the whole of the historic Greater Israel ("Eretz Yisrael ha-Shelemah").

Settlement localities and population, 2001		
Settlement type	Number of settlements (West Bank and Gaza Strip)	Population
Rural	10	9,700
Rural communal	69	41,700
Rural Kibbutzim	9	1,800
Rural Moshavim	32	8,800
Total rural population	**120**	**62,000**
Urban 2,000–9,999	14	57,500
Urban 10,000–19,999	4	63,000
Urban 20,000–49,999	1	25,800
Total urban population	**19**	**146,300**
Grand total	**139**	**208,300**

SOURCE: Central Bureau of Statistics, *Statistical Abstract of Israel,* 2002, Table 2.9.

TABLE BY GGS INFORMATION SERVICES, THE GALE GROUP.

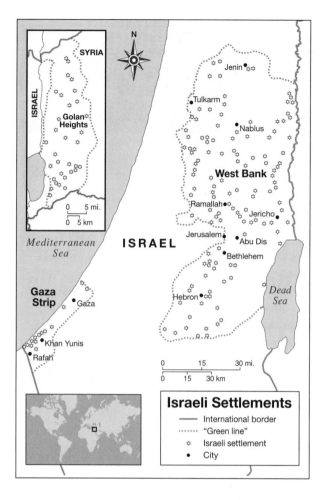

MAP BY XNR PRODUCTIONS, INC. THE GALE GROUP.

They criticized the Allon plan for being minimalist and too compromising in its territorial claims. Their settlement blueprint was rejected by the Rabin government of the time, but was later accepted in 1977 following the rise to power of Israel's first right-wing Likud government under the leadership of Menachem Begin.

Settlement activity took off vigorously in the early 1980s when the planning regulations and restrictions were lifted to make it easier to create suburban communities as an alternative to agricultural and socially controlled small settlements. Under the slogan of "five minutes from Kfar Saba," Israelis were now able to build detached houses on large land plots which they received at a low cost and, at the same time, retain their places of employment in the Tel Aviv and Jerusalem metropolitan centers. During the 1980s and 1990s, the road and transportation infrastructure linking Israel to the West

Bank was improved, thus enhancing the appeal of the region for many Israelis who were attracted to settle there for economic rather than ideological or political reasons.

Following the first National Unity government of 1984, the Israeli cabinet announced a freeze on all new settlement activity. But, despite this and similar announcements by subsequent governments, settlement activity continued unabated, even under the pro-peace administrations of Yitzhak Rabin and Ehud Barak. At the most, there were periods in which no new settlements were constructed, but the expansion and consolidation of existing communities to allow for "natural growth" never ceased. Under the Ariel Sharon administration after February 2001, militant settlers constructed new settlement outposts on their own initiative. These were deemed illegal by the government as a means to differentiate them from the so-called "legal" settlements and were forcibly removed in an attempt to appease international criticism of settlement activity.

The settlements are organized in a system of small towns (some of them, such as Ariel, Emanuel, and Maʿaleh Adumim, consist of over 20,000 inhabitants each) and villages. A system of municipal regional and local councils, similar to that in operation inside Israel itself, caters to their daily needs in the areas of public services, schools, health clinics, and welfare services. This system of local government operates totally independently and separately from the parallel, but much poorer, system that continued to function for the majority Palestinian population of the region.

The establishment of the settlements has resulted in the expropriation of much Palestinian land in both the public and private domain. Israeli high court rulings at the end of the 1970s warned against the use of private land for such purposes, but there are differences of opinion concerning just what is private and what is public land. Under international law, even the use of public land in occupied territories can only be justified for bona fide defensive purposes, not for the sake of civilian settlement activity. Security problems during the Al-Aqsa intifada that broke out in September 2000 led Israel to destroy Palestinian olive groves, orchards, and other agricultural assets in attempts to enhance the safety of the settlers and their families. Similar concerns have also resulted in the construction of by-pass and controlled-access roads throughout the region, enabling settlers to reach their homes without having to drive through the Palestinian towns and villages while causing disruptions to the normal movement of Palestinians.

The issue of settlements has been a major point for discussion in all negotiations aimed at bringing an end to the conflict. Most observers agree that any future peace agreement between Israel and the Palestinians based on territorial compromise will necessitate the evacuation and removal of most, if not all, of these settlements. The inconclusive territorial negotiations that accompanied the Oslo Accords either ignored the settlement issue altogether or attempted to redraw the borders in such a way as to include as many settlements on the Israeli side of the border—whether in exchange for territory elsewhere or as out-and-out annexation. The building of a unilaterally imposed security wall begun in 2002 in effect implemented this policy on the ground.

See also ALLON, YIGAL; GUSH EMUNIM.

Bibliography

Newman, David. "The Evolution of a Political Landscape: Geographical and Territorial Implications of Jewish Colonization in the West Bank." *Middle Eastern Studies* 21, no. 2 (1985), 192–205.

Newman, David. "The Territorial Politics of Exurbanisation: Reflections on Thirty Years of Jewish Settlement in the West Bank." *Israel Affairs* 3, no. 1(1996): 61–85.

DAVID NEWMAN

ISRAEL LABOR PARTY

See ISRAEL: POLITICAL PARTIES IN

ISTANBUL

Largest city of Turkey; capital of the Byzantine and Ottoman empires.

Istanbul is the only city in the world straddling two continents (Europe and Asia). Its situation at the southern end of the Bosporus Strait and on the Golden Horn (an inlet of the Bosporus bisecting the European side) provides the city with excellent harbors. When the Ottoman sultan Mehmet II conquered the city in 1453, he took the title "Master of the Two Seas and Lord of Two Lands," glorifying his new capital at the junction of land routes from Asia and Europe, and of sea routes from the Black Sea and the Mediterranean (through the Dardanelles Strait).

Istanbul's roots date to a short-lived Mycenean settlement in the second millennium B.C.E. and the foundation of Byzantium as a Megaran colony in the seventh century B.C.E. The city rose to greatness when the Roman emperor Constantine I chose this "New Rome" as his capital in 324 C.E., renaming it Constantinopolis and extending its area over seven hills on the peninsula between the Golden Horn and the Sea of Marmara. The most imposing Byzantine monuments of the city date from the reigns of early emperors who followed Constantine, and throughout its eleven centuries as capital, the city continuously was adorned by fine examples of Byzantine architecture. By the mid-fifteenth century, however, the once mighty Byzantine Empire had shrunk to such an extent that it held only the city and its immediate environs, surrounded on all sides by the rising Ottoman state. Mehmet II conquered the city in 1453 and set about to rebuild and repopulate his new capital. Within a century, Istanbul had a cosmopolitan population that reflected its international status and the multiethnic character of the empire. Of the two Greek names of the city, Kustantaniyye remained an official designation, but the colloquial eis ten polein, Turkified as Istanbul, was firmly established as the city's name.

In the seventeenth century Pera, located on the heights above Galata, became the site of European embassies and merchants' mansions, leading to the Europeanization of the city's municipal administration, architecture, banking, and trading. Greater Istanbul covered a large area beyond the walled city. However, the population was concentrated in the walled city and across the Golden Horn in Galata; fishing villages along the Bosporus became fashionable summering suburbs, expanding with the advent of steam ferry service. Railway lines constructed late in the nineteenth century led to the further development of European and Asian suburbs along the Sea of Marmara. In the last days of the Ottoman Empire, the city and its suburbs had a total population

Istanbul's impressive Blue Mosque was completed in 1616 during the reign of Sultan Ahmet I. The architecture is classic Ottoman, with a perfect proportion of domes and semidomes, and the interior is covered by twenty thousand blue ceramic tiles that give the landmark its nickname. © ROSE HARTMAN/CORBIS. REPRODUCED BY PERMISSION.

of about 900,000: 560,000 Muslims, 205,000 Greeks, 73,000 Armenians, 52,000 Jews, and several thousand Europeans, according to a 1914 census.

During World War I, the Ottoman capital was defended successfully at the Dardanelles (Gelibolu/Gallipoli). Despite this victory, the city suffered typical wartime deprivations, and after the armistice it was occupied by the Allied powers. It was the only defeated capital to be subjected to occupation, primarily because of its strategic position and the international importance of the Turkish Straits. The Turkish nationalist movement that defeated the occupation was directed from Ankara, then a secondary city on the Anatolian plateau. After victory, the sultanate and the caliphate were abolished (in 1922 and 1924, respectively), and the Turkish republic (founded in 1923) chose Ankara as its capital, because it was both easier to defend against

foreign powers and untainted by the Ottoman past. During the occupation, Istanbul experienced an influx of White Russians fleeing Bolshevik rule. Most of these Russians, along with many of the local Greeks and Armenians, left in the early years of the republic. Istanbul became much more Turkish, albeit at the cost of a reduced population. The prewar population level was regained only after 1950, when an explosive rate of growth began. Much of this new growth was due to the migration of the rural poor to the industrializing urban areas. By the 2000 census, Istanbul's population had reached 9,119,135.

With the population explosion, the city has suffered the breakdown of transport, electricity, gas, and water supply. Temporary shantytowns, or *gecekondus*, gradually have transformed into permanent tenements. In older quarters of the city, graceful wooden houses have given way to blocks of characterless

Istanbul boasts many forms of public transportation, including trams. The tram line, managed by the Istanbul Municipality, was renovated in the early 1990s, and tickets between the tram system and bus system are conveniently interchangeable. © Chris Hellier/Corbis. Reproduced by permission.

apartments. Nevertheless, this ancient capital of two great empires retains a rich architectural heritage and extraordinary setting, so that Istanbul remains one of the great cities of the world. Two bridges across the Bosporus connect the European and Asian suburbs, and a new business center has developed further to the north. Istanbul has regained its historical role as the region's international trading and financial capital.

See also GECEKONDU.

Bibliography

Celik, Zeynep. *The Remaking of Istanbul: Portrait of an Ottoman City in the Nineteenth Century.* Seattle: University of Washington Press, 1986.

Freely, John. *Istanbul,* 2d edition. New York: Norton, 1987.

Mansel, Philip. *Constantinople: City of the World's Desire, 1453–1924.* New York: St. Martin's, 1996.

I. METIN KUNT
UPDATED BY ERIC HOOGLUND

ISTANBUL TECHNICAL UNIVERSITY

Oldest engineering college in Turkey.

Istanbul Technical University (ITU) is one of the oldest engineering colleges in the world; it traces its origins to 1773, when the Ottoman Empire established a military engineering school in Constantinople as part of a modernization effort. In 1884 a separate department in the school was set up for civilian students. That department was transferred to the Ministry of Public Works in 1909 and was spread over several campuses in Istanbul until 1920, when its present campus was established on a hill overlooking the Turkish Straits. After Turkey was proclaimed a republic in 1923, additional departments were added to provide training in railroad construction, electro-mechanics, civil engineering, and architecture. In 1944 the school was reorganized and named Istanbul Technical University. Its eleven faculties offer instruction in thirty-three departments, including engineering, architecture, management, and the sciences. The university has also expanded its programs in research and development.

Bibliography

Lewis, Bernard. *Istanbul and the Civilization of the Ottoman Empire.* Norman: University of Oklahoma Press, 1989.

NIYAZI DALYANCI

ISTANBUL UNIVERSITY

Largest and oldest public university in Turkey.

Founded in 1900 and reorganized in its present form in 1933, Istanbul University comprises the faculties of letters, science, law, economics, forestry, pharmacy, dentistry, political science, business administration, veterinary science, engineering, and two faculties of medicine, as well as schools of fisheries, journalism, paralegal studies, and tobacco specialist education. With 3,500 teaching staff and 60,000 students (46 percent female) in 2002, it is Turkey's biggest university.

Istanbul University sometimes claims descent from the complex of eight madrasa colleges (religious schools) endowed by Mehmet II soon after the conquest of Constantinople (now Istanbul) in 1453. However, a university in the European sense was first proposed in the era of Tanzimat, the Ottoman Empire's reform period in the 1860s. After some abortive attempts, the university was launched in 1900, incorporating newly established faculties and colleges founded in the previous two decades. After the establishment of the Republic of Turkey in 1923, the staff as well as the programs of Istanbul University were suspected in Ankara, the new capital, of resistance to republican reform. Finally, in 1933 a complete overhaul of the academic programs and a purge of the staff brought it in line with republican thinking. This era of reestablishment was facilitated by the influx of large numbers of German and other European scholars, many of them Jewish, fleeing Nazi intimidation or persecution. The refugee scholars were especially active in the fields of law and economics, but other programs, including Islamic studies, benefited from a substantial European presence.

In spite of the government's attempts to promote Ankara University during the 1950s, Istanbul University remained the country's biggest and most prestigious academic establishment. Its academic staff and students were in the forefront of political protests in the late 1950s and during the 1970s. Its legal experts were influential in the preparation of the 1961 constitution, promulgated after the 1960 military coup. Its economists have been champions of Turkish membership in the European Union since the mid-1980s.

See also ANKARA UNIVERSITY; MADRASA.

Bibliography

Higher Education in Turkey. UNESCO, European Centre for Higher Education. December 1990.

The World of Learning, 2000. Available at <http://www .worldoflearning.com>.

I. METIN KUNT
UPDATED BY ERIC HOOGLUND

ISTIQLAL PARTY

This entry consists of the following articles:

ISTIQLAL PARTY: LIBYA
ISTIQLAL PARTY: MOROCCO
ISTIQLAL PARTY: PALESTINE
ISTIQLAL PARTY: SYRIA

ISTIQLAL PARTY: LIBYA

Political party of Tripolitania, Libya, 1948–1952.

Istiqlal (Independence party) was founded in 1948 by Salim al-Muntasir, former leader of the United National Front of Libya, from which many members were drawn. One of several political parties that briefly flourished under the British military administration at a time of intense debate about the future of Libya, the Istiqlal's influence belied a small following. It came under the patronage of a powerful lobby advocating renewed Italian rule in Tripolitania, activity the British authorities eventually suppressed. The party was a divisive element in Tripolitanian politics at a time when most of the province's leaders were trying to make a coherent case for Libyan unity and independence. It was one of four Tripolitanian political groups whose views on Libyan independence were heard by the United Nations in 1949. Like all other officially sanctioned parties, the Istiqlal was suppressed as a result of the disturbances that followed the first postindependence elections of February 1952.

See also LIBYA; TRIPOLITANIA.

Bibliography

Wright, John L. *Libya, a Modern History.* Baltimore: Johns Hopkins University Press, 1982.

JOHN L. WRIGHT

ISTIQLAL PARTY: MOROCCO

Leading party in the Moroccan nationalist movement, 1946–1956, and chief competitor of the monarchy during the first postindependence decades.

Istiqlal was founded in 1943 by the core leadership of the banned Parti National. Headed by Ahmed Balafrej and Allal al-Fasi, it drew its strength from the traditional bourgeois elites of the northern cities, particularly Fez, the emerging national bourgeoisie, and more leftist urban professionals. Its charter, issued on 11 January 1944, demanded independence from France with a constitutional monarchy under the sultan. The publication of the charter and the resulting arrest of Balafrej provoked serious urban unrest in January and February 1944. Fasi returned to Morocco in 1946 after nine years in Gabon and assumed undisputed leadership of the party. By 1950 Istiqlal's membership was 100,000. After 1951 Istiqlal supported the sultan against the French authorities. In 1952 the party was suppressed following riots in Casablanca, but it played an important role in the negotiations for independence (1953–1956).

Istiqlal assumed a dominant position in the initial postindependence Moroccan governments, but internal splits and competition from the palace prevented it from establishing lasting dominance. In 1959 Istiqlal was weakened by the secession of some of its more dynamic leaders (for example, Prime Minister Abdullah Ibrahim, Mehdi Ben Barka, Mahjoub Ben Seddiq, and Muhammad al-Basri), who formed the Union Nationale des Forces Populaires (UNFP), which favored far-reaching social reforms and vigorous development programs through nationalization of key economic sectors.

The monarchy refused to acquiesce to Istiqlal's efforts to reduce its powers. From the end of 1962 to 1977, King Hassan II repelled challenges to his rule and consolidated his political supremacy. Like the other opposition parties, Istiqlal was harnessed into service by Hassan during the mid-1970s in support of his Western Sahara policy. In Istiqlal's case, that was hardly unexpected, since it had been the original standard-bearer of the claim of historical rights to "Greater Morocco," which in the doctrine's purest form included all of Mauritania and parts of Algeria, Senegal, and Mali, as well as the Spanish enclaves of Ceuta and Melilla.

Fasi died in 1974 while in Romania to explain the king's Western Saharan policy; Muhammad Boucetta replaced him as secretary-general. Boucetta and other Istiqlal leaders were co-opted into the government in 1977, but following the 1984 elections, Istiqlal returned to opposition ranks. Although no longer the leader of the nationalist movement, Istiqlal maintained a significant place in the political landscape, thanks in part to its affili-

The Istiqlal Party was formed by Moroccan nationalists in 1943 and supported Sultan Muhammad V in his quest to bring self-rule to the country. The sultan was deposed in 1953, but the French allowed him to return to power in 1955, and the Istiqlal Party was able to hold its first public meeting in Rabat two months later. © BETTMANN/CORBIS. REPRODUCED BY PERMISSION.

ated labor confederation, the Union Générale des Travailleurs Marocains (UGTM), and its influential daily newspapers, *Al-Alam* and *L'opinion*. In May 1992, with the Union Socialiste des Forces Populaires (USFP), the Parti du Progrès et du Socialisme (PPS), the rump UNFP, and the tiny Organisation pour l'Action Démocratique et Populaire (OADP), Istiqlal formed the "Democratic Bloc" (*al-kutla*) to press for constitutional and electoral reform. Istiqlal won forty-three seats in Parliament in the direct balloting portion of the 1993 elections, a gain of nineteen seats from 1984, but only eight seats in the indirect portion of the vote, a decline of nine seats. Along with the USFP, Istiqlal was now roughly equal in size to the pro-palace Union Constitutionelle and the Mouvement Populaire as the largest parliamentary factions. They refused the terms offered to them for joining a new government, and thus remained in opposition. In the 1997 elections the Istiqlal received nearly the same number of votes as the leading vote-getter, the USFP, but owing to the vagaries of the system, declined to thirty-two seats. Charging widespread fraud, the party's congress called for the election's annulment and rejected participation in any new government. Two months later, however, the USFP was chosen to lead the new government, and the Istiqlal, under the newly elected secretary-general, Abbas al-Fasi, joined the forty-one-member cabinet, receiving six posts, with Fassi becoming minister of health. The USFP-Istiqlal relationship in government was frequently rocky. In the 2002 elections, the party increased its strength in parliament to forty-eight seats, and eight cabinet seats in the new government headed by the king's loyalist Driss Jettou. Fasi's new position was minister of state without portfolio. However, many in the party were disappointed with the party's junior status in the government, and unhappy with Fasi's leadership. One focal point of internal opposition was led by Abd al-Razzak Afilal, the leader of the UGTM.

See also BALAFREJ, AHMED; BEN BARKA, MEHDI; BEN SEDDIQ, MAHJOUB; BOUCETTA, MUHAMMAD; CEUTA; FASI, ALLAL AL-; FEZ, MOROCCO; HASSAN II; IBRAHIM, ABDULLAH; MELILLA; MOUVEMENT POPULAIRE (MP); PARTI NATIONAL; UNION GÉNÉRALE DES TRAVAILLEURS MAROCAINS (UGTM); UNION NATIONALE DES FORCES POPULAIRES (UNFP); UNION SOCIALISTE DES FORCES POPULAIRES (USFP).

Bibliography

Mossadeq, Rkia el-. "Political Parties and Power-Sharing." In *The Political Economy of Morocco*, edited by I. William Zartman. New York: Praeger, 1987. pp. 59–83.

Pennell, C. R. *Morocco since 1830.* New York: New York University Press, 2000.

Waterbury, John. *The Commander of the Faithful.* London: Weidenfeld & Nicholson, 1970.

BRUCE MADDY-WEITZMAN

ISTIQLAL PARTY: PALESTINE

Important political party established in Palestine, August 1932.

The party's creation was spurred by the Husayni–Nashashibi split, which had almost paralyzed the Palestinian national movement. Its founders, most of whom hailed from the Nablus area, called for the adoption of new methods of political action, including noncooperation with the British Mandate authorities and nonpayment of taxes. The party also called for total Arab independence, pan-Arab unity, the abrogation of the Mandate and the Balfour Declaration, and the establishment of Arab parliamentary rule in Palestine.

After reaching its maximum degree of influence, especially among the young and the educated, in the first half of 1933, the party began to decline very rapidly. Among the factors responsible for its decline were the active hostility of the Husayni camp, the lack of financial resources, and the differences between the pro-Hashimite and pro-Saʿudi elements within the party. A distinctive mark of the party was its espousal of the idea that British imperialism was the principal enemy of the Palestinians; thus the party urged them to focus their struggle not simply on Zionism, but on British colonialism as well.

See also BALFOUR DECLARATION (1917); HUSAYNI FAMILY, AL-; HUSAYNI, MUSA KAZIM AL-; NASHASHIBI FAMILY; ZIONISM.

Bibliography

Porath, Yehoshua. *The Emergence of the Palestinian–Arab National Movement, 1918–1929.* London: Cass, 1974.

MUHAMMAD MUSLIH

ISTIQLAL PARTY: SYRIA

The Independence party, officially founded in Damascus on 5 February 1919.

Also known as Hizb al-Istiqlal al-Arabi (Arab Independence party), the party was established after the demise of the Ottoman Empire and during the Arab kingdom of Syria under Faisal I ibn Hussein. Its core members were drawn from the committee of the secret Arab society al-Fatat (Young Arab Society). The founding members of the Istiqlal were Saʿid Haydar, Asʿad Daghir, Fawzi al-Bakri, Abd al-Qadir al-Azm, Salim Abd al-Rahman, Faʾiz al-Shihabi, and Muhammad Izzat Darwaza, its secretary who was at the same time the secretary of al-Fatat. They decided to come into the open and form a political party under a new name. Al-Fatat continued to exist as the mother party of the Istiqlal, which was considered its spokesman. Members from the other Arab secret society, al-Ahd (the Covenant), also joined the Istiqlal. Party adherents, known as al-Istiqlaliyyun (the Independentists), were active in the towns of Syria, where the party had branches during the early years of the French Mandate. Istiqlal also included Palestinian members, who were active against the British Mandate authority in Palestine, 1923–1948.

Istiqlal called for Arab unity and independence; it was secular rather than religious. Faisal had supported it financially and politically while he ruled Syria (1918–1920). The party supported the Great Syrian Revolt of 1925 and party members supported the Palestine Arab Revolt of 1936–1939. It is not known whether the Syrian party was still functioning in 1936.

See also AHD, AL-; DARWAZA, MUHAMMAD IZ-ZAT; FAISAL I IBN HUSSEIN; FATAT, AL-; PALESTINE ARAB REVOLT (1936–1939).

Bibliography

Khoury, Philip. *Syria and the French Mandate: The Politics of Arab Nationalism, 1920–1945.* Princeton, NJ: Princeton University Press, 1987.

Khoury, Philip. *Urban Notables and Arab Nationalism: The Politics of Damascus, 1860–1920.* Cambridge, U.K., and New York: Cambridge University Press, 1983.

Muslih, Muhammad. "The Rise of Local Nationalism in the Arab East." In *The Origins of Arab Nationalism*, edited by Rashid Khalidi et al. New York: Columbia University Press, 1991.

ABDUL-KARIM RAFEQ

ITALY IN THE MIDDLE EAST

The Italian presence in North Africa loomed large in the nineteenth and twentieth centuries.

Modern Italian dreams of an empire along the southern rim of the Mediterranean long predated the achievement of Italian reunification. As early as 1838, Giuseppe Mazzini, the great theoretician of the *Risorgimento,* had argued that Tunisia, the key to the central Mediterranean, would have to belong to Italy. By 1861, with the first achievement of the *Risorgimento* of an independent Italian kingdom, some were already looking toward the recovery of former territory from the Roman Empire and for a Mediterranean role for the new nation. By the mid-1860s,

Italian dictator Benito Mussolini (1883–1945) holds the Sword of Islam, given to him by Muslims as a sign of allegiance. © BETTMANN/CORBIS. REPRODUCED BY PERMISSION.

there were public expressions of concern over the danger of Italy being excluded from the region altogether by powers such as France and Great Britain.

The opening of the Suez Canal in 1869 and the recovery of Papal Rome the following year spurred Italian mercantilist and classical dreams. On the one hand, they wished to benefit from the commercial advantages offered by empire, on the other, many Italians wished to re-create the greatness of classical Rome. The latter sentiment was particularly acute as far as Tunisia was concerned, where there were already 25,000 Italians in the Regency by 1881. Furthermore, Italian aspirations had been lulled into a false sense of security by a twenty-year-long treaty with the Beylik after 1868. The French annexation of Tunisia as a protectorate in 1881 came, therefore, as a very unpleasant surprise.

As a result, Italy rushed to join other European powers in trying to carve out a colonial empire in Africa during 1882, as part of the scramble for Africa. Italian troops landed at Assab, on the Red Sea coast, and in 1882 began the process of creating a colony in Eritrea—an attempt that was to last fourteen years—and of establishing its presence in Somalia. Italian attempts to occupy Ethiopia, however, were to be unsuccessful, culminating in the catastrophic Italian defeat at Adwa in 1896.

By the start of the twentieth century, however, Italian self-confidence had been restored and attention was being directed toward North Africa once again. The new wave of Italian colonial interest was signaled by the Italian–French agreement of December 1902, which recognized Italian interests in Libya. Peaceful penetration began thereafter, as Italian commercial houses and banks began to appear along the Libyan coast. In 1911, Italy declared war on the Ottoman Empire in Libya and invaded the coastal regions.

A concerted intellectual and journalistic effort conducted in Italy persuaded public opinion that a colony in Libya would be a worthwhile endeavor: Not only would it re-create the dream of imperial Rome (frustrated by France's annexation of Tunisia in 1881) but it was believed that Libya was potentially very fertile. It was argued as well that Tripoli was still the crucial endpoint of trans-Saharan trade and, thus, a source of immense wealth. Such arguments were opposed by the socialists, who saw the national crusade for Libya as a diversion from the essential task of revivifying Italy itself.

In reality, however, there were immense pressures building up inside Italy for the development of settler colonies as demographic growth threw into stark relief the problems faced by poverty-stricken regions. Only Libya was left as a potential destination for Italy's excess population, apart from migration to the Americas. As a result, the illusory claims of journalists over the potential offered by Libya were reinforced by the hard realities of domestic economic crises.

The difficulties of establishing a firm grasp on Libya, after the 1911 invasion, were revealed by the two Italo–Sanusi wars, and it was only in 1932 that the new colony was declared pacified. Italy soon discovered that Libya's agricultural potential was a myth, and the new colony turned out to be a constant drain on the metropole's resources. By 1942, 110,000 Italians resided in Libya, of whom 40,000 were involved directly in agriculture; the development of an infrastructure and of colonial settlement had cost the vast sum of 1.8 billion Italian lire, and Italy had little to show for its colonial experiment.

Nonetheless, Libya had been molded into the Fascist vision, which, during the 1930s, had in addition sought to avenge the defeat of Aduwa in Ethiopia. The definitive military pacification of Libya had occurred directly after the Fascists had come to power in Rome, in October 1922. Libya was also seen by the Fascist Party as an ideal testing ground for their ideas of racial development, where Libyans were to become Italian Muslims and Italy, under Mussolini, would become the protector of the Muslim world. All these ambitions were to be destroyed by Allied victory in Libya in 1943.

The one other major Fascist experience in Africa was to be the Italian attempt, once again, to conquer Ethiopia. Despite Italian military superiority, the conquest was never completed. It also led to Italy's ostracism by the League of Nations. Finally, the Italian presence there was ended during World War II by British troops, who restored the emperor, Haile Selassie Miriam, to his throne.

Italy's African experiences have, however, left some traces on the modern scene. In 1935, France offered concessions over Libya's southern international border as part of a complex attempt to satisfy Italian claims in Tunisia and in Nice—as well as trying to prevent Italy from joining Nazi Germany as an ally. Although the proposal was never realized, it still remains to bedevil modern international relations, as a result of the competing claims between Libya and Chad to the Aozou Strip.

See also FOURTH SHORE, THE; LIBYA; TURKISH–ITALIAN WAR (1911–1912).

Bibliography

Ahmida, Ali Abdullatif. *The Making of Modern Libya: State Formation, Colonization, and Resistance, 1830–1932.* Albany: State University of New York Press, 1994.

Nyrop, Richard F., et al., eds. *Libya: A Country Study,* 3d edition. Washington, DC: American University, 1979.

Wright, John. *Libya.* London: Benn; New York: Praeger, 1969.

Wright, John. *Libya: A Modern History.* Baltimore, MD: Johns Hopkins University Press, 1982.

Wright, John. "Libya: Italy's 'Promised Land.' " In *Social and Economic Development of Libya,* edited by E. G. H. Joffe and K. S. McLachlan. Wisbech, U.K.: Middle East and North African Studies Press, 1982.

GEORGE JOFFE

IZLANE

See GLOSSARY

İZMIR

Third largest city in Turkey and seaport on the Aegean Sea.

İzmir (formerly known in English as Smyrna) is situated at the head of a long bay. With mountains in the Aegean region of western Anatolia stretching east to west, the river valleys from the Anatolian plateau leading to the Aegean Sea allow easy communication with a considerable hinterland. Due to these advantages, the city has been an important trading center over a long period of time: Its origins go back to the third millennium B.C.E., and it maintained its prominence during Hittite, Greek, Roman, and Byzantine domination. During the fourteenth century, İzmir was held by the Turkish Aydin *Beyliği* (emirate), and when Aydin—like other Anatolian Turkish emirates—was incorporated into the rising Ottoman state around 1400, İzmir became an Ottoman city.

During the early nineteenth century, İzmir's European trade was disrupted first by the Napoleonic Wars and then, in the 1820s, by the war of Greek independence. However, beginning in the 1830s, industrializing Europe's demand for Anatolian raw cotton and wool soon restored trade. Dried fruits (raisins and figs), tobacco, olive oil, and animal hides were also exported at unprecedented levels. Its population increased considerably, as the city attracted not only foreigners but also an influx of population from both Anatolia and the Aegean islands. The first railroad to be built in Anatolia was laid between İzmir and Aydin to facilitate the exports of its rich hinterland. Just before World War I, İzmir and its vicinity had a total population of

Turkey's port city of İzmir, known before 1923 as Smyrna, a name derived from an ancient myth involving Aphrodite and the daughter of the king of Cyprus. Excavations in 1948 uncovered mudbrick defense walls that suggest İzmir was already a city-state as early as the eighth century B.C.E. © YANN ARTHUS-BERTRAND/ CORBIS. REPRODUCED BY PERMISSION.

210,000, of which 100,000 were Muslims, 74,000 Greeks, 10,000 Armenians, 24,000 Jews, and 2,000 Europeans.

After the defeat of the Ottoman Empire in 1918, the victorious allies allowed Greek occupation of the city and its hinterland. But Greek occupation sparked a nascent Anatolian resistance, and the Turkish war of independence ended with the recapture of İzmir in September 1922. The city was devastated by a huge conflagration as the Greek forces and population withdrew to the Aegean; its burgeoning industry was wrecked and its foreign trade sharply declined. The new Turkish Republic, however, was determined to restore İzmir's prominent commercial role and held its first national congress there in 1923 to set economic policy. Although İzmir became a much more Turkish city than it had been in Ottoman times, Muslims immigrating from Crete, the Aegean islands, and Salonika replaced the Greek population and helped preserve a relatively cosmopolitan atmosphere; the city quickly regained its historic role as Turkey's leading exporter and it was second only to Istanbul in imports.

Since the 1950s, İzmir has experienced a significant degree of industrialization, establishing strong automotive and food processing sectors and modernizing its traditional textile production. In 2002, it produced 13.5 percent of Turkey's gross domestic product and employed 9.7 percent of the country's total labor force. İzmir has grown faster than any other Turkish city except Istanbul; its population reached 3,370,866 in 2000. In addition to its commercial importance, İzmir serves as the focus of a hinterland rich in classical and Turkish cultural heritage. Among the nearby sites of importance are Ephesus, Pergamum, and Sardis.

See also AEGEAN SEA; ANATOLIA; OTTOMAN EMPIRE.

Bibliography

Güvenç, Bozkurt, ed. *Social Change in Izmir: A Collection of Five Papers.* Ankara: Social Science Association, 1975.

Kasaba, Reşat. "İzmir." *Review: Fernand Braudel Center for the Study of Economies, Historical Systems, and Civilizations* XVI, no. 4 (Fall 1993).

Taylor Saçlioğlu, Virginia. *Three Ages of İzmir: Palimpsest of Cultures.* İstanbul: Yapi Kredi Yayinlari, 1993.

Turkish Ministry of Culture. Information available at <http://www.kultur.gov.tr/portal/default_en.asp?belgeno=2069>.

I. METIN KUNT
UPDATE BY BURÇAK KESKIN-KOZAT

İZMIR ECONOMIC CONGRESS

Turkish economic summit meeting, 1923.

Convened in February 1923 during a recess in the Lausanne Peace Conference, the İzmir Economic Congress consisted of more than 1,100 Turkish delegates representing agriculture, trade, artisans, and labor, as well as top political leaders, including Mustafa Kemal Atatürk. The resolutions adopted were referred to as the Economic Pact (*Misak-i Iktisadi*), signifying that the government considered them as important as the previously promulgated Turkish National Pact (*Misak-i Milli*), which enunciated the goal of political independence. These resolutions proclaimed the intention of developing the nation's economy by relying on the free activity of Turkish entrepreneurs. Foreign capital was to be welcome provided it adhered to Turkish law. Monopolies were opposed. Thus, the congress inaugurated a phase of reliance on private enterprise. This phase ended after the consolidation of the republican regime and the onset of the worldwide depression in the late 1920s. It was replaced by a concerted policy of state initiatives on the economy, including ownership and operation of major enterprises.

See also ATATÜRK, MUSTAFA KEMAL; TURKISH NATIONAL PACT.

Bibliography

Bianchi, Robert. *Interest Groups and Political Development in Turkey.* Princeton, NJ: Princeton University Press, 1984.

FRANK TACHAU

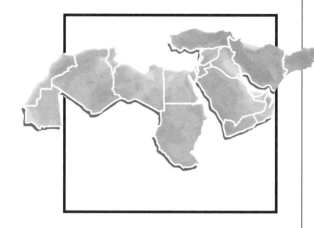

JABABDI, LATIFA
[1955–]

Moroccan women's rights advocate; founder of L'Union de L'Action Feminine (FUA).

Latifa Jababdi was born in Tiznit of Berber heritage. She received a degree in sociology and feminist studies from Mohammed V University in Rabat, and in 2003 was preparing a doctorate in sociology at the Université du Québec à Montréal, Canada, on the integration of women in development.

At the age of fourteen Jababdi joined the Party of Liberation and Socialism (PLS) and took part in the student movement in the 1960s that campaigned for greater democracy in Morocco. This group was associated with the New Left, and Jababdi herself became a member of the PLS, the Communist Party of Progress. She was condemned in 1977 for threatening state security and spent two-and-a-half years in prison with other well-known Moroccan feminists such as Fatna el-Bouih because of her participation in the illegal Marxist-Leninist group "March 23."

In 1984 Jababdi ran for office, but no women were elected. Disappointed, she went on to serve as editor of the *8 Mars* newspaper, named after International Women's Day (8 March, or *Thamaniya Mars*) and written by and for Moroccan women interested in feminist issues. She later founded L'Union de L'Action Feminine (FUA) in 1987. The FUA has seventeen offices throughout Morocco and one in Paris. It offers literacy classes and workshops, seminars, festivals, and publications such as *8 Mars*.

In 1993 Jababdi launched a campaign to change the *mudawana*, the female-status code of Moroccan family law that reduces all women to legal minors. She collected one million signatures for a petition given to King Hassan II requesting the abolition of marital tutorship and polygamy, recognition of women's full maturity at age twenty-one, gender equality in marriage, and judicial divorce. The king convened a committee of women to examine these issues further. Revisions to the *mudawana* concluded that women could no longer be repudiated by their husbands without their knowledge. No sweeping changes to the *mudawana* have been made, but

Moroccans hope that Muhammad VI will soon do so.

See also BOUIH, FATNA EL-; *8 MARS* NEWSPAPER; GENDER: GENDER AND LAW; GENDER: GENDER AND POLITICS; MOROCCO: POLITICAL PARTIES IN.

Bibliography

Fernea, Elizabeth Warnock. *In Search of Islamic Feminism: One Woman's Global Journey.* New York: Doubleday, 1998.

Morocco Trade and Development Services. "Union de L'Action Féminine." Available from <http://www.mtds.com/uaf>.

Slymovics, Susan. "This Time I Choose When to Leave: An Interview with Fatna El-Bouih." *Morocco in Transition, Middle East Report* 218 (Spring 2001).

The Tamaniya Mars Collective. "Journal for an Emerging Women's Movement (Morocco)." In *Alternative Media: Linking Global and Local,* edited by Peter Lewis. *Reports and Papers on Mass Communication* 107 (1993): 61–72.

MARIA F. CURTIS

JABAL AL-AKHDAR, LIBYA

Eastern "green mountain" region.

An area of Libya in the hinterland of the eastern city of Benghazi, with mountains of nearly 3,300 feet (1,000 m). It is one of the few parts of Libya with relatively good rainfall (98–118 in/yr; 250–300 cm/yr) but with difficult terrain and soil conditions, characterized by grain cultivation with modest yields and livestock grazing.

Bibliography

Allan, J. A., ed. *Libya since Independence: Economic and Political Development.* New York: St. Martin's, 1982.

LAURENCE MICHALAK

JABAL AL-AKHDAR, OMAN

The highest and best-watered region in the western Hajar Mountains of Oman.

About ninety-five miles southwest of Muscat, the highest peak of the Jabal al-Akhdar ("green mountain" in Arabic) region is Jabal Shams, which rises to nearly 10,000 feet. The region received its name from the relatively abundant vegetation found on its slopes and valleys. Because it receives up to twenty-eight inches of rain per year, and portions of it have suitable soil in its valleys, plateaus, and man-made terraces, a variety of agricultural products can be grown in Jabal al-Akhdar, including wheat, legumes, and a variety of fruits such as grapes, pomegranates, and peaches. Irrigation is provided by the *falaj* system, an ancient technique using channels to direct water from sources underground to crops some distance away. The main region of habitation is the Sayq plateau. The seaward side of Jabal al-Akhdar faces the Gulf of Oman, and the main towns are al-Rustaq, al-Awabi, and Nakhl. On the interior-facing slopes lie Nizwa, Manah, and Izki. Jabal al-Akhdar is part of the once nearly inaccessible area of Oman proper to which Muslim minority groups such as the Ibadi sect fled as a result of conflicts in Arabia during the late seventh and early eighth centuries C.E. After converting much of the local population, Ibadi imams rose to power in 751 C.E., and Jabal al-Akhdar remained a stronghold of the Ibadi imamate until 1959.

See also OMAN.

Bibliography

Allen, Calvin H., Jr. *Oman: The Modernization of the Sultanate.* Boulder, CO: Westview Press; London: Croom Helm, 1987.

Held, Colbert C. *Middle East Patterns: Places, Peoples, and Politics.* Boulder, CO: Westview Press, 1989.

ANTHONY B. TOTH

JABAL AL-KHALIL

Group of mountains constituting the southernmost part of the Judean mountains, surrounding the town of Hebron (Khalil), about twenty miles south of Jerusalem.

Jabal al-Khalil forms the tallest part of the mountain ridge extending north to Tiberias. The ridge was where most villages of Palestine were concentrated during the nineteenth century. While agricultural cultivation increased under Jordan's rule, between 1948 and 1967, many villagers of the relatively congested and unindustrialized Jabal al-Khalil migrated for work to the east bank of the Jordan River. Since the 1967 Arab-Israel War, Jabal al-Khalil has been part of the Israeli-occupied West Bank and the site of a growing number of Israeli settlements, such as Kiryat Arba.

The Oslo Accords, signed on 13 September 1993, provided for a transitional period not exceeding five years to Palestinian interim self-government in the Gaza Strip and the West Bank. On 15 January 1997 a joint protocol provided for the redeployment of Israeli troops and the handing over of 80 percent of the Hebron area to the Palestinian Authority. The area remained, however, in continuous strife and instability.

ELIZABETH THOMPSON
UPDATED BY YEHUDA GRADUS

JABAL, BADAWI AL-

[1905–1981]

Pen name of Muhammad Sulayman al-Ahmad, a Syrian poet of high reputation in the Arab world.

Badawi al-Jabal was born in the village of Difa in the district of al-Haffa, in Latakia province, to Sulayman al-Ahmad, the head of a distinguished Alawite family. His pen name was given to him, according to the compiler of his poetry, Midhat Akkash, by the editor of the Damascus newspaper *Alif Ba,* apparently in 1920. The editor liked the poetry, but because the poet was not well known, the editor agreed to publish the poetry under the pseudonym of Badawi al-Jabal, a reference to the cloak *(aba'a)* and the headband *(iqal)* the poet wore at the time—like a *badawi* (bedouin) coming from al-Jabal (the Alawite mountain).

Badawi al-Jabal practiced politics and poetry at an early age. As a nationalist, he joined the National Bloc, and later on the National Party. He was imprisoned by the French mandatory authorities in Syria, and in 1939 he sought refuge in Baghdad. While there, he taught Arabic at the University of Baghdad and also supported the revolt of Rashid Ali al-Kaylani against the British in 1941. Upon returning to Syria, he was apprehended by the French authorities in 1942. Later on, he was twice elected to parliament, in 1943 and 1947. In the 1950s, he became minister of health. The defeat of the Arabs in the 1967 Arab–Israel War was a great shock to him; he wrote much poetry inspired by it. He adhered to the old school of Arabic literature and po-

etry, which upholds the classical mode. His poetry was also influenced by a mystical orientation. Selections from his poetry were published in Damascus in 1968 by Midhat Akkash. A full anthology appeared in Beirut in 1978 with an introduction by Akram Zu'aytir.

See also ARAB–ISRAEL WAR (1967); KAYLANI, RASHID ALI AL-; LITERATURE: ARABIC; NATIONAL PARTY (SYRIA).

Bibliography

Jayyusi, Salma Khadra, ed. *Modern Arabic Poetry: An Anthology.* New York: Columbia University Press, 1987.

ABDUL-KARIM RAFEQ

JABAL DRUZE

A volcanic massif in southern Syria, between the plain of Hawran and the Eastern desert.

This mountain region has a curved, conelike surface, its highest peak rising to 5,915 feet (1,803 m). On the west, the basalt upland is surrounded by lava, which tapers into the fertile plains of Hawran and Jawlan, famed since Roman times for their abundance in grain. The western slopes of the mountain receive an average annual rainfall of about 11.7 inches (300 mm). The soil is especially suitable for vine and fruit trees.

The term *Jabal Druze* was first applied to the Shuf region of Mount Lebanon where the people of the Druze community predominate. Under the Mamluk sultanate (1260–1517), some Druze, suffering from Mamluk punitive expeditions against them, took refuge in Jabal Hawran. After the Qaysi–Yamani war at Ayn Dara in Lebanon in 1711, the Yamanis, most of whom were Druze, who were overpowered in the fighting, fled to Jabal Hawran, where they formed the bulk of the Druze community. Later on, more Druze fled from Mount Lebanon to the Hawran in the wake of the 1860 events, when punitive measures were taken against them. Others went there during World War I to avoid Ottoman Empire conscription and the famine. Because of this considerable Druze settlement in Jabal Hawran, it became known in the latter part of the nineteenth century as Jabal Druze. In the 1930s, Jabal Druze was also referred to as Jabal al-Arab to avoid the sectarian term of *Druze* and also in recognition of the nationalist role played by the Druze, headed by Sultan al-Atrash, in leading the Great Syrian Revolt against the French (1925–1927).

See also ATRASH, SULTAN PASHA AL-; DRUZE; LEBANON, MOUNT; MAMLUKS; SHUF.

Bibliography

Lewis, Norman. *Nomads and Settlers in Syria and Jordan, 1800–1980.* Cambridge, U.K., and New York: Cambridge University Press, 1987.

ABDUL-KARIM RAFEQ

JABAL NABLUS

Group of low mountains in the Nablus region.

Located about 30 miles (48.3 km) north of Jerusalem, Jabal Nablus forms the northern edge of the Central Highlands that extend south to Hebron (Arabic: al-Khalil). The region, dotted with hillside agricultural villages, has been known particularly for its olives and olive oil soap. For much of the Ottoman era, Jabal Nablus was ruled as part of Damascus province, and dominated for centuries by the Tuqan family. The area became known in Palestinian folklore as Jabal al-Nar (Mountain of Fire) for its resistance to Britain's rule in the mandate period (1922–1948).

See also TUQAN FAMILY.

Bibliography

Doumani, Beshara. *Rediscovering Palestine: Merchants and Peasants in Jabal Nablus, 1700–1900.* Berkeley: University of California Press, 1995.

Graham-Brown, Sarah. "The Political Economy of Jabal Nablus, 1920–48." In *Studies in the Social and Economic History of Palestine in the 19th and 20th Centuries,* edited by Roger Owen. London: Macmillan, 1982.

ELIZABETH THOMPSON

JABAL SHAMMAR

A mountainous region in northwestern Saudi Arabia.

Named for the Shammar tribal confederation, Jabal Shammar consists of the Aja Mountains, which are mainly granite; the basaltic Salma Mountains; the high sand dunes of al-Nafud; and scattered oases. A mixed economy of pastoral nomadism, oa-sis agriculture, and urban crafts and trade prevailed until the modern era. The region's principal city, the oasis of Ha'il, has been for centuries an important stopping place for persons traveling between the holy cities of Mecca and Medina and the towns and cities of Iraq and Iran. Hail continues to be an important regional center of transportation, commerce, and administration, as well as one of the principal agricultural areas in Saudi Arabia.

See also SAUDI ARABIA.

Bibliography

Al Rasheed, Madawi. *Politics in an Arabian Oasis: The Rashidi Tribal Dynasty.* New York and London: I.B. Tauris, 1991.

Vassiliev, Alexei. *The History of Saudi Arabia.* New York: New York University Press, 2000.

ELEANOR ABDELLA DOUMATO
UPDATED BY ANTHONY B. TOTH

JA'BARI FAMILY

Prominent Palestinian family from Hebron.

The Ja'bari family dominated political posts in the Hebron district from the 1940s to the 1970s. They rose to prominence in Palestinian politics through their support of Jordanian rule in the West Bank. In the 1970s and 1980s, the family's political support declined as their cooperation with the governments of Israel and Jordan came under increasing criticism.

See also WEST BANK.

Bibliography

Sahliyeh, Emile. *In Search of Leadership: West Bank Politics since 1967.* Washington, DC: Brookings Institution, 1988.

Smith, Pamela Ann. *Palestine and the Palestinians, 1876–1983.* New York: St. Martin's, 1984.

ELIZABETH THOMPSON

JABARTI, ABD AL-RAHMAN AL-
[1753–1825]

Egyptian historian and scholar.

Abd al-Rahman al-Jabarti is best known as the fore-most Egyptian Muslim chronicler of Napoléon

Bonaparte's invasion and occupation of Egypt from 1798 to 1801. His family was originally from the village of Jabart on the Red Sea coast, but al-Jabarti himself was born in Cairo to a wealthy family whose economic base included *iltizams* (tax farms) and a *waqf* (religious endowment). Both he and his father were educated at al-Azhar University.

Al-Jabarti's studies included medicine and arithmetic, but his main scholarly activity was writing histories of Egypt. His principal works were *Aja'ib al-Athar fi al-Tarajim wa al-Akhbar* (Wondrous seeds of men and their deeds), *Muzhir al-Taqdis bi Dhahab Dawlat al-Faransis* (The demonstration of piety in the demise of French society), and *T'arikh Muddat al-Faransis bi Misr* (History of the French presence in Egypt).

There is debate over whether *T'arikh Muddat al-Faransis* is an earlier version of *Muzhir al-Taqdis*. Both are short works dealing only with the period of French occupation. *T'arikh Muddat al-Faransis* appears to be an eyewitness account of the events, probably written in 1798; *Muzhir al-Taqdis* was probably completed in 1801. *Aja'ib* is a longer work covering Egyptian history from 1688 to 1821 in four volumes. There are also questions about the relative dating of the first three volumes of *Aja'ib*, which include the events of the French occupation, and *Muzhir al-Taqdis*. The parts of *Aja'ib* relevant to the French occupation are now thought to have been completed in 1805 or 1806, after *Muzhir al-Taqdis*. The issue of the relative dating of the two works is considered important because *Muzhir al-Taqdis* is more critical of the French than *Aja'ib*, which, if it were indeed written after *Muzhir al-Taqdis*, suggests that it could have been a "revisionist" work reflecting the real opinions of al-Jabarti, as opposed to "official" versions of the events related in the other works.

Although al-Jabarti is a key figure in late eighteenth- and early nineteenth-century Egyptian history, historians have reevaluated the period itself. In particular, they question the idea that the French invasion marked the definitive onset of modernity in the Middle East. Both historians Peter Gran and Kenneth Cuno argue, from otherwise different perspectives, that the French invasion is best understood as an event in the larger processes of Egyptian history. In the same vein, the nature of al-Jabarti's histories has been reexamined. Jack Crabbs, for example, argues that al-Jabarti was an

outstanding, but typical, medieval Egyptian historian who happened to have recorded extraordinary events. In contrast, Gran claims that al-Jabarti's accounts of the French invasion, and his historiography in general, were cultural manifestations of a nascent capitalist transformation already underway before the first European attempts to colonize the region. But aside from such issues, there is general consensus that al-Jabarti's histories were the best account of the French invasion from an Egyptian or Arab perspective, and generally above the standards for accuracy and detail common in late Ottoman historical writing. Al-Jabarti remains one of the principal sources for historians interested in early modern Egypt.

See also BONAPARTE, NAPOLÉON.

Bibliography

Ayalon, David. "The Historian al-Jabarti and His Background." *Bulletin of the Society of Oriental and African Studies* 23 (1960): 217–249.

Crabbs, Jack A., Jr. *The Writing of History in Nineteenth-Century Egypt: A Study in National Transformation.* Detroit, MI: Wayne State University Press, 1984.

Cuno, Kenneth. *The Pasha's Peasants: Land, Society, and Economy in Lower Egypt, 1740–1858.* Cambridge, U.K., and New York: Cambridge University Press, 1992.

Gran, Peter. *Islamic Roots of Capitalism: Egypt, 1760–1840.* Austin: University of Texas Press, 1979.

Jabarti, Abd al-Rahman al-. *Napoleon in Egypt: Al-Jabarti's Chronicle of the French Occupation, 1798,* translated by Shmuel Moreh. Princeton, NJ: M. Wiener, 1993.

WALTER ARMBRUST

JABHA AL-WATANIYYA, AL-

Tripolitanian nationalist movement.

The political movement, al-Jabha al-Wataniyya (United National Front), was established by Tripolitanian notables during the British military administration of Tripolitania after World War II to oppose the return of Tripolitania to Italian trusteeship. Instead they advocated the resolution that eventually prevailed: the independence of all the provinces of Libya together under the leadership of the amir of the Sanusi order.

See also SANUSI ORDER.

LISA ANDERSON

JABOTINSKY, VLADIMIR ZE'EV
[1880–1940]

Founder and leader of Zionism's Revisionist movement.

Vladimir Ze'ev Jabotinsky was a man whose talents, charismatic personality, and Revisionist movement attracted a large and passionate following and polarized Zionism. Born in Odessa on 18 October 1880, he studied law in Switzerland and Italy. He became a journalist at a young age, serving as a correspondent for Russian dailies writing under the pseudonym "Altalena." He was a prolific writer and essayist in several languages. He wrote the historical novel *Samson the Nazarite* (1926) as well as numerous short stories, poems, songs, plays, and political and autobiographical tracts. He translated Hebrew poetry into Russian and translated Dante Alighieri's *Inferno* into Hebrew, and he was the author of Hebrew dictionaries and textbooks. He continued his literary work even as he became a major political leader.

Following the Kishinev pogroms of 1903, Jabotinsky became a leading figure in Russian Zionism and a strong advocate of Jewish self-defense. With the onset of World War I, he sided with Britain and lobbied for the creation of a Jewish Legion within the British Army. He saw the Legion as a means for furthering the Zionist cause by linking it to British aspirations in the Middle East. The creation of the Legion was announced in 1917, and in 1918, Lieutenant Jabotinsky entered Jerusalem with his Legionnaires as part of General Edmund Allenby's army. To his dismay, Britain disbanded the Jewish Legion at war's end. Jabotinsky helped lead the Yishuv's resistance to Arab rioters in Jerusalem in April 1920, and following the riots he was arrested by the British and sentenced to fifteen years in prison. After intense lobbying by the Zionist leadership, High Commissioner Herbert Samuel granted amnesty, and upon Jabotinsky's release from jail he received a hero's welcome in the Yishuv.

From 1921 to 1923, Jabotinsky served as an increasingly controversial member of the Zionist Executive. He publicly criticized official Zionist policy for being overly moderate in pursuit of Zionist goals. In January 1923, he resigned from the Executive. From this point onward he would be a polarizing figure, adored by his followers and despised by his detractors. Jabotinsky had long demanded that the World Zionist Organization (WZO) openly declare the final aim of Zionism to be the establishment of a Jewish state with a Jewish majority on both sides of the Jordan River, to be facilitated by massive, unlimited immigration. According to Jabotinsky, Zionism should return to the grand political vision of Theodor Herzl and reject the incremental Zionism embraced by Chaim Weizmann and the socialism of the Labor movement. He also wanted the Mandate to be "revised" to its original, pre-1922 status that included Transjordan as part of Palestine. These demands became the platform of Revisionist Zionism.

The Revisionist movement was composed of three main organizations, all headed—at least symbolically—

Zionist leader Jabotinsky promoted an assertive and nationalistic approach to the rebuilding of the Jewish homeland. In 1925, Jabotinsky formed the Union of Zionist Revisionists, which advocated massive immigration to form a Jewish state on both sides of the Jordan River. © GOVERNMENT PRESS OFFICE (GPO) OF ISRAEL. REPRODUCED BY PERMISSION.

by Jabotinsky: a political party, a youth movement, and an underground military organization. Jabotinsky founded the party, the Union of Zionist Revisionists (ha-Histadrut ha-Zionit ha-Revisionistit, or ha-Zohar), on 25 April 1925 in Paris. He led the party until his death. Betar (Brit Trumpeldor) was Jabotinsky's youth movement. It began its activities in Riga in 1923. Betar's primary emphasis was on formal military training and discipline. Jabotinsky defined Betar's values and structure to the smallest details, wrote its charter and anthem, designed its brown-shirt uniform, and served as its spiritual and organizational leader. Many Betarim, including Menachem Begin, eventually made their way into the Irgun Zva'i Le'umi, the militant underground founded in 1937 and inspired by Jabotinsky's ideas and positions. Although Jabotinsky was technically its "supreme commander," he was able to exert only limited control over the Irgun from its inception.

Jabotinsky believed that the Arabs would never accept the Zionist project, and he proposed that an "iron wall" be constructed to drive home to them the inevitability of the Jewish state. The British accused the Revisionists of provoking the Arab riots of 1929, and Jabotinsky was barred from reentering Palestine. From 1929 until his death in 1940, he would never again set foot in the country, a fact that greatly hindered the success of his movement in the Yishuv. But despite his strong criticism of British anti-Zionist policies, Jabotinsky maintained a pro-British orientation. He believed that Zionist goals meshed with Britain's own interests and that once the British were convinced of this they would live up to the promises of the Balfour Declaration and the Mandate.

Jabotinsky tried but failed to get the WZO to adopt the Revisionist program at the biannual Zionist Congresses. He denounced Labor's call for class struggle and argued that Zionism should focus on the needs of the Jewish nation in its entirety, and everything else, including class and the individual, should be subordinated to the nation. His rhetoric was often similar to Benito Mussolini's and his followers were denounced by Laborites as "Jewish fascists." The animosity between Revisionists and Labor Zionists occasionally led to physical clashes, and in October 1934, Jabotinsky and David Ben-Gurion met in London to discuss a rapprochement. The resulting accords were angrily rejected in a La-

bor referendum in March 1935. In April, Jabotinsky and his party withdrew from the WZO and founded the New Zionist Organization (NZO). Following this act, support for Revisionism declined within the broader Zionist movement.

Jabotinsky died on 4 August 1940 while visiting a Betar camp in New York. Many of his positions that were rejected as "extremist" during the 1920s and 1930s became part of mainstream Zionism by the 1940s, including the open demand for a Jewish state with a Jewish majority and unlimited immigration. Jabotinsky was the intellectual and political father of the Zionist right. Begin called himself "Jabotinsky's disciple," although the two men openly disagreed on tactics. Jabotinsky's territorial maximalism and rejection of any partition of Eretz Yisrael can be found in several contemporary Israeli parties and movements.

See also BEGIN, MENACHAM; IRGUN ZVA'I LE'UMI (IZL); ZIONIST REVISIONIST MOVEMENT.

Bibliography

Cohen, Mitchell. *Zion and State: Nation, Class and the Shaping of Modern Israel.* New York: Columbia University Press, 1992.

Jabotinsky Institute in Israel. "Biography." Available from <http://www.jabotinsky.org>.

Schechtman, Joseph B. *The Vladimir Jabotinsky Story*, Vol. 1: *Rebel and Statesman: The Early Years.* New York: Thomas Yoseloff, 1956.

Schechtman, Joseph B. *The Vladimir Jabotinsky Story*, Vol. 2: *Fighter and Prophet: The Last Years.* New York: Thomas Yoseloff, 1961.

Shapiro, Yonathan. *The Road to Power: Herut Party in Israel*, translated by Ralph Mandel. Albany: State University of New York Press, 1991.

Shavit, Yaacov. *Jabotinsky and the Revisionist Movement, 1925–1948.* Totowa, NJ; London: Frank Cass, 1988.

PIERRE M. ATLAS

JABR, SALIH

[c.1896–1957]

Iraqi politician.

Salih Jabr was born in al-Nasiryya, in southern Iraq, to a Shi'ite Muslim family of limited means. He learned to speak Turkish early in life. During the

British occupation of al-Nasiriyya, he worked for the British revenue officers as a petty clerk and learned to speak English. In the early 1920s, Jabr graduated from Baghdad Law College. He was appointed judge shortly after graduation because the government of Iraq was dominated by Sunni Muslims and the demand for educated Shiʿa was great. His professional and public career advanced rapidly. He was elected a deputy senator; appointed governor of several provinces; and served as minister of education, justice, finance, social work, the interior, and foreign affairs numerous times. During the Rashid Ali al-Kaylani uprising, Jabr was governor of Basra. Because he sided with the regent and helped him to escape from Iraq, he was dismissed as governor, arrested, released a short time later, and allowed to go to Iran. With the collapse of the uprising, he returned to Iraq and was appointed minister of the interior.

On 29 March 1947 the regent invited Jabr to form a new government and appointed him prime minister, the first Shiʿite to hold this post. The regent hoped that Jabr, being a Shiʿite, would secure support for the revision of the Anglo–Iraqi Treaty of 1930. The treaty gave Britain numerous privileges, including the right to have two military bases in Iraq over the next twenty-five years. Many Iraqis were not enthusiastic about Jabr and did not welcome him. The nationalists resented him for his support of the British during the Rashid Ali uprising and for sending hundreds of people to prisons and detention camps when he became minister of the interior after the uprising. The leftists disliked him for marrying the daughter of al-Jaryan, one of the largest landlords in southern Iraq.

Jabr announced a sweeping and ambitious program for his government. On the domestic scene, he called for social, economic, and cultural development. On the international scene, he called for a revision of the Anglo–Iraqi Treaty of 1930, ratification of the Iraq–Transjordan Treaty, and the signing of the Turkish–Iraqi Agreement. As prime minister, Jabr proved to be less liberal than his predecessors. His term in office was marred by violent demonstrations. In less than six months in office, he banned the two moderately Left parties and put their leaders, Kamil Chadirchi and Abd al-Fattah Ibrahim, on trial. Three leaders of the Communist Party were sentenced to death. The Portsmouth Treaty—the revision of the Anglo–Iraqi Treaty of 1930—was signed in January 1947. Public dissatisfaction and resentment among the masses led to what came to be known as the Wathba uprising. Violent demonstration erupted against Jabr for several weeks in Baghdad and across Iraq. Virtually every element of Iraq's society—students, teachers, lawyers, doctors, artisans, members of parliament and of political parties—demanded his resignation. Several people lost their lives.

The Wathba uprising underlined the people's resentment of and dissatisfaction with the government and its foreign connections. Several factors contributed: the nationalist resentment over the continuous British interference in Iraq's affairs; the British role in creating the problems in Palestine by the establishment of Israel; and the high cost of living and inflation aggravated by a bad crop year. The Wathba forced Jabr to resign on 27 January 1947. He fled to his home on the Euphrates, then later to Jordan and England. The succeeding government repudiated the treaty.

Jabr was rehabilitated and became minister of the interior in the government of Tawfiq al-Suwaydi in 1950. During his term in office, he introduced a law permitting Iraqi Jews to leave the country, provided they gave up their nationality and property. Over 130,000 Jews left the country.

In 1951, Jabr formed a conservative party, Hizb al-Umma al-Ishtiraki (National Socialist party), to challenge Nuri al-Saʿid. The principles of the party were democracy and nationalism. But in reality, the party was neither democratic nor nationalist, drawing its members largely from tribal and feudal elements. Most of the support came from the Middle Euphrates—Jabr's birthplace—and from the Shiʿite community.

Jabr died of a heart attack while giving a speech opposing Prime Minister Nuri al-Saʿid.

See also ANGLO–IRAQI TREATIES; EZRA AND NEHEMIAH OPERATIONS; KAYLANI, RASHID ALI AL-; SUWAYDI, TAWFIQ AL-.

Bibliography

Khadduri, Majid. *Independent Iraq 1932–1958: A Study in Iraqi Politics,* 2d edition. London and New York: Oxford University Press, 1960.

Marr, Phebe. *The Modern History of Iraq.* Boulder, CO: Westview Press, 1985.

AYAD AL-QAZZAZ

JACIR, EMILY
[1970–]

Palestinian multimedia artist.

Emily Jacir is a multimedia artist whose work represents the Palestinian contribution to the international avant-garde trend, at the turn of the twenty-first century, of exploring issues of borders and displacement. Dividing her time between Ramallah and New York, Jacir uses her personal experience and that of many displaced and exiled Palestinians to explore the voluntary and forced movement of people, and its relationship to real or imagined borders between places. She works in a variety of media, including photography, installation, performance, video, and sculpture. Two noteworthy examples of her work include a refugee tent stitched with the names of the Palestinian villages destroyed by Israel in 1948, executed by a large number of Palestinian-rights supporters. For another piece, she asked Palestinian exiles around the world what they would like her to do for them upon arrival, with her U.S. passport, in their native land. Jacir documented the various requests and her attempts to fulfill them, and then exhibited these testimonies to the pain of displacement and memory. Jacir received her M.F.A. from the Memphis College of Art and studied at the Whitney Independent Study Program. She has exhibited widely in the United States, Europe, and the Middle East, and maintains especially active ties with the art scene in Palestine.

Bibliography

Cotter, Holland. "Emily Jacir." *New York Times,* 9 May 2003.

Jacir, Emily. "Where We Come From." Debs & Co. Available from <http//:www.debsandco.com/jacir .html>.

Stoeckler, Jacqueline S. "Exiles and Cosmopolitans." *Afterimage* volume 20 (January/February, 2001).

JESSICA WINEGAR

JADID, SALAH
[1926–1993]

Syrian army officer and politician.

Salah Jadid was an Alawi Muslim born in the village of Duwayr Ba'abda. After attending the Syrian military academy at Homs, he rose to be director of Officers' Affairs at the army's General Staff in 1963 and, from 1963 to 1965, chief of staff of the army. Jadid joined the Syrian Social Nationalist Party as a youth, along with his brother Ghassan, but later became a member of the Ba'th party. Along with air force officer and fellow Ba'thist Hafiz al-Asad, Jadid was a key member of the secret Military Committee of Ba'thist officers formed in 1959 when Syria was part of the United Arab Republic (UAR) along with Egypt. Jadid served as chair of the committee on two occasions until it was superseded by the Ba'th Regional (Syrian) Command's Military Bureau in August 1965.

Jadid rose to become assistant secretary-general of the party from 1965 to 1970, but this modest title belied the fact that he was really the leader of the Ba'th in Syria, particularly its military wing. While not a deeply ideological man, Jadid headed the party during the period of the "radical Ba'th" from February 1966 to November 1970. He increasingly came into rivalry with Asad, who was close to the "pragmatic" civilian wing of the party. Asad eventually seized power in 1970 and threw Jadid into prison, where he died in August 1993.

See also ASAD, HAFIZ AL-; BA'TH, AL-; SYRIAN SOCIAL NATIONALIST PARTY; UNITED ARAB REPUBLIC (UAR).

Bibliography

Batatu, Hanna. *Syria's Peasantry, the Descendants of Its Lesser Rural Notables, and Their Politics.* Princeton, NJ: Princeton University Press, 1999.

MICHAEL R. FISCHBACH

JAFFA

An ancient port on the central coast of the eastern Mediterranean, south of modern Tel Aviv, Israel.

Jaffa, known as Joppa in biblical times, became an important entrepôt in the nineteenth century when the local rulers constructed walls, planned markets, established a central mosque, and built a road leading to Jerusalem. Occupied by the Egyptian Ibrahim Pasha in 1831, Jaffa prospered because the Egyptians encouraged trade, immigrated to the city, and relaxed restrictions against minorities. With the return of Ottoman rule after 1840, the port became a stop for steamships plying the eastern Mediterranean and, after the opening of the Suez Canal in 1869, for oceangoing liners. The port was expanded to accommodate grain, olive, and citrus exports. Jaffa was linked to Jerusalem by road and rail to serve pilgrims and tourists. German Templar and American colonies were established near the city.

The population expanded from 5,000 in the mid-nineteenth century to nearly 40,000 in 1914, of whom 15,000 were Jews. They made Jaffa the center for the first and second *aliya* until the development of Tel Aviv just to the north of Jaffa. The city was deserted during World War I because the port was closed, citizens were conscripted into the Ottoman army, and the Turks forced many of the inhabitants to leave the city. Under the British mandate, as Tel Aviv developed into an almost exclusively Jewish city, Jaffa expanded. Its population, the majority of whom were Palestinians, reached more than 30,000 in 1922.

A center of opposition to Zionism, Jaffa suffered during the strike called during the 1936 to 1939 Arab rebellion. The rebellion paralyzed the port; it did not recover, and the port of Tel Aviv replaced it. Most of the Jews left Jaffa at that time.

Riots broke out after the United Nations decision to partition Palestine in 1947 and, in the fighting that ensued, the Jews took the city (May 1948). Most of the 65,000 Palestinians abandoned the city—only 4,000 remained. A large number of Jewish immigrants were housed in the city, and in 1950, Jaffa was incorporated into the Tel Aviv municipality, officially called Tel Aviv-Yafo. Jaffa remains a religiously mixed section of the larger metropolitan area.

In 1968, a plan to reconstruct Jaffa and renovate its old buildings was undertaken. The city is noted for its gardens, artists' studios and galleries, the old fishing harbor and ancient site of the original port, and modern boat docks. The city is also known for its export of oranges.

See also ALIYAH; IBRAHIM IBN MUHAMMAD ALI.

Bibliography

Kark, Ruth. *Jaffa: A City in Evolution, 1799–1917*, translated by Gila Brand. Jerusalem: Yad Izhak Ben-Zvi Press, 1990.

REEVA S. SIMON

JALLUD, ABD AL-SALAM
[1941 or 1944–]

Libya's former second in command.

A childhood friend of Muammar al-Qaddafi, Abd al-Salam Jallud became the second most powerful figure in Libya after the military coup that brought Qaddafi to power on 1 September 1969. Born into a nomadic tribe of the Fezzan region, he is, like Qaddafi, a graduate of the Libyan military academy. Jallud was a captain when he joined in planning the coup against the Libyan monarchy; after its success, he was promoted to major and made the de facto deputy chair of the ruling Revolutionary Command Council. He was the country's prime minister from 1972 to 1977, when the establishment of the *jamahiriya* was proclaimed; in 1979, both he and Qaddafi resigned their formal government positions but they remained in full control of the affairs of state. Jallud also occupied, sometimes simultaneously, the posts of interior minister, minister of economy, and minister of finance. He held the post of prime minister during the abduction in Tripoli of the Lebanese Shi'ite leader Imam Musa al-Sadr. Jallud is considered more pragmatic, less ideological, and a more skilled negotiator than Qaddafi. His loyalty to the Libyan regime was the subject of speculation. Despite his allegiance to a radical revolutionary ideology, Jallud occasionally criticized the "demagogic" tone of Qaddafi's discourse. The latter's reorganization of the Libyan security services in 1993 partially confirmed the fall from grace of Jallud and his family tribe, the Migariha. In 1994 he was temporarily placed under house arrest. Since then, and particularly after the Libyan regime entered into negotiations with the United Kingdom and the United States over resolution of the Lockerbie case and the lifting of the United Nations–imposed economic embargo over Libya, Jallud has occupied a marginal place in Libyan politics.

See also QADDAFI, MUAMMAR AL-.

Bibliography

Bianci, Steven, ed. *Libya: Current Issues and Historical Background.* New York: Nova Science Publishers, 2003.

El-Kikhia, Mansour O. *Libya's Qaddafi: The Politics of Contradiction.* Gainesville: University Press of Florida, 1997.

LISA ANDERSON
UPDATED BY VANESA CASANOVA-FERNANDEZ

JALLULI FAMILY

A family important in the commercial elite of nineteenth-century Tunisia.

The Jalluli family was influential at the bey's court, and thus secured *iltizam* (tax farms), monopolies, and supply contracts. They were also *qa'ids* of Sfax, and thereby responsible for the collection of taxes and security in that city.

Important members of the family in the nineteenth century were Mahmud (d. 1839), Muhammad (d. 1849), and Hassuna. In the 1830s Mahmud made his fortune as a corsair. Between 1805 and 1808, he had been chief customs collector, one of the most lucrative concessionary posts; he was also a prominent figure at the bey's court under Hammuda Pasha (ruler of Tunisia, 1777–1814). Muhammad ran the *qiyada* of Sfax for a number of years. In 1829, the Jallulis saved the government of Husayn Bey from bankruptcy. In 1864, Hassuna gained the *qiyada* of Sfax. Following the insurrection of 1864, the family was regarded by Muhammad al-Sadiq Bey as a stabilizing force.

The Jallulis' tradition of state service continued into the twentieth century. Many Jallulis are prominent in Tunisia's commercial and political elite.

See also MUHAMMAD AL-SADIQ; SFAX.

Bibliography

Brown, L. Carl. *The Tunisia of Ahmad Bey, 1837–1855.* Princeton, NJ: Princeton University Press, 1974.

Perkins, Kenneth J. *Historical Dictionary of Tunisia,* 2d edition. Lanham, MD: Scarecrow Press, 1997.

LARRY A. BARRIE

JAMAHIRIYYA

In Libya, "rule of the masses."

This new word was coined by Muammar al-Qaddafi and adopted by the Libyan General People's Congress in 1977 as part of the country's official name: the Socialist People's Libyan Arab Jamahiriyya. It is designed to convey the abolition of "government" and the beginning of the "era of people's authority" in Libya.

See also GENERAL PEOPLE'S CONGRESS (GPC); QADDAFI, MUAMMAR AL-.

LISA ANDERSON

JAMALI, MUHAMMAD FADHIL AL-
[1903–1997]

Iraqi educator, diplomat, and prime minister.

A Shi'ite born in the al-Kazimiyya quarter of Baghdad to a lower-middle-class family, Muhammad Fadhil (also Fadil) al-Jamali received a religious education at al-Najaf. He attended the newly established Teachers Training College in Baghdad, and then was sent to the American University of Beirut, receiving a B.A. in 1927. He did postgraduate work at Teachers College, Columbia University, in New York, where he wrote on the problems of bedouin education. He returned to Iraq in 1932 and served in the ministry of education until 1942.

Touring Europe in 1937, Jamali made arrangements for an Iraqi delegation to attend the Nuremburg rally the following year. His admiration of Germany was expressed in a published comparative study of education, *Ittijahat al-Tarbiyya wa al-Ta'lim fi Almaniya wa Inkiltira wa Faransa* (Modern ways of training and culture in Germany, England, and France). When later asked about his support for Germany, he replied that he was not a socialist, not a capitalist, but a Muslim Arab. In the late 1930s, he also invited teachers from Syria and Palestine to write textbooks and to teach in Iraq.

Jamali encouraged Shi'a to attend the Teachers College and he used his position as director-general in the ministry of education to establish schools in Iraq's rural south and to provide scholarships for Shi'a to study abroad. Because he was not directly involved in Prime Minister Rashid Ali al-Kaylani's government, Jamali retained his post in the ministry of education after the government was brought down in 1941. From 1942 until the end of the monarchy in 1958, he held various posts for the ministry of foreign affairs, including in Washington, D.C., in the United Nations, and in the Arab League, except during his brief tenure as prime minister from September 1953 to April 1954. Jamali served during a period of disastrous floods. Dissatisfaction with his flood-relief program and his involvement in the regent's intervention in Syrian politics led to a change of government.

After the violent overthrow of the monarchy in the revolution of 1958, Jamali was tried by a revolutionary military tribunal and sentenced to death. This was commuted to a fifty-five-year sentence, but he only spent three years in prisons. After he was pardoned in 1961 he moved to Tunis, Tunisia, and taught at Tunis University. He died there in 1997.

See also AMERICAN UNIVERSITY OF BEIRUT (AUB); *FUTUWWA*; KAYLANI, RASHID ALI AL-; NAJAF, AL-.

Bibliography

Simon, Reeva S. *Iraq Between the Two World Wars: The Creation and Implementation of a Nationalist Ideology.* New York: Columbia University Press, 1986.

REEVA S. SIMON
UPDATED BY MICHAEL R. FISCHBACH

JAMALZADEH, MOHAMMAD ALI
[1892–1997]

Iranian short story writer.

Mohammad Ali Jamalzadeh was born in Isfahan, Iran, and studied in Tehran, Beirut, and Paris. From 1916 to 1930, he worked for the Iranian embassy in Berlin and participated with a group of Iranian intellectuals there to publish the journal *Kaveh.* Jamalzadeh is known as the pioneer of Iranian short stories in the Western style. In 1921, he published *Yeki bud yeki nabud* (Once upon a time), a collection of six stories with a simple and flowing narrative style characteristically distinct from classic Iranian written prose. Later, Jamalzadeh moved to Switzerland as the representative for the International Employment Agency in Geneva. His autobiographical work, *Sar-o tah yek karbas* (Cut from the

same cloth), was published in English as *Isfahan Is Half the World: Memories of a Persian Boyhood* in 1983. Jamalzadeh died in 1997 in Geneva, Switzerland.

See also LITERATURE: PERSIAN.

Bibliography

Moayyad, Heshmat, ed. *Stories from Iran: A Chicago Anthology, 1921–1991.* Washington, DC: Mage, 1991.

PARDIS MINUCHEHR

JAMI'A AL-ARABIYYA, AL-

See NEWSPAPERS AND PRINT MEDIA: ARAB COUNTRIES

JAMI'A AL-ISLAMIYYA, AL-

Loosely organized network of neofundamentalist Islamist groups in Egypt.

When Egyptian president Gamal Abdel Nasser outlawed the Muslim Brotherhood in 1954, some of its members formed splinter groups and adopted more radical tactics to achieve their goal of an Islamic state. The Brotherhood developed its own secret armed wing during its most violent period, between 1945 and 1965, and was associated with numerous assassinations. Under presidents Anwar Sadat and Husni Mubarak, it was revitalized and brought back into the mainstream, and its ideology and objectives are now different from those of al-Jami'a al-Islamiyya. It has undertaken a policy of nonviolence and formed coalitions with the secular Wafd Party in 1984 and the Socialist Labor Party and the Liberal Party in 1987 to form the Islamic Alliance (al-Tahaluf al-Islami).

Al-Jami'a al-Islamiyya (also al-Gama'a al-Islamiyya, Islamic Society) was established as a faction of al-Jihad (holy war) by a local leader (amir), Gamal Farghali Haridi. It is a network of approximately twenty small groups whose members sometimes cross-participate. The groups emerged in the 1970s and 1980s as branches of the Muslim Brotherhood's youth movement; the most notorious, al-Jihad, led by Muhammad Abd al-Salam Faraj, claimed responsibility for Sadat's assassination in 1981. This group has been linked to various violent incidents and Muslim–Christian confrontations in Upper

Egyptian towns such as Asyut, Minya, and Bani Suwayf.

Other affiliate groups are the Islamic Liberation Organization (also known as the Technical Military Academy Group, TMA), the Samawiyya, Saved from the Inferno (al-Najun min an-Nar), the Islamic Vanguard, the New Islamic Jihad, Excommunication and Emigration (al-Tafkir wa al-Hijra), and Muhammad's Youth (Shabab Muhammad). Although it is no longer thought to exist, Muhammad's Youth dates back to 1965, when some of its members wanted a gradual creation of an Islamic state and others supported immediate confrontation. Its leader, an agriculture student from Asyut, Shukri Mustafa, was sentenced to death in 1977 for kidnapping and murder. Its members were absorbed into Saved from the Inferno and Repose and Meditation (al-Tawaqqufwa al-Tabayyun). Another group, the al-Qutbiyyan, was influenced by the teachings of Sayyid Qutb of the Muslim Brotherhood, who was sentenced to death in 1965. In 1990 members of the al-Aqsa Martyrs of the World Islamic Front for Liberation assassinated the speaker of the National Assembly, Rif'at al-Mahjub. In 1992 al-Jami'a attacked tourists, prompting the government to enact strict antiterrorism measures. In 1995 Husni Mubarak accused Sudan of having ties to the Jami'a al-Islamiyya after an assassination attempt on his life in Ethiopia.

Research from around the Middle East indicates that instances of neofundamentalist terrorism are increasingly a youth phenomenon. Islamists recruit among high school students and teachers. Between 1970 and 1990 the average age of young Islamists caught in police sweeps dropped from 27 to 21. Leaders in southern Egypt are often university students, while those in Cairo and the delta region are generally professionals. Recognizing the lack of opportunity among disenfranchised youth, the government has promised to expand resources in youth and sporting centers throughout the country.

See also JIHAD; MUBARAK, HUSNI; QUTB, SAYYID; SADAT, ANWAR AL-; WAFD.

Bibliography

Shaikh, Farzana. "Egypt." In *Islam and Islamic Groups: A Worldwide Guide.* Essex, U.K.: Longman Group, 1992.

Starrett, Gregory. *Putting Islam to Work: Education, Politics, and Religious Transformation in Egypt.* Berkeley: University of California Press, 1998.

MARIA CURTIS

JAMI'AT-E ISLAMI

Afghan Islamist political party.

Jami'at-e Islami (Islamic Society) was formed in Kabul in 1971 in reaction to the increasing secular and leftist trends in Afghanistan at the time. In 1975, after the government of Muhammad Daud came to power, the organization moved its headquarters to Peshawar, Pakistan, and became a political and guerrilla resistance organization dedicated to the overthrow of the Afghan government. In 1978, Burhanuddin Rabbani became its leader. Advocating the establishment of an Islamic government in Afghanistan and strict adherence to *shari'a* (Islamic law), Jami'at-e Islami has connections with other international Islamist movements, including the Muslim Brotherhood and the Jami'at-e Islami of Pakistan.

Jami'at-e Islami's greatest following has been among Afghanistan's northern ethnolinguistic groups, particularly the Tajiks, in part because the leader, Rabbani, is a Tajik. Jami'at-e Islami commanders have included the martyred Ahmad Shah Mas'ud (1953–2001) and Isma'il Khan, who controls Herat province. In 1992, the Jami'at-e Islami returned to Kabul along with the other resistance groups to form an Islamic government, and in 1993 Rabbani became president of Afghanistan. Forced from power when the Taliban captured Kabul in 1996, the remnants of Jami'at-e Islami, including Rabbani and Mas'ud, fled to the north of Afghanistan, where they formed the United Front to resist Taliban control. When, in turn, the Taliban were forced from Kabul in December 2001, the United Front was the first group into Kabul. As a result, the leaders of the Jami'at-e Islami now hold most of the key positions in the interim government of Hamid Karzai.

See also RABBANI, BURHANUDDIN; *SHARI'A.*

Bibliography

Farr, Grant. "The Failure of the Mujahedin." *Middle East International* 476 (1994): 19–20.

Rubin, Barnett R. *The Fragmentation of Afghanistan: State Formation and Collapse in the International System.* New Haven, CT: Yale University Press, 2002.

GRANT FARR

JANGALI

A nationalist and reformist movement in Iran in the early twentieth century.

The Jangali movement was formed in the forests (*jangal*) of northwestern Iran. Its members, under the leadership of Mirza Kuchek Khan and Ehsan Allah Khan, were intent on eradicating foreign influence in the country.

The Jangalis were active in the constitutional revolution of 1905–1911, and their aim was to restore the sovereignty and autonomy of Iran under a broad Islamic framework. They established a revolutionary council, Ettehad-e Eslam (Islamic unity), published a newspaper called *Jangal,* and enlisted the help of Ottoman and German military advisers. The Jangalis stole from the rich landowners of Gilan to give to the poor and to support their movement. The 1917 Bolshevik revolution in Russia enhanced their standing in Iran. The movement spread to Mazandaran, another Caspian province, and in 1918 the Jangalis nearly took Qazvin. In that year, the British signed an agreement with Mirza Kuchek Khan, in which Britain would recognize Jangali autonomy in Gilan in return for a cessation of hostilities between the two camps and the expulsion of all German and Ottoman Jangali advisers. The agreement was seen as a compromise by the more radical faction of the movement under the leadership of Ehsan Allah Khan, and their split enabled the Cossack Brigade, dispatched from Tehran, to temporarily quell the uprising. Following the Russian revolution of 1917, Russian troops invaded Rasht, the capital of the province of Gilan, in 1920, and Mirza Kuchek Khan proclaimed the Socialists Republic of Gilan. The Soviet–Iranian treaty of 1921 stopped Soviet aggression in the country; the Soviets withdrew their troops and Reza Khan, later to become the first Pahlavi monarch, obliterated the Jangalis by October 1921. Mirza Kuchek Khan was executed, and Ehsan Allah Khan fled to the USSR.

See also COSSACK BRIGADE; KUCHEK KHAN-E JANGALI; PAHLAVI, REZA.

Bibliography

Browne, Edward G. *The Persian Revolution of 1905–1909,* revised edition, edited Abbas Amanat. Washington, DC: Mage, 1995.

NEGUIN YAVARI

JANISSARIES

Military corps in the Ottoman Empire's army from the late fourteenth century to 1826.

The term *janissary* is the anglicized form of the Turkish *yeni çeri* (new troops). The Janissary corps was established in the late fourteenth century. The Janissaries' first recruits were from the ranks of young Christian prisoners of war; they were converted to Islam, taught Turkish, and given a rigorous military training. At the end of the sixteenth century, the Janissary corps began to admit untrained, mostly Muslim-born, recruits. The admission of untrained recruits marked the beginning of the janissaries' decline as a fighting force and their growing corruption. The basic regulations that had preserved the special character of the corps for some two centuries were treated with growing laxity, until they were abandoned altogether. The janissaries were allowed to marry and have families; then, in order to support their dependents, they were permitted to engage in gainful activities. Over the years, an ever-increasing number of janissaries gave up the practice of living at the barracks and training regularly, and the corps became largely a poorly trained and undisciplined militia. Commissions were sold to the highest bidders, and numerous civilians seeking to enjoy tax exemptions and other privileges bought their way into the corps. Consequently, the number of janissaries steadily increased from 12,000 in the early sixteenth century to 140,000 around 1820. The great majority of these men were not soldiers, but shopkeepers, artisans, porters, and followers of other trades, who rarely performed any military duties but zealously defended their privileged position. Identified with large segments of the urban population, they became a powerful caste resisting change.

The janissaries consistently opposed attempts to introduce military reforms because those required training and submission to discipline. They also objected to any attempts to create a new military force that might replace them or threaten their privileged position. In the last decade of the eighteenth century, Selim III (r. 1789–1807) hesitatingly introduced a new infantry corps known as the *Nizam-i Cedit.* The janissaries objected to the new force, and they eventually led a coalition of conservative forces that overthrew Selim and abolished his reforms (May 1807). An attempt by the grand vizier, Bayrakdar (Alemdar) Mustafa Paşa, to reintroduce the Nizam-i Cedit also was foiled by the janissaries, and Bayrakdar himself was killed (November 1808).

Following Bayrakdar's death, Mahmud II (r. 1808–1839) concluded a pact with the janissaries, known as *Sened-i Ita'at* (Deed of Obedience), promising not to introduce military reforms in return for a janissary commitment not to intervene in political affairs. However, the Greek war of independence that broke out in 1821 (and lasted until 1830) confronted the Ottoman Empire with new and dangerous challenges, including the possibility of European intervention. The janissaries proved ineffective against the Greek insurgents, and the sultan was forced to enlist the support of his governor of Egypt, Muhammad Ali Pasha, who had a new, European-style, modern army. The contrast between the ineffectual janissaries and the disciplined, successful Egyptian troops softened public opinion toward military reform. Capitalizing on this new mood, early in 1826 Mahmud proposed a plan (the Eşkinci/Eşkenci project) to reform a small segment of the Janissary corps, transforming it into a regular, modern, European-style force. Although most of the senior officers approved the plan, soon after its implementation the janissaries once again rose in rebellion. The sultan, however, had taken precautions against such a threat. With the support of the *ulama* (body of Islamic scholars) and the general public, loyal forces including artillery and naval units quickly suppressed the rebellion with considerable bloodshed (15 June 1826). Mahmud seized the opportunity to abolish completely the Janissary corps and the Bektashi sufi order affiliated with it.

Thus ended an institution that had existed for almost five centuries and that had become a hallmark of Ottoman power, in both its greatness and decline. The suppression of the janissaries, which became known in Ottoman history as the Beneficial Event (Vaka-i Hayriye), made a great impression on

The janissaries were the standing army of the Ottoman empire, formed in the late fourteenth century. The corps began as an elite and highly disciplined fighting force, but lax recruitment policy, an overabundance of privileges, and an aversion to reform led to a severe decline in its effectiveness by the early nineteenth century. © HISTORICAL PICTURE ARCHIVE/CORBIS. REPRODUCED BY PERMISSION.

contemporaries in the Ottoman Empire and abroad. It also cleared the way for comprehensive, European-style military and administrative reforms that, in the long run, affected every aspect of society, and extended the life of the Ottoman Empire into the twentieth century.

See also BAYRAKDAR, MUSTAFA; VAKA-I HAYRIYE.

Bibliography

Levy, Avigdor. "The Eşkenci Project: An Ottoman Attempt at Gradual Reform (1826)." *Abr-Nahrain* 14 (1974): 32–39.

Shaw, Stanford J., and Shaw, Ezel Kural. *History of the Ottoman Empire and Modern Turkey,* Vol. 2: *Reform, Revolution, and Republic: The Rise of Modern Turkey, 1808–1975.* New

York and Cambridge, U.K.: Cambridge University Press, 1979.

AVIGDOR LEVY
UPDATED BY ERIC HOOGLUND

JARALLAH FAMILY

Prominent Palestinian family from Jerusalem.

The Jarallahs belonged to Jerusalem's old Muslim elite, and were counted among the city's *ashraf* or descendants of the prophet Muhammad. Family members held religious posts in Jerusalem for hundreds of years and emerged at the end of the nineteenth century among the local Ottoman bureaucratic-landowning class, although less influential than the Husaynis and Nashashibis.

In 1921, Husam al-Din Jarallah (1884–1954), a graduate of al-Azhar, received the highest number of votes in an election for mufti (canon lawyer) of Jerusalem. But the rival Husaynis organized a petition campaign and succeeded in placing their candidate, al-Hajj Amin al-Husayni, in the post. Husam nonetheless served as chief justice of the religious courts, and in 1948 was finally appointed mufti by Jordan's King Abdullah, to replace the anti-Hashimite Husayni. While Husam al-Din was a pro-Hashimite moderate, other family members took stronger stands against Zionism. Hasan Jarallah, for example, in 1918 helped found an organization that took violent action against Arabs who sold land to Jews, called Jamʿiyyat al-Ikha wa al-Afaf (Association of Brotherhood and Purity).

See also ABDULLAH I IBN HUSSEIN; HUSAYNI, MUHAMMAD AMIN AL-.

Bibliography

Mattar, Philip. *The Mufti of Jerusalem: Al-Hajj Amin al-Husayni and the Palestinian National Movement,* revised edition. New York: Columbia University Press, 1992.

Muslih, Muhammad Y. *The Origins of Palestinian Nationalism.* New York: Columbia University Press, 1988.

ELIZABETH THOMPSON

JARASH

Jordanian town and archaeological site.

Lying 29 miles (47 km) north of Jordan's capital city, Amman, the ruins at Jarash are some of the most famous in the Middle East and, along with Petra, one of Jordan's two main tourist attractions.

Founded as part of Alexander the Great's empire (c. 334 B.C.E.), Jarash became a thriving Roman provincial city during the first to third centuries C.E. It was one of the ten cities of the Decapolis, a commercial federation in Roman Syria. After its decline from shifting trade routes, Jarash lay in ruins until about 1884, when the Ottoman Empire introduced Circassians (Muslims from the Caucasus mountains fleeing Russian rule) as settlers. The town later grew to incorporate Arabs as well. By 1994, the population stood at 21,300; 2002 estimates put it at 26,300.

The first European to report on Jarash's Roman ruins was the German Ulrich J. Seetzen in 1806. Serious restoration and archaeological work were undertaken by the Transjordanian government in the 1920s on the city's amphitheater, forum, colonnaded road, temples, churches, and other buildings. The ruins now offer one of the best examples of provincial architecture from the Roman Empire, and serve as the backdrop for Jordan's most celebrated cultural event, the internationally known Jarash Festival for music and dance.

Bibliography

Harding, G. Lankester. *The Antiquities of Jordan,* 2d edition. London: Lutterworth, 1959.

Showker, Kay. *Fodor's Jordan and the Holy Land.* New York: McKay, 1989.

MICHAEL R. FISCHBACH

JARIDA, AL-

See NEWSPAPERS AND PRINT MEDIA: ARAB COUNTRIES

JARRING, GUNNAR
[1907–2002]

Swedish diplomat; UN special envoy to the Middle East (1967–1971).

After studying linguistics at Lund University, Gunnar Jarring joined the Swedish foreign ministry and served in Asia. He was Sweden's UN ambassador (1956–1958) and ambassador to the United States

(1958–1964). In November 1967, when he was serving as Sweden's ambassador to Moscow, he was appointed by UN Secretary-General U Thant as special envoy to promote an Arab-Israel peace settlement based on Security Council Resolution 242. In 1968 he embarked on shuttle diplomacy and addressed a series of notes to the parties. But they displayed little trust in his judgment and ability to promote peace, and turned elsewhere. Jarring's mission was suspended temporarily when UN representatives of the four powers began talks. It resumed briefly after the August 1970 cease-fire agreement ended the war of attrition along the Suez Canal, and again was suspended because of Egyptian violations of that agreement. It was restarted in December 1970. In February 1971 Jarring presented Israel and Egypt identical notes proposing a peace settlement. Egypt expressed readiness to consider peace in return for total Israeli withdrawal and a resolution of the Palestinian problem. Israel said it was ready to enter into peace talks but would not return to the 4 June 1967 lines. Israel felt Jarring had exceeded his mandate and role by conducting negotiations instead of letting the parties negotiate directly. His mission effectively lapsed and was not formally terminated until 1990.

See also UNITED NATIONS AND THE MIDDLE EAST.

Bibliography

Bar-Siman-Tov, Yaacov. *The Israeli-Egyptian War of Attrition, 1969–1970: A Case-Study of Limited Local War.* New York: Columbia University Press, 1980.

Eban, Abba. *Personal Witness: Israel through My Eyes.* New York: Putnam, 1992.

Heikal, Mohamed. *The Road to Ramadan.* New York: Ballantine, 1975.

Rafael, Gideon. *Destination Peace: Three Decades of Israeli Foreign Policy: A Personal Memoir.* New York: Stein and Day; London: Weidenfeld and Nicolson, 1981.

Touval, Saadia. *The Peace Brokers: Mediators in the Arab-Israeli Conflict, 1948–1979.* Princeton, NJ: Princeton University Press, 1982.

MERON MEDZINI

JAWAHIRI, MUHAMMAD MAHDI AL-
[1900–1997]

The leading neoclassical poet of modern Iraq.

Muhammad Mahdi al-Jawahiri, born in al-Najaf, became a teacher in the 1920s. His poetry brought him to the notice of King Faisal I, who became his patron and protector. Closely associated with the Communist Party, al-Jawahiri became president of the Journalists' Association after the Revolution of 1958, and was Iraq's ambassador to Czechoslovakia until 1963. He returned to Iraq in the early 1970s but went into exile in Damascus a few years later. He was famous for his forceful revolutionary poetry.

See also FAISAL I IBN HUSSEIN.

PETER SLUGLETT

JAZEERA, AL-

Arab satellite television based in Qatar.

Al-Jazeera is a pan-Arab satellite television station founded in 1996, shortly after the failure of the Arabic British Broadcasting Corporation (BBC) experiment, with funding from the amir of Qatar. On 1 November 1996, al-Jazeera started broadcasting six hours a day. It expanded to twelve hours in 1999, and to twenty-four hours in 2001. In 2003 it had 500 employees, twenty-seven bureaus worldwide, and 35 million viewers. Only 40 percent of its revenue comes from advertising; the rest comes from selling programs, footage, and other services. Al-Jazeera is a leader in providing news. Its self-proclaimed ethic is "independence, objectivity, and freedom of expression." In 1999 it won the Ibn Rushd Prize for Freedom of Thought. Al-Jazeera's independent programming has angered many Arab governments, especially its news, commentary, and call-in and debate shows such as "The Opposing View" that are critical of Arab regimes.

Al-Jazeera scooped all competition, including Cable News Network and BBC, with exclusive interviews and videos of the bombing of Kabul in October 2001. During the war on Iraq in 2003, al-Jazeera angered the U.S. government by airing pictures of U.S. prisoners of war as well as reports critical of the occupation. Its web site occasionally has been hacked. Al-Jazeera is both praised and vilified. Arab viewers clamor for al-Jazeera when governments shut down its signal, while critics denounce it as a "sinister salad of sex, religion and politics, topped with sensationalist seasoning." With its commanding viewer following, however, al-Jazeera has become a major media player in the Arab region.

Bibliography

Zednik, Rick. "Perspectives on War: Inside Al Jazeera." *Columbia Journalism Review*, March/April 2002. Available from <http://www.cjr.org/year/02/2/zednik.asp>.

LES ORDEMAN
UPDATED BY KARIM HAMDY

JAZIRA, AL-

See NEWSPAPERS AND PRINT MEDIA: ARAB COUNTRIES

JAZRAWI, TAHA AL-

See RAMADAN, TAHA YASIN

JEHAD-E SAZANDEGI

Postrevolutionary organization in Iran for developing rural areas of the country.

The leaders of the Iranian Revolution believed that the deposed monarchy of Mohammad Reza Shah Pahlavi had neglected both agriculture and rural economic development in its program to create an urban and industrialized society. Therefore, government attention to the "deprived" rural sector became an ideological pillar of the Islamic Republic. A special government organization, the Jehad-e Sazandegi (literally, the Construction Crusade), was set up with the mandate to provide basic infrastructure to all of the country's 70,000 villages. The Jehad's projects included road construction, rural electrification, provision of piped potable water, building waste water systems, and implementing numerous programs to enhance agricultural productivity. The philosophy of Jehad stressed local participation in development projects, and its trained cadres mobilized thousands of villagers in cooperative efforts that eventually brought modern amenities to and transformed the appearance of most villages. Its achievements included the construction of 60,000 kilometers of rural roads between 1979 and 1999 and the extension of piped

water to 850,000 rural households in the same period.

Jehad's successes raised its profile and it became a cabinet-level ministry in the mid-1980s. As a ministry, its hands-on approach to agricultural productivity problems sometimes clashed with the more bureaucratically inclined approach of the ministry of agriculture. Rivalry between Jehad and the ministry of agriculture prompted the government of President Ali Akbar Hashemi Rafsanjani (1989–1997) to streamline state rural development programs by merging the two ministries, a policy that both resisted. Eventually, Jehad was incorporated as an organization within the ministry of agriculture, but it has maintained a separate identity and its focus on rural development.

See also AGRICULTURE; IRANIAN REVOLUTION (1979); PAHLAVI, MOHAMMAD REZA; RAFSANJANI, ALI AKBAR HASHEMI.

Bibliography

Azkia, Mostafa. "Rural Society and Revolution in Iran." In *Twenty Years of Islamic Revolution: Political and Social Transition in Iran since 1979*, edited by Eric Hooglund. Syracuse, NY: Syracuse University Press, 2002.

ERIC HOOGLUND

JELLABA

See CLOTHING

JENIN

Palestinian city in the West Bank.

Jenin (also Janin) is one of three Palestinian towns (the others being Nablus and Tulkarm) that formed the "Triangle" region of north-central Palestine. The city was noted in history for the bounty of its agriculture, particularly fruits and vegetables. Both the Ottomans and the British made Jenin the administrative center of an administrative sub-governorate bearing its name as well.

The Arab–Israel War (1948) changed the town's fortunes drastically. It was noteworthy for the fact that, although the Haganah captured Jenin briefly in June 1948, it quickly withdrew after fighting with Palestinian and Iraqi forces. The eventual cease-fire lines left the city within the Jordanian-controlled West Bank, and cut it off from the traditional markets for its agricultural exports to the north and west, in what now had become Israel. Beyond this, the war caused the population to increase from 3,990 in 1945 to 10,000 as Palestinian refugees swelled the town's ranks. From June 1967 until November 1995, Jenin lay under Israeli military occupation until it came under the control of the Palestinian Authority. By 1997, Jenin's population stood at 26,650.

During the al-Aqsa Intifada that began in 2000, the Israeli army reoccupied parts of the city on several occasions. The eleven-day Israeli assault on the nearby Jenin refugee camp in April 2002, populated by some 10,000 refugees, devastated the camp. The destruction prompted international outrage, and "Jenin" became a symbol of the violence of the second Intifada.

See also AQSA INTIFADA, AL-; ARAB–ISRAEL WAR (1948); WEST BANK.

Bibliography

Fischbach, Michael R. "Jenin." In *Encyclopedia of the Palestinians*, edited by Philip Mattar. New York: Facts On File, 2000.

MICHAEL R. FISCHBACH

JERICHO

Modern Palestinian oasis town, resting on the ruins of the ancient city.

Jericho dates archaeologically to about 9000 B.C.E. It is best known from the Bible as the city conquered by Joshua (c. 1400 B.C.E.) leading the Hebrew tribes and as the site where Zacchaeus spoke with Jesus from a tree.

Jericho is about 15 miles (22.5 km) northeast of Jerusalem, and some 825 feet (250 m) below sea level. The 2003 population estimate was 19,140 (not counting the Palestinian refugee camps). After the Ottoman Empire was defeated and dismembered in World War I, Jericho became part of the British mandate over Palestine, which began in 1922. The town became a winter resort. When Israel became a state in 1948, Jericho fell under Jordanian rule after the first Arab–Israel War. The

United Nations Relief and Works Agency built three large Palestinian refugee camps near it and, shortly before the Arab–Israel War of 1967, the population of the city and the camps was estimated at 80,000. Almost all the inhabitants of those refugee camps became refugees yet again in 1967, crossing the Jordan River into Jordan. On 13 September 1993, Israel and the Palestine Liberation Organization signed an agreement under which Jericho, along with the Gaza Strip, became an area of Palestinian autonomy beginning in 1994.

See also ARAB–ISRAEL WAR (1948); ARAB–ISRAEL WAR (1967); PALESTINE; PALESTINE LIBERATION ORGANIZATION (PLO).

BENJAMIN JOSEPH

JERICHO CONGRESS (1948)

Conference of Palestinians organized by King Abdullah.

Held in Jericho on 1 December 1948, the Jericho Congress was convened in response to the establishment of the State of Israel and the corresponding loss to the Arabs of most of Palestine. This provided the legal basis for the union of central Palestine (the West Bank and East Jerusalem) with Transjordan (East Bank). The conference was presided over by Shaykh Muhammad Ali Ja'bari, mayor of Hebron, and included leaders from Jerusalem, Hebron, Bethlehem, Nablus, and Ramallah, as well as representatives of refugees from Israeli-occupied cities and towns. It was attended by 1,000 delegates, including mayors, tribal chiefs, *mukhtars,* and military governors from all over Palestine. The conferees voted unanimously to request unity with Jordan; proclaimed Abdullah I ibn Hussein to be king of all Palestine; affirmed faith in the unity of Palestine; called for the return of Palestinian refugees to their homes; called on Arab states to continue the fight to save Palestine; and asked King Abdullah to hold elections for legitimate Palestinian representatives for consultations on affairs of Palestine. It was understood that the union would not compromise Arab rights to Palestine. The conference also repudiated the All-Palestine Government in Gaza sponsored by the Arab Higher Committee. On 7 December, the Jordanian cabinet under Tawfiq Abu al-Huda approved the resolutions, and parliament ratified them 13 December.

The Jordanian election law was amended, doubling the number of seats in the lower house of parliament to forty, designating half for representatives from the West Bank and Jerusalem and the other half from Jordan. Elections to the new, expanded parliament were held in 1950, and unity was ratified unanimously on 24 April 1950.

Egypt strongly opposed the union. Syria criticized it but did not oppose it outright. Britain approved of the congress and its resolutions. Israel's recognition of the union was implicit in the armistice agreement between the two countries. The United States granted *de jure* recognition on 31 January 1949.

See also ABDULLAH I IBN HUSSEIN; ABU AL-HUDA, TAWFIQ; ALL-PALESTINE GOVERNMENT; ARAB HIGHER COMMITTEE (PALESTINE).

Bibliography

Dann, Uriel. *King Hussein and the Challenge of Arab Radicalism: Jordan, 1955–1967.* New York: Oxford University Press in cooperation with the Moshe Dayan Center for Middle Eastern and African Studies, Tel Aviv University, 1989.

Nevo, Joseph. *King Abdallah and Palestine: A Territorial Ambition.* New York: St. Martin's, 1966.

Shlaim, Avi. *Collusion across the Jordan: King Abdullah, the Zionist Movement, and the Partition of Palestine.* New York: Columbia University Press, 1988.

Wilson, Mary. *King Abdullah, Britain, and the Making of Jordan.* Cambridge, U.K., and New York: Cambridge University Press, 1987.

JENAB TUTUNJI

JERUSALEM

City that is sacred to Jews, Christians, and Muslims, and that has become embroiled in the politics of the Arab–Israel conflict.

Located in the Judaean mountains, on the watershed between the Judaean hills and the Judaean desert, Jerusalem (in Hebrew, *Yerushalayim*; in Arabic, *Bayt al-Maqdis* or *al-Quds al-Sharif*) overlooks the Dead Sea to the east and faces Israel's coastal plain to the west. It has warm, dry summers and cool, rainy winters. Jerusalem was inhabited as far back as the fourth millennium B.C.E. By the late Bronze Age, it was occupied by the Jebusites. The city became the Jewish national and religious center after its conquest by King David (c. 1000 B.C.E.) from the Jebusites until the destruction of the second Jewish temple (70 C.E.) and the rebellions against Roman occupation, which resulted in the Jews' exile from the city and their dispersion. The Western Wall of the temple complex was the only remnant to survive destruction and over the course of time became the focus of Jewish veneration. As the scene of the last ministry, death, and resurrection of Jesus, Jerusalem emerged as one of the five original Christian patriarchates and has remained a center of Christian pilgrimage since the reign of the Roman emperor Constantine, when it was rebuilt as a Christian city. After the Muslim conquest (638 C.E.), the construction of the al-Aqsa mosque and the Dome of the Rock (part of the complex known as al-Haram al-Sharif) to commemorate the Night Journey of the prophet Muhammad focused Muslim attention on the city. It became the first *qibla* (direction of prayer), and is the third holiest city of Islam.

Nineteenth-Century Jerusalem

Conquered by the Ottomans in 1517, Jerusalem remained a backwater town in the province of Syria until the nineteenth century, when Europeans and Ottomans refocused on its religious significance. During the brief reign of Ibrahim ibn Muhammad Ali (1832-1840), relaxed restrictions against the *dhimmi* (non-Muslim) population and renewed interest by Western Christians in the Holy Land resulted in an increase in tourism, the installation of European consulates, the beginnings of biblical archaeology, and the establishment of Protestant institutions adjoining those of the Roman Catholic (Latin), Greek Orthodox, Coptic, Armenian, and other Christian denominations. Communal conflicts over the religious jurisdiction of the Christian holy places led to the Crimean War (1854–1856), after which the keys to the Church of the Holy Sepulchre were entrusted to the Muslim Nusayba family.

The city plan at the time remained as it was when it was rebuilt by the Romans as Aelia Capitolina. Walled, with a system of principal streets, it was dominated by the holy sites and divided into Muslim, Christian, Jewish, and Armenian residential quarters with maze-like streets, bazaars, churches, synagogues, and mosques. It was the residence of Muslim Arab notables and, later, members of the Ottoman official class. The Khalidi, Nashashibi, and Husayni families played important roles in local politics and Muslim religious administration. The Jewish population included the Mizrahi Jews (Jews from the Middle East, North Africa, and Western Asia) who had lived there since ancient times or who had migrated after the expulsion of Spanish (Sephardic) Jewry in 1492. Some of their leading families included the Navon, Amzalak, Antebi, and Valero families, who became important as translators, bankers, and merchants. Ashkenazic (European) Jews began to immigrate to Jerusalem during the early nineteenth century, including Hasidim (called *haredim* in the late twentieth century), who were dependent upon philanthropy from abroad to support them while they lived a life of full-time study. In the 1860s, at the invitation of British consul James Finn and philanthropist Sir Moses Montefiore, who donated money for the construction of residential areas outside the walls, Jews, some Muslims, and the Russian Orthodox Church began to build new neighborhoods along the roads to the Old City. By 1860 the city's population stood at approximately 40,000, which grew to 55,000 by 1900.

In 1873 Jerusalem was placed under direct Ottoman rule from Constantinople (now Istanbul), and during the reign of Abdülhamit II, who championed its Islamic significance, it underwent major expansion. A municipal council, dominated by Muslim Arabs, was established. Jerusalem became a major provincial city with new courts, a modern water system, mosques, and public offices. New residential and commercial construction, both inside and outside the walls, was undertaken by the local population and by Europeans who established banks and built schools, hospitals, and hospices. Roads were paved, the city was linked by rail to Jaffa on the Mediterranean coast, and Ottoman secondary schools were set up close to new Muslim neighborhoods. The visit to Jerusalem by Kaiser Wilhelm II of Germany (1898) heralded the city's emerging importance in the Ottoman Empire. In 1917 Jerusalem was occupied by the British army under the command of General Edmund Allenby; it later became the capital of what the British called Palestine. The British ruled Palestine within the rubric of the mandate system from 1922 to 1948. The New City

The Christian Quarter of Jerusalem is situated in the northwest section of the city and has a population of around five thousand people. The area is home to the Church of the Holy Sepulchre, which is built over the remains of Golgatha, where Christ was crucified, and the tomb he rose from. Pilgrims from across the world journey to worship at this holy site. © RICHARD T. NOWITZ/CORBIS. REPRODUCED BY PERMISSION.

expanded with the development of additional Palestinian Arab and Jewish neighborhoods. The British improved the water-supply system, paved roads, planted gardens, and encouraged the repair and construction of buildings. More significantly, they allowed large-scale Jewish immigration into Palestine. Indeed, the terms of the mandate included the Balfour Declaration (1917), which obligated Britain to foster Jewish immigration, land purchases, and institution building. This quickly led to a growth in the population in the city from just over 91,000 in 1922 to almost 133,000 in 1931. By 1944, according to the American Committee of Inquiry, the Jewish population in the city was 97,000, with 30,630

Muslims and 29,350 Christians (the overwhelming majority of Muslims and Christians were Palestinians).

Zionism and Palestinian Nationalism under British Mandate

Jerusalem became the center of both Zionist and Palestinian nationalist institutions and aspirations during the British mandate. The Supreme Muslim Council was located in Jerusalem, headed by the Jerusalem mufti, Hajj Muhammad Amin al-Husayni (who then also controlled the considerable *waqf* income that under Ottoman rule had gone directly to Constantinople). Palestinian political life was complicated by the bitter rivalry between the Husaynis and the Nashashibis for control of the Palestinian nationalist movement. Jerusalem's mayors were Arab notables active in the nascent Palestinian nationalist movement, and once again included members from the Husayni and Nashashibi families, including Musa Kazim al-Husayni, Raghib al-Nashashibi, Husayn Fakhri al-Khalidi, and Mustafa al-Khalidi. The Arab Executive was also headed by Musa Kazim al-Husayni. With the Arab and Jewish populations governed by the British under separate systems, the Zionists developed economic, social, educational, and political institutions of their own, including the Hadassah Hospital and the Hebrew University of Jerusalem. The Jewish Agency was headquartered in the city as well. Nationalist passions, and Palestinian fears of political and demographic displacement in the face of continued Zionist immigration, led to violence as early as April 1920. The more serious Western (Wailing) Wall Disturbances of 1929 were a result of the politicization of religious shrines. During the Palestine Arab Revolt (1936–1939) Palestinian guerrillas actually occupied the Old City for a time. Both incidents were suppressed by overwhelming British police and military force.

The Arab–Israel Wars and Aftermath

During the Arab–Israel War of 1948, Jerusalem was the scene of bitter fighting. Fighting between Palestinians and the Jewish Haganah began in late November 1947, and by late April 1948, Imost Palestinian neighborhoods in West Jerusalem had been captured by Jewish forces and depopulated, and the vacant houses handed over to Jews. Jordan

and other Arab states entered the fray on 15 May 1948. Although the Jordanian Arab Legion waited three days to enter Jerusalem, it ended up engaging in fierce fighting with Jewish forces for control of the Old City. The surrender of the Jewish Quarter after ten days' fighting, and the expulsion of its remaining Jewish population, left the city divided into Israeli-controlled West Jerusalem and Jordanian-controlled East Jerusalem, including the Old City. Despite United Nations General Assembly Resolution 181 (II) of 29 November 1947, that called for the city to be controlled neither by Jews nor Arabs, as well as later proposals for its internationalization supervised by the United Nations Trusteeship Council, the city remained divided between Jordan and Israel. Access between the two sectors was via the Mandelbaum gate. Both sectors of the city had been emptied of inhabitants belonging to the other side, and both the Jordanian and Israeli governments neglected, destroyed, and/or allowed the desecration of captured cemeteries and religious sites.

East Jerusalem was officially incorporated into Jordan in 1950 and remained subordinate to Amman throughout the period of Jordanian rule, despite protestations by mayors Arif al-Arif and Ruhi al-Khatib. Requests to establish an Arab university in Jerusalem were denied. Many of the Palestinian elite left the city; they were replaced by notables from Hebron invited to the city by Jordan. Though the city expanded northward, plans to incorporate the neighboring villages in the direction of Ramallah into the city never crystallized. Hotels were built, and construction began on a royal palace at Tall al-Full.

In 1950 Israel proclaimed Jerusalem as its capital even though almost all governments maintained embassies in Tel Aviv, where the real work of the state was done. Institutions such as the Hebrew University and Hadassah Hospital, which had come under Jordan's rule, were rebuilt in West Jerusalem. Christians, including Palestinian Christian citizens of Israel, were allowed to cross through the gate to visit the shrines in East Jerusalem on Christmas. Jews, however, were denied access to their holy places. In general, Jerusalem became a backwater for both Palestinians and Israelis alike.

In the Arab–Israel War of June 1967 another round of fierce fighting broke out. Jordanian forces shelled West Jerusalem on 5 June and two days later Israeli paratroopers assaulted East Jerusalem, including the Old City. The Arab Legion and local Palestinians put up a stiff resistance, but were defeated. Israelis were jubilant at being able to pray at the Western Wall for the first time since 1948; Palestinians were mortified to see Muslim and Christian holy sites under Jewish control. Israel immediately began effecting significant changes to the newly unified city. It placed East Jerusalem under its legal and administrative jurisdiction on 28 June, thereby effectively annexing it and uniting it with West Jerusalem. Following on Jordanian procedure, Israel dramatically expanded the municipal city limits into the West Bank. On 30 July 1980 the Israeli Knesset declared the newly expanded city to be the "eternal" capital of Israel. Israeli authorities also confiscated Palestinian land in the Old City to rebuild the destroyed Jewish Quarter, and destroyed 135 Palestinian homes and two historic mosques to build an expansive pilgrims' plaza facing the Western Wall. Finally, new Jewish settlements like Pisgat Ze'ev were constructed in East Jerusalem surrounding the Old City. The acceleration of settlement building for Jews under the Likud governments starting in 1977 resulted, by the mid-1980s, in 12 percent of the Jewish population of Jerusalem residing in East Jerusalem beyond the 1948 armistice line (Green Line). By contrast, the Palestinian neighborhoods in West Jerusalem that were captured in 1967 were not resettled, and remain inhabited by Jews. By 2000, the city's population stood at 670,500 in the expanded city: 454,600 Jews and 215,400 Palestinians. Under the administration of Jewish mayor Teddy Kollek (1965–1992), all barriers dividing the city were removed. The city underwent a major beautification program that included the construction of a ring of parks around the Old City. Other green spaces, combined with zoning regulations, also served to prevent the expansion of Palestinian built-up areas while Jewish settlement construction continued and, in general, Kollek neglected development of the Palestinian parts of the city.

Unified Jerusalem

Jerusalem is the seat of the government of the state of Israel, and the site of the Knesset, Supreme Court, Chief Rabbinate, and the offices of many Jewish institutions. Most countries of the world,

The Jewish Quarter of Jerusalem was heavily damaged during the Arab–Israel War of 1948. Restoration began after the Israeli conquest of the city in 1967. Located in the southeast section of the city, with a population of approximately 2,300, the Jewish Quarter contains the Western Wall (once Wailing Wall) of the Temple Mount, the holiest site in Judaism. © DANIEL LAINE/CORBIS. REPRODUCED BY PERMISSION.

however, maintain their embassies in Tel Aviv, in deference to United Nations General Assembly Resolution 181 (II) of 1947 and the unsettled international legal status of the city. Since 1967, Muslim and Christian holy places have been under the jurisdiction of their respective religious authorities, with the al-Haram al-Sharif under the administration of the *waqf* and *shari'a* courts. Jerusalem Palestinians were also granted Israeli permanent residency cards, and thus treated differently from West Bank Palestinians.

The unification of Jerusalem in 1967 revived the religious and political competition for control of the city. Some of the new Israeli neighborhoods in

East Jerusalem have been settled by *haredi* (ultra-orthodox) Jews, for whom Jerusalem is the center of their religious worldview that calls for strict observance of the Sabbath rest. Their opposition, at times violent, to secular vehicular traffic through these neighborhoods has renewed the religious-secular conflict among Jews in Israel. *Haredi* votes enabled the Likud candidate, Ehud Olmert, to become mayor of Jerusalem in 1993 and to place *haredi* members on the Municipal Council. In 2003 the city voted in its first *haredi* mayor, Uri Lupolianski. Through immigration and natural increase, the *haredi* population will soon exceed that of the secular Jewish residents of the city. For the Jewish religious nationalist settlers, who also have a presence in these neighborhoods and have bought or leased housing in Palestinian neighborhoods in the Old City or in villages such as Silwan that have Jewish historic significance, Jerusalem is holy land never to be relinquished.

For the Palestinians, Jerusalem remains their spiritual and national capital. They have viewed these political and demographic changes with great alarm, and have been angered by violent threats to their shrines. In August 1969 an Australian Christian set fire to the al-Aqsa mosque, destroying a twelfth-century pulpit. Israeli police thwarted several Jewish attempts to blow up the shrines in al-Haram al-Sharif in the early 1980s. In April 1982 a U.S.-born Israeli began shooting inside the Dome of the Rock, killing two Palestinians.

To bolster the Arab-Islamic nature of East Jerusalem, the Jordanian and Saudi governments have helped to fund the more than 2,000 Muslim endowments in the city—Islamic schools, colleges, mosques, welfare services, and commercial enterprises, as well as the repair of Islamic holy sites. Archaeological excavations also carry political ramifications in Jerusalem and have led to violence. Palestinian disturbances broke out in September 1996, prompted by Israel's opening of an ancient tunnel running adjacent to al-Haram al-Sharif. Intra-Jewish confrontations sometimes occur over archaeological digs that *haredi* Jews claim desecrate ancient Hebrew burial grounds.

The signing of the Oslo Accord in 1993 has accelerated the political struggle over the city as both Israel and the Palestinians prepare for the "final status talks" that were slated to determine the future of the city. Despite Israel's insistence that the unified city is its eternal capital, Palestinians continue to maintain that it (or at least East Jerusalem) is the capital of a future Palestinian state, as stated in the 1988 declaration of independence by the Palestine Liberation Organization (PLO). Indeed, the city has become the Palestinian religious, cultural, and intellectual center, and, through the establishment of the Arab Studies Society (1979) by Faysal al-Husayni at Orient House, the site of Palestinian archives collected to build and transmit Palestinian nationalism. After the onset of the Israeli–Palestinian peace process after 1993, the PLO gave al-Husayni responsibility for assessing municipal functions of a Palestinian part of the city, and the Orient House began to play the de facto role of a municipal institution with national functions. For their part, Israeli authorities in the 1990s began tightening residency requirements for Palestinians in East Jerusalem, a process that led to hundreds of them losing their residency rights. Israel's decision to build a Jewish settlement at Har Homa (in Arabic, *Jabal Abu Ghunaym*) in Jerusalem's southern suburbs angered Palestinians and threatened the peace process. Even Arab-Arab friction grew in 1994 when Israel's peace treaty with Jordan maintained Jordan's role in Islamic religious affairs in the city, to the outrage of Palestinians.

These political struggles witnessed the intensification of the level and degree of violence in the city. In October 1990 Israeli security forces opened fire on Palestinians in al-Haram al-Sharif who were stoning Jewish worshippers at the Western Wall below, killing seventeen. The violent opposition to the peace process by Islamic fundamentalist groups such as HAMAS and Islamic Jihad, who operated within the Palestinian Authority, led to numerous terrorist attacks on Jewish civilian targets that killed dozens. An unnerving development in this regard was the beginning of suicide bombings by members of the two groups. These suicide bombings on buses in Jerusalem led directly to the election victory of the Likud in 1996, and soured many Israelis to the idea of the peace process. The visit of the controversial Likud politician Ariel Sharon to al-Haram al-Sharif in September 2000 led to a particularly intense outbreak of the violence of the al-Aqsa Intifada, which has prompted Israeli authorities to close Orient House and restrict non-Jerusalem resident Palestinians from entering the city, while HAMAS and Islamic Jihad carry out more suicide bombings, including in non-Zionist religious Jewish neighborhoods. In response, Israel began constructing a barrier cutting off Palestinian population centers from Jewish areas. In January 2004, Israeli authorities began extending the wall so that it cut off the Palestinian suburb of Abu Dis from the city proper. Jerusalem remained a city on the edge by early 2004.

See also ABDÜLHAMIT II; ALLENBY, EDMUND HENRY; AQSA INTIFADA, AL-; ARAB–ISRAEL WAR (1948); ARAB–ISRAEL WAR (1967); ARAB LEGION; ARIF, ARIF AL-; ASHKENAZIM; BALFOUR DECLARATION (1917); CRIMEAN WAR; DEAD SEA; HAGANAH; HAMAS; HARAM AL-SHARIF; HASIDIM; HEBREW UNIVERSITY OF JERUSALEM; HOLY SEPULCHRE, CHURCH OF THE; HUSAYNI FAMILY, AL-; HUSAYNI, MUHAMMAD AMIN AL-; HUSAYNI, MUSA KAZIM AL-; IBRAHIM IBN MUHAMMAD ALI; ISLAMIC JIHAD; ISRAEL; JEWISH AGENCY FOR PALESTINE; KHALIDI, HUSAYN FAKHRI AL-; KOLLEK, TEDDY; LIKUD; MANDATE SYSTEM; MONTEFIORE, MOSES; NASHASHIBI FAMILY; NUSAYBA FAMILY; OSLO ACCORD (1993); PALESTINE ARAB REVOLT (1936-1939); PALESTINE LIBERATION ORGANIZATION (PLO); PALESTINIAN AUTHORITY; SHARON, ARIEL; SUPREME MUSLIM COUNCIL; WEST BANK; WESTERN WALL; WESTERN WALL DISTURBANCES.

Bibliography

Armstrong, Karen. *Jerusalem: One City, Three Faiths.* New York: Ballantine, 1997.

Asali, K. J., ed. *Jerusalem in History.* New York: Interlink, 1990.

Ben-Arieh, Y. *Jerusalem in the Nineteenth Century: The Emergence of the New City.* New York: St. Martin's Press, 1987.

Ben-Arieh, Y. *Jerusalem in the Nineteenth Century: The Old City.* Jerusalem: Yad Izhak Ben-Zvi, 1984.

Benvenisti, Meron. *City of Stone: The Hidden History of Jerusalem.* Berkeley: University of California Press, 1997.

Dumper, Michael T. *The Politics of Jerusalem Since 1967.* New York: Columbia University Press, 1997.

Elon, Amos. *Jerusalem: City of Mirrors.* Boston: Little, Brown, 1989.

Friedland, Roger, and Hecht, Richard. *To Rule Jerusalem.* Cambridge, U.K.: Cambridge University Press, 1996.

Irani, George E. *The Papacy and the Middle East: The Role of the Holy See in the Arab-Israeli Conflict, 1962–1984.* South Bend, IN: University of Notre Dame Press, 1986.

Kraemer, Joel, ed. *Jerusalem: Problems and Prospects.* New York: Praeger Publishers, 1981.

REEVA S. SIMON
UPDATED BY MICHAEL R. FISCHBACH

JERUSALEM POST

See NEWSPAPERS AND PRINT MEDIA: ISRAEL

JEWISH AGENCY FOR PALESTINE

Established in 1929 to enlist non-Zionist Jewish support for the national home in Palestine.

The League of Nations mandate for Palestine, awarded in the Treaty of Sèvres (1920), called for a Jewish agency that would be expected to provide Britain with advice and aid in discharging its duties in the establishment of a Jewish nation. Chaim Weizmann insisted that this agency be used to broaden Jewish support for economic development in Palestine, particularly among those ambivalent about Zionism's political aims. To mobilize that kind of support, Weizmann offered non-Zionists a measure of power over the development of Palestine's Jewish national home. Eastern European Zionists were reluctant to share power with those not fully committed to the Zionist political cause, so the founding of the Jewish Agency was delayed until 1929, when the World Zionist Organization (WZO) faced a severe financial crisis.

When the sixteenth congress of the WZO created the Jewish Agency, it accepted the principle of parity in membership between Zionists and non-Zionists on its three governing bodies—the 224-member council, the administrative committee, and the executive. The president of the WZO was to serve as Jewish Agency head unless opposed by 75 percent of the council. Of the non-Zionists on the council, 40 percent were Americans, and many had international reputations. The nature of the agency's

David Ben-Gurion, chairman of the Jewish Agency for Palestine and Israel's future prime minister, with Israeli troops at Haganah. After World War II, Ben-Gurion was a supporter of the 1947 United Nations partition plan, which proposed separate Jewish and Arab states in Palestine. © BETTMANN/CORBIS. REPRODUCED BY PERMISSION.

economic and social mission allowed both non-Zionists and Zionists to participate without compromising or altering their divergent principles: Economic aid could be provided to Palestinian Jewry either on the grounds that it was a community in distress or as a means to building the infrastructure of a Jewish state. Parity in the agency was not sustained. Because the agency never created effective links with non-Zionist philanthropic organizations, non-Zionists continually lost positions to Zionists and the balance of political alignment shifted in favor of the Zionists.

The Jewish Agency initially opened offices in Jerusalem, London, and Geneva. During World War II, it opened an office in New York City. Its political department conducted negotiations with Britain, particularly over annual immigration quotas. Functioning as the equivalent of a foreign office, the political department established contacts with a number of Palestinian leaders and organizations. The agency supervised the transfer of Jewish capital from Germany to Palestine during the 1930s, as well as the emigration—legal and illegal—of thousands of Jews from Nazi-dominated Europe. The agency also assumed partial control over the Yishuv's defense forces.

At the end of World War II, the agency helped prepare Palestine's Jewish population for war (the Arab-Israel War of 1948) by uniting, at least for a short period, the Haganah, Irgun, and Lohamei Herut Yisrael (LEHI). During that time, members of the agency's executive served in the central ministries of what became Israel's government—as prime minister and treasurer, and in the departments of Foreign Affairs and Defense. In the first years of statehood, the agency undertook primary responsibility for the settlement of Israel's immigrants from Europe and Islamic countries, and it later supervised the mass immigration of Jews from the former Soviet Union and Ethiopia into Israel.

Although a government ministry was eventually created to manage the process of immigrant absorption, the Jewish Agency retains significant control over organizing the rescue of diaspora Jews in danger. While some authority pertinent to agricultural settlement still resides with its offices, the agency's major tasks are now cultural and charitable. The agency expends a major portion of its budget on Jewish education and serves as the main fund-raising organization linking Israel to diaspora Jewry.

See also SÈVRES, TREATY OF (1920); WORLD ZIONIST ORGANIZATION (WZO).

Bibliography

Arbel, Andrea S. *Riding the Wave: The Jewish Agency's Role in the Mass Aliyah of Soviet and Ethiopian Jewry to Israel, 1987–1995.* Hewlett, NY; Jerusalem: Gefen, 2001.

Dowty, Alan. *The Jewish State a Century Later.* Berkeley: University of California Press, 1998.

Elazar, Daniel J., and Dortort, Alysa M., eds. *Understanding the Jewish Agency: A Handbook.* Philadelphia; Jerusalem: Jerusalem Center for Public Affairs, 1985.

Halpern, Ben. *The Idea of the Jewish State.* Cambridge, MA: Harvard University Press, 1961.

Stock, Ernest. *Partners and Pursestrings: A History of the United Israel Appeal.* Lanham, MD: University Press of America; Jerusalem: Jerusalem Center for Public Affairs/Center for Jewish Community Studies, 1987.

DONNA ROBINSON DIVINE

JEWISH BRIGADE

Established by the British war cabinet in 1944 as the only Jewish military unit to fight the Axis powers.

The Jewish Brigade represented the culmination of efforts by Jews in both Palestine and the United States to create an independent Jewish fighting force. In 1939, Jews in Palestine began to volunteer for military service, and after repeated pressure from the Jewish Agency and other Jewish organizations, in 1942 the British agreed to form a Palestine Regiment. The Palestine Regiment was sent to serve in the Middle East, although its responsibilities there were primarily restricted to guard duty.

Finally, in September 1944, the British created the Jewish Brigade (in Hebrew, *Ha-Hayil*) out of the Palestine Regiment, a field artillery regiment, and other auxiliary service units. The men, numbering approximately 5,000, were placed under the command of a Canadian-born Jew, Brigadier Ernest Frank Benjamin of the Royal Engineers, and they continued their training with the Eighth Army in Italy. In early 1945, the soldiers of the Jewish Brigade saw their first fighting at Alfonsine, and in April 1945 they led the offensive across the Senio River.

As they moved into northern Italy, the Jewish soldiers met Holocaust survivors for the first time; thereafter they provided them with food, clothing, and assistance immigrating to Palestine. They continued these activities in Belgium, Austria, Germany, and Holland and also assisted the Allied authorities in searching for Holocaust survivors.

In 1946, the Jewish Brigade was disbanded, partly because of increasing tension between the Yishuv and the mandatory authorities.

See also JEWISH AGENCY FOR PALESTINE; YISHUV.

Bibliography

Beckman, Morris. *The Jewish Brigade: An Army with Two Masters, 1944–1945.* Staplehurst: Spellmount, 1998.

Blum, Howard. *The Brigade: An Epic Story of Vengeance, Salvation and World War II.* New York: HarperCollins, 2001.

Rabinowitz, Louis. *Soldiers from Judaea, Palestinian Jewish Units in the Middle East, 1941–1943.* New York: American Zionist Emergency Council, 1945.

BRYAN DAVES

JEWISH COLONIAL TRUST

Financial organ of the Zionist movement.

The Jewish Colonial Trust (JCT) was established in England in 1899. The first Zionist Congress (1897) had created the World Zionist Organization; the JCT was one of two subsidiaries subsequently set up in order to promote Jewish settlement in Palestine. The JCT was in charge of banking operations and of colonization projects in Palestine. It set up the Anglo–Palestine Bank, which virtually became the official bank of the Jewish national home, as a subsidiary. By 1936 it was the second largest bank in Palestine (after Barclay's). The other subsidiary, the Jewish National Fund, was responsible for the purchase of land that was to become the inalienable property of the Jewish people.

See also BANKING; JEWISH NATIONAL FUND; WORLD ZIONIST ORGANIZATION (WZO).

JENAB TUTUNJI

JEWISH COLONIZATION ASSOCIATION

Philanthropic organization (also known as the ICA and the PICA, or Palestine Jewish Colonization Association) founded in 1891.

Baron Maurice de Hirsch founded the ICA to assist Jews in Europe and Asia to flee persecution and go to countries in the Western Hemisphere. He initially endowed it with $10 million as a joint stock company, and the amount was eventually increased fourfold. The ICA assisted Jews by establishing agricultural settlements; most of these were in Argentina but there were also some in Brazil. It also helped Jewish farmers in Canada and the United States and provided assistance to Jews who were still living in Russia and the newly created states of Eastern Europe after World War I. In Palestine, the ICA took over the support and consolidation of colonies Baron Edmond de Rothschild had created.

Since Israeli statehood, the ICA has helped support settlements as well as research and training in agriculture. It also works with the Hebrew Immigrant Aid Society and the Joint Distribution Committee in providing relief aid.

See also JOINT DISTRIBUTION COMMITTEE.

Bibliography

Winsberg, Morton D. *Colonia Baron Hirsch: A Jewish Agricultural Colony in Argentina.* Gainesville: University of Florida Press, 1964.

BRYAN DAVES

JEWISH LEGION

Four battalions of Jewish volunteers in the British army during World War I.

On the urging of Russian Zionist Vladimir Ze'ev Jabotinsky, Jewish units were formed to serve in the British army during World War I. The "Zion Mule Corps" consisted of 650 Palestinian Jews; it served in Gallipoli and was disbanded in 1916. The Thirty-eighth Battalion Royal Fusiliers (800 men) was recruited in England mainly from Russian immigrants, and was sent to Egypt and then Palestine in February 1918. The Thirty-ninth Battalion Royal Fusiliers enlisted some 2,000 men in the United States under the leadership of David Ben-Gurion, Yizhak Ben-Zvi, and Pinhas Rutenberg. It arrived in Egypt in August 1918 and was sent to Palestine. The Fortieth Battalion Royal Fusiliers was recruited from Palestinian Jews in British-controlled southern Palestine in July 1918. Commanded by Lieutenant Colonel John Henry Patterson, these units of the Jewish Legion participated in Edmund Allenby's campaigns in Palestine and Syria in 1918. At the end of the war, the Thirty-eighth and Thirty-ninth battalions were disbanded, but the 1,000 men of the Fortieth Battalion remained in active service as part of the British forces in Palestine until after the riots of May 1921.

Proponents of Zionism believed that if their volunteers supported Britain in World War I, it would reflect favorably on their aspirations for a national home in Palestine. A decidedly practical result was that members of the Jewish Legion—including Berl Katznelson, Shmuel Yavnieli, Dov Hos, Eliahu Golomb, and Levi Eshkol—gained valuable organizational and military experience and later formed the nucleus of the future Jewish army in Palestine, the Haganah.

Bibliography

Ben-Gurion, David. *Letters to Paula,* translated by Aubrey Hodes. Pittsburgh: University of Pittsburgh Press; London: Vallentine Mitchell, 1971.

Fromkin, David. *A Peace to End All Peace: The Fall of the Ottoman Empire and the Creation of the Modern Middle East.* New York: Henry Holt, 1989.

Schechtman, Joseph B. *The Vladimir Jabotinsky Story,* vol. 2: *Rebel and Statesman: The Early Years.* New York: T. Yoseloff, 1956.

ZACHARY KARABELL
UPDATED BY NEIL CAPLAN

JEWISH NATIONAL FUND

Land-purchase and development fund of the World Zionist Organization.

The Jewish National Fund (JNF), or Keren Kayemet le-Yisrael in Hebrew, was set up in 1901. Its primary aim was to buy land in Palestine for the "eternal possession" of the Jewish people. The concept of public ownership was based on the biblical injunction that the land of Israel belongs to God and that it may be leased for forty-nine years.

Funds raised by Jews all over the world were used to buy land in Palestine for Jewish settlements. The first land was bought in 1904 at Kfar Hittim in lower Galilee. The first forest was planted by the JNF in 1908; this became a major activity of the JNF after the establishment of the State of Israel. By 1960 the JNF had 637,000 acres of land, and control of these was passed to a body set up by the government of Israel. This constituted 10 percent of the area of Israel. Since the 1990s the JNF has built reservoirs and has become involved in river rehabilitation in addition to its traditional functions of afforestation and the creation of parks. In 1997, the JNF opposed proposals set forth in a government-sponsored report to privatize the ownership of its land, on which hundreds of thousands of Israelis live.

Bibliography

Zvi Shilony. "Ideology and Settlement: The Jewish National Fund 1887–1914." Available at <http//:www.jnf.org>.

PAUL RIVLIN

JEWISH SETTLEMENTS

See ISRAELI SETTLEMENTS

JEWS IN THE MIDDLE EAST

History of Jewish presence in the area from 2000 B.C.E.

The origins of the Jewish people are in the Middle East. Earliest Jewish history dates from the second millennium B.C.E.and its echoes appear in the Hebrew Bible. The Bible also recounts the vicissitudes of national life in ancient Israel and the evolution of Judaism. By the time of the Romans' expansion and their destruction of the Second Jewish Commonwealth in 70 C.E., Jews were living in much of the Middle East and some had moved into the western Roman Empire—Europe. The foundations of post–Second Temple Judaism were then laid by rabbis in Roman Palestine and in Parthian and Sassanian Babylonia. They canonized the Scripture, redacted the liturgy, and created the Talmud and Midrash.

Beginnings of Muslim Rule

With the conquests of Islam from the seventh century on, the majority of world Jewry came under Muslim rule. The demographic centers of world Jewry were located in the Middle East and the Maghrib, which included North Africa and Muslim regions of the Iberian Peninsula. Jewish merchants kept records in Arabic rendered in Hebrew script, and major rabbinic works in Judeo-Arabic were written by luminaries such as Saʿadyah Gaon in Iraq or Maimonides in Egypt. Jews in Persia also developed a Judeo-Persian literature.

In the later Middle Ages, the quality of Jewish life in the Middle East declined following transformed economic, social, and intellectual climates in the region. Native Christianity disappeared from the Maghrib and general attitudes toward non-Muslims hardened both there and further east. The laws of differentiation (in Arabic, *ghiyar*) were enforced with greater vigor and consistency than in earlier periods. Over time, Jews were increasingly confined by law or custom to restricted quarters, called *mellah* in Morocco, *qaʿat al-Yahud* in Yemen, *mahallat* in Iran, and *harat al-Yahud* elsewhere.

The arrival, beginning in the fifteenth century, of Sephardim—Jewish refugees from Christian Spain, Portugal, and Sicily—and the Ottoman conquest of much of the region in the early sixteenth century

After World War II, many Jewish emigrants fled to Israel to escape physical and religious persecution. Between 1948 and 1951, over 650,000 Jews immigrated to Israel, many, such as these Yemenite Jews, from other Middle Eastern countries. © PHOTOGRAPH BY DAVID ELDAN. GOVERNMENT PRESS OFFICE (GPO) OF ISRAEL. REPRODUCED BY PERMISSION.

breathed new demographic, economic, and cultural life into Middle Eastern Jewry. Jews in many eastern Mediterranean cities continued to speak Judeo-Spanish (Ladino). Some wealthy Sephardic families were intermediaries linking European commerce with local economies, but in time this niche was lost to Armenians, Greeks, and Levantine Christians. Most Jews, artisans and petty merchants, were poor. Culturally, Sephardic rabbinic codification and mystical exploration continued to evolve.

In the nineteenth century expanding European economies in the area enabled Jewish and Christian merchants to link up with European consular interests or seek foreign protection that became available under the Capitulations (in Turkish, *imtiyazat*). At the same time, many came to enjoy improved civil status in the Ottoman Empire under the Tanzimat reforms. They also availed themselves of Western education provided by foreign cultural and religious missionaries. From 1862 on, the Alliance Israélite Universelle (AIU) was the main propagator of the French language and European-style education among Jews from Morocco to Iran. By 1900 more than 100,000 students had studied

Jews attend a synagogue in Baghdad. Until 1947, over one hundred thousand Jews lived in Iraq, but after Arab-Jewish hostilities mounted over the creation of the State of Israel in 1948, most fled to Israel. © FANCOISE DE MULDER/CORBIS. REPRODUCED BY PERMISSION.

in AIU schools. The AIU stressed Enlightenment values, created new expectations, and aroused feelings of international Jewish solidarity. It produced cadres of Westernized Jews with a social advantage over Muslims who lacked such education, as the Middle East was drawn into world capitalism. Educational mobility led to geographical mobility as Jews in the region moved from areas of lesser economic opportunity such as Morocco, Syria, and the Turkish Aegean isles to areas of European economic concentration such as Algeria and Egypt. Others emigrated to Europe and South America. Jews from Iraq settled in ports in India, Burma, Malaysia, and China.

Against the backdrop of these trends, Jews were incorporated into different political frameworks during the nineteenth and twentieth centuries. In Algeria they were French citizens from 1870; in Tunisia, after the French Protectorate in 1883,

some could apply for citizenship, and eventually about one-third of them did so; Syrian Jews lived under a French mandate after World War I; in Iraq, they were citizens of an independent Arab state from 1932; and in Yemen, Jews retained the status of *dhimmi* in a Muslim polity until they began to migrate to Israel after 1948. Within these diverse conditions Jews exhibited a range of cultural and political responses.

AIU education partially separated Jews from local Muslims and heightened their receptivity to French colonialism in the Maghrib, Syria, and Lebanon. With some exceptions, such as Ya'qub Sanu, the father of modern Arab theater and political journalism in Egypt, and Albert Carasso, active in the Young Turk movement, Jews were not prominent in the intellectual and political currents developing in the Islamic world. In Iraq, only a handful of Jewish writers wrote in literary Arabic.

Rise of Zionism

A small number of Jews were touched by the Haskala, the Hebrew-language Enlightenment of mid- to late-nineteenth-century Europe. Books and newspapers in Hebrew circulated throughout Middle Eastern communities. A Judeo-Arabic press was active in some countries, notably Tunisia. Newspapers made Jews of the region aware of currents sweeping others parts of the Jewish world, including migration, religious reform, and Zionism.

From its very earliest days, Zionism made modest inroads into major urban centers in the Middle East. Sympathy for the movement was often philanthropic rather than political. Zionism did arouse popular enthusiasm in the wake of the 1917 Balfour Declaration, the Allied victory in World War I, and the San Remo Conference in 1920. In 1917 thousands of Jews gathered in Cairo and Alexandria in support of the Balfour Declaration, and similar scenes greeted Chaim Weizmann and the Zionist Commission for Palestine when they passed through Egypt the following year. Several hundred Jewish families emigrated from Morocco to mandatory Palestine between 1919 and 1923, to the chagrin of French colonial authorities. About 1,000 Jews from Iraq and smaller numbers from Syria settled in Palestine at this time. Others arrived from Libya in the 1930s as part of sports events, and stayed in the country. There had been a stream of Jews from Yemen to Palestine, totaling several thousand from 1880 to 1929, when the imam of Yemen ordered an end to the emigration.

The initial enthusiasm for Zionism subsided due to opposition from colonial authorities, members of the Jewish upper classes, and, most importantly, growing Arab and pan-Islamic nationalist movements. With rare exceptions, such as Sasson Heskayl, who served as Iraq's first finance minister; Joseph Aslan Cattaoui, who was Egypt's minister of finance in 1923 and minister of communications in 1925; or Léon Castro, editor of the Egyptian Wafd Party's French-language daily *La Liberté,* Jews in the Muslim world were studiously apolitical, especially in Arab countries. From the time of the Western Wall riots in Jerusalem in 1929, Arab nationalism became increasingly anti-Zionist, and, despite frequent disclaimers, both nationalist leaders and followers often merged anti-Zionism with antisemitism.

A Jewish wedding ceremony in Syria in 1988. Syrian Jews, referred to by the government as "follows of Moses" rather than "Jews," were treated as a suspicious religious community and are under constant surveillance by the police. © Corbis Sygma. Reproduced by permission.

In the 1930s and 1940s the growing admiration among Arabs for German national socialism and Italian fascism, which stood in opposition to the colonial powers of Great Britain and France, discouraged Jews from finding a place in the societies that Arab nationalists wanted to create. In Turkey, too, some Jews were affected by the Axis sympathies of the government that at times was paralleled by discrimination against nonethnic Turks.

World War II affected Jews in the Muslim world in various ways. In June 1941, at the end of the short-lived pro-Axis regime of Rashid Ali a-Kaylani, Iraqi Jewry suffered a pogrom called the Farhud; Jews in Libya became subject to racial laws enacted in Italy;

and Vichy, France, rescinded the citizenship of Jews in Algeria. Jews in Egypt and Mandatory Palestine felt deeply threatened by the German Afrika Korps advancing into western Egypt. Throughout the Middle East, Jews had heard the mufti of Jerusalem, Hajj Muhammad Amin al-Husayni, broadcast in Arabic from Berlin, calling upon listeners to "kill the Jews wherever you find them, for the love of God, history, and religion." Many Jews began to ponder their future in the region both in relation to European colonial powers and to the local Muslim societies.

Post–World War II

The postwar years witnessed a renewal of pan-Islam and pan-Arabism on the one hand and Jewish nationalism on the other. A rapid chain of events undermined the weakened underpinnings of Jewish life in the Arab countries. Anti-Jewish riots occurred in Egypt and Libya in November 1945. In December 1947, following the United Nations partition vote on Palestine, riots rocked Jewish communities in Aden, Bahrain, and Aleppo. With the establishment of the state of Israel in May 1948, restrictive administrative measures were imposed on Jews in Egypt, Syria, and Iraq, both during and after the Arab–Israel War of 1948. From May 1948 through 1951 more than 650,000 Jews migrated to Israel, half of them from the Middle East. Major migrations from Morocco and Tunisia arrived in the mid-1950s and early 1960s. By 1967 the majority of the 800,000 Jews in Arab countries at mid-twentieth century had left. During this period, half of Turkey's 80,000 Jews and about one third of Iran's 100,000 Jews departed for Israel, but others, including nearly half of Maghribi Jewry, went to France and elsewhere.

By the 1980s Jews of Middle Eastern origin—*adot ha-mizrah*—comprised well over half of Israel's Jewish population. Migration to Israel by Jews from the former Soviet Union made the percentages of Middle Eastern and European origin groups equal in the 1990s. By 2000 the Jewish community in Turkey stood at about 20,000. Iranian Jewry functioned actively until the revolution of 1979 that established the Islamic republic. Jews then immigrated to Israel, Europe, and the United States, and in 1989 about 22,000 remained in Iran. Very few Jews now reside in the Arab world; the largest group—

about 3,500—lives in Morocco. Since the 1980s Morocco has encouraged Jewish tourists from Israel and elsewhere, and Tunisia has done the same since the 1990s.

See also ADOT HA-MIZRAH; ALLIANCE ISRAÉLITE UNIVERSELLE (AIU); ANTISEMITISM; ARAB–ISRAEL WAR (1948); BALFOUR DECLARATION (1917); CAPITULATIONS; DHIMMA; FARHUD; HASKALAH; HESKAYL, SASSON; JUDAISM; LADINO; MIZRAHI MOVEMENT; SAN REMO CONFERENCE (1920); SANU, YA'QUB; TALMUD; UNITED NATIONS AND THE MIDDLE EAST; WEIZMANN, CHAIM; ZIONISM; ZIONIST COMMISSION FOR PALESTINE.

Bibliography

Goldberg, Harvey E., ed. *Sephardi and Middle Eastern Jewries: History and Culture in the Modern Era.* Bloomington: Indiana University Press, 1996.

Lewis, Bernard. *The Jews of Islam.* Princeton, NJ: Princeton University Press, 1984.

Simon, Reeva S.; Laskier, Michael M.; and Reguer, Sara, eds. *The Jews of the Middle East and North Africa in Modern Times.* New York: Columbia University Press, 2002.

Stillman, Norman. "Fading Shadows of the Past: Jews in the Islamic World." In *Survey of Jewish Affairs 1989,* edited by William Frankel. Oxford, U.K.: Oxford University Press, 1989.

Stillman, Norman. *The Jews of Arab Lands: A History and Source Book.* Philadelphia: Jewish Publication Society, 1979.

Stillman, Norman. *The Jews of Arab Lands in Modern Times.* Philadelphia: Jewish Publication Society, 1991.

NORMAN STILLMAN
UPDATED BY HARVEY E. GOLDBERG

JEZREEL VALLEY

A major internal plain stretching almost 30 miles (48 kilometers) across northern Israel, from the northwestern base of Mount Carmel to the Jordan Valley.

The Jezreel Valley is called, in Hebrew, *Emek Yizre'el*; in Arabic, *Marj ibn Amir*; and in English, the Plain of Esdraelon. Its larger, western portion is based on the westward flowing Kishon (Muqatta) River, while its smaller, eastern portion is based on the eastward flowing Harod (Jalud) River. Separating the hills of the lower Galilee in the north from the Carmel ridge and Samarian hills (Jabal Nablus) in the south, the valley has been a natural route for travelers, merchants, nomads, and armies for thousands of years. Its agricultural land has consistently been cultivated by surrounding hill settlements.

Named for the ancient Israelite city of Yizreʿel (Hebrew for "may god sow"), the valley has supported varying levels of population throughout history. The dense habitation of pre-Crusader times later gave way to a thinner population and the emergence of marshland, both of which fluctuated historically and seasonally. During British rule in Palestine, Zionist organizations purchased parts of the valley and undertook Jewish settlement and marshland drainage, resulting in the rapid increase of its predominantly European-born Jewish population alongside the local Arab population. The events surrounding the 1948 war and the establishment of Israel resulted in a sharp decrease in the valley's Arab population and another increase in its Jewish population. The 1949 Israeli-Jordanian armistice lines cut across the southeastern valley just north of Jenin, leaving most of the valley within the borders of Israel and a small portion in the West Bank.

Bibliography

Naor, Mordechai. *The Jezreel Valley, 1900–1967: Sources, Summaries, Selected Episodes and Material.* Jerusalem: Yad Izhak Ben-Tzvi, 1993.

Smith, George Adam. *The Historical Geography of the Holy Land: Especially in Relation to the History of Israel and the Early Church,* 22d edition. London: Hodder and Stoughton, 1896.

GEREMY FORMAN

JIBRIL, AHMAD

[1935–]

Palestinian militant.

Born in Ramla, Ahmad Jibril found himself in Syria after the Palestinian refugee exodus of 1948. He served in the Syrian army and was the national chess champion of Syria in 1956. He left the army in 1958 and formed the Palestinian Liberation Front in 1961. The organization began military operations in 1965, and merged with the Popular Front for the Liberation of Palestine (PFLP) in December 1967.

Jibril left the PFLP in November 1968 out of frustration at the group's preoccupation with ideological debates, and formed the Popular Front for the Liberation of Palestine–General Command, a nonpolitical, armed organization dedicated to fighting Israel. Jibril helped form the Rejectionist Front in 1974 along with the PFLP and several other groups.

Jibril's PFLP–GC was responsible for the April 1974 terrorist attack against the Israeli town of Kiryat Shmona, in which eighteen Israelis died. A 1987 operation in which a fighter flew into Israel on a hang-glider and killed six Israeli soldiers helped spark the first Intifada. Jibril's group also fought against Palestine Liberation Organization (PLO) loyalists in Lebanon in 1983 in support of a Syrian-backed mutiny, and has consistently opposed PLO policy ever since from his headquarters in Damascus.

See also PALESTINE LIBERATION ORGANIZATION (PLO); POPULAR FRONT FOR THE LIBERATION OF PALESTINE–GENERAL COMMAND.

Bibliography

Sayigh, Yezid. *Armed Struggle and the Search for State: The Palestinian National Movement, 1949–1993.* London and New York: Oxford University Press, 1997.

LAWRENCE TAL
UPDATED BY MICHAEL R. FISCHBACH

JIDDA

Saudi Arabian port on the Red Sea.

Jidda is the second largest city of Saudi Arabia, with a population of some two million. It is also the largest city of the Hijaz, located in the country's western region, along the Red Sea. Its prosperity dates from its designation by the early Islamic state as the port of nearby Mecca. Jidda was occupied by the first Saudi state at the beginning of the nineteenth century, then Muhammad Ali of Egypt restored it to nominal Ottoman authority in 1811. It was the last city in the short-lived Hashimite kingdom of Hijaz to resist the Al Saʿud, finally surrendering after a long siege in 1925. Jidda is important as the commercial and banking center of the country, the site of the Islamic Port of Jidda (Saudi Arabia's largest port) and King Abd al-Aziz Airport, through which most of the pilgrims pass during the annual *hajj* (pilgrimage). The centuries-old immigration of Muslims from around the world makes Jidda one of the most cosmopolitan of Saudi Arabia's cities.

Bibliography

Farsy, Fouad al-. *Modernity and Tradition: The Saudi Equation.* London: Kegan Paul International, 1991.

J. E. PETERSON

JIHAD

A term that derives from the Arabic word jahada, *meaning "to strive."*

The Arabic nouns *juhd, mujahid, jihad,* and *ijtihad* mean endeavor, training, exertion, effort, diligence, and fighting. "Traditionally jihad was understood to be justified for three reasons: to repel invasion or its threat, to punish those who had violated treaties, and to guarantee freedom for the propagation of Islam" (Abedi). According to Iranian ayatollah Morteza Mutahhari, Jihad as a defensive act is explained in the *Hajj sura* 22:38–41, where it is said that God gives permission (for warfare) to those who have been attacked. In an Islamic legal context, the term *jihad* is most often used to refer to a martial campaign in the cause of religion and is therefore frequently translated as "holy war." Many now would argue that there is no such thing as a holy war, and that Islam does not sanction war but rather defense of Islamic values (this is certainly the case in the longest conventional war between two Muslim nations, Iran and Iraq, 1980–1988). Iran called the war a sacred defense rather than a jihad.

According to classical Muslim legal theory, the only kind of lawful military conflict is jihad, and a jihad can only be used to fulfill at least one of two main objectives. The first is the effective spread of Muslim ideals and values into a region of society unmoved by the call to Islam. The second is defense of the Muslim community from external threats. In addition to discussing the conditions necessary to establish these objectives, Muslim teachings on jihad also deal with important related issues such as the immunity of noncombatants, ethical restrictions on the applications of destructive force, and the circumstances warranting armistice. In fact, the doctrine of jihad is probably best understood as being

similar to the "just war" theory in Western Christian contexts. Over the course of the twentieth century, jihad discourse was polarized by modernists like Muhammad Shaltut (died 1963) who argue that, in the modern era, offensive jihad should only take the form of a peaceful propagation of Islam, and revolutionary Islamist groups such as Islamic Jihad, HAMAS, and Hizbullah, which maintain that Muslims around the world are obliged to use any available means to fight against the forces of Western imperialism.

Bibliography

Abedi, Mehdi, and Legenhausen, Gary, eds. *Jihād and Shahādat: Struggle and Martyrdom in Islam.* Houston, TX: Institute for Research and Islamic Studies, 1986.

Mutahhari, Morteza. *Jihad: The Holy War in Islam and the Legitimacy in the Qur'an,* translated by Mohammad Salman Tawhidi. Tehran, Iran: Islamic Propagation Organization, 1998.

SCOTT ALEXANDER
UPDATED BY ROXANNE VARZI

JINNAH, MUHAMMAD ALI
[1876–1948]

Founder and first governor-general of Pakistan.

Muhammad Ali Jinnah was born in Karachi in 1876 and died in the same city in 1948, while serving as governor-general of Pakistan. Originally, Jinnah had stood for a united India, but when Muhammad Iqbal, the poet-philosopher, articulated the two-nation theory in 1930, Jinnah adopted the theory as his own political ideology. He helped to achieve the foundation of the state of Pakistan in 1947 through negotiations with the All-India National Congress and the British government.

Jinnah went to London in 1893, studied law at Lincoln's Inn, and qualified as a barrister (attorney) on 11 May 1896. He settled in Bombay, India, actively practicing law through the 1930s. His political career can be divided into phases. In the first phase, from 1906 to 1937, Jinnah was a member of the National Congress and called himself "an Indian first, and a Muslim afterwards." He was opposed initially to the Muslim demand for separate electorates, but in 1926 he shifted his support to the principle of separate electorates that guaranteed fixed proportional representation for Hindus and

Muslims in legislatures. Despite this shift, Jinnah asserted that Muslims' rights and interests would be protected in a united India. In the second phase, from 1937 to 1947, Jinnah's position reversed completely. His dissatisfaction started with Mohandas (Mahatma) Gandhi's position at the London Round-table Conference (1939) and spread to frustration with the Muslim League, the British government's communal award based on the principle of separate electorates, the ultimatum to the Muslim League to merge with the National Congress in order to participate in provincial governments in 1937, and the suggestion of majority rule to the neglect of the Muslims, which probably convinced Jinnah that the National Congress was determined to establish majority Hindu rule in a united India.

In the second phase of his career Jinnah endeavored to create a separate Pakistani state with the approval of the British and the National Congress. In March 1942 at Lahore the Muslim League adopted the Pakistan Resolution, which demanded the partitioning of India into two states. In February 1942 the British government sent to India a prominent minister, Sir Stafford Cripps, to secure the cooperation of the Indian leaders for the defense of India. Muslims were assured that "dissident provinces" would be free to leave an independent and united India. Cripps's mission failed, but Jinnah saw Pakistan in Cripps's proposals.

In May 1946 the British sent the cabinet mission to India to negotiate a constitutional formula for the transfer of power to India. The cabinet mission plan divided India into three zones: Hindu majority provinces (present-day India); Muslim provinces in the Northwest (Pakistan); and Bengal and Assam, where Muslims would have a slim majority. Provinces could opt out of the plan to form a new federation after ten years. Jinnah accepted the proposal, and so did the congress. When the congress president publicly expressed reservations in implementing the plan, Jinnah rejected the plan, making the state of Pakistan a reality on 14 August 1947.

See also IQBAL, MUHAMMAD; PAKISTAN AND THE MIDDLE EAST.

Bibliography

Malik, Hafeez. *Muslim Nationalism in India and Pakistan.* Washington, DC: Public Affairs Press, 1963.

Mujahid, Sharif al-. *Quaid-i-Azam Jinnah: Studies in Interpretation.* Karachi: Quaid-i-Azam Academy, 1981.

Wolpert, Stanley. *Jinnah of Pakistan.* New York: Oxford University Press, 1984.

HAFEEZ MALIK

JIZYA

A poll tax.

Several poll taxes were levied throughout the Middle East from the time of the Muslim conquests (seventh century). Caliph Umar II (717–720 C.E.) established the principle that they should be levied only on non-Muslims. Islam exempted women, children, and the disabled or unemployed from the tax.

In 1855, the Ottoman Empire abolished the tax, as part of reforms to equalize the status of Muslims and non-Muslims. It was replaced, however, by a military-exemption tax on non-Muslims, the Bedel-i Askeri.

See also BEDEL-I ASKERI.

Bibliography

Lapidus, Ira M. *A History of Islamic Societies,* 2d edition. Cambridge, U.K., and New York: Cambridge University Press, 2002.

Lewis, Bernard. *The Emergence of Modern Turkey,* 3d edition. New York: Oxford University Press, 2002.

ELIZABETH THOMPSON

JMA'A TRIBAL COUNCIL

North African Berber political unit.

In precolonial North Africa, Jma'a represented the highest political authority in the tribe, led by an *amghar* (chief). During periods of war, the *amghar* became the chief of war (*amghar n-l-baroud*). Each subtribe had its representative in the Jma'a. In the contemporary period, although some villages still have a Jma'a, its functions have been, however, reconciled to the management of collective social events.

RAHMA BOURQIA

JOHNSON–CROSBIE COMMITTEE REPORT (1930)

A survey in Palestine.

The Johnson–Crosbie committee collected data from 25,573 Palestinian Arab families in 104 villages. The report calculated that Arab peasant debt per family averaged 27 Palestinian pounds, the equivalent of a year's income. It also found that the average cultivator held a mere 56 *dunums* (14 acres; 6 ha) whereas 75 *dunums* (18.5 acres; 7.5 ha) were required for basic economic maintenance. The survey was conducted by William Johnson and Robert Crosbie, officials in the British administration in Palestine.

Bibliography

Khalaf, Issa. *Politics in Palestine: Arab Factionalism and Social Disintegration, 1939–1948.* Albany: State University of New York Press, 1991.

ELIZABETH THOMPSON

JOHNSON, LYNDON BAINES

[1908–1973]

U.S. president, 1963–1969.

Lyndon Baines Johnson succeeded to the presidency after the assassination of John F. Kennedy in November 1963. Although a long-time member of the U.S. House of Representatives (1937–1949) and U.S. Senate (1949–1961), and a most effective legislative leader, he had little experience in foreign affairs. With an escalating war in Vietnam, the Middle East had low priority for him.

He was unable to persuade Egypt to limit its armament program; to balance U.S.S.R. arms sales to Egypt, Syria, Iraq and elsewhere, Johnson authorized increased military sales to Israel and to conservative Arab regimes, particularly to King Hussein ibn Talal of Jordan. When Egypt blocked the Strait of Tiran to Israeli shipping in May 1967, Johnson denounced the act as illegal. During the Arab–Israel War of June 1967, Johnson kept the United States neutral, although American sympathies were clearly with Israel. Through his ambassador to the United Nations, Arthur Goldberg, Johnson gave crucial support to UN Resolution 242, passed in November 1967, which has been the keystone of Arab–

Israeli diplomacy since then. In 1968, Johnson declined renomination for another term.

See also ARAB–ISRAEL WAR (1967); HUSSEIN IBN TALAL.

Bibliography

Safran, Nadav. *Israel: The Embattled Ally.* Cambridge, MA: Belknap Press, 1981.

Spiegel, Steven. *The Other Arab–Israeli Conflict: Making America's Middle East Policy, from Truman to Reagan.* Chicago: University of Chicago Press, 1985.

ZACHARY KARABELL

JOHNSTON PLAN (1953)

Development plan for the Jordan River.

This comprehensive plan was drawn up by U.S. Special Ambassador Eric Johnston in 1953, for regional development of the Jordan River system. The hope was that it would reduce regional conflicts by promoting cooperation and economic stability. The two major riparians—Israel and the Kingdom of Jordan—had their own plans for water development, but each objected to the other's plan. Eric Johnston attempted to reach a unified plan through negotiations that dealt with water quotas, use of Jordan water for outside the water-basin area, use of the Sea of Galilee (also called Lake Tiberias or Lake Kinneret) as a storage area, incorporating the Litani River into the Jordan system, and international supervision.

Negotiations lasted from 1953 to 1955 and the Unified Plan was negotiated, with Johnston playing the key role in pushing the compromises along. The Unified Plan was accepted by the technical committees of the League of Arab States (Arab League) and Israel. Israel's government informed the United States that it would accept the plan, but in October 1955, the Arabs decided not to ratify it. In fact, there has been implementation of the Johnston Plan on the part of Israel and separately by Jordan.

See also GALILEE, SEA OF; LEAGUE OF ARAB STATES.

Bibliography

Reguer, Sara. "Controversial Waters: Thirty Years of Exploitation of the Jordan River, 1950–1980." *Middle Eastern Studies* (spring 1993).

Sherman, Martin. *The Politics of Water in the Middle East: An Israeli Perspective on the Hydro-Political Aspects of the Conflict.* New York: St. Martin's, 1999.

SARA REGUER

JOHN XIX

113th Coptic patriarch of Egypt, 1928–1942.

The successor of Cyril V (1874–1927), John XIX had an uneventful patriarchate. He had been chosen by Cyril to be the *abuna* (archbishop) of the Ethiopian Orthodox Church but declined the offer. For many years metropolitan (chief bishop) of the Egyptian provinces of Behariya and Minufiyya, in 1892 he went into exile after a dispute with the Coptic Community Council but eventually regained its favor for his part in reforming the church's handling of bequests and administration of educational institutions. As patriarch, John established near Cairo a theological college to improve their education. He appointed the *abuna* and several bishops of the church in Ethiopia.

See also COPTS; CYRIL V.

Bibliography

Meinardus, Otto F. A. *Christian Egypt: Faith and Life.* Cairo: American University in Cairo Press, 1970.

Shoucri, Mounir. "John XIX." In *The Coptic Encyclopedia,* vol. 4, edited by Aziz S. Atiya. New York: Macmillan, 1991.

DONALD SPANEL

JOINT DISTRIBUTION COMMITTEE

Charitable organization that assists Jews in distress.

The Joint Distribution Committee (JDC) was established in 1914 by a committee of relief agencies, including the American Jewish Relief Committee (affiliated with the American Jewish Committee), the Central Relief Committee (part of the Orthodox movement), and the People's Relief Committee (affiliated with American labor groups). Initially, the JDC assisted Jews in central and eastern Europe before, during, and after World War I, and later it helped reconstruct the Jewish communities in those regions. Before and during World War II, the JDC worked to rescue Jews from Nazi-occupied Europe;

after the war, it assisted in the resettlement of displaced persons. Thereafter, the JDC focused its attention on helping the Jews of central and eastern Europe and those in Muslim countries. In 1991 it helped the Israeli government airlift nearly 15,000 Ethiopian Jews from Ethiopia to Israel.

In the early years of the twenty-first century the JDC, in response to a rising level of terrorist attacks in Israeli cities, funded activities for Israeli children who were left alone in the afternoon while their parents worked. It also became active in helping the Jewish community in Argentina, hit by the economic crisis there, setting up a soup kitchen for Jewish and non-Jewish children.

Bibliography

Handlin, Oscar. *A Continuing Task: American Jewish Joint Distribution Committee, 1914–1964.* New York: Random House, 1964.

BRYAN DAVES
UPDATED BY PAUL RIVLIN

JORDAN

A small Arab kingdom east of the Mediterranean Sea.

Jordan is bordered on the north by Syria, on the east by Iraq, on the south by Saudi Arabia, and on the west by Israel and the West Bank. The Gulf of Aqaba, an extension of the Red Sea, abuts its southernmost tip. To the west, it shares the Dead Sea (an inland salt lake) with Israel and the West Bank. Jordan is a crossroads in the region: The hajj (Islamic pilgrimage) route from Turkey and Syria passed through Jordan to the Hijaz and the holy cities of Mecca and Medina. A major trunk road runs from Iraq to Jordan's only port, Aqaba. Oil pipelines, now nonfunctioning, were built from Iraq and Saudi Arabia across Jordan to Mediterranean ports. Prior to the establishment of the State of Israel (1948), Jordan (called Transjordan from 1920–1946) was the transit route from Palestinian ports to Iraq, Saudi Arabia, and the Persian/Arabian Gulf. With a population that is about 50 percent Jordanian Arabs and 50 percent Palestinian (most refugees from the first Arab–Israel War of 1948), and a location between Israel and the powerful Arab states, Jordan is frequently buffeted by Middle Eastern and international political currents.

The site of Petra, the ancient city of Arabia, in southwestern Jordan. Once the stronghold city of the Nabataens, Petra was conquered successively by the Romans, the Muslims, and the Crusaders before it fell into ruins after the twelfth century. The fortress was rediscovered in 1812 by the Swiss explorer Johan Burckhardt. REDONDO, CARMEN, PHOTOGRAPHER. FROM A PHOTOGRAPH IN THE ATLAS OF PEOPLE & PLACES, BY PHILIP STEELE. ALADDIN BOOKS LTD., 2002. PHOTOGRAPH © CARMEN REDONDO/CORBIS. REPRODUCED BY PERMISSION.

Geography and Climate

Jordan's landmass, almost 90,649 square kilometers (38,000 square miles), is marked by three distinct geological systems: the Jordan rift valley, the Transjordan plateau, and the Arabian/Syrian desert. At 397 meters (1,302 feet) below the level of the Mediterranean Sea, the Jordan valley contains the Dead Sea, the lowest surface point on the planet (the lowest actual point being beneath the ocean). Since the 1960s, the Jordanians have developed a sophisticated irrigation system in the valley, because it receives little rain. Given the topography and low rainfall, most of Jordan is a classic desert, with only 3 percent arable (partly under irrigation) and 1 percent forested. The Jordan valley is, however, warm in winter, so off-season fruits and vegetables can be produced for temperate markets. To the east of the rift valley, the Transjordan plateau runs like a wedge from the Syrian border to Ma'an in the south of the country. The plateau is composed of broad rolling plains, cut by precipitous valleys or wadis (streambeds that have water only during the rainy season). Rain-fed agriculture and animal husbandry are practiced here. To the east and south of the plateau,

lies the Arabian/Syrian desert, a wasteland only sparsely populated by Bedouin.

Jordan possesses few natural resources; its only significant mineral deposits consist of phosphates, which are mined, and potash, which is extracted from evaporation of Dead Sea water. Jordan has very few petroleum deposits and no coal. Its important rivers are the Yarmuk River (shared with Syria and Israel), the Jordan River, (shared with Israel and the West Bank), and the Zarqa. Except for the small oasis of Azraq in the northeastern desert, Jordan has no natural freshwater lakes. An artificial lake was established behind the King Talal dam on the Zarqa River.

Jordan has a pleasant warm climate with little humidity, but also little precipitation. In the winter in the capital of Amman, the average high temperature is 11 degrees C (52 degrees F) and the average low is 4.4 degrees C (40 degrees F); in the summer they are 30 degrees C (86 degrees F) and 18 degrees C (64 degrees F). In the northern part of the Transjordan plateau, precipitation averages

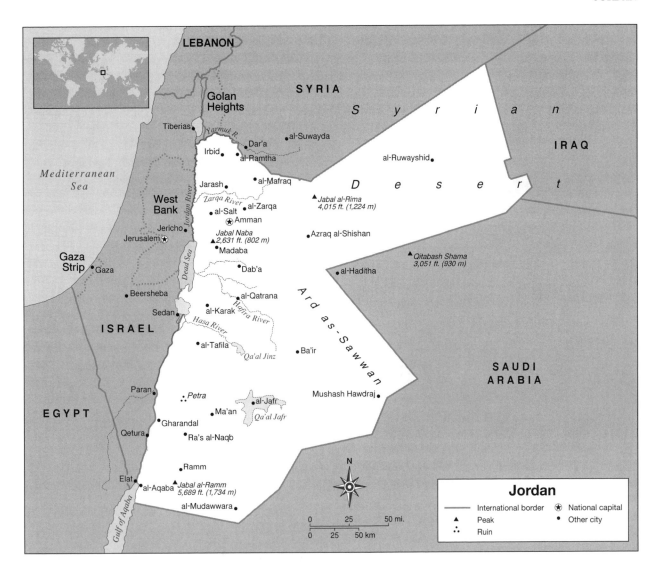

MAP BY XNR PRODUCTIONS, INC. THE GALE GROUP.

64 centimeters (25 inches), but in the southern part it falls to an erratic 25 to 35 centimeters (10 to 14 inches)—barely enough to raise a wheat crop. The desert and the Jordan valley receive 0 to 25 centimeters (0–10 inches) of rain. Typical of the eastern Mediterranean, the precipitation falls only during the late autumn, winter, and early spring—the rainy season.

The People, Language, and Religion

Jordan's population of 5,460,265 (mid-2003 estimate), lives largely in the fertile highlands of the Transjordan plateau. Smaller numbers live in the Jordan valley, where they practice agriculture or mining, and in the desert, where they herd sheep,

goats, and camels or enlist in the military. About 50 percent of the population are Jordanians who originate from the land east of the Jordan river. Most of the balance have their origins in Palestine. Many arrived as refugees in Jordan following the establishment of the State of Israel and the Arab–Israel Wars of 1948 and 1967. Other Palestinians moved to Jordan beginning in the 1950s. As a result of the Gulf Crisis and war, about 300,000 Palestinians with Jordanian citizenship moved from Kuwait back to Jordan, where they increased the population by 9 percent. While relations between the refugees and other Jordanians are relatively amicable today, Palestinian guerrilla organizations did conduct an unsuccessful civil war against the Jor-

A semidesert region in southern Jordan, Wadi Rum boasts sweeping vistas, spectacular rock formations, and towering granite and sandstone cliffs. Once a holy place for Nabataens, Wadi Rum is now inhabited by several Bedouin tribes. © PETER M. WILSON/CORBIS. REPRODUCED BY PERMISSION.

danian regime in 1970 ("Black September"). Both groups are of Arab stock and think of themselves as part of the larger Arab nation.

In terms of minorities, about 5 percent of the population are Arab Christians, mostly Greek Orthodox. They have positive relations with the Muslim majority and hold responsible and high-level positions in business, industry, commerce, banking, and government. Ethnic minority groups are even smaller; among these are Armenian Christians, Chechen Muslims, and Circassian Muslims. Some Circassians are royal palace guards.

The official language of Jordan is Arabic. Throughout the Arab world, although the written language is virtually the same, spoken dialects have developed. The Arabic spoken in Jordan conforms to the general eastern Mediterranean dialect; however, one finds some variations in the spoken lan-

guage between the rural and urban regions, the older and younger generations, and the Jordanians and Palestinians. The influence of modern communications and education is causing many of these differences to be tempered or to disappear. Among the ethnic minority groups, Arabic is spoken in public but their mother tongue is often spoken at home.

Islam is Jordan's official religion. Ninety-five percent of the population are of that faith and almost all are Sunni Muslims. The government supports the established religion through its ministry of Awqaf (Waqf) and Islamic affairs. (Religious pluralism is also officially countenanced; the state recognizes and respects the rights of religious minorities.) Islam deeply affects the lives and behavior of many Jordanians. Praying five times a day, attendance at mosque on Fridays, tithing, fasting during Ramadan, and the Hajj to Mecca are aspired to and practiced by many. The wave of popular Islamic fundamentalism that has affected the Middle East since the 1970s has had its influence in Jordan. Some practice their religion more diligently and demonstrably. Islamic classes and discussions, including informal and formal organizational activities, are popular; some women follow the religious dress code characterized by modest long coats and head scarves.

Jordan is a highly urbanized country. Seven out of every ten Jordanians live in towns of 5,000 or more; the balance resides in villages and encampments. With the return of the Palestinian Jordanians from Kuwait in 1990 and 1991, many of whom settled in Amman, 1,864,500 people lived in that city by 1999. In the 1970s, there was a great contrast between urban and rural living standards. Urbanites enjoyed basic services, such as drinking water and electricity in their homes, with schools and clinics in close proximity to their residences. By the late 1980s, those differences had substantially, but not entirely, disappeared. In urban areas, 99 percent have electricity in their residences; in the rural areas, the figure is 81 percent. For drinking water, the figures are 92 percent and 78 percent respectively. In terms of living space, while there are certainly some crowded quarters in the urban regions, they do not approach the crowded conditions often associated with developing countries. About 10 percent of the people reside in Palestinian refugee camps, where living conditions are congested. In rural areas, around 25 percent live in stone and mud houses; a diminishing number (less than 5 percent) follow the traditional life of the Arab Bedouin, living in tents and tending camels, sheep, and goats.

Jordan is substantially overpopulated, given its limited natural resources, because of the influx of Palestinian refugees and the very high birth rate. This overpopulation is a major reason for the degree of urbanization in the country. Low rainfall and a growing population put pressure on the very limited water supply. Some significant cuts in irrigation have already occurred and more are expected. In addition, as of the early twenty-first century, some 52 percent of the population is below 20 years of age—a heavy burden on the economy and service sector, especially in education.

Economy

Jordan's economy is highly skewed by its growing population and its dependence on the economies and politics of the Middle East. From the period of its gradual independence from Great Britain in the late 1940s and early 1950s, development has been the watchword of Jordan's economy. Beginning from a modest base, it grew by 11 percent per year from 1954 to 1967. During this period, Jordan received considerable economic and financial assistance first from Britain and later from the United States. After a period of decline caused by wars, civil strife, and international and regional constraints, it recommenced steady growth in 1974. This was stimulated by substantial aid and remittances from the oil-rich states of the region, plus a period of relative stability in Jordan and the region. By the mid-1980s, along with the Middle East economy generally, growth slowed to the point of stagnation. In 1988, the Jordanian currency, the dinar, was considered to be overvalued by international financial circles and devalued by 40 percent. This economic decline was exacerbated by the Gulf Crisis and war (1990–1991). Among other things, Jordan lost most of the remittances from the returned Jordanians who had been working in the Persian (Arabian) Gulf states as well as the direct financial aid from those countries.

In terms of both labor force and share of gross national product (GNP), Jordan's economy is dominated by the service sector (over 60 percent in both categories), followed by mining and manufacturing, construction, and agriculture. The service sector overshadows the economy because of the country's relatively large population, high birth rate, number of government employees in both the civilian and military sectors, and the government's successful efforts at extending essential services throughout the country. The mining and manufacturing sector is composed of five large companies—phosphate mining, potash extraction, fertilizer and cement facilities, and an oil refinery (that refines imported oil)—as well as many small factories and artisans. Agriculture, which is usually important in developing countries, claims less than 10 percent of both GNP and the labor force in Jordan.

In the 1990s, Jordan started moving in another economic direction: free trade. After the 1994 peace treaty with Israel, the United States and Jordan established "Qualified Industrial Zones" (QIZs) in the country. Under this system, manufacturers in the twelve QIZs use a combination of Israeli, Jordanian, and West Bank–Gaza materials to manufacture goods that are then exported to the United States duty free. Jordan's exports to the United States grew from $20 million in 1999 to $200 million in 2002. However, only 20 percent of these manufacturers are Jordanian firms, and only one-half of the 20,000 work force in the QIZs are Jordanians. Then in 2000, Jordan signed a Free Trade Agreement with the United States, according to which the two nations pledged to phase out their respective import tariffs over ten years. Jordan's commitment to U.S.–led free trade was symbolized by Jordan's hosting of the World Economic Forum meeting in June 2003. There has been another side of these close economic ties: The United States has provided $3 billion in financial and military aid since 1993, including $700 million as payment for Jordan's role in the 2003 Iraq war. Still, unemployment was about 20 percent in 2003.

History

Throughout most of recorded history, Jordan (formerly Transjordan) was not a distinct geographical or political entity. Rather it was usually just a provincial area of a larger state or empire. The exceptions might be the biblical Moabite kingdom centered in what is now Karak, the Nabatean trading state ruled from its unique capital carved out of the rose-colored stone cliffs of Petra, and the Crusader state led by Renard de Châtillon, who built a large citadel in Karak. Otherwise, the area was ruled successively by the Hittites, Egyptians, Assyrians, Babylonians, Persians, Israelites, Greeks, Seleucids, Ptolemies, Romans, Byzantines, and the Muslim dynasties (Umayyads, Abbasids, Fatimids, Ayyubids, and Mamluks). In 1517 the Ottoman Empire established control in the region that would endure until the last days of World War I.

After World War I, Transjordan came under the British-sponsored rule of King Faisal I ibn Hussein and the short-lived United Syrian Kingdom. In July 1920, France drove Faisal out of Syria and took control of most of the Arab kingdom, while Britain continued to claim Transjordan, as prescribed in the secret French–British Sykes-Picot Agreement. In the meantime, Faisal's brother, Amir Abdullah I ibn Hussein, arrived in Maʿan with an entourage of followers in the fall of 1920. In 1921, British colonial secretary Winston Churchill accepted Abdullah as the ruler of Transjordan under the League of Nations Mandate System for Britain (while Faisal was made ruler of Iraq). Amir Abdullah, with the crucial cooperation and financial help of Britain, established the basic institutions of the state—a government, parliament (Council of Notables, later replaced by the Legislative Council in 1928), a constitution (the Organic Law in 1928), and a security force (the Arab Legion). After World War II, in 1946, an Anglo-Jordanian treaty was signed, to be revised in 1948—after which the emirate of Transjordan became the Hashimite Kingdom of Jordan and Abdullah was crowned king.

In May 1948, Jordan, along with several other Arab states, entered Palestine and joined the Arab–Israel War of 1948 six months after fighting first broke out between Jewish forces and local Palestinians. In 1949, at the end of the war, Jordan was in military possession of that portion of central Palestine that came to be called the West Bank. Following considerable political maneuvering and parliamentary elections on the East Bank (of the Jordan river—the old Transjordan) and the West Bank, the two entities were coupled via a parliamentary vote as a unitary kingdom. On 20 July 1951, angered by Jordan's secret negotiations with Israel, a Palestinian assassinated King Abdullah in Jerusalem's al-Haram al-Sharif, whose shrines are the third holiest Islamic sites in the world. He was succeeded by his son Talal ibn Abdullah. By constitutional means, Talal was removed from the throne in 1952 due to mental illness. He was succeeded that year by his son, Hussein ibn Talal, who was then a minor. King Hussein did not officially take up his duties until he reached the age of eighteen in 1953.

Jordan's history during King Hussein's long reign (1952–1999) may be divided into three major periods. The first two decades were marked by internally and externally generated crises and threats to Hashimite rule and the very existence of the country: Radical Arab nationalism stimulated street riots, challenges to the regime from Jordan's Prime Minister Sulayman al-Nabulsi in 1956 and 1957, destabilization by larger and stronger Arab states, and the devastating loss of the West Bank to Israel in the Arab–Israel War of June 1967. In addition, the Palestinian guerrilla organizations confronted Jordan in the bloody Black September civil war in 1970. Nonetheless, while relying on his loyal military to survive, King Hussein and his circle helped put in place the bases for social and economic development.

The second phase, starting after the Arab–Israel War of October 1973, is distinguished by quieter political conditions within Jordan, rapid development fueled by funds (direct grants, loans, individual remittances) derived from the oil boom in neighboring states, and improved relations with most of Jordan's Arab neighbors in a relatively less radical regional atmosphere. Despite Jordan's problems with the Palestinians and its frequently strained relations with the Palestine Liberation Organization (PLO), the country became an accepted player and the king came to be a respected leader in most Arab capitals. Indeed, Jordan hosted two Arab summits—1980 and 1987—in Amman.

The third phase was dominated by the end of the Cold War and the alteration of regional relationships. In a sense, as a precursor to these changes, King Hussein decided to disengage Jordan politically and administratively from the West Bank in July 1988, in response to the pressures from the Palestinian Intifada (uprising), which began in late 1987. More important was the withdrawal of the Soviet Union as an active player in the region (1989–1990), the United States's ensuing dominance in areas of its perceived interests, and the resulting polarization of the Arab world. The 1990–1991 Gulf Crisis and war left Jordan (then diplomatically allied with Saddam Hussein's Iraq) and a few other poor Arab states politically, economically, and regionally isolated.

On the domestic level, though, Jordan began a gradual democratization process; its parliament had been recalled in 1984 after a hiatus that began in 1970, and in 1989, elections (generally considered to be the freest in the Arab Middle East) were held. Subsequently, under a mandate from King Hussein, leaders from all political streams wrote a national charter defining the general principles for political life in the country. They include democracy, pluralism, and the recognition of the legitimacy of the Hashimite throne. A special general

Fourteen miles from Jordan's capital city of Amman lies Baqʻa, the country's largest refugee camp. Some 120,000 Palestinians left the West Bank and flooded into Baqʻa after the Arab–Israel War of 1967. Approximately 10 percent of Jordan's population lives in camps such as this, and the influx of refugees has contributed to the country's severe overcrowding problem. © OWEN FRANKEN/CORBIS. REPRODUCED BY PERMISSION.

congress, of 2,000 representatives, ratified the document on 9 June 1991. Democratization initially led to significant parliamentary gains by opposition Islamic candidates and parties, although non-ideological, pro-regime politicians dominated the parliament by the early 2000s.

Jordan fully embraced the United States–sponsored Middle East peace process and, along with other Arab states and the Palestinians, participated in direct negotiations with Israel beginning at the October 1991 Madrid Conference. In the wake of the September 1993 Oslo Accord between Israel and the PLO, Jordan signed its own peace treaty with Israel in October 1994, the second Arab state to do so. In November 1995, King Hussein traveled to Jerusalem for the first time since 1967 to attend the funeral of assassinated Israeli prime minister Yitzhak Rabin.

Hussein's own death in January 1999 from cancer devastated Jordanians, many of whom had never known any leader but him, and who had come to associate him with the very existence of Jordan. Two weeks prior to his death, Hussein had shocked the nation by ousting his brother, Hassan, from the post of crown prince that he had held since 1965, and replacing him with his eldest son, Abdullah II ibn Hussein. The young king quickly assumed the throne upon his father's death, and faced monumentally large shoes to fill. Since then, he has pulled Jordan even closer to the United States and its vision of the Middle East. In addition to developing bilateral free trade agreements, Jordan also allowed the United States to station troops in the country before and during the American invasion of Iraq in March 2003. With the Jordanian economy still in trouble, the Israeli–Palestinian peace process stalled, and a new regional balance of power given the direct intervention of the United States in Iraq, King Abdullah faced some serious challenges by late 2003.

See also ABDULLAH I IBN HUSSEIN; ABDULLAH II IBN HUSSEIN; AMMAN; AQABA; ARAB–ISRAEL WAR (1948); ARAB–ISRAEL WAR (1967); ARAB–ISRAEL WAR (1973); BLACK SEPTEMBER; HUSSEIN IBN TALAL; INTIFADA (1987–1991); JORDINIAN CIVIL WAR (1970–1971); REFUGEES: PALESTINIAN.

Bibliography

Brand, Laurie A. *Jordan's Inter-Arab Relations: The Political Economy of Alliance Making.* New York: Columbia University Press, 1994.

Fischbach, Michael R. *State, Society, and Land in Jordan.* Leiden and Boston: Brill, 2000.

Gubser, Peter. *Jordan: Crossroads of Middle Eastern Events.* Boulder, CO: Westview, 1983.

Massad, Joseph A. *Colonial Effects: The Making of National Identity in Jordan.* New York: Columbia University Press, 2001.

Piro, Timothy J. *The Political Economy of Market Reform in Jordan.* Lanham, MD: Rowman & Littlefield, 1998.

Salibi, Kamal. *The Modern History of Jordan.* New York: St. Martin's Press, 1999.

Shlaim, Avi. *Collusion across the Jordan: King Abdullah, the Zionist Movement and the Partition of Palestin.* New York: Columbia University Press, 1988.

Vatikiotis, P. J. *Politics and the Military in Jordan: A Study of the Arab Legion, 1927–1957.* London: Cass, 1967.

Wilson, Mary C. *King Abdullah, Britain and the Making of Jordan.* Cambridge, U.K. and New York: Cambridge University Press, 1987.

PETER GUBSER
UPDATED BY MICHAEL R. FISCHBACH

JORDANIAN CIVIL WAR (1970–1971)

Fighting between the Jordanian army and Palestinian guerrillas in 1970 and 1971.

Between 1967 and 1970, Palestinian guerrilla groups associated with the Palestine Liberation Organization (PLO) established a strong presence in Jordan. By the summer of 1970, their attacks against Israel, which prompted Israeli counterattacks, and their activities within Jordan posed a significant threat to the stability, if not the existence, of the Jordanian monarchy. As a complicating factor, in the aftermath of the Arab defeat in the 1967 Arab–Israel War, Iraqi troops were stationed in Jordan. They, along with a strong Syrian military presence just north of Jordan's border, constituted an additional security threat to the regime of King Hussein ibn Talal.

In June 1970, guerrillas and the Jordanian army clashed in the capital, Amman, but fighting ceased after an agreement was struck allowing Palestinian fighters to continue their presence. In early September, another round of clashes erupted, with serious new complications. The Popular Front for the Liberation of Palestine (PFLP), led by George Habash, hijacked four international airplanes, forcing three to land in Jordan with their hostages. After Jordanian authorities negotiated an evacuation of the passengers and an end to the standoff, the PFLP blew up the empty planes. This spectacle, in the full glare of the international media, drove King Hussein to appoint a military cabinet, signaling his intent to confront the guerrillas once and for all. Jordanian troops began a major assault against PLO targets on 17 September. Iraqi troops, by minor repositioning, indicated they would not interfere; but on 19 September as many as 200 Syrian tanks, along with Syrian-controlled Palestine Liberation Army forces, invaded to assist PLO forces. Jordan requested help from the United States, and Israel made moves indicating it might intervene. Because of internal Syrian politics and direct communications between King Hussein and Hafiz al-Asad, then Syrian air force commander, Syrian planes did not join the battle. Bereft of air cover, the Syrian force was driven back by Jordanian planes and tanks on 22 September. Subsequently, Jordan's army defeated the Palestinian guerrillas on the ground after ten days' fighting and thousands of casualties, including heavy civilian losses in Palestinian refugee camps.

With considerable assistance from Egypt's President Gamal Abdel Nasser, King Hussein and PLO Chairman Yasir Arafat (who had escaped from Jordan) signed a peace accord in Cairo dated 27 September, which called for the withdrawal of the Palestinian forces from Amman. In July 1971, the army undertook extensive and harsh mopping-up operations in northern Jordan, driving the PLO completely out of Jordan. As punishment for its actions against the Palestinians, Kuwait and Libya ended financial aid to Jordan, and Syria closed its border and airspace to Jordanian traffic. Although Jordan suffered economically and politically for its defeat of the guerrillas, it eventually renormalized relations with the Arab world, especially after the October 1973 Arab–Israeli War.

See also ARAFAT, YASIR; HABASH, GEORGE; HUSSEIN IBN TALAL; NASSER, GAMAL ABDEL; PALESTINE LIBERATION ORGANIZATION (PLO); POPULAR FRONT FOR THE LIBERATION OF PALESTINE.

Bibliography

Gubser, Peter. *Jordan: Crossroads of Middle Eastern Events.* Boulder, CO: Westview Press, 1983.

Sayigh, Yezid. *Armed Struggle and the Search for State: The Palestinian National Movement, 1949–1993.* Oxford: Oxford University Press, 1997.

PETER GUBSER
UPDATED BY MICHAEL R. FISCHBACH

JORDANIAN OPTION

A term used to describe the foreign policy of the Israeli Labor Party; a preference for reaching a settlement with the Hashimite rulers of Jordan rather than with the Palestinians.

The origins of the Jordanian Option can be traced to the contacts between the Jewish Agency (the official link between the Jews in Palestine and the British mandate authorities) and King Abdullah I ibn Hussein of Jordan, which culminated in a secret agreement to partition Palestine between themselves in 1947. After the attainment of Israel's independence, on 15 May 1948, Israeli leaders saw the survival of the Hashimite monarchy in Jordan as essential to their own nation's security.

After Israel captured the West Bank of the Jordan River during the 1967 Arab–Israel War, Labor Party leaders opposed the creation of a Palestinian state and strove, unsuccessfully, for a territorial compromise with Jordan. The Jordanian Option ceased to be Israel's official policy following the rise to power of the Likud Party in 1977. Later, whether in opposition or as the Likud's coalition partner, the Labor Party continued to advocate the Jordanian Option. By cutting the links between Jordan and the West Bank in July 1988, Jordan's King Hussein announced, in effect, that a Jordanian Option no longer exists—if it ever did.

See also ABDULLAH I IBN HUSSEIN; ARAB–ISRAEL WAR (1967); HUSSEIN IBN TALAL; JEWISH AGENCY FOR PALESTINE.

Bibliography

Shlaim, Avi. *Collusion across the Jordan: King Abdullah, the Zionist Movement, and the Partition of Palestine.* New York: Columbia University Press, 1988.

AVI SHLAIM

JORDANIAN PRESS AGENCY

See NEWSPAPERS AND PRINT MEDIA: ARAB COUNTRIES

JORDAN RIVER

River that forms the boundary between Israel, the Palestinian Authority, and Jordan; it flows south from Syria to the Dead Sea.

The Jordan River rises from the confluence of three major springs and streams located on the southern and western slopes of Mount Hermon (Arabic, *Jabal al-Shaykh*). The largest is the Dan and the other two are the Hasbani (Hebrew, *Nahal Senir*) and the Baniyas (Hebrew, *Nahal Hermon*) streams. The streams unite about 4 miles south of the Lebanon-Israel border. These springs usually provide 50 percent of the water of the upper Jordan, the rest coming from surface runoff in the rainy winter months. The discharge flows into the northern end of the Ghawr, which is the valley of the Dead Sea and the northern extremity of the Great Rift Valley that runs south to Africa, ending at Mozambique.

The upper Jordan River flows swiftly through the Hula Valley, additional water coming to it from minor springs and Wadi Barayghit (Hebrew, *Nahal Iyyon*). Four miles south of the Jordan's outlet from Lake Hula, the water course deepens and the river runs for 10 miles, plunging 850 feet. The central Jordan river begins north of the Sea of Galilee (also called Lake Tiberias or Lake Kinneret), leaving the southern exit of the lake, where it meets up with a few more streams and most importantly with its main tributary, the Yarmuk River. The Yarmuk originates in the eastern rift and forms the border between Syria and the Kingdom of Jordan as it flows westward to enter the Jordan River 6 miles south of the Sea of Galilee at 985 feet below sea level. The lower Jordan River flows southward, dropping to 1,310 feet below sea level, emptying into the Dead Sea, a great salt lake whose surface level is the lowest point on Earth's surface.

The Jordan and Agriculture

The water of the Jordan is freshest at the headwaters and becomes more saline as it enters the Sea of Galilee; the salinity rises rapidly as it moves south to the Dead Sea. Agriculture depends in part on water quality (freshness) and in part on soil quality (organic matter and minerals). Over the years, and after much intensive study and advice, during the British Mandate (1922–1948) the Zionists in Palestine determined that the northern Negev Desert had fertile soil and that all it needed was a good supply of water. At that time, the only large-scale development plan for the Jordan River was carried out by the Zionist leader and hydroelectric engineer Pinhas Rutenberg; even that was limited by the British

Mandate administration to the construction of one power station to supply hydroelectric power to Palestine west of the Jordan. All Rutenberg's plans for irrigation and electrification of the area east of the Jordan River came to nothing.

When the state of Israel came into existence in 1948, plans were drawn for the diversion of water from Jisr Banat Ya'qub, on the upper Jordan, to be taken via massive pipelines across the Jezreel Valley and south along the coastal plain, terminating in Beersheba, where it could be used most effectively. When work began on this diversion scheme in 1952, Syria complained to the United Nations that it violated the demilitarized zone agreement of the 1949 armistice (which ended the 1948 Arab–Israel War). Israel was ordered to cease construction, and U.S. Special Ambassador Eric Johnston was appointed to devise a scheme for regional development of the Jordan River system. Johnston's Unified Plan, worked out from 1953 to 1955, was never formally ratified by the League of Arab States but has been implemented by Israel and by the Hashimite Kingdom of Jordan in separate schemes.

Israel has constructed the Cross Israel Water Carrier, which was its original idea, but the carrier was started at the northern end of the Sea of Galilee—a costly modification, considering that the water had to be pumped up to the level of the Jezreel Valley. Across Israel, the government built smaller pipelines radiating out over the farmland to bring water for irrigation. The entire system forms a water grid, easily controlled and measured; it was completed in 1964.

The Kingdom of Jordan has constructed the East Ghawr Project, hooking up a pipeline to the Yarmuk above Adassiya, which parallels the flow of the Jordan River. The pipeline is on a much higher level than the river, just below the high ridges, and the radiating smaller pipelines flow by gravity to the rich Jordan Valley soil, irrigating the farms. The final stage of the project, under Jordan Valley Authority control (created in 1973), was completed in 1980 when the pipeline reached the Dead Sea.

Hydropolitics

After the 1967 Arab–Israel War, new issues complicated an already complex situation, since Israel took and occupied Jerusalem and the West Bank of the Jordan. Discovering the existence of the huge aquifer under the spine of the mountains of the West Bank, Israel began to pump winter floodwaters into the aquifer to use it as a better water storage area than the Sea of Galilee. Israel refuses to allow the Palestinians in the West Bank to drill deeply for new wells lest they tap this vital storage area. By taking the Golan Heights from Syria, Israel also gained complete control over the Galilee, the upper Jordan River, and even part of the Yarmuk River. This gave Israel effective control over the Jordan River, preventing water diversion downstream by either Jordanians or Palestinians. Indeed, securing control over the water supply was one of several Israeli motivations in launching the 1967 war in the first place.

Throughout the 1970s, 1980s, and 1990s, Israel continued to build settlements in the West Bank, diverting surface water from the Jordan and more groundwater from underground aquifers, in each case lessening the amount of water available for Palestinian towns and cities. The 1973 Arab–Israeli War did nothing to change this situation, nor did the wars of the 1980s in Lebanon and in the Persian Gulf. The situation for Palestinians and Jordanians, suffering from chronic water shortages, grew steadily more desperate.

The post–Gulf War atmosphere included a return to the regional peace process, beginning in 1991 with meetings in Madrid. These were followed by specialized rounds of multilateral talks, including negotiations over water and environmental issues. By 1993, Israel and the Palestine Liberation Organization began direct negotiations at Oslo. This was followed by the 1994 peace treaty between Jordan and Israel, in which water rights loomed large. The treaty returned the Wadi Araba (a major source of groundwater) to Jordanian control, while leasing the same land back to an Israeli kibbutz for twenty-five years. It is not accidental that the treaty was signed at the Wadi Araba. The two states agreed that Jordan could build a dam and divert water from the Yarmuk River, while Israel would consider Jordan's water needs when releasing waters from the Galilee to the lower Jordan. Since Jordan had no capacity for storing Yarmuk floodwaters, Israel agreed to pump winter water from the Yarmuk for storage in the Sea of Galilee, which would then be sent back to Jordan in the summer.

In practice, however, repeated summer droughts and overuse of water resources together have depleted the regional water supplies, even lowering the water level of the Galilee. As a consequence, Israel has tended to send Jordan less water than expected. This has led Jordan to obtain supplemental and emergency supplies from Syria and has also led Jordan and Syria to finally begin construction of a decades-old project: the Wihda, or Unity, Dam (also called the Maqarin Dam) on the Yarmuk River. In the West Bank, Israeli reoccupation, the Palestinian uprising (since September 2000), and the collapse of much of the regional peace process has at least delayed any hope of more equitable access to surface or groundwater supplies. Hence the water situation for the Palestinian Authority remains dire and will be a vital point of negotiation with Israel.

Hydropolitics are vitally important to Israel, Jordan, Syria, and the Palestinian Authority as they approach the point when they will be using all their available water and yet have rapidly growing populations. Unless there is a major technological breakthrough, and unless greater levels of cooperation can be arranged between these riparian peoples, hydropolitics may precipitate ecological disaster and possibly the next war.

See also ARAB–ISRAEL WAR (1948); ARAB–ISRAEL WAR (1967); ARAB–ISRAEL WAR (1973); BEERSHEBA; DEAD SEA; GOLAN HEIGHTS; JEZREEL VALLEY; JOHNSTON PLAN (1953); LEAGUE OF ARAB STATES; MAQARIN DAM; NATIONAL WATER SYSTEM (ISRAEL); NEGEV; OSLO ACCORD (1993); PALESTINIAN AUTHORITY; RUTENBERG, PINHAS; WEST BANK; YARMUK RIVER.

Bibliography

Borthwick, Bruce. "Water in Israeli-Jordanian Relations: From Conflict to the Danger of Ecological Disaster." *Israel Affairs* 9, no. 3 (2003): 165–186.

Haddadin, Munther J. *Diplomacy on the Jordan: International Conflict and Negotiated Resolution.* Boston: Kluwer Academic Publishers, 2001.

Lowi, Miriam. *Water and Power: The Politics of a Scarce Resource in the Jordan River Basin.* New York and Cambridge, U.K.: Cambridge University Press, 1993.

Naff, Thomas, and Matson, Ruth C., eds. *Water in the Middle East: Conflict or Cooperation?* Boulder, CO: Westview Press, 1984.

Reguer, Sara. "Controversial Waters: Thirty Years of Exploitation of the Jordan River, 1950–1980." *Middle Eastern Studies* 29, no. 1 (1993) pp. 53–90.

Rouyer, Alwyn R. *Turning Water into Politics: The Water Issue in the Palestinian-Israeli Conflict.* New York: St. Martin's Press, 1999.

Wolf, Aaron T. *Hydropolitics along the Jordan River: Scarce Water and Its Impact on the Arab-Israeli Conflict.* New York and Tokyo: United Nations University Press, 1995.

SARA REGUER
UPDATED BY CURTIS R. RYAN

JORDAN TIMES

See NEWSPAPERS AND PRINT MEDIA: ARAB COUNTRIES

JOSEPH, DOV
[1899–1980]

Israeli lawyer and cabinet member.

Dov (Bernard) Joseph was born in Montreal, where he began his Zionist activity as a teen. In 1917 he became the first editor of the *Judaean,* a prominent Canadian Zionist publication. In 1918 he joined the Jewish Legion. He emigrated to Palestine in 1921 and became a lawyer. He received a doctorate from the University of London in 1929. From 1936 to 1945 he was a legal adviser in the political department of the Jewish Agency for Palestine. This brought him into close contact with the department's head, Moshe Sharett. In 1945 he was appointed to the Jewish Agency Executive, where he continued his leadership of the political department. During the fall of 1947 he was dispatched by the World Zionist Organization to the United States to push for a United Nations vote in support of partition. During Israel's War of Independence he was military governor of Jerusalem. On 17 September 1948 the United Nations mediator Count Folke Bernadotte was assassinated by Lohamei Herut Yisrael (LEHI)—the "Stern Gang," led by Abraham Stern—on his way to an appointment with Joseph. Joseph took the lead in the arrest of the responsible LEHI members.

Joseph served in various ministerial capacities between 1949 and 1955, and was a member of Knesset (MAPAI) until 1956. From 1957 to 1961 Joseph served as treasurer of the Jewish Agency, and as Israel's minister of justice from 1961 to 1965. He died in Jerusalem in 1980.

See also BERNADOTTE, FOLKE; LOHAMEI HERUT YISRAEL; SHARETT, MOSHE; STERN, ABRAHAM.

Bibliography

Bernard, Joseph. *British Rule in Palestine.* Washington, DC: Public Affairs Press, 1948.

Bernard, Joseph. *The Faithful City.* New York: Simon and Schuster, 1960.

CHAIM I. WAXMAN

JUBAYL, AL-

A small port on the Gulf coast of Saudi Arabia.

Al-Jubayl traditionally served the Najdi hinterland, especially al-Qasim district. The kingdom's Second Five-Year Development Plan (1975–1980) teamed al-Jubayl with Yanbu on the Red Sea coast in an ambitious industrial development scheme involving crude oil refining, petrochemical complexes, and steel-manufacturing industries, linked by trans–Saudi Arabian oil and gas pipelines. The development of the two sites was expected to take ten years and cost in excess of $70 billion. Al-Jubayl was to be the bigger of the two, with three petroleum refineries, six petrochemical plants, an aluminum smelter, and a steel mill, as well as support industries and an industrial seaport. By 1999, seventeen basic industrial plants had been established and the city had an estimated population of 101,000, projected to grow to 290,000 by 2010. It also had acquired an industrial college and an airport.

Bibliography

Farsy, Fouad al-. *Modernity and Tradition: The Saudi Equation.* London: Kegan Paul International, 1991.

J. E. PETERSON

JUDAISM

The religion of the Jewish people.

Judaism developed out of scripture (the Torah) and an oral tradition of legal and ethical conduct as inscribed in the Talmud, codes, mystical literature, and rabbinic commentaries. Although traditional

Jews assume that Judaism has remained unchanged from the revelation at Sinai to the present, most scholars agree that it has been transformed by the vicissitudes of Jewish history since the days of the Bible.

A significant turning point in Judaism occurred when the wandering Israelites entered into the Promised Land and later when they built their Holy Temple in Jerusalem. For much of this time, the religion was essentially a temple cult, organized around regular ritual sacrifices and a series of three pilgrimages to Jerusalem, and practiced by a people ruled by kings, guided by prophets, and ministered to by priests.

After the Babylonian destruction of the First Temple in 586 B.C.E. and even more so following the Roman destruction of the Second Temple in 70 C.E., Judaism became a religion of exile. Replacing the temple and temple rites were synagogues, regular prayer, and an emphasis on the lifelong study of sacred texts in the Torah. Rabbis and teachers replaced the priests and prophets, and Jewish community leaders, the kings. This new Judaism was a more portable religion, appropriate to a wandering people. Moral and ethical laws became central, but ritual praxis, governed by strict codes and guided by rabbinic interpretation of the law, was also crucial. The Torah became the focus of Judaism, the yeshiva its most important sanctuary, and a return to the Promised Land Zion and a rebuilding of the temple in Jerusalem remained abiding hopes and part of the promise of messianic redemption.

The Diaspora has led to a nuancing of Jewish tradition into distinct customs. Among the most outstanding have been the custom variations between Sephardic Jews, whose expatriation occurred in the Middle East, North Africa, and the Iberian Peninsula, and Ashkenazic Jews, who trace their origins to France and the German-speaking countries but who emigrated ultimately to almost all of Europe and later to the Americas. Sephardic Jews and Ashkenazic Jews share a belief in Scripture and a dependence on the Talmud, but they have evolved variations in custom and ritual praxis based upon their varying ethnic experiences and the disparate rabbinic authorities by whom they have been guided over the years. Nevertheless, many of the rabbis and their commentaries have, through time, acquired a religious legitimacy that supersedes these differences. Thus, for example, Rashi, an eleventh-century Ashkenazic exegete, and Maimonides, a twelfth-century Sephardic rabbinic codifier, are recognized by all Jewish traditions to be authoritative interpreters of Judaism.

By and large, Judaism defines a Jew as someone born of a Jewish mother or someone who has submitted to religious conversion. Although there is debate about what constitute the minimal requirements of conversion, the *halakhic* (Judeo–legal) minimum requirement consists of circumcision for males, immersion in the waters of a ritual bath (*mikveh*), a period of Torah study, and a commitment to be bound by all the laws of Judaism. During the twentieth century, some non-Orthodox Jews expanded this religious definition to include children of either a Jewish father or mother and do not require a commitment to keep all the laws. The definition is a crucial one in Israel, which guarantees full citizenship rights to all Jews.

Through most of the period of the Diaspora, Judaism has tended to focus on matters of praxis more than on principles of faith, because, it was argued, the former better guaranteed the religion's continuity while ensuring the integrity of belief. Since the eighteenth century and especially in the twentieth century, however, a large-scale move away from praxis has occurred. A result of religious reform and social changes that brought Jews out of their status as pariahs and into the mainstream of Western societies, this development has led to a Judaism that focuses more on its moral and ethical principles and on some vague notions of ethnicity than it does on ritual praxis. Accordingly, in contemporary Judaism, those who strictly maintain traditions, ritual praxis, and time-honored Jewish codes of conduct now constitute a growing minority.

Although the principles of Jewish faith have been the subject of much discussion and debate among Jewish philosophers and rabbinic commentators, among the most commonly cited essentials are thirteen principles listed by Maimonides. These include a belief in a single Creator, a unique and everlasting God, who is incorporeal, who existed before time began and will last after it has passed, and who alone is worthy of worship. It also includes a belief in the utterances of the prophets, and especially the words of Moses; a conviction that the entire Torah was divinely revealed to Moses at Sinai and passed on intact to the Jewish people, who may not replace it with another set of teachings; and a belief that God is omniscient and that He creates all life, rewards the good, and punishes the bad. Finally, it includes a faith in the promise of messianic redemption. In the same way that only a minority of Jews today abide by all the rules of Jewish law and praxis, so is it likely that only a few Jews today hold all of the thirteen beliefs.

Although Judaism has demonstrated a remarkable capacity to survive the vicissitudes of Jewish history and the vagaries of existence in the Diaspora, including persecution and pogrom (most recently during the European Holocaust), some observers are anxious about its future in the context of an open society like America's and that of a secular state like Israel, the two largest population centers of Jewry today. Pointing to a decline in numbers of Jews in America as well as a diminution of Jewish education, practice, and faith, these observers argue that Judaism's days as a vital religion are numbered in America and throughout the Diaspora. On the other hand, looking at Israel's large-scale redefinition of Jews as secular Israelis, other observers worry no less about the future of the religion in the Jewish homeland. To some of these observers, the answer to these anxieties is to press for the coming of the Messiah. To others, the answer is a revitalization of Jewish education and a return to Jewish tradition.

See also DIASPORA; HOLOCAUST; POGROM; YESHIVA.

Bibliography

Finkelstein, L., ed. *The Jews: Their History,* 4th edition. New York: Schocken Books, 1970.

Glatzer, Nahum N., ed. *In Time and Eternity: A Jewish Reader.* New York: Schocken Books, 1946.

Heilman, Samuel C., and Cohen, Steven M. *Cosmopolitans and Parochials: Modern Orthodox Jews in America.* Chicago: University of Chicago Press, 1990.

SAMUEL C. HEILMAN

JUDEO-ARABIC

The various forms of Arabic spoken or written by Jews from before the rise of Islam to modern times.

Like all Diaspora Jewish languages, Judeo-Arabic is distinguished from its non-Jewish cognate, Arabic, in the use of the Hebrew alphabet, a significant number of Hebrew and Aramaic loanwords and elements, and its own distinguishing grammatical, syntactical, and phonological forms.

In the Middle Ages, written Judeo-Arabic, which depending upon the subject matter ranged from Classical to Middle Arabic in style, became a primary medium of Jewish intellectual creativity for theologians, philosophers, grammarians, lexicographers, and legal scholars, and was also the primary medium of correspondence. Only for poetry (which in Islamic society is considered the supreme national art form) was Hebrew the principal language of expression. Owing to the decline of Hellenistic humanism after the High Middle Ages and the increased social isolation of Jews within the context of a larger Arab world after the thirteenth century, the regional varieties of modern Judeo-Arabic that emerged in the late fifteenth century were characterized by their vernacular nature.

During the nineteenth and early twentieth centuries, Judeo-Arabic books and newspapers were published from Morocco to India (where there was an Iraqi Jewish mercantile colony). Many of the books were translations or adaptations of European popular literature and, in some instances, works of Haskalah Hebrew writers. By the 1920s, Judeo-Arabic publication was declining in many places as French became the main language of high culture for many Jews, because of the Alliance Israélite Universelle schools. Nevertheless, it remained the spoken language for the great majority of Jews until their mass exodus to Israel in the mid-1950s. Judeo-Arabic is dying out among the second and third generations born in Israel, France, and the Americas, who tend to speak their national languages (Hebrew, French, and English, Spanish, or Portuguese).

See also ALLIANCE ISRAÉLITE UNIVERSELLE (AIU); HASKALAH.

Bibliography

Stillman, Norman A. "Language Patterns in Islamic and Judaic Societies." In *Islam and Judaism: 1400 Years of Shared Values,* edited by S. Wasserstrom. Portland, OR: Institute for Judaic Studies in the Pacific Northwest, 1991.

Stillman, Norman A. *The Language and Culture of the Jews of Sefrou, Morocco: An Ethnolinguistic Study.* Manchester, U.K.: University of Manchester, 1988.

NORMAN STILLMAN

JUMAYYIL, AMIN
[1942–]

President of Lebanon, 1982–1988.

Amin Jumayyil (or Gemayel) studied law at St. Joseph University in Beirut, and is noted for his oratorical skills in Arabic. A moderate who was not active in the Phalange party, founded by his father, Pierre Jumayyil, he concentrated on his political career after being elected to parliament in 1970, the youngest deputy in the body. Jumayyil was named president on 23 September 1982 after the assassination of his brother Bashir Jumayyil, through consensus among the various political factions, key Arab states, and Western powers. He based his policies on his alliance with the United States, which ultimately led to the unraveling of his presidency. Under pressure from Syria, he abrogated the U.S.–brokered 1983 security agreement with Israel. On 17 February 1984, the last of the multinational force withdrew from Beirut. Without support, Jumayyil was a lame-duck president. He remained in office until the end of his term in 1988. Minutes before leaving office, he violated the terms of the 1943 National Pact (which required a Sunni Muslim serve as prime minister) by appointing fellow Maronite Christian Gen. Michel Aoun to the post. Given his poor relations with Syria, he left Lebanon and went into exile.

Jumayyil taught at Harvard University, wrote, and lectured. The death of Syrian president Hafiz al-Asad in June 1990 paved the way for his return to Lebanon. Jumayyil found an ally in Druze leader Walid Jumblatt, who forsook his traditionally pro-Syrian line to join what had been the Maronite campaign against Syria.

See also AOUN, MICHEL; JUMAYYIL, BASHIR; JUMAYYIL, PIERRE; JUMBLATT, WALID; NATIONAL PACT (LEBANON); PHALANGE.

Bibliography

Jumayyil, Amin. *Rebuilding Lebanon's Future.* Lanham, MD: University Press of America, 1992.

MAJED HALAWI
UPDATED BY MICHAEL R. FISCHBACH

JUMAYYIL, BASHIR
[1947–1982]

Militia leader; later president of Lebanon.

Bashir Jumayyil (also Gemayel) was the son of Pierre Jumayyil, a right-wing, militant Maronite leader who founded the fascist Phalange party. Bashir Jumayyil grew up in Beirut and joined the Phalange early in his youth. He studied law at Saint Joseph University and was very active in the militarized youth branch of the Phalange. He supervised the anti-Palestinian armed branch of the movement and provoked clashes with Palestinian organizations in Lebanon after forming the BG (his initials, using the French spelling of his name) militia in 1974, a year before the eruption of the Lebanese Civil War. Jumayyil became a key militia leader in the Civil War. He rose to prominence in the battle against the Palestinian refugee camp in Tall al-Zaʿtar in 1976 and was appointed president of the Military Council after the mysterious death of William Hawi. He formed the Lebanese Forces in 1976 as an umbrella group for the right-wing Christian militias under his command. He ruthlessly eliminated his rivals in 1980 and expelled fighters belonging to the National Liberal Party, his former allies. His name is associated with the bloodiest day of the Civil War, Black Saturday, when he and his followers massacred hundreds of innocent Muslim civilians to avenge the death of four members of the party. He led the fight against Syrian forces in 1978 and struck a close alliance with Israel, which propelled him to the presidency after Israel invaded Lebanon in 1982. He was assassinated in a massive car bomb in September 1982, weeks after assuming the presidency. His son Nadim has become active in Lebanese politics in alliance with the forces loyal to General Michel Aown.

See also JUMAYYIL, PIERRE; LEBANESE FORCES; NATIONAL LIBERAL PARTY; PHALANGE.

Bibliography

Hiro, Dilip. *Lebanon: Fire and Embers: A History of the Lebanese Civil War.* New York: St. Martin's Press, 1993.

ASʿAD ABUKHALIL

JUMAYYIL, PIERRE
[1905–1984]

Lebanese nationalist; founder of al-Kataʾib (Phalange) party.

Pierre Jumayyil was born in Bikfayya, Mount Lebanon, into a Maronite family. He completed his education at Jesuit schools and obtained a degree in pharmacy. In 1936 Jumayyil attended the Berlin Olympics, where he was impressed by the youth movement of the National Socialist (Nazi) Party. He decided, upon his return to Lebanon, to form a similar group, al-Kata'ib (the Phalange). Initially, al-Kata'ib stood at the divide between the two main currents of Christian public opinion: that of Emile Eddé, which favored the consolidation of France's hegemony in Lebanon, and that of Bishara al-Khuri, which called for Lebanon's independence with close ties to the Arab world.

After a failed attempt in 1951, Jumayyil was elected deputy from Beirut in 1960. He had led the opposition to President-elect Fu'ad Chehab, the candidate of the consensus between President Gamal Abdel Nasser of Egypt and the United States that ended the 1958 civil war; nevertheless, he joined a four-member national reconciliation cabinet that was formed on 24 September 1958. He subsequently participated in most cabinets formed by Chehab and by his protégé successor, Charles Hilu.

In 1968, Jumayyil entered into al-Hilf al-Thulathi (Tripartite Alliance) with former President Camille Chamoun and Deputy Raymond Eddé, gradually distancing himself from Chehab. In 1970, the Hilf candidate, Sulayman Franjiyya, was elected president.

Jumayyil staunchly opposed Nasserism and Arab nationalism. He was particularly hostile to the armed Palestinian fighters in Lebanon. The Kata'ib repeatedly clashed with Palestinian fighters in the early 1970s. In January 1975, Jumayyil denounced the Palestine Liberation Organization for sowing anarchy in Lebanon, and the following month demanded a referendum on Palestinian presence in the country. The Ayn al-Rimmani incident of 13 April 1975, which ignited Lebanon's civil war, occurred between Kata'ib members and Palestinian fighters.

During the Lebanese Civil War, with the Kata'ib as his base, Jumayyil was at the center of the Christian right camp. He played a key role in obtaining the introduction into Lebanon of troops from Syria, who initially helped the Christians to achieve a reversal of the successes of the Palestinian–leftist alliance. His relations with Syria, however, deteriorated as the Kata'ib's military cooperation with Israel, which culminated in Israel's invasion of Lebanon in 1982, grew ever stronger.

During the civil war, Jumayyil worked with the traditional Muslim leadership to create a right-wing Christian–Muslim alliance. With the failure of these efforts, he began advocating political decentralization, which many considered a call for the de facto partition of Lebanon. At the time of his death, Jumayyil was a minister in the National Unity government of Rashid Karame.

See also CHAMOUN, CAMILLE; CHEHAB, FU'AD; EDDÉ, EMILE; EDDÉ, RAYMOND; FRANJIYYA, SULAYMAN; HILU, CHARLES; KARAME, RASHID; KHURI, BISHARA AL-; LEBANESE CIVIL WAR (1958); LEBANESE CIVIL WAR (1975–1990); NASSER, GAMAL ABDEL; PALESTINE LIBERATION ORGANIZATION (PLO); PHALANGE.

Bibliography

Cobban, Helena. *The Making of Modern Lebanon.* London: Hutchinson, 1985.

MAJED HALAWI

JUMBLATT FAMILY

Prominent Druze family in Lebanon.

The Jumblatts are one of two rival Druze family confederations in Lebanon (the other being the Yazbaki). The family traces back to a Kurdish family from Janbulad, Syria, and to the chieftain Ali Janbulad, from Aleppo. They came to Lebanon in the seventeenth century after a failed rebellion against the Ottomans. With the support of Prince Fakhr al-Din II al-Ma'hi, the family was invited to settle in the Shuf, establishing itself in Mukhtara. After their conversion to the Druze religion, the extinction of the Ma'nid dynasty enabled them to become shaykhs of the Shuf. They extended their feudal domain south of the Shuf, coming to rival in power, and later forming the opposition to, the Chehab dynasty. In the nineteenth century, the Jumblatt family became one of the most prominent political (zu'ama) families in Lebanon. In the twentieth century, the history of the family is indistinguishable from the history of the Druze in Lebanon. In the 1920s, during the French mandate, the political leadership of the family was assumed by Nazira Jumblatt, who succeeded her husband Fu'ad after his assassination in 1921. She cooperated with the French authorities to prevent the Druze from defying the mandate government.

The political prominence of the family was boosted by the emergence of Kamal Jumblatt (Nazira's son), who until his death in 1977 dominated Lebanon's political life. The nature of the Jumblatt leadership changed when Kamal promoted progressive and socialist policies that extended his leadership beyond the confines of the Druze family confederation. He also succeeded in marginalizing, perhaps more than at any other time in the modern history of the Druze in Lebanon, the role of the Yazbaki Arslan family. This was especially true under the leadership of the highly ineffective Prince Majid, whose close association with Maronite Christian leader Camille Chamoun discredited him, particularly after the outbreak of the Lebanese Civil War of 1975. Kamal emerged as the spokesperson of the leftist/Muslim coalition that he had helped found before the outbreak of civil war. The death of the Yazbaki *shaykh al-aql* (the highest religious authority among the Druze) also helped the Jumblatt family, whose *shaykh al-aql* became the Druze religious leader in Lebanon, thereby unifying, for the first time in modern times, the religious leadership of the community.

Upon Kamal's assasination, his son, Walid, assumed leadership of the family and of the Progressive Socialist Party it led. He played an important role in the Lebanese Civil War of 1975 through 1990 and in postwar Lebanese politics, continuing the family's significance in that country.

See also ARSLAN FAMILY; CHAMOUN, CAMILLE; DRUZE; JUMBLATT, KAMAL; JUMBLATT, WALID; LEBANESE CIVIL WAR (1975–1990); PROGRESSIVE SOCIALIST PARTY; SHUF.

Bibliography

AbuKhalil, As'ad. *Historical Dictionary of Lebanon.* Lanham, MD: Rowan and Littlefield, 1998.

AS'AD ABUKHALIL
UPDATED BY MICHAEL R. FISCHBACH

JUMBLATT, KAMAL
[1917–1977]

Lebanese Druze politician.

Kamal Jumblatt was the son of Fu'ad (assassinated when Kamal was a boy) and Nazira Jumblatt. A bright young man, he showed deep interest in academic matters and distanced himself from the political affairs of the Druze community, of which his mother was the political leader. He studied at St. Joseph University and attended the Sorbonne. As a student Jumblatt was far from the radical politics with which he was later associated. He was sympathetic to the French mandate in his youth but became a supporter of Bishara al-Khuri after independence. His first prominent political role was in 1952, when he was instrumental in the formation of the opposition block that worked for the ouster of President al-Khuri.

Over the years, Jumblatt became identified with socialist and pro-Palestinian politics. He initially tried to mobilize non-Lebanese Druze, and he founded the Progressive Socialist Party in the late 1940s. The party, however, gradually lost its non-Druze leaders and became a political tool for Jumblatt political leadership. Jumblatt was inconsistent: He championed secularization of politics in Lebanon while cultivating sectarian support among Druze followers, and he promoted socialist policies while remaining a large landowner. He emerged as a prominent pan-Arabist in 1958, when he was one of the key leaders of the popular uprising against the rule of Camille Chamoun. He became a staunch supporter of Gamal Abdel Nasser.

In his political career, Jumblatt maintained the roles of both insider and outsider. He held ministerial posts in cabinets beginning in the 1940s, although he always spoke as the representative of the antiestablishment. In the 1960s, Jumblatt formed a loose coalition of leftist and Muslim organizations and parties to champion support for the Palestine Liberation Organization (PLO) in Lebanon and to call for major reforms of the political system in Lebanon. By 1975, Jumblatt had become one of the most effective and popular leaders in the country. He headed the Lebanese National Movement (which comprised leftist and Muslim organizations) and aligned himself with the PLO. His conflict in 1976 with the regime in Syria over the future course of the Lebanese Civil War of 1975, which Jumblatt wanted to end with a decisive victory for his coalition, led to his death the following year at the hands of assassins believed to be working for Syria.

Although Jumblatt's critics question his motivations during the civil war (he was often accused of frustration at not being able to run for president, an office reserved for Maronites), he succeeded in playing a role that far exceeded the historical role of the Jumblatt family. Some say that he solidified the ties between the Druze and Arabism, at the same time that others within the community wanted him to focus more on the affairs of the community.

See also CHAMOUN, CAMILLE; DRUZE; JUMBLATT FAMILY; KHURI, BISHARA AL-; LEBANESE CIVIL WAR (1975–1990); LEBANESE NATIONAL MOVEMENT (LNM); NASSER, GAMAL ABDEL; PALESTINE LIBERATION ORGANIZATION (PLO); PROGRESSIVE SOCIALIST PARTY.

Bibliography

Cobban, Helena. *The Making of Modern Lebanon.* London: Hutchinson, 1985.

AS'AD ABUKHALIL

JUMBLATT, WALID

[1949–]

Lebanese politician.

Like his father, Kamal, Walid Jumblatt did not seek the political leadership of the Druze community in Lebanon or of the Jumblatt family. It was thrust upon him in the wake of his father's assassination in 1977. Jumblatt studied at the American University of Beirut and seemed uninterested in politics. In his first years as leader, he was uncomfortable with his new role and merely followed his father's path. However, he quickly made peace with the regime in Syria. He later abandoned his father's pan-Arab vision and decided to focus more on the affairs of the community. Following Israel's 1982 invasion of Lebanon, Walid reorganized the Progressive Socialist Party, making it a purely Druze fighting force. He led the defense of the predominantly Druze mountain areas against the encroachments of the Maronite-led Lebanese Forces. His

stand within the community was strengthened when he allowed his militias to fight an all-out war against the Lebanese Forces, aided by some Palestine Liberation Organization factions. The fighting, in what became known as the War of the Mountains in 1983, was accompanied by bloody massacres, committed by both sides.

Jumblatt survived a 1982 assassination attempt that soured his relationship with the regime of Amin Jumayyil. He later formed the nucleus of the opposition to Jumayyil after the agreement of 17 May 1983 between Israel and Lebanon, which was rejected by Syria. Jumblatt dissolved his militia after the election of Ilyas al-Hirawi as president in 1989. He ran in the 1992 elections and won. His party also won another seat in parliament, bringing its total to ten. Jumblatt was named minister for the affairs of the displaced peoples in 1994 and served in several other cabinet positions.

Jumblatt's close relations with Syria, dating back to the 1980s, began to change in autumn 2000, when he joined his voice to what had been a largely Christian call for a reduction of the Syrian troop presence in Lebanon. He and his political allies, including Christians, did well in parliamentary elections, indicating a shift in his long-held political strategy.

See also AMERICAN UNIVERSITY OF BEIRUT (AUB); DRUZE; HIRAWI, ILYAS AL-; JUMAYYIL, AMIN; JUMBLATT FAMILY; LEBANESE FORCES; PALESTINE LIBERATION ORGANIZATION (PLO); PROGRESSIVE SOCIALIST PARTY.

Bibliography

AbuKhalil, As'ad. *Historical Dictionary of Lebanon.* Lanham, MD: Rowman and Littlefield, 1998.

AS'AD ABUKHALIL
UPDATED BY MICHAEL R. FISCHBACH

JUMHURIYYAH, AL-

See NEWSPAPERS AND PRINT MEDIA: ARAB COUNTRIES

JUSTICE AND DEVELOPMENT PARTY

See AKP (JUSTICE AND DEVELOPMENT PARTY)

JUSTICE PARTY

Turkish political party.

The Justice Party (JP) was founded in early 1961 by the former chief of the general staff, Ragip Gümüspala and ten associates, four of whom had been active in the Democrat Party (DP). The JP was created as a continuation of the DP and absorbed the latter's provincial party organization. Three groups comprised the JP in the early years and vied for its leadership: a group of officers centered around Gümüspala; a right-wing group led by Gökhan Evliyaoğlu; and a liberal wing, which succeeded in making Süleyman Demirel head of the party in 1964. The JP received 43.8 percent of the vote in the October 1961 elections and formed a coalition government with the Republican People's Party (RPP) that lasted until May 1962. In the October 1965 general elections, the Demirel-led JP received 53 percent of the vote and 240 out of 450 seats in the National Assembly. The JP also won the 1965 and 1969 elections, but despite a rapidly growing economy, expanding political instability led the military to threaten to intervene. On 13 March 1971 the Demirel government resigned.

When civilian politics resumed in 1973, Demirel refused to form a coalition with the RPP, and the JP became the main opposition party. In 1975, Demirel formed a coalition government, known as the Nationalist Front, with three other parties and independents. Although the coalition lasted more than two years, members of the coalition seldom cooperated, preferring to work to infiltrate supporters into the bureaucracy. In addition, during these years, the JP became associated with the extremist right-wing positions of one of its partners, the Nationalist Action Party. The 1977 elections were held in the midst of increasing street violence. Following the elections, the RPP formed a minority government that lasted less than one month, and Demirel attempted to form a government. The second JP-dominated Nationalist Front government lasted only through 1977. The JP formed a third government in December 1979: It was in power at the time of the Black September coup. One of the first acts of the new military government was to close down all existing parties, putting an end to the JP. In 1983, the True Path Party was established as a continuation of the JP.

Like the DP, the Justice Party won support from peasants in the wealthier regions of the country, commercial farmers, and the business community. In addition, the party won the votes of many workers and residents of the squatter districts of the cities, but in the 1970s, the RPP began to win the loyalty of these two groups. Like the DP, the JP sought to expand the private sector but also intervened widely in the economy through the public sector, controls over trade, and other regulations. Through 1970, the JP pursued a policy of import-substituting industrialization. Beginning in 1970, the government attempted to reorient the economy toward exporting, a move resisted by many industrialists.

Despite similarities with the DP, a number of changes in Turkey prevented the JP from replicating its predecessors' electoral success. First, the proliferation of smaller parties made it necessary to form coalition governments in the 1970s. Second, the RPP made many inroads into the urban coalitions that had supported the DP in the 1950s and the JP in the 1960s. Third, in 1967, a more militant workers' union was formed, which refused to cooperate with the government. Fourth, small businessmen in the party were alienated by JP policies that favored large businessmen, particularly in Istanbul. Many small-business owners supported the National Order Party, led by Necmeddin Erbakan, which captured a portion of JP votes. Fifth, the JP continued the DP policy of closely allying with the West. But, particularly after American condemnation of the Turkish intervention in Cyprus in 1974, many people criticized the JP for being too close to the West. Finally, in the 1960s, rising tensions led to escalating political violence. All of these factors combined to make it more difficult for the JP to form stable governments than it had been for the DP.

See also DEMIREL, SÜLEYMAN; ERBAKAN, NECMEDDIN; NATIONALIST ACTION PARTY; REPUBLICAN PEOPLE'S PARTY (RPP); TRUE PATH PARTY.

Bibliography

Ahmad, Feroz. *The Making of Modern Turkey.* London and New York: Routledge, 1993.

Levi, Ayner. "The Justice Party, 1961–1980." In *Political Parties and Democracy in Turkey,* edited by Metin Heper and Jacob M. Landau. London and New York: I.B. Tauris, 1991.

Sherwood, W. B. "The Rise of the Justice Party in Turkey." *World Politics* 20 (1967–1968): 54–65.

DAVID WALDNER

KA'BA

The most important shrine of Islam.

The Ka'ba is a sanctuary consecrated to the worship of God. A simple cubic structure (12.6 m by 13.1 m by 11.3 m by 11.2 m with a height of 13 m), it stands at the center of Mecca. It constitutes the *qibla,* the direction to which Muslims must orient themselves in prayer, and it is at the heart of the hajj, the pilgrimage prescribed at least once in their lifetime for the faithful. The doors are situated in the northern wall and the whole structure is covered with a black cloth embroidered with golden Qur'anic calligraphy and replaced with a new one every year.

The Ka'ba in pre-Islamic times was the main temple of Associationist Mecca and a pilgrimage site for all Arabians. Associationism, the pre-Islamic religious tradition of Arabia, and later the Qur'an itself, attributed the construction of the Ka'ba to Abraham, to whom most Arabian tribes traced their ancestry through his son Ishmael. According to tradition, the Black Stone, which was and to this day remains encased in one of the walls of the Ka'ba, was believed to be the only remnant of the original construction; and some traditions report that it had originally fallen from the sky. The pre-Islamic temple housed symbols of the various deities worshiped in association with the creator Allah, as well as representations of Mary and Jesus and Jewish symbols. Tradition reports that when Mecca surrendered to the Prophet, the latter's first act after granting amnesty to all Meccans was to ride to the Ka'ba, empty it of all representations and re-dedicate it to the worship of the one God.

Although in principle fighting is not allowed in its vicinity, the Ka'ba was destroyed and rebuilt more than once in Muslim history, and the Black Stone stolen but eventually returned. Today, political demonstrations around the Ka'ba and during the hajj are not allowed. Over time, a large mosque (al-Masjid al-Haram) was built around it. Though neither in itself an object of worship nor considered as having a "sacred" nature, the Ka'ba remains to the Muslim the holiest place on earth.

K

Bibliography

Nomachi, Ali K., and Nasr, Seyyed Hossein. *Mecca the Blessed, Medina the Radiant.* New York: Aperture Foundation, 1997.

MAYSAM J. AL FARUQI

KABAK, AARON ABRAHAM

[1880–1944]

Hebrew novelist.

Born near Vilna (now Vilnius, Lithuania), Aaron Abraham Kabak studied at universities in Berlin and Switzerland and settled in Palestine in 1911. He left in 1914 but returned in 1921. As a teacher at Jerusalem's Rehaviah Gymnasium (secondary school), he had great influence on the literary and educational dynamics of the city.

In 1905 Kabak wrote the first Zionist novel in Hebrew, *Levaddah* (By herself). His *Shelomo Molkho* (1928–1929), a three-volume work about the sixteenth century pseudo-messiah, was the first historical novel in Hebrew. *Ba-Mishʿol Ha-Zar* (In the narrow path), written in 1937 after his return to Orthodox Judaism, describes the teachings of Jesus of Nazareth, the Jew. Although he retained its Jewish content, Kabak modernized the Hebrew novel by ridding it of its hitherto conventional protagonists, motifs, and settings.

See also LITERATURE: HEBREW.

ANN KAHN

KABUL

Afghan city and province.

Kabul is both Afghanistan's largest city and national capital and the name of the province that surrounds the city. Kabul is at nearly 1828 meters (6,000 feet) above sea level and situated near the Khyber Pass, a major route between Afghanistan and Pakistan. Strategically located on north-south and east-west trade routes, Kabul has been a major city for thousands of years; the oldest reference to it is found in the *Rig Veda,* an ancient Sanskrit text (1500 B.C.E.). The city now holds more than 2 million people; an accurate census has not been taken.

Since 1980 Kabul has suffered considerable physical, social, and economic damage. Bombs or artillery have destroyed many of the main buildings, particularly during the civil war of the early 1990s, and many of the educated elite have fled Kabul. Since the Taliban fell in December 2001, the city has been crowded with returning refugees and Afghans who are internally displaced because of fighting, the drought, or the general collapse of the rural economy. In 2003, Kabul was controlled by the Afghan interim government of Hamid Karzai, but remained without basic services. Security remained problematic and an international peacekeeping force policed Kabul.

Bibliography

Adamec, Ludwig. *Historical Dictionary of Afghanistan,* 2d edition. Lanham, MD: Scarecrow Press, 1997.

GRANT FARR

KABUL UNIVERSITY

Afghan university.

Founded in 1932 during the reign of Nadir Shah, Kabul University began as a medical school with Turkish and French faculty. In 1959, dormitories were built to house students from rural or outlying areas. By 1963, the university had eight faculties, including faculties of law and political science, natural sciences, economics, home economics, education, engineering, and pharmacy.

As student demand increased, a quota system was imposed in 1964 that fixed the urban-to-rural ratio at 60 to 40 percent. In the late 1960s and early 1970s Kabul University became a center of political activity, although the government officially banned such activity on campus in 1968. Many of the future leaders of Afghanistan, from both the left and the right of the political spectrum, began their political careers by engaging in campus politics during this time. When the communist government came to power in 1978 many of the faculty left Afghanistan. In the period after 1992 fighting between various militia groups destroyed many of the university buildings, the remaining faculty fled, and the university was essentially closed.

The government of Hamid Karzai reopened the university in 2002, but the lack of basic facilities created hardships and led to student demonstrations.

Bibliography

Farr, Grant. "New Afghan Middle Class: Refugees and Insurgents." In *Afghan Resistance: The Politics of Survival,* edited by Grant M. Farr and John G. Merriam. Boulder, CO: Westview, 1987.

GRANT FARR

KABYLIA

Berber-speaking mountainous area in northern Algeria east of Algiers.

Kabylia, derived from the French Kabylie, is based on the Arabic *qabila* (tribe; pl., *qabail*). The region is traditionally divided into two parts: the Djurdjura Mountains (highest point 7,565 ft.) separating the Great Kabylia, to the north and centering on the regional capital, Tizi-Ouzou, and the Lesser Kabylia, to the south and east. Population density in this very hilly and not very fertile region is quite high. Though the area produces much of Algeria's olive oil and dried figs, the agricultural economy cannot support the total population. Thus historically the Kabylia has been a region of emigration to the Algerian port cities and the manufacturing centers of France. Although difficult to count accurately, the current Berber (Tamazight)-speaking population of the region is estimated at roughly four million.

Kabyle participation in Algeria's war of independence (1954–1962) was strong and determined. Upon independence, however, the Arab leadership of the National Liberation Front declared Algeria to be an Arab-Muslim nation. It broke up Berberist organizations and repressed the use of Tamazight, deeming it a threat to national unity. In 1980 largely peaceful, student-led demonstrations protesting the government's suppression of Berber cultural events broke out at Tizi-Ouzou—the administrative, commercial, and cultural center of the region—and then spread to other parts of the Kabylia. Violently repressed by the regime, these events came to be known as Berber Spring. Since then, and despite the strong opposition of Muslim fundamentalists and dominant sectors of the Algerian regime, Kabyles slowly have been able to obtain limited recognition for their cultural traditions and language: Tamazight was recognized as one of the languages of the country in 1989, and a Berber culture

curriculum has been developed at the University of Tizi-Ouzou. However, censorship against Berber cultural demonstrations continues at different levels. Kabyles pride themselves in their distinct cultural achievement and traditions, which include poetry, jewelry, and music.

During the events known as the Black Spring of April 2001, Kabyle youth protested the *hogra,* a Tamazight word signifying the abuse of authority and the violation of citizens' rights on the part of the authorities. Structural unemployment fueled by International Monetary Fund policies, continued Islamist and state-sponsored violence, and lack of prospects for the youth contributed to the revolt.

In March 2002 the Algerian government finally decided to include Tamazight as a national language. Nevertheless, under the slogan "no forgiveness, no vote," the Kabyle citizens' movement called for a boycott of the Algerian legislative elections of May 2002; voter turnout in Tizi-Ouzou was 2 percent. In another concession in 2003, President Abdelaziz Bouteflika agreed to include the Tamazight language in the national education system.

See also BERBER SPRING; BLACK SPRING.

Bibliography

Movement for the Autonomy of the Kabylia (MAK). Available from <http://www.makabylie.info>.

United Nations High Commissioner for Human Rights. "United Nations Committee on Economic, Social and Cultural Rights Starts Review of Report of Algeria." Press Release. Available from <http://www.unhchr.ch>.

THOMAS G. PENCHOEN
UPDATED BY VANESA CASANOVA-FERNANDEZ

KACH

See ISRAEL: POLITICAL PARTIES IN

KADIVAR, MOHSEN
[1959–]

Iranian cleric who rejects the notion of political rule by the clergy.

Mohsen Kadivar was born in Fasa, a small town in the southern province of Fars, Iran. He studied electrical and electronic engineering at the University of

Shiraz prior to the Iranian Revolution of 1979. With the onset of the revolution, Kadivar started studying at the seminary in Shiraz, and in 1981 he went to Qom, where he studied *fiqh* (Islamic jurisprudence) and the related principal sciences (*usul*), as well as Islamic philosophy under Ayatollah Hosainali Montazeri. Kadivar concurrently studied in the university system and received a Ph.D. in Islamic philosophy and theology from Tehran's Teachers' Training College.

In his writings, Kadivar has strived to reveal a harmony between reason (*aql*) and revelation by analyzing and interpreting classical Islamic and Shi'ite texts. In his two books, *Nazariyeha-ye Dulat dar Fiqh-e Shi* (1997; Theories of state in Shi'ite law) and *Hukumat-e Velayi* (1998; Government by the guardian), Kadivar has criticized the notion of *velayat-e faqih* (guardianship of the jurist) by attempting to show the lack of Qur'anic, rational, and *fiqh* grounds for the idea of political rule by the clergy headed by a supreme jurisprudent. As a result, the Special Court for the Clergy charged Kadivar with propaganda against the Islamic Republic, dissemination of lies, and creating confusion in public opinion, for which he served a prison term of eighteen months. He was released in July 2000.

See also VELAYAT-E FAQIH.

FARZIN VAHDAT

KADRI, MUFIDE

[1889–1911]

Turkish modern artist.

Mufide Kadri was one of the earliest female modern artists in the Middle East. She was born in Turkey and trained in private lessons under Osman Hamdi Bey and Salvatore Venery of the Istanbul Fine Arts Academy, an institution that did not admit women for a number of years. Despite an early death, at the age of twenty-two, many of her works survive and are on display at the Istanbul Art Museum. They include portraits done in the impressionist style, a trend common among Middle Eastern artists at the beginning of the twentieth century.

See also ART; GENDER: GENDER AND EDUCATION.

JESSICA WINEGAR

KAFIYYA

See CLOTHING

KAFR QASIM

Arab village in Israel, site of 1956 massacre.

On the eve of the 1956 Arab–Israel War, 29 October 1956, Israeli border police deliberately shot and killed forty-nine Israeli Arabs—workmen, women, and children—who were returning to Kafr Qasim, for the violation of a curfew of which they were not aware. A commission of inquiry was formed on 1 November 1956, which established the extent of responsibility and compensation.

Eight of the eleven military personnel brought to trial were convicted of murder and given sentences of up to seventeen years. All were released by 1960 through a partial pardon.

See also ARAB–ISRAEL WAR (1956).

Bibliography

Hirst, David. *The Gun and the Olive Branch*. London: Faber and Faber, 1977.

Rolef, Susan Hattis, ed. *Political Dictionary of the State of Israel*, 2nd edition. New York: Macmillan, 1993.

ELIZABETH THOMPSON

KAHAN COMMISSION (1983)

Israeli judicial commission that investigated the 1982 massacres at the Sabra and Shatila refugee camps in Beirut.

The Israeli government established the Commission of Inquiry into the Events at the Refugee Camps in Beirut (the Kahan Commission) in response to a massive public outcry following the killing of an estimated 800 to 1,200 Palestinian civilians in the Sabra and Shatila refugee camps on the outskirts of Beirut by right-wing Christian militiamen, primarily of the Lebanese Phalange Party, on 16 and 18 September 1982. The massacres occurred in territory under the control of the Israel Defense Force in the wake of Israel's June 1982 invasion of Lebanon, and the perpetrators were Israeli allies. On 24 September 1982, some 400,000 Israelis demonstrated in Tel Aviv against their country's continuing involvement in Lebanon and in favor of an official investigation into the massacres. The three-person commission was chaired by Yitzhak Kahan, president of the Supreme Court; the other members were Aharon Barak, a Supreme Court justice, and retired army general Yona Efrat.

The commission issued its report on 7 February 1983. It noted that the Phalange had secured the permission of Major General Amir Drori, of the Northern Command, to enter the camps. This was approved by Israel's chief of staff, Lieutenant General Rafael Eitan, and Minister of Defense Ariel Sharon. The commission found that Israel's leaders and commanders bore indirect responsibility for the massacre by not anticipating Phalange revenge attacks against the unprotected Palestinians and by not acting to halt the killings soon enough, once indications of the bloodletting began to emerge from the camps. The commission chastised Prime Minister Menachem Begin, Foreign Minister Yitzhak Shamir, and the (unnamed) head of the Mossad for their indifference to the events at the time, but it found particular fault with Drori, Eitan, the director of military intelligence General Yehoshua Saguy, and Division Commander General Amos Yaron. Most seriously, the commission found that Ariel Sharon bore personal responsibility for the tragedy and recommended that the prime minister consider removing him from office. On 10 February 1983, the cabinet voted to remove Sharon from his position as defense minister, although he remained as minister without portfolio.

Given the dread with which most Israelis came to regard the Lebanese quagmire in which Israel remained embroiled for the next seventeen years, Sharon's election as prime minister in February 2001 constituted a remarkable case of political rehabilitation. But the disaster in Lebanon dogged his premiership when, in June 2001, a group of Sabra and Shatila survivors filed a war-crimes complaint against him in a Belgian court under a 1993 Belgian law allowing claimants to bring cases against foreigners accused of crimes against humanity, regardless of where they occurred. One year later, however, a Belgian appeals court dismissed the case on the grounds that Sharon was not domiciled in Belgium, so the case never went to trial. No Lebanese inquiry into the massacre was ever carried through to completion.

See also BEGIN, MENACHEM; EITAN, RAFAEL; LEBANESE CIVIL WAR (1975–1990); MOSSAD; PHALANGE; SABRA AND SHATILA MASSACRES; SHAMIR, YITZHAK; SHARON, ARIEL.

Bibliography

The Beirut Massacre: The Complete Kahan Commission Report. Princeton, NJ: Karz-Cohl, 1983.

Schiff, Ze'ev, and Ya'ari, Ehud. *Israel's Lebanon War.* New York: Simon and Schuster, 1984.

JENAB TUTUNJI
UPDATED BY LAURIE Z. EISENBERG

KAHANE, MEIR
[1932–1990]

Rabbi, founder of U.S. Jewish Defense League and the Kach Party in Israel.

Born in New York, Meir Kahane was active in youth movements before becoming a rabbi and writer for Jewish nationalist journals. He founded the Jewish Defense League (JDL) in 1968 to combat antisemitism. The JDL soon became known as a militant Jewish self-defense organization, and it encountered difficulties with the government because of its violent tactics.

In 1969 Kahane moved to Israel, where he began to speak out against the Black Jews in Dimona. In 1972 his Kach (also Kakh; "thus" in Hebrew) Party became a proponent of inducing Palestinians to leave the West Bank voluntarily; if they would not leave, Kahane proposed expelling them. He believed that Israel should become a theocratic state, and wanted the government to pass laws formally entrenching Orthodox Judaism as the official state religion. He ran for the Knesset unsuccessfully in 1973 and 1977. In 1980 he was sentenced to six months in prison for plotting to attack Muslim shrines on the Temple Mount (al-Haram al-Sharif). After his release he ran for the Knesset in the 1984 election and won a seat, but in 1988 Kach was outlawed on the grounds that it was a racist party. Kahane was assassinated in New York in November 1990.

Kahane's son, Binyamin Kahane, founded the organization Kahane Hai ("Kahane Lives") after his father's assassination. In March 1994 it was declared by the Israeli cabinet to be a terrorist organization and was therefore banned, as Kach had been. Binyamin was assassinated, too, by some Palestinians in a drive-by shooting in December 2000 in the West Bank. According to a 2003 U.S. Department of State report, the group has continued organized protests against the Israeli government and has harassed Palestinians in the West Bank. Kach members have also threatened to attack Israeli government officials and have vowed revenge for the death of Binyamin Kahane and his wife. They have also been suspected of involvement in a number of attacks on Palestinians since the start of the al-Aqsa Intifada.

See also ISRAEL: OVERVIEW OF POLITICAL PARTIES IN.

Bibliography

Ben-David, Calev. "The Life of Meir Kahane: A Cautionary Tale." *Jerusalem Post.* 22 October 2002.

Kahane, Meir. *Never Again! A Program for Survival.* Los Angeles: Nash Publishing, 1971.

Kahane, Meir. *Our Challenge: The Chosen Land.* Radnor, PA: Chilton Book Co., 1974.

Kahane, Meir. *The Story of the Jewish Defense League.* Radnor, PA: Chilton Book Co., 1975.

WALTER F. WEIKER
UPDATED BY GREGORY S. MAHLER

KAID, AHMED
[1927–1978]

Algerian officer and government minister.

Ahmed Kaid was born near Tiaret. He attended the French military school at Hussein-Dey and then the Normal School for teacher training in Algiers. Before the Algerian War of Independence (1954–1962), he aligned with the moderate nationalist Union Démocratique du Manifeste Algérien (UDMA) of Ferhat Abbas. He joined the Front de Libération Nationale (FLN) and rose to assistant chief of staff of the Armée de Libération Nationale (ALN). Kaid sided with the Ahmed Ben Bella–Houari Boumédienne faction after the war. He was elected to the National Assembly and served as minister of tourism (1963). He resigned in 1964, though he retained his seat on the Central Committee of the FLN. After Boumédienne's coup, he became minister of finance (1967) and then was chosen to head FLN. He resigned in 1972, critical of the party's bureaucracy

and of the Agrarian Revolution. In March 1976 while in France, he publicly criticized the Boumédienne government. Given his anti-Boumédienne position, suspicion rose over his death, reportedly from a heart attack. Thousands attended his funeral in Tiaret.

See also ABBAS, FERHAT; ALGERIAN WAR OF INDEPENDENCE; ARMÉE DE LIBÉRATION NATIONALE (ALN); BEN BELLA, AHMED; BOUMÉDIENNE, HOUARI; FRONT DE LIBÉRATION NATIONALE; UNION DÉMOCRATIQUE DU MANIFESTE ALGÉRIEN (UDMA).

Bibliography

Ottaway, David, and Ottaway, Marina. *Algeria: The Politics of a Socialist Revolution.* Berkeley: University of California Press, 1970.

PHILLIP C. NAYLOR

KALEMIYYE

Ottoman hierarchy of scribes, clerks, and accountants headed by the reis ül-küttap.

Aside from the sultan's own staff, the *kalemiyye* (scribal institution) was one of three powerful bureaucracies in the Ottoman government, the others being the *seyfiyye* (military) and *İlmiyye* (religious). From 1794, the *kalemiyye* was headquartered in the Sublime Porte, and while the grand vizier was nominally its head, the *reis ül-küttap* held the real power. In the early nineteenth century, the major Tanzimat reformers emerged from the *kalemiyye,* the most prominent of them Mustafa Reşid Paşa, who was *reis ül-küttap* in 1827–1830. In 1835, the *kalemiyye* was joined with the sultan's imperial bureaucracy. Later renamed the *mülkiyye,* it would be reformed several times during the nineteenth century, as former patronage systems were replaced with regular salaried employees and formal departments and ministries were organized. It would come to include the finance, commerce, interior, foreign affairs, and other ministries.

See also İLMIYYE; MUSTAFA REŞID; SUBLIME PORTE; TANZIMAT.

Bibliography

Shaw, Stanford, and Shaw, Ezel Kural. *History of the Ottoman Empire and Modern Turkey.* 2 vols. Cambridge,

U.K., and New York: Cambridge University Press, 1976–1977.

ELIZABETH THOMPSON

KALISCHER, HIRSCH
[1795–1874]

Rabbi and precursor of Zionism.

Born in western Poland in a region acquired by Prussia in 1793, Hirsch Kalischer was aware of nationalist struggles from an early age, perhaps sensitizing him to the misery of European Jewry. He was engaged early in his career in a defense of traditional Judaism against the Reform movement. Subsequently, he began to argue that the redemption would only come after action was taken by the Jewish people on their own behalf. He elaborated these ideas in *Derishat Tziyon* (1862; Seeking Zion), a book about modern Jewish agricultural settlement in Palestine.

Kalischer was successful in persuading the Alliance Israélite Universelle, a French organization for the international defense of Jewish rights, to found an agricultural school in Jaffa, Palestine, in 1870. He made numerous visits to wealthy Jews in Germany to recruit their support for Jewish settlement in Palestine.

See also ALLIANCE ISRAÉLITE UNIVERSELLE (AIU).

Bibliography

Hertzberg, Arthur, ed. *The Zionist Idea: A Historical Analysis and Reader*. Philadelphia: Jewish Publication Society, 1997.

MARTIN MALIN

KALVARYSKI, CHAIM MARGALIUT-
[1868–1947]

Land-purchase agent and adviser on Arab–Jewish relations in Palestine.

Chaim Margaliut-Kalvaryski was born in Poland and emigrated to Palestine in 1895, after completing studies in agronomy in France. Between 1900 and 1922 he served as an administrator of the Jewish Colonization Association in the Galilee, helping to acquire extensive areas for Jewish settlement. Beginning in 1913 he became involved in political discussions with Arab nationalists in Beirut and Damascus. Between 1923 and 1927 Kalvaryski was employed by the Palestine Zionist Executive as an adviser on Arab affairs. Despite controversies over his methods and doubts about his financial management, he was recalled to head the Joint Bureau of Jewish Public Bodies that was formed to coordinate relations with the Arabs following the 1929 Palestine riots.

Kalvaryski was a member of the Palestine government's first Advisory Council (1920–1923) and the Vaʿad Leʾumi (National Council of the Jews) beginning in 1920, and was active in Jewish groups promoting binationalism and rapprochement with the Arabs of Palestine and the neighboring countries. He also devised several of his own peace plans, which he discussed with Arab leaders.

Kalvaryski's articles and speeches were published in various Hebrew newspapers and periodicals and in a collection entitled *Al Parshat Darkeinu* (At the parting of our ways; Jerusalem, 1939).

See also JEWISH COLONIZATION ASSOCIATION.

Bibliography

Caplan, Neil. "Arab-Jewish Contacts in Palestine After the First World War." *Journal of Contemporary History* 12, no. 4 (1977): 635–668.

Caplan, Neil. *Futile Diplomacy*, Volumes 1 and 2. London: Frank Cass, 1983, 1986.

Cohen, Aharon. *Israel and the Arab World*. New York: Funk and Wagnalls, 1970.

NEIL CAPLAN

KAMAL, AHMAD
[1849–1923]

The first prominent Egyptian archaeologist and Egyptologist.

Ahmad Kamal Pasha studied under Heinrich K. Brugsch (1827–1894), a German archaeologist, a scholar of hieroglyphics and demotic Egyptian, and the director of the short-lived school of Egyptology in Cairo in the 1870s. Kamal made his career in the Egyptian Antiquities Service and helped open professional archaeology and Egyptology to Egyptians (they were dominated by Europeans). His long campaign succeeded when immediately after his death, the department that evolved into today's Faculty of Archaeology of Cairo University was established.

See also ARCHAEOLOGY IN THE MIDDLE EAST.

Bibliography

Dawson, Warren R., and Uphill, Eric P. *Who Was Who in Egyptology,* 2d edition. London: Egypt Exploration Society, 1972.

DONALD MALCOLM REID

KAMAL, ZAHIRA
[1945–]

Palestinian activist.

Director of the Gender Department of the Palestinian Authority's Ministry of Planning and International Cooperation as of 2003, Zahira Kamal has represented Palestinians through her writing and activism for more than thirty years. Trained as a physics teacher, she founded and, from 1978 to 1992, led the Women's Work Committee (later the Union of Palestinian Women's Action Committees), an organization serving professional, clerical, and industrial women workers and closely affiliated with the Democratic Front for the Liberation of Palestine (DFLP). Originally a member of the political leadership of the DFLP, she was imprisoned in 1979 and held under town arrest in Jerusalem from 1980 to 1986. She left the party for FIDA, the Palestinian Democratic Union, when that group split from the DFLP in support of the Madrid and Oslo peace negotiations with Israel. With Yasir Abd Rabbo, who led the split from the DFLP, Kamal was a delegate to the 1991 Madrid Conference. She also headed the Women's Affairs Technical Committee, which monitored women's issues as a component of the interim peace negotiations. Kamal was appointed head of the Ministry of Planning and International Cooperation (MOPIC) Gender Planning and Development Directorate in 1995. A noted writer on issues of gender and Israeli–Palestinian relationships, she has engaged in active dialogue with Israeli groups, particularly women's groups, for years, and is cofounder of the Jerusalem Link, an organization which supports women's participation, awareness-raising, and leadership development within the context of the peace process.

See also GAZA STRIP; GENDER: GENDER AND EDUCATION; GENDER: GENDER AND LAW; GENDER: GENDER AND POLITICS; INTIFADA (1987–1991); MADRID CONFERENCE (1991); OSLO ACCORD (1993); PALESTINE; WEST BANK.

Bibliography

Ashrawi, Hanan. *This Side of Peace: A Personal Account.* New York: Simon and Schuster, 1995.

Berger Gluck, Sherna. "Shifting Sands: The Feminist-Nationalist Connection in the Palestinian Movement." In *Feminist Nationalism,* edited by Lois A. West. New York: Routledge, 1997.

Jerusalem Center for Women (Jerusalem Link). Available from <http://www.j-c-w.org/index.htm>.

RACHEL CHRISTINA

KAMIL, KIBRISH MEHMET
[1832–1913]

Ottoman grand vizier.

The son of a military officer, Kibrish Mehmet Kamil was born in Nicosia on the island of Cyprus (in Turkish, Kibris). He was graduated from the military academy in Cairo and served as adjutant to Abbas Paşa. Between 1860 and 1879, he held various positions in the Ottoman provincial bureaucracy, rising to the position of governor of Kosovo and Aleppo. In 1879, he became a cabinet minister, serving for short periods as minister of education and of religious foundations until becoming grand vizier on 25 September 1885, replacing Küçük Sait Paşa who became a rival and regular replacement. Between 1885 and 1891, he successfully stabilized Ottoman finances while encouraging foreign investment in Ottoman railroads and industries. In 1895, at the start of a second stint as grand vizier, he fell into the sultan's disfavor and was sent into exile, serving eleven years as governor of İzmir. Although an opponent of the Committee for Union and Progress, he was appointed grand vizier for a third time on 5 August 1908, serving until 14 February 1909. During this period, when Abdülhamit II was still sultan, Kamil Paşa worked to balance the budget, reorganize the bureaucracy and armed forces, and put an end to the millet system and the privileges enjoyed by foreigners according to the capitulations.

See also ABDÜLHAMIT II; CAPITULATIONS; COMMITTEE FOR UNION AND PROGRESS; MILLET SYSTEM.

Bibliography

Shaw, Stanford, and Shaw, Ezel Kural. *History of the Ottoman Empire and Modern Turkey,* Vol. 2: *Reform, Revolution, and Republic: The Rise of Modern Turkey, 1808–1975.* Cambridge, U.K., and New York: Cambridge University Press, 1977.

DAVID WALDNER

KAMIL, MUSTAFA

[1874–1908]

Egyptian nationalist leader, orator, and editor.

Mustafa Kamil, the son of an army officer from an ethnic Egyptian family, was educated in government schools, the French School of Law in Cairo, and the University of Toulouse, France, where he received his law degree in 1895. A strong opponent of the British occupation of Egypt, he soon became closely associated with Khedive Abbas Hilmi II and with Ottoman Sultan Abdülhamit II, both of whom supported him materially as well as morally in his campaigns to persuade European governments and peoples to demand the evacuation promised by successive British governments. He also worked closely with Muhammad Farid and other Egyptians to form a secret society, initially under the aegis of the *khedive,* to inculcate resistance to the British among the people of Egypt. This society, known from its inception as al-Hizb al-Watani (the National Party), became a public political party, open to all Egyptians, in December 1907. He also founded a popular daily newspaper, *al-Liwa* (The banner), in 1900, which became the official party organ, and a boys' school that bore his name. He wrote many articles for the French press, for *al-Mu'ayyad* under Shaykh Ali Yusuf, and for *al-Liwa,* as well as a book on the Eastern Question called *al-Mas'ala al-Sharqiyya,* in which he strongly supported the Ottoman Empire. He delivered many stirring speeches in French and in Arabic, of which the best remembered was translated into English as "What the National Party Wants." He died of tuberculosis (but some think he was poisoned) in the thirty-fourth year of his life, and his funeral was the occasion for a massive demonstration of popular grief. Remembered as a fervent patriot and occasional supporter of pan-Islam, he called for the British evacuation of Egypt and a constitutional government but showed little interest in economic or social issues.

See also ABBAS HILMI II; ABDÜLHAMIT II; EASTERN QUESTION; NATIONAL PARTY (EGYPT).

Bibliography

Goldschmidt, Arthur. "The Egyptian Nationalist Party, 1892–1919." In *Political and Social Change in Modern Egypt: Historical Studies from the Ottoman Conquest to the United Arab Republic,* edited by P. M. Holt. London: Oxford University Press, 1968.

Sayyid-Marsot, Afaf Lutfi. *Egypt and Cromer: A Study in Anglo–Egyptian Relations.* London: Murray, 1968.

ARTHUR GOLDSCHMIDT

KANAFANI, GHASSAN

[1936–1972]

Palestinian writer and political activist.

A native of Acre, Palestine, Ghassan Kanafani published the Arab National Movement's official organ, *al-Ra'y* (Opinion), with George Habash. Kanafani was also a prominent spokesman and ideologue for the Popular Front for the Liberation of Palestine. Believed by Israel's intelligence service, Mossad, to have been involved in planning terrorist operations, Kanafani was assassinated by a hit team from Israel who detonated a car bomb outside his home in Hazmiyya, near Beirut, killing him and his seventeen-year-old niece, Lamis Najim. Kanafani's Danish wife, small son, and daughter escaped unhurt. Kanafani's successor, Bassam Abu Sharif, also was targeted by Israel's intelligence; he lost the sight in one eye and several fingers when a letter bomb exploded in his Beirut office.

At his death, Kanafani had already established himself as a prolific writer and commentator. Among his best-known works is *Rijal fi al-Shams* (1963; Men in the sun), based on his traumatic experiences as a refugee. Some of his other books include *The Middle of May, The Land of Sad Oranges,* and *That Which Is Left Over for You.*

See also ARAB NATIONAL MOVEMENT (ANM); HABASH, GEORGE; MOSSAD; NEWSPAPERS AND PRINT MEDIA: ARAB COUNTRIES;

POPULAR FRONT FOR THE LIBERATION OF PALESTINE.

Bibliography

Cooley, John K. *Green March, Black September: The Story of the Palestinian Arabs.* London: Cass, 1973.

Rabbani, Muin. "Kahafani, Ghassan." In *Encyclopedia of the Palestinians,* edited by Philip Mattar. New York: Facts On File, 2000.

LAWRENCE TAL

KANDAHAR

Afghan city and province.

Located in southern Afghanistan, the province of Kandahar has a population of approximately 700,000, most of whom are Durrani Pushtuns. The city of Kandahar is the provincial capital and the second largest city in Afghanistan, with a population of about 200,000. It was Afghanistan's original capital. Centrally situated on trade routes between the Iranian plateau and the Indian subcontinent, Kandahar has been an important city for centuries and has played a major role in the history of Afghanistan. Most of the leaders of Afghanistan have come from the Pushtun tribes in the Kandahar area.

During the War of Resistance (1978–1992), Kandahar was the scene of intense fighting and much of the city was destroyed. Almost half of the population of the province fled to neighboring Pakistan during the war, but most subsequently returned.

Kandahar played a central role in the Taliban movement (1996–2001). Although Kabul remained the capital of Afghanistan, Mullah Omar, the leader of the Taliban government, kept his residence in Kandahar.

Bibliography

Adamec, Ludwig. *Historical Dictionary of Afghanistan,* 2d edition. Lanham, MD: Scarecrow, 1997.

Rubin, Barnett R. *The Fragmentation of Afghanistan: State Formation and Collapse in the International System.* New Haven, CT: Yale University Press, 2002.

GRANT FARR

KANIUK, YORAM
[1930–]

Israeli author.

Born in Tel Aviv into a family deeply involved in the cultural life of that city (his father was one of the founders of the Tel Aviv Museum), Yoram Kaniuk served in the Haganah, the underground army of Jewish Palestine, and fought in the 1948 War. A painter, journalist, and theater critic, he is best known as a novelist. He is the author of many works of fiction, including children's books, and a few works of nonfiction. Although his works have been translated into twenty languages, only some of his books have appeared in English, and most of these are earlier works; his later ones, notably the remarkable if painful *Post-Mortem* (1992) and *Ahavat David* (1990), remain unavailable in English. Kaniuk's distinguishing trademark is the fiercely lucid—some might say cruel—literary eye he brings to bear on life in contemporary Israel. Indeed, Israel itself and the price it has exacted from the Jewish soul is the ever-present, overriding theme of all his novels. The uncompromising truths of his fiction, at times personally and nationally autobiographical, bring the reader face to face with the white-hot paradox of life and Jewish history. Kaniuk has been the recipient of the Bialik Prize, the French Prix de Droits de l'Homme, the Prix Méditerranée Etranger, and the Israel President's Prize for Literature. As of 2004, he continued to live in his native city of Tel Aviv.

See also LITERATURE: HEBREW.

Bibliography

Kaniuk, Yoram. *The Acrophile,* translated by Zeva Shapiro. New York: Atheneum, 1960.

Kaniuk, Yoram. *Commander of the Exodus,* translated by Seymour Simckes. New York: Grove, 1999.

Kaniuk, Yoram. *Confessions of a Good Arab: A Novel,* translated by Dalya Bilu. New York: G. Braziller; London: P. Halban, 1984.

Kaniuk, Yoram. *His Daughter,* translated by Seymour Simckes. New York: G. Braziller, 1989; London: P. Halban, 1987.

Kaniuk, Yoram. *Rockinghorse,* translated by Richard Flantz. New York: Harper and Row, 1977.

Kaniuk, Yoram. *The Story of Aunt Shlomzion the Great*, translated by Zeva Shapiro. New York: Harper and Row, 1978.

ZEVA SHAPIRO
UPDATED BY STEPHEN SCHECTER

KAN, SUNA
[1936–]

Turkish violinist.

A born violinist, Suna Kan attracted her audiences with a stage presence of serene statuesque beauty combined with a serene beauty of tone she produced from her instrument. Kan was born in Adana, Turkey, in 1936. Her extraordinary talent was recognized when she started playing the violin at the age of five. Walter Gerhard, Gilbert Back, Licco Amar, and Izzet Albayrak were among her teachers in Ankara. She played Mozart's A major and Viotti's A minor violin concertos with the Ankara Presidential Symphony Orchestra when she was nine years old. In 1949 she was sent to France by the Turkish government to study at the Paris Conservatory, where she was a pupil of Gabriel Bouillon. She graduated in 1952, winning the first prize. Kan won first prizes at the Geneva Competition in 1954 and the Viotti Competition in 1955, second prize at the Munich Competition in 1956, and the City of Paris Prize in the Marguerite Long/Jacques Thibaud Competition in 1957.

She had a brilliant international concert career between 1958 and 1977, during which she performed with most of the world's greatest orchestras under the direction of the most famous conductors. She also performed double concertos with legendary musicians such as Yehudi Menuhin, Piérre Fournier, André Navarra, and Frederick Riddle. She toured all over Europe, Russia, Canada, Japan, China, South America, Ethiopia, United Arab Republic, Kenya, and Iran.

Kan was a founding member and principal soloist of the Turkish Radio-Television's Ankara Chamber Orchestra, with which she toured Turkey, Europe, and Russia between 1977 and 1986. Since 1986 she has devoted herself to the music education of her countrymen, conducting masterclasses and summer schools. She has not retired from the concert stage and continues to perform regularly. She has recorded all of Mozart's violin concertos and Ulvi Cemal Erkin's violin concerto. She received Chevalier dans l'ordre du Mérite from the government of France, and is also the State Artist of the Turkish Republic.

See also GENDER: GENDER AND EDUCATION; MUSIC.

FILIZ ALI

KARACAN, ALI NACI
[1896–1955]

Turkish journalist and publisher.

Born in Istanbul, Ali Naci Karacan attended Galatasaray Lycée. He began working as a reporter at a young age, before World War I, first at *Tasvir-i Efkar* and then at the oppositional paper *Ikdam*. Later, he worked as an editor for famous newspapers such as *Vakit*. He was cofounder, in 1918, of *Akşam*, with well-known journalists Salih Rifki Atay and Kazim Şinasi Dersan. In 1935, Karacan became editor of Turkey's newly founded leftist daily *Tan*.

Karacan's greatest success was founding the daily paper *Milliyet* in 1950. Karacan and his son Ercüment quickly carved a place among a number of new newspapers of the period, including Sedat Simavi's *Hürriyet*, founded two years before. Carrying the slogan "Independent Political Newspaper" on its masthead, *Milliyet* matched *Hürriyet*'s slick style, but also managed to appeal to intellectuals with a well-respected staff of writers. Under the editorial leadership of Abdi İpekci, it became an influential player in Turkey's political arena in the 1960s and 1970s. By then, the Karacan family, including grandson Ali Naci Karacan, controlled a publishing syndicate that included printing and book and magazine publishing companies.

See also ATAY, SALIH RIFKI; GALATASARAY LYCÉE; NEWSPAPERS AND PRINT MEDIA: TURKEY; SIMAVI, SEDAT.

ELIZABETH THOMPSON

KARAGÖZ

See THEATER

KARAITES

Religious sect that was formed in Babylonia in the eighth century C.E.

The Karaites hold to a literal interpretation of scripture, rejecting Talmudic and rabbinic interpretations that are based on an oral tradition. In twentieth-century Israel, there were two small communities of several hundred persons in Galilee and Jerusalem. The Jewish status of Karaites is ambiguous; in Israel, they have the option of holding identity cards that label them either as "Karaite" or "Karaite-Jew."

Bibliography

Birnbaum, Philip, ed. *Karaite Studies.* New York: Hermon Press, 1971.

SAMUEL C. HEILMAN

KARAK, AL-

A provincial capital in the central part of Jordan.

During the Bronze Age, starting about 2400 B.C.E., the region surrounding Karak supported sedentary agriculturalists. Semitic tribes settled there in 1200 B.C.E. and, in 850 B.C.E., the great King Mesha consolidated what came to be known as the Moabite kingdom. Then, atop a small mountain, Karak was settled and fortified. Nearby on the plains of Mu'ta, the first battle between the Arab Muslims and the Byzantine Empire was fought in 629 C.E. The Crusader Renauld de Châtillon ruled the broad region east of the Jordan rift from the massive fortress he built at Karak.

After World War I, Karak was a southern province of the short-lived Syrian Kingdom. Following its demise at the hands of the French in July 1920, the local tribal shaykhs declared the Karak region to be the independent Arab Government of Moab, led by Rufayfan al-Majali. In 1921, it became part of the Emirate of Transjordan. In 2003, Karak is an agricultural market town of 23,200 people and the government center for the Karak district of Jordan. The majority are Sunni Muslim, but a significant minority are Christian. One of Jordan's institutions of higher education, the University of Mu'ta, is located nearby in the village of that name.

See also MAJALI FAMILY.

Bibliography

Gubser, Peter. *Politics and Change in al-Karak, Jordan: A Study of a Small Arab Town and its District.* London and New York: Oxford University Press, 1973.

PETER GUBSER
UPDATED BY MICHAEL R. FISCHBACH

KARAKUL

See GLOSSARY

KARAMA, BATTLE OF (1968)

Battle (also known as Karameh) in the Jordan valley in which Yasir Arafat and his Fatah faction successfully resisted Israeli forces.

After the Arab–Israel War of 1967, although repeated artillery shelling by Israel had driven Palestinian refugees from the Jordan valley to the Biqa and Marka refugee camps outside Amman, there were still 25,000 to 35,000 refugees in Karama. In early March 1968, information on an impending attack by Israel had come from Arafat's agents in the occupied territories and Jordan's intelligence services under the command of Colonel Ghazi Arabiyyat. The Palestinians and Jordan's army decided to take a stand. President Gamal Abdel Nasser of Egypt offered to send air power, but Jordan's King Hussein refused because he feared another disaster like that of 1967.

On 21 March about 15,000 troops began the assault from Israel in three armored brigade formations using M-48 Patton tanks. Their main columns hit the Shuna–Karama area near the King Abdullah Bridge, north of the Dead Sea and Ghawr Safi. A smaller attack took place in neighboring al-Himma, but Jordan's army command believed that the main thrust was taking place in Karama. Jordan's artillery stopped Israel's tank column at the Allenby Bridge, near the crossroads of the main road from Shuna to Karama. Palestinian commandos (*fida'iyyun*) were able to destroy several of Israel's tanks and armored cars, and engaged Israel's airborne troops entering the town of Karama. The town was destroyed after fierce fighting between Israel's troops and approximately 200 to 300 Palestinian commandos. Israel admitted losing 21 soldiers, but the Palestinians claimed the real figure was over 200.

The significance of the battle lay in the fact that, for the first time, Palestinian fighters had successfully engaged Israel's army, scoring a major symbolic victory. Although Jordan's military sources indicated that Jordan's troops did the bulk of the fighting, King Hussein allowed Arafat and al-Fatah to take credit for the victory, thus boosting the prestige of the Palestine Liberation Organization (PLO). After Karama, thousands of young Palestinians flocked to the PLO's guerrilla wings and began paramilitary training.

See also ARAB–ISRAEL WAR (1967); ARAFAT, YASIR; FATAH, AL-; HUSSEIN IBN TALAL; NASSER, GAMAL ABDEL; PALESTINE LIBERATION ORGANIZATION (PLO).

Bibliography

Cooley, John K. *Green March, Black September: The Story of the Palestinian Arabs.* London: Cass, 1973.

LAWRENCE TAL

KARAME, ABD AL-HAMID
[1890–1947]

Lebanese politician; prime minister (1945).

Abd al-Hamid Karame was born into a prominent Sunni family of Tripoli, whose scions traditionally held the office of mufti of the city. He himself served in that post until France's mandatory power replaced him with a man more agreeable to them. A socially conservative and very devout man, he vehemently opposed the creation of Greater Lebanon in 1920. During the 1920s and 1930s, Karame repeatedly clashed with the authorities, demanding the annexation of Tripoli and its hinterland to Syria. Although he was the dominant political figure in Tripoli, he never developed a national base, and thus failed to pose a real challenge to France. A pragmatic politician, he established a close relationship with Britain in the early 1940s, when he joined the movement for Lebanon's independence, reconciling himself to the concept of Lebanon as an entity separate from Syria. Although Karame initially supported President Bishara al-Khuri, under whom he served as prime minister between January and August 1945, he eventually became the leader of an opposition group first called the Independent

Bloc and, after April 1946, the Reform Bloc. Following his death in 1947, his son Rashid inherited his political mantle.

See also KARAME, RASHID; KHURI, BISHARA AL-.

Bibliography

Hudson, Michael C. *The Precarious Republic: Political Modernization in Lebanon.* Boulder, CO: Westview, 1985.

Zamir, Meir. *The Formation of Modern Lebanon.* Ithaca, NY: Cornell University Press, 1988.

GUILAIN P. DENOEUX

KARAME, RASHID
[1921–1987]

Lebanese politician; prime minister at various times from the 1950s through the 1980s.

Rashid Karame, the son of Abd al-Hamid Karame, received a law degree from Cairo University in 1947. He was elected deputy for Tripoli in 1951 and remained a member of parliament until his death. A staunch Arab nationalist and an advocate of political and social reforms, he gained influence through patronage and his ability to function within a confessional political system.

Karame became prime minister in 1955 but resigned in 1956 to protest President Camille Chamoun's refusal to sever diplomatic relations with France and Britain in the wake of the Suez crisis. He became a major opponent of the Chamoun regime and was a leader of the uprising against Chamoun in 1958. After the Lebanese Civil War (1958), President Fu'ad Chehab appointed him prime minister. Karame held the premiership regularly under both Chehab (1958–1964) and his successor, Charles Hilu (1964–1970).

In the late 1960s and early 1970s, Karame supported the presence of armed Palestinians in Lebanon and a radical restructuring of the country's political system. Such positions brought him into conflict with key Maronite politicians, including President Sulayman Franjiyya. In June 1975, when he appeared to be the only politician who might overcome the growing polarization in the country, President Franjiyya appointed him prime minister; he resigned in June 1976.

After Israel's invasion of Lebanon in 1982, Karame emerged as a leading opponent to President Amin Jumayyil's government. With Druze leader Walid Jumblatt and former President Franjiyya, he founded the National Salvation Front in July 1983. In April 1984, Jumayyil bowed to pressures and appointed him prime minister of a government of national unity. Although he formally remained premier until he resigned in May 1987, his authority was limited. He was assassinated on 1 June 1987, when a bomb exploded aboard his helicopter.

See also CHAMOUN, CAMILLE; CHEHAB, FU'AD; FRANJIYYA, SULAYMAN; HILU, CHARLES; JUMAYYIL, AMIN; JUMBLATT, WALID; KARAME, ABD AL-HAMID; LEBANESE CIVIL WAR (1958); NATIONAL SALVATION FRONT (LEBANON); SUEZ CRISIS (1956–1957).

Bibliography

Hudson, Michael C. *The Precarious Republic: Political Modernization in Lebanon.* Boulder, CO: Westview, 1985.

Petran, Tabitha. *The Struggle over Lebanon.* New York: Monthly Review Press, 1987.

GUILAIN P. DENOEUX

KARAM, YUSUF
[1822–1889]

Lebanese hero known for his opposition to Ottoman rule in Lebanon.

Born to a Maronite family in Ehden, north Lebanon, Yusuf Karam had an eclectic education. He wrote and spoke fluent Arabic, Syriac, Italian, French, and English. He also learned the art of fighting and horse riding.

In 1841, he participated in his first battle against the Ottomans to lift the siege against the town of Dayr al-Qamar. At the age of twenty-three, he succeeded his father as governor of Ehden. During the conflicts between Maronite Christians and Druze from 1840 to 1845, he was appointed by the Ottomans to become governor of the Christian district headquartered in Juniya. In 1860, Karam refused the Ottomans' offers that he lead a small contingent of Lebanese soldiers. Exiled from Lebanon by the Ottomans, Karam returned in 1864, but he was exiled again in 1867 and died in Italy in 1889.

GEORGE E. IRANI

KARBALA

Site of sanctuary honoring Husayn ibn Ali's martyrdom.

Karbala is the name of a plain located in Iraq, approximately 55 miles (88.5 km) south-southwest of modern Baghdad and close to the west bank of the Euphrates. The plain is the recorded site of the infamous mass killing, in 680 C.E. (A.H. 61), of the prophet Muhammad's grandson Husayn ibn Ali and his small band of supporters by the forces of Yazid ibn Mu'awiya, the second Umayyad caliph. According to tradition, the decapitated body of Husayn was buried in a spot not far from the battlefield. As a result, Karbala and its environs quickly became known as Mashhad al-Husayn (the tomb shrine of Husayn), and today it is still one of the principal pilgrimage centers for Twelver Shi'ite Muslims, who revere Husayn as one of the great imams, or divinely inspired leaders, of the Muslim community.

Each year, for example, beginning on the first and culminating on the tenth of the Muslim month of Muharram, large numbers of pilgrims gather at the shrine complex at Karbala and perform solemn passion plays and other commemorations of Husayn's great martyrdom (other Twelver Shi'ites around the world do the same). According to the common belief of Twelver Shi'ites, Husayn's suffering and death constitute a source of redemption for all who are sincerely devoted to Husayn and his fellow imams. Many Twelvers believe that such practices as ritual visitation to Karbala as well as to other sacred tombs are excellent means of realizing this devotion to the imams and the salvific blessings it entails.

Throughout its long history, Karbala has generally prospered as a richly endowed pilgrimage site. A few notable exceptions to this sanctuary's history of good fortune include its destruction by the Abbasid caliph al-Mutawakkil in 850 C.E. (A.H. 236), its storming and looting by the *muwahhidun* (wahhabis) in 1801 C.E. (A.H. 1215), and the widespread devastation it suffered as a consequence of the confrontation after the Gulf War between Iraq's Republican Guard and Shi'ite rebel forces in March 1991.

See also GULF WAR (1991); HUSAYN IBN ALI; MUHARRAM.

SCOTT ALEXANDER

KARBASCHI, GHOLAMHOSAIN

[1953–]

Governor of Isfahan and mayor of Tehran in the 1980s and 1990s.

Born in 1953 into the family of a high-ranking cleric, Gholamhosain Karbaschi attended Haqani Seminary in Qumand and was arrested in 1975 for his antishah activities. After his release from prison in 1978, he left the seminary and put himself at the service of the Iranian Revolution. He was appointed the representative of Ayatollah Ruhollah Khomeini in the gendarmerie, then the Islamic Republic News Agency, and finally as the governor of Isfahan province—a position in which Karbaschi demonstrated his strong managerial capabilities. In 1989, when Ali Akbar Hashemi Rafsanjani became president, he appointed Karbaschi the mayor of Tehran—an expanding metropolitan city that had experienced years of neglect, war economy, and mismanagement.

Karbaschi transformed Tehran by planning for control of waste and air pollution and by building highways, parks, libraries, art galleries, and cultural centers. He established *Hamshahri,* a daily newspaper with a new look and the largest circulation in the country, which advocated Rafsanjani's economic-development policies. With support from Rafsanjani, Karbaschi and fifteen other pragmatic technocrats founded the Executives of Construction Party (ECP) in 1996 in order to counter the conservative candidates from the Militant Clergy Association (MCA) in the fifth parliamentary election. Karbaschi was the first secretary-general for the party, serving until 1998. In 1997 Karbaschi helped to engineer the election of Mohammad Khatami as president.

Karbaschi's policy of taxing the rich for urban public projects and building chain stores around the city earned him the nickname Robin Hood, and angered the conservative merchants in the bazaar and their clerical allies in the MCA. His efforts to block some land transfers among major players of the MCA—and his participation in Khatami's election—prompted his opponents from the MCA and the Society of Islamic Coalition to use their political influence in the judiciary to stop Karbaschi's political machine.

In April 1998 Karbaschi was arrested and tried by the conservative judiciary for alleged embezzlement and mismanagement of state funds. His controversial trial, which was broadcasted publicly, captivated the nation, generated public debate and agitation, and led to his conviction. His original sentence of five years' imprisonment, twenty lashes, and a twenty-year ban from political activities was reduced on appeal to two years' imprisonment, a cash fine, and a ten-year ban from politics. After serving nine months in prison, he was pardoned through Rafsanjani's intervention. Since his release from jail, he has been leading a quiet life with occasional public appearances and nonpolitical interviews.

See also IRANIAN REVOLUTION (1979); ISFAHAN; KHATAMI, MOHAMMAD; KHOMEINI, RUHOLLAH; RAFSANJANI, ALI AKBAR HASHEMI; TEHRAN.

ALI AKBAR MAHDI

KARIYUKA, TAHIYA

[1915–1999]

Dancer and actress on stage, radio, and screen.

Born Badawiya Muhammad Karim Ali al-Sayyid, in Manzala, Egypt, Tahiya Kariyuka debuted as a carioca dancer in Badiah Masabni's famous Cairo casino. The carioca, a tango variation performed by Fred Astaire and Ginger Rogers in the 1933 film *Flying Down to Rio,* had become wildly popular. Kariyuka's solo version of a dance intended for a couple can only be imagined; however the moniker stuck, although its pseudo-Brazilian/Hollywood connotations did not. Among Kariyuka's fellow dancers at the Casino was Samiya Jamal (also Gamal), another accomplished dancer and actress. The two women remained rivals until Samiya's death in 1994.

Kariyuka's first role was a small appearance in a short 1935 film; her first starring role was in 1946, with actor Najib al-Rihani, known as the Molière of Egypt, in the film *Li'bat al-sitt* (The woman's game). She eventually appeared in over 190 films as well as numerous stage plays and radio serials. She is best known for her role as the seductress Shafa'at in the 1956 film *Shabab imra'a* (A woman's youth). She was also politically active, and her call for a return to democracy after the Free Officers' coup of 1952 led to her being jailed for three months in 1953. In 1981 she served as president of the Egyptian Actors Union. She allegedly married more than a dozen times but was unmarried at the time of her death from heart failure.

See also ART; GAMAL, SAMIYAH.

Bibliography

Amin, Shahira. "Tahia Carioca: Serious Dancing." *Arabesque: A Magazine of International Dance* 20, no.1 (1994): 14–16.

Said, Edward. "Homage to a Belly-Dancer." In *Reflections on Exile and Other Essays,* by Edward Said. Cambridge, MA: Harvard University Press, 2001.

ROBERTA L. DOUGHERTY

KARMAL, BABRAK
[1929–1996]

President of Afghanistan, 1980–1986.

Babrak Karmal was a founder of the Marxist movement in Afghanistan and the president of Afghanistan and secretary-general of the People's Democratic Party of Afghanistan (PDPA) from 1980 to 1986. He was born in 1929 in Kamari, a village near Kabul, into the family of Mohammad Hossayn, an army general and one-time governor of Paktika. Karmal received his high-school education in Kabul at Nejat School, from which he graduated in 1948. He entered Kabul University in 1951 and became active in student politics and in the Afghan communist movement. Known as a gifted orator, in 1954 he adopted the name *Karmal,* which in Persian means "friend of labor."

From 1953 to 1956, Karmal was imprisoned for his political activism, but he was well treated in jail because of his family connections. In 1965 and 1969, during the period of constitutional reforms (1963–1973), he was elected to the Afghan parliament. He was a founding member of the PDPA in 1965. When the party split into two factions in 1967, he led the Parcham (flag) faction. Karmal's background in the Kabul elite put him at odds with other members of the Marxist movement in Afghanistan.

At the time of the Saur Revolution (April 1978), the two rival factions of the PDPA united and swept into power. Karmal was elected vice-chairman of the Revolutionary Council and deputy prime minister of Afghanistan. In July 1978, the Parcham members of the party were purged, and Karmal was named ambassador to Czechoslovakia.

On 27 December, 1979, Soviet troops entered Kabul and Hafizullah Amim, the president of Afghanistan at that time, was assassinated. Karmal returned to Kabul with the Soviet forces and was installed as president of Afghanistan on that date. Karmal was unable to unite Afghanistan or to win the trust of the resistance fighters, and the country spiraled into civil war during his term. Although he was a gifted orator, Karmal was never an effective leader. He was more a thinker than a doer, more an ideologue than a politician. In addition, his aristocratic urban background often worked against his Marxist rhetoric, especially in a country such as Afghanistan, which is mostly rural and largely populated by peasants.

In 1986, in part because of his failing health, Karmal was replaced by strongman Mohammed Najibullah and left Afghanistan for Moscow. He returned to Kabul in 1989, only to leave for Moscow again when the Najibullah government fell in 1992. He died of cancer in Moscow on 1 December 1996.

See also AMIN, HAFIZULLAH; COMMUNISM IN THE MIDDLE EAST; NAJIBULLAH; PARCHAM.

Bibliography

Arnold, Anthony. *Afghanistan's Two-Party System: Parcham and Khalq.* Stanford, CA: Hoover Institution Press, 1983.

Male, Beverley. *Revolutionary Afghanistan: A Reappraisal.* New York: St. Martin's Press, 1982.

GRANT FARR

KAR, MEHRANGIZ
[1944–]

Iranian lawyer, writer, and women's rights activist.

Mehrangiz Kar was born in Ahvaz, Iran, in 1944. She studied law at the School of Law and Political Science, Tehran University. After graduation, she worked for the Social Security Department and also wrote for the press, publishing more than 100 articles on current social and political issues in newspapers and magazines. She obtained her attorney's license in 1978, shortly before the Iranian Revolution, but she did not start her own practice until the early 1990s. In 1992 Kar began collaboration with *Zanan,* a monthly journal (launched the same year) with an Islamic feminist agenda. Her advocacy of political, legal, and constitutional reform, including the promotion of civil society and democracy and the dismantling of legal barriers to women's rights, made her a target of the antireformist backlash that followed the massive reformist victory in the February 2000 parliamentary elections. In April 2000, Kar was arrested for participating in the Berlin conference on the future of reforms in Iran, charged with acting against national security and disseminating propaganda against the Islamic regime. Released after six weeks, then tried in closed hearings in January 2001, she was convicted and sentenced to four years' imprisonment. Granted bail to leave the country for medical treatment, she moved to the United States. The appeal court later reduced her sentence to a fine, but meanwhile her husband, Siyamak Pourzand, was jailed. She has published several books in Persian and has received many international awards, including the 2002 Ludovic-Trarieux Award.

Bibliography

Kar, Mehrangiz. "Women's Strategies in Iran from 1979 Revolution to 1999." In *Globalization, Gender, and Religion: The Politics of Women's Rights in Catholic and Muslim Contexts,* edited by Jane H. Bayes and Nayereh Tohidi. New York and Hampshire, U.K.: Palgrave, 2001.

ZIBA MIR-HOSSEINI

KARNOUK, LILIANE
[1944–]

Egyptian-Canadian artist, writer, and educator.

Liliane Karnouk is an Egyptian-Canadian visual artist, writer, and arts educator who has also worked in theater and furniture design. She was trained at the Academy of Fine Arts in Rome and at the University of British Columbia. She is well known as one of the few authors who have introduced modern Egyptian art to an English-speaking audience, producing two authoritative volumes on the subject. She was also instrumental in shaping the art department at the American University in Cairo. Karnouk is the recipient of prestigious Ford Foundation grants to further the knowledge of contemporary Egyptian art, and her paintings and installations have been exhibited extensively in her native Egypt and Canada, as well as in Europe. Working in a range of materials from the industrial to the or-

ganic, her conceptual works have dealt with themes related to the desert, ancient Egypt, plants and organic designs, and Islamic philosophy regarding the functional and the aesthetic. Her work is primarily concerned with exploring her own experience between East and West.

Bibliography

Karnouk, Liliane. *Contemporary Egyptian Art.* Cairo: The American University in Cairo Press, 1995.

Karnouk, Liliane. *Modern Egyptian Art: The Emergence of a National Style.* Cairo: The American University in Cairo Press, 1988.

JESSICA WINEGAR

KARP REPORT (1984)

Report into irregularities in police investigations of violence by Jewish settlers against Palestinians in the Occupied Territories.

The Karp Report was issued by a committee of Israeli jurists headed by Deputy Attorney General Judith Karp. The committee was appointed by Attorney General Yitzhak Shamir in 1981 in response to Israeli law professors who expressed concern over the deterioration of the rule of law in the territories occupied by Israel since the 1967 war.

The committee examined seventy cases, fifty-three of which had been left unsolved, in which Israeli settlers were charged with harassing Palestinian residents in the Hebron region who had refused to sell their land. The report found "serious shortcomings" in investigations when Arabs were victims: investigations of complaints lodged by Palestinians were inadequate. It criticized the police for failing to seriously investigate charges, noted delays in pursuing cases, and faulted the separation between the regular and military police. The report advised a reassessment of the instructions given to Israeli soldiers for opening fire on civilians, recommended an increase in the number of civilian police in the West Bank, and criticized the refusal of Jewish witnesses—especially settlers in the West Bank—to cooperate with police in investigations related to Arab victims.

The Israeli right wing charged that the investigation had failed to examine cases in which Palestinian Arabs went unpunished for attacks on Jews.

Karp resigned after the Likud-led government neglected the report's findings.

See also ARAB–ISRAEL WAR (1967); LIKUD; WEST BANK.

Bibliography

The Karp Report: An Israeli Government Inquiry into Settler Violence against Palestinians on the West Bank. Washington, DC: Institute for Palestine Studies, 1984.

"West Bank: Study Cites West Bank Police Failings." In *Facts On File,* accession no. 1984004260. New York: Facts on File News Services, 7 February 1984.

MARTIN MALIN
UPDATED BY GREGORY S. MAHLER

KARZAI, HAMID
[1957–]

President of the transitional government of Afghanistan.

Hamid Karzai, born 24 December 1957 in Kandahar, Afghanistan, the fourth of seven sons of a chief of the Popalzai tribe, was a leader in efforts to reconstitute Afghanistan after the demise of the Taliban in 2001. After being educated in Kabul, he earned a postgraduate degree in political science in Shimla, India. During the war against the Communist regime in Afghanistan (1980–1992) Karzai was an active supporter of the opposition, contributing money and serving as political advisor to certain resistance leaders. In 1992 he served as deputy foreign minister in the government of Burhanuddin Rabbani, but he resigned in 1994. Soon after the Taliban arose as a force in Kandahar in 1994 Karzai began to support them, donating $50,000 and a large hoard of weapons in hopes they would quell the fighting among the various commanders. The Taliban leadership wanted him to be their envoy to the United Nations (UN), but he refused. He came to believe that the Taliban were mere proxies for Pakistani and Arab radical Islamists, and in 1997 he joined family members in Quetta, where he worked for the reinstatement of the former king, Mohammad Zahir. In the next year he collaborated with other Pushtun chiefs in inciting an anti-Taliban movement; in response, in 1999 the Taliban murdered Karzai's father. Elected chief of the Popalzai tribe in his father's place, Karzai immediately defied Taliban warnings by organizing a 300-vehicle convoy of Pushtun mourners to carry his father's remains back to Kandahar, an act that won him wide respect.

Soon after the 11 September 2001 attacks against the United States, Karzai began to organize a tribal militia to fight the Taliban. His request for help from the U.S. ambassador in Islamabad was refused, but he won support from the British. On 8 October 2001, one day after the United States started bombing the Taliban, he led militia into the Kandahar area. The Taliban almost captured him, but he was rescued by U.S. helicopters. The U.S. government only reluctantly came to see him as a key Pushtun leader. When a body of prominent Afghans assembled in Bonn, Germany, to constitute a new regime, the United States and representatives of the Northern Alliance, now the main political instrument of U.S. policy in Afghanistan, induced the attendees to name him leader of a provisional administration. Installed on 22 December 2001, Karzai's task was to organize a *Loya-Jirga* (national assembly) that would elect a temporary head of state who would form a permanent government. In the summer of 2002 the *Loya-Jirga* elected him president of the Afghan Transitional Authority, commissioning him to draft a new constitution, form a national army, and set up a national election by 2004. As transitional president his main achievement by the summer of 2003 was the securing of commitments from other countries of more than $4 billion for reconstruction. Early in his regime, his greatest difficulty was the incorrigibility and truculence of local commanders, many of whom paid no remittances to the Kabul government. There have been several attempts on his life, the most notable on 5 September 2002, when a gunman missed him at point-blank range.

See also AFGHANISTAN: POLITICAL PARTIES IN; AFGHANISTAN: U.S. INTERVENTION IN; TALIBAN; ZAHIR SHAH.

ROBERT L. CANFIELD

KASAP, TEODOR
[1835–1905]

Turkish Ottoman journalist, dramatist, and publisher.

Teodor Kasap, the son of a manufacturer, was born in Kayseri, Turkey. When he was eleven, his father died and he moved to Istanbul, where he was apprenticed to a Greek merchant and studied at a Greek school. While working in the merchant's store, he met a French officer who had come to Turkey during the Crimean War. Under the patronage of this officer, he went to France in 1856 to complete his studies. Upon his return to Istanbul, Kasap gave private French lessons, through which he entered the Istanbul literary circuit.

On 24 November 1870 Kasap published the first issue of the first Ottoman humor magazine, *Diyojen*. *Diyojen* quickly became famous for its caricatures and high-quality articles; among the regular contributors were Namik Kemal and Ebüzziya Tevfik. *Diyojen* also featured translations from French literature: Kasap's translation of Alexandre Dumas's *The Count of Monte Cristo* was one of the first Turkish translations of a French novel.

The caustic humor that was featured in *Diyojen* led the government to order it temporarily closed after only four issues. Kasap eventually published 183 issues of *Diyojen* before it was ordered permanently closed in 1873. Following this, he published two other magazines, *Cingirakli Tatar* and *Hayal* (both in 1873), and a daily political newspaper, *Istikbal* (1875). In 1877, Kasap was sentenced to three years in prison for a cartoon criticizing censorship of the press that appeared in *Hayal*. He was released from prison on the condition that he cease publishing *Hayal* and *Istikbal*; upon his release, he went into exile in Europe. Following a stay in Europe of several years, he was pardoned by Sultan Abdülhamit II and allowed to return to Istanbul where he was employed in the sultan's private library.

In addition to his publishing and journalistic activities, Kasap is known for his plays. His first play, *Pinti Hamit,* was performed at the Gedikpaşa Theater in 1873; this was followed by *Iskilli Memo* in 1874 and *Para Meselesi* in 1875. The first two were based on plays written by Molière, the last, on a play written by Dumas. Kasap believed that Turkish theater had to draw upon local sources and customs; his play *Iskilli Memo* was based on Turkish folk theater (Ortaoyunu). He was opposed to unreflective adoption of Western theatrical genres, and he defended local traditions of drama: "Theater, like civilization, does not enter a country from the outside, but must come from within."

See also ABDÜLHAMIT II; NAMIK KEMAL; NEWSPAPERS AND PRINT MEDIA: TURKEY; ORTAOYUNU.

DAVID WALDNER

KASHANI, ABU AL-QASEM
[1882–1962]

Iranian religious leader and political activist, important for his role in the events of 1945–1955, the postwar decade.

Born in Tehran, Abu al-Qasem Kashani was taken at an early age by his father to al-Najaf in Iraq, where he began his formal religious education in Islam. With his father, he fought against the British in the battle of Kut al-Amara in 1916. Hostility to British imperialism was destined to remain the chief emphasis of his political life. Kashani also participated in the anti-British uprising of 1921, as a result of which he was compelled to return to Persia (Iran). He remained politically inactive until 1941, when the British forces occupying Iran arrested him for alleged contacts with agents. Released in 1945 (after World War II), he was placed under house arrest in 1946 for opposing a new press law.

In 1948, he organized demonstrations that called for volunteers to fight the Zionists in Palestine (Israel was established in May 1948) and also began collaborating with the militant organization Feda'iyan-e Islam. In 1949, he was exiled to Beirut on charges of involvement in a failed attempt on the life of the shah, Mohammad Reza Shah Pahlavi. He returned in triumph in 1950 and was elected to the *majles* (Iran's legislature), where he worked with Mohammad Mossadegh in bringing about the nationalization of the Iranian oil industry. From the fall of 1952 on, relations between the two men declined, and Kashani stood aside when Mossadegh was overthrown by the U.S.-sponsored royalist coup of August 1953. Kashani nonetheless resumed his own oppositional activities in 1954 and was arrested anew in 1955. He was released in January 1956 and, intimidated by the death of his son under questionable circumstances, remained politically inactive until his death in March 1962.

See also FEDA'IYAN-E ISLAM; KUT AL-AMARA; MOSSADEGH, MOHAMMAD; PAHLAVI, MOHAMMAD REZA.

Bibliography

Richard, Yann. "Ayatollah Kashani: Precursor of the Islamic Republic?" In *Religion and Politics in Iran,* edited by Nikki R. Keddie. New Haven, CT: Yale University Press, 1983.

HAMID ALGAR

KASHIF AL-GHITA FAMILY

A family of Shi'ite ulama *and* mujtahidun *originating in the Shi'ite holy city of al-Najaf in southern Iraq.*

The founder of the family, Ja'far ibn Khidr al-Najafi (1743–1812), was an *alim* (singular of *ulama*) who wrote the *fiqh* (Islamic jurisprudence) textbook *Kashif al-Ghita* (The uncoverer of the error), from which the family surname was derived. In 1807, he led the defense of Najaf against the raiding Wahhabis, a Sunni fundamentalist and purist movement led by amirs of the house of Al Sa'ud, based in Najd.

Ja'far's sons, Shaykh Musa ibn Ja'far (1766–1827), Shaykh Ali ibn Ja'far (d. 1837), and Shaykh Hasan ibn Ja'far (1776–1848), were *mujtahidun* (senior Shi'ite religious authorities empowered to issue religious decrees based on primary sources; singular *mujtahid*) in Najaf, where they were involved in political developments. Shaykh Musa ibn Ja'far Kashif al-Ghita mediated between the Ottoman Empire and the Persians during the 1820s.

The most prominent scion of the Kashif al-Ghita family in the twentieth century was Muhammad Husayn Kashif al-Ghita (1877–1954), who received the title and status of *marja* (supreme religious authority). He was the author of numerous books on religious topics, printed in Arabic and Persian, and had adherents throughout the Shi'a world. In his books he showed the need for Islamic unity and expressed his views about the ideal Islamic society. He maintained a correspondence with the Maronite intellectual Amin Rihani. He traveled to Hijaz, Syria, and Egypt, and lectured at al-Azhar University in Cairo. In 1909, he published a book, *al-Din wa al-Islam aw al-Da'wa al-Islamiyya* (Religion and Islam, or The Islamic call), which called for a revival of Islam and its purification from recent trends of extremism and superstition.

During the 1920s and 1930s, Muhammad Husayn was an active Shi'ite politician in Iraq. In the period of unrest and tribal rebellions (1934–1935), he formulated the Shi'ite demands, but refused—due to the strife among the Shi'ite tribes and politicians—to commit himself to the tribal rebellion under Abd al-Wahid Sikkar, which was backed and manipulated by Sunni Baghdadi politicians of the Ikha al-Watani Party. Starting from the late 1930s, he introduced moderate reforms and modernization in his *madrasa* (religious college) in Najaf.

In 1931, Muhammad Husayn Kashif al-Ghita attended the Muslim Congress in Jerusalem—the first Shi'ite *mujtahid* to take part in a Muslim Congress—and led the prayers at the opening ceremony at the al-Aqsa Mosque.

Following World War II Muhammad Husayn began to warn against the dangers of communism. In 1953, he held talks with the British and American ambassadors on the communist influences among young Shi'ites in Iraq.

See also AL SA'UD FAMILY; IKHA AL-WATANI PARTY.

Bibliography

Momen, Moojan. *An Introduction to Shi'i Islam: The History and Doctrines of Twelver Shi'ism.* New Haven, CT: Yale University Press, 1983.

Nakash, Yitzhak. *The Shi'is of Iraq.* Princeton, NJ: Princeton University Press, 1994.

MICHAEL EPPEL

KASHWAR KAMAL, MEENA
[1956–1987]

Afghan feminist, poet, and political activist.

Meena Kashwar Kamal was born in 1956 in Kabul. Her husband, Faiz Ahmad, a physician, was a member of the Afghan Maoist Communist political movement, Sho'la-i-Jawid (Eternal flame); however, it is not clear whether Kashwar Kamal adhered to the same political ideology. Kashwar Kamal's political and feminist ideas were shaped during the late 1960s and early 1970s, a period of intense student involvement in politics in Kabul and other major cities in Afghanistan. After her husband's assassination in 1976, she abandoned her studies at Kabul University and devoted her time to social and political activities. In 1977, at age twenty-one, she organized the Revolutionary Association of Women of Afghanistan (RAWA) in Kabul as an alternative platform to the Marxist-Leninist Democratic Organization of Afghan Women, to fight against the fundamentalism of radical Islamists.

After the Soviet intervention in Afghanistan in 1979, Kashwar Kamal shifted her focus to the liberation of Afghanistan. She declared, "To fight against the Russian aggressors is inseparable from struggle against the fundamentalists. Nevertheless, for the time being we should give priority to the former." In October 1981, she was invited to attend the congress of the anti-Soviet Socialist Party of French President François Mitterrand as a representative of the Afghan resistance. From there, she visited other European countries, speaking in support of the Afghan resistance. Her strong anti-Soviet and antifundamentalist feminist stance earned her the animosity of both radical Islamists in Pakistan and the pro-Soviet regime in Afghanistan. She was killed in her home in Quetta, along with two close associates, on 4 February 1987, allegedly at the instigation of Gulbuddin Hekmatyar, leader of the radical Islamic Party of Afghanistan. Her work, however, has continued under the banner of the Revolutionary Afghan Women's Association.

See also AFGHANISTAN; DEMOCRATIC ORGANIZATION OF AFGHAN WOMEN (1965); GENDER: GENDER AND LAW; GENDER: GENDER AND POLITICS; HEZB-E ISLAMI; REFUGEES: AFGHAN; REVOLUTIONARY ASSOCIATION OF THE WOMEN OF AFGHANISTAN (RAWA); SAMAR, SIMA; TALIBAN.

Bibliography

"Imperialist Hypocrisy over Afghan Women's Rights: RAWA Afghan Feminists Back Imperialist Reaction." *Workers Vanguard* 776, (8 March 2002). Available from <http://www.icl-fi.org/ENGLISH/Rawa.htm>.

Shahin, Juhi. "Revolution of the Afghan Women." *The Daily Pioneer*, 12 November 2000. Available from <http://www.geocities.com/Wellesley/3340/pioneer.htm>.

SENZIL NAWID

KASRAVI, AHMAD
[1890–1946]

Iranian writer and reformer.

Born into a religious family in Tabriz, Ahmad Kasravi received a religious education and for a brief time was a preacher. As a young man, he joined the Tabriz branch of the reformist Democrat party, which had acquired a reputation in the national assembly for being anticlerical. Kasravi was expelled from the party in 1917 for his opposition to a growing trend among Tabriz Democrats to emphasize provincial concerns over national concerns. In 1921, he moved to Tehran, where he spent the remainder of his life working as a social reformer, activist, and historian. Kasravi was one of the most prolific and influential writers of early twentieth-century Iran. His important works include *History of Iran's Constitutional Revolution, An Eighteen-Year History of Iran, Shiʿigari,* and *Piramun-e Islam* (all of them in Arabic). Kasravi often criticized the Shiʿite clergy in his writings, especially in the two latter works, both of which were condemned by some clergy. He was assassinated by a member of the radical Fedaʾiyan-e Islam.

See also FEDAʾIYAN-E ISLAM.

Bibliography

Kasravi, Ahmad. *On Islam and Shiʿism,* translated by M. R. Ghanoonparvar. Costa Mesa, CA: Mazda Publishers, 1990.

ERIC J. HOOGLUND

KASSALLAH

Commercial and agricultural center of eastern Sudan.

Founded in 1840, Kassallah grew rapidly, and within a few decades became the most important commercial and agricultural center in eastern Sudan. During the Mahdiya revolt, its Turko–Egyptian defenders withstood the siege by the Mahdists from 1883 until 1885, when the garrison surrendered after the Mahdi had captured Khartoum. In 1894 the Italians, who had occupied Eritrea, captured the town; they did so again for a few months in 1940, before Kassallah was liberated by Allied forces under British command. As the gateway to Eritrea and Ethiopia and the *entrepôt* for the rich agricultural lands in the Gash River delta of the Sudan, Kassallah became the center for road and rail traffic between Port Sudan and Khartoum. Its strategic location has made it the sanctuary for the thousands of refugees who have fled from the Eritrean–Ethiopian war since the mid-1960s. The influx of refugees has swollen the population beyond any accurate assessment, but Kassallah has become the largest city in the Sudan after the Three Towns (Khartoum, Khartoum North, and Omdurman).

ROBERT O. COLLINS

KASZTNER AFFAIR

Dramatic and highly politicized slander trial in Israel from January 1954 to June 1955.

Gossip journalist Malkiel Grunwald stood accused of defaming Dr. Rudolf Kasztner, director of public relations for the ministry of commerce and industry and hero of Holocaust rescue efforts on behalf of Hungarian Jewry. Kasztner's role in the failed 1944 negotiations to "buy" the survival of Hungary's Jews from Adolf Eichmann was portrayed by the defense as collaboration with the Nazis in exchange for the freedom of a handpicked few of Kasztner's friends and relatives who were transported to Switzerland as an agreed-upon "good faith" gesture. According to defense counsel Shmuel Tamir, whose Herut Party's political agenda was to associate Kasztner's "war-crimes" with the Jewish Agency and by extension with MAPAI party, it was to ensure this "delivery" that Kasztner kept from Hungarian Jewry the truth about its expected fate and encouraged Palestinian Jewish parachutists to surrender to the authorities. He was also disparaged for testifying on behalf of one of his Nazi interlocutors, Kurt Becher, at the Nuremberg trials after World War II. Grunwald was acquitted. Reverberations of the trial led to the resignation of Prime Minister Moshe Sharett's government in June 1955. Kasztner was assassinated in March 1957 by three youths associated with the extreme right, ten months before Israel's Supreme Court overturned the ruling in the Grunwald case.

See also HOLOCAUST; ISRAEL: POLITICAL PARTIES IN; JEWISH AGENCY FOR PALESTINE; SHARETT, MOSHE; TAMIR, SHMUEL.

Bibliography

Hecht, Ben. *Perfidy.* Jerusalem and New London, NH: Milah, 1997.

ZEV MAGHEN

KATEB, YACINE
[1929–1989]

A leading Algerian literary figure.

Born in Constantine, Algeria, Yacine Kateb was marked by the 1945 massacres that French colonial troops committed in eastern Algeria. He was imprisoned during those years of repression and then went into exile in France, where he survived by taking low-paying jobs. He joined the National Liberation Front (FLN) during the 1950s and served as FLN representative in various countries. He earned fame with *Nedjma* (1956), a love story. Three years later he published *Le cercle des représailles* in Paris. After Algeria's independence, Kateb devoted his time to writing and theater. His political views angered the regime. Kateb's position that dialectal Arabic and Berber should be the only national languages conflicted with the regime's all-out campaign to make Arabic the only national language. In response, the authorities sought to marginalize him. Modest, Kateb worked with his theater troupe and wrote plays and books, including *Le polygone étoilé* (1966) and *L'homme aux sandales de caoutchouc* (1970). Because he was spurned by the authorities who controlled the national publishing house, most of Kateb's works were published in France. Kateb also wrote plays in dialectal Arabic and French, the most famous being *Mohammed prends ta valise* (1971), *Saout Ennisa* (1972), *La guerre de 2000 ans* (1974), and *La Palestine trahie* (1972–1982). He was awarded France's Grand Prix National des Lettres in 1987. He died of leukemia on 28 October 1989 in Grenoble, France.

Bibliography

Kamal, Salhi. *The Politics and Aesthetics of Kateb Yacine: From Francophone Literature to Popular Theatre in Algeria and Outside.* Lewiston, NY: Edwin Mellen Press, 1999.

YAHIA ZOUBIR

KATTANI, MUHAMMAD IBN ABD AL-KABIR AL-
[?–1909]

Idrisi sharif; head of the Kattaniya Sufi brotherhood; anticolonial leader in the period of the Moroccan Question.

As head of the Kattaniya Brotherhood, in 1904 Muhammad ibn Abd al-Kabir al-Kattani led the notables of Fez in opposition to France's reform plan presented to Morocco's sultan Abd al-Aziz. Disappointed with the sultan's acquiescence to French pressure, in 1907–1908 he led demonstrations at Fez in favor of deposing Abd al-Aziz and proclaiming Abd al-Hafid as sultan. He also sought to impose conditions on the latter when he assumed the throne, committing him to a program of unwavering opposition to European rule.

In 1909, Kattani's unrelenting public attacks on Abd al-Hafid led to the former's arrest and execution. Subsequent generations of Moroccan nationalists have, however, viewed him as a hero for his staunch opposition to French colonial rule.

See also ABD AL-AZIZ IBN AL-HASSAN; ABD AL-HAFID IBN AL-HASSAN; KATTANIYA BROTHERHOOD.

Bibliography

Burke, Edmund, III. *Prelude to Protectorate in Morocco: Precolonial Protest and Resistance, 1860–1912.* Chicago: University of Chicago Press, 1976.

EDMUND BURKE III

KATTANIYA BROTHERHOOD

A Moroccan Sufi order, formally intended to enhance the spirituality of its adherents, which played a major political role in the early twentieth century.

The Kattaniya brotherhood (in Arabic, *tariqa*) was founded in Fez, Morocco, in 1890 by Muhammad ibn Abd al-Kabir al-Kattani—known popularly as Muhammad al-Kabir. Al-Kabir was inspired by the Sufi doctrines and practices of the established Darqawi *tariqa*.

The Kattani family, known for its scholars and jurists, claimed descent from the prophet Muhammad through Morocco's Idrisi dynasty. The Kattaniya rapidly gained adherents in Fez, Meknes, and Morocco's rural regions, but the brotherhood was condemned by reformist *ulama* (religious scholars). In 1909, Muhammad al-Kabir fled Fez to sanctuary with a neighboring tribe when the new ruler, Sultan Mulay Abd al-Hafid (ruled 1908–1912), ordered his arrest and closed all Kattaniya *zawiyas* (Islamic compounds). Pursued and beaten, he was executed soon after he was brought back to Fez.

Once the French protectorate was established (1912–1956), the Kattaniya again flourished under Shaykh Muhammad Abd al-Hayy al-Kattani—a scholar, popular religious leader, implacable foe of the Alawite dynasty, and a beneficiary of French colonial rule. In 1953, Abd al-Hayy joined other antinationalists in calling for the deposition of Sultan Muhammad V, and the Kattaniya brotherhood rapidly collapsed.

See also ALAWITE DYNASTY; KATTANI, MUHAMMAD IBN ABD AL-KABIR AL-; MUHAMMAD V.

DALE F. EICKELMAN

KATZNELSON, BERL
[1887–1944]

Labor Zionist leader, writer, and publisher.

Berl Katznelson was born in Belorussia and went to Palestine in 1909. He became a farm laborer and a friend of A. D. Gordon. In World War I, he was in the Jewish Legion with David Ben-Gurion and Yizhak Ben-Zvi. With them, and as a theoretician in Labor Zionism, he created the platform for bringing together the several Labor Zionist (socialist) parties into a unified framework. He was a founder of Ahdut Ha-Avodah in 1919, the Histadrut labor organization in 1920, and the MAPAI political party in 1930. In 1925, he founded the Histadrut's daily newspaper, *Davar*, which he edited until 1936, and its publishing house, Am Oved.

Central to Katznelson's outlook was the notion that Zionism would not be achieved without socialism because of the need to direct investment. He called his socialism "constructive" to signal both its preference for the interests of the workers and its priority for building the infrastructure necessary in a state. During World War II, the knowledge of the Holocaust changed his rigid stance against the Arabs and inclined him toward compromise.

See also AHDUT HA-AVODAH; BEN-GURION, DAVID; BEN-ZVI, YIZHAK; HISTADRUT; ZIONISM.

Bibliography

Shapira, Anita. *Berl: The Biography of a Socialist Zionist.* Cambridge, U.K., and New York: Cambridge University Press, 1981.

DONNA ROBINSON DIVINE

KAWAKIBI, ABD AL-RAHMAN AL-
[1854–1902]

Central figure in the development of Arab nationalist thought.

Abd al-Rahman al-Kawakibi was born in Aleppo but grew up in Antioch, where he studied a variety of subjects in Arabic, Turkish, and Persian under the supervision of a prominent scholar related to his mother. He then returned to Aleppo and served as an editor of the Ottoman-sponsored newspaper *al-Furat* during the latter half of the 1870s. In 1878, he founded the city's first privately published Arabic-language newspaper, the weekly *al-Shadaba*. He played active roles in the then newly established Chamber of Commerce, the municipal administration, and the government-owned Tobacco Corporation. His outspoken advocacy of programs to help the poor won him the nickname Abu al-Duʿafa (Father of the Weak). His willingness to challenge the authorities eventually brought him into conflict with the provincial governor, who arrested him for sedition and confiscated his property. An appeals court ordered his release but refused to return his possessions, so around 1898 he emigrated to Egypt and entered the service of the Khedive Abbas Hilmi II. He died in Cairo.

Al-Kawakibi is best known for two short treatises, written in Aleppo but first published in Cairo. The first, *Umm al-Qura* (The mother of towns, i.e., Mecca), appeared in print in 1899 under the pseudonym al-Sayyid al-Furati. Structured in the form of a discussion among twenty-two Muslims planning to set up a secret society to revitalize the Islamic world, the book's thesis is that Islam will remain incapable of resisting the intellectual and political challenges emanating from Europe unless the leadership of the faith (*khalifa*) is returned to the Arabs from the (Ottoman) Turks. If a new *khalifa* were to be established in Mecca and were accorded authority only in religious matters, then the political position of all Muslims would be greatly strengthened. Despite its controversial if not explosive argument, this book went virtually unnoticed until it was serialized in Rashid Rida's journal *al-Manar* in 1902 and 1903.

The second treatise, *Tabaʾi al-Istibdad wa Masari al-Istiʿbad* (The attendants of despotism and the destruction of subjugation), is a spirited critique of tyranny in all its myriad forms: political, intellectual, economic, spiritual, and national/racial. For al-Kawakibi, each of these despotisms can be traced to earthly rulers' refusal to acknowledge the rule of Allah. Bringing an end to tyranny thus entails recognizing the supremacy and oneness of God (*tawhid*). But in order to prevent despotism from reemerging, governments must be made fully accountable to the people and wealth must be distributed equitably. Al-Kawakibi thus presents a program for social reform that is sharply at variance with that advocated by contemporaneous Islamic thinkers, who generally considered both democracy and socialism to be antithetical to Islam. There are indications that al-Kawakibi outlined several other writings during his years in Aleppo, but the notes for these works were seized and destroyed by the Ottoman police.

See also ABBAS HILMI II; RIDA, RASHID.

FRED H. LAWSON

KAYLANI, ABD AL-RAHMAN AL-
[1841–1927]

First prime minister of Iraq.

Scion of an ancient aristocratic family, Abd al-Rahman al-Kaylani was the head of the Qadiri (Sufi) mystical order, established by his ancestor, Abd al-Qadir al-Kaylani (or al-Jilani) (1077–1166). He was also the *naqib al-ashraf* (a noble title denoting responsibility for the genealogical records listing the descent of a city's families from the prophet Muhammad; the title conveys the status of titular head of those families) of Baghdad.

Sir Percy Cox, British civil commissioner after World War I, regarded the Kaylani family as the most aristocratic and monarchial in Baghdad, and suggested that Abd al-Rahman al-Kaylani be made amir of Iraq. In November 1920, al-Kaylani was appointed president of the Iraqi Council of Ministers, the nucleus of the future Iraqi administration. In 1921, as a candidate for the planned throne of Iraq, al-Kaylani objected to the choice of Faisal I ibn Hussein of Hijaz as king of Iraq, but gradually resigned himself to the idea, realizing that the British insisted on Faisal. Al-Kaylani resigned from the Council of Ministers on Faisal's accession in August 1921. Subsequently he was appointed by Faisal as head of the cabinet and became the first prime minister of Iraq. Al-Kaylani conducted talks with Britain about the Anglo–Iraqi Treaties and also objected to the Mandate. In 1922, as the official representative of Iraq, al-Kaylani signed the treaty with Britain but on condition that it would be ratified by the Constituent Assembly.

See also ANGLO–IRAQI TREATIES; COX, PERCY; FAISAL I IBN HUSSEIN.

Bibliography

Batatu, Hanna. *The Old Social Classes and the Revolutionary Movements of Iraq: A Study of Iraq's Old Landed and Commercial Classes and of Its Communists, Ba'thists, and Free Officers.* Princeton, NJ: Princeton University Press, 1978.

MICHAEL EPPEL

KAYLANI, RASHID ALI AL-

[1892–1965]

Four-time prime minister of Iraq in the 1930s and 1940s and a symbol of Arab nationalist resistance.

Rashid Ali al-Kaylani (also al-Gilani) was born in Baghdad in 1892. Although a member of one of the oldest local families, Rashid Ali's personal circumstances were quite modest, as a family disagreement had deprived his father of the stipend from the Qadiriyya *waqf* to which he was entitled as a Kaylani family member.

In 1924 he was appointed minister of justice in the cabinet of Yasin al-Hashimi, probably his closest political colleague; they were cofounders, in 1930, of Hizb al-Ikha al-Watani (Party of National Brotherhood), which spearheaded the opposition to the Anglo–Iraqi treaty of that year. By 1933, however, when the treaty had taken effect, both men acquiesced to the new situation, and Rashid Ali accepted his first premiership (20 March–28 October).

Out of office between October 1933 and March 1935, Rashid Ali and Hashimi spent much of this period encouraging the Middle Euphrates tribes to rebel against the governments of Ali Jawdat al-Ayyubi and Jamil al-Midfa'i. By March 1935, they had succeeded to the extent that Jawdat and Midfa'i could no longer form cabinets; Hashimi became prime minister and Rashid Ali minister of interior in a government that lasted until the coup d'état by Bakr Sidqi in October 1936.

By the late 1930s, Britain and France had become increasingly unpopular in the Arab Middle East. In addition, while pan-Arab nationalism had little following in Iraq outside the officer corps, anti-British—and to some extent pro-Axis—feeling was heightened by the combination of the general weakness of the institutions of the state after the death of King Faisal I; the existence of widely shared aspirations for independence from Britain; the arrival of al-Hajj Amin al-Husayni, the *mufti* of Jerusalem, in Baghdad in October 1939; and the fact that a small clique of nationalist officers, the so-called Golden Square, had come to exercise a pivotal influence on Iraqi politics.

Rashid Ali became the chief political ally of the nationalist officers of the Golden Square and became prime minister in March 1940 after the fall of Nuri al-Sa'id's fifth ministry. Sa'id, unpopular because of his staunch support for Britain, considered, somewhat overoptimistically, that Rashid Ali, who had opposed the Anglo–Iraqi treaty, was both less compromised than himself and better able to resist the Golden Square's more extreme demands.

Under the terms of the 1930 treaty, the Iraqi government agreed to allow the transit of British troops across its territory in time of war. Britain sought to take advantage of this provision in June 1940, and permission in principle was given in mid-July. However, in spite of requests from Britain, Iraq refused to break off relations with Italy when Italy declared war on Britain in June 1940, and in consequence, the Italian legation in Baghdad developed into a center of anti-British intrigue. In addition, in August 1940 Rashid Ali and the mufti entered into secret negotiations with Berlin.

Matters rapidly came to a head, since Rashid Ali, who had the support of most of the armed forces, would not yield to British pressure to resign because of his refusal to allow troops to land in Iraq and pass through the country to Palestine in November 1940. By January 1941, he had been forced to step down as prime minister, but he returned to power on 12 April. In consequence, the regent Abd al-Ilah, Sa'id, and other pro-British politicians fled to Transjordan (now Jordan).

British troops landed at Basra a few days later; while this showed that Britain meant business, it became clear that Rashid Ali and his government enjoyed widespread popular support. Given the balance of forces, the defeat of the Iraqi army by British troops after the thirty days war (May 1941) was very much a foregone conclusion. The much-heralded German support never materialized, and Rashid Ali fled the country with some of his closest supporters, reaching Germany in November 1941. He stayed there until May 1945, subsequently taking refuge in Saudi Arabia, where he remained until 1954.

After the overthrow of the Iraqi monarchy, Rashid Ali returned to Baghdad in September 1958, apparently hoping that his previous services to the state would be properly acclaimed. When adequate recognition was not forthcoming, he set about inciting rebellion among the tribes of the Middle Euphrates in a quixotic attempt to unseat the government of Abd al-Karim Qasim. He was arrested in December 1958, tried and condemned to death, but subsequently pardoned by Qasim. He died in Beirut on 30 August 1965.

See also AYYUBI, ALI JAWDAT AL-; FAISAL I IBN HUSSEIN; GOLDEN SQUARE; HASHIMI, YASIN AL-; HUSAYNI, MUHAMMAD AMIN AL-; IKHA AL-WATANI PARTY; MIDFA'I, JAMIL AL-; QASIM, ABD AL-KARIM; SIDQI, BAKR; WAQF.

Bibliography

Khadduri, Majid. *Independent Iraq, 1932–1958: A Study in Iraqi Politics.* New York: Oxford University Press, 1960.

PETER SLUGLETT

KAZA

See GLOSSARY

KEBAN DAM

Dam built on the Euphrates River in eastern Turkey.

In 1974, near the provincial capital city of Elazığ (1980 population about 143,000), the Keban Dam was opened by Turkey's Prime Minister Bülent Ecevit, after eight years of construction. A future prime minister, Turgut Özal, had been an engineer on the project. When it was completed, the Keban Dam was the world's eighteenth-tallest dam at 680 feet (207 m); it created Turkey's third-largest lake.

The Keban Dam is part of Turkey's Southeastern Anatolia Project, a long-term hydroelectric program designed to increase the country's electrical generating capacity by 45 percent. It includes two other dams—one on the Tigris River and a second, the Atatürk Dam, completed in 1990, on the Euphrates. The project is intended to increase irrigable land in the region by 700,000 acres (283,000 ha) and to stimulate the economy of the region, largely inhabited by Kurds. The project has been a source of political tension with Syria and Iraq, since both depend on the same rivers for water.

See also ECEVIT, BÜLENT; ÖZAL, TURGUT; SOUTHEASTERN ANATOLIA PROJECT.

Bibliography

Metz, Helen Chapin, ed. *Turkey: A Country Study,* 5th edition. Washington, DC: U.S. Government Printing Office, 1996.

ELIZABETH THOMPSON

KEINAN, AMOS
[1927–]

Israeli writer and satirist.

Amos Keinan helped create Israeli culture and served as one of its severest critics. A member of the generation that fought for an independent Jewish state, he soon accused Israel of moral and political decline particularly with regard to its military actions. Influenced by the Canaanite movement, Keinan also argued that Israel lacked a genuine national identity. As a regular columnist for two of Israel's leading newspapers, *Yediot Aharonot* and *Haaretz,* Keinan was widely known for his caustic satire. Keinan's writings are pessimistic and preoccupied with the possibility of destruction. Among his works are *Shoah II* (Holocaust II; 1975); *Ba-Derekh Le-En Harod* (On the road to En Harod; 1984, recounting the destruction of Israel); *Mi-Tahat La-Perahim* (Under the flowers; 1979), an anthology of short stories describing attitudes toward death during war; and *Sefer ha-Satirot* (Book of satires; 1984). A collection of his plays appeared in 1979.

Bibliography

Almog, Oz. *The Sabra: The Creation of the New Jew,* translated by Haim Watzman. Berkeley: University of California Press, 2000.

Shaked, Gershon. *Modern Hebrew Fiction,* translated by Yael Lotan. Bloomington: University of Indiana Press, 2000.

ANN KAHN
UPDATED BY DONNA ROBINSON DIVINE

KEMALETTIN BEY

[1870–1927]

Turkish architect.

Kemalettin was born in Istanbul into a middle-class family; his father was a naval captain. After graduating from the School of Civil Engineering in 1891, he became the assistant to the German architect A. Jasmund, who designed Istanbul's Sirkeci railroad station. Kemalettin later studied at Germany's Charlottenburg Technische Hochschule. Upon returning to Istanbul in 1900, he worked as chief architect in the ministry of war and taught at the School of Civil Engineering. He was a founder of the First National Architectural Movement in the early part of the twentieth century. The style developed by him and his contemporary Vedat Bey has been termed Ottoman Revivalism, because it incorporated the architectural elements of the classical Ottoman period over basically neo-Renaissance structures. When in 1909 he was appointed to the architectural department at the ministry of religious foundations, he began to apply his ideas of a national architecture. Architects trained under his guidance at the ministry helped to spread his vision throughout the Ottoman Empire.

Kemalettin was responsible for the restoration of historical monuments and the design of new buildings, including new mosques, mausoleums, office buildings, prisons, hospitals, schools, and train stations. His buildings were characteristically symmetrical with reference to the entrance, while protrusions at the two ends and at the central axis served to highlight this symmetry. These protrusions were often towers covered with domes, in the classical Ottoman style. He emulated Renaissance architecture by dividing his facades into three sections separated by continuous molding; he used different window orders in each section to render the three sections as distinct entities. The facades had rich carvings, tile panels, and carved moldings, composed in careful symmetry.

One of Kemalettin's most important works is a complex of 124 apartment houses and 25 shops he designed in 1918, the first examples of reinforced concrete construction in Turkey. The Republic of Turkey, established in 1923, recruited Kemalettin to design the portal of the new Turkish Grand National Assembly building and to complete the design of the Ankara Palace Hotel across from the new parliament building. In addition, he designed a series of housing projects for civil servants.

Bibliography

Sey, Yildiz. "To House the New Citizens: Housing Policies and Mass Housing." In *Modern Turkish Architecture,* edited by Renata Holod and Ahmet Evin. Philadelphia: University of Pennsylvania Press, 1984.

Yavuz, Yildirim. "Turkish Architecture during the Republican Period (1923–1980)." In *The Transformation of Turkish Culture: The Atatürk Legacy,* edited by Günsel Renda and C. Max Kortepeter. Princeton, NJ: Kingston Press, 1986.

Yavuz, Yildirim, and Özkan, Suha. "The Final Years of Ottoman Empire" and "Finding a National Idiom: The First National Style." In *Modern Turkish Architecture,* edited by Renata Holod and Ahmet Evin. Philadelphia: University of Pennsylvania Press, 1984.

DAVID WALDNER
UPDATED BY ERIC HOOGLUND

KEMALISM

The official present-day political ideology of the Republic of Turkey.

Kemalism refers variously to the thought of Mustafa Kemal Atatürk (1881–1938); the ideology and regime of the single-party period (1920–1950) in the Republic of Turkey; the official Turkish political ideology to date (semiofficial in the 1961 constitution, fully official and imperative in the 1982 constitution); the principles of national education and citizenship training; the hegemonic public philosophy in contemporary Turkey; and finally to the name of the persistent Turkish personality cult.

Westernist Reforms in Turkey

Kemal derived his legitimacy from the commandership in chief of the successful war of independence (1919–1922), which ended up in the

---

Encyclopedia of **THE MODERN MIDDLE EAST AND NORTH AFRICA**

foundation of the republican Turkish nation-state on the ruins of the Ottoman Empire (1299–1922). No less important, this legitimacy was reinforced by his extreme qualities of charismatic leadership. Kemal and his followers, after abolishing the sultanate and the caliphate, proceeded to build up an authoritarian, single-party state, with discernable totalitarian characteristics in certain ideological and institutional spheres. The Kemalists implemented, alternately gradually and forcefully, a series of radical reforms in the political, legal, educational, and cultural fields, including adoption of Western legal codes (some liberal, such as the Swiss civil code; some fascistic, such as the penal and labor codes); latinization of the Ottoman alphabet; adoption of the Western calendar and units of measurement and imposition of Western clothing and headwear; the closing down of social and associational institutions of Islamic sects; unification of education in the sense of prohibiting schools of religious instruction and creating a new system of secular national education; and disestablishment of Islam in general beyond the narrow laicist sense of separation of religion and politics, but at the same time bringing religion under the control and supervision of the state through a Directorate of Religious Affairs.

The main thrust of these reforms was Westernization and secularization of the society, based on a rejection of the Ottoman Islamic past and on a synthesis of Western values with the virtues of old, original, Turkish "national character," not excluding a tertiary element of the purified, pre-Arabic-Persian-Ottoman version of Islamic morality. Many of these reforms constituted the completion of a long process of Westernist modernization, some inaugurated by the "Re-Ordering" (Tanzimat, 1838) and the First and Second Constitutional periods (1876 and 1908), some others formulated by Ziya Gökalp and partially implemented by the Unionists (1908–1918). Whether the Kemalist reforms constitute a revolution or radical reform is the subject of an ongoing debate, but the Kemalists identified themselves as "transformist" (inkilapi).

Interpretation and Classification of Kemalism

Partly impressed by the Westernist reformist and laicist character of "cultural Kemalism," most interpreters—Turkish and foreign alike—have designated Kemalism as a tutelary democracy overlooking or playing down the severely antidemocratic essence of "political Kemalism" both as an ideology and as a regime. This standard interpretation of Kemalism has also been partly guided by an imputation of false causality, in the sense that the development of the single-party regime after the end of World War II into a sort of multiparty parliamentary system (1946–1950), as a result of external pressures, was attributed to the unfolding of the internal dynamics of the first thirty formative years of the Turkish republic. As a matter of fact, this rootless parliamentarianism has been thrice interrupted by military coups (1960, 1971, 1980) of varying degrees of violence—all declared to be staged, among but above all other things, in the cause of Kemalism.

Kemalism as a "Third Way" Ideology

Kemalism was an early brand of those "third way" (tertium genus) ideologies and regimes of the post–World War I world of late-modernizing capitalist countries which were to borrow further elements, especially in the 1930s and early 1940s, from the full fascisms of interbellum Europe. Kemalism was antisocialist and anti-Marxist, antiliberal but not anticapitalist; that is, it was corporatist capitalist. It belonged more to the solidaristic species of corporatism formulated by the Turkish social and political thinker Ziya Gökalp, only later assuming partial fascistic overtones in certain ideological and institutional spheres. The Kemalist single-party regime rested on a class alliance of civilian-military petite bourgeoisie, big landowners, a nationalistic commercial bourgeoisie, and an incipient and subordinate industrial bourgeoisie, which it was the explicit ideology of the Kemalists to create and strengthen through neomercantilist policies of economic statism (etatism). This developmentalist objective required accelerated capital accumulation through labor policies which provided a cheap and disciplined labor force for private enterprises, for state economic enterprises, and for joint ventures between the two and through fiscal policies that called for transfer of resources from the agricultural countryside to industry and the urban centers, especially after the Great Depression.

"Transformation" Becomes Repression

The Kemalist regime, aiming at the creation of a bourgeois society without liberal politics, was not a *de jure* but a *de facto* dictatorial regime. Mustafa Kemal Atatürk, as the "greatest father" (*Ata-Türk*) of the nation, as the "eternal chief" of the single party, as the president of the republic, as the effective head of the executive branch (in breach of the 1924 Constitution that formally called for a sort of cabinet system) which governed in accordance with his directives, sat at the apex of this system. The parliamentary facade but thinly veiled the fact that the legislature (the Grand National Assembly) was regularly "packed" by Atatürk and his lieutenants, second-degree electors rubber-stamping the candidates handpicked by the former. The parliament, in Kemal Atatürk's own words, was coterminous with the parliamentary group of his Republican People's Party.

In other words, Kemalism was a plebiscitary, Bonapartist-charismatic "chief-system" in whose ideology the identity of the charismatic leader, the nation and its will, the state, and the party was emphatically expressed. Opposition, pluralism, and freedom of press and association, among others, were suppressed in the name of "transformationism" as against the overstretched category of reactionary forces. This attitude and its attendant formal and informal arrangements were to leave a durable imprint on the political culture, political-legal regime, and institutional structures of contemporary Turkey—the most recent fortification of which was to be made after the 1980 military coup in the form of the 1980 Constitution, the new Political Parties Act, the Higher Education Act, the Associations Act, and so forth. Certain liberalizations of the 1950s and 1960s had already been reversed immediately after the semicoup of 1971, restorationist reorderings and preparations of which were to culminate in the systemic overhauling executed by the 1980 coup.

The Six Arrows

The Kemalist ideology is summed up by, but cannot be reduced to, the Six Arrows: (1) Republicanism, meaning antimonarchism rather than democratic res publica; (2) Nationalism, aiming at linguistic and cultural identity-building rather than being an expansionist or irredentist political program; with a less known second face that has racist undertones; (3) "Peopleism," not in the common sense of populism but one which postulates a unified, indivisible, harmonious "whole people"; (4) Statism/etatism; (5) Laicism; and (6) "Transformism," meaning radical, especially cultural, reformism in contradistinction to both revolutionism and evolutionism—all seminally formulated by Gökalp, subsequent distortions notwithstanding.

Technically a rightist ideology, Kemalism in the Turkish context, however, proved to be very pervasive and all-embracing, thanks to characteristics typical of most "third way" ideologies, which try to "reconcile the incompatibles" in order to have a catchall appeal. Hitherto all Turkish political groups, from the extreme right to the center, and more interestingly, to many gradations of the left, have professed (and had to profess) allegiance to Kemalism. Its appeal to the right and center parties is more opaque in view of its authoritarian, "above-parties" and "above-classes," corporatist context. It has been and continues to be very functional in this sense, being the "grund-norm" of political legitimacy in Turkish politics, reproduced by the intelligentsia and forcefully guarded by the military. As for the left, most have incorrectly taken Kemalism's developmentalist statism for a form of state socialism, its anti-imperialism for a kind of anticapitalism, and some of its political reforms for a variant of bourgeois revolution (that would mechanically lead into a socialist revolution)—forgetting the profoundly antidemocratic character of political Kemalism. This consensus, surviving the 1990s despite the foregoing, excludes only a very marginal sector of academe and the nonauthoritarian left, as well as the fringes of the fundamentalist—but not the orthodox, statist-religious right. The former is excluded for obvious reasons; the latter less because of the authoritarian aspects of Kemalism than for its, in their view, excessive Westernism. It should also be noted that the much-spoken-of revival of Islam in Turkey in the 1980s was not initiated by the fundamentalist groups—certainly one of the beneficiaries—but by the military (1980–1983) and civilian (1983–) governmental policies of granting religion a far greater domain of legitimacy than hitherto seen in the history of the Republic of Turkey. The military-imposed Constitution of 1982 provided for compulsory courses on "religious culture and morality" in elementary and secondary education "under the control and supervision of the state." This constituted the first significant deviation from the otherwise intact Kemalist orthodoxy of Turkish establishment politics. In breaking, in this instance, with the classical Kemalist principle of laicism, which has excluded religious instruction from the national education and citizenship training system, the military sought to add Islam to Kemalism in its program of depoliticization, control, and ideological manipulation of Turkey's youth and society, paralleling measures it has taken in many other spheres.

Works on Kemalism, interchangeably called Atatürkism, are legion. Attempts at differentiating the two are polemical and unfounded; Atatürk and his followers baptized their own ideology as Kemalism. A great many of these works, however, are hagiography or are based on secondary or tertiary evidence, whether they be belletristic or academic. In academe, too, Kemalism remains the social scientific official ideology—the obvious contradiction in terms notwithstanding.

See also ATATÜRK, MUSTAFA KEMAL; GÖKALP, ZIYA; REPUBLICAN PEOPLE'S PARTY; TANZIMAT.

TAHA PARLA

KENAZ, YEHOSHUA
[1937–]

Israeli author.

Born in Petah Tikvah, a small town outside Tel Aviv, in 2004 Yehoshua Kenaz lived in Tel Aviv, where he worked on the editorial staff of the Hebrew daily *Haaretz.* A graduate of the Hebrew University and the Sorbonne, he translates works from French in addition to being a literary, film, and theater critic. Kenaz has authored both short stories and novels, and has had four of his works translated into English. Characterized by a harrowing beauty, his fiction captures something of the dark sadness of life, mirroring in the stories' various settings Israel's hemmed-in horizons. He skillfully turns his characters' dilemmas into situations of comic pathos and ironic heroism, thereby transforming Israeli conundrums into universal literature, much as Joyce did with his native Ireland. Kenaz has been awarded the Bialik Prize, the Prime Minister Eshkol Prize, the Alterman Prize, the Agnon Prize, and the Bar Ilan University Newman Prize. The film *On the Edge* was based on his book *After the Holidays.*

See also LITERATURE: HEBREW.

Bibliography

Kenaz, Yehoshua. *After the Holidays,* translated by Dalya Bilu. San Diego, CA: Harcourt Brace Jovanovich, 1987.

Kenaz, Yehoshua. *Musical Moment and Other Stories,* translated by Dalya Bilu. South Royalton, VT: Steerforth, 1995.

Kenaz, Yehoshua. *Returning Lost Loves,* translated by Dalya Bilu. South Royalton, VT: Steerforth, 2001.

Kenaz, Yehoshua. *The Way to the Cats,* translated by Dalya Bilu. South Royalton, VT: Steerforth, 1994.

ZEVA SHAPIRO
UPDATED BY STEPHEN SCHECTER

KENNEDY, JOHN FITZGERALD
[1917–1963]

U.S. President, 1961–1963.

Born in Brookline, Massachusetts, John Fitzgerald Kennedy was the son of Joseph P. Kennedy, first chairman of the U.S. Securities and Exchange Commission and ambassador to Britain from 1937 to 1940. After a Harvard University education, Kennedy served in the navy during World War II, then served as U.S. congressman (1947–1953) and senator (1953–1960) from Massachusetts.

As a senator, Kennedy supported Algeria's independence from France. After taking office as president in 1961, Kennedy's policy toward the Middle East shifted from that of previous administrations. He initially supported Egypt's President Gamal Abdel Nasser, whom he saw as a progressive leader, favoring nationalism, who might keep the Arab world out of the Soviet Union's orbit. Nasser's conflict with Saudi Arabia over the Yemen Civil War undermined Kennedy's policy, however. At the same time that he was attempting to woo Nasser, Kennedy also strengthened U.S. ties with Israel, and he approved the sale of Hawk antiaircraft missiles to Israel in 1962—the first advanced U.S. weapons system sold to Israel. Yet he was plagued by Israel's attempts to develop nuclear weapons at its Dimona nuclear facility, and his attempts to press the Israelis on the matter damaged his relationship with Israeli prime minister David Ben-Gurion.

Kennedy also made some timid diplomatic efforts aimed at resolving the Palestinian refugee problem. He dispatched Joseph E. Johnson to the region in

1961 and 1962 to develop a plan aimed at making progress on the issue, under the aegis of the United Nations Conciliation Commission for Palestine. In the end, however, he failed to support Johnson's recommendations after Israel objected. The "informal talks" launched in the spring and summer of 1963 similarly made no progress.

See also NASSER, GAMAL ABDEL; UNITED NATIONS CONCILIATION COMMITTEE FOR PALESTINE (UNCCP); YEMEN CIVIL WAR.

Bibliography

Cohen, Avner. *Israel and the Bomb.* New York: Columbia University Press, 1998.

Gazit, Mordechai. *President Kennedy's Policy toward the Arab States and Israel: Analysis and Documents.* Tel Aviv: Shiloah Center for Middle Eastern and African Studies, Tel Aviv University, 1983.

ZACHARY KARABELL
UPDATED BY MICHAEL R. FISCHBACH

KENTER, YILDIZ
[1928–]

Turkish actress and director.

Yidiz Kenter, born in Istanbul, is the older sister of Musfik Kenter. After graduating from the Ankara State Conservatory in 1948, she won recognition for her work in small theaters in Ankara and soon began to perform in Turkey's State Theater. In 1959/60, she and her brother left the State Theater to form their own performance company, the Kent Actors. She has twice won the prestigious İlhan İskender award—for her role in the play *Salincakta İki Kişi* (Two people on a wwing) in the 1959/60 season, and for her play *Nalinlar* (Clogs) in the 1961/62 season.

DAVID WALDNER

KEREN HAYESOD

Fundraising division of the World Zionist Organization.

Keren Hayesod (also Keren ha-Yesod), the Palestine Foundation Fund, was established by the London Zionist Conference in 1920 to serve as the major fundraising division and financial institution of the World Zionist Organization (WZO), administered by a board of trustees appointed by the Zionist Executive and Jewish Agency. Its main office was moved in 1926 to Jerusalem, where it has been ever since.

During its inception, Keren Hayesod was the subject of a disagreement between the U.S. and European branches of the WZO. The former, headed by Louis Brandeis, argued for an economic approach in which the Keren Hayesod would raise funds for specific, economically practical projects. The Europeans, headed by Chaim Weizmann, argued for a broader approach in terms of participants and projects that would encourage the support of the Jewish masses and include a range of settlement activity. In the end, the European faction prevailed and the fund had the dual goals of settlement and fostering private-enterprise ventures. Until the establishment of Israel, Keren Hayesod was the major agency involved in financing immigration, absorption, housing, and rural settlement in the *yishuv.* It also purchased arms and paid for other expenses involved in Israel's War of Independence (1948). Since then, Keren Hayesod has encouraged business development in partnership with the private sector. In the United States, it functions as part of the United Jewish Appeal, raising funds for immigration and absorption and for services to the underprivileged in Israel.

See also JEWISH AGENCY FOR PALESTINE; JEWISH NATIONAL FUND; UNITED JEWISH APPEAL (UJA).

Bibliography

Berkowitz, Michael. *Western Jewry and the Zionist Project, 1914–1933.* New York: Cambridge University Press, 1997.

Berman, Morton Mayer. *The Bridge to Life: The Saga of Keren Hayesod, 1920–1970.* Tel Aviv: Shifrin and Naaman, 1970.

Stock, Ernest. *Partners and Pursestrings: A History of the United Israel Appeal.* Lanham, MD: University Press of America, 1987.

CHAIM I. WAXMAN

KERMAN

A province and its capital city in south-central Iran.

The province of Kerman is in south-central Iran. The construction of the town of Kerman probably began in pre-Islamic times. When Marco Polo visited the city in 1271 it had become a major trade emporium linking the Persian Gulf with Khorasan and Central Asia. Subsequently, however, the city was sacked many times by various invaders. The present city of Kerman, 661 miles southeast of Tehran, and the capital of the modern province of Kerman, was rebuilt in the nineteenth century to the northwest of the old city, but it did not recover until the twentieth century. Carpet weaving is one of the main industries of the city, and the carpets produced there are renowned internationally. A number of modern establishments such as textile mills and brickworks also have been constructed. The province's mineral wealth includes copper and coal. The population of the city in 1996 was 385,000. The total population of the province in 1996 was 2,004,328.

Bibliography

Fisher, W. B., ed. *The Cambridge History of Iran,* Vol. 1: *The Land of Iran.* Cambridge, U.K.: Cambridge University Press, 1968.

Islamic Republic of Iran Today. Tehran: Islamic Propagation Organization, 1987.

PARVANEH POURSHARIATI

KESSAR, ISRAEL
[1931–]

Israeli trade union leader; member of the Knesset.

Israel Kessar was born in Yemen and immigrated to Mandatory Palestine in 1933. His education focused on sociology and economics; he received a master's degree from Tel Aviv University. Employed first as a teacher of new immigrants, Kessar then worked in the Ministry of Labor. His work in the Histadrut, Israel's trade union, began in 1966, and he held many positions: treasurer from 1973 to 1977, chairman of the Trade Union Department and deputy secretary-general from 1977 to 1984, and secretary-general from 1984 to 1992. He was elected to the Knesset in the same year and served in the Eleventh, Twelfth, and Thirteenth Knessets (serving as minister of transportation from 1992 to 1996). His cooperation with the government while he was secretary-general of the Histadrut was important to the ultimate success of the emergency economic stabilization plan, which while fighting

to keep real wages from falling too steeply also guarded against policies that would increase unemployment.

See also HISTADRUT.

MARTIN MALIN
UPDATED BY GREGORY S. MAHLER

KGB

Soviet espionage organization.

KGB, or Komitet Gosudarstvennoi Bezopasnosti (Committee for State Security), was the Soviet Union's state security and political police agency, serving as the main internal and external intelligence and counterintelligence bureau, and external espionage and counterespionage organization from 1954 to 1991. It was somewhat similar to the U.S. Central Intelligence Agency (CIA) and British MI-6. Under Communist Party control, it was the world's largest secret police and espionage organization, with seven directorates including foreign operations; internal political control; military counterintelligence; surveillance; and border guards. The latter included 300,000 personnel dispersed in Eastern Europe and the Central Asian Republics. Turkey, Iran, and Afghanistan were special targets.

Bibliography

Yost, Graham. *The KGB: The Russian Secret Police from the Days of the Czars to the Present.* New York: Facts On File, 1989.

CHARLES C. KOLB

KHADDAM, ABD AL-HALIM
[1932–]

Syrian politician.

Born in 1932 to a Sunni family of modest means from the coastal town of Jabla, just north of Banyas, Abd al-Halim Khaddam became active in Ba'th party politics while attending secondary school in Latakia in the late 1940s. During his student days, he forged a fast friendship with another young firebrand, Hafiz al-Asad. After graduating from the Faculty of Law at Damascus University, he practiced law and taught school before devoting himself to a career inside the party apparatus. He married into a prominent Alawi family in 1954.

By 1964 Khaddam had become governor of the troubled city of Hama, whose citizenry rose in rebellion against the Baʿth-dominated regime that April. He was governor of Qunaytra when the Israelis overran the Golan three years later. He then served as governor of Damascus city, before assuming the post of minister of the economy and foreign trade during the turbulent final years of the Salah Jadid period (1966–1970). When his old friend Hafiz al-Asad seized power in November 1970, Khaddam was promoted to the post of foreign minister. President al-Asad entrusted him with the thankless duty of negotiating the May 1974 disengagement agreement with Israel and with the difficult task of mediating among rival Lebanese factions during the tense period between the outbreak of the civil war in April 1975 and Syria's intervention in the conflict the following June. He was also given the delicate assignment of lobbying Arab leaders to reject the Egyptian–Israeli peace initiative of 1977–1978 and the tricky role of emissary between Damascus and Tehran during the uncertain months immediately following the 1978–1979 Iranian revolution.

When President al-Asad fell ill at the end of November 1983, Khaddam was appointed to the six-person committee charged with keeping affairs of state in order. Four months later, in a move clearly intended to counterbalance the influence of the president's ambitious brother Rifʿat, al-Asad named Khaddam as one of Syria's first three vice presidents, forcing him to relinquish the foreign ministership. Shortly thereafter, one of his sons married a daughter of the venerable al-Atasi clan in a lavish ceremony at the Damascus Sheraton Hotel. By the mid-1990s, some felt that his evident astuteness and longevity made him the most likely candidate to succeed Hafiz al-Asad as president of the republic. Yet al-Asad began grooming his youngest son Bashshar al-Asad for the job, and Bashshar assumed the presidency when his father died in June 2000. Khaddam remained a vice president, but not being a protegé of the younger al-Asad, slipped into a largely ceremonial role in Syrian politics.

Bibliography

Batatu, Hanna. *Syria's Peasantry, the Descendants of Its Lesser Rural Notables, and Their Politics.* Princeton, NJ: Princeton University Press, 1999.

Seale, Patrick. *Asad: The Struggle for the Middle East.* London: Tauris, 1988.

FRED H. LAWSON
UPDATED BY MICHAEL R. FISCHBACH

KHADER, ASMA
[1952–]

Jordanian lawyer, human-rights activist, and a founder of Sisterhood Is Global Institute in Jordan.

Asma Khader (also Khadr), a Jordanian lawyer and human-rights activist, is founder and president of Mizan: The Law Group for Human Rights in Jordan and a founding member of the Arab Association for Human Rights. She served for two terms as president of the Jordanian Women's Union. Khader is a member of the Jordanian and Arab Lawyers' Unions and was recently appointed to the Executive Committee of the International Commission of Jurists.

Khader played an instrumental role in developing a legal literacy program for Jordanian women, as well as establishing the Jordanian Children's Parliament. She was instrumental in conducting human-rights education workshops in 1984 in different areas of Jordan and launched a program to integrate human-rights education within the school curricula. Khader is the founder and reporter of the National Network for Poverty Alleviation. Sponsored by the United Nations Development Program (UNDP) Poverty Strategy Initiative, the network was established in October 2000 in cooperation with the Families Development Association. Encompassing more than ninety participants from governmental and nongovernmental organizations as well as independent individuals, the network focuses on tackling poverty in Jordan and is also involved in the preparation of the Millennium Development Goals Report in Jordan. In 2003, Khader was the recipient of the UNDP's Poverty Eradication Award in the Arab states.

Khader served in 1999 as legal counsel to the Jordanian National Campaign Committee to Eliminate So-called Crimes of Honor in Jordan. She also served as a counsel to the Permanent Arab Court on Violence against Women in 1996 and as a judge in the Court's public hearings in Lebanon in 1997. She serves on the advisory committee of various national and international women's and human-rights organizations, including the Advisory Committee of the Women's Rights Division of Human Rights Watch and Equality Now. In addition, and at the request of prominent international and regional human-rights organizations such as Amnesty International, she has monitored trials and served on various human-rights fact-finding missions. Khader has maintained a private legal practice for over twenty-three years and was recently appointed minister of state and spokesperson for the Jordanian government.

Bibliography

Afkhani, Mahnaz, and Friedl, Erika. *Muslim Women and the Politics of Participation: Implementing the Beijing Platform.* Syracuse, NY: Syracuse University Press, 1998.

Ismail, Ghena. "An Interview with Asma Khader." *Al-Raida* 70–71 (1996).

ISIS NUSAIR

KHALAF, ABDULHADI
[1945–]

Bahraini political activist and academic who has lived in Sweden since 1990.

Abdulhadi (also Abd al-Hadi) Khalaf was born in Bahrain in 1945. He received his primary and secondary education there, then went abroad for college. He obtained a doctorate in sociology from Sweden's University of Lund in 1972. Returning to Bahrain, he became a candidate for the country's first National Assembly and was elected in December 1973. The assembly was an advisory body with limited powers to approve laws drawn up by the government. Several months after the National Assembly convened, Khalaf was expelled and arrested on charges of supporting one of several banned political groups that called for a constitutional monarchy. He was released from prison in 1975, then rearrested in 1976, again because of his political activities on behalf of democratic government.

Between 1975 and 1990, Khalaf was among the small group of Bahraini intellectuals who developed the country's fledgling system of higher education. In 1990, he accepted an appointment to teach sociology at the University of Lund and moved to Sweden. He continues to write articles about Bahrain's politics and society for Arabic and English publications.

See also BAHRAIN.

Bibliography

Khalaf, Abdulhadi. *An Unfinished Business: Contentious Politics and State Building in Bahrain.* Lund, Sweden: University of Lund, 2000.

EMILE A. NAKHLEH
UPDATED BY ERIC HOOGLUND

KHALAF, SALAH
[1933–1991]

Palestine Liberation Organization leader, also known as Abu Iyad.

Born in Jaffa to a religious Muslim family, Salah Khalaf fled to Gaza during the 1948 Arab–Israel War. After 1951, he attended the University of Cairo, where he joined Yasir Arafat's Palestinian Students Union. He and Arafat founded the al-Fatah organization in Kuwait, where Khalaf was working as a schoolmaster in the 1960s. Khalaf played a leading role in the fighting of Black September in 1970, participated in the Lebanese Civil War in the late 1970s, and was linked to several violent and terrorist incidents in the 1970s and 1980s. By the late 1980s he had emerged as the second most powerful leader of the Palestine Liberation Organization (PLO), in charge of intelligence and security.

Khalaf was killed 14 January 1991 in the Tunis suburb of Carthage at the villa of Abd al-Hamid Ha'il (Abu al-Hawl) (the Fatah security chief). The gunman was Hamza Abu Zayd, a guard stationed at the villa. Khalaf had married the daughter of a wealthy Palestinian businessman, with whom he had six children. He was author of a widely read memoir, *My Home, My Land,* written with Eric Rouleau.

See also ARAFAT, YASIR; BLACK SEPTEMBER; FATAH, AL-; LEBANESE CIVIL WAR (1975–1990); PALESTINE LIBERATION ORGANIZATION (PLO).

Bibliography

Becker, Jillian. *The PLO: The Rise and Fall of the Palestine Liberation Organization.* London: Weidenfeld and Nicolson, 1984.

Livingstone, Neil C., and Halevy, David. *Inside the PLO: Covert Units, Secret Funds, and the War against Israel and the United States.* New York: Morrow, 1990.

ELIZABETH THOMPSON

KHALDUNNIYYA

Tunisian educational society.

Khaldunniyya was founded by the Young Tunisians in 1896 and named in honor of the fourteenth-century Tunisian intellectual Ibn Khaldun. Intended to acquaint Tunisians who were illiterate in European languages with the contemporary European world, it offered instruction in Arabic in a wide variety of subjects. The organizers of the Khaldunniyya especially sought to reach Zaytuna University students in order to enhance their still largely traditional curriculum.

See also ZAYTUNA UNIVERSITY.

KENNETH J. PERKINS

KHALED, LEILA

[1948–]

Palestinian hijacker, feminist, and activist.

Leila Khaled (also Layla Khalid), long-time activist and Central Committee member of the Popular Front for the Liberation of Palestine (PFLP), was born on 9 April 1944 in Haifa, Palestine. Her family left Haifa as refugees to Lebanon on 13 April 1948, just before the State of Israel was established. Khaled joined a Lebanese cell of the Arab Nationalists Movement (ANM) in 1958. She was a student and activist at the American University of Beirut (AUB) in 1962 to 1963, but left because of financial difficulties and was employed as a teacher in Kuwait for a number of years. In Kuwait she became active with al-Fatah, which did not grant her request to join its military wing. In 1968 Khaled made contacts with PFLP cadres in Kuwait, and in 1969 she was accepted for military training in its Special Operations Squad. She left Kuwait for Amman, Jordan in 1969 in order to undertake resistance activities. Khaled became infamous when she and a male colleague hijacked a TWA airplane headed for Tel Aviv on 29 August 1969, forcing the flight to land in Damascus, where they blew it up after emptying it of passengers. Khaled underwent a number of clandestine plastic-surgery operations in Lebanon to transform her world-renowned face. In 1970 she commandeered another flight with a male colleague (who was killed in the operation) on behalf of the PFLP. This hijacking, of an Israeli El Al airplane, was thwarted, and the plane was forced to land in England, where Khaled was held by the British government and eventually released in a prisoner exchange. Khaled repeatedly stated that the aim of the hijackings was to gain international recognition of the plight of Palestinians as an issue of national dislocation and desire for self-determination rather than a refugee problem to be resolved through charity. Her well-known biography, *My People Shall Live* (1971), demonstrates a combined feminist and nationalist orientation, and provides a leftist analysis of the Palestinian-Israeli conflict. Khaled survived a number of assassination attempts—in one, Israeli forces killed her sister. She attended university in the Soviet Union in the early 1980s, married her second husband in 1982, and worked with the PFLP-affiliated Palestinian Popular Women's Committees in Damascus following its establishment in the mid-1980s. She is a member of the Palestine National Council and a high-ranking leader in the General Union of Palestinian Women. Khaled's stances have not softened with age. In the 1990s she denounced the Oslo Accords, calling them fundamentally flawed because they did not address the status of Jerusalem, the ending of the Israeli occupation of territories occupied in June 1967, the right of return for Palestinian refugees, or Palestinian sovereignty. Although her actions are considered terrorism by many in the West, she has achieved the status of political icon throughout much of the Arab world.

See also PALESTINE NATIONAL COUNCIL; POPULAR FRONT FOR THE LIBERATION OF PALESTINE.

Bibliography

Khaled, Leila, and Hajjar, George. *My People Shall Live: Autobiography of a Revolutionary.* Toronto: NC Press, 1975.

MacDonald, Eileen. *Shoot the Women First.* New York: Random House, 1991.

Mohan, Rajeswari. "Loving Palestine: Nationalist Activism and Feminist Agency in Leila Khaled's Subversive Bodily Acts." *Interventions* I, no. 1 (1998): 52–80.

FRANCES HASSO

KHAL, HELEN
[1923–]

Lebanese painter.

Born in the United States to Lebanese parents, Helen Khal studied at the Lebanese Academy of Fine Arts and returned to study at the Art Students League in New York. She returned to Lebanon to live and work, and in the 1960s she opened and directed the first permanent art gallery in that country, Gallery One. She continues to paint and write art criticism for Lebanese journals and newspapers. She is also the author of *The Woman Artist in Lebanon* (1987). Khal's paintings are primarily an exploration and expression of the emotive capacities of color, a theme inspired by the intense light of Lebanon. A notable portion of her work examines the relationship between color and the human figure. Her later work plays with relationships between fields of color in a way similar to Rothko and the New York color field painters. Khal's work was part of the major *Forces of Change* exhibit of Arab women artists in the United States and has also been included in the biennials of Sao Paulo and Alexandria.

See also GENDER: GENDER AND EDUCATION; LEBANESE CIVIL WAR (1958); LEBANESE CIVIL WAR (1975–1990); LEBANON.

Bibliography

Khal, Helen. *The Woman Artist in Lebanon*. Beirut: Institute for Women's Studies in the Arab World, 1987.

Nashashibi, Salwa Makdadi. *Forces of change: Artists of the Arab World*. Lafayette, CA: National Museum of Women in the Arts, 1994.

JESSICA WINEGAR

KHALIDI, AHMAD AL-SAMIH AL-
[1896–1951]

Palestinian educator, writer, and social reformer.

Ahmad al-Samih al-Khalidi studied pharmacy at the American University of Beirut until 1917. After a brief stint in the Ottoman military, he worked for the education department of the British Palestine Government between 1919 and 1925. From 1925 until 1948 he headed a teacher-training school in Jerusalem, which was renamed the Arab College. It was the best secondary school in the country. He was appointed in 1941 assistant director of education for the British Mandate in Palestine. While he was director of the Arab College he issued one of the earliest proposals for the partition of Palestine, which called for dividing the country into Arab and Jewish cantons.

Khalidi wrote works on education, psychology, and history, some of which became textbooks in a number of Arab countries, including *Anzimat al-Ta'lim wa al-Hukm fi rif Filastin* (Systems of learning and leadership in the rural areas of Palestine, 1968). In addition, he translated a number of foreign works into Arabic, including those of Viennese psychoanalyst Wilhelm Stekel and American psychologist Robert Sessions Woodworth. In the early 1940s Khalidi became interested in Palestinian orphans. He established the General Arab Committee for Orphans and opened a school in Dayr Amr, Jerusalem, for sons whose fathers were killed in the Palestine Arab Revolt of 1936 to 1939. Later he added a girls' school nearby. After the 1948 Arab–Israel War, Khalidi established a school for orphaned Palestinian refugees in Hinniyya, southern Lebanon.

See also ARAB COLLEGE OF JERUSALEM.

MICHAEL R. FISCHBACH

KHALID IBN ABD AL-AZIZ AL SA'UD
[1912–1982]

King of Saudi Arabia, 1975–1982.

Khalid ibn Abd al-Aziz Al Sa'ud was born in 1912 in Riyadh, the seventh son of King Abd al-Aziz Al Sa'ud (known as Ibn Sa'ud in the West), the founder of Saudi Arabia. Khalid's only full brother was Muhammad ibn Abd al-Aziz Al Sa'ud, two years his elder.

Khalid was educated in the royal court, studying the Qur'an, Islamic history, and a limited range of several practical subjects, together with firsthand observation of court politics. He did not pursue an overtly political career. Nonetheless, from early adulthood he played an important part in family councils and by his thirties had become part of the small circle of princes that would guide Saudi Arabia's affairs. Of all his brothers he was, perhaps, the closest to the aloof Faisal. When only nineteen, Khalid acted as viceroy in Hijaz during Faisal's absences, and he later accompanied Faisal to the United States in 1943 and was deputy prime minister in the cabinet that Faisal, acting as the Saudi prime minister, appointed in October 1962. Following Faisal's accession as king in November 1964, the senior princes and he pressed the reluctant Khalid to become crown prince. After several months of resistance, Khalid yielded to their pressure.

Khalid rose to the throne three days after the assassination of Faisal in 1975. Although the period of his rule was characterized by tremendous economic wealth generated by oil exports, and rapid development in nearly all sectors of the economy and society, Khalid's reign included some of the most turbulent episodes in recent Saudi history. Contradictions in Saudi society that had begun to develop during the reign of Faisal broke to the surface during the Khalid years. For example, although Khalid's regime supported the spread of religious education and encouraged a conservative Islamic worldview, many members of the ruling family espoused or at least tolerated Western values and lived a lavish lifestyle untrammeled by religious restrictions. This and other factors led to deep resentments among segments of the population and open opposition, which broke out most dramatically in the seizure of the Grand Mosque of Mecca in 1979 and uprisings in the Eastern Province among the Shi'ite population.

Khalid acknowledged the legitimacy of some complaints that those who seized the Grand Mosque had raised and sought to address them. Following the disturbances among the long-mistreated Shi'ia of the Eastern Province (al-Hasa) in 1979 and 1980, he launched a major new development project in the principal Shi'ite area and made a personal visit—the first time a reigning Saudi monarch had done so. His 1976 tour of the other conservative Arab Gulf states to discuss common security concerns initiated the process that led to creation of the Gulf Cooperation Council in 1981.

See also AL SA'UD FAMILY; FAISAL IBN ABD AL-AZIZ AL SA'UD; GULF COOPERATION COUNCIL.

Bibliography

Al-Rasheed, Madawi. *A History of Saudi Arabia.* New York and Cambridge, U.K.: Cambridge University Press, 2002.

Bligh, Alexander. *From Prince to King: Royal Succession in the House of Sa'ud in the Twentieth Century.* New York: New York University Press, 1984.

Holden, David, and Johns, Richard. *The House of Sa'ud: The Rise and Rule of the Most Powerful Dynasty in the Arab World.* New York: Holt, Rinehart, and Winston, 1981.

MALCOLM C. PECK
UPDATED BY ANTHONY B. TOTH

KHALIDI, HUSAYN FAKHRI AL-
[1894–1962]

Palestinian politician who hailed from a prominent Jerusalem family.

Born in Jerusalem, Husayn Fakhri al-Khalidi studied medicine at the American University of Beirut and Istanbul University. After service in the Ottoman army, he joined the Arab Revolt and later worked for the department of health in Aleppo during the short-lived rule (1918–1920) of King Faisal I ibn Hussein in Syria. He was mayor of Jerusalem from 1934 to 1937, the last time that the city's mayor was elected by the entire population. In 1935 he founded the Reform Party (Hizb al-Islah). He was elected member of the Arab Higher Committee, a Palestinian political body formed in 1936 to direct the Palestinian national struggle. Al-Khalidi was then exiled by British authorities to the Seychelles islands from 1937 to 1942 along with other nationalist leaders. In 1946 he was a member of the reconstituted Arab Higher Committee. As a senior politician, al-Khalidi participated in the London Roundtable Conference (St. James Conference) of 1939.

After 1948 he served as Jordan's foreign minister in the cabinets of Fawzi al-Mulqi (1953) and Samir Rifa'i (1955). In April 1957 al-Khalidi was appointed prime minister of Jordan during the political crisis brought on by the dismissal of Prime Minister Sulayman al-Nabulsi, but his cabinet lasted only one week. Al-Khalidi spent the rest of his life in Jericho where he wrote articles for the Jerusalem daily *al-Jihad* and authored a book entitled *al-Khuruj al-Arabi* (The Arab exodus). Al-Khalidi's unpublished autobiography illuminates many aspects of Arab and Palestinian politics.

See also ARAB HIGHER COMMITTEE (PALESTINE); LONDON (ROUNDTABLE) CONFERENCE (1939); NABULSI, SULAYMAN AL-.

Bibliography

Fischbach, Michael R. "Khalidi Family." In *Encyclopedia of the Palestinians,* edited by Philip Mattar. New York: Facts On File, 2000.

MUHAMMAD MUSLIH
UPDATED BY MICHAEL R. FISCHBACH

KHALIDI, WAHIDA AL-
[1900–?]

First president of the Arab Women's Executive Committee, the coordinating committee of the women's movement in Palestine during the British Mandate.

Wahida al-Khalidi completed her high school education in a school run by nuns and spoke six languages. She married Dr. Husayn Fakhri al-Khalidi, who was active in the Palestinian national movement during the British Mandate. He served as mayor of Jerusalem in 1934 and as a member of the Islah (Reform) Party. Wahida al-Khalidi was a founding member and president of the Arab Women's Executive Committee (AWE) in the late 1920s and early 1930s. She was active in demanding a political role for women and in distributing aid to the revolutionaries in the 1936 through 1939 revolt. She was a member of the Palestinian delegation to the Eastern Women's Conference on Palestine, held in Cairo in 1938. In 1939 she stopped working with the AWE, possibly due to her husband's deportation to the Seychelles islands in 1937.

See also ARAB WOMEN'S ASSOCIATION OF PALESTINE; ARAB WOMEN'S EXECUTIVE COMMITTEE; JERUSALEM.

Bibliography

"First Time in the History of Palestine, Conference of Palestinian Arab Ladies." *Filastin* 29: 27 October 1929.

Mogannam, Matiel. *The Arab Woman and the Palestine Problem.* London: Herbert Joseph, 1937.

ELLEN L. FLEISCHMANN

KHALIDI, WALID
[1925–]

Palestinian intellectual and strategist.

Walid Khalidi has devoted much of his life to research and writing on the Palestine question. In 1963 he cofounded the Institute for Palestine Studies, an independent nonprofit Arab research and publication center. He has taught at the American University in Beirut, as well as at Oxford and Harvard, and has been a research associate at the Center for International Affairs and the Center for Middle East Studies at Harvard University. He has written and edited several articles and books including *From Haven to Conquest* (1970); *Conflict and Violence in Lebanon: Confrontation in the Middle East* (1979); *Before Their Diaspora, A Photographic History of the Palestinians 1876–1948* (1984); and *All That Remains: The Palestinian Villages Occupied and Depopulated by Israel in 1948* (1992). A consummate expert on the Palestinian question and the Arab–Israeli conflict, he played an important role in shaping the Palestine Liberation Organization's (PLO) peace strategy toward Israel, and was a member of the Jordanian delegation to the peace talks with Israel (1991–1992). Despite Khalidi's role in developing PLO policy, he has never been affiliated with the PLO.

See also INSTITUTE FOR PALESTINE STUDIES; PALESTINE LIBERATION ORGANIZATION (PLO).

MUHAMMAD MUSLIH

KHALID, KHALID MUHAMMAD
[1920–1996]

Egyptian political and religious thinker and writer.

Born to a modest family, Khalid Muhammad Khalid studied Islamic law at al-Azhar University. He was influenced greatly by the liberal ideology of the Wafd Party as championed by authors such as Ahmad Amin and Taha Husayn. He joined the opposition group al-Hay'a al-Sa'diyya, founded by Ahmad Mahir and Mahmud Fahmi al-Nuqrashi, who had split from the Wafd Party, and he wrote critically of the government of Mustafa al-Nahhas, whom his party opposed. He was jailed and released, but imprisoned again in 1950 after the publication of his widely successful book *From Here We Start,* which was banned by the government. The book advocated a representative government and socialist economic policies such as nationalization of means of production and limited private property, and it is said to have greatly influenced Gamal Abdel Nasser, whose government Khalid strongly supported. His opposition to the role of religion in the state and his call for the suspension of *shariʿa* led to a strong condemnation from al-Azhar theologians and to a rebuttal by Muhammad al-Ghazali in a book entitled *From Here We Know*. Khalid also opposed the Muslim Brotherhood, and especially the violent policies followed by one of the Brotherhood's branches. But his disenchantment with the failed economic policies of Nasser's government—and the transformation of the government into a totalitarian regime—gradually led Khalid to join the Islamic revivalist movement. In 1989 he published *Islam and the State*, in which he declared that he had misrepresented the historical and political role of Islam, and advocated political solutions closer to the ideology of the Muslim Brotherhood. He wrote more than thirty books and his writings remain influential in Egypt.

See also AZHAR, AL-; GHAZALI, MUHAMMAD AL-; MAHIR, AHMAD; NAHHAS, MUSTAFA AL-; NASSER, GAMAL ABDEL; NUQRASHI, MAHMUD FAHMI AL-; WAFD.

MAYSAM AL FARUQI

KHALIFA, SAHAR
[1941–]

Palestinian novelist and short-story writer.

Sahar Khalifa (also Khalifeh), a leading Palestinian author of novels, short stories, and plays, was born in Nablus, where most of her stories are set. Khalifa attended high school in Amman and, shortly after graduating, entered into an arranged marriage at the age of eighteen. Thirteen years and two daughters later, Khalifa divorced her husband, began working, and pursued a post-secondary education. She received her bachelor's degree in English and American literature at Bir Zeit University in the West Bank, and then traveled to the United States for her graduate studies. She received her doctorate in American Studies at the University of Iowa. Khalifa is best known in the English-speaking world for her 1984 novel *Wild Thorns* (first published in Arabic in 1976), which portrays the conflict between occupied Palestinians and the Israeli army from a variety of perspectives and in different voices, both male and female, young and old, Arab and Israeli. Khalifa's other works include *We Are Not Your Slave Girls Anymore* (1974), which was serialized and made into a radio program; *The Sunflower* (1980); *Memoirs of an*

Unrealistic Woman (1986), a novel said to be based on her own bitter experience of a loveless, arranged marriage; *The Door of the Courtyard* (1990); and *The Inheritance* (1997). Khalifa's works have been translated into Hebrew, Dutch, Russian, and Swedish, in addition to English. She has taught literature at the University of Iowa and Bir Zeit University, and founded the Women's Affairs Center in Nablus, an organization focusing on women's economic and political empowerment, which now has additional branches in Gaza City and Amman.

Bibliography

Khalifeh, Sahar. "My Life, Myself, and the World." *Al Jadid* 8, no. 39 (Spring 2002).

Khalifeh, Sahar. Selected writings. Available from <http://www.sakakini.org>.

Nazareth, Peter. "An Interview with Sahar Khalifeh." *Iowa Review* 11, no. 1 (1980): 67–86.

LAURIE KING-IRANI

KHALIL, SAMIHA SALAMA
[1923–1999]

Founder of the Palestinian charitable society Inʿash al-Usra (Rejuvenation of the Family).

Samiha Salama Khalil (Umm Khalil) was born in Anabta, near Tulkarm. A strong, resourceful, and proactive natural leader, she is best known as the founder of the Palestinian charitable society Inʿash al-Usra (Rejuvenation of the Family), as well as for her bold though unsuccessful attempt to stand for election for the presidency of Palestine, running against Yasir Arafat in 1996. Khalil mounted a presidential campaign centering on democratization, justice, and equality for all, and received nearly 10 percent of the vote. A firm believer in empowerment and self-sufficiency in the face of the adversities that history had visited upon Palestinians, Khalil inspired many others, primarily women, through her life of community and national service. In 1948 Khalil became a refugee, fleeing to the Gaza Strip, where she remained until sailing to Beirut in 1952. Soon thereafter, she returned to Palestine, this time to the West Bank, where, in 1965, she became president of the Women's Federation Society, al-Bira, as well as of the Union for Voluntary Women's Societies and the General Union of Palestinian Women (GUPW). That year she also founded, with the help of many local women volunteers, the In'ash al-Usra Society in a garage in Ramallah. The society's empowering message of self-sufficiency and communal dignity became indispensable as the Israeli occupation became increasingly oppressive in the 1970s and 1980s. At the time of Khalil's death, In'ash al-Usra had a monthly operating budget of $500,000 and successfully administered vocational embroidery, nursing, and beauty programs, as well as offering nursery facilities and residential child care. In'ash al-Usra was closed down several times by the Israeli military during the 1970s until the early 1990s, and Khalil was arrested on a number of occasions. She died on 26 February 1999 at the age of 76.

Bibliography

In'ash al-Usra Society. Available from <http://www.inash.org>.

Jad, Islah. "From Salons to the Popular Committees: Palestinian Women, 1919–1989." In *Intifada: Palestine at the Crossroads,* edited by Jamal Nassar and Roger Heacock. New York: Praeger, 1990.

LAURIE KING-IRANI

KHALIS, MOHAMMAD UNIS
[1919–]

Afghan resistance leader.

The leader of one branch of the Hezb-e Islami party, Mohammad Unis Khalis was born in 1919 in Gandamak among the Khugiani Pushtun and studied Islamic law and theology. He fled Afghanistan in 1973 at the time of the coup led by Muhammad Daud. At first he joined the Hezb-e Islami party led by Golbuddin Hekmatyar, but he left to form his own party of the same name in 1978. During the war of resistance (1978–1992), his men fought in the Khugiani area, and Khalis, despite his advanced age, often accompanied them.

In 1992, he returned to Kabul with the other Islamic leaders to play a role in the attempt to form an Islamic government. He is strongly Muslim and anti-Western and opposes universal suffrage as well as the participation of the Shi'a in Afghanistan politics.

See also DAUD, MUHAMMAD; HEKMATYAR, GOLBUDDIN; HEZB-E ISLAMI.

Bibliography

Roy, Olivier. *Islam and Resistance in Afghanistan,* 2d edition. Cambridge, U.K., and New York: Cambridge University Press, 1990.

GRANT FARR

KHAL, YUSUF AL-
[1917–1987]

Lebanese poet; founder of the poetry review Shi'r.

A Protestant born in Tripoli, Lebanon, Yusuf al-Khal was educated in literature and philosophy at the American University at Beirut (AUB). After World War II, he spent several years in the United States, where he worked as publishing director at *al-Huda,* a New York–based magazine catering to Lebanese emigrants. The years spent at AUB and in the United States provided him with a great familiarity with Western (particularly Anglo-Saxon) literature, and he even edited an anthology of American poetry.

Back in Lebanon, he became a leading figure in an emerging group of young modernist Lebanese poets who were determined to break away from the traditional poetic forms that had prevailed in the Arab world since al-Nahda, the cultural awakening of the late nineteenth century. In January 1957, drawing on his experience as a journalist and publisher, he founded the poetry review *Shi'r,* which remained a rallying point for avant-garde Arab poets—including Khalil Hawi, Adonis, and Badr Shakir al-Sayyab—until it ceased to exist in the early 1970s.

In *Shi'r,* al-Khal pressed for the opening up of Arab poetry to the influence of the new poetic current emanating from the West. He advocated making colloquial Arabic the basis of literature as a way of reviving and widening the appeal of Arabic poetry, which, he thought, would otherwise be condemned to die out slowly. His own poetry was written in a language that approached that of everyday conversation. Its rhythm and skillful manipulation of images and sounds established him as the most prominent Lebanese member of the group of poets belonging to the free verse movement. Unlike many of his contemporaries, however, he always refrained from mixing poetry and politics; he even condemned "engagement literature," which he saw as a source of cultural decay.

See also ADONIS; HAWI, KHALIL; NAHDA, AL-; SAYYAB, BADR SHAKIR AL-.

Bibliography

Allen, Roger, ed. *Modern Arabic Literature*. New York: Ungar, 1987.

Boullata, Issa J., ed. and tr. *Modern Arab Poets, 1950–1975*. Washington, DC: Three Continents Press, 1976.

GUILAIN P. DENOEUX

KHAMENEHI, ALI
[1939–]

Leader (rahbar) *of the Islamic Republic of Iran and successor to the constitutional functions of Ayatollah Ruhollah Khomeini.*

Born in the northeastern Iranian city of Mashhad, Khamenehi began his advanced studies in Islam in 1958, with a year's attendance at courses on Islamic jurisprudence in al-Najaf, Iraq. He received most of his training in Qom, where he studied with ayatollahs Damad, Haeri, Tabatabai, and most importantly Khomeini.

During the uprising in Iran of June 1963, inspired by Khomeini, Khamenehi acted as liaison between Qom and his native city of Mashhad; he was jailed twice for this in 1964. Released in 1965, he resumed propagating the revolutionary vision of Khomeini in Mashhad while teaching the Qur'an and Islamic law. These activities earned him further periods of imprisonment as well as banishment in 1968, 1971, 1972, 1975, and 1978. After the Iranian Revolution in February 1979, Khamenehi emerged as a key figure in the elite of clerical activists who founded the Islamic Republican Party and came to dominate the Iranian parliament during its first postrevolutionary term. In July 1979 he was appointed undersecretary for defense in the Mehdi Bazargan cabinet, becoming acting minister of defense after Bazargan's resignation.

Among the most determined opponents of Abolhasan Bani Sadr, the first president of the Islamic republic, Khamenehi played an important role in the events leading to his dismissal in June 1981. On 27 June, while delivering the Friday sermon at Tehran University, Khamenehi was injured in one

Ali Khamenehi was elected president of Iran for two successive terms, in 1981 and 1985. Following the death of Ayatollah Ruhollah Khomeini in 1989, an elected council of religious law experts chose Khamenehi to succeed Khomieni as Iran's chief faqih (religious jurist). © AP/WIDE WORLD PHOTOS. REPRODUCED BY PERMISSION.

of the numerous assassinations of leading government figures that followed the disgracing of Bani Sadr. When Mohammad Ali Rajai, the next president, was assassinated in August 1981, Khamenehi was appointed head of the Islamic Republican Party. On 2 October 1981, he was elected president of the Islamic Republic. He also served as deputy minister of defense and commander of the Revolutionary Guards. Khomeini appointed him in 1980 to be the leader of the Friday congregational prayers in Tehran. He was also elected as a deputy of the Islamic Consultative Assembly (Majles) in the same year. He was elected for a second term as president, with an overwhelming majority, on 16 August 1985.

After the death of Khomeini on 4 June 1989, Khamenehi was swiftly chosen as his successor, despite his lack of seniority in the learned hierarchy of Iranian Shiʿism; this choice received popular ratification in August 1989, when the modifications to the constitution were approved. For example, because of Khamenehi's policies regarding the freedom of the press (he has approved the judiciary's shutdown of more than 100 reformist newspapers) he and the conservatives have come to be known as "hard-liners" in most Western political writings. Khamenehi continues to hold an important place in the leadership of the Islamic Republic and has followers outside Iran, as witnessed in the many Web sites dedicated to his teachings and speeches.

KHAN

Bibliography

Bakhash, Shaul. *The Reign of the Ayatollahs: Iran and the Islamic Revolution.* New York: Basic Books, 1984.

HAMID ALGAR
UPDATED BY ROXANNE VARZI

KHAN

See GLOSSARY

KHANJAR

See GLOSSARY

KHANOUM

See GLOSSARY

KHARG ISLAND

Island off the coast of Iran in the Persian Gulf.

Kharg Island, located about 30 miles from the Iranian mainland, historically has been associated with Iran, although the British occupied it briefly in 1838. The discovery of an offshore oil field in the waters around Kharg in the early 1960s stimulated the development of the island as a site for major petroleum and petrochemical installations. Connection by pipelines to the underwater oil fields, as well to the oil fields in Khuzistan, transformed Kharg into Iran's largest oil-loading terminal by the early 1970s. During the Iran–Iraq war (1980–1988), Kharg repeatedly was bombed, and its oil facilities suffered extensive damage, but they were reconstructed in the early 1990s.

Bibliography

Ramazani, R. K. *Revolutionary Iran: Challenge and Response in the Middle East.* Baltimore, MD: Johns Hopkins University Press, 1986.

NEGUIN YAVARI
UPDATED BY ERIC HOOGLUND

KHARRAZI, KAMAL
[1944–]

Iranian foreign minister.

Kamal Kharrazi was born into a clerical family in Tehran in 1944. He attended Alavi high school in Tehran, where he met many of his future political colleagues in the Islamic Republic. He holds B.A. and M.A. degrees in Persian language and literature from Tehran University. He studied in the United States and received his Ph.D. in education from the University of Houston, where he joined the first generation of Iranian Moslems, such as Ibrahim Yazdi and Mostafa Chamran (1932–1981), who had established the Islamic Student Association in the United States. Kharrazi also maintained an active profile in the Muslim Students Association in Canada and the Islamic Research Institute in London.

Returning to Iran after the Iranian Revolution (1979), he was appointed by his Houston colleague and the then foreign minister, Ibrahim Yazdi, as deputy foreign minister for political affairs. Given his close association with clerics, he was assigned to several other positions: vice president for planning at the Islamic Republic of Iran Broadcasting (1979), director of the Islamic Republic News Agency (1980–1989), member of the Supreme Defense Council of Iran, head of the War Information Headquarters (1980–1988), and ambassador and permanent representative of the Islamic Republic at the United Nations (1989–1997). In 1997 President Mohammad Khatami appointed him minister of foreign affairs.

Kharrazi's tenure has been marked by Khatami's efforts to de-ideologize Iranian foreign policy, improve relationships with Iran's neighbors, and develop constructive relationships with Western countries. Despite conservative objections, he divorced his government from Ayatollah Ruhollah Khomeini's 1989 *fatua* condoning Salman Rushdie's death for writing *The Satanic Verses,* made an official visit to Iraq in 2000, and made many conciliatory gestures toward the United States. There have been a number of contacts between delegations from Iran and the United States since the removal of the Taliban regime in Afghanistan in 2001.

In the absence of any real power associated with his position, Kharrazi has been a moderate pragmatist. He has tried to promote the interest of his country while minimizing the negative international reactions to policies of the Islamic Republic at home and abroad. His appointment as foreign minister was a compromise. Although he attracts criticisms

1300 *Encyclopedia of* THE MODERN MIDDLE EAST AND NORTH AFRICA from both reformists and conservatives on issues dear to each camp, his pragmatic moderation has saved his long career in the foreign ministry. In 2003, shortly before the U.S. invasion of Iraq, he was summoned to a closed session of the parliament by reformist deputies and asked to explain his policies toward Iraq and his passive policy on the division of Caspian Sea resources among the five shoreline states. He was also criticized for his hiring practices in the ministry, especially the employment of several family members.

See also CHAMRAN, MOSTAFA; KHATAMI, MOHAMMAD; KHOMEINI, RUHOLLAH; YAZDI, IBRAHIM.

Bibliography

Iran Foreign Policy and Government Guide. USA International Business Publications, 2000.

Tarock, Adam. *Iran's Foreign Policy Since 1990: Pragmatism Supersedes Islamic Ideology.* New York: Nova Science Publishers, 1999.

ALI AKBAR MAHDI

KHARTOUM

Capital of Sudan.

The Three Towns—Khartoum, Omdurman, and Khartoum North—together comprise the political, commercial, and administrative center for Sudan. Located where the Blue Nile and White Nile join to flow north toward Egypt, the capital city is the largest urban complex in the country. Its population of 850,000 in 1980 swelled to nearly 4 million by 2002, as the result of the influx of migrants from drought areas in the west and displaced persons from the war-torn south. Their immigration has transformed the character of the Three Towns from largely Arab, with Nubian enclaves, into a polyglot mix of peoples and cultures.

Khartoum, the political capital, means "elephant trunk" in Arabic. It was a small village called al-Jirayf, on the south shore of the Blue Nile, before the Turko-Egyptian conquest of 1821. The invading force established a small garrison near Mogren village, which became the government center in 1826. The government provided free building materials to encourage the residents to replace their straw huts with permanent brick houses; built a dockyard, military storehouse, barracks, and large mosque; and encouraged commerce by steamer on the Nile and overland to the west and east. A telegraph line linked Khartoum to Egypt by 1874 and, later, to the Red Sea coast and the west. The town remained relatively small, however, peaking at 30,000. The Mahdiyya forces captured Khartoum on 26 January 1885, which signaled the demise of Turko-Egyptian rule and was dramatized by the death of the British officer Charles Gordon on the steps of the Turkish governor-general's palace.

Khartoum was sacked by the Mahdists (1885–1898), but was restored as the capital after the British forces seized Omdurman and Khartoum on 1 September 1898. During the Anglo-Egyptian condominium (1898–1956), the British rebuilt Khartoum and constructed a series of stone government buildings along the Nile waterfront, flanking the imposing governor-general's house. They planned the city streets to resemble Union Jacks, built distinct residential quarters for Europeans and Sudanese, opened Gordon Memorial College in 1903, and established an industrial zone. A railway bridge across the Blue Nile was opened in 1909. The population grew rapidly from 30,000 in 1930 to 96,000 at the time of independence.

Since independence the principal government offices, embassies, European-style hotels, airport, offices, shops, and villas have been located in Khartoum; so has the University of Khartoum (known until independence on 1 January 1956 as Gordon Memorial College). By 1973, a third of a million people lived in Khartoum; in 2003 the total exceeded two million. Wealthy merchants live in palatial houses in al-Riyadh district, just across the highway from impoverished slums and squatter housing.

Omdurman, located on the southern side of the junction of the White and Blue Niles, served as the capital of the Sudan during the Mahdist period. As many as a quarter million people lived there during the 1890s. As the place where the Mahdi died, it had a special sanctity. The British initially emptied the city, but it grew to a sprawling residential area with some one million inhabitants. It has traditional-style housing: The wealthier areas have stone and brick villas with courtyards and gardens hidden from the street by high walls, and the poorer

Sudan's capital city, Khartoum, was founded in 1821 as an Egyptian army camp and quickly grew to become a trade center and slave market. Today Khartoum is one of the country's largest cities and is Sudan's chief administrative and transportation center. © NEEMA FREDERIC/CORBIS SYGMA. REPRODUCED BY PERMISSION.

areas consist of mud-brick huts in walled-off compounds along dirt roads. Different ethnic groups tend to live in distinct quarters, with a large public market serving the entire city. The government periodically razes districts filled with migrants from the west and internally displaced people from the south, in an attempt to force them out of the city. The parliament building, television and radio stations, and major academic institutions such as Omdurman Islamic University and al-Ahfad College for Women are located there. The headquarters of the leading political parties and religious movements, notably the Ansar and its Umma party and the Khatmiyya brotherhood and its Democratic Unionist party, are in Omdurman. The skyline is dominated by the silver-colored dome of the Mahdi's tomb and its adjacent great mosque, destroyed by British gunboats in 1898 but rebuilt in the 1940s.

Khartoum North (Halfaya, Khartoum Bahri), located on the north bank of the Blue Nile, was the site of two small villages before the Turko-Egyptian occupation. It contained the encampment of the Khatmiyya sufi order during that period. Destroyed by the Mahdists, it was completely rebuilt by the British and contained the terminus for the railway from Egypt, which reached the capital in 1899. Spurs to Port Sudan in the east and to Sennar, farther south, opened in 1909. The railway was extended west to al-Ubayd in 1911. Today, two bridges link Khartoum North to Khartoum and Omdurman. Khartoum North's location at the junction of those lines provided a base for the rapid growth of industry and residential areas. The main manufacturing industries are located there as well as extensive middle-class and squatter housing areas. By 2002, about a half million people lived in Khartoum North, as against 40,000 in 1956 and 151,000 in 1973.

Bibliography

Hall, Marjorie, and Ismail, Bakhita Amin. *Sisters under the Sun: The Story of Sudanese Women.* London: Longman, 1981.

Holt, P. M., and Daly, M. W. *The History of the Sudan.* Boulder, CO: Westview Press, 1979.

Lobban, Richard A., Jr.; Kramer, Robert S.; and Fluehr-Lobban, Carolyn. *Historical Dictionary of the Sudan,* 3d edition. Lanham, MD: Scarecrow Press, 2002.

Simone, T. Abdou Maliqalim. *In Whose Image? Political Islam and Urban Practices in Sudan.* Chicago: University of Chicago Press, 1994.

ANN M. LESCH

KHARTOUM ARAB SUMMIT

See ARAB LEAGUE SUMMITS

KHATAMI, MOHAMMAD

[1943–]

President of Iran, elected in 1997 and re-elected in 2001.

Mohammad Khatami was born in Ardakan, central Iran, in 1943. His father was a widely respected Shiʿite cleric and raised his children in a religious household. Khatami attended the University of Tehran and obtained a B.A. in philosophy before going to the seminary to study Shiʿite theology. In the late 1970s, he went to Hamburg as manager of the Islamic Center, which served the large number of Iranian students in West Germany. Following the Iranian Revolution, he was appointed supervisor of the newly nationalized Keyhan Publishing Company. In 1980, he was elected to the First Majles al-Shura (parliament) as a deputy from Ardakan. Khatami was associated with the progressive faction of clergy, which advocated a liberal interpretation of Islam and the implementation of economic and social polices that would promote the welfare of middle- and low-income groups. As minister of culture and Islamic guidance from 1989 to 1992, he angered conservatives by relaxing censorship on the press and cinema. After resigning under pressure, he became director of the National Library and participated in several academic seminars where he called for democratization of the political system.

Khatami entered the 1997 presidential election and won nearly 70 percent of the popular vote on the strength of his promises to initiate social reforms, create a civil society, and promote a dialogue of civilizations. His victory launched the reform movement, the most notable characteristic of which was the proliferation of newspapers that championed accountable government and launched investigations of political institutions and politicians suspected of abusing civil rights. The activities of the reformists prompted a backlash from conservatives, who felt threatened by the reforms. By 2000, the conservatives had proven adept at using the judicial system to stymie many reform policies and even to send some reform politicians to prison on charges of slander. Khatami, who disliked confrontations, publicly expressed frustration with his office's limited authority to counteract judicial decisions. Nevertheless, he agreed to run for a second term in 2001 and was re-elected with 70 percent of the vote. During his second term, although Khatami remained the titular head of the reform movement, many reformist politicians openly criticized him for failing to actively support them and for effectively allowing the opponents of reform to gain the political initiative.

See also IRANIAN REVOLUTION (1979); MAJLES AL-SHURA.

Bibliography

Hooglund, Eric. "Khatami's Iran." *Current History* 98, no. 625 (February 1999): 59–64.

ERIC HOOGLUND

KHATIBI, ABDELKABIR

[1938–]

Moroccan sociologist, literary critic, and writer.

Abdelkabir Khatibi, born in al-Jadida, Morocco, received a doctorate in sociology from the Sorbonne in 1965. He is both a professor of sociology at Muhammad V University in Rabat and a researcher at the Centre de Recherche Scientifique de Rabat.

Khatibi writes in French. One of his early works is a play titled *La mort des artistes* (The death of the artists), which was staged in Paris in 1963. Khatibi's work is distinguished by a double identity that results from his double culture, which he perceives positively, as revealed in his book *Amour bilingue* (1983), translated by Richard Howard and published in the United States as *Love in Two Languages* (1990). The diversity of the Maghrib is studied and analyzed with lucidity and realism in *Maghreb pluriel* (1983; Plurality of the Maghrib). Khatibi's first work of fiction was *La memoire tatotée* (1971; Tattooed memory), a highly autobiographical novel. Another of his novels, *Un été à Stockholm* (1990; A summer in Stockholm), explores human relations within the context of love. This theme is also the subject of a collection of poetry, *Dédicace à l'année qui vient* (1986; Dedication to the upcoming year).

Khatibi's well-known *La blessure du nom propre* (1974; The wound of the proper name) reveals his interest in the popular culture of Morocco. No matter how removed his philosophical thinking is from his culture, he almost unfailingly links it to his Arab Islamic roots and elevates it to a universal precept. This is obvious in *Le livre de sang* (1979; The book of blood) and *Ombres japonaises* (1988; Japanese shadows), where he studies the seductive power of the narrative based on the *Arabian Nights*. His study of the concept of the false prophet in his play *Le prophète voilé* (1979; The veiled prophet) uses examples from Arab Islamic history.

Some of Khatibi's writings reveal his interest in the political situation of the contemporary Arab world, particularly the Palestinian problem. Although he criticizes Zionism in *Vomito blanco* (1974; White vomit), his *Le même livre* (1985; The same book) stresses the similarities between Arabs and Jews in a correspondence with his Jewish friend Jacques Hassoun.

Khatibi's production is prolific as well as varied. His writings cover a wide range of topics, some purely literary, such as *Le roman maghrébin* (1958; The Maghribi novel), *Ecrivains Marocains, du protectorat à 1965. Anthologie* (1974; Moroccan writers, from the protectorate to 1965, an anthology), and *Figures de l'étranger* (1987; Faces of the foreigner). Khatibi is also interested in art and has written on calligraphy (with Mohammed Sijilmassi) in *L'art calligraphique arabe* (1976; Art of Arabic calligraphy) and painting (with M. el-Maleh Maraini) in *La peinture de Ahmed Cherkaoui* (1976; The painting of Ahmed Cherkaoui). His book *Le livre de l'aimance* (1995; The book of love) explores love and passion among women and men. Khatibi returns to his native Morocco in *Triptyque de Rabat* (1993; A Rabat triptych) after having expanded the limits of territoriality in *Un été à Stockholm* (A summer in Stockholm). He tackles political restrictions, women's emancipation, and a critical look at the self.

See also LITERATURE: ARABIC, NORTH AFRICAN.

Bibliography

Berger, Anne-Emmanuelle, ed. *Algeria in Others' Language.* New York: Cornell University Press, 2002.

Mortimer, Mildred, ed. *Maghrebian Mosaic: A Literature in Transition.* Boulder, CO, and London: Lynne Rienner Publishers, 2001.

AIDA A. BAMIA

KHATTABI, MUHAMMAD IBN ABD AL-KARIM AL-
[c. 1880–1963]

Moroccan leader of resistance to Spanish and French colonial conquest.

Muhammad ibn Abd al-Karim al-Khattabi was born in the Rif mountains, a Berber region of northern Morocco, sometime in the 1880s. His father was appointed *qadi* of the largest and most powerful tribe of the central Rif, the Banu Waryaghal (Aith Waryaghar in Berber) by sultans Hassan I and Mulay Abd al-Aziz, although neither had much influence over day-to-day affairs in the region. His father, like many other people in the area, also had an association with the Spanish military in the enclaves of Melilla and Alhucemas island, the latter immediately offshore from the village of Ajdir, where the Khattabi family lived. The Spanish authorities hoped to use their influence with him, and with other local notables, to ease their path in occupying the northern zone of Morocco.

Abd al-Karim's early life was a mixture of Moroccan and Spanish influences. He studied at the Qarawiyyin University in Fez, where he was influenced by teachers of the Salafiyya movement. In 1907 he went to Melilla where he became, in rapid succession, teacher, military interpreter, and *qadi*, and finally *qadi qudat* (chief judge) of the Moroccan community in the Spanish enclave. He also wrote and translated articles for *El Telegrama del Rif,* the local newspaper. In 1913, the year after the joint Franco–Spanish protectorate was declared over Morocco, he was decorated for his services to Spain.

During World War I, this relationship with the Spanish authorities broke down because of Abd al-Karim's impatience with Spanish cooperation with France and his corresponding sympathy for Germany, despite his desire to marry the benefits of European technical modernization with Islamic reform. In 1915 he was arrested and imprisoned in Melilla on suspicion that his German sympathies had taken the form of subversive activities. Although he was released quite quickly, the Spanish authorities never regained his trust or sympathy.

In 1919, as the Spanish army began a slow march westward from Melilla toward the central Rif, his father broke relations with the Spanish garrison in Alhucemas island and joined a slowly growing resistance movement centered in the Banu Waryaghal. At the same time, Abd al-Karim left Melilla and returned to Ajdir. This resistance movement was based upon an unstable unity between the various tribal subdivisions and depended on the continued functioning of customary legal and political systems. When his father died—or was murdered—in 1920, Abd al-Karim succeeded in taking the leadership of the resistance and secured a more stable unity by insisting on the imposition of the *shariʿa*. At the same time he trained a military nucleus using European methods and weapons.

This military nucleus enabled him to defeat the Spanish forces in the eastern part of the Spanish protectorate in July 1921. He went on to set up a government in the central Rif that united his two aims of modernization and Islamic reform. In February 1923 he received *bayʿas* (formal declarations of allegiance) from various central Rifi tribes that justified his leadership in terms of fulfilling requirements for the caliphate—justice, unity, order, and the preservation of *shariʿa*—and referred to him as imam. On other occasions he referred to himself as *amir al-muʾminin,* a title that, despite its caliphal connotations, reflected not so much a claim to universal leadership as a statement of the religious nature of his movement. The official title of the Rif state was al-Dawla al-Jumhuriyya al-Rifiyya (State of the Rifi Republic), although the Rifis themselves referred to it as *al-jabha al-rifiyya* (the Rifi front) reflecting its temporary nature. The confusion of titles reflected the fluidity of the political structures in the Rif. Nevertheless, they were strong enough for Rifi forces to again defeat the Spanish in northwestern Morocco in 1924 and the French in 1925, before the combined strength of the two European armies put an end to his state.

After his surrender in May 1926, Abd al-Karim was exiled on the French island of Réunion, where

Moroccan leader Muhammad ibn Abd al-Karim al-Khattabi (ca. 1880–1963) spent much of his life building resistance to French and Spanish colonialism in Morocco. He and his followers fought many successful battles until his forced surrender during Franco-Spanish retaliation in 1927. © BETTMANN/CORBIS. REPRODUCED BY PERMISSION.

he stayed until 1947. In that year he escaped from a ship taking him back to France while it was traveling through the Suez Canal. He spent the rest of his life in Egypt, where he became the titular leader of the North African Defense League, the umbrella organization for Maghribi nationalists. He refused to return to Morocco at independence in 1956 saying that, since there were still foreign (American) troops on Moroccan soil, the country was not truly independent. He died in Cairo in 1963.

Abd al-Karim has been described by both French colonialist and modern Moroccan nationalist writers as a typical example of Berber resistance to outside authority. But others have seen him as a great guerrilla leader, part of a tradition including China's Mao Tse-tung and North Vietnam's Ho Chi Minh. Abd al-Karim himself situated his ideological stance in religious and nationalist terms. Despite the clear religious feeling of his followers, he told Léon Gabrielli, a French intelligence officer, that he specifically rejected the label of a jihad, saying that such medieval concepts were not relevant to the modern world. In an interview in the Egyptian Islamic journal *al-Manar* after the war, however, he admitted that he had made use of religious sensibilities as a rallying cry, although he presented himself in the context of the Salafiyya movement and modern Moroccan and Arab nationalism, and blamed his defeat on the opposition of the *tariqas* (Sufi religious brotherhoods), particularly the Darqawiyya, which was one of the biggest in the Rif, and on the failure of many of his supporters to accept his long-term political objective of replacing tribal systems with central government control and the absolute rule of the *shariʿa*. It is true, however, that other *tariqas* did support him, and in fact, the Rif was too small and too poor to resist the combined force of two European armies.

See also ABD AL-AZIZ IBN AL-HASSAN; FEZ, MOROCCO; HASSAN I; JIHAD; QADI; RIF; SALAFIYYA MOVEMENT; *SHARIʿA*.

Bibliography

Hart, David M. *The Aith Waryaghar of the Moroccan Rif: An Ethnography and History.* Tucson: University of Arizona Press, for Wenner-Gren Foundation for Anthropological Research, 1976.

Pennell, C. R. *Morocco since 1830.* New York: New York University Press, 2000.

C. R. PENNELL

KHAWAJA

See GLOSSARY

KHAWR

See GLOSSARY

KHAYR AL-DIN

[c. 1822–1890]

Prime minister of Tunisia (1873–1877) and grand vizier of the Ottoman Empire (1878–1879).

Khayr al-Din, a Circassian from the Caucasus Mountains, was sold as a slave in Constantinople at a young age; he was then resold to an agent of the bey of Tunis. As a teenager he arrived as a Mamluk at the court of Ahmad Bey. After receiving an education at the military school established by Ahmad Bey, Khayr al-Din rose through the military ranks to cavalry commander (*fariq*). He spent the years 1853–1857 in Paris arguing Tunisia's position against Mahmud ibn Ayad, who had defrauded the government of millions of dinars. Under Ahmad Bey's successor, Muham-

mad Bey, Khayr al-Din served as minister of marine (*wazir al-bahr*) from 1857 to 1859. He later presided over the Majlis al-Akbar (Great Council), a parliamentary body established in 1860.

In conflict with Prime Minister Mustafa Khaznader (his father-in-law), whose ruinous policy of incurring foreign loans was just beginning, Khayr al-Din resigned in 1862 and spent the next seven years in Europe. In response to his European experience, and in hopes of reforming the political system in Tunisia, he wrote *The Surest Path to Knowledge Concerning the Condition of Countries* (1868). In it he discussed the economic superiority of the West and offered a practical guide for improving the political system in Tunisia. He saw the *ulama* as the key guarantors of the political system who would ensure that the *shura* ideal of Islam would be upheld, and urged them to fulfill this role.

Khayr al-Din returned to Tunisia in 1869 in order to preside over the International Debt Commission. In his new political capacity, he conspired to discredit and replace Khaznader as prime minister. Faced with mounting pressures from foreign consuls and the disastrous state of Tunisia's finances, the bey retired Khaznader in 1873 and made Khayr al-Din prime minister. As prime minister, Khayr al-Din had to contend with the machinations of foreign consuls (particularly those of France, Britain, and Italy), the press campaign of his father-in-law to discredit him, his Mamluk rivals, and the economic downturn of the mid-1870s. Furthermore, he had lost faith in the pact of security of 1857 and the constitution of 1861. He realized that these liberal reforms were merely camouflage behind which Khaznader had been able to hide his ambition to become the wealthiest and most powerful member of the bey's government, and that they had been implemented to enhance foreign influence in Tunisia. Having witnessed firsthand Europe's aggressive intentions toward Africa, as well as the machinations of the foreign consuls in Tunis, Khayr al-Din had come to perceive that Europe was the paramount threat to Tunisia's existence and that the reincorporation of Tunisia into the Ottoman Empire was perhaps the country's one hope to avoid being occupied.

Khayr al-Din's disillusionment with constitutionalism led him to conclude that reforms should be directed to a wise elite in cooperation with an enlightened *ulama*. These two groups could limit the arbitrariness of absolutist rule and implement principles of justice and freedom according to the *shari'a* (Islamic religious law). He then advocated a selective incorporation of those elements of Western civilization compatible with Islam. His final goal was the implementation of the Islamic concept of *maslaha* (the public good).

To help him introduce his reforms, Khayr al-Din appointed his Circassian and military school colleagues to positions of authority. He was also supported by Muhammad Bayram V, whom he appointed to direct the Hubus Administration, the government press, and *al-Ra'id al-Tunisi,* the official gazette of the government.

Khayr al-Din tackled administrative, financial, and tax reform, and ended the expensive *mahalla* military taxation expeditions against the tribes. To improve the country's economy, he expanded land under cultivation from 60,000 to 1 million hectares (132,000–2.2 million acres), reformed the customs system to protect Tunisia's handicraft and other industries, and launched public works projects such as paving the streets of Tunis. He founded Sadiqi College in 1875, and established a public library (al-Abdaliya). He briefly instituted a complaint box for citizens and sought to introduce a mixed judicial system to prevent foreign efforts to protect minorities in Tunisian courts. In his attempts to limit tyranny, he tried to persuade the bey to acquiesce to Ottoman claims of sovereignty and to restrictions on his arbitrary rule.

Khayr al-Din's efforts turned Muhammad al-Sadiq Bey against his reformist minister. Khayr al-Din's support of the Ottomans in the Russian–Turkish War of 1877 provided the bey with an excuse to dismiss him. Complicating his pro-Ottoman stance and loss of the bey's confidence were economic and financial difficulties, intrigues of foreign consuls and of the bey's favorite, Mustafa ibn Isma'il, and Khaznader's vilification campaign. All of these factors finally forced Khayr al-Din to resign on 2 July 1877. He went into self-imposed exile in Constantinople, where, because of his pro-Ottoman viewpoint, he was rewarded with a brief appointment as Ottoman grand vizier in 1878 and 1879. After his removal as grand vizier, Khayr al-Din retired to private life and spent his final years in Constantinople, where he died.

Khayr al-Din's legacy in Tunisia proved an inspiration for later reformers such as the Young Tunisians. Sadiqi College was the most enduring of his accomplishments. Young Tunisians and later Tunisian nationalists, including Habib Bourguiba, were educated there.

See also AHMAD BEY HUSAYN; BAYRAM V, MUHAMMAD; BOURGUIBA, HABIB; KHAZNADER, MUSTAFA; MUHAMMAD AL-SADIQ; SADIQI COLLEGE; *SHURA; ULAMA;* YOUNG TUNISIANS.

Bibliography

Anderson, Lisa. *The State and Social Transformation in Tunisia and Libya, 1830–1980.* Princeton, NJ: Princeton University Press, 1986.

Khayr al-Din al-Tunisi. *Surest Path: The Political Treatise of a Nineteenth-Century Muslim Statesman,* translated by Leon Carl Brown. Cambridge, MA: Harvard University Press, 1967.

LARRY A. BARRIE

KHAZ'AL KHAN
[c. 1880–1936]

Shaykh of Muhammara, independent tribal chieftain in Iran.

In 1897, Khaz'al became chief to the Muhaysin, a powerful Arab tribe whose territory, mostly in Persia (now Iran), extended into Iraq. Confirmed as march-warden by the weak Qajar shah, he expanded his sway over the Ka'b and other local tribes. As de facto ruler of Khuzistan, with a potential army of 20,000 tribesmen, he was courted as a strategic ally by the British; when oil was discovered at Masjed Soleyman in 1908, Khaz'al granted them the necessary rights of way for a pipeline to the Persian/Arabian Gulf and port facilities at Abadan. In the 1920s, however, after Reza Shah Pahlavi came to the throne and began centralization—which was also seen to be in Britain's interest—Khaz'al's British patrons were unwilling to support him and defy the shah. The Iranian army, having subjugated neighboring Luristan, advanced on Khuzistan; in 1925, Khaz'al was arrested at Muhammara (now Khorramshahr) and kept in Iran's capital, Tehran, until his death.

See also PAHLAVI, REZA.

JOHN R. PERRY

KHAZNADER, MUSTAFA
[1817–1878]

State treasurer (1837–1861) and prime minister (1861–1873) of Tunisia.

Mustafa Khaznader was born Georges Kalkias Stravelakis, on the island of Chios. In 1821, during the Greek rebellion against the Turks, he was seized, taken to Constantinople, and sold into slavery. In 1827 he was sent to Tunis, where he was sold again. He converted to Islam and took the name Mustafa.

Mustafa became a close friend of Ahmad ibn Mustafa, future bey of Tunis. When Ahmad became bey in 1837, he named Mustafa *khaznader* (state treasurer). (His long tenure in this office led to the use of Khaznader as his surname.) The centralization of governmental authority under Ahmad Bey and the combination of an increasingly complex tax structure and a rudimentary tax collection apparatus obliged the government to farm out the various taxes in *iltizam*.

Mahmud ibn Ayad, the top tax farmer, conspired with Khaznader to fleece the government of millions of dinars by transferring funds to France and acquiring French citizenship. In 1852, having transferred the equivalent of 50 million francs, he fled to France and acquired French citizenship; he was unable to secure citizenship for Khaznader. The latter's involvement in the affair apparently did not lessen the bey's ultimate faith in his finance minister.

Khaznader built up a powerful patronage network through his own marriage into the bey's family and marriage of his children into prominent political and business families. He encouraged Ahmad Bey in his reforms because these enabled him to profit from new tax farms and other financial ventures. Under Muhammad Bey (1855–1859) and Muhammad al-Sadiq Bey (1859–1882), Khaznader supported the reforms of the Fundamental Pact (1857) and the constitution of 1861 because these sought to restrict the power of the bey and increase the power of his ministers.

Between 1859 and 1869, Khaznader and his associates virtually ran and ruined the Tunisian state. The Grand Council, established as a kind of Parliament to implement the 1861 Constitution, was staffed with his cronies. Beginning in 1863, Khaznader floated a series of foreign loans that bankrupted the government by 1868. To pay for these loans, he authorized the doubling of the personal income tax, the *majba*. When this went into effect in 1864, there arose a widespread tribal revolt. It was severely repressed, the constitution was suspended, and Khaznader ran the state even more firmly. But in the long term, his financial policies destroyed the state's financial viability. Bad harvests, famines, and epidemics compounded Tunisia's financial plight and led to the International Finance Commission of 1869, set up by foreign creditors to ensure that Tunisia paid its debts.

Khaznader's son-in-law Khayr al-Din used his position on this commission to discredit Khaznader and to force the bey to dismiss him. In 1873, Muhammad al-Sadiq Bey reluctantly agreed to retire Khaznader and confiscate some of his wealth. In his place, the bey appointed Khayr al-Din prime minister. During the latter's tenure of office (1873–1877) Khaznader continually attacked him and sought his removal. Finally, in 1877, the bey discharged him. Khaznader's triumph was short-lived, however; he died the following year.

See also AHMAD BEY HUSAYN; FUNDAMENTAL PACT; KHAYR AL-DIN; MUHAMMAD AL-SADIQ.

Bibliography

Brown, L. Carl. *The Tunisia of Ahmad Bey, 1837–1855.* Princeton, NJ: Princeton University Press, 1974.

LARRY A. BARRIE

KHEMIR, SABIHA
[1959–]

Tunisian painter, illustrator, and writer.

Sabiha Khemir was born in Tunisia. She is a painter, illustrator, writer, and historian of Islamic art, based in London. She studied at the University of Tunis and received a Ph.D. from the School of Oriental and African Studies at the University of London. Most of her works are highly detailed pieces, executed in pen and ink, and often explore legendary figures and events from Islamic history. They appear on the covers of some important translations of Arabic novels, especially by Naguib Mahfouz and Alifa Rifaat. Khemir has described her illustrations as rooted in the history of Islamic book illustration, especially miniatures. She sees the simplicity, purity, and precision of black-and-white pointillism as reflecting the ethos of Islamic art. Like many Arab artists of her generation, Khemir recreates the past treasures of art from her part of the world as a way to transform the present. In her essay "Mobile Identity and the Focal Distance of Memory," she described this practice as an attempt to "animate our present reality with the timeless values of our civilisation" (p. 46). In this essay and others, Khemir writes about issues of identity, history, and memory in the Arab world and the Arab diaspora, drawing on her personal experience. She has also written and presented two documentaries on Islamic art for British television. She published her first novel, *Waiting in the Future for the Past to Come,* in 1993.

See also ART; TUNISIA.

Bibliography

Khemir, Sabiha. "Mobile Identity and the Focal Distance of Memory." In *Displacement and Difference: Contemporary Arab Visual Culture in the Diaspora,* edited by Fran Lloyd. London: Saffron Books, 2001.

Lloyd, Fran, ed. *Contemporary Arab Women's Art: Dialogues of the Present.* London: Women's Art Library, 1999.

JESSICA WINEGAR

KHIDER, MOHAMED
[1912–1967]

Algerian revolutionary.

The son of a poor family from Biskra, Mohamed Khider was born in Algiers, the capital of Algeria, and became a bus driver/fare collector. He joined the Etoile Nord Africaine (ENA; Star of North Africa) of Messali al-Hadj and the Parti du Peuple Algérien (PPA; Algerian People's Party). He favored armed rebellion against the French, although he tried to reconcile Messalists and centralists of the Mouvement pour le Triomphe des Libertés Démocratiques (MTLD; Movement for the Triumph of Democratic Liberties). As a cofounder, Khider was known as an historic chief of the Front de Libération Nationale (FLN; National Liberation Front). During the Algerian War of Independence (1954–1962), he served with the "external" FLN and in 1956 was involved with initial French government contacts. He was seized along with other historic chiefs (Ahmed Ben Bella, Hocine ait Ahmed, Mohamed Boudiaf, and Rabah Bitat) in the infamous skyjacking of an Air Maroc airplane in October 1956.

After the war, he became secretary-general of the FLN but later disagreed with Ben Bella concerning the relationship between the party and the army in independent Algeria. Thereupon, he resigned and went into exile but kept a substantial sum of the party funds (to be used by the Algerian opposition), which was invested in a Swiss account. Khider was assassinated in Madrid in 1967, but the Algerian government failed to recover the funds. Khider's reputation was later officially rehabilitated in 1984.

See also AIT AHMED, HOCINE; ALGERIAN WAR OF INDEPENDENCE; BEN BELLA, AHMED; BITAT, RABAH; BOUDIAF, MOHAMED; FRONT DE LIBÉRATION NATIONALE; HADJ, MESSALI AL-; MOUVEMENT POUR LE TRIOMPHE DES LIBERTÉS DÉMOCRATIQUES; PARTI DU PEUPLE ALGÉRIEN (PPA).

Bibliography

Horne, Alistair. *A Savage War of Peace: Algeria, 1954–1962,* revised edition. New York: Penguin, 1987.

PHILLIP C. NAYLOR

KHIDHIR, ZAHRA
[1895–1955]

Pioneer of women's rights and education in Iraq.

Zahra Khidhir was born in Baghdad to a prominent scholarly and religious family, and was the eldest daughter. Her father, Mullah Khidhir al-Kutubchi, was a scholar at one of the most prestigious Sunni educational centers in Baghdad, Abu Hanifa's Mosque. After his retirement in 1870, he established the first bookshop in Baghdad, al-Zawra, which pioneered the publication of Iraqi literary and political works and the distribution of Arab literary and political journals. The bookshop became a hub of Iraqi intellectual and nationalist discourse in the early twentieth century. The tradition was carried on by his youngest son, Abd al-Karim, who took over the bookshop in 1920 and changed its name to Maktabat al-Sharq. Abd al-Karim was assassinated in the nationalist uprising of 1941. All of Mullah Khidhir's five children played important roles in Iraq's emergence as a modern nation state.

In 1918, Zahra opened a private school for girls in Iraq and enrolled forty students in three classes—Qur'anic studies, mathematics, and home economics. As the first school for girls in Iraq, it was applauded by progressives and opposed by conservatives who sought to forestall change. After the First World War, she took an active part in Iraqi resistance to British occupation, and following Iraq's independence in 1921 was one of the first women appointed to head a public school for girls. She continued her struggle for women's rights and was one of the founders of the Young Women's Muslim Association (YWMA) of Iraq in the early 1950s. She remained active for the rest of her life.

See also COLONIALISM IN THE MIDDLE EAST; GENDER: GENDER AND EDUCATION; GENDER: GENDER AND LAW; GENDER: GENDER AND POLITICS; IRAQ.

Bibliography

Daoud, Sabiha al-Sheikh. *Awal al-Tariq.* Baghdad: al-Rabitah Press, 1958.

Rao'f, Aimad Abdul Salam. *Maktabat al-Sharq: Tarikhuha wa Makhtutatuha.* Baghdad: Zain al-Naqshabandi, 1999.

Interview by author with a relative of Zahra Khifhir, Dr. Ghazi A. Karim. 27 October 2002.

JACQUELINE ISMAEL

KHOMEINI, RUHOLLAH

[1902–1989]

Leader of the Iranian revolution of 1979.

Ruhollah Musavi Khomeini was born in Khomein, central Iran, in 1902. His early religious education was in Khomein as a student of Akhund Molla Abolqasem, Aqa Shaykh Ja'far, Mirza Mahmud Eftekhar al-Olama, Mirza Mehdi Da'i, Aqa Najafi, his brother-in-law, and Ayatollah Morteza Pasandideh, his older brother. Khomeini left for Arak, a religious center in central Iran, in 1920. In 1922, when Ayatollah Abd al-Karim Ha'eri left Arak for

Qom and founded the Feyziyeh religious seminary, Khomeini accompanied him to study there. In 1929, Khomeini went to Tehran to marry Khadijeh Saqafi, the daughter of a prominent ayatollah. Their first son, Mostafa, was born in 1930 and died under mysterious circumstances in 1977 in Iraq; three daughters, Sediqeh, Farideh, and Fahimeh, and another son, Ahmad, who died in 1995, followed.

Ayatollah Ha'eri died in 1937, and by that time Khomeini, who had completed his formal education in 1928, had established himself as one of the more active and prominent religious scholars of Qom. Ha'eri was succeeded by Ayatollah Hosayn Borujerdi. Khomeini also studied with Borujerdi, serving as his special assistant. Borujerdi's primary preoccupation, however, was the expansion and strengthening of the Feyziyeh and preserving its autonomy from governmental supervision. To do so, Borujerdi generally assumed an apolitical and quietist stance throughout his tenure as director. In deference to his mentor, Khomeini did not openly participate in the political movement over oil nationalization in the early 1950s. Following the death of Borujerdi in 1962, however, activist *ulama* at the Feyziyeh openly pursued an oppositional stance regarding Mohammad Reza Shah Pahlavi's policy of alliance with Western countries, secularization, and centralization of the state.

Khomeini's first direct involvement with the country's political affairs took place in October 1962, when the government drafted a law that would grant diplomatic immunity to U.S. military personnel stationed in Iran. Khomeini expressed his opposition in sermons that became increasing strident in their criticism of the shah's foreign policies, including his tacit support of Israel, which pious Muslims opposed because of the way it had been created out of Palestine. Khomeini's criticisms increased after the shah launched the White Revolution in January 1963. Khomeini was arrested, along with several other prominent clergymen, on 5 June 1963 after delivering a fiery sermon denouncing the shah for taking a pro-Zionist, pro-U.S., and anti-Islamic stance. His arrest sparked several days of demonstrations in Qom and several other cities, which were suppressed forcibly and with scores of deaths. Khomeini was incarcerated in Tehran and released under pressure from other prominent clerics in early 1964. That July, he again was in the vanguard of the religious opposition decrying final passage of the bill granting diplomatic immunity to all U.S. military representatives and their families. Khomeini was imprisoned and subsequently exiled to Turkey. In 1965, he was allowed to take up residence in al-Najaf, Iraq, a Shi'ite shrine city with Shi'ite Islam's most important religious seminary. In exile, Khomeini continued to draw supporters from among Iranian clerics and the bazaar middle class, and he continued to criticize the shah's policies, notably in 1971 when the shah lavishly celebrated the 2,500th anniversary of monarchy and in 1975 when the shah inaugurated Iran's single party, the Rastakhiz.

During the late 1960s and early 1970s, while in al-Najaf, Khomeini formulated his concept of *velayat-e faqih,* or the governance of the religious jurist. Essentially, the doctrine called for an Islamic government supervised by the clergy to ensure that it did not violate Islamic principles. Khomeini already had a network of supporters inside Iran, including Mehdi Bazargan, Mortaza Motahhari, and Mahmud Taleqani, and he spent these years fostering his ties with Iranian oppositional groups abroad, including the Islamic student associations. Leaders of the latter included Ibrahim Yazdi, Sadeq Qotbzadeh, Abolhasan Bani Sadr, and Mostafa Chamran, all of whom rose to prominence after the Iranian Revolution of 1979.

In January 1978, when the first antigovernment protests occurred in Iran as a direct response to official media efforts to slander Khomeini, the ayatollah had access to a well-established and influential infrastructure inside the country. As the demonstrations intensified during the spring and summer, Khomeini rejected all pleas for compromise and instead heightened his anti-shah declarations. In October 1978, under pressure from the Iranian government, the then vice president of Iraq, Saddam Hussein, expelled Khomeini. The ayatollah obtained political asylum in Paris, where he not only enjoyed attention from the Western media but also gained access to wider communication with Iran. In January 1979, the shah, failing to quell the strikes and demonstrations, left Iran after having installed National Front leader Shapur Bakhtiar as prime minister. Khomeini returned to Iran amid widespread celebrations on 1 February 1979 but refused to acknowledge legitimacy of Bakhtiar's government. On 11 February 1979, Bakhtiar's government,

Khomeini was expelled from Iran in 1964 and and given refuge first in Turkey and then in al-Najaf, Iraq, where he continued to criticize the shah and spread his political ideas through a network of students. Due to pressure from the Iranian government, Saddam Hussein, then the vice president of Iraq, expelled Khomeini from the country in October 1978. © BETTMANN/CORBIS. REPRODUCED BY PERMISSION.

the last royalist cabinet in Iran, fell, marking the success of the Iranian Revolution. Bazargan, appointed by Khomeini, assumed office as leader of the provisional government.

After the revolution, the new constitution incorporated the concept of *velayat-e faqih* and named Khomeini as the first *faqih* and leader of the revolution (*rahbar-e enqelab*). But Khomeini did not exercise a direct role in the operation of the government. Rather, his domestic policies in the initial post-revolutionary period were marked by subtle compromises undertaken to consolidate the revolution. Political opposition was tolerated, and a noncleric, Abolhasan Bani Sadr, emerged as his choice for Iran's first president. However, his break with Bani Sadr, the eight-year war with Iraq (1980–1988), the severing of diplomatic ties with the United States, international isolation, the armed uprising by the internal opposition (1981–1982), and factional strife within Islamic circles combined to radicalize his political views.

An Iranian student gives a speech during the occupation of the U.S. embassy in Tehran, backed by posters of Ayatollah Ruhollah Khomeini. Khomeini criticized the West's political influence on his country and staunchly opposed Mohammad Reza Shah Pahlavi's alliance with the United States. © AP/WIDE WORLD PHOTOS. REPRODUCED WITH PERMISSION.

Khomeini died on 5 June 1989. Although his former student and revolutionary ally Ayatollah Hosayn Ali Montazeri had been designated as his successor in 1983, the two men increasingly differed over policies after 1985. Montazeri's open criticisms in 1988 about the lack of human rights protections for opponents of the regime led Khomeini to demand his resignation in early 1989. Thus when Khomeini died several weeks later there was no designated successor. However, before his death, he had authorized the formation of a committee to revise the constitution, especially the articles pertaining to *velayat-e faqih*. The amendments made it possible to consider for the position of paramount *faqih* a person with appropriate political qualifications even if he lacked superior religious credentials. It seems that Khomeini had concluded near the end of his life that a proper political perspective was more critical for ensuring the long-term viability of the Islamic state than expertise in the nuances of Islamic law.

See also BAKHTIAR, SHAPUR; BANI SADR, ABOLHASAN; BAZARGAN, MEHDI; BORUJERDI, HOSAYN; CHAMRAN, MOSTAFA; IRANIAN REVOLUTION (1979); MONTAZERI, HOSAYN ALI; MOTAHHARI, MORTAZA; NAJAF, AL-; PAHLAVI, MOHAMMAD REZA; QOM; QOTBZADEH, SADEQ; SHIʿISM; VELAYAT-E FAQIH; WHITE REVOLUTION (1961–1963); YAZDI, IBRAHIM.

Bibliography

Abrahamian, Ervand. *Khomeinism: Essays on the Islamic Republic.* Berkeley: University of California Press, 1993.

Moin, Baqer. *Khomeini: Life of the Ayatollah.* New York: St. Martin's Press, 1999.

Moslem, Mehdi. "Ayatollah Khomeini's Role in the Rationalization of the Islamic Government." *Critique* 14 (spring 1999).

NEGUIN YAVARI
UPDATED BY ERIC HOOGLUND

KHORASAN

Province in northeastern Iran.

The northeasternmost province (*ostan*) of Iran, with its capital at Mashhad, Khorasan is dominated by a zone of mountain ranges, a continuation of the Alborz Mountains in northern Iran, running roughly northwest to southeast. It is the longest province in the country, covering 194,700 square miles. Khorasan is bounded on the north by the steppes and deserts of Turkmenistan and on the east by Afghanistan; to the west and south lie extensive landlocked deserts such as the Dasht-e Kavir and Dasht-e Lut. Khorasan receives adequate rainfall only in the more northerly mountain zone, where there is a relatively flourishing agricultural and pastoral economy and the population is quite dense. The southern region typically has an oasis pattern of life sustained by wells and irrigation systems called *qanats* (underground canals).

Khorasan's strategic position as a corridor between the steppe and the settled parts of the Middle East endowed it with a rich cultural and political history up until the modern period. Through Khorasan, armies of Alexander the Great of Macedonia (356–323 B.C.E.) passed to Central Asia and India, and Turkish people moved into the Middle East. In

Built in 1418, the Shrine of Imam Reza stands in Mashhad, the capital city of the Khorasan province. Reza was an early ninth century Shiʿite religious leader, and his shrine is considered by Shiʿa as the holiest one in Iran. © CORBIS. REPRODUCED BY PERMISSION.

the pre-Islamic times Khorasan was one of the four great provinces of Iran. In the early Islamic period Tus was one of the great cities of Central Asia. The seventh Shiʿa Imam, Reza, came to Tus in the early ninth century. He died in a nearby village, and his tomb then developed into a pilgrimage site. The village eventually developed into the city of Mashhad.

During the second half of the eighteenth century, parts of Khorasan passed into the hands of the Durrani Afghan chief Ahmad Shah for a short period of time. But in the late eighteenth century, Khorasan was fully restored to the newly established Qajar dynasty. As a result of continuous wars with the Uzbeks (Ozbegs) and Turkmens, however, life in the northern regions of Khorasan continued to be precarious. Commerce and agriculture declined, and many Iranians were captured as slaves by the central Asian emirates. Only Russian intervention and annexation of Khiva in 1873 and the crushing of the Turkmens in 1881, actions motivated by Russian political ambitions, finally ended the insecurity.

Meanwhile, relations with the amirs of Afghanistan continued to deteriorate. Yet another super-power intervention, this time British, put a halt to this hostility. Herat, also a part of Khorasan, was ceded to Afghanistan after a brief war between the Qajar ruler Naser al-Din Shah and the British in 1856 and 1857. The boundary dispute between Iran and Afghanistan was not settled until 1934 to 1935.

Variegated political and cultural influences on Khorasan have created a heterogeneous population in the region, including tribes such as Turkmens, Kurds, Baluchi, Arabs, and others. The population of Khorasan in 2002 was over 6 million, with over 1.8 million people living in Mashhad.

See also MASHHAD.

PARVANEH POURSHARIATI

KHRAIEF, BECHIR
[1917–1983]

Tunisian novelist and short story writer.

Bechir Khraief, born in Nefta, is considered the father of fiction writing in Tunisia. He first worked in trade, selling fabrics during the day while attending night school. His occupation gave him an excellent insight into the life of the Tunisian people and enhanced the realism of his writings. When Khraief went into teaching, he looked back on those years as the best of his life. His writings reveal his strong attachment to his Tunisian roots. Like other writers of his generation, Khraief published his writings first in the journal *Al-Fikr* (founded in 1955).

Khraief, noted for his realistic approach, simple style, and use of dialect in dialogue, gives a truthful and interesting depiction of Tunisian life while shying away from philosophical themes. His efforts to endow his short story "Al-murawwid wa al-thawr" (The trainer and the bull), in his collection *Mashmum al-full* (Smelling the Arabian jasmine [Tunis, 1971]), with a specific theme failed. Another story in the same collection, "Khalifa al-aqraʾ" (Khalifa the bald), reveals his skill as a fiction writer.

Khraief's writings provided a panorama of Tunisian life in its different settings. His novel *Al-dajla fi arajiniha* (Dates on the branch [Tunis, 1969]) reveals various aspects of desert life, although he often uses too many details, a weakness that characterizes some of his other works. *Iflas aw hubbak darbani* (Being penniless or your love hit me [Tunis, 1959]), on the other hand, paints a picture of the Zaytuna University circles as well as of the middle class when Tunisia was undergoing the social transition from a traditional to a modern society.

Motivated by the same nationalist feeling that influenced his fiction, Khraief wrote two historical novels, *Barq al-layl* (Night's lightning [Tunis, 1961]) and *Ballara* (Tunis, 1992), which was published posthumously.

See also LITERATURE: ARABIC, NORTH AFRICAN; ZAYTUNA UNIVERSITY.

AIDA A. BAMIA

KHRIMIAN, MKRTICH
[1820–1907]

Patriarch of Constantinople, 1869–1873; catholicos of all Armenians, 1892–1907.

Born in the city of Van, Mkrtich Khrimian joined the church in 1845, after the death of his wife and child. He was ordained a *vardapet* (celibate priest) in 1854. He began publishing the periodical *Ardsvi Vaspurakan* (The eagle of Vaspurakan) in 1855 and a year later returned to Van as the prior of the monastery of Varak. In 1858 he resumed publication of *Ardsvi Vaspurakan*. In 1862 he became prelate of Daron and prior of the monastery of Surp Karapet.

Khrimian was ordained a bishop in 1868 and elected Armenian patriarch of Istanbul in 1869. Because of his efforts to document the exploitation of the Armenian populace and to register official complaints with the Sublime Porte, he was forced to resign in 1873. Five years later, he led an Armenian delegation that hoped to appeal to the conferring powers at the Congress of Berlin. Unsuccessful, Khrimian returned to Istanbul and delivered the homily for which he is most remembered, the "Sermon of the Iron Ladle," in which he stated that each power at Berlin took a share of the contents of a great soup bowl with an iron ladle, whereas he had only a paper petition and thus could bring nothing back to the Armenian people. It marked a turning point in Armenian political consciousness.

In 1879 Khrimian was elected prelate of the Armenians in Van. Suspected of associating with Armenian resistance groups, he was recalled to Istanbul and in 1890 was exiled to Jerusalem. In 1892 he was elected catholicos (supreme patriarch) of all Armenians at Echmiadzin. Khrimian's refusal to obey the Russian imperial edict of 1903, which authorized seizing the properties of the Armenian church, galvanized the Armenian communities of Russia to protest the decision, resulting in the eventual rescinding of the edict in an effort to reduce the turmoil in the Transcaucasus.

See also SUBLIME PORTE.

Bibliography

Walker, Christopher J. *Armenia: The Survival of a Nation*, 2d edition. New York: St. Martin's, 1990.

ROUBEN P. ADALIAN

KHRUSHCHEV, NIKITA S.
[1894–1971]

Soviet politician; premier of the USSR, 1958–1964.

Before the Communist revolution, Nikita S. Khrushchev, son of a Russian villager, worked in the Ukrainian coal region of Donbas. He joined the Communist Party (CPSU) in 1918 and rose rapidly through its ranks. After Josef Stalin's death in 1953, Khrushchev became first secretary of the CPSU, retaining this position until 1964, when he was ousted by opponents led by Leonid Brezhnev.

In contrast to Stalin, Khrushchev adopted the policy of peaceful coexistence with the West. In the Middle East, however, he engaged in political competition with the United States. Arguing the advantages of "scientific socialism" and offering military and economic assistance, Khrushchev hoped to persuade the neutralist leaders of Egypt, Syria, Iraq, and Algeria to join the USSR in an anti-Western "zone of peace," as he called it. While several accepted Soviet assistance, no Arab leader took seriously Khrushchev's ideological arguments. Consequently, Moscow established relatively close relations with several Arab states and supported them in the 1956 war with Israel but was not able to sway them from their independent course.

See also ARAB–ISRAEL WAR (1956).

Bibliography

Smolansky, Oles M. *The Soviet Union and the Arab East under Khrushchev*. Lewisburg, PA: Bucknell University Press, 1974.

OLES M. SMOLANSKY

KHUBAR, AL-

Port of Saudi Arabia.

Located in the Eastern Province, on the Persian Gulf coast of Saudi Arabia, al-Khubar (also al-Khobar) was founded in 1923 as a fishing and pearling village by members of the Dawasir tribe fleeing from Bahrain. It thrived as a terminal for the first crude oil that was shipped from Saudi Arabia to Bahrain for refining, until a deep-water port was constructed at nearby al-Dammam. A causeway and four-lane highway link Bahrain and Saudi Arabia at al-Khubar. In June 1996 an explosive device attached to a vehicle was detonated outside an al-Khubar apartment complex in which U.S military personnel lived; nineteen U.S. servicemen were killed and 400 persons (including 109 Americans and 147 Saudis) were injured. No group or person claimed responsibility for the attack, but by 1998 it was widely assumed to be the work of operatives affiliated with Osama bin Ladin's al-Qaʿida group.

Bibliography

Chapman, Simon. "Saudi Arabia: History." In *The Middle East and North Africa 1999*, 45th edition. London: Europa Publications, 1998.

LES ORDEMAN
UPDATED BY ERIC HOOGLUND

KHURI, BISHARA AL-

[1890–1964]

Prime minister of Lebanon under the French mandate; first president of independent Lebanon (1943–1952).

Bishara al-Khuri (also Khoury, Khouri) was born into a Maronite family and studied law in Paris. After spending World War I in Egypt, he returned to Lebanon and in 1922 was appointed secretary of Mount Lebanon. He served as prime minister in 1927–1928 and 1929. During the 1930s, his rivalry with Emile Eddé dominated Maronite politics. Al-Khuri strove to develop good relations with moderate Sunni circles, gambling that since they had opposed the establishment of Greater Lebanon, they would abandon their demand for unity with Syria if the Christians asserted their independence from France. He created the Constitutional Bloc Party in 1934 and cooperated closely with a group of Sunni politicians, led by Riyad al-Sulh.

After being elected president of the republic in 1943, al-Khuri chose Sulh as prime minister, and they concluded the oral agreement known as the National Pact. It defined the terms of the Maronite–Sunni partnership that provided the framework of Lebanon's politics until the outbreak of the Lebanese Civil War in 1975. In 1947, al-Khuri rigged the parliamentary elections in an effort to obtain passage of a constitutional amendment that would allow him to run for reelection in 1949. After 1949, he faced a powerful coalition including the Druze leader Kamal Jumblatt and the Maronite politicians Pierre Jumayyil, Camille Chamoun, and Raymond Eddé. In September 1952 a general strike compelled al-Khuri to step down.

See also CHAMOUN, CAMILLE; CONSTITUTIONAL BLOC; EDDÉ, EMILE; EDDÉ, RAYMOND; JUMAYYIL, PIERRE; JUMBLATT, KAMAL; LEBANESE CIVIL WAR (1975–1990); NATIONAL PACT (LEBANON); SULH, RIYAD AL-; SUNNI ISLAM.

Bibliography

Hudson, Michael C. *The Precarious Republic: Political Modernization in Lebanon.* Boulder, CO: Westview Press, 1985.

Salibi, Kamal. *The Modern History of Lebanon.* New York: Praeger, 1965.

GUILAIN P. DENOEUX

KHUTBA

Sermon delivered from an elevated pulpit (minbar) *by a* khatib, *or Muslim preacher, at Friday prayers and at special celebrations.*

The Friday *khutba* precedes the noon prayers that bring local Muslim communities together at the mosque. The *khatib* usually follows a formula in which he admonishes those present to be pious, conducts a prayer on behalf of the faithful, and recites part of the Qurʾan.

The *khutba* has also traditionally included an expression of loyalty to the sovereign. This practice has at times carried political significance, as in 1953, when the French deposed the Moroccan sultan Muhammad V. Many *khatibs* refused to invoke the name of his French-appointed replacement and even suspended prayers, a protest that ultimately led to his return and the independence of Morocco in 1956.

Khatibs also address public issues, and many governments today circulate suggested themes on public health, political issues, and other topics for the weekly *khutba*. In recent years, the *khutbas* of famous religious leaders have been distributed directly to the faithful on cassette tape, thereby reaching a wide audience, often across national boundaries.

See also MOROCCO; MUHAMMAD V.

Bibliography

Antoun, Richard T. *Muslim Preacher in the Modern World: A Jordanian Case Study in Comparative Perspective.* Princeton, NJ: Princeton University Press, 1989.

Eickelman, Dale. *Knowledge and Power in Morocco: The Education of a Twentieth-Century Notable.* Princeton, NJ: Princeton University Press, 1985.

ELIZABETH THOMPSON

KHUZISTAN

A province in southwestern Iran with its capital at Ahvaz.

The Iranian province of Khuzistan is in a fertile southwestern region of alluvial plains made by two

Completed in 1962, the Diz River Dam has provided water for both irrigation and electricity in this southwestern Iranian province for more than 40 years. © ROGER WOOD/CORBIS. REPRODUCED BY PERMISSION.

rivers, the Karkheh and Karun. It is situated between the Zagros Mountains and the sea. On the north Khuzistan borders Lorestan (Luristan) province; on the south, the Persian Gulf. The Iran-Iraq border forms the western part of its boundaries, and on the east lies the Hindiya or Hindijan River.

Khuzistan's climate is hot and very humid in the summer due to a lack of altitude—averaging only 10 meters (33 feet) and in the south and 100 meters (328 feet) in the central parts of the region; the southerly inclination of the land (which makes it susceptible to maximum effects of the sun); the hot winds from the Syrian Desert and Saudi Arabia; and the lack of snow-covered mountains, forests, or open water to ease the effect of these winds. In spite of its heat and humidity, Khuzistan has always been amply provided with water by the Karkheh, Diz, and Karun rivers, and noted from earliest times for its prosperity. Thriving agriculture produces plentiful grain, rice, sugarcane, citrus fruits, melons, and dates, as well as cotton. The Persian Gulf provides abundant seafood.

Arabs form a substantial portion of the Khuzistani population. The local Arab Shiʿite dynasty of the Mushaʿsha (who established their rule in the region for a short period in the fifteenth century and acted as powerful governors of the region until the nineteenth century), and other Arab tribes such as the Banu Kaʿb and Banu Lam (who immigrated from Arabia and the lower course of the Tigris in the eighteenth and nineteenth centuries), generally referred to the region as Arabistan, especially the western parts of the province. In 1925, under Reza Shah Pahlavi, the ancient name of the region, Khuzistan, was established as the official, legal name.

The prosperity of Khuzistan declined after the eighteenth century primarily beause of Iranian–Arab hostility, damage to agriculture by migrations and nomadism, raiding of trade caravans (especially by the Banu Lam), and lack of central authority. Prosperity returned to Khuzistan in the twentieth century because of various factors: the discovery of oil at Masjed Soleyman in 1908; the construction and growth of the Abadan oil refinery by the 1950s; the construction of the Trans-Iranian railway in 1938; the 1962 construction of the Muhammad Reza Pahlavi Dam on the Diz River (which provided the

MAP BY XNR PRODUCTIONS, INC. THE GALE GROUP.

region not only with hydroelectricity but also with water for market gardening and other agricultural projects on a large scale); the development of the natural-gas industry (which exported 28 billion cubic feet of natural gas to the U.S.S.R. in 1973); and the development of Khorramshahr as one of the major ports of entry on the Persian Gulf. The Iran–Iraq War (1980–1988) was largely fought in Khuzistan, causing extensive damage. According to the 1996 census, the population of the province was 3,746,772.

PARVANEH POURSHARIATI

KHYBER, MIR AKBAR
[1925–1978]

Afghan Marxist leader.

Mir Akbar Khyber was an Afghan poet and a cofounder of the Marxist movement in Afghanistan. He was born in Logar Province in 1925 and graduated from military high school in 1947. He was im-

prisoned for his political activities in 1950 and spent the next five years in jail, where he met other leftist inmates including Babrak Karmal, later president of Afghanistan. Although he became a career police officer, he also was a leading member of the Parcham faction of the People's Democratic Party of Afghanistan and the editor of its newspaper, *Parcham.*

By the late 1970s he found himself at odds with other Marxist leaders, in part because he believed that the Marxist movement could not rule Afghanistan even if it took power. In addition, he had strong nationalist beliefs that were unpopular with his Marxist comrades. Khyber was killed by an unknown assassin who shot from a passing Jeep on 17 April 1978. Ironically, it was his assassination that sparked a major demonstration that led to the Saur Revolution and the Marxist takeover of Afghanistan.

Bibliography

Arnold, Anthony. *Afghanistan's Two-Party Communism: Parcham and Khalq.* Stanford, CA: Hoover Institution Press, 1983.

GRANT FARR

KHYBER PASS

Pakistani pass into Afghanistan.

The Khyber Pass begins about 10 miles outside the Pakistani city of Peshawar in the northwest frontier province and ends on the Afghan border at Torkham. Because it is the main connection between Afghanistan and the Indian subcontinent, the route through the Khyber Pass constitutes one of the major means of access to Central Asia. The pass, which narrows at one point to 200 yards, reaches an altitude of 3,500 feet. The pass is situated in the Afridi tribal areas, where the government has little authority; as a result, kidnapping and smuggling are common occurrences along the route. The British built a narrow-gauge railroad that passes from Peshawar to Torkham.

After 1980 the pass became a major route for refugees leaving, or later returning to, Afghanistan, and for guerrilla fighters entering Afghanistan. Pakistan has periodically closed the border crossing at the Afghan side of the pass in an attempt to control the movement of unwanted refugees.

Bibliography

Adamec, Ludwig. *Historical Dictionary of Afghanistan,* 2d edition. Lanham, MD: Scarecrow, 1997.

GRANT FARR

KIANURI, NUR AL-DIN
[1916–1999]

First secretary of Iran's Tudeh Party, 1978 to 1983.

Nur al-Din Kianuri was born in the village of Nur in Mazandaran. His grandfather was Ayatollah Fazlollah Nuri, the famous archconservative clerical leader executed during the Constitutional Revolution. Kianuri's father, however, was a prominent proconstitutionalist, later killed in a street shootout. Kianuri received his schooling in Tehran, studied architecture in Germany during the late 1930s, and joined the faculty of Tehran University in 1941. He became a member of the Tudeh Party, Iran's communist organization, in 1942 and was elected to its central committee in 1948. In the mid-1940s, he married Maryam Firuz, the head of the Tudeh women's organization. Maryam Firuz is the daughter of Prince Nasrat al-Dowleh (Farmanfarmayan), a well-known Qajar dynasty aristocrat killed by Reza Shah Pahlavi.

Kianuri fled Iran after the 1953 coup and spent over twenty-six years in exile—mostly in East Germany. He was elected first secretary of the Tudeh Party in late 1978, because he headed the wing of the party that supported the Iranian Revolution—a policy favored by the then Soviet Union. In 1983, however, when the Tudeh criticized the Islamic Republic of Iran for prolonging the war against Iraq, much of their leadership, including Kianuri, were arrested and tortured into "confessing" that they were spies and traitors plotting to overthrow Ayatollah Ruhollah Khomeini. Although most of his colleagues were executed, Kianuri and Maryam Firuz were not. Kianuri died in 1999 while still under house detention.

ERVAND ABRAHAMIAN

KIAROSTAMI, ABBAS
[1940–]

Internationally acclaimed Iranian film director and screenplay author.

Abbas Kiarostami was born in Tehran and educated in fine arts. He is best known for his Kokar film trilogy (*Where's the Friend's House, Life Goes On,* and *Under the Olive Trees*), which documents daily life in a mountain village in the Caspian. The trilogy is credited as the apex of the Iranian new wave, a form of cinema with which Kiarostami is closely identified. The Iranian new wave came about in the 1960 when directors such as Kamran Shirdel and Forugh Farokhzad, influenced by Italian neorealism, the French new wave, and the poetics of surrealism, began to blur the line of documentary and fiction. The struggle of children is the central theme of many of Kiarostami's films (and he was the founder of the film department at the Institute for Intellectual Development of Children and Young Adults, which he ran during the first years after the Iranian Revolution of 1979), but it is his films *Close-Up* (1990), about an adult who impersonates fellow director Mohsen Makhmalbaf, and *Taste of Cherry* (1998), about a middle-class Tehrani man on the verge of suicide (for which he won the Palm d'Or at Cannes), to which most film critics refer when labeling him an auteur. His most recent films, *ABC Africa* and *Ten,* have moved away from his signature style of deep landscape photography, long takes, little plot, and lush photography, toward the digital medium and women characters (until the movie *Ten,* the only women in Kiarostami's films were village mothers and off-camera workers, never leading roles).

See also FILM; MAKHMALBAF, MOHSEN.

Bibliography

Dabashi, Hamid. *Close-up Iranian Cinema Past, Present and Future.* London and New York: Verso, 2001.

The New Iranian Cinema, Politics, Representation, and Identity, edited by Richard Tapper. London and New York: I.B. Tauris Publishers, 2002.

ROXANNE VARZI

KIBBUTZ

A collective community in Israel.

The kibbutz (also *kevutza*; pl. kibbutzim, *kevutzot*) has long been the symbol and embodiment of socialist Zionism, which defined it as the most effective way to settle the land and build a new society. Never involving more than a small minority of the Israeli population, kibbutz members were promoted as the elite of Israeli society and the kibbutz was presented as the model of the new, egalitarian society. It became one of most effective fund-raising symbols among diaspora communities and has always been a priority sightseeing attraction for visitors from abroad. A prominent American Jewish social scientist once quipped that there were probably many more books and articles written about the kibbutz than there were actual kibbutzim. This is in large measure true and indicates the exalted status of the kibbutz and its members in a society whose political elite viewed it as beneficial to the country's development.

The first kibbutz, Deganya, was founded by a group of pioneers from Russia in December 1909, in the Jordan River Valley just off the southern shore of the Sea of Galilee. By the end of 1948 there were 177 kibbutzim whose population of 54,200 comprised 6 percent of the Israeli population. By 2000, only about 2 percent of the Israeli population, or 118,000 individuals, lived on its 270 kibbutzim.

The various streams of socialist Zionism devised different types of kibbutzim but at least originally all adhered to the basic tenets of collectivism, namely that all property was communal and the kibbutz provided for the needs of all of its members. Everyone worked in and for the kibbutz and all jobs were, ostensibly, of equal status. Members shared in the goods and services according to their needs as defined by democratically decided criteria. The kibbutz functioned as a populist democracy, with all members having equal voice in the operation of the community. Until the 1970s, kibbutzim were overwhelmingly involved in agricultural production.

The more ideologically socialist kibbutzim practiced strong age segregation, with adults and children—even young infants—living separately, not only during the daytime hours but at night as well. An original motivating factor for this type of living arrangement was to foster the notion that the kibbutz was more important than the family. Over time, commitment to this ideology dwindled and traditional family patterns, including that of children living with their parents, reasserted themselves in the overwhelming majority of kibbutzim.

Agriculture is the second largest branch of employment on kibbutzim. Advanced farming methods and hard work help kibbutz members coax remarkable crop yields from what is often dismissed as nonarable land. © PAUL A. SOUDERS/CORBIS. REPRODUCED BY PERMISSION.

Each kibbutz is essentially autonomous, both socially and economically. They do, however, belong to movements with political affiliations, which provide a wide range of services to them. In principle, the kibbutz is committed to accepting the decisions of its political movement, but there have been a number of exceptions.

The kibbutz movements themselves have undergone a variety of transformations. The vast majority are secular socialist movements. The Hashomer Hatzair kibbutzim federated into the Kibbutz Artzi movement in 1927. Two other kibbutz federations, representing somewhat different ideological commitments, were ha-Kibbutz ha-Meʾuhad and Ihud ha-Kibbutzim. In 1980, these latter two merged into the United Kibbutz Movement (Takam). In October 2000, a decision was taken to merge the United Kibbutz Movement and Kibbutz Artzi into the Kibbutz Movement, a movement which, in mid-2003, represented 244 of the existing 267 kibbutzim. Another, much smaller, secular federation contains the five kibbutzim that belong to the Zionist Workers (ha-Oved ha-Zioni) movement.

Eighteen religious Zionist kibbutzim also exist. Of these, sixteen are affiliated with the Religious

Kibbutz members weave a fishing net. Members rotate job assignments, and all jobs are open to everyone, regardless of gender, though women typically choose to work in education and health services rather than agriculture and industry. © PHOTOGRAPH BY ZOLTAN KLUGER. GOVERNMENT PRESS OFFICE (GPO) OF ISRAEL. REPRODUCED BY PERMISSION.

Kibbutz (ha-Kibbutz ha-Dati) movement, and two national-haredi (ultra-orthodox) kibbutzim belong to the Poalei Agudat Israel movement.

Since the 1980s, many of the basic tenets of the kibbutzim have undergone radical transformation, such as the commitment to agricultural production and the ban on employing non-kibbutz members. Kibbutzim are now heavily engaged in manufacturing, and some have opened large shopping centers.

The kibbutz population is aging. This is due both to declining birth rates and to the greater rate of younger people leaving the kibbutz. Between 1988 and 1998, kibbutzim witnessed a 30 percent decrease in the number of children below the age of four and a 10 percent increase in the number of members sixty-five and older.

The educational level of the kibbutz population continues to be higher than that of the larger Jewish population in Israel. In 1998, 47 percent of kibbutz residents above the age of fifteen had more than thirteen years of formal education, as compared to 39 percent of the Jewish population of Israeli society as a whole. Likewise, 20 percent of the kibbutz population have post–high school certificates, as compared to 12 percent of those in the Jewish population of Israeli society as a whole.

By 1990, industry replaced agriculture as the largest branch of employment on kibbutzim; agri-culture is now the second largest branch and education the third.

A variety of factors lie at the root of the transformation and decline of the kibbutz. These include a growing desire on the part of parents to be the primary socializers of their children, increased educational aspirations for youth, and the increased industrialization of the larger Israeli society. Most significantly, as a result of the end of Labor hegemony within Israel with the election of Menachem Begin and the Likud alliance in 1977, the kibbutzim no longer retain the elite status they once enjoyed in the political economy of the country. This has forced them to become much more self-sufficient. Some of those that were not successful were forced to disband or reorganize in a noncommunal form.

Bibliography

Ben-Rafael, Eliezer. *Crisis and Transformation: The Kibbutz at Century's End.* Albany: State University of New York Press, 1997.

Spiro, Melford E. *Kibbutz: Venture in Utopia,* augmented edition. Cambridge, MA: Harvard University Press, 1975.

CHAIM I. WAXMAN

KIBBUTZ MOVEMENT

Association representing agricultural collectives.

The kibbutz movement (Ha-Tnu'ah Ha-Kibbutzit Ha-Meuhedet; acronym, TAKAM) is an association comprising three of the four federations of agricultural collectives in Israel that operated in Palestine before independence, including Hever Ha-Kvutzot, Ha-Kibbutz Ha-Meuhad, and Ha-Kibbutz Ha-Artzi. The consolidation of the separate kibbutz federations, to an extent, reflected both bureaucratic realignments since the 1948 independence of Israel and the changing balance of political party power in the election arena.

The kibbutz is a socialist community without private ownership and was first improvised in 1909 at Degania, in Ottoman Palestine, by young Jewish immigrants devoted to the establishment of a highly egalitarian society. Theirs was a small agricultural community, concentrating on a single crop. After World War I, immigrants from Europe and Russia brought ambitious schemes for an organization based on the Bolshevik Revolution, postulating that Palestine might only be developed by an all-embracing commune of Jewish workers. In 1921, they founded the first large kibbutz in the Jezreel valley at Ein Harod, with a diversified crop base and, eventually, with industries.

In 1924, a third form of collective was founded at Beit Alpha, by Ha-Shomer Ha-Tzaʿir (Young Guard), rooted in egalitarian principles and the possibilities for self-fulfillment in a small community. An association of religious (Orthodox Jewish) kibbutzim, Ha-Kibbutz Ha-Dati, has not affiliated with the all-embracing kibbutz movement federation.

See also JEZREEL VALLEY; KIBBUTZ.

Bibliography

Drezon-Tepler, Marcia. *Interest Groups and Political Change in Israel.* Albany: State University of New York Press, 1990.

DONNA ROBINSON DIVINE

KIKHYA FAMILY

Political family of Cyrenaica (Libya).

Umar Mansur al-Kikhya was educated at the Ottoman Empire's capital, Constantinople. His first official post under the Turkish administration of Cyrenaica was as *qaʾimmaqam* (district officer) of Gialo oasis. In 1905, the sultan gave him the title of pasha, and in 1908 he was one of three Cyrenaican representatives in the Ottoman parliament. After the 1911 Italian invasion of Libya, he went into exile in Egypt and practiced law in Alexandria to raise funds for the resistance in Libya. In 1920, he returned to Cyrenaica and became native-affairs adviser to Governor Giacomo di Martino. At a time when Italy was trying to put a Cyrenaican constitution and an elected parliament into effect, Umar Mansur acted as liaison between the Italian authorities and the head of the Sanusi order, Sayyid (Amir) Idris. He was particularly active in the negotiations leading to the accord of al-Rajma in October 1920. When, however, these arrangements broke down in 1923 and Amir Idris al-Sanusi went into exile, Umar Mansur was tried on charges of misleading the Italian government and spent many years in prison and in exile.

After the Allies liberated most of North Africa during World War II, the British brought Umar Mansur back to Benghazi, where he began to campaign for the recognition of Idris as ruler of a self-governing Cyrenaican emirate, assisted by and formally allied to Great Britain. His was an important voice in keeping international public opinion aware of the Cyrenaican case at a time when it could easily have been ignored. On the declaration of Cyrenaican autonomy in July 1949, Umar Mansur was appointed head of the amir's *diwan* (royal court). In November 1949, he became prime minister of the first Cyrenaican government after his son, Fathi, had resigned as the designated prime minister. He also held the interior, foreign affairs, defense, and education portfolios. Although he initiated a vigorous program, he came into increasing conflict with the younger opposition leaders grouped around the Omar Mukhtar Club, largely on the emotive issue of a purely Cyrenaican independence (which Umar Mansur and others of his generation favored) or the independence of a united Libya. Opposition to his administration also grew within the sole legal political organization, the Cyrenaican National Congress, and in March 1950 he was forced to resign. He was appointed president of the upper house of the all-Libyan parliament, the Senate, in March 1952, but was dismissed in October 1954 for his public criticism of the new base-leasing agreement with the United States.

Omar Mansur's son Fathi first entered public service as justice secretary in the new British military administration in Cyrenaica in 1943. In July 1949, Fathi had been named prime minister of the first Cyrenaican government, which took office in September, during his absence abroad. Fathi never took office, however, resigning on the grounds that his powers would have been too restricted. He returned to his law practice in Egypt.

In 1949, Hajj Rashid al-Kikhya was president of the Cyrenaican Legislative Assembly and was one of seven Cyrenaican representatives on the preparatory committee of twenty-one Libyan members, set up in July 1950, to decide the composition of the Libyan National Assembly and to draft the constitution.

See also CYRENAICA; IDRIS AL-SAYYID MUHAM-
MAD AL-SANUSI; OMAR MUKHTAR CLUB.

Bibliography

Khadduri, Majid. *Modern Libya: A Study in Political Development.* Baltimore, MD: Johns Hopkins Press, 1963.

Pelt, Adrian. *Libyan Independence and the United Nations: A Case of Planned Decolonization.* New Haven, CT: Yale University Press, 1970.

JOHN L. WRIGHT

KIKHYA, RUSHDI AL-
[1900–1988]

Syrian politician and founder of the People's Party.

Rushdi al-Kikhya was born in Aleppo, where he was elected deputy in 1936, 1943, 1947, 1949, and 1954. In 1948, together with other Aleppo leaders such as Nazim al-Qudsi and Mustafa Barmada, al-Kikhya formed the People's Party. This party represented the interests of the business community in Aleppo and northern Syria. It won the support of the prominent Atasi family of Homs against the head of the National Bloc headed by Shukri al-Quwatli and other notables from Damascus. In August 1949, al-Kikhya was appointed minister of interior in the cabinet headed by Hashim al-Atasi. In December 1949, he was elected speaker of the Syrian parliament. In September 1954, following the overthrow of the Shishakli dictatorship, the People's Party participated in the first free elections in post-independence Syria. Al-Kikhya firmly believed in the union of Iraq and Syria under Hashimite rule.

See also ATASI, HASHIM AL-; HASHIMITE HOUSE (HOUSE OF HASHIM); NATIONAL BLOC; QUWATLI, SHUKRI AL-.

Bibliography

Seale, Patrick. *The Struggle for Syria: A Study of Post-War Arab Politics, 1945–1958.* New Haven, CT: Yale University Press, 1987.

GEORGE E. IRANI

KIMCHE, DAVID
[1928–]

Israeli intelligence officer, diplomat, and writer.

"Dave" Kimche was born in London in 1928, and emigrated to Israel in 1948 and fought in the Arab–Israel War of 1948. He attended the Hebrew University in Jerusalem (where he earned a Ph.D.) and the Sorbonne in Paris. He was employed as a journalist by the *Jerusalem Post* before joining Israel's foreign intelligence service, the Mossad, in 1953, and worked under journalistic "cover" in Paris, specializing in clandestine links with countries such as Morocco and Iran, and from 1976, with Lebanon's Christians. He rose in the ranks of the Mossad to be deputy head (for external relations) under Yitzhak Hofi.

In 1980 Kimche left the Mossad because of disagreements with Hofi over Lebanon policy. He was appointed director-general of the Foreign Ministry under Prime Minister Menachem Begin, and was the chief Israeli delegate at Khalda, outside Beirut, in the December 1982 talks with Lebanon and the United States discussing Israel's withdrawal from Lebanon following the 1982 invasion. In 1985 he played a key early role in the Iran-Contra Affair, in which Israel worked secretly with the United States to supply antitank missiles to Iran as part of an effort to free U.S. hostages held by Iranian-inspired Islamic militants in Lebanon.

Following retirement from government service in 1987 Kimche was a guest lecturer at Tel Aviv and Bar-Ilan universities and president of the Israel Council on Foreign Relations. Kimche authored several books, among them *The Secret Roads, Both Sides of the Hill* (with his brother Jon), *The Afro-Asian Movement,* and *The Last Option.*

See also ARAB–ISRAEL WAR (1982); IRAN-CONTRA AFFAIR.

Bibliography

Black, Ian, and Morris, Benny. *Israel's Secret Wars: A History of Israel's Intelligence Services.* New York: Grove Press, 1991.

Kimche, David. *The Last Option: After Nasser, Arafat, and Saddam Hussein—The Quest for Peace in the Middle East.* New York: Charles Scribner's Sons; Maxwell Macmillan International, 1991.

ANN KAHN
UPDATED BY IAN BLACK

KING–CRANE COMMISSION (1919)

A U.S. commission of inquiry sent to Syria and Palestine in 1919 to investigate the wishes of the populace regarding the political future of the territories.

U.S. president Woodrow Wilson opposed British and French plans to annex territories conquered from the Ottomans during World War I. The proposed League of Nations provided a formula, the mandate system, that would allow these territories to be taken over temporarily, until they were guided to self-determination, by the power to whom the mandate was awarded. The covenant of the league stipulated that "the wishes of these communities must be a principal consideration in the selection of a mandatory power." At the Council of Four, the United States proposed an Allied commission consisting of representatives from France, Great Britain, Italy, and the United States to ascertain the wishes of the inhabitants of Syria, Palestine, and Iraq. The British and French, at odds with each other and interested in dividing up the spoils of war, declined to join. President Wilson then sent two U.S. representatives, Henry C. King and Charles R. Crane, to interview Syrians and Lebanese regarding Syria and Palestinians and Jews regarding Palestine. The two envoys spent June and July 1919 in the region but did not go to Iraq.

The King–Crane Commission found that the inhabitants of Syria and Palestine opposed being placed under a mandate, which they perceived as a disguised form of colonial rule. They wanted independence for a united Greater Syria, including Lebanon and Palestine, with Faisal I ibn Hussein as king; but if they had to accept tutelage, their first choice of guardian would be the United States, which had no history of imperialism, and their second would be Great Britain. The Syrians were opposed to any French rule.

The King–Crane Commission also looked into Zionist claims and demands, which it had initially supported. It concluded that Zionist leaders anticipated "complete dispossession of the present non-Jewish inhabitants of Palestine, by various forms of purchase." General opposition to Zionism led the King–Crane Commission to recommend limiting Jewish immigration, reducing the Zionist program, and giving up on the project of a Jewish commonwealth in Palestine.

The British and French ignored the report and occupied and divided up the territories between themselves. As the British historian Elizabeth Monroe points out: The "report came to nothing because of Wilson's failure to grasp that consultation is a virtue only if the consulting authority has the will and the ability to act on what it finds."

See also CRANE, CHARLES R.; FAISAL I IBN HUSSEIN; WILSON, WOODROW.

Bibliography

Hurewitz, J. C., ed. *The Middle East and North Africa in World Politics: A Documentary Record,* 2d edition, Vol. 2: *British–French Supremacy, 1914–1945.* New Haven, CT: Yale University Press, 1979.

Monroe, Elizabeth. *Britain's Moment in the Middle East, 1915–1956.* Baltimore, MD: Johns Hopkins University Press, 1963.

Palestine Government. *A Survey of Palestine, Prepared in December 1945 and January 1946 for the Information of the Anglo–American Committee of Inquiry.* 2 vols. Jerusalem, 1946–1947. Reprint, Washington, DC: Institute for Palestine Studies, 1991.

Smith, Charles D. *Palestine and the Arab–Israeli Conflict,* 4th edition. Boston: Bedford/St. Martin's, 2001.

PHILIP MATTAR

KING DAVID HOTEL

Famous hotel and landmark in Jerusalem.

The "King David," the most prestigious hotel in Israel, was established by Ezra Mosseri, an Egyptian Jewish banker, in the late 1920s. It was opened to the public in January 1931, and over the years became the site of many important historical events. It is located in the center of Jerusalem overlooking the ramparts of the 3,000-year-old city and an impressive landscape of the Judean Desert, the Dead Sea, and the mountains of Moab in Jordan. The simple symmetric rectangular edifice, clad in reddish stone, was designed by Emile Vogt, with interior decoration by G. H. Hufschmidt, both Swiss architects. While the exterior, with its roof crenellations, echoes the old city walls, the interior is an eclectic mix of motifs from Ancient Near Eastern and Islamic art, meant to evoke the atmosphere of a biblical palace.

During its first two decades it hosted myriad international dignitaries such as Winston Churchill, Haile Selassie (then exiled emperor of Ethiopia), King George II of Greece, Amir Abdullah of Transjordan, King Faisal of Iraq, and many other kings, princes, artists, generals, and diplomats. In 1938, with a world war on the horizon, the British sequestered more then half of the space to house the Military Area Command and the Secretariat of the Mandatory administration. On 22 July 1946 the Irgun Zva'i Le'umi (IZL), a Zionist extremist underground organization, blew up the entire southern part of the hotel's six stories, which housed the Secretariat, killing ninety-one people—British, Arabs, and Jews. This bloody operation put an end to the loose coalition of the three Zionist underground movements and triggered severe repressive measures by the British authorities. The entire hotel was then put to the use by the British and remained so until their departure from Palestine on 14 May 1948.

During the Arab–Israel War of 1948 the King David Hotel briefly housed various officials of the Red Cross and the United Nations, including Count Folke Bernadotte, the United Nations mediator, and eventually the Israeli army, which used it as a front-line stronghold. After that war the hotel, which remained on the Israeli side of the divided city, was rebuilt and once again became a luxury residence that hosted many state guests of Israel, UN and U.S. peace mediators (such as U.S. secretaries of state Henry Kissinger, George Shultz, and James Baker), and prominent writers and journalists. In 1977 it played host to President Anwar al-Sadat and many of the diplomatic meetings that led to peace between Israel and Egypt.

See also IRGUN ZVA'I LE'UMI; TERRORISM.

Bibliography

Clarke, Thurston. *By Blood and Fire: The Attack on the King David Hotel.* New York: Putnam, 1981.

Comay, Joan. "Fifty Years of the King David Hotel." *The Jerusalem Post Supplement,* 14 October 1981.

"Notes on the Interior Decorations of the King David Hotel." *The Jerusalem Post,* 9 August 1975.

MORDECHAI BAR-ON

KING SA'UD UNIVERSITY

The oldest and largest university in Saudi Arabia.

Established in 1957 as the University of Riyadh and renamed in 1982, King Sa'ud University has about 31,000 students, one-fourth of the country's total.

In addition, it has some 2,700 instructors working in thirteen colleges, most on the large and modern Riyadh campus and others on smaller campuses in al-Qasim and Abha. The language of instruction for most subjects is Arabic, except for engineering and medicine, which are taught in English. During the 1961–1962 academic year, women were permitted to enroll as external students (taking correspondence courses from their homes) in the colleges of arts and administrative sciences for the first time. On-campus instruction became available to them beginning with the 1975–1976 academic year. As in other areas of Saudi society, women in higher education were given separate facilities and unequal access to areas of study. In the 1990s the university offered majors in sixty-one subjects and doctoral programs in Arabic, geography, and history.

Bibliography

Al Salloom, Hamad I. *Education in Saudi Arabia,* 2d edition. Beltsville, MD: Amana Publications, 1995.

Metz, Helen Chapin, ed. *Saudi Arabia: A Country Study,* 5th edition. Washington, DC: Library of Congress, 1993.

ANTHONY B. TOTH

KIRKBRIDE, ALEC SEATH
[1897–1978]

British army officer, colonial administrator, and diplomat.

Alec Seath Kirkbride was born in Leeds and moved with his parents to Egypt in 1906. In 1916 he enlisted in the Royal Engineers and was commissioned in the same year. In early 1918 he was posted to the Arab army, which was commanded by Amir Faisal bin Hussein of the Meccan Hashimite family. This put him in touch with a number of experts who would help shape British policy in the Middle East, including Wyndham Deedes, T. E. Lawrence, and David G. Hogarth.

After World War I Kirkbride was sent to Transjordan with some other British political officers (including his brother, Alan Logan Kirkbride) to assist the local chiefs in administering their territories, which the British in Palestine were reluctant to control directly. He was posted to al-Karak (the biblical Wall of Moab) and, with a sense of history, he called his administration the National Government of Moab. He was the first British official to meet the amir, Abdullah I ibn Hussein (Faisal's brother) upon the latter's arrival in Transjordan in March 1921.

Between 1921 and 1939 Kirkbride served in various posts in the administration of Palestine and Transjordan. Until 1927 he was a member of the high commissioner's secretariat in Jerusalem. From 1927 to 1937 he was assistant British resident in Amman. Between 1937 and 1939 he served as district commissioner of Galilee and Acre. In 1939 he was nominated British resident in Transjordan, and when the country won its independence in 1946 he was upgraded to become the first British minister in Amman. Kirkbride was a lifelong friend of Amir (later king) Abdullah and became one of his closest advisers and confidants. Abdullah's assassination in 1951 had a traumatic impact on Kirkbride, and he asked to be transferred to another post. In late 1951 he was appointed the first British minister to Libya, a position he held until his retirement in 1954.

See also ABDULLAH I IBN HUSSEIN; DEEDES, WYNDHAM; JORDAN; KARAK, AL-; LAWRENCE, T. E.

Bibliography

Kirkbride, Sir Alec Seath. *Crackle of Thorns: Experiences in the Middle East.* London: John Murray, 1956.

Kirkbride, Sir Alec Seath. *From the Wings: Amman Memoirs, 1947–1951.* London: Frank Cass, 1976.

JENAB TUTUNJI
UPDATED BY JOSEPH NEVO

KIRKUK

A city in northeastern Iraq at the foot of the Zagros Mountains.

Historically a Kurdish city, Kirkuk today has an Arab plurality. According to the 1977 census, the population was 535,000; in 2004, it was estimated to be 784,100. The city is in the heartland of the Kurdish region; the Kirkuk oil field, the largest oil field in Iraq, is also the center of the Iraqi petroleum industry. Refineries and major oil pipelines lead from Kirkuk to Syria, Lebanon, and Turkey.

See also ZAGROS.

REEVA S. SIMON

KIRYAT ARBA

Jewish settlement outside of Hebron (Khalil).

The name of Kiryat Arba is taken from the biblical description of the place where Abraham is reputed to have purchased a plot of land to bury his wife, Sarah. One of the oldest and largest Jewish settlements in the occupied West Bank, Kiryat Arba was established in 1968, after Rabbi Moshe Levinger and his followers checked into a Hebron hotel and refused to leave. By 2002, the population of Kiryat Arba numbered 6,000, with an industrial area and a number of educational—mostly religious—institutions.

Although many settlers came to Kiryat Arba for purely economic reasons, the community is particularly known for its militant leadership, committed to an ideology of extending Jewish sovereignty over the territories occupied by Israel in 1967 and provoking Arabs to emigrate. Many of the leaders of the Kach movement are residents of Kiryat Arba. Violent encounters with Palestinians in Hebron have continued through the years. Jewish settlers have been killed while on their way to worship at the Tomb of the Patriarchs (Machpelah Cave), and in 1994 a resident of Kiryat Arba, Dr. Baruch Goldstein, massacred Muslim worshipers in the al-Ibrahimi Mosque. Residents of Kiryat Arba formed the core of the Jewish settlers who took up residence in the city of Hebron itself, concentrating around a former Jewish property known as Bet Hadassah.

Under the terms of the 1997 Hebron Agreement negotiated by then prime minister Benjamin Netanyahu, Kiryat Arba retained a territorial link to the site of the Tomb of the Patriarchs in Hebron, although the rest of the city was transferred to the Palestinian Authority as part of the Oslo Accord.

See also HEBRON; KACH; LEVINGER, MOSHE; OSLO ACCORD (1993).

Bibliography

Benvenisti, Meron. *The West Bank Data Project: A Survey of Israel's Policies.* Washington, DC: American Enterprise Institute for Public Policy Research, 1984.

Benvenisti, Meron; Abu-Zayed, Ziad; and Rubinstein, Danny. *The West Bank Handbook: A Political Lexicon.* Jerusalem: Jerusalem Post, 1986.

Hirst, David. *The Gun and the Olive Branch: The Roots of Violence in the Middle East,* 2d edition. Boston and London: Faber and Faber, 1984.

Lustick, Ian S. *For the Land and the Lord: Jewish Fundamentalism in Israel.* New York: Council on Foreign Relations, 1988.

ELIZABETH THOMPSON
UPDATED BY DAVID NEWMAN

KISAKÜREK, NECIP FAZIL
[1905–1983]

Turkish Islamist publisher and writer.

Born in Istanbul, Necip Fazil Kisakürek began his writing career at a Kemalist monthly youth magazine in the late 1920s. He wrote for other magazines, like Sedat Simavi's *Yedigün* (Seven days), and in 1936 started his own arts and ideas journal, *Ağaç*, which he published for one year. Kisakürek also published three volumes of poetry in those years and began writing plays about materialism and despair in modern life. Although his works in this period expressed the mystical turn of mind that would later inform his Islamist politics, in the 1930s, he joined Western-influenced artistic movements like the D-Group.

In 1945, he became editor of *Büyük Doğu* (Great east), an Islamist magazine whose anti-Westernization message carried influence particularly in rural areas. From 1950, the ruling Democrat party provided financial support to the magazine, but in a twist of politics, Kisakürek was jailed in 1952 in a crackdown on politically oriented Islamist publications. He resumed publication of *Büyük Doğu* and turned it into a daily paper in 1957. In the 1960s and 1970s, he alternatively lent his influence in religious circles to the National Salvation Party and to the neofascist National Movement Party of Colonel Alparslan Türkes. Kisakürek continued writing plays (several of which were made into films), poetry, and political memoirs in the 1960s and 1970s.

See also SIMAVI, SEDAT; TÜRKES, ALPARSLAN.

Bibliography

Ahmad, Feroz. *The Turkish Experiment in Democracy.* Boulder, CO: Westview, 1977.

ELIZABETH THOMPSON

KISCH, FREDERICK HERMANN
[1888–1943]

British career officer; director of the Political Department and chairman of the Palestine Zionist Executive (PZE), 1923–1931.

Frederick Hermann Kisch was born in India, the son of a British civil servant. He served in military intelligence in Paris during and after the World War I peace conference (1919–1922). In 1923, Kisch's Anglo–Jewish background was put to use in efforts at improving the tense relations in Palestine between the Yishuv (Palestine's Jewish community) and the British mandate administration. Another of his priorities as PZE chairman was to convince both his superiors and local Jewish leaders of the importance of devoting more attention and funds to dealing with Arab–Jewish relations. He cultivated contacts with Amir Abdullah of Transjordan and others; supported C. M. Kalvaryski's attempts to organize a pro-Zionist Arab movement in Palestine; and sought to influence Arab opinion through press subsidies. He frequently criticized the British attitude of encouraging "extremist" Arab leaders while discouraging those who might have taken a more "moderate" view of Zionism. Throughout his tenure, he enjoyed the complete confidence of Dr. Chaim Weizmann, president of the World Zionist Organization, and was seen by many as "Weizmann's man" in Palestine.

After leaving his Zionist post in 1931, Kisch resided and worked in Haifa and continued to advise the Yishuv on security matters. In 1938, he published an edited version of the extensive diaries that he had kept during his period as political secretary and chairman of the PZE. In addition to detailing the day-to-day complexities of Anglo–Zionist and Arab–Jewish relations, his *Palestine Diary* offers a colorful portrait of the political parties and personalities of the Yishuv during a formative period of its development.

Kisch returned to active military service in World War II as an army engineer with the rank of brigadier. He was killed while inspecting a minefield in Tunisia.

See also ABDULLAH I IBN HUSSEIN; KALVARYSKI, CHAIM MARGALIUT-; WEIZMANN, CHAIM; WORLD ZIONIST ORGANIZATION (WZO); YISHUV.

Bibliography

Bentwich, Norman, and Kisch, Michael. *Brigadier Frederick Kisch, Soldier and Zionist.* London: Vallentine, Mitchell, 1966.

Caplan, Neil. "Britain, Zionism and the Arabs, 1917–1925." *Wiener Library Bulletin* 31 (1978): 4–17.

Caplan, Neil. *Palestine Jewry and the Arab Question, 1917–1925.* London: Frank Cass, 1978.

Kisch, Frederick Hermann. *Palestine Diary* (1938). New York: AMS Press, 1974.

NEIL CAPLAN

KISSINGER, HENRY
[1923–]

American diplomat.

Born in Fürth, Germany, Henry Alfred Kissinger moved with his Jewish middle-class family to the United States in 1938 trying to escape from Hitler's antisemitic regime. They settled in New York and were naturalized U.S. citizens in June 1943. Kissinger studied at City College, joining the U.S. Army in 1943, serving as an interpreter and intelligence officer in Europe. Once back in the United States in 1947, he received a bachelor of arts degree, summa cum laude, at Harvard in 1950, a master of arts degree in 1952, and a doctorate in 1954, both at Harvard, where in 1957 he became a professor of government and international affairs. As a scholar, Kissinger contributed to the realist school of international relations, which argued that foreign policy should be based on rational calculations of state interests, not on ideals of freedom and democracy.

During the administrations of presidents John Fitzgerald Kennedy and Lyndon Baines Johnson, Kissinger played the role of part-time consultant, and he was the main intellectual force in engineering Kennedy's "flexible response" strategy, which aimed at maintaining both conventional and nuclear forces to react against Communist aggression, instead of using massive nuclear retaliation. As his biographer Robert Schulzinger has pointed out, Kissinger "engineered the most significant turning point in United States foreign policy since the beginning of the cold war." Kissinger founded his foreign policy on two ideas: the raison d'état, in which the national interest justified any means to pursue a country's aim; and the balance of power, in which no country is dominant, and in its independence can choose to align or oppose other nations, always according to its national interest. During the Cold War, Kissinger criticized the U.S. view that "the So-

U.S. secretary of state Henry Kissinger, left, speaks with Egyptian president Anwar al-Sadat. © CORBIS. REPRODUCED BY PERMISSION.

viet Union was an ideological rather than a geopolitical threat." Considering that the world's trend was competition instead of cooperation, it was necessary for the United States to continue to be present in two critical theatres, Europe and Asia, but in a moderate role.

From 1969 to 1975, Kissinger served as national security adviser. He completely changed the role of the secretary of state and the professional foreign service, transferring their power to the White House. This decentralization led him to personally conduct secret negotiations with North Vietnam, negotiating the Paris agreements of 1973 that ended the U.S. involvement in Vietnam; with the Soviet Union, designing the first détente; and with China, reviving their relations, first with his secret trip to Beijing in July 1971, followed by President Richard Nixon's visit in February 1972. Unfortunately, in the short run Kissinger's diplomacy, based on force and realism, did not see the results of its efforts. The Communist victory in Vietnam in 1975 and the end of détente with the Soviet Union diminished Kissinger's previous foreign policy achievements. Moreover, the role that he played in the bombing of Cambodia in 1969 and in Chile's coup d'état backed by the Central Intelligence Agency (CIA), which led to the death of President Salvador Allende in 1973, still overshadow his reputation as a statesman.

As secretary of state from 1973 to 1977, he was the chief architect of the so-called "shuttle diplomacy" to the Middle East. For much of Nixon's first

Henry Kissinger (b. 1923) served as secretary of state under both Gerald Ford and Richard Nixon. Although his actions in the Cambodian and Vietnam wars have been heavily debated, he commanded a great deal of respect, and in 1973 was awarded the Nobel Peace Prize, along with Vietnamese leader Le Duc Tho. Kissinger, right, is pictured with Israeli prime minister Yitzhak Rabin. © MOSHE MILNER. GOVERNMENT PRESS OFFICE (GPO) OF ISRAEL. REPRODUCED BY PERMISSION.

term, the Middle East was a marginal area; in fact Kissinger, as national security adviser, did not support Secretary of State William P. Rogers's 1969 Middle East peace plan, even after Egypt's President Gamal Abdel Nasser accepted it as a framework for negotiations. Kissinger suggested that a prolonged stalemate "would move the Arabs toward moderation and the Soviets to the fringes of Middle East diplomacy." But in 1973 the Arab–Israeli conflict moved from the periphery to center stage of American strategic interests. Kissinger, appointed secretary of state that September, was determined to use the war to start a peace process. He immediately realized that if either Israel or the Arabs achieved a decisive victory, it would be difficult to reach a compromise solution during peace negotiations. His strategy was therefore to seek a return to the prewar situation, thereby preventing either side from winning the war while creating momentum for a peace process. His gradualist approach lasted a good twenty-three months, in the course of which five agreements were concluded. Negotiations commenced immediately following the cease-fire of 22 October 1973, on 23 October at Kilometer 101 on the Cairo-Suez road. Kissinger believed it would be a mistake to seek a comprehensive settlement that

could not be attained and that, by leading to frustrated expectations, would result in an enhanced role for the Soviet Union in the Middle East. Instead, he elected to pursue a step-by-step approach: achieving more modest goals that, by producing results, would create the momentum needed to tackle the bigger issues. This strategy led to the formal signing of the so-called Six-Point Agreement, signed by Egyptian and Israeli military representatives at Kilometer 101 on 11 November 1973, when the two countries exchanged prisoners of war. The second agreement was to convene a conference in Geneva under joint American-Soviet auspices with the participation of Israel and the Arab States. The conference lasted two days (21–22 December 1973) and was attended by the United States, the Soviet Union, Israel, Egypt, and Jordan, and the secretary-general of the United Nations, Kurt Waldheim; it turned out to be nothing more than a symbolic event. In January 1974 Kissinger began the third episode of his shuttle diplomacy: a series of flights between Aswan, Tel Aviv, and Jerusalem, during which he hammered out the terms of Sinai I, a disengagement agreement separating the armies of Israel and Egypt, signed on 18 January at Kilometer 101. In May 1974 Kissinger undertook a fourth round of shuttle diplomacy, this time between Damascus and Tel Aviv, to reach a disengagement agreement between Syria and Israel. The armistice was signed on 31 May. After negotiations between Jordan and Israel, and between Israel and Egypt, failed in March 1975, Kissinger, as President Gerald Ford's secretary of state, embarked on the fifth and last round of shuttle diplomacy; he negotiated Sinai II, signed on 1 September, which called for further withdrawal of Israel's troops into the Sinai desert.

See also UNITED STATES OF AMERICA AND THE MIDDLE EAST.

Bibliography

Garrity, Patrick J. "How to Think about Henry Kissinger." John M. Ashbrook Center for Public Affairs, Ashland University, Ohio. Available from <http://www.ashland.edu/>.

Kissinger, Henry. *Years of Upheaval.* Boston: Little, Brown, 1982.

Schulzinger, Robert D. *Henry Kissinger: Doctor of Diplomacy.* New York: Columbia University Press, 1989.

Touval, Sadia. *The Peace Brokers: Mediators in the Arab–Israeli Conflict, 1948–1979*. Princeton, NJ: Princeton University Press, 1982.

DAVID WALDNER
UPDATED BY PAOLA OLIMPO

KITCHENER, HORATIO HERBERT
[1850–1916]

First earl of Khartoum, British field marshal, and colonial administrator in the Sudan, 1899–1900, and in Egypt, 1911–1914.

Horatio Herbert Kitchener was born in Ireland, the second son of Henry Horatio Kitchener, an eccentric Anglo–Irish landowner. Educated at home, then in Switzerland (where he became fluent in French), and at the Royal Military Academy, Woolwich, England, Kitchener was commissioned in 1871 into the Royal Engineers. He devoted most of the rest of his life to sustaining the British Empire in Egypt, the Sudan, South Africa, and India. He never married.

While working on land surveys in Palestine, Cyprus, and the Sinai Peninsula between 1874 and 1883, he learned Arabic and acquired a passion for porcelain and old furniture. He joined the reconstituted Anglo–Egyptian army in 1883, after Britain had occupied the country in 1882 because of Suez Canal debts and the Urabi revolt. He participated in Lord Wolseley's tardy expedition of 1885 that failed to rescue the hapless British General Charles ("Chinese") Gordon at the siege of Khartoum in the Egyptian Sudan. He also helped delimit the territory of the sultan of Zanzibar and served as governor-general of the Eastern Sudan before returning to the Anglo–Egyptian army as adjutant general in 1888.

Kitchener's exploits in battle against the Mahdi and his followers and his reputation as a methodical and penurious military organizer captured the attention of the British public and ruling elite. He was promoted to *sirdar* (commander in chief) of the Anglo–Egyptian army in 1892. Under control of the Foreign Office and Lord Cromer, Kitchener brilliantly organized the River War campaigns of 1896–1898, which ousted the followers of the Mahdi from the Sudan. His desecration of the Mahdi's remains failed to harm his extraordinary popularity in England, and the mustachioed Kitchener of Khartoum became the symbol of Great Britain at her imperial zenith.

At Fashoda, in 1898, he repulsed France's efforts to control the Nile's headwaters. In South Africa, he organized the ruthless crushing of the Boers. Then, while commanding the Indian Army, he deviously wrecked the political career of India's viceroy, Lord Curzon. When Sir Eldon Gorst (the former British foreign office agent and consul-general in Egypt) died in 1911, the Liberal government sent Kitchener back to Egypt as agent and consul-general, with instructions to keep Egypt quiet while seeing to its economic health.

Kitchener was regal in style, where Gorst had been self-effacing. Egypt was relatively quiet politically during Kitchener's tenure, and he worked to improve the lot of the Egyptian *fellah* (peasant) and extended the irrigation system. He banned nationalist newspapers and excluded certain Egyptian leaders, including Saʿd Zaghlul, from office. At least two attempts by nationalists to assassinate him failed. He cut Khedive Abbas Hilmi II's finances, trying, unsuccessfully, to force him to abdicate. As the Ottoman Empire waned, he kept Egypt "neutral." Hoping to bring it and the Sudan under formal British control, he sought to end the Capitulations and opened anti-Ottoman discussions with various Arab leaders, especially the son of Sharif Husayn ibn Ali of Mecca.

When World War I began, British Prime Minister Herbert H. Asquith insisted Kitchener join the British cabinet as war minister. He grasped the nature of modern war, but his popularity and prestige were not enough to compensate for his deficiencies as a politician, administrator, and organizer. He died midway through the war.

See also ABBAS HILMI II; AHMAD, MUHAMMAD; BARING, EVELYN; CAPITULATIONS; GORDON, CHARLES; GORST, JOHN ELDON; ZAGHLUL, SAʿD.

Bibliography

Magnus, Philip. *Kitchener: Portrait of an Imperialist.* New York: Dutton, 1959.

Royle, Trevor. *The Kitchener Enigma.* London: M. Joseph, 1985.

PETER MELLINI

KLÉBER, JEAN-BAPTISTE
[1753–1800]

French general.

Jean-Baptiste Kléber accompanied General Napoléon Bonaparte to Egypt in 1798, and was placed in command of the expeditionary force of France after Napoléon's departure in 1799. Kléber then negotiated the terms of the French evacuation with Britain's Admiral Sidney Smith, but when the British government refused the terms, Kléber attempted to reconquer Egypt. He defeated an Anglo–Turkish army at Heliopolis in 1800 and took Cairo, but was then assassinated by an Egyptian.

See also BONAPARTE, NAPOLÉON.

Bibliography

Anderson, M. S. *The Eastern Question, 1774–1923: A Study in International Relations.* London: Macmillan; New York: St. Martin's, 1966.

ZACHARY KARABELL

KNESSET

The parliament of Israel.

The Knesset is unicameral, with 120 members who are elected for a term of four years. A majority may call for early elections. The Knesset's power of judicial review is limited, but it can, with special majorities (that is, fixed numerical requirements that may be more than a majority of those present and voting on a given occasion), change the Basic Laws—the constitution. (Only simple majorities—more than half of those present in the Knesset at any given time, which could be less than half of the 120 Members of Knesset—are necessary to make ordinary legislation.) The Knesset chooses the prime minister, the cabinet, and the symbolically important president of the state, and it can dismiss the government through a no-confidence vote. In addition to legislative duties, it has broad investigative powers. It must be in session for at least eight months of each year. Members enjoy wide legislative immunity.

Most of the Knesset's work is done by standing committees. The legislative process is similar to those of most other countries. After a first reading, a bill is sent to committee where it may be studied and amended, after which it returns to the full Knesset for second and third readings. Israel has a classical parliamentary system; the Knesset has relatively little political independence. Committee membership corresponds to party strength in the Knesset, and deputies are restrained by their parties under tight discipline. Knesset members may introduce private bills, question members of the government, and present motions for debate of subjects not on the government's agenda. However, these rarely have a significant impact.

Knesset members are subordinate to political parties because of the electoral system, a single national constituency in a proportional representation system. Voting is by party lists. Until 1992 parties needed only 1 percent of the votes to win a seat, and the result of this system was the presence of numerous small parties. There has never been a time when a single party had a majority in the Knesset; coalitions have always been necessary. When the threshold was raised to 1.5 percent in 1992, the number of parties dropped markedly.

Structural characteristics strengthen the role of the executive at the expense of parliamentary independence. It has been estimated that 95 percent of the bills are introduced into the Knesset by the government. Knesset debate on them, both in committees and on the floor, seldom leads to any outcome other than that desired by the coalition members.

See also ISRAEL: POLITICAL PARTIES IN.

Bibliography

Arian, Asher. "Politics in Israel. The Second Generation." In *Encyclopedia Judaica*, Vol. 10. Chatham, NJ: 1985.

Hazan, Reuven. *Reforming Parliamentary Committees: Israel in Comparative Perspective.* Columbus: Ohio State University, 2001.

Mahler, Gregory. *The Knesset: Parliament in the Israeli Political System.* Rutherford, NJ: Fairleigh Dickinson University Press, 1981.

WALTER F. WEIKER
UPDATED BY GREGORY S. MAHLER

KOCHI

See GLOSSARY

KOÇ, VEHBI
[1901–1996]

Turkish businessman.

Born in Ankara, Vehbi Koç entered trade in 1917 at a grocery store in Karaoğlan. In the 1920s he founded his own company and accumulated businesses steadily, emphasizing assembly industries for import substitution, including cars and trucks. By the 1970s he was called the wealthiest man in Turkey. Koç's group sales doubled in the 1970s to $1.1 billion, profiting particularly from increased demand for consumer goods. In 1987, he controlled 117 firms. Koç Holding A.S. remained in the early 1990s the largest of an elite group of conglomerates that dominate Turkey's private economy. These companies have benefited from government ties and foreign capital.

Koç remained a member of the original state Republican People's Party through the 1950s, when many businessmen were attracted to the new Democrat Party and its call for free enterprise. But he resigned from his party in 1960, opposing the growing violence between the two, which harmed the business environment. After the military coup of 1960, Koç advocated strong government against anarchy, although in the 1970s he opposed efforts by the employers' union to allow government to intervene in collective bargaining. As a leading member of the Turkish Industrialists and Businessmen's Association (Tüsiad), he advocated social reform in conjunction with promoting Turkey's entrance into the European Economic Community. His son Rehmi M. Koç took over as chairman of the vast Koç Holding A.S., which in 2001 employed some 39,800 people.

See also REPUBLICAN PEOPLE'S PARTY.

Bibliography

Bianchi, Robert. *Interest Groups and Political Development in Turkey.* Princeton, NJ: Princeton University Press, 1984.

ELIZABETH THOMPSON

KOLLEK, TEDDY
[1911–]

Israeli politician; mayor of Jerusalem, 1965–1993.

Teddy Kollek was born in Hungary and moved to Mandatory Palestine in 1934. In 1935 he became a founding member of Kibbutz En Gev. In 1942 he was recruited by the Jewish Agency to serve as an intelligence officer in Istanbul, where he maintained contact with Jewish communities in Europe. After returning from Istanbul in 1943, Kollek worked for the intelligence branch of the Jewish Agency and was frequently sent to Cairo, where he arranged for stolen British weaponry to be smuggled to Palestine for the Haganah.

During the 1940s his principal contribution to the Zionist movement was the acquisition of armaments, primarily in the United States. After returning to Jerusalem following World War II, Kollek supported David Ben-Gurion in the formative years of Israel's independence. He was sent back to the United States to work with Abba Eban in the Israeli embassy and was responsible for liaison with Jewish groups and the U.S. State Department. In 1949 he was made head of the United States desk of Israel's Foreign Ministry and from 1952 to 1964 served as director general of the prime minister's office.

Shimon Peres first recommended that Kollek run for mayor of Jerusalem in 1965. He wanted Kollek to represent his new party, Rafi, which was primarily made up of Ben-Gurion supporters who were unhappy with MAPAI. Although Kollek did not want the position, he accepted the assignment to support Ben-Gurion. Kollek won, and soon afterward began working for the social, political, and geographical unification of Jerusalem after the eastern part of the city was conquered from Jordan in the June 1967 war. He made overtures to the city's Palestinian population and strove to make all religious groups, orthodox as well as secular, feel that they had a place in the city. One of Kollek's initiatives involved establishing the Jerusalem Foundation, the goal of which was to raise money for the beautification and cultural enhancement of the city. The foundation was an enormous success and was instrumental in a great number of cultural and recreational initiatives.

During his later years in office Kollek was criticized by many, including his deputy mayor, Meron Benvenisti, for paying much more attention to the development of Jewish Jerusalem than he did to Palestinian (East) Jerusalem. Palestinians were especially frustrated by bureaucratic hurdles placed in the way of their building and developing their land, while Jewish developers received government encouragement.

Although Kollek was offered other positions over the years, including the ministry of tourism, the Weizmann Institute of Science, and the Jewish Agency, he remained as mayor of Jerusalem. In 1988 he was awarded the Israel Prize for his accomplishments. Five years later, after serving as mayor for more than twenty-five years, he was defeated by Likud candidate Ehud Olmert.

See also ARAB–ISRAEL WAR (1967); BEN-GURION, DAVID; EBAN, ABBA (AUBREY); HAGANAH; ISRAEL: POLITICAL PARTIES IN; JERUSALEM; PERES, SHIMON; ZIONISM.

Bibliography

Kollek, Teddy, with Kollek, Amos. *For Jerusalem: A Life.* New York: Random House; London: Weidenfeld and Nicolson, 1978.

Sachar, Howard M. *A History of Israel,* Vol. 1: *From the Rise of Zionism to Our Time.* New York: Knopf, 1981.

"Teddy Kollek." Jewish Virtual Library. Available from <http://www.us-israel.org/>.

GREGORY S. MAHLER

KOL, MOSHE
[1911–1989]

Israeli cabinet minister and political leader.

Moshe Kol was one of the signers of Israel's Declaration of Independence and a member of the provisional government. He was born on 28 May 1911 in Pinsk, Belorussia. He attended a Hebrew secondary school, founded a local Zionist youth movement, edited a Hebrew newspaper, and was one of the founders of the World General Zionist Organization.

Kol arrived in Palestine in 1932 and was active in many Zionist organizations. He became a member of the Histadrut's Executive, a post which he held until 1947. He was active in youth *aliyah* (immigration) activities, and in 1948, just before the formation of the state of Israel, he was elected world head of Youth Aliyah.

Kol was elected to the First Knesset and chaired its Education Committee. He headed the Progressive Party from 1949 and was chairman of the Liberal Party from 1961 to 1965, when the Progressives joined the Liberals. After the 1965 split in the Liberal Party, Kol founded and led the Independent Liberal Party. He held many Jewish Agency and cabinet posts during his lifetime, and served as minister of development and tourism (1965) and minister of tourism (1969). He died on 7 July 1989.

Bibliography

Information about Moshe Kol can be found at the Knesset Web page: <http://www.knesset.gov.il/mk/eng/exmk_eng.asp?id=593>.

MARTIN MALIN
UPDATED BY GREGORY S. MAHLER

KOMITEH

See GLOSSARY

KONYA

Large city in central Turkey and capital of Konya province.

Konya is located in a large fertile plain in Anatolia. A town has existed on its site since at least 1200 B.C.E. When the area was part of the Roman Empire, the town was known as Iconium. Konya was the capital of the Seljuk Turks' kingdom in Anatolia between 1081 and 1334 and contains several historical monuments dating from that period, most notably the monastery and tomb of Celaleddin Rumi (d. 1273), a leading founder of Sufism and Sufi Orders. Modern Konya is a major industrial center and one of Turkey's largest cities, with a population of approximately 1.3 million. Konya province ranks as the country's major grain-producing region. The total population of the province (including the city of Konya) was 2,192,166, according to the census of 2000.

See also SUFISM AND THE SUFI ORDERS.

ERIC HOOGLUND

KONYA, BATTLE OF

Victory of Egyptian forces over the Ottoman army in December 1832.

An army sent by Egypt's Muhammad Ali and led by his son Ibrahim Paşa occupied Konya on 21 November 1832 after sweeping through Palestine and Syria during the previous year. On 21 December, outside of Konya, Ibrahim Pasha defeated the army sent by Sultan Mahmud II and led by Mehmet V Reşat, opening the way for conquest of all of Anatolia. Russian, British, and French intervention forced an Egyptian retreat to Syria and Cilicia, which was formalized in an agreement in March 1833.

See also IBRAHIM IBN MUHAMMAD ALI; MAHMUD II; MEHMET V REŞAT; MUHAMMAD ALI.

Bibliography

Sayyid-Marsot, Afaf Lutfi. *Egypt in the Reign of Muhammad Ali.* Cambridge, U.K., and New York: Cambridge University Press, 1984.

ELIZABETH THOMPSON

KOOK, ABRAHAM ISAAC HACOHEN
[1865–1935]

Religious Zionist theoretician.

Born in Latvia, Abraham Isaac Hacohen Kook received his early education was in the local *cheder* (Jewish day school). His father was a scholar who gave him a great love for Eretz Yisrael, the Land of Israel. He then studied privately with several well-known Jewish scholars and, later, in the yeshiva in Volozhin. In addition to the traditional Talmud, he studied literature, philosophy, and kabbalah (Jewish mysticism), during his young adult years; he also began writing on Talmudic literature, philosophy, and poetry. He served as a rabbi in Lithuania from 1888 to 1904 and immigrated to Palestine in 1904, where he was appointed rabbi of Jaffa. His enthusiastic support of Zionism, which he perceived as part of messianic redemption, antagonized much of the rabbinic leadership, whose members opposed, on religious grounds, both the notion and the movement. In 1914, he traveled to Europe and, prevented from returning by the outbreak of World War I, assumed the temporary position of rabbi in a London congregation; there he also attempted to establish a movement for spiritual renewal, Degel Yerushalayim (Flag of Jerusalem), which was to supplement the secular Zionist movement. He returned to Palestine after the war, was appointed chief rabbi of Jerusalem and, when Palestine's rabbinate was established in 1921, he was selected as the Ashkenazic chief rabbi.

Kook's personal warmth and his interaction with all Jews, regardless of their degree of religiosity, as well as his attribution of holiness to all participants in the Zionist endeavor, became legendary and won him admiration even among the most secular Zionists; they mistook his individual acceptance of them as acceptance of their secularism in principle, however. Although firmly entrenched in traditional learning, he was also well versed in modern Western thought. He manifested simultaneously the sensitivity of the mystic and the intellectual sharpness that took cognizance of the rational. As a communal rabbi, he was attuned to contemporary difficulties and attempted to accommodate his rabbinic decisions to both his interpretation of religio-legal decision making and the contemporary situation. This was, at times, another source of tension in his relations with various Orthodox Jewish sects. Another manifestation of his relatively modern perspective was his view of higher Jewish education. He established a school, the yeshiva Merkaz ha-Rav, which was unique in its incorporation of Bible studies and Jewish thought with traditional Talmudic studies, to promote a deep commitment to Zionism. The yeshiva was small and remained so after his death, when it was headed by his son, Rabbi Zvi Yehuda Kook, and his son-in-law, Rabbi Shalom Natan Raʿanan. It became a major institution only after the Arab–Israel War of June 1967.

Kook's voluminous writings are available in Hebrew, but only a few have been translated into English.

See also ARAB–ISRAEL WAR (1967); KOOK, ZVI YEHUDA.

Bibliography

Kook, Abraham Isaac. *Lights of Holiness; The Lights of Penitence; The Moral Principles; Essays, Letters, and Poems,* translated by Ben Zion Bokser. New York: Paulist Press, 1978.

Kook, Abraham Isaac. *Rav A. Y. Kook: Selected Letters,* translated by Tsvi Feldman. Maʾaleh Adumim, Israel: Maʾaliot Publications of Yeshivat Birkat Moshe, 1986.

Metzger, Alter B. Z. *Rabbi Kook's Philosophy of Penitence.* New York, 1968.

CHAIM I. WAXMAN

KOOK, ZVI YEHUDA
[1891–1982]

Lithuanian-born rabbi, teacher, and leader of Gush Emunim, the religious Zionist settlement movement.

Zvi Yehuda Kook was born in Kovno, Lithuania, the son of Rabbi Abraham Isaac Hacohen Kook. The family immigrated to Palestine in 1904, and Zvi studied in yeshiva (Jewish religious school) in Jerusalem. Later, he administered his father's yeshiva, Merkaz ha-Rav. When his father died, in 1935, he began editing his father's extensive writings. He retained his father's mystical tradition and devotion to Zionism.

After the Arab–Israel War of June 1967, Kook's messianic approach to Zionism attained new levels of political significance. He advocated that Israel keep all the territories captured in that war, which made him a nationally known figure instead of the relatively quiet scholar he had been. He became the spiritual leader of the dominant nationalist wing of the religious Zionist movement. Following the October 1973 Arab–Israel War, he led the settlement movement called Gush Emunim into the new administered territories and opposed the evacuation of settlers from the Sinai, as was agreed by Israel and Egypt in the Camp David Accords.

Most of his writings, which include traditional essays on the Talmud and volumes on contemporary public issues, were edited by students and published posthumously.

See also ARAB–ISRAEL WAR (1967); ARAB–ISRAEL WAR (1973); CAMP DAVID ACCORDS (1978); GUSH EMUNIM; KOOK, ABRAHAM ISAAC HACOHEN.

Bibliography

Lustick, Ian S. *For the Land and the Lord: Jewish Fundamentalism in Israel.* New York: Council on Foreign Relations, 1988.

CHAIM I. WAXMAN

KOOR INDUSTRIES

Major Israeli industrial conglomerate.

Koor Industries was founded by the Histadrut in 1944, and until 1958 it was part of the Solel Boneh group. Its main areas of activity are building materials, electronics, telecommunications, and chemicals.

Koor's biggest component is Tadiran, one of Israel's largest companies, a producer of electrical, electronic, and telecommunication equipment. It also owns Telrad, another major telecommunications producer. Other large companies in the group include the Nesher cement company and Soltam, an armaments firm, which has incurred financial losses as a result of declining military purchases. Among the older companies in the group are Phoenicia, a glassmaking company, and Koor's metal production subsidiary.

Between 1987 and 1989, Koor suffered a major financial crisis and accumulated losses of US$845 million. In 1989 alone, its losses came to US$303 million. After protracted negotiations between Hevrat Ovdim, the government, and the banks of Israel and abroad to whom Koor was in debt, the company was rescued by a government loan, made on condition that it implement a radical restructuring program. This involved reducing the labor force, selling subsidiaries, and closing unprofitable production lines. Koor's workforce fell from 31,000 in 1987 to about 17,000 in 1992. It has shares in 35 companies, compared with 130 in 1989.

In 1991 and 1992, Koor's financial position improved and its net profits in 1992 came to 375 million shekels. It has raised funds on the stock exchange and has been able to repay debts owed to the banks.

Given that the company was owned by the Histadrut, this posed serious ideological problems, but reforms were implemented. Koor's admission to the manufacturers' association of private sector employers in 1992 was an indication of the extent of these changes. It remains one of the largest industrial groups in the economy, although its share in total industrial output declined sharply from about 25 percent in the early 1980s to about 8 percent in 1992. In that year, Koor's sales came to 6.1 billion shekels ($2.5 billion), of which 1.8 billion shekels ($725 million) were exports. Its operating profits equaled 630 million shekels. Koor is now considering investments in the tourist and retailing sectors.

Koor's shares are owned by the Israeli bank, Hevrat Ovdim, the government of Israel, and others. In 1993 the government sold shares that it acquired in exchange for loans made to Koor.

See also HISTADRUT.

Bibliography

Kleinman, Ephraim. "The Histadrut Economy of Israel: In Search of Criteria." *Jerusalem Quarterly* 41 (1987).

PAUL RIVLIN

KOPRÜLÜ, MEHMET FUAT
[1890–1966]

Turkish literary scholar, historian, and statesman.

Born in Istanbul during the last decades of the Ottoman Empire, Mehmet Fuat Koprülü was descended from a family of viziers and taught at the Ottoman University (reorganized as Istanbul University) from 1913 to 1943. He was a prolific scholar, best known for his many fundamental contributions to the study of Turkish and Ottoman classical and folk literature, religion and political and institutional history. Koprülü was also prominent in public life. He was elected to the Turkish Grand National Assembly in 1935, representing Kars and, later, Istanbul until 1957. He was a cofounder of Turkey's new opposition Democrat Party in 1946; following the party's 1950 electoral victory, he served as foreign minister (1950–1956), except for a brief period as a minister of state and deputy prime minister (1955).

See also DEMOCRAT PARTY; TURKISH GRAND NATIONAL ASSEMBLY.

ULI SCHAMILOGLU

KORDOFAN

Region and administrative province of Sudan.

Kordofan (Kurdufan) is bounded by the White Nile on the east, Darfur in the west, the Bahr al-Arab River in the south, and desert in the north. In the southeast corner of the plain the Nuba Mountains (2,000–4,000 feet; 610–1220 meters) rise dramatically from the surrounding plain inhabited by the Nuba people (unrelated to the Nubians of the Nile Valley in northern Sudan). The Nuba are farmers who have crafted complex terraces on their hillsides and cultivated fields on the plains below. Known for their complex body decoration, musical performance, and wrestling (which is an obsessive pastime), each hill community has its own culture. They speak more than a dozen Kordofanian languages and the Arabic of the Baggara Arabs, with whom they have an historic and hostile relationship. The Baggara are cattle-owning nomads who roam widely over the plains surrounding the Nuba Mountains. They were the first and most fervent followers (*al-Ansar*) of Muhammad Ahmad al-Mahdi and remain firm supporters of the Mahdi's great-grandson, the leader of the Umma Party, Sadiq al-Mahdi. Since the 1980s the Baggara Arabs, supported by the Sudanese government, have seized the opportunity presented by the civil war to drive the insurgent Nuba from the plains and destroy their sanctuaries in the hills in the name of Islam. This has aroused the concern and intervention of the international community, which aims to preserve the Nuba and their culture.

See also ANSAR, AL-; *MAHDI*; SUDAN; SUDANESE CIVIL WARS.

Bibliography

Stiansen, Endre, and Kevane, Michael, eds. *Kordofan Invaded: Peripheral Incorporation and Social Transformation in Islam Africa.* Leiden, Netherlands: Brill, 1998.

ROBERT O. COLLINS

KOSHER

In Judaism, refers to dietary regulations for daily life.

Kosher is a Yiddish word, from Hebrew *kasher*, "proper" or "fit." The laws of *kashrut* (dietary laws) define foods fit for use, those that are kosher for Jews. They are mentioned in numerous verses of the Bible (especially in Deuteronomy), but they were interpreted for daily use by the sages of the Talmud (in the commentaries called the Mishnah, c. 200 C.E., and in the Gemarah, commentaries on the Mishnah). They went into effect, for the most part, during the early Diaspora, and they helped establish both a religious and a folk sense of community among a dispersed nation. Those who traveled, who were engaged in international trade, or who were dispossessed from century to century could seek others who shared a sense of proper food handling.

The laws of kashrut define how to kill, handle, and prepare meat and dairy products. They define which animals may be considered food at all, and which parts of kosher animals may be used. For example, fish without fins and scales may not be eaten, and animals without horns and cloven hooves may not be eaten. Animals that eat carrion are unfit, as is the eating of meat with dairy products. Vegetables, fruits, and grains are never unfit. Thus, out of necessity, many Jews who travel without kosher food available become vegetarians in order to keep the kashrut tradition.

See also DIASPORA; TALMUD.

Bibliography

Fishbane, Michael. *Judaism: Revelation and Traditions.* San Francisco, CA: Harper and Row, 1987.

Gilbert, Martin, ed. *The Illustrated Atlas of Jewish Civilization: Four Thousand Years of Jewish History.* New York: Macmillan, 1990.

ZACHARY KARABELL

KOVNER, ABBA
[1918–1987]

Organizer of Vilna ghetto revolt, World War II partisan leader, and acclaimed Hebrew poet.

Born in Sevastopol, Russia, and raised in Vilna, Poland. Kovner joined ha-Shomer ha-Tzaʿir and planned immigration to Eretz Yisrael (Palestine) but was prevented by the German invasion of 1941. His wartime resistance activities—notably in founding an umbrella resistance force in the Vilna ghetto, the United Partisans Organization—made him a symbol of the heroism of Jewish fighters in the Holocaust to generations of Israelis. Kovner cofounded the Jewish Museum in Vilna in 1944, then helped to organize clandestine Jewish immigration to Eretz Yisrael, cofounding the Brichah, and was briefly imprisoned by the British in Egypt. On his release, he joined the Givʿati brigade and fought in the Arab–Israel War of 1948. Books of Kovner's poetry, which focuses on the Holocaust and Zionism, were published in Israel in the 1940s (reprinted from partisan newsletters), 1950s and 1960s. At the Eichmann trial in 1961, Kovner testified to the brutality of Germans and their collaborators in the Vilna ghetto, as well as to reprisals meted out by Jewish partisans against captured German soldiers.

Kovner's poetry, mimicking the epics of the Russian symbolists, focused on his experience of the Holocaust in Vilna and his sense of isolation as a survivor thereafter. For Kovner, postwar Jewish and Israeli experience was also part of the ongoing experience of the Holocaust. His work thus traced reflections of the Holocaust in the present and was not solely a lament of the losses and pain of the past—for example, his 1970 poem "Huppa bamidbar'" (A canopy in the desert," Kovner, 1973).

Kovner cofounded the Holocaust journal *Yalkut Moreshet* in 1963, and was awarded the coveted Israel Prize for literature in 1970, though few of his Israeli contemporaries shared his focus on Jewish resistance, viewing European Jews instead as predominantly passive victims of the Nazis.

Bibliography

Cohen, Rich. *The Avengers: A Jewish War Story.* New York: Knopf, 2000.

Ginor, Zvia. "'Meteor-Yid': Abba Kovner's Poetic Confrontation with Jewish History," *Judaism* 48, no.1 (Winter 1999): 83–98.

Kovner, Abba. *A Canopy in the Desert,* translated by Shirley Kaufman, with Ruth Adler and Nurit Orchan. Pittsburgh, PA: University of Pittsburgh Press, 1973.

Segev, Tom. *The Seventh Million: The Israelis and the Holocaust,* translated by Haim Watzman. New York: Hill and Wang, 1993.

ZEV MAGHEN
UPDATED BY GEORGE R. WILKES

KRIM, BELKACEM
[1922–1970]

Algerian revolutionary leader.

A Kabyle (a Berber group), Belkacem Krim was born near Dra-el-Mizan and was an employee of the Mirabeau mixed commune. In 1945 he joined Messali al-Hadj's Parti du Peuple Algérien and then the Organisation Spéciale. Following the assassination of a forest ranger in 1947, Krim was always on the run from French authorities. In 1954 he assisted in the organization of the Comité Révolutionnaire d'Unité et d'Action, which led to the formation of the Front de Libération Nationale (FLN) and became one of the nine "historic chiefs" of the revolution (the Algerian War of Independence,

1954–1962). During the Gouvernement Provisoire de la République Algérienne years, he served as war minister (1958), vice president of the Council of Ministers (1958), foreign minister (1960), and minister of the interior (1961). He was the chief FLN negotiator with the French, resulting in the Evian agreement (March 1962). He opposed Ahmed Ben Bella and was eventually forced to leave Algeria, given his opposition to Houari Boumédienne, who took over the government in June 1965. In 1969 he organized in opposition the Mouvement Démocratique de Renouveau Algérien. He was assassinated, probably by Boumédiennist agents, in Frankfurt in 1970. Krim was officially rehabilitated in 1984.

See also ALGERIAN WAR OF INDEPENDENCE; BEN BELLA, AHMED; BERBER; BOUMÉDIENNE, HOUARI; COMITÉ RÉVOLUTIONNAIRE D'UNITÉ ET D'ACTION (CRUA); EVIAN ACCORDS (1962); FRONT DE LIBÉRATION NATIONALE; HADJ, MESSALI AL-; PARTI DU PEUPLE ALGÉRIEN (PPA).

Bibliography

Horne, Alistair. A Savage War of Peace: Algeria, 1954–1962, revised edition. New York: Penguin, 1987.

PHILLIP C. NAYLOR

KUCHEK KHAN-E JANGALI
[1888–1921]

Iranian revolutionary fighter.

Mirza Kuchek Khan-e Jangali was born in Rasht, Iran. He attended religious school in Tehran and was in contact with Russian revolutionaries in Baku and Tbilisi. He cooperated with the constitutional revolution of 1905–1911 but he espoused a religious pan-Islamist worldview. From 1909 to 1911, he collaborated with the constitutionalists in fighting the despotic Qajar monarch, Mohammad Ali Qajar. In 1913, Mirza Kuchek Khan was exiled to Tehran, where he frequented political and pan-Islamist religious meetings. In 1914 he returned to his native Gilan and rose in rebellion against the central government with the help of Ottoman and German military advisers. The movement's official organ, *Jangal,* was published in 1917. Following the Bolshevik revolution of 1917 and the Anglo–Iranian Agreement of 1919, Mirza Kuchek Khan sided with the Russian Bolshevik regime and, in 1920, proclaimed the Socialist Republic of Gilan. The Soviet–Persian Agreement of 1921 reversed all czarist policy in Persia, and Mirza Kuchek Khan was hence deprived of Soviet support. He was executed in 1921. During the lifetime of the Gilan republic, he initiated a land-reform policy and was intent on eradicating foreign influence, even that of the Russians, in Iran. Mirza Kuchek Khan was also a poet and wrote under the pen name of "Gomnam," which means "unknown."

See also ANGLO–IRANIAN AGREEMENT (1919); MOHAMMAD ALI SHAH QAJAR.

NEGUIN YAVARI

KUDSI, NAZIM AL-
[1906–1998]

Syrian lawyer-politician, born in Aleppo, from landowning, scholarly Sunni family.

During the French mandate, Nazim al-Kudsi (or al-Qudsi) was one of the leaders of the Nationalist Youth (al-Shabab al-Watani), an elitist organization that began to take shape in Damascus at the encouragement of Fakhri Bey al-Barudi, a Damascene notable. Al-Kudsi's class origin and the advanced Western education he received in Beirut and Geneva enabled him to acquire a number of political positions: leader of the Aleppo-based People's party; member of the Syrian parliament; foreign minister and prime minister for brief intervals in 1949, 1950, and 1951; president of the Syrian parliament from 1951 to 1953 and from 1954 to 1957; and president of Syria following the dissolution of the Egyptian-Syrian union in 1961. Following the Baʿth party coup of March 1963, al-Kudsi withdrew from political life and left Syria to live in Lebanon from 1963 to 1986, later taking up residence in France. He died in Jordan in February 1998.

Bibliography

Seale, Patrick. The Struggle for Syria. A Study of Post-War Arab Politics, 1945–1958. London: Tauris, 1986.

MUHAMMAD MUSLIH
UPDATED BY MICHAEL R. FISCHBACH

KUFTA

See FOOD: KUFTA

KURD ALI, MUHAMMAD

[1876–1953]

Syrian historian, literary critic, and educator.

Muhammad Kurd Ali was a man of letters who began his career during the Ottoman Empire as a pioneer journalist and then devoted his mature years to scholarship as a historian, literary critic, and memoirist. His writings embraced a wide range of subjects, but he paid special attention to the historical achievements of Arab–Islamic civilization and to a comparison of those achievements with the ascendancy of Western Europe.

Kurd Ali's father was from a long-established Damascene (Syria) family of Kurdish ancestry, while his mother's family was Circassian (from the Caucasus region of Russia). The family was of modest means. Kurd Ali's upbringing took place during a period of intellectual ferment in Damascus. Therefore, he was the beneficiary of a considerable range of educational opportunities, both formal and informal. After completing his secondary studies at a standard government school, he spent two years at the Lazarist school in Damascus where he acquired fluent French and began a lifelong appreciation of French literature and culture. He was also profoundly influenced by his personal contact with the Damascus circle of religious reformers and studied under their most prominent member, Tahir al-Jazaʾiri. In addition, he was a friend of Rashid Rida and an admirer of Muhammad Abduh, whose lectures he attended at Cairo's venerable institution of Islamic learning, al-Azhar University. Kurd Ali's outlook was further shaped by two lengthy visits to Europe (1908 and 1913), which convinced him that Western society possessed certain attributes that were worth emulating.

In 1901, Kurd Ali took up residence in Cairo, where he honed his journalistic skills in the lively Egyptian press, writing and editing for such well-known publications as *al-Muqtataf* and *al-Muʾayyad.* He founded his own journal, *al-Muqtabas,* in 1906 and transferred it to Damascus in 1909. It was as the publisher, editor, and principal correspondent of *al-Muqtabas* that Kurd Ali rose to prominence in Damascene society. *Al-Muqtabas* was an outspoken reformist journal that addressed such sensitive issues as Ottoman misrule, the stagnation of the Islamic world, and the special role the Arabs had to play in the revival of Islam. Despite his criticism of the Ottoman government, Kurd Ali favored Syria's continued affiliation with the empire. During World War I, he supported the government by serving on the editorial board of an Ottoman-sponsored newspaper, *al-Sharq.*

Following the Ottoman defeat and the establishment of a separate Syrian state, Kurd Ali abandoned political journalism. Although he served two terms as Syrian minister of education (1920–1922 and 1928–1931), he generally eschewed politics and devoted his energies to scholarship. He played a leading role in the establishment of the Arab Academy of Damascus in 1919 and served as its director until his death. Modeled on the Académie Française, the Arab Academy facilitated the publication of classical and contemporary works in Arabic and generally sought to encourage a public interest in literature. Kurd Ali's personal contributions to this endeavor were substantial. He edited several classical texts, compiled a six-volume history of Syria *(Khitat al-Sham),* and wrote other works on literature and on the achievements of Arab–Islamic civilization. He also published four volumes of memoirs.

Kurd Ali's historical studies were intended not only to inform readers about the past but also to demonstrate the positive achievements of Arab–Islamic civilization. He believed that European progress was generated by the rediscovery of ancient knowledge during the Renaissance, and he argued that Arab Muslims must become aware of the achievements of their ancestors in order to experience their own awakening and renewal.

See also ABDUH, MUHAMMAD; ARAB ACADEMY OF DAMASCUS; RIDA, RASHID.

Bibliography

Kurd Ali, Muhammad. *Memoirs: A Selection,* translated by Khalil Totah. Washington, DC: American Council of Learned Societies, 1954.

Seikaly, Samir. "Damascene Intellectual Life in the Opening Years of the 20th Century: Muhammad Kurd ʾAli and al-Muqtabas." In *Intellectual Life in the Arab East, 1890–1939,* edited by Marwan R. Buheiry. Beirut: American University of Beirut, 1981.

WILLIAM L. CLEVELAND

KURDISH AUTONOMOUS ZONE

Region of northern Iraq where Iraqi Kurds have been living under de facto autonomy since 1991.

At the instigation of France, on 5 April 1988 the United Nations Security Council produced Resolution 688 condemning "the repression of the Iraqi civilian population in many parts of Iraq, including most recently in Kurdish populated areas" and demanding "an immediate end to this repression" and immediate access to all parts of Iraq for humanitarian organizations. Given this international awareness of the plight of the Kurds, the collapse of the Kurdish uprising in March 1991 that followed the Gulf War and the flight of hundreds of thousands of Kurds to the borders of Turkey and Iran shocked Westerners. On 10 April, under pressure from his own constituents, U.S. president George Bush prohibited Iraqi planes from flying north of the 36th parallel, creating the so-called No-Fly Zone, and on 17 April he announced the creation of a "safe haven" inside Iraqi Kurdistan. At first, the Allies created three protection zones: around Zakho, Amadia, and Shila Diza. The signing of a Memorandum of Understanding between the UN and the Iraqi government on 18 April 1991 allowed the repatriation of thousands of Kurdish refugees within the framework of Operation Provide Comfort.

While Masʿud Barzani, Jalal Talabani, and the other leaders of the Kurdistan Front, a coalition of Kurdish parties, were negotiating with Iraq's President Saddam Hussein in Baghdad, an uneasy military situation prevailed in Kurdistan. The Kurdish *peshmergas* ("those who face death," i.e., fighters) were able to enter the cities of Erbil and Sulaymaniyya, which were theoretically still controlled by the Iraqi army. On 20 August 2002 Barzani returned to Kurdistan with a draft agreement that was rejected by the other parties, ending the negotiations. In October 2002 the Iraqi armed forces and the Iraqi administration evacuated Irbil and Sulaymaniyya, maintaining their presence in what is called the "useful Kurdistan": Kirkuk, Khanakin, and Sinjar.

For the first time in their history, the Kurds controlled a large area of Kurdistan—more than 15,400 square miles—in which they planned to set up their own institutions, organizing elections in May 1992 and forming a Kurdish government in July 1992.

But in May 1994 fighting resumed between the Democratic Party of Kurdistan, Iraq (DPK) and the Patriotic Union of Kurdistan (PUK), and in spite of the diplomatic efforts of the French and British governments, this fratricidal war continued until the U.S. government imposed the Washington Agreement in September 1998. The Kurdish Autonomous Zone remains divided into two regions, each ruled by a Kurdish regional government, based in Irbil (DKP) and Sulaymaniyya (PUK). In spite of these problems, the Kurdish Autonomous Zone has made tremendous progress since 1996 thanks to the implementation of UN Security Council Resolution 986—the Oil for Food resolution—and the injection of hundreds of million of dollars in the region. On 8 September 2002 Barzani and Talabani reached an agreement in Sari Rash on the normalization of relations between the two warring parties, which led to meetings of the Kurdish parliament in full session in Irbil and Sulaymaniyya in October 2002 and the adoption of a draft federal constitution.

During the Iraq War (2003), Kurdish forces placed themselves under the authority of the invading American-led coalition forces, and constituted a major part of the coalition's northern front. They also helped capture Mosul and Kirkuk from Iraqi forces.

See also BARZANI, FAMILY; DEMOCRATIC PARTY OF KURDISTAN (IRAQ); GULF WAR (1991); HUSSEIN, SADDAM; KURDISH REVOLTS; KURDISTAN; KURDS; PATRIOTIC UNION OF KURDISTAN (PUK); TALABANI, JALAL.

Bibliography

McDowell, David. *A Modern History of the Kurds.* London: I. B. Tauris, 1996.

Randal, Jonathan C. *After Such Knowledge, What Forgiveness?: My Encounters with Kurdistan.* New York: Farrar, Straus, and Giroux, 1997.

CHRIS KUTSCHERA

KURDISH REVOLTS

The organized efforts of stateless Kurds to form a Kurdish state or achieve autonomy.

Since the late nineteenth century, the Kurds have made ceaseless efforts to achieve statehood or self-

Iraqi Kurdish refugees relocate to Iran after the failure of their 1991 uprising against the government of Iraq. During the rule of Saddam Hussein, the Iraqi government often sought to suppress the Kurds, most notably in 1988 when he authorized a poison gas attack on Halabja, Iraq, which killed five thousand Kurds. © THIERRY ORBAN/CORBIS SYGMA. REPRODUCED BY PERMISSION.

rule. These efforts have been identified, from a state-centered perspective, as "rebellion," "revolt," "insurrection," "insurgency," "sabotage," "treason," "turmoil," "religious fanaticism," "subversion," "banditry," "tribal feud," "secessionism," "sedition," "conspiracy," "unrest," "foreign agitation," "plot," or "intrigue," and, more recently, "terrorism." By contrast, the Kurds themselves and a body of less partisan literature use terms such as "resistance," "revolution," "patriotism," "national liberation," "independence movement" or "nationalist movement," "autonomy movement," "emancipation," "uprising," "(armed) struggle," and "self-determination." Western powers, such as Russia, Britain, France, Germany, and the United States, as well as states in the region have intervened in these revolts either as supporters or adversaries of the Kurds.

Although labeled as the world's largest "stateless nation," most Kurds lived under the direct rule of independent and autonomous Kurdish principali-

ties, often nominally dependent on the overlord states of Ottoman Turkey and Iran. As part of their administrative-military modernization and centralization projects, the two states overthrew the last remaining principalities in the mid-nineteenth century.

The fall of the principalities brought the extension of state power to all parts of Kurdistan. The leadership of revolts then transferred, according to some historians, to the sheikhs, or leaders of religious orders, although tribal and feudal lords continued to rebel. The most important revolt, occurring in 1879–1880 against Turkey and Iran, was undertaken by Shaykh Ubaydullah. Some scholars see this revolt as the first stage of Kurdish nationalism because Ubaydullah tried to unite the Kurds in an independent Kurdish state. However, he and many other leading sheikhs were part of the landed feudal aristocracy motivated by class and clan interests.

Modernist nationalist ideas were first expressed by the Kurdish poet Hajji Qadiri Koyi (1818–1897). However, the modernist nation-building and state-building projects of Iran and Turkey, powerfully expressed in the Constitutional Revolution of 1906–1911 and the Young Turk Revolution of 1908, denied the Kurds any degree of self-rule.

World War I led to the redivision of Ottoman Kurdistan among the new states of Turkey, Iraq, and Syria. Together with Iran, they emerged as centralized nationalist regimes that used violence to assimilate autonomy-seeking minority groups such as the Kurds. Kurdish nationalist resistance emerged, in part, as a reaction to modernist state violence.

A series of revolts shocked republican Turkey soon after its formation in 1923: the Shaykh Saʿid revolt (1925), the Ararat revolt (1927–1931, led by Khoybun, a nationalist party), and the Dersim revolt (led by religious leader Sayyid Riza). Some historians see the Shaykh Saʿid revolt as a new stage in the history of Kurdish nationalism because it was planned by a nationalist party although led by a religious leader. In Iran a series of tribal revolts in the 1920s and early 1930s reacted to Reza Shah Pahlavi's harsh centralization project. The most serious (1918–1930) was led by tribal leader Ismaʿil Agha Simko. In the unstable post–World War I Iraq, the British occupying administration allowed religious leader Shaykh Mahmud autonomous rule as a bulwark against Turkish military incursions. He revolted and declared himself "King of Kurdistan" in 1922, only to be removed after a series of battles in 1923–1924.

During World War II and soon after, the hegemonic rule of tribal, feudal, and religious leaders gradually gave way to modern-style, secular, nationalist, party-centered politics of urban intellectuals and activists, while the peasantry remained the main fighting force, now called *peshmarga*, "those who face death." In the absence of civil society, political parties often had to work clandestinely and were forced into armed confrontation in mountainous countryside, but urban civil forms of dissidence began to emerge. The most important party, Komeley J. K (Society for the Revival of Kurdistan, 1942), aimed at the creation of a greater Kurdistan, reorganized as the Democratic Party of Kurdistan, Iran, and established the first modern Kurdish government, the Kurdish Republic of 1946, in northwestern Iran.

The longest Kurdish revolt in Iraq (1961–1975) was launched by Mulla Mustafa Barzani, leader of both the Barzani tribe and the Kurdish Democratic Party, Iraq (KDP; also known as the Democratic Party of Kurdistan, DPK). It resumed in 1976 under the newly formed Patriotic Union of Kurdistan and the reorganized KDP, which in the wake of the 1991 U.S.-led war against Iraq formed the Kurdish Regional Government in the "Safe Haven" created and protected by the United States and the United Kingdom. Both parties participated in the 2003 U.S.-led war against the Ba'thist regime of Saddam Hussein.

In Turkey dissidence resumed in the 1960s with the participation and leadership of students, urban intellectuals, and political activists, who were, as of the 1970s, part of the leftist social movements of the country. The Kurdistan Workers Party (PKK, in Kurdish acronym) launched an armed struggle for Kurdish independence in 1984. It gradually shifted to political struggle, especially after the abduction in Kenya of its leader Abdullah Öcalan by Turkish commandos in 1998, and reorganized into the Freedom and Democracy Congress of Kurdistan (KADEK, in Kurdish acronym) in 2002.

In Iran the Kurds demanded autonomy during the Iranian Revolution and after the Islamic Re-

The Kurds are a non-Arabic people, who speak a language closely related to Persian. Kurds are Muslims but adhere to different Islamic sects, and include Sunni, Shi'a, Alevi, and Ahl-e Haqq Kurds. There are eight to ten million million Kurds living in the border areas of Armenia, Turkey, Syria, Iran, and Iraq (an area known as Kurdistan), with another eight million living in southwest Turkey. © HULTON|ARCHIVE BY GETTY IMAGES. REPRODUCED BY PERMISISON.

public assumed power in 1979. Faced with Tehran's large-scale military offensive, the traditional nationalist KDP of Iran and the newly formed radical Komele (the Revolutionary Organization of the Toilers of Kurdistan), together with other groups, engaged in armed resistance, which continues to this day.

The transition from patriarchal-tribal-feudal to democratic politics has been going on since the 1890s. The nationalist movement has become increasingly urbanized, has embraced secularism, socialism, and liberalism, and has allowed the more visible participation of women. Nevertheless, a radical rupture between tribal-feudal and democratic politics—especially in Iraqi Kurdistan—has not yet occurred.

See also CONSTITUTIONAL REVOLUTION; DEMOCRATIC PARTY OF KURDISTAN (IRAN; KDP); DEMOCRATIC PARTY OF KURDISTAN (IRAQ); IRANIAN REVOLUTION (1979); KURDISH AUTONOMOUS ZONE; KURDISTAN; KURDISTAN WORKERS PARTY (PKK); KURDS; PAHLAVI, REZA; PATRIOTIC UNION OF KURDISTAN (PUK); YOUNG TURKS.

Bibliography

Bruinessen, Matin van. *Agha, Shaikh and State: The Social and Political Structures of Kurdistan.* London: Zed Books, 1992.

Eagleton, William. *The Kurdish Republic of 1946.* London: Oxford University Press,1963.

Levene, Mark. "Creating a Modern 'Zone of Genocide': The Impact of Nation- and State-Formation on Eastern Anatolia, 1878–1923." *Holocaust and Genocide Studies* 12, no. 3 (1998): 393–433.

McDowall, David. *A Modern History of the Kurds.* London: I. B. Tauris, 2000.

Olson, Robert. *The Emergence of Kurdish Nationalism and the Sheikh Said Rebellion, 1880–1925.* Austin: University of Texas Press, 1989.

AMIR HASSANPOUR

KURDISTAN

The land of the Kurds.

Kurdistan does not have boundaries on any map, but it extends over five Middle Eastern states: Turkey, Iraq, Iran, Syria, and parts of the former Soviet Armenia. It is a 620-mile (1,000 km) strip of land that, stretching from the southeast to the northwest, extends from Kermanshah (Iran) to the Gulf of Iskenderun (or Alexandretta, Turkey). Its width varies from about 150 miles (250 km) to 250 miles (400 km) between Mosul and Mount Ararat. The heart of Kurdistan is two long chains of mountains, the Taurus and the Zagros, which have many summits towering over 9,800 feet (3,000 m), while Mount Ararat reaches 16,900 feet (5,157 m).

Two long rivers, the Tigris and the Euphrates, have their sources in Kurdistan, which is also watered by two huge lakes—Van in Turkey and Urmia in Iran. Despite its harsh climate, Kurdistan is very fertile and rich in natural resources, particularly petroleum (especially in Kirkuk). Sulaymaniya, Diyarbakir, and Sanandaj have long been considered the "capitals" of Iraqi Kurdistan, Turkish Kurdistan, and Iranian Kurdistan, respectively. Iran is the only country where the word *Kurdistan* officially appears on the map, as a province.

There are no official statistics, but it is estimated that the Kurds number more than 25 million. Sharing a common culture (although they speak three different Kurdish dialects—Kurmanji, Sorani, and Zaza) and artifically divided by international borders that were imposed on them after World War I, the Kurds have not been able to develop a single and unified Kurdish national movement. They have fought separately in Turkey (Öcalan's Kurdistan Workers Party), in Iraq (KDP and Patriotic Union of Kurdistan), and in Iran (KDPI, Iran), sometimes even allowing the neighboring countries to play upon their divisions. Long considered an obscure minority problem, the Kurdish issue has become an international question since the invasion of Kuwait (1990), the Gulf War (1991), and the creation in northern Iraq of a Kurdish Autonomous Zone, which is now shown on all maps of the Middle East.

See also DIYARBAKIR; GULF CRISIS (1990–1991); KURDISH AUTONOMOUS ZONE; KURDISH REVOLT; KURDS; SULAYMANIYA.

Bibliography

McDowall, David. *A Modern History of Kurds,* 2d revised and updated edition. New York; London: I. B. Tauris, 2000.

Randal, Jonathan C. *After Such Knowledge, What Forgiveness?: My Encounters with Kurdistan.* New York: Farrar, Straus and Giroux, 1997.

Van Bruinessen, Martin. *Aghas, Shaikhs, and State.* London: Zed Books, 1992.

CHRIS KUTSCHERA

KURDISTAN WORKERS PARTY (PKK)

Kurdish party in Turkey that fought a guerrilla war for Kurdish independence, 1984–1998.

The PKK (*Partiya Karkeren Kurdistan,* or Workers' Party of Kurdistan) has been, both ideologically and in its emphasis on violence, the most radical Kurdish political movement ever. During the last two decades of the twentieth century, the PKK was the most formidable opposition force in Turkey, where it was established, waging a bloody guerrilla war from 1984 to 1999 that cost perhaps 35,000 lives. It was and still is also active among the Kurds in the neighboring states, and it became a prominent factor in the Kurdish diaspora.

The PKK came out of one of the radical left tendencies in the Turkish student movement of the early 1970s, when a handful of students at Ankara University, including some Turks as well as Kurds, decided to take up the Kurdish issue and to devote themselves, as they claimed, to the liberation of the oppressed Kurdish people from both national and class oppression. Seeking proximity to the masses they left the university and went to eastern Turkey, where they attempted to mobilize disaffected Kurdish youth against tribal and feudal leaders as well as against the state. In 1978 they formally organized the party, of which they became the political bureau. Abdullah Öcalan (c. 1946–), himself born in the village of Omerli to a poor Kurdish peasant family, became the chairman and soon assumed dictatorial powers in the organization.

At the time of the 1980 military coup in Turkey, the PKK was one of about a dozen Kurdish nationalist organizations and had become notorious through a series of violent conflicts with several of these rival organizations as well as with tribal chieftains. It was the only one of these organizations that was not virtually wiped out in the wake of the coup. The largest mass trials and the heaviest sentences concerned PKK activists, but small armed groups kept resisting arrest and clashing with army and police. Öcalan himself earlier had escaped to Syria; with Palestinian and Syrian support he began organizing proper guerrilla training for his followers, in camps in the Biqa Valley in Lebanon and later in northern Iraq.

In 1984 PKK bands, probably operating from Iraq, carried out their first raids on military positions inside Turkey. In spite of massive counterinsurgency operations, including air raids on suspected PKK camps and repeated invasions of Iraq by ground troops, the PKK managed to expand its area of operations and strike increasingly forcefully deep inside Turkey. Guerrilla bands stayed inside the country for extended periods and locally recruited numerous young fighters. The government mobilized Kurdish militia forces—mostly tribesmen under their own leaders—to fight the PKK; these ultimately numbered over 65,000. The countryside became polarized as both the PKK and the government pressured villagers to take sides and responded brutally to suspected disloyalty.

The 1990s brought great ideological and strategic changes, in part as a result of the PKK's military successes, in part in response to changes in the environment. The party, which had found new supporters and sympathizers among broader strata of Kurdish society, shed its Marxism and adopted a more accommodating attitude toward Islam. It renounced the struggle for a united and independent Kurdistan and aimed instead at a far more modest compromise with the Turkish authorities. It strongly supported such civil society initiatives as human-rights associations, legal pro-Kurdish parties, and village or neighborhood committees, and it attempted, without complete success, to bring them under its control. Realizing that Turkey never would give in to Kurdish demands without pressure from Europe, the PKK gave up its earlier violent protest demonstrations abroad and concentrated on developing an effective international lobby instead. A satellite television station (MED-TV, later Medya-TV) with studios in Belgium that broadcast to the Middle East and Europe provided the PKK with an effective modern means of propaganda and nation-building.

The PKK made various unsuccessful efforts to engage the Turkish authorities in negotiations and several times declared a unilateral cease-fire, but it failed to make a transition from military to political struggle. Counterinsurgency operations in the mid-1990s targeted especially the civilian wing of the Kurdish movement and forced a separation of the PKK from its potential supporters through massive village evacuations. Turkey put increasing political and military pressure on Syria, which had continued supporting the PKK, and secured in 1998 the expulsion of Öcalan. After unsuccessful efforts to find asylum in various European countries, he was hunted down in Kenya in 1999 by Western intelligence services (and according to some accounts, Israeli agents as well) and handed over to Turkish commandos, who flew him to Turkey, which put him on trial for high treason.

During the trial Öcalan renounced most of the ideas the PKK had stood for and ordered the PKK guerrilla fighters to lay down arms. Some disappointed followers turned their back on him, but the remaining political bureau members continued to consider him to be the supreme leader and to follow his orders. Most guerrilla units withdrew from Turkey into northern Iraq; significant numbers later gave themselves up to the Turkish authorities.

Öcalan was convicted and sentenced to death in 1999, but this was commuted to life imprisonment in 2002. At a party congress in 2002 the PKK was formally dissolved and transformed into a new organization, KADEK (Congress for Freedom and Democracy in Kurdistan), which vowed to be nonviolent and democratic. The congress duly elected Öcalan again as its president. In early 2003 the party still had several thousand armed men and women in Iraqi Kurdistan and at least tens of thousands of active supporters in Kurdistan and the diaspora.

See also KURDISH REVOLTS; KURDISTAN; KURDS.

Bibliography

Barkey, Henri J., and Fuller, Graham E. *Turkey's Kurdish Question.* Lanham, MD: Rowman and Littlefield, 1998.

White, Paul. *Primitive Rebels or Revolutionary Modernizers? The Kurdish National Movement in Turkey.* London: Zed Books, 2000.

MARTIN VAN BRUINESSEN

KURDS

People of Aryan origin who live in an area that embraces the highlands of eastern Anatolia and the northwest Zagros Mountains.

Kurds have been living for millennia in the region they call Kurdistan, which is divided today among five countries: Turkey (15 million), Iraq (5 million), Iran (8 million), Syria (1.5 million), and the Caucasus of the former Soviet Armenia (500,000).

History

Scholars debate whether the Kurds originally belonged to a group of Iranian (Indo-European-speaking) populations living around Lake Urmia who migrated westward during the seventh century B.C.E.; others emphasize the indigenous character of the Kurds living in the Taurus and Zagros mountain ranges since antiquity. Clearly, they have always been seen by their neighbors as a people apart, as documented by the medieval geographer Abu Ishaq al-Farsi some thousand years ago.

Their history becomes clear after the conquest of Tikrit by Islam, when Caliph Omar's troops pre-

vailed in 637 C.E. Arab chronicles detail Kurdish revolts against their successive masters; they also tell of the rise of Kurdish dynasties—the Shahdids, the Hasanwayhids, and the Merwanids.

Playing upon the rivalry between the Ottoman Turks and the Iranians, the Kurds managed a measure of autonomy in the nineteenth century, and Amir Bedir Khan (1805–1870) ruled as the "uncrowned king of Kurdistan" over a large portion of Ottoman Kurdistan in the 1840s. After World War I and the demise of the Ottoman Empire, Kurdistan was apportioned to Iran, Iraq, Syria, and Turkey (the Caucasus region had been within Russia since the beginning of the early 1800s). There were numerous Kurdish revolts led by religious or tribal leaders including Simko in Iran, Shaykh Mahmud Barzinji in Iraq, and Shaykh Said Piran in Turkey.

Kurdish Culture

Despite the influence of the neighboring cultures and the displacements of populations, and despite the campaigns of open or covert assimilation, Kurdish identity asserted itself by use of the Kurdish language, although the majority of the population is illiterate. Kurdish is not a dialect of Persian as some writers have claimed, but an Indo-European language of the western Indo-Iranian branch. Kurdish (or Kurdi) is characterized by a distinct grammar and syntax and by its own rich vocabulary.

Linguists working in France at the Paris-based Institut Kurde have been editing a dictionary of 50,000 words. There are three main Kurdish dialects: the Kurmandji, spoken in Turkey and in the northern part of Iraqi Kurdistan; the Sorani, used in Iran and in southern Iraqi Kurdistan; and the Zaza, also spoken in Turkey. Since the Kurdish people are subjected to national borders, the Kurdish language is written in three different types of characters: the Latin, or Roman, alphabet in Turkey and Syria; the Arabic alphabet in Iraq and Persia; and the Cyrillic alphabet in the former Soviet Union. Although, or because, Kurds are forbidden by many governments of the region to study their own language at school, they demonstrate a passion for their own idiom. There is a Kurdish proverb or saying for every situation, and daily life inspires popular songs (often about love and death, but also about war and hunting). Stirred by the feats of their leaders, poets have written epics that are memorized and transmitted from generation to generation; one of these is Ahmad Khani's *Mem o Zin,* the Kurdish *Romeo and Juliet.*

Religion

Most of the Kurds adhere to Sunni Islam, save for some districts of Turkey where they are Alevis and the southern part of Iranian Kurdistan where they are Shi'a and Ahl-e Haqq (which, both in Turkey and in Iran, negatively affects their relationship to the Kurdish national movement). Sufism is traditionally very strong in Kurdistan. After the demise of the principal Kurdish feudal leaders, the Kurdish revolts of the late nineteenth century and early twentieth century were led by religious shaykhs belonging to one or another of the great dervish orders, particularly the Qadiriyya order or the Naqshbandi.

Observing a tolerant Islam that is marked by holdovers from Zoroastrianism such as the celebration of the new year (*Nowruz*) on 21 March, Sunni Kurds have coexisted for centuries with a number of Kurdish minorities, including Yazidis, who live around Jabal Sinjar; Ahl-e Haqq in the region straddling the border between Iraq and Iran; Shi'a in the Kermanshah region of Iran; Jews in Badinan, Iraq (until the 1950s) and Kermanshah Iran; and Nestorians—Christian Assyrians, by far the largest group. This coexistence is mostly peaceful, but it has been marred by some conflicts that contributed to a negative opinion of the Kurds in the West. In 1846, Amir Badr Khan invaded the Nestorian districts, provoking a violent reaction in Europe and a punitive Ottoman expedition that led to his capture. At the end of the nineteenth century and during World War I, the Kurds participated in the Turks' mass killing of Armenians. In February 1918 Simko, the leader of the Kurdish revolt in Iran, assassinated the Mar Sham'un, the Nestorian patriarch—an act that was condemned by other Kurdish leaders such as the Barzani family.

Anthropology, Ethnography, Sociology

At the beginning of the twentieth century, Kurdish society was not very different from the Kurdistan depicted in eighteenth- or nineteenth-century European travelers' narratives: Feudal chiefs were living in castles in relative luxury while peasants lived in natural caves or in mud huts, cultivating wheat and barley, tobacco and rice; most Kurds were nomads or seminomads, spending the summers with their herds of sheep and goats in the mountains and migrating back with them to the lowlands in the winters. The big tribes—the Herki, the Jaf, and the Shikak—were known by their number of tents (1,600 tents for such a tribe, and so many guns for one tent). The Kurds lived outside the towns, which were inhabited mainly by Turkish soldiers, officials, and merchants, as well as by Jews, Armenians, and other Christian minorities.

There were a few historical cities that served as trade centers for many centuries. These included Diyarbakir, Sulaymaniyya, and Bitlis in Ottoman Kurdistan, and Kermanshah and Sanandaj in Iranian Kurdistan. In Kurdish villages land tenure was conservative, with aghas owning the land—sometimes several villages—on which the poor peasants were working and paying a rent of as much as half their annual crop. Traditional Kurdish society has been seriously eroded by the exploitation of petroleum in Kirkuk and by Saddam Hussein's wars in Iraqi Kurdistan; by the policy of systematic destruction of the tribal system by the Pahlavi shahs of Iran; and by Turkey's policy of repression and assimilation, in particular during the fifteen-year-long war against the Kurdistan Workers Party (1984–1999). Most Kurds live now in the villages and in the big cities of Kurdistan, although a number of them have looked for refuge in Istanbul, Tehran, Baghdad, or Western Europe, where the Kurdish diaspora (over half a million Kurds in Germany alone) has prompted calls for a political solution to the Kurdish issue.

See also ALEVI; DIYARBAKIR; KURDISH REVOLTS; KURDISTAN; NAQSHBANDI; QADIRIYYA ORDER; SHI'ISM; SUFISM AND THE SUFI ORDERS; SULAYMANIYA; SUNNI ISLAM; ZOROASTRIANISM.

Bibliography

Ghassemlou, Abdul Rahman. *Kurdistan and the Kurds.* Prague: Czechoslovak Academy of Sciences, 1965.

McDowall, David. *A Modern History of the Kurds,* 2d revised and updated edition. New York and London: I. B. Tauris, 2000.

Olson, Robert. *The Emergence of Kurdish Nationalism and the Sheikh Said Rebellion, 1880–1925.* Austin: University of Texas Press, 1989.

Van Bruinessen, Martin. *Aghas, Shaikhs, and State.* London: Zed Books, 1992.

CHRIS KUTSCHERA

KÜTAHYA, PEACE OF

An 1833 pact granting Ottoman Empire territories, including Egypt, to Muhammad Ali Pasha and his son, Ibrahim Pasha.

In 1831, Muhammad Ali Pasha, the Ottoman governor of Egypt, attacked Syria, also part of the Ottoman Empire. Commanded by his son Ibrahim Pasha, Muhammad Ali's forces were successful. The empire's sultan, Mahmud II, responded to this rebellion, only to be soundly defeated by Ibrahim near Konya on 21 December 1832. Ibrahim continued his advance through Anatolia and occupied Kütahya in early February 1833. With Ibrahim so near Constantinople (now Istanbul), seat of the empire, Mahmud turned in desperation to Russia. Czar Nicholas I sent Russian ships to the Bosporus in late February, and Russian troops encamped at Hunkâr–Iskelesi soon after. At this point, the other European powers intervened. Egypt's ally France pressured Ibrahim to settle with the sultan, and Britain wished to defuse the crisis before Russian troops became involved in hostilities. On orders from his father, Ibrahim demanded the provinces of Syria and Cilicia, as well as Crete and Egypt for his father. At the end of March 1833, an agreement was concluded between Ibrahim and the sultan's representative, Mustafa Raşit Paşa. Ibrahim and Muhammad Ali were granted the aforementioned territories, and the Egyptian army then withdrew from Kütahya. The Peace of Kütahya was not an official treaty, but rather a pact between the sultan and his vassal. It concluded the First Egyptian Crisis and left Muhammad Ali in an extremely strong position, so strong that Britain's foreign minister, Lord Palmerston, was determined that he would not be allowed to maintain that position permanently. Eight years later, in the Second Egyptian Crisis, Muhammad Ali lost much of what was gained at Kütahya. After the First Crisis, Russia and the Ottoman Empire signed a mutual-defense agreement, the Treaty of Hunkâr–Iskelesi.

See also HUNKÂR–ISKELESI, TREATY OF (1833); IBRAHIM IBN MUHAMMAD ALI; KONYA, BATTLE OF; MAHMUD II; MUHAMMAD ALI; PALMERSTON, LORD HENRY JOHN TEMPLE.

Bibliography

Anderson, M. S. *The Eastern Question, 1774–1923: A Study in International Relations.* London: Macmillan; New York: St. Martin's, 1966.

Shaw, Stanford, and Shaw, Ezel Kural. *History of the Ottoman Empire and Modern Turkey.* 2 vols. Cambridge, U.K., and New York: Cambridge University Press, 1976–1977.

ZACHARY KARABELL

KUT AL-AMARA

Town in Iraq.

Kut al-Amara is approximately 100 miles (160 km) southeast of Baghdad on the left bank of the Tigris, opposite the mouth of the Shatt al-Hayy, the old canal connecting the Tigris with the Euphrates. The name Kut al-Amara, often shortened to Kut, derives from the Hindi word *kot,* meaning fortress.

Kut al-Amara's main claim to fame—or rather notoriety—is the decimation of several thousand British and Indian Allied forces stranded there during World War I by the advancing Turkish forces on 29 April 1916, after a five-month-long siege. The whole affair boiled down to a miscalculation on the part of the British commander, Major General Charles Townshend, who thought he could take Baghdad. Repulsed at Ctesiphon by the Turkish forces in late November 1915, Townshend was forced to retreat to Kut. In the end, after all attempts to redeem the situation failed, the Allied forces surrendered. According to the records, approximately 2,000 Allied soldiers lost their lives during the siege, and almost 12,000 were taken as prisoners of war.

Bibliography

Millar, R. W. *Kut: The Death of an Army.* London: Secker and Warburg, 1969.

KAREN PINTO

KUTTAB

Basic school in Islamic education.

The *kuttab* was originally attached to a mosque, and the school taught children and new converts to be true believers of Islam. In the morning, students would recite and memorize passages from the Qur'an. In the afternoon, they would learn to write, study Islamic prayers and rituals, and, particularly in the Arab East, study Arabic grammar and poetry.

Beginning in the mid-nineteenth century, secular studies were introduced in many *kuttabs,* especially in cities, where they faced competition from new Western-style primary schools. In 1926, the Republic of Turkey abolished the *kuttabs* and instituted secular education and society.

Throughout the Middle East, most religious education is now taught in government schools, but *kuttabs* have remained an important vehicle of rural education, particularly in Saudi Arabia and Egypt.

See also QUR'AN.

ELIZABETH THOMPSON

KUWAIT

Arab country situated at the northern end of the Persian/Arabian Gulf.

The state of Kuwait *(dawlat al-Kuwayt)* is located at the northern tip of the Persian Gulf. Its name in Arabic means "small fort," perhaps referring to an outpost left by sixteenth-century Portuguese sailors. Kuwait borders Iraq and Saudi Arabia.

Land and People

Kuwait's 7,800 square miles of territory are mostly flat except for a ridge in the north overlooking the Bay of Kuwait and a hill about 300 meters high in the southwest. The bay is Kuwait's most distinctive geographic feature, providing a sheltered harbor that many regard as the best port in the Persian Gulf. Kuwait has little available freshwater but, with 96.5 billion barrels of proven petroleum reserves, it produces most of its freshwater supplies from seawater in conjunction with electricity generation.

Summers are hot, with temperatures regularly topping 45 °C (113 °F) and sometimes exceeding 50 °C (122 °F). During other times of year, temperatures are moderate, especially at night, and, occasionally in winter may dip below freezing. Annual rainfall is about three inches per year, but varies locally from mere traces to downpours averaging several inches at a time. There is frequent wind and dust

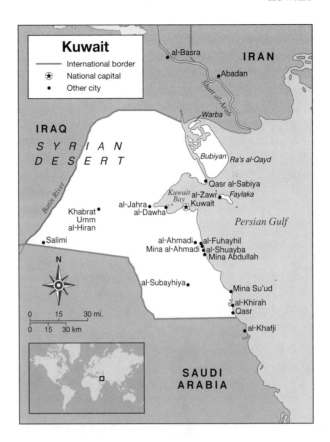

MAP BY XNR PRODUCTIONS, INC. THE GALE GROUP.

storms are common, especially during the spring and summer.

Before Iraq invaded Kuwait in August 1990, Kuwaiti citizens made up about 28 percent of the population of 2.1 million. Palestinians, peaking at about 400,000 persons, constituted the largest immigrant community, many having come to Kuwait after the 1948 and 1967 Arab–Israel wars. Kuwait also hosted an estimated quarter-million stateless Arabs, the *bidun* ("without"—for without citizenship). *Bidun* worked primarily as police and military personnel and were treated almost as citizens. When oil prices collapsed in 1986, the government tried to curb guest-worker immigration and encouraged *bidun* to emigrate. Following liberation in February 1991, most Palestinians were deported in retaliation for Yasir Arafat's support of Saddam Hussein's invasion, while *bidun* continued to suffer discrimination. Guest workers came increasingly from Egypt and South Asia. By 2003 the population had returned to 2.1 million but the proportion of citizens was approximately 40 percent. Nearly all native

Triumphant citizens of Kuwait City celebrate the liberation of the country from Iraqi forces in 1991. The invasion began in August 1990 with Iraq shelling the main bases of the Kuwati Army and Air Force. The United Nations issued an ultimatum to Saddam Hussein to withdraw his troops, and when he refused, U.S.-led coalition forces were deployed. © PATRICK DURAND/CORBIS SYGMA. REPRODUCED BY PERMISSION.

Kuwaitis are Muslim; approximately 15 to 20 percent are Shiʿite and the rest Sunni. Most guest workers also are Muslim.

Few nomads remain in Kuwait. Most of the population is urban, concentrated in Kuwait City and its closely adjoining suburbs. Suburbs also are burgeoning in what formerly were called "outlying areas" farther from the city center. Building is booming south of the city, inland as well as along the coast; in Ahmadi, home of the Kuwait Oil Company; and in the rapidly urbanizing zone between Kuwait City and Jahra.

History

During the third millennium B.C.E., what is now Kuwait was part of a highly developed culture based on maritime commerce and linked to ancient Sumer. Kuwait's modern history began in the early eighteenth century when several clans of the al-Utub

tribal grouping (part of the Aniza tribal confederation to which the Al Saʿud belong), left drought- and famine-stricken central Arabia and settled on the northern Gulf coast. The Al Sabah were formally established as rulers in 1756. They directed Kuwait's affairs in consultation with members of other paramount clans who, like them, had become merchants.

Throughout the eighteenth and nineteenth centuries, the Al Sabah proved adept at the maneuvering necessary for a small state to survive next to powerful Saudi and Rashidi neighbors. They were especially successful in capitalizing on the rivalry between the imperialist Ottomans and British. In 1899 Mubarak Al Sabah (Mubarak the Great) reached the first in a series of secret agreements with the British relinquishing authority over Kuwait's foreign relations and potential oil reserves to Britain in exchange for protective services and secret subventions. The

Kuwaiti-British bond remained in effect until 1961. It ensured that the succession to the rulership would remain with Mubarak's direct descendants. The British helped to set up and run the state's administration but neglected to demarcate Kuwait's borders when states in its region were created by the victors of World War I. A general agreement on Kuwait's boundaries was reached by British, Saudi, and Iraqi representatives at the Uqayr Conference (1922), shrinking Kuwait's territory. But the ambiguity of Kuwait's borders invited attempts by both the Saudis and Iraqis to shrink Kuwait further and, with the 1990 Iraqi invasion, to extinguish its independent existence altogether.

Economics

Nineteenth-century Kuwait enjoyed enviable prosperity from maritime trade, pearling, and fishing. Its economy was devastated by World War I, Saudi raids, and the introduction of Japanese cultured pearls in the late 1920s. The Great Depression in the United States also affected Kuwait, but oil was discovered in 1938, promising a new prosperity. Amir Ahmad al-Jabir had granted the concession to develop Kuwait's oil to the Kuwait Oil Company (KOC), a joint venture between British Petroleum (formerly the Anglo-Iranian Oil Company) and the American-owned Gulf Oil Corporation. Kuwait's oil production expanded rapidly following the nationalization of Iranian oil by Prime Minister Mohammad Mossadegh in 1951. Conflicts with KOC's operators underlay Kuwait's decision to become a founding member of OPEC in 1960. It nationalized foreign oil properties in the 1970s and, in 1980, established a holding company, the Kuwait Petroleum Corporation (KPC), for all its hydrocarbon assets, including those located abroad. In the 1990s Kuwaitis began debating the wisdom of inviting foreign oil companies back to produce oil in Kuwait on a contract basis and, by the turn of the century, debate over oil privatization had become a staple of parliamentary politics.

The government invested Kuwait's oil income directly, by expanding domestic and foreign oil holdings through KPC and its various subsidiaries; indirectly, it made large purchases of foreign blue-chip securities. Most of the latter are held by the Reserve Fund for Future Generations (RFFG), established in 1976 to ensure Kuwait's post-hydrocarbon prosperity. By law, the RFFG receives 10 percent of annual government revenue; it is the only reserve of its kind anywhere in the Gulf. By the early 1980s, Kuwait's portfolio income exceeded its income from oil and gas.

This changed following the 1990 Iraqi invasion. RFFG funds were tapped to provide approximately $26 billion toward liberation efforts. Billions more were spent during the war to support Kuwaitis in and outside the country and, after the war, to extinguish 732 oil well fires, to repair or replace industrial and civilian infrastructure, and to indemnify Kuwaitis through direct payments and large salary increases. Even before the invasion, financial misappropriations through insider trading, sweetheart contracts, and alleged embezzlement had eaten into Kuwait's financial reserves. This continued following liberation despite parliamentary oversight and a strengthened audit bureau. Whereas before the invasion Kuwait held approximately $100 billion in the RFFG and in the state's General Reserve Fund, its postliberation assets were estimated at only $30 to $35 billion. Owing to these financial reversals, Kuwait today is more dependent on oil revenues than it was twenty years ago.

Other investments had equally ambiguous results. Kuwait has made extensive indirect investments in human capital, offering citizens generous social services, medical benefits, and free education from kindergarten through postgraduate school. Literacy rates grew rapidly, and life expectancy in 2003 reached seventy-seven years. Full employment was a government goal but, like social services, became harder to provide after liberation because of straitened capital availability and soft oil markets. Kuwaiti economic policy also is affected by changing attitudes toward personal responsibility, including policies affecting the private sector, curtailing subsidies, and imposing user fees.

Kuwait's foreign aid history has undergone a similar transition over the past four-plus decades since the 1960s. Oil-rich Kuwait invested in projects in other Muslim countries, but few were profitable. It also pioneered direct assistance through foreign-aid programs. It hosts university students from abroad and was the first developing country to establish its own international aid organization, the Kuwait Fund for Arab Economic Development. Yet

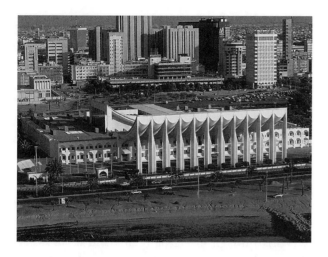

Kuwait's National Assembly Building was designed by Jørn Utzon, the man responsible for the iconic Sydney Opera House. Construction on the massive edifice was completed in 1985. The building sustained heavy damage during the Iraqi invasion in 1990 and extensive renovations were needed. © YANN ARTHUS-BERTRAND/CORBIS. REPRODUCED BY PERMISSION.

as with direct investment projects, Kuwait (along with its OPEC peers) found itself criticized by aid recipients for demanding that they adhere to international standards of compliance with loan and grant requirements. Even before Kuwait incurred large economic liabilities from the Iraqi invasion and occupation, Kuwaitis had begun to reconsider their foreign aid policies.

Government and Politics

Kuwait's dynastic, patriarchal system of government remains firmly in the hands of the Al Sabah, strengthened first by British support and then by Kuwait's oil wealth. Merchant attempts to recover their authority continue to be stymied. Although the 1962 constitution established an elected National Assembly, the parliament's ability to curb the rulers' power was undermined by two multiyear amiri suspensions of civil liberties guarantees. The parliament's power is diluted in several other ways: The amir's cabinet appointments are ex officio members; and an informal tradition gave a monopoly on the prime ministry to the crown prince until 2003. Elections are enthusiastically contested. Native-born Kuwaitis and sons of naturalized Kuwaiti citizens who are twenty-one years of age or older may vote in parliamentary elections but, despite an equal rights provision in the constitution, women are for-

bidden by law to vote or run for parliamentary office.

The two constitutional suspensions provided opportunities for the amir to manipulate the voter base. Elections held in 1981 after a five-year parliamentary hiatus were run in redrawn districts incorporating thousands of newly naturalized bedouin. Four years into the second suspension, the amir tried to quash the parliament altogether, holding new elections in June 1990 for an extraconstitutional "National Council" lacking the National Assembly's legislative powers. The Iraqi invasion ended this experiment; a new National Assembly was elected in October 1992.

The 1992 election marked a significant political watershed for Kuwait. Antigovernment candidates, about half of them Islamists, won thirty-five of the fifty seats. The ideological balance between Islamist and secularist parliamentarians (there are no legal parties in Kuwait, although a minority of candidates associate themselves with political clubs whose stands on issues they share) brought policy making to a virtual halt through much of the 1992 parliament's four-year term. Its successor, the 1996 parliament, was equally deadlocked on major issues, prompting the amir to dismiss the body in 1999 and call for new elections within sixty days, the first constitutional transition of this kind. The 1999 parliament also reflected a close balance between liberal and Islamist forces, but members of both coalitions were notably more flexible than their predecessors. Cross-coalitions centered mainly on economic issues were occasionally able to mobilize parliamentary majorities.

The most serious domestic political problem faced by Kuwait and other Gulf monarchies is uncertainty over ruler succession. Rulers and heirs apparent are mostly old and ailing, and the size of ruling families, along with evidence of clashing personal ambitions, heightens insecurity about future governance.

Foreign Relations

Kuwait's foreign relations reflect its changing economic circumstances and the resumption of direct intervention by major powers from outside the region. Prior to the Iraqi invasion, Kuwait used "checkbook diplomacy," hoping to buy off enemies and win friends among its neighbors. The 1990–1991 Iraqi invasion and widespread Arab popular support for it illustrated the failure of that strategy. Kuwait's long-standing nonaligned policy was undermined by the collapse of the Soviet Union. Kuwait's current strategic dependence on the United States, which spearheaded the coalition of forces liberating Kuwait in 1991, leaves it vulnerable to direct pressure to conform to U.S. policy wishes. Since then, Kuwait has since faced pressure to increase arms purchases and provide access to more than a third of its territory as a platform for the 2003 U.S. and British invasion of Iraq. Given rising prospects for violent conflict in the Middle East, should the absence of regionally based security arrangements continue, Kuwaiti near-term foreign policy autonomy is, for all practical purposes, foreclosed.

See also AL SABAH FAMILY; AL SABAH, MUBARAK; GULF CRISIS (1990–1991); KUWAIT FUND FOR ARAB ECONOMIC DEVELOPMENT; KUWAIT PETROLEUM CORPORATION; MOSSADEGH, MOHAMMAD.

Bibliography

Anscombe, Frederick F. *The Ottoman Gulf: The Creation of Kuwait, Saudi Arabia, and Qatar.* New York: Columbia University Press, 1997.

Al-Assiri, Abdul Reda. *Kuwait's Foreign Policy: City-State in World Politics.* Boulder, CO: Westview, 1990.

Crystal, Jill. *Kuwait: The Transformation of an Oil State.* Boulder, CO: Westview, 1992.

Herb, Michael. *All in the Family: Absolutism, Revolution, and Democracy in the Middle Eastern Monarchies.* Albany: State University of New York Press, 1999.

Tétreault, Mary Ann. *Stories of Democracy: Politics and Society in Contemporary Kuwait.* New York: Columbia University Press, 2000.

MALCOLM C. PECK
UPDATED BY MARY ANN TÉTREAULT

KUWAIT CITY

Capital of Kuwait.

The origins of modern Kuwait appear to date to a settlement generally identified on early maps as *Grane,* a phonetic spelling of of *Qurayn* (Arabic for either "hillock" or "little horn," both describing features of the coast). By the last third of the eigh-teenth century, the name *Kuwait* ("little fort") also was used by the migrating clans from central Arabia who had settled there. In the nineteenth century, Kuwait developed into a significant entrepôt, the home port of large trading vessels. Shipbuilding was a major industry, along with pearl fishing, which employed some 700 ships and 15,000 men by the early twentieth century. The town was walled in 1920 during four months of furious preparation to defend it against bedouin marauders, an event laying the groundwork for the state's current definition of citizenship. Residents of the town in 1920 and their descendants became "first category" citizens under the nationality law of 1959.

With the influx of oil wealth in the 1950s, the town was transformed. Under a master plan drawn up by a British firm, most of the old city was razed and rebuilt to contemporary Western tastes. Between 1960 and 1964 the Palestinian-American architect and city planner Saba George Shiber sought to reincorporate elements of Kuwait's past into the city's urban landscape. His influence is visible in the National Assembly building and the seafront water towers.

The 1990 to 1991 Iraqi occupation and war inflicted extensive damage on buildings and infrastructure in the city. Remnants of the wall and its gates were almost totally lost, the Dasman and Sief Palaces were damaged extensively, and the old suq was destroyed. Much of the new Kuwait was trashed as well. Public and private buildings, including homes, were filled with broken furniture, damaged books and papers, and occasional strategic deposits of human waste. An appalling wreckage was left in the Kuwait Museum, a complex housing a notable collection of Islamic art whose courtyard on the seafront had been home to a now-missing old Kuwaiti dhow.

Postwar rehabilitation proceeded rapidly and has been overtaken by new construction. The city center has acquired new high-rises. There is an explosion of growth in the suburbs, especially in Salmiya, which now sports American-style malls and a seafront aquarium. Prior to the invasion, urban sprawl spilled primarily southward, along the coast beyond Salmiya and inland to suburbs such as Jabriya and Rumaythiya. Now the city is spreading north and west as well, past the health and science complexes lying beyond the university's Shuwaykh campus, and inland, toward Jahra.

What has not changed is the traffic. The city hub is surrounded by a series of concentric arcs—the Ring Roads—connected by major thoroughfare and highway "spokes." On and off the highways, the city is beset by traffic congestion with its associated noise, pollution, accidents, and parking problems. The population of Kuwait in 2004 was 2,257,549 residents.

See also KUWAIT.

Bibliography

Bonine, Michael E. "The Urbanization of the Persian Gulf Nations." In *The Persian Gulf States: A General Survey*, edited by Alvin J. Cottrell. Baltimore, MD: Johns Hopkins University Press, 1980.

Crystal, Jill. *Kuwait: The Transformation of an Oil State.* Boulder, CO: Westview Press, 1992.

MALCOLM C. PECK
UPDATED BY MARY ANN TÉTREAULT

KUWAIT FUND FOR ARAB ECONOMIC DEVELOPMENT

Organization set up in 1961 to extend foreign aid to Arab, Islamic, and Third World countries, primarily in Asia and Africa.

The Kuwait Fund for Arab Economic Development (KFAED) was the first foreign-aid vehicle entirely financed by a developing state. Established to aid other Arab countries, KFAED's recipient list grew following the rapid rise in world oil prices in the early 1970s to include developing countries around the world. KFAED supplies project aid, mostly in the form of concessional loans, technical assistance, and training. Its capitalization reached KD 2 billion in 1981 and, since then, it has been self-financing: repayments serve as the source of funds for subsequent loans and grants. Kuwait's foreign assistance effort through KFAED and other agencies averaged more than 5 percent of GDP per year from the mid-1960s until oil prices collapsed in the mid-1980s.

Between January 1962 and March 2003, KFAED made 631 loans to 99 countries for a total of KD 3.345 billion, and it supplied KD 73 million in grants and technical assistance to 163 countries. Slightly more than one-half of the commitments in each category went to other Arab states. KFAED also contributed KD 335 million to eight development institutions.

The 1990 Iraqi invasion of Kuwait exposed the ineffectiveness of foreign aid as a generator of diplomatic support for Kuwait among its neighbors and peers. Since then, Kuwait's economic circumstances have become more straitened and Kuwaitis have grown cynical about the utility of foreign aid either to themselves or to populations in recipient countries. In April 2003, responding to sharp criticism and political pressure from other Arab governments and mass publics regarding Kuwait's position on the U.S.-led war in Iraq, several proposals were made in parliament to limit KFAED's autonomy. One sought to amend KFAED's charter to require its awards to support Kuwait's foreign policy goals; another to forbid KFAED to award assistance to any country whose government had attacked Kuwait's support for the 2003 U.S.-led attack on Iraq; a third to require that every new KFAED loan be approved by a parliamentary vote. Despite support for KFAED from the government and liberal elites, and the budget autonomy which offers KFAED fiscal independence from domestic critics in and outside of parliament, the lack of correspondence between the national interests of Kuwait and those of the recipients of its foreign aid leave KFAED vulnerable to a reevaluation of foreign policy tools that could diminish its future role.

See also KUWAIT.

Bibliography

Annual Report 2001–2002. Kuwait: Kuwait Fund for Arab Economic Development, 2002.

"Highlights of the Activities of the Fund, 1st January 1962–31st March 2003." Kuwait: Kuwait Fund for Arab Economic Development, 2003.

Stephens, Robert H. *The Arab's New Frontier.* London: T. Smith, 1973.

EMILE A. NAKHLEH
UPDATED BY MARY ANN TÉTREAULT

KUWAIT PETROLEUM CORPORATION

National oil company of the State of Kuwait.

The Kuwait Petroleum Corporation (KPC) was formed in 1980 as a holding company for most of the state's hydrocarbon assets. These had been acquired through the nationalization of foreign-owned equities in the 1970s and through the purchase of domestic investors' shares of state-private joint ventures. Major subsidiaries include the Kuwait Oil Company (KOC), which develops and produces domestic oil and gas; the Kuwait National Petroleum Company, which refines and exports oil and gas products and markets them directly domestically; the Kuwait Oil Tanker Company, which operates crude, product, and gas carriers; the Petrochemical Industries Company, which produces, distributes, and markets petrochemicals; and the Kuwait Foreign Petroleum Exploration Company, which engages in exploration, development, and production of hydrocarbons outside of Kuwait, mostly through joint ventures. Among KPC's foreign subsidiaries are KPC International, parent of Kuwait Petroleum International (KPI), which supervises overseas refining and marketing operations.

KPC acquired refining, storage, and marketing assets in Europe during the 1980s to extend its vertical integration. It also acquired a U.S.-based firm, Santa Fe Braun, with drilling, construction, and production assets, but KPC gradually sold most of these operations as incompatible with its long-term corporate goals. The Iraqi invasion and occupation of Kuwait demonstrated the usefulness of KPC. Its character as the parent of European subsidiaries and affiliates attracted support from host governments; KPI's London offices ran operations outside of Iraqi control and coordinated planning for reentry and reconstruction following liberation. Reconstruction was made more difficult by Iraqi sabotage, which left 727 oil wells damaged, most of them on fire. The fires were extinguished and all the wells capped within nine months by nearly forty teams of firefighters from around the world, including from KOC.

In recent years, KPC has been planning for the privatization of some of its assets. Deciding what should be privatized and how has been contentious. Kuwait's constitution vests ownership of mineral assets in the state but does not prohibit foreign ownership of other than production assets. One model was worked out when Equate, a subsidiary of Petroleum Industries Company, itself a subsidiary of KPC, was established. Equate is owned 45 percent each by the government and Union Carbide and 10 percent by local shareholders, who have very little say in how the company is run. Other models include the direct sale of selected operations to a group of investors and the sale of a portion of equity in existing companies through an initial public offering, with or without restrictions on the nature and number of buyers. International oil companies are eager to acquire production interests in countries with high reserves, like Kuwait, which faces competition for their investment dollars from Russia, the central Asian republics, and Africa. With the privatization of Iraqi oil a likely legacy of the 2003 U.S.-British invasion, additional privatization of KPC's operations is highly likely, too.

See also KUWAIT.

Bibliography

Tétreault, Mary Ann. *The Kuwait Petroleum Corporation and the Economics of the New World Order.* Westport, CT: Quorum Books, 1995.

Tétreault, Mary Ann. "Pleasant Dreams: The WTO as Kuwait's Holy Grail," *Critique: Critical Middle Eastern Studies* 12, no. 1 (spring 2003): 75–93.

MARY ANN TÉTREAULT

KUWAIT UNIVERSITY

Kuwait's principal institution of higher education, established in 1966 and geared to prepare Kuwaitis for professional careers in a variety of fields.

When it opened in 1966, Kuwait University consisted of colleges of science, art, and education, and a college for women. It had 31 faculty members and 418 students. During the Iraqi invasion of Kuwait in 1991, occupation forces looted and damaged the university and used some of its buildings to hold prisoners. Much of the war's damage was repaired within a year of the country's liberation, and by the mid-1990s enrollments had attained prewar levels. The student body has always had a Kuwaiti majority, and in the late 1990s there were 13,261 Kuwaitis and 1,397 non-Kuwaitis enrolled. The student body consists of about twice as many women as men.

By the early twenty-first century, the number of colleges had expanded from the original four to twelve, including colleges of dentistry, engineering, law, medicine, and *shariʿa* and Islamic studies. The number of students reached 19,000, with 1,297 teaching staff. In mid-2003, plans were being implemented to establish a college of marine science. Most of the colleges are coeducational; the college of women provides a same-sex environment and courses of study in nutrition, food and family studies, information science, and communication science and languages.

See also KUWAIT; *SHARIʿA*.

Bibliography

Lesko, John P. "Kuwait." In *World Education Encyclopedia: A Survey of Educational Systems Worldwide,* vol. 2, edited by Rebecca Marlow-Ferguson. Detroit, MI: Gale Group, 2002.

MALCOLM C. PECK
UPDATED BY ANTHONY B. TOTH